THIRD EDITION

Gender in Cross-Cultural Perspective

Edited by

Caroline B. Brettell

and

Carolyn F. Sargent

Southern Methodist University

Prentice Hall

Upper Saddle River, New Jersey 07458

Library of Congress Cataloging–in–Publication Data

Gender in cross-cultural perspective / edited by CAROLINE B. BRETTELL and CAROLYN F.
SARGENT.—3rd ed.
   p. cm.
  Includes bibliographical references.
  ISBN 0-13-017487-4
  1. Sex role—Cross-cultural studies. I. Brettell, Caroline. II. Sargent, Carolyn Fishel,
[date]

GN479.65.G4634 2000
305.3—dc21   00-028571

VP/ Editorial Director: *Laura Pearson*
Managing Editor: *Sharon Chambliss*
Director of Marketing: *Beth Gillette Mejia*
Editorial/production supervision: *Edie Riker*
Prepress and Manufacturing Buyer: *Benjamin D. Smith*
Cover Director: *Jayne Conte*
Cover design: *Bruce Kenselaar*
Cover photo: *Robert Neubecker*

This book was set in 10/11.5 New Baskerville by East End Publishing Services, Inc.,
and was printed and bound by Hamilton Printing Company.
The cover was printed by Phoenix Color Corp.

 © 2001, 1997, 1993 by Prentice-Hall, Inc.
A Division of Pearson Education
Upper Saddle River, New Jersey 07458

Printed in the United States of America

10 9 8 7 6 5 4 3 2 1

ISBN 0-13-017487-4

Prentice-Hall International (UK) Limited, *London*
Prentice-Hall of Australia Pty. Limited, *Sydney*
Prentice-Hall Canada Inc., *Toronto*
Prentice-Hall Hispanoamericana, S.A., *Mexico*
Prentice-Hall of India Private Limited, *New Delhi*
Prentice-Hall of Japan, Inc., *Tokyo*
Pearson Education Asia Pte. Ltd., *Singapore*
Editora Prentice-Hall do Brasil, Ltda., *Rio de Janeiro*

Contents

Preface

The initial idea for this reader came from the experience of teaching undergraduate courses in gender and anthropology. In reviewing the textbooks available for an introductory course, we came to the conclusion that there was a need for a readable text that built on the classic contributions of the 1970s while also incorporating the more recent and diverse literature on gender roles and ideology around the world. Although a number of sophisticated theoretical works devoted to this subject existed, we felt there was a dearth of classroom material available in one volume and appropriate for less advanced students, whether undergraduates or beginning graduate students.

We have had five goals in mind as we selected materials for the third edition. First, as in previous editions, we want to introduce students to the most significant topics in the field of the anthropology of gender. These include the study of men and women in prehistory; the relationship between biology and culture; the cultural construction of masculinity, femininity, and sexuality; variations in the sexual division of labor and economic organization; women's involvement in ritual and religion; and the impact on gender issues of various forces of change such as colonialism, the rise of the state, and the global economy.

Second, we think it is important to maintain the broad cross-cultural coverage evident in earlier editions. This breadth encourages comparative analysis of the themes under discussion and allows us to address issues of gender in industrial society as well as in developing societies.

Third, we have expanded our efforts to complement research on women's lives with articles that deal with masculinity and male gender roles. Although a truly balanced reader may not yet be possible, feminist theory is increasingly being applied to the study of men. We think this edition includes some of the most exciting new research in this domain.

Fourth, we have always been committed to combining theoretically and ethnographically based articles in each section of the book. We hope that we have compiled a volume that can stand alone or, if the instructor so desires, can be complemented by the use of full ethnographies.

Fifth, in every edition we have included introductions to each section that review as clearly as possible some of the significant issues debated in particular subject areas in the anthropology of gender. These introductions, updated for the current edition, are intended to orient students to the articles in the section and to provide a context in which readers can more fully understand each article. Each introduction concludes with a list of references that can be used by teachers and students to examine further the questions raised in that section.

We do not expect all instructors to assign the sections in the order that they appear in the text. This order makes sense to us, but our ultimate goal is to provide for maximum flexibility in teaching. We also have no intention of imposing a particular theoretical perspective, although our own predilections may be apparent to some readers. We include readings that reflect a variety of theoretical orientations to enable instructors to emphasize their own approach to the subject.

The text concludes with an updated list of recommended films organized by sections of this book. We have reviewed many of these films, and we hope that all of them will successfully complement the readings in the text.

ACKNOWLEDGMENTS

Many people have contributed substantially to the preparation and development of this book. For the first edition, Andrew Webb provided invaluable clerical and organizational assistance. The undergraduate students in Professor Sargent's Sex Roles course during the fall semester of 1990 and the fall semester of 1995 offered valuable criticisms of selected articles. Their opinions continue to influence us enormously in the final selection process. John Phinney acted as an invaluable library of knowledge for obscure references; Sue Linder-Linsley offered indispensible computer advice and tirelessly scanned in text to save us time in the preparation of the second edition; and Sue Racine and Scott Langley contributed clerical assistance. Tim Benner and Louann Miller worked conscientiously to help us complete the third edition. We are also grateful to Southern Methodist University for various forms of support over the years.

We want to thank the reviewers of the original manuscript, and the professors around the world who have used previous editions and offered valuable suggestions for improvements to the third edition. We thank our project assistant Angela Stone who answered numerous queries during the summer and fall of 1999. Finally, we are grateful to Nancy Roberts and Sharon Chambliss of Prentice Hall for their confidence in our judgment and their constant support of this project. We have a wonderful partnership!

Caroline B. Brettell
Carolyn F. Sargent

I

Biology, Gender, and Human Evolution

What is the role of biology in human behavior? To what extent are differences between men and women explained by biology, by culture, or by an interaction between the two? Is there a biological basis for the sexual division of labor? These questions are hotly debated in the United States as we struggle with such issues as why men dominate the fields of math and science, whether women are equipped for war and combat, and the implications for child development of female participation in the labor force. When issues of gender are considered in a cross-cultural context, we explore whether women are universally subordinated to men and to what extent biological differences explain the allocation of roles and responsibilities between men and women.

The relative importance of biology, or nature, versus culture, or nurture, is an enduring dilemma. This issue was addressed by anthropologist Margaret Mead several decades ago. Using data drawn from her fieldwork in Samoa and New Guinea, Mead (1928, 1935) set out to establish the significance of culture or environment in molding gender differences. She wanted to offer an alternative to the powerful intellectual principles of biological determinism and eugenics (biological engineering) that dominated academic circles in the 1920s. She also hoped to demonstrate to North American women that a range of possibilities was open to them and that the social roles of housework and childrearing were not their inevitable lot. In her view, anatomy was not destiny.

Mead's work was challenged in the 1980s by Derek Freeman (1983). Freeman accused Mead of cultural determinism (that is, giving priority to culture over biology) and opened a lively debate within academic and nonacademic circles (Holmes 1987; Leacock 1993; Orans 1996; Rensberger 1983; Scheper-Hughes 1987; Schneider 1983). For some, Freeman's book was taken (erroneously) as new support for the sociobiological approach to an understanding of human behavior, an approach formulated by Edward Wilson (1975) that contends that there is a genetic basis for all social behavior.

Although few people deny the anatomical and hormonal differences between men and women, they disagree about the importance of these differences for gender roles and personality attributes. A significant body of research, much of it conducted by psychologists, suggests that male and female infants cannot be significantly distinguished by their degree of dependence on parents, their visual and verbal abilities, or their aggression as measured by activity level (Bleier 1984; Fausto-Sterling

1985; Renzetti and Curran 1989). These characteristics tend to emerge later in the development process, indicating the importance of environment.

One controversy centers on how the brain is organized and to what extent brain lateralization is related to sex differences. One position holds that women are left-brain dominant, giving them superior verbal skills, while men are right-brain dominant, giving them superior visual-spatial skills. While research on variations in the structure and development of male and female brains continues, there are those who contend that to date "there is little evidence indicating that the sexual differentiation of the brain, if it occurs in humans, consequently predisposes males and females to behave in gender-specific ways" (Renzetti and Curran 1989: 33; see also Fausto-Sterling 1985: 44-53).

Within anthropology the role of biology in explaining differences between men and women, including social behaviors such as the division of labor and the tendency for women to be subordinated to men, has been explored within an evolutionary framework. Evolutionary theories fall roughly into four categories: male strength hypotheses, male aggression hypotheses, male bonding hypotheses, and women's childbearing hypotheses. Male strength hypotheses argue that men are physically stronger than women and this gives them superiority. They are larger, and they have stronger muscles and less fat, a pelvis better adapted for sprinting, larger hearts and lungs, and so forth. These physical differences between the males and females of a species are referred to as sexual dimorphism.

Several anthropologists have studied nonhuman primates in order to explore the evolutionary origins of sexual dimorphism (differences in morphology, such as weight and body dimensions) and, by analogy, sexual asymmetry, the sexual division of labor, and the emergence of the nuclear family (Fedigan 1992; Zihlman 1993). This research is part of a large body of literature that uses animals as models for understanding human behavior. One of the earliest statements was Leibowitz's (1975) discussion of the evolution of sex differences. Leibowitz challenged the tendency to link sexual dimorphism to particular sex role patterns by demonstrating enormous variations among different species of primates. Rather than explaining greater male size and strength solely as an adaptation to the roles of protection and provisioning associated with hunting, Leibowitz urged consideration of the reproductive advantage to women of the cessation of growth soon after sexual maturity is reached. In the process, she asked us to reconsider what we mean by strength. She also cautioned that our stereotypes of human male attributes have been drawn from one of the most sexually dimorphic species of nonhuman primates, the plains baboon. As Sperling observed, "This use of the baboon troop as model for ancestral human populations was very influential in forming both sexist and anthropomorphic views of monkeys in popular culture" (1991: 210). Sperling, Fedigan (1986), and Leibowitz have all emphasized the inappropriateness of the "baboonization" of early human life, given the distant relationship between humans and baboons. If we are going to draw comparisons with nonhuman primates, it would be preferable to draw analogies with the great apes, particularly the chimpanzees.

A second line of argument attempts to explain male dominance with reference to the biological basis of aggression. Many studies of aggression contend that men are more aggressive than women (Wilson 1975; see Fedigan 1992:71ff for a critique of this position), and often link this difference to levels of male hormones (testosterone). According to Fausto-Sterling (1985: 126), "Many societies, including our own, have tested this belief by castrating men who have a history of violent or antisocial behavior." Scientific research has demonstrated that there is no connection between castration and aggression.

It has also been argued that male aggressive tendencies are an adaptation to the male role in defense (Martin and Voorhies 1975) among both human and nonhuman primates. The problem with any line of argument that links male dominance or male social roles to male aggression is that it ignores the wide variation in behaviors and personalities not only between the sexes, but also within them (Renzetti and Curran 1989: 38). Smuts (in this book) draws on nonhuman primate examples to explore these variations in the relationship between gender and aggression. Based on the evidence, she argues that no consistent sex differences in the frequency of agonistic interactions exists. Both males and females in various species are capable of opportunistic alliances and defense of victims, depending on the circumstances.

Cross-cultural ethnographic data indicate that human societies also differ in culturally appropriate levels of aggression expressed by men and women (Burbank 1994; Counts, Brown, and Campbell 1992). Richard Lee's (1979) study of conflict and violence among the !Kung San, a relatively egalitarian and peace-loving people, addresses the issue of aggression among men and women. He lends support to the argument that both men and women are aggressive in different ways. !Kung women engage in verbal abuse, but homicides are disproportionately committed by men. Lee compares trends in !Kung violence to those in several other societies. Although his statistics are from the 1950s and 1960s, more recent research indicates that the patterns remain similar. For example, although the percentage of recorded offenses of "violence against the person" committed by women in England and Wales increased by 58 percent between 1975 and 1985, the increase in such crimes by men was 40 percent; the absolute number of crimes committed by men in 1985 remained much higher than that for women, and the male-to-female ratio for violent crimes was 9:1 (Morris 1987: 35). In 1991, 24 percent of male prison inmates and 20 percent of female prison inmates in England and Wales were incarcerated for "violence against a person" (Lynch et al. 1994). Similarly, research on criminal activity in the United States indicates that while violent offenses committed by women increased between the mid-1970s and the mid-1980s, they were still predominantly committed by men (Morris 1987: 35). Between 1986 and 1991, the proportion of violent offenses among female prison inmates declined from 40.7 percent to 32.2 percent. Corresponding figures for males were from 55.2 percent and 47.4 percent (U.S. Department of Justice 1991). A comparison between the !Kung and modern industrial societies suggests that the reasons for gender differences in aggressive behavior are complex. In addition to biological factors, access to weapons, culturally approved expressions of hostility, and the role of the state in the evolution of social control should also be considered.

Among the !Kung the victims of violent crimes tend to be other men, a finding that supports Maccoby and Jacklin's (1974) observation that primate males in general demonstrate more aggression against one another than against females. Dominance of men over women through aggression is thereby brought into question, as is the concept of aggression itself. As Fedigan (1992: 89) suggests, aggression "is such a heterogeneous category of behaviors and interactions that 'amount of aggression' is not a very useful concept." Fausto-Sterling (1985: 129) concurs and points to the fact that no studies on hormone levels and aggression use female subjects or compare men and women. She raises fundamental questions regarding the causal relationship between testosterone levels and aggression.

In her essay in this book, Smuts also deals with the bonding relationships among males and females in various species of nonhuman primates. A third body of evolutionary theory attempts to explain male domination in terms of their supposedly greater ability to form social bonds among themselves (Tiger 1969). This ability is presumed to be genetically programmed and associated with the evolutionary adaptation to hunting. Women, conversely, are thought to lack the genetic code for bonding and are therefore unsuited to the kinds of cooperative and political endeavors that give men power and prestige.

Ehrenberg (in this book) explores this bonding issue in its relation to the development of the sexual division of labor among early humans. She suggests that women were often the social center of groups. They fostered sociability and sharing. Ehrenberg also addresses a much wider debate about the relative contributions of men and women to human evolution. She provides an alternative to what has been labeled the "coattails theory" of biological evolution—"Traits are selected for in males and women evolve by clinging to the men's coattails" (Fedigan 1986: 29). The male bias reflected in this approach has been equally evident in analyses of cultural development, especially in the emphasis on hunting, a male activity, as the distinctive human activity (Lee and DeVore 1968). In her reevaluation of a discussion that essentially omitted half of humanity from the story of evolution, Ehrenberg suggests that hunting probably evolved from the physical, technological, and social innovations associated with gathering (a female activity).

In this book, Lucinda Peach explores how the ideas about male strength, male bonding, and male aggression have shaped the debate in the United States about women in the military. Women are barred from almost all assignments involving the operation of offensive, line-of-sight weapons as well as from all positions involving ground fighting. She suggests that such exclusions are based on assumptions and stereotypes about female "nature" rather than on verifiable gender differences that clearly demonstrate women's inability to perform competently specific combat duties. Warfare is a masculine arena; women need to be protected; women lack the necessary physical strength to perform adequately; the presence of women in combat units would undermine unit cohesion by disrupting male bonding—these are some of the arguments that are put forward to justify the banishment of women from specific military activities. One result, by extension, is that women are denied certain opportunities for promotion that are predicated on active combat service.

A fourth body of theory linking biology to gender difference and gender hierarchy explains the absence of women from cooperative and political activity in the nondomestic sphere (hence their subordination) in terms of their reproductive roles. A corollary of this argument is the idea that women possess a maternal instinct. The fact that women bear children and lactate has been the basis of assertions that women innately experience an attachment to their children that forms the foundation of effective mothering, while men lack a similar capacity to nurture (Peterson 1983; Rossi 1977, 1978). This attachment may be the result of such factors as hormone levels (O'Kelly 1980: 30) or of the experiences of pregnancy, labor, and nursing (Whitbeck 1983: 186). In contrast, Collier and Rosaldo (1981: 315) argue that "there are no facts about human sexual biology that, in and of themselves, have immediate social meanings or institutional consequences. Mothering is a social relation, much like fathering, judging, or ruling, whose meaning and organization must be understood with reference to a particular configuration of relationships within a complex social whole."

The articles by Etienne and by Scheper-Hughes (in this book) illustrate this assertion. Etienne's case study focuses on the adoption of children by urban Baule women in the Ivory Coast, West Africa. Etienne shows that to be without children is considered a regrettable fate, but rights to children are not determined by reproductive capacity alone. While all women are supposed to desire children, the Baule recognize unequal distribution of talent for motherhood. Thus, some women receive many children to adopt because of their childrearing skills, while others give their children to kin because they do not like raising children. Emotional ties to adoptive parents tend to be strong, although children remain in contact with their birth parents. Etienne's research contests the assumption that paternity is inherently social, while maternity is essentially natural.

Similarly, Scheper-Hughes (1987) examines the inevitability of maternal-infant attachment among mothers in the shantytowns of northeast Brazil. In an environment of poverty, chronic hunger, and economic exploitation, Scheper-Hughes finds that mothers adopt a strategy of delayed attachment and neglect of weaker children thought unlikely to survive. Such attitudes of resignation and fatalism toward the death of children are documented in historical studies of other cultures as well; for example, Ransel's account of child abandonment in Russia relates the passive attitude toward childhood death to child death rates in the 50 percent range (1988: 273; see also Boswell 1988). Parental attitudes are reflected in an entire category of lullabies with the motif of wishing death on babies; women sang these lullabies to infants who were sickly, weak, or crippled (Ransel 1988: 273). Thus, mother love seems less a "natural and universal maternal script" than a luxury reserved for the strongest and healthiest children. In the context of frequent infant death, maternal attachment means grief, and mother love emerges as culturally and socially constructed, rather than as an innate emotion.

Hewlett (in this book) offers a somewhat different perspective on the question of maternal instinct by exploring the role of fatherhood among the Aka pygmies, a group of foragers who live in the tropical forest regions of central Africa. Aka fathers spend a significant portion of their day caring for and nurturing their children. A good father, among the Aka, is a man who stays near his children, shows them affection, and assists the mother with her work. Indeed Aka male-female relations are very egalitarian. Women and men each contribute significantly to subsistence; while Aka men hold all the named positions of status, women challenge men's authority regularly and play a decisive role in all kinds of decision making; physical violence is infrequent, and violence against women is rare (Hewlett 1991). Hewlett suggests that strong father-infant attachment among the Aka can be explained by a range of ecological, social, ideological, and demographic factors. The implications of the Aka example, especially for alternate parenting models in the United States, are clear. As Hewlett argues, "The Aka demonstrate that there are cultural systems where men can be active, intimate and nurturing caregivers" (Hewlett 1991: 171).

Research on nonhuman primates has shown that role variability and plasticity are deeply rooted in the evolutionary history of primates. Cross-cultural data suggest a similar plasticity among humans. The evidence from this section should support the argument that biology merely sets the parameters for a broad range of human behaviors. Thus, biological differences between men and women have no uniform and universal implication for social roles and relations. As Rosaldo and Lamphere (1974: 4) contend, biology, for humans, takes on meaning as it is interpreted in human culture and society.

REFERENCES

Bleier, Ruth. 1984. *Science and Gender: A Critique of Biology and Its Theories on Women.* New York: Pergamon Press.

Boswell, John. 1988. *The Kindness of Strangers: The Abandonment of Children in Western Europe from Late Antiquity to the Renaissance.* New York: Pantheon Books.

Burbank, Victoria Katherine. 1994. *Fighting Women. Anger and Aggression in Aboriginal Australia.* Berkeley: University of California Press.

Collier, Jane E., and Michelle Z. Rosaldo. 1981. *The Politics of Gender in Simple Societies.* In Sherry S. Ortner and Harriet Whitehead (eds.). *Sexual Meanings,* pp. 275–330. Cambridge: Cambridge University Press.

Counts, D, J. Brown, and J. Campbell (eds.). 1992. *Sanctions and Sanctuary: Cultural Perspectives on the Beating of Wives.* Boulder: Westview Press.

Fausto-Sterling, A. 1985. *Myths of Gender.* New York: Basic Books.

Fedigan, Linda Marie. 1986. The Changing Role of Women in Models of Human Evolution. *Annual Review of Anthropology* 15:25–66.

———.1992. *Primate Paradigms: Sex Roles and Social Bonds.* Chicago: University of Chicago Press.

Freeman, Derek. 1983. *Margaret Mead and Samoa: The Making and Unmaking of an Anthropological Myth.* Cambridge: Harvard University Press.

Hewlett, Barry S. 1991. *Intimate Fathers: The Nature and Context of Aka Pygmy Paternal Infant Care.* Ann Arbor: University of Michigan Press.

Holmes, Lowell D. 1987. *Quest for the Real Samoa: The Mead/Freeman Controversy and Beyond.* South Hadley, MA: Bergin Garvey

Leacock, Eleanor. 1993. "Women in Samoan History: A Further Critique of Derek Freeman." In Barbara Diane Miller (ed.). *Sex and Gender Hierarchies,* pp. 351–365. Cambridge: Cambridge University Press.

Lee, Richard. 1979. *The !Kung San: Men, Women, and Work in a Foraging Society.* Cambridge: Cambridge University Press.

Lee, Richard S., and Irven DeVore (eds.). 1968. *Man the Hunter.* New York: Aldine.

Leibowitz, Lila. 1975. "Perspectives on the Evolution of Sex Differences." In Rayna Rapp (ed.). *Toward an Anthropology of Women,* pp. 20–35. New York: Monthly Review.

Lynch, James P., Steven K. Smith, Helen A. Graziadei, and Tanutda Pittayathikhun. 1994. "Profiles of Inmates in the United States and in England and Wales." U.S. Department of Justice, Office of Justice Programs, Bureau of Justice Statistics, NFJ-145863.

Maccoby, E.E., and C.N. Jacklin. 1974. *The Psychology of Sex Differences.* Stanford: Stanford University Press.

Martin, M. Kay, and Barbara Voorhies. 1975. *Female of the Species.* New York: Columbia University Press.

Mead, Margaret. 1928. *Coming of Age in Samoa.* New York: Dell.

———.1935. *Sex and Temperament in Three Primitive Societies.* New York: Dell.

Morris, Allison. 1987. *Women, Crime and Criminal Justice.* Oxford: Basil Blackwell.

O'Kelly, Charlotte. 1980. *Women and Men in Society.* New York: D. Van Nostrand Co.

Orans, Martin. 1996. *Not Even Wrong: Margaret Mead, Derek Freeman and the Samoans.* New York: Chandler and Sharp.

Peterson, Susan Rae. 1983. "Against 'Parenting'" In Joyce Trebilcot (ed.). *Mothering: Essays in Feminist Theory,* pp. 41–62. Totowa, NJ: Rowman and Allanheld.

Ransel, David L. 1988. *Mothers of Misery: Child Abandonment in Russia.* Princeton: Princeton University Press.

Rensberger, Boyce. 1983. "Margaret Mead: The Nature-Nurture Debate: From Samoa to Sociobiology." *Science* 83: 28–46.

Renzetti, Clair M., and Daniel J. Curran. 1989. *Women, Culture and Society.* Stanford: Stanford University Press.

Rosaldo, Michelle Z., and Louise Lamphere (eds.). 1974. *Woman, Culture, and Society.* Stanford: Stanford University Press.

Rossi, Alice. 1977. "A Biosocial Perspective on Parenting." *Daedalus* 106: 1–31.

———.1978. "The Biosocial Side of Parenthood. *Human Nature* 1: 72–79.

Scheper-Hughes, Nancy. 1987. "The Margaret Mead Controversy: Culture, Biology and Anthropological Inquiry." In Herbert Applebaum (ed.). *Perspectives in Cultural Anthropology*, pp. 443–454. Albany: State University of New York Press.

Schneider, David. 1983. "The Coming of a Sage to Samoa." *Natural History* 92(6): 4–10.

Sperling, Susan. 1991. "Baboons with Briefcases vs. Langurs in Lipstick. Feminism and Functionalism in Primate Studies." In Micaela di Leonardo (ed.). *Gender at the Crossroads of Knowledge: Feminist Anthropology in the Postmodern Era*, pp. 204–234. Berkeley: University of California Press.

Tiger, Lionel. 1969. *Men in Groups.* New York: Random House.

Trebilcot, Joyce (ed.). 1983. *Mothering: Essays in Feminist Theory.* Totowa, NJ: Rowman and Allenheld.

U.S. Department of Justice. 1991. *Women in Prison*, Bureau of Justice Statistics, Special Report. Washington D.C.: U.S. Department of Justice.

Whitbeck, Caroline. 1983. "The Maternal Instinct." In Joyce Trebilcot (ed.). *Mothering: Essays in Feminist Theory*, pp. 185–192. Totowa, NJ: Rowman and Allenheld.

Wilson, Edward O. 1975. *Sociobiology: The New Synthesis.* Cambridge: Harvard University Press.

Zihlman, Adrienne L. 1993. Sex Differences and Gender Hierarchies among Primates: An Evolutionary Perspective. In Barbara Diane Miller (ed.). S*ex and Gender Hierarchies*, pp. 32–56. Cambridge: Cambridge University Press.

Gender, Aggression, and Influence

Barbara B. Smuts

Nonhuman primates often exhibit striking sex differences in behavior. Individual differences in behavior are widespread among primates, and, they involve many characteristics, including age, status, and kinship as well as sex. Sex differences in behavior, however, often carry special significance because of controversy about the origins and meaning of human sex differences. The belief that observations of animals can illuminate this controversy has stimulated a search for generalizations about behavioral sex differences, especially in nonhuman primates. Some of the generalizations that have emerged reflect cultural stereotypes: male primates are more aggressive than females; males dominate females; females are more

From *Primate Societies* edited by Barbara Smuts, Dorothy L. Cheney, Robert Seyfarth, Richard Wrangham and Thomas Struhsaler. University of Chicago Press. 1986.

passive than males (e.g., Tiger 1969). Others represent attempts to counteract such cultural biases: female primates are more influential than males; females are more likely than males to form affiliative social bonds (e.g., French 1985).

Widespread acceptance of these types of generalizations has two unfortunate consequences. First, inter-and intraspecific variation in male and female behavior are often ignored. Second, insufficient attention is paid to the functional significance of sex differences in behavior. This chapter stresses the importance of these two issues for understanding behavioral sex differences in nonhuman primates. It makes no attempt to review sex differences in all aspects of behavior but focuses instead on how gender relates to social bonds, aggression, and influence. This chapter examines contextual factors that influence sex differences in social behavior.

BEHAVIORAL SEX DIFFERENCES

Impact of the Social System

Among nonhuman primates, patterns of intergroup transfer appear to have important effects on intrasexual relationships within groups (Wrangham 1980; Harcourt and Stewart 1983). First consider female-female relationships. In species in which females usually remain in their natal groups, females develop strong bonds with other females, revealed by frequent association and grooming. Examples include macaques, vervets, and savanna baboons; gelada baboons (Dunbar 1984); gray langurs and Nilgiri langurs (Poirier 1970); squirrel monkeys and capuchins; and sifakas and ring-tailed lemurs. In some of these species, females develop highly differentiated dominance relationships, in macaques, vervet monkeys, and baboons, these relationships are based largely on coalitions among female kin.

In species in which females usually transfer out of their natal groups, female-female relations lack such cohesion. Females rarely rest in close proximity or groom one another. Dyadic agonistic interactions and female-female coalitions against other females are uncommon, and female dominance relationships remain ill defined. Examples include red colobus monkeys, gorillas, and chimpanzees. Female hamadryas baboons also fit this pattern, except that female dominance relationships appear more clearly defined in this species.

Similarly, male-male relationships also reflect transfer patterns. In chimpanzees and red colobus, males remain in the natal group and form strong bonds characterized by grooming, proximity, and coalitionary support. Among hamadryas baboons, males born in the same band associate and groom until they acquire their own females. After this they no longer groom or sit together, but coordinated travel, respect for one another's females, and mutual support against males from other bands indicate their continuing bonds with one another. In all of these species, male-male bonds appear to be stronger than female-female bonds (with the exception of mother-daughter relationships).

Conversely, in species in which males typically transfer, males rarely associate closely or groom one another. Examples include savanna baboons, gelada baboons, squirrel monkeys, capuchins, and ring-tailed lemurs. There are some exceptions to these generalizations. however. In macaques and vervets, brothers sometimes transfer together and maintain close relationships (Meikle and Vessey 1981; Cheney and Seyfarth 1983), and in seasonally breeding species, male-male relations are typically more relaxed outside the mating season. Nevertheless, male-male bonds are generally weaker in these species than female-female bonds.

Thus, in male-transfer species, female-female bonds are most apparent, whereas in female-transfer species male-male bonds are more prominent (Wrangham 1980). This general finding vividly demonstrates the value of a broad-based, comparative approach to the study of sex differences (Hrdy 1981; Fedigan 1982; Harcourt and Stewart 1983). If, for example, data were available only for macaques, vervets, and savanna baboons, one would conclude that female nonhuman primates are more affiliative than males; if data were available only for chimpanzees, red colobus, and hamadryas one would conclude just the opposite. Although we can now clearly see the pitfalls of any investigation of sex differences that fails to include species with different transfer patterns, the importance of this variable went unrecognized for many years due to the lack of data. There are probably other social or ecological variables of which we are not yet aware that are equally critical for understanding sex differences in behavior. For this reason, the ideal method for investigating any aspect of behavioral sex differences involves comparison of many species that differ in a wide variety of ways (e.g., social system, ecology, demography, phylogeny, size, and so on), both because this reduces the chances of invalid generalizations and because it is likely to reveal new and important factors influencing gender-related behaviors.

Even within species, female-female and male-male relationships can vary dramatically, depending on the context. For example, in some male-transfer species, such as gray langurs, extragroup males who are not competing directly over females form stable friendly associations that involve proximity, grooming, and coalitional support (Moore 1985). However, once these males succeed in replacing the breeding male of a bisexual group, they fight among themselves until only one male remains with the females. Similarly, in experiments with captive macaques, the introduction of females severely disrupts male-male affiliative relationships (Bernstein, Gordon, and Rose 1974; Coe and Rosenblum 1984).

Another example of intraspecific variation in social relationships comes from de Waal's study of captive female chimpanzees. In the wild, adult females spend most of their time alone and rarely associate with unrelated females. When brought into prolonged, close proximity in captivity, however, females form close, stable bonds and support one another through agonistic interventions (de Waal 1982).

Several behaviors, however, appear to vary by sex in consistent ways across a wide variety of nonhuman primate species with different social systems. As illustrated later, these behaviors are closely tied to fundamental differences in the reproductive strategies of males and females.

Sex Differences in Aggression

Since the first systematic field studies of nonhuman primates, researchers have often claimed that males are more aggressive than females (e.g., Tiger 1969; Nagel and Kummer 1974). However, this hypothesis has received little systematic attention since relatively few studies have provided quantitative comparisons of aggression in the two sexes. The available data suggest that, in terms of the frequency of agonistic interactions (supplants, threats, chases, and fights), no consistent sex differences exist. In some studies, males engaged in agonistic interactions more often than did females, but in others the reverse was true (table 1).

TABLE 1. Sex Differences in the Frequency of Agonistic Interactions of Adults

SPECIES	*MEASURE USED*	*SEX SHOWING MORE AGONISM*
Cebus apella (w)	Frequency of threats[a]	F
Presbytis johnii (w)	Frequency of aggressive encounters[a]	M
P. entellus (w)	Frequency of agonistic interactions[a]	M
Macaca mulatta (c)	Number of fights[a]	F
M. nemestrina (c)	Frequency of all agonistic interactions[b]	F
	Frequency of damaging aggression[b]	M
M. arctoides (c)	Frequency of threats and bites[b]	F
	Frequency of chases and contact aggression[b]	F=M
	Frequency of initiation of agnostic interactions[b]	M
M. sinica (w)	Frequency of threats given, corrected for age-sex composition of group[b]	M
Papio cynocephalus anubis (w)	Time spent in agnostic interactions[b]	F
P. c. ursinus (w)	Mean number approach-retreat interactions per dyad per hour[a]	F
	Mean number agressive interactions per dyad per hour[a]	M
Pan troglodytes	Frequency of aggression[b]	M

NOTE: w = wild; c = captive
[a] Includes only agonism between adults of the same sex.
[b] Includes agonism between adult and all other age-sex classes.

A few studies, however, suggest intriguing sex differences in the quality of agonistic interactions. During encounters with other males, male baboons, vervet monkeys, and macaques use ritualized threats such as yawns and teeth grinding that normally are not shown by females (macaques: Blurton-Jones and Trollope 1968; vervets: Durham 1969; baboons: Smuts, personal observation), and male chimpanzees routinely use a ritualized charging display to intimidate rivals, whereas females do so only occasionally (Bygott 1979). In addition, several observers have noted that ritualized threats nearly always precede male attacks on other males, whereas females often attack other females without warning (captive patas monkeys and captive Sykes's monkeys: Nagel and Kummer 1974; captive chimpanzees: de Waal 1982; savanna baboons: Smuts, personal observation; vervet monkeys: Cheney and Seyfarth, personal communication). One possible explanation for these differences is that males attempt to settle conflicts through ritualized signals more often than do females because the risks of injury through physical combat are greater for males.

Since observers rarely witness infliction of wounds, it is difficult to test directly the hypothesis that males injure one another during fights more often than do females. Instead, researchers have relied on comparisons of the frequency in males and females of fresh wounds or scars indicating previous wounds (table 2). What can such comparisons tell us? In most species, observations of fights indicate that most, and in some cases all, male wounds are inflicted by other males. Thus, when males have more wounds than females,

TABLE 2. Sex Differences in the Frequency of Wounds in Adults

SPECIES	MEASURE USED	SEX WITH MORE WOUNDS
Arctocebus calabarensis (w)	Traces of serious wounds in captured animals	M
Perodicticus potto (w)		
Galago elegantulus (w)		
G. alleni (w)		
G. demidovii (w)		
Propithecus verreauxi (w)	Fresh wounds during breeding season	M
Lemur catta (w)	Fresh wounds during breeding season	M
Alouatta seniculus (w)	Lip injuries, scars, and missing fingers	M
A. Palliata (w)	Scars and freshly torn lips	M
Presbytis entellus	Fresh wounds	M
Cercopithecus aethiops (w)	Fresh wounds	M
Macaca mulatta (p)	Fresh wounds	M
(p)	Fresh wounds during breeding season	M
(p)	Fresh wounds: posterior	F
	Fresh wounds: anterior	M
(w)	Fresh wounds	M
(c)	Fresh wounds	F
(c)	Fresh wounds	M
M. arctoides (c)	Fresh wounds	M
M. nemestrina (c)	Fresh wounds	M
Cercoebus atys (c)	Fresh wounds	M
Papio cynocephalus anubis (w)	Fresh wounds	M

NOTE: w = wild; p = provisioned; c = captive

it usually indicates higher levels of severe aggression among males than among females. However, since males injure females, if females show more wounds than males, we cannot assume that this indicates higher levels of severe aggression among females than among males. In all but two of the comparisons shown in table 2, males have more wounds than females, and thus we can conclude that severe aggression is more common among males.

Why should males injure one another more often than females? First, sex differences in rates of wounding may reflect, at least in part, sexual dimorphism in canine size and shape. In all of the species listed in table 2, adult males have longer, sharper canines than do females (Harvey, Kavanagh, and Clutton-Brock 1978). However, because female teeth can also inflict serious wounds, this is unlikely to be the whole explanation (it also, of course, begs the question of why males have evolved longer, sharper canines to begin with).

A second hypothesis argues that the potential payoffs of escalated aggression (i.e., aggression in which individuals risk injury) are greater for males than for females because of differences in the resources over which they compete (Clutton-Brock, Guinness, and Albon 1982). Among males, the outcome of a single interaction or of a series of interactions over brief periods of time can result in great differences in access to females and thus in reproductive success (e.g., olive baboons: Sapolsky 1983; rhesus macaques: Chapais 1983a; chimpanzees: Riss and Goodall 1977; gray langurs: Hrdy 1977; mantled howlers: Clarke 1983). Among females, however, the outcome of a single interaction rarely leads to large variations in reproductive success because female reproductive performance depends mainly on the ability to sustain investment in offspring over long periods of time. Also, females may have more to lose from defeat in an escalated encounter since in many cases they risk not only injury to themselves but also harm to a fetus or an infant. Thus, although intrasexual competition plays

a critical role in the reproductive success of both sexes, in females relatively small payoffs accumulate over long periods of time so that competition is generally low-key and chronic, while for males the payoffs are often large but short-term so that competition tends to be intense and episodic.

This does not mean, however, that females will always be more circumspect and males always more belligerent. It suggests, instead, that the contexts that provoke aggression will differ for each sex, and that given particularly high and immediate stakes, females will fight intensely and risk injury as much as will males. The following examples illustrate this point.

First, although females seldom initiate aggression against higher-ranking females. they will sometimes do so in order to protect vulnerable offspring (e.g., Kaplan 1978; Silk 1980; Bernstein and Ehardt 1985; de Waal 1982). Females have even been known to attack adult males twice their size to protect close relatives. For example, Collins, Busse, and Goodall (1984) describe how an old female baboon attacked an adult male when he bit her grandchild.

Second, although female rank reversals rarely occur in cercopithecines, when they do occur, they often involve intense female-female fights that sometimes result in injuries (e.g., Koyama 1970; Marsden 1968; Witt, Schmidt, and Schmidt 1981). High rank sometimes leads to higher reproductive success for females, and, since females usually inherit ranks from their mothers in these species, the benefits of high rank can accumulate through more than one generation. Thus, in the rare instances in which low-ranking females have an opportunity to raise their dominance status, the stakes may be high, and we might expect females to engage in escalated aggression. In one troop of wild baboons undergoing a series of dramatic shifts in female dominance relationships, females showed three types of behavior that were otherwise observed exclusively among males (Smuts and Nicolson, unpublished observation). First, females fought face to face and inflicted facial lacerations similar to the wounds males inflict on one another, although these were less deep. Second, to intimidate opponents, females used ritualized threats such as repeated circling, tooth grinding, and deep yawns that exposed the canines. Third, females solicited aid from one another through a combination of rapid head flagging, hip grasping, and mounting of potential allies—all tactics employed in male-male coalitions.

Finally, females in several female-bonded species engage in escalated aggression against females from other groups during intergroup encounters. For example, during intergroup encounters in olive baboons and rhesus monkeys, females from one group repeatedly hit, pushed, jumped on, and bit females from the other group (Nicolson and Smuts, unpublished observation. The outcome of such encounters can have long-term reproductive consequences for females in different groups.

The three examples discussed above concern cases in which the payoffs of intense aggression seemed to be unusually high. A fourth example concerns situations in which the costs of intense aggression appear to be unusually low: gang attacks on single females, often by a group of closely allied female relatives. These attacks occur occasionally in female-bonded species in the wild (e.g., Wasser 1983), but they are more common in captivity when the victim can neither escape nor effectively fight back once she is cornered (e.g., de Waal 1978; Alexander and Bowers 1969). In the wild, such attacks may be more costly both because they often require repeated chasing and because a male relative or long-term associate of the victim may intervene and attack the perpetrators (e.g., Kaplan 1978; Watanabe 1979; Smuts 1985). Because group membership is often unstable in captive groups, male intervention on behalf of relatives and associates may be less common in the wild.

These examples indicate that the lower frequency of intense intrasexual aggression among females than among males depends, at least in part, on differences in the context of male-male versus female-female conflicts

rather than on inherent sex differences in the potential for violent combat.

Sex Differences in Types of Agonistic Interventions

In addition to sex differences in the context and frequency of aggression, researchers have also considered sex differences in patterns of aggression. One such pattern involves interference by third parties in dyadic disputes. It takes two forms: (1) intervention on behalf of a victim (loser support), and (2) support for the aggressor (winner support). In a study of captive chimpanzees, de Waal (1984) reported that adult male interventions involved a significantly higher proportion of winner support than those of adult females, who generally supported losers. Furthermore, females usually supported relatives and friends, whereas males sometimes intervened against their closest associates. Based on these quantitative findings and qualitative observations of the outcomes of interventions, de Waal concluded that males used interventions to form opportunistic alliances that might increase status, whereas females intervened to protect vulnerable group members and to maintain peaceful relations within the group.

Although these sex differences are intriguing, no evidence indicates that they hold for primates in general. Both males and females show winner support and loser support, depending on the circumstances. For example, young adult male baboons sometimes support winners in an opportunistic manner, but older males tend to support their stable coalition partners, whether or not the partner is winning or losing a dispute (Smuts 1985). Similarly, male macaques tend to support winners (Bernstein and Ehardt 1985) except when they intervene to protect matrilineal kin who are the victims of aggression (e.g., Kaplan 1978). In baboons and macaques, adult males consistently support losers when the victim is a close female associate or one of her offspring (e.g., Kurland 1977; Chapais 1983b; Seyfarth 1978; Smuts 1985). Finally, even among the chimpanzees studied by de Waal, patterns of male intervention varied depending on the circumstances. When vying for rank, males supported winners, but once a male had firmly established the alpha position, he shifted toward loser support (de Waal 1984).

Females, like males, may support either winners or losers, depending on the context. In cercopithecines, females intervene on behalf of relatives most often, and when they do so, they support both winners and losers (e.g., Datta 1983a, 1983b). However, females also support unrelated females against other females. When this occurs, they generally support higher-ranking aggressors. These alliances with higher-ranking females appear to help females maintain or enhance their own status. Finally, females sometimes support unrelated females and immatures when they are victims of aggression by adult males.

Thus, both males and females are capable of opportunistic alliances and defense of victims, depending on the circumstances. It is therefore inappropriate to conclude that males in general are more concerned with winning than are females or that females are more concerned with protecting friends and relatives than are males.

Observed Behavior versus Behavioral Potentials

The examples discussed earlier clearly demonstrate, in both females and males, a potential for agonistic behaviors typically shown by the opposite sex. Observations of nonhuman primates suggest that, as among humans, expression of behavioral potentials may be inhibited in the presence of members of the opposite sex and released in their absence. Two sets of findings illustrate this point.

First, experiments with captive macaques and squirrel monkeys have shown that, in the absence of females, males exhibit a wide variety of infant caretaking behaviors that rarely occur when females are present (Vaitl 1977; Snowdon and Suomi 1982). For instance, when male and female rhesus macaques were individually exposed to a distressed infant, both responded

with equal solicitude. When the experiment was repeated with male-female pairs, the females showed caretaking behaviors but the males did not, and some actively avoided the infants (Gibber 1981). Second, in the absence of males, some females in all-female groups adopt behavior typical of the male or males in bisexual groups. Examples include wild rhesus females who displayed at strange males (Neville 1968), immature rhesus females who showed the typical male foot-clasp mount (Goldfoot, Wallen, and Neff 1984), and female hamadryas who adopted the centripetal social role normally taken by the single breeding male (Stammbach 1978). Thus, the fact that a behavior has been observed only among males or only among females does not necessarily imply that members of the opposite sex are unable to perform the behavior or lack the motivation to do so.

Conclusion: The Study of Sex Differences

There is a widespread tendency to interpret sex differences in terms of qualities or traits inherent to males and females. So, for example, if males are observed to injure one another more often than females, and if females are observed to support victims more often than males do, this difference is attributed to the fact that males are more aggressive than females and that females are more protective than males. In other words, intrinsic sex differences in temperament are used to explain sex differences in behavior. This is circular reasoning, analagous to "explaining" a behavior in terms of instinct, which, to use a memorable phrase, "is just another name for an inscrutable behavior" (Itani and Nishimura 1973:23).

The examples discussed earlier suggest that, in studying behavioral sex differences, it is useful to shift attention away from intrinsic properties of individuals and toward social interactions and the contexts in which they take place (see also Fedigan 1982). By examining how, and in what situations, the behaviors of females and males are similar and different, primatologists can begin to develop testable hypotheses about why these patterns occur.

BIBLIOGRAPHY

Alexander, B. K., and J. M. Bowers. 1969. Social Organization of a Troop of Japanese Monkeys in a Two-qcre Enclosure. *Folia Primatologica* 10:230-42.

Bercovitch, F. B. 1983. Time Budgets and Consortships in Olive Babboons (*Papio Anubis*). *Folia Primatologica* 41:180-190.

Bernstein, I. S. 1971. Activity Profiles of Primate Groups. In *Behavior of Nonhuman Primates*, vol. 3, eds. A. M. Schrier and F. Stollnitz. New York: Academic Press.

Bernstein, I. S., and C. L. Erhardt. 1972. Daily Activity Cycles and Weather Influences on a Pigtail Monkey Group. *Folia Primatologica* 18:390-415.

———. 1980. Activity Patterns in a Stumptail Macaque Group (*Macaca artoides*). *Folia Primatologica* 33:20-45.

———. 1985. Agonistic Aiding : Kinship, Rank, and Sex Influence. *American Journal of Primatology* 8:37-52.

Bernstein, I. S., L. Williams, and M. Ramsay. 1983. The Expression of Aggression in Old World Monkeys. *International Journal of Primatology* 4:113-25.

Bernstein, I. S., T. P. Gordon, and R. M. Rose. 1974. Aggression and Social Control in Rhesus Monkey (*Macaca mulatta*) Groups Revealed in Group Formulation Studies. *Folia Primatologica* 21:81-107.

Boggess, J. 1980. Intermale Relations and Troop Male Membership Changes in Langurs *Presbytis entellus* in Nepal. *International Journal of Primatology* 1:233-74.

Burton-Jones, N. G., and J. Trollope. 1968. Social Behavior of Stump-tail Macaques in Captivity. *Primates.* 9:365-94.

Bygott, J. D. 1979. Agonistic Behavior, Dominance, and Social Structure in Wild Chimpanzees of the Gombe National Park. In *The Great Apes*, edited by D. A Hamburg and E. R. McCown. Menlo Park, CA: Benjamin/Cummings.

Chapais, B. 1983a. Reproductive Activity in Relation to Male Dominance and the Likelihood of Ovulation in Rhesus Monkeys. *Behav. Ecol. Sociobiol.* 12:215-28.

———. 1983b. Structure of the Birth Season Relationship Among Adult Male and Female Rhesus Monkeys. In *Primate Social Relationships: An Integrated Approach,* edited by R. A. Hinde. Oxford: Blackwell.

Charles-Dominique, P. 1974. Aggression and Territoriality in Nocturnal Prosimians. In *Primate Aggression, Territoriality, and Xenophobia,* ed. Ralph L. Holloway. New York: Academic Press.

Cheney, D.L., and R. M. Seyfarth. 1983. Non-random Dispersal in Free-ranging Vervet Monkeys: Social and Genetic Consequences. *American Naturalist* 122:392-412.

Chivers, D. J. 1969. On the Daily Behavior and Spacing of Howling Monkey Groups. *Folia Primatologica* 10:48-102.

Clarke, M. R. 1983. Infant-killing and Infant Disappearance Following Male Takeovers in a Group of Free-ranging Howling Monkeys (*Alouatta Palliata*) in Costa Rica. *American Journal of Primatology* 5:241-47.

Clutton-Brock, T. H., F. E. Guinness, and S. D. Albon. 1982. *Red Deer: Behavior and Ecology of Two Sexes.* Chicago: University of Chicago Press.

Coe, C. L., and L. A. Rosenblum. 1984. Male Dominance in the Bonnet Macaque: A Malleable Relationship. In *Social Cohesion: Essays Toward a Sociophysiological Perspective,* edited by P. Barchar and S. P. Mendoza. Westport, CT: Greenwood Press.

Collins, D. A., C. D. Busse, and J. Goodall. 1984. Infanticide in Two Populations of Savannah Baboons. In *Infanticide: Comparative and Evolutionary Perspectives,* edited by G. Hausfater and S. B. Hrdy. Hawthorne, NY: Aldine.

Datta, S. B. 1983a. Patterns of Agonistic Interference. In *Primate Social Relationships: An Integrated Approach,* edited by R. A. Hinde. Oxford: Blackwell.

———. 1983b. Relative Power and the Acquisition of Rank. In *Primate Social Relationships: An Integrated Approach,* edited by R. A. Hinde. Oxford: Blackwell.

Dittus, W. 1977. The Social Regulation of Population Density and Age-sex Distribution in the Toque Monkey. *Behaviour* 63:281-322.

Drickamer, L. C. 1974. Quantitative Observation of Behavior in Free-ranging *Macaca mulatta*: Methodology and Aggression. *Behaviour* 55:209-36.

Dunbar, R. I. M. 1984. *Reproductive Decisions.* Princeton: Princeton University Press.

Durham, N. M. 1969. Sex Differences in Visual Threat Displays of West African Vervets. *Primates* 10:91-95.

Fedigan, L. 1982. *Primate Paradigms: Sex Roles and Social Bonds.* Montreal: Eden Press.

French, M. 1985. *Beyond Power: On Women, Men, and Morals.* New York: Summit.

Gibber, J. R. 1981. Infant-directed Behaviors in Young Rhesus Monkeys. Ph.D. dissertation, University of Wisconsin-Madison.

Goldfoot, D. A., K. Wallen, and D. A. Neff. 1984. Social Influences on the Display of Sexually Dimorphic Behavior in Rhesus Monkeys: Isosexual Rearing. *Archives of Sexual Behavior* 13:395-412.

Harcourt, A. H., and K. J. Stewart. 1983. Interactions, Relationships, and Social Structure: The Great Apes. In *Primate Social Relationships: An Integrated Approach,* edited by R. A. Hinde. Oxford: Blackwell.

Harvey, P. H., M. Kavanagh, and T. H. Clutton-Brock. 1978. Sexual Dimorphism in Primate Teeth. *Journal Zool. Soc. Lond.* 186:475-85.

Hausfater, G. 1972. Intergroup Behavior of Free-ranging Rhesus Monkeys (*Macaca mulatta*). *Folia Primatologica* 18:78-107.

Henzi, S. P., and J. W. Lucas. 1980. Observations on the Intergroup Movement of Adult Vervet Monkeys (*Cercopithecus aethiops*). *Folia Primatologica* 33:220-35.

Hrdy, S. B. 1977. *The Langurs of Abu.* Cambridge: Harvard University Press.

———. 1981. *The Woman that Never Evolved.* Cambridge: Harvard University Press.

Itani, J., and A. Nishimura. 1973. The Study of Infrahuman Culture in Japan. *In Symposia of the Fourth Congress of the International Primatological Society,* vol. 1: *Precultural Primate Behavior,* edited by E. Menzel. Basel: S. Karger.

Izawa, K. 1980. Social Behavior of the Wild Black-caped Capuchin (*Cebus apella*). *Primates* 20:443-67.

Jolly, A. 1966. *Lemur Behavior.* Chicago: University of Chicago Press.

Kaplan, J. N., A. Winship-Ball, and L. Sim. 1978. Maternal Discrimination of Infant Vocalizations in the Squirrel Monkey. *Primates* 19:187-93.

Kaplan, J. R. 1978. Fight Interference and Altruism in Rhesus Monkeys. *American Journal of Physical Anthropology* 47:241-49.

Koyama, N. 1970. Changes in Dominance and Rank and Division of a Wild Japanese Monkey Troop in Arishiyama. *Primates* 11:335-90.

Kurland, J. A. 1977. Kin section in Japanese Monkey. In *Contributions to Primatology,* vol. 12. Basel: S. Karger.

Lindburg, D. G. 1971. The Rhesus Monkey in Northern India: An Ecological and Behavioral Study. In *Primate Behavior,* vol. 2, ed. L. A. Rosenblum. New York: Academic Press.

Loy, J. K., G. Keifer, and C. Conoway. 1984. The Behavior of Gonadectomized Rhesus Monkeys. In *Contributions to Primatology,* vol. 20. Basel: S. Karger.

Marsden, H.M. 1968. Agonistic Behavior of Young Rhesus Monkeys After Changes Induced in Social Rank of Their Mothers. *Animal Behavior.* 16:38-44.

Meikle, D. B., and S. H. Vessey. 1981. Nepotism Among Rhesus Monkey Brothers. *Nature* 294:160-61.

Moore, J. 1985. Demography and Sociality in Primates. Ph.D. dissertation, Harvard University.

Nagel, U., and H. Kummer. 1974. Variation in Cercopithecoid Aggressive Behavior. In *Primate Aggression, Territoriality, and Xenophobia,* edited by R. L. Holloway. New York: Academic Press.

Neville, M. K. 1968. A Free-ranging Rhesus Monkey Troop Lacking Males. *Journal of Mammology* 49:771-78.

Poirier, F. E. 1970. The Nilgiri Langur (*Presbytis johnii*) of South India. In *Primate Behavior: Developments in Field and Laboratory Research,* vol. 1, edited by L. A. Rosenblum. New York: Academic Press.

———. 1974. Colobine Aggression: A Review. In *Primate Aggression, Territoriality, and Xenophobia: A Comparative Perspective,* ed. R. H. Holloway. New York: Academic Press.

Riss, D. C., and J. Goodall. 1977. The Recent Rise to Alpha Rank in a Population of Free-living Chimpanzees. *Folia Primatologica* 27:134-51.

Sapolsky, R. M. 1983. Endocrine Aspects of Social Instability in the Olive Baboon (*Papio anubis*). *American Journal of Primatology* 5:365-79.

Sekulic, R. 1981. The Significance of Howling in the Red Howler Monkey (*Alouatta seniculus*). *Folia Primatologica* 38:217-32.

Seyfarth, R. M. 1976. Social Relationships Among Adult Female Baboons. *Animal Behavior* 24:917-38.

————. 1978. Social Relationships Among Adult Male and Female Baboons, 2: Behaviour Throughout the Female Reproductive Cycle. *Behaviour* 64:227-47.

Silk, J. B. 1980. Kidnapping and Female Competition Among Female Bonnet Macaques. *Primates* 21:100-110.

Smuts, B. B. 1985. *Sex and Friendship in Baboons.* Hawthorne, NY: Aldine.

Snowdon, C. T., and S. J. Suomi. 1982. Paternal Behavior in Primates. In *Child Nurturance,* vol. 3: *Studies of Development in Nonhuman Primates,* edited by H. Fitzgerald, J. Mullins, and P. Gage. New York: Plenum Press.

Stammbach, E. 1978. On Social Differentiation in Groups of Captive Female Hamadryas Baboons. *Behaviour* 67:322-38.

Sussman, R. W., and A. F. Richard. 1974. The Role of Aggression Among Diurnal Prosimians. In *Primate Aggression, Territoriality, and Xenophobia,* ed. R. L. Holloway. New York: Academic Press.

Tiger, L. 1969. *Men in Groups.* New York: Vintage Books.

Vaitl, E. 1977. Social Context as a Structuring Mechanism in Captive Groups of Squirrel Monkeys *(Saimiri sciureus). Primates* 18:861-74.

Vandenbergh, J. G., and S. H. Vessey. 1968. Seasonal Breeding of Free-ranging Rhesus Monkeys and Related Ecological Factors. *Journal of Reproduction and Fertility* 15:71-79.

de Waal, F. B. M. 1978. Exploitative and Familiarity-Dependant Support Strategies in a Colony of Semi-free-living Chimpanzees. *Behaviour* 66:268-312.

————. 1982. *Chimpanzee Politics.* New York: Harper and Row.

————. 1984. Sex Differences in the Formulation of Coalitions among Chimpanzees. *Ethnol. Sociobiol.* 5:239-55.

Wasser, S. K. 1983. Reproductive Competition and Cooperation Among Female Yellow Baboons. In *Social Behavior of Female Verebrates,* edited by S. K. Wasser. New York: Academic Press.

Watanabe, K. 1979. Alliance Formation in a Free-ranging Troop of Japanese Macaques. *Primates* 20:459-74.

Whitten, P. L., and E. O. Smith. 1984. Patterns of Wounding in Stumptail Macaques *(Macaca arctoids). Primates* 25:326-36.

Wilson, A. P., and R. C. Boelkins. 1970. Evidence for Seasonal Variation in Aggressive Behavior by *Macaca mulatta. Animal Behavior* 18:719-24.

Witt, R., C. Schmidt, and J. Schmidt. 1981. Social Rank and Darwinian Fitness in a Multimale Group of Barbary Macaques *(Macaca sylvanus Linnaeus, 1758). Folia Primatologica* 36:201-11.

Wrangham, R. W. 1980. An Ecological Model of Female-bonded Primate Groups. *Behaviour* 75:262-300.

The Role of Women in Human Evolution

Margaret Ehrenberg

Human evolution has traditionally been discussed in terms of the role which "Man the Hunter" played in devising weapons and tools for catching and slaughtering animals for food, how he needed to walk upright on two feet to see his prey above the tall savanna grass, and how he was more successful than other species in his hunting exploits because he teamed up with other men and learnt the value of co-operation. And what of "woman", meanwhile? Was she sitting at home, twiddling her thumbs, waiting for "man" to feed her and increase his brain capacity and abilities until he became *"Homo sapiens sapiens?"* The argument went that as human evolution progressed, more and more time was needed to look after infants, so females no longer had time to hunt, and male co-operative hunting became essential in order that the men could bring enough food home to feed the family. As a result, male-female bonding in monogamous unions was an essential and a very early development. While most accounts of human evolution have assumed that all the advances in human physical and cultural development were led by men, a number of recent studies suggest alternative possibilities and have pointed out the vital role which must have been played by women.

Research into the earliest stages of human evolution is based on three strands of evidence. Physical anthropologists study the remains of early human skeletons, to assess the way in which they developed. For example, it is possible to tell from the structure of the legs and back whether an individual would have walked upright on two legs, or used the forearms for balance. Changes in the size of the skull through time give an indication of brain capacity. Secondly, the study of the behaviour of other animals, and especially primates, particularly those species closest to humans such as apes and chimpanzees, reveals some patterns which may have been shared by the earliest humans before cultural norms began to play an overriding part. For example, chimpanzees may be studied to see if males and females eat or collect different foods, or to find out whether they share any of the differences in child-care practices seen in human women and men. Thirdly, archaeological evidence for tools, settlements, environment and diet sheds light on the social and cultural development of the earliest humans.

Some scholars within all these three areas have turned away from the traditional male-dominated view of evolution and have begun to formulate an alternative model, allowing that female primates and hominids have played an important part, if not the key role, in the development of human behaviour. Different authors have stressed different factors in this development. Adrienne Zihlman[1] argues that changes in the environment were crucial in necessitating social and economic changes in human populations in order to exploit this environment efficiently. Sally Slocum[2] points out that the only division of labour by sex amongst other primates is that females take primary care of their young, while males tend to dominate in protecting the group. She argues that a division of labour in food collecting is therefore unlikely to have been a key feature of early human behaviour. Other feminist writers[3] suggest that the female's choice of a co-operative and gentle mate was a critical factor in human evolution, as the chances of survival were improved by caring more closely for near relatives; in all mammals, and especially in primates, this is much more a female task or trait.

Among the physical changes which took place in the early stages of human evolution were increases in the size of the brain and the teeth; a decrease in sexual dimorphism (difference in size between males and females); increased hairlessness over the body; and bipedalism, or walking on two feet, rather than using the forelimbs for support, as chimpanzees and apes do. While an infant chimpanzee can cling to its mother's cover of body hair, leaving her hands free for walking or carrying food, a young human or early hairless hominid would need to be carried by the mother: this seems a much more likely stimulus both to bipedalism and to the invention of tools for carrying the infant as well as food than is the need to see prey animals over tall savanna grass and to throw simple weapons at them, which has been the traditional explanation for these changes.

A key aspect of the debate about the evolution of sex-role behaviour centres on food collection, and the way in which females and males may have foraged for different foods. Many discussions, including those written by some feminist anthropologists, assume that from a very early stage in evolution females primarily gathered plant foods, while males mainly hunted animals, the pattern usual in modern hunter-gatherer societies. Many recent arguments about other aspects of the role played by females in human social and technological evolution depend on this belief, even though it is rarely argued out fully. At one end of the scale other primates show little evidence for differences in food collecting behaviour between females and males, while at the other all modern foragers apparently divide subsistence tasks on the basis of sex. The question, therefore, is when and why this difference came about, and whether looking after young offspring would have a limiting effect on hunting by females. One view[4] suggests that although males unburdened by young might have caught meat more often than females, a regular division of labour would probably have come

quite late in human evolution, as the physical differences between females and males are insufficient to make one sex or the other more suitable for either task. Recent work has also questioned whether meat actually filled a significant part of the early human diet, suggesting that this would have been far more like that of other primates, based almost entirely on a wide range of plant foods. What meat was eaten in the earliest phases of the Palaeolithic was probably scavenged, rather than hunted. Both these factors are problematic for the traditional view, as they suggest that hunting was neither an important factor in physical evolution, nor in the social and economic balance between female and male activities. Both sexes would have obtained vegetable foods and occasional meat, and brought some of their day's collection back to the homebase for sharing.

If there was little division of labour in the earliest phase of human development, when and why did it become usual? Two chronological points may have provided possible contexts. Initially, hominids would have been content to catch small game or to scavenge meat caught by other animals, or to collect those that had died naturally, but perhaps around 100,000 years ago they developed suitable tools and techniques for hunting large animals. While hunting small game would not have been hazardous, big-game hunting might often have resulted in death or injury to the hunter rather than the hunted. In small societies, such as these early human groups and present-day forager societies, every unexpected death is a serious blow to the viability of the community, particularly the death of women of child-bearing age. Mobility would also have been more important in hunting large game; the hunter would have to move rapidly and quietly, with hands free to throw a spear or shoot an arrow. It would not be possible to do this while carrying a bag or basket of gathered food, nor a young child, who might cause an additional hazard by making a noise at a crucial moment. Thus gathering and hunting become incompatible as simultaneous occupations; pregnant women and those carrying very small infants would have found hunting difficult, though gathering is quite easily combined with looking after young children. It is therefore possible that at this stage women began to hunt less, until a regular pattern of dividing subsistence tasks was established.[5]

Another possible context for the origin of the division of labour[6] is the change in environment which hominids found when they first entered Europe. It is argued that this spread could not have occurred until the perceptual problems of coping with a new environment had been resolved, by splitting food foraging into separate tasks. During the Lower Palaeolithic in East Africa, plants and animals would have been abundant, so vegetable foods and small game would have provided plenty of easily obtainable food with only the occasional large game caught to supplement the diet. As the hominid population increased and went in search of new territory, some hominids moved north into Europe. There they encountered colder conditions in which plant foods were harder to come by, so meat would have formed a more significant part of their diet. If this problem was not serious enough to necessitate a solution when hominids first moved into Europe, it would have become so with the onset of the last glaciation when conditions became very much colder and vegetation more sparse (this period equates archaeologically with the Upper Palaeolithic). The time and danger involved in hunting large animals became more worthwhile, but would not have provided a regular, guaranteed source of food, and would have been more dangerous. A solution might have been for only part of the community to concentrate on hunting, while the rest continued gathering plants and small animals. It is likely that this division would usually have been on a female-male basis for the reasons already suggested.

On the other hand, more detailed studies of chimpanzee behaviour suggest that there may be slight differences in the food collecting behaviour of females and males of non-human primates, which could argue for an early gathering/hunting division.[7] Although chimpanzees eat very little animal flesh, males make nearly all the kills and eat more of the meat; however, termite fishing, involving the use of sticks as fishing rods to poke into the termite mounds, a skilled task requiring patience and simple tool use, is far more commonly carried out by females. Whether the "changing environment" theory or the latter argument is preferred, both hypotheses suggest that a division of labour on the basis of sex would have been an early development in human history.

Tool-using was once thought to be a distinctly human attribute, but in simple form it is now known to be shared with several of the higher primates, and even other animals and birds. Most early theories suggested that tool-using by humans was intimately linked with hunting, which in turn was assumed to be a male task, and that the earliest tools would have been spears for hunting animals and stone knives or choppers for butchery. This idea was partly encouraged by the archaeological evidence of the early stone tools, most of which are thought to have had such functions. However, this is partly a circular argument, as on the one hand the function of these tools is far from certain, and many would have been just as useful for cracking nuts or digging roots, and on the other, the very earliest tools would almost certainly have been made of wood, skins or other perishable material. Artefacts such as digging sticks, skin bags, nets, clubs and spears can be made entirely of organic materials, and would not have survived, so the extant stone tools are probably quite late in the sequence of hominid tool use. The evidence of tool use by other primates and by modern foragers, combined with a more balanced theoretical view, suggests that other factors and possibilities need to be considered.

One of the most significant human tools must be the container. Whether it be a skin bag, a basket, a wooden bowl or pottery jar, it allows us to carry items around or store them safely in one place. The container may have been one of the earliest tools to be invented, though unfortunately there is little archaeological evidence to demonstrate this. Chimpanzees can carry things in the skinfold in their groin, but when hominids became bipedal this skin was stretched and the fold was lost. The use of a large leaf or an animal skin, carried over one arm or the developing shoulder, or tied to the waist, might have replicated this lost natural carrier.[8] One of the most important things that a female hominid would need to carry would be her young offspring. The complex interaction of bipedalism, food gathering, the loss of hair for the infant to cling to, and changes in the structure of the toes which made them useless for clinging to its mother would have made it necessary for the mother to carry the child. The development of a sling for supporting the infant, found in almost all modern societies, including foraging groups, is likely to have been among the earliest applications of the container.

The first tools to aid in foraging and preparing foodstuffs are perhaps more likely to have been used in connection with plant foods and small animals than in the hunting of large mammals. The tools and actions required for termite fishing, for example, are not unlike those required for digging up roots more easily. Modern foraging groups often choose a particularly suitable stone to use as an anvil for cracking nuts, which they leave under a particular tree and then return to it on subsequent occasions. Higher primates also use stones for cracking nuts, so it is very likely that early hominids would have done this even before tools were used for hunting. The role of women as tool inventors, perhaps contributing many of the major categories of tools which are most essential even today, cannot be dismissed.

The introduction of food gathering, as opposed to each individual eating what food was available where it was found, was another significant advance which would both have necessitated and been made possible by the invention of the container. More food might be gathered than was needed immediately by one individual, either for giving to someone else or for later consumption. With the exception of parents feeding very young offspring, this behaviour is unusual among other animals and presumably would not have been common amongst the very earliest hominids, but gradually developed to become a hallmark of human behaviour. Another change would have involved carrying this food to a base, which would imply both conceptual and physical changes, made possible by the use of containers, and may also have made it necessary to walk on two legs, leaving the hands free to carry the food, either directly or in containers. The development of consistent sharing, not only with offspring but with others in the group, and exchanging food brought from different environments of savanna and forest would have been a stage towards living in regular social groups.

Environmental changes would also have led to social changes within early hominid groups. In savanna grassland, as opposed to forest, it would have been more difficult to find safe places to sleep overnight, and water would have been harder to obtain. Once a suitable location was discovered, there would have been a greater tendency to remain there as long as possible rather than sleeping in a different place each night, thus introducing the idea of a homebase.

Women also played a key role in social development. A major difference between human development and that of other animals is the greater length of time during which infants need to be cared for and fed: this has probably contributed to a number of human characteristics, including food sharing and long-term male-female bonding. The sharing of food between mother and offspring would necessarily have continued for longer in early hominids than in other primates, and it is argued that when a mammal too large to be consumed by the hunters alone was killed, the males would have shared it with those who had shared with them in their youth, that is their mothers and sisters, rather than with their sexual partners. This argument is supported by a primate study[9] which shows that banana sharing almost always takes place within matrifocal groups rather than between sexual partners. This has important implications for the primacy or otherwise of monogamy and marriage. Several scholars have also pointed out that in this situation the female would choose to mate with a male who was particularly sociable and willing to share food with his partner while she was looking after a very young infant. As well as preferring those most willing to share, females would choose those males who appeared to be most friendly. Not surprisingly, female chimpanzees will not mate with males who are aggressive towards them. The more friendly-looking males would probably have been smaller, or nearer in size to the female, and would have had less pronounced teeth, and therefore have been less aggressive-looking. Over thousands of years this female sexual preference would have led to gradual evolutionary changes in favour of smaller, less aggressive, males.

The stronger tie between mother and offspring caused by the longer period of time during which human infants need to be cared for would have resulted in closer social bonds than are found in other species. The primary bond between mother and offspring would be supplemented by sibling ties between sisters and brothers growing up together. Older offspring would be encouraged or socialised to contribute towards the care of younger siblings, including grooming, sharing food, playing and helping to protect them. The natural focus of such a group would clearly be the mother rather than, as is so often supposed, any male figure. Moreover, this group behaviour would lead to increased sociability in the male as well as in the species in general. The role of the female, both in fostering this increased sociability in the species and as the primary teacher of technological innovations during this long period of caring, must be recognised.

An increase in human sociability, and particularly female sociability, would have had a number of other positive side-effects. As a result of a mutual willingness to share food and food resources, each individual would have had more access to overlapping gathering areas when a particular resource was abundant. This in turn might greatly increase the chances of the offspring being well fed and therefore surviving, and thus of the survival of the species in general. As the ability to communicate precisely increased with the development of language, it would have become possible for humans to have ordered social relationships with more individuals and other groups. This would have evolved into a pattern very similar to that found in modern foraging groups, many of which include distant relations who regularly meet up with other groups in the course of their annual movements. Males who had moved out of the matrifocal group in order to mate would have learnt a pattern of friendly contact with their ancestral females when they met them in the course of their foraging.

It can therefore be argued that the crucial steps in human development were predominantly inspired by females. These include economic and technological innovations, and the role of females as the social centre of groups. This contrasts sharply with the traditional picture of the male as protector and hunter, bringing food back to a pair-bonded female. That model treats masculine aggression as normal, assumes that long-term, one-to-one, male-female bonding was a primary development, with the male as the major food provider, and that male dominance was inherently linked to hunting skills. None of these patterns, however, accords with the behaviour of any but the traditional Western male. Other male primates do not follow this pattern, nor do non-Western human groups, in particular those foraging societies whose lifestyle in many ways accords most closely with putative early human and Palaeolithic cultural patterns.

NOTES

1. Zihlman, 1981.
2. Slocum, 1975.
3. For example, Tanner, 1981; Martin and Voorhies, 1975.
4. Zihlman, 1981; Isaac and Crader, 1981.

5. Zihlman, 1978; the same arguments are used by Friedl, 1975 and 1978, who explains in more detail than here why present-day foragers divide food collecting tasks along gender lines.
6. Dennell, 1983, 55.
7. McGrew, 1981; Goodall, 1986.
8. Tanner and Zihlman, 1976.
9. McGrew, 1981, 47.

REFERENCES

Dennell, R. 1983. *European Economic Prehistory.* London: Academic Press.
Friedl, E. 1975. *Women and Men: An Anthropologist's View.* New York: Holt, Rinehart and Winston.
———. 1978. "Society and sex roles." *Human Nature* 1: 68–75.
Goodall, J. 1986. *The Chimpanzees of Gombe: Patterns of Behavior.* Cambridge, MA: Harvard University Press.
Isaac, G. and Crader, D. 1981. "To what extent were early hominids carnivorous?" In Teleki, G. (ed.). *Omnivorous Primates: Gathering and Hunting in Human Evolution.* New York: Columbia University Press.
Martin, M. K. and Voorhies, B. 1975. *Female of the Species.* New York: Columbia University Press.
McGrew, W. 1981. "The female chimpanzee as a human evolutionary prototype." In Dahlberg, Frances (ed.). *Woman The Gatherer.* New Haven: Yale University Press.
Slocum, S. 1975. "Woman the gatherer: male bias in anthropology." In Reiter, Rayna R. (ed.). *Toward an Anthropology of Women.* New York: Monthly Review Press.
Tanner, N. 1981. *On Becoming Human.* Cambridge: Cambridge University Press.
Tanner, N. and Zihlman, A. 1976. "Woman in evolution. Part 1: Innovation and selection in human origins." *Signs* 1(3): 585–608.
Zihlman, A. 1978. "Women in evolution. Part 2: Subsistence and social organization among early hominids." *Signs* 4: 4–20.
———. 1981. "Woman as shapers of human adaption." In Dahlberg, Frances (ed.). *Woman the Gatherer.* New Haven: Yale University Press.

Gender and War:
Are Women Tough Enough for Military Combat?
Lucinda J. Peach

INTRODUCTION

Women's participation in the U.S. military was spotlighted during the Persian Gulf War. Since that time, military personnel, government officials, public policy makers, and members of the public have given increased scrutiny to the issue of whether women should participate in military combat.

A number of arguments have been made over the years to justify the exclusion of women from military combat. Although certain positions in the military designated as

Original material prepared for this text.

"combat" have been opened up to women in recent years, especially on combat aircraft and naval vessels (except for submarines), the vast majority of combat positions remain closed to them.

The definition of "direct ground combat" that was adopted in 1993 bars women from units that engage the enemy with weapons on the ground while exposed to hostile fire *and* which involve substantial probability of direct physical contact with hostile forces (see Schmitt 1994a; Schmitt 1994b: A18; Lancaster 1994: A1; Pine 1994: A5). Under the new policy, exposure to risk, *alone,* is an insufficient ground for excluding women from a particular assignment. Nevertheless, women are barred from almost all assignments that involve operating offensive, line-of-sight weapons, and from all positions involving ground fighting. This includes armor, infantry, and field artillery, the three specialities that are considered the core of combat (see Schmitt 1994b; Schmitt 1994: A7). In consequence, women have been excluded from certain benefits and opportunities for promotion and advancement within (and outside) the military that are available only to those with combat experience. The exclusion also functions to limit the numbers of women who can participate in military service (because of the relatively small percentage of positions that *are* available to them). In addition, the exclusion of women from combat contributes to other forms of discrimination against women, both within and outside of the military.

In this essay, I will argue that all of these arguments have been based more on "gender ideology"—that is, on assumptions, prejudices, stereotypes and myths about male and female "natures" and "natural" or "proper" sex roles and behaviors (see Code 1991: 196)—than on empirically verifiable gender differences that demonstrate women's inability to competently perform combat roles in the U.S. military.

Two ideological myths about gender in particular underlie many of the arguments against according combat positions to women. First, identification of the military as masculine makes males the standard by which females are assessed. The male standard operates, sometimes explicitly, but more often implicitly, to perpetuate the stereotype that women are out of place in the military, particularly in combat. Throughout history, war has been a theater in which men could prove their masculinity, and in which masculinity has been deemed a necessary prerequisite to success. During his 1992 presidential election campaign, for example, Bill Clinton's lack of military experience received a lot of attention, some of it based on the view that Clinton's lack of exposure to war made him unfit for presidential leadership. The perception that the virtues of "manliness" are necessary for effective combat soldiering, and that women are incapable or ill-suited to the development of these virtues, has contributed to the maintenance of women's exclusion from most combat assignments.

The second myth used as a rationale to exclude women from combat duty suggests that the purpose for which men fight is to protect women (see Stiehm 1989: 6–7; Kornblum 1984). Women, according to the myth, are the weaker sex and need to be protected by strong men; they are victims dependent upon men rather than autonomous agents who are competent to defend themselves. Members of the military have expressed "a special regard for women who must be protected as the symbolic vessel of femininity and motherhood" (Karst 1991: 536).

These myths are supported by the argument that integrating women into combat would be deleterious to combat effectiveness and the military's ability to mobilize in time of war (Hooker 1989: 36; Kelly 1984: 103; Mitchell 1989: 159; Marlowe 1983: 194; Rogan 1981: 21). Women's supposed physical, physiological, and psychological characteristics are offered as the basis for this argument. Although none of these rationales, alone or combined, provides an adequate ethical basis for maintaining the combat restrictions for women, their popularity and prominence makes it important to note how each of them is based on ideological notions of gender that frequently are inconsistent with the realities of gender difference.

The most common arguments in support of the view that the inclusion of women would diminish combat readiness and effectiveness are that: (1) women lack the necessary physical strength to perform adequately; (2) their capacity for pregnancy and childbearing makes them inappropriate combatants; and (3) women's participation in combat units would reduce unit cohesion by disrupting male bonding and promoting sexual fraternization. Let us examine each of these arguments in greater detail.

PHYSICAL STRENGTH

Military effectiveness is often said to be compromised by women's lack of physical strength and stamina relative to men (Mitchell 1989: 156–62; Kantrowitz 1991; Gordon and Ludvigson 1991: 20–22, D'Amico 1990: 6). Military personnel have testified before Congress that few women would meet the physical standards for combat duty (Hackworth 1991: 25; Appropriations Hearings 1991; Cramsie 1983: 562). Women's purported inferior physical capability is voiced especially loudly by enlisted men, who deny that women have the strength necessary for fighting on the front lines (see Kantrowitz 1991: 23). For example, one of the reasons integrated basic training was ended in the Army in 1982 was because of enlisted men's complaints that women were holding them back (see Coyle, 1989; Stiehm 1985b: 209; Rogan 1981: 27). A study of enlisted service personnel's attitudes toward women in the Army in 1975 indicated that only about 50 percent of men interviewed thought women had the physical strength for combat (see Mitchell 1989: 157–58; Stiehm 1989: 102).

There is no question that, in general, *most* men are physically stronger than *most* women. Military studies document that men have some advantages in upper body and leg strength, cardiovascular capacity, and lean muscle, which make men "more fitted for physically intense combat" (see Mitchell 1989: 157; Kelly 1984: 100–101; Marlowe 1983: 190; Hooker 1989: 44). However, these tests generally do not also indicate the fact that some women *are* capable of meeting the standards established for men. Nor do they typically take into consideration the disparities in prior physical training and physical conditioning that men and women have undergone. Army reports reveal that some women *do* have the requisite upper body strength to qualify for combat. In addition, *some* women are stronger than *some* men. Women have performed well in the limited number of combat-type situations in which they have been tested. However, because the

combat exclusion has precluded the possibility of obtaining data about women's physical performance under actual combat conditions, gender-based assumptions and prejudices have dominated policy discussions.

The assumption that women lack the physical strength necessary for combat is ideological because it often persists in the face of direct evidence to the contrary. The nature of modern combat, with its emphasis on high-technology equipment, makes the issue of physical strength far less important than it was in an era when war involved primarily hand-to-hand combat. Physical size and strength are of minimal, if any, consideration, when weapons are being fired at the touch of a button from a location far removed from the combat theatre. As Judith Stiehm argues, the question should not be "how strong women are, but how strong they need to be" (1989: 219). The positive experiences with using women in traditionally all-male fields, such as police and fire fighting forces, which require similar skills to combat, support the conclusion that women are capable of performing satisfactorily in physical defense of self and others in situations involving the use of lethal force (see McDowell 1992; Segal 1982: 286; Karst 1991: 539; Kornblum 1984: 392–93).

Nonetheless, skeptics point out that "there is no real evidence that technology has in fact reduced the need for physical strength among military men and women. What evidence there is shows that many military jobs still require more physical strength than most women possess" (Mitchell 1989: 157). To the contrary, although there are some combat positions that most women are unable to perform satisfactorily because of inadequate physical strength, there is a considerable range of combat positions that many, if not most, women *are* qualified to perform. Although sheer physical strength may occasionally be an issue when technology fails to function properly, more often than not, the physical strength issue is no longer a legitimate reason for excluding women from combat duty. In addition, physical strength is only one of many factors that needs to be assessed in determining the capability of persons for military combat.

Several proposals have been forwarded, by military personnel and others, to assign combat positions on the basis of the physical strength required to perform them, as at least one of several relevant criterion, rather than exclusively on the basis of gender (Appropriations Hearings 1991: 865; Roush 1990: 11–12; Coyle 1989: 31; Proxmire 1986: 110; Segal 1983: 110; Segal 1982: 270–71; Nabors 1982: 51; Rogan 1981: 306).[1] Such proposals would result in a fairer and more accurate measure of "fit" between persons and assignments than the current reliance on gender difference. The main rationale used by military officers for their failure to implement such a gender-neutral scheme is that it may not be "cost-effective" (see Association 1991: 54; Rogan 1981: 20). However, the military's failure to demonstrate how gender-neutral standards for assignments would be financially infeasible suggests that the maintenance of the combat exclusion is based more on the continuing force of gender ideology than on financial expense or damage to military effectiveness.

Sometimes the protection myth serves to reinforce the physical strength argument by portraying women as "the weaker sex" who need to be protected from the risks of being raped and physically violated in war. It is sometimes argued that the presence of women in combat would cause male soldiers to respond by becoming more concerned about protecting them than fighting the enemy, thus compromising combat effectiveness (see Barkalow 1990: 260 (quoting Colonel Houston's comment that men's emotional commitment to recapture POW women would be so intense and extreme as to cause fighting to escalate); Beecraft 1989: 43; Van Creveld 1993). Here, the protection rationale is dominant.

During the Gulf War, the press raised the argument that women soldiers would be psychologically unable to handle being taken as prisoners of war, especially because of the greater possibility that they would be raped and otherwise sexually abused (see Nabors 1982: 59; Rogan 1981: 26). Here, the assumption is that women are less stable than men emotionally, and are thus less well equipped to handle the extreme psychological stresses of combat (Mitchell 1989: 7, 182–92; Marlowe 1983: 195).

There is no factual basis for the conclusion that female combatants would be any weaker or more vulnerable than men under such circumstances. To the contrary, the experience of military women such as Air Force Major Rhonda Cornum, a flight surgeon whose aircraft was shot down during the Gulf War, reveals a very matter-of-fact attitude about survival in the face of physical injury and sexual abuse at the hands of her captors. Cornum's response stands as a testament to the ability of military women to cope as POWs (see Cornum 1992).

The notion that women in the military are in *need* of protection is based on stereotypes of male machismo and female weakness and vulnerability. Further, the assumption that males are *able* to protect military women is itself a myth, since women are too integrated throughout the armed forces to be protected by their exclusion from combat. (Providing women soldiers with arms and training in self-defense would provide a measure of protection against sexual violence that they would not otherwise have.) The rationale that women need to be protected from becoming POWs because of the risk that their torture would include sexual abuse ignores the reality that men as well as women are raped in war, and that women are already subject to such sexual violence at home or by their fellow soldiers on or near the field of combat. In addition, military women are susceptible to being captured and raped during war, regardless of whether they are themselves engaged in combat.

Also related to the physical strength argument is the assumption that men are naturally more aggressive than women, and that the "natural aggressiveness" of males would be "softened" by women's participation in battle (Mitchell 1989: 7; Marlowe 1983: 191; Tuten

1982: 255). More recently, some scholars have challenged the argument that women are innately less aggressive than men (see Rosoff 1991; Sunday 1991; Marquit 1991), while others observe the lack of evidence regarding women's psychological weakness (see Gordon and Ludvigson 1991; Dillingham 1990: 227–28; Kornblum 1984: 398–99).

Many of those who conclude that men are "naturally" more aggressive than women rely on incomplete studies of *primates,* not humans, conducted by anthropologist Lionel Tiger. Tiger observed that male primates in the wild spend much of their time in groups organized to fight with outsiders, whereas female primates were engaged in grooming activities in pairs. Tiger's research has since been largely discredited by further research. Subsequent studies have revealed that females also engaged in collective aggressive action to protect their young, and that both males and females spend much of their time grooming (see Appropriations Hearings 1991: 981; Holm 1982: 95).

The evidence to support the claim of women's lesser aggression is very tenuous, especially after women soldiers demonstrated their competence in performing the psychologically demanding tasks required in combat duty during the Gulf War. But even assuming that women are less aggressive than men, there is still no evidence that it stems from biological causes rather than culture and socialization, which are malleable. The military has not offered empirical evidence to demonstrate that women cannot be trained to exhibit the same degree of aggressiveness that men exhibit. Nonetheless, the assumption that women are less aggressive continues to strengthen the myth of combat as a masculine institution of which only men are capable.

PREGNANCY AND MOTHERHOOD

One specific aspect of women's physiology that some have argued disrupts unit cohesion and consequently hampers combat effectiveness is pregnancy (Nabors 1982: 56–58; see Barkalow 1990: 238–41; Shields 1988: 108; Stiehm 1985b: 226; Rogan 1981: 256). The Army has expressed concern with the effects of pregnancy on "readiness," "mission accomplishment," and "deployability" (Mitchell 1989: 6, 166–71; see Tuten 1982: 251; Rogan 1981: 26; Stiehm 1985a). Until 1975, women were automatically discharged from the military as soon as their pregnancy was discovered. This contributed to high attrition rates for women in the armed services. In 1975, the Department of Defense (DOD) made such discharge for pregnancy voluntary (see Segal 1983: 207; Treadwell 1954: 200).

Pregnancy also arguably interferes with the ability of the armed forces to rapidly mobilize troops for combat, since it cannot be predicted in advance which women will be pregnant, and thus unavailable for deployment. Pregnancy continues to be an issue of concern, both in the military and among the public. A *Newsweek* poll conducted in 1991 revealed that 76 percent of the public is concerned about military women becoming pregnant and putting the fetus at risk (Hackworth 1991: 27). Pregnancy does account for a significant percentage of women's lost time, although military women lose *less* service time overall than do men for illness, drug and alcohol abuse, and disability (see D'Amico 1990: 8; Coyle 1989: 39; Shields 1988: 109; Kornblum 1984: 417–18).

Because of the way military units are currently structured, pregnancy does present a genuine difficulty in the full integration of all women into combat forces. Since military policy, at least in the Army, does not provide temporary replacements for pregnant personnel, the presence of pregnant women in a unit increases everyone else's work load, and consequently brings with it the risk of breeding resentment among coworkers. In addition, although there is no certainty that women desiring to get pregnant will be successful, some opponents of women combatants contend that enlisted women will use pregnancy as a means of avoiding combat duty.

Therefore, pregnancy may be a legitimate reason to exclude women from actually engaging in some forms of combat. However,

excluding *all* women from *all* positions designated as combat is far too extreme a
response. Most women are not pregnant most
of the time. Only about ten percent of service-
women are pregnant at any given time (see
Gordon and Ludvigson 1991: 22–23; Hackworth 1991: 27). Further, the experience of
pregnancy varies widely in affecting a
woman's job performance. Some women are
able to carry on their normal activities into
the latter stages of pregnancy. Most logistical
problems relating to pregnancy, such as
deployment plans, etc., can be satisfactorily
surmounted by careful planning.

The protection myth also operates here to
call into question the propriety of risking the
safety of the nation's child bearers by exposing them to the risks of combat. As with the
lack of data on gender-integrated units, there
have been no studies of the actual impact of
pregnancy on military effectiveness because
the combat exclusion has precluded the possibility of gathering data. Pregnancy is *one*
consideration that needs to be factored into
the analysis of how and whether to integrate
women into certain combat roles. But it does
not justify the stringency of the current
restrictions.

Related to the pregnancy issue is the symbolic, if not actual, role of women as mothers.
Motherhood and women's responsibilities to
their families are viewed as antithetical to
effective combat soldiering. The assumption
underlying this view is that women's proper
role is to be the center of family life. According to this perspective, women not only bear
the children, but are also primarily responsible for their care and nurture (see Mitchell
1989: 6, 171–76; Rogan 1981: 26; Segal 1982:
274–75, 281–82; Costin 1983: 305). The
media's promulgation of images of women
soldiers kissing their infants goodbye before
going off to the Gulf War, and its stories
about fathers left at home to care for children emphasized the unnaturalness of
female soldiers going off to combat (see
Enloe 1993: 201–27).

The influence of gender ideology on this
issue is evident in the view of Alexander

Webster, a chaplain for the Army National
Guard, who speculates about the "identity
confusion that must confront any would-be
woman warrior who pauses for a moment to
consider her potential for motherhood."
Webster also surmises that the paradigm of
the citizen soldier may have been destroyed
by the "social disruption and havoc among
families wreaked by the mobilization and
deployment of mothers of young children to
the theater of operations in the Persian Gulf"
(1991: 29). Webster continues: "Disturbing
images on television and in the print media
of mothers wrenched from their offspring
may be the most enduring from the Persian
Gulf War" (24–25). According to these ideological notions of gender, women need special protection because they are responsible,
in turn, for protecting their children. Notably
missing from this assessment is consideration
of the consequences of *fathers* being
"wrenched from their offspring," thus perpetuating the identification of women as the primary parent. Such testimony assumes that
mothers are more responsible for family life
than are fathers, so that it is women's military
involvement that is questionable, not men's,
whenever families are concerned.

Such ideological assumptions about the
gender of parenthood are widespread. Surveys reveal that the public continues to be
more willing to send young fathers into combat than young mothers. Even supporters of
combat roles for women have assumed that
mothers would be more reluctant to risk their
lives in combat than would men (see Campbell 1992: 18; Lieberman 1990: 219). Attrition
and reenlistment data for women indicate
that motherhood is a primary reason why
women leave the military. And surveys indicate that the large majority of service women
do want to have children (see Shields 1988:
109). Former Secretary of Defense Richard
Cheney argued that exempting all single parents and dual service-career couples from
deployment would weaken military capability
(see Campbell 1992: 18, 20). This problem
impacts more heavily on women, who comprise the larger percentage of single parents

in the military. Women's family obligations may thus present a practical problem for women's ability to carry out combat assignments, particularly for single mothers.

Several other factors need to be considered, however. Many military women are not mothers, and have no plans to become mothers. Most women entering the military are not (yet) mothers. The belief that women *are* essentially mothers is an outdated ideological assumption. It leads to the irrational result that men who are fathers can be required to participate in combat whereas women who are *not* mothers cannot (see Association 1991: 25; Segal 1982: 283). Such beliefs underlie the former Army prohibition on the enlistment of women who had children in certain age groups (see Treadwell 1954: 496).[2]

Further, although most women traditionally *have* taken primary responsibility for protecting and providing for their children, not all mothers are primary caretakers. Many families include alternative arrangements for child care that do not make the mother primarily responsible. Finally, tradition should not determine who *should* be responsible for national defense in time of war. Fathers have equal responsibility for protecting and providing for their children. Yet, since the Korean War, they have not been exempted from combat duty. In addition, the legislation mandating women's exclusion from combat does not exempt them from military *service* in time of war. Children of military parents are just as much in need of care and protection during wartime, regardless of whether their mothers are assigned to combat duty or some other position. In the absence of evidence indicating that combat jobs are more incompatible with being a wife and mother than a husband and father, families should be entitled to make their own decisions about child care in the event that the mother is called to serve in combat duty. Current military policy provides that if both parents are in the services, one can claim an exemption in the event that troops are deployed. There is no rational basis for the government to preempt the parents' right to choose based on a set of assumptions about motherhood.

UNIT COHESION AND MALE BONDING

Unit or troop "cohesion" is a function of interpersonal relationships between military leaders and their troops, and the leader's ability to create and sustain "those interpersonal skills that allow him to build strong ties with his men" (Gabriel 1982: 172–73). The argument that male soldiers will lose the camaraderie and team spirit necessary for unit cohesion if they are required to share their duties with women has been advanced as a reason to exclude women from military combat. For example, former Marine Corps Commandant Robert Barrows defends the notion of male bonding as a "real ... cohesiveness," a "mutual respect and admiration," and a "team work" that would be destroyed by the inclusion of women. "If you want to make a combat unit ineffective," he said, "assign some women to it" (Appropriations Hearings 1991: 985–96).

Although the argument about the indispensability of cohesion to effectiveness is persuasive, the view that the presence of women will damage the "male bonding" linked to that cohesion is exaggerated by the influence of gender ideology. This "influence" is often supported by outdated and anecdotal evidence, such as Tiger's largely discredited research (Mitchell 1989; Golightly 1987; Rogan 1981: 25; Hooker 1989: 45). In addition, the military has not studied the impact that integration of the forces has had on "male bonding" in actual combat for the past several years, nor has it made efforts to instill male–female or female–female bonding in its soldiers (see Stiehm 1989: 236; Stiehm 1985a:172).

The experience with female soldiers in the Persian Gulf War, as well as the limited studies that have been done in simulated combat and field conditions, indicate that the presence of women in combat units does not adversely affect combat effectiveness. The Army Research Institute conducted two of these studies, labelled "REFWAC" and "MAXWAC" (Johnson 1978; United States

Army Research Institute 1977). MAXWAC results showed that female ratios varying from 0 to 35 percent had no significant effect on unit performance. REFWAC results similarly showed that the presence of 10 percent female soldiers on a REFORGER ("Return of Forces to Germany") ten-day field exercise made no difference in the performance of combat support and combat service support units.

In addition, Navy Commander Barry Boyle, participating in Navy squadron preparations, Charles Moskos, observing an Army exercise in Honduras, and Constance Devilbliss, participating in rigorous Army exercises, reached similar conclusions that integrated units performed as effectively, if not more so, than all-male units (see Coyle 1989; Moskos 1985; Devilbliss 1985). Experience with women in combat in other nations, as well as the successful integration of women into police and other traditionally male-only professions, also provide useful analogies indicating that the participation of American military women in combat would not hamper unit or troop cohesion (Association 1991; Appropriations 1991; Goldman 1982a, b).

FRATERNIZATION

Women in uniform represent an anomaly to traditional social ordering based on traditional sex-gender distinctions, and thus to traditional sexual morality. Thus, in addition to their supposedly detrimental effect on male bonding, including women in combat roles is sometimes alleged to diminish troop effectiveness because of the inevitable sexual attraction and behavior that would follow from having mixed-gender units. Some express a fear that men will be preoccupied with winning the sexual favors of women rather than concentrating on their mission (Mitchell 1989: 176–78; Golightly 1987: 46; Rogan 1981: 27).

The fraternization argument ignores the capability of the sexes to interact with one another in nonsexual ways, particularly under the exigent circumstances of combat. The limited studies that have been conducted under simulated combat conditions indicate that fraternization does not hamper combat readiness or troop effectiveness. Studies show that gender-integrated combat units are as effective as all-male units, and that members of gender-integrated units develop brother-sister bonds rather than sexual ones.

Fraternization is most likely to be a problem where there is ineffective leadership. It is likely that unit bonding depends more on shared experiences, including sharing of risks and hardships, than on gender distinctions (see Karst 1991: 537, 543; Devilbliss 1985: 519; Opinion 1988: 138). Experience has shown that actual integration diminishes prejudice and fosters group cohesiveness more effectively than any other factor. It is thus likely that women's integration into combat forces would parallel that of black men into previously all-white forces during the 1950s and 1960s (see Moskos 1990: 74; Kornblum 1984: 412, 422; Segal 1983: 203–04, 206; Holm 1982: 257).

As the preceding discussion reveals, none of the primary rationales that have been forwarded to exclude women from combat roles provides a legitimate basis for maintaining the current restrictions on women's participation in combat. The analysis of these rationales suggests that the resistance of Congress, the courts, the military, and the public to removing the combat restrictions results more from gender ideology than from demonstrated evidence of women's inability to perform combat roles effectively.

Once outdated stereotypes and myths about women's capabilities and deficiencies are eliminated from consideration of the ethics of women in military combat, the current restrictions on combat roles for women are revealed to lack persuasive foundations. Only when the military begins assigning women to positions on the basis of gender-neutral standards for evaluating the degree of physical strength, psychological fortitude, bonding and troop cohesiveness necessary to perform combat roles can the issue of women in combat be addressed without the undue influence of ideological notions of gender.

NOTES

1. A standard based on physical strength rather than gender could be waived in emergency situations where rapid mobilization is necessary and individual testing would be inefficient (see Segal 1982: 270–71).
2. This policy was reversed in *Crawford v. Cushman*, 531 F.2d 1114 (2d Cir. 1976).

REFERENCES

Association of the Bar of the City of New York, "The Combat Exclusion Laws: An Idea Whose Time Has Gone," *Minerva*, Vol. 9, No. 4 (Winter, 1991), pp. 1–55 (Association).

Barkalow, Carol, *In the Men's House* (New York: Poseidon Press, 1990).

———. "Women Have What It Takes," *Newsweek* (August 5, 1991), p. 30.

Beecraft, Carolyn, "Personnel Puzzle," *Proceedings (of the U.S. Naval Institute)*, Vol. 115, No. 4 (April, 1989), pp. 41–44.

Campbell, D'Ann, "Combatting the Gender Gulf," *Temple Political and Civil Rights Law Review*, Vol. 1, No. 2 (Fall, 1992), reprinted in *Minerva*, Vol. X, Nos. 3–4 (Fall/Winter 1992), pp. 13–41.

Code, Lorraine, *What Can She Know? Feminist Theory and the Construction of Knowledge* (Ithaca, NY: Cornell University Press, 1991).

Cornum, Rhonda, *She Went to War: The Rhonda Cornum Story* (Novato, CA: Presidio Press, 1992).

Costin, Lela, "Feminism, Pacifism, Nationalism, and the United Nations Decade for Women," in Judith Stiehm (ed.), *Women and Men's Wars* (Oxford: Pergamon Press, 1983), pp. 301–16.

Coyle, Commander Barry, U.S. Navy, "Women on the Front Lines," *Proceedings (of the U.S. Military Institute)*, Vol. 115, No. 4 (April, 1989), pp. 37–40.

Cramsie, Jodie, "Gender Discrimination in the Military: The Unconstitutional Exclusion of Women From Combat," *Valparaiso Law Review*, Vol. 17 (1983), pp. 547–88.

D'Amico, "Women at Arms: The Combat Controversy," *Minerva*, Vol. 8, No. 2 (1990), pp. 1–19.

Devilbliss, M. C., "Gender Integration and Unit Deployment: A Study of G.I. Jo," *Armed Forces and Society*, Vol. 11, No. 3 (1985), pp. 523–52.

Dillingham, Wayne, "The Possibility of American Military Women Becoming Prisoners of War: Justification for Combat Exclusion Rules?" *Federal Bar News and Journal*, Vol. 37, No. 4 (1990), pp. 223–30.

Enloe, Cynthia, *The Morning After: Sexual Politics at the End of the Cold War* (Berkeley, CA: University of California Press, 1993).

Gabriel, Richard, *To Serve With Honor: A Treatise on Military Ethics and the Way of the Soldier* (Westport, CT: Greenwood Press, 1982).

Goldman, Nancy Loring (ed.), *Female Soldiers—Combatants or Noncombatants? Historical and Contemporary Perspectives* (Westport, CT: Greenwood Press, 1982a).

———. *The Utilization of Women in Combat: An Historical and Social Analysis of Twentieth-Century Wartime and Peacetime Experience* (Alexandria, VA: U.S.A.R.I., 1982b).

Golightly, Lieutenant Neil L., U.S. Navy, "No Right to Fight," *Proceedings (of the U.S. Naval Institute)*, Vol. 113, No. 12 (1987), pp. 46–49.

Gooch, Master Chief Sonar Technician Robert H., U.S. Navy, "The Coast Guard Example," *Proceedings (of the U.S. Naval Institute)*, Vol. 114, No. 5 (May, 1988), pp. 124–33.

Gordon, Marilyn and Mary Jo Ludvigson, "A Constitutional Analysis of the Combat Exclusion for Air Force Women," *Minerva: Quarterly Report on Women and the Military*, Vol. 9, No. 2 (1991), pp. 1–34.

Hackworth, Colonel David, "War and the Second Sex," *Newsweek* (August 5, 1991), pp. 24–28.

Holm, Maj. Gen. Jeanne, U.S.A.F. (Ret.), *Women in the Military* (Novato, CA: Presidio Press, 1982).

Hooker, Richard, "Affirmative Action and Combat Exclusion: Gender Roles in the U.S. Army," *Parameters: U.S. War College Quarterly*, Vol. 19, No. 4 (1989), pp. 36–50.

Hunter, Anne E. (ed.), *Genes and Gender VI: On Peace, War, and Gender: A Challenge to Genetic Explanations* (New York: Feminist Press, 1991).

Johnson, Cecil, et al., *Women Content in the Army: REFORGER (REFWAC 77)* (Alexandria, VA: U.S.A.R.I., 1978).

Kantrowitz, Barbara, "The Right to Fight," *Newsweek* (August 5, 1991), pp. 22–23.

Karst, Kenneth, "The Pursuit of Manhood and the Desegregation of the Armed Forces," *U.C.L.A. Law Review*, Vol. 38, No. 3 (1991), pp. 499–581.

Kelly, Karla, "The Exclusion of Women From Combat: Withstanding the Challenge," *Judge Advocate General Journal*, Vol. 33, No. 1 (1984), pp. 77–108.

Kornblum, Lori, "Women Warriors in a Men's World: The Combat Exclusion," *Law and Inequality*, Vol. 2 (1984), pp. 351–445.

Lancaster, John, *Washington Post* (January 13, 1994), pp. A1, A7.

Lieberman, Jeanne, "Women in Combat," *Federal Bar News and Journal*, Vol. 37, No. 4 (1990), pp. 215–22.

Marlowe, David, "The Manning of the Force and the Structure of Battle: Part 2—Men and Women," in Robert Fullinwider (ed.), *Conscripts and Volunteers: Military Requirements, Social Justice, and the All-Volunteer Force* (Totowa, NJ: Rowman & Allanheld, 1983), pp. 189–99.

Marquit, Doris and Erwin Marquit, "Gender Differentiation, Genetic Determinism, and the Struggle for Peace," in Anne E. Hunter (ed.), *Genes and Gender VI: On Peace, War, and Gender: A Challenge to Genetic Explanations* (New York: Feminist Press, 1991), pp. 151–62.

McDowell, Jeanne, "Are Women Better Cops?" *Time* (February 17, 1992), pp. 70–72.

Mitchell, Brian, *The Weak Link: The Feminization of the American Military* (Washington, DC: Regnery Gateway, 1989).

Moskos, Charles, "Female GI's in the Field," *Society*, Vol. 22, No. 6 (1985), pp. 28–33.

———. "Army Women," *Atlantic Monthly*, Vol. 266, No. 2 (August, 1990), pp. 70–78.

———, "How Do They Do It? *The New Republic* (August 5, 1991), pp. 16–20.

Nabors, Major Robert, "Women in the Army: Do They Measure Up?" *Military Review* (October, 1982), pp. 50–61.

Newsweek Staff, "Women in the Armed Forces," *Newsweek*, Vol. 95 (February 18, 1980), pp. 34–42.

"No Right to Fight?" *Proceedings (of the U.S. Naval Institute)*, Vol. 114, No. 5 (May, 1988), pp. 134–39.

Pine, Art, "Women Will Get Limited Combat Roles," *Los Angeles Times* (January 14, 1994), p. A5.

Proxmire, Senator William, "Three Myths About Women and Combat," *Minerva*, Vol. 4, No. 4 (Winter, 1986), pp. 105–19.

Rogan, Helen, *Mixed Company: Women in the Modern Army* (New York: G.P. Putnam's Sons, 1981).

Rosoff, Betty, "Genes, Hormones, and War," in Hunter (ed.), *Genes and Gender VI: On Peace, War, and Gender: A Challenge to Genetic Explanations* (New York: Feminist Press, 1991), pp. 39–49.

Roush, Paul, "Combat Exclusion: Military Necessity or Another Name For Bigotry?" *Minerva*, Vol. 13, No. 3 (Fall, 1990), pp. 1–15.

Schmitt, Eric, "Generals Oppose Combat by Women" *Newsweek* (June 17, 1994a) pp. A1, A18.

Schmitt, Eric, "Army Will Allow Women in 32,000 Combat Posts" *New York Times* (July 28, 1994b), p. A5.

Segal, Mady Wechsler, "The Argument for Female Combatants," in Goldman (ed.), *Female Soldiers—Combatants or Noncombatants? Historical and Contemporary Perspectives* (Westport, CT: Greenwood Press, 1982), pp. 267–90.

———. "Women's Roles in the U.S. Armed Forces: An Evaluation of Evidence and Arguments for Policy Decisions," in Robert Fullinwider (ed.), *Conscripts and Volunteers: Military Requirements, Social Justice, and the All-Volunteer Force* (Totowa, NJ: Rowman & Allanheld, 1983), pp. 200–13 .

Shields, Patricia, "Sex Roles in the Military," in Charles Moskos and Frank Wood (eds.), *The Military—More Than Just a Job?* (Washington, DC: Pergamon Basseys, 1988), pp. 99–111.

Stiehm, Judith Hicks, "Women's Biology and the U.S. Military," in Virginia Sapiro (ed.), *Women, Biology, and Public Policy* (Beverly Hills: SAGE Publications, 1985a), pp. 205–32.

———. "Generations of U.S. Enlisted Women," *Signs: Journal of Women in Culture and Society*, Vol. 11, No. 1 (1985b), pp. 155–75.

———. *Arms and the Enlisted Woman* (Philadelphia: Temple University Press, 1989).

Sunday, Suzanne R., "Biological Theories of Animal Aggression," in Hunter (ed.), *Genes and Gender VI: On Peace, War, and Gender: A Challenge to Genetic Explanations* (New York: Feminist Press, 1991), pp. 50–63.

Treadwell, Mattie, *The Women's Army Corps*, in *World War II Special Studies*, Vol. 8 (Washington, DC: Office of the Chief of Military History of the Army, 1954).

Tuten, Jeff, "The Argument Against Female Combatants," in Goldman (ed.), *Female Soldiers—Combatants or Noncombatants? Historical and Contemporary Perspectives* (Westport, CT: Greenwood Press, 1982), pp. 237–66.

United States Army Research Institute, *Women Content in Units Force Deployment Test (MAXWAC)* (Alexandria, VA: U.S.A.R.I., 1977).

United States Senate, Hearings before the Committee on Appropriations, DOD Appropriations, 102d Cong., 1st Sess., H.R. 2521, Pts. 4 & 6, *Utilization of Women in the Military Services* (Washington, DC: Government Printing Office, 1991) (Appropriations Hearings).

Van Creveld, Martin, "Why Israel Doesn't Send Women into Combat," *Parameters,* Vol. 23, No. 1 (Spring, 1993), pp. 5–9.

Webster, Alexander, "Paradigms of the Contemporary American Soldier and Women in the Military," *Strategic Review* (Summer 1991), pp. 22–30.

The Case for Social Maternity: Adoption of Children by Urban Baule Women

Mona Etienne

In interpreting the adoption of children by urban Baule women of the Ivory Coast,[1] I will focus on such transactions in parenthood as evidence that maternity, like paternity is social as well as natural.[2] In analyzing the data, I will also try to emphasize the ways in which Baule women behave as autonomous social agents, controlling their own destiny— and often determining that of others. I suggest that this autonomy, like the adoption phenomenon itself, is not specific to the contemporary postcolonial urban context, but is rooted in precolonial Baule society.

That history and structure can be summarized as follows:

Colonized in the late nineteenth century and conquered only in the early twentieth, Baule society could hardly be characterized as "egalitarian," in the reductive sense, but there was no centralized political authority and there were no clear-cut principles of stratification, certainly no class structure. Early administrators were impressed by the independent spirit of the Baule in general and by what one described as "the preponderant role of women."[3] The Baule were primarily farmers and land was accessible to all, a woman normally farming in partnership

From *Dialectical Anthropology* 4:237–242, 1979. Reprinted by permission of Kluwer Academic Publishers.

with a man, typically her husband, *and having rights to the surplus production of specific crops.*

Craft production, trade, and gold-prospecting were major sources of wealth. In all of these activities, the woman had her share, both of the labor and of the profits.[4]

Physical warfare was the province of men, but it was supported by a women's ritual that constituted magical warfare. It is said that men who went to war against the will of village women would die in combat.

Political authority was limited, only magico-religious sanctions were in effect, but such authority as existed was vested in women as well as men; there is ample evidence that the almost total disappearance of women chiefs was due to colonization. The one clear indication of a limit on women's access to positions of authority is the principle of virilocality. A married woman normally resided in her husband's household and this prevented her from being household head or kin group elder. Baule society was not however strongly gerontocratic. There was leeway for the acquisition of wealth by all adults. Differential wealth and status were made possible both by individual enterprise and by the access an individual had to the labor of dependents— mainly children, junior kin and captives.

A head of household or kin group elder had more ready access to the labor of dependents than others. There is however clear evidence that even within her husband's household a woman could have her own dependents and profit by their labor. Besides her daughters, she could also have captives of her own, along with junior female kin living and working with her. Junior members of a woman's kin group were acquired more or less definitively by fosterage or adoption. There was in fact an established custom whereby a married woman who went to reside with her husband was accompanied by a sister, a classificatory sister or a classificatory daughter, who remained with her if she had no daughter of her own at the time of marriage.

Although this usage can be seen to reflect a concern with maintaining a married woman's kin ties, my data also suggest the concern with a woman's having her own personal dependent, a child of her own, *who is not shared with the husband,* and also a concern with maintaining precise interindividual bonds with the mother, aunt or older sister who gives her the child.

Baule marriage is marked by brideservice and symbolic gifts of consumable goods; there is no bridewealth that gives a father and paternal kin undisputed rights in children.

Descent is cognatic with matrilineal emphasis,[5] and, although there are some rules governing the relationship between a child and its maternal and paternal kin, conflicting rights in children tend to make the option of the mother herself decisive. This shows up in adoption transactions although consent of the father is required.

It is perhaps significant that in pre-colonial Baule society, where pawning of persons existed, only maternal kin, including the mother herself, could pawn a child.

Another pertinent aspect of Baule society is that, although natural maternity, like natural paternity, is highly valued, sterility does not carry with it the onus described for some other African societies and sterility does not justify divorce. To be alone, without children, without dependents, is the saddest of conditions. It is also a threat for the future, since children are a guarantee of security in old age. Rights in children, however, are not determined by reproductive capacity alone. As I shall explain, sterility can even be a positive advantage for the urban woman.

Since early colonization, Baule women have been migrating to urban centers. Although some come to town as wives of male migrants, many come as single women, on their own initiative. Their principal motivation is to seek wealth and status. For the most part, urban migrants maintain active ties with the village; and status is a function not only of wealth, but of the network of social relations wealth facilitates and is facilitated by. To return to the village well-dressed and with gifts is essential. To build a house there, even though one may never live in it, is a much sought-after goal. To leave an inheritance that will make for an important funeral and remembrance after death is an ultimate achievement. Without people, however, without dependents who will live in the house, carry out the funeral, take the inheritance, speak your name after death, wealth is futile. To fulfill these needs, children, whether natural or social, are indispensable, just as they are indispensable to constitute the wealth itself and to build relationships in the present and the future.

It is necessary here to indicate the ways in which illiterate women acquire wealth in town. To a certain extent they try to appropriate the advantage of men, who have greater access to the cash economy. Baule women are rarely prostitutes in the European sense, but they may try to profit by their sexual relationships or enter into temporary marriages with a man who is at least generous enough to assume all household expenses and make occasional gifts, leaving the woman free to trade and keep her profits. A woman who has established herself in petty trade can eventually maintain both herself and dependents without a man's support. Women who are unsuccessful return to the village, often with the hope of trying again. For reasons that I shall not elaborate on here, fertility is often an obstacle to urbanization. Pregnancy favors a return to the village that, with further pregnancy, may become definitive. It is therefore not surprising that successful urban women tend to be sterile or of low fertility.

In addition to property in the village, these women acquire their own urban compounds and can maintain dependents who consolidate their ties with the village and eventually serve their interests in many ways. They have the advantage of being able to acquire children either temporarily or permanently when the most burdensome period of motherhood is past, at an age when a child starts to become an asset rather than a liability, and at a moment in their own lives when they are economically capable of taking responsibility for a child. Sterile women are also preferential candidates as adoptive mothers because the adoptee will not be in competition with natural children.

Transfers of parental rights and obligations range from minimal to maximal and can involve children and partners of both sexes and of varying degrees of kinship, as well as non-kin and, sometimes, non-Baule. Rather than review all of these variables and the combinations in which they appear, I will describe the different forms of transfer briefly and then focus on quasi-total transfer, or *adoption,* with women as the principal participants. (Rural to urban is today the preferential direction of adoption. Although urbanization may have intensified transfers of children, it is also possible that the lower incidence of rural-to-rural transfers may be only a recent phenomenon, a result of the draining toward the city of children who would formerly have been transferred between rural kin.)

Clear-cut cases of temporary transfer always refer to a specific reason. A child may be sent to a guardian or foster parent for schooling or as a temporary household aid. When these transfers take place between distant kin or non-kin, the child is often treated as a servant. As in all rural-urban transfers there is nevertheless the idea that the child, even when taken on as a household aide and treated as a servant, is receiving an education in the ways of the city and thus a chance at

success. Children themselves may enter into such relationships on their own initiative. Baule children, in any case, *are not forced into such fosterage situations against their will,* nor are they exploited in the sole interest of their parents. These transfers may however relieve the burden on a fertile and economically disadvantaged family and, at the same time, create ties with the city that can serve in the future.

A child may also be sent on a temporary basis to remain with an older sister or other close kin for a specified period of time or for a given task, for example to help after childbirth. This kind of transfer is, to a certain extent, part of the normal rights and obligations of close kin. If however the arrangement has not been precise enough or the foster parent begs time and again to keep the child a little longer and the child wants to remain, the ensuing relationship may be interpreted after the fact as a case of adoption, the foster mother ultimately assuming all the rights and obligations of an adoptive mother.

Cases in which the child is given simply to go with the woman, to accompany her, are the object of contradictory interpretations by informants, who refer sometimes to the closeness of kinship, sometimes to the age of the child as criteria of whether there is fosterage or adoption. Again the nature of the transfer will often be defined *a posteriori.*

In the clear-cut case of adoption, the child is given with the words "This is your own child," "Take this child for yourself," or even "Here is a child to put in your belly." Ideally the adopted is a baby and may even be promised before birth, although the actual transfer will take place only after weaning, sometimes very much later. In this type of transfer, the emphasis is on the relationship between the natural and the adoptive parent. In the case of close kin such as sisters, beyond the obligations they normally have to each other and to each other's children, the gift of a child is supposed to mark something extra, a special bond of affection. But a child can also be given to a more distant kinswoman, an affine, or even a stranger "to show that you love her." Here any suggestion that the child may be considered a burden, and given for that reason is inadmissible. When a fertile woman gives a child to a sterile woman or an older woman who has no young children, the gift is seen in terms of generosity and sharing. It would be selfish to do otherwise.

The fact remains that adoption here serves to adjust the imbalance of natural maternity. It may also serve to adjust the imbalance between natural maternity and a woman's desire to raise children, either at a given moment in her life or in general. Although all women are supposed to desire their children, the Baule recognize an unequal distribution of both the penchant, and the talent for active motherhood. Some women receive many children in adoption because they are considered to raise children well, while others systematically give their children to sisters or mothers because they simply do not like raising children.

If these cases make it appear that, in spite of the ideology, adoption serves to get rid of unwanted or excess children, many others appear to confirm the ideology and reveal the importance of the bond between natural and adoptive parents. A much-desired first-born, often promised before birth, may be given to an adoptive mother as proof of the natural mother's special affection for her. This can occur as a form of indirect exchange following a previous adoption. When a young woman has been given a younger sister to accompany her in marriage, she may later give her first-born to this adoptive daughter. Where this is not possible, because the original adoptive mother is old or sterile, one finds reinforcement and perpetuation of the original bond by duplication: An adoptee, as proof of her affection for her adoptive mother, is supposed to replace herself when she leaves to marry, ideally by the gift of her first-born. Not to offer a child to one's adoptive mother is a way of saying that the adoptee does not love her, is not happy with the way she was raised. In one case of a very old woman I found duplication of adoption over several generations.

In true adoption, life-long rights and obligations of the natural parent are transferred. An adoptive mother will assume all expenses for the child in health and in illness, perhaps send her/him to school; and she can authorize marriage without consulting the natural parents. The adult adoptee will maintain ties with the adoptive parent, returning to her in case of divorce or difficulty, caring for her in old age, eventually burying her, and possibly becoming her heir.

Ties with the natural parents are not, however, broken. A child adopted in babyhood must be taught who its natural parents are, and incest prohibitions are defined through them. They receive visits and gifts from the child, and they must be informed, if not consulted, when the child is married.[6]

It is particularly interesting, however, that, juridically at least, the bond between adoptee and adoptive parent is in some ways stronger than the bond between a child and its natural parents. As noted, Baule children have considerable autonomy and often leave home on their own. If a child insists, the natural parent cannot object. The bond between adoptee and adoptive parent, however, has the character of a sacred gift. The child must not leave, especially to return to the natural parents. If she/he does, both natural and adoptive parents must do everything possible to see that the child returns. To act otherwise would suggest that the former want to take the child back and the latter want to return it. A child will, of course, especially in cases of extreme mistreatment, sometimes return to its natural parents; but this is never accomplished easily or without conflict and bad feelings.

While there are such cases of returned children, there are also others in which women who give their first-born in adoption subsequently have no other children and are in dire straits for lack of a child helper. In such cases, the child may be sent temporarily to help the natural mother, but there can be neither a request nor an offer that she/he be given back permanently.

In another sense, the rights of an adoptive parent are stronger than those of natural parents. As suggested previously, in natural parenthood, rights in the child are considered to be shared between mother and father, although mother-right is stronger, especially in the case of girl children and babies of both sexes. The adoptive parent, however, who is most often a woman, receives the child in her name only. Her husband, if she has one, may sometimes create ties with the child by contributing to its welfare, but the transfer itself gives rights only to the woman. The adoptive mother therefore acquires, even within her husband's household, a child that is hers alone, that materializes her personal bond with the child's natural family, and, if she raises the child to successful adulthood, guarantees her future security.

Transactions involving males follow, as might be expected, similar rules.[7] Whereas a girl is traditionally considered the appropriate adoptive child for a woman because of the sexual division of labor, and women still adopt more girls for their labor value and for rights in their future children, a boy who is sent to school may become part of the urban educated elite, even the modern political power structure. If this happens, he will not forget his adoptive mother—or his natural parents. Particularly foresighted women therefore tend to give and receive a certain number of boy children as urban adoptees. Further, in spite of the generally stronger rights of mothers and maternal kin, precisely the most prestigious urban women frequently receive adoptive children both through male kin and on the initiative of fathers themselves.

These cases are important, because they show that networks constituted by urban women through adoption are not strictly female networks. Rather, while they appear to be female-dominated, they include male elements. Here the adoption data correlate with my observations of compounds, where one finds men as well as women among the urban woman's constituency of dependents.[8]

Let me note finally that further exploration of similar material will contribute to

undermining the assumption that, whereas paternity is eminently social, maternity is irrevocably natural. The biological fact that only women give birth to children is seen by some as the theoretical key to male dominance—dominance that is perhaps too easily considered to be amply demonstrated by the empirical data. At the same time, the tendency of male-centered anthropology to assume that, when women's reproductive capacity is controlled or manipulated, the agents of this social action are necessarily men, is but another instance of the more general tendency to see only men as social actors. Thus the empirical data feed back into the theoretical orientation that posits the universal subordination of women.

When a contemporary theorist who has also done fieldwork in Africa—I am referring here to Meillassoux—says: "Woman, in spite of her irreplaceable function in reproduction, never intervenes as a vector of social organization. She disappears behind the man; her father, her brother, her husband"[9] we must ask ourselves to what extent the theory accounts for the reality of other societies, and its incarnation in an anthropology that makes women disappear behind fathers, brothers and husbands. I believe that only systematic attempts to make women visible, to determine whether in fact they do or do not appear as vectors of social organization, can begin to answer this question. And if they do, as among the Baule, what are the occasions for their visibility and their autonomy?

NOTES

1. This is a paper presented at the 76th annual meeting of the American Anthropological Association, Houston, Texas, 1977. An extended version of this article will be published in French: *L'Homme*, XIX (3/4, Juin/ Décembre, 1979). Data are based on 1962–63 fieldwork among rural Baule, supported by the Ivory Coast government (Ministère de Plan) in the context of the Bouaké Regional Study (Etude régionale de Bouaké), and on 1974–75 fieldwork among urban Baule of Abidjan, supported by Grant No.

3067 from the Wenner-Gren Foundation. I thank the Ivory Coast Ministère de la Recherche Scientifique and the Institut d'Ethnologie of the University of Abidjan for authorizing 1974–75 research, and the Institut de Linguistique for use of audio equipment.

2. See Nicole-Claude Mathieu, "Paternité biologique, maternité sociale," in Andrée Michel (ed.). *Femmes, sexisme et société.* (Paris: Presses universitaires de France, 1977), pp. 39–48. A critique of male bias in anthropological views of reproduction, this article strongly influenced not only the present analysis, but also my 1974–75 fieldwork. Written in 1974, it explicitly suggests adoption as one insufficiently explored object of research and as a "sign of the social manipulation of biological engendering" ("signe de la manipulation sociale de l'engendrement biologique", pp. 43–44).

3. ". . . le rôle prépondérant des femmes ...", p. 139 in J. F. Bouet, "Quelques opérations militaires á la Côte d'Ivoire en 1909," *Revue des troupes coloniales*, IX (1910), 2ème sem., pp. 134–153. Early observers are unanimous in noting the high status of Baule women.

4. Concerning women's control of cloth, an important item in long-distance trade, see Mona Etienne. "Women and Men, Cloth and Colonization: The Transformation of Production—Distribution Relations among the Baule (Ivory Coast)", *Cahiers d'Etude Africaines*, vol. 65, XVII (1), (1977), pp. 41–64.

5. Baule kinship nomenclature is of the "generation" or "Hawaiian" type. The correlation of institutionalized adoption with this type of nomenclature and cognatic descent is frequently noted, usually with reference to non-African societies and especially Polynesia. For excellent case studies, see Vern Carroll (ed.), *Adoption in Eastern Oceania* (Hawaii: University of Hawaii Press, 1970). The only serious exploration of the subject by an Africanist is Esther Goody, "Some Theoretical and Empirical Aspects of Parenthood in West Africa," in C. Oppong, G. Adaba et al. (eds.), *Marriage, Fertility and Parenthood in West Africa* (Papers from the XVth Seminar of the International Sociological Association Committee on Family Research, Lomé, Togoland, January 1976). Changing African Family No. 4, Canberra: Australian National University; n.d., pp. 227–271.

6. An adoptee's relationship to the ancestors is determined by birth and must be maintained. In disagreement with Goody (*op. cit.*) and in accord with the Oceanists (Carroll, *op. cit.*), I use the term "adoption," in spite of its different connotations in our own society, to mark the specificity of a form of transfer significantly distinct from those that can be called "fosterage."

7. Of the three positions involved in a transfer: giver, adoptee and recipient, males appear least frequently as recipients in true adoption, although they often receive older children in fosterage, especially for schooling. The raising of young children is woman's work and creates strong emotional ties. The giver would not want such ties to develop with an unrelated woman (the wife of the recipient) and eventually cause problems in case of divorce.

8. During my 1974–75 fieldwork, the suggestions of Naomi Quinn, "Asking The Right Question: A Re-examination of Akan Residence," Wm. M. O'Barr, David H. Spain and Mark Tessler (eds.), *Survey Research in Africa* (Evanston, IL: Northwestern University Press, 1973), pp. 168–183, proved invaluable in establishing relationships of dependency in general and adoption in particular. The questions, "By whom is she/he here?" and "Who takes care of (is responsible for) her/him?" applied to all inhabitants of each compound studied, revealed relationships that genealogical and "head of household" bias would have obscured. For example, a woman residing in her brother's compound could be the autonomous head of a sub-group, a child residing in the same compound as its mother could be the adoptee of another woman.

9. ". . . la femme, malgré sa fonction irremplaçable dans la reproduction, n'intervient jamais comme vecteur de l'organisation sociale. Elle disparait derrière l'homme: son père, son frère ou son époux." See Claude Meillassoux, *Femmes, Greniers et Capitaux* (Paris: Maspéro, 1975), p. 116. It is interesting that Meillassoux and Marvin Harris give explanations of "male dominance" that are diametrically opposed, but founded on similar assumptions. For Meillassoux (*op. cit.*), women become subordinate with the development of horticulture because their reproductive capacity is *so valuable* to societies that rely on increased population to increase production; for Harris, male dominance emerges in the first moments in human history because women's reproductive capacity is *so dangerous* to a world threatened by overpopulation. (see "Why Men Dominate Women," *The New York Times Magazine*, November 13, 1977, p. 46ss., and W. T. Divale and

M. Harris, "Population, Warfare and the Male Supremacist Complex," *American Anthropologist,* vol. 78, no. 3 (1976), pp. 521–538.)

Both theorists assume that men are the social actors, that men manipulate women's reproductive capacity but women do not (even in infanticide!). It must be noted to Meillassoux's credit that he does attempt to explain why men are the actors and women the objects in the earliest struggle to control their childbearing potential; but his argument begs the question, reifying women to explain their reification. It belongs to the realm of anthropological mythology and, if one accepts the ground rules, could easily be converted into its opposite, an argument for matriarchy.

Lifeboat Ethics: Mother Love and Child Death in Northeast Brazil

Nancy Scheper-Hughes

I have seen death without weeping.
The destiny of the Northeast is death.
    Cattle they kill.
To the people they do something worse.
—Anonymous Brazilian singer (1965)

"Why do the church bells ring so often?" I asked Nailza de Arruda soon after I moved into a corner of her tiny mud-walled hut near the top of the shantytown called the Alto do Cruzeiro (Crucifix Hill). I was then a Peace Corps volunteer and a community development/health worker. It was the dry and blazing hot summer of 1965, the months following the military coup in Brazil, and save for the rusty, clanging bells, of N. S. das Dores Church, an eerie quiet had settled over the market town that I call Bom Jesus da Mata. Beneath the quiet, however, there was chaos and panic. "It's nothing," replied Nailza, "just another little angel gone to heaven."

Nailza had sent more than her share of little angels to heaven, and sometimes at night I could hear her engaged in a muffled but passionate discourse with one of them, two-year-old Joana. Joana's photograph, taken as she lay propped up in her tiny cardboard coffin, her eyes open, hung on a wall next to one of

Nailza and Ze Antonio taken on the day they eloped.

Nailza could barely remember the other infants and babies who came and went in close succession. Most had died unnamed and were hastily baptized in their coffins. Few lived more than a month or two. Only Joana, properly baptized in church at the close of her first year and placed under the protection of a powerful saint, Joan of Arc, had been expected to live. And Nailza had dangerously allowed herself to love the little girl.

In addressing the dead child, Nailza's voice would range from tearful imploring to angry recrimination: "Why did you leave me? Was your patron saint so greedy that she could not allow me one child on this earth?" Ze Antonio advised me to ignore Nailza's odd behavior, which he understood as a kind of madness that, like the birth and death of children, came and went. Indeed, the premature birth of a stillborn son some months later "cured" Nailza of her "inappropriate" grief, and the day came when she removed Joana's photo and carefully packed it away.

More than fifteen years elapsed before I returned to the Alto do Cruzeiro, and it was anthropology that provided the vehicle of my return. Since 1982 I have returned several times in order to pursue a problem that first attracted my attention in the 1960s. My involvement with the people of the Alto do Cruzeiro now spans a quarter of a century and three generations of parenting in a community where mothers and daughters are often simultaneously pregnant.

The Alto do Cruzeiro is one of three shantytowns surrounding the large market town of Bom Jesus in the sugar plantation zone of Pernambuco in Northeast Brazil, one of the many zones of neglect that have emerged in the shadow of the now tarnished economic miracle of Brazil. For the women and children of the Alto do Cruzeiro the only miracle is that some of them have managed to stay alive at all.

The Northeast is a region of vast proportions (approximately twice the size of Texas) and of equally vast social and developmental problems. The nine states that make up the region are the poorest in the country and are representative of the Third World within a dynamic and rapidly industrializing nation. Despite waves of migrations from the interior to the teeming shantytowns of coastal cities, the majority still live in rural areas on farms and ranches, sugar plantations and mills.

Life expectancy in the Northeast is only forty years, largely because of the appallingly high rate of infant and child mortality. Approximately one million children in Brazil under the age of five die each year. The children of the Northeast, especially those born in shantytowns on the periphery of urban life, are at a very high risk of death. In these areas, children are born without the traditional protection of breast-feeding, subsistence gardens, stable marriages, and multiple adult caretakers that exists in the interior. In the hillside shantytowns that spring up around cities or, in this case, interior market towns, marriages are brittle, single parenting is the norm, and women are frequently forced into the shadow economy of domestic work in the homes of the rich or into unprotected and oftentimes "scab" wage labor on the surrounding sugar plantations, where they clear land for planting and weed for a pittance, sometimes less than a dollar a day. The women of the Alto

may not bring their babies with them into the homes of the wealthy, where the often-sick infants are considered sources of contamination, and they cannot carry the little ones to the riverbanks where they wash clothes because the river is heavily infested with schistosomes and other deadly parasites. Nor can they carry their young children to the plantations, which are often several miles away. At wages of a dollar a day, the women of the Alto cannot hire baby sitters. Older children who are not in school will sometimes serve as somewhat indifferent caretakers. But any child not in school is also expected to find wage work. In most cases, babies are simply left at home alone, the door securely fastened. And so many also die alone and unattended.

Bom Jesus da Mata, centrally located in the plantation zone of Pernambuco, is within commuting distance of several sugar plantations and mills. Consequently, Bom Jesus has been a magnet for rural workers forced off their small subsistence plots by large landowners wanting to use every available piece of land for sugar cultivation. Initially, the rural migrants to Bom Jesus were squatters who were given tacit approval by the mayor to put up temporary straw huts on each of the three hills overlooking the town. The Alto do Cruzeiro is the oldest, the largest, and the poorest of the shantytowns. Over the past three decades many of the original migrants have become permanent residents, and the primitive and temporary straw huts have been replaced by small homes (usually of two rooms) made of wattle and daub, sometimes covered with plaster. The more affluent residents use bricks and tiles. In most Alto homes, dangerous kerosene lamps have been replaced by light bulbs. The once tattered rural garb, often fashioned from used sugar sacking, has likewise been replaced by store-bought clothes, often castoffs from a wealthy *patrão* (boss). The trappings are modern, but the hunger, sickness, and death that they conceal are traditional, deeply rooted in a history of feudalism, exploitation, and institutionalized dependency.

My research agenda never wavered. The questions I addressed first crystallized during a veritable "die-off" of Alto babies during a severe drought in 1965. The food and water shortages and the political and economic chaos occasioned by the military coup were reflected in the handwritten entries of births and deaths in the dusty, yellowed pages of the ledger books kept at the public registry office in Bom Jesus. More than 350 babies died in the Alto during 1965 alone—this from a shantytown population of little more than 5,000. But that wasn't what surprised me. There were reasons enough for the deaths in the miserable conditions of shantytown life. What puzzled me was the seeming indifference of Alto women to the death of their infants, and their willingness to attribute to their own tiny offspring an aversion to life that made their death seem wholly natural, indeed all but anticipated.

Although I found that it was possible, and hardly difficult, to rescue infants and toddlers from death by diarrhea and dehydration with a simple sugar, salt, and water solution (even bottled Coca-Cola worked fine), it was more difficult to enlist a mother herself in the rescue of a child she perceived as ill-fated for life or better off dead, or to convince her to take back into her threatened and besieged home a baby she had already come to think of as an angel rather than as a son or daughter.

I learned that the high expectancy of death, and the ability to face child death with stoicism and equanimity, produced patterns of nurturing that differentiated between those infants thought of as thrivers and survivors and those thought of as born already "wanting to die." The survivors were nurtured, while stigmatized, doomed infants were left to die, as mothers say, a mingua, "of neglect." Mothers stepped back and allowed nature to take its course. This pattern, which I call mortal selective neglect, is called passive infanticide by anthropologist Marvin Harris. The Alto situation, although culturally specific in the form that it takes, is not unique to Third World shantytown communities and may have its correlates in our own impoverished urban communities in some cases of "failure to thrive" infants.

I use as an example the story of Zezinho, the thirteen-month-old toddler of one of my neighbors, Lourdes. I became involved with Zezinho when I was called in to help Lourdes in the delivery of another child, this one a fair and robust little tyke with a lusty cry. I noted that while Lourdes showed great interest in the newborn, she totally ignored Zezinho who, wasted and severely malnourished, was curled up in a fetal position on a piece of urine- and feces-soaked cardboard placed under his mother's hammock. Eyes open and vacant, mouth slack, the little boy seemed doomed.

When I carried Zezinho up to the community day-care center at the top of the hill, the Alto women who took turns caring for one another's children (in order to free themselves for part-time work in the cane fields or washing clothes) laughed at my efforts to save Ze, agreeing with Lourdes that here was a baby without a ghost of a chance. Leave him alone, they cautioned. It makes no sense to fight with death. But I did do battle with Ze, and after several weeks of force-feeding (malnourished babies lose their interest in food), Ze began to succumb to my ministrations. He acquired some flesh across his taut chest bones, learned to sit up, and even tried to smile. When he seemed well enough, I returned him to Lourdes in her miserable scrap-material lean-to, but not without guilt about what I had done. I wondered whether returning Ze was at all fair to Lourdes and to his little brother. But I was busy and washed my hands of the matter. And Lourdes did seem more interested in Ze now that he was looking more human.

When I returned in 1982, there was Lourdes among the women who formed my sample of Alto mothers—still struggling to put together some semblance of life for a now grown Ze and her five other surviving children. Much was made of my reunion with Ze in 1982, and everyone enjoyed retelling the story of Ze's rescue and of how his mother had given him up for dead. Ze would laugh the loudest when told how I had had to force-feed him like a fiesta turkey. There was no hint of guilt on the part of Lourdes and no resentment on the part of Ze. In fact, when questioned in private as to who was the best friend he ever had in life, Ze took a long drag on his cigarette and answered without a trace of irony, "Why my mother, of course!" "But of course," I replied.

Part of learning how to mother in the Alto do Cruzeiro is learning when to let go of a child who shows that it "wants" to die or that it has no "knack" or no "taste" for life. Another part is learning when it is safe to let oneself love a child. Frequent child death remains a powerful shaper of maternal thinking and practice. In the absence of firm expectation that a child will survive, mother love as we conceptualize it (whether in popular terms or in the psychobiological notion of maternal bonding) is attenuated and delayed with consequences for infant survival. In an environment already precarious to young life, the emotional detachment of mothers toward some of their babies contributes even further to the spiral of high mortality—high fertility in a kind of macabre lock-step dance to death.

The average woman of the Alto experiences 9.5 pregnancies, 3.5 child deaths, and 1.5 stillbirths. Seventy percent of all child deaths in the Alto occur in the first six months of life, and 82 percent by the end of the first year. Of all deaths in the community each year, about 45 percent are of children under the age of five.

Women of the Alto distinguish between child deaths understood as natural (caused by diarrhea and communicable diseases) and those resulting from sorcery, the evil eye, or other magical or supernatural afflictions. They also recognize a large category of infant deaths seen as fated and inevitable. These hopeless cases are classified by mothers under the folk terminology "child sickness" or "child attack." Women say that there are at least fourteen different types of hopeless child sickness, but most can be subsumed under two categories—chronic and acute. The chronic cases refer to infants who are born small and

wasted. They are deathly pale, mothers say, as well as weak and passive. They demonstrate no vital force, no liveliness. They do not suck vigorously; they hardly cry. Such babies can be this way at birth or they can be born sound but soon show no resistance, no "fight" against the common crises of infancy: diarrhea, respiratory infections, tropical fevers.

The acute cases are those doomed infants who die suddenly and violently. They are taken by stealth overnight, often following convulsions that bring on head banging, shaking, grimacing, and shrieking. Women say it is horrible to look at such a baby. If the infant begins to foam at the mouth or gnash its teeth or go rigid with its eyes turned back inside its head, there is absolutely no hope. The infant is "put aside"—left alone—often on the floor in a back room, and allowed to die. These symptoms (which accompany high fevers, dehydration, third-stage malnutrition, and encephalitis) are equated by Alto women with madness, epilepsy, and worst of all, rabies, which is greatly feared and highly stigmatized.

Most of the infants presented to me as suffering from chronic child sickness were tiny, wasted famine victims, while those labeled as victims of acute child attack seemed to be infants suffering from the deliriums of high fever or the convulsions that can accompany electrolyte imbalance in dehydrated babies.

Local midwives and traditional healers, praying women, as they are called, advise Alto women on when to allow a baby to die. One midwife explained: "If I can see that a baby was born unfortuitously, I tell the mother that she need not wash the infant or give it a cleansing tea. I tell her just to dust the infant with baby powder and wait for it to die." Allowing nature to take its course is not seen as sinful by these often very devout Catholic women. Rather, it is understood as cooperating with God's plan.

Often I have been asked how consciously women of the Alto behave in this regard. I would have to say that consciousness is always shifting between allowed and disallowed levels of awareness. For example, I was awakened early one morning in 1987 by two neighborhood children who had been sent to fetch me to a hastily organized wake for a two-month-old infant whose mother I had unsuccessfully urged to breast-feed. The infant was being sustained on sugar water, which the mother referred to as *soro* (serum), using a medical term for the infant's starvation regime in light of his chronic diarrhea. I had cautioned the mother that an infant could not live on *soro* forever.

The two girls urged me to console the young mother by telling her that it was "too bad" that her infant was so weak that Jesus had to take him. They were coaching me in proper Alto etiquette. I agreed, of course, but asked, "And what do *you* think?" Xoxa, the eleven-year-old, looked down at her dusty flip-flops and blurted out, "Oh, Dona Nanci, that baby never got enough to eat, but you must never say that!" And so the death of hungry babies remains one of the best kept secrets of life in Bom Jesus da Mata.

Most victims are waked quickly and with a minimum of ceremony. No tears are shed, and the neighborhood children form a tiny procession, carrying the baby to the town graveyard where it will join a multitude of others. Although a few fresh flowers may be scattered over the tiny grave, no stone or wooden cross will mark the place, and the same spot will be reused within a few months' time. The mother will never visit the grave, which soon becomes an anonymous one.

What, then, can be said of these women? What emotions, what sentiments motivate them? How are they able to do what, in fact, must be done? What does mother love mean in this inhospitable context? Are grief, mourning, and melancholia present, although deeply repressed? If so, where shall we look for them? And if not, how are we to understand the moral visions and moral sensibilities that guide their actions?

I have been criticized more than once for presenting an unflattering portrait of poor Brazilian women, women who are, after all, themselves the victims of severe social and institutional neglect. I have described these women as allowing some of their children to die, as if this were an unnatural and inhuman act rather than, as I would assert, the way any one of us might act, reasonably and rationally, under similarly desperate conditions. Perhaps I have not emphasized enough the real pathogens in this environment of high risk: poverty, deprivation, sexism, chronic hunger, and economic exploitation. If mother love is, as many psychologists and some feminists believe, a seemingly natural and universal maternal script, what does it mean to women for whom scarcity, loss, sickness, and deprivation have made that love frantic and robbed them of their grief, seeming to turn their hearts to stone?

Throughout much of human history—as in a great deal of the impoverished Third World today—women have had to give birth and to nurture children under ecological conditions and social arrangements hostile to child survival, as well as to their own well-being. Under circumstances of high childhood mortality, patterns of selective neglect and passive infanticide may be seen as active survival strategies.

They also seem to be fairly common practices historically and across cultures. In societies characterized by high childhood mortality and by a correspondingly high (replacement) fertility, cultural practices of infant and child care tend to be organized primarily around survival goals. But what this means is a pragmatic recognition that not all of one's children can be expected to live. The nervousness about child survival in areas of northeast Brazil, northern India, or Bangladesh, where a 30 percent or 40 percent mortality rate in the first years of life is common, can lead to forms of delayed attachment and a casual or benign neglect that serves to weed out the worst bets so as to enhance the life chances of healthier siblings, including those yet to be born. Practices similar to those that I am describing have been recorded for parts of Africa, India, and Central America.

Life in the Alto do Cruzeiro resembles nothing so much as a battlefield or an emergency room in an overcrowded innercity public hospital. Consequently, morality is guided by a kind of "lifeboat ethics," the morality of triage. The seemingly studied indifference toward the suffering of some of their infants, conveyed in such sayings as "little critters have no feelings," is understandable in light of these women's obligation to carry on with their reproductive and nurturing lives.

In their slowness to anthropomorphize and personalize their infants, everything is mobilized so as to prevent maternal overattachment and, therefore, grief at death. The bereaved mother is told not to cry, that her tears will dampen the wings of her little angel so that she cannot fly up to her heavenly home. Grief at the death of an angel is not only inappropriate, it is a symptom of madness and of a profound lack of faith.

Infant death becomes routine in an environment in which death is anticipated and bets are hedged. While the routinization of death in the context of shantytown life is not hard to understand, and quite possible to empathize with, its routinization in the formal institutions of public life in Bom Jesus is not as easy to accept uncritically. Here the social production of indifference takes on a different, even a malevolent cast.

In a society where triplicates of every form are required for the most banal events (registering a car, for example), the registration of infant and child death is informal, incomplete, and rapid. It requires no documentation, takes less than five minutes, and demands no witnesses other than office clerks. No questions are asked concerning the circumstances of the death, and the cause of death is left blank, unquestioned and unexamined. A neighbor, grandmother, older sibling, or common-law husband may register the death. Since most infants die at home, there is no question of a medical record.

From the registry office, the parent proceeds to the town hall, where the mayor will give him or her a voucher for a free baby coffin. The full-time municipal coffinmaker cannot tell you exactly how many baby coffins are dispatched each week. It varies, he says, with the seasons. There are more needed during the drought months and during the big festivals of Carnaval and Christmas and São Joao's Day because people are too busy, he supposes, to take their babies to the clinic. Record keeping is sloppy.

Similarly, there is a failure on the part of city-employed doctors working at two free clinics to recognize the malnutrition of babies who are weighed, measured, and immunized without comment and as if they were not, in fact, anemic, stunted, fussy, and irritated starvation babies. At best the mothers are told to pick up free vitamins or a health "tonic" at the municipal chambers. At worst, clinic personnel will give tranquilizers and sleeping pills to quiet the hungry cries of "sick-to-death" Alto babies.

The church, too, contributes to the routinization of, and indifference toward, child death. Traditionally, the local Catholic church taught patience and resignation to domestic tragedies that were said to reveal the imponderable workings of God's will. If an infant died suddenly, it was because a particular saint had claimed the child. The infant would be an angel in the service of his or her heavenly patron. It would be wrong, a sign of a lack of faith, to weep for a child with such good fortune. The infant funeral was, in the past, an event celebrated with joy. Today, however, under the new regime of "liberation theology," the bells of N. S. das Dores parish church no longer peal for the death of Alto babies, and no priest accompanies the procession of angels to the cemetery where their bodies are disposed of casually and without ceremony. Children bury children in Bom Jesus da Mata. In this most Catholic of communities, the coffin is handed to the disabled and irritable municipal gravedigger, who often chides the children for one reason or another. It may be that the coffin is larger than expected and the gravedigger can find no appropriate space.

The children do not wait for the gravedigger to complete his task. No prayers are recited and no sign of the cross made as the tiny coffin goes into its shallow grave.

When I asked the local priest, Padre Marcos, about the lack of church ceremony surrounding infant and childhood death today in Bom Jesus, he replied: "In the old days, child death was richly celebrated. But those were the baroque customs of a conservative church that wallowed in death and misery. The new church is a church of hope and joy. We no longer celebrate the death of child angels. We try to tell mothers that Jesus doesn't want all the dead babies they send him." Similarly, the new church has changed its baptismal customs, now often refusing to baptize dying babies brought to the back door of a church or rectory. The mothers are scolded by the church attendants and told to go home and take care of their sick babies. Baptism, they are told, is for the living; it is not to be confused with the sacrament of extreme unction, which is the anointing of the dying. And so it appears to the women of the Alto that even the church has turned away from them, denying the traditional comfort of folk Catholicism.

The contemporary Catholic church is caught in the clutches of a double bind. The new theology of liberation imagines a kingdom of God on earth based on justice and equality, a world without hunger, sickness, or childhood mortality. At the same time, the church has not changed its official position on sexuality and reproduction, including its sanctions against birth control, abortion, and sterilization. The padre of Bom Jesus da Mata recognizes this contradiction intuitively, although he shies away from discussions on the topic, saying that he prefers to leave questions of family planning to the discretion and the "good consciences" of his impoverished parishioners. But this, of course, sidesteps the extent to which those good consciences have been shaped by traditional church teachings in Bom Jesus, especially by his recent predecessors. Hence, we can begin to see that the seeming indifference of Alto mothers toward the death of some of their infants is but a pale reflection of the official indifference of church and state to the plight of poor women and children.

Nonetheless, the women of Bom Jesus are survivors. One woman, Biu, told me her life history, returning again and again to the themes of child death, her first husband's suicide, abandonment by her father and later by her second husband, and all the other losses and disappointments she had suffered in her long forty-five years. She concluded with great force, reflecting on the days of Carnaval '88 that were fast approaching:

> No, Dona Nanci, I won't cry, and I won't waste my life thinking about it from morning to night.... Can I argue with God for the state that I'm in? No! And so I'll dance and I'll jump and I'll play Carnaval! And yes, I'll laugh and people will wonder at a *pobre* like me who can have such a good time.

And no one did blame Biu for dancing in the streets during the four days of Carnaval—not even on Ash Wednesday, the day following Carnaval '88 when we all assembled hurriedly to assist in the burial of Mercea, Biu's beloved *casula,* her last-born daughter who had died at home of pneumonia during the festivities. The rest of the family barely had time to change out of their costumes. Severino, the child's uncle and godfather, sprinkled holy water over the little angel while he prayed: "Mercea, I don't know whether you were called, taken, or thrown out of this world. But look down at us from your heavenly home with tenderness, with pity, and with mercy." So be it.

The Cultural Nexus of Aka Father-Infant Bonding

Barry S. Hewlett

Despite a steady increase in the quantity and quality of studies of infants, young children and motherhood in various parts of the world (e.g., LeVine et al. 1994), we know relatively little about the nature of father–child relations outside of the U.S. and Western Europe (see Hewlett 1992 for some exceptions). In general, mother-oriented theories of infant and child development have guided cross-cultural research. The majority of these theories view the mother-infant relationship as the prototype for subsequent attachments and relationships (Ainsworth 1967, Bowlby 1969, Freud 1938, and Harlow 1961). According to Freud and Bowlby, for instance, one had to have a trusting, unconditional relationship with his or her mother in order to become a socially and emotionally adjusted adult. These influential theorists generally believed that the father's role was not a factor in the child's development until the Oedipal stage (3–5 years old). The field methods to study infancy reflected this theoretical emphasis on mother. Observations were either infant or mother-focused and conducted only during daylight hours; father-focused and evening observations were not considered. Also, standardized questionnaires and psychological tests were generally administered only to the mother. One consistent result from the cross-cultural studies was that fathers provided substantially less direct care to infants than mothers. In fact, all cross-cultural studies to date indicate that a number of other female caretakers (older female siblings, aunts, grandmothers) provide more direct care to

infants than do fathers. Since fathers are not as conspicuous as mothers and other females during daylight hours researchers tend to emphasize a "deficit" model of fathers (Cole and Bruner 1974); that is, fathers are not around much and therefore do not contribute much to the child's development.

Given the paucity of systematic research outside of the U.S. on father's interactions with children, it is ironic that this variable (i.e., the degree of father vs. mother involvement with children) should be so consistently invoked as an explanatory factor in the literature. It is hypothesized to be related, for example, to gender inequality (Chodorow 1974), universal sexual asymmetry (Rosaldo and Lamphere 1974), and the origin of the human family (Lancaster 1987).

FATHER-INFANT BONDING

Bowlby's (1969) theory, mentioned above, suggested that an early secure attachment (or "bonding") between infant and caregiver (usually mother) was crucial for normal development. Lack of bonding between mother and infant led to the infant's protest, despair, detachment, and eventual difficulty in emotional and social development. Most studies of attachment have focused on mother–infant bonding, but an increasing number of studies in the U.S. and Europe have tried to understand if and when infants become attached to fathers. Numerous psychological studies now indicate that infants are attached to their fathers and that the infants become attached to fathers at about the same age as they do to mothers (8–10 months of age) (Lamb 1981).

But how does this bonding take place if infant bonding to mother is known to develop through regular, sensitive, and responsive care? American fathers are seldom around to provide this type of care. The critical factor that has emerged in over 50 studies of primarily middle-class American fathers is vigorous play. The physical style of American fathers is distinct from that of American mothers, is evident three days after birth, and continues throughout infancy. The American data have been so consistent that some researchers have indicated a biological basis (Clarke-Stewart 1980). The idea is that mother–infant bonding develops as a consequence of the frequency and intensity of the relationship, while father–infant bonding takes place because of this highly stimulating interaction. British, German, and Israeli studies generally support this hypothesis. This chapter examines the process of father–infant bonding among the Aka, a hunter-gatherer group living in the tropical forest of central Africa.

THE AKA

There are about 30,000 Aka hunter-gatherers in the tropical rain forests of southern Central African Republic and northern Congo-Brazzaville. They live in camps of 25–35 people and move camp every two weeks to two months. Each nuclear family has a hut, and each camp generally has 5–8 huts arranged in a circle. The circle of huts is about 12 meters in diameter and each hut is about 1.5 meters in diameter. Each hut has one bed of leaves or logs on which everyone in the family sleeps. The Aka have patriclans and many members of a camp belong to the same patriclan (generally a camp consists of brothers, their wives and children, and unrelated men who are doing bride service for the sisters of the men in camp). The Aka have high fertility and mortality rates: A woman generally has five to six children during her lifetime, and one-fifth of the infants die before reaching 12 months and 43 percent of children die before reaching 15 years.

Life in the camp is rather intimate. While the overall population density is quite low (less than one person per square kilometer), living space is quite dense. Three or four people sleep together on the same 4-feet-long by 2-feet-wide bed, and neighbors are just a few feet away. The 25–35 camp members live in an area about the size of a large American living room. The Aka home represents the "public" part of life, while time outside of camp tends to be relatively "private." This is the reverse of the American pattern (i.e., home is usually considered private). The camp is relatively young as half of the members of the camp are under 15 and most women have a nursing child throughout their childbearing years.

The Aka use a variety of hunting techniques, but net hunting, which involves men, women, and children, is the most important and regular hunting technique. Women generally have the role of tackling the game in the net and killing the animal. Game captured is eventually shared with everyone in camp. Some parts of the game animal are smoked and eventually traded to Bantu and Sudanic farmers for manioc or other domesticated foods. The Aka have strong economic and religious ties to the tropical forest. The forest is perceived as provider and called friend, lover, mother, or father.

Sharing and cooperation are pervasive and general tenets of Aka camp life. Food items, infant care, ideas for song and dance, and material items such as pots and pans are just some of the items that are shared daily in the camp. An Ngandu farmer describes Aka sharing:

> Pygmies [the Ngandu use the derogatory term Babinga to refer to the Aka] are people who stick together. Twenty of them are able to share one single cigarette. When a pygmy comes back with only five roots she shares them all. It is the same with forest nuts; they will give them out to everybody even if there are none left for them. They are very generous.

The Aka are also fiercely egalitarian. They have a number of mechanisms to maintain individual, intergenerational, and gender equality. The Ngandu villager mentioned above describes his concerns about Aka intergenerational egalitarianism:

> Young pygmies have no respect for their parents; they regard their fathers as their friends... There is no way to tell whether they are talking to their parents because they always use their first names. Once I was in a pymgy camp and several people were sitting around and a son said to his father "Etobe your balls are hanging out of your loincloth" and everyone started laughing. No respect, none, none, none. . . . It's real chaos because there is no respect between father and son, mother and son or daughter. That's why pygmies have such a bad reputation, a reputation of being backward.

Three mechanisms that promote sharing and egalitarianism are prestige avoidance, rough joking and demand sharing. The Aka try to avoid drawing attention to themselves, even if they have killed an elephant or cured someone's life-threatening illness. Individuals who boast about their abilities are likely to share less or request more from others in the belief that they are better than others. If individuals start to draw attention to themselves, others in the camp will use rough and crude jokes, often about the boastful person's genitals, in order to get the individuals to be more modest about their abilities. Demand sharing also helps to maintain egalitarianism: if individuals like or want something (cigarettes, necklace, shirt) they simply ask for it, and the person generally gives it to them. Demand sharing promotes the circulation of scarce material goods (e.g., shoes, shirt, necklaces, spear points) in the camp.

Gender egalitarianism is also important. For instance, there are male and female roles on the net hunt, but role reversals take place daily and individuals are not stigmatized for taking the roles of the opposite sex. If one does the task poorly, regardless of whether it is a masculine or feminine task, then one is open to joking and teasing by others (e.g., when the anthropologist chases the game in the wrong direction).

The rough joking mentioned above is also linked to another feature of Aka culture—playfulness. There is no clear separation between "work" and "play" time. Dances, singing, net hunting, male circumcision, sorcery accusations all include humorous mimicking, practical jokes, and exaggerated storytelling. Aka life is informal because of egalitarianism and the playful activity that occurs throughout the day by both adults and children. Play is an integral part of both adult and child life and contributes to enhanced parent–child and adult–child communication. Parents and adults have an extensive repertoire of play, and can and do communicate cultural knowledge to children through their playful repertoire.

Greater ethnographic detail on the Aka can be found in Hewlett (1991) or Bahuchet (1985).

AKA INFANCY

The infant lives with a relatively small group of individuals related through his or her father (unless the infant is the first born in which case the family is likely to be in the camp of the wife for the purposes of bride service) and sleeps in the same bed as mother, father, and other brothers and sisters.

Cultural practices during infancy are quite distinct from those found in European and American cultures. Aka parents are indulgent as infants are held almost constantly, nursed on demand (breast-fed several times per hour), attended to immediately if they fuss, and are seldom, if ever, told "no! no!" if they misbehave (e.g., get into food pots, hit others, or take things from other children). An Aka father describes Aka parenting and contrasts it with parenting among his Ngandu farming neighbors:

> We, Aka look after our children with love, from the minute they are born to when they are much older. The villagers love their children only when they are babies. When they become children they get beaten up badly. With us, even

if the child is older, if he is unhappy, I'll look after him, I will cuddle him.

Older infants are allowed to use and play with knives, machetes, and other "adult" items. They are allowed to crawl into a parent's lap while the parent is engaged in economic (e.g., butchering animal, repairing net) or leisure (e.g., playing a harp or drum) activity. While older infants are given considerable freedom to explore the house and camp, parents do watch infants to make sure they do not crawl into the fire.

Extensive multiple caregiving of 1–4-month-old infants (Hewlett 1989) exists, especially while the Aka are in the camp. Individuals other than mother (infant's father, brothers, sisters, aunts, uncles, grandmothers) hold the infant the majority of the time (60 percent) in this context, and the infant is moved to different people about seven times per hour. Mothers' holding increases to 85 percent and the transfer rate drops to two transfers per hour outside of the camp (i.e., on net hunt or in fields).

Infancy is very active and stimulating. Infants are taken on the hunt and are seldom laid down. They are held on the side of the caregiver rather than on the caregiver's back as in many farming communities so there are opportunities for caregiver–infant face-to-face interaction and communication. The infant can also breast feed by simply reaching for the mother's breast and can nurse while mother walks. While out on the net hunt the infant sleeps in the sling as the caregiver walks, runs, or sits.

THE STUDY

I started working with the Aka in 1973 so by the time I started the father–infant study in 1984 I was familiar with specific Aka families and Aka culture in general. Since I wanted to test some of the psychological hypotheses regarding father–infant relations, I incorporated psychological methods into my research. The quantitative psychological methods consisted of systematically observing 15 Aka families with infants from 6 A.M. to 9 P.M. (the observations focused either on the father or the infant). This enabled me to say precisely how much time Aka versus American fathers held or were near their infants and precisely describe how American versus Aka styles of interaction were similar or different. Informal discussions while on the net hunt and in camp were also utilized to develop structured interviews. Men and women, young and old, were asked about their feelings regarding relations with their mothers, fathers, and other caregivers.

The study focused on two domains important for trying to understand father-infant bonding: the degree of father involvement and mother's versus father's parenting style. For degree of father involvement I wanted to know: How often do fathers actually interact with their infants, how often are fathers available to their infants, if fathers are not involved with infants what other activities are they involved in, how do children characterize the nature of their involvement with their father? Questions regarding paternal versus maternal parenting style included: Are there distinctions between the mother's and the father's play behavior with their infants, do mothers and fathers hold their infants for different purposes, what do mothers and fathers do while they hold the infant, do infants show different types of attachment behavior to mothers and fathers, how do children view their mother's and father's parenting styles?

WHY ARE AKA FATHERS SO INVOLVED WITH THEIR INFANTS? THE CULTURAL NEXUS OF FATHER-INFANT BONDING

Although few cross-cultural studies of father-child relations have been conducted, Aka father involvement in infancy is exceptional, if not unique. Aka fathers are within an arm's reach (i.e., holding or within one meter) of their infant more than 50 percent of 24-hour periods. Table 1 demonstrates that Aka

TABLE 1 Comparison of Father Holding in Selected Foraging Populations

POPULATION	AGE OF INFANTS (MOS.)	FATHER HOLDING (PERCENT OF TIME)	SOURCE
Gidgingali	0–6	3.4	Hamilton (1981)
	6–18	3.1	
!Kung	0–6	1.9	West and Konner (1976)
	6–24	4.0	
Efe Pygmies	1–4	2.6	Winn et al. (1990)
Aka Pygmies	1–4	22.0	Hewlett (1991)
	8–18	14.0	

Note: All observations were made in a camp setting (Table from Hewlett 1991).

fathers hold their very young infants during the day at least five times more than fathers in other cultures, while Table 2 indicates Aka fathers are available to their infants at least three times more frequently than fathers in other cultures. American and European fathers hold their infants, on average, between 10 and 20 minutes per day (Lamb et al. 1987) while Aka fathers, on average, hold their infants about one hour during daylight hours and about 25 percent of the time after the sun goes down. At night fathers sleep with mother and infant, whereas American fathers seldom sleep with their infants. While Aka father care is extensive, it is also highly context dependent—fathers provide at least four times as much care while they are in the camp setting than they do while out of camp (e.g.,

TABLE 2 Comparison of Father Presence with Infants or Children Among Selected Foraging and Farming Populations

POPULATION	LOCATION	SUBSISTENCE	PERCENT TIME FATHER PRESENT/IN VIEW	PRIMARY SETTING OF OBSERVATIONS	SOURCE
Gusii	Kenya	farming	10	house/yard & garden	1
Mixteca	Mexico	farming	9	house/yard	1
Ilocano	Philippines	farming	14	house/yard	1
Okinawan	Japan	farming	3	public places & house/yard	1
Rajput	India	farming	3	house/yard	1
!Kung	Botswana	foraging	30	camp	2
Aka Pygmies	Central African Republic	foraging	88	forest camp	3
Logoli	Kenya	farming	5	house/yard	4
Newars	Nepal	farming	7	house/yard	4
Samoans	Samoa	farming	8	house/yard	4
Carib	Belize	farming	3	house/yard	4
Ifaluk	Micronesia	farm-fish	13	house/yard	5

Sources (Table from Hewlett 1991):
1. Whiting and Whiting 1975
2. West and Konner 1976
3. Hewlett 1991
4. Munroe and Munroe 1992
5. Betzig, Harrigan, and Turke 1990

out on the net hunt or in the villagers' fields). What factors influence this high level of paternal emotional and physical involvement among the Aka?

Aka father-infant bonding is embedded within a cultural nexus—it influences and is influenced by a complex cultural system. This brief overview describes some of the cultural facets linked to Aka father-infant bonding.

Like many other foragers, the Aka have few accumulable resources that are essential for survival. "Kinship resources," the number of brothers and sisters in particular, are probably the most essential "resource" for survival, but are generally established at an early age. Food resources are not stored or accumulated, and Aka males and females contribute similar percentages of calories to the diet. Cross-cultural studies have demonstrated that in societies where resources essential to survival can be accumulated or where males are the primary contributors to subsistence, fathers invest more time competing for these resources and, consequently, spend less time with their children. In contrast, where resources are not accumulable or men are not the primary contributors to subsistence, men generally spend more time in the direct care of their children. Katz and Konner (1981: 174) found that father–infant proximity (degree of emotional warmth and physical proximity) is closest in gathering-hunting populations (gathered foods by females are principal resources, meat is secondary) and most distant in cultures where herding or advanced agriculture is practiced. In the latter cultures, cattle, camels, and land are considered the essential accumulable resources necessary for survival. These findings are consistent with Whiting and Whiting's (1975) cross-cultural study of husband–wife intimacy. They found husband–wife intimacy to be greatest in cultures without accumulated resources or capital investments. While there are other factors to consider (the protection of resources and the polygyny rate), there is a strong tendency for fathers/husbands to devote more time to their children/wives if there are no accumulable resources.

Three additional factors seem to be especially influential in understanding the extraordinarily high level of Aka paternal care. First, the nature of Aka subsistence activity is rather unique cross-culturally. Usually mens' and womens' subsistence activities take place at very different locations. The net hunt and other subsistence activities, such as caterpillar collecting, involve men, women, and children. If men are going to help with infant care on a regular basis they have to be near the infant a good part of the day. The net hunt makes this possible. The net hunt also requires that men and women walk equal distances during the day. In most foraging societies, females do not travel as far from camp as males. Older siblings are not useful for helping their mothers because of the extensive labor involved in walking long distances with an infant. If a mother is to receive help on the net hunt, it needs to come from an adult. Most of the other adult females carry baskets full of food and have their own infants or young children to carry since fertility is high. Fathers are among the few alternative caregivers regularly available on the net hunt to help mothers. While fathers do carry infants on the net hunt, especially on the return from the hunt when the mothers' baskets are full of meat, collected nuts, and fruit, father–infant caregiving is much more likely to occur in the camp.

Another influential factor is the nature of husband–wife relations. The net hunt contributes substantially to the time husband and wife spend together and patterns the nature of that time spent together. Observations in the forest and village indicate husbands and wives are within sight of each other 46.5 percent of daylight hours. This is more time together than in any other known society, and it is primarily a result of the net hunt. This percentage of course increases in the evening hours. But, husbands and wives are not only together most of the day, they are actively cooperating on the net hunt. They have to know each other well to communicate and cooperate throughout the day. They work together to set up the family net, chase game into the net, butcher and divide the game and take care of the children. Husbands and wives help each other out in a number of domains, in part because they spend so much time together. Husband–wife relations are many-stranded; that is, social, economic, ritual, parenting, and leisure activities are shared and experienced in close proximity. When they return to camp the mother has a number of tasks—she collects firewood and water, and prepares the biggest meal of the day. The father has relatively few tasks to do after returning from the hunt. He may make string or repair the net, but he is available to help with infant care. He is willing to do infant care, in part, because of the many-stranded reciprocity between husband and wife. In many societies men have fewer tasks to do at the end of the day, while women have domestic tasks and prepare a meal. Men are available to help out with child care, but seldom provide much assistance, in part, due to the more distant husband–wife relationship.

The third important factor in understanding Aka fathers' involvement with infants is father-infant bonding. Father and infant are clearly attached to each other. Fathers seek out their infants and infants seek out their fathers. Fathers end up holding their infants frequently because the infants crawl to, reach for, or fuss for their fathers. Fathers pick up their infants because they intrinsically enjoy being close to their infants. They enjoy being with them and carry them in several different contexts (e.g., out in the fields drinking palm wine with other men).

While the factors described above are especially influential, other cultural factors also play a part. Gender egalitarianism pervades cultural beliefs and practices: Men do not have physical or institutional control over women, violence against women is rare or nonexistent, both women and men are valued for their different but complementary roles, there is flexibility in these gender roles, and holding infants is not perceived as being feminine or "women's work." Sharing, helping out, and generosity are central concepts in Aka life; this applies to subsistence and

parenting spheres. Aka ideology of good and bad fathers reiterates the importance of father's proximity—a good father shows love for his children, stays near them, and assists mother with caregiving when her workload is heavy. A bad father abandons his children and does not share food with them. There is no organized warfare and male feuding is infrequent, so men are around camp and help with subsistence rather than being away at battle. Fertility is high, so most adult women have nursing infants and there are few other adult women around to help out. Finally, the Aka move their camps several times a year and consequently do not accumulate material goods that need to be defended.

The point here is that Aka father-infant relations have to be viewed in a complex cultural nexus. Some cultural factors are somewhat more influential than others—net hunting, husband-wife relations, for instance—but even these cultural features take place in a web of other cultural beliefs and practices that contribute to the intimate nature of Aka father-infant relations.

FATHER–INFANT BONDING IN THE AKA AND UNITED STATES

Over 50 studies of European and American fathers indicate that father's interactions with infants and young children are clearly distinguished from mother's interactions in that fathers are the vigorous rough and tumble playmates of infants and young children, while mothers are sensitive caregivers. The American literature suggests that this rough and tumble play is how infants become attached to fathers ("bond") and develop social competence (Lamb et al. 1987). The Aka father–infant study is not consistent with the American studies that emphasize the importance of father's vigorous play. Aka fathers rarely, if ever, engage in vigorous play with their infants; only one episode of vigorous play by a father was recorded during all 264 hours of systematic observation. Informal observations during more than 10 field visits over the last 20 years are also consistent with this finding. The quantitative data indicate that by comparison to mothers, Aka fathers are significantly more likely to hug, kiss, or soothe a fussy baby while they are holding the infant.

While Aka fathers do not engage in vigorous play with their infants, they are slightly more playful than mothers; fathers are somewhat more likely to engage in minor physical play (e.g., tickling) with their one- to four-month-old infants than are mothers. But characterizing the Aka father as the infant's playmate would be misleading. Other caretakers, brothers and sisters in particular, engage in play with the infant while holding much more frequently than fathers or mothers. Mothers have more episodes of play over the course of a day than fathers or other caretakers because they hold the infant most of the time. The Aka father-infant relationship might be better characterized by its intimate and affective nature. Aka fathers hold their infants more than fathers in any other human society known to anthropologists, and Aka fathers also show affection more frequently while holding than do Aka mothers.

So how can vigorous play be a significant feature in American studies of father-infant bonding, but not among the Aka? Four factors appear to be important for understanding the process of Aka father–infant bonding: familiarity with the infant; knowledge of caregiving practices (how to hold an infant, how to soothe an infant); the degree of relatedness to the infant; and cultural values and parental goals.

First, due to frequent father-holding and availability, Aka fathers know how to communicate with their infants. Fathers know the early signs of infant hunger, fatigue, and illness as well as the limits in their ability to soothe the infant. They also know how to stimulate responses from the infant without being vigorous. Unlike American fathers, Aka wait for infants to initiate interaction. Aka caregivers other than mothers and fathers are less familiar with the infants and the most physical in their play, suggesting a relationship between intimate knowledge of the infant's cues and the frequency of vigorous play while holding. Consistent with this is the finding that working mothers in the U.S. are more likely to engage in vigorous play than are stay-at-home mothers.

Second, knowledge of infant caregiving practices seems to play a role in determining how much play is exhibited in caretaker-infant interactions. Child caretakers were the most physical and the loudest (singing) in their handling of infants. Children were not restricted from holding infants, but they were closely watched by parents. While "other" caretakers were more playful than mothers or fathers, younger fathers and "other" caretakers were more physical than older ones, probably because they did not know how to handle and care for infants as well as adult caretakers.

A third factor to consider is the degree of relatedness of the caretaker to the infant. If vigorous play can assist in developing attachment, more closely related individuals may have a greater vested interest in establishing this bond than distantly related individuals. Attachment not only enhances the survival of the infant, but it can potentially increase the related caretaker's survival and fitness. Aka mothers and fathers establish attachment by their frequent caregiving; vigorous play is not necessary to establish affective saliency. Brothers and sisters, on the other hand, might establish this bond through physical play. Aka brothers and sisters, in fact, provided essentially all of the physical play the focal infants received; cousins and unrelated children were more likely to engage in face-to-face play with the infant instead of physical play.

Finally, cultural values and parental goals of infant development should be considered. American culture encourages individualistic aggressive competition; Aka culture values cooperation, nonaggression, and prestige avoidance (one does not draw attention to oneself even, for instance, if one kills an elephant). Apparently, Americans tolerate—if not actually encourage—

aggressive rough-and-tumble types of play with infants. Also, due to the high infant mortality rate, the primary parental goal for Aka is the survival of their infants. The constant holding and immediate attention to fussing reflect this goal. In the United States, infant mortality rates are markedly lower and, as a result, parental concern for survival may not be as great. The Aka infant is taken away from a caretaker who plays roughly with the infant, in part because it could be seen as aggressive behavior, but also because the pervasive aim of infant care practices is survival of the infant, and rough-and-tumble play could risk the infant's safety.

These factors tentatively clarify why Aka fathers do not engage in vigorous play like American fathers, but do participate in slightly more physical play than Aka mothers (but not more than other caretakers). American fathers infrequently participate directly in infant care and consequently are not as familiar with infant cues. To stimulate interaction and (possibly) bonding, they engage in physical play. Aka brothers and sisters are also much less physical in their play with infants than America fathers (Aka never tossed infants in the air or swung them by their arms), again suggesting that Aka children know their infant brother or sister and the necessary infant caregiving skills better than American fathers. These observations are obviously speculative and need further empirical study.

Sociologists LaRossa and LaRossa (1981) also describe stylistic differences between American mothers' and fathers' interactions with their infants. They list a number of male–female role dichotomies that reflect different parenting styles. One distinction they make is role distance versus role embracement. Fathers are more likely to distance themselves from the parenting role while mothers are more likely to embrace the parenting role. American women generally want to remain in primary control of the children, and while fathers may show interest in caregiving, they are more likely to distance themselves from caregiving while embracing their

roles as the breadwinners. LaRossa and LaRossa also suggest that fathers generally have low intrinsic value and relatively high extrinsic value, while mothers have the reverse.

> The intrinsic value of something or someone is the amount of sheer pleasure or enjoyment that one gets from experiencing an object or person. The extrinsic value of something or someone is the amount of social rewards (e.g., money, power, prestige) associated with having or being with the object or person. (64)

They use this dichotomy to explain why fathers are more likely to carry or hold an infant in public than in private. Fathers receive extrinsic rewards from those in public settings, while this does not happen in the home. According to LaRossa and LaRossa,

> Fathers will roughhouse with their toddlers on the living-room floor, and will blush when hugged or kissed by the one-year-olds, but when you really get down to it, they just do not have that much fun when they are with their children. If they had their druthers, they would be working at the office or drinking at the local pub. (65)

These role dichotomies may be useful for understanding American mother–father parenting styles, but they have limited value in characterizing Aka mother–father distinctions. Aka mothers and fathers embrace the parenting role. Generally, mothers and fathers want to hold their infants, and certainly they derive pleasure from infant interactions. As indicated earlier, fathers were in fact more likely to show affection while holding than mothers. Fathers also offered their nipples to infants who wanted to nurse, cleaned mucus from their infants' noses, picked lice from their infants' hair, and cleaned their infants after they urinated or defecated (often on the father). Fathers' caregiving did not appear any more or less perfunctory than mothers'. Aka fathers are not burdened with infant care; if a father does not want to hold or care for the infant he gives the infant to another person. Overall, Aka fathers embrace their parenting role as much as they embrace their hunting role.

The intrinsic–extrinsic role dichotomy does not fit well with Aka mother–father parenting styles either. Again, both Aka mothers and fathers place great intrinsic value and little extrinsic value on parenting. The fathers' intrinsic value is demonstrated above, but the lack of extrinsic value among the Aka can best be seen by comparing Aka and Ngandu fathers (the Ngandu are the horticulturalist trading partners of the Aka). When a Ngandu father holds his infant in public he is "on stage." He goes out of his way to show his infant to those who pass by, and frequently tries to stimulate the infant while holding it. He is much more vigorous in his interactions with the infant than are Aka men. The following experience exemplifies Ngandu fathers' extrinsic value towards their infants. An Ngandu friend showed me a 25-pound fish he had just caught, and I asked to take a photograph of him with his fish. He said fine, promptly picked up his nearby infant, and proudly displayed his fish and infant for the photograph. His wife was also nearby but was not invited into the photograph. Aka fathers, on the other hand, are matter-of-fact about their holding or transporting of infants in public places. They do not draw attention to their infants. Aka fathers also hold their infants in all kinds of social and economic contexts.

CONCLUSION

This paper has examined the cultural nexus of Aka father–infant bonding and has made some comparisons to middle-class American father–infant relations. American fathers are characterized by their vigorous play with infants, while Aka fathers are characterized by their affectionate and intimate relations with their infants. Aka infants bond with their fathers because they provide sensitive and regular care, whereas American infants bond to their fathers, in part, due to their vigorous play. The purpose of this paper is not to criticize American fathers for their style of interaction with their infants; physical play is important in middle-class American context because it is a means for fathers who are seldom around their infants to demonstrate their love and interest in the infant. Vigorous play may also be important to American mothers who work outside the home; studies indicate they are also more likely than stay-at-home mothers to engage in vigorous play with their infants. The Aka study does imply that father–infant bonding does not always take place through physical play, and it is necessary to explore a complex cultural nexus in order to understand the nature of father-infant relations.

Aka fathers are very close and affectionate with their infants, and their attachment processes, as defined in Western bonding theory, appear to be similar to that of mothers. While Aka mother- and father–infant relations are similar they are not the same. Fathers do spend substantially less time with infants than do mothers, and the nature of their interactions is different. Aka and American fathers bring something qualitatively different to their children; father's caregiving pattern is not simply a variation of mother's pattern. More research is needed on the unique features of father involvement so we can move away from a "deficit" model of fathering.

Finally, this paper identifies cultural factors that influence father-infant bonding; biological forces are not considered. This is unusual in that mother-infant bonding generally mentions or discusses the biological basis of mother's attachment to the infant. The release of prolactin and oxytocin with birth and lactation is said to increase affectionate feelings and actions toward the infant. These same hormones exist in men but endocrinologists generally believe they have no function in men. Is there a biology of fatherhood, or is motherhood more biological and fatherhood more cultural? This is a complex question as both men and women probably have evolved ("biological") psychological mechanisms that influence their parenting, but if one just focuses on endocrinology, few data exist on the endocrinology of fatherhood. For instance, Gubernick et al. (unpublished paper) found that men's testosterone levels decreased significantly two weeks after the birth of their children; the decrease was not linked to decline in sexual behavior, increased stress, or sleep deprivation. Another small study of American fathers indicated significant increases in plasma prolactin levels after fathers held their 3-month-old infants on their chest for 15 minutes (Hewlett and Alster, unpublished data). The few biological studies that do exist suggest that biology can and does influence fatherhood. More studies of the biocultural nexus of fatherhood are needed.

While biology probably influences both mothers' and fathers' parenting to some degree, this chapter has demonstrated that the cultural nexus is a powerful force that profoundly shapes the nature and context of father-infant bonding. Aka father-infant bonding takes place through regular and intimate (i.e., hugging, kissing, soothing) care while American father-infant bonding takes place through vigorous play. American fathers often do not know their infants very well and try to demonstrate their love and concern through vigorous play. American mothers that work outside the home also tend to be more vigorous with their infants. American fathers are not necessarily "bad" fathers because they do not do as much direct caregiving as the Aka fathers. Fathers around the world "provide" and enrich the lives of their children in diverse ways (e.g., physical and emotional security, economic well-being). The Aka data do suggest that there are alternative processes by which father-infant bonding can and does take place and that Americans and others might learn from this comparative approach as policy decisions about parental leave and other topics are considered.

REFERENCES

Ainsworth, M.D.S. 1967. *Infancy in Uganda: Infant Care and the Growth of Love.* Baltimore: Johns Hopkins Press.

Bahuchet, S. 1985. *Les Pygmees Aka et la Foret Centrafricaine.* Paris: Selaf.

Betzig, L., A. Harrigan, and P. Turke. 1990. "Childcare on Ifaluk." *Zeitscrift fur Ethnologie* 114.

Bowlby, J. 1969. *Attachment and Loss Vol. 1: Attachment.* New York: Basic Books.

Chodorow, N. 1974. "Family Structure and Feminine Personality." In *Woman, Culture, and Society,* ed. Michelle Zimbalist Rosaldo and Louise Lamphere. Stanford, CA: Stanford University Press.

Clarke-Stewart, K.A. 1980. "The Father's Contribution to Children's Cognitive and Social Development in Early Childhood." In *The Father-Infant Relationship,* ed. S.A. Pedersen. New York: Praeger.

Cole, M., and J.S. Bruner. 1974. "Cultural Differences and Inferences about Psychological Processes." In *Culture and Cognition,* ed. J.W. Berry and P.R. Dasen. London: Methuen.

Freud, S. 1938. *An Outline of Psychoanalysis.* London: Hogarth.

Gubernick, D.J., C.M. Worthman, and J.F. Stallings. "Hormonal Correlates of Fatherhood in Men." Unpublished paper.

Hamilton, A. 1981. *Nature and Nurture: Aboriginal Child-Rearing in North-Central Arnhem Land.* Canberra: Australian Institute of Aboriginal Studies.

Harlow, H.F. 1961. "The Development of Affectional Patterns in Infant Monkeys." In *Determinants of Infant Behavior,* Vol. 1, ed. B.M. Foss. London: Methuen.

Hewlett, B.S. 1989. "Multiple Caretaking Among African Pygmies. *American Anthropologist* 91: 186–191.

———. 1991. *Intimate Fathers: The Nature and Context of Aka Pygmy Paternal-Infant Care.* Ann Arbor, MI: University of Michigan Press.

———. 1992 (ed.). *Father-Child Relations: Cultural and Biosocial Perspectives.* NY: Aldine de Gruyter.

Hewlett, B.S. and D. Alster. "Prolactin and Infant Holding among American Fathers." Unpublished manuscript.

Katz, M.M., and Melvin J. Konner. 1981. "The Role of Father: An Anthropological Perspective." In *The Role of Father in Child Development,* ed. Michael E. Lamb. New York: John Wiley and Sons.

Lamb, M.E., ed. 1981. *The Role of the Father in Child Development* 2nd ed. New York: John Wiley & Sons.

Lamb, M.E., J.H. Pleck, E.L. Charnov, and J.A. LeVine. 1987. "A Biosocial Perspective on

Paternal Behavior and Involvement." In *Parenting Across the Lifespan,* ed. J.B. Lancaster, J. Altmann, A. Rossi, L.R. Sherrod. Hawthorne, NY: Aldine.

Lancaster, J.B., and C.S. Lancaster. 1987. "The Watershed: Change in Parental-Investment and Family Formation Strategies in the Course of Human Evolution." In *Parenting Across the Life Span,* ed. J.B. Lancaster, J. Altmann, A.S. Rossi, and L.R. Sherrod. Hawthorne, NY: Aldine.

LaRossa, R., and M.M. LaRossa. 1981. *Transition to Parenthood: How Infants Change Families.* Beverly Hills: Sage Publications.

LeVine, R.A., S. Dixon, S. LeVine, A. Richman, P.H. Leiderman, C.H. Keefer, and T.B. Brazelton. 1994. *Child Care and Culture: Lessons from Africa.* New York: Cambridge University Press.

Munroe, R.H., and R.L. Munroe. 1992. "Fathers in Children's Environments: A Four Culture Study." In *Father-Child Relations: Cultural and Biosocial Contexts,* Barry S. Hewlett, ed. New York: Aldine de Gruyter.

Rosaldo, M.Z., and L. Lamphere, eds. 1974. *Woman, Culture and Society.* Stanford, CA: Stanford University Press.

West, M.M., and M.J. Konner. 1976. "The Role of Father in Anthropological Perspective." In *The Role of the Father in Child Development.* 2nd ed., M.E. Lamb, ed. New York: John Wiley and Sons.

Whiting, B.B., and J.W.M. Whiting. 1975. *Children of Six Cultures.* Cambridge, MA: Harvard University Press.

Winn, S., G.A. Morelli, and E.Z. Tronick. 1990. "The Infant in the Group: A Look at Efe Caretaking Practices." In *The Cultural Context of Infancy,* J.K. Nugent, B.M. Lester, and T.B. Brazelton, eds. Norwood, NJ: Ablex.

II
Gender and Prehistory

A popular introductory archaeology text began its career 15 years ago with the title *Men of the Earth* (Fagan 1974). For the last several editions (Fagan 1977–1991) it has been called *People of the Earth*. This change is deliberate and illustrates a growing sensitivity on the part of some archaeologists to the importance of considering the contribution of women, as well as men, to the history of our species (Wylie 1991, 1992; Gero and Conkey 1991; Seifert 1991). An archaeological focus on gender provides a lens for reassessing myths about the past that glorify men as the agents of cultural change. As some archaeologists seek to reinstate women as agents and as subjects, widely held assumptions about "mankind" and "man's past" are challenged by a focus on women's involvement in production, politics, and the generation of symbol systems in past societies. In contrast to earlier archaeological orientations (see Conkey and Spector 1984 for a review of archaeological approaches), an "engendered" archaeology assumes that the process of survival throughout human history has of necessity involved a collaborative effort between men and women. Those who advocate a feminist-informed archaeology have explored such issues as women's participation in the creation of wealth (for example, women's production of textiles or ceramics), consequences of women's rule in state societies, images of powerful women in prehistoric art, and women's roles in the development of agriculture (Spielmann 1995; Simon and Ravesloot 1995).

Questions of fundamental importance regarding the sexual division of labor in past societies may benefit from an archaeological perspective that includes women's interests. Rather than assuming that the "earliest human groups were conscious of and elaborated sex differences into differentially valued, gender-exclusive task groups," Spector and Whelan (1989: 73) suggest that an archaeology of gender needs to begin by raising questions about the origins of a sexual division of labor and by determining what gender differentiation might have accomplished among early human populations (Spector and Whelan 1989: 72–73; see also Ehrenberg 1989).

As Conkey (this book) suggests, in the study of gender in archaeology, we are reminded of the importance of confronting presuppositions and values that guide our work, however "scientific" we presume our methodologies to be. Conkey outlines a number of challenges for future archaeological research. First, archaeologists must recognize and eliminate biased reconstructions of past gender roles that derive from our own cultural assumptions. Second, they must pay more attention to theories about gender in analyzing their data. Third, archaeologists need to use their data to make explicit inferences about men and women in prehistory. Finally, Conkey points out biases not only in analysis but also in the very practice of archaeology. Eliminating gender bias from archaeology, as Conkey suggests, will require a major commitment to the same critical reflection that has characterized other branches of anthropology. As Nelson and Kehoe (1990: 4) observe, "disentangling our culture-bound assumptions from the actual archaeological record will be a long and wrenching procedure."

Similarly, Galloway (in this volume) argues that ethnocentric bias has shaped archaeological interpretations of menstrual seclusion structures in late prehistoric Southeastern Indian societies. Like Conkey, she advocates "engendering archaeology," and suggests that the search for evidence of menstrual practices is a direct route to finding women in the archaeological record. Menstrual seclusion may be an important correlate of social organization, indicating the probability of matrilineal kinship. Accordingly, investigation of menstrual structures may provide a means of testing for matriliny archaeologically. In spite of the likelihood that there are thousands of menstrual structures in the Southeast, so far none has been reliably reported from an archaeological context. Galloway argues that discomfort with the topic has produced its erasure from scientific discourse, and urges archaeologists both to reinterpret existing data and search for new evidence on these "women's houses," and the artifactual evidence of ritual elements and requirements of daily life associated with them.

Nelson's discussion of Upper Paleolithic "Venus" figurines in archaeology textbooks (in this book) also illustrates Conkey's point about the potential for distortion in the archaeological record when cultural values affect archaeological analysis. Nelson demonstrates that most textbooks convey the same ideological message in their treatment of Venus figurines—that adult male humans are fascinated by women's bodies and view them as signs of fertility. The widely held assumption that Upper Paleolithic figurines possibly depicting human females are fertility fetishes is, according to Nelson, poorly founded. Feminist analysis of the figurines suggests alternative explanations regarding their production, functions, and symbolism, and serves as a warning that "reinforcing present cultural stereotypes by projecting them into the past allows whole generations of students to believe that our present gender constructs are eternal and unchanging" (Nelson 1990: 19; see also Rice 1991).

In an effort to better explain contemporary gender relations, archaeological evidence has offered a means of understanding the present by reconstructing our evolutionary past. Scholarly and public imaginations have been drawn to the possibility that archaeological data might document the existence of a matriarchal society in which women occupied a privileged position as rulers. If powerful women could be found in history or prehistory, this would serve as evidence that male dominance is not inevitable.

Images of matriarchy exist in both western and nonwestern societies. Nineteenth-century evolutionists such as J.J. Bachofen (1967) described a history of humankind that passed from a state of primitive communal marriages, through mother right, or a rule of women, to patriarchy. Similar myths of matriarchy have been recorded in several South American societies (Bamberger 1974: 266). According to Bamberger these myths share a common theme, that of women's loss of power through moral failure. The myths describe a past society in which women held power; however, through their inability to handle power when they had it, the rule of women was eventually replaced by patriarchal leadership.

Rather than representing historical events, the myths of matriarchy serve as a tool to keep woman bound to her place. They reinforce current social relations by justifying male dominance (Bamberger 1974: 280). There is no historical or archaeological evidence of matriarchal societies in which women systematically and exclusively dominated men. In spite of the absence of such evidence the idea remains popular, precisely because it conveys the possibility of a future society characterized by female dominance that is reminiscent of the matriarchal past.

Culturally based assumptions can be avoided by paying more careful attention to a range of sources at our disposal in the archaeological record. The reconstruction of gender roles and relations in past societies may be facilitated by representations of women and men in burials, images, and written texts. Literary texts pertaining to early Sumer, for instance, portray women in supportive, nurturing roles, acting to further the interests of male political rulers or heroes (Pollock 1991). In some texts, women are also described as political officeholders, or queens. Pollock concludes that some women seem to have had significant political and economic power, although few of them were written about, compared to the number of men in such positions whose lives were more fully recorded. Women also held offices in the temple hierarchy as priestesses; it is possible that these were the primary positions of power available to women. An informative example is that of the priestess Enheduanna, installed at Ur by her father King Sargon. Literary texts suggest that she acted to further her father's political ambitions as well as her own authority (Pollock 1991). These texts, as well as other representations such as burials and images, suggest that Sumerian women were not pawns to be manipulated by men, but were able to attain positions of high status and power.

Similarly, recent access to Maya history by decipherment of glyphic texts on public monuments has shown that some royal women played politically central roles in their kingdoms. Hypogamy, or the marriage of higher-status women to lower-status men, insured the alliance of these lower-status men to higher-status men of their wives' families. Hypergamy, or the marriage of lower-status women to higher-status men, also occurred. More importantly, the women involved in marriage alliance and royal politics were anything but passive pawns in the games of men. Freidel and Schele (in this book) look at the lives and exploits of powerful Maya women in two classic-period kingdoms to show that generalities based on limited data often fail in the face of detailed information. They also show that royal women can emerge as extraordinarily heroic figures and great politicians when their stories are known. In the case of two important royal Maya women, whose stories are told in glyphs, Freidel and Schele explore what happened when one revived a failing kingdom and the other, whose own child was passed over for heirship to the throne, was permitted to raise a beautiful temple in her city that memorialized her in perpetuity. The various forms of power exercised by these women suggest that although there were no matriarchies in the past, women could control important resources and influence the course of public events. Little is known about the lives of commoner women, whose exploits are less visible in texts and other representations. The limited information available on commoner Maya women highlights the need for innovative conceptual and methodological approaches to the archaeological record that will help reconstruct gender roles in past societies.

Conkey and Spector discuss the general problem of the "archaeological invisibility" of women (1984: 5), which, they contend, is more the result of a false notion of objectivity and of the gender paradigms archaeologists use than of an inherent invisibility of such data (Conkey and Spector 1984:6). Questions that would elicit information about prehistoric gender behavior or organization are too infrequently asked, while researchers "bring to their work preconceived notions about what each sex ought to do, and these notions serve to structure the way artifacts are interpreted" (for example, the presumption of linkages between projectile points with men and pots with women) (Conkey and Spector 1984: 10). In contrast, goals for a feminist archaeology would include gender-inclusive reconstructions of past human behavior, the development of a specific paradigm for the study of gender, and an explicit effort to eliminate androcentrism in the content and mode of presentation of archaeological research (Conkey and Spector 1984: 15).

REFERENCES

Bachofen, Johann. 1967. *Myth, Religion and Mother Right* [Die Mutterrecht 1861 orig.]. London: Routledge and Kegan Paul.

Bamberger, Joan. 1974. "The Myth of Matriarchy: Why Men Rule in Primitive Society." In Michelle Z. Rosaldo and Louise Lamphere (eds.). *Woman, Culture, and Society*, pp. 263–281. Stanford: Stanford University Press.

Conkey, Margaret W. and Janet Spector. 1984. "Archaeology and the Study of Gender." In Michael B. Schiffer (ed.). *Advances in Archaeological Method and Theory*, Vol. 7, pp. 1–29. New York: Academic Press.

Ehrenberg, Margaret. 1989. *Women in Prehistory.* Norman, Oklahoma: University of Oklahoma Press.

Fagan, Brian. 1974. *Men of the Earth.* Boston: Little, Brown and Co.

Gero, J.M. and Margaret W. Conkey (eds.). 1991. *Engendering Archaeology: Women in Prehistory.* Oxford: Basil Blackwell.

Nelson, Sarah M. 1990. "Diversity of the Upper Paleolithic Venus Figurines and Archeological Mythology." In Sarah M. Nelson and Alice B. Kehoe (eds.). *Powers of Observation: Alternative Views in Archeology*, pp. 11–23. *Archeological Papers of the American Anthropological Association*, Number 2.

Nelson, Sarah M. and Alice B. Kehoe. 1990. "Introduction." In Sarah M. Nelson and Alice B. Kehoe (eds.). *Powers of Observation: Alternative Views in Archeology*, pp. 1–10. *Archeological Papers of the American Anthropological Association*, Number 2.

Pollock, Susan. 1991. "Women in a Men's World: Images of Sumerian Women." In Joan Gero and Margaret Conkey (eds.). *Engendering Archaeology: Women and Prehistory.* Oxford: Basil Blackwell.

Rice, Patricia. 1991. "Prehistoric Venuses: Symbols of Motherhood or Womanhood?" *Journal of Anthropological Research* 37 (4): 402–414.

Seifert, Donna J. (ed.). 1991. "Gender in Historical Archaeology." *Historical Archeology* (special issue) 25 (4): 1–132.

Simon, Arleyn W. and John C. Ravesloot. 1995. "Salado Ceramic Burial Offerings: A Consideration of Gender and Social Organization." *Journal of Anthropological Research* 51 (2): 103–124.

Spector, Janet D. and Mary K. Whelan. 1989. "Incorporating Gender into Archaeology Courses." In Sandra Morgen (ed.). *Gender and Anthropology: Critical Reviews for Research and Teaching*, pp. 65–95. Washington, DC: American Anthropological Association.

Spielmann, Katherine A. 1995. "Glimpses of Gender in the Prehistoric Southwest." *Journal of Anthropological Research* 51 (2): 91–102.

Wylie, Alison, 1991. "Feminist Critiques and Archaeological Challenges." In D. Walde and N. Willows (eds.). *The Archaeology of Gender*, pp. 17–23. Calgary: The Archaeological Association of Calgary.

———. 1992. "The Interplay of Evidential Constraints and Political Interests: Recent Archaeological Research on Gender." *American Antiquity* 57 (1): 15–35.

Men and Women in Prehistory: An Archaeological Challenge

Margaret W. Conkey

When we close our eyes and think about the human societies and groups that lived thousands of years ago, what kinds of men and women do we "see"? What are they doing? What kinds of roles and relationships do we imagine? When we think about this we realize that there must have been many different roles and relationships. There must have been men of power and women of power, men with children and women as decision makers, men making pots and women making stone tools, men and women working together in the fields, men in trance and women as healers.

Yet, all too often archaeological accounts and the popular reconstructions of past societies that appear in magazines or coffeetable books suggest a much simpler picture: men hunting, women gathering plants, men making tools, women with children carrying firewood. Why do we have such simple and yet very familiar kinds of reconstructions? Certainly part of the explanation is that archaeologists have not done much that explicitly asks about gender, yet they have developed models or reconstructions that involve gender. These reconstructions derive from a variety of problematic sources: from ethnographic accounts that are gender biased (such as the previous quote from Levi-Strauss) or from the beliefs that twentieth century (mostly western, white, male)

Original material prepared for this text.

archaeologists hold about gender, about men and women, and about how prehistoric societies "worked" and changed. We are all, of course, quite susceptible to our own cultural ideas, ideals, and ideologies. Most North American archaeologists have taken somewhat longer to be as reflexive and self-critical about this than some of their anthropological colleagues.

Thus, to think about men and women in prehistoric societies and to think about their gender roles, gender ideologies, and gender relations raises several archaeological challenges. First, there is the challenge of recognizing and stripping away the biased or implied gender reconstructions. Second, there is the challenge of understanding more explicitly what gender is about so we can develop a theory of gender that is useful in archaeological research. Third, there is the challenge of making explicit inferences about gender and about men and women, using archaeological data to help answer questions concerning what might have happened in prehistory.

On one hand, archaeologists have not taken gender as an important research question; they have, in fact, come quite late to the field of gender studies or to any kind of insights from feminist theory. The first major paper that reviewed archaeology and the study of gender (Conkey and Spector 1984) came more than ten years after the first major books in sociocultural anthropology, and most archaeology in North America is housed in departments of anthropology. On the other hand, archaeology has not been silent about gender. Our accounts of prehistoric societies have been "saturated" with gender, but most of these accounts are—as we will see—male-centered, or androcentric. At this point in the development of gender studies within archaeology, at least half of the task of thinking about men and women in prehistory is to question the gendered accounts that pervade our reconstructions of past societies and of how cultures have changed with time.

CHALLENGING GENDER BIAS

Although many archaeologists maintain that it is very difficult to know, or to make inferences, about gender relations or even about male and female activities in prehistoric societies, gender assertions are made regularly in interpretations. Often these assertions are so implicit that archaeologists don't really "see" them as specific ideas that need to be confirmed or tested. Most ideas about gender have come from the implicit and stereotypical gender models of our own sociopolitical lives (e.g., women at home) or from the androcentric ethnographies of sociocultural anthropology. In the early 1970s when anthropology "discovered" the widespread androcentric biases in ethnographic accounts, most of archaeology—which really *depends* on ethnographic analogies—was not paying much attention!

To take apart, or deconstruct, archaeological interpretations can be very useful, but this should not be taken as an end in itself. Rather, this critical scrutiny is part of the way in which we come to see not just *that* research and "results" can be biased, but exactly *how* they are biased and in what ways. This historical analysis of archaeological accounts is a necessary part of the process whereby we transform what we do. In reviews of the treatment of gender in the archaeological literature of the 1960s through the early 1980s, Mary Kennedy, Janet Spector, and I found some significant problems that are worth summarizing to understand how bias works (Conkey and Spector 1984).

First, we found that women—if they are present at all in reconstructions of prehistory—are usually depicted in a narrow range of passive, home-oriented tasks; they are often

"exchanged" as wives, the objects of art and image-making, and symbols of fertility and sexuality. In contrast prehistoric men are shown as very public, far-ranging (adventurous), productive, active, and responsible for most of the significant changes in human evolution, especially technological innovations. These kinds of representations led Ruth Hubbard (1982) to write an article entitled, "Have only men evolved?"

Second, archaeologists often go through interpretive "contortions" to avoid suggesting that some prehistoric women might actually have been strong, active, or determining people in cultural life. For example one archaeological account of burials interpreted the same artifacts quite differently when they were found in a woman's grave than when found in a man's (Winters 1968). A pestle buried with a woman was there because in life she had done foodprocessing and grinding with it; the same kind of pestle in a man's grave was there because he had *made* it. If a spear-thrower (*atlatl*) was found in a man's grave, it was because he had used it; if found in a woman's grave, it was a gift to her, or, the archaeologist speculated, there really were (female) "Amazons" in this river valley. If trade goods were buried with a man, it was because he controlled the trading; if in a woman's grave, it was because she simply "had" the items. Thus, bias and differential representations of men and women can emerge in archaeological interpretations. Men, in prehistoric societies, often performed (various) "activities"; women (more passively) engaged in "tasks." Male activities are often described in more detail, and they are portrayed more frequently than female ones.

Ethnographers have noted that in many horticultural societies (those that cultivate plants with a simple technology) women do most of the field labor; they are often associated with plants. Archaeologists have long been fascinated with how and why some prehistoric people developed horticulture, which predominated over hunting-gathering-fishing as a way of life and as a subsistence system. In one study of how archaeologists account for the cultural innovation of "horticulture" (the domestication of plants) in the eastern woodlands of the United States, the analysts—Pat Watson and Mary Kennedy (1991)—show how the two major accounts have suggested some of the most obscure or contorted ways in which horticulture was developed to avoid suggesting that women might have been the innovators. One account accepts the idea that women were extremely familiar with plant resources when these societies were primarily collecting wild foods for their resources and the idea that *after* the "invention" of agriculture, women were the primary crop tenders. However, according to this account invention happened because shamans—men, of course— came to control the production and reproduction of the squashes that they used for gourd rattles in their ceremonies. Indeed, squashes were among some of the early cultivated plants in this region, but it is very difficult to link the speculative notion about shamans in one narrow context to such a major change in subsistence practices.

The other account suggests that because human occupation sites are areas of soil disturbance, this would have been a likely place for stray seeds from wild plants to have been "naturally" encouraged to the point of deliberate further modifications by humans. In other words the plants just about domesticated themselves. As Watson and Kennedy argue these two primary interpretations seem to go to considerable extremes to avoid disrupting the "sacred association" of women-passive-plants.

From this and other critiques it is clear that unexamined and present assumptions about gender have crept into archaeological interpretation. Explicit attention to women as active and as having varied roles and positions is usually absent. There is also a lack of consideration of other kinds of gender relations than those of the idealized mid-twentieth century—white, western, middle-class—with a sexual division of labor and a male-dominated, androcentric society. The reconstructions of our most ancient hominid ancestors, more

than 2 million years ago, show a monogamous nuclear family unit: The male strides ahead across the savannah landscape, carrying a pointed stick as tool and/or as weapon. The female is several steps behind, carrying a young child on her hip.

The most widely touted version (Lovejoy 1981) of the social life of early hominids is that of men (mobile, risk taking, and adventurous), who "provision" the females and young with the most desirable resources (especially meat); the waiting women cluster for protection at a "home base," while making limited forays for gathered foods. Clearly, this is a familiar picture to us, not because it has been well demonstrated with archaeological (or other) data, but because it represents a culturally idealized (yet culturally limited) view of gender and socioeconomic relationships.

Such an interpretation is problematic. It invites and reifies the idea that there are deep and specific *continuities* in how men and women relate to each other in gender roles and gender positions. By suggesting that mobile men have been provisioning dependent and relatively constrained women and children for more than 2 million years, this account strongly implies that this is "natural" and therefore legitimate. Specific and narrow gender relations are universalized—"it's always been this way"—and convey the (mistaken) idea that these relationships and gender stereotypes are inevitable and immutable (unchanging and unchangeable).

The kinds of biased archaeological views I have discussed are promoted and reinforced by androcentric ethnographic and ethnoarchaeological accounts.[1] When John Yellen (1977) reported on his ethnoarchaeological studies of the !Kung people of the Kalahari desert of southern Africa, he first noted how research has shown that the female gathering of food accounts for most of the !Kung diet (60 to 80 percent). In writing about his observations based on living with and interviewing various !Kung people, however, he finds that "in practice, it is much easier to talk to the men because each day is in some way unique and stands out in the hunter's mind. Asking women where they went produces much less detailed and reliable information" (Yellen 1977:62–63).

Although this kind of reporting raises another central issue—the relationship between the observer and the people being studied—the *effects* of this kind of statement on the reader are insidious and powerful. This is particularly because ethnoarchaeological studies of contemporary people like the !Kung have been carried out specifically to build models for interpreting prehistoric hunter-gatherers. If women are never named and if they are portrayed as somehow wandering around the Kalahari with no clear recollection of what they did or where they have been, how can we avoid using these impressions in our visions of past social life?

So far we have seen how bias can creep into archaeological accounts when the analysts do not consciously reflect on their assumptions or explicitly use some theoretical models about gender. The differential use of language to describe men and women has further contributed to problematic accounts of their activities and contributions to human societies. Further archaeology, like all other research, is influenced by and embedded in the social and political worlds within which it is practiced. At this point in the development of our field the topic with which we are concerned is just as much the gender of archaeology as the archaeology of gender.

There is now a very well established body of literature that shows how the values, cultural assumptions, and social contexts of the researchers can and do strongly affect the kind of science that is practiced.[2] *All* sciences are social; every fact has a factor, a maker, who is a person of a certain nationality, race, class, ethnicity, and gender. In many instances some of these factors do affect their research (e.g., Latour and Woolgar 1986). For example, to draw further on the !Kung case given previously, it is more likely that Yellen did not get precise information from the women because he is a western, foreign man than because they didn't know where they go and what they do. As an ethnographer Yellen was admittedly attracted to male information because !Kung men would and could speak to him and give him information in *his* terms. This needs to be recognized before an ethnographer writes in a way that creates gender differences, in this case in knowledge between !Kung men and women, that perpetuate androcentric accounts to be accepted and applied by other researchers.

In archaeology it is also true that women tend to be relegated to or take up what are considered to be more marginal positions and jobs. Usually this is the lab analysis or "housework" of archaeology (Gero 1985). In Americanist archaeology the statistics confirm that it has been predominantly a white male enterprise; Robert Ascher (citing Kidder 1949) discusses the two types of archaeologists as being either "hairy-chested" or "hairy-chinned" (Ascher 1960). *Who* the practitioners are affects the kinds of questions that are given priority in research and thus the interpretations of the past.

Gero (1991a) has shown, for example, that when archaeologists replicate various prehistoric tools and technologies through experiments, male archaeologists do all the manufacturing (and they especially manufacture the finished tools, the projectile points thought central to the hunting of wild game), and female archaeologists do much of the edge-wear or use-wear analysis. For this they study in the laboratory the polishes left on the edges of tools and used pieces from the various activities, such as hide working and plant or wood processing. Furthermore, Gero (1991b) has also shown how the studies of American Paleoindian cultures have been dominated by male archaeologists and how the primary picture of Paleoindian lifeways is one that focuses almost exclusively on activities presumed to be male, especially the hunting of big game, with all the associated tools and strategies.

The point of studies like Gero's is not merely to "expose" and critique androcentric thinking. It is a serious charge to note that the nature of archaeological knowledge about the past is directly created by the topics that are given research priority and that these are very much influenced by the gender, class, race, ethnicity, and nationality of the practitioners (and of those who fund archaeology). Rather, the point of such studies is to understand how such factors work and to ask critical questions, such as "where *do* archaeologists get the assumptions about gender and social life that underlie their interpretations?"[3]

MAKING GENDER EXPLICIT IN ARCHAEOLOGICAL RESEARCH

I have already noted how ideas about gender drawn from ethnography or ethnoarchaeology must be critically evaluated because of long-standing biases (Moore 1988). Additionally, archaeologists have been drawing primarily on specific theoretical frameworks in the last several decades that have very little to offer in terms of making inferences about social processes and social life, except in a general way. That is, the preferred—and in many ways very productive—theories have been cultural ecology (how humans relate to their environment), cultural evolution (how societies and cultures change), and systems theory (how societies and cultures "work" on a grand scale). There is very little in these theories about social *relations* and much less about gender. Even most materialist approaches have never looked at how cultural materials are part of gender relations; until recently, most material culture studies in archaeology have not viewed artifacts as active means through which social relations are produced. If archaeologists thought materials could be used to "say" something about past societies, it was usually a direct "reflection" of relatively static social phenomena, such as status (e.g., a burial item reflects the status of the deceased) or "group" (e.g., an artifact style reflects the existence of a specific "ethnic group"). When material culture and artifacts are understood as an active part of the definition and transformation of social relationships, we can then ask how the artifacts have

been part of these social processes, including gender relations. For example, one ethnoarchaeological study (Braithwaite 1982) has shown how, among the Azande of the Sudan (Africa), the decorated ceramics (not the plainware) are used by women to serve food to men because this exchange and interface between men and women is considered potentially dangerous and ambiguous. The use of decorated ceramics is integral to, and signifies, the tensions and the enactments of these male/female gender relations.

However, although gender, like many other aspects of social life, was probably present in past societies (at least since the establishment of modern humans), it may not be something we can always "get at."[4] We know there were both men and women (as well as children) in prehistory, and we suspect that gender often may have been a powerful—but highly variable—dimension of social life. Just because gender inquiry is enjoying some popularity now, it should not necessarily become the goal of most archaeological research. Whether gender is considered in analyses will depend on the questions being asked, the particular archaeological contexts being studied, and the kinds of archaeological data involved. As in *all* archaeological research the kinds of questions asked successfully will be closely linked to, if not somewhat constrained by, each case. However, it is clear that by taking gender as an explicit focus, there can be important and rich insights into past human lives.

In all societies it is not just gender *per se* that is of anthropological interest, but gender relations, because gender identity, roles, and ideologies are established in relation to others of similar and different genders, roles, and classes.[5] We have seen what problems arise in archaeological interpretation when certain assumptions about gender and gender roles are not made explicit or questioned. Many archaeologists think that gender studies in archaeology are simply linking certain artifacts and activities to men or women, which is a limited view. Even then, as in the different interpretations of grave goods discussed previously, they often do not question or consider the assumptions they are making about roles and activities.

By *not* taking gender seriously archaeologists often miss powerful evidence and rich interpretations. For example, some anthropologists (e.g., Silverblatt 1987) have shown how the development of complex societies, such as the state, were often partly accomplished by a shift from societies based on kinship to relations based more on economics and politics. This means there were significant changes in gender relations. How then could archaeologists possibly explain the "rise of the state" *without* analysis of the role of gender in the successful transformations and subsequent maintenance of the state itself?

Brumfiel's (1991) recent analysis of the Aztec state in the Valley of Mexico has shown how the tribute system (the collection and redistribution of textiles), the fundamental politicoeconomic basis for state maintenance, was in large part based on female labor: Women either made textiles directly or cooked and prepared food for market "sale" to obtain the textiles for the tribute payments. How did these gender roles emerge and become established? When gender relations are viewed as one of the (many) processes "at work" in cultural change and in how humans cope and live their daily lives, we *do* get a much more human picture and a more detailed picture of the past.

There have been a number of important attempts to take gender and gender relations seriously in archaeological interpretation, and some of these are worth reviewing. For example, the traditional view on hunter-gatherers is that they lived their lives more or less dictated by their environments because they did not produce their own food. This has easily led to interpretations of hunter-gatherers either in ecological terms (focusing on such things as "resource-procurement strategies") or in biological terms (that they had to be involved in "viable mating networks"). There is little room in such characterizations for real people with social and interpersonal lives and relationships.

One archaeologist has taken a different perspective on some California hunter-gatherers (Jackson 1991). Archaeology and ethnography have shown that as a group California hunter-gatherers had much more complex social relations, alliances, and trade networks than the more "stereotypically simple" hunter-gatherer societies. Usually such phenomena as alliances and trade are viewed as ways to move resources and not to be too controlled by the environment. Although many of these people knew about the practices of agriculture (from some of their southwestern neighbors), this was not a part of their ways; however, we know that they did control the production of some resources, such as the deliberate burning of wild grasses, which could increase productivity. Often the location of their sites is described in terms of "maximizing" their access to desired or necessary resources.

But instead of thinking about these people primarily in economic terms (and terms derived from the "maximization" principles of western capitalism), we could think about them through the lens of gender. Jackson, using historic, ethnohistoric, and archaeological data on the Western Sierra Mono people, came up with a model for their food-getting and food-preparation (which are standard archaeological topics) that features women doing most of the processing of the staple crop—acorns. When he asked what the *implications* of this might be for other aspects of Mono life, he arrived at some interesting observations. For one thing much of this acorn processing (and storage) occurred in locations where outcrops of bedrock lay exposed because they created mortars, or places *in* the bedrock, for grinding acorns. Often "granaries" were built over the bedrock mortars to store the acorns. These mortars are thus "fixed" on the landscape, and it was at these locales that other activities—of men, women, and children—were often focused. Thus, these locations of women's work structured settlement patterns and social relations. In this case Jackson suggested that women's production served as an economic and social focus for Mono daily life. As a result we get a glimpse into how gender roles and relations were integral to prehistoric lifeways.

As suggested previously the many instances of large-scale cultural change, which are a favorite topic of archaeological inquiry, can be better understood if we understand how gender roles and relations were involved. Christine Hastorf (1991) studied what happened in an area of highland Peru when the Inka tried to move in and establish sociopolitical control. The study shows how changing gender relations and changes in something as mundane as food preparation and consumption have much to do with large-scale sociopolitical transformations. Hastorf's research is a powerful example, not just because it involves explicit attention to gender, but because several lines of evidence converge to reinforce the interpretation. This kind of archaeological reasoning is particularly important because one line of evidence (such as changes in location of food processing) might not be adequate to make a strong case, in this instance for shifts in gender roles and relations.

First Hastorf analyzed the pollen found in soil samples from dwelling areas or "patios," and she documented changes in the kinds of plant foods processed, including an increase in corn. Her analysis of the spatial distribution of food processing and consumption suggests that food processing, for example, was becoming more focused in certain patios. This more concentrated food production seemed to occur within individual domestic units primarily associated with women. This insight is reinforced by ethnohistoric information about sexual and spatial divisions of labor.

Second Hastorf looked at the bone chemistry of skeletons buried at different phases in the transformation to greater control by the Inka. From bone chemistry we can infer certain aspects of people's dietary intake (because the chemical composition of food leaves some "signatures" during the growth of human bone). Corn is one food product that leaves a quite distinctive signature because of its carbon content. The bone

chemistry analysis showed that the diets of men and women were about the same at the beginning of the transformation, but by the time the Inka had taken over the region, there were marked differences in male and female diets. The consumption of corn in some form increased in the men. Drawing on ethnohistoric accounts of the political life of the Inkas, Hastorf suggests that men consumed corn mostly in the form of a corn-based beer, which was central to the feasting offered as tribute and as a political symbol of Inka control. The general picture of the transformation is one whereby household food production increased and men consumed increasingly more corn, probably in the form of beer.

Hastorf's study is an archaeological inquiry into what happens with the "rise of a state:" How did the Inka expand their territory and get other people to give in to them? In daily lives how does this happen? Most archaeological accounts tend to invoke large-scale processes, such as ecological pressure, warfare, and mobilization of labor for public works. Again we might ask, what happens if we inquire into how such a sociopolitical change impacts on, and was affected by, gender roles and relations? As with Brumfiel's work with the Aztecs it appears as if changing gender roles and women's labor are crucial to the establishment and maintenance of the political tributes that sustain some empires. Furthermore, archaeology performed at the level of the household—which has not been as popular as studying the big ceremonial centers and public buildings of complex societies—can be not at all marginal to answering large questions about political power and the "rise of states."

Much of the archaeological research that asks about gender and about the implications of gender for other sociocultural processes has drawn on ethnohistoric records about male and female activities and positions in society. Such data have been used to make archaeological inferences about gender more credible. It may not be possible to have such strong culturally specific starting assumptions about gender in many prehistoric situations, although as we have seen this has not always deterred archaeologists from assuming a lot about gender in prehistory. Regardless of the source or the relative strength of starting assumptions, it is, as with all archaeological interpretations, up to us to make our assumptions explicit and to make our inferences "tight." They must be as well grounded as possible.

Archaeologists may not be able to consider gender in every instance. However, the one thing to be learned from both social and gender theory and from archaeological studies in which gender has been taken seriously is that gender can be one of many powerful relations that embody the dialectics of human life. Also the one thing to be learned from studies of gender in archaeology is that the human past was also full of tensions, conflicts, and cooperation between men and women (and other possible genders). Without attention to this when possible we will have an impoverished and often mechanistic view of human lives.

We have learned in anthropology, history, archaeology, sociology, and other fields of the tremendous range and variability in gender relations, meanings, and gendered lives, even within a single society or culture. We have also learned of variations in archaeological contexts in which we are specifically inquiring into gendered social lives. It is thus increasingly unlikely that we will be able to account for hundreds of societies for long periods of time and in wide geographic areas with just one "account" or story of gender—whether that is a story of androcentric or gynecentric (women-centered) social life. We are beginning to appreciate how dynamic and fluid gender relations can be and how diverse the possibilities and practices are that existed for, and were engaged in by, men and women for tens of thousands of years of past human lives.

NOTES

1. I make a distinction here between research and interpretation that is "sexist" and that which is androcentric or gynecentric. Sexism involves statements, attitudes, and theories that presuppose, assert, or imply inferiority (of one sex or the other), that accept as legitimate the subordination of one sex to the other, and that view prescriptions for defining roles on the basis of sex as legitimate and unproblematic. Androcentrism or gynecentrism is less intentional. Human life is perceived from a male (androcentrism) or female (gynecentrism) perspective without considering or describing the activity or position of the other sex or gender.

2. Within archaeology, there is an increasing amount of work being done that not only documents the different status of men and women in the field (Gero 1985; Kramer and Stark 1988; and a range of papers in Walde and Willows 1991), but also shows how the "profile of practitioners" substantively affects the kind of interpretations we develop (see also in Hastorf 1991). Also there are accounts about how the preferred topics for discussion and explanation (e.g., technological innovations as crucial to culture change) are also highly gendered (usually male) (see for example, Conkey and Williams 1991; Wylie 1991).

3. There is a rich and important literature on the concept of gender that I cannot discuss here. It is important to recognize the distinction between sex, which is biologically based, and gender. Gender is, at one level, the cultural and social construction of sex, but it is more complex than merely mapping cultural constructs onto one sex or another. There can be, for example, more than two genders, such as in the *berdache* of some native American people. Because there is often some relation between sex and whatever genders develop, some analysts have referred to this area of inquiry as the "sex/gender system" (see Fausto-Sterling 1985; Harding 1983).

   Archaeologists who wish to make inferences about gender need to consider the rich theoretical literature and understand that gender is not just another static variable for which we can find a material correlate in the archaeological record (see the critique by Stacey and Thorne 1985; Conkey 1991).

4. Archaeologists continue to debate what our "objects of knowledge" can be, especially in terms of what we call the "level of resolution." With reference to gender research there are those who are not convinced we can make

inferences about individual human behavior in the past (e.g., Hayden 1991) and those who argue that "ethnographic variables" (such as gender relations) are outside the scope of a "scientifically credible" archaeology (e.g., Binford 1983, 1986; but see Wylie 1991 for a critique of these views with particular reference to gender).

5. Gender is a complex social process, involving such aspects as gender roles (what people do, what is considered appropriate), gender ideology (what meanings are assigned to male, female, or other genders; these are not universal in the sense that there are some essential, unchanging notions of male and female), and gender identity (feelings about one's own gender). Gender is, above all, highly variable; it is a social and cultural way of marking differences, and it is entangled with other social and cultural phenomena, such as (in our current western societies) ethnicity, class, and religion.

REFERENCES

Ascher, Robert. 1960. Archaeology and the public image. *American Antiquity* 25(3):402–403.

Binford, Lewis R. 1983. *Working at Archaeology*. New York: Academic Press.

———. 1986. Data, relativism, and archaeological science. *Man* (n.s.) 22:391–404.

Braithwaite, Mary. 1982. Decoration as ritual symbol: A theoretical proposal and an ethnographic study in southern Sudan. In Ian Hodder (ed.). *Symbolic and Structural Archaeology*, pp. 80–88. Cambridge, England: Cambridge University Press.

Brumfiel, Elizabeth. 1991. Weaving and cooking: Women's production in Aztec Mexico. In Joan Gero and Margaret Conkey (eds.). *Engendering Archaeology: Women and Prehistory*, pp. 224–254. Oxford: Basil Blackwell.

Conkey, Margaret W. 1991. Does it make a difference? Feminist thinking and archaeologies of gender. In Dale Walde and Noreen Willows (eds.). *The Archaeology of Gender*. Chacmool Archaeological Association. Calgary, Alberta: Department of Archaeology, University of Calgary.

Conkey, Margaret W. and Janet Spector. 1984. Archaeology and the study of gender. In Michael B. Schiffer (ed.). *Advances in Archaeological Method and Theory*, Vol. 7, pp. 1–38. New York: Academic Press.

Conkey, Margaret and Sarah H. Williams. 1991. Original narratives: The political economy of gender in archaeology. In M. DiLeonardo (ed.). *Gender at the Crossroads of Knowledge: Feminist Anthropology in the Post-Modern Era*. Berkeley and Los Angeles: University of California Press.

Eichler, Margrit and Jeanne Lapointe. 1985. *On the Treatment of the Sexes in Research*. Ottawa: Social Sciences and Humanities Research Council of Canada.

Fausto-Sterling, Anne. 1985. *Myths of Gender: Biological Theories about Women and Men*. New York: Basic Books.

Gero, Joan M. 1985. Socio-politics of archaeology and the woman-at-home ideology. *American Antiquity* 50:342–350.

———. 1991a. Genderlithics: Women's roles in stone tool production. In Joan Gero and Margaret Conkey (eds.). *Engendering Archaeology: Women and Prehistory*, pp. 163–193. Oxford: Basil Blackwell.

———. 1991b. The social world of prehistoric facts: Gender and power in knowledge construction. Paper presented at "Women in Archaeology" conference, Albury, New South Wales, Australia, February 1991. (To be published by the Australian National University, Department of Anthropology and Prehistory; Laurajane Smith and Hilary DuCros, editors.)

Harding, Sandra. 1983. Why has the sex/gender system become visible only now? In Sandra Harding and Merrill B. Hintikka (eds.). *Discovering Reality: Feminist Perspectives on Epistemology, Metaphysics, Methodology, and Philosophy*, pp. 311–324. Boston: Reidel.

Hastorf, Christine A. 1991. Gender, space, and food in prehistory. In Joan Gero and Margaret Conkey (eds.). *Engendering Archaeology: Women and Prehistory*, pp. 132–162. Oxford: Basil Blackwell.

Hayden, Brian. 1991. Observing prehistoric women. Paper presented at Anthropology and Archaeology of Women Conference, Appalachian State University, Boone, NC (May 1991).

Hubbard, Ruth. 1982. Have only men evolved? In R. Hubbard, M. S. Henfin, and B. Fried (eds.). *Biological Woman—the Convenient Myth*, pp. 17–46. Cambridge: Schenkman.

Jackson, Thomas L. 1991. Pounding acorn: Women's production as social and economic focus. In Joan Gero and Margaret Conkey (eds.). *Engendering Archaeology: Women and Prehistory*, pp. 301–328. Oxford: Basil Blackwell.

Kidder, A. V. 1949. Introduction. *Prehistoric South-westerners from Basketmaker to Pueblo,* by Charles Amsden. Los Angeles: Southwest Museum.

Kramer, Carol and Miriam Stark. 1988. The status of women in archaeology. *Anthropology Newsletter* 29(9):11–12. Washington, DC: American Anthropological Association.

Latour, Bruno and Stephen Woolgar. 1986. *Laboratory Life: The Construction of Scientific Facts,* 2nd ed. Princeton: Princeton University Press.

Levi-Strauss, Claude. 1936. Contribution à l'étude de l'organization sociale des Indiens Bororo. *Journal de la Societe des Americanistes de Paris* 28:269–304.

Lovejoy, Owen. 1981. The origin of man. *Science* 211:341–350.

Michard-Marshale, Claire and Claudine Ribery. 1982. *Sexisme et Science Humaine.* Lille: Presses Universitaires de France.

Moore, Henrietta. 1988. *Feminism and Anthropology.* Oxford: Polity Press.

Silverblatt, Irene. 1987. *Moon, Sun, and Witches: Gender Ideologies and Class in Inca and Colonial Peru.* Princeton: Princeton University Press.

Stacey, Judith and Barrie Thorne. 1985. The missing feminist revolution in sociology. *Social Problems* 32(4):301–316.

Trigger, Bruce G. 1984. Alternative archaeologies: Nationalist, colonialist, imperialist. *Man* (n.s.) 19:355–370.

Walde, Dale and Noreen Willows (eds.). 1991. *The Archaeology of Gender.* Proceedings of the Chacmool Conference, 1989. Calgary, Alberta: Chacmool Archaeological Association, Department of Archaeology.

Watson, Patty Jo and Marcy C. Kennedy. 1991. The development of horticulture in the eastern woodlands of North America: Women's role. In Joan Gero and Margaret Conkey (eds.). *Engendering Archaeology: Women and Prehistory,* pp. 255–275. Oxford: Basil Blackwell.

Winters, Howard. 1968. Value-systems and trade cycles of the late archaic in the Midwest. In S.R. Binford and L. R. Binford (eds.). *New Perspectives in Archaeology,* pp. 175–222. Chicago: Aldine.

Wylie, M. Alison. 1991. Gender theory and the archaeological record: Why is there no archaeology of gender? In Joan Gero and Margaret Conkey (eds.). *Engendering Archaeology: Women and Prehistory,* pp. 31–54. Oxford: Basil Blackwell.

Yellen, John. 1977. *Archaeological Approaches to the Present.* New York: Academic Press.

Where Have All the Menstrual Huts Gone? The Invisibility of Menstrual Seclusion in the Late Prehistoric Southeast

Patricia Galloway

OVERTURE

. . . she invariably had three things with her on the ledge of her ground-floor box: her opera-glass, a bag of sweets, and a bouquet of camellias. For twenty-five days of the month the camellias were white, and for five they were red; no one ever knew the reason for this change of

From C. Claussen and R. Joyce, eds. *Women in Prehistory: North America and Mesoamerica,* pp. 47–62. 1997, University of Pennsylvania Press.

colour, which I mention though I can not explain it.

Alexandre Dumas fils

"She," of course, was Alexandre Dumas fils's Camille, the Lady of the Camellias, a very expensive Parisian courtesan who renounced everything for love. Today the best-selling line of French "sanitary napkins" is brand-named "Camellia," but then that is the kind of mildly smutty public discourse that straitlaced

Americans would expect from the French. And it is a far cry, indeed, from a high-flown literary allusion to the grubby term "menstrual hut"—or is it? Both terms were coined by Western cultures, and both share the tendency to hide female practices accommodating the "wound that does not heal." As archaeologists we are deluding ourselves if we think our own professional practice is unaffected by that same tendency. If the most basic move toward engendering archaeology is finding women in the archaeological record, the search for evidence of menstrual practices is about as direct a way to do it as there could be. Yet it is a search that pretty clearly has not been made. This is unfortunate, since anthropological studies suggest that menstrual seclusion may be an important correlate of social organization, and social organization is just what researchers concerned with the late prehistoric Southeast have all been claiming to be interested in.

LITERATURE REVIEW

The term "menstrual hut" is already very evocative; why not "house" or simply "structure"? We know in a general way that in historic period Southeastern nonstate societies women subject to rules of ritual seclusion during menses withdrew to specific structures for the duration of their period of "pollution." But Southeastern archaeologists do not find menstrual huts routinely, even when investigating settlements; they have apparently assumed that the structures reserved for that purpose were too squalid and temporary to leave evidence worth looking for, and the term "hut" is an index of that assumption. But why have such assumptions been made? Is this really the reliable import of the ethnographic literature?

In the first place, "the ethnographic literature" for the early historic period in the Southeast is almost exclusively limited to the work of John R. Swanton. We should remember in dealing with the information he provides that this is the same John Swanton who presented the explicit sexual material in *Myths and Tales of the Southeastern Indians* (1929) in Latin, and his reticence in dealing with reproductive matters with most of his contemporary informants is reflected in the fact that his sources on the topic of menstruation are mostly limited to the fortuitous testimonies of eighteenth-century male European missionaries and colonists and (for the Creeks) other ethnologists of his own time. Neither Swanton nor his colleagues obtained information about menstrual huts from female informants, so all that we have regarding this matter, even now, amounts to external observation at best. A sample of Swanton's evidence for menstrual practices and taboos follows:

1. *Timucua:* fish and venison food restrictions, prohibition of fire kindling; similar food restrictions after childbirth (Swanton 1946:713). Note that Swanton's source for making of "a separate fire" by women during menses is its listing as a superstitious sin in the 1613 *Confessionario of Francisco Pareja* (Milanich et al. 1972:25).
2. *Creek:* menstrual seclusion in house "by herself" for four days (as at childbirth); utensils for food preparation and consumption reserved for use during menses; prohibition on consumption of meat from large animals and on presence in garden; bathing required downstream from men, prohibition on presence upwind of men; required bath and change of clothes for purification at the end of menses. Early-twentieth-century informants and ethnologists referred to "a house," a "seclusion lodge," "a separate tent or house," and "a small house near some spring or stream" (Swanton 1928:358–360, 1947:714).
3. *Chickasaw:* menstrual huts, built far from dwellings but near enough to the village to be safe from enemies, used monthly and at childbirth; required bath and change of clothing afterward; food restrictions during pregnancy, also *couvade* practices (abstention from work, avoidance by other men) by the husband after birth. Adair refers to the relevant structures as "small huts" (Swanton 1928:358–359, 1946:715–716).
4. *Choctaw:* small cabin "apart" monthly and for childbirth; food restrictions at childbirth;

covade practices (food restrictions) (Swanton 1946:716). Note that this comes from only one source, the ca. 1730s French "Anonymous Relation."

5. *Natchez:* A brief remark taken from the descriptions of marriage by the missionary Father Le Petit notes that during menstruation there was a prohibition on marital intercourse; Swanton notes nothing further for the Natchez on this subject (1911:97).

Thus where information is available for Southeastern Indian groups, it all definitely points to ritual seclusion during menses carried out publicly, generally in a structure specifically reserved for the purpose, with accompanying taboos. It is relevant that where such ritual seclusion took place for menstruation, it was also required along with many of the same taboos for childbirth, often apparently in the same structure. Unfortunately the evidence is rather vague on the details of such structures, suggesting that many of those who reported them may not have seen one. The overwhelming evidence for such structures makes it all the more curious that none has been found by archaeologists.

THE ANTHROPOLOGY OF MENSTRUATION

The topic of menstrual practices has served along with female puberty initiations and childbirth practices as a hobbyhorse for nearly every strain of anthropological thought (see Buckley and Gottlieb 1988b). Lately, as a result of attention from feminists, menstrual practices have come in for a good deal of popularizing "anthropological" and "psychological" treatment, being linked with the old notion of primal matriarchies and the New Age "goddess" movement in several popular books (cf. Delaney et al. 1976; Shuttle and Redgrove 1978; even Weideger 1976 overgeneralizes from very poor anthropological evidence). However praiseworthy a clear-eyed look at menstruation as experienced by modern women is, these books have not clarified

matters by viewing menstrual seclusion as "universal" and a "cruelty" imposed by patriarchal authority jealous of "women's mysteries," and in any case they all virtually ignore prehistoric cultures.

Several relatively recent serious anthropological studies are, I think, much more helpful in thinking about prehistory because they grapple with the problem of how menstrual seclusion works within cultures and its possible correlation with social organization. Paige and Paige (1981) have treated the topic as part of an analysis of the sociopolitical functioning of "fraternal interest groups" under a version of exchange theory; Douglas (1966) and Schlegal (1972) have analyzed menstrual seclusion as part of cross-cultural studies of pollution and male domination, respectively; several of the essays edited by Buckley and Gottlieb (1988a) focus on the experience of the practice itself and on its advantages to women; while Martin's (1992) work on Western female embodiment stresses the usefulness of menstrual taboos to modern women. These rather heterogeneous studies appear to agree that menstrual seclusion and its accompanying practices are advantageous to women and are characteristic of societies where husbands and males in general are not particularly dominant, especially matrilineal societies where residence rules are generally matrilocal. Paige and Paige (1981) go on to generalize that such societies—societies with "weak fraternal internal groups"—are characterized by a subsistence base that is not valuable enough to require defense, such as shifting agriculture with hunting and gathering. This is not inappropriate as a description of the historic tribes of the Southeast, but it is more problematic as a characterization of the rather aggressive chiefdom model now accepted for the late prehistoric societies that preceded them.

Kinship and residence in Mississippian societies have been more assumed about than understood. Knight (1990) has recently discussed the relation of kinship to sociopolitical structure in some detail, foregrounding the problematic nature of ethnohistorically attested kinship forms in the early colonial Southeast, but concludes that archaeological correlates "are yet to be worked out." And although Paige and Paige (1981:121) argue generally that matrilineal, matrilocal societies do not have an abundant and rich resource base, they have discussed one example of an advanced agricultural society, the Nayar of India (which is matrilineal and matrilocal), that practices menstrual seclusion and is even characterized by nonresident husbands.

Clearly much more work remains to be done in understanding whether menstrual seclusion does actually correlate reliably with matrilineality/matrilocality, since the cross-cultural sample used by Paige and Paige (1981) was based on largely androcentrically biased ethnographies and coding practices (cf: Buckley 1988:192–193). It is, for example, quite possible that matrilineality/matrilocality in the Southeast was an artifact of the protohistoric disease holocaust period: Harris (1988:34–37) suggests that warfare or other disruption is a strong pressure for matrilocality, and it stands to reason that since matrilineages would select for female children to expand the lineage and attract bridewealth, they would also favor population increase and prove an ideal vehicle for post-catastrophe population recovery.

Still, it is not beyond the bounds of possibility that the known population expansion of the Mississippian period might also be explained in this manner; that the Natchez model, at least for matrilines, is correct for the Mississippian period; and that Mississippian societies might thus be characterized by the same practices—which should be marked materially by the presence of "menstrual huts." If, on the other hand, Mississippian societies did not practice menstrual seclusion, it is quite possible that their kinship organization was not matrilineal, and their residence practice not matrilocal. If that possibility is admitted, then a thorough reexamination of our dependence on post-contact ethnographies is in order. The point is that the correlation between menstrual seclusion and matrilineal kinship seems to be good enough that it should be possible to test for matrilineal kinship archaeologically if we can just figure out what a "menstrual hut" ought to look like in the ground.

MENSTRUAL TABOOS AND MODERN ARCHAEOLOGY

If the ethnographic evidence and the matrilineal model are correct, there must have been thousands of menstrual huts constructed in the Southeast, just from the colonial period from which they are certainly attested. Yet so far no menstrual hut has been reliably reported from a Southeastern archaeological context. The few identifications from elsewhere are unfortunately problematic. J. Heilman's identification of a "women's house" (House II/77) at the Fort Ancient Sunwatch site is the right period, but it remains unpublished and details are lacking (J. Heilman, personal communication, 1992); furthermore, the structure in question is located within the village, which would contradict the need for spatial separation. Robson Bonnichsen (1973:281) suggested a "menstrual retreat" as one possible explanation for apparently female-occupied tent remains at a contemporary multiple-structure Cree camp, but this and the other two candidate explanations proved false when the camp owner was interviewed. Finally, Lewis Binford's half-hearted identification of a possible menstrual hut in the Hatchery West report (1970:40–41), was based solely on the fact that it was a small and anomalous structure. Why "anomalous"? Perhaps simply because menstruation is marked as "polluting" and "dangerous" in our own society's dominant male discourse, and that prejudice is transferred to other societies, including prehistoric ones, without much reflection. I am suggesting, in short, that the influence of modern taboos on ethnocentric archaeologists, whether male or female, should not be ignored; just as women rarely menstruate in Western literature, so menstruation is generally ignored in considering women's lives archaeologically, as though women in all times and places similarly hid the condition of menstruation—indeed hid it so effectively that it became invisible in the archaeological record.

The symptoms of this ethnocentricity are not far to seek. Charles Hudson, in his influential normative summary of Southeastern menstrual seclusion practices in 1976, matter-of-factly drew on uniformitarian generalization when he offered the following assertion, now discounted by cross-cultural studies (Hudson's reference in this passage is to Paige's 1973 popular article, which was actually about how Western women are *socialized* to suffer during menstruation):

> The Southeastern Indians may have recognized at least implicitly some sound social and psychological principles. Psychologists have amply verified what folk knowledge tells us about menstruation, namely that women become depressed, hostile, anxious, and even socially disruptive just before and during menstruation. (Hudson 1976:320)

There is very good reason for anthropologists and archaeologists enculturated in Western societies to believe assertions like Hudson's and to experience "negative affect" associated with the very topic of menstruation, despite mounting evidence for the social origin of most of the negative behavioral correlates observed in Western societies (Martin 1992:92–138). Because Western societies practice the hiding of menstruation (as do many "primitive" societies like the Manus of New Guinea [Mead 1939:157–158]), the topic itself is treated with reticence by females, discomfited derision by males, and with pollution anxieties, in many instances, by both. Being seen in public to bleed from the vagina is still one of the most profound humiliations a Western female can experience, despite the fact that at least a majority of American women value their menstrual periods as a sign of their identity as women and of their continuing fertility (Martin 1992).

Beginning with the commodification of disposable "sanitary" supplies in 1921, advertisements for them have stressed invisibility, security of protection from staining, and suppression of menstrual odor, without once using the word "menstruation." These advertisements have frequently featured women wearing white or light-colored clothing (though white clothing is the very last thing a menstruating Western woman would choose to wear or especially the expensive formal clothing worn on highly public (and therefore dangerously exposed) occasions. Even in the 1990s, very little has changed in terms of the language used (menstruation and blood are almost never mentioned explicitly), although much more frankness in the portrayal of the product (particularly comparative photographs of sanitary napkins, for example) is evident. The fact remains that despite all the pop-psychology discussion of premenstrual syndrome, or PMS, menstruating Western women are still not supposed to betray the fact in public and may still be subject to specific restrictions in private on grounds of religious or other belief (Martin 1992:97–98). And although most Western males do not go so far as John Milton, whose wife had to sleep on the floor while menstruating rather than pollute the marriage bed, many are reluctant to have sexual intercourse with menstruating women.

This is not a trivial issue. The whole topic of menstruation in modern Western cultures is still so avoided by women through shame, or trivialized by men through PMS jokes (even scientific ones), that our discomfort with it may blind us even to paying attention to its significance in other cultures or in subcultures within our own. Modern Miccosuki women use paper plates and plastic utensils in the tribal cafeteria during their periods, while men and nonmenstruating women use china and stainless steel (Pat Kwachka, personal communication, 1992), and the same practice is followed in conservative Creek households (Bell 1990:334). Orthodox Jewish women around the world are forbidden to prepare food while menstruating and are required to take a ritual bath at the termination of the menstrual cycle. I suggest, therefore, that discomfort with the topic and its resulting erasure from scientific discourse are the simple reasons that no one has proposed a model for the archaeological correlates of menstrual seclusion practices.

Cultural practices that deal with areas of life that the dominant culture does not mark as shameful (and that are the domain of men and, therefore, "unmarked") can be looked at in public, and this is nowhere more graphically obvious than in the treatment of blood: we have become accustomed to gallons of blood and gore from wounds inflicted by (generally male) violence, whether on the evening news or in our entertainment, and even we as archaeologists have exhibited endless fascination with evidence for wounds on skeletal remains. Yet advertisements depicting the absorptive capabilities of "sanitary" supplies prudishly use a thin *blue* liquid for demonstration. Examples of treatment of blood from the female genital area in current entertainment media include horror films (both *Carrie* and *The Exorcist* treat the alleged enormously magnified telekinetic powers of young girls at menarche) and decidedly unusual European films (in both Ingmar Bergman's *Cries and Whispers* and the soft-porn French film *Going Places*, women mutilate their vaginas, in the first case possibly to simulate menstruation and avoid intercourse, and in the second to recover menstrual function lost during a prison sentence). In none of these films is menstruation treated as something that happens ordinarily to every woman, and in the very few television shows that have treated it so (*All in the Family, Cosby Show, I'll Fly Away*), the theme is taken up only once or twice, and blood has been notable for its invisibility.

CONSIDERATIONS FOR AN ARCHAEOLOGICAL MODEL

The same kind of gender discrimination, I suggest, carries over into the treatment of archaeological features. Features created by male-dominated or gender-neutral activities,

even if they were designed for purification from ritual pollution, do not suffer from invisibility. Indeed several instances of putative sweat lodges are reported in the Southeastern literature (for example, the Fredericks site sweat lodge reported in Ward and Davis 1988). Yet for at least half of the population, the so-called menstrual huts were equally important for ritual purification, both monthly and after childbirth. This helps make an argument for their being more than flimsy "huts."

To suggest something of the possible existential force of the taboos connected with the menstrual-seclusion practice in the prehistoric Southeast, let me offer a specific example from the early eighteenth century, in which a male adult Creek was observed to vomit the *sagamité* he had eaten before learning that it had been prepared by a menstruating woman; he then claimed to see red specks in the remaining food in the pot (Swanton 1931). His European guest thought he was overreacting, but the nineteenth- and twentieth-century Creek materials that Swanton presented and that Bell has confirmed by recent fieldwork—which indicate persistent beliefs that menstruating women should not touch men or gardens and that it was dangerous for men to smell menstruating women, to bathe downstream of them, or to walk where they had walked—indicate that this was likely normal behavior, however androcentrically interpreted. If people in Southeastern societies indeed believed that menstruating women were capable of introducing disruption and disaster at frequent and regular intervals, it was cost-effective for the societies to be serious about their precautions and to provide substantial structures for containing the danger, as other societies have done.

Because of this fear of pollution, the location where menstruating women should be secluded, according to all the testimony offered, had to be at a distance from where men carried on their ordinary activities, and ought to have been downstream from the primary village or hamlet water source (Swanton 1928). Restrictions on contact with males and with agricultural fields dictated that historic period menstrual huts were placed on the outskirts of the villages, at what might be seen as the village/fields boundary, and the taboo was observed no matter what. In the 1750s, Chickasaw women who so isolated themselves in the face of attacks by pro-French enemies were recognized as valorous, because their action helped to preserve their husbands' virility (Bossu 1962:171). This locational practice can be compared with an example from the South Seas, the Ulithi, who placed the communal menstrual structure parallel to the shore (Paige and Paige 1981:213), thus also at the village/subsistence-source boundary.

Another issue that needs to be addressed when considering how many menstrual huts there were, and how substantial they were, is the average frequency of menstruation for late prehistoric Southeastern women. There is still great difficulty in addressing the issue of birth regulation archaeologically, but modern studies of women without access to medicalized birth control measures show that women can and do regulate birth frequency by means of extended lactation after a birth and complex socially institutionalized practices of abstention from intercourse. Although it is finally being recognized that the Western frequency of regular menstrual periods is unusual and perhaps unprecedented, it is not true that fertile non-Western women were always pregnant. Thus it is possible that if menstrual seclusion was practiced in the late prehistoric Southeast, at any given time as many as one-eighth to one-tenth of the fertile adult female population might have been so secluded. What the women did during their ritual seclusion from village life should be of interest, both because it would suggest what kind of structure was involved and because it would account for a significant expenditure of time. Pollution restrictions would have meant that there were many things menstruating women could not do (evidence for which would therefore not be found): produce household necessities like pottery or cloth, work at cultivation, perhaps take care of children, or cook for the household. With a wide range of activities barred, most of them the very activities that constituted the enormous visible economic contribution of women to Southeastern societies, what was left?

Although, most frequently, "menstrual huts" were also used for all the other activities related to female biological reproduction—including puberty rituals, childbirth, and the purification rituals following it—details of what went on inside them are noticeably missing for the colonial period Southeast as elsewhere (cf. Buckley and Gottlieb 1988b:12–13). Yet it is unlikely that fertile women spent one-fourth to one-fifth of their time while not pregnant or lactating sleeping or looking at the wall. Part of that notion may arise from the general assumption that women were alone in their huts.

There is another possibility worth considering, which is that more than one woman from the same household might be spending the same time in ritual seclusion. The tendency of women who live together or work together in close proximity to synchronize menses is now widely attested medically as well as anecdotally (see McClintock 1971 for the *locus classicus*; Knight 1988:233 lists references from recent medical literature; Knight 1991 builds an entire theory of the origins of culture on the phenomenon). Menstrual synchrony would surely have been experienced by the menstruating women, all of them related, in the extended matrilineage households postulated as the dominant residential mode in the late prehistoric Southeast. The ethnographic evidence from historic Southeastern tribes is not at all clear on how many of these huts there were at any given time, but the possibility of menstrual synchrony suggests that perhaps each lineage had its own women's house, a structure as substantial as any other.

Much has been made of the hard and unremitting work of women in the aboriginal agricultural Southeast, as opposed, to the episodic hunting and defense activities of men. Although that picture is surely skewed, no one who works hard is going to mind getting up to a week off once a month, as Hudson has suggested (1976:320; cf. Martin 1992:98). But it is likely that such time would be spent doing something. Even if societies themselves articulate the male-segregated activities as "sacred" and the female-segregated activities as "polluting" (though this is usually attributable to a Western reading of the evidence), that does not mean that there are no activities at all. Instead, it would seem reasonable to suggest that a similar range of activities might take place in the structures dedicated to both and that archaeological correlates might be suggested for them. Buckley's (1988) work on Yurok menstrual practices suggests that they could be seen as directly parallel to the male purification activities aimed at the accumulation of spiritual power, and that the structures used for menstrual seclusion could be as important as men's houses.

Since male ethnographers have been invited to partake of the activities in "men's houses," we do know something of what goes on in them. Men carry out ritual activities or preparation for ritual activities, tell stories about hunting and women, sleep, and make ceremonial items, weapons or boats, or items of personal adornment. Although not restricted to the interior of the men's house by pollution restrictions, the ceremonial items are frequently restricted to use within the men's house because of secrecy requirements. And because male ethnographers are telling the tale, the talking that goes on is usually dignified as instructive for younger men or as reinforcing societal conventions (or, in case the stories go beyond societal conventions, as encouraging innovation). It is rarely trivialized as gossip.

If activities in the women's house paralleled such men's house activities, certainly women must have spent time resting as men did; certainly they also spent time talking and telling stories that could be similarly dignified as instruments of societal regulation. Other social activities, such as gambling, are

documented ethnographically (Underhill 1936). We know they ate, because there is evidence that they had to use special vessels that could not be used elsewhere; indeed the Beng women of the Ivory Coast prepare a particularly prized and delectable dish only when menstruating (Gottlieb 1988:71–72). Because they did bleed, they may have had blood-stained breechcloths or other absorbent materials to dispose of by burning or burial. Is there any reason why it would have been unlikely that they participated in ritual activities? Certainly the sun worship that dominated Southeastern ritual practice is connected with fertility, and women in their period of ritual seclusion would at a minimum be concerned with the continuing fertility that their very seclusion proclaimed.

At this point I take a side trip into Southeastern myth to emphasize the connections between women, blood, and fertility by retelling the common story from the region of the origin of corn, with its overtones of the dominance of hunting-gathering by agriculture. In this tale there is a family consisting of a father, Hunter; a mother, Corn; and two boys, one a son of Hunter and Corn and one an adopted son who had been made from discarded deer's blood. After the boys had in mischief released game animals from the secret place where their father kept them, thereby making them scarce and hard to find, they became interested in how it was that their mother was able to provide corn and beans for them to eat instead. One day they spied on her activities within the storehouse and discovered that the corn and beans came from her body. Thinking her a witch, they decided to kill her. Seeing them refuse the food she offered, which they now considered polluted, she guessed their plan and instructed them on how they should do it: clear a large piece of ground and drag her dead body over it seven times. The boys killed her after having cleared only small patches of ground and then dragged her body over it only twice. As a result, corn sprang up only where her blood touched the cultivated earth, and it would make only two crops per year ever after (paraphrased from the Cherokee version as presented in Lankford 1987:148–151; cf. Bell 1990:335 for the relevance of this myth to Creek social reproduction).

This is as clear a connection as could be desired between female fertility, of which blood is the sign, and agricultural fertility, of which female blood is the cause. I would suggest that it may even include a mythical explanation of the origin of menstrual seclusion in the Southeast. I take the liberty of imagining that this connection would have been celebrated and ritualized somehow and, further, that it must have been part of at least some rites connected with the "women's house." It seems to me that the widespread attestation of the existence of "women's languages" in the Southeast (cf. Bell 1990:341 n. 1), correlated as it is with the practice of menstrual seclusion from the community, may also argue for the existence of a "women's house" institution with ritual characteristics that has simply been missed in the ethnohistorical literature for the reasons suggested above.

What might this possibility of ritual activity mean for archaeological correlates? We have had a hard time trying to decide how to identify other structures connected with Southeastern ritual; temple structures are known not only by their division into multiple rooms and the presence of a hearth, but almost indispensably by location on a mound. Clearly a "women's house" would be distinguished by the locational considerations I have discussed, and structurally it would require a hearth, because women would be staying there for several days, but little else of a structural nature can be suggested.

The story would, however, be different with reference to artifacts. If ritual artifacts such as statuettes or pipes or everyday items like pottery vessels, which might have been specially decorated to ensure their recognition and avoidance by others, were used inside the women's house, pollution restrictions would keep them there, where they would likely be found.

ARCHAEOLOGICAL IMPLICATIONS

What we have to look for, therefore, would be much like any other Mississippian house of wattle and daub or thatch. It would be spatially distinguished because it would be at whatever distance from living areas and field or forest that ritual purity demanded. The pattern of its location might select for nearness to running water because of its requirement for ritual cleansing. It would be downstream from the village or hamlet. If the disposal of soiled garments or pads had to be provided for by burning or burial—as we know was the case with the placenta—evidence of such disposal would be found within the house or nearby. Furthermore, if we reconceive the "menstrual hut" as a "women's house," then the complex of artifactual evidence would be much expanded to include ritual elements—structures, artifacts—and more of the long-term requirements of daily life. The presence of artifacts symbolically associated with females, fertility, and agriculture would fit this scenario, as would a distinctive ceramic assemblage with limited distribution. Both sorts of evidence are habitually assigned to (male) ritual contexts, as at the BBB Motor site (Emerson 1989; Pauketat and Emerson 1991) and the Sponemann site (Jackson et al. 1992) in the America Bottom, but in light of this discussion it might be worth reevaluating the evidence to see if another explanation might deal equally parsimoniously with the evidence.

I am suggesting, of course, that the red bauxite Birger and Keller figurines at the BBB Motor site, portraying kneeling women occupied in agricultural pursuits, and the similar Sponemann, Willoughby, and West figurines from Sponemann may be a clue that there is another possible interpretation not only for the "temple" complexes on both sites but for Ramey ceramics as well. Emerson's (1989:65) interpretation of Ramey motifs as "involving fertility and life forces" could hardly be more apposite to such an interpretation. Pauketat and Emerson interpret the symbolism of the Ramey jar, seen from above, as the cosmos (the decorative field) surrounding an orifice symbolizing the Underworld, such that the contents of the jar were seen as "associated with feminine life forces—earth, fertility, Under World—or female activities (e.g., agriculture, food preparation)" (Pauketat and Emerson 1991:933) But why not then see the orifice as the vaginal opening, and the contents of the pots (perhaps that dangerous red-flecked *sagamité*?) as coming from the body of the Corn Mother? Certainly pottery with "broad, simple designs . . . highly visible at a distance" (Pauketat and Emerson 1991:922) would be easily avoidable; designs "meant for a special purpose rather than simply being decorations for the elite" (Emerson 1989:63) could be meant to warn of pollution. The care taken in the execution of Ramey pottery, which Emerson (1989:66–67) argues was by "potters who were associated with each specific lineage/community ritual group," would be appropriate to a ware made by women not burdened by daily tasks (note that there is enough variation in Ramey ceramics that highly restricted specialist production is not suggested), and its relative scarcity fits well with a ware used for periodic seclusion. Such a "'utilitarian' ritual ware" (Emerson 1989:65) might well be included in mortuary offerings (especially for childbirth deaths), would appear in midden and garbage deposits, and would be distributed through all levels of the social hierarchy (since all women menstruate and most give birth).

It is worth noting that the BBB Motor site also exhibited other finds that could be reinterpreted in the direction of women's house practices: systematically reexcavated pit features; red ocher pigment and a large quartz crystal with a dramatic red impurity (which Emerson compares to a Cherokee story of a man who regularly fed such a crystal with blood!); and *Datura stramonium*, which could have been used for abortion or difficult childbirths. Finally, the site was separated from the surrounding land by water and marshes dur-

ing the period of its use. None of this evidence is conclusive, but I suggest that it is worth a thorough revaluation, especially the sexing of the burials.

The occurrence of figurines similar to those at BBB Motor made a "ceremonial" interpretation inevitable for the Sponemann "Ceremonial Complex" of architectural and pit remains, which includes a "temple" and an adjoining structure interpreted as the temple-keeper's lodging. Because the figurines were evidently intentionally "killed" by being broken into fragments, and because the spread of those fragments coincides closely with the burned "temple," Fortier argues that the figurines had been broken outside the structure and most of the fragments placed within it before its intentional destruction by fire. This destruction supposedly marked a final "purification" step in an episode of "busk" ceremonialism focused on this "household temple" structure, which Fortier identifies by analogy with temples described by Du Pratz for the Natchez (Jackson et al. 1992:52–70).

Again, however, it would seem that an alternative interpretation connected with women's house ceremonialism and especially purification practices might be appropriate, at least for the "Ceremonial Complex" portion of the site. Fortier suggests that the destruction of the figurines and the "temple" building was part of a ritual act terminating a "year-end busk celebration" and representing "a symbolic act of regeneration and perhaps purification of the sacred busk complex." Further, he suggests that the "sanctity of this act and the busk ground itself" is signified by the fact that the site was not reoccupied after the destruction episode (Jackson et al. 1992:303). Yet if the "temple" and adjoining "lodging" were interpreted as a women's house complex accommodating menstrual-seclusion facilities and fertility ceremonialism, it would seem that abandonment might be as much the product of notions of pollution as of sacredness, and the apparently inauspicious location of the site in a low clayey swale (Jackson et al. 1992:49) would then suggest that it was chosen because of its proximity to water needed for purification.

In both the "ceremonial" and "residential" precincts of the Sponemann site small quantities of Ramey ceramics were found, although the concentration of small sherds in pits, especially in the "ceremonial" precinct, gave Fortier grounds for the suggestion that they were part of assemblages that represented the sweeping out of structures as another part of a "purification" practice. Certainly this kind of distribution for Ramey ceramics—whether associated with menstrual practices or not—helpfully raises the question of whether a possible distinctive "menstrual ware " might not also appear in an ordinary domestic setting, where vessels might be stored or used to obtain cooked foods destined for women in menstrual seclusion. This last surmise shows that finding evidence of distinctive women's houses will not be uncomplicated, but it will not be done at all unless we ask the questions.

There is no way we are going to understand late prehistoric Southeastern cultures until we come to grips with the basic issues of kinship organization and the role of women. Nor can we completely ignore a substantial portion of Southeastern women's lives, particularly one so strikingly connected with the central arcana of Mississippian ceremonialism. Ethnohistorical evidence can only take us so far back; after that, archaeology must serve as time machine. Here, however, ethnographic analogy gives us an actual structure to look for, and it is time we stopped being too ethnocentric to do so.

ACKNOWLEDGMENTS

I am indebted to Cheryl Claassen for inviting me to reprise and polish this essay, which was first presented in a less developed form at the 1990 Southeastern Archaeological Conference meeting in Jackson, Mississippi. Since that presentation, I have received many helpful suggestions from colleagues and friends, including Amy Bushnell, Penelope Drooker, James Heilman, Bonnie McEwan, Charles McNutt, LeAnne Howe, Pat Kwachka, Mary Powell, John Scarry, and Bruce Smith. It is interesting to note that whereas female colleagues took this essay seriously from the outset, some male colleagues initially behaved as though they considered it a joke. I am happy to say that they no longer seem to do so.

REFERENCES

Bell, Amelia Rector. 1990. "Separate People: Speaking of Creek Men and Women." *American Anthropologist* 92:332–345.

Binford, Lewis R. 1970. "Archaeology at Hatchery West." *Memoirs of the Society for American Archaeology* 24.

Bonnichsen, Robson. 1973. "Millie's Camp: An Experiment in Archaeology." *World Archaeology* 4:227–291.

Bossu, Jean-Bernard. 1962. *Travels in the Interior of North America, 1751–1762.* Translated and edited by Seymour Feiler. Norman: University of Oklahoma Press.

Buckley, Thomas. 1988. "Menstruation and the Power of Yurok Women." In *Blood Magic: The Anthropology of Menstruation,* edited by Thomas Buckley and Alma Gottlieb, 188–209. Berkeley: University of California Press.

Buckley, Thomas, and Alma Gottlieb (editors). 1988a. *Blood Magic: The Anthropology of Menstruation.* Berkeley: University of California Press.

———. 1988b. "A Critical Appraisal of Theories of Menstrual Symbolism." In *Blood Magic: The Anthropology of Menstruation,* edited by Thomas Buckley and Alma Gottlieb, 3–50. Berkeley: University of California Press.

Delaney, Janice, Mary Jane Lupton, and Emily Toth. 1976. *The Curse: A Cultural History of Menstruation.* New York: E. P. Dutton.

Douglas, Mary. 1966. *Purity and Danger.* London: Pelican.

Emerson, Thomas E. 1989. "Water, Serpents, and The Underworld: An Exploration into Cahokian Symbolism." In *The Southeastern Ceremonial Complex: Artifacts and Analysis,* edited by Patricia Galloway, 45–92. Lincoln: University of Nebraska Press.

Gottlieb, Alma. 1988. "Menstrual Cosmology among the Beng of Ivory Coast." In *Blood Magic: The Anthropology of Menstruation,* edited by

Thomas Buckley and Alma Gottlieb, 55–74. Berkeley: University of California Press.

Harris, Marvin. 1988. *Culture, People, Nature: An Introduction to General Anthropology.* 5th ed. New York: Harper and Row.

Hudson, Charles. 1976. *The Southeastern Indians.* Knoxville: University of Tennessee Press.

Jackson, Douglas K., Andrew C. Fortier, and Joyce A. Williams. 1992. *The Sponemann Site 2: The Mississippian Oneota Occupations (II-Ms-517).* American Bottom Archaeology, FAI-270 Site Reports, No. 24. Urbana: University of Illinois Press.

Knight, Chris. 1988. "Menstrual Synchrony and the Australian Rainbow Snake" In *Blood Magic: The Anthropology of Menstruation,* edited by Thomas Buckley and Alma Gottlieb, 232–255. Berkeley: University of California Press

———. 1991. *Blood Relations: Menstruation and the Origins of Culture.* New Haven: Yale University Press.

Knight, Vernon James. 1990. "Social Organization and the Evolution of Hierarchy in Southeastern Chiefdoms." *Journal of Anthropological Research* 46:1–23.

Lankford, George. 1987. *Native American Legends.* Little Rock: August House.

Martin, Emily. 1992. *The Woman in the Body: A Cultural Analysis of Reproduction.* 2nd ed. Boston: Beacon Press.

McClintock, Martha K. 1971. "Menstrual Syndrome and Suppression." *Nature* 229(5282):244–245.

Mead, Margaret. 1939. *From the South Seas: Studies of Adolescence and Sex in Primitive Societies.* New York: William Morrow and Company.

Milanich, Jerald, William C. Sturtevant, and Emilio Moran (editors and translators). 1972. *Francisco Pareja's 1613 Confessionario: A Documentary Source for Timucuan Ethnography.* Tallahassee: Florida Division Archives, History, and Records Management.

Paige, Karen Ericksen, and Jeffrey M. Paige. 1981. *The Politics of Reproductive Ritual,* Berkeley: University of California Press.

Pauketat, Timothy R., and Thomas E. Emerson. 1991. "The Ideology of Authority and the Power of the Pot." *American Anthropologist* 93:919–941.

Schlegal, Alice. 1972. *Male Dominance and Female Autonomy.* New Haven: HRAF Press.

Shuttle, Penelope, and Peter Redgrove. 1978. *The Wise Wound: Eve's Curse and Everywoman.* New York: Richard Marek.

Swanton, John R. 1911. *Indians of the Lower Mississippi Valley and Adjacent Coast of the Gulf of Mexico.* Bureau of American Ethnology Bulletin 43. Washington, D.C.

———. 1928. "Social Organization and Social Usages of the Indian of the Creek Confederacy." Bureau of American Ethnology 42nd Annual Report (1925), 43–472. Washington, D.C.

———. 1929. *Myths and Tales of the Southeastern Indians.* Bureau of American Ethnology Bulletin 88. Washington, D.C.

———. 1931. *Source Material for the Social Ceremonial Life of the Choctaw Indians.* Bureau of American Ethnology Bulletin 103. Washington, D.C.

———. 1946. *Indians of the Southeastern United States.* Bureau of American Ethnology Bulletin 137. Washington, D.C.

Underhill, Ruth. 1936. *The Autobiography of a Papago Woman.* Memoir 46, American Anthropological Association.

Ward, Trawick, and Steve Davis. 1988. "Archaeology of the Historic Occaneechi Indians." *Southern Indian Studies* 36–37.

Weideger, Paula. 1976. *Menstruation and Menopause: The Physiology and Psychology, The Myth and Reality.* New York: Knopf.

Diversity of the Upper Paleolithic "Venus" Figurines and Archeological Mythology

Sarah M. Nelson

Among the earliest depictions of human beings, dating back to perhaps 30,000 years ago, are small figurines of nude females, which are found across a broad belt in Europe from the Pyrenees in southern France to the Don river in the USSR, with outliers in Siberia. Every anthropologist is familiar with these Upper Paleolithic "Venus" figurines. They are used to titillate freshman classes, and photographs or drawings, especially of the figurines from Willendorf and Dolni Vestonice, routinely enliven introductory textbooks.

Current trends in literary criticism lean toward deconstruction of "texts," in which both words and situations may serve as the text for analysis. In this [reading], I would like to deconstruct some texts in a narrower sense, using the example of the Venus figurines to demonstrate that introductory textbooks of archeology and physical anthropology produce gender metaphors which, by ignoring much of the scholarship on the figurines, reaffirm the folk model of gender preferred by our culture.

FIGURINE DESCRIPTIONS

The figurines themselves have only gender in common. They are diverse in shape, in pose, in the somatic details depicted, and in ornamentation (Soffer 1988, Fleury 1926, Abramova 1967, Luquet 1926, Delporte 1979). They seem to represent differences in age as well (Rice 1981). Yet the textbooks

tend to represent the figurines as all the same, and then to leap from this purported sameness to a supposed function for all figurines over their 3000-mile and perhaps 10,000-year spread (Soffer [1988], although Gamble [1986, 1987] asserts that most figurines fall within a 2000-year range). We need to explore this phenomenon of perceiving sameness in the diverse figurines, and ask why it occurs.

The texts our students read describe the figurines and frequently ascribe a function to them. There is little indication in the bibliographies that the authors of the texts have read any primary sources about the figurines, or that they are conversant with the rich literature which explores the variation in both the figurines themselves and the possible meanings and functions of the figurines. Rather, it seems that a kind of folklore is repeated, a folklore of the anthropology profession, too well known to require documentation.

The textbooks utilized in this study represent an unsystematic nonrandom sample—all that happen to be on my bookshelves, supplemented with those of my colleagues. Of twenty introduction to archeology or archeology and physical anthropology textbooks thus examined, eight concentrate on methodology and do not mention the figurines, while the other twelve contain cursory remarks on one to three pages. It is these twelve texts which constitute the study sample.

Table 1 shows the distribution of what is written regarding the physical characteristics of the figurines. Six of the textbooks mention exaggerated sexual characteristics as a prominent feature, whether or not they specify which traits are meant. The most common feature to be singled out is the breasts,

TABLE 1 Description of Figurines

AUTHOR	SEXUAL	ABDOMEN	BREASTS	BUTTOCKS	HIPS	PREGNANT	FAT
Barnouw (1978)	X	X	X		X	X	
Campbell (1988)		X	X	X			X
Chard (1975)			X	X	X	X	X
Clark (1977)			X	X	(thighs)		X
Eddy (1984)	X		X	X			
Fagan (1986)	X		X				
Hester & Grady (1982)			X		X		
Jurmain et al. (1981)	X						
Pfeiffer (1985)	(stylized)						
Poirier (1987)		X	X	X			
Smith (1976)	X		X	X		X	
Wenke (1984)	X						

described as "large," "generous," or "pendulous." All but one of the texts characterize the figurines as having either exaggerated sexual characteristics or large breasts, and four include both. Buttocks are mentioned five times, once described as "protruding," while hips, once with the adjective "broad," are specified three times. Only one author mentions both, showing that he makes a distinction between hips and buttocks. We are left to guess whether these terms are intended to refer to hindquarters in general in the other cases, or whether one set of authors indeed has protruding buttocks in mind (i.e., steatopygia), and the other really means broad hips (i.e., steatomeria) (Boule and Vallois 1957:318). In one confusing case, an illustration of Willendorf, without a trace of steatopygia but with undoubted steatomeria, is pictured side by side with a Khoi-San woman, of whom the reverse is clearly the case—that is, protruding buttocks without broad hips (Campbell 1988:508).

The assertion that pregnancy is depicted in the figurines occurs in the textbook sample three times, and one additional author points out the exaggerated "belly," allowing him the satisfying alliteration of "breasts, belly, and buttocks." Three of the authors describe the figurines as fat. The only author to refrain from asserting or implying fatness does not describe the figurines at all, but contents himself with an illustration of Willendorf (Pfeiffer 1985:203). Reading these descriptions, one would suppose that the Willendorf statuette, easily the most familiar, was typical or normal or modal. Instead, it is one of the least stylized and the most obese—referred to in another context with admiration as representing "resplendent endomorphy" (Beller 1977:78).

The generalizations in the textbooks do some violence to the facts. Few of the statuettes represent gross obesity, and some are quite slender (Fig. 1). Even the first figurines found in the 1890s were classified by Piette into svelte and obese classes (Delporte 1979:73). Half a century ago Passemard (1938) examined all the then-known figurines to see whether they were steatopygous, a description quite popular at that time, and came to the conclusion that most were not. Saccasyn Della Santa (1947:9–13) reviewed the literature on the figurines again, and also concluded that they were not meant to represent steatopygia.

An unpublished statistical study of the variation in body shapes made 22 measurements on each figurine for which both frontal and profile photographs could be found—24 measurable figurines in all. The statuettes sorted into distinct groups of 10 obese (wide hips and thick body), 3 steatopygous (protruding buttocks), and 11 normal (Nelson n.d.). Another study shows that only

Figure 1 Slender figurines from a. Petrokovie, Czechoslovakia; b. Elisevitchi, USSR; and c. Sireul, France.

39 percent of these figurines could possibly represent pregnancy, slightly over half (55 percent) have pendulous breasts, 45 percent have broad hips, and 13 percent have protruding buttocks. Twenty-two percent have none of these characteristics, (Nelson and Bibb n.d.). Bodyshapes depicted in the figurines have been divided into three or four categories by intuitive studies as well, such as those by Fleury (1926), Abramova (1967), and Luquet (1926).

Rice (1981) has suggested that this variability in body shape reflects different age groups, and has shown that different body characteristics can be so interpreted, with a high correlation between ratings. The distribution of the figurines in these age categories corresponds to the expected age pyramid for foraging societies.

Failure to acknowledge the variability of the figurines makes it easier to produce sweeping generalizations about their proba-

ble meaning or function. This is evident in the textbook interpretations. By far the most common function ascribed to the figurines is that of "fertility" (Table 2), specifically so designated in seven of the 12 texts, and called "procreation" and "maternity" by one text each. This ascription is usually not explained at all, or weakly expressed at best. For example, "It seems unlikely that Upper Paleolithic women actually looked like that, but perhaps it was an ideal type or expressed a wish for fertility" (Barnouw 1978:176). Apparently in conjunction with the fertility function is the idea of a "cult" or "Mother Goddess," since the five authors who use one or both of these expressions attach them to the fertility notion. Only one author rejects fertility as an explanation, on the grounds that hunters are not concerned with human fertility. Rather he explicitly suggests that the figurines are erotic: "Pleistocene pinup or centerfold girls" (Chard 1975:182).

TABLE 2 Functions of Figurines

AUTHOR	FERTILITY	GODDESS/CULT	EROTIC	ARTISTIC/STYLIZED
Barnouw (1978)	X			
Campbell (1988)	X	X		
Chard (1975)	rejects		X	
Clark (1977)	X (maternity)			ö
Eddy (1984)	X	X	X	
Fagan (1986)	X	X		
Hester & Grady (1982)	X			X
Jurmain et al. (1981)	X	X	X	ö
Pfeiffer (1985)				X
Poirier (1987)	X	X		
Smith (1976)	X		X	X
Wenke (1984)			ö	X

HIDDEN ASSUMPTIONS

The brief descriptions and interpretations of the female figurines contain and to some extent conceal unexamined assumptions about gender. Among them are: that the figurines were made *by* men, that the figurines were made *for* men, that nakedness is necessarily associated with eroticism, and that depiction of breasts is primarily sexual.

Underlying the description of the female figurines as erotic or reproductive is a masculist construction of the world, in which females are assumed to exist primarily for the use of males, sexually or reproductively. The scholarly literature is replete with explicit examples of this worldview, which the textbooks reflect.

A few quotations from the scholarly literature will demonstrate that males are usually assumed to be the sculptors of the figurines. The italics are mine throughout. "How did the artist's vision, which reflected the ideal of *his* time, see her? For as with man, we can never know what she really looked like ... so we have to make do with the version her comparison, man, had of her" (Berenguer 1973:48). The possibility that it was *her* version appears not to have crossed Berenguer's mind. Although this mindset focuses on males exclusively, it is not confined to males only, as shown from this quote from a woman, "He [the artist] desired only to show the female erotically and as the source of all abundance—in her he portrayed not woman but fertility" (Hawkes 1964:27). Referring to the not uncommon find of broken-off legs, Campbell (1982:410) suggests that "they may have cracked off in the baking, or when the ancient ceramicist tossed aside a work that failed to please *him*." (Most of the figurines of course are carved.) In case there is any doubt about the use of the specific rather than the generic use of the term "man," Leroi-Gourhan (1967:90) makes it crystal clear that "prehistoric man" doesn't include females, speaking of "the first figurines representing prehistoric man—or at least *his wife.*"

If the figurines are assumed to have been made by men, then it follows that they were created for male purposes. Even when they were first discovered, the Abbé Breuil (1954, cited in Ucko and Rosenfeld 1973:119) said they were for "pleasure to Paleolithic man during his meals" (do we have a euphemism here?). Berenguer (1973:52) focuses on reproductivity: "we may deduce man's obsessive need for women who would bear *him* lots of children to offset the high mortality rate caused by the harsh living conditions." Von Königswald worried about other possessions, "It certainly is an old problem: how could man protect *his* property, mark a place as 'his home,' 'his living site' so that others would recognize and respect it, especially in a period where there were no houses, just *abris* and caves?" He concludes that men made the "grotesque" figurines to guard their property, and scare off intruders! Delporte (1979:308) muses more philosophically, "for [paleolithic men] as for us ... the mother who gives and transmits life is also the woman who gives and shares pleasure: could the paleolithic have been insensitive to this novel duality?" [my translation]. Could the present be insensitive to the fact that there were paleolithic women as well as men? Are women to be denied their own sensitivity, or indeed their own existence as sentient beings?

The fact that the figurines were unclothed, or scantily clothed, for several wear belts and other decorations (a fact that is noted only by Clark [1977:105] among our textbook sample), surely has been essential to the interpretation of eroticism, in spite of the fact that there are many other possible reasons for the depiction of nudity. For example, people may have been usually unclothed inside the cave or hut, so that nakedness was not a special condition. The figurines could have been teaching devices for girls' puberty rites, as Marshack (1972:283) has suggested.

Nakedness frequently has different connotations when men rather than women are the sculptor's subject. For example, a naked male torso from Harappa is shown under the heading "Figures of Authority," in *The First Cities,* a widely used book from the Time-Life series (Hamblin 1973:133). The text tells us:

> Although male figures rarely appear among sculptures dug up at Mohenjo-Daro and Harappa, the few that do all seem to represent men of importance. In the three works reproduced here, there is a common theme, however varied the pieces themselves may be: regality or godliness.

As Conkey and Spector (1985:11) point out in another context, changing the rules of interpretation according to sex will not reveal anything about prehistoric gender roles. Rather it comforts us in supposing that things have always been the same.

In spite of being naked, however, it would seem that the fat figurines have little sex appeal to modern male scholars. This has called forth various explanations, ranging from assertions that they are stylized, to a suggestion that you cannot tell *what* might have turned on those prehistoric men (you can almost see the shrug and the wink), to a rejection of the erotic argument on the grounds that the figurines are simply too grotesque! In all of this discussion, passivity of women is assumed.

It is deserving of some comment that breasts are equated with eroticism in the textbooks, more by juxtaposition of words than by explicit statements. Sometimes, though, the equation is specified. There is one carving, referred to as the "rod with breasts," which evoked the following paean: "This statuette shows us that the artist has neglected all that did not interest *him,* stressing *his* sexual libido only where the breasts are concerned—a diluvial plastic pornography." (Absolon 1949). Surely anthropologists of all people know that exposed breasts are not at all uncommon in the warmer parts of the world, and cause little comment or excitement except for visiting tourists and perhaps a segment of the readership of *National Geographic.*

The "rod with breasts" is an interesting example of the extension of the underlying attitude toward women that is revealed in some generalizations about the figurines. Enigmatic carvings are declared to represent breasts, buttocks, or vulvae, reducing women to their "essentials" (Fig. 2). Especially the notion of the "vulvae" (some of which look rather like molar teeth), "has become an *idée fixe* and one of the most durable myths of prehistory" (Bahn 1986:99). The "rods" from Dolni Vestonice could be as easily perceived as stylized male genitalia, but if they were so described the eloquence would probably be in a different vein. It is hard to imagine exchanging the genders in the quote by Absolon above.

Alternative explanations, based on variability rather than generalizations, are not lacking in the scholarly literature. The figurines have been argued to represent priests or ancestors or clan-mothers, to show women as

(a)   (b)

Figure 2 "Rod with breasts from Dolni Vestonice, Czechoslovakia

actors with a ritual function (Klima 1962:204, Abramova 1967:83, Hancar 1940). These possibilities are not even hinted at in the texts, with one sole exception (Campbell 1988:481).

ARCHEOLOGICAL MYTHOLOGY

What are the possible reasons for the selective reporting found in the textbooks? First, to be fair, is the summary nature of the texts. Little space is given to the figurines, and it is necessary to paint a broad picture with a few strokes. But the selection of this particular

way of viewing the Upper Paleolithic figures as fat, as sexual, and as representing fertility, can be linked to our own cultural stereotypes and assumptions about the nature of men, women, sexuality, and reproduction. I suggest that our own culture makes these generalizations seem so natural, so satisfying, that there is no reason to examine them. The "text" read into the figurines is ours.

Several archeologists have commented on the problems of reading our unconscious assumptions about the present into the past. "History and prehistory constitute bodies of knowledge used to legitimize social policies and to validate social trajectories" (Moore and Keene 1983:7). This tendency has been traced to the dominant paradigm in archeology: "Because of the logic of empiricist epistemology, theories rising on empiricist foundations potentially serve only to recreate in the past the dominant cultural ideologies of the present" (Saitta 1983:303). We must recognize "the importance of taking into account the conceptions we hold of our own society which inevitably mediate our understanding of the past" (Miller and Tilley 1984:2).

Recent research on gender roles in cultural anthropology proposes that "male and female, sex and reproduction, are cultural or symbolic constructs" (Ortner and Whitehead 1981:6). These constructs are often reflected in origin stories as "metaphors for sexual identity" (Sanday 1981:56), which Sanday calls "scripts." I am suggesting that culturally constructed gender roles, and our attitudes and beliefs about sex and reproduction, enter into the selectivity of reporting on the Upper Paleolithic figurines. The reading of the metaphors of the figurines derives from a masculist script.

I do not wish to impute either evil intentions or inferior scholarship to the authors of these textbooks. It is important to note the unconscious nature of the acceptance of cultural scripts. But that does not make them less pernicious. Reinforcing present cultural stereotypes by projecting them into the past allows whole generations of students to believe that our present gender constructs are eternal and unchanging. Especially those who deal in prehistory need to be alert to our cultural biases, and not imply that present gender roles are external verities.

Marvin Harris points out that "our ordinary state of mind is always a profoundly mystified consciousness. . . . To emerge from myth and legend to mature consciousness we need to compare the full range of past and present cultures" (Harris 1974:5). The trick is to examine the past without the mystification.

I am not proposing that alternative explanations are necessarily better, only that the diversity of the figurines should be taken into account. Maybe women made some of the figurines. Maybe the figurines were used for women's purposes. Maybe it isn't relevant whether men find them sexy or not. If an explanation feels intuitively right, perhaps that is the best reason to reexamine it.

REFERENCES

Abramova, Z. A. 1967. Paleolithic Art in the USSR. *Arctic Anthropology* 4(2):1–179.

Absolon, K. 1949. The Diluvial Anthropomorphic Statuettes and Drawings, Especially the So-called Venus Statuettes Discovered in Moravia. *Artibus Asiae* 12:201–220.

Bahn, P. G. 1986. No Sex Please, We're Aurignacians. *Rock Art Research* 3(2):99–105.

Barnouw, V. 1978. *Physical Anthropology and Archaeology.* 3rd ed. Homewood, IL: The Dorsey Press.

Beller, A. S. 1977. *Fat and Thin.* New York: Farrar, Strauss and Giroux.

Berenguer, M. 1973. *Prehistoric Man and His Art.* M. Heron, trans. London: Souvenir Press.

Boule, M., and H. Vallois. 1957. *Fossil Man.* New York: Dryden Press.

Campbell, B. G. 1982. *Humankind Emerging.* 3rd ed. Boston: Little, Brown.

———. 1988. *Humankind Emerging.* 5th ed. Glenview, IL: Scott, Foresman and Company.

Chard, C. 1975. *Man in Prehistory.* 2nd ed. New York: McGraw-Hill.

Clark, G. 1977. *World Prehistory in New Perspective.* 3rd ed. Cambridge: Cambridge University Press.

Conkey, M. and J. Spector. 1985. Archaeology and the Study of Gender. In *Advances in Archaeological Method and Theory.* Vol. 7. M. B. Schiffer, ed., pp. 1–38. New York: Academic Press.

Delporte, H. 1979. *l'Image de la Femme dans l'Art Préhistorique.* Paris: Picard.

Eddy, F. W. 1984. *Archaeology, A Cultural-Evolutionary Approach.* Englewood Cliffs: Prentice Hall.

Fagan, B. 1986. *People of the Earth: An Introduction to World History.* 5th ed. Boston: Little, Brown.

Fleury, C. 1926. Quelques Considerations sur la Pseudo-steatopygie des Venus Aurignaciennes. *Archives Suisses d'Anthropologie Generale* 11(1):137–141.

Gamble, C. 1986. *The Paleolithic Settlement of Europe.* Cambridge: Cambridge University Press.

———. 1987. Interaction and Alliance in Palaeolithic Society. *Man* (n.s.) 17:92–107.

Hamblin, D. J. 1973. *The First Cities.* New York: Time-Life Books.

Hancar, F. 1940. Problem der Venus Statuetten im Eurasiatischen Jung-Palaolithikum. *Praehistorische Zeitschrift:* 30–31.

Harris, M. 1974. *Cows, Pigs, Wars and Witches: The Riddles of Culture.* New York: Random House.

Hawkes, J. 1964. The Achievements of Paleolithic Man. In *Man Before History.* C. Gabel, ed., pp. 21–35. Englewood Cliffs: Prentice Hall.

Hester, J. J. and J. Grady. 1982. *Introduction to Archaeology,* 2nd ed. New York: Holt, Rinehart and Winston.

Jurmain, R., H. Nelson, H. Kurashina, and W. Turnbaugh. 1981. *Understanding Physical Anthropology and Archaeology.* St. Paul: West Publishing Co.

Klima, B. 1962. The First Ground-Plan of an Upper Paleolithic Loess Settlement in Middle Europe and its Meaning. In *Courses Toward Urban Life.* R. Braidwood and G. Willey, eds., pp. 193–210. Chicago: Aldine.

Koenigswald, G. H. R. von. 1972. Early *Homo sapiens* as an Artist: The Meaning of Paleolithic Art. In *The Origin of Homo sapiens, Ecology and Conservation,* Vol. 3. F. Bordes, ed., pp. 133–139. Proceedings of the Paris Symposium 1969.

Leroi-Gourhan, André. 1967. *Treasures of Prehistoric Art.* Translated by N. Guterman. New York: Henry N. Abrams.

Luquet, G. H. 1926. *L'Art et la Religion des Hommes Fossiles.* Paris: Masson et Cie.

Marshack, A. 1972. *The Roots of Civilization.* New York: McGraw-Hill.

Miller, D. and A. Tilley. 1984. Ideology, Power and Prehistory: An Introduction. In *Ideology, Power and Prehistory.* Daniel Miller and Christopher

Tilley, eds., pp. 1–15. Cambridge: Cambridge University Press.

Moore, J. A. and A. S. Keene. 1983. Archaeology and the Law of the Hammer. In *Archaeological Hammers and Theories*. J. A. Moore and A. S. Keene eds., pp. 3–13. New York: Academic Press.

Nelson, S. M. n.d. "Venus" Figurines as Evidence of Sedentism in the Upper Paleolithic. (On file, Department of Anthropology, University of Denver.)

Nelson, S. M., and L. Bibb. n.d. Notes and Statistics on Venus Figurines. (On file, Department of Anthropology, University of Denver.)

Ortner, S. B., and H. Whitehead (eds.). 1981. *Sexual Meanings: The Cultural Construction of Gender and Sexuality*. Cambridge: Cambridge University Press.

Passemard, L. 1938. *Les Statuettes Feminines Paléolithiques Dites Venus*. St. Nîmes: Libraire Teissier.

Pfeiffer, J. 1985. *The Emergence of Humankind*. 4th ed. New York: Harper and Row.

Poirier, F. E. 1987. *Understanding Human Evolution*. Englewood Cliffs, NJ: Prentice Hall.

Rice, P. C. 1981. Prehistoric Venuses: Symbols of Motherhood or Womanhood? *Journal of Anthropological Research* 37(4):402–416.

Saccasyn Della Santa, E. 1947. *Les Figures Humaines du Paléolithique Superior Eurasiatique*. Paris: Amberes.

Saitta, D. J. 1983. The Poverty of Philosophy in Archaeology. In *Archaeological Hammers and Theories*. James A. Moore and Arthur S. Keene, eds., pp. 299–304. New York: Academic Press.

Sanday, P. R. 1981. *Female Power and Male Dominance: On the Origins of Sexual Inequality*. Cambridge: Cambridge University Press.

Smith, J. W. 1976. *Foundations of Archaeology*. Beverly Hills: Glencoe Press.

Soffer, O. 1988. Upper Paleolithic Connubia, Refugia and the Archaeological Record for Eastern Europe. In *Pleistocene Old World: Regional Perspectives*. O. Soffer, ed., pp. 333–348. New York: Plenum Publishing Co.

Ucko P.J. and A. Rosenfeld. 1973. *Palaeolithic Cave Art*. New York: McGraw-Hill.

Wenke, R. 1984. *Patterns in Prehistory, Humankind's First Three Million Years*. 2nd ed. New York: Oxford University Press.

Maya Royal Women: A Lesson in Precolumbian History

David Freidel and Linda Schele

The lowland Maya civilization flourished on the Yucatan peninsula for 2,000 years before the Spanish arrived on their shores in the early sixteenth century. What particularly distinguishes the Maya civilization from the others of Mesoamerica is its literature. Some other cultures, such as the Zapotec of Oaxaca, Mixe societies of Veracruz, and the early highland Maya of Guatemala, had written scripts that approximated spoken language as did the Maya script. Yet only the lowland Maya have left posterity a sizable collection of texts. Together these texts on carved stone,

Original material prepared for this text.

painted walls, pottery vessels, and other small artifacts are a bare remnant from a civilization that mostly wrote on screen-fold books of bark paper sized with lime plaster. Nevertheless, they reveal dimensions of ancient society in the New World that are barely hinted at in other regions known primarily or exclusively through their archaeological remains.

One of the lessons from textual history is that women were much more than pawns in Maya power politics. In three cases already documented (and with the prospect of more to come with continued decipherment), the performance of royal women proved decisive to the destiny of particular late Classic period

(A.D. 600 to A.D. 900) kingdoms.[1] We will briefly summarize one of these dramatic episodes in Maya history that shows how women propelled themselves to the center stage of an ancient civilization. We think there is a basic lesson to be learned by archaeologists who must deal with the remains of past complex societies without the guide of written texts detailing state politics. Despite some lip service to the contrary, current introductory archaeology texts relate the rise and fall of such ahistorical civilizations as if women did not exist and as if only men ruled and made the critical decisions guiding governments. We think, on the basis of our experience with the ancient Maya, that in some early class-structured societies with hereditary elites, such as the Maya classes of *ahaw* (supreme lord) or *sahal* (noble vassal), women ruled with men in the context of court politics revolving around family alliances and feuds. Governments ruled by royal dynasties did not merely profit by the participation of women, such participation was mandatory and necessary. The political reproduction of power required the physical reproduction of rulers, a process in which women played a clear role. Beyond this biological fact, Maya rulers inherited the social, political, and religious potential for power from their mothers and their fathers. Our cases illustrate these points.

THE GREAT CLASSIC MAYA WARS

The seventh century witnessed bloody and endemic wars of conquest between the great houses of the Maya in the interior forests of the Yucatan peninsula. On the one side were the kings of Tikal and their allies and on the other were the kings of Calakmul and theirs. Ruler 1 of Dos Pilas (Balah-Kan-K'awil),[2] a member of the Tikal royal family, established a new offshoot capital south of Tikal in A.D. 645. He joined the Calakmul alliance, warred against Tikal, and rapidly transformed his small city into one of the great Maya conquest states. Ruler 1 consolidated his hold over the southern forest region not only through battle, but also through judicious polygamous marriage to several princesses from smaller kingdoms in the area. His ambition stretched across the vast and rich farmlands of the interior forest now called Peten in Guatemala. He engaged in the wars embroiling the Tikal and Calakmul alliances, capturing and sacrificing the contemporary king of Tikal on behalf of Calakmul.

The basic military strategy of the Calakmul alliance was to surround the centrally situated Tikal state with enemy capitals. To that end Calakmul established an alliance with the city of Naranjo, to the northeast of Tikal. The king of Naranjo, however, evidently betrayed Calakmul, so that great city and another allied city called Caracol together attacked and captured Naranjo, sacrificing its king. At the same time, the son of the Tikal king captured by Ruler 1 of Dos Pilas came to power at Tikal. He prepared to rise in vengeance against the Calakmul alliance. Calakmul needed new partners on Tikal's northeastern flank at Naranjo, ready to attack in coordination with the rest of the circle of capitals.

The Princess of Dos Pilas and the Revival of Naranjo

The Calakmul alliance then called on Ruler 1 of Dos Pilas for assistance and he sent his daughter to Naranjo to rededicate the sacred center and establish a new, loyal, dynastic family there. The new Tikal king came to the throne on May 6, A.D. 682, readying his war with his enemies. By August 30 of that same year the Dos Pilas princess had successfully crossed the forest past Tikal without being captured and had arrived at Naranjo. It takes little imagination to know the courage and resolve of this woman, riding in her sedan chair as a living declaration of war more than 100 kilometers over jungle paths through enemy territory. Every moment of that journey she faced capture and death by sacrifice at the hands of the Tikal king and his allies.

No doubt to the people of Naranjo her arrival was nothing short of miraculous, and her three-day ceremonial was precisely that. Her duty was to rededicate the sacred temple of the city. In the thinking of the Maya she reopened the Naranjo portal to the Other-world, allowing communication and magical power to pass from the world of the ancestors to the world of the living. The usual way to accomplish this for a royal woman was to pierce her tongue in self-sacrifice with a lancet of black volcanic glass and then to pull a cord through it as she entered an ecstatic trance and brought forth the spirit of her ancestor to bless the place.

The royal princess of Dos Pilas, named Wak-Kanal-Tzuk, probably married a prince of the defeated dynasty. That man's only role was to beget a son who would take his throne and rule in the name of the Calakmul alliance. The son of the princess became king as a small child. His mother, and his mother's brother from Dos Pilas, fought wars in his name against Tikal and Tikal's allies. From the texts of this city, we know that she fought the wars and not her husband, whose name is never mentioned in the histories of Naranjo. The ignominious defeat of Naranjo by the Calakmul alliance during his early reign, or during that of his father, stripped him of the privilege of history. Without the Dos Pilas princess the kingdom of Naranjo would have slipped quietly into obscurity.

The Naranjo Wars

After her dedication of the Naranjo royal temple, the Dos Pilas princess gave birth to a royal heir, Butz-Tilwi' in ancient Mayan, nick-named Smoking-Squirrel by scholars, on January 6, A.D. 688. There is little doubt that although her husband may have been alive, she ruled during this period, because she was the only one with a royal history from Naran-jo at this time. Clearly, however, Ruler 1 of Dos Pilas was anxious to see his daughter's command of this strategic city consolidated. When the boy was only 5 years old he ascend-ed to the throne of Naranjo on May 31, A.D. 693. Out of deference to the humiliated royal house of Naranjo, the scribes of the city never explicitly announced the parentage of

the new king. But the systematic way that they linked the arrival of the princess at Naranjo, the birth of her son, and the declaration of the princesses' parentage in Ruler 1 of Dos Pilas in a single text makes it certain that she is the mother of the young king of Naranjo.

Soon after the boy became king, on June 20, A.D. 693, Naranjo went to war against the allies of Tikal to the southwest of their realm. Obviously, a 5-year-old child had little to do with this bloody work. The princess and her brother successfully prosecuted war against the kingdom of Ucanal, capturing a high lord there. On a retrospective carved stone monument celebrating this victory, the princess shows herself standing upon this prostate captive in the time honored stance of conquest taken by Maya kings. This was only the opening battle in a protracted series of campaigns by the newly refurbished dynasty of Naranjo against the Tikal state. One hundred days later Naranjo attacked Ucanal again, and on February 1, A.D. 695, Naranjo delivered a major defeat against this border kingdom ally of Tikal. This victory involved an unnamed lord from Dos Pilas, probably a relative of the princess, and it shows that Dos Pilas played an active military role in the success of Naranjo.

Naranjo continued to attack to the south and east under the aegis of Smoking-Squirrel and his mother for many years. Between them, they wreaked havoc on Tikal and other cities for two generations. The princess from Dos Pilas clearly played the key role in this success in the early and critical years of the fledgling new dynasty at Naranjo. The result of her success was a mixed blessing for her father, Ruler 1. The victories against Tikal and its allies invited counter-attacks from the city against Naranjo. Eventually, Tikal would defeat Naranjo and capture high lords there. And enemies of Dos Pilas, no doubt fueled by Tikal, would in time lay siege to the city and bring down the dynasty Ruler 1 worked so hard to establish. Still, in her lifetime the princess from Dos Pilas was a formidable leader in the great alliance wars of the ancient Maya.

The Queens of Yaxchilan

Far to the west and a few years later in the drainage of the mighty "Xokol Ha," now called the Usumacinta River, two queens nearly tore their kingdom asunder in their struggle to determine who would inherit the throne. The kingdom was Yaxchilan, its capital, a city graced with white temples, carved and terraced on a mountain facing northeast over the forested swamps of the interior. On August 24, A.D. 709, Lady Eveningstar, daughter of the royal house of Calakmul and wife to Shield-Jaguar, Holy lord of Yaxchilan, gave birth to a son named Bird-Jaguar after his illustrious grandfather. The event brought no happiness to Lady Shark, cowife to Lady Eveningstar and the senior wife of the Yaxchilan King. Lady Shark's family was local to the kingdom, a vassal lineage to the house of Yaxchilan. Lady Shark was, technically, Shield-Jaguar's mother's father's sister's daughter—or first cousin once removed. Lady Shark had every reason and precedent to support her claim to give birth to the heir to the throne, but now there was a rival claimant. The logic of Lady Eveningstar's claim no doubt derived from the powerful alliance that was sustained if the heir was from two great royal houses strategically spanning the great forest.

We don't know exactly when the old king first declared for his younger son, but we do know that the consequences were to thrust Yaxchilan to the brink of civil war. Some noble families supported the precedent that the heir should come from the union of the dynasty with a vassal noble house of Yaxchilan and others supported the king's alliance to Calakmul. Shield-Jaguar went out among his noble vassals and performed public sacrifices at their provincial capitals to cement their loyalty to him and his heir. The king attempted to settle the struggle by conceding to Lady Shark an extraordinary privilege: She was to dedicate a new royal temple in the most important location in the city. This beautiful temple contained carved stone lintels over the doorways featuring portraits of Lady Shark with Shield-Jaguar and with his ancestor. Shield-Jaguar went to war to bring back sacrificial victims to bless this temple. There was a catch, however. The text of one of the lintels celebrates a hierophany, a conjunction of planets in the sky; this conjunction occurs a magic number of days, 52, after the birth of Bird-Jaguar to Lady Eveningstar. In this indirect and discrete fashion Lady Shark was required to acknowledge through her dedication of a royal temple that the dynastic heir was to be Bird-Jaguar. In this way Lady Shark won the privilege of writing sacred history for herself in one of the most beautiful set of Maya carvings, but she had to inscribe against the starfield that her rival's son would rule the kingdom.

On the other hand, while Lady Eveningstar won the crown for her son, she forfeited her claim to history all through the lifetime of her husband. Never once in all of his inscriptions does Shield-Jaguar mention Lady Eveningstar's existence. It is only because Bird-Jaguar won his struggle for the throne and inscribed retrospective history about his mother that we know of her. It was not an easy fight. All through his waning years Shield-Jaguar worked to confirm and sanctify his son's claim to succeed him. After his death there were ten long years before Bird-Jaguar actually acceded to the throne. We surmise that Bird-Jaguar was battling against rival claimants derived from Lady Shark and her patriline. Although he does not mention the civil wars we find him out in the provincial capitals cementing alliances with noble vassals and celebrating victory in wars by sacrificing captives. It was not until Lady Shark died on April 3, A.D. 749, and her rival Lady Eveningstar died on March 13, A.D. 751, that Bird-Jaguar could finally take his throne on February 10, A.D. 752.

Despite his success, the civil war had taught Bird-Jaguar a bitter lesson. He made sure his own heir was born to a noble woman from one of his own vassal lineages. His wife, Lady-Great-Skull, and her brother, Great-Skull, figure prominently in his official history in ceremonies carved on lintels, along with his son Chel-Te. In light of the events we can document from Bird-Jaguar's life we think his attribution by modern scholars as "Bird-Jaguar the Great" is well earned. He was clearly a charismatic and very able military and political leader. Without such skill he may have failed to repair the breach caused by his father's decision to choose him for heir. A struggle of great women underscored that the fate of major Maya kingdoms depended on them as much as their husbands and sons.

The role of Maya royal women in the history of this ancient civilization is beginning to come into focus. We have had clues for some time in the form of sumptuous tomb furniture accompanying some elite women. Slowly we have moved in our understanding of the texts from initial hypotheses that the exchange of women between dynasties strengthened alliances between their male rulers to more subtle and complicated scenarios in which Maya women have emerged as powerful personalities and active politicians. As the archaeologists continue to excavate and as the epigraphers continue to decipher texts more completely, we expect the role of royal women to become even more central in our interpretations of this New World civilization.

NOTES

1. As in any other historical inquiry, our interpretations are subject to change with new information. The present description was originally based on our book *A Forest of Kings* (Linda Schele and David Freidel, Wm. Morrow & Co., Inc. 1990). Already in this outline of the complex events surrounding the life of the Dos Pilas princess, we have changed many interpretations given in our book. We are drawing on new evidence supplied by the Vanderbilt University research in the Petexbatun region and at the site of Dos Pilas. This research is directed by Arthur Demarest and Stephen Houston. We are also drawing on collaborative research by Nikolai Grube and Linda Schele and Nikolai Grube with Simon Martin. Simon Martin, in particular, is an expert on the texts of Naranjo.

2. The name given this Holy Lord, k'ul ahaw, which is what the Maya called kings, is a decipherment of the main elements of his glyphs. He is called Ruler 1 of Dos Pilas in the scholarly literature, and also Flint-Sky-God K.

III
Domestic Worlds and Public Worlds

In 1974, in an attempt to document a universal subordination of women, Michelle Rosaldo (1974: 18) proposed a paradigm relating "recurrent aspects of psychology and cultural and social organization to an opposition between the 'domestic' orientation of women and the extradomestic or 'public' ties, that, in most societies, are primarily available to men." The domestic-public model led Rosaldo to suggest that women's status is highest in societies in which the public and domestic spheres are only weakly differentiated, as among the Mbuti pygmies. In contrast "women's status will be lowest in those societies where there is a firm differentiation between domestic and public spheres of activity and where women are isolated from one another and placed under a single man's authority, in the home. Their position is raised when they can challenge those claims to authority ..." (Rosaldo 1974: 36). Accordingly, women may enhance their status by creating a public world of their own or by entering the men's world. In addition, the most egalitarian societies will be those in which men participate in the domestic domain.

Correspondingly, Sanday (1974) suggests that women's involvement in domains of activity such as subsistence or defense may be curtailed because of their time and energy commitment to reproduction and mothering. Men, on the other hand, are free to form broader associations in the political, economic, and military spheres that transcend the mother-child unit. While the linkage of women with the domestic and men with the public domains may imply a biological determinism based on women's reproductive roles, Rosaldo (1974: 24) argues that the opposition between domestic and public orientations is an intelligible but not a necessary arrangement.

One aspect of women's domestic responsibilities is that it is women who primarily raise children. Nancy Chodorow (1974) develops a theory linking adult sex role behavior to the fact that children's early involvement is with their female parent. Chodorow argues that girls are integrated through ties with female kin into the world of domestic work. Age, rather than achievement, may define their status, while boys must "learn" to be men. Unlike girls, boys have few responsibilities in childhood and are free to establish peer groups that create "public" ties. To become an adult male a boy is often obliged to dissociate himself from the home and from female kin. According to Rosaldo (1974: 26), "the fact that children virtually everywhere grow up with their mothers may well account for characteristic differences in male and female psychologies" as well as set the stage for adult organization of activities.

As scholarship devoted to an understanding of gender issues has evolved, the influential domestic-public model has been the focus of considerable controversy, revolving around three related issues: whether male domination is universal, whether male domination is explained by the domestic-public dichotomy, and whether the concept of domestic-public has relevance in all cultures.

Lamphere (in this book) reviews the formulation of the domestic-public model, and discusses the subsequent critiques of its applicability. Rosaldo herself, rethinking her original position, said that although male dominance appears widespread, it does not "in actual behavioral terms assume a universal content or a universal shape. On the contrary, women typically have power and influence in political and economic life, display autonomy from men in their pursuits, and rarely find themselves confronted or constrained by what might seem the brute fact of male strength" (1980: 394). Although the domestic-public opposition has been compelling, Rosaldo suggests that the model assumes too much rather than helping to illuminate and explain.

As Lamphere observes, it has become increasingly clear that the domestic-public opposition is the heir to nineteenth-century social theory rooted in a dichotomy contrasting home and woman, with a public world of men, and reflecting an understanding of political rights based on sex. It has also been noted that conceptualizing social life as dichotomized into domestic and public domains does not make sense in societies in which management of production occurs within the household and in which household production itself involves the management of the "public" economy (Leacock 1978: 253).

In contrast, in an industrial society, where home and workplace are clearly demarcated, the domestic-public opposition may have explanatory value. For example, Murcott (in this book) analyzes one domestic task, cooking, as part of an exploration of economic relations in the family and of the division of labor between spouses. Interviews with Welsh housewives indicate that ideas about home cooking reflect understandings of the relationship between domestic and paid labor. An analysis of the production of meals illuminates the allocation of responsibility for different aspects of family living, the gendered control of decision making and the distribution of power and authority in marriage. The informants shared the view that proper eating must occur at home and that a cooked dinner is necessary to family health and well-being. Murcott suggests that the emphasis on having a proper dinner waiting for the husband when he comes in from work underscores the symbolic importance of the return home: "the cooked dinner marks the threshold between the public domains of school or work and the private sphere behind the closed front door" (Murcott, this volume).

In his analysis of fatherhood in the United States, Townsend (in this volume) contends that in this industrial society, it is often assumed that parenting represents a simple division of labor in which men are engaged in the public sphere of paid labor and politics, while women are involved in the domestic sphere of childcare and reproduction. His research demonstrates, however, that the domestic and public spheres interpenetrate and that arrangements made in one sphere influence behavior in another. Parenting, he argues, is deeply gendered. This means not only that fathers and mothers "do" different things, but that fatherhood has different meanings for men and women. Men interviewed in his research claimed to want greater involvement as fathers than their own fathers had experienced. They saw "marriage and children" as a package deal; for these men, a relationship with a woman was necessary for a man to see himself as a father. Correspondingly, Townsend shows that women are often influential in men's decisions about when to have children; that women are the "default parent" while men are in a more "optional" position with their role as disciplinarian or "fun dad" shaped by their children's mother. Thus women, as wives and mothers, mediate and facilitate fatherhood. Moreover, the structural division of labor placing men in the labor force and women at home has been maintained by strong cultural themes that continue to emphasize women's involvement in their children's lives, even with women's increasing labor force participation.

Just as Townsend shows that in the United States, an ideological association of men with the public and women with the domestic does not accurately represent the interpenetration of these spheres. In Andalusia, in southern Spain, women are ideologically associated with the home, and men with public places, yet the reality is more complex (Driessen 1983). According to widely held ideals, the woman should be virtuous, docile, and devoted to husband and children; the ideal man is the head of the household, tough, but seldom at home. However, in actuality, the involvement of men in the private sphere and women in the public sphere varies according to social class. Among agricultural laborers, women's labor is critical to the household economy. It is common for women to be employed, while their men are unemployed. This contradiction produces tensions that are reflected in men's sociability patterns. The bar offers men the opportunity to display their masculinity by heavy drinking and sexual banter. Men's sociability is best understood as a response to the vulnerability of unemployed men to women who contribute substantially to the family income through wage labor. This results in blurred idealized distinctions between male and female identity.

Research on the public/private distinction has implications for the interplay among gender, status, and power. Whereas traditional conceptions of power emphasized formal political behavior and authority associated with a status conferring the "right" to impose sanctions (Lamphere 1974: 99), informal power strategies such as manipulation and maneuvering are also important aspects of political activity. Cynthia Nelson (1974) examines the concept of power, focusing on images of women and power in the domestic and public domains in the societies of the Middle East. Ethnographies of the Middle East have commonly differentiated two social worlds, a woman's private world and a man's public world. Women's concerns are domestic, men's political. Nelson argues that the assignment of private and public reflects the imposition of western cultural categories on the Middle East; the meaning of power is influenced by these categorizations, as well as by the limitations of data obtained by male ethnographers from male informants.

This is a point made forcefully by Annette Weiner (1976) in her reanalysis of Trobriand exchange. She argues that "we unquestioningly accept male statements about women as factual evidence for the way a society is structured.... Any study that does not include the role of women—as seen by women—as part of the way the society is structured remains only a partial study of that society. Whether women are publicly valued or privately secluded, whether they control politics, a range of economic commodities, or merely magic spells, they function within that society, not as objects, but as individuals with some measure of control" (228).

Similarly, Nelson argues that by asking such questions as "How do women influence men?" "Who controls whom about what?" "How is control exercised?" it becomes apparent that women exercise a greater degree of power in social life than is often appreciated. In addition, she challanges the idea that the social worlds of men and women are reducible to private and public domains, with power limited to men and women in the public arena. Nelson's review of ethnographies addressing the role and position of women in Middle Eastern society suggests that women play a crucial role as structural links between kinship groups in societies in which family and kinship are fundamental institutions. Women are in a position to influence men through ritual means, to channel information to male kin, and to influence decision making about alliances; consequently, women do participate in "public" activities, and women's exclusive solidarity groups exercise considerable social control and political influence. The conceptions of power as defined by the western observer are particularly challenged by literature on women written by women who offer a perspective on the position of Middle Eastern women derived from the actors themselves.

In the course of her critique of the application of the domestic-public opposition to social organization in the Middle East, Nelson challenges longstanding assumptions regarding women's subordination and male dominance and calls into question the association between political power and a public domain that excludes women. Similarly, in studies of peasant societies Rogers (1975) and others (Friedl 1967; Riegelhaupt 1967) contend that the sector of life over which peasant women have control—the household—is in fact the key sphere of activity, socially, politically, and economically. Men occupy public and prestigious positions of authority within the village sphere, but these activities do not have the impact on daily life that household activities have. In light of these analyses demonstrating women's power and influence, we are reminded that the universality of male dominance appears untenable.

Similarly, Brenner (in this volume) questions the value of totalizing models of gender-based power and prestige in her study of gender ideologies in Java. Her analysis critiques the stereotyped, male-centered visions of male power pervasive in Javanese cultural representations and in ethnographic accounts. The ethnographic record has emphasized male-focused gender ideologies while neglecting alternative conceptions of gender voiced by women. She shows that the home and market, both associated with women in Javanese thought, are not only sites of economic production, but also sites where conflicting understandings of male and female nature are symbolically negotiated. According to the gendered division of domestic power, the wife should defer to her husband as head of the household but in reality, women's power may far outweigh that of their husbands. Moreover, the dominance of women in the household is often linked to economic power within and outside the home. Yet in spite of their economic power, central ideologies devalue women precisely because of their commercial pursuits, which are held to detract from prestige. These ideologies stress men's stability and self-discipline and women's emotionality and lack of control. Nonetheless, Brenner argues that in many situations, a very different conceptualization of human nature prevails, one that emphasizes women's self-control and men's inability to master their passions. This analysis of gender, desire, and economic practice subverts any straightforward association of women with the domestic and men with the public spheres. Insofar as women are identified with the domestic, their activities are central to the production of the family's status in the broader society; they move easily between the household and the public domain.

In reflecting on feminist research in anthropology, Rosaldo critiques the very tendency to look for universal truths and origins. Rather, anthropologists need to develop theoretical perspectives that analyze the relationships of men and women in a broader social context (Rosaldo 1980: 414), involving inequality and hierarchy. As Henrietta Moore emphasizes, although women in many societies share some experiences and problems, women have had very different encounters with racism, colonialism, the penetration of capitalism, and international development. We need to move from assumptions of the shared experience of "women" to a critical analysis of the differences among women (1988:9).

REFERENCES

Chodorow, Nancy. 1974. "Family Structure and Feminine Personality." In Michelle Z. Rosaldo and Louise Lamphere (eds.). *Woman, Culture, and Society*, pp. 43–67. Stanford: Stanford University Press.

Driessen, Henk. 1983. "Male Sociability and Rituals of Masculinity in Rural Andalusia." *Anthropological Quarterly* 56(3): 125–133.

Friedl, Ernestine. 1967. "The Position of Women: Appearance and Reality." *Anthropological Quarterly* 40: 97–108.

Lamphere, Louise. 1974. "Strategies, Cooperation, and Conflict Among Women in Domestic Groups." In Michelle Z. Rosaldo and Louise Lamphere, (eds.). *Woman, Culture, and Society*, pp. 97–113. Stanford: Stanford University Press.

Leacock, Eleanor. 1978. "Women's Status in Egalitarian Society. Implications for Social Evolution." *Current Anthropology* 19(2): 247–275.

Moore, Henrietta L. 1988. *Feminism and Anthropology*. Minneapolis: University of Minnesota Press.

Nelson, Cynthia. 1974. "Public and Private Politics: Women in the Middle Eastern World. *American Ethnologist* 1(3):551–563.

Riegelhaupt, Joyce. 1967. "Saloio Women: An Analysis of Informal and Formal Political and Economic Roles of Portuguese Peasant Women." *Anthropological Quarterly* 40: 109–126.

Rogers, Susan Carol. 1975. "Female Forms of Power and the Myth of Male Dominance: A Model of Female/Male Interaction in Peasant Society." *American Ethnologist* 2: 727–756.

Rosaldo, Michelle Z. 1974. "Theoretical Overview." In Michelle Z. Rosaldo and Louise Lamphere (eds.). *Woman, Culture, and Society*, pp. 17–43. Stanford: Stanford University Press.

———. 1980. "The Use and Abuse of Anthropology: Reflections on Feminism and Cross-Cultural Understanding." *Signs* 5(3): 389–418.

Sanday, Peggy R. 1974. "Female Status in the Public Domain." In Michelle Z. Rosaldo and Louise Lamphere (eds.). *Woman, Culture, and Society*, pp. 189–207. Stanford: Stanford University Press.

Weiner, Annette B. 1976. *Women of Value, Men of Renown: New Perspectives in Trobriand Exchange*. Austin: University of Texas Press.

The Domestic Sphere of Women and the Public World of Men: The Strengths and Limitations of an Anthropological Dichotomy

Louise Lamphere

Since 1974 there has been a burgeoning interest within anthropology in the study of women, sex roles, and gender. Anthropology has long been a discipline that contained important women (Elsie Clews Parsons, Ruth Benedict, and Margaret Mead among the most famous) and a field in which women have been studied as well (e.g., Kaberry 1939, 1952; Landes 1938, 1947; Leith-Ross 1939; Underhill 1936; and Paulme 1963). However, with the publication of *Woman, Culture, and Society* (Rosaldo and Lamphere 1974) and *Toward an Anthropology of Women* (Reiter 1975a) women scholars, many of whom were identified as feminists, began to critique the androcentric bias in anthropology, to explore women's status in a wide variety of societies, and to provide explanatory models to understand women's position cross-culturally.

One of the most powerful and influential models was proposed by Michelle Rosaldo in her introductory essay to *Woman, Culture, and Society* (1974). Her argument began by asserting that although there is a great deal of cross-cultural variability in men's and women's roles, there is a pervasive, universal asymmetry between the sexes. "But what is perhaps most striking and surprising," Rosaldo writes, "is the fact that male, as opposed to female, activities are always recognized as predominantly important, and cultural systems give authority and value to the roles and activities of men" (Rosaldo 1974:19).

One of the quotes we chose to appear at the beginning of the book, a passage from

Original material prepared for this text.

Margaret Mead's *Male and Female,* sums up what we saw in 1974 in all the ethnographies and studies we examined. "In every known society, the male's need for achievement can be recognized. Men may cook, or weave, or dress dolls or hunt hummingbirds, but if such activities are appropriate occupations of men, then the whole society, men and women alike, votes them as important. When the same occupations are performed by women, they are regarded as less important" (Mead 1949:125). Not only were there differential evaluations of women's activities, but, Rosaldo argues, "everywhere men have some *authority* over women, that [is] they have culturally legitimated right to her subordination and compliance" (1974:21).

Having argued for a pervasive sexual asymmetry across cultures, not just in terms of cultural values, but also in terms of power and authority, Rosaldo accounted for this difference between men and women in terms of a dichotomy.[1] She argued that women are associated with a "domestic orientation," while men are primarily associated with extradomestic, political, and military spheres of activity. By "domestic" Rosaldo meant "those minimal institutions and modes of activity that are organized immediately around one or more mothers and their children." In contrast, the "public" referred to "activities, institutions, and forms of association that link, rank, organize, or subsume particular mother-child groups. Put quite simply, men have no single commitment as enduring, time-consuming, and emotionally compelling—as close to seeming necessary and natural—as the relation of a woman to her infant child; and so men are free to form those broader associations that we call 'society,' universalistic systems of order, meaning, and commitment that link particular mother-child groups."

Rosaldo, along with Sherry Ortner and Nancy Chodorow who also wrote essays in *Woman, Culture, and Society,* insisted that the connection between women's role in reproduction (the fact that women everywhere lactate and give birth to children) and their domestic orientation is not a necessary one. In other words biology is not destiny. Women's domestic orientation was structurally and culturally constructed and "insofar as woman is universally defined in terms of a largely maternal and domestic role, we can account for her universal subordination" (Rosaldo 1974:7).

"Although" Rosaldo writes, "I would be the last to call this a necessary arrangement or to deny that it is far too simple as an account of any particular empirical case, I suggest that the opposition between domestic and public orientations (an opposition that must, in part, derive from the nurturant capacities of women) provides the necessary framework for an examination of male and female roles in any society" (Rosaldo 1974:24).

For Rosaldo, then, women were involved in the "messiness" of daily life; they were always available for interruption by children. Men could be more distanced and may actually have separate quarters (such as men's houses) away from women's activities. Men could thus "achieve" authority and create rank, hierarchy, and a political world away from women. The confinement of women to the domestic sphere and men's ability to create and dominate the political sphere thus accounted for men's ability to hold the greater share of power and authority in all known cultures and societies.

At the time Rosaldo wrote her overview and in the introduction we both wrote, we were faced with building a framework where none existed. Despite the number of monographs on women, Margaret Mead's work and that of Simone de Beauvoir (1953) were the most provocative, and perhaps the only, theoretical works we knew.[2] The argument for universal sexual asymmetry followed in a long tradition in anthropology where scholars have sought to look for what is broadly "human" in all cultures. In addition to language, anthropologists have discussed the universality of the incest taboo, marriage, and the family. The notion that women might be universally subordinate to men thus made sense as a first attempt at theory building in this newly revived "subfield" within anthropology.

Although Rosaldo argued for universal subordination, she was careful to make clear that women are not powerless. They exercise informal influence and power, often mitigating male authority or even rendering it trivial (Rosaldo 1974:21). In addition, there are important variations in women's roles in different cultures, and variation was discussed in most of the rest of the articles in the collection. For example, Sanday and Sacks compared women's status in a number of different societies, while Leis examined the structural reasons why women's associations are strong in one Ijaw village in Nigeria, yet absent in another. Finally, in my own article I examined the differences in women's strategies within domestic groups in a number of societies, which related to the relative integration or separation of domestic and political spheres.

Since 1974 the hypothesis of universal subordination of women and the dichotomous relationship between women in the domestic sphere and men in the public sphere have been challenged and critiqued by a number of feminist anthropologists. As appealing as this dichotomy seemed in the abstract, it turned out to be difficult to apply when actually looking at examples of women's activities in different cultures. For example, in an important article written about the same time as Rosaldo's introduction, Rayna Reiter (now Rayna Rapp) described women's and men's distinct lives in a small French village in the south of France. "They inhabited different domains, one public, one private. While men fraternized with whomever they found to talk to in public places, women were much more enmeshed in their families and their kinship networks" (Reiter 1975b:253). However, two categories of public space fell into women's domain: the church and three shops, including the local bakery. Men tended to avoid women's places, entering the bakery, for example, only when several men were together and joking, "Let's attack now" (Reiter 1975b:257).

Reiter argues that men and women use public space in different ways and at different times. "The men go early to the fields, and congregate on the square or in the cafes for a social hour after work. Sometimes they also fraternize in the evenings. These are the times when women are home cooking and invisible to public view. But when the men have abandoned the village for the fields, the women come out to do their marketing in a leisurely fashion. The village is then in female hands. In the afternoon, when the men return to work, the women form gossip groups on stoops and benches or inside houses depending on the weather" (Reiter 1975b:258). Despite the powerful imagery—women associated with the private or domestic domain and men with public space—the description also shows that the dichotomy is not neat. After all women are in public a great deal; they have taken over, in some sense, the Church and the shops and even the public square in the middle of the day.

In Margery Wolf's description of women in a Taiwanese village based on data she collected in the late 1950s, she emphasizes that because researchers have focused on the dominance of patrilineal descent in the family, they have failed to see women's presence. "We have missed not only some of the system's subtleties but also its near-fatal weaknesses" (Wolf 1972:37). Women have different interests than men and build uterine families—strong ties to their daughters, but primarily to their sons who give their mothers loyalty and a place in the patrilineal extended family. Outside the

family in the community women formed neighborhood groups—around a store, at a platform where women washed their clothes in the canal, or under a huge old tree. In a village strung out between a river and a canal, there was no central plaza dominated by men as in the South of France.

In Peihotien Wolf did not describe a cultural geography where women were in a private sphere and men in the public one; rather there was more of a functional separation— men and women had different activities and interests. They were often located in the same places but had a different relationship to the patrilineal extended family and the male-dominated community. Women's lack of power led them to different strategies, different tactics that often undermined male control of the household and even the community. As Sylvia Yanagisako (1987:111) has pointed out the notion of domestic-public entails both a spatial metaphor (of geographically separated or even nested spaces) and a functional metaphor (of functionally different activities or social roles) in the same conceptual dichotomy. Analysts often "mix" these different metaphors in any particular analysis— sometimes using domestic-public spatially and at other times functionally.

Even in the Middle East, the association of women with a private domain (and a lack of power) and men with a public domain (and the center of politics) was too simple, as Cynthia Nelson pointed out in her article, "Public and Private Politics: Women in the Middle Eastern World" (1974). Because they are born into one patrilineal group and marry into another, women are important structural links between social groups and often act as mediators. Because there are segregated social worlds, all-female institutions are important for enforcing social norms: Women fill powerful ritual roles as sorceresses, healers, and mediums; women are important sources of information for their male kin; and women act as "information brokers," mediating social relations within both the family and the larger society.

From Rosaldo's point of view, these aspects of women's power are primarily "informal" and very different from the public, legitimate roles of men. Nevertheless, even though Nelson affirms the separation of male and female worlds (both spatially and functionally), what is "domestic" has public ramifications (the arrangement of a marriage, the transmission of highly charged political information) and the shadow of the family and kin group (the "domestic") is present in even the most "public" of situations. What at first seemed like a simple straightforward dichotomy, in light of actual case material seems very "slippery" and complex.

Furthermore, in many cultures, particularly those with an indigenous band or tribal structure, a separation of "domestic" and "public" spheres makes no sense because household production was simultaneously public, economic, and political. Leacock pointed out the following after reviewing the literature on the Iroquois during the seventeenth and eighteenth century:

> Iroquois matrons preserved, stored, and dispensed the corn, meat, fish, berries, squashes, and fats that were buried in special pits or kept in the long house. Brown (1970:162) notes that women's control over the dispensation of the foods they produced, and meat as well, gave them de facto power to veto declarations of war and to intervene to bring about peace.... Women also guarded the "tribal public treasure" kept in the long house, the wampum quill and feather work, and furs.... The point to be stressed is that this was "household management" of an altogether different order from management of the nuclear or extended family in patriarchal societies. In the latter, women may cajole, manipulate, or browbeat men, but always behind the public facade; in the former case, "household management" was itself the management of the "public economy." (Leacock 1978:253)

Sudarkasa has made much the same point about women in West African societies such as the Yoruba. She argues that many of the politi-

cal and economic activities anthropologists discuss as public are actually embedded in households (Sudarkasa 1976, as quoted in Rapp 1979:509). Furthermore, "in West Africa, the 'public domain' was not conceptualized as 'the world of men.' Rather, the public domain was one in which both sexes were recognized as having important roles to play" (Sudarkasa 1986:99).

A more appropriate conception would be to recognize two domains, "one occupied by men and another by women, both of which were internally ordered in a hierarchical fashion and both of which provided 'personnel' for domestic and extradomestic (or public) activities" (Sudarkasa 1986:94).

Furthermore, a careful examination of "domestic domain" indicates that the categories of "woman" and "mother" overlap in Western society, but the meaning of motherhood may be vastly different in another society. Women may not be exclusively defined as mothers and childrearers in terms of their status and cultural value (see Moore 1988:20–29 for a discussion of this point).

In addition to the issue of whether the domestic-public dichotomy can provide an adequate *description* of men's and women's spatial and functional relationships in our own and other societies, the model has problems as an *explanation* of women's status. One of these problems is the inherent circularity of the model. A central point is to account for the nature of these domains, yet they are already assumed to exist widely and are treated as categories in terms of which women's activities (such as food preparing, cooking, childcare, washing) can be classified (as opposed to male hunting, warfare, political councils). Comaroff says that the model "can only affirm what has already been assumed—that is, that the distinction between the domestic and politico-jural is an intrinsic, if variable, fact of social existence" (Comaroff 1987:59). When the model is used to explain women's positions in different societies in relation to these two orientations, the reasoning is equally circular. To put it in the words of Yanagisako and Collier, "The claim that women become absorbed in domestic activities because of their role as mothers is tautological given the definition of 'domestic' as 'those minimal institutions and modes of activity that are organized immediately around one or more mothers and their children'" (Yanagisako and Collier 1987:19).

Finally, we have come to realize that the concepts of domestic and public were bound up in our own history and our own categories grounded particularly in a Victorian heritage. Rosaldo, in a thoughtful reevaluation of her model, came to argue this position herself.

> The turn-of-the-century social theorists whose writings are the basis of most modern social thinking tended without exception to assume that women's place was in the home. In fact, the Victorian doctrine of separate male and female spheres was, I would suggest, quite central to their sociology. Some of these thinkers recognized that modern women suffered from their association with domestic life, but none questioned the pervasiveness (or necessity) of a split between the family and society. (Rosaldo 1980:401–402)

Rosaldo traced the historical roots of domestic-public from the nineteenth century evolutionists through twentieth-century structural functionalists to her own work. Instead of two opposed spheres (different and apart), Rosaldo suggested an analysis of gender relationships, an examination of inequality and hierarchy as they are created particularly through marriage (Rosaldo 1980:412–413).

The dichotomy has been usefully employed in several ways since 1974. First, several authors have shown us how it works in Western societies (e.g., France and the United States, where it arose historically and still has an important ideological function) (Reiter 1975b; Collier, Rosaldo, and Yanagisako 1982). In a related way, analysts have explored the meanings surrounding domestic activities of women, putting together a much more complex picture of women's relation to men in this sphere (Chai 1987; and Murcott 1983, reprinted in this book).

Second, anthropological analysis has helped us to understand the historical development of domestic-public spheres in societies under colonialism. John Comaroff's analysis of the Tshidi chiefdom in South Africa during the early twentieth century is an excellent example of this approach (1987:53–85). Finally, some analysts have used the cultural concepts of other societies to critique our own model of domestic-public orientations. Sylvia Yanagisako's essay on the clear separation of "inside-outside" domains (a spatial metaphor) and "work-family" activities (a functional dichotomy) in Japanese American culture demonstrates how the anthropological model of domestic-public mixes these metaphors, which has made analysis confusing and difficult (Yanagisako 1987).

Despite these useful attempts at examining women's lives through the lens of a domestic-public opposition, many of us would agree with Rayna Rapp's 1979 summary of the problems with this dichotomy.

> We cannot write an accurate history of the West in relation to the Rest until we stop assuming that our experiences subsume everyone else's. Our public/private conflicts are not necessarily the same as those of other times and places. The specific oppression of women cannot be documented if our categories are so broad as to decontextualize what "womanness" means as we struggle to change that definition. A Tanzanian female farmer, a Mapuche woman leader, and an American working-class housewife do not live in the same domestic domain, nor will the social upheavals necessary to give them power over their lives be the same. We must simultaneously understand the differences and the similarities, but not by reducing them to one simple pattern. (Rapp 1979:511)

Thus, many of us have tired of the domestic-public dichotomy. We feel it is constraining, a "trap," while new approaches try to get away from dichotomous thinking. These approaches do one of several things. Often they take history seriously, examining women's situation as it has evolved, often in a colonial context. Furthermore, they treat women as active agents and following Collier

(1974), as people who have interests, often divergent from men, and who act on them. Third, they often focus on gender relationships, rather than only on women. Finally, they do not treat all women as part of a single universal category of "woman." Rather women are usually analyzed in terms of their social location. Age, class, race, ethnicity, and kinship are all likely to divide women, so newer analyses examine women's strategies and identities as they are differently shaped. Several examples will illustrate some of the different approaches taken in recent years.

Collier's examination of Comanche, Cheyenne, and Kiowa gender relationships (1988) illustrates the recent focus on gender and on the multiple positions that men and women hold in societies in which the domestic-public dichotomy seems inappropriate. This is because these "spheres" are integrated, and there is no firm line between domestic and public space (see Lamphere 1974 and Leacock 1978).

The Comanche are an example of a bride service society in which, like many hunter-gatherer societies, men and women were relatively autonomous, the concept of femininity was not elaborated, and the greatest status differences were between unmarried and married men. Marriage established men as having something to achieve (e.g., a wife), leaving women without such a cultural goal. Young men, through providing meat for their in-laws (bride service), become equal adults, and older men, through egalitarian relations and generosity, become the repositories of wisdom and knowledge. Politics focused on the issue of sexuality and on male–male relationships, which often erupted in conflict and violence. Women celebrated their health and sexuality, and hence the roles of "woman the gatherer" or even "woman the mother" did not emerge as cultural themes.

Among the Cheyenne, an equal bridewealth society, and among the Kiowa, an unequal bridewealth society, marriage relationships were structured in a much different way in the nineteenth century, so gender relationships had a much different

content, politics were more hierarchical, and ideology played a different role. Collier's interest is not in the subordination of women in these three societies, because in all three there are several kinds of inequality: between men and women, between older women and girls, between unmarried men and married men, and between kin and affines. An interest in "spheres" and "domains" has been replaced by an emphasis on relationships and an analysis that focuses on the ways in which inequality gets reproduced through marriage transactions, claims on the labor of others, and giving and receiving of gifts. Dominance and subordination become a much more layered, contextualized phenomenon—more interesting than the simple assertion that women are universally subordinated. The processes through which women's inequality (and that of young men) is constructed are laid bare, rather than flatly asserted.

Mary Moran's study of civilized women (1990) explores the historical beginnings and present-day construction of the category "civilized," which does confine educated women among the Glebo of southeastern Liberia to a "domestic sphere." The dichotomy between "civilized" and "native" (or even tribal or country) is a result of missionization and has created a status hierarchy differentially applied to men and to women. Men, once educated and with a history of paid wage work, never lose their status as "civilized," while women, even though married to a "civilized man," may lose their status if they do not dress correctly, keep house in specific ways, and refrain from farming and marketing. Native women, who market or have farms, are more economically independent but occupy positions of lower prestige. Here we see not only the importance of historical data in examining how cultural categories evolve, but also the ways in which both civilized and native women actively manage their status positions. Civilized women, through the practice of fosterage, recruit younger women to their households to carry out the more elaborate household routines in which they must engage and to train these fostered daughters to become civilized themselves.

The civilized-native dichotomy represents the juxtaposition of two systems. One is a parallel-sex system in which native men and women are represented by their own leaders in two linked but relatively autonomous prestige hierarchies (as suggested by Sudarkasa 1986). The other is a single-sex system (based on a Western model) in which men in political positions represent both sexes, and women have little access to prestige except through their husbands. Thus, this is a much more complex system than one based on a domestic-public dichotomy. There are dichotomous categories—civilized-native, male-female—but they do not fit neatly together. Moran speaks of categories as "gender sensitive" and suggests that "The Glebo have inserted gender into the civilized/native dichotomy to the point that women's status is not only more tenuous and vulnerable than men's but also very difficult to maintain without male support." In some respects civilized women trade off dependency for prestige, but Moran provides a sympathetic picture of how both civilized and native women manage their lives.

Lila Abu-Lughod's study (1986) of Bedouin women's ritual poetry gives us further insights into the complexity of women who in 1974 we would have simply thought of as "confined to a domestic sphere." Among the Bedouin, women's marriages are arranged; wives wear black veils and red belts (symbolizing their fertility); and women must behave within a code of behavior that emphasizes family honor and female modesty and shame. When confronted with loss, poor treatment, or neglect, the public discourse is one of hostility, bitterness, and anger. In the case of lost love the discourse is of militant indifference and denial of concern. In contrast, Bedouin poetry, a highly prized and formally structured art, expresses sentiments of devastating sadness, self-pity, attachment, and deep feeling (Abu-Lughod 1986:187). Although both men and women recite poetry for women, it may express conflicting feelings concerning an arranged marriage, a sense of loss over a divorce, or sentiments of betrayal

when a husband marries a new wife. The poems are used to elicit sympathy and get help, but they also constitute a dissident and subversive discourse. Abu-Lughod sees ritual poetry as a corrective to "an obsession with morality and an overzealous adherence to the ideology of honor.... Poetry reminds people of another way of being and encourages, as it reflects, another side of experience.... And maybe the vision [offered through poetry] is cherished because people see that the costs of this system, in the limits it places on human experiences, are just too high" (Abu-Lughod 1986:259). Bedouin women in this portrait are not simply victims of patriarchy confined to a domestic sphere; they are active individuals who use a highly valued cultural form to express their deepest sentiments, acknowledge an alternative set of values, and leave open the possibility of subverting the system in which they are embedded.

A large number of studies have been conducted in the United States that loosely focus on what used to be termed the domestic sphere and the public world of work. As in the Native American, African, and Middle Eastern cases cited previously, when one begins to examine a topic in detail, global notions like domestic-public seem too simple to deal with the complexities of women's lives. Clearly work and home are distinctly separated spheres in the United States. Women who have been employed in the paid labor force have experienced the disjunction of spending eight or more hours of the day in a place of employment where they are "female workers" and the rest of their time in the home where they are daughters, wives, and/or mothers. With this comes responsibilities for cooking, cleaning, and providing nurturance, care, and intimacy for other family members. Several recent studies have examined the contradictions women face when combining work and family, the impact of paid employment on family roles, and vice versa. I will refer to only three examples of this growing literature.

Patricia Zavella's research on Chicana cannery workers examines women's networks that link the workplace and the family (Zavella 1987). Calling these "work-related networks," Zavella describes groups of friends who saw each other outside work and who were members of a kin network employed in the same cannery. Women used work-related networks as sources of exchange for information, baby sitters, and emotional support. Networks operated in more political ways as workers organized a women's caucus and filed a complaint with the Fair Employment Practices Commission. Women's cannery work was seasonal and had relatively little impact on power relations in the family or the household division of labor. On the other hand work-related networks of friends or kin were an important "bridging mechanism" helping women to deal with the contradictions and demands that came from two different spheres.

Karen Sacks' study of hospital workers at the Duke Medical center examines the ways in which black and white women brought family notions of work, adulthood, and responsibility to work with them and used these values to organize a walk out and subsequent union drive (1988). Sacks focuses on the activities of "center women"—leaders in the union drive. Unlike the men who were often the public speakers at rallies and events, the center women organized support on an interpersonal, one-to-one basis. Rather than emphasizing the bridging aspect of women's networks, Sacks shows how the family is "brought to work" or in the old terminology how the "domestic" influences the "public."

In my own research I have traced the changes in the relationship between women, work, and family historically through the study of immigrant women in a small industrial community, Central Falls, Rhode Island (Lamphere 1987). Using the twin notions of productive and reproductive labor, I examined the rise of the textile industry in Rhode Island and the recruitment of working daughters and later of working mothers to the textile industry and to the other light industries that have replaced it since World War II. Rather than seeing production and reproduction as a rigid dichotomy (like public and domestic), I have used these categories to study relationships and to examine the kinds of strategies that immigrant women and their families forged in confronting an industrial system where wage work was a necessity and where working-class families had no control over the means of production. Such an approach revealed a great deal of variability both between and within ethnic groups—the Irish, English, French-Canadian, and Polish families who came to Central Falls between 1915 and 1984 and the more recent Colombian and Portuguese immigrants. Examination of strikes and walkouts in the 1920s and 1930s and my own experience as a sewer in an apparel plant in 1977 led me to emphasize the strategies of resistance the women workers used on the job, as well as the impact of women's paid labor on the family itself. When daughters were recruited as workers in textile mills, the internal division of labor within the household did not materially change because wives and mothers continued to do much of the reproductive labor necessary to maintain the household. Fathers, teenage sons, and daughters worked for wages. In the current period, in contrast, as more wives have become full-time workers, immigrant men have begun to do some reproductive labor, particularly child care. Immigrant couples often work different shifts and prefer to care for children themselves rather than trust baby sitters from their own ethnic group. In my study I argue that "the productive system as constituted in the workplaces has shaped the family more than issues of reproduction have shaped the workplace" (Lamphere 1987:43).

More recently Patricia Zavella, Felipe Gonzalez, and I have found that young working mothers in sunbelt industries have moved much further than Cannery women or New England industrial immigrant women in changing the nature of the household division of labor (Lamphere, Zavella, Gonzalez, and Evans 1993). These new committed female workers have been employed since high school and do not drop out of the labor force for long periods of time to have children. Thus, they and their husbands construct a family life around a two-job household. Although some couples have a "traditional" division of housework (women do the cooking and the majority of the cleaning and husbands take out the garbage, do minor repairs, and fix the car), many husbands participate in "female chores" and do substantial amounts of childcare (often caring for children while the wife is at work). Here we see the impact of what we used to call the "public sphere" on the domestic one, but in our analysis we have focused more on the varied ways that Anglos and Hispanics (including single mothers) have negotiated household and childcare arrangements, viewing husbands and wives as mediating contradictions. Subtle similarities and differences among and between working class Anglo and Hispanic women have emerged from this analysis, making it clear that the impact of work in the public world is not a monolithic but a variegated process.

In summary the dichotomy between the public world of men and domestic world of women was, in 1974, an important and useful starting point for thinking about women's roles in a cross-cultural perspective. As anthropologists have written more detailed and fine-grained studies of women's lives in a wide variety of other cultures and in our own society, we have gone beyond the use of dichotomies to produce analyses of the complex and layered structure of women's lives. We now treat women more historically, viewing them as social actors and examining the variability among women's situations within one culture and in their relationship to men.

NOTES

1. Rosaldo says that "the opposition does not *determine* cultural stereotypes or asymmetries in the evaluations of the sexism, but rather underlies them, to support a very general ... identification of women with domestic life and of men with public life" (Rosaldo 1974:21–22). Thus, I would

argue, Rosaldo did not attempt to *explain* women's subordination through the dichotomy, but saw it as an underlying structural framework in any society that supported subordination and that would have to be reorganized to change women's position.

2. It is interesting that we did not know of Elsie Clews Parsons' extensive feminist writing during 1910 to 1916, much of which is reminiscent of the kind of position we took in *Woman, Culture, and Society*. In another article I have noted the similarities between Shelly's prose and that of Parsons (see Lamphere 1989 and Parsons 1913, 1914, 1915).

REFERENCES

Abu-Lughod, Lila. 1986. *Veiled Sentiments: Honor and Poetry in a Bedouin Society*. Berkeley and Los Angeles: University of California Press.

Brown, Judith. 1970. Economic organization and the position of women among the Iroquois. *Ethnohistory* 17(3/4):131–167.

Chai, Alice Yun. 1987. Freed from the elders but locked into labor: Korean immigrant women in Hawaii. *Women's Studies* 13:223–234.

Collier, Jane. 1974. Women in politics. In Michelle Z. Rosaldo and Louise Lamphere (eds.). *Woman, Culture, and Society*. Stanford: Stanford University Press.

———. 1988. *Marriage and Inequality in Classless Societies*. Stanford: Stanford University Press.

Collier, Jane, Michelle Rosaldo, and Sylvia Yanagisako. 1982. Is there a family? New anthropological views. In Barrie Thorne and Marilyn Yalom (eds.). *Rethinking the Family: Some Feminist Questions*. New York and London: Longman.

Comaroff, John L. 1987. Sui genderis: Feminism, kinship theory, and structural "domains." In Jane Fishburne Collier and Sylvia Junko Yanagisako (eds.). *Gender and Kinship: Essays Toward a Unified Analysis*. Stanford: Stanford University Press.

de Beauvoir, Simone. 1953. *The Second Sex*. New York: Alfred A. Knopf. Originally published in French in 1949.

Kaberry, Phyllis M. 1939. *Aboriginal Women, Sacred and Profane*. London: G. Routledge.

———. 1952. *Women of the Grassfields*. London: H. M. Stationery Office.

Lamphere, Louise. 1974. Strategies, cooperation, and conflict among women in domestic groups. In Michelle Z. Rosaldo and Louise

Lamphere (eds.). *Woman, Culture, and Society*. Stanford: Stanford University Press.

———. 1987. *From Working Daughters to Working Mothers: Immigrant Women in a New England Industrial Community*. Ithaca, NY: Cornell University Press.

———. 1989. Feminist anthropology: The legacy of Elsie Clews Parsons. *American Ethnologist* 16(3):518–533.

Lamphere, Louise, Patricia Zavella, Felipe Gonzales and Peter Evans 1993. *Sunbelt Working Mothers: Reconciling Family and Factory*. Ithaca, NY: Cornell University Press.

Landes, Ruth. 1938. *The Ojibwa Woman, Part 1: Youth*. New York: Columbia University. Contributions to Anthropology, Vol. 31.

———. 1947. *The City of Women: Negro Women Cult Leaders of Bahia, Brazil*. New York: Macmillan.

Leacock, Eleanor. 1978. Women's status in egalitarian society: Implications for social evolution. *Current Anthropology* 19(2):247–275.

Leith-Ross, Sylvia. 1939. *African Women: Study of the Ibo of Nigeria*. London: Faber and Faber.

Mead, Margaret. 1949. *Male and Female*. New York: William Morrow and Co.

Moran, Mary H. 1990. *Civilized Women: Gender and Prestige in Southeastern Liberia*. Ithaca, NY: Cornell University Press.

Moore, Henrietta L. 1988. *Feminism and Anthropology*. Minneapolis: University of Minnesota Press.

Murcott, Anne. 1983. "It's a pleasure to cook for him": Food, mealtimes and gender in some South Wales households. In Eva Gamarnikow, D. H. J. Morgan, June Purvis, and Daphne Taylorson (eds.). *The Public and the Private*. London: Heinemann Educational Books.

Nelson, Cynthia. 1974. Public and private politics: Women in the Middle East. *American Ethnologist* 1:551–563.

Ong, Aihwa. 1987. *Spirits of Resistance and Capitalist Discipline*. Albany, NY: State University of New York Press.

Parsons, Elsie Clews. 1913. *The Old Fashioned Woman*. New York: G. P. Putnam's Sons.

———. 1914. *Fear and Conventionality*. New York: G. P. Putnam's Sons.

———. 1915. *Social Freedom: A Study of the Conflicts Between Social Classifications and Personality*. New York: G. P. Putnam's Sons.

Paulme, Denise (ed.). 1963. *Women of Tropical Africa*. Berkeley: University of California Press.

Rapp, Rayna. 1979. Anthropology. *Signs* 4(3): 497–513.

Reiter, Rayna (ed.). 1975a. *Toward an Anthropology of Women*. New York: Monthly Review Press.

———. 1975b. Men and women in the South of France: Public and private domains. In Rayna Reiter (ed.). *Toward an Anthropology of Women*. New York: Monthly Review Press.

Rosaldo, Michelle. 1974. Woman, culture and society: A theoretical overview. In Michelle Z. Rosaldo and Louise Lamphere (eds.). *Woman, Culture, and Society*. Stanford: Stanford University Press.

———. 1980. The uses and abuses of anthropology. *Signs* 5(3): 389–417.

Rosaldo, Michelle Z. and Louise Lamphere (eds.). 1974. *Woman, Culture, and Society*. Stanford: Stanford University Press.

Sacks, Karen. 1988. *Caring by the Hour: Women, Work, and Organizing at the Duke Medical Center*. Urbana and Chicago: University of Illinois Press.

Sudarkasa, Niara. 1976. Female employment and family organization in West Africa. In Dorothy McGuigan (ed.). *New Research on Women and Sex Roles*. Ann Arbor: Center for Continuing Education of Women.

———. 1986. The status of women in indigenous African Societies. *Feminist Studies* 12: 91–104.

Underhill, Ruth. 1936. *Autobiography of a Papago Woman*. Supplement to *American Anthropologist* 38(3), Part II. Millwood, NY: American Anthropological Association.

Wolf, Margery. 1972. *Women and the Family in Rural Taiwan*. Stanford: Stanford University Press.

Yanagisako, Sylvia Junko. 1987. Mixed metaphors: Native and anthropological models of gender and kinship domains. In Jane Fishburne Collier and Sylvia Junko Yanagisako (eds.). *Gender and Kinship: Essays Toward a Unified Analysis*. Stanford: Stanford University Press.

Yanagisako, Sylvia Junko and Jane Fishburne Collier. 1987. Toward a unified analysis of gender and kinship. In Jane Fishburne Collier and Sylvia Junko Yanagisako (eds.). *Gender and Kinship: Essays Toward a Unified Analysis*. Stanford: Stanford University Press.

Zavella, Patricia. 1987. *Women's Work and Chicano Families: Cannery Workers of the Santa Clara Valley*. Ithaca, NY: Cornell University Press.

"It's a Pleasure to Cook for Him": Food, Mealtimes, and Gender in Some South Wales Households

Anne Murcott

INTRODUCTION

I think it lets him know that I am thinking about him—as if he knows that I am expecting him. But it's not as if "oh I haven't got anything ready" ... Fair play, he's out all day ... he doesn't ask for that much ... you know it's not as if he's been very demanding or—he doesn't come home and say "oh, we've got chops again," it's really a pleasure to cook for him, because whatever you ... oh I'll give him something and I think well, he'll like this, he'll like that. And he'll always take his plate out ... and he'll wash the dishes without me even asking, if I'm busy with the children. Mind, perhaps his method is not mine.

Every now and then an informant puts precisely into words the results of the researcher's analytic efforts—providing in the process a quotation suitable for the title! The extract reproduced above, explaining the importance of having the meal ready when her husband arrives home, comes from one of a series of interviews on which this paper is based.[1] The discussion starts by remembering that "everyone knows" that women do the cooking: all the women interviewed—and the few husbands/boyfriends or mothers who came in and out—took it for granted that cooking was women's work. Informants may not enjoy cooking, or claim not to be good at it; they may not like the arrangement that it is women's work, or han-

Reprinted with permission from Eva Gamarnikow, David H. J. Morgan, June Purvis, and Daphne Taylorson (eds.), The Public and the Private (London: Heinemann Educational Books, Ltd., 1983), pp. 78–90. Copyright © 1983 British Sociological Association.

ker after modifying it. But all recognise that this is conventional, some volunteer a measure of approval, most appeared automatically to accept it, a few resigned themselves and got on with it.

Studies of the organisation of domestic labour and marital role relationships confirm that cooking continues to be a task done more by women than men; this is also the case cross-culturally (Stephens, 1963; Murdock and Provost, 1973). Emphasis in the literature has shifted from Young and Willmott's (1975) symmetrical view of sharing and marital democracy. Now rather more thoroughgoing empirical study suggests their assessment is little more than unwarranted optimism (Oakley, 1974a and b; Edgell, 1980; Leonard, 1980; Tolson, 1977). This work improves on earlier studies of the domestic division of labour by going beyond behaviourist enquiry about "who does which tasks" to consider the meanings attached to them by marital partners. The distribution of work turns out not to correlate neatly with assessments of importance or allocation of responsibility. (Oakley, 1974b; Edgell, 1980).

Part of this effort (in particular, Oakley, 1974a and b) has in addition attempted to analyse domestic work as a "job like any other," considering housewives' work satisfaction, routines, supervision and so on. While this line of enquiry has undoubtedly made visible much of women's lives conventionally rendered invisible, it has perhaps not gone far enough. The study of housework as an occupation needs to attend in addition to features such as quality control, timekeeping, client as well as worker satisfaction, and perhaps further consideration of who, if anyone, is a housewife's boss. As will be seen, each of these is implicated in the discussion that follows.

These occupational aspects of housework provide, moreover, additional means of examining the relationship of the domestic division of labour to the economic structure as a whole. Recent commentary has also proposed that the view of the family as stripped of all but the residual economic function of consumption is ill-conceived and over-simplified. Domestic labourers refresh and sustain the existing labour force and play a key part in reproducing that of the future—as well as providing a reserve of labour themselves. The precise manner in which the political economy is to be accounted continues to be debated (West, 1980; Fox, 1980; Wajcman, 1981). For the moment, however, the general drift of that discussion can be borne in mind by recalling the everyday terminology of eating; food is consumed, meals have to be produced. The language favoured in cookbooks echoes that of industry and the factory (Murcott, 1983a). Homecooking may nicely embody the terms in which the family and household's place in the division of labour has to be seen. It may also provide a convenient arena for the further exploration of the economic and labour relations in the family and the relation of the marital partners to the means of production of domestic labour (Middleton, 1974).

Examination of the household provision of meals in these terms is, however, some way in the future. This paper does no more than offer some empirical foundation on which such study might build. It brings together informants' ideas about the importance of cooking, their notions of propriety of household eating, and indicates their relation to gender. It starts with views of the significance of good cooking for home life, and goes on to deal with the place of cooking in the domestic division of labour. The familiar presumption that women are the cooks is extended to show that their responsibility in

this sphere is tempered with reference to their husband's, not their own, choice. The paper concludes with brief comment on possible ways these data may illuminate some of the questions already raised.

HOME COOKING

> Aside from love, good food is the cornerstone of a happy household . . . (Opening lines of a 1957 cookbook called *The Well Fed Bridegroom*).

Right through the series of interviews three topics kept cropping up; the idea of a proper meal, reference to what informants call a "cooked dinner" and the notion that somehow home is where proper eating is ensured. Moreover, mention of one like as not involved mention of another, sometimes all three. The composite picture that emerges from the whole series suggests that these are not merely related to one another in some way, but virtually equated.

It first needs to be said that informants seemed quite comfortable with a conception of a proper meal—indeed the very phrase was used spontaneously—and were able to talk about what it meant to them. Effectively a proper meal is a cooked dinner. This is one which women feel is necessary to their family's health, welfare and, indeed, happiness. It is a meal to come home to, a meal which should figure two, three, or four times in the week, and especially on Sundays. A cooked dinner is easily identified—meat, potatoes, vegetables and gravy. It turns out that informants displayed considerable unanimity as to what defines such a dinner, contrasting it to, say, a "snack" or "fried." In so doing they made apparent remarkably clear rules not only for its composition but also its preparation and taking. I have dealt with their detail and discussed their implications in full elsewhere (Murcott, 1982). But in essence these rules can be understood as forming part of the equation between proper eating and home cooking. And, as will be noted in the next section, they also provide for the symbolic expression of the relationship between husband and wife and for each partner's obligation to their home.

The meal for a return home is, in any case, given particular emphasis—a matter which cropped up in various contexts during the interviews. Thus, for some the very importance of cooking itself is to be expressed in terms of homecoming. Or it can provide the rationale for turning to and making a meal, one to be well cooked and substantial—not just "beans on toast ... thrown in front of you."

The actual expression "home cooking"—as distinct from "cooking for homecoming"—received less insistent reference. Informants were straightforward, regarding it as self-evident that people preferred the food that they had at home, liked what they were used to and enjoyed what they were brought up on. Perhaps untypically nostalgic, one sums up the point:

> When my husband comes home ... there's nothing more he likes I think than coming in the door and smelling a nice meal cooking. I think it's awful when someone doesn't make the effort... I think well if I was a man I'd think I'd get really fed up if my wife never bothered...

What was prepared at home could be trusted—one or two regarded the hygiene of restaurant kitchens with suspicion, most simply knew their chips were better than those from the local Chinese take-away or chippy. Convenience foods had their place, but were firmly outlawed when it came to a cooked dinner. In the ideal, commercially prepared items were ranged alongside snacks, and light, quick meals: lunches and suppers in contrast to proper dinners. Informants talked about home cooking, but used this or some such phrase infrequently; the following is an exception:

> I'd like to be able to make home-made soups and things, it's just finding the time and getting organised, but at the moment I'm just not organised... I think it would probably be more

good for us than buying... I suppose it's only—I'd like to be—the image of the ideal housewife is somebody who cooks her own food and keeps the household clean and tidy.

The sentiments surrounding her valuation of home-made food are not, however, an exception. Time and again informants linked not only a view of a proper meal for homecoming, but a view of the proper parts husband and wife are to play on this occasion. So cooking is important when you are married.

> you must think of your husband ... it's a long day for him at work, usually, ... even if they have got a canteen at work, their cooking is not the same as coming home to your wife's cooking... I think every working man should have a cooked meal when he comes in from work...

Cooking is important—though not perhaps for everybody "like men who don't cook"—for women whose "place [it is] to see the family are well fed."

In this section, I have indicated that informants virtually treat notions of proper meals, home-based eating, and a cooked dinner, as equivalents. The stress laid on the homecoming not only underlines the symbolic significance attached to both the meal and the return home. It simultaneously serves as a reminder of the world beyond the home being left behind for that day. Put another way, the cooked dinner marks the threshold between the public domains of school or work and the private sphere behind the closed front door. In the process of describing these notions of the importance of cooking in the home, it becomes apparent that the familiar division of labour is assumed.

COOKING IN THE DOMESTIC DIVISION OF LABOUR

As noted in an earlier section, all those interviewed took it for granted that it is the women who cook. What they had to say refers both to conventions in general, and themselves and their circumstances in particular.[2] There are two important features of their general presumption that women are the cooks; one indicates the terms in which it is modifiable, the other locates it firmly as a matter of marital justice and obligation. The upshot of each of these is to underline the manner in which the domestic preparation of meals is securely anchored to complementary concepts of conduct proper to wife and husband.

To say that women cook is not to say that it is only women who ever do so. It is, however, to say that it is always women who daily, routinely, and as a matter of course are to do the cooking. Men neither in the conventional stereotype nor in informants' experience ever cook on a regular basis in the way women do.[3] Husband/boyfriends/fathers are "very good really"; they help informants/their mothers with carrying the heavy shopping, preparing the vegetables, switching the oven on when told, doing the dishes afterwards (cf. Leonard, 1980). Such help may be offered on a regular enough basis, notably it is available when the women are pregnant, dealing with a very young infant, unwell or unusually tired. But none of this is regarded as men doing the cooking.

More significantly, it is not the case that men do not cook—in the strict sense of taking charge of the transformation of foodstuffs to some version of a meal. They may make breakfast on a Sunday, cook only "bacon-y" things, can do chips or "his" curries: all examples, incidentally, of foods that do *not* figure in the proper cooked dinner (Murcott, 1983c).

For some, however, competence in the kitchen (and at the shops) is suspect: he'll "turn the potatoes on at such and such a time ... but leave him he's hopeless" and another just "bungs everything in." For others, it is men who make better domestic cooks than women, are more methodical, less moody. Another couple jokingly disagree: she "not taken in" by Robert Carrier on TV, he claiming that "the best chefs are men." The point is that either way, of course, informants do regard gender as relevant to the question of who is to cook.

It is not even the case that all men cannot cook the proper, homecoming meal. One or two, when out of work for a while, but his wife still earning (this only applied to those having a first baby) might start the meal or even have it ready for her return. But once he is employed again he does not continue to take this degree of responsibility, reverting either to "helping" or waiting for her to do it. Now and again, wives have learned to cook not at school or from their mothers, but from their husbands. But it was still assumed that it was for the woman to learn. This was even so in one instance where the informant made a "confession ... my husband does the cooking." But now that she was pregnant and had quit paid work she would take over; "it would be a bit lazy not to." Like others for whom the cooking may have been shared while both were employed, cooking once again became the home-based wife's task (cf. Bott, 1957, p. 225; Oakley, 1980, p. 132).

The issue is, however, more subtle than an account of who does what, or who takes over doing what. Men and women's place involve mutual obligation. "I think a woman from the time she can remember is brought up to cook... Whereas most men are brought up to be the breadwinner." The question of who does the cooking is explicitly a matter of justice and marital responsibility. A woman talks of the guilt she feels if she does not, despite the greater tiredness of late pregnancy, get up to make her husband's breakfast and something for lunch—"he's working all day." Another insists that her husband come shopping with her so he knows the price of things—he's "hopeless" on his own—but she has a clear idea of the limits of each person's responsibility: each should cook only if the wife *has* to earn rather than chooses to do so.

Here, then, I have sought to show that informants subscribed in one way or another to the convention that it is women who cook. In the process it transpired that it is certain sorts of cooking, i.e., routine, homecoming cooking, which are perennially women's work. The meal that typically represents "proper" cooking is, of course, the cooked dinner. Its composition and prescribed cooking techniques involve prolonged work and attention; its timing, for homecoming, prescribes when that work shall be done. To do so demands the cook be working at it, doing wifely work, in time that corresponds to time spent by her husband earning for the family (Murcott, 1982). This is mirrored in Eric Batstone's (1983) account of the way a car worker's lunch box prepared by his wife the evening before is symbolic of the domestic relationship which constitutes the rationale for his presence in the workplace; he endures the tedium of the line in order to provide for his wife and family. It transpired also that men do cook in certain circumstances, but such modification seems to reveal more clearly the basis for accounting cooking as part of a wife's responsibility (to the family) at home corresponding to the husband's obligation (to the family) at work, i.e., their mutual responsibilities to each other as marriage partners.

WHO COOKS FOR WHOM?

At this point I introduce additional data which bear on cooking's relation to the question of marital responsibility. Repeatedly informants indicated that people do not cook for themselves; evidently it is not worth the time and effort.[4] But the data suggest implications beyond such matters of economy. Two interrelated features are involved: one is the distinction already alluded to in the previous section, between cooking in the strict sense of the word and cooking as preparation of a particular sort of meal. The other enlarges on the following nicely. To observe that people do not cook for themselves can mean two things. First it can imply that a solitary person does not prepare something for themselves to eat while on their own. But it can also imply that someone does not do the cooking on their own behalf, but in the service of some other(s). Examination of the transcripts to date suggests that not only could informants mean either or both of these, but also that

each becomes elided in a way that underlines the nuances and connotations of the term cooking.

The question of a lone person not cooking themselves a meal unsurprisingly cropped up most frequently with reference to women themselves, but men, or the elderly, were also thought not to bother.

Informants are clear, however, that not cooking when alone does not necessarily mean going without. Women "pick" at something that happens to be in the house, have a bar of chocolate or packet of crisps later in the evening or a "snack." Men will fry something, an egg or make chips. No one said that a man would go without altogether (though they may not know), whereas for themselves—and women and girls in general—skipping a meal was thought common enough. Men—and occasionally women—on their own also go back to their mother's or over to their sister's for a meal. One informant was (the day of my interview with her) due to go to her mother's for the evening meal, but fearful of being alone in the house at night, she was also due to stay there for the next few days while her husband was away on business.

The suggestion is, then, that if a person is by themselves, but is to have a proper meal, as distinct from "fried" or a "snack" then they join a (close) relation's household. The point that it is women who cook such meals receives further emphasis. Indeed, when women cook this particular meal, it is expressly *for* others. In addition to the temporary lone adults just noted who return to mothers or sisters, women in turn may cook for the older generation, as well as routinely cooking for children or for men home at "unusual" times if unemployed or temporarily or a different shift.

This conventional requirement that women cook for others is not always straightforward in practice. At certain stages in an infant's life the logistics of producing meals for husband *and* child(ren) there as well meant the woman felt difficulties in adequately meeting the obligations involved. And not all informants enjoyed cooking; most just accepted that it needed doing, though there were also those who took positive, creative pleasure in it (cf. Oakley, 1974b). Part of this is expressed in the very satisfaction of providing for others something they should be getting, and in turn will enjoy.

More generally cooking can become tiresome simply because it has to be done day-in, day-out. The pleasure in having a meal prepared for you becomes all the more pointed if routinely you are cooking for others.[5] In the absence of any data for men, it can only be a guess that going out for a meal is thus specially enjoyable for women. But for those who on occasion did eat out this clearly figures in their pleasure. Even if it rarely happened, just the idea of having it put in front of you meant a treat: "it's nice being spoiled."

The question "who cooks for whom?" can now begin to be answered. Apparently it is women who cook for others—effectively, husbands and children. If husbands and children are absent, women alone will not "cook," indeed many may not even eat. It is the others' presence which provides the rationale for women's turning to and making a proper meal—that is what the family should have and to provide it is her obligation. Men—and children—have meals made for them as a matter of routine: but for women it is a treat. That solitary men do not "cook" for themselves either, and may go to a relative's for meals (cf. Rosser and Harris, 1965; Barker, 1972), or that a woman on her own may also do so does not detract from the main proposal that it is women who cook for others. For it is not only that informants or their husbands will go temporarily back to their mother's, not their father's, home-cooking. It is also that both men and women revert to the status of a child for whom a woman, a mother, cooks. The mother may actually be the adult's parent, but they—and I with them—may stretch the point and see that she may be mother to the adult's nieces or nephews or indeed, as in the case of cooking for the elderly, she may be mother to the adult's grandchildren.

The appreciation that it is women who cook for others elaborates the more familiar convention, discussed above, that in the domestic division of labour cooking is women's work. First of all it indicates that this work is service work. Cooking looks increasingly like a task quite particularly done for others. Second, when cooking for others women are performing a service to those who are specifically related (sic) rather than for a more generalised clientele known only by virtue of their becoming customers. The marital—and parental—relationship defines who is server, who served.

That said, there remains the question of deciding what the server shall serve. As already discussed in an earlier section, the conventional expectation shared, it seems, by both woman and man, is that meals shall be of a certain sort—a cooked dinner for a certain occasion, most commonly the return home from work, or the celebration of Sunday, a work-free day. The "rules" involved are not entirely hard and fast, or precisely detailed. Cooked dinners are neither daily nor invariable affairs (Murcott, 1982). And the cooked dinner itself can properly comprise a number of alternative meats (and cuts) and range of different vegetables. What then, determines the choice of meat and vegetables served on any particular day? Some of the factors involved, as will be seen in the next section, once again echo ideas of responsibility and mutual obligation.

DECIDING WHAT TO HAVE

A number of factors feature in deciding what to have for a particular day's meal.[6] First, a question of cost was taken for granted. This does not necessarily mean keeping expenditure to a minimum—eating in the customary manner despite hard times was highly and expressly valued by some. Second, the conventional provision of proper dinners itself contributed to the determination of choice. These two factors present themselves as marking the limits within which the finer decisions about what the precise components of the day's dinner are to be. Here reference to their husband's—and, to a lesser extent, children's—preferences was prominent in informants' discussion of such detailed choices.

It was indicated earlier that in an important sense women's cooking is service work. This sort of work has two notable and interrelated aspects affecting decisions and choice: is it the server or served who decides what the recipient is to want? Exploring the mandate for professionals' work, Everett Hughes (1971, p. 424) highlights a key question: "professionals do not merely serve: they define the very wants they serve." Servants, and service workers such as waitresses (Whyte, 1948; Spradley and Mann, 1975) compliantly provide for the wants identified by the served. On the face of it, then, the professional has total and the waitress nil autonomy. Examples reflecting this sort of range occurred among informants, varying from one woman apparently always deciding, through to another always making what he wants for tea. But in the same way that the maximum autonomy of the professional is continually, to a certain degree, a matter of negotiation and renegotiation with clients, and that, similarly, the apparent absence of autonomy is modified by a variety of more or less effective devices waitresses use to exert some control over customers, so a simple report of how meal decisions are reached can, I propose, either conceal negotiations already complete, or reveal their workings.

Thus informants interested in trying new recipes still ended up sticking to what they usually made because their husbands were not keen. Others reported that "he's very good" or "never complains" while some always asked what he wanted. A non-committal reply however did not necessarily settle the matter, for some discovered that being presented with a meal she had then decided on could provoke adverse and discouraging remarks. But it was clear that even those who claimed not to give their husbands a choice were still concerned to ensure that he agreed to her suggestion. It is almost as if they already knew what he would like, needed to check out a specific possibility every now and then but otherwise continued to prepare meals within known limits. Deciding what to have already implicitly took account of his preferences so that the day-to-day decision *seemed* to be hers.

The material presented in this section provides only a glimpse of this area of domestic decision-making. Other aspects need consideration in future work. For instance, what degree of importance do people attach to the matter (cf. Edgell, 1980, pp. 58–9)? Attention also needs to be paid to wider views of the legitimacy of choice in what one eats. In what sense do restaurant customers choose and mentally subnormal patients not? Does a child that spits out what it is fed succeed in claiming a choice or not? And in apparently acquiescing to their husband's choice, are wives circumscribing their own? But it looks as if deciding what to have is of a piece with a shared view of marital responsibility whereby he works and so deserves, somehow, the right to choose what she is to cook for him.

GENDER AND THE PRODUCTION OF MEALS

> I know a cousin of mine eats nothing but chips, in fact his mother-in-law had to cook him chips for his Christmas dinner and she went berserk...

This "atrocity story" recapitulates various elements of the preceding discussion. Such unreasonableness is, no doubt, unusual but its artless reporting emphasises a number of points already made. Not only do chips break the rules of what should properly figure in a Christmas meal, superior even to the Sunday variant of a cooked dinner, but it remains, however irksome, up to the woman to prepare what a man wants. The burden of this paper, then, may be summarised as revealing allegiance to the propriety of occasion such that a certain sort of meal is to mark home (male) leisure versus (male) work-time, and that such meals are cooked by women for others, notably husbands, in deference, not to the woman's own, but to men's taste.

This examination of cooking, mealtimes and gender within the household has implications for the continuing analysis of domestic work as work. While it does not shed light on why such work is women's, only reasserting that conventionally this is so, it clearly casts the work of meal provision as service work.

The everyday way of describing dishing up a meal as serving food is embedded in a set of practices that prescribe the associated social relationships as of server and served. As already observed this involves two interrelated matters: control over the work, and decisions as to what are the "wants" the worker shall serve, what the work shall be. Each is considered in turn.

Oakley (1974a and b) reports that one of the features of housewifery that women value is the feeling of autonomy. Care is needed, though, not to treat such attitudes as tantamount to their analysis. Just because housewives express their experiences in terms of enjoying being their own boss does not mean that their conditions of work can be analysed in terms of a high degree of autonomy. The material presented in this paper suggests that doing the cooking is not directed by the woman herself, but is subject to various sorts of control.

First of these is the prescription for certain kinds of food for certain occasions. The idea of the cooked dinner for a homecoming is just such an example of cultural propriety. Related to this is a second control, namely that the food is to be ready for a specific time. Mealtimes construed in this way may exert just the same sort of pressure on the cook as any other production deadline in industry. Third, control is also exerted via the shared understanding that it is the preferences of the consumer which are to dictate the exact variant of the dinner to be served. What he fancies for tea constrains the cook to provide it. These kinds of control in the domestic provision of meals find their counterpart in the industrial concerns of quality control, time-

keeping and market satisfaction. A woman cooking at home may not have a chargehand "breathing down her neck" which is understandably a source of relief to her. But this does not mean to say that she enjoys autonomy—simply perhaps that other controls make this sort of oversight redundant. Evidence either way is extremely sparse, but Ellis (1983) suggests that failing to cook according to her husband's wishes can contribute to a wife's battering.

Linked to the issue of control of domestic cooking is the question of decision-making. Edgell (1980) has drawn attention to the degree of importance couples attach to different aspects of family living about which decisions have to be made. He distinguishes assessments of importance from, first, whether the decision is mainly the wife's or husband's responsibility and second, from the frequency with which the decision has to be made. So, for instance, moving is the husband's decision, perceived to be very important and infrequent, a contrast to the matter of spending on food. What Edgell does not make clear, however, is quite what either his informants or he mean by "importance." As an analytic device, the idea does not distinguish between family matters which partners may identify as both important and somehow major or permanent such as moving, and those identified as mundane, or fleeting but important nonetheless, such as daily eating. Like refuse collection or sewage work which is regarded as vital but low-status, the importance attached to meals may not be remarked in the general run of things, though noticed particularly if absent. But that does not necessarily mean that both husband and wife regard it as unimportant. And, harking back to the question of autonomy in decision-making, reports such as Edgell's that food spending, cooking or whatever is regarded as the wife's responsibility, cannot, of itself, be seen as evidence of her power and freedom from control in those areas. For as Jan Pahl (1982, p. 24) has so cogently observed, "being able to offload certain decisions and certain money-handling chores on to the other spouse can itself be a sign of power." The delegate may be responsible for execution of tasks, but they are answerable to the person in whom the power to delegate is originally vested.

The preliminary analysis offered in this paper has theoretical and political implications concerning power and authority in marriage and the relation between domestic and paid work. The exploration of ideas about cooking and mealtimes starts to provide additional approach to detailing the means of domestic production. And the sort of work women are to do to ensure the homecoming meal provides a critical instance of the juncture between the control of a worker and the (his) control of his wife. The meal provides one illustration not only of a point where the public world of employment and the private world of the home meet one another; it also shows how features of the public take precedence within the private. For the stress informants lay on this mealtime offers an interesting way of understanding how the industrial rhythms which circumscribe workers are linked to the rhythms which limit women's domestic work (cf. Rotenberg, 1981). And women's continual accommodation to men's taste can also be seen as a literal expression of wives' deference to husbands' authority (Bell and Newby, 1976; Edgell, 1980, p. 70). This acquiescence to his choice provides the cultural gloss to the underlying economic relationship whereby industry produces amongst other things both the wage, and the raw materials it buys, for the domestic to produce what is needed to keep the industrial worker going. Part of the conjugal contract that each in their own way provide for the other, it does indeed become "a pleasure to cook for him."

ACKNOWLEDGEMENTS

I am very grateful to all those necessarily anonymous people who made the research possible and who generously gave their time to answer my questions. I should like to record my appreciation of conversations with Tony Coxon, Sara Delamont, Robert Dingwall, Rhian Ellis, Bill Hudson and Phil Strong at various stages during the preparation of this paper and of the computing help and advice Martin Read provided. Only I and not they are to blame for its deficiencies. And I must thank Lindsey Nicholas, Joan Ryan, Sheila Pickard, Myrtle Robins and Margaret Simpson very much, despite flu all round, and an unusually scrawly manuscript, for their help in typing both drafts.

NOTES

1. In order to begin remedying sociology's neglect (Murcott, 1983b) of food beliefs and of the social organisation of eating, I conducted a single-handed exploratory study (supported by a grant from the SSRC) holding unstructured tape-recorded interviews with a group of 37 expectant mothers attending a health centre in a South Wales valley for antenatal care (22 pregnant for the first time), 20 of whom were interviewed again after the baby's birth. No claim is made for their representativeness in any hard and fast sense, though they represent a cross-section of socio-economic groups. For present purposes the data are treated as providing a composite picture. The prime concern here is to indicate the range and variety of evidence gathered. An instance that occurs once only thus becomes as interesting as one occurring 30 times. This is reflected in the discussion by the deliberate use of phrases such as "some informants" rather than "6 out of 37." In any case reference to numbers of instances is no more exact, and risks implying a spurious representativeness.

   These qualifications are most important. But for the sake of a tolerably readable account I do not hedge every other sentence with reminder of these limitations. Yet they do actively have to be taken as read.
2. Informants referred not only to themselves but also to mothers, sisters, sisters-in-law and women friends doing cooking.
3. No informant who had children old enough to cook currently shared the household with them.
4. Market researchers know how to trade on such reports. During the period of interviewing a TV commercial was running which sought to

persuade busy housewives not to neglect themselves but have a frozen ready-cooked meal at lunchtime.

5. Interestingly, no one talked of hospital meals put in front of them as a treat. (None had a home delivery.) Rather it was the quality of the food provided which informants concentrated on. Institution cooking could not be home cooking.

6. It might have been expected that nutritional criteria would figure in these decisions. Analysis so far suggests that cultural prescriptions for proper eating at home override what is known about healthy eating. (Murcott, 1983d).

REFERENCES

Barker, D. L. 1972. "Keeping close and spoiling," *Sociological Review*, 20(4), 569–590.

Batstone, E. 1983. "The hierarchy of maintenance and the maintenance of hierarchy: Notes on food and industry," in A. Murcott (ed.), *The Sociology of Food and Eating*, Gower.

Bell, C. and Newby, H. 1976. "Husbands and wives: The dynamics of deferential dialectic," in D. L. Barker and S. Allen (eds.), *Dependence and Exploration in Work and Marriage*, Longmans.

Bott, E. 1957. *Family and Social Network*, Tavistock.

Edgell, S. 1980. *Middle Class Couples: A Study of Segregation, Domination and Inequality in Marriage*, Allen and Unwin.

Ellis, R. 1983. "The way to a man's heart ... ," in A. Murcott (ed.), *The Sociology of Food and Eating*, Gower.

Fox, B. (ed.). 1980. *Hidden in the Household*, Toronto: Women's Press.

Hughes, E. C. 1971. "The humble and the proud," in *The Sociological Eye: Selected Papers*, Aldine-Atherton.

Leonard, D. 1980. *Sex and Generation*, Tavistock.

Middleton, C. 1974. "Sexual inequality and stratification theory," in E. Parkin (ed.), *The Social Analysis of Class Structure*, Tavistock.

Murcott, A. 1982. "On the social significance of the 'cooked dinner' in South Wales," *Social Science Information*, 21(4/5), 677–695.

———. 1983a. "Women's place: Cookbook's image of technique and technology in the British Kitchen," *Women's Studies International Forum*, 6(1): 33–40.

———. (ed.) 1983b. *The Sociology of Food and Eating*, Gower.

———. 1983c. "Cooking and the cooked," in A. Murcott (ed.), *The Sociology of Food and Eating*, Gower.

———. 1983d. "Menus, meals and platefuls," *International Journal of Sociology and Social Policy* (forthcoming).

Murdock, G. P. and Provost, C. 1973. "Factors in the division of labour by sex: A cross-cultural analysis," *Ethnology*, XII(2), 203–225.

Oakley, A. 1974a. *Housewife*, Penguin.

———. 1974b. *The Sociology of Housework*, Martin Robertson.

———. 1980. *Women Confined: Towards a "Sociology of Childbirth,"* Martin Robertson.

Pahl, J. 1982. "The allocation of money and the structuring of inequality within marriage," *Board of Studies in Social Policy and Administration*, University of Kent, mimeo.

Rosser, C. and Harris, C. 1965. *The Family and Social Change*, Routledge and Kegan Paul.

Rotenberg, R. 1981. "The impact of industrialisation on meal patterns in Vienna, Austria," *Ecology of Food and Nutrition*, 11(1), 25–35.

Spradley, J. O. and Mann, B. J. 1975. *The Cocktail Waitress: Women's Work in a Man's World*, John Wiley.

Stephens, W. N. 1963. *The Family in Cross-Cultural Perspective*, Holt, Rinehart and Winston.

Tolson, A. 1977. *The Limits of Masculinity*, Tavistock.

Wajcman, J. 1981. "Work and the family: Who gets "the best of both worlds?"" in Cambridge Women's Studies Group, *Women in Society*, Virago.

West, J. 1980. "A political economy of the family in capitalism: Women, reproduction and wage labour," in T. Nichols (ed.), *Capital and Labour: A Marxist Primer*, Fontana.

Whyte, W.F. 1948. *Human Relations in the Restaurant Industry*, McGraw-Hill.

Young, M. and Willmott, P. 1975. *The Symmetrical Family*, Penguin.

Fatherhood and the Mediating Role of Women

Nicholas W. Townsend

In this chapter I confront an apparent paradox in men's accounts of fatherhood. Men say they want to be involved fathers but they do not seem to be acting that way.

Nearly all the men I talked to in my research said they wanted to be more involved as fathers than their own fathers had been, and this stated desire is very common for men in the United States. But men in the United States do not put much time into domestic work or child care (Coltrane, 1996), and after divorce many men in the United States pay very little or nothing in child support and frequently maintain no contact with their children (Furstenberg and Cherlin, 1991; Arendell, 1995). I argue that we can understand some of this paradox if we consider what men do as fathers as well as what they do not do, and if we listen to what they have to say about being fathers.

Parenting is deeply gendered. And by this I do not mean only that fathers and mothers do different things, though that is clearly the case, but also that being a parent means different things to mothers and fathers, and that being a father means different things to men and women. Parenting is also gendered in other ways, such as men's stated preference for sons and the ways they treat daughters and sons differently. I have discussed these aspects of fatherhood elsewhere (Townsend, n.d.). In this chapter, I am focusing on the gendered relationship between fathers and mothers. Seeing men and their accounts as gendered in this way helps us to understand how men think about being fathers and about relationships in general.

In the first section below I describe how men see "marriage and children" as elements of a "package deal" which cannot be easily separated. Conceptually, a relationship with a

Original material prepared for this text

woman is necessary for a man to see himself as a father or "family man." In the subsequent sections, I show how women are often the "driving force" behind men's decisions about when to have children; that a structural division of labor that places men in the labor force and women at home is maintained and supported by cultural work in the face of women's increasing labor force participation; and that parenting itself is gendered, with women being the "default parents" who maintain schedules and routines, while men are in a more "optional" position, with their participation as "fun dads" or "enforcers" mediated by their children's mothers.

It has been easy to see the gendered division of labor in parenting as a simple division in which men are engaged in the public sphere of paid work and politics and women are involved in the domestic sphere of child care and reproduction.[1] What my description shows, however, is that these two spheres interpenetrate, and that arrangements made in one sphere influence behavior in another. For instance, we shall see that cultural ideas about the division of paid labor and about who should provide for families have an impact on ideas about who should do what for children.

My discussion in this chapter is based on talking to men who graduated from the same high school in 1972 and were in their late thirties when I interviewed them.[2] Because they all graduated from the same high school, I was able to learn a lot a about the community in California in which they grew up, the events of their youth, and the opportunities they faced as adults. I can speak with confidence about the attitudes these men shared, and about the differences between them, and I would argue that these men are in many ways typical of men in the United States, but these men's experiences and meanings cannot be used to support universal or essential ideas about "male" experience or fathering as a universal pattern of behavior.[3]

What emerged from my conversations is that, for the men I talked to, the father–child relationship could not be described or thought about independent of the relationship between husband and wife. When I ask men about their parents, they talk mostly about their fathers, but when I ask them about becoming fathers they talk about their wives. Some of the paradoxes of men's relations to their children may be resolved by understanding the relative positions of men, women, and children, and specifically the crucial linking or mediating role of women.

Appreciating the linking role of women is not the same as saying that men do not care about children, or that they think that children are entirely women's business. Certainly becoming a parent is more separated from biological reproduction for men than for women. One can scarcely imagine a woman saying, as one of my male informants did: "Actually I have had a child before, although through very strange circumstances I didn't know I had a child before he was a year old and someone sent me a Christmas card saying: 'This is your baby.'" Equally certainly, men consider childbearing and child rearing to be predominantly women's responsibility. This is not to say that men are indifferent to having children. They have strong feelings about the number, timing, and kind of children they want, but at crucial points in their lives they find that their paternity depends on the cooperation of women. The men are not passively dependent on women's motivations—they actively select and try to persuade, pressure, and coerce women, but the mediating link provided by women remains crucial.

It is not just that men need, and realize that they need, a woman's physical cooperation in order to become fathers. There is also an asymmetry in the ways that men and women *think* about becoming parents. For instance, many women are prepared to think about single parenthood as a possible, though usually less desirable, route to motherhood; the men I talked to, on the other hand, do not even register it as a possibility. Many single, childless women are able to think and talk directly about whether they want to have children. In doing so, and in reading the advice and examples they are offered in books and magazines, it is clear that they see having a child on one's own as an option. It is an option with definite emotional, social, and financial drawbacks as well as opportunities, and it is an option that they may well reject, but it remains a possibility. That having a child on her own is a possibility to be considered means that women are able to weigh and articulate their specific desire for children outside the matrix of family and relationship with a man. The relationship between mother and child, the activity of mothering, and the transformation of self into a mother, are things women can think about directly and in isolation. The men I talked to could not talk about having children without talking about "having a family" or "being a family man." For these men, "having children" is part of "being married and having a family." They can only conceptualize the relationship between father and children within the matrix of family relationships.

Of course, the relationships between men and their wives are very important in their own right, but my interest here is in the way that marital relationships are structurally important for men's relationships with their children. Women, as wives and mothers, mediate and facilitate fatherhood. The word "mediate" describes women's role in the relationship between men and children because it captures, in its various meanings, some of the complexity of that role. Women are in the middle of this relationship, they frequently do mediate in the most literal sense of operating as go-betweens or negotiators between their husbands and their children, and their presence and activity makes possible the reproduction, both biological and social, that is at the heart of fatherhood.

For men, having children is a reproduction of fatherhood—a patrilineal process of the movement of males through the statuses of son, father, and grandfather and of child, adult, and old man (Townsend, 1998). There are five moments, phases, or aspects of reproduction at which women's mediating role is most apparent: at marriage, when decisions are made about the timing and number of children, in the structural division of labor after children are born, in gendered parenting, and after divorce.

MARRIAGE AND CHILDREN: WIFE AND MOTHER

"We always knew we wanted to get married and have a family" was a frequent comment of men who married women they had known in high school. For my informants, marriage is almost always considered to be a relationship that will involve having children. In most first marriages, husbands say they either "knew" or "assumed" that their wives would want children. For the men, marriage meant getting a "wife and family" as a sort of package deal.

As is often the case, it is when obstacles to meeting a norm arise that its existence is made most clear. Several men told me that they did not marry women with whom they had "good relationships" because those women did not want or could not have children. Conversely, men who had actually wanted to have children told me that they had ended relationships with women they did not want to marry by telling them that they did not want to have children. That this was an excuse is made clear by the rapidity with which they subsequently met, married, and had children with other women. Regardless of whether the particular men or women in any relationship or marriage really wanted children or not, the point is that the cultural idea that marriage and children go together was so clear to all that it could be used as a reason to end a relationship without rejecting the other person by saying: "I don't want to marry you." Men are making a simultaneous decision about "a wife and a mother to my children."

Greg, an earnest man with two children who worked as a programmer in a software company, had married at age twenty-nine, a fact that was very significant to him and to which he returned repeatedly. To him, twenty-nine was old to be getting married, and he did not want to be too old to be a vigorous father to his children. He felt, however, that waiting until he was twenty-nine had not been a bad thing:

I kind of got everything out of my system before I got married. And then, when I did get married I wanted it to be forever, as they say, and I was ready to have kids. When I got married I was ready to have kids. I probably had it planned in my mind. "We'll get married and we'll have children."

Although Greg linked marriage with having children, he said that he and his wife had not talked explicitly before their marriage about having children, but that it was "Just something you kind of know."

I had seen a lot of women over a period of years. You see all kinds of women out there. I mean, there are some smart ones, but most of them are—they don't know if they're coming or going, you know. Maggie's very intelligent, which I like, very kind, and very funny. That's very important to me, a sense of humor. It is kind of hard to explain exactly why you know that that's the person, but she had all the factors that I was looking for. I remember telling myself: "I can live with this girl for the rest of my life. I mean I can actually do it through the day to day." I just had the inner feeling that I could be comfortable with her for basically the rest of my life.

Greg's choice of a wife was, however, not based simply on personal compatibility: "If I knew that she did not want to have children," he added, "I would not have married her."

Gordon, an engineer with three sons, had married his wife two years after they met, and two years later, while he was still in college, his first son was born. Gordon told me early on that: "before we got married we had a goal of three and when we finally got three, I just said: 'I don't have enough for any more.'" Later, when I asked him if he had always wanted children, he replied, after a pause: "I never felt that I would *not* have children. But, you know, up until I found the person I wanted to marry and live with, I never thought 'I really want kids.' I don't think I consciously said that." And when I asked him if children are needed to complete a family he immediately responded: "That's not the reason we had children, but I believe that's a true statement. Not to say that a couple is incomplete, but I think you're *more married* if you have children." His predisposition to have children, and his liking for children (he taught Sunday School before he was married) had not gelled into a firm plan to have children of his own until he met the person he wanted to marry. Marriage and children were inextricably linked in his thinking, as they were in another man's comment that "Getting married and not having kids at all, seems kind of incomplete. I can see you being a single person and not having kids. I can understand that more now. If you're married it would be odd not having children."

A deliberately childless marriage is definitely a thing to be negotiated beforehand. At least normatively, inability to bear children is not grounds for divorce, but one partner's unwillingness to have them might cause the other partner to hesitate or to refuse to enter into marriage in the first place. Several men said that in order to marry a woman who did not want children "you would have to love her a lot." There is an implication here that a marriage without children requires a stronger love than a marriage with children. But I think it is closer to these men's meanings that children provide structure and cohesion to a marriage, and that romantic love alone, without the cement of shared parenting and the economic partnership of working to support home and family, is a slender thread on which to hang a lifetime together.

During the 1970s and early 1980s, when the men I interviewed were aged between eighteen and thirty, the divorce rate for childless couples was higher than for couples who had children (Wienberg, 1988). Divorces of childless couples also proceeded more rapidly than the divorces of couples with children (White, et al., 1986). Conversely, the birth of a first child within marriage drastically reduced the divorce rate for the next year (Waite, et al., 1985). Although subsequent births did not have this effect, the presence of children in a marriage did appear to slow the process of divorce (White, et al., 1986).[4] Of the men I talked to, those who had been through divorces in which children had been involved reported more protracted divorces, with separations and reconciliations, whereas the divorces that did not involve children were more rapid and clear-cut. The direction of causation in these relationships between fertility and divorce is not always clear. It may be that having children makes a marriage less likely to end in divorce, but it may also be that couples who think their marriage is in trouble are less likely to embark on childbearing.

The men I talked to recognized that having a child may both strengthen and undermine the relationship between husband and wife. On the one hand, they appreciated the problems of fatigue, busy schedules, and restrictions on shared leisure that children create for marriages. On the other hand, they stressed the responsibility they felt toward maintaining an intact family and also mentioned the new connections with their wives that came from enjoying their children and from sharing activities with them. Having children certainly made divorce harder to think about. They would, they said, stay married through hard times and routine times.

The comments I heard are consistent with the statistical picture that fertility within marriage reduces the incidence and slows the process of divorce. They also indicate that childlessness within marriage is not a common goal, and would demand of a marriage something qualitatively different than is expected in a reproductive union. Several men described a couple they knew who were married soon after high school graduation but deliberately had no children. After their divorce, both partners remarried and had children. The interpretation put on this by their friends is that the marriage without children could not sustain itself, but that subsequent marriages to people with whom they were ready to have children were likely to be satisfying and successful. Childlessness, in this account, is presented as both a consequence of doubts about the marriage and a cause of its failure.

The men I spoke to depend on a marital relationship with a woman for a paternal relationship with children. In the contemporary United States, the availability of effective contraception and a relaxation of the standard of sexual chastity for brides means that a man's girlfriend, his premarital sexual partner, the woman he lives with, and his wife may all be the same person, but are not necessarily so—the roles and the individuals filling them are uncoupled. A wife, however, is unique in the formalization of her social position and in the way that she links a man to other social persons by virtue of that social position and not merely by virtue of her personal qualities and associations.

Barry, balding and hospitable, lived in a new house in a new subdivision. As we sat on his deck, watching his young children from his second marriage play in the wading pool, he told me a story that encapsulated the connection between marriage and children:

> It's funny, I knew this one girl that I worked with. She was living with her boyfriend. She never took any birth control. For probably years, she never did. Never got pregnant. But they finally got married, and like their wedding night, she got pregnant. It was kind of a psychological thing, you know? Like: "Geez, I can't get pregnant, I'm not married. Well, now I'm married, it's OK."

In both his own marriages, Barry had drawn the same distinction between living together (and therefore not having children) and being married (and having or planning children).

> The first time, you just get married because it was the thing to do, so to speak. The second time you're a little bit wiser and more cautious.

> The first time I was twenty-one and my wife had just turned nineteen. We were married for a couple of years. And what's interesting is that she was raised in a very strict Catholic background so living together was kind of taboo. So we never lived together. We basically got married and we found out that what she wanted and what I wanted were really different. We talked about children. Nothing real serious, but like: "Down the road here, we should have children." So it's a good thing that we didn't. We were using birth control. It wasn't to the point where we decided "Let's try" and we weren't successful. We weren't ready at that time.

The second time he got married, Barry proceeded very differently. Even his sentence structure and word choice when telling me about it expressed his greater deliberation:

> We both had our own separate homes and lifestyles when we first met and we spent a lot of time together. We decided we had a pretty lasting relationship going and that we should live together and consolidate. That way we could really tell, by living together, whether or not we could live together forever. Because you just don't know people until you actually live with them. So we lived together for a while. And then we decided to get married and have children. In fact, that was kind of interesting. My wife—one of her comments that kind of surprised me was: "Geez, we don't need to get married to have children." And that really kind of took me by surprise because I've kind of had different morals than that. If you're going to have children, at least *plan* children, then you need to be married. Obviously there are times when things are not planned and you're not married. But the way I believe, if you're going to plan to have children, you should be married. She was very insistent that that didn't need to be the case. . . . She likes children, and I like children, so it was kind of a—We discussed it and decided "Let's get married and we'll have children" instead of just having children and not getting married.

Barry attributed his surprise at his wife's suggestion that they did not need to get married to have children to "different morals," but when his comments are taken as a whole, we can see that his association of children and marriage is not so much moral as conceptual. His picture of family life, his conceptual framework for social relationships, was one that included the possibility of living together and that separated sexual relations from procreation, but equated having children with being married. In this, and in the difference between him and his wife, Barry was typical. In order to be a father, he had to be married. His fatherhood, therefore, conceptually depends on his having a marital relationship with a woman. Once married, the timing of his children's births would depend on his wife's willingness and initiative.

"THE DRIVING FORCE": WOMEN, TIMING, AND BIRTH CONTROL

In general, the men I talked to assumed that, in their own lives, conception and birth were events that could be controlled. They assumed that sexual intercourse without pregnancy was a reasonable expectation, so that premarital sex, a space of time between marriage and their first birth, a controlled space between their children's births, and a cessation of childbearing were all things to be reasonably expected and planned for. Their confidence in their ability to plan was, to a certain extent, justified by the technological innovations of the birth control pill, the IUD, and safe and easy techniques for male and female sterilization.

Previous fertility declines and control, at the level of populations and of couples, have depended on a mix of methods, including heavy reliance on abstinence and withdrawal (Schneider and Schneider, 1996). These are methods that involve at least the participation, if not the active initiation, of men. The Pill and the IUD, by contrast, are methods that are used by women and that do not require contraceptive action by men or women at the time of intercourse. They are, particularly for men, much less psychically costly than withdrawal or abstinence. For men in the United States, these methods have had the double effect of enabling a conceptual

and physical separation between sexual activity and reproduction and of moving control over reproduction to women. Control over reproduction was seen as not only technically, but also morally, women's responsibility.

Barry, for example, does not say the decision about when to have children was his wife's alone, but he does put the primary responsibility on her.

> She was probably the driving force. Again, I wanted children too. So it wasn't like: "OK, I'll just give in. If you want children, we'll have children." But she was probably more the driver of that issue than myself. I could have been content to wait a couple years. But again, we both wanted children. It wasn't just because she wanted children. If she would have been very insistent against it, it would have been something we probably would have had to talk about. It's really hard to say, but I think I wanted to have children also, but not to the same degree as she did. It would have been nice to have them, but if I didn't, I could have lived without them. It wouldn't have been a decision I may have regretted.

Notice that while she is the "driving force" behind the timing, he also makes it clear that he too wanted children. But he then questions his own desire when he says "I *think* I wanted to have children" and "I could have lived without them." In the face of this uncertainty, he placed the initiative with his wife.

The norm expressed by all the men I talked to is that there should be a period at the beginning of married life when the couple have "time for themselves as a couple." This norm may be violated by early conception, or by a period of living together followed by marriage and rapid subsequent conception.

Marvin, a large, easygoing man, who worked in purchasing, told me that he and his wife had children sooner than he would have liked. His plan had been to graduate from college and buy a house before having children. His wife had taken the initiative and had persuaded him that they should have children while he was still in college.

I wasn't all that hot about the idea. I was not sure I could handle all the responsibilities. I probably thought, in fact I did think, about how they develop and how you grow along with them. It's "Oh gosh, what am I gonna do when they're teenagers?" that sort of thing. So I wasn't all that hot about having kids. My wife convinced me that yeah, it's probably not all that tough. I should say now I know how tough it is. It's very hard. It's a never-ending challenge. But we finally agreed that we'd go ahead and have kids. And so we did. I wanted to make sure I had a house, which we didn't at the time. And go ahead and have college for me, which I didn't. So that was a kind of unsettling thing, to go from following this nice neat path to success. And here's the time to have kids. Here's the time to do this, to do that. I couldn't do that. So that kind of bothered me.

In the event, Marvin had not finished college, but he told me that had not been a real obstacle in his career, and he and his wife had bought a house with help from his wife's parents.

Men discuss their decisions about timing in terms of their "readiness" to become fathers.[5] Readiness is presented as a psychological state that does not necessarily coincide with the birth of the first child. Men may realize that they are "ready" when their first child is born, but they may also feel "not ready," causing personal anxiety and strain on their marriage. Several men told me that they only became ready to be fathers some time after the birth of their first child, usually at a point when they felt they could relate to their children.[6] On the other hand, other men have reported "being ready" before their wives were, and then embarking on campaigns to persuade them to become pregnant. For these men, it was not women's enthusiasm that drove the decision, but their reluctance or hesitation that put women in a position to control the realization of men's plans for fatherhood.

The men I talked to discussed the timing of births as if they were under perfect control, and difficulties getting pregnant, as well as unplanned pregnancies, were seen as surprising. From my perspective as an observer who knows something about the variability of human biology, this sense of being in perfect control was itself surprising. But being in control is a central organizing element of my informants' stories in all areas. Being out of control is an explanation for the bad things that happen, and a good deal of rhetorical effort is expended to create a life story characterized by control and the realization of intentions.[7] Men are actively involved in decisions about timing, but contraception during the childbearing years is overwhelmingly by female methods and men are dependent on the cooperation of their wives. But their dependence is not inevitable or driven simply by the use of female contraceptive methods. These men are actually *relinquishing* control and presenting the situation as if their wives were the only ones responsible.

Alfred, for instance, had wanted only one child, but he delayed his vasectomy after the birth of his first child. He reported that his wife then "surprised" him with a set of twins, but he delayed his vasectomy again. He only got around to sterilization after she "surprised" him with a second set. He is an exceptional example only because of the extreme personal and demographic consequences of his dependence on imperfect methods and his reluctance to assume responsibility for birth control. Alfred's position, however, underlines the centrality of effective birth control for the realization of these men's fertility plans and life plans in general. With five children under the age of six, he found himself living in too small a house, with bills higher than he had expected, and with no financial leeway. He worked as a skilled technician, but his skills were being made obsolete by technological change, and he was not in a position to make the expenditure, or take the cut in pay, necessary to acquire new skills or to move into a job with prospects of promotion. His high fertility, in fact, had effects on his work, his place of residence, and the division of labor in his marriage, and will continue to have effects in the future.

MEN AT WORK, WOMEN AT HOME: THE STRUCTURAL DIVISION OF LABOR

The archetypical picture of family life in the United States has been of a nuclear household, composed of a married heterosexual couple and their children, in which the man is the breadwinner and the woman is the homemaker. This has not, of course, been an accurate picture of the family lives of many people, but it has been a cultural archetype, or hegemonic image, that shapes people's perceptions even when it does not represent their reality.[8] Even when they become very common, however, behaviors that do not conform to hegemonic cultural norms continue to be perceived as "exceptions." When people's lives diverge from cultural norms they have to do cultural work to deny, explain, or reinterpret, this divergence. Some husbands of employed women who wanted to emphasize that they were the primary providers for their families explained that their wives' incomes were used for "extras" or "luxuries." Others described their wives' work as something they did mainly for variety, social contacts, or to "get away from the kids." But in either case they were doing cultural work to interpret their arrangements as conforming to a hegemonic picture of the structural division of labor in marriage. In support of this division of labor, the men I talked to made three interlocking arguments: that they liked or chose the arrangement, that it was best for the children, and that it was natural.

Gordon, the engineer with three sons who felt "more married" once he had children, expressed very clearly the structural division of labor between parents: one parent should stay home to raise the children, and it should be the mother.

> I think it's wrong to have kids and then lock them in daycare centers while you're working. That's why I'm really grateful that my wife can stay home. And although at times we were real tight for money, and I told her she might have to start looking for a job if we were going to make ends meet, I was grateful when things

worked out and she didn't have to. Because this is really the place the kids need a full-time mother, to watch them.

This arrangement works, Gordon says, because "She's not the working type." This gendered division of labor between husband and wife is a reproduction of his parents' pattern. His father had been a skilled machinist, his mother, with a college degree, had stayed home and not worked outside the home until her children were in high school. Gordon explains the arrangement he has with his wife as the result of their "choice" and in accord with his wife's personality. Although Gordon described both the division of labor and the fact that he followed his father into working on machines as "natural," this couple is an instance of a social fact: in the overwhelming number of cases where one of a couple works full time, it is the husband.

Like Gordon, Marvin attributes the division of labor in his marriage to his wife's preference. She has worked off and on, he says, selling products from the home and working as a teacher's aide for the local school district, which "gives her a lot of flexibility." When I asked him if she had ever wanted to work full-time, he said:

> She seems to have wanted more to be a good mother. And she was the type of person that when we got married, she had this view of herself as not "Super Mom," but "Nice Mom" that does the things that Moms do and takes the kids and gets involved in things. And that was a really big thing to her.

Marvin is articulating what Garey (1999) points to as a dominant cultural image of mothers as oriented either to work or to family. Garey argues that many employed mothers downplay their aspirations to "career"or to being "Super Mom" and practice "maternal visibility" by making a point of being seen as doing "the things that Moms do."

Paul went a step beyond Gordon and Marvin in his defense of a structural gendered division of labor, turning it into a timeless and natural pattern. Paul is a serious, almost intense man who talks quietly but displays a fierce protectiveness of his family. He works a night shift with lots of overtime and shift differential pay. He and his wife, who was employed full time, lived with their two sons, ages six and eight, in a townhouse near his work. The children were cared for by his wife's mother during the day, but she was about to move away and Paul's plan was for his wife to reduce her hours of employment and work part time.

> I was thinking about trying to buy a [single family] house over here, but if it's going to cause me to be away from the family, or cause [my wife] to have to work all the time, I think we're gonna back out. If I can't afford a house on my pay alone, and make it, if we can't do it on my paycheck alone, we're not gonna do it. Because that's just basic. It's just the way it's been since time began. Women stay home. I'm not trying to be chauvinist by any—but if you're gonna have a family, that's the way it works best.

The gendered division of labor, then, puts women in the home as the mothers of men's children, and this division of labor is reinforced by cultural work that emphasizes men's responsibility as providers and women's involvement in their children's lives. Such a division of labor is presented as natural and equal, but it is a product of a particular economic structure and social organization of work, and it works to the advantage of men in giving them more control over their leisure time (though less over the large amount of their lives they spend at work). The gendered division of labor at the structural level also has profound implications for the daily activity of parenting.

DISCIPLINE, CARING, AND PROVIDING: GENDERED PARENTING

In parenting and child rearing men once again place women between themselves and their children. Their interactions with their children are controlled, arranged, or supervised by their wives. Women have most of the responsibility for arranging and enforcing children's activities, with men exerting their influence through their wives. Some men do put a lot of energy into their children's activities, especially into their athletic activities, and even more express the desire to do so, especially to do more with their children than their fathers did with them. But studies of time use continue to find differences between working husbands and wives in the total number of hours worked when paid labor, childcare, and housework are combined.[9]

Not only is there a difference in the number of hours men and women spend in child rearing, but fathers and mothers approach parenting very differently. The men I talked to express the belief that mothers are the "default parent." They act on this belief and by their actions make it true. Being the default parent means being on terms of greater intimacy, being the one to whom a child turns first, and being the one with the responsibility for knowing what the child's needs and schedules are. The default parent, ultimately, is the one who has to be there, to whom parenting is in no sense optional (Walzer, 1998). For example, fathers may go to meetings at their children's schools or take their children to sports practice, but it is usually mothers who keep track of when the meetings and practices are, and who are, therefore, the default parents. Lareau (2000a, 2000b) reports that fathers are very vague and general in their accounts of their children's daily routine, in contrast to the detailed and specific responses of mothers. In general, my informants indicated that it was their wives who kept the mental and physical calendar, and I would simply add that the person who keeps track of scheduling has a good deal of control over what is scheduled.

Even in the area of discipline and punishment, where it would seem that the father's position as ultimate authority was secure, mothers are the gatekeepers or mediators. Consider the proverbial threat of mothers to their children: "Just you wait until your father gets home!" This expression was used as an example by a number of men to express that they were deeply involved in their children's lives. It was meant to indicate that they were the source of discipline even if they were not in a position of direct supervision most of the time. On closer examination, however, the expression indicates a very different relationship, for it is the mother who decides when and what the father is told, and thus when he can act. Rather than being in an immediate disciplinary relationship with his children, he is a resource to be mobilized by his wife in her dealings with the children, and thus in a relationship mediated by his wife.

The disciplinary dynamic in families can take several forms, but two are common. While they may seem very different, in both of them the wife and mother is ultimately responsible for discipline. In the first, the husband is an authority figure and disciplinarian who sees himself as supporting or backing up his wife. In the second, the husband is allowed to be fun because his wife is the disciplinarian.

Both Ralph and Terry used the word "enforcer" to describe their role in their children's discipline. Neither of them liked this, though both accepted it as their responsibility to support their wives. Ralph had two children and was one of the most impressive men I met doing this research. He had had a troubled adolescence, but since then he had worked his way to a highly responsible job in public service and was universally admired by his former classmates. Ralph told me that there had been one disciplinarian in his family when he was growing up, and that it was the same in his marriage:

One parent seems like the disciplinarian and the other one is not. And in my family I am. And my wife doesn't understand: "Why won't the children listen to me?" Because it's always: "I'm gonna tell your father." She had to call me here [at work]. I've had to talk to them on the phone. And they straighten right up.

Ralph felt that his wife should be more consistent in her discipline so that the children would not ignore her threats and make her lose her temper. She, on the other hand, sometimes felt overwhelmed and told him that if she were to hit the children instead of threatening: "I'd beat them to death. I'd be constantly hitting them."

Terry, the father of two boys, is also critical of his wife's treatment of the children, but he too accepts his role as enforcer.

The thing is, you've gotta be the enforcer. The man has to be the enforcer and that's the only thing that sometimes irritates me. I come home from working a hard day and my wife right off "Terry, he's done this, he's done that." And I get mad and I go in there and yell at him. That's where a lot of times I would like to say "You're the mother. Handle it. If you want to restrict him, restrict him. If you want him to be whupped, do it." She's home every day. She knows exactly what's going on. I think she ought to handle it more herself.

For both Ralph and Terry, the structural division of labor, their position at work, and their wives' presence at home, means that their wives are the ones who determine what is expected of their children and who know what they are doing. The women then decide what to tell their husbands and so determine the kinds of interactions fathers and children will have. Terry yells at his children and Ralph spanks his, but their wives, as the default parents, mediate the flow of information and expectation between fathers and children. Women's mediation should not, however, be seen as deliberately manipulative. The gendered division of discipline is not an individual choice or decision, but part of a whole gendered system of division of labor.

Gordon's situation is a rather different manifestation of the same gendered system. In Gordon's family, he is the one who can relax and have fun with his sons because his wife is protective and strict. When it comes to parenting, he says:

My wife does a better job. Although she is very protective of the kids. Like my eleven-year-old, she won't drop off at baseball practice. She'll stay and wait until it's over. And even though sitting in a car, she's always there. She won't leave the kids anywhere alone. . . . I think she's just worried about something happening to them. Not having an accident, like falling off of something, but with all the crazies out there, she's just worried about losing one of them. Which is—I mean, it's a real-life concern. I can't blame her for that, but it gets a little excessive sometimes. And she does discipline them better, they mind her better, she's more sensitive to their feeling and that kind of thing. It's the insensitive dad, sometimes. . . . I don't treat my kids the way [my father] treated us. He was a *very* heavy disciplinarian and we were afraid of him when we grew up. I don't want my kids to be afraid of me.

Partly because he does not want his children to fear him as he feared his father, and partly because his wife is watching over them, protecting them, and disciplining them, he feels he can let them run a little wild: "When they're just goofing off and it's Friday night, I'm not going to crack the whip and put them to bed." He laughs, "It wouldn't work anyway."

Edward's position as a "fun dad" to his three children is also mediated by his wife, who ran a child care business in her home when the youngest was a toddler and now teaches at the private school the children attend. She is very involved in the lives of children in general and her own children in particular, and part of her involvement is in scheduling her husband's time with his children. Edward says that: "When there are three there, it's tough. They're all vying for your attention." So his wife intervened and he now says to his children: "'Your Mom says it's your turn.' So each time I do something I take a different child with me. And it works out two ways. It's a lot cheaper for one. And also I get that one-on-one with my kids." Many of the things he does with his children are recreational activities that he enjoys, such as baseball and basketball games. While his wife is orchestrating this activity, Edward gets to be the fun father, spending quality time with his children doing something they can enjoy together. Edward also gets to be spontaneous with the whole family. Several times he told me that he would, "on the spur of the

moment," sweep the family up and drive to the beach:

> Like I get them going at seven in the morning up to Santa Cruz and I'll bring my camping stuff and we'll cook breakfast and we'll just have breakfast and when other people are coming, we're leaving and coming back home. We do stuff off the wall like that. Spur-of-the-moment type things. On Friday afternoon I'll tell everyone to pack their suitcase and we'll go to Monterey for a night and things like that. I think that's pretty neat.

Overall, Edward emphasized the fun and spontaneity of his relations with his children: "Age wise, I'm probably considered an adult, but you talk to my kids and I'm probably the biggest kid around. I'm not kidding. I'm a big kid at heart. I love sports. I love my kids." It is important to notice that Edward's ability to be spontaneous and to have fun with his children, just like his one-on-one time with his children, is dependent on the routine, day-by-day, planned, and conscientious work of his wife.

The gendered division of labor in parenting not only distributes work and fun differentially between fathers and mothers, it also distributes who gets taken for granted, and who gets the credit for what they do. Hochschild shows how couples negotiate not only a material division of labor, but also an economy of gratitude (1989): people do not just want to be appreciated, they want to be appreciated for the contributions *they* think are important. Psychologists Carolyn and Philip Cowan (1999) observed that, for men, paid employment "counts" as childcare—when men work they are seen as doing something for their children. In addition, wives see their husbands' attention to their children as contributions to the marriage relationship. Women's employment, on the other hand, is seen as detracting from their mothering, and their husbands do not see the care mothers give their children as couple time or as building the marriage. For the men I talked to, their fathers' employment was remembered and appreciated, while their mothers' employment was minimized or forgotten. In addition, their mothers' parenting was taken for granted, while their fathers' more occasional attention was treasured.

Even though he said his father did not spend much time with him— "Dad was working. I remember when my father worked three jobs"—Edward appreciated the hard work his father had done to build a financially stable foundation for his family: "My Dad's helped me out financially, he's helped every single one of his kids out. Financially and every other way." Edward also remembered "the *few* vacations we had" with his father. His fond memories of those rare occasions was one motivation for his own spontaneous family trips. But his memories of his mother are less precise and more matter-of-fact. I asked him if his mother had worked:

> I know she worked off and on because she worked at [an electronics company] for the longest time. Yeah, she did work. I'm just trying to remember. There was a time when I know she didn't because I know when I was in elementary school I remember coming home at lunchtime and she would have lunch for me. So maybe when the kids were smaller she didn't work. And then she started working. I remember her working at [the electronics company] a long time. Then went to [a computer manufacturer] and retired from there.

In fact, his mother had also worked full-time before the family moved to Orchardtown when Edward was six, but the point to notice is not so much whether she worked or not as that her son did not see her work as part of her identity, and certainly not as part of her parenting, which was represented by that daily routine of having lunch ready. On the other hand, for her husband work was central to his being a father. The financial help Edward received from his parents (both of whom were working full time when he was a young man) is reported as coming from his father, and the family activities he points to are a handful of family vacations with his father.

Mothers who are supervising and caring for their children may well know more about those children, about their hopes and insecurities, than fathers who are there to have occasional fun. They are then in a position to relay or to hold back knowledge about their children, and mothers are the ones who both fathers and children talk to about the other. Edward told me a typical story of an incident between him and his daughter about which both of them had, independently, talked to his wife. Their communication about the event, and its resolution in Edward's mind, was very directly mediated by the mother.

> I just talked to my wife the other night. My oldest daughter, somehow I felt like she wasn't communicating with me lately, the last couple weeks. I was asking my wife if there was anything wrong. What particular things had happened at school. I went to pick up my son and she was gonna go somewhere else and I saw her and I know she saw me, but she didn't acknowledge me being there. So I was kind of hurt because usually they'll come up "Hi Dad!" And my wife goes "It had nothing to do with her not wanting—" What it was, I guess, her friends were wearing makeup and she knows I'm against girls at this age wearing makeup and I guess that was why she didn't come and talk to me. So that's fine. I can see why she didn't want to talk to me.

These examples illustrate that the structural division of labor, in which men are seen as providers and women as homemakers, is connected to a gendered division of parenting. Mothers not only do more child care and domestic work, they also know more about what their children are doing and feeling, they talk to them more, and they control the flow of information between fathers and children. They also schedule their children's lives and the interactions they have with their fathers. As part of this gendered system, the relationship that mothers have with their children even influences the quality of the interactions men have with their children. Mothers may invoke their husbands as disciplinarians and enforcers, so that the fathers are stricter or sterner than they might otherwise be. Or mothers may maintain the structure of family life, giving men the space to be spontaneous and fun.

Within this gendered system of parenting, men and women act out and reinforce gender stereotypes. Men are expected to play more actively with children than women do, and as a general rule they do so. Mothers, so I was told, control male exuberance, calming people down and discouraging dangerous or over-exuberant play. It is mothers, I am told, who set limits on the activity of men and children. By doing so, they constrain themselves or, rather, are constrained by an entire system of expectations from being "fun" in quite the same way that men are. Men's playfulness and men's anger, their distance and their sense of inadequacy, are reproduced in the daily interactions of family life. A crucial element of these interactions is the mediating position of women, as wives and mothers.

CONCLUSION

The question arises of whether women jealously guard their control over the family or whether men relegate women to the less prestigious area of domestic work and child care. At the level of family life and the lives of individual men and women, clearly both are going on (Coltrane, 1989; Cowan and Cowan, 1999; Hertz, 1986: 64-65; Walzer, 1998: 45 ff). The gendered division of labor in parenting is part of an "arrangement between the sexes" (Goffman, 1977)—a constructed and continually reinforced division of being between men and women. Men certainly develop a learned or deliberate incompetence in certain areas. It is a joke among both men and women that after a man has once done the laundry with mixed whites and coloreds and turned everything pink, or fixed a meal and turned the kitchen into a disaster area, or looked after the children for a weekend during which they ate nothing but pizza and never bathed, it is easier for women to do these things themselves. But men also develop different ways of

doing things—playing more aggressively, teasing, and challenging children to take risks or break out of routines. Both men and women live out and perform stereotypes, frequently performing them while acknowledging that, in some sense at least, they should not do so. So a woman who says: "I know I should learn how to check the oil in the car, but I let my husband do it," or a man who, like me, sheepishly excuses himself from making social arrangements because "My wife keeps track of the calendar," is perpetuating a particular gendered division of labor at the same time that his words are explicitly criticizing it.

This process of negotiating gender, which is often referred to as "doing gender" (West and Zimmerman, 1987) to describe gender as an activity rather than an intrinsic quality that people have, is complex and often internally contradictory. In this chapter I have shown how the cultural norm of men's public labor force participation and their role in the domestic sphere as family providers is maintained by cultural work done by men (and women) to emphasize the importance of fathers' earnings although mothers are also playing vital roles in the work force and public sphere. I have also shown that, within the domestic area, there is a gendered division of parenting, and of the meaning of being a parent, that continues to be very important even when both parents are involved in the day to day activities of their children. Fathering, like all human activity, is both a pattern of behavior and a set of meanings. Behavior and meaning sometimes reinforce each other, sometimes contradict each other, and sometimes work together to cover over contradictions or to make sense of changing circumstances.

In family life in the United States, as men, women, and children move back and forth between the public areas of employment and school and the domestic areas of home life and care giving, cultural ideas of what is gender-appropriate function to make sense of change and to provide meaningful continuity and coherence.

NOTES

1. A large amount of human activity is carried on in an area that is neither strictly domestic nor public. Areas of life such as friendship, visiting, kinship, and socializing cut across the public/domestic divide. In a study of community in nineteenth-century New England, Hansen (1994) proposes the term "social" for this third sphere of action.

2. The interviews involved an interaction between my personal situation, the perceptions of the men I talked to, and my conclusions (Townsend, 1999). I refer to all the men by pseudonyms. The quotations are taken from the transcripts of tape-recorded interviews. I have not changed or added to what men said, but because I do not want to distract attention from the content of what they told me, I have not presented all the "ers," "ums," and "you knows" with which real speech is studded. In the quotations, a dash (–) indicates an incomplete sentence or change of topic, ellipsis (. . .) indicates that I have omitted words or sentences from a quotation.

3. I do not mean to imply that all men, or all women, think and feel alike. Certainly, fatherhood means something different to men in the contemporary United States than it does to men in India, in the Congo basin, or in New Guinea. Fatherhood also has different meanings to men in the United States now than it did to men in the nineteenth century or in the colonial period. Fatherhood also means different things to different groups of men in the contemporary United States. Fathers in the upper classes, for instance, have concerns about inheritance and family status that are very different from those of fathers in the middle class who are worried about their children's college education and the dangers of downward mobility, or from working class fathers whose positions in families are being transformed by declining real wages and an increasing family dependence on two incomes.

4. The birth of children before marriage is associated with a marital disruption rate 57 to 80 percent higher than for couples without premarital births for cohorts of white women married between 1970 and 1985 (Martin and Bumpass, 1989: 42). This association may be because of greater strains on the early marriage, because couples who have a child before marriage have less normative commitment to marriage, or because some of the births were the biological children of men other than the husband and so do not have an "own children" effect on his behavior. My assertion of the connectedness of marriage and children is bolstered, however, by the lack of association between premarital *conception* and marital disruption (Billy, et al., 1986).

5. Leone's (1986) discussion of the key values invoked by middle class white women in the United States to describe and explain their childbearing decisions reveals the importance of "readiness" for women as well as for men.

6. Ehrensaft (1990: 119–122) interviewed couples who had decided to share the work of parenting their children. She describes the men's reactions of "falling in love with" their children. For women, "the gap between the anticipation and the reality [of children] was smaller" and the major surprise was the absorbing day-to-day reality of parenthood. For men, the anticipation was more anxious and the realization of parenthood marked a greater break. In the terms of my discussion, the paternal relationship, the paternal sentiment, and the sense of *being* a father is something that is brought about, that happens, and that is not taken for granted or inevitably linked to the biological events of conception or birth. (In an absolute sense, the same is true of women. "Maternal bonding" is a cultural event also, but it is an unquestioned event of our culture in a way that "paternal bonding" is not.)

7. Langer (1983) has analyzed the psychology of "perceived control" and its importance for both a sense of well-being and the actual outcome of events.

8. The "father breadwinner, mother homemaker" family has been both historically recent and short-lived as a dominant pattern. From 1850 until the Second World War, the decline of farm families was matched by an increase in the percentage of children in "father breadwinner, mother homemaker, nonfarm families" which reached almost 60 percent by 1930 and then fluctuated around that level until 1960, when it began a rapid drop to 27 percent by 1989. From 1950 onward, the declines in farm and father breadwinner families has been matched by a rise in the percentage of children in dual-earner and one-parent families, which was approaching 70 percent by 1990. Since 1970, less than half of the children in the United States have been in families of the father breadwinner, mother homemaker type (Hernandez, 1993: 103).

9. Hochschild (1989: 3–4 and 271–273) summarized studies that concluded that there was a difference of ten to twenty hours of total work between working husbands and wives. Other studies have found that men and women spend approximately equal amounts of time on the combination of housework and paid work (Ferree, 1991; Pleck, 1985; Schor, 1991), but certain domestic tasks continue to be overwhelmingly women's work (Coltrane, 1996; Shelton, 1992), and men's contribution to housework still tends to be thought of, by both husbands and wives, as helping (Coltrane, 1989; Walzer, 1998). When married couples have children, the division of domestic labor tends to become more traditionally gendered (Cowan and Cowan, 1999) and women spend less time in the paid labor force while men spend more (Shelton, 1992).

REFERENCES

Arendell, Terry. 1995. *Men and Divorce.* Thousand Oaks, CA: Sage.

Billy, John H. G., Nancy S. Landale, and Steven D. McLaughlin. 1986. "The Effect of Marital Status at First Birth on Marital Dissolution Among Adolescent Mothers." *Demography* 23:329–49.

Coltrane, Scott. 1989. "Household Labor and the Routine Production of Gender." *Social Problems* 36:473-90.

———. 1996. *Family Man: Fatherhood, Housework, and Gender Equity.* New York: Oxford University Press.

Cowan, Carolyn Pape and Philip A. Cowan. 1999. *When Partners Become Parents: The Big Life Change for Couples.* Mahwah, NJ: Lawrence Erlbaum.

Ehrensaft, Diane. 1990. *Parenting Together: Men and Women Sharing the Care of Their Children.* Urbana: University of Illinois Press.

Ferree, Myra Marx. 1991. "The Gender Division of Labor in Two-Earner Marriages: Dimensions of Variability and Change." *Journal of Family Issues* 12:158–80.

Furstenberg, Frank F. and Andrew Cherlin. 1991. *Divided Families: What Happens to Children When Parents Part.* Cambridge: Harvard University Press.

Garey, Anita Ilta. 1999. *Weaving Work and Motherhood.* Philadelphia: Temple University Press.

Goffman, Erving. 1977. "The Arrangement Between the Sexes." *Theory and Society* 4:301-36.

Hansen, Karen V. 1994. *A Very Social Time: Crafting Community in Antebellum New England.* Berkeley: University of California Press.

Hernandez, Donald J. 1993. *America's Children: Resources from Family, Government, and the Economy.* New York: Russell Sage Foundation.

Hertz, Rosanna. 1986. *More Equal Than Others: Women and Men in Dual-Career Marriages.* Berkeley: University of California Press.

Hochschild, Arlie. 1989. *The Second Shift: Working Parents and the Revolution at Home.* New York: Viking.

Langer, Ellen J. 1983. *The Psychology of Control.* Beverly Hills: Sage.

Lareau, Annette. 2000a. "Vague Answers: Reflections on Studying Fathers' Contributions to Children's Care." Paper presented at "Work and Family, Expanding the Horizons," University of California, Berkeley.

———. 2000b. "Social Class and the Daily Lives of Children: A Study from the United States," *Childhood* 7 (2): 155–171.

Leone, Catherine L. 1986. "Fairness, Freedom, and Responsibility: The Dilemma of Fertility Choice in America," Unpublished Ph.D. dissertation in Anthropology, Washington State University.

Martin, Teresa Castro and Larry L. Bumpass. 1989. "Recent Trends in Marital Disruption." *Demography* 26:37–51.

Pleck, Joseph. 1985. *Working Wives/Working Husbands.* Beverly Hills, CA: Sage.

Schneider, Jane C. and Peter Schneider. 1996. *Festival of the Poor: Fertility Decline and the Ideology of Class in Sicily, 1860–1980.* Tucson: University of Arizona Press.

Schor, Juliet B. 1991. *The Overworked American: The Unexpected Decline of Leisure.* New York: Basic Books.

Shelton, B. A. 1992. *Women, Men, Time.* New York: Greenwood.

Townsend, Nicholas W. 1998. "Fathers and Sons: Men's Experience and the Reproduction of Fatherhood," pp. 363–76 in *Families in the U.S.: Kinship and Domestic Politics*, edited by Karen V. Hansen and Anita Ilta Garey. Philadelphia: Temple University Press.

———. 1999. "Fatherhoods and Fieldwork: Intersections Between Personal and Theoretical Positions." *Men and Masculinities* 2(1):89–99.

———. n.d. *The Package Deal: Marriage, Work, and Fatherhood in Men's Lives.*

Waite, Linda, Gus Haggstrom, and David Kanouse. 1985. "The Consequences of Parenthood for the Marital Stability of Young Adults." *American Sociological Review* 50:850-57.

Walzer, Susan. 1998. *Thinking About the Baby: Gender and Transitions Into Parenthood*. Philadelphia: Temple University Press.

West, Candace and Don H. Zimmerman. 1987. "Doing Gender." *Gender & Society* 1(2):125-51.

White, Lynn, Alan Booth, and John Edwards. 1986. "Children and Marital Happiness: Why the Negative Relationship?" *Journal of Family Issues* 7:131-48.

Wienberg, Howard. 1988. "Duration Between Marriage and First Birth and Marital Stability." *Social Biology* 35:91-102.

Why Women Rule the Roost: Rethinking Javanese Ideologies of Gender and Self-Control

Suzanne A. Brenner

The ethnographic literature on Java has referred repeatedly over the years to a concept that can be glossed as "spiritual potency" (see Keeler 1987, 1990; C. Geertz 1960; Anderson 1972; Hatley 1990; S. Errington 1990). According to a number of ethnographic accounts, there is a common belief among Javanese people that individuals have the potential to develop a concentration of inner spiritual strength through the sustained practice of emotional and behavioral self-control. Individuals who have amassed this mystical power are said to be recognizable through their constantly calm demeanor, their refined speech styles and comportment, and their ability to elicit deferential behavior from others without apparent coercion or effort. Such individuals are lauded for achieving the goal of self-mastery, ultimately leading to the ability to master others (Anderson 1972; Keeler 1987).

Ideas about spiritual potency do seem to be widespread in Java. It is clear, however, that these ideas have been most highly elaborated and systematically perpetuated among

From: *Bewitching Women, Pious Men: Gender and Body Politics in Southeast Asia.* Aihwa Ong and Michael Peletz, eds. Berkeley: University of California, 1995. Reprinted by permission of the publisher

the ranks of the traditional Javanese aristocratic-cum-bureaucratic elite, the *priyayi* (see C. Geertz 1960; J. Errington 1984, 1988; Sutherland 1979). The concept of spiritual potency and the practices associated with it reinforce the ethical codes, behavioral norms, and linguistic styles that uphold *priyayi* claims to high status and cultural superiority. This concept is thus part of a larger ideological system that legitimates the deeply entrenched social hierarchies of Javanese society, especially those that have developed in the environs of the courtly centers of Solo and Yogyakarta. The ideology of spiritual potency supports the notion that people of high social status are inherently deserving of that status, and deserving of the deferential behavior and language that high status commands, because of their superior spiritual strength and moral worth.

Although the elite *priyayi* class includes females as well as males, I suggest that these ideologies of spiritual potency reinforce the superiority of *priyayi* males in particular, while placing all females, regardless of social class, in a categorically inferior spiritual, moral, and social position. The assertion that males are spiritually stronger than females is used to justify *priyayi* declarations that women should defer to and faithfully serve men, whether their husbands, fathers, or rulers. Within this ideological framework, it is often said that men have greater self-control than women over their emotions and behavior, suggesting that men are "naturally" stronger than women in a spiritual sense, and that women should "naturally" defer to them as a result. The fact that these ideologies are not confined to the ranks of the *priyayi* alone, but are also commonly voiced among other elements of the Javanese population, indicates that their influence on gender relations and identities in Javanese society deserves some attention.

Several types of linguistic and behavioral "evidence" are used to support the idea that men have greater self-control, and therefore greater spiritual potency, than women. It is said, for example, that men have greater mastery over the hierarchical intricacies and etiquette of the Javanese language,[1] thereby indicating their superior personal refinement; that men are more able and more inclined than women to perform various sorts of ascetic practices, which both reflect upon and augment their power and self-control; and that men's sexual prowess and potency is linked to a more spiritual kind of potency that women lack.

While Javanese women sometimes express their agreement with these assertions of male power and self-control, they frequently give accounts of male and female behavior that directly contradict the same notions. This paper will explore conflicting Javanese representations of gender, drawing into question the stereotyped, male-centered visions of male potency—inevitably suggesting female impotency—that pervade Javanese cultural representations, and which have in turn shaped ethnographic accounts of how gender "works" in Java. It will focus on ideas about human passions and the ability to control those passions, and how these ideas underlie the negotiation of male and female identities and statuses within the broader social order. The marketplace and the home—two places that are closely associated with women in Javanese thought—will be seen not only as

sites of economic production and of social and biological reproduction, but also as sites where conflicting understandings of male and female nature are symbolically and ideologically negotiated.

Although many scholars have recognized the need to draw a distinction between ideologies of gender and the actual social practices that may belie those ideologies (e.g., Tsing 1990; Keeler 1990), there remains a persistent tendency for ethnographic accounts to privilege dominant or hegemonic representations of gender.[2] By "dominant" or "hegemonic" representations or ideologies, I refer to those models that support the claims of a particular category of people to superior status and power, models which are most likely to be invoked in formal discourse and which are most often accorded a position of supremacy among other, potentially competing models. Ideologies, particularly the clearly articulated gender ideologies that many people seem to have ready at the tips of their tongues, tend to have a simplicity and even elegance to them that is difficult to resist. These dominant representations have a way of taking over studies of gender even when the writer is fully aware that they do not exhaust the full range of cultural discourses or social practices.

As a result, the ethnographic record presents a somewhat uneven picture of gender in Java—a topic that has been treated quite shallowly to date. It emphasizes certain prevalent, generally male-focused gender ideologies, while paying scant attention to less systematically articulated conceptions of gender, especially those that are voiced more often by women. In this paper I will point to an alternative, sometimes submerged view of male and female nature that presents a counterpoint to more conventional depictions of gender in Java. In the final analysis, however, no single configuration of gender relations can be considered absolutely "correct" or total, because constructions of gender invariably encode conflicting and ambivalent meanings that can never be fully reconciled (Ong 1987, 1990; Flax 1990).

CONTESTED AUTHORITY IN THE JAVANESE HOUSEHOLD

At a certain point in many Javanese wedding ceremonies, the bride and groom approach each other. When a few paces still remain between them, each one takes up a small quantity of betel *(sirih)* and throws it at the other, the idea being that the one whose betel hits the other person first will be the dominant partner in the marriage. It is often said that the bride should make sure that she loses the contest, but apparently the outcome is not always predictable. In a tone of mild amusement, Augusta de Wit describes this nuptial ritual as she observed it early in this century:

> With measured steps, the two advanced towards each other; and whilst yet at some distance paused. Two small bags of sirih-leaves containing chalk and betel-nuts were handed them; and with a quick movement each threw his at the other's head. The bride's little bag struck the groom full in the face. "It is she that will rule the roost," said one of the women, chuckling. And I fancied I saw a gleam of satisfaction pass over the bride's demure little face, half hidden though it was by the strings of beads and jessamine flowers dependent from her head dress. The next moment however, she had humbly knelt down on the floor. One of the bridesmaids handed her a basin full of water and a towel; and she proceeded to wash her husband's feet, in token of loyalty and loving submission (De Wit [1912] 1984:306–307).

This small ritual seems to epitomize the ambivalence with which the gendered division of domestic power is viewed in Java. On the one hand, the dominant ideology dictates that the wife should defer to her husband's greater prestige and authority as the nominal head of the household; thus, the bride is supposed to make sure that the groom wins the betel battle, and washes his foot "in token of loyalty and loving submission." On the other hand, the reality of the situation is that in many Javanese households, women enjoy a de facto power which far outweighs that of their husbands. Consequently, no one is too

surprised if the bride's betel strikes the groom first.[3]

The observations of a host of anthropologists confirm that in the majority of homes, the woman does indeed "rule the roost"; Robert Jay puts it quite bluntly when he writes that married men in rural Java are "probably among the most henpecked lot of husbands anywhere in the world" (Jay 1969:92). Scholars have remarked in particular on the prominent economic roles of women and their central position in the household (H. Geertz 1961; Jay 1969; Stoler 1977; Koentjaraningrat 1985; Siegel 1986; Papanek and Schwede 1988; Keeler 1987, 1990; Hatley 1990). The dominance of women in the household is almost invariably linked to their economic power, often both inside and outside the home. In *The Javanese Family*, for example, Hildred Geertz notes that within the domestic domain, "The wife makes most of the decisions; she controls all family finances, and although she gives her husband formal deference and consults with him on major matters, it is usually she who is dominant" (1961:46). Much earlier accounts of Javanese society reveal that women's economic clout is not a modern development; in 1817, Sir Thomas Stamford Raffles wrote, "It is usual for the husband to entrust his pecuniary affairs entirely to his wife. The women alone attend the markets, and conduct all the business of buying and selling. It is proverbial to say that the Javanese men are fools in money concerns" ([1817] 1965:353).

In most Javanese families today, regardless of social class or occupation, the wife continues to manage household finances.[4] Javanese women often voice the opinion that men are incompetent in managing money, and many men seem to agree (cf H. Geertz 1961; Jay 1969). Husbands are expected to turn over most or all of their income to their wives, who in turn allocate it as they see fit for household expenditures, sometimes giving their husbands only pocket money with which to buy cigarettes or snacks. Although one hears complaints on both sides—the wife grumbling that her husband keeps more for himself than he should, while the husband feels that his wife demands too much from him—this financial arrangement is generally accepted as the proper one between husband and wife. At a wedding that I attended in a village in Central Java, the village headman delivered a typical lecture of fatherly advice to the bride and groom, amplified through the public address system for all the guests present to hear, during the course of which he drew attention to "the notion that we Javanese have of 'female money,'" *(dhuwit wédok)*. "This means," he instructed the young couple, "that the husband should set aside a portion of his wage every month to turn over to his wife." However, many people—women in particular—would argue that a man should give his entire salary to his wife, not just a portion of it.

With regard to patterns of inheritance and property ownership, women also fare quite well relative to men. Both descent and inheritance are reckoned bilaterally in Java (as is true in many parts of Indonesia and in Southeast Asia more generally). Javanese custom prescribes that daughters and sons should inherit equal shares of property from their parents; this can include land, houses, jewelry, money, and other valuables.[5] Women often own property separately from their husbands, particularly property that they have inherited from their own parents, and they may dispose of it as they please (H. Geertz 1961). Husbands have no claim over their wives' property and, in the event of divorce, a woman may take with her whatever she inherited or otherwise brought with her into the marriage. Property that has been owned jointly by a husband and wife is usually divided evenly between them if they are divorced.

Women not only manage their husbands' incomes and control their own inherited property; they are also very important economic contributors to their households in their own right. In many households women earn as much as or more than their husbands. In fact, they are often the main or even sole breadwinners for their families. This is certainly the case in households where men are absent (many households are headed by women alone, in part because of the high divorce rate in Java), but it is also true in some households where both husband and wife are present. Women's earnings through agricultural or other wage labor, craft manufacture, trade, or employment in the informal sector (for instance, as domestic servants or sidewalk food vendors) not infrequently exceed their husbands' economic contributions to the household. Many Javanese women also pursue careers as civil servants, teachers, doctors, and owners or employees of shops and other private businesses.

In the merchant community of Solo, the city in Central Java where I conducted research, women were quite commonly the major providers for their families as textile merchants or market traders, while their husbands took a back seat to them in running the family businesses and in managing household finances.[6] What Raffles observed in the early nineteenth century continues to be true in Solo today: among the Javanese, women dominate the markets, from petty retail trade up to the lucrative large-scale wholesale trade in agricultural products, textiles, and other commodities.[7] In the region of Central Java that includes the court cities of Solo and Yogyakarta, it is a commonplace that a market stall entrusted to a Javanese man is doomed to failure (cf. Atmowiloto 1986). The prevailing stereotype in Solo is that while the wife goes off each day to the market to earn a living for her family, her husband stays at home, amusing himself by whistling to his songbirds.[8] In this sense, the relationship of men and women to money at the marketplace closely parallels the situation found in the home: just as men are deemed ill suited to handling household finances, they are also considered incapable of competently managing many kinds of businesses.

THE RELATIVE STATUSES OF WOMEN AND MEN

The dominance of women in their households, combined with their economic strength and autonomy, would seem to suggest a degree of social and economic status for women in Java which is comparable to that of men. To the extent that status can be measured by financial independence, influence in the family, and the freedom to make one's own decisions, women do indeed enjoy, at least in some respects, nearly equal standing to men.

Yet the notion of "status" itself is a very complex one in Java, not reducible to economic position or to any other simple factor.[9] Considerations of status shape every interpersonal encounter and linguistic utterance (C. Geertz 1960; Siegel 1986; Keeler 1987; J. Errington 1988). Status, always relative, is determined by a remarkably intricate set of considerations. These considerations include, but are not limited to, age and seniority, whether one is of noble descent, education, occupation, wealth, ethnicity, place of origin (e.g., village versus city), and gender. Status is also measured on the basis of somewhat less tangible qualities—for example, degree of cultural refinement, mastery of elaborate linguistic etiquette and social skills, and the reputed possession of spiritual strength. The concept of prestige is important in the evaluation of status, but is sometimes divorced from other determinants of status, such as wealth. For example, certain occupations, such as palace retailer, Muslim religious leader, or petty civil servant, are poorly paid but are still considered prestigious, at least in some circles. On the other hand, ethnic Chinese, many of whom are quite well-to-do, are categorically disrespected by many Javanese in spite of their wealth, due to the pervasive stereotypes that hold them to be unrefined, greedy, and incapable of mastering proper Javanese linguistic etiquette.[10]

Scholars of Javanese society are generally quick to point out that while women have economic power and considerable control over household affairs, in the realm of prestige they fall far short of men (Jay 1969; Hatley 1990; Keeler 1987, 1990). This detracts markedly from society's overall evaluation of their status. According to key ideological formulations, women have certain inborn character traits that doom them to an inferior station in life no matter how much money they earn or how much power they wield in the household (Hatley 1990; Keeler 1987, 1990). As these representations have it, most women are lacking in the qualities that lead individuals to be designated as "high status" even when they control substantial economic resources and domestic authority.

What is it about women that relegates them to this (ideologically, at least) inferior position? Ironically, one of the very characteristics that appears to give women so much autonomy and power in the household— their economic prowess—is also one of the main factors detracting from their prestige. In the central ideologies of Javanese society, there is an undeniable devaluation of the economic activities for which women and traders are known. Excessive attention to financial matters and the pursuit of wealth is said to indicate low status, lack of refinement, and a corresponding lack of spiritual potency (Anderson 1972; Keeler 1987, 1990; Djajadiningrat–Nieuwenhuis 1987; Hatley 1990; S. Errington 1990). Matters of money, especially where bargaining or the open pursuit of profit are involved, are seen as *kasar*—unrefined, uncivilized, coarse, and of low status.[11] Individuals who are mindful of their prestige must be careful never to show too much concern with money, lest they be seen as *kasar* too.

The idea that a preoccupation with money points to low status—an idea that is strongest among *priyayi* elites but which is also held, to some extent, by nonelites— shows how deeply ingrained *priyayi* ideologies are in Javanese society. *Priyayi* ideologies can be traced to the marriage of Javanese aristocratic values with nineteenth-century codes of proper conduct for indigenous servants of the colonial bureaucracy, espoused by Dutch and Javanese elites and legitimated by reference to Javanese tradition. It was in the interest of the well-entrenched colonial state and its Javanese functionaries, the members of the *priyayi* class, to support ideologies that made service to the state, rather than independent wealth, the primary source of prestige in Javanese society. The view that trade was inherently coarse protected *priyayi* and colonial interests against those of a monied elite that might otherwise have rivaled them for status and power (see Brenner 1991a). Particularly in the court centers of Solo and Yogyakarta, trade among the Javanese was considered the proper domain only of women and low-status men, as well as members of "foreign" ethnic groups such as Chinese, Arabs, or Europeans. While some *priyayi* women did engage in trade in order to supplement their husbands' incomes, their *priyayi* status was not questioned as long as their husbands were not openly involved in business. Dutch observers claimed that the Javanese were generally ill suited to trade (e.g., van Deventer 1904), noting that "only" the women seemed to have any business sense. It has been argued convincingly that the colonial dismissal of trade as an insignificant sideline activity for women served ideologically to legitimate state policies that limited Javanese participation in the most profitable areas of commerce (Alexander and Alexander 1991:373).

The broad influence of *priyayi* values in Javanese society has often been noted. This influence did not stop with the end of colonial rule, but has continued on into the present period, in a process that has been referred to as "priyayization," whereby *priyayi* norms and values are adopted by other elements of the population (see Djajadiningrat–Nieuwenhuis 1987). While Javanese men are increasingly involved in business, especially in the more modern sectors of the economy, and although wealth is, in practice, a very important source of status in Indonesian society, there remains a certain taint to business matters and to the handling of money, and a continued association of the less savory aspects of monetary and mercantile pursuits with women and ethnic minorities, all of which indicate that *priyayi* ideologies have not lost their hold upon the Javanese population.

Women, then, appear to be destined to inhabit the low-status, "coarse" realm of the social hierarchy. Their firm obligation as wives and mothers is to attend to financial matters: they are supposed to see to it that every last *rupiah* of the family's money is wisely spent. Those who are traders must bargain and calculate shrewdly in order to compete successfully in the overcrowded marketplace, where acting refined is out of the question. Other aspects of women's conduct also seem to support the conclusion that women are more *kasar*, and therefore of lower status, than men. Women are quicker than men to use low, or *kasar*, forms of Javanese language (*Jawa kasar, ngoko*), and to otherwise display behavior without embarrassment that many men would feel to be beneath their dignity. In the marketplace, even the wealthiest women traders can be seen slapping each other on the arm in a gesture of friendliness, shouting and laughing boisterously, and hurling pieces of cloth or wads of money across the aisles at each other. Few men of similar socioeconomic position would be willing to comport themselves this way in a public setting; they would consider such behavior demeaning and damaging to their prestige.

Men's interactions with each other, in contrast to women's, tend to be stiff and formal, marked by an attention to social and linguistic decorum that is almost painful to watch when one has become accustomed to the earthier, more relaxed styles of women (see H. Geertz 1961). The higher a man's social standing, the more circumscribed his range of behavioral and speech styles must be in order to protect and regenerate his status, style being a critical element of an individual's status image (cf. Keeler 1987, 1990; J. Errington 1988). Although this is also true for women, the latter are not expected to control their language and conduct to the same degree as men.[12] Ward Keeler (1990) remarks that "Women can disaggregate status and style more than men can in part because . . . women's status is defined in considerable measure by that of their husbands" (Keeler

1990:144; cf. Hatley 1990:184). As he also observes, to the extent that women's behavior and speech styles are accorded less weight than men's, women have the freedom to engage with relative impunity in behavior that would be compromising to men's status. Women are not thought *incapable* of speaking or behaving in an *alus* or refined manner—indeed, it is primarily women, not men, who are given the task of educating their female and male children in linguistic and behavioral politesse—but the wider range of social styles deemed acceptable for women gives them the reputation for behaving erratically, and not always in accordance with common standards of refined behavior.

IDEOLOGIES OF GENDER AND SELF-CONTROL

In a highly influential article entitled "The Idea of Power in Javanese Culture," Benedict Anderson (1972) explores Javanese ideologies of spiritual potency, which he terms "Power." To grossly simplify his more elaborate explanation: this form of Power goes beyond ordinary worldly power as it is generally understood in the West. It is a kind of divine energy and mystical inner strength that enables an individual to control himself, other people, and his environment without the use of crude physical, political, or material force. This Power is said to be accumulated and concentrated through ascetic exercise and through other forms of self-discipline that involve sustained control over one's personal passions and desires. The more self-discipline an individual has, the more spiritual power he amasses, which in turn leads to further self-control as well as the ability to master supernatural forces and the wills of human beings.

A calm, refined *(alus)* demeanor is taken to indicate that an individual possesses a large store of personal Power. Achieving high status is contingent upon having this Power, and consequently upon projecting an image of having total but effortless mastery over the inner passions. Powerful persons can thus be recognized from their poise, restraint, and equanimity in all situations. Conversely, those who are unable to control their emotions, speech, or behavior demonstrate their lack of spiritual potency (Anderson 1972; see also Keeler 1987; Hatley 1990). Excessive attention to the pursuit of personal gain, including economic profit, is seen as a sign of greed and self-interest, betokening lack of Power and low status.

Anderson does not directly address the issue of gender in his article, which, as he writes in a later retrospective paper, was intended primarily to offer an alternative, culturally unique perspective to Weber's concept of charisma (Anderson 1990). Whether this model of Power might apply differently to women or men is beyond the scope and intent of the article: the relationship of women to Power is not specifically discussed (see Djajadiningrat–Nieuwenhuis 1987:46). The article does draw some clear linkages between male sexual potency and spiritual potency, however, and the examples cited of Powerful figures are all male.

Later studies of Javanese gender relations have been more explicit in revealing the male-centered focus of the ideology of spiritual potency. In particular, several authors have noted that, according to the rhetoric of spiritual potency, women find it much harder than men to harness the self-control and mental discipline needed to acquire spiritual power. Ascetic exercise, which Anderson identifies as one of the primary means of acquiring Power, is said to be especially difficult (although not impossible) for women. In Hatley's words, "Though women may perform ascetic exercise, it is not considered usual for them to do so. Thus they are seen as incapable of refined controlled speech and of the emotional control that is the outward reflection of accumulated spiritual strength" (Hatley 1990:182). This view is shared by other scholars, such as Madelon Djajadiningrat–Nieuwenhuis, who writes, "According to the Javanese idea of the woman's role, she is more bound to her social and material context and consequently less suited for asceticism, which after all means distancing oneself from one's social environment. Only in very exceptional cases can women muster sufficient kekuwatan batin (mental strength) to acquire Power" (Djajadiningrat–Nieuwenhuis 1987:47; see also C. Geertz 1960:329).

Whether or not women actually do engage in ascetic practice is an issue to which I shall return presently. What *is* clear, however, is that women rarely make the extreme effort that men do to suppress strong affect and emotion, or to present an ever cool, refined demeanor to others. Hence it is less common for them to adhere to the codes of outward behavior that are portrayed by the dominant ideologies as reflective of high status and an inner spiritual strength.

When visiting a marketplace in Solo, I witnessed an especially amusing bout of bargaining between two experienced traders that brought home to me the difference between women's and men's styles of interaction, especially where self-control and refinement are concerned. One of the traders, Bu (Mrs.) Sita, was a friendly woman, quite successful in business, who had owned a stall in the market for a number of years. The other trader was a self-assured woman who wanted to buy a quantity of batik cloth wholesale from Bu Sita to sell again elsewhere. The pace of their bargaining was fast and furious, and the language used by the women, all low *(kasar)* Javanese, was rough, their tone almost a growl. The buyer was pointing out imperfections in the cloth and making low offers, while the seller, Bu Sita, kept refusing, insisting on a higher price. The bargaining became more and more intense, and the two of them seemed to be getting angrier and angrier with each other, to the point where I was beginning to wonder if they would actually come to blows. All of a sudden, before I knew what was happening, they both broke into broad grins, slapped each other on the arm jovially, and the sale was made, with sounds of disgust and exasperation, obviously exaggerated, coming from the buyer as she looked at the prices on the receipt that Bu Sita was writing for her. They chuckled together, chatted amicably and inquired about each other's families, the tone of their conversation changing dramatically from what it had been just moments earlier. It was only at that point that I realized the women were old friends who had been doing business together for years.

Two Javanese men would have been much less apt to put on such a display. Even a semblance of a strong emotion like anger would be construed as a lack of control, threatening their status as well as their friendship. Many Javanese men in Solo—even those of the trading class, remarkably enough—are reluctant to bargain at all. Although they often claim disdain for the marketplace and dislike of its *kasar* atmosphere (in keeping with the ideology of spiritual potency), it appears that what they fear most is the possibility of losing the image of self-control, equanimity, and disinterest in personal gain that is so important for maintaining men's status. They therefore avoid the marketplace, where it is especially hard to maintain linguistic propriety and an image of perpetual composure. The majority of Javanese men are more than happy to leave the business of buying and selling to their wives (cf. Siegel 1986).

Sudden shifts in language and behavior are quite common in the marketplace, and in women's interactions more generally. As women, the traders that I observed had the flexibility to switch stylistic registers abruptly without fearing loss of face or loss of friendship, although the sharp swings that sometimes characterize women's speech and behavior are also seen by the dominant representations as indicating their inability to master their emotions and behavioral style. Keeler (1990) observes that women's lability in style is considered by some Javanese as a sign that women are by their very nature lacking in self-control. Dominated by their impulses and emotions, their behavior is never fully predictable.[13] This broad categorization of women, he adds, has negative implications for their social status. Building on Anderson's earlier argument, which ties refinement to spiritual potency and status, Keeler suggests that these generalizations about women's lack of self-control ultimately point to their lack of spiritual potency and consequent lower status relative to men.

The Javanese ideological declaration that men are better able than women to control themselves also dovetails well with Islamic gender ideologies. These pan-Islamic conceptions of male and female nature, which are found in Indonesia and Malaysia as well as in the Middle East and elsewhere in the Islamic world, portray men as innately more capable than women of controlling their base passions and instincts, *nafsu*.[14] Although men as well as women have natural desires that threaten to overcome them, it is believed that men have greater rationality and reason, *akal,* which enables them to suppress those desires and to hold fast to the guidance of the Qur'an (see, e.g., Siegel 1969; Rosen 1984; Abu–Lughod 1986; Mernissi 1987; Ong 1987, 1990). Women are said to be more emotional, sexual, and irrational than men by nature; hence they must be carefully controlled by men so that they do not lead the latter astray from the proper path, thereby wreaking havoc on the social and religious order. Although I did not encounter this explicitly Islamic interpretation of human nature during the course of my research in Solo (where the majority of the population, although professing adherence to Islam, heavily mixes Islamic beliefs and practices with those of Javanese origin, often making it difficult and perhaps irrelevant to distinguish clearly between "Javanese" and "Islamic"), I would conjecture that it has been incorporated into the Javanese ideologies that associate women with irrationality and emotionality and men with self-control and a superior capacity for reason.

These two sets of gender ideologies, Javanese and Islamic, present an unproblematic image of men as potent, self-controlled, and in possession of the higher mental and spiritual faculties that allow them to maintain order in their own lives and in the social and supernatural world. Women, on the other hand, are depicted as spiritually impotent, less rational than men, and lacking in self-control. Such categorical statements about the nature of the sexes are well in keeping with an ideological system that places men at the center of the social, moral, and symbolic order. This ideological system has been generated and reinforced not only by the values of the Javanese *priyayi* elite, as mentioned earlier, but also by the patriarchal tendencies of Dutch colonial rule (in which male dominance was taken for granted in both political and domestic life, and which itself had a marked influence on the development of nineteenth- and twentieth-century *priyayi* rhetoric), of Islamic doctrine, and of the postcolonial Indonesian state.

Almost everyone I knew in Java, men and women alike, paid lip service to the notion that the father is the head of the household, and therefore deserving of deferential behavior from every other member of the family. Men also dominate the political order, from the community level up to the national level, and tend to serve as the representatives of their households in matters concerning the local and state bureaucracies. It is hardly surprising, then, to find gender stereotypes that associate women with low-status behavior—capriciousness, lack of control, emotionality—and men with the positive, high-status qualities of behavioral stability and self-discipline.

A CONTRARY VIEW: THE DANGER OF MEN'S DESIRE

I stress the *ideological* nature of these constructs, however, because in many situations, one finds an entirely different conceptualization of human nature in Java. This alternative, sometimes submerged view is also formulaic, but it contradicts the dominant ideological premise that to be male is to have greater self-control, whereas to be female is to be lacking in self-control. According to this vision of male and female nature, *men* find it much more difficult to restrain their innate passions and desires (*nafsu* or *hawa nafsu*) than do women. While both men and women are subject to the sometimes overwhelming influence of their own desires, it is women, not men, who can better control themselves. Although this idea is expressed more openly and more often by women than by men, as one might expect, it is not a view held exclusively by women, for men, too, often make statements or engage in actions that support this belief. I would argue, in fact, that this conception of the nature of the sexes underlies key roles that men and women play in the household, and that it forms the basis for their practices in other spheres of social life.

By underscoring this alternate understanding of gender and self-control, I do not intend to offer it as a "female countercultural" model that undermines male views. Nor do I propose that this is the "true" Javanese model, to be accorded absolute primacy over competing models, be they Islamic, *Priyayi*, or other. Rather, this is a view of human nature that is invoked in specific contexts by males as well as females, devout Muslims and non-Muslims, *priyayi* and non-*priyayi*. To the extent that it contradicts the dominant gender ideologies, it may be seen as counterhegemonic, yet its proponents include people who in other situations would uphold the dominant ideology of male potency without hesitation. Even to characterize this contradiction as a conflict between ideology and practice, or between thought and action (Gramsci 1957) misses the mark, because both these conflicting representations of gender and self-control are verbalized as axiomatic truths *and* expressed implicitly in people's actions. The key to understanding these contradictory views of gender is to see them as alternative paradigms that can be called upon to legitimate and to interpret the actions of males and females in different contexts. In formal discourse, the hegemonic view of male potency and self-control is more likely to be emphasized, while the view that men have less self-control than women often comes to the fore in casual discourse where there is less at stake ideologically.

Because ethnographers have highlighted the dominant model for so long, in the remainder of this essay I will focus on the subordinate perspective in order to demonstrate its significance for understanding gender relations. To start, it is important to look at the way the concept of desire, *nafsu*, is figured in a specifically Javanese sense. Many Javanese believe that to experience desire is normal to the human condition, but to be governed by it is dangerous, not only to the individual, but also to the family and to society. Here, one should distinguish between ordinary desires, and those that are excessive and therefore potentially disturbing both to an individual's internal equilibrium and to the social relationships in which he or she participates. *Nafsu* connotes ardent longing or passionate desire which, if left uncontrolled, causes people to behave in an unbalanced, irrational, or socially unacceptable manner.

Nafsu may take many forms, but the most powerful, and therefore potentially most dangerous, desires are those for sex and money—lust and greed, which are often seen as intrinsically related. Many Javanese men and women seem to take it as a given that men have an innately greater desire for sex than women, and that this desire is extremely difficult for them to suppress. Although this notion seems to run counter to both Javanese and Islamic ideologies that hold males to have greater control of their instincts and emotions than females, I encountered it often enough to be convinced that it was not just the idiosyncratic opinion of a few individuals. The degree to which it actually contradicts the ideology of male potency is debatable, however, since it reaffirms male sexual potency—a concomitant of male spiritual potency (see Anderson 1972)—even as it challenges men's ability to master their passions.

In relation to economic practices, this alternative view of the inherent differences between women and men leads people in Solo to conclude that women are naturally better suited to managing household finances, the family firm, or the marketplace. But what is the connection between controlling money and controlling one's passions? The words of one unusually candid Javanese man in his seventies summed it up: "Women make better traders and entrepreneurs than men, because men have greater lust *(syahwat)* than women. Men can never hold onto money for long, because if you give them money, they'll spend it on getting women. Give 'em enough money, and they'll have more than one wife, either out in the open or on the sly.[15] Men have greater desires than women *(nafsuné niku, gedhé wong lanang)*. It's always men who spend money on women, who 'buy' women. Who ever heard of a woman buying a man?" A female textile merchant made a similar remark: "When men get hold of money, they use it to take another wife, or to gamble." Yet another woman commented, "You can tell if a man is keeping a woman on the side—eventually he gets found out because he's spending money too quickly." A man's lust requires money, I was told, because few women will sleep with a man illicitly unless they can derive some financial benefit from it. Moreover, men's natural proclivity to give in to their desires, it is said, leads them to squander money in the process; they will stop at nothing to find satisfaction for their passions.

One often hears lower-class women in particular, such as household servants or batik workers, complain about the financial drain that their husbands' sexual indulgence, gambling, and general irresponsibility and lack of consideration for the family's welfare create for them and their children. Stories of husbands who abandon their wives and children to run off with other women are everyday fare, but many women feel that this is preferable to having a husband who stays around and continues to sap the family's already strained resources, without contributing anything in return.

Inem, a village woman who worked as a housekeeper for a family in Solo, often grumbled about the problems that her husband's womanizing caused for her and her two children. Not untypically, it was Inem, not her husband, who supported the family; her husband only worked about one month in ten, she figured, but he continued to come to her for money when he needed it. He spent most of his time with another woman in a nearby village, only making an appearance at home once every week or so. Fed up with the situation, Inem asked her husband for a divorce, but he refused, as did the local village authorities, who had the final say in the matter. She told me that she would have been happy to divorce him, and would not want to marry again. She already had two children, lived close to her mother, and got along well with her mother-in-law, with whom she and her children shared a house. What did she need a husband for? She was better off without one, she said. That way, she could devote herself and her limited money exclusively to her two children.

The "official" view that has been emphasized in the ethnographic literature is that men are too concerned with their prestige to bother themselves with petty and demeaning monetary matters. They turn their wages over to their wives and leave all the marketing to their wives as well, because they consider financial affairs to be beneath their dignity. This is consistent with the ideology of male potency, for undue concern with financial gain is considered to be detrimental to an individual's spiritual power and social standing. However, the alternative view, that men cannot hold onto money because they cannot control their desires, suggests that the accepted "official" line is not sufficient to explain why women take charge of financial affairs while men tend to avoid them. The alternative view of men's lack of control relative to women's is invoked often enough to take on an authority of its own, encouraging as well as explaining certain types of behavior for men and women.

Although anecdotes and warnings about men's lack of self-control frequently focus on their lust, men are also accused of (and admit their own guilt over) uncontrolled gambling, extravagant consumption, and other spendthrift practices. However, since lust is considered one of the most potent forms of *nafsu* it seems to stand as a figure for all forms of desire, representing the power of base passions over the will to be self-disciplined. Money tempts men to various forms of profligacy, but lust serves as the ultimate symbol of human—especially male —weakness. Money is thus seen as the gateway to the fulfillment of desire, and sex comes to represent all desires that money can fulfill, which may explain why discussions of men's inability to handle money so commonly refer to their lustfulness. The desire for money and the things that money can buy is thought to exert a powerful influence on both women and men, but women are expected (by women and men alike) to be able to keep their desire under control for the sake of the family. While such self-discipline is an ideal for men as well, it is widely believed that a man's passion-ridden nature sorely taxes his ability to exercise restraint, which becomes, of course, a self-fulfilling prophecy. While this flies in the face of the ideology of superior male self-control, it is worth noting that many men appear to take a perverse pride in the unquenchable lust and "naughtiness" of those of their sex—suggesting, once again, that the positive associations of sexual potency and of generally "manly" behavior offset any shame that might accompany their inability to exercise self-control.

A friend related the story of a young village man who had made off with all the gold jewelry that his wife, who was expecting a child, had borrowed from his mother to wear for a ritual ceremony *(mitoni)* that is held during a woman's first pregnancy. Several months after abandoning his wife and unborn child, he showed up destitute on a relative's doorstep in the city, having spent all the money from the sale of the jewelry, everyone assumed, on gambling and prostitutes. His parents came to pick him up and brought him back to the village, where he resumed life in their home with his wife and new baby. The young man, who had never had much money of his own, had been unable to overcome the temptation that was presented

when be suddenly had access to a considerable amount of wealth, in the form of his mother's jewelry. However, it is not too surprising that his parents and wife were willing to accept their prodigal son and husband back into their home, since his behavior, although certainly reproachable, was in keeping with common Javanese beliefs about male nature. From infancy on, males are expected to be "naughty" *(nakal)*, and the attainment of adult status does nothing to change this expectation (see H. Geertz 1961).

Women's control over their own desires serves to compensate for men's lack of control (as the alternative representation has it), and by so doing preserves the assets that should properly be used to ensure the family's security. It is the wife's responsibility to do her utmost to make sure that her husband's desires do not drain the family's resources, while also doing everything in her means to *increase* those resources, thereby contributing to the improvement of her family's social status. By taking charge of the family's financial affairs and keeping her husband away from matters of money, the wife prevents her husband from squandering the family's wealth. She also protects her husband's dignity and status, which by association (since he is considered to be the main representative of the family) protects her own status and that of her children.

In accepting control of the family's finances, a woman is entrusted, in a sense, with her husband's desires, his *nafsu*. In other words, she must control not only her own passions, but also, to whatever extent possible, those of her husband. Women realize that there are limits to how far they can restrain their husbands' desires, but by controlling the family purse, they do what they can to keep in check a major source of temptation: money.

Just as women conserve material resources for the family by restraining desire, they also conserve spiritual resources through a similar, but more intensive, form of self-discipline. Although several authors have reported that few women engage in ascetic practices, my own research in Solo did not support this finding. Many people told me that when a child is sick, or is taking exams in school, it is the child's mother, not the father, who fasts, gets up to pray in the middle of the night, and deprives herself of sleep (all considered forms of asceticism) in order to help her child. I repeatedly encountered women who fasted—sometimes twice a week—or engaged in other ascetic practices on a regular basis, primarily, they said, for the benefit of their children and future descendants. In fact, several women told me point-blank that many men, in contrast to women, do not have the strength of will to carry out ascetic practices, contradicting the ethnographic commonplace that asceticism is predominantly a male undertaking in Java.[16]

The ability to control *nafsu* is considered integral to conserving money for the family and to the production of the more abstract benefits that accrue through ascetic exercise. Although men as well as women engage in ascetic practices, men's asceticism seems usually to be directed toward the fulfillment of personal goals, whereas women's ascetic practices are typically carried out on behalf of their families. This is not to say that men take no interest in the welfare of their children. However, women believe that they have a naturally stronger bond with their offspring than their husbands do, which leads them to take the burden of securing their descendants' futures more heavily on their own shoulders. Most men appear to be more than willing to turn this responsibility over to their wives. Moreover, it is generally believed that if men cannot sufficiently curb their ordinary desires to accumulate material wealth for the family, they can scarcely be expected to exert the additional self-control required to engage in asceticism on their children's behalf.

Men's tendency to avoid the marketplace, which scholars have often attributed to their deep concern with prestige and spiritual potency, can also be understood in terms of this alternative model of gender and self-control. As a prime site for the accumulation of money and the acquisition of commodities, the marketplace seems to incite desire and at the same time advertise the potential for its satisfaction. The priority of an economic logic of commodity exchange in the marketplace, moreover, leads to a partial breakdown of the boundaries that conventionally order and circumscribe social relations in Java, thereby creating a situation in which the social mechanisms for the suppression of desire are weak. Women believe they are better able than men to restrain themselves from giving in to the desires of the marketplace, and many men seem, whether tacitly or explicitly, to concur. Hence, the Solonese say that the market is a woman's world, *donyané wong wédok*. Most women *and* men believe that, aside from concerns of prestige, Javanese men are ill suited to trading in the marketplace because they lack the self-discipline needed to bring money home at the end of the day instead of squandering it.

In the large textile market that I frequented in Solo, few Javanese men were to be found, either as consumers or traders (there were, I should mention, plenty of men of Chinese and Arab descent among the traders; the rules for Javanese men do not hold for members of other ethnic groups). One notable exception, however, was a Javanese transvestite *(banci)* who ran one of the largest rotating cooperative credit associations *(arisan)* among the traders in the market.[17] Every day Pak (Mr.) Hardjo (some people called him *Bu* Hardjo because of his inclination to cross-dress) went around the market collecting money from participating traders, and he was responsible for picking the winners of that day's pot and distributing their shares to them. This was a job that the traders felt required tremendous self-control, because handling several million *rupiah* (well over a thousand dollars) each day was a source of temptation that even those of the strongest character might find difficult to resist. My sense was that as far as the women traders were concerned, Pak Hardjo's ambiguous gender made him an acceptable person to fill the role of *arisan* coordinator (from what I could tell, all the other *arisan* managers in the market were women), whereas a "straight" man would have been distrusted. His female-ness suggested trustworthiness, a self-discipline of which an unambiguously gendered male would not have been assumed capable. By taking on the mannerisms and clothing of a woman, Pak Hardjo also acquired the reputation that women have for being able to control their desires.

THE DANGER OF AUTONOMOUS WOMEN

The relationships between gender, desire, and economic practice are further complicated by the ambivalence with which women's self-control, and their control over money, is viewed. On the one hand, women are considered to be ever mindful of their families and less lustful than men, which keeps them in control of their desires. These are some of the factors which are said to make them "naturally" better traders than men. On the other hand, the more money a woman controls, the more autonomous she is, and an autonomous women is always suspect. Self-control over one's desires is evaluated positively in Java, but a woman who is not subject to any *man's* control is potentially threatening to the male-dominated social order. Widows and divorcées, for example, are frequently the objects of gossip and suspicion for their sexual activities because they are no longer under the supervision or control of fathers or husbands (cf. Ong 1987:89).

The connections between economic independence and sexual license are often made explicit, as in the following passage from an Indonesian newspaper article entitled "Hunting for Satisfaction: Sex among the Ranks of Javanese Women":

> At 8:30 in the morning, Hartini, 27, a tall, slender, beautiful woman, steps supplely. Her hips sway, fully confident. "There's a diamond deal in Tawangmangu," she remarks as she says goodbye to her husband and children and makes for the Mazda 323 Trendynamic that's ready to go.
> The metallic black Mazda hits the road without a moment's hesitation. And, at a plush villa,

the car comes to a stop. Soon the attractive woman who was driving it gets out, and, as if quite at home, enters the villa. A man with the air of a big shot, who appears to have been waiting for some time, greets her, "Hello dear."
> How intimately this man takes Ms. Hartini by the shoulder. And, as if by plan, they jokingly go into a bedroom. Ah . . . must a diamond deal take place inside a closed room between two human beings of different sex?

The above illustration is one incident that was recorded during a field study conducted for almost a year among women traders between the ages of 25-40, in one center of trade in Solo. The conclusions from that study were truly startling: "The higher the degree of a woman trader's economic independence, the greater her degree of sexual freedom." Might there be something amiss in the study, for instance, that the respondents were chosen incorrectly?[18]

This "field study" merely seemed to confirm rumors about female market traders that were already rife in Solo. There were stories, for instance, that some traders participated in a magical practice that required having sexual relations with someone other than their own spouse as a means of ensuring success in business. Others said that a few of the traders were actually prostitutes or madams who used their market stalls in order to find clients from among out-of-town male traders or customers, especially when sales of textiles and other goods were slow. It was said of market women that their "sarongs are loose" (*tapihé kendho*)—in other words, that they "come off easily" (*gampang dicopot*). In short, women traders had a reputation in the wider society for being willing to sell more than just their wares. One man recounted an anecdote to illustrate the allure of female traders in Solo, a city already infamous for its *femmes fatales:* "A man was on his way to Solo from another city, when he ran into a friend. When his friend found out where he was going, he said that he would like to go along, too, so that he could visit the market in Solo. 'I'll go to a batik trader there, and ask to see all her goods,' said the man. 'After she's laid out the last sarong in stock for me, I'll ask her for the *very* last one—the one she's wearing.'"

To say that "sexual freedom" for Solonese market women is the norm would clearly be an exaggeration. Like most stereotypes, this one was clearly blown out of proportion. What is significant, however, is the extent to which such generalizations prevail, and their implications for understanding the logics of gender in Java. These stories suggest that the marketplace, a domain controlled by women, is also a place where women cannot be controlled by men. But can market women control *themselves?* At first glance, stories about the "looseness" of women traders seem to contradict the notion that women have more control over their desires than men, making them better suited to handling money. For if it is indeed the case that the women who have the most dealings with money are also perceived as being the most widely involved in illicit sexual affairs, then it would appear that there is no clear connection between the control of money and the control of desire.

I should point out, however, that I never heard anyone in Solo attribute women's engagement in extramarital affairs to their uncontrollable desires. Sometimes it was attributed to women's dissatisfaction or boredom with their husbands, the wish to "get even" with husbands who had been unfaithful, or even the "need for recreation." More commonly, though, women's infidelity was imputed to economic need or ambition; for instance, a way to compensate for a slow period in the market. As I mentioned earlier, there was a general belief that few women would be willing to have adulterous relations were there not some financial gain to be had in the bargain. When a neighbor told me that a married woman with children she knew was driven by economic hardship to seek out liaisons with men, for example, I asked her if she was sure that the woman was being paid by the men she was seeing. "Well, if they didn't give her money, do you think she'd do it? Of course not," my neighbor answered matter-of-factly. Since a double standard in Javanese society makes it less acceptable for women to engage in extramarital relations than men, it is felt that most

women will not take part in such activities lightly.[19]

Prevalent ideas about the dissimilar natures of men and women often lead people to conclude that whereas men are driven by their concupiscence to seek out extramarital relationships, women are more apt to be motivated by other factors, especially concern for the family's financial welfare. Women may be the objects of *men's* sexual desire, but they are not thought likely to succumb to their *own* sexual desires. This notion contradicts the idea that men are ruled by reason and women by their passions, but it should not be taken at face value, for it, too, constitutes a prescription for, rather than a description of, reality. I stress the formulaic nature of both the dominant and alternative conceptions of gender and self-control lest one or the other be taken as a statement of "fact" or "practice." Nonetheless, it should be kept in mind that these normative prescriptions often *do* have a real effect on individuals' everyday practices and their reactions to the behavior of others. In my observation, the belief that women have more self-control than men in matters of sex and money leads women and men to have very different expectations of themselves and of each other, and frequently to fulfill those expectations through particular modes of action.

Despite the definitiveness with which categorical assertions about gender and self-control are made, the stories about the sexual activities of market traders point to the underlying *ambivalence* with which the notion of self-control itself is viewed in Java. When a man controls his desires, it is commonly believed, he makes himself potent. When he lets his self-control lapse, he is a danger to the family. When a woman controls *her* desires, she accumulates economic and spiritual value for the family, more than personal potency. But a woman with too much control over her own person, it appears, is considered a threat to society. The woman merchant occupies an especially ambiguous position in Javanese society. She is thought better able than a man to suppress her own desires, but she is also seen as manipulating the desires of others toward her own ends. At home, she is entrusted with the safekeeping of her husband's desires and the welfare of her family, yet her success in business depends on her capacity to arouse the desires of her customers, to make them willing to spend money. It is this ambiguity that is reflected in the stories about the "sexual freedom" of women traders. Their "danger" lies in their ability to control their own passions, but to awaken those of others.

CONCLUSIONS

Aihwa Ong has noted that gender is a "potentially contradictory configuration of meaning that codes alternative structures of morality, control, and power" (Ong 1990:422). In this paper, I have attempted to demonstrate that Javanese discourses and practices of gender embody contradictory representations that sometimes confound the ideological association of males with a higher degree of self-control, potency, and morality than females. Why is this important? It is important, I propose, because the dominant ideologies of male potency serve to legitimate male control over women and over the society more broadly. By throwing these ideologies into question, the Javanese "cultural" insistence on male superiority and control is also brought into question. For too long the ethnography of Java has reproduced the rhetoric of male potency without discussing its alternatives. By failing to give adequate expression to contradictory representations of gender, these studies have implicitly taken men's claims to superior status and power as unshakable facts of Javanese culture, which, I am arguing here, they are not.

A one-sided approach to the relationships between gender, self-control, and potency, then, obscures the ambiguities, paradoxes, and multiple layers of meaning that attach to ideas about maleness and femaleness in Java. Although describing and analyzing the impact of dominant gender ideologies is worthwhile, to grant them too central a posi-

tion in analysis may obscure subtler but equally important ways that people think and talk about gender. Furthermore, it is clear that both men *and* women in Java make pronouncements and engage in practices that support as well as contradict the dominant ideologies of spiritual potency and self-control. As I stated earlier, to assume that any of the viewpoints offered here represents "the male point of view" or "the female point of view," would be incorrect (cf. Yanagisako and Collier 1987), even if one perspective seems to privilege men over women (or vice versa), or is voiced more often by men or women.

Javanese women give tacit approval to ideologies of superior male potency and status by deferring to their husbands in both private and public contexts and by helping them to avoid situations in which their prestige might be compromised (see Keeler 1990 for a nice illustration of this point). At the same time, women freely express the opinion that most men have uncontrollable passions and childlike dispositions which prevent them from acting in the best interests of their families. Women, they add, must rely on their own superior strength of will in order to compensate for their husbands' lack of control. Many Javanese men also admit openly that members of their sex are less capable than women of controlling their base desires (especially lust), even while they make categorical statements about women's inability to manage their emotions and behavior. In formal or public interactions, where male dominance and prestige tend to be highlighted, men attempt to project an image of equanimity and total self-mastery, but in private, they may give rein to their passions, thus fulfilling other cultural expectations for male behavior. Conversely, in public situations Javanese women sometimes appear cheerfully unconcerned with conveying a dignified, self-controlled image (though they are every bit as capable as men of assuming an air of refinement when the situation requires it), but at home they take the injunction to be self-controlled utterly seriously in order to accumulate economic and spiritual resources for themselves and their families.

We need not seek to reconcile these conflicting images of female and male nature and behavior. All cultural systems embody such contradictions and ambiguities, and to try to resolve or to ignore the contradictions gives priority to our own desire for order rather than to the realities of complex social phenomena. Although ethnographers of Java have recognized the marked discrepancies that exist between patently ideological formulations and actual day-to-day practices (see Keeler 1990; Hatley 1990), some of the alternative perspectives on gender have remained largely unexplored. My intention has been to bring to light some of these less prominently articulated, but nonetheless significant, views of gender relations in Javanese society. I am here advocating what Gayatri Spivak refers to as "an espousal of, and an attention to, marginality—a suspicion that what is at the center often hides a repression" (Spivak 1987:104). By paying too much attention to the ideologies of the center, one runs the risk of relegating to the margins of scholarly inquiry perspectives that have already been suppressed because of their subordinate status, but which are still crucial to an understanding of social relations and cultural logics.

Even when ideology seems to be borne out by practice—as, for instance, when Javanese men avoid the marketplace, claiming that they do so because of their disinterest in petty material matters that are best left to women— there may be more going on than meets the eye. Attention to peripheral discourses may reveal fundamental views of women's and men's natures that bypass or reconfigure the idioms of potency and prestige. In this case, as I have shown, an alternative perspective is that men stay clear of the marketplace because they cannot control their desires to the degree that women can. To be sure, both the dominant and alternative views are highly conventionalized, and should not be taken to explain in themselves why market trade tends to be marked as women's, not men's, work. A deeper understanding of why men in parts of

Java shun the marketplace, and why women do not, would have to take into account, among other factors, the historical developments that have shaped Java's social, political, and economic landscape, and not just the modern-day cultural pronouncements that attempt to explain or to justify the end products of those developments.[20]

Nevertheless, to the extent that women's and men's interpretations of gender guide and give meaning to their social actions, they deserve attention. The key is not to give so much weight to one set of interpretations that one overlooks others because they are not voiced as formally or as insistently. As Jane Flax writes, advocating a rapprochement between feminist and postmodernist theoretical approaches, "Perhaps reality can have structure only from the falsely universalizing perspective of the dominant group. That is, only to the extent that one person or group can dominate the whole will reality appear to be governed by one set of rules or be constituted by one privileged set of social relations" (Flax 1990:49). The "rules" that are frequently invoked for Javanese society only represent "reality" as it exists within the limited framework of a particular ideological system—one that grants superior status to men and their domains of activity.

Writing about traditional ideological conceptions of gender in Java, Barbara Hatley comments: "Women's economic activities outside the home, in market trade particularly, are seen as an extension of the natural female household concern with money matters. The association of women with money brings more disparagement than esteem, as men complain of their wives' tightfistedness and rather contemptuously attribute to women a *jiwa dagang*, 'soul of a trader'" (Hatley 1990:182). From this perspective, women's transactions of money and goods inevitably detract from their prestige and lead to their devalued position in Javanese society. But another possibility should be considered. Outside the dominant ideologies, women's dealings with money can be viewed in a different, more positive light: as a means by which they domesticate the antisocial forces of desire so as to ensure the property and status of their families. By accumulating wealth and investing it in the material and social welfare of the family, they generate prestige for their husbands, their children, and, of course, themselves (cf. Djajadiningrat–Nieuwenhuis 1987). Men and women alike directly or indirectly acknowledge the importance of women's economic activities in this regard. *Both* sexes are invested in generating status for themselves and for their families, and their roles in this endeavor are complementary. The common assumption that Javanese women are relatively indifferent to matters of status and prestige, then, is misguided, a result of paying undue attention to ideologies that privilege men and their activities.

This suggests that focusing on "prestige systems" as a diagnostic of gender relations (Ortner and Whitehead 1981) may lead to an analysis that is both too narrow and too ideological if one does not take into account the inherent complexities embodied in the notion of prestige itself. For example, Shelly Errington has proposed that in island Southeast Asia,

> differences between people, including men and women, are often attributed to the activities the people in question engage in or the spiritual power they exhibit or fail to exhibit. If we want to understand gender there, we . . . must understand local ideas of power and prestige; the next step . . . is to ask how people defined as male, female, or something else are mapped onto, as it were, the prestige and power systems (S. Errington 1990:58).

I would caution, however, that "the prestige and power system" may represent, in Flax's words, "the falsely universalizing perspective of the dominant group," which, while defining a certain structure of reality, may not represent the entire range of cultural discourses or actual practices in a given society. Sherry Ortner and Harriet Whitehead (1981) observe that almost all prestige systems accord males superior status to females. Should we, then, accept at face value the hegemonic constricts that privilege males, without investigating the possibility that there might be competing ideas that do not always assume female inferiority?

In a recent essay, Ortner (1989-90) has reevaluated her own earlier model of prestige systems, now recognizing the limitations of approaches to prestige that do not consider the multiple logics and conflicting practices of power and prestige that are inevitably at play. Avoiding totalizing models of prestige systems, she observes, can lead to a very different picture of gender and status—one that may call into question the universality and absoluteness of male dominance. Bearing these issues in mind, I maintain that the ideology of spiritual power does not underlie all notions of prestige and hierarchy in Java, nor does it define all aspects of gender; it is a dominant, but not an exhaustive, cultural model. Furthermore, in response to Shelly Errington's statement above, I would add that the notion that males and females can be "mapped onto" a prestige and power system seems to presuppose the unitary nature of such a system, as a rigid grid that allocates fixed coordinates for males and females. Social systems, and ideas about gender, are far more complex than such a "mapping on" would permit. As prevalent as ideologies of spiritual power and prestige are in Java, they only represent one facet of the social and cultural dynamic. Even though women are allotted an inferior position in the "official" Javanese model of prestige and potency, this model, it turns out, is not the sole indicator of cultural value, nor of the respective positions of women and men in the social order.

As Sylvia Yanagisako and Jane Collier point out, the concept of a "male prestige system" rests on the assumption of an encompassing (superior) male sphere and an encompassed (subordinate) female sphere, the latter generally identified as the domestic sphere (1987:28). In Java, the ideologies of the center do tend to identify women with the "mundane" matters of running the household and child rearing; even their activities as traders in the very public domain of the marketplace are seen, as Hatley mentions, as extensions of their "natural" female household concern with matters of money. Since the dominant ideologies often devalue as unprestigious those activities that are associated with what we might refer to as "the domestic sphere" (in particular, the household and the family), as well as those that involve transactions of money and commodities, one might easily assume that women and their activities are uniformly considered to be of low status.

What I have proposed here is an alternative configuration of gender relations and/or women's association with the household: one which grants women the role, at least in some contexts, of domesticator (of men, money, and desire, among other things) rather than domesticated, and which sees women's activities as central to the production of the family's status in the wider society. Seen from this angle, neither the household nor women's spheres of activity more broadly should be seen as subordinate domains: they are, rather, crucially important sites of cultural production and social reproduction in their own right.

Yet the linkage between women and "the domestic," I wish to emphasize, is by no means absolute. Since many Javanese women work outside the home, in the marketplace and elsewhere, they move easily between the household and the public domain (cf. Djajadiningrat–Nieuwenhuis 1987:45). In the case of Javanese merchants, it is women's freedom to move between the home and the public sphere—in particular, their willingness to expose themselves to the desires of the marketplace while controlling their own desires—that enables them to accumulate wealth for the family. Even in their forays outside the conjugal bond, women are thought to keep the best interests of their families in mind; they thus retain their status as domesticators. Whereas men's extramarital sexual activity is associated with uncontrolled desire and the dispersion of family resources, female sexuality remains conceptually bound to economic accumulation and the production of status for the family. A shift away from the ideologies to

the center reveals that women do not only participate tangentially in the status systems of men—they themselves play a central role in defining and reproducing the status hierarchies of Javanese society.

NOTES

A shorter version of this paper, entitled "Sex and the Marketplace, or: Why Men Can't Control Themselves," was presented at the Ninth Annual Berkeley Conference on Southeast Asia Studies, February 29, 1992, at the University of California, Berkeley. I am grateful to two anonymous readers as well as to the following people for their comments on this paper and earlier versions of this work: Benedict Anderson, Nancy Florida, Paschalis Laksono, Aihwa Ong, Michael Peletz, Vicente Rafael, P. Steven Sangren, Saya Shiraishi, Takashi Shiraishi, James Siegel, Budi Susanto, G. G. Weix, and Astri Wright. In formulating the ideas presented here, I have also benefited from many conversations with Leslie Morris, Ward Keeler, and Tinuk Yampolsky.

The research on which this article is based was conducted in Solo, Central Java, Indonesia, from February 1986 to August 1988. It was funded by a Social Science Research Council Dissertation Research Grant, a Fulbright-Hays Dissertation Research Fellowship and a Woodrow Wilson Research Grant in Women's Studies. Research was carried out under the auspices of the Indonesian Institute of Sciences (LIPI) and the Cultural Studies Center of Gadjah Mada University, under the directorship of Professor Umar Kayam.

1. The Javanese language is structured around a remarkably complex system of language levels that indicate the relative status of interlocutors and the degrees of formality and politeness that they wish to express. A fluent command of the full range of speech levels is usually considered by Javanese people to be a sign of high status, good breeding, and personal refinement. For detailed explanations of the workings of the Javanese language and its place in social life, see C. Geertz 1960; Keeler 1984; Siegel 1986; J. Errington 1988.
2. See Peletz (1995). See Ortner 1989–90 on the subject of gender hegemonies more broadly.
3. Some Javanese grooms seem to fear this possible outcome. One man described to me a wedding

he had attended where the groom had ducked out of the way when the bride threw her betel. Then, grasping his chance, he took careful aim at his wife-to-be and flung his betel at her as hard as he could.

4. The nuclear family is the basic unit of kinship in Java and a "typical" household is often thought of as consisting of a husband, wife, and their unmarried children. However, other arrangements are also very common. Many households contain only a woman and her children; in other cases, a household may include other relatives or nonkin from outside the nuclear family. For further discussion of Javanese household arrangements, see H. Geertz 1961; Hart 1986.

5. Some strict Muslims prefer to follow Islamic rules of inheritance, whereby a brother receives two shares for every one share that his sister receives. Although the majority of the Javanese population professes at least nominal adherence to Islam, my impression in Solo was that more people preferred to follow the prescription of "Javanese custom" (adat Jawa), i.e., equal inheritance for males and females, than that of "Islamic law" (hukum Islam), which some people felt was unfair to women.

6. Although the city of Solo, the site of my research, does have a reputation in Java for having especially independent women who contribute more than their share to the family financially, the pattern of women contributing substantially to their households' incomes is certainly not limited to this city alone.

7. I stress that this is the case among the *Javanese*, because many traders of other ethnic groups— Chinese, Arab, Indian, and other indigenous Indonesian groups, such as the Minangkabau— are men. As trade in Java has for centuries (particularly since colonization) been in the hands of non-Javanese as well as Javanese people, it is important to make this qualification. In inland Central Java, where the court cities of Solo and Yogyakarta are located, male traders are relatively scarce among the ethnic Javanese. In other parts of the island, they are found more commonly. On the north coast of Java, for instance, where Islam has had a more pervasive influence on people's lifestyles and where long-distance trade has been carried on for many centuries, more Javanese men participate in trade than in the inland regions. For further discussion of the ethnic division of trade in Java and the dominance of women traders among

ethnic Javanese, see Alexander and Alexander 1991, and Brenner 1991a and 1991b.

8. Collecting and caring for songbirds of various types is a favorite hobby of members of the traditional *priyayi* aristocracy, primarily males. Many non-*priyayi* men, usually men of means, also devote their leisure time, and often considerable sums of money, to the cultivation of birds.

9. The Javanese term *dradjad* (*derajat* in Indonesian) can be glossed as "status." However, numerous other terms are used to refer to status in its different aspects.

10. These stereotypes remain in place even in the face of evidence to the contrary. Many ethnic Chinese in Solo actually do have an excellent command of Javanese language and etiquette, but they tend to be pointed to by Javanese as "exceptions to the rule." In general, ethnic Chinese in Java speak Indonesian (the national language, which has relatively few status indicators) or low Javanese on a day-to-day basis, but many have also learned high or refined (*alus*) Javanese and speak it with their Javanese acquaintances or customers.

11. On the definition and cultural significance of the term *kasar* and its polar opposite *alus,* see C. Geertz 1960.

12. For a specific analysis of gender differences with regard to speech styles in Java, see Smith-Hefner 1988: 535–54.

13. Keeler points out quite appropriately that women are certainly as capable as men of speaking and behaving in a refined and dignified manner when they choose to do so, and women who do behave in a consistently refined manner are accorded due respect. But the relative lack of constraints on women's speech compared to men's permits them to use a wider range of styles in various contexts, and it is this latitude that leads to the stereotypes about women's "lack of control" over their speech. For further discussion of the interplay of speech, gender, and potency, see Keeler 1990.

14. The term *nafsu* (a term of Arabic origin) or *hawa nafsu,* is used in Javanese as well as Malay and Indonesian. In *The Rope of God* (1969), James Siegel shows that the Islamic concept of *hawa nafsu* (human beings' instinctive nature, their passions and desires) and its opposite, *akal* (also derived from Arabic), reason or rationality, form the basis for conceptualizing both internal experience and social relations

among the Acehnese of North Sumatra, Indonesia. Although all human beings have the capacity to control their *hawa nafsu* with *akal*, which is developed and guided through prayer and religious practice, Acehnese men believe that they possess more *akal* than women, giving them greater self-control and a moral superiority legitimated by God. This paradigm of human nature appears to accord with mainstream Muslim gender ideologies, according to Rosen (1984), who found these ideas to be widespread in Morocco. Similar ideas are also found among Bedouins of Egypt (Abu–Lughod 1986), Malays (Ong 1987, 1990), and other Muslim populations, such as the Mombasa Swahili (Swartz 1991).

15. Under Indonesian and Islamic law, Muslim men may have up to four wives at the same time, although polygyny is officially discouraged by the government.

16. Whether Solo represents the norm or an exception to the general rule in this sense is a question that deserves further investigation.

17. For a description of the *arisan* in Java, see C. Geertz 1962.

18. "Memburu Kepuasan: Seks di Kalangan Wanita Jawa," *Wawasan*, April 3, 1988, p. 1.

19. Hildred Geertz found during her fieldwork in the 1950s that adultery was widespread among the Javanese, but carried little moral weight. She observes that, "each partner is constantly on the watch to catch the other in a misstep, and both are also looking out for a chance for an illicit affair—although women are less likely either to have such a chance or to take advantage of it after they have children" (1961: 128).

20. A discussion of the historical factors that shaped the gendered and ethnic division of trade in Java is beyond the scope of the present paper, though these are discussed in Brenner 1991a and 1991b, and in Alexander and Alexander 1991. Further exploration of why men avoid the marketplace would also involve consideration of the broader ethnographic setting, and the fact that women rather than men dominate the marketplace not only in Java, but also in many other parts of Indonesia and Southeast Asia. The prevalence of women traders throughout Southeast Asia does not invalidate or make irrelevant specifically Javanese understandings of this gendered division of labor, however, for in each region the meanings of trade, money, and gender are interpreted within the framework of local histories and cultural constructions.

REFERENCES

Abu-Lughod, Lila. 1986. *Veiled Sentiments: Honor and Poetry in a Bedouin Society.* Berkeley: University of California Press.

Alexander, Jennifer, and Paul Alexander. 1991. "Protecting Peasants from Capitalism: The Subordination of Javanese Traders by the Colonial State." *Comparative Studies in Society and History* 33(2):370–394.

Anderson, Benedict R. O'G. 1972. "The Idea of Power in Javanese Culture." In C. Holt, B. Anderson, and J. Siegel, eds., *Culture and Politics in Indonesia,* pp. 1–69. Ithaca: Cornell University Press.

———. 1990. "Further Adventures of Charisma." *In Language and Power: Exploring Political Cultures in Indonesia,* pp. 78–93. Ithaca: Cornell University Press.

Atmowiloto, Arswendo. 1986. *Canting.* Jakarta: PT Gramedia Press.

Brenner, Suzanne A. 1991a. "Competing Hierarchies: Javanese Merchants and the *Priyayi* Elite in Solo, Central Java." *Indonesia* 52:55–83.

———. 1991b. "Domesticating the Market: History, Culture, and Economy in a Javanese Merchant Community." Ph.D. diss. Cornell University.

Deventer, C. Th. van. 1904. *Overzicht van den Economischen Toestand der Inlandsche Bevolking van Java en Madoera.* The Hague: Martintis Nijhoff.

De Wit, Augusta. [1912] 1984. *Java: Facts and Fancies.* Singapore: Oxford University Press.

Djajadiningrat—Nieuwenhuis, Madelon. 1987. "Ibuism and Priyayization: Path to Power?" In Elsbeth Locher-Scholten and Anke Niehof, eds., *Indonesian Women in Focus,* pp. 43–51. Dordrecht: Foris Publications.

Errington, J. Joseph. 1984. "Self and Self-Conduct among the Traditional Javanese." *American Ethnologist* 11:275–290.

———. 1988. *Structure and Style in Javanese: A Semiotic View of Linguistic Etiquette.* Philadelphia: University of Pennsylvania Press.

Errington, Shelly. 1990. "Recasting Sex, Gender, and Power: A Theoretical and Regional Overview." In Jane M. Atkinson and Shelly Errington, eds., *Power and Difference: Gender in Island Southeast Asia,* pp. 1–58. Stanford: Stanford University Press.

Flax, Jane. 1990. "Postmodernism and Gender Relations in Feminist Theory." In Linda Nicholson, ed., *Feminism/Postmodernism,* pp. 39—62. New York: Routledge.

Geertz, Clifford. 1960. *The Religion of Java.* Chicago: University of Chicago Press.

———. 1962. "The Rotating Credit Association: A 'Middle Rung' in Development." *Economic Development and Cultural Change* 10(3):241–263.

Geertz, Hildred. 1961. *The Javanese Family: A Study of Kinship and Socialization.* Glencoe, Ill.: Free Press.

Gramsci, Antonio. 1957. *The Modern Prince and Other Writings.* Trans. Louis Marks. New York: International Publishers.

Hart, Gillian. 1986. *Power, Labor, and Livelihood: Processes of Change in Rural Java.* Berkeley: University of California Press.

Hatley, Barbara. 1990. "Theatrical Imagery and Gender Ideology in Java." In Jane M. Atkinson and Shelly Errington, eds., *Power and Difference: Gender in Island Southeast Asia,* pp. 177–207. Stanford: Stanford University Press.

Jay, Robert. 1969. *Javanese Villagers: Social Relations in Rural Modjokuto.* Cambridge, Mass.: MIT Press.

Keeler, Ward. 1984. *Javanese: A Cultural Approach.* Monographs in International Studies, Southeast Asia Series, no. 69. Athens, Ohio: Ohio University.

———. 1987. *Javanese Shadow Plays, Javanese Selves.* Princeton: Princeton University Press.

———. 1990. "Speaking of Gender in Java." In Jane M. Atkinson and Shelly Errington, eds., *Power and Difference: Gender in Island Southeast Asia,* pp. 127–152. Stanford: Stanford University Press.

Koentjaraningrat. 1985. *Javanese Culture.* Singapore: Oxford University Press.

Mernissi, Fatima. 1987. *Beyond the Veil. Male-Female Dynamics in Modern Muslim Society.* Rev. ed. Bloomington: Indiana University Press.

Ong, Aihwa. 1987. *Spirits of Resistance and Capitalist Discipline: Factory Women in Malaysia.* Albany: SUNY Press.

———. 1990. "Japanese Factories, Malay Workers: Class and Sexual Metaphors in West Malaysia." In Jane M. Atkinson and Shelly Errington, eds., *Power and Difference: Gender in Island Southeast Asia,* pp. 385–422. Stanford: Stanford University Press.

Ortner, Sherry. 1989–90. "Gender Hegemonies." *Cultural Critique* 14:35–80.

Ortner, Sherry, and Harriet Whitehead. 1981. "Introduction: Accounting for Sexual Meanings," In Sherry Ortner and Harriet Whitehead, eds., *Sexual Meanings: The Cultural Construction of Gender and Sexuality,* pp. 1–27. Cambridge: Cambridge University Press.

Papanek, Hanna, and Laurel Schwede. 1988. "Women Are Good with Money: Earning and Managing in an Indonesian City." In D. Dwyer and J. Bruce, eds., *A Home Divided: Women and Income in the Third World,* pp. 71–98. Stanford: Stanford University Press.

Peletz, Michael. 1995. "Neither Reasonable Nor Responsible: Contrasting Representations of Masculinity in Malay Society." In Aihwa Ong and Michael Peletz, eds., *Bewitching Women, Pious Men,* pp. 76–123. Berkeley: University of California Press.

Raffles, Thomas Stamford. [1817] 1965. *The History of Java.* 2 vols. Kuala Lumpur: Oxford University Press.

Rosen, Lawrence. 1984. *Bargaining for Reality: The Construction of Social Relations in a Muslim Community.* Chicago: University of Chicago Press.

Siegel, James T. 1969. *The Rope of God.* Berkeley: University of California Press.

———. 1986. *Solo in the New Order: Language and Hierarchy in an Indonesian City.* Princeton: Princeton University Press.

Smith-Hefner, Nancy J. 1988. "Women and Politeness: The Javanese Example." *Language in Society* 17:535–554.

Spivak, Gayatri Chakravorty. 1987. "Explanation and Culture: Marginalia." In *In Other Worlds: Essays in Cultural Politics,* pp. 103–117. New York: Routledge.

Stoler, Ann L. 1977. "Class Structure and Female Autonomy in Rural Java." *Signs* 3(1):74–89.

Sutherland, Heather. 1979. *The Making of a Bureaucratic Elite.* ASAA Southeast Asia publications series. Singapore: Heinemann.

Swartz, Marc J. 1991. *The Way the World Is: Cultural Processes and Social Relations among the Mombasa Swahili.* Berkeley: University of California Press.

Tsing, Anna L. 1990. "Gender and Performance in Meratus Dispute Settlement." In Jane Atkinson and Shelly Errington, eds., *Power and Difference: Gender in Island Southeast Asia,* pp. 95–125. Stanford: Stanford University Press.

Yanagisako, Sylvia, and Jane Collier. 1987. "Toward a Unified Analysis of Gender and Kinship." In Jane Collier and Sylvia Yanagisako, eds., *Gender and Kinship: Essays toward a Unified Analysis,* pp. 14–50. Stanford: Stanford University Press.

IV

The Cultural Construction of Gender and Personhood

We all live in a world of symbols that assign meaning and value to the categories of male and female. Despite several decades of consciousness raising in the United States, advertising on television and in the print media perpetuates sexual stereotypes. Although "house beautiful" ads are less prominent as women are increasingly shown in workplace contexts, "body beautiful" messages continue to be transmitted. In children's cartoons, women are still the helpless victims that the fearless male hero must rescue. Toys are targeted either for little boys or little girls and are packaged appropriately in colors and materials culturally defined as either masculine or feminine.

To what extent are these stereotypes of men and women and the symbols with which they are associated universal? If they are universal, to what extent are they rooted in observed differences in the biological nature of men and women that are made culturally significant? These questions have interested scholars as they have attempted to account for both similarity and difference among the people of the world. Making the assumption that the subordination of women exists in all societies—a "true universal"—Ortner (1974: 67) sought to explain the pervasiveness of this idea not in the assignation of women to a domestic sphere of activity, but in the symbolic constructions by which women's roles are evaluated. Ortner argues that women, because of their reproductive roles, are universally viewed as being closer to nature while men are linked with culture. She defines culture as "the notion of human consciousness, or...the products of human consciousness (i.e., systems of thought and technology), by means of which humanity attempts to assert control over nature" (72). That which is cultural and subject to human manipulation is assigned more worth than that which is natural; hence, women and women's roles are denigrated or devalued, whether explicitly or implicitly.

The nature–culture dichotomy is a useful explanatory model in the United States where, according to Martin (1987: 17), "Women are intrinsically closely involved with the family where so many 'natural,' 'bodily' (and therefore lower) functions occur, whereas men are intrinsically closely involved with the world of work where (at least for some) 'cultural,' 'mental,' and therefore higher functions occur. It is no accident that 'natural' facts about women, in the form of claims about biology, are often used to justify social stratification based on gender."

Although this model may be applicable in some cultures, its universality has been challenged not only by those who point out that nature–culture is a dichotomy of western thought in particular (Bloch and Bloch 1980; Jordanova 1980; Moore 1988), but also by those who provide ethnographic data to indicate its lack of salience in other cultures around the world (Strathern 1980). Similarly, the assumption that women are universally subordinated while men are dominant (Ortner 1974: 70) appears questionable when viewed through the lens of recent ethnographic reanalyses. The critique of the concepts of universal subordination and of the nature–culture dichotomy has stimulated significant research on how gender identity and gender roles are constructed in particular cultural contexts (Errington and Gewertz 1987; Ortner and Whitehead 1981; Weiner 1976). Whether and under what conditions social asymmetry between men and women emerges in the process of this construction is open to empirical investigation.

The cultural construction of gender in a particular society involves definitions of what it means to be masculine or feminine, and these definitions vary cross-culturally. Although masculinity is thought to have a powerful biological component in the United States, among the Sambia of New Guinea it is constructed in the context of ritual. The Sambia, like many other societies in New Guinea (Brown and Buchbinder 1976; Herdt 1982; Meigs 1984), are characterized by a high degree of segregation and sexual antagonism between men and women, both of which are reinforced by powerful taboos. These taboos, and other facets of Sambian male identity including that of the warrior, are inculcated during a series of initiation rituals whereby boys are "grown" into men. As Herdt (in this book) observes, the Sambia "perceive no imminent, naturally driven fit between one's birthright sex and one's gender identity or role" (1982: 54). Indeed, Sambian boys and men engage in what some societies would label homosexual activity, yet they do it to create masculinity. It is precisely for this reason that an analytical distinction is often made between "sex" as a biological classification and "gender" as a set of learned social roles.

Through the rituals of manhood Sambian boys are progressively detached from the world of women, a world they occupied for the first six or seven years of their lives and which they must now learn to both fear and devalue. This process of detachment has been identified by Chodorow (1974) as a major phase of human male development. If it is unmarked and therefore ambiguous in most western cultures, it is marked in many nonwestern cultures and often associated with male circumcision. Among the Mende of Sierra Leone (Little 1951), for example, boy initiates are seized from their homes by the force of spirits—men wearing masks and long raffia skirts. In this act they are dramatically and suddenly separated from their childhood, and carried into the bush where they will spend several weeks in seclusion and transition before they reemerge as men.

Initiation rituals that prepare girls for their roles as women and instruct them in what it means to be a woman in a particular cultural context can also be found in various societies around the world (Brown 1963; Richards 1956). However, the transition to womanhood is often part of a more subtle and continuous process of enculturation and socialization. In a description of Hausa socialization Callaway (1987) demonstrates how girls in this society learn how to behave in culturally appropriate ways. The Hausa are an Islamic people who live in northern Nigeria.

Historically, ruling-class Hausa women had significant authority and social standing, but with the expansion of Islam this position was eroded and a sexually segregated society characterized by female subordination emerged. Hausa girls marry young, generally upon reaching puberty. At that time they enter *kulle*, or seclusion. In seclusion, the social roles of women are specifically defined and their sexual activities are limited. Though a Hausa woman becomes part of her husband's family, her place is secured only by bearing sons, and all her children belong to her husband. Hausa women are taught the expected life course from early childhood. In Hausa society, Callaway (1987: 22) claims, "the reproduction of 'masculine' and 'feminine' personalities generation after generation has produced psychological and value commitments to sex differences that are tenaciously maintained and so deeply ingrained as to become central to a consistent sense of self." This self is defined by reproductive roles and by deference to men; thus a good daughter-in-law gives her first-born child to her husband's mother, an act that strengthens family ties.

Conceptions of the self or personhood are, as Henrietta Moore (1988: 39) has observed, "cross-culturally as variable as the concepts of 'woman' and 'man.'" Personhood is constituted by a variety of attributes. In addition to gender, it may comprise age, status in the family and in the community, and physical appearance or impairment. In many cultures naming is also an important mechanism for constructing personhood. In the United States, for instance, the use of Ms. to replace Mrs. and Miss is an acceptable option. It is increasingly common for married women to retain the name that they were born with rather than replace it with one that only gives them an identity in relation to someone else—their husband.

Among the Chambri of New Guinea, initial identity or personhood is gained through a totemic name given by a child's patrilineal and matrilateral relatives. According to Errington and Gewertz (1987: 32, 47), "these names both reflect and affect the transactions which constitute a person's fundamental social relationships and identity....Totemic names allow both men and women to pursue respectively their culturally defined preoccupations of political competition and the bearing of children. The totemic names available to men, however, convey different sorts of power and resources than do those available to women....Men seek to augment their own power through gaining control of the names of others....The power conveyed by [women's] names cannot shape social relationships as does the power of names men hold, but, instead, ensures reproduction."

Women's names among the Chambri work in different ways from those of men, but they nonetheless enable women to claim personhood in Chambri society. The married Chinese women described by Watson (in this book) have an entirely different experience. They are denied individuating names, and through this denial their personhood is in question. They remain, says Watson, "suspended between the anonymous world of anybodies and the more sharply defined world of somebodies." In contrast with the namelessness of Chinese women, men in Chinese culture acquire numerous names as they pass through the life cycle. Nowhere is the difference more apparent than at marriage—a time when a man acquires a name that symbolizes his new status and public roles and a woman loses her girlhood name and becomes the "inner person." Like the Hausa women who assume an identity with respect to their husbands, Chinese women begin newly married life by learning the names and kinship terms for all their husbands' ancestors and relatives. Namelessness follows them to the grave—anybodies in life, they become nobodies at death.

In many societies personhood for women is also associated with conceptions of the body and often centers on reproductive functions. One reproductive process that has particular salience is menstruation. Understandings of the symbolic meanings of menstruation influence men's and women's ideologies of gender. Buckley and Gottlieb (in this book) review symbolic analyses of menstrual taboos built on the concept of "pollution." These analyses contend that menstrual blood and menstruating women are widely viewed as dangerous; accordingly, taboos have been devised to contain women's symbolic contamination. Douglas (1966) proposes that "pollutants" represent matter out of place. Menstrual blood, for example, is out of place in that it breaches the boundaries of the body, does not issue accidentally from a wound, and is one of the rare acts in which women normatively let blood. As an anomaly, menstruation carries a certain symbolic power. Douglas also posits a close relationship between ideas about the physical and social body. Thus, menstrual blood might be seen as polluting when it reflects an underlying structural ambiguity or contradiction regarding women and women's power. Buckley and Gottlieb access the limits of these influential pollution theories, and critique the notion that women are passive recipients of male-created cultures. The treatment of pollution concepts may reflect male domination of the ethnographic record as researchers and as informants. They argue that there is a need to consult female informants before reaching conclusions about the status of menstruation as polluting in any given society.

Buckley (1982) addresses male bias and the female perspective on menstruation in his discussion of menstrual beliefs and practices among the Yurok Indians of North America. In his reanalysis of Yurok data Buckley found that while precontact Yurok men considered women, through their menstrual blood, to be dangerous, Yurok women viewed menstruation as a positive source of power. Rather than looking on the forced monthly seclusion as isolating and oppressive, women viewed it as a source of strength and sanctuary.

By contrast, among numerous groups in New Guinea, men perceive menstrual blood as dangerously polluting and engage in a range of symbolic behaviors to cleanse themselves of what they believe are the harmful effects of contact with women—for example, tongue scraping and smokehouse purification. The Mae Enga, for example, believe that "contact with [menstrual blood] or a menstruating woman will, in the absence of appropriate counter-magic, sicken a man and cause persistent vomiting, turn his blood black, corrupt his vital juices so that his skin darkens and wrinkles as his flesh wastes, permanently dull his wits, and eventually lead to a slow decline and death" (Meggitt 1964: 207).

Male beliefs about the dangers of menstrual blood can be found in a number of other cultures around the world (Buckley and Gottlieb 1988). In some contexts men appear to devalue female reproductive roles by defining menstruation as the unfortunate lot of women. For example, a creation story of a group of pastoral nomads in northern Iran goes as follows: "In the beginning men had menstruation and not women. But blood would go down their pants and it was very uncomfortable. So they went to God and complained about their situation, asking Him to give menstruation to women who had skirts. At the time of childbirth, it used to be men who had pains. Again they complained to God, and He gave the pain to women, as He had done with menstruation" (Shahshahani 1986: 87).

This creation story, like many beliefs about menstrual pollution, represents a male view that not only associates women with nature and men with culture, but also helps to explain and support sexual asymmetry in that culture. However, Rosaldo

(1974: 38) and others (Gottlieb 1982; Keesing 1985; Lawrence 1988; Powers 1986) have suggested that pollution beliefs can provide a source of power and form the basis for solidarity among women. This body of work suggests that the male point of view is not wrong or unimportant, but that it is only a partial representation. Gender roles and gender identities are constructed by both men and women in any society.

REFERENCES

Bloch, Maurice and Jean Bloch. 1980. "Women and the Dialectics of Nature in Eighteenth-Century French Thought." In Carol MacCormack and Marilyn Strathern (eds.). *Nature, Culture and Gender,* pp. 25–41. Cambridge: Cambridge University Press.

Brown, Judith K. 1963. "A Cross-Cultural Study of Female Initiation Rites Among Pre-Literate Peoples." *American Anthropologist* 65(4): 837–853.

Brown, Paula and Georgeda Buchbinder. 1976. *Man and Woman in the New Guinea Highlands.* Washington, DC: American Anthropological Association, Special Publication, number 8.

Buckley, Thomas. 1982. "Menstruation and the Power of Yurok Women: Methods in Cultural Reconstruction." *American Ethnologist* 9: 47–60.

Buckley, Thomas and Alma Gottlieb (eds.). 1988. *Blood Magic: The Anthropology of Menstruation.* Berkeley: University of California Press.

Callaway, Barbara J. 1987. *Muslim Hausa Women in Nigeria: Tradition and Change.* Syracuse: Syracuse University Press.

Chodorow, Nancy. 1974. "Family Structure and Feminine Personality." In Michele Z. Rosaldo and Louise Lamphere (eds.). *Woman, Culture, and Society,* pp. 43–67. Stanford: Stanford University Press.

Douglas, Mary. 1966. *Purity and Danger: An Analysis of Concepts of Pollution and Taboo.* London: Routledge and Kegan Paul.

Errington, Frederick and Deborah Gewertz. 1987. *Cultural Alternatives and a Feminist Anthropology: An Analysis of Culturally Constructed Gender Interests in Papua New Guinea.* Cambridge: Cambridge University Press.

Gottlieb, Alma. 1982. "Sex, Fertility and Menstruation Among the Beng of the Ivory Coast: A Symbolic Analysis." *Africa* 52(4): 34–47.

Herdt, Gilbert. 1982. *Rituals of Manhood: Male Initiation in Papua New Guinea.* Berkeley and Los Angeles: University of California Press.

Jordanova, L. J. 1980. "Natural Facts: A Historical Perspective on Science and Sexuality." In Carol MacCormack and Marilyn Strathern (eds.). *Nature, Culture and Gender,* pp. 42–69. Cambridge: Cambridge University Press.

Keesing, Roger. 1985. "Kwaio Women Speak: The Micropolitics of Autobiography in a Solomon Island Society." *American Anthropologist* 87: 27–39.

Lawrence, Denise. 1988. "Menstrual Politics: Women and Pigs in Rural Portugal." In Thomas Buckley and Alma Gottlieb (eds.). *The Anthropology of Menstruation,* pp. 117–136. Berkeley: University of California Press.

Little, Kenneth L. 1951. *The Mende of Sierra Leone: A West African People in Transition.* London: Routledge and Kegan Paul.

Martin, Emily. 1987. *The Woman in the Body: A Cultural Analysis of Reproduction.* Boston: Beacon Press.

Meggitt, M. J. 1964. "Male-Female Relationships in the Highlands of Australian New Guinea." *American Anthropologist* 66(4, part 2): 204–224.

Meigs, Anna S. 1984. *Food, Sex, and Pollution: A New Guinea Religion.* New Brunswick, NJ: Rutgers University Press.

Moore, Henrietta. 1988. *Feminism and Anthropology.* Minneapolis: University of Minnesota Press.

Ortner, Sherry. 1974. "Is Female to Male as Nature to Culture?" In Michelle Z. Rosaldo and Louise Lamphere (eds.). *Woman, Culture, and Society*, pp. 66–87. Stanford: Stanford University Press.

Ortner, Sherry and Harriet Whitehead. 1981. *Sexual Meanings: The Cultural Construction of Gender and Sexuality*. Cambridge: Cambridge University Press.

Powers, Marla. 1986. *Oglala Women*. Chicago: University of Chicago Press.

Richards, Audrey I. 1956. *Chisungu: A Girls' Initiation Ceremony among the Bemba of Northern Rhodesia*. London: Faber and Faber.

Rosaldo, Michelle. 1974. "Woman, Culture, and Society: A Theoretical Overview." In Michelle Z. Rosaldo and Louise Lamphere (eds.). *Woman, Culture, and Society*, pp. 17–42. Stanford: Stanford University Press.

Shahshahani, Soheila. 1986. "Women Whisper, Men Kill: A Case Study of the Mamasani Pastoral Nomads of Iran." In Leela Dube, Eleanor Leacock, and Shirley Ardener (eds.). *Visibility and Power: Essays on Women in Society and Development*, pp. 85–97. Delhi: Oxford University Press.

Strathern, Marilyn. 1980. "No Nature, No Culture: The Hagen Case." In Carol MacCormack and Marilyn Strathern (eds.). *Nature, Culture and Gender*, pp. 174–222. Cambridge: Cambridge University Press.

Weiner, Annette. 1976. *Women of Value, Men of Renown*. Austin: University of Texas Press.

Rituals of Manhood: Male Initiation in Papua New Guinea

Gilbert H. Herdt

Sambia are a mountain-dwelling hunting and horticultural people who number some 2,000 persons and inhabit one of New Guinea's most rugged terrains. The population is dispersed through narrow river valleys over a widespread, thinly populated rain forest; rainfall is heavy; and even today the surrounding mountain ranges keep the area isolated. Sambia live on the fringes of the Highlands, but they trace their origins to the Papua hinterlands; their culture and economy thus reflect a mixture of influences from both of those areas. Hunting still predominates as a masculine activity through which most meat protein is acquired. As in the Highlands, though,

Reprinted with permission from Gilbert H. Herdt, *Rituals of Manhood: Male Initiation in Papua New Guinea* (Berkeley, University of California Press, 1982), pp. 50–57. Copyright ©1982 The Regents of the University of California.

sweet potatoes and taro are the staple crops, and their cultivation is for the most part women's work. Pigs are few, and they have no ceremonial or exchange significance; indigenous marsupials, such as possum and tree kangaroo, provide necessary meat prestations for all initiations and ceremonial feasts (cf. Meigs 1976).

Sambia settlements are small, well-defended, mountain clan hamlets. These communities comprise locally based descent groups organized through a strong agnatic idiom. Residence is patrivirilocal, and most men actually reside in their father's hamlets. Clans are exogamous, and one or more of them together constitute a hamlet's landowning corporate agnatic body. These men also form a localized warriorhood that is sometimes allied with other hamlets in matters of fighting, marriage, and ritual.

Each hamlet contains one or two men's club-houses, in addition to women's houses, and the men's ritual life centers on their club-house. Marriage is usually by sister exchange or infant betrothal, although the latter form of prearranged marriage is culturally preferred. Intrahamlet marriage is occasionally more frequent (up to 50 percent of all marriages in my own hamlet field site) than one would expect in such small segmentary groupings, an involutional pattern weakened since pacification.

Sambia male and female residential patterns differ somewhat from those of other Highlands peoples. The nuclear family is an important subunit of the hamlet-based extended family of interrelated clans. A man, his wife, and their children usually cohabit within a single, small, round hut. Children are thus reared together by their parents during the early years of life, so the nuclear family is a residential unit, an institution virtually unknown to the Highlands (Meggitt 1964; Read 1954). Sometimes this unit is expanded through polygyny, in which case a man, his cowives, and their children may occupy the single dwelling. Girls continue to reside with their parents until marriage (usually near the menarche, around fifteen to seventeen years of age). Boys, however, are removed to the men's clubhouse at seven to ten years of age, following their first-stage initiation. There they reside exclusively until marriage and cohabitation years later. Despite familial cohabitation in early childhood, strict taboos based on beliefs about menstrual pollution still separate men and women in their sleeping and eating arrangements.

Warfare used to be constant and nagging among Sambia, and it conditioned the values and masculine stereotypes surrounding the male initiatory cult. Ritualized bow fights occurred among neighboring hamlets, whose members still intermarried and usually initiated their sons together. At the same time, though, hamlets also united against enemy tribes and in staging war parties against them. Hence, warfare, marriage, and initiation were interlocking institutions; the effect of this

political instability was to reinforce tough, strident masculine performance in most arenas of social life. "Strength" (*jerundu*) was—and is—a pivotal idea in this male ethos. Indeed, strength, which has both ethnobiological and behavioral aspects, could be aptly translated as "maleness" and "manliness." Strength has come to be virtually synonymous with idealized conformity to male ritual routine. Before conquest and pacification by the Australians, though, strength had its chief performative significance in one's conduct on the battlefield. Even today bitter reminders of war linger on among the Sambia; and we should not forget that it is against the harsh background of the warrior's existence that Sambia initiate their boys, whose only perceived protection against the inconstant world is their own unbending masculinity.

Initiation rests solely in the hands of the men's secret society. It is this organization that brings the collective initiatory cycle into being as jointly performed by neighboring hamlets (and as constrained by their own chronic bow fighting). The necessary feast-crop gardens, ritual leadership, and knowledge dictate that a handful of elders, war leaders, and ritual experts be in full command of the actual staging of the event. Everyone and all else are secondary.

There are six intermittent initiations from the ages of seven to ten and onward. They are, however, constituted and conceptualized as two distinct cultural systems within the male life cycle. First-stage (*moku*, at seven to ten years of age), second-stage (*imbutu*, at ten to thirteen years), and third-stage (*ipmangwi*, at thirteen to sixteen years) initiations—bachelorhood rites—are collectively performed for regional groups of boys as age-mates. The initiations are held in sequence, as age-graded advancements; the entire sequel takes months to perform. The focus of all these initiations is the construction and habitation of a great cult house (*moo-angu*) on a traditional dance ground; its ceremonialized building inaugurates the whole cycle. Fourth-stage (*nuposha:* sixteen years and onward), fifth-stage (*taiketnyi*), and sixth-stage (*moondangu*) initiations are, conversely, individually centered events not associated with the confederacy of interrelated hamlets, cult house, or dance ground. Each of these initiations, like the preceding ones, does have its own ritual status, social role, and title, as noted. The triggering event for the latter three initiations, unlike that for the bachelorhood rites, is not the building of a cult house or a political agreement of hamlets to act collectively but is rather the maturing femininity and life-crisis events of the women assigned in marriage to youths (who become the initiated novices). Therefore, fourth-stage initiation is only a semipublic activity organized by the youths' clansmen (and some male affines). Its secret purificatory and other rites are followed by the formal marriage ceremony in the hamlet. Fifth-stage initiation comes at a woman's menarche, when her husband is secretly introduced to additional purification and sexual techniques. Sixth-stage initiation issues from the birth of a man's wife's first child. This event is, de jure, the attainment of manhood. (The first birth is elaborately ritualized and celebrated; the next three births are also celebrated, but in more truncated fashion.) Two children bring full adulthood (*aatmwunu*) for husband and wife alike. Birth ceremonies are suspended after the fourth birth, since there is no reason to belabor what is by now obvious: a man has proved himself competent in reproduction. This sequence of male initiations forms the basis for male development, and it underlies the antagonistic tenor of relationships between the sexes.

It needs stating only once that men's secular rhetoric and ritual practices depict women as dangerous and polluting inferiors whom men are to distrust throughout their lives. In this regard, Sambia values and relationships pit men against women even more markedly, I think, than occurs in other Highlands communities (cf. Brown and Buchbinder 1976; Meggitt 1964; Read 1954). Men hold themselves as the superiors of women in physique, personality, and social position. And this dogma of male supremacy permeates all social relationships and institutions, likewise coloring domestic behavior among the sexes

(cf. Tuzin 1980 for an important contrast). Men fear not only pollution from contact with women's vaginal fluids and menstrual blood but also the depletion of their semen, the vital spark of maleness, which women (and boys, too) inevitably extract, sapping a man's substance. These are among the main themes of male belief underlying initiation.

The ritualized simulation of maleness is the result of initiation, and men believe the process to be vital for the nature and nurture of manly growth and well-being. First-stage initiation begins the process in small boys. Over the ensuing ten to fifteen years, until marriage, cumulative initiations and residence in the men's house are said to promote biological changes that firmly cement the growth from childhood to manhood. Nature provides male genitals, it is true; but nature alone does not bestow the vital spark biologically necessary for stimulating masculine growth or demonstrating cold-blooded self-preservation.

New Guinea specialists will recognize in the Sambia belief system a theme that links it to the comparative ethnography of male initiation and masculine development: the use of ritual procedures for sparking, fostering, and maintaining manliness in males (see Berndt 1962; Meigs 1976; Newman 1964, 1965; Poole 1981; Read 1965; Salisbury 1965; Strathern 1969, 1970). Sambia themselves refer to the results of first-stage collective initiation—our main interest—as a means of "growing a boy"; and this trend of ritual belief is particularly emphatic.

Unlike ourselves, Sambia perceive no imminent, naturally driven fit between one's birthright sex and one's gender identity or role.[1] Indeed, the problem (and it is approached as a situation wanting a solution) is implicitly and explicitly understood in quite different terms. The solution is also different for the two sexes: men believe that a girl is born with all of the vital organs and fluids necessary for her to attain reproductive competence through "natural" maturation. This conviction is embodied in cultural perceptions of the girl's development beginning with the sex assignment at birth. What distinguishes a girl (*tai*) from a boy (*kwulai'u*) is obvious: "A boy has a penis, and a girl does not," men say. Underlying men's communications is a conviction that maleness, unlike femaleness, is not a biological given. It must be artificially induced through secret ritual; and that is a personal achievement.

The visible manifestations of girls' fast-growing reproductive competence, noticed first in early motor coordination and speech and then later in the rapid attainment of height and secondary sex traits (e.g., breast development), are attributed to inner biological properties. Girls possess a menstrual-blood organ, or *tingu*, said to precipitate all those events and the menarche. Boys, on the other hand, are thought to possess an inactive tingu. They do possess, however, another organ—the *kere-ku-kereku*, or semen organ—that is thought to be the repository of semen, the very essence of maleness and masculinity; but this organ is not functional at birth, since it contains no semen naturally and can only store, never produce, any. Only oral insemination, men believe, can activate the boy's semen organ, thereby precipitating his push into adult reproductive competence. In short, femininity unfolds naturally, whereas masculinity must be achieved; and here is where the male ritual cult steps in.

Men also perceive the early socialization risks of boys and girls in quite different terms. All infants are closely bonded to their mothers. Out of a woman's contaminating, life-giving womb pours the baby, who thereafter remains tied to the woman's body, breast milk, and many ministrations. This latter contact only reinforces the femininity and female contamination in which birth involves the infant. Then, too, the father, both because of postpartum taboos and by personal choice, tends to avoid being present at the breast-feedings. Mother thus becomes the unalterable primary influence; father is a weak second. Sambia say this does not place girls at a "risk"—they simply succumb to the drives of their "natural" biology. This maternal attachment and paternal distance clearly jeopardize the boys' growth,

however, since nothing innate within male maturation seems to resist the inhibiting effects of mothers' femininity. Hence boys must be traumatically separated—wiped clean of their female contaminants—so that their masculinity may develop.

Homosexual fellatio inseminations can follow this separation but cannot precede it, for otherwise they would go for naught. The accumulating semen, injected time and again for years, is believed crucial for the formation of biological maleness and masculine comportment. This native perspective is sufficiently novel to justify our using a special concept for aiding description and analysis of the data: masculinization (Herdt 1981:205 ff). Hence I shall refer to the overall process that involves separating a boy from his mother, initiating him, ritually treating his body, administering homosexual inseminations, his biological attainment of puberty, and his eventual reproductive competence, as *masculinization*. (Precisely what role personal and cultural fantasy plays in the negotiation of this ritual process I have considered elsewhere: see Herdt 1981: chaps. 6, 7, and 8.)

A boy has female contaminants inside of him which not only retard physical development but, if not removed, debilitate him and eventually bring death. His body is male: his tingu contains no blood and will not activate. The achievement of puberty for boys requires semen. Breast milk "nurtures the boy," and sweet potatoes or other "female" foods provide "stomach nourishment," but these substances become only feces, not semen. Women's own bodies internally produce the menarche, the hallmark of reproductive maturity. There is no comparable mechanism active in a boy, nothing that can stimulate his secondary sex traits. Only semen can do that; only men have semen; boys have none. What is left to do, then, except initiate and masculinize boys into adulthood?

NOTE

1. I follow Stoller (1968) in adhering to the following distinctions: the term *sex traits* refers to

purely biological phenomena (anatomy, hormones, genetic structure, etc.), whereas *gender* refers to those psychological and cultural attributes that compel a person (consciously or unconsciously) to sense him- or herself, and other persons, as belonging to either the male or female sex. It follows that the term *gender role* (Sears 1965), rather than the imprecise term *sex role,* refers to the normative set of expectations associated with masculine and feminine social positions.

REFERENCES

Berndt, R. M. 1962. *Excess and Restraint: Social Control among a New Guinea Mountain People.* Chicago: University of Chicago Press.

Brown, P., and G. Buchbinder (eds.). 1976. *Man and Woman in the New Guinea Highlands.* Washington, D.C.: American Anthropological Association.

Herdt, G. H. 1981. *Guardians of the Flutes: Idioms of Masculinity.* New York: McGraw-Hill.

Meggitt, M. J. 1964. Male-female relationships in the Highlands of Australian New Guinea. In *New Guinea: The Central Highlands,* ed. J. B. Watson, *American Anthropologist,* 66, pt. 2 (4):204–224.

Meigs, A. S. 1976. Male pregnancy and the reduction of sexual opposition in a New Guinea Highlands society. *Ethnology* 15 (4):393–407.

Newman, P. L. 1964. Religious belief and ritual in a New Guinea society. In *New Guinea: The Central Highlands,* ed. J. B. Watson, *American Anthropologist* 66, pt. 2 (4):257–272.

———. 1965. *Knowing the Gururumba.* New York: Holt, Rinehart and Winston.

Poole, F. J. P. 1981. Transforming "natural" woman: female ritual leaders and gender ideology among Bimin-Kuskumin. In *Sexual Meanings,* ed. S. B. Ortner and H. Whitehead. New York: Cambridge University Press.

Read, K. E. 1954. Cultures of the Central Highlands, New Guinea. *Southwestern Journal of Anthropology* 10 (1):1–43.

———. 1965. *The High Valley.* London: George Allen and Unwin.

Salisbury, R. F. 1965. The Siane of the Eastern Highlands. In *Gods, Ghosts, and Men in Melanesia,* P. Lawrence and M. J. Meggitt, pp. 50–77. Melbourne: Melbourne University Press.

Sears, R. R. 1965. Development of gender role. In *Sex and Behavior,* ed. F. A. Beach, pp. 133–163. New York: John Wiley and Sons.

Stoller, R. J. 1968. *Sex and Gender.* New York: Science House.

Strathern, A. J. 1969. Descent and alliance in the New Guinea Highlands: some problems of comparison. Royal Anthropological Institute, *Proceedings,* pp. 37–52.

———. 1970. Male initiation in the New Guinea Highlands societies. *Ethnology* 9(4):373–379.

Tuzin, D. F. 1980. *The Voice of the Tambaran: Truth and Illusion in Ilahita Arapesh Religion.* Berkeley, Los Angeles, and London: University of California Press.

The Named and the Nameless: Gender and Person in Chinese Society

Rubie S. Watson

In Chinese society names classify and individuate, they have transformative powers, and they are an important form of self-expression. Some names are private, some are chosen for

Reproduced by permission of the American Anthropological Association from *American Ethnologist* 13:4, November 1986. Not for further reproduction.

their public effect. Many people have a confusing array of names while others are nameless. The theory and practice of personal naming in Chinese society is extremely complex and unfortunately little studied.

For the male villagers of rural Hong Kong, naming marks important social transitions: the more names a man has the more "socialized" and also, in a sense, the more "individuated" he becomes. To attain social adulthood a man must have at least two names, but most have more. By the time a male reaches middle age, he may be known by four or five names. Village women, by contrast, are essentially nameless. Like boys, infant girls are named when they are one month old, but unlike boys they lose this name when they marry. Adult women are known (in reference and address) by kinship terms, teknonyms, or category terms such as "old woman."

In Chinese society personal names constitute an integral part of the language of joking, of boasting, and of exhibiting one's education and erudition. The Chinese themselves are fascinated by personal names: village men enjoy recounting stories about humorous or clumsy names, educated men appreciate the elegance of an auspicious name, and all males worry about the quality of their own names and those of their sons. To a large extent women are excluded from this discourse. They cannot participate because in adulthood they are not named, nor do they name others. Until very recently the majority of village women were illiterate and so could not engage in the intellectual games that men play with written names. Women were not even the subjects of these conversations.

The namelessness of adult women and their inability to participate in the naming of others highlights in a dramatic way the vast gender distinctions that characterize traditional Chinese culture. The study of names gives us considerable insight into the ways in which gender and person are constructed in Chinese society. Judged against the standard of men, the evidence presented here suggests that village women do not, indeed cannot, attain full personhood. The lives of men are punctuated by the acquisition of new names, new roles, new responsibilities and new privileges; women's lives, in comparison, remain indistinct and indeterminate.

In his essay "Person, Time, and Conduct in Bali," Clifford Geertz argues that our social world "is populated not by anybodies ... but by somebodies, concrete classes of determinate persons positively characterized and appropriately labeled" (1973:363). It is this process by which anybodies are converted into somebodies that concerns me here. Do men and women become "somebodies" in the same way? Are they made equally determinate, positively characterized and labeled?

Although this discussion is based primarily on field research carried out in the Hong Kong New Territories, examples of naming practices have been drawn from other areas of Chinese culture as well. It is difficult to determine the extent to which the patterns described in this paper are indicative of rural China in general.[1] Available evidence suggests that there is considerable overlap between Hong Kong patterns of male naming and those of preliberation Chinese society and present-day rural Taiwan (see for example Eberhard 1970; Kehl 1971; Sung 1981; Wu 1927). Unfortunately, there have been no studies that specifically examine the differences between men's and women's naming, although brief references in Martin Yang's study of a Shantung village (1945:124) and in Judith Stacey's account of women in the People's Republic (1983:43, 131) suggest that the gender differences discussed here are not unique to Hong Kong. In making these statements I do not wish to suggest that there are no substantial differences in personal naming between rural Hong Kong and other parts of China. A general survey of personal naming in China, especially one that takes the postrevolution era into account, has yet to be done.

This paper draws heavily on ethnographic evidence gathered in the village of Ha Tsuen, a single-lineage village located in the northwest corner of the New Territories. All males in Ha Tsuen share the surname Teng and trace descent to a common ancestor who settled in this region during the 12th century (see R. Watson 1985). For most villagers postmarital residence is virilocal/patrilocal. The Ha Tsuen Teng practice surname exogamy, which in the case of a single-lineage village means that all wives come from outside the community. These women arrive in Ha Tsuen as strangers and their early years of marriage are spent accommodating to a new family and new community. The Teng find this completely natural; "daughters," they say, "are born looking out; they belong to others."

Patrilineal values dominate social life in Ha Tsuen. Women are suspect because they are outsiders. As Margery Wolf points out, Chinese women are both marginal and essential to the families into which they marry (1972:35). They are necessary because they produce the next generation, yet as outsiders their integration is never complete. Women are economically dependent on the family estate, but they do not have shareholding rights in that estate. Half the village land in Ha Tsuen is owned by the lineage (see R. Watson 1985:61–72), and the other half is owned by private (male) landlords. Women have no share in this land; they do not own immovable property nor do they have rights to inherit it. Few married women are employed in wage labor, and since the villagers gave up serious agriculture in the 1960s, most women are dependent on their husbands' paychecks for family income. At the time I conducted my research (1977–78) Ha Tsuen had a population of approximately 2500—all of whom are Cantonese speakers.

NAMING AN INFANT

Among the Cantonese a child's soul is not thought to be firmly attached until at least 30 days after its birth. During the first month of life the child and mother are secluded from all but the immediate family. After a month has passed, the child is considered less susceptible to soul loss and is introduced into village life. The infant is given a name by his or her father or grandfather at a ceremony called "full month" (*man yueh*). If the child is a son, the "full month" festivities will be as elaborate as the family can afford; if, on the other hand, a girl is born, there may be little or no celebration (except, perhaps, a special meal for family members). The naming ceremony for

a boy normally involves a banquet for neighbors and village elders, along with the distribution of red eggs to members of the community. The first name a child is given is referred to as his or her *ming*.[2]

This name (*ming*) may be based on literary or classical allusions. It may express a wish for the child's or family's future, or it may enshrine some simple event that took place at or near the time of the child's birth. Examples of this kind of naming are found not only in Ha Tsuen but in other areas of China as well. Arlington, in an early paper on Chinese naming, describes how the name "sleeve" was given to a girl of his acquaintance who at the time of her birth had been wrapped in a sleeve (1923:319). In the People's Republic of China, people born during the Korean War might be called "Resist the United States" (Fan-mei) or "Aid Korea" (Pang-ch'ao). Alternatively, children may be given the name of their birthplace, for example, "Born in Anhwei" (Hui-sheng) or "Thinking of Yunnan" (Hsiang-yun). In the past girl babies might be named Nai ("To Endure"). This name was given to infant girls who survived an attempted infanticide. One way of killing an infant was to expose it to the elements. If a girl survived this ordeal, she might be allowed to live. In these cases the name Nai commemorated the child's feat of survival.[3]

A child's name may express the parents' desire for no more children. For instance, in Taiwan a fifth or sixth child may be named Beui, a Hokkien term meaning "Last Child." Alternatively, a father may try to ensure that his next child will be a son by naming a newborn daughter "Joined to Brother" (Lien-ti). There are several girls with this name in Ha Tsuen. A father or grandfather might express his disappointment or disgust by naming a second or third daughter "Too Many" (A-to)[4] or "Little Mistake" (Hsiao-t'so) or "Reluctant to Feed" (Wang-shih). A sickly child might be given the name of a healthy child. My informants told me that a long-awaited son may be given a girl's name to trick the wandering ghosts into thinking the child had no value and therefore could be ignored (see also Sung 1981:81–82). For example, a Ha Tsuen villager, who was the only son of a wealthy family (born to his father's third concubine), was known by everyone as "Little Slave Girl" (in Cantonese, Mui-jai).

In most cases the infant receives a *ming* during the full month ceremony but this name is little used. For the first year or two most children are called by a family nickname ("milk name" or *nai ming*). Babies are sometimes given milk names like "Precious" (A-pao), or A-buh (mimicking the sounds infants make) or "Eldest Luck," or "Second Luck," indicating sibling order.

Some care and consideration is given to a child's *ming*, especially if it is a boy. By referring to the Confucian classics or by alluding to a famous poem, the name may express the learning and sophistication of the infant's father or grandfather. The name, as we will see, may also save the child from an inauspicious fate. Commonly girls' names (*ming*) are less distinctive and less considered than are boys' names. And, as we have seen, girls' names may also be less flattering: "Too Many" or "Little Mistake." Often a general, classificatory name is given to an infant girl; Martin Yang reports from rural Shantung that Hsiao-mei ("Little Maiden") was a "generic" girls' name in his village (1945:124).

Most Chinese personal names are composed of two characters, which follow the one character surname (for example, Mao Tse-tung or Teng Hsiao-ping). One of the characters of the *ming* may be repeated for all the children of the same sex in the family or perhaps all sons born into the lineage during one generation (for example, a generation or sibling set might have personal names like Hung-hui, Hung-chi, Hung-sheng, and so on). Birth order may also be indicated in the child's name. In these cases part of the name indicates group affiliation and sibling order. However, one of the characters is unique to the individual and so the child is distinguished from his siblings. A variation on this theme occurs when a parent or

grandparent selects a name for all sons or grandsons from a group of characters that share a single element (known as the radical—a structured component found in every Chinese character). For example, Margaret Sung (1981:80) in her survey of Chinese naming practices on Taiwan notes that in some families all son's names may be selected from characters that contain the "man" radical (for example, names like "Kind" [Jen], "Handsome" [Chun], or "Protect" [Pao]).

Individuation of the name, Sung points out, is very strong in Chinese society (1981:88). There is no category of words reserved specifically for personal names and care is taken to make names (particularly boys' names) distinct. The Chinese find the idea of sharing one's given name with millions of other people extraordinary.[5] In Taiwan, Sung notes that individuation of one's name is so important that the government has established a set of rules for name changes (1981:88). According to these regulations a name can be changed when two people with exactly the same name live in the same city or county or have the same place of work. "Inelegant" names or names shared with wanted criminals can also be changed.

In Ha Tsuen a boy might be named, in Cantonese, Teng Tim-sing, which translates Teng "To Increase Victories"; another person could be called Teng Hou-sing, "Reliably Accomplish" (Teng being the shared surname). Parents, neighbors, and older siblings will address the child or young unmarried adult (male or female) by his or her *ming* or by a nickname. Younger siblings are expected to use kin terms in addressing older siblings. It should be noted that, in contrast to personal names, Chinese surnames do not convey individual meaning. When used in a sentence or poem, the character *mao* (the same character used in Mao Tse-tung) means hair, fur, feathers, but when it is used as a surname it does not carry any of these connotations.

THE POWER OF NAMES: NAMES THAT CHANGE ONE'S LUCK

Names classify people into families, generational sets, and kin groups. Ideally, Chinese personal names also have a unique quality. Personal names carry meanings; they express wishes (for more sons or no more daughters), mark past events ("Sleeve" or "Endure"), and convey a family's learning and status. Beyond this rather restricted sense there is, however, another level of meaning. According to Chinese folk concepts each person has a unique constitution—a different balance of the five elements (fire, water, metal, earth, and wood). When the child is about one month old a family will usually have a diviner cast the child's horoscope. The horoscope consists of eight characters (*pa tzu*)—two each for the hour, day, month, and year of birth. The combination of these characters determines in part what kind of person one is (what kind of characteristics one has) and what will happen in future years. However, the *pa tzu* do not represent destiny; one is not bound to act out this fate.

By means of esoteric knowledge a person's fate can be changed. Perhaps the most common method of accomplishing such a change is through naming. For example, if one of the five elements is missing from a person's constitution or is not properly balanced with other elements, the name (*ming*) may then include a character with the radical for that element. In the event of illness the diviner may suggest that the patient suffers from an imbalance of wood and that the radical for this element be added to the child's name. In such a case the character *mei* (plum), for example, may replace one of the original characters of the *ming* and thus save the child from a bad fate, illness, or perhaps death. *Mei* achieves this astounding feat not because there is anything intrinsically wood-like about *mei* but because the written character *mei* has two major components: *mu*, the radical for wood and another symbol that is largely phonetic. It is the written form of the character

that is important here; in spoken Chinese there is nothing that suggests that *mei* has within it the element wood. I will return to this point later.

Significantly, it is not only one's own horoscope that matters; one must also be in balance with the horoscopes of parents, spouses, and offspring. It is particularly important that the five elements of mother and child be properly matched to ensure mutual health.[6] If conditions of conflict arise and nothing is done to resolve this conflict, the child may become ill and even die. A name change, however, can rectify the situation. It is obvious that Chinese personal names *do* things: they not only classify and distinguish but also have an efficacy in their own right.

GENDER DIFFERENCES AND THE WRITTEN NAME

As noted above, even in childhood there are important gender distinctions in naming. Girls nearly always have less elaborate full month rituals than their brothers, and less care is taken in choosing girls' names. The greatest difference between the sexes, however, pertains not to the aesthetics of naming but to the written form of the name.

Until the 1960s in Ha Tsuen and in rural Hong Kong generally births were seldom registered with government agencies. Except in cases of a bad fate, there was no compelling reason for girls' names ever to appear in written form. There was rarely any need to attach their names to legal documents. Girls did not inherit land, they had no rights in property, and their given names were not entered in genealogies (on this point see also Hazelton 1986) or on ancestral tablets (see below). Until the 1960s girls rarely attended primary schools. Consequently, nearly all village women born prior to 1945 cannot write or recognize their own names.

Commenting on the role of nicknames, Wolfram Eberhard makes the point that in spoken Chinese with its many homonyms, a two-word combination may fail to express clearly what the speaker wants to convey. The intended meaning of a name (that is, the two-character *ming*) is only apparent when it is written. Nicknames, Eberhard notes, are not normally meant to be written and, hence, are usually longer (often three or four characters) than a person's *ming* (1970:219). Given the ambiguities, a great deal of play is possible with the spoken form of names. For example, Hsin-mei can mean "New Plum" or "Faithful Beauty" depending on the tones that one uses in pronouncing the characters. In the written form the meaning of this name is perfectly clear, but in the spoken form it can be misunderstood or misconstrued, sometimes with disastrous consequences. The Manchu (Ch'ing) authorities played the naming game when they changed the written form of one of Sun Yat-sen's many names. During Sun's long political career, he used a variety of names and aliases (see Sharman 1934), one being Sun Wen (*wen* translates as "elegant," "civil," "culture"). In Manchu attacks on Sun the character *wen* pronounced with a rising tone (elegant, culture) was replaced by another character *wen* pronounced with a falling tone (which translates as "defile"). The change was effected simply by adding the water radical to the term for elegant. *Wen* (defile), it should be noted, was also the name of a famous criminal in southern China during the last years of Manchu rule.

Upon seeing a person's written name, the beholder may comment on the beauty, the refinement, the auspicious connotations of the characters. As long as it is simply spoken, however, it is in a sense "just a name." Although women have names, these do not convey as much information as do men's names, for the obvious reason that the former were rarely written. Until recently New Territories women were not given names with a view to their written effect. The written form of "Too Many" may be offensive or unpleasant in a way that the spoken form is not.

Given that it is the written form of names that has force, that informs, that can be used to change a bad fate, there is justification for

thinking that those whose names are rarely or never written are at some disadvantage. Girls, it would appear, did not have names in the same way that boys did.[7] It is also clear that girls' names are less expressive, less individuating than their brothers' names are. Fathers strove to make son's names distinctive, unique—whereas girls' names tended to classify (for example, Endure, Little Maiden) or to be used as a vehicle for changing circumstances external to the girl herself (for example, Joined to Brother). Many girls of course had names like Splendid Orchid, Morning Flower, Resembling Jade, but in general they were more likely than were their brothers to be given negative names, stereotypic names, or goal-oriented names. These gender distinctions are significant, but the contrast between men and women becomes even more dramatic when we consider adult naming practices.

MEN'S NAMING

When a Ha Tsuen man marries, he is given or takes (often he chooses the name himself) a marriage name, or *tzu*. Considering the importance of the written name it is significant that *tzu* is the same character that is commonly used for "word" or "ideograph." The marriage name is given in a ceremony called *sung tzu,* which literally means "to deliver written characters." This ceremony is an integral part of the marriage rites and is held after the main banquet on the first day of wedding festivities.

In Ha Tsuen, the marriage name (always two characters) is written on a small rectangular piece of red paper and is displayed in the main reception hall of the groom's house (alternatively, it may be hung in the groom's branch ancestral hall). This name is chosen with regard to its effect in the written form. Great care is taken in choosing the characters; they often have origins in the Confucian classics. In Ha Tsuen one of the two characters of this marriage name is usually shared by a lineage generational set. In some kin groups a respected scholar may be asked to choose a poem or aphorism to be used in generational naming. Each generation will then take in turn one character of the poem as part of their (*tzu*) name. Of course, this makes the selection of an auspicious, learned name more difficult and also more intellectually challenging. Naming at this level can become a highly complicated game.

In choosing a marriage name (*tzu*) the groom demonstrates his sophistication, learning, and goals. Among the people I studied, the possession of a marriage name is essential for the attainment of male adulthood, which gives a man the right to participate in important lineage and community rituals. In Ha Tsuen the correct way to ask whether a man has full ritual rights in the lineage is to inquire, "Does X have a *tzu*?" not "Is X married?" Marriage names are not used as terms of address; they may, however, appear in lineage genealogies and in formal documents.

By the time a man is married he will have acquired a public nickname (*wai hao*, literally an "outside name"). This is usually different from the family nickname he had in infancy or the "school name" given to him by a teacher.[8] Nicknames are widely used as terms of address and reference for males in the village; in fact, a man's birth and marriage names may be largely unknown.

In a discussion of naming among the Ilongot, Renato Rosaldo emphasizes the process by which names come into being (1984:13). Rosaldo argues that names are negotiated, and that naming, like other aspects of Ilongot social life, is a matter of give and take, challenge and response (1984:22). Rosaldo's approach is particularly useful for understanding Chinese nicknaming. *Ming* (birth names) are formally bestowed by one's seniors, one chooses the *tzu* (marriage name) and, as we will see, the *hao* (courtesy name) oneself. Nicknames (*wai hao*), however, are negotiated; both the namer and the named play the game. By setting up this dichotomy between nicknames and other given names, I do not mean to suggest that these two categories have no common features or that *ming*, marriage names, and courtesy names

are simply the consequence of a set of rigidly applied rules and structures. It is clear, however, that nicknames fit into the transactional world of local politics, friendship, and informal groups more comfortably than do formal names.

In Chinese society, one can gain a reputation for cleverness by giving nicknames that are particularly apt or make witty literary allusions. Chinese nicknames are highly personalized and often refer to idiosyncratic characteristics. They may also be derogatory or critical, whereas one's formal names would never be intentionally unflattering (especially for a man). Nicknames may refer to a physical quality (for example, "Fatty") or a personal quality ("Stares at the Sky" for someone who is a snob). Nicknames may also protect ("Little Slave Girl") or they may equalize, at least temporarily, unequal relationships. The richest and most powerful man in one New Territories village was nicknamed "Little Dog." In one respect this was a useful nickname for an extremely wealthy man whose political career depended on being accepted by everyone in the community. Rather than rejecting his derogatory nickname he embraced it.

In Ha Tsuen when a man reaches middle age or when he starts a business career, he usually takes a *hao*—"style" or "courtesy" name. A man chooses this name himself. Sung notes that such names are "usually disyllabic or polysyllabic, and [are] selected by oneself bas[ed] upon whatever one would like to be" (1981:86). Some people have more than one courtesy name. The *hao* is a public name par excellence. Such names, Eberhard points out, are often used on occasions when a man wants "to make his personal identity clear without revealing his personal name (*ming*)" (1970:219). In the past, and to some extent today,[9] the *ming* was considered to be too intimate, too personal to be used outside a circle of close friends and kin (Eberhard 1970:218). "The Chinese I know hide their names," writes Maxine Hong Kingston in *Woman Warrior;* "sojourners take new names when their lives change and guard their real names with silence" (1977:6).

Sung notes that *hao* names are no longer popular in present-day Taiwan except among high government officials (1981:86). However, in Hong Kong *hao* are still widely used; they are commonly found, for example, on business cards, and of course many painters or writers sign their work with a *hao*.

In one sense courtesy names are different from birth and marriage names. One achieves a courtesy name. They are a mark of social and economic status, and a poor man who gives himself such a name may be accused of putting on airs. Any man may take a *hao* but if he is not a "man of substance," the *hao* is likely to remain unknown and unused. With poor men or politically insignificant men these names, if they have them at all, may appear only in genealogies or on tombstones.

Some Ha Tsuen men have posthumous names (*shih-hao*) that they take themselves or have conferred upon them by others. Among the imperial elite posthumous names or titles were given to honor special deeds. In the village, however, taking or giving a *shih-hao* is left to individual taste. The practice has declined in recent years.

The preceding discussion suggests that names mark stages in a man's social life. The possession of a birth name, school name, nickname, marriage name, courtesy name, and posthumous name attest to the fact that a man has passed through the major stages of social adulthood. By the time a man reaches middle age he has considerable control over his names and naming. He names others (his children or grandchildren, for example) and he chooses his own marriage, courtesy, and posthumous names. He also has some control over the use of these names. This is especially true of a successful businessman or politician whose business associates may only know his courtesy name, his drinking friends one of his nicknames, his lineage-mates his birth name, and so on. The use of names is situational and involves some calculation both on the part of the named and those with whom he interacts.

Beidelman, in an article on naming among the Kaguru of Tanzania, emphasizes the point that the choice of name reflects the relation between the speaker and the person to whom he speaks (1974:282; see also Willis 1982). The choice of one name or another, or the use of a kin term rather than a personal name, is a tactical decision. In Ha Tsuen the use of nicknames, pet names, birth names, courtesy names is, like the use of kin terms, highly contextual. Intimates may address each other by a nickname when they are among friends but not when strangers are present; family nicknames may be used in the household but not outside of it; birth names and surnames with titles may be used in formal introductions but not in other settings. A man might be addressed by a kin term or a nickname depending on the speaker's goals. One can give respect by using a courtesy name or claim intimacy by using a nickname. In a single lineage village like Ha Tsuen, where all males are agnatic kinsmen, the strategic use of kin terms and personal names provides a fascinating glimpse into social relationships.

Surprisingly, however, this flexibility does not continue into old age. When a man reaches elderhood at age 61, his ability to control his names diminishes just as his control over his family and corporate resources weakens. In Ha Tsuen and in China generally men often hand over headship of the family when they become elders. The village code of respect requires that male elders be addressed by a kin term (for example, in Cantonese *ah baak*, FeB, or a combination of the given name and kin term, for example, *ah Tso baak*). Only an exceptional man, a scholar or wealthy businessman, will continue to be called by one of his personal names after his 60th birthday. For example, no villager would dare refer to or address the 93-year-old patriarch of the wealthiest family in Ha Tsuen as *ah baak*. In general, however, with advancing age the playful aspects of names and naming are taken away as is a man's power to transact his name. In old age a man has little control over what he is called, and in this respect his situation is similar to that of a married woman. As with wives, old men have left (or are leaving) the world of public and financial affairs to become immersed in the world of family and kinship where they are defined not by a set of distinctive names but by their relationship to others.

"NO NAME" WOMEN

At one month a Ha Tsuen girl is given a name (*ming*); when she marries this name ceases to be used. Marriage is a critical rite of passage for both men and women, but the effect of this rite on the two sexes is very different. Just as a man's distinctiveness and public role are enhanced by his marriage and his acquisition of a marriage name, the marriage rites relegate the woman to the inner world of household, neighborhood, and family. On the one hand, the marriage rites seek to enhance the young bride's fertility, but on the other hand, and in a more negative vein, they also dramatize the bride's separation from her previous life and emphasize the prohibitions and restrictions that now confine her. When the young bride crosses her husband's threshold, what distinctiveness she had as a girl is thrust aside. It is at this point that she loses her name and becomes the "inner person" (*nei jen*), a term Chinese husbands use to refer to their wives.

While the groom is receiving his marriage name on the first day of marriage rites, his bride is being given an intensive course in kinship terminology by the elderly women of Ha Tsuen. Marriage ritual provides a number of occasions for the formal, ritualized exchange of kin terms (for a description of marriage rites in Ha Tsuen see R. Watson 1981). These exchanges, which always feature the bride, instruct the new wife and daughter-in-law in the vast array of kin terms she must use for her husband's relatives. The prevalence of virilocal/patrilocal residence means that the groom remains among the kin with whom he has always lived. It is the bride who must grasp a whole new set of kin terms and learn to attach these terms to what must seem a bewildering array of people. Two women residents in the groom's village (called in Cantonese *choi gaa*, "bride callers") act as the bride's guides and supporters during the three days of marriage rites, and it is their responsibility to instruct the bride in the kin terminology she will need in order to survive in her new environment.

These ritualized exchanges of kin terms do more, however, than serve as a pedagogic exercise; they also locate and anchor the bride in a new relational system. As the groom acquires his new marriage name—a name, it should be noted, that denotes both group or category membership *and* individual distinctiveness—the bride enters a world in which she exists only in relation to others. She is no longer "grounded" by her own special name (*ming*), however prosaic that name might have been; after marriage she exists only as someone's eBW or yBW or as Sing's mother, and so on. Eventually even these terms will be used with decreasing frequency; as she approaches old age, she will be addressed simply as "old woman" (*ah po*) by all but her close kin.

When I first moved into Ha Tsuen, I quickly learned the names of the male residents (mostly nicknames). But for the women I, like other villagers, relied on kin terms or category terms. Significantly, the rules that govern the use of these terms are not dependent on the age of the women themselves, but rather are a function of the lineage generation of their husbands. Women married to men of an ascending generation to the speaker (or the speaker's husband) may be addressed as *ah suk po* (a local expression meaning FyBW) or by the more formal *ah sam* (also meaning FyBW). For women married to men of one's own generation (male ego) the terms *ah sou* (eBW) or, if one wanted to give added respect, *ah sam* (FyBW) may be used.

A woman may also be referred to by the nickname of her husband plus "leung" (for example, ah Keung leung), or by a teknonym. For their part married women ordinarily use kin terms for their husbands' agnates and for other women in the village. I was told that a woman must use kin terms for men older in age or generation than her husband. Between husband and wife teknonyms are often used so that the father of Tim-sing might address his wife as *ah Sing nai* (*ah* is a prefix denoting familiarity, *Sing* is part of the son's *ming, nai* is "mother" or, literally, "milk"). In addressing their husbands, women might use nicknames; my neighbor always called her husband "Little Servant."[10]

Although there is some flexibility in deciding what to call a woman, the reference and address terms used for women in Ha Tsuen are very rigid compared to those employed for men. Furthermore, among women there is no possibility of self-naming. Men name themselves, women are named by others. Similarly, Ha Tsuen women are more restricted than their husbands in the tactical use they can make of names and kin terms. Whereas a man may refer to or address his neighbor by his nickname ("Fatty"), his *ming* (*ah Tim*), or by a kin term, decorum dictates that his wife use either a kin term appropriate to her husband's generation or one appropriate to her children. In Cantonese society, and presumably in China generally, adults often address and refer to each other by a version of the kin term their children would use for that person. I suspect, but at this point cannot document, that women are far more likely to do this than are men.

While it is true that a man has little choice in the reference or address terms he uses for women, he does have considerable freedom in distinguishing among his male acquaintances, friends, and kin. Women, as outlined previously, have a restricted repertoire for both sexes. In this sense adult women may be said to carry a particularly heavy burden for guarding the kinship and sexual order. No adult woman is free to act alone or to be treated as if she were independent. The terms by which she is addressed and the terms she uses to address others serve as constant reminders of the hierarchical relations of gender, age, and generation.

As men grow older, as they become students, marry, start careers, take jobs, and eventually prepare for ancestorhood, their new names anchor them to new roles and privileges. These names are not, however, only role markers or classifiers. Ideally, they assign people to categories and at the same time declare their uniqueness. The pattern of naming in Chinese society presents an ever changing image of men. Viewed from this perspective Chinese males are always growing, becoming, accumulating new responsibilities and new rights.

Peasant women, on the other hand, experience few publicly validated life changes, and those that they do undergo link them ever more securely to stereotyped roles. Women's naming leaves little room for individuation or self-expression. Unlike males, whose changes are marked by both ascribed (for example, elderhood) *and* achieved criteria (such as student, scholar, businessman, writer, politician), a woman's changes (from unmarried virgin to married woman, from nonmother to mother, from reproducer to nonreproducer) are not related to achievement outside the home. Instead of acquiring a new name at marriage or the birth of a first child, women's changes are marked by kin terminology or category shifts. At marriage the bride loses her *ming* and becomes known by a series of kin terms. At the birth of a child she may add a teknonym ("Sing's mother"), and as she approaches and enters old age more and more people will address her simply as "old woman" (*ah po*).

The most dramatic changes that women make are the shift from named to unnamed at marriage and the gradual shift from kin term to category term as their children mature and marry.[11] It would appear that as a woman's reproductive capacity declines, she becomes less grounded in the relational system. She becomes, quite simply, an "old woman" much like any other old woman. Of course, family members continue to use kin terms for these elderly women, especially in reference and address, but gradually their anonymity increases. Unlike men, women do not become elders. There is no ceremony marking their entry into respected old age. They move from reproductively active mother to sexually inactive grandmother with no fanfare and with little public recognition of their changed status.

Even in death a woman has no personal name. On the red flag that leads the spirit of the deceased from the village to the grave is written the woman's father's surname (for example, *Lin shih,* translated "Family of Lin"); no personal name is added. For men, the deceased's surname plus his courtesy and/or posthumous name is written on the soul flag. Neither do women's personal names appear on the tombstone where, here again, only the surname of the woman's father is given ("Family of Lin"). In Ha Tsuen women do not have separate ancestral tablets; if they are commemorated at all, they appear as minor appendages on their husbands' tablets. And, once more, they are listed only under the surnames of their fathers. In subsequent generations whatever individuating characteristics a woman might have had are lost—not even a name survives as testimony of her existence as a person.

CONCLUSIONS

If one were to categorize Ha Tsuen villagers on a social continuum according to the number and quality of their names, married peasant women would stand at the extreme negative pole.[12] To my knowledge they share this dubious distinction with no other group. In the past even male slaves (*hsi min*) and household servants had nicknames (see J. Watson 1976:365). They may not have had *ming* or surnames as such but they did possess names that distinguished them from others. It is important to note that it is not only the possession of multiple names that matters but also the fact that, at one end of the continuum, people have no control over their own names while, at the other end, they name themselves and others.

At marriage women find themselves enmeshed in the world of family and kinship. It is a world, as noted in the introduction, that they belong to but do not control. In Ha Tsuen brides arrive as outsiders but quickly,

one might even say brutally, they become firmly entrenched in their new environment. Village women can only be identified within the constellation of male names or within the limits of kinship terminology. Unlike their husbands and brothers, women—having no public identity outside the relational system—are defined by and through others.

In Ha Tsuen women are excluded from participation in most of the formal aspects of lineage or community life and they are not involved in decision making outside the home. Ha Tsuen women do not inherit productive resources; they are also restricted in the uses to which they can put their dowries (R. Watson 1984). Furthermore, women in Ha Tsuen cannot become household heads and, even today, they do not vote in local elections. They do not worship in ancestral halls nor do they join the cult of lineage ancestors after death. Although individual peasant women may attain considerable power within their households, they are said to have gained this power by manipulation and stealth. Women by definition cannot hold positions of authority.

In a discussion of male and female naming among the Omaha Sioux, Robert Barnes writes: "The names of Omaha males provide men with distinctive individuality, while also linking each unmistakably to a recognized collectivity. The possibility of acquiring multiple names in adulthood enhances individual prominence for men" (1982:220). Barnes goes on to say that women's names "barely rescue them from a general anonymity, neither conferring uniqueness nor indicating group membership" (1982:22). As among the Sioux, personal naming among Chinese men is a sign of both individual distinctiveness and group membership, while naming practices among village women simply confirm their marginality.

In Ha Tsuen the practice of personal naming reflects and facilitates the passage from one social level to another. Names establish people in social groups and give them certain rights within those groups. With each additional name, a man acquires new attributes.

Maybury-Lewis has argued that among many Central Brazilian societies names give humans their "social persona and link [them] to other people" (1984:5; see also Bamberger 1974). Names, Maybury-Lewis writes, "transform individuals into persons" (1984:7). Naming may not be as central to Chinese social organization and ideology as it is among the societies of Central Brazil, yet there is no doubt that, for Chinese men, names have a transformative power that binds them as individuals to society.

In Ha Tsuen the ultimate goal of all males is to produce an heir, to have a grandson at one's funeral, to leave property that guarantees the performance of one's ancestral rites. The possession of many names testifies to the fact that a man has completed the cycle of life. Full personhood is not acquired at birth, at marriage, or even at the death of one's father. It is a process that continues throughout life and is punctuated by the taking and bestowing of names. One might argue that it is a process that extends even beyond death as the named ancestor interacts with the living. If, as Grace Harris suggests, personhood involves a process of social growth "in the course of which changes [are] wrought by ceremony and ritual" (1978:49), then Chinese women never approximate the full cycle of development that their menfolk experience.[13] In stark contrast to men, women become less distinct as they age. The changes they undergo remain largely unrecognized and unnoticed.

In Chinese society, as in other societies, there is a tension between the notion of the unique individual (the individual as value) and the notion of the person tied to society.[14] In some sense the great philosophical systems of Taoism and Confucianism represent these two poles. Among men, naming involves a dual process through which they achieve personhood by being bound to society, while at the same time they acquire an enhanced sense of individuality and distinctiveness. The peasant women described in this paper seem to have been largely excluded from the individuating, individualizing world of personal naming. The situation with regard to personhood is, however, another matter. It would be wrong to say that peasant wives are nonpersons; rather, they are not persons in the same sense or to the same degree as are husbands and sons. Viewed from the perspective of names, peasant women are neither fully individuated nor "personed." In life as in death they remain suspended between the anonymous world of anybodies and the more sharply defined world of somebodies.

NOTES

Acknowledgments. The research for this study was conducted in 1977–78 and was made possible by a grant from the Social Science Research Council (Great Britain) and by the University of London Central Research Fund. An earlier version of this paper was presented at the 1984 American Anthropological Association Annual Meetings. Versions of this paper were also presented at the University of London Intercollegiate Anthropology Seminar and at the University of Rochester's Anthropology Colloquium. I thank the members of those seminars for their suggestions and criticisms. I owe a special debt to Jack Dull, Hsu Cho-yun, Sun Man-li, Roderick MacFarquhar, and James Watson, all of whom have helped in this project. Deborah Kwolek, Judy Tredway, and Martha Terry of the Asian Studies Program at the University of Pittsburgh helped in the preparation of the manuscript and I thank them for their assistance.

Cantonese terms are in Yale romanization and Mandarin terms follow the Wade-Giles system.

This paper is dedicated to the memory of my friend and fellow anthropologist Judith Strauch (1942–85).

1. There are bound to be regional, temporal, urban-rural, and class differences in Chinese naming practices. A general discussion of Chinese naming awaits further research.
2. In Taiwan the *ming* is the legal name (it appears in the official household register) and is sometimes called the *cheng ming* (correct name) (Sung 1981:70). In Hong Kong this name may or may not be the name used on legal documents.
3. I am grateful to Professor Jack Dull for pointing out to me the significance and frequency of the personal name Nai among Chinese women.

4. In a similar vein a fifth or sixth child might be named "To End" or "To Finish." One can find such names in the Hong Kong and Taipei telephone directories (see also Sung 1981:81).

5. In China there are no given names like John that are shared by millions of people; on this point see Sung 1981:85.

6. In a discussion of the cosmic relationship between mother and child Marjorie Topley writes of her Cantonese informants:

The constitutional imbalance of a child with a queer fate may also involve other parties. First, the child may be polarized in the same direction as someone with whom it has a continuous relationship. Then both parties may suffer from continual illness. This may be corrected by adding an element to the child's name so it is compatible with that of the other party [1974:240].

7. This is changing now that girls go to school and their births are registered.

8. In the past when village boys started school at age five or six (girls did not attend school until the 1960s), the schoolmaster gave each student a school or "study name" (hsueh-ming). School names are no longer very important in the New Territories.

9. In the past officials' ming could not be used except by intimates (see Eberhard 1970 and Sung 1981).

10. After I gained some insight into the micropolitics of my neighbor's household, the name seemed well chosen.

11. Once a son marries reproduction becomes a matter for the younger generation, and in Ha Tsuen it was considered shameful for the mother of a married son to become pregnant.

12. It should be noted here that men do not constitute a uniform category in this regard. Highly literate men make up one extreme but many poorly educated or uneducated men fall somewhere between the two extremes. Like the names of their sisters, their names may be inelegant and rarely seen in written form, but unlike adult women, they do retain their names after marriage.

13. On this point see also LaFontaine 1985:131.

14. For discussions of the concept of the individual as value and the self in Chinese society see for example de Bary 1970; Shiga 1978:122; and more recently Elvin 1985; Munro 1985 (especially essays by Hansen, Yu, Munro, and de Bary).

REFERENCES

Arlington, L. C. 1923. The Chinese Female Names. *China Journal of Science and Arts* 1(4):316–325.

Bamberger, Joan. 1974. Naming and the Transmission of Status in a Central Brazilian Society. *Ethnology* 13:363–378.

Barnes, Robert B. 1982. Personal Names and Social Classification. In *Semantic Anthropology*. David Parkin, ed., pp. 211–226. London: Academic Press.

Beidelman, T. O. 1974. Kaguru Names and Naming. *Journal of Anthropological Research* 30:281–293.

de Bary, William Theodore. 1970. Individualism and Humanitarianism in Late Ming Thought. In *Self and Society in Ming Thought*. Wm. Theodore de Bary, ed., pp. 145–247. New York: Columbia University Press.

Eberhard, Wolfram. 1970. A Note on Modern Chinese Nicknames. In *Studies in Chinese Folklore and Related Essays*. Wolfram Eberhard, ed., pp. 217–222. Indiana University Folklore Institute Monograph Series, Vol. 23. The Hague: Mouton.

Elvin, Mark. 1985. Between the Earth and Heaven: Conceptions of the Self in China. In *The Category of the Person*. Michael Carrithers, Steven Collins, Steven Lukes, eds., pp. 156–189. Cambridge: Cambridge University Press.

Geertz, Clifford. 1973. Person, Time, and Conduct in Bali. In *The Interpretation of Cultures*. pp. 360–411. New York: Basic Books.

Harris, Grace. 1978. *Casting Out Anger: Religion among the Taita of Kenya*. Cambridge: Cambridge University Press.

Hazelton, Keith. 1986. Patrilines and the Development of Localized Lineages: The Wu of Hsiu-ming City, Hui-chou, to 1528. In *Kinship Organization in Late Imperial China*. Patricia B. Ebrey and James L. Watson, eds., pp. 137–169. Berkeley: University of California Press.

Kehl, Frank. 1971. Chinese Nicknaming Behavior: A Sociolinguistic Pilot Study. *Journal of Oriental Studies* 9:149–172.

Kingston, Maxine Hong. 1977. *The Woman Warrior: Memories of a Girlhood among Ghosts*. New York: Vintage Books. (Originally published in hardcover by Alfred Knopf, 1976.)

La Fontaine, Jean. 1985. Person and Individual: Some Anthropological Reflections. In *The Category of the Person*. Michael Carrithers, Steven Collins, and Steven Lukes, eds., pp. 123–140. Cambridge: Cambridge University Press.

Maybury-Lewis, David. 1984. Name, Person, and Ideology in Central Brazil. In *Naming Systems.* Elisabeth Tooker, ed., pp. 1–10. 1980 Proceedings of the American Ethnological Society. Washington, DC: American Ethnological Society.

Munro, Donald (ed.). 1985. *Individualism and Holism: Studies in Confucian and Taoist Values.* Ann Arbor: University of Michigan Press.

Rosaldo, Renato. 1984. Ilongot Naming: The Play of Associations. In *Naming Systems.* Elisabeth Tooker, ed., pp. 11–24. 1980 Proceedings of the American Ethnological Society. Washington, DC: American Ethnological Society.

Sharman, Lyon. 1934. *Sun Yat-sen: His Life and Its Meaning.* Stanford, CA: Stanford University Press.

Shiga, Shuzo. 1978. Family Property and the Law of Inheritance in Traditional China. In *Chinese Family Law and Social Change.* David Buxbaum, ed., pp. 109–150. Seattle: University of Washington Press.

Stacey, Judith. 1983. *Patriarchy and Socialist Revolution in China.* Berkeley: University of California Press.

Sung, Margaret M. Y. 1981. Chinese Personal Naming. *Journal of the Chinese Language Teachers Association* 16(2):67–90.

Topley, Marjorie. 1974. Cosmic Antagonisms: A Mother-Child Syndrome. In *Religion and Ritual in Chinese Society.* Arthur Wolf, ed., pp. 233–249. Stanford, CA: Stanford University Press.

Watson, James L. 1976. Chattel Slavery in Chinese Peasant Society: A Comparative Analysis. *Ethnology* 15:361–375.

Watson, Rubie S. 1981. Class Differences and Affinal Relations in South China. *Man* 16:593–615.

———. 1984. Women's Property in Republican China: Rights and Practice. *Republican China* 10(12):1–12.

———. 1985. *Inequality Among Brothers: Class and Kinship in South China.* Cambridge: Cambridge University Press.

Willis, Roy. 1982. On a Mental Sausage Machine and other Nominal Problems. In *Semantic Anthropology.* David Parkin, ed., pp. 227–240. London: Academic Press.

Wolf, Margery. 1972. *Women and the Family in Rural Taiwan.* Stanford, CA: Stanford University Press.

Wu, Ching-chao. 1927. The Chinese Family: Organization, Names, and Kinship Terms. *American Anthropologist* 29:316–325.

Yang, Martin C. 1945. *A Chinese Village: Taitou, Shantung Province.* New York: Columbia University Press.

A Critical Appraisal of Theories of Menstrual Symbolism

Thomas Buckley and Alma Gottlieb

MENSTRUATION AND POLLUTION

An abundance of symbolic analyses of menstrual taboos has been built on the concept of "pollution"—symbolic contamination. These studies posit (correctly or incorrectly) that

Reprinted with permission from Thomas Buckley and Alma Gottlieb (eds.), *Blood Magic: Explorations in the Anthropology of Menstruation* (Berkeley: University of California Press, 1988), pp. 25–40. Copyright 1988 The Regents of the University of California.

menstrual blood and menstruous women are culturally defined as dangerous to established order (in various senses)—if not universally then at least widely enough to constitute a justifiable generalization. Because menstrual blood and menstruous women are perceived as dangerous, taboos have been devised to contain their energies and keep these from spreading beyond a limited place in the order of things. Among anthropologists utilizing a pollution model in the study of menstrual customs and beliefs two lines of analysis have been followed, independently or in conjunction with each other. The first of these stresses the symbolic structures of pollution concepts in diverse cultures; the second emphasizes the sociological correlates of such symbolic structures.

Both lines of analysis have been pursued by Mary Douglas, an anthropologist perhaps best known for her work in general pollution theory. Although Douglas has written no extended work solely on the topic of menstrual pollution, her broader investigations of pollution (1966, 1972) and of body symbolism (1968, 1970) place her foremost among theoretical contributors to the comparative cultural-anthropological study of menstruation.

THE SYMBOLISM
OF MENSTRUAL POLLUTION

In *Purity and Danger* (1966) Douglas proposes that the cultural coding of a substance as a pollutant is based in a shared perception of that substance as anomalous to a general symbolic, or cultural, order. Pollutants are coded as "dirt," symbolic "matter out of place." As such, pollutants are at once a product of a specific symbolic order and a danger to it. As dangers to symbolic order, pollutants are also perceived as dangers to social order given that for Douglas—following Durkheim—the symbolic system has functional goals in the maintenance of society. Hence the acknowledgment of pollutants in cultural systems is accompanied by prohibitions the intent of which is the protection of *social* order from disruptive forces symbolized by culturally defined anomalous substances.

Menstrual blood is a particularly apt candidate for analysis in terms of this theory. As blood itself, menstrual discharge is "out of place," breaching the natural bounds of the body that normally contain it. All forms of human bloodshed may be coded as polluting (and are in many cultures; see Durkheim 1897:48 ff.), but menstruation is generally

found especially so. Menstrual blood does not issue randomly or accidentally, as does the blood of wounds, but from a single source and to some extent regularly and predictably (but see later discussion)—if, unlike other products of elimination, uncontrollably. Again, in flowing from the reproductive organs of women such blood, rather than signaling a threat to life, is recognized by most peoples as signaling its very possibility. Finally, in the vast majority of the world's societies men have a virtual monopoly on routine or ritual forms of bloodletting: hunting, butchering, warfare, rituals involving sacrifice, mutilation, and scarification alike (Rosaldo and Atkinson 1975). Thus the fact that menstruation may be the only act in which women normatively and routinely let blood may, depending on the culture, constitute a symbolic anomaly. In all of these senses, then, there is a compelling tendency to perceive menstrual blood as "out of place," and more so than other sorts of blood. Hence in terms of Douglas's theory, menstrual blood is perceived as a dire pollutant whose effects must be contained through stringent taboos.

In a follow-up article to *Purity and Danger,* Douglas (1972) revised her initial theory of pollution somewhat. Responding to the work of Tambiah (1969) and Bulmer (1967), Douglas argued that although all pollutants are anomalous in terms of a given symbolic order, not all symbolic anomalies must be coded as polluting. Rather, anomalies are simply "powerful," according to Douglas, their power being granted a negative or positive valence to be determined through specific cultural analysis rather than being attributed cross-culturally. An entity deemed polluting in one culture might, for example, be deemed holy in another.

In either case, however, the issue remains "power" and is therefore, as in Douglas's original scheme, an essentially religious matter (1966:49). Two issues are thereby addressed. First, the constitution of laws regarding pollution as supernaturally sanctioned taboos, rather than as mundane rules, becomes comprehensible through recognition of "power" as a concept grounded in spiritual notions (as, for instance, is the case in Polynesian *mana*). Second, in keeping with Durkheim's theory of the relationship between religion and society (1915), the matter of containment of extrahuman power links neatly with the social functions of taboos such as menstrual ones. For Douglas consideration of a symbolic anomaly and religious attention to it lead directly to a consideration of sociological functionality.

THE SOCIOLOGY OF MENSTRUAL POLLUTION

The social functions of religious symbolism were broadly explored early on by Durkheim (1915), and his student Marcel Mauss went on to outline a specific model for a sociological analysis of human body symbolism (1979). Mauss's premise was that symbolically elaborated body concepts mirror the society in which they occur. This insight has been further developed by investigators working on a variety of specific problems in body symbolism, including menstruation.

Other than Durkheim himself (1897), one of the first proponents of a Durkheimian perspective in menstruation studies was Meggitt (1964). Meggitt pointed out that the Mae Enga of New Guinea place unusually strong emphasis on the polluting nature of menstruation, in comparison to other nearby peoples. Meggitt proposed that menstrual pollution serves the Mae Enga as a metaphor for their distrust of outsiders, of which a man's wife is, in this virilocal society, the prototype, as the Enga "marry their enemies."

This kind of analysis, which posits a close relationship between ideas about the body social and the body physical, was greatly extended in the work of Mary Douglas (especially 1970). Pollutants such as menstrual blood that are given meanings within religious systems bespeak, for Douglas, the sociosymbolic logic primary to religion itself

(1966:6 ff). By this route Douglas moves firmly back from arbitrary symbolic processes to the determination of those processes by social facts.

In particular Douglas hypothesizes that beliefs about menstrual pollution are found in a restricted number of societies and take on analogous meanings throughout these societies. Menstrual blood is seen as polluting when it symbolically encodes an underlying social-structural ambiguity regarding women and things female. On the one hand a society may have a consciously developed *ideology* of male superiority but, on the other, it may also permit women access to at least some kinds of power, thereby in a sense undermining its own ideology of male dominance. The common fact of menstruation among all women challenges the social order of a male-dominated society and defines and bounds a female subgroup within the society, thereby creating a new separate and dangerous order. Here is a social situation, then, that contains a powerful contradiction, and Douglas suggests that it is in such societies that a strong concept of menstrual pollution will arise, signaling the contradiction.

Most recently Balzer (1981) has taken up Douglas's theory, documenting subtly and precisely just how this theory can be used to explain Siberian Khanty menstrual taboos in the wider context of Khanty society. Others have drawn on Douglas's central insight as well, offering variations on its theme. Raymond Kelly (cited in Ortner and Whitehead 1981:20–21) suggests that women are viewed as polluting in societies in which men are dependent on them as sources of prestige— economic, political, or social. Sanday (1981) has also been influenced by Douglas and by Meggitt as well. She proposes that a society will view menstruation as dangerous and polluting if it holds a negative view of its environment as dangerous—threatening starvation—and a concomitant negative relationship with neighboring groups in that environment. Like Meggitt, Sanday predicts that the view of menstrual blood as dangerous mirrors ideas about the outside world, with those ideas being projected onto women's bodies.

Finally, a recent book on reproductive ritual by Karen and Jeffrey Paige (1981) makes further use of Douglas's interpretation. Like Douglas, these authors seek to predict what types of social structures will generate menstrual taboos with (supposedly) concurrent notions of pollution. Paige and Paige postulate that in tribal and band societies one finds the seclusion of menstruous women when there is an unstable economy and, hence, an unstable political base. In this situation, the Paiges hypothesize, men attempt both to maintain control over and to dissociate themselves from women's reproductive cycles. These men seek to demonstrate that they have more of an interest in the society as a whole and in keeping it together in the face of economic hazard than they do in their own narrow conjugal concerns (Paige and Paige 1981:209–254).

The paired theories of menstrual pollution—symbolic and sociological—that have been summarized here have been crucial in shaping current anthropological understanding of menstrual customs and beliefs. How justified is this influence, and in what ways might anthropology now be ready to move on to new theoretical approaches to the topic?

THE LIMITS OF POLLUTION THEORY

Pollution theory, and especially Mary Douglas's initial foray into it (1966), has made notable contributions to knowledge both in anthropology and in other fields, such as the history of religions. Its usefulness, however, is not unbounded. To begin with, there is a clear limit to the fruitfulness of analyses of menstrual blood as "matter out of place," and not recognizing this leaves the replicative analyst open to the dreadful inquiry, "So what?" What, for example, lies beyond the structural grasp of symbolic grammars in the lived experiences of people, once these grammars and

their anomalies have been fully explored (see Bruner and Turner 1986)?

The anomalies themselves pose further problems. Although Douglas, in her 1972 article "Self-Evidence," agreed with her critics that symbolic anomalies themselves were of neutral valence, to be "swung" either positively or negatively by the cultural system that determined their anomaly, the possibility that symbols anomalous to one subsystem within a culture could find a securely structured place within an alternate subsystem was not taken up. Analyses following Douglas in finding menstrual blood, for instance, polluting because it is anomalous to *the* symbolic system can thus be both overly idealistic and simplistic.

As regards the sociological components of Douglas's overall theory of pollution, the one most frequently utilized by other investigators, there are equivalent problems. The focus on solidarity in male-dominated analytic domains of social action reflects a methodological prejudice, in classic social anthropology, for formal social structures as against informal modes of social organization. "Real" society has been located in large-scale analytic domains—politics, economics, kinship, religion—that are seen as dominated by men occupying named statuses imbued with authority. The often informal structures through which the influence of women may be exercised have customarily been disregarded as inconsequential to this "real" society, as have been formal structures dominated by women (but see, e.g., Weiner 1976). When they have been acknowledged at all, such female-dominated formal structures, and the seemingly more frequent informal ones, have usually been viewed as comprising futile "shadow" societies, generated by male domination and alienated from "real" society (e.g., Wolf 1972). In short, until recently society has been analytically treated as a result of and vehicle for male action.

This effect constitutes the sociological dimension of the cultural theory critiqued earlier: that women are the passive recipients of male-created cultures. It is this male-focal vision of culture and society that underlies analyses of pollution as an index of social-structural tension. The social vision itself, as well as the way in which pollution ideas have been related to it, may reflect the relative domination of the ethnographic record by men, to some extent as anthropologists and, even more, as informants. It is men who have by and large defined menstruation as polluting, and the typical ethnography rarely tells us what the women of the culture at hand think of their own menstrual periods, and those of other women. Thus there hardly seems much solid cross-cultural evidence to support a generalization such as the following, found in a popular text: "There is everywhere a sense that menstruation is unclean. And everywhere women seem to have internalized this attitude to feel shame or unease concerning the natural workings of their own bodies" (Hammond and Jablow 1976:7).

In two of the rare studies that do report the attitudes of individual women toward their menstrual cycles, we find much more variation than this sort of generalization indicates. The Syrian Orthodox Jewish women studied by Kharrazi (1980) express deep ambivalence, while a portion of Skultans's Welsh sample (1988) apparently feel entirely positive about their periods: far from perceiving them as being polluting, these women find in their periods confirmation of their own positively valued womanhood. There is a clear need, then, to consult female informants before reaching any conclusions regarding the status of menstruation as an accepted pollutant in any given society.

However careful Mary Douglas herself may have been in attributing the notion of menstrual pollution only to certain types of societies (those in which there is evidence for strong structural ambiguity regarding women), others have not been so careful. Indeed, when one consults the index of an ethnography, if reference to menstruation is included at all, it is almost invariably included under the rubric of "menstrual pollution." One has the impression that most, if not all, societies view menstruation as a source of pollution, in extension of Douglas's general theory, and that there is no more to be said. Yet it is clear that the situation is hardly that simple, and that the very power of pollution theory, coupled with Western societies' own codings of menstrual blood as a pollutant, has perhaps created "dirt" where none previously existed, or existed only for some people and/or in some contexts in a given culture. The elegance of pollution theory itself can thus manufacture the illusion of overwhelming negativity in symbolic systems where menstruation may be coded ambiguously or even positively.

In the West we are accustomed to thinking of menstruation as largely negative. It is "the curse" or, more fully, "the curse of Eve": a part of God's punishment of women for Eve's role in the Biblical Fall (Wood 1981).[1] We are not alone in holding such a view, but it is hardly a universal one. Niangoran-Bouah (1964:52) reports, for instance, that among the Ebrié of Ivory Coast it is forbidden to collect fruits of trees protected by their owners with certain mystically powerful objects. If a man disobeys this taboo he is afflicted with impotence until he confesses to the owner; if a woman picks the fruit she is afflicted with amenorrhea—*losing* her period (rather than enduring it for eternity like the daughters of Eve) until she confesses. In this case menstruation would appear to be the female counterpart of the masculine erection: associated with fertility, not pollution; desirable, and traumatic to lose. As the Ebrié case shows, menstruation is by no means coded as a universal negative.

Moreover, the widespread exclusive use of males as ethnographic informants tends to place analytic stress on the vulnerability of men to female pollution and the consequent efforts of men to distance themselves from the sources of such pollution. Yet the consistency of reported male testimony regarding menstrual pollution disguises complexities of various kinds.

First, where there is a documented ideology of menstrual pollution, close reading often reveals that not all men are deemed vulnerable to a woman's polluting influence, but only certain classes of men—for example, husbands (e.g., Thompson 1985:706) or old men (Gottlieb, 1988). Second, women are not alone in being suspected of contaminating influence during their periods; often their husbands must share the ritual restrictions incumbent upon their menstruating wives, as among the Hadza of Tanzania (in Douglas 1968:23). The !Gwi of southern Africa, by the same token, initiate the husbands of menarcheal women together with their young wives, the two being scarified and decorated in identical manner (Silberbauer 1963:21–22). Such cases as those of the Hadza and !Gwi suggest that although pollution may be an issue in a given culture, other matters may be equally of concern. Most pertinent here is a notion of *shared substance* between husband and wife, which is quite similar to that shared substance stressed by anthropologists in analyses of the *couvade* (symbolic joint pregnancy and birth labor) which the menstrual practices of the Hadza and !Gwi resemble (see Rivière 1974–75).[2]

Both Hadza and !Gwi men (at least) do view menstruation as polluting. The meanings of menstruation cannot be exhausted in either case through a simple theory of pollution, however, for in both there is at least one other constituent—the idea of shared substance. As we suggested for "taboo," culturally constituted symbolic anomalies such as menstrual blood may gather meaning from two directions at once to be both negative, or polluting, and positively powerful. The shortcoming of pollution theory in the analysis of menstrual meanings is that it can too easily obscure, through its own elegance, such potential multivalence. In explanations of menstrual symbolism through it, understanding too easily escapes us. We illustrate this crucial point through further ethnographic examples.

Ritual Uses of Menstrual Blood

The heuristic value of interpreting menstrual blood as an anomalous substance whose power is gained through its relationship to other items in a symbolic structure is clear (Gottlieb 1990); again and again menstrual discharge has indeed been granted the extraordinary powers of the anomalous, or "liminal" (Turner 1969). The symbolically constituted power of menstrual blood makes it, "naturally," in Douglas's terms (1970), a prime substance for manipulation in rituals. At the same time, its frequently multiple meanings as well as its symbolic arbitrariness suit it for use in a variety of rituals with diverse and even contradictory intent, both intra- and cross-culturally.

As a culturally specified pollutant, menstrual blood is an obvious candidate for ritual use with the negative intent of bringing harm to others, especially through witchcraft. Thus among the Mae Enga, it is held that "menstrual blood introduced into a man's food ... quickly kills him, and young women crossed in love sometimes seek their revenge in this way" (Meggitt 1964:207). Similar alleged uses of menstrual blood may be cited for any number of cultures, in most of which—as in New Guinea—avoidance of this substance is conjoined with a fear of those who are reputed to *seek* contact with it for unscrupulous purposes. Menstrual witchcraft, where it is reported, need not necessarily be voluntary. For example, in China, according to Ahern (1975:194–195), people say that menstrual blood adheres to the ground, making it dangerous to walk on the streets. The use of menstrual blood in witchcraft thus seems to exist within a continuum of negative effects and manipulations all reflecting a clear underlying notion of pollution. Quite opposite effects and ritual manipulations have also been reported, however, that cannot be resolved through pollution theory.

Probably the most commonly reported *positive* use of menstrual blood is in the manufacture of various kinds of love charms and potions. These occur in cultures as diverse as the medieval farmers and shepherds of southwestern France (Ladurie 1979:32), the Beng of Ivory Coast (Gottlieb, 1988), and rural whites in the United States. Kirksey (1984:32) gives the following fictional but ethnographically informed rendering of a conversation in Southern Illinois:

> "You remember your Uncle Skinny and your Aunt Jac, don't you?"
>
> "Yes, ma'am," Ward said. "I remembers them pretty well."
>
> "Maybe you don't remember this, but your Uncle Skinny snuck around on your aunt a lot. That is, till she come to me, said that Skinny was stepping out on her, said she wanted to keep him at home. So I told her to put a spoonful of her 'time of the month' in his coffee regularly. If she did, he'd never leave her. Of course, you know what happened, I'm sure. Your uncle died in your aunt's arms, loving her to the very end."
>
> Ward was shocked to hear the tale, but he remembered his Uncle Skinny's often docile, loving manner toward Aunt Jac.

We also find accounts of *men* using menstrual blood to ensure the fidelity of their wives, as Pliny reported for Imperial Rome (in Novak 1916:273). These accounts seem better analyzed in terms of a theory of shared substance, as discussed earlier, than one of pollution. Their sense would not seem exhaustible by this or any other single cross-cultural theory, however, for the accounts themselves arise within a literature replete with positive uses of menstrual blood that cannot be explained through a notion of shared substance—such as the medicinal uses described earlier—but, rather, seem to have in common only the general theme of "power."

Such power has been specified through a variety of metaphors—"pollution," "shared substance," and others. Among such metaphors that of "life force" (Kuper 1947:107) is perhaps most striking. In this case menstrual blood is viewed as an emblem or manifestation of creative power, particularly in the sense of fertility. Thus the use of menstrual blood in fertility rituals is widespread (and, it would seem, conceptually linked to the use of this substance in love charms). The Nigerian Tiv use menstrual blood in the *imborivungu* ("owl pipe") ritual, which also involves human sacrifice (Lincoln 1975:51 ff.) Menstrual blood is mixed with

that of a sacrificial child in a ritual pipe as a central act in an elaborate ritual through which the farms surrounding a ritual center are blessed, and their fertility—and that of the women who inhabit them—ensured. (For other examples see Poole 1982:105; Jetté 1911:257, 403; Yalman 1964:135.)

The use of menstrual symbols in the enhancement of life force (in the sense of fertility) seems to point in two directions at once: toward a better understanding of pollution, when it is manipulated toward the protection of life, and toward an appreciation of folk-biological components in culturally specific menstrual meanings. This complex, even dialectical, situation may again be illuminated through ethnographic examples.

Menstrual blood is often used in symbolically powerful objects the purpose of which is to keep life-threatening forces at bay. Among the Kwakiutl, for example, "the malignant power which menstrual blood was believed to have for human beings extended to monsters; therefore when women were traveling, they kept some menstrual blood in a bit of shredded bark to be used to poison a monster should one appear" (Ford 1941:35). In this instance the polluting powers of menstruation are linked with its status as a symbol of life force to be manipulated in such a way that its very negativity protects life itself.

We suspect that such a dialectical relationship between the negative and positive poles of symbolic menstrual power is found more commonly than has been remarked upon. An example is provided by the well-studied Asante of Ghana. According to Rattray (1927:74–75, 211, 234, 271), menstruating Asante women are subject to numerous taboos, some of which are kept under pain of immediate, automatic death. The strength of menstrual pollution may, however, be used by priests in assuring their own safety. Asante priests manufacture fetishes (*kunkuma*) of brooms defiled with menstrual blood, and "a priest is supposed to be safe without any other protective charm provided he has with him his *kunkuma*" (Rattray 1927:14). The logic appears simple enough: potent, negatively valued substances such as menstrual blood may be manipulated for positive ends by those who are themselves spiritually potent enough to reverse the valence and make it positive. Yet the Asante case exhibits further complications.

Although the Asante view menstrual blood as definitively polluting, subject to "one of the greatest and deadliest taboos in Ashanti" (Rattray 1927:13), they also celebrate menarche with an elaborate ritual for individual girls in which the menarcheal girl, among other things, sits in public view beneath an umbrella (a symbol generally reserved for kings and other dignitaries), receiving gifts and congratulations and observing singing and dancing performed in her honor (Rattray 1927:69–74). Within Asante society, then, menstrual symbolism is highly complex. Menstrual blood itself causes dire pollution (especially to ancestral altars), yet menarche is celebrated with profound honors and, moreover, priests use menstrual blood toward positive ends. Among the Asante as among comparable peoples, we are in a realm far beyond the grasp of any single model of menstruation-as-pollution.

We suggest that such diversity in meaning is strongly tied to indigenous conceptions of the biological function of menstruation in the reproductive cycles of women. Though this has been symbolized in different ways among different peoples, particularly widespread conceptions focus on the symbolic role of menstruation in human fertility. When they are found these ideas further undermine the utility of a simple pollution model of menstruation.

Menstruation and Gestation

In the medieval European interpretation of Aristotle's biology, menstrual blood was held to be the "matter" to which semen supplied "form," creating the fetus (Wood 1981:715–719). In this system excess menstrual blood was retained in the womb, providing the basis for lactation at parturition (Wood 1981). The basic elements of this folk-biological theory of conception and lactation are widespread, found in many cultures that, like medieval Europe, also view menstrual blood as a pollutant.

For example, the Paiela of New Guinea have a highly elaborate theory of conception in which menstrual blood is held to be "bound" slowly by semen introduced into the womb through repeated intercourse (Biersack 1983). (Also see Evans-Pritchard 1932:407 on the Azande of the Sudan; O'Flaherty 1980:42 on fourth-century India; and Laqueur 1986 on Europe through the Renaissance.) The Mohave Indians of southern California give an added twist to this general theory, viewing the blood of parturition as "a sort of supermenstruation, expelling all at once the accumulated menstrual blood of ten missed periods" (Devereux 1950:253), and deeming this blood polluting, as they do menstrual blood.

Such folk theories—and they are both numerous and widely distributed (see Ford 1945)[3]—both complicate efforts to analyze menstrual symbolism purely in terms of a theory of pollution and, at the same time, inform that theory. The negativity of menstruation is necessarily made ambiguous by the inclusion of the menstrual cycle among the reproductive processes, which is generally viewed quite positively. Ernestine Friedl (1975:29) remarks that the very occurrence of menstruation can be interpreted as a sign of death, insofar as it is a signal that a new life has not been conceived. Friedl finds an explanation of menstrual taboos and notions of menstrual pollution in this connection between menstruation and death (but see Gottlieb 1988 for a different view).

We hypothesize that where the fetus is held to be menstrually constituted, one will find strong menstrual taboos and assertions of pollution. This is based on the supposition that such taboos and ideologies reflect a notion that the proper role of menstrual blood is in the formation of new life, and that its flow beyond the boundaries of women's bodies marks a missed opportunity for procreation. Our hypothesis would illuminate the observation of Vosselmann (1935:79) that "without a doubt this blood that is so useful ... when it was retained in the womb lost these [useful] qualities as soon as it began to escape from it" (our translation). In this way the presence of menstrual taboos and notions of menstrual pollution, far from signaling the inherent pollution of the female principle as has so often been postulated, may instead point toward a more complex and far-reaching conceptual system that includes elements of folk-biology to constitute the basis for the meaning of the taboos themselves.

This would seem to be the case in Swazi culture, as reported by Kuper (1947; also see Wright 1982 on the Navajo): "menstrual blood is ... considered part of the foetus that grows within the womb—its discharge is analogous to a miscarriage" (Kuper 1947:107). In keeping with our hypothesis, the Swazi say that menstrual blood can pollute crops, cattle, and men alike. However, Kuper continues (1947:107),

> In certain situations ... menstrual blood is not destructive, but is considered a life symbol or rather a life force; thus the recurrence of menstruation after a woman gives birth "washes her" and enables her to cohabit again with her husband, and after a death in the family circle, a man should not cohabit with his wife until she has menstruated.

In this case menstruation both pollutes and purifies: "The verb (Z[ulu]) *geza*, to wash, purify after death, is a euphemism for menstruation. The flow of blood pollutes women yet also cleanses after death or bearing a child" (Kuper 1947:107). (A parallel understanding occurs in certain rabbinical commentaries among Orthodox Jews, as in this Talmudic scholar's verse: "As yeast is good for dough, / so is menstruation good for women"—cited in Vosselmann 1935:121.)

Our hypothesis may explain a certain percentage, but undoubtedly not all, of those cases in which notions of menstrual pollution are found. That is, it should explain those societies in which are found an idea both of menstrual pollution *and* of the menstrual constitution of the fetus. We hope future researchers will pursue this line of inquiry. They will need to take into account indigenous perceptions of biological processes.

NOTES

1. The Christian tradition is not entirely negative in its view of menstruation. Jesus, for example, is said to have cured a woman of the "plague" of "an issue of blood" that had lasted twelve years, making her "whole" (Mark 5:25–29). According to Mark, the incident occurred between Jesus's casting out of "unclean spirits" and "the devil" from the possessed (Mark 5:1–19), and his raising of the daughter of Jairus from death (Mark 5:23–24, 35–43). It is emphasized, however, that Jairus's daughter "was of the age of twelve years" (Mark 5:42), and the structural sense of the juxtaposition of the twelve years of dysmenorrhea, in the sick woman, and the girl's age—when coupled with other Judeo-Christian references to the age of women at menarche—is that Jesus restored the daughter of Jairus to life in the sense of full, fecund womanhood; that is, that "life" in this instance is equated positively with menarche (Jorunn Jacobsen Buckley, personal communication, 1984).

    Ambivalence may well be embedded in the very way Westerners talk about menstruation. In an early study of menstrual euphemisms in several European languages, Joffe found that such expressions fall into five general categories of metaphor: time, color, visitors, other persons, and disabilities (1948:184). Terence Hays (n.d.) is currently researching this subject, and when combined with Joffe's work, Hays's preliminary findings make it clear that in English and other European languages women express diverse perceptions of their own menstrual periods though euphemisms.

2. The notion of shared substances is not only pertinent to the analysis of some menstrual customs, such as joint husband/wife restrictions and rituals, but also to other types of beliefs regarding menstruation. The ideology that menstrual blood is inherited from the mother is widespread, especially in matrilineal societies. Mary Douglas (1969) and Wyatt MacGaffey (1969), however, have both pointed out that it is not just menstrual blood that is thought to be so inherited but veinous blood as well, and that such beliefs are not restricted to matrilineal societies.

Here the topic of shared substance—an underinvestigated one, we think—connects with a wide variety of ideas regarding the composition of fetuses, examined below.

3. Ford (1945:44–46) gives nine examples of societies that hold the fetus to be composed wholly or in part from menstrual blood. Richards (1950:222–223) and Wilson (1957:299) both propose that such a view is found in societies in which descent is reckoned matrilineally. But in accord with Douglas and MacGaffey (see note 2), we do find evidence of this notion being associated with patrilineal descent as well, as it is among the Azande of the Sudan, the Kwoma of New Guinea, and the Lepcha of Tibet and Mongolia (Ford 1945:44).

REFERENCES

Ahern, Emily Martin. 1975. "The power and pollution of Chinese women." In *Women and the Family in Rural Taiwan,* M. Wolf and R. Witke, eds., pp. 193–214. Palo Alto: Stanford University Press.

Balzer, Majorie Mandelstam. 1981. "Rituals of gender identity: markers of Siberian Khanty ethnicity, status and belief." *American Anthropologist* 83: 850–867.

Biersack Aletta. 1983. "Bound blood: Paiela "conception" theory interpreted." *Mankind* 14: 85–100.

Bruner, Edward M. and Victor W. Turner, eds. 1986. *The Anthropology of Experience.* Urbana: University of Illinois Press.

Bulmer, Ralph. 1967. "Why is the cassowary not a bird: A problem in zoological taxonomy among the Karam of the New Guinea Highlands." *Man* 2: 5–25.

Devereux, George. 1950. "The psychology of feminine genital bleeding." *International Journal of Psycho-Analysis* 31: 237–257.

Douglas, Mary. 1966. *Purity and Danger: An Analysis of Concepts of Pollution and Taboo.* London: Routledge & Kegan Paul.

———. 1968. "The relevance of tribal studies." *Journal of Psychosomatic Research* 12: 21–28. Reprinted as "Couvade and menstruation: The relevance of tribal studies." In *Implicit Meanings,* M. Douglas, ed., pp. 60–72. London: Routledge & Kegan Paul.

———. 1969. "Correspondence: Virgin Birth." *Man* 4: 133–134.

———. 1970. *Natural Symbols.* London: Barrie & Rockliff.

———. 1972. "Self-Evidence." The Henry Myers Lecture. Proceedings of the Royal Anthropological Institute for 1972: 27–43. Reprinted in *Implicit Meanings,* M. Douglas, ed., pp. 276–318. London: Routledge & Kegan Paul.

Durkheim, Emile. 1897. "La prohibition de l'inceste et ses origines." *L'Annee Sociologique* 1: 1–70.

———. 1915. *The elementary forms of the religious life,* trans. Joseph Ward Swain. London: George Allen & Unwin. (Original publication: *Les formes elementaires de la vie religieuse, le systeme totemique en Australie.* Paris: F. Alcan, Travaux de l'Annee Sociologique, 1911.)

Evans-Pritchard, E. E. 1932. "Heredity and gestation as the Zande see them." *Sociologus* 8: 400–413.

Ford, Clellan. 1941. *Smoke from Their Fires.* New Haven: Yale University Press.

———. 1945. *A Comparative Study of Human Reproduction.* New Haven: Yale University Press.

Friedl, Ernestine. 1975. *Women and Men: An Anthropologist's View.* New York: Holt, Rinehart & Winston.

Gottlieb, Alma. 1988. "Menstrual cosmology among the Beng of Ivory Coast." In *Blood Magic: The Anthropology of Menstruation,* Thomas Buckley and Alma Gottlieb, eds., pp. 55–74. Berkeley: University of California Press.

———. 1990. "Rethinking Female Pollution: The Beng Case (Cote d'Ivoire)." In *Beyond the Second Sex: Essays in the Anthropology of Gender,* Peggy Sanday, ed., pp. 113–138. Philadelphia: University of Pennsylvania Press.

Hammond, Dorothy and Alta Jablow. 1976. *Women in Cultures of the World.* Menlo Park, CA: Benjamin Cummings.

Hays, Terence E. n.d. *Menstrual Expressions and Menstrual Attitudes.* Unpublished manuscript.

Jette, A. Julius. 1911. "On the superstitions of the Ten'a Indians (middle part of the Yukon Valley, Alaska.)" *Anthropos* 6: 95–108, 241–259, 602–615, 699–723.

Joffe, Natalie F. 1948. "The Vernacular of Menstruation." *Word* 4(3): 181–186.

Kharrazi, Lily. 1980. "State of separation: Syrian Jewish women and menstruation." *National Women's Anthropology Newsletter* (2): 13–14, 27.

Kirksey, Matthew. 1984. "Dying." *Grassroots 1984* (Southern Illinois University at Carbondale), 32–35.

Kuper, Hilda. 1947. *An African aristocracy: Rank among the Swazi.* London: Oxford University Press for the International African Institute.

Ladurie, Emmanual Le Roy. 1979. *Montaillou: The Promised Land of Error.* New York: Random House.

Laqueur, Thomas. 1986. "Orgasm, generation, and the politics of reproductive biology." *Representations 14* (Spring): 1–41. "Special Issue: Sexuality and the Social Body in the Nineteenth Century."

Lincoln, Bruce. 1975. "The religious significance of woman's scarification among the Tiv." *Africa* 45: 316–326.

MacGaffey, Wyatt. 1969. Correspondence: virgin birth. *Man* 4: 457

Mauss, Marcel. 1979. "Body techniques." In *Sociology and Psychology, Essays by Marcel Mauss,* trans. Ben Brewster, pp. 95–123. London: Routledge & Kegan Paul. (Original French publication 1935.)

Meggitt, Mervyn J. 1964. "Male-female relationships in the Highlands of Australian New Guinea." *American Anthropologist* 66, (4), pt. 2: 204–224.

Niangoran-Bouah, Georges. 1964. *La division du temps et le calendrier ritual des peuples lagunaires de Cote- d'Ivoire.* Paris: Institut d'Ethnologie.

Novak, Emil, M. D. 1916. "The superstition and folklore of menstruation." *Johns Hopkins Hospital Bulletin* 27 (307): 270–274 (26 September).

O'Flaherty, Wendy Doniger. 1980. *Women, Androgynes, and Other Mythical beasts.* Chicago: University of Chicago Press.

Ortner, Sherry B. and Harriet Whitehead. 1981. "Introduction: accounting for sexual meanings." In *Sexual Meanings,* S. B. Ortner and H. Whitehead, eds., pp. 1–27. Cambridge: Cambridge University Press.

Paige, Karen Ericksen and Jeffrey M. Paige. 1981. *The Politics of Reproductive Ritual.* Berkeley, Los Angeles, London: University of California Press.

Poole, Fitz John Porter. 1982. "The ritual forging of identity: aspects of person and self in Bimin-Kuskusmin male initiation." In *Rituals of Manhood,* G. H. Herdt, ed., pp. 9–154. Berkeley, Los Angeles, London: University of California Press.

Rattray, R. S. 1927. *Religion and Art in Ashanti.* Oxford: Clarendon Press.

Richards, Audrey I. 1950. "Some types of family structure amongst the Central Bantu." pp. 207–251. In *African Systems of Kinship and Marriage,* A. R. Radcliffe-Brown and Daryll Forde, eds. London: Oxford University Press.

Riviere, Peter G. 1974–1975. "Couvade: a problem reborn." *Man* 9: 423–435; 10: 476.

Rosaldo, Michelle Zimbalist and Jane Monnig Atkinson. 1975. "Man the hunter and woman: metaphors for the sexes in Ilongot magical spells." In *The Interpretation of Symbolism,* Roy Willis, ed., pp. 43–75. London: J. M. Dent & Sons, Ltd.; New York: John Wiley & Sons.

Sanday, Peggy. 1981. *Female Power and Male Dominance: On the Origins of Sexual Inequality.* Cambridge: Cambridge University Press.

Silberbauer, George B. 1963. "Marriage and the girl's puberty ceremony of the G/wi Bushmen." *Africa* 33 (4): 12–26.

Skultans, Vieda. 1988. "Menstrual Symbolism in South Wales." In B*lood Magic: the Anthropology of Menstruation,* pp. 137–160. Thomas Buckley and Alma Gottlieb, eds. Berkeley: University of California Press.

Tambiah, S. J. 1969. "Animals are good to think and good to prohibit." *Ethnology* 8, (4): 423–459.

Thompson, Catherine. 1985. "The power to pollute and the power to preserve: perceptions of female power in a Hindu village." *Social Science and Medicine* 21 (6): 701–711.

Turner, Victor. 1969. *The Ritual Process: Structure and Anti-Structure.* Chicago: Aldine.

Vosselmann, Fritz. 1935. "La menstruation: legendes, coutumes et superstitions." Lyon: Faculte de Medicine et de Pharmacie de Lyon. *Annee Scolaire* 1935–1936, no. 23. Theses de Docteur en Medicine.

Weiner, Annette B. 1976. *Women of Value, Men of Renown: New Perspectives in Trobriand Exchange.* Austin: University of Texas Press.

Wilson, Monica. 1957. *Rituals of Kinship among the Nyakyusa.* London: Oxford University Press.

Wolf, Margery. 1972. *Women and the Family in Rural Taiwan.* Stanford: Stanford University Press.

Wood, Charles T. 1981. "The doctors' dilemma: sin, salvation, and the menstrual cycle in medieval thought." *Speculum* 56: 710–727.

Wright, Anne. 1982. "Attitudes toward childbearing and menstruation among the Navajo." In *Anthropology of Human Birth,* Margarita Artschwager Kay, ed., pp. 377–394. Philadelphia: F. A. Davis Co.

Yalman, Nur. 1964. "Sinhalese healing rituals." *Journal of Asian Studies* 23: 115–150.

V

Culture and Sexuality

The study of sexuality in anthropology is a relatively recent research emphasis. Classic anthropological monographs have reported exotic sexual practices in the course of ethnographic description (for example, we learn in Malinowski's *The Sexual Life of Savages* (1929) that the Trobriand islanders may bite each others' eyelashes in the heat of passion), but other than occasional esoterica, the naturalistic, biological bias has dominated the study of sexuality. However, as Vance observes (1984: 8), "although sexuality, like all human cultural activity, is grounded in the body, the body's structure, physiology, and functioning do not directly or simply determine the configuration or meaning of sexuality." Rather, sexuality is in large part culturally constructed. Just as we may inquire into the culturally variable meanings of masculinity and femininity, we may examine the ways in which sexuality is invested with meaning in particular societies (Ortner and Whitehead 1981: 2).

Sexuality, as a topic of analysis, links the personal and the social, the individual and society. To Americans sex may imply medical facts, Freud, and erotic techniques, but all of these aspects of sexuality are socially shaped and inevitably curbed. Within every culture there are measures for the management of sexuality and gender expression (Ortner and Whitehead 1981: 24-25) and sanctions for those who break the rules.

These sanctions may be imposed at the level of the family, the lineage, the community, or the state. Indeed, Foucault (1981) has suggested that a feature of the recent past is the increasing intervention of the state in the domain of sexuality. In this regard Ross and Rapp (1981: 71) conclude that it is not accidental that contemporary western culture conceptualizes sex as a thing in itself, isolated from social, political, and economic context: "The separation with industrial capitalism of family life from work, of consumption from production, of leisure from labour, of personal life from political life, has completely reorganized the context in which we experience sexuality.... Modern consciousness permits, as earlier systems of thought did not, the positing of 'sex' for perhaps the first time as having an 'independent' existence." However, Caplan (1987: 24) warns that while western culture may have a concept of sexuality divorced from reproduction, marriage, or other social domains, it is not possible to analyze sexuality without reference to the economic, political, and cultural matrix in which it is embedded.

A comparative perspective informs us that the attributes of the person seen as sexual and erotic vary cross-culturally. For example, scarification, the corseted waist, bound feet, and the subincised penis are admired and provocative in particular cultures. Such attributes as these are not only physical symbols of sexuality, but indicators of status. Similarly, Sudanese women enforce infibulation, or pharaonic circumcision, causing serious pain and health risks to young women, for the honor of the lineage. In the name of power, young men applied as recruits to the palace eunuch staff in Imperial China carrying their genitals in jars (Ortner and Whitehead 1981: 24). These examples are reminders of the impact of social concerns and cultural meanings in the domain of sexuality.

Abu-Lughod (in this book) explores the cultural construction of sexuality and local meanings of Islam through an analysis of wedding rituals in a Bedouin community in Egypt's Western Desert. Weddings produce and transform people's experiences of sexuality and gender relations, and serve as a marker of cultural identity. Whereas sexuality in North America is considered something essentially private, separate from society and social power, to these Bedouin the wedding involves sexuality that has a public and participatory element. Connections to kin and control of the kinship group are symbolized in wedding rites. The sexual politics of gender relations were formerly portrayed in women's wedding songs and dances. Changing power relations have led to a deemphasis of this mechanism for challenging male power. As Bedouins are drawn into the wider Egyptian state and economy, weddings increasingly are seen as entertainment and spectacle, rather than as the ritual reproduction of the social and political dynamics of the community.

Research in hunting and gathering societies also shows that sexual intercourse, while personal, can also be a political act. In such societies, claims to women are central to men's efforts to achieve equal status with others (Collier and Rosaldo 1981: 291). Through sexual relations with women, men forge relationships with one another and symbolically express claims to particular women. Shostak (1981) presents the perspective of a !Kung woman, Nisa, on sex, marriage, and fertility in the broader context of a hunting and gathering society in which women have high status.

In !Kung society children learn about sex through observation. Boys and girls play at parenthood and marriage. If they are caught playing at sex, they are scolded but are not severely punished. No value is placed on virginity, and the female body need not be covered or hidden. A girl is not expected to have sex until the onset of menstruation, usually age 16. During adolescence, both heterosexual and homosexual sex play is permitted, and sexual liaisons outside of marriage are also permissible.

The !Kung believe that without sex, people can die, just as without food, one would starve. Shostak observes that "talk about sex seems to be of almost equal importance [to eating]. When women are in the village or out gathering, or when men and women are together, they spend hours recounting details of sexual exploits. Joking about all aspects of sexual experience is commonplace" (1981: 265). According to Nisa, "If a woman doesn't have sex ... her thoughts get ruined and she is always angry" (Shostak 1981: 31).

From Nisa, Shostak elicits the history of her relationships with men, in particular her former husband and constant admirer, Besa, who abandons her while she is pregnant but later tries to persuade her to return and live with him as his wife. Although he seeks the intervention of the headman, Nisa refuses to return to him, and the headman supports her decision. Nisa's characterization of sexuality among the !Kung suggests that for both men and women, engaging in sex is necessary to maintaining good health and is an important aspect of being human.

In contrast, for the past 150 years Anglo-American culture has defined women as less sexual than men. This represents a major shift from the widespread view prior to the seventeenth century that women were especially sexual creatures (Caplan

1987: 3). By the end of the nineteenth century the increasingly authoritative voice of male medical specialists argued that women were characterized by sexual anesthesia (Caplan 1987: 3). Victorian ideas about male sexuality emphasized the highly sexed and baser nature of men. In contrast, Muslim concepts of female sexuality (Mernissi 1987: 33) cast the woman as aggressor and the man as victim. Imam Ghazali, writing in the eleventh century, describes an active female sexuality in which the sexual demands of women appear overwhelming and the need for men to satisfy them is a social duty (Mernissi 1987: 39). Women symbolize disorder and are representative of the dangers of sexuality and its disruptive potential.

The example of the Kaulong of New Guinea further illustrates the extent to which understandings of male and female sexual natures are cultural products (Goodale 1980). Both sexes aspire to immortality through the reproduction of identity achieved through parenting. Sexual intercourse, which is considered animal-like, is sanctioned for married people. Animals are part of the forest and nature, so the gardens of married couples are in the forest. The only sanctioned purpose of sex and marriage is reproduction; sex without childbearing is viewed as shameful. Suicide was formerly considered an acceptable recourse for a childless couple. Sexual activity is thought to be dangerous to men and women in different ways: polluting for men and leading to dangers of birth for women. Goodale notes that girls are encouraged to behave aggressively toward men, to initiate sex, and to choose a husband. In contrast, men are reluctant to engage in sex, are literally "scared to death of marriage," and rarely take the dominant role in courtship (1980: 135). Thus, the Kaulong view seems to reverse the western idea of the passive woman and the active man (Moore 1988: 17).

Attempting to explain such variations in cultural constructions of sexuality, Caplan (1987) suggests that when desire for children is high, fertility and sexuality are hardly distinguished; biological sex is important and impediments to procreation (e.g., contraception, homosexuality) are viewed as wicked. Caplan shows that Hindu tradition values celibacy, although there may be a life stage in which an individual is sexually active. The spirit is valued over the flesh, and celibacy represents a purer and higher state than sexual activity. In contrast, a spirit–flesh dichotomy is less common in Africa and the Caribbean, where sexual activity is thought to be a part of healthy living (Nelson 1987: 234-235). When fertility is less valued, sexual activity is more open and less regulated, and sexuality becomes an aspect of self, not of parenthood. Thus, control of female fertility is linked to control of sexual behavior; when sexual activity is thought to be a prerequisite for good health, there tends to be greater sexual autonomy for women.

Gender, referring to sociocultural designations of behavioral and psychosocial qualities of sexes (Jacobs and Roberts 1989), is commonly contrasted with sex, or the observable biophysiological, morphological characteristics of the individual. Gilmore (in this book) examines the relationship between sex and gender in his analysis of the often dramatic ways in which cultures construct appropriate manhood. He finds a recurring notion that "real manhood is different from simple anatomical maleness, that it is not a natural condition that comes about spontaneously through biological maturation but rather is a precarious or artificial state that boys must win against powerful odds" (1990: 11).

To Gilmore the answer to the manhood puzzle lies in culture. He examines a post-Freudian understanding of masculinity as a category of self-identity, showing how boys face special problems in separating from their mother. A boy's separation and individuation is more perilous and difficult than a girl's, whose femininity is reinforced by the original unity with her mother. Thus, to become separate the boy must pass a test, breaking the chain to his mother. Ultimately, Gilmore concludes that manhood ideologies force men to shape up "on penalty of being robbed of their identity." Men are not innately different from women, but they need motivation to be assertive.

Gilmore notes that some cultures also provide for alternative gender constructs. Popular thinking in the United States dichotomizes two sexes, male and female, and corresponding gender identities, masculinity and femininity, leaving little room for culturally defined variance. Some research suggests at least three phenotypic sexes in human cultures: female, male, and androgynous or hermaphroditic people. This classification refers to characteristics observable to the naked eye rather than to medical classifications of sex types based on chromosomal evidence (Jacobs and Roberts 1989: 440). Linguistic markers for gender reveal culturally specific epistemological categories (Jacobs and Roberts 1989: 439). Accordingly, in English one may distinguish woman, lesbian, man, or gay male. The Chuckchee counted seven genders—three female and four male—while the Mohave reportedly recognize four genders—a woman, a woman who assumes the roles of men, a man, or a male who assumes the roles of women (Jacobs and Roberts 1989: 439–440). Thus, cross-cultural research suggests that we need to use categories of sex and gender that reflect the evidence of diversity rather than rigid classification systems.

In any culture genders are recognized, named, and given meaning in accordance with the culture's rules or customs (Jacobs and Roberts 1989: 446). When a baby is born people generally rely on the appearance of the infant's external genitalia to determine whether that child will be treated as female or male. As a child grows, more criteria come into play, such as the phenotypic expression of sex—facial hair, voice, and breast development. In some societies spiritual development and interests may be used as criteria for gender attribution. One such example is the hijras of Indian society. The hijra role attracts people who in the West might be called eunuchs, homosexuals, transsexuals, transvestites, or hermaphrodites.

The hijra role is deeply rooted in Indian culture, and it accommodates a variety of sexual needs, gender behaviors and identities, and personalities. Nanda (1990) shows that Hinduism encompasses ambiguities and contradictions in gender categories without trying to resolve them. In Hindu myths, rituals, and art, the theme of the powerful man-woman is significant; mythical figures who are androgynes figure in popular Indian culture. Thus the hijra represents an institutionalized third gender role.

Hinduism holds that all people contain both male and female principles, and in some sects male transvestism is used as a way of achieving salvation. There are many references in Hinduism to alternative sexes and sexual ambiguity. However, hijras are viewed ambivalently and can inspire both fear and mockery. Ancient writings indicate criticism of homosexuality, but in actuality homosexuals were tolerated, following the counsel of the classic Hindu text, the Kamasutra, that in sex one should act according to the custom of one's country and one's own inclination. Hijras see themselves as humans, neither man nor woman, calling into question basic social categories of gender. The accommodation of the hijras reflects the extent to which contradictions are embraced and tolerated in Indian culture.

Additional examples of cultures that tolerate gender ambiguity are found in Native American societies, in which a male who felt an affinity for female occupation, dress, and attributes could choose to become classified as a two-spirit, sometimes known as a berdache. Williams (1986) discusses alternative gender identities for Native American women whom he calls amazons; others refer to them as "cross-gender females" or female berdache. According to Williams' use of the term, an amazon is a woman who has manifested an unfeminine character from infancy, has shown no interest in heterosexual relations, and might have expressed a wish to become a man. Such women were known for their bravery and skill as warriors. For example, Kaska Indians would select a daughter to be a son if they had none; after a transformation ritual the daughter would dress like a man and be trained for male tasks. Ingalik Indians also recognize such a status; in this society the amazons even participated in male-only sweat baths. The woman was accepted as a man on the basis of her gender behavior (Williams 1986).

The assignment of this changed gender "operates independently of a person's morphological sex and can determine both gender status and erotic behavior" (Williams 1986: 235). In some societies a woman could choose to be a man, as among the Kutenai Indians. The "manlike woman" was greatly respected, although the Kutenai did not recognize a similar status for men. A tribe with an alternative gender role for one sex did not necessarily have one for the other, and the roles were not seen as equivalent. The Mohave also recognized the status of amazons, subjecting these women to a ritual that authorized them to assume the clothing, sexual activity, and occupation of the opposite, self-chosen sex. It is sometimes believed that such women do not menstruate because menstruation is a crucial part of the definition of a woman. However, the category of amazon is distinct from that of men or women. It is another gender status. Thus, some Native American cultures have a flexible recognition of gender variance, and they incorporate fluidity in their world view.

Sexuality, as differentiated from sex and gender, refers to sexual behaviors, feelings, thoughts, practices, and sexually based bonding behaviors (bisexuality, heterosexuality, homosexuality) (Jacobs and Roberts 1989: 440). Sexual identity, involving an individual's self-attribution of sex preferences and practices, is both a response to and an influence on sexuality. In western culture today sexuality is thought to comprise an important part of one's identity, the core of self (Caplan 1987: 2).

The complex ways in which sexuality acts as a medium for the construction of identities as well as an instrument for the exercise of power are explored in Yelvington's analysis of flirting between female workers and male co-workers and supervisors in a factory in Trinidad (in this volume). Flirting, defined as indirect behavior intended to indicate a possible sexual interest in another individual and to elicit the other's interest, is best understood in the context of the pervasive public display of sexuality in the Caribbean region. Yelvington argues that men's stylized repartee and "sweet talking" marks power relations between men and women. His ethnographic analysis of flirting in a Trinidad factory illustrates how ethnicity, gender, and age shape sexualized relationships among workers and supervisors. Flirting in this work environment recapitulates the discourses and practices of gender relations and ethnic preferences in Trinidad more broadly. Flirting serves as a means for men to control women; in the factory, flirting by supervisors enhances their authority and diminishes younger women's status. For women, flirting serves as a means to resist and mitigate men's control. Both men and women engaged in flirting behavior and discourse become sexual objects, Yelvington argues, but in unequal ways. Thus flirting, as an expression of sexuality, represents an instrument for exercising power and constructing identity along lines of ethnicity, class and gender.

In her discussion of women's intimate friendships (this volume), Blackwood notes that while although a Western viewpoint, sexuality and sexual identity are held to comprise stable, coherent categories, comparative evidence from other cultures challenges this assumption. Based on case studies of women's same sex relations in southern Africa, aboriginal Australia, China, New Guinea, Surinam and Sumatra, she argues that human sexuality takes its form through social processes such as religion, ethnicity, class, family, and reproduction, as well as the material conditions of everyday life. The ethnographic data suggest that sexuality is neither a static state nor a fixed identity. In Lesotho, for example, intimate schoolgirl friendships called "mummy-baby" relationships draw on a tradition of girls' initiations, strong social networks for women, and cultural notions of women's agency in their own sexuality. Close bonds between young women are constructed as an aspect of maturing, and are believed to shape girls' sexuality as they enter into heterosexual relations. Blackwood contends that cultural systems of gender construct different sexual beliefs and practices for men and women, and frame sexual desire within cultural systems of meaning.

As Blackwood points out, in American society sexuality is an integral part of identity on a personal and a social level. Sexuality not only classifies one as male or female, but is an aspect of adult identity. In the United States, where heterosexual relations are the norm, the dominant ideology suggests that heterosexuality is innate and natural. Correspondingly, lesbianism may be threatening to male dominance, while male homosexuality threatens male solidarity and the sense of masculine identity. In other cultures, however, gender and sexuality are conceptually separate. For example, Shepherd (1987) shows that for Swahili Muslims of Mombasa, Kenya, being in a homosexual relationship does not change one's gender, which is essentially assigned by biological sex.

The linkage of sexual identity and gender leads to an identification of gay men and lesbians in terms of their homosexuality, although they do not necessarily change their gender. In this culture a lack of fit between sex, gender, and sexuality causes suspicion. In addition, the conflating of sexuality and gender makes it hard to conceptualize homosexual parents. Bozett (1987) points out that there is almost no scientific literature on this subject, although there is somewhat more discussion of lesbian mothers than of gay fathers. Custodial gay fathers are less common and have been less accessible for research, although there may be as many as three million gay men who are natural fathers, not including those who adopt children, are stepfathers, or are foster parents.

Recent interest in gay families and gay parenting reflects the awareness that the "traditional" nuclear family now describes fewer than one-third of families with children (Bozett 1987: 40). Bozett's research on children of gay fathers suggests that the father–child relationship does not significantly change when the child becomes aware of the father's homosexuality. Although the children may not approve, the bond to their father remains. Because of embarrassment or concern that others will think they too are gay, the children may seek to use social control strategies that will protect their public image of themselves. Gay fathers attempt to prevent homophobic harassment of their children and to prevent them from being socially marginalized. Fathers' homosexuality does not seem to influence children's sexual orientation.

The articles in this section reveal that there are a number of possible combinations of sex, gender, and sexuality, leading to different and culturally acceptable identities (Caplan 1987: 22). Although western categorizations impose a particular rigidity on gender concepts, cross-cultural data demonstrate that these identities are not fixed and unchangeable. This realization necessitates a critique of these western classifications and provokes a number of stimulating questions: Are heterosexuality and homosexuality equally socially constructed? Is there cross-cultural variation in the extent to which sexuality represents a primary aspect of human identity? Is desire itself culturally constituted?

REFERENCES

Bozett, Frederick W. 1987. *Gay and Lesbian Parents.* New York: Praeger Publishers.

Caplan, Pat. 1987. "Introduction." In Pat Caplan (ed.). *The Cultural Construction of Sexuality,* pp. 1–31. London: Tavistock.

Collier, Jane E. and Michelle Z. Rosaldo. 1981. "Politics and Gender in Simple Societies." In Sherry Ortner and Harriet Whitehead (eds.). *Sexual Meanings: The Cultural Construction of Gender and Sexuality,* pp. 275–330. Cambridge: Cambridge University Press.

Foucault, Michel, 1981. *The History of Sexuality.* Harmondsworth: Penguin.

Goodale, Jane C. 1980. "Gender, Sexuality and Marriage: a Kaulong Model of Nature and Culture." In Carol P. MacCormack (ed.). *Nature, Culture and Gender,* pp. 119–143. Cambridge: Cambridge University Press.

Jacobs, Sue-Ellen and Christine Roberts. 1989. "Sex, Sexuality, Gender, and Gender Variance." In Sandra Morgen (ed.). *Gender and Anthropology: Critical Reviews for Research and Teaching,* pp. 438–462. Washington, DC: American Anthropological Association.

Malinowski, Bronislaw. 1929. *The Sexual Life of Savages in Northwestern Melanesia.* New York: Harvest Books.

Mernissi, Fatima. 1987. *Beyond the Veil: Male–Female Dynamics in Modern Muslim Society.* Bloomington and Indianapolis: Indiana University Press.

Moore, Henrietta L. 1988. *Feminism and Anthropology.* Minneapolis: University of Minnesota Press.

Nanda, Serena. 1990. *Neither Man Nor Woman: The Hijras of India.* Belmont, California; Wadsworth, Inc.

Nelson, Nici. 1987. "'Selling her Kiosk': Kikuyu Notions of Sexuality and Sex for Sale in Mathare Valley, Kenya." In Pat Caplan (ed.). *The Cultural Construction of Sexuality,* pp. 217–240. London: Tavistock.

Ortner, Sherry B. and Harriet Whitehead. 1981. "Introduction: Accounting for Sexual Meanings." In Sherry Ortner and Harriet Whitehead (eds.). *Sexual Meanings: The Cultural Construction of Gender and Sexuality,* pp. 1–29. Cambridge: Cambridge University Press.

Ross, E. and R. Rapp. 1981. "Sex and Society: A Research Note from Social History and Anthropology." *Comparative Studies in Society and History* 20: 51–72.

Shepherd, Gill. 1987. "Rank, Gender, and Homosexuality: Mombasa as a Key to Understanding Sexual Options." In Pat Caplan (ed.). *The Cultural Construction of Sexuality,* pp. 240–271. London: Tavistock.

Shostak, Marjorie. 1983. *Nisa: The Life and Words of a !Kung Woman.* Cambridge, MA: Harvard University Press.

Vance, Carole S. 1984. "Pleasure and Danger: Toward a Politics of Sexuality." In Carole S. Vance (ed.). *Pleasure and Danger: Exploring Female Sexuality,* pp.1–29. Boston: Routledge and Kegan Paul.

Williams, Walter L. 1986. *The Spirit and The Flesh.* Boston: Beacon Press.

Is There a Muslim Sexuality?
Changing Constructions of Sexuality
In Egyptian Bedouin Weddings

Lila Abu-Lughod

The project of defining the nature of Muslim Arab sexuality—what it is or what it should be—has engaged many people with different stakes and interests. Western discourses have tended to contrast the negative sexuality of "the East" with the positive sexuality of the West. French colonial settlers in Algeria depicted Algerian women in pornographic postcards that suggested a fantastic Oriental world of perverse and excessive sexuality (Alloula 1986). Western feminists concerned with global issues dwell on veiling and other practices like clitoridectomy found in the Muslim Arab world as signs of the repressive control over or exploitation of women's sexuality (e.g., Daly 1978).

From the Muslim world itself come other discourses on Arab Muslim sexuality. These include religious and legal texts and pronouncements, but also, more recently, some critical studies by intellectuals and scholars. How different the understandings can be is clear from two important books. One, by a Tunisian scholar with a background in psychoanalytic thought, argues that the misogynist practices of sexuality in the Muslim world are corruptions of the ideals of the Quran and other religious texts (Bouhdiba 1985). The second, by a Moroccan sociologist, argues from a feminist perspective that the legal and sacred texts themselves, like the erotic texts that flourished in the medieval period, carry negative messages about and perpetuate certain consistent attitudes toward the bodies and behavior of Muslim women (Sabbah 1984).

Original material prepared for this text.

What these various discourses on Arab Muslim sexuality, by outsiders and insiders, defenders and critics, share is the presumption that there is such a thing as a "Muslim sexuality." An anthropologist like myself, familiar with the tremendous variety of communities to be found in the regions composing the Muslim Arab world, would have to question this presumption. Neither Islam nor sexuality should be essentialized—taken as things with intrinsic and transhistorical meanings. Rather, both the meaning of Islam and the constructions of sexuality must be understood in their specific historical and local contexts.[1]

To show why I argue this, I will analyze wedding rituals in a community of Awlad 'Ali Bedouin in Egypt's Western Desert—a community I worked in over a period of twelve years. Weddings are the highlight of social life, awaited with anticipation and participated in with enthusiasm. Each wedding is different. And each wedding is a personal affair of great moment for the bride and groom, even if only one dramatic event in what will be their marriage, lasting for years. Yet public rituals in face-to-face societies are also arenas where people play out their social and political relations. There are other discourses and practices related to sexuality in this Bedouin community but none so powerfully seek to produce, and are now transforming, people's experiences of sexuality and gender relations as weddings do. Without pretending that a symbolic analysis exhausts the meaning of weddings for the individuals involved, I would still insist that such an analysis of Awlad 'Ali weddings is useful: It reveals both how sexuality is constructed by the symbols and practices of members of particular communities and how these symbols and practices themselves are open to change and political contestation. Islam, it will be seen, figures not so much as a blueprint for sexuality as a weapon in changing relations of power.

SEXUALITY AND CULTURAL IDENTITY

In the twelve years between 1978 and 1990 that I had been regularly returning to this community of Arab Muslim sedentarized herders in Egypt, the same questions had been asked of me, sometimes even by the same people, as were asked in the first month of my stay. Usually in the context of a gathering of older women, one old woman would lean toward me and ask if I were married. After a short discussion of the fact that I was not, she or another older woman would ask me the next intense question: "Where you come from, does the bridegroom do it with the finger or with 'it'?" The first time they asked me this, I did not know what they meant by "it" and they had a good laugh. The question that followed inevitably in such conversations was, "And do they do it during the daytime or at night?" They were asking about weddings and particularly about the defloration of the virgin bride, which is for them the central moment of a wedding.[2]

In the obsessive concern with whether they do it with the finger or "it," at night or during the daytime, is a clue to one of the things the discourse on this aspect of sexuality has become as the Awlad 'Ali Bedouins have greater contact and interaction with outsiders, primarily their Egyptian peasant and urban neighbors. Whatever its former or current meaning within the community, meanings I will analyze in the following section, the central rite of weddings has now also become a marker of cultural identity—essential to the Awlad Ali's self-defining discourse on what makes them distinctive.

Individuals vary in how they evaluate their differences from their compatriots. When I met the Bedouin representative to the Egyptian Parliament, a sophisticated man in sunglasses whose long contact with other Egyptians showed in his dialect, he assured me that there were a few Bedouin practices that were wrong: One was that they used the finger in the daytime. But he defended the practice by saying that it reminded girls to be careful. Another respected man of the community explained to me that "entering" with the finger was wrong. "We're the only ones who do it this way," he noted. Then he added, "Nothing in our religion says you should." By way of excuse, though, he said, "But the faster the groom does it, the better—the more admired he is because it means he wasn't timid or cowardly." Even women occasionally complained that it was stupid how the female wedding guests waited and waited, just to see that drop of blood. But they too defended the ceremony, saying that the defloration had to take place in the afternoon so that everyone could see and there would be no doubts about the reputation of the girl. Their horror at the idea that the groom would use "it" came from their fear that it would be more painful for the bride.

Besides asking whether they do it with the finger or "it," day or night, the women I knew often asked whether, where I came from, there was anyone with the bride to hold her down. They were surprised to hear that she needed no one and marveled that she wasn't afraid to be alone with the man. Among themselves, they almost always had a few older women, usually aunts or close neighbors of the groom and bride, in the room with the bride when the groom came to her. There in theory to hold the bride, these women also end up giving advice to the groom and making sure that he knew what to do so that everything—the display of the blood on the cloth—would turn out right.

For their part, somewhat like most Europeans and Americans, non-Bedouin Egyptians and assimilated Awlad 'Ali from the agricultural areas find Bedouin weddings scandalous and distasteful. Bedouin women are not unaware of these views and the men discussed previously were probably reacting defensively to them. These outsiders may laugh at some customs but they are embarrassed by others. After one wedding in the community in which I was living, the bride's aunt, who had spent most of her life in a non-Bedouin provincial town, talked about the wedding and some of the customs she had witnessed that made her laugh "until her stomach hurt." She obviously considered her new in-laws backward.[3]

What seemed to disturb her most was the public nature of what she felt should be private. She thought it humiliating, for example, that at night, the young men from the community (peers of the bridegroom) hung around the room, listening, shining a flashlight under the door and through the window, and generally being disruptive. More horrible to her was the public display of the blood-stained cloth. "It was incredible," she exclaimed. "After the defloration didn't you hear my son saying to his aunt when she went to hang the cloth on the tent ropes, 'It's shameful, my aunt, it's shameful to put the cloth out for people to see.'" Like other urban and rural Egyptians, she thought that the bride and groom should be brought together at night and left alone.

Although other Egyptians and Americans might feel that such privacy is more civilized, the Awlad 'Ali women I knew did not see it that way. Bedouin women were scandalized by the secrecy of night deflorations, the immediate and explicit link such weddings make between marriage and sexual intercourse, and what they view as either the total vulnerability of the poor bride forced to be alone with a man or, even worse, the bride's immodest desire for a man. They knew that instead of struggling, the Egyptian bride has her photo taken with her husband-to-be, she sits with him at weddings where the sexes mix, and she dresses in makeup and fancy clothes for all to see. Because poorer Bedouin men sometimes marry young women from peasant areas, whether they are of Egyptian stock or long-sedentarized Bedouin involved in agriculture, the Bedouin

women also knew that unmarried sisters accompanied the bride. They interpreted this practice as a shameful attempt to display and "sell" marriageable daughters. They also knew that such brides sometimes arrived bringing a cooked duck or goose to feed a new husband; they took this as a sign of the bride's unseemly eagerness to please the groom.

Egyptian weddings, much like American ones, construct the couple as a separate unit, distinct from families or ties to members of the same gender group. At their center is a sexual joining that is private and intimate. For the Awlad 'Ali, this is a strange thing. The secrecy of private sex, in the dark, behind closed doors, and preferably in the foreign or anonymous setting (for the honeymoon) produces sexuality as something personal, intensely individual, apparently separate from society and social power. It produces sexuality as something belonging in an inviolable private sphere—the bedroom—a sphere in which others cannot interfere with whatever pleasure or violence and coercion accompanies it. One of the consequences of this construction of sexuality is that we, and perhaps Egyptians, come to think there is a part of oneself that is not social or affected by the prevailing power relations in society.[4]

The three crucial elements in the Bedouin discourse on differences between their weddings and those of other groups are (1) whether the defloration is public and participatory, (2) whether it involves sexual intercourse, and (3) whether it is seen as a contest, especially between bride and groom. These elements also had meaning within the local context. In Bedouin weddings the ways in which sexuality is related to power relations and the social order were clear. Marriages have been the occasion for people to collectively enact and reproduce this social order and the individual's place in it. And the individual's place was, until recently, very much a part of the group—whether the kin group or the group defined by gender.

WEDDINGS AS PUBLIC RITES: THE POWER OF KINSHIP AND GENDER

The participants in Awlad 'Ali Bedouin weddings instantiate, by means of a bride and groom, the relations between families or kin groups on the one hand, and the relations between men and women on the other. A symbolic analysis of the central rite, the defloration, enacted in a homologous fashion on the bodies of the bride and groom and on the collective bodies of the gathered kin and friends, reveals that it produces an understanding of sexuality as something public and focused on crossing thresholds, opening passages, and moving in and out. There are no strong messages of mingling or joining or even interchange in a private sexual act. The emphasis is on opening the bride's vagina by breaking the hymen and bringing out or making visible what was in there. And although people say that deflorations should be done during the daytime so everyone can see the cloth, the fact that in the rhythm of daily life morning and daytime generally are times of opening and going out from home or camp, while evening is a time of returning inward, cannot but reinforce the auspiciousness of this time for opening and taking outward.[5]

That this opening is a prelude to the insemination which should eventuate in childbirth is suggested by some practices associated with the blood-stained virginity cloth. It is taken out of the room by the groom and thrown to the women gathered just outside. It is said that if the cloth is then brought back into the room without the bride having exited first—if, as they say, the cloth enters upon her—it will block her from conceiving.[6] Young women are told to save their virginity cloths; if they have trouble conceiving, they must bathe in water in which they have soaked the cloth.

Everything in the rites and the songs that accompany them suggests that the individuals engaged in this opening and being opened, taking out and showing, and having something taken out and shown, embody both their kin groups and their gender groups. The connection to kin, and control by the kin group, is clear in the key role they have in arranging and negotiating marriages and is reflected in the songs the groom's female relatives sing as they go to fetch the bride from her father's household. It is also reinforced in the songs the bride's female kin sing to greet these people. Most of the songs compliment the social standing of the families of the bride and groom.

Even the practices and movements of the wedding itself perpetuate the identifications with kin groups. Most brides, even today, are brought from their fathers' households completely covered by a white woolen woven cloak (*jard*) that is the essential item of men's dress. The cloak must belong to the girl's father or some other male kinsman. So, protected and hidden by her father's cloak, she is brought out of her father's protected domain and carried to her husband's kin group's domain. There she is rushed, still hidden, into the room (or in the past, the tent) which she will share with her husband. Although nowadays the woven cloak is usually removed once she enters the room, in the past the bride remained under her father's cloak and was not revealed even to the women gathered around her until after the defloration.

The virginity of the bride is also constructed as something inseparable from her family's honor. Although one unmarried girl explained the importance of the blood-stained cloth in terms of her own reputation, she stressed the effect it would have on others.

> For us Bedouins, this is the most important moment in a girl's life. No matter what anyone says afterward, no one will pay attention as long as there was blood on the cloth. They are suspicious of her before. People talk. "She went here, she went there." "She looked at So-and-so." "She said hello to So-and-so." "She went to the orchard." But when they see this blood the talk is cut off.... When they see the cloth, she can come and go as she pleases. They love her and everything is fine.

The best way to get a sense of who has a stake in the girl's virginity and why is to listen to the conventional songs sung wildly outside the door of the bride's room as the defloration is underway. Unmarried girls and some young married women clap and sing rhyming songs that refer to the effect of the proof of the bride's virginity on various members of her family and community.

Make her dear Mom happy, Lord
Hanging up her cloth on the tent ropes

O Saint 'Awwaam on high
Don't let anyone among us be shamed

Older women sing more serious songs that take up similar themes:

When the people have gathered
O Generous One favor us with a happy ending
. . .

Behind us are important men
who ask about what we are doing ...

Relatives of the bride show their support and faith in the bride in songs like this:

I'm confident in the loved one
you'll find it there intact ...

Even the groom's behavior during the defloration reflects on his relatives. One song a relative of his might sing as he arrives or is inside with the bride is the following:

Son, be like your menfolk
strong willed and unafraid ...

After the virginity cloth is brought out by the groom and thrown to the women, a different set of songs is sung. These praise the cloth and the honor of the girl who had remained a virgin. The songs reflect on who is affected by her purity and who is proud. At one wedding a female relative of the bride sang to a nephew nearby:

Go tell your father, Said
the banner of her honor is flying high ...

About the bride a woman might sing:

Bravo! She was excellent
she who didn't force down her father's
eyelashes ...

Given this group investment in the bride's virginity, the central rite of the wedding becomes a drama of suspense and relief that must powerfully shape people's experiences of sexuality as something that belongs to the many, and especially to one's family. The wedding is also, importantly, an occasion when families find themselves in some rivalry, the honor of each at stake. This was more apparent in the past when the young men celebrated all night on the eve of the wedding and expressed the rivalry through singing contests that sometimes broke out into actual fights between lineages.

Kinship is not the only power-laden aspect of social life that finds itself reflected and reinforced in the wedding. The second set of power relations weddings play with are those of gender. The bride and groom in the wedding rite enact the charged relations between men and women as distinct genders in a kind of battle of the sexes. Although most activities in the community are informally segregated by gender, at weddings—in part because there are non-family members present—the sexual segregation is more obvious and fixed, women and men forming highly separate collectivities for nearly all events.

Given this separation of the sexes, the defloration, taking place in the middle of the day when all are gathered in their distinct places, becomes a ritualized and extreme form of encounter between both the bride and groom and the women and men who surround each of them. The movements of the groom and his age-mates as they penetrate the crowd of women surrounding the bride mirror the groom's penetration of his bride, who forms a unit with the women in the room with her. The young men stand just outside the door, sometimes dancing and singing, ready to fire off guns in celebration when the groom emerges. They rush him back away from the women. This mirroring is expressed in the ambiguity of the term used for both moments of this event: the entrance (*khashsha*) refers both to the entry with the finger and the whole defloration process when the groom enters the bride's room, which can be thought of as his kin group's womb.

The encounter between male and female takes the form of a contest. The groom is encouraged to be fearless. He is expected to finish the deed in as short a time as possible. The bride is expected to try valiantly to fight him off. Taking the virginity she has been so careful to guard and thus opening the way for his progeny is the groom's victory; the bride doesn't give it up without a struggle. Calling this, as the literature often does, a virginity test is a misnomer in that it misses this combative dimension of the ritualized act. The way people describe what happens even on the wedding night suggests again that the groom and bride are involved in a contest. The rowdy young men who listen outside the marital chamber want to know "who won." They know this, some adolescent girls informed me, not just by whether the groom succeeds in having intercourse with his bride (a rare event), but by whether the groom succeeds in making his bride talk to him and answer his questions. This is, perhaps, another kind of opening up.

There is other evidence that weddings provoke a heightened attention to issues of gender and sexual mixing. One of the most revealing and intriguing is the spontaneous cross-dressing that sometimes happens at weddings. At several weddings I attended one woman in our community actually put on men's clothes, a fake mustache and beard, and covered her head in a man's headcloth. Amidst much hilarity she came out to dance in front of the bride. Others expressed some disapproval and called this woman a bit mad. But they laughed riotously anyway. One woman who thought it excessive described someone else who she thought was quite funny: All she did was dance in front of the bride with a shawl bunched up in front like

male genitalia. Sometimes it was reported that the unmarried men and young boys had celebrated the night before the wedding by dressing up a boy with women's bracelets and a veil and dancing in front of him as if he were a bride.

SEXUAL TRANSFORMATIONS

Many Awlad 'Ali claim that their rituals are changing. In this final section, I want to explore how in these changed wedding practices we can begin to track changes in the nature of power and social relations. This is further support for my initial argument that constructions of sexuality cannot be understood apart from understandings of particular forms of social power. Most people talked about changes in weddings over the last twenty years or so in terms of what had been lost. Many said weddings were not fun any more. As far as I could determine, the main element that seems to have been lost is the celebration the night before the wedding (*saamir*). Not only do the young men no longer sing back and forth, but no longer is it even thinkable that a young woman from the community would come out to dance in front of them. This is what used to happen and the change is crucial for Bedouin gender relations.

What happened in the past was that an unmarried sister or cousin of the groom would be brought out from among the women by a young boy. She would dance amidst a semi-circle of young men. Her face veiled and her waist girded with a man's white woven cloak, like the one the bride would come covered in the following day, she danced with a stick or baton in her hands. According to one man who described this to me, the young men tried to "beg" the stick from her, sometimes using subterfuges like pretending to be ill; she would often bestow the stick, he said, on someone she fancied. But according to the women I spoke with, the young men would sometimes try to grab the stick from her and she would, if they were too aggressive, get angry with them and leave.

The young men took turns singing songs that welcomed the dancer and then described her every feature in flattering terms. The standard parts praised in such songs were her braids, her eyes, her eyebrows, her cheeks, her lips, her tattoos, her neck, her breasts, her arms, her hands, and her waist—most of which, it should be remembered, because of the way she was dressed were not actually visible. Thus in a sense the dancer was, through men's songs, made into the ideal woman, attractive object of men's desires.

The dancer must be seen as the bride's double or stand-in, an interpretation supported by the other occasion on which a young woman danced in front of men. In the days before cars, brides were carried from their fathers' households to their husbands' on camel-back, completely cloaked and sitting hidden inside a wooden litter (*karmuud*) covered in red woven blankets. Another woman always preceded her on foot, dancing as young men sang to her and shot off guns near her.

In both cases, the dancer as bride and as ideal womanhood went out before men who complimented and sought her. What is crucial to notice is how the women described the dancer. They attributed to her a special bravery and described her actions as a challenge to the young men. One wedding in which a young woman was accidentally wounded by a poorly aimed gun was legendary. The wedding went on, the story went, as a second dancer who had been near her merely wiped the blood from her forehead and continued to dance. More telling is the ritualized struggle over the stick, which one anthropologist who worked with a group in Libya has argued is associated with virginity (Mason 1975). A woman explained to me, "If the dancer is sharp they can't take the stick from her. They'll be coming at her from all sides but she keeps it."

But perhaps some of the short songs traditionally exchanged between the women (gathered in a tent some distance away from the young men standing in a line near the dancer) and the young men, make clearest the ways in which a challenge between the sexes was central to weddings. One especially memorable competitive exchange was the following. As her sister danced a woman sang of her:

A bird in the hot winds glides
and no rifle scope can capture it ...

A man responded with the song:

The heart would be no hunter
if it didn't play in their feathers ...

In the loss and delegitimation of this whole section of the wedding ritual, an important piece of the construction of Bedouin sexual relations has disappeared. Today, all that is left in a ritual that was a highly charged and evenly matched challenge between the sexes is the enactment of the men's hunt. The groom is the hunter, the bride his prey. Decked out in her make-up and white satin dress, she is brought from her father's house and her "virginity" taken by her groom in a bloody display.

Wedding songs, only sung by women now, reinforce this construction of the bride as vulnerable prey. They liken the bride to a gazelle. This is a compliment to her beauty but also suggests her innocence and defenselessness. Other songs liken the groom to a falcon or hunter. This is no longer balanced by women's former powers to create desire but elude capture.

The disappearance of the female dancer can thus be seen to have shifted the balance such that women's capacities to successfully challenge men have been de-emphasized. Although the sexes are still pitted against each other, the contest is no longer represented as even.

There is a second important point to be made about the dancer that relates to some transformations in constructions of power and sexuality. For it is not completely true that women no longer dance in front of men at Awlad 'Ali weddings. It has become unacceptable for respectable young kinswomen to dance, but there are now some professional dancers. They accompany musical troupes hired to entertain at weddings of the Bedouin nouveau riche. These women may or may not be prostitutes but they are certainly not considered respectable.[7] In that sense, and in the fact that ordinary women go nowhere near the areas where these musicians and dancers perform, one cannot any longer claim that the dancer represents Woman or enacts women's challenge of men. The opposite may be true. This new kind of wedding may be introducing a new view of women, one quite familiar to us in the United States but quite strange to the Awlad 'Ali: women as sexual commodities stripped of their embeddedness in their kin groups or the homosocial world of women.

The professionalization of weddings as entertainment and spectacle (if spectacles that retain vestiges of the participatory in that young men seize the microphone to sing songs) may also be signaling a fundamental shift in the relationship of the construction of sexuality and the construction of the social order. What seems to be disappearing is the participation of the whole community in the responsibility of ritually reproducing the fundamental social and political dynamics of the community. Does this indicate the emergence of a new kind of power? One that works differently? One whose nexus is perhaps the individual rather than the kin group or gender group? This new form of wedding is not being adopted universally in the Bedouin region since the poor cannot afford it and the respectable condemn it as undignified and inappropriate for pious Muslims. Nevertheless, as a public discourse it must enter and shape the field of sexuality for all.

The third and final historical shift I will discuss comes out in the comments women made about what had happened to weddings. One old woman reminisced about weddings of the past. She shook her head and laughed, "No, the things they did before you can't do anymore. Nowadays weddings are small, like a shrunken old man. People used to really celebrate, staying up all night, for days! But they

have become like the Muslim Brothers now." The younger woman she was talking to had explained for me. "They say it is wrong. Now everything is forbidden. People before didn't know. They were ignorant." She used a term with connotations of the pre-Islamic era.

These women's invocations of Islam and the proper behavior of the pious in the contexts of weddings mark some significant changes in power relations. It has always been important to the Awlad 'Ali that they are Muslims and that they are good Muslims. And these two women themselves were devout. They prayed regularly and the old one had been on the pilgrimage to Mecca. Yet when they and other women brought up the religious wrongness of their traditional wedding practices, it was with some ambivalence since they were also nostalgic for the richer days of the past. After one wedding there was a hint of disapproval in women's gossip about one aunt in the community. Someone with a good voice who usually sang at weddings, she had just returned from the pilgrimage to Mecca and had refused this time. "It is wrong," she told them. They thought she was being self-righteous—and selfish.

What is really at stake comes out clearly from women's discussions of a happy wedding that had taken place in my absence. I was told that, as usual, for days before the wedding the women and girls had been celebrating by themselves every evening, drumming and singing. The older men of the community wanted them to stop and instructed them that at least once the guests (non-relatives) had begun to arrive, they would have to stop. It was shameful to sing in front of people, the men insisted. On the eve of the wedding as the women and girls gathered and began to sing and dance in celebration, the groom's father came in to greet his visiting female relatives. He also wanted to try to silence the group of women. When he entered the tent, he saw his own older sister, a dignified woman in her sixties, dancing. "Hey, what's this?" he said. "Rottenest of days, even you, Hajja?" He called her by the respectful title reserved for those who have performed the pilgrimage to

Mecca. "That's right," she answered definitely, "even me!" Everyone laughed, then and each time they retold the story.

Women still refuse to be stopped from celebrating weddings. But the older men, armed with religious righteousness, are clearly trying to assert authority over them in domains that were previously inviolable. Weddings, like the discontinued sheep-shearing festivities to which they are often likened, were always before classified as occasions where young men and young women could express desires. Elder men were not to interfere. At sheep-shearing festivities young men used to sing with impunity oblique sexual songs to flirt with the women present. The songs often insulted the patriarch whose herds the young men were shearing. Similarly, at weddings young men sang to women, not just the dancer. Even more important, women sang back—songs of love and desire. Older men made sure they were not in the vicinity.[8]

Now, not only have the exchanges between young men and women stopped but older men seem to be trying to assert control over the separate women's festivities. Their motives for this intervention are irrelevant. They may genuinely believe they are encouraging their families to live up to an interpretation of Islam that denounces such frivolity as impious. The effect, however, on women and young men, is that by means of this discourse of Islamic propriety wielded by older men, they are being displaced as the prime actors in the rites that produced and reproduced Bedouin constructions of sexuality and desire.

If, as I have tried to show, in a small Bedouin community in Egypt, sexuality can come to be a crucial marker of cultural identity, and if the construction of sexuality is so closely tied to the organization of kinship and gender and changes as the community is transformed by such broad processes as its incorporation into the wider Egyptian nation and economy, then it seems impossible to assert the existence of a Muslim sexuality that can be read off texts or shared across communities with very different histories and ways of life. Instead, we need to think about specific constructions of sexuality and, in the case of the Muslim Arab world, about the variable role discourses on religion can play in those constructions.

Author's Note: Most of the research in Egypt on which this article is based was supported by an NEH Fellowship for College Teachers and a Fulbright Award under the Islamic Civilization Program. I am grateful to Samia Mehrez for inviting me to present an early version at Cornell University. I am more grateful to the women and men in the Awlad 'Ali community who shared their lives, including their weddings, with me.

NOTES

1. The literature, especially the feminist literature, on sexuality has become vast in the last decade or two. A helpful early text is Vance (1984). Anthropologists have recently begun to pay more attention to constructions of sexuality and their cross-cultural perspective should contribute to our understanding of the way that sexuality is constructed. For a good introduction to some of that work, see Caplan (1987).
2. For this reason the weddings of divorcees or widows are not celebrated with as much enthusiasm and are considered somewhat ordinary affairs.
3. For example, she described what is known as the *dayra* (the circling). On the evening of the wedding day, they had seated the bride and groom on a pillow, back to back. A neighbor carrying a lamb on his back, holding one foreleg in each of his hands, had walked around and around them—seven times. She mimicked the audience counting: "Hey, did you count that one? One, two, three, four." "Thank God," she said at one point, "there were no outsiders (non-relatives) from back home with us. How embarrassing it would have been."
4. The theorist who has most developed this notion of the effects on subjectivity and sense of individuality of the Western discourses on sexuality is Michel Foucault (1978, 1985).
5. For an analysis of similar kinds of symbolic constructions of gender and sexuality, see Bourdieu's (1977) work on Algerian Kabyles. My analysis of the meaning of this rite differs significantly from that of Combs-Schilling (1989), who worked in Morocco.

6. For more on rituals related to fertility and infertility, see my *Writing Women's Worlds* (1993). Boddy (1989) has analyzed for Muslim Sudanese villagers the extraordinary symbolic stress on women's fertility over their sexuality.
7. As Van Nieuwkerk (1995) has documented, this is generally true about professional dancers in Egypt.
8. Peters (1990) describes a similar avoidance by elders of wedding celebrations among the Bedouin of Cyrenaica in the 1950s.

REFERENCES

Abu-Lughod, Lila. 1993. *Writing Women's Worlds: Bedouin Stories.* Berkeley and Los Angeles: University of California Press.

Alloula, Malek. 1986. *The Colonial Harem.* Myran and Wlad Godzich, trans. Minneapolis: University of Minnesota Press.

Boddy, Janice. 1989. *Wombs and Alien Spirits: Women, Men, and the Zar Cult in Northern Sudan.* Madison, WI: University of Wisconsin Press.

Bouhdiba, Abdelwahab. 1985. *Sexuality in Islam.* London and Boston: Routledge & Kegan Paul.

Bourdieu, Pierre. 1977. *Outline of a Theory of Practice.* Cambridge: Cambridge University Press.

Caplan, Patricia, ed. 1987. *The Cultural Construction of Sexuality.* London and New York: Tavistock Publications.

Combs-Schilling, M.E. 1989. *Sacred Performances: Islam, Sexuality and Sacrifice.* New York: Columbia University Press.

Daly, Mary. 1978. *Gyn/ecology, the Metaethics of Radical Feminism.* Boston: Beacon Press.

Foucault, Michel. 1978. *The History of Sexuality: Volume 1: An Introduction.* New York: Random House.

———. 1985. *The Use of Pleasure.* Vol. 2 of *The History of Sexuality.* New York: Pantheon.

Mason, John. 1975. "Sex and Symbol in the Treatment of Women: The Wedding Rite in a Libyan Oasis Community." *American Ethnologist* 2: 649–61.

Peters, Emrys. 1990. *The Bedouin of Cyrenaica.* Edited by Jack Goody and Emanuel Marx. Cambridge: Cambridge Univeristy Press.

Sabbah, Fatna A. 1984. *Woman in the Muslim Unconscious.* New York and Oxford: Pergamon Press.

Vance, Carole. 1984. *Pleasure and Danger: Exploring Female Sexuality.* Boston and London: Routledge & Kegan Paul.

Van Nieuwkerk, Karin. 1995. *"A Trade Like Any Other": Female Singers and Dancers in Egypt.* Austin, TX: University of Texas Press.

The Manhood Puzzle

David D. Gilmore

> There are continuities of masculinity that transcend cultural differences.
>
> —*Thomas Gregor, Anxious Pleasures*

Are there continuities of masculinity across cultural boundaries, as the anthropologist Thomas Gregor says (1985:209)? Are men everywhere alike in their concern for being "manly?" If so, why? Why is the demand made upon males to "be a man" or "act like a man" voiced in so many places? And why are boys and youths so often tested or indoctrinated before being awarded their manhood? These are questions not often asked in the growing literature on sex and gender roles. Yet given the recent interest in sexual stereotyping, they are ones that need to be considered if we are to understand both sexes and their relations.

Regardless of other normative distinctions made, all societies distinguish between male and female; all societies also provide institutionalized sex-appropriate roles for adult men and women. A very few societies recognize a third, sexually intermediary category, such as the Cheyenne *berdache,* the Omani *xanith,* and the Tahitian *mahu* ... but even in these rare

Reprinted with permission from David D. Gilmore, *Manhood in the Making* (New Haven: Yale University Press, 1990), pp. 9–29. Copyright © 1990 Yale University Press.

cases of androgynous genders, the individual must make a life choice of identity and abide by prescribed rules of sexual comportment. In addition, most societies hold consensual ideas—guiding or admonitory images—for conventional masculinity and femininity by which individuals are judged worthy members of one or the other sex and are evaluated more generally as moral actors. Such ideal statuses and their attendant images, or models, often become psychic anchors, or psychological identities, for most individuals, serving as a basis for self-perception and self-esteem (D'Andrade 1974:36).

These gender ideals, or guiding images, differ from culture to culture. But, as Gregor and others (e.g., Brandes 1980; Lonner 1980; Raphael 1988) have argued, underlying the surface differences are some intriguing similarities among cultures that otherwise display little in common. Impressed by the statistical frequency of such regularities in sexual patterning, a number of observers have recently argued that cultures are more alike than different in this regard. For example, Gregor (1985:200) studied a primitive Amazonian tribe and compared its sex ideals to those of contemporary America. Finding many subsurface similarities in the qualities expected of men and women, he concludes that our different cultures represent only a symbolic veneer masking a bedrock of sexual thinking. In another study, the psychologist Lonner (1980:147) echoes this conclusion. He argues that culture is "only a thin veneer covering an essential universality" of gender dimorphism. In their comprehensive survey of sex images in thirty different cultures, Williams and Best (1982:30) conclude that there is "substantial similarity" to be found "panculturally in the traits ascribed to men and women."

Whether or not culture is only a thin veneer over a deep structure is a complicated question: as the rare third sexes show, we must not see in every culture "a Westerner struggling to get out" (Munroe and Munroe 1980:25). But most social scientists would agree that there do exist striking regularities in standard male and female roles across cultural boundaries regardless of other social arrangements (Archer and Lloyd 1985: 283–84). The one regularity that concerns me here is the often dramatic ways in which cultures construct an appropriate manhood—the presentation or "imaging" of the male role. In particular, there is a constantly recurring notion that real manhood is different from simple anatomical maleness, that it is not a natural condition that comes about spontaneously through biological maturation but rather is a precarious or artificial state that boys must win against powerful odds. This recurrent notion that manhood is problematic, a critical threshold that boys must pass through testing, is found at all levels of sociocultural development regardless of what other alternative roles are recognized. It is found among the simplest hunters and fishermen, among peasants and sophisticated urbanized peoples; it is found in all continents and environments. It is found among both warrior peoples and those who have never killed in anger.

Moreover, this recurrent belief represents a primary and recurrent difference from parallel notions of femaleness. Although women, too, in any society are judged by sometimes stringent sexual standards, it is rare that their very status as woman forms part of the evaluation. Women who are found deficient or deviant according to these standards may be criticized as immoral, or they may be called unladylike or its equivalent and subjected to appropriate sanctions, but rarely is their right to a gender identity questioned in the same public, dramatic way that it is for men. The very paucity of linguistic labels for females echoing the epithets "effete," "unmanly," "effeminate," "emasculated," and so on, attest to this archetypical difference between sex judgments worldwide. And it is far more assaultive (and frequent) for men to be challenged in this way than for women.

Perhaps the difference between male and female should not be overstated, for "femininity" is also something achieved by women who seek social approval. But as a social icon, femininity seems to be judged differently. It usually involves questions of body ornament or sexual allure, or other essentially cosmetic behaviors that enhance, rather than create, an inherent quality of character. An authentic femininity rarely involves tests or proofs of action, or confrontations with dangerous foes: win-or-lose contests dramatically played out on the public stage. Rather than a critical threshold passed by traumatic testing, an either/or condition, femininity is more often construed as a biological given that is culturally refined or augmented.

TESTS OF MANHOOD: A SURVEY

Before going any further, let us look at a few examples of this problematic manhood. Our first stop is Truk Island, a little atoll in the South Pacific. Avid fishermen, the people of Truk have lived for ages from the sea, casting and diving in deep waters. According to the anthropologists who have lived among them, the Trukese men are obsessed with their masculinity, which they regard as chancy. To maintain a manly image, the men are encouraged to take risks with life and limb and to think "strong" or "manly" thoughts, as the natives put it (Marshall 1979). Accordingly, they challenge fate by going on deep-sea fishing expeditions in tiny dugouts and spearfishing with foolhardy abandon in shark-infested waters. If any men shrink from such challenges, their fellows, male and female, laugh at them, calling them effeminate and childlike. When on land, Trukese youths fight in weekend brawls, drink to excess, and seek sexual conquests to attain a manly image. Should a man fail in any of these efforts, another will taunt him: "Are you a man? Come, I will take your life now" (Marshall 1979:92).

Far away on the Greek Aegean island of Kalymnos, the people are also stalwart seafarers, living by commercial sponge fishing (Bernard 1967). The men of Kalymnos dive into deep water without the aid of diving equipment, which they scorn. Diving is therefore a gamble because many men are stricken and crippled by the bends for life. But no matter: they have proven their precious manhood by showing their contempt for death (119). Young divers who take precautions are effeminate, scorned and ridiculed by their fellows.

These are two seafaring peoples. Let us move elsewhere, to inland Africa, for example, where fishing is replaced by pastoral pursuits. In East Africa, young boys from a host of cattle-herding tribes, including the Masai, Rendille, Jie, and Samburu, are taken away from their mothers and subjected at the outset of adolescence to bloody circumcision rites by which they become true men. They must submit without so much as flinching under the agony of the knife. If a boy cries out while his flesh is being cut, if he so much as blinks an eye or turns his head, he is shamed for life as unworthy of manhood, and his entire lineage is shamed as a nursery of weaklings. After this very public ordeal, the young initiates are isolated in special dormitories in the wilderness. There, thrust on their own devices, they learn the tasks of a responsible manhood: cattle rustling, raiding, killing, survival in the bush. If their long apprenticeship is successful, they return to society as men and are only then permitted to take a wife.

Another dramatic African case comes from nearby Ethiopia: the Amhara, a Semitic-speaking tribe of rural cultivators. They have a passionate belief in masculinity called *wand-nat*. This idea involves aggressiveness, stamina, and bold "courageous action" in the face of danger; it means never backing down when threatened (Levine 1966:18). To show their wand-nat, the Amhara youths are forced to engage in whipping contests called *buhe* (Reminick 1982:32). During the whipping ceremonies, in which all able-bodied male adolescents must participate for their reputations' sake, the air is filled with the cracking of whips. Faces are lacerated, ears torn open, and red and bleeding welts appear (33). Any sign of weakness is greeted with taunts and mockery. As if this were not enough, adolescent Amhara boys are wont to prove their virility by scarring their arms with red-hot embers (Levine 1966:19). In these rough ways the boys actualize the exacting Amhara "ideals of masculinity" (Reminick 1976:760).

Significantly, this violent testing is not enough for these virile Ethiopians. Aside from showing physical hardihood and courage in the buhe matches, a young man must demonstrate his potency on his wedding night by waving a bloody sheet of marital consummation before the assembled kinsmen (Reminick 1996: 760–61). As well as demonstrating the bride's virginity, this ceremonial defloration is a talisman of masculinity for the Amhara groom. The Amhara's proof of manhood, like that of the Trukese, is both sexual and violent, and his performances both on the battlefield and in the marriage bed must be visibly displayed, recorded, and confirmed by the group; otherwise he is no man.

Halfway around the world, in the high mountains of Melanesia, young boys undergo similar trials before being admitted into the select club of manhood. In the New Guinea Highlands, boys are torn from their mothers and forced to undergo a series of brutal masculinizing rituals (Herdt 1982). These include whipping, flailing, beating, and other forms of terrorization by older men, which the boys must endure stoically and silently. As in Ethiopia, the flesh is scored and blood flows freely. These Highlanders believe that without such hazing, boys will never mature into men but will remain weak and childlike. Real men are made, they insist, not born.

PARALLELS

To be sure, there are some contextual similarities in these last few examples. The Amhara, Masai, and New Guinea Highlanders share one feature in common beyond the stress on manhood: they are fierce warrior peoples, or were in the recent past. One may argue that their bloody rites prepare young boys for the idealized life of the warrior that awaits them. So much is perhaps obvious: some Western civilizations also subject soft youths to rough hazing and initiations in order to toughen them up for a career of soldiering, as in the U.S. Marines (Raphael 1988). But these trials are by no means confined to militaristic cultures or castes. Let us take another African example.

Among the relatively peaceful !Kung Bushmen of southwest Africa (Thomas 1959; Lee 1979), manhood is also a prize to be grasped through a test. Accurately calling themselves "The Harmless People" (Thomas 1959), these nonviolent Bushmen have never fought a war in their lives. They have no military weapons, and they frown upon physical violence (which, however, sometimes does occur). Yet even here, in a culture that treasures gentleness and cooperation above all things, the boys must earn the right to be called men by a test of skill and endurance. They must single-handedly track and kill a sizable adult antelope, an act that requires courage and hardiness. Only after their first kill of such a buck are they considered fully men and permitted to marry.

Other examples of stressed manhood among gentle people can be found in the New World, in aboriginal North America. Among the nonviolent Fox tribe of Iowa, for example, "being a man" does not come easily (Gearing 1970:51). Based on stringent standards of accomplishment in tribal affairs and economic pursuits, real manhood is said to be "the Big Impossible," an exclusive status that only the nimble few can achieve (51–52). Another American Indian example is the Tewa people of New Mexico, also known as the Pueblo Indians. These placid farmers, who are known today for their serene culture, gave up all warfare in the last century. Yet they subject their boys to a severe hazing before they can be accounted men. Between the ages of twelve and fifteen, the Tewa boys are taken away from their homes, purified by ritual means, and then whipped mercilessly by the Kachina spirits (their fathers in disguise). Each boy is stripped naked and lashed on the back four times with a crude yucca whip that draws blood and leaves permanent scars. The adolescents are expected to bear up impassively under the beating to show their fortitude. The Tewa say that this rite makes their boys into men, that otherwise manhood is doubtful. After the boys' ordeal, the Kachina spirits tell them, "You are now a man.... You are made a man" (Hill 1982:220). Although Tewa girls have their own (nonviolent) initiations, there is no parallel belief that girls have to be *made* women, no "big impossible" for them; for the Tewa and the Fox, as for the other people above, womanhood develops naturally, needing no cultural intervention, its predestined arrival at menarche commemorated rather than forced by ritual (Hill 1982:209–10).

Nor are such demanding efforts at proving oneself a man confined to primitive peoples or those on the margins of civilization. In urban Latin America, for example, as described by Oscar Lewis (1961:38), a man must prove his manhood every day by standing up to challenges and insults, even though he goes to his death "smiling." As well as being tough and brave, ready to defend his family's honor at the drop of a hat, the urban Mexican, like the Amhara man, must also perform adequately in sex and father many children. Such macho exploits are also common among many of the peasant and pastoral peoples who reside in the cradle of the ancient Mediterranean civilizations. In the Balkans, for instance, the category of "real men" is clearly defined. A real man is one who drinks heavily, spends money freely, fights bravely, and raises a large family (Simic 1969). In this way he shows an "indomitable virility" that distinguishes him from effeminate counterfeits (Denich 1974:250). In eastern Morocco, true men are distinguished from effete men on the basis of physical prowess and heroic acts of both feuding and sexual potency; their manly deeds are memorialized in verses sung before admiring crowds at festivals, making manhood a kind of communal celebration (Marcus 1987:50). Likewise, for the Bedouin of Egypt's Western Desert, "real men" are contrasted with despicable weaklings who are "no men." Real Bedouin men are bold and courageous, afraid of nothing. Such men assert their will at any cost and stand up to any

challenge; their main attributes are "assertiveness and the quality of potency" (Abu-Lughod 1986:88–89). Across the sea, in Christian Crete, men in village coffee shops proudly sing paeans to their own virility, their self-promotion having been characterized as the "poetics of manhood" by Michael Herzfeld (1985:15). These Cretans must demonstrate their "manly selfhood" by stealing sheep, procreating large families, and besting other men in games of chance and skill.

Examples of this pressured manhood with its almost talismanic qualities could be given almost indefinitely and in all kinds of contexts. Among most of the peoples that anthropologists are familiar with, true manhood is a precious and elusive status beyond mere maleness, a hortatory image that men and boys aspire to and that their culture demands of them as a measure of belonging. Although this stressed or embattled quality varies in intensity, becoming highly marked in southern Spain, Morocco, Egypt, and some other Mediterranean-area traditions, true manhood in other cultures frequently shows an inner insecurity that needs dramatic proof. Its vindication is doubtful, resting on rigid codes of decisive action in many spheres of life: as husband, father, lover, provider, warrior. Because it is a restricted status, there are always men who fail the test. These are the negative examples, the effete men, the men-who-are-no-men, held up scornfully to inspire conformity to the glorious ideal.

Perhaps these stagy routes to manhood seem bizarre to us at first glance. But none of them should surprise most Anglophone readers, for we too have our manly traditions, both in our popular culture and in literary genres. Although we may choose less flamboyant modes of expression than the Amhara or Trukese, we too have regarded manhood as an artificial state, a challenge to be overcome, a prize to be won by fierce struggle: if not "the big impossible," then certainly doubtful.

For example, let us take a people and a social stratum far removed from those above: the gentry of modern England. There, young boys were traditionally subjected to similar trials on the road to their majority. They were torn at a tender age from mother and home, as in East Africa or in New Guinea, and sent away in age sets to distant testing grounds that sorely took their measure. These were the public boarding schools, where a cruel "trial by ordeal," including physical violence and terrorization by elder males, provided a passage to a "social state of manhood" that their parents thought could be achieved in no other way (Chandos 1984:172). Supposedly, this harsh training prepared young Oxbridge aristocrats for the self-reliance and fortitude needed to run the British Empire and thereby manufactured "a serviceable elite as stylized as Samurai" (346). Even here, in Victorian England, a culture not given over to showy excess, manhood was an artificial product coaxed by austere training and testing.

Similar ideas motivated educators on both sides of the Atlantic, for example, the founders of the Boy Scouts. Their chartered purpose, as they put it in their pamphlets and manuals, was to "make big men of little boys" by fostering "an independent manhood," as though this were not to be expected from nature alone (cited by Hantover 1978:189). This obsessive moral masculinization in the English-speaking countries went beyond mere mortals of the day to Christ himself, who was portrayed in turn-of-the-century tracts as "the supremely manly man," athletic and aggressive when necessary, no "Prince of Peace-at-any-price" (Conant 1915:117). The English publicist Thomas Hughes dilated rhapsodically about the manliness of Christ (1879), while his colleagues strove to depict Christianity as the "muscular" or "manly" faith. Pious and articulate English Protestants loudly proclaimed their muscular religion as an antidote to what Charles Kingsley derided as the "fastidious maundering, die-away effeminacy" of the High Anglican Church (cited in Gay 1982:532). Boys, faiths, and gods had to be made masculine; otherwise there was doubt. The same theme runs through much British literature of the time, most notably in Kipling, as for example in the following lines from the poem "If":

If you can fill the unforgiving minute
With sixty seconds worth of distance run,
Yours is the Earth, and everything that's in it,
And—which is more—you'll be a Man, my son!

Consequent only to great deeds, being a Kiplingesque man is more than owning the Earth, a truly imperial masculinity consonant with empire building. The same theme of "iffy" heroism runs through many aspects of popular middle-class American culture today. Take, for example, the consistent strain in U.S. literature of masculine *Bildungsroman*— the ascension to the exalted status of manhood under the tutelage of knowledgeable elders, with the fear of failure always lurking menacingly in the background. This theme is most strongly exemplified by Ernest Hemingway, of course, notably in the Nick Adams stories, but it is also found in the work of such contemporaries as William Faulkner and John Dos Passos, and in such Hemingway epigones as Studs Terkel, Norman Mailer, James Dickey, Frederick Exley, and—the new generation—Robert Stone, Jim Harrison, and Tom McGuane. This "virility school" in American letters (Schwenger 1984:13), was sired by Papa Hemingway (if one discounts Jack London) and nurtured thereafter by his acolytes, but it is now in its third or fourth generation and going strong (for a feminist view see Fetterly 1978).

In contemporary literary America, too, manhood is often a mythic confabulation, a Holy Grail, to be seized by long and arduous testing. Take, for example, this paradigmatic statement by Norman Mailer (1968:25): "Nobody was born a man; you earned manhood provided you were good enough, bold enough." As well as echoing his spiritual forebears, both British and American, Mailer articulates here the unwritten sentiments of the Trukese, the Amhara, the Bushmen, and countless other peoples who have little else in common except this same obsessive "quest for male validation" (Raphael 1988:67). Although some of us may smile at Mailer for being so histrionic and sophomoric about it, he nevertheless touches a raw nerve that pulsates through many cultures as well as our own. Nor is Mailer's challenge representative of only a certain age or stratum of American society. As the poet Leonard Kriegel (1979:14) says in his reflective book about American manhood, "In every age, not just our own, manhood was something that had to be won."

Looking back, for instance, one is reminded of the cultural values of the antebellum American South. Southerners, whatever their class, placed great stress on a volatile manly honor as a defining feature of the southern character, a fighting principle. Indeed, Bertram Wyatt-Brown, in his book *Southern Honor* (1982), has argued convincingly that this touchy notion was a major element behind southern secessionism and thus an important and underrated political factor in U.S. history. A defense of southern "manliness" was in fact offered by Confederate writers of the time, including the South Carolina firebrand Charles C. Jones, as one justification for regional defiance, political separation, and, finally, war (cited in McPherson 1988:41). And of course similar ideals are enshrined in the frontier folklore of the American West, past and present, as exemplified in endless cowboy epics.

This heroic image of an achieved manhood is being questioned in America by feminists and by so-called liberated men themselves (Pleck 1981; Brod 1987). But for decades, it has been widely legitimized in U.S. cultural settings ranging from Italian-American gangster culture to Hollywood Westerns, private-eye tales, the current Rambo imagoes, and children's He-Man dolls and games; it is therefore deeply ingrained in the American male psyche. As the anthropologist Robert LeVine (1979:312) says, it is an organization of cultural principles that function together as a "guiding myth within the confines of our culture." But given the similarities between contemporary American notions of manliness and those of the many cultures discussed above, can we drop LeVine's qualifying phrase about "the confines of our culture"? Can we speak instead of an archetype or

"deep structure" of masculinity, as Andrew Tolson (1977:56) puts it? And if so, what explains all these similarities? Why the trials and the testing and the seemingly gratuitous agonies of man-playing? Why is so much indoctrination and motivation needed in all these cultures to make real men? What is there about "official" manliness that requires such effort, such challenge, and such investment? And why should manhood be so desirable a state and at the same time be conferred so grudgingly in so many societies? These are some of the questions I want to consider here. Only a broadly comparative approach can begin to answer them.

MANHOOD AND GENDER ROLE

Let us pause at this point to take stock. What do we know so far about the origins of such gender imagery? Until very recently, studies of male and female were wedded to a persistent paradigm derived from mechanistic nineteenth-century antecedents. Most pervasive was the idea of generic types, a Universal Man counterposed to a Universal Woman—a sexual symmetry supposedly derived from self-evident dualisms in biology and psychology (Katchadourian 1979:20). Freud, for example, held that anatomy was destiny, and Jung (1926) went so far as to develop universal principles of masculinity and femininity which he conveyed as "animus" and "anima," irreducible cores of sexual identity. Western literature and philosophy are full of such fundamental and supposedly immutable dualisms (Bakan 1966); they are also found in some Asian cosmologies, for example, the Chinese Yin and Yang, and in countless sets of binary oppositions both philosophical and scientific (e.g., Ortner 1974). What could be a neater polarity than sex? Our view of manhood in the past was often a simple reflection of these polar views of male and female "natures" or "principles." This view had some scientific support among biologists and psychologists, many of whom held that the aggressiveness of masculinity, including the testing and proving, was merely a conse-quence of male anatomy and hormones: men seek challenges because they are naturally aggressive. That is simply the way they are; women are the opposite. Period.

The way we look at sex roles, however, has changed drastically in the past two decades. Although appealing to many, sex dualisms and oppositions are definitely out of fashion, and so are sexual universals and biological determinisms. Part of the reason, aside from the recent movement away from static struc-tural dualisms in the social sciences generally, lies in the feminist revolution of the past twenty years. Starting in the 1960s, the femi-nist attack on the bipolar mode of sexual thinking has shaken this dualistic edifice to its roots; but to be fair, it was never very sturdy to begin with. For example, both Freud and Jung accepted an inherent mixture of mas-culinity and femininity within each human psyche. Although he distinguished male and female principles, Jung to his credit admitted the existence of animus and anima to degrees in all people; bisexuality was in fact one of the bedrocks of Freud's psychological reasoning. In every human being, Freud (1905:220) remarks, "pure masculinity or femininity is not to be found either in a psychological or a biological sense. Every individual on the con-trary displays a mixture."

Moreover, feminists of various back-grounds and persuasions (see, for example, Baker 1980; Sanday 1981; Otten 1985) have convincingly demonstrated that the conven-tional bipolar model based on biology is invalid and that sex (biological inheritance) and gender (cultural norms) are distinct cate-gories that may have a relationship but not an isomorphic identity. Most observers would agree that hormones and anatomy do have an effect on our behavior. The biological anthro-pologist Melvin Konner has convincingly shown this in his book, *The Tangled Wing* (1982). Assessing the latest scientific and clin-ical literature in this highly acclaimed survey, Konner concludes that testosterone (the main male sex hormone) predisposes males to a slightly higher level of aggressivity than

females (see also Archer and Lloyd 1985; 138–39). But, as Konner freely admits, biolo-gy does not determine all of our behavior, or even very much of it, and cultures do indeed vary to some degree in assigning sex roles, measured in jobs and tasks. Discrete con-cepts of masculinity and femininity, based on secondary sex characteristics, exist in virtual-ly all societies, but they are not always con-structed and interfaced in the same way. Gender is a symbolic category. As such, it has strong moral overtones, and therefore is ascriptive and culturally relative—potentially changeful. On the other hand, sex is rooted in anatomy and is therefore fairly constant (Stoller 1968). It is now generally accepted, even among the most traditional male researchers, that masculine and feminine principles are not inherent polarities but an "overlapping continuum" (Biller and Borstelmann 1967: 255), or, as Spence and Helmreich put it (1979:4), "orthogonal dimensions."

Still, as we have seen from the previous examples, there exists a recurrent cultural tendency to distinguish and to polarize gen-der roles. Instead of allowing free play in sex roles and gender ideals, most societies tend to exaggerate biological potentials by clearly dif-ferentiating sex roles and by defining the proper behavior of men and women as oppo-site or complementary. Even where so-called "third sexes" exist, as for example the Plains Indian *berdache* and the Omani *xanith*, con-ventional male and female types are still strongly differentiated. So the question of continuities in gender imaging must go beyond genetic endowment to encompass cultural norms and moral scripts. If there are archetypes in the male image (as there are in femininity), they must be largely culturally constructed as symbolic systems, not simply as products of anatomy, because anatomy deter-mines very little in those contexts where the moral imagination comes into play. The answer to the manhood puzzle must lie in cul-ture; we must try to understand why culture uses or exaggerates biological potentials in specific ways.

PREVIOUS INTERPRETATIONS

Some feminists and other relativists have perceived the apparent contradiction between the theoretical arbitrariness of gender concepts and the empirical convergence of sex roles. Explanations have therefore been offered to account for it. The existing explanations are interesting and useful, and I do not argue against them on the grounds of logical consistency. Rather, I think that the wrong questions have been asked in this inquiry. Most explanations have been phrased in one of two ways, both ideologically satisfying depending upon one's point of view, but neither getting us very far analytically.

First, the question has been phrased by the more doctrinaire Marxists and some radical feminists in an idiom of pure conflict theory. They see gender ideology as having a purely exploitative function. Thus they ask, inevitably, cui bono? Since many male ideologies include an element of gender oppressiveness, or at least hierarchy (in the view of liberated Western intellectuals), some of these radicals regard masculine ideologies as masks or justifications for the oppression of women. They see male ideologies as mystifications of power relationships, as examples of false consciousness (see, for example, Ortner 1981; Godelier 1986). This explanation is probably true for some cases, at least as a partial explanation, especially in some extreme patriarchies where male dominance is very pronounced. But it cannot be true as a universal explanation, because it cannot account for instances in which males are tested for manhood but where there is relative sexual equality. We have seen one example of this in the African Bushmen (Thomas 1959; Lee 1979; Shostak 1981). Although these nonsexist foragers are often held up by feminists as a model of sexual egalitarianism (Shostak 1981), Bushmen boys must prove their manhood by hunting prowess. They must also undergo tests of hardiness and skill from which girls are excluded.... Their manhood is subject to proof and, conceptually, to diminishment or loss. The same is true of the Fox and the Tewa of North America. So if a conception of manhood has no oppressive function in these societies, what is it doing there? It seems that the conflict theorists are missing something.

The second idiom of explanation is equally reductionistic. Here, biological or psychological processes are given analytical priority. There are two forms of biopsychological reductionist argument. The first is biological/evolutionary à la Lionel Tiger in *Men in Groups* (1971). Tiger holds that men worry about manhood because evolutionary pressures have predisposed them to do so. Once we were all hunters, and our success and therefore the survival and expansion of the group depended upon our developing genetically determined "masculine tendencies," aggression and male bonding being principal among them. This sociobiological argument is useful in certain cases, again, most notably in the violent patriarchies. But it is demonstrably false as a universal explanation because there are many societies where "aggressive" hunting never played an important role, where men do not bond for economic purposes, where violence and war are devalued or unknown, and yet where men are today concerned about demonstrating manhood. Further, this argument commits the historical fallacy of proposing a historical explanation for a cultural trait that persists under changed circumstances.

The second genetic reductionism is the standard psychoanalytic one about male psychic development. It is based squarely on an orthodox reading of Freud's Oedipus complex and its derivative, castration anxiety. This orthodoxy has been challenged recently with a neo-Freudian viewpoint stressing other aspects of male development, which I find much more powerful.... The standard psychoanalytic view holds that men everywhere are defending against castration fears as a result of identical oedipal traumas in psychosexual development. Masculinity cults and ideals are compensations erected universally against such fears (Stephens 1967; Kline 1972).

In this view, the norms of masculinity are projected outward from the individual psyche onto the screen of culture; public culture is individual fantasy life writ large. I think this explanation is useful in some cases but supererogatory. More damaging, it fails to give proper weight to social constraints that enforce male conformity to manhood ideals; as we shall see, boys have to be encouraged— sometimes actually forced—by social sanctions to undertake efforts toward a culturally defined manhood, which by themselves they might not do. So the explanation cannot be one based solely on psychic projections. Moreover, the orthodox psychoanalytic view can also be demonstrated to be false at a universal level, for there are empirical exceptions to the culture of manhood. There are a few societies that do not place the usual stress on achieving a masculine image; in these exceptional "neuter" societies, males are freed from the need to prove themselves and are allowed a basically androgynous script, which, significantly, they find congenial. As these exceptions do exist, ... the answer to the masculinity puzzle must have a social side to it, because formal variation cannot be explained on the basis of a psychological constant such as castration anxiety.

SOME HELP FROM THE POST-FREUDIANS

At this point we have to call upon some alternative models of male psychosexual development that accommodate social and relational factors. A psychological theory of masculinity that I find useful derives in part from recent work by the post-Freudian ego psychologists. The list of relevant theorists and their works is long but may be reduced here to Erik Erikson, Ralph Greenson, Edith Jacobson, Margaret Mahler, Gregory Rochlin, Robert Stoller, and D. W. Winnicott.

The basic idea here concerns the special problems attached to the origin of masculinity as a category of self-identity distinct from femininity. The theory begins with the assumption that all infants, male and female, establish a primary identity, as well as a social bond, with the nurturing parent, the mother. This theory already departs from the classic Freudian assumption that the boy child has from the first a male identity and a natural heterosexual relationship with his mother that culminates in the oedipal conflict, that the boy's identity as male is axiomatic and unconflicted. This new theory goes on to posit an early and prolonged unity or psychic merging with the mother that Freud (1914) discussed under "primary narcissism," a period when the infant fails to distinguish between self and mother. The argument is that the physical separation of child and mother at birth does not bring with it a psychological separation of equivalent severity or finality.

As the child grows, it reaches the critical threshold that Mahler (1975) has called separation-individuation. At this juncture its growing awareness of psychic separateness from the mother combines with increased physical mobility and a motoric exercise of independent action, for example, walking, speaking, manipulating toys. These independent actions are rewarded socially both by parents and by other members of the group who want to see the child grow up (Erikson 1950). Boys and girls alike go through these same trial stages of separation, self-motivation, encouragement and reward, and proto-personhood; and both become receptive to social demands for gender-appropriate behavior. However, according to this theory, the boy child encounters special problems in the crucible of the separation-individuation stage that impede further progression toward independent selfhood.

The special liability for boys is the different fate of the primal psychic unity with the mother. The self-awareness of being a separate individual carries with it a parallel sense of a gender identity—being either a man or a woman, boy or girl. In most societies, each individual must choose one or the other unequivocally in order, also, to be a separate and autonomous person recognizable as such by peers and thus to earn acceptance. The special problem the boy faces at this point is in overcoming the previous sense of unity with the mother in order to achieve an independent identity defined by his culture as masculine—an effort functionally equivalent not only to psychic separation but also to creating an autonomous public persona. The girl does not experience this problem as acutely, according to this theory, because her femininity is reinforced by her original symbiotic unity with her mother, by the identification with her that precedes self-identity and that culminates with her own motherhood (Chodorow 1978). In most societies, the little boy's sense of self as independent must include a sense of the self as different from his mother, as separate from her both in ego-identity and in social role. Thus for the boy the task of separation and individuation carries an added burden and peril. Robert Stoller (1974:358) has stated this problem succinctly:

> While it is true the boy's first love object is heterosexual [the mother], he must perform a great deed to make this so: he must first separate his identity from hers. Thus the whole process of becoming masculine is at risk in the little boy from the day of birth on; his still-to-be-created masculinity is endangered by the primary, profound, primeval oneness with mother, a blissful experience that serves, buried but active in the core of one's identity, as a focus which, throughout life, can attract one to regress back to that primitive oneness. That is the threat latent in masculinity.

To become a separate person the boy must perform a great deed. He must pass a test; he must break the chain to his mother. He must renounce his bond to her and seek his own way in the world. His masculinity thus represents his separation from his mother and his entry into a new and independent social status recognized as distinct and opposite from hers. In this view the main threat to the boy's growth is not only, or even primarily, castration anxiety. The principal danger to the boy is not a unidimensional fear of the punishing

father but a more ambivalent fantasy-fear about the mother. The ineradicable fantasy is to return to the primal maternal symbiosis. The inseparable fear is that restoring the oneness with the mother will overwhelm one's independent selfhood.

Recently, armed with these new ideas, some neo-Freudians have begun to focus more specifically on the puzzle of masculine role modeling cults. They have been less concerned with the questions of gender identity and castration anxiety than with the related questions of regression and its relation to social role. In a recent symposium on the subject, the psychoanalyst Gerald Fogel (1986:10) argues that the boy's dilemma goes "beyond castration anxiety" to a conflicted effort to give up the anaclitic unity with the mother, which robs him of his independence. In the same symposium, another psychoanalyst (Cooper 1986:128) refers to the comforting sense of omnipotence that this symbiotic unity with the mother affords. This sense of omnipotence, of narcissistic completeness, sensed and retained in fantasy as a blissful experience of oneness with the mother, he argues, is what draws the boy back so powerfully toward childhood and away from the challenge of an autonomous manhood. In this view, the struggle for masculinity is a battle against these regressive wishes and fantasies, a hard-fought renunciation of the longings for the prelapsarian idyll of childhood.

From this perspective, then, the manhood equation is a "revolt against boyishness" (Schafer 1986:100). The struggle is specifically "against regression" (100). This revisionist theory provides us with a psychological key to the puzzle of manhood norms and ideals. Obviously, castration fear is also important from an individual point of view. But manhood ideologies are not only intrapsychic; they are also collective representations that are institutionalized as guiding images in most societies. To understand the meaning of manhood from a sociological point of view, to appreciate its social rather than individual functions and causes, regression is the more important variable to consider. The reason for this is that, in aggregate, regression poses a more serious threat to society as a whole. As we shall see, regression is unacceptable not only to the individual but also to his society as a functioning mechanism, because most societies demand renunciation of escapist wishes in favor of a participating, contributing adulthood. Castration anxiety, though something that all men may also need to resolve, poses no such aggregate threat to social continuity. In sum, manhood imagery can be interpreted from this post-Freudian perspective as a defense against the eternal child within, against puerility, against what is sometimes called the Peter Pan complex (Hallman 1969).

REFERENCES

Abu-Lughod, Lila. 1986. *Veiled Sentiments: Honor and Poetry in a Bedouin Society.* Berkeley: University of California Press.

Archer, John, and Barbara Lloyd. 1985. *Sex and Gender.* Cambridge: Cambridge University Press.

Bakan, David. 1966. *The Duality of Human Existence.* Chicago: University of Chicago Press.

Baker, Susan W. 1980. Biological influences on human sex and gender. *Signs* 6:80–96.

Bernard, H. Russell. 1967. Kalymnian sponge diving. *Human Biology* 39:103–30.

Biller, Henry B., and Lloyd Borstelmann. 1967. Masculine development: An integrative view. *Merrill-Palmer Quarterly* 13:253–94.

Brandes, Stanley H. 1980. *Metaphors of Masculinity: Sex and Status in Andalusian Folklore.* Philadelphia: University of Pennsylvania Press.

Brod, Harry (ed.). 1987. *The Making of Masculinities: The New Men's Studies.* Boston: Allen and Unwin.

Chandos, John. 1984. *Boys Together: English Public Schools, 1800–1864.* New Haven: Yale University Press.

Chodorow, Nancy. 1978. *The Reproduction of Mothering.* Berkeley: University of California Press.

Conant, Robert W. 1915. *The Virility of Christ.* Chicago: no publisher.

Cooper, Arnold M. 1986. What men fear: The facade of castration anxiety. In *The Psychology of Men: New Psychoanalytic Perspective,* ed. Gerald Fogel, F. M. Lane, and R. S. Liebert, pp. 113–30. New York: Basic Books.

D'Andrade, Roy G. 1974. Sex differences and cultural institutions. In *Culture and Personality: Contemporary Readings,* ed. Robert A. LeVine, pp. 16–39. Chicago: Aldine.

Denich, Bette. 1974. Sex and power in the Balkans. In *Women, Culture, and Society,* ed. Michelle Rosaldo and Louise Lamphere, pp. 243–62. Stanford: Stanford University Press.

Erikson, Erik. 1950. *Childhood and Society.* New York: Norton.

Fetterly, Judith. 1978. *The Resisting Reader: A Feminist Approach to American Fiction.* Bloomington, Ind.: Indiana University Press.

Fogel, Gerald I. 1986. Introduction: Being a man. In *The Psychology of Men: New Psychoanalytic Perspectives,* ed. Gerald Fogel, F. M. Lane, and R. S. Liebert, pp. 3–22. New York: Basic Books.

Freud, Sigmund. 1905. Three Essays on the Theory of Sexuality, III: The Transformations of Puberty. *Standard Edition,* ed. James Strachey 7:207–30. London: Hogarth Press (1975).

———. 1914. On narcissism. *Standard Edition,* ed. James Strachey, 14:67–102. London: Hogarth Press (1975).

Gay, Peter, 1982. Liberalism and regression. *Psychoanalytic Study of the Child* 37:523–45. New Haven: Yale University Press.

Gearing, Frederick O. 1970. *The Face of the Fox.* Chicago: Aldine.

Godelier, Maurice. 1986. *The Making of Great Men.* Cambridge: Cambridge University Press.

Gregor, Thomas. 1985. *Anxious Pleasures: The Sexual Life of an Amazonian People.* Chicago: University of Chicago Press.

Hallman, Ralph, 1969. The archetypes in Peter Pan. *Journal of Analytic Psychology* 14:65–73.

Hantover, Jeffrey P. 1978. The Boy Scouts and the validation of masculinity. *Journal of Social Issues* 34:184–95.

Herdt, Gilbert H. 1982. Fetish and fantasy in Sambia initiation. In *Rituals of Manhood,* ed. Gilbert H. Herdt, pp. 44–98. Berkeley: University of California Press.

Hertzfeld, Michael. 1985. Gender pragmatics: agency, speech and bride-theft in a Cretan mountain village. *Anthropology* 9:25–44.

Hill, W. W. 1982. *An Ethnography of Santa Clara Pueblo, New Mexico,* ed. and annotated by Charles H. Lange, Albuquerque, N. Mex.: University of New Mexico Press.

Hughes, Thomas. 1879. *The Manliness of Christ.* London: Macmillan.

Jung, Carl. 1926. *Psychological Types.* New York: Harcourt, Brace and Co.

Katchadourian, Herant A. 1979. The terminology of sex and gender. In *Human Sexuality: Comparative and Developmental Perspectives,* ed. Herant A. Katchadourian, pp. 8–34. Berkeley: University of California Press.

Kline, Paul. 1972. *Fact and Fantasy in Freudian Theory.* London: Methuen.

Konner, Melvin. 1982. *The Tangled Wing: Biological Constraints on the Human Spirit.* New York: Harper Colophon Books.

Kriegel, Leonard, 1979. *On Men and Manhood.* New York: Hawthorn Books.

Lee, Richard B. 1979. *The !Kung San: Men, Women, and Work in a Foraging Society.* Cambridge: Cambridge University Press.

Levine, Donald N. 1966. The concept of masculinity in Ethiopian culture. *International Journal of Social Psychiatry* 12:17–23.

LeVine, Robert A. 1979. Anthropology and sex: Developmental aspects. In *Human Sexuality: Comparative and Developmental Perspectives,* ed. Herant A. Katchadourian, pp. 309–31. Berkeley: University of California Press.

Lewis, Oscar. 1961. *The Children of Sanchez.* New York: Random House.

Lonner, Walter J. 1980. The search for psychological universals. In *Handbook of Cross-Cultural Psychology,* ed. Harry C. Triandis and William W. Lambert, 1:143–204. Boston: Allyn & Bacon.

McPherson, James M. 1988. *Battle Cry of Freedom: The Civil War Era.* New York: Oxford University Press.

Mahler, Margaret, et al. 1975. *The Psychological Birth of the Human Infant.* New York: Basic Books.

Mailer, Norman. 1968. *Armies of the Night.* New York: New American Library.

Marcus, Michael. 1987. "Horsemen are the fence of the land": Honor and history among the Ghiyata of eastern Morocco. In *Honor and Shame and the Unity of the Mediterranean,* ed. David D. Gilmore, pp. 49–60. Washington, D.C.: American Anthropological Association, Special Pub. no. 22.

Marshall, Mac. 1979. *Weekend Warriors.* Palo Alto, CA: Mayfield.

Munroe, Robert L. and Ruth H. Munroe. 1980. Perspectives suggested by anthropological data. In *Handbook of Cross-Cultural Psychology,* ed. Harry C. Triandis and William W. Lambert 1:253–317. Boston: Allyn and Bacon.

Ortner, Sherry B. 1974. Is female to male as nature is to culture? In *Woman, Culture, and Society,* ed. Michelle Z. Rosaldo and Louise Lamphere, pp. 67–88. Stanford: Stanford University Press.

———. 1981. Gender and sexuality in hierarchical societies: The case of Polynesia and some comparative implications. In *Sexual Meanings,* ed. Sherry B. Ortner and Harriet Whitehead, pp. 359–409. Cambridge: Cambridge University Press.

Otten, Charlotte M. 1985. Genetic effects on male and female development and on the sex ratio. In *Male-Female Differences: A Bio-Cultural Perspective,* ed. Roberta L. Hall, pp. 155–217. New York: Praeger.

Pleck, Joseph. 1981. *The Myth of Masculinity.* Cambridge, Mass.: MIT Press.

Raphael, Ray. 1988. *The Men from the Boys: Rites of Passage in Male America.* Lincoln, Nebr.: University of Nebraska Press.

Reminick, Ronald A. 1976. The symbolic significance of ceremonial defloration among the Amhara of Ethiopia. *American Ethnologist* 3:751–63.

———. 1982. The sport of warriors on the wane: a case of cultural endurance in the face of social change. In *Sport and the Humanities,* ed. William H. Morgan, pp. 31–36. Knoxville, Tenn.: Bureau of Educational Research and Service, University of Tennessee Press.

Sanday, Peggy R. 1981. *Female Power and Male Dominance: On the Origins of Sexual Inequality.* Cambridge: Cambridge University Press.

Schafer, Roy. 1986. Men who struggle against sentimentality. In *The Psychology of Men: New Psychoanalytic Perspectives,* ed. Gerald I. Fogel, L. M. Lane, and R. S. Liebert, pp. 95–110. New York: Basic Books.

Schwenger, Peter. 1984. *Phallic Critiques: Masculinity and Twentieth-Century Literature.* London: Routledge and Kegan Paul.

Shostak, Marjorie. 1981. *Nisa: The Life and Words of a !Kung Woman.* Cambridge, Mass.: Harvard University Press.

Simic, Andrei. 1969. Management of the male image in Yugoslavia. *Anthropological Quarterly* 42: 89–101.

Spence, Janet, and Robert L. Helmreich. 1979. *Masculinity and Femininity: Their Psychological Dimensions, Correlates and Antecedents.* Austin, Tex.: University of Texas Press.

Stephens, William N. 1967. A cross-cultural study of menstrual taboos. In *Cross-Cultural Approaches*, ed. Clellan S. Ford, pp. 67–94. New Haven: HRAF Press.

Stoller, Robert. 1968. *Sex and Gender*. New York: Science House.

———. 1974. Facts and fancies: An examination of Freud's concept of bisexuality. In *Women and Analysis*, ed. Jean Strousse, pp. 343–64. New York: Dell.

Thomas, Elizabeth Marshall. 1959. *The Harmless People*. New York: Vintage Books.

Tiger, Lionel. 1971. *Men in Groups*. New York; Random House.

Tolson, Andrew. 1977. *The Limits of Masculinity: Male Identity and the Liberated Woman*. New York: Harper and Row.

Williams, John E., and Deborah L. Best. 1982. *Measuring Sex Stereotypes: A Thirty-Nation Study*. Beverly Hills: Sage Publications.

Wyatt-Brown, Bertram. 1982. *Southern Honor: Ethics and Behavior in the Old South*. New York: Oxford University Press.

Flirting in the Factory

Kevin A. Yelvington

Generally speaking, the erotic question between the sexes is that of offer and refusal. Its objects are, of course, infinitely varied and graduated, and by no means either-ors, much less exclusively physiological. The nature of feminine coquetry is to play up, alternately, allusive promises and allusive withdrawals-to attract the male but always to stop short of a decision, and to reject him but never to deprive him of all hope (Simmel 1950: 50).

Si cocinas como caminas, me como hasta la raspita ("If you cook like you walk, I'll even eat the dregs")—Cuban *piropo*[1]

INTRODUCTION

One day, at afternoon break time, the factory workers filed out of the factory and made their way across the street to the "snackette," a small shop that sells fast food and cold drinks. In this factory in Trinidad, nearly all of the line workers are women and every line worker is either of African or of East Indian descent. On their way out, the workers passed the supervisors who were leaning up against the front wall of the building, chatting to each other

while watching the women. All of the supervisors are men, and nearly all of them are White. Lloyd, a 41-year-old White supervisor who was known to have sources of income in addition to his factory position, and Patricia, a nineteen-year-old East Indian worker, had been "flirting" for the previous three months, since Patricia started working at the factory. When Patricia walked past the men, Lloyd smiled and said to her "Come here you hot bucket of food, you." Patricia smiled back and kept on walking. "She love every bone in he body," said Winston, a thirty-year-old East Indian supervisor, loud enough for Patricia to hear. Lloyd, grabbing his crotch, said equally loud, "There's one bone I *know* she'd love." The men chuckled. Patricia made no indication that she heard Winston's comment or Lloyd's second comment. When break time was over, Patricia walked past the men, smiled at them, and went towards the factory entrance. After commenting to one of the men on her propensity to wear tight jeans, Lloyd said, ostensibly to the other men but in a voice loud enough for Patricia to hear as she was about to round a corner of the building. "Ooh, I would love to fuck she." With various sounds and gestures, the other men indicated

J. Roy. anthrop. Inst. (N.S.) 2, 313–333, Vol. 2 (2) 1996.

that it would indeed be a good thing to do. After this incident, the flirting between Lloyd and Patricia became even more intense and obvious. Together they attended a worker's wedding some weeks later. However, at the reception Lloyd got drunk and became angry with Patricia for dancing with one of the bride's cousins. Lloyd's and Patricia's relationship subsequently cooled.[2]

This incident shows that what I will call flirting is more than simple coercion. Lloyd was not Patricia's direct supervisor, although he did enjoy a position of general authority over her and, of course, enjoyed the status that "whiteness" and "maleness" bring in Trinidad in general. But the incident also shows that flirting is more than some sort of sociologically empty "game." Flirting is not only an idiom for expressing one's sexuality and sexual desire, but is also an instrument for exercising (and resisting) power along various axes and, in the process, for constituting and constructing gendered, ethnic and "classed" identities.

By flirting I mean indirect behaviour designed to indicate a possible sexual interest in another individual as well as to inquire, through this indirection, as to the other's possible interest. It is also a way of attracting interest in oneself. We may know when we are being flirted with, but what we do not know is what is meant by the flirting or what the flirt's exact intentions are. When we flirt we may not know what our own exact intentions are, for that matter. Flirting not only entails the creation of an aura of uncertainty on the part of the flirt—as observers from Simmel (1984) to Phillips (1994) have noted—but it is also risk-taking behaviour.

Though indirect, flirting is "directed" behaviour, that is, it does not always have to be reciprocal or reciprocated. In addition, it may or may not reveal a "serious" interest in forming a sexual relation. At times it can indicate a more abstract interest in forming a liaison while simultaneously acknowledging the existence of social obstacles that make such a liaison impossible or undesirable. The Trinidadian term that comes closest to describing this kind of behaviour is "tracking," also sometimes referred to as "making track" (Mendes 1986: 149). This refers to actions associated with sustained pursuit of a serious sexual or romantic interest of which flirting could be part. Given the nature of flirting, it was not always clear to me (much less to some of the participants) just when flirting in the factory was carried on as part of serious "tracking" or as a more immediate attempt to exercise power or utilize sex in order to acquire other kinds of resources. The expression of sexuality is involved not only with qualities such as physical attractiveness and personality but, perhaps more overtly so in the Caribbean, with position and power. As we will see below, the indeterminacy implicit in flirting guarantees its effectiveness as an instrument of domination. When combined with unequal gender relations in an industrial setting flirting can deflect critiques grounded in the class consciousness of the disempowered.

Analysing flirting as a channel for sexual desires, as the establishment, as it were, of uncertainty, as an objectified and reified social form and as an exercise of power, echoes Simmel's analysis of *die Koketterie*. For Simmel, flirting depends on a vacillation between "having" and "not having":

> . . . flirtation must make the person for whom it is intended feel the variable interplay between consent and refusal; the unwillingness to submit oneself that could be an indirect way to self-surrender; the surrender of the self behind which the withdrawal of the self stands as a background, a possibility and a threat.

> Every conclusive decision brings flirtation to an end. The sovereign peak of its art is exhibited in its apparent approximation to a definitive condition, while at every moment balancing this condition by its opposite (Simmel 1984:135–6).

We can take on board Simmel's extraordinary insights only with caution. For Simmel, flirtation as sociability is at best narrowly and at worst tautologically defined. It suspends status differences, it is derived from "life" but permits none of life's exigencies to enter, it is democratic, and it is artificial. Otherwise, "the game becomes a lie [. . .] when sociable action and speech are made into mere instruments of the intentions and events of practical reality" (1950: 49). Part of the reason for this deficiency can be traced to Simmel's view of male and female essential natures as influenced and even developed by, but in the end independent of, the historical and cultural forms that give rise to them. Except in rare instances (1984: 136–7, 139–40), Simmel does not provide a cross-cultural perspective on flirting. He does not discuss men's flirting. Absent, as well, is a consideration of women's participation—although on unequal terms—in the division of labour. Finally, viewing flirting as a game removed from life and power relations is quite idealistic. While he acknowledges that women derive power from flirting, this notion remains underdeveloped.

CARIBBEAN SEXUAL POLITICS

Gender relations and the public display of sexuality pervade all aspects of life in the Caribbean. The flirting in the factory must be understood in this context. Historical studies of Caribbean women's general subordination (Bush 1990; Mathurin 1974; Morrissey 1989; Reddock 1994) have informed recent sociological and anthropological research on their contemporary status (Douglass 1992; Mohammed & Shepherd 1988; Momsen 1993; Safa 1995; Senior 1991; Yelvington 1995) as well as on Caribbean male–female sexual behaviour in general (Chevannes 1993; Dann 1987). The nature and quality of male–female relations have become a topic of analysis not only by historians and anthropologists, but also by ethnomusicologists, linguists, literary critics, novelists and journalists. An important focus has been on men's stylized repartee and oratorical eloquence and on the way that speech constructs and marks power relations between men and women.

Differing from "cat calls" *per se,* these speech acts perhaps reach their poetic apogee in the Cuban *piropo*: for instance, "*Te llevo de rama a rama como Tarzán lleva a Juana*" ("I'll swing you from branch to branch like Tarzan swings Jane") (Carbajo 1968: 21). These are in most cases spoken aloud by men, apparently to no-one in particular. Men's speech acts such as the *piropo* are part of a general Caribbean-wide pattern. The "man of words" has been most notably documented by Abrahams (1983) for several Afro-Caribbean contexts. Rhyming performances in licentious play and joking, such as "talking broad," which is associated with the use of Creole, and artful speech that connotes decorum, order and hierarchy, such as "sweet talking," associated with the use of standard English, are means by which masculinity is constructed. In Guadeloupe, "If a man provokes or addresses a woman on the street, he does it in Creole. When he undertakes to court her . . . it is always in a polite fashion, keeping the sexual at a distance; and in order to set the sexual act apart, he expresses himself in French" (Schnepel 1993: 254). Boys grow up learning Creole, the language of the streets, while girls are taught French, the language of propriety. Practices such as the *piropo* and the use of Creole are seen as exclusively male provinces. Women who engage in this sort of speech face community sanctions.

At first glance, the properties of gendered speech seem to affirm Wilson's (1969; 1973) duality of "reputation" and "respectability" (see Abrahams 1979; 1983: 161–4), which "came close to becoming the master trope of Caribbean anthropology" (Trouillot 1992: 26). For Wilson, men's worlds are imbued with the ethos of "reputation," an egalitarian value system of local origin which emphasizes virility, sexual conquests and public swearing and fighting. Respectability, by contrast, is rooted in social and class stratification and colonially-derived notions of status and comportment exemplified by the established European churches, Eurocentric culture, legal marriage and the official ideology of education. Respectability is seen by Wilson as primarily the domain of women. While Wilson's schema is theoretically somewhat deficient (as we shall see), it is descriptively evocative, especially with regards to men's activities. Within the field of music, for example, sexual and verbal performance are purposefully conflated by men. The *double-entendre* technique and "the battle of the sexes" theme are part of the Trinidadian calypso tradition (Austin 1976; Elder 1968; Rohlehr 1985; 1988; 1990) and pervade the contemporary Jamaican dance hall. Cooper argues that in the Jamaican dance hall "verbal and sexual skills are often indistinguishable," (1993: 142).

Pervading such speech acts is the "indirection" characteristic of what Brenneis calls "occasionally egalitarian communities," those in which "egalitarian notions strongly inform local social life, but the face-to-face community is embedded within a larger stratified society" (1987: 500). These include Afro-Caribbean as well as Indo-Caribbean communities (on the latter see Jayawardena 1963). Pointing to egalitarian norms and practice, Brenneis is, however, careful to state that "While for some members no relations of subordinate and superordinate are present, such equivalence rarely extends throughout the entire community; women and younger males are often excluded" (1987: 500–1). Such indirection entails the speaker meaning more or other than what is said; it allows the speaker to avoid full responsibility for what is said; it compels listeners, including, and especially, an audience of those other than to whom the remark was addressed, to arrive at their own interpretations and within all this are nestled formal codes that indicate that there are hidden meanings and relationships (Brenneis 1987: 504–5). Indirect speech can be seen as a form of roundabout confrontation in which the chance of retaliation is minimized or avoided altogether.

A widely reported phenomenon, called by Trinidadians "dropping words," corresponds to "throwing words" in Jamaica, "dropping remarks" in Barbados (see Fisher 1976), and *indirectas* in Cuba and Puerto Rico. In "dropping words" the word dropper might make a

disparaging comment about someone by talking apparently to no-one or by ostensibly talking to a third party. To gain status, the victim must remain "cool-cool" and pretend not to hear. If he or she is provoked into the slightest response, this is taken as proof by the audience that the comments or accusations are in fact true. Fisher (1976: 240) reports that men rarely "drop remarks" in Barbados. Yet, at least in flirting, men are able to use this technique to do what Trinidadians call "put question" to women, that is, to proposition them, to enquire as to their interest in a sexual liaison. In rural Jamaica:

Men do not always "talk straight" regarding sex "because shyness": women might reject them. Out of need, one man explained, men developed a rich vocabulary describing sex and the vagina—a vocabulary full of words and phrases with many meanings. Women accepting male offers acknowledge one meaning. Those who would not comply take another.

Since men always want sex, women need not fear misinterpretation. Yet, if a woman interprets a statement as a sexual overture and shows scorn or otherwise irritates her suitor/aggressor, he can "throw" immorality accusations back on her. He can tell her he meant no such thing—that her own "bad mind" and propensity for prostitution caused her to think in terms of sexual solicitation (Sobo 1993: 174–5).

Indirection, then, is essential to playing what Freilich (1968: 48) calls the "sex-fame game," in which Trinidadian villagers "believe that everyone has a sexual appetite the satisfaction of which is natural and pleasurable," and that men's object is to "sweet-talk" women and make sexual "conquests." The more women and the more sexual involvement, the more "fame" is achieved. "Famous" men are known as "hot boys," "sweet men" and "wild men." In urban Trinidad their counterparts are "saga boys," good-looking, masculine, well-dressed men who have numerous girlfriends. Men receive "fame" for their ability to "fool" women in order to obtain sex.

A related activity is what Trinidadians refer to as "sooting" (Mendes 1986: 137). This occurs when men "liming" (passing the time in idle conversation [Eriksen 1990]) on a street corner call out to women with a loud hiss. This is usually followed by "Hey dahrlin" and comments about the woman's appearance. One letter of complaint to a newspaper stated:

> On the roads, I am Psst'd at by many males ranging from ages eight to 50. If I ignore them, I am then addressed as Dahlin, or nice Thing or whatever suits their fancy. I am given a complete run down on every part of my body, including my most private parts. At the supermarkets and banks I am addressed (by guards, customers and so on) to the effect: Mornin' sweets: or "sis" or "sexy" or some other suggestive and derogatory term. I am constantly invited to "go up by de beach" to engage in sexual activity by men whose wives, I am certain, are at home attending to household chores and material responsibilities *(Trinidad Guardian,* 11 March 1988, cited in Miller 1994: 178).

This is a verbal activity that men do not receive status for, except, perhaps, from their "liming" partners. As Terry, a nineteen-year-old East Indian factory worker, said:

> Youths who lime on the street are the least respected. They may soot a girl and she don't look they say "I don't want a wife, I want a shit cleaner," and they do big women that. But I classin' myself in that category too, 'cause I do that.[3]

Despite a societal emphasis on respectability, women's sexuality is not constructed as passive nor are their domains constructed as solely domestic. Caribbean women participate, and have always participated, in wage-labour, although they are incorporated into the division of labour in a disempowered way. Emic (and etic) stereotypes of the fiercely independent Black "matriarch" abound, based to a large extent on women's actual experience of relative economic independence (Safa 1986) but they obscure the stark necessity behind this independence. Almost all non-kin male-female relationships are defined by men as sexual ones. In a study of Blacks in business in Trinidad and Tobago, one Black female entrepreneur complained that her Black male business associates wanted to mix her business with their pleasure. But her remarks could be generalized to other Caribbean ethnic groups as well:

> I have problems dealing with Black men in business. You are dealing with them at a business level and they will always have to let some sort of sexual thing come into it. It is as if we have not grown up and realise business is business and something else is something else. We have to play carnival everyday. You speak to a man on the telephone and address him as Mr. X and he in the middle of the conversation will call you "dear, sweetheart." When you stop him, he will get very upset and we immediately get to a point where he is saying: "Weh yuh playing? Yuh believe yuh so special that ah carh call yuh sweetheart" (Ryan & Barclay 1992: 125).

In most cases women have little choice but to accept this definition of the situation. They then make use of their own "sexualization" (cf. Allison 1994: 61) as part of tactics of resistance and power-seeking.

The subject of flirting invokes the Cuban principle of *sandunga. Sandunga* is more than women's "sexiness." In the pantheon of the syncretic *santería* religion, Ochún is the Yoruba *orisha*, or deity, whose Cuban Catholic manifestation of the Virgin Mary is *La Caridad del Cobre,* the patron saint of Cuba. Ochún is a coquette. In an article on post-evolutionary Cuban women's aesthetics in the New York-based beauty magazine Allure, Ochún, speaking through a possessed medium, calls *sandunga* a way of walking, an undulating sway that involves the whole body, her gift to Cuban women: "A silent song that begins with the ankle and continues just past the ass" (Hanly 1991: 47). Self- and other-objectification meet in the display and emphasis on parts of the body.

In Trinidad, at Carnival time the local newspapers are full of pages upon pages devoted to photographs of the street celebrations. These photographs are carried daily for weeks after the annual pre-Lenten event. By far the majority of these photographs are of scantily clad women—the ratio of women to men participating is estimated to be of the order of eight to one. Almost always light-skinned, "Mixed" (mulatto), or East Indian women, with straight or straightened hair are featured in these photo montages. Women who are unequivocally Black are hardly ever featured in this way, except to poke fun at individuals considered to be overweight. When captured by the lenses, women are in sexually provocative poses, or doing sexually provocative dances, such as "wining," which involves a gyrating of the hips (Miller 1991), "de dog," "the butterfly," or others. These women are never identified by name, unless they happen to be local celebrities. Instead, the photographs are captioned (to take only a few recent examples) with references such as: "Carnival is woman," the [calypso] song goes. In all shapes, colours and sizes, they graced the streets of Port-of-Spain and the Queen's Park Savannah stage yesterday to formally start the Carnival celebrations" *(Trinidad Guardian,* 28 February 1995, p. 1); "These women of the Southland are indeed "Hot Hot Hot" and they seem to depict the name of their band better than their costumes do" *(Trinidad Guardian,* 1 March 1995, p. 15); "In a band filled with shapely women, this Poison reveller still stood out" *(Trinidad Guardian,* 3 March 1995, p. 19); "...women play a great part in all the fun and revelry. Carnival and our pretty gals go hand in glove," and "She exalted in the sweet Carnival moment. What's more, she demonstrated for all to see—"The Iwer Dance." Go ahead, baby!" *(Sunday Punch,* 20 February 1994, pp. 1, 3).

Carnival is deemed to be an overturning of the established order, a period of licensed expression.[4] Women "freeing-up" in Carnival and "winning," and especially the image of the so-called "Bacchanal women" (Miller 1991), have come to be interpreted by Trinidadians as part of a duality of which Carnival is perhaps the most exemplary: the expression of a rampant sexuality not possible in normal times. The term "bacchanal," referring to scandal and acrimony (Mendes

1986: 7), is often heard in Trinidad and is often associated with women. In their focus on women, Trinidadian men are apt to tell stories of a certain ostensibly respectable woman who "wine and get on bad" during Carnival, but on Ash Wednesday "she pass you straight" (pretends not to know you) in the street, and returns to being "social" (that is, anti-social) and straight-laced. As a male Trinidadian friend in his sixties often says, "Dey say in de day she can't say prunes," pursing his lips, "but at night she say guava-aaaaaa," opening his mouth wide. While men mock this "freeing-up" behaviour, what is taken to be women's licensed expression of sexuality during Carnival is tolerated because it is restricted and ritualized.[5]

Sexuality, gender relations and flirting are related to particular Caribbean kinship arrangements whereby male–female relationships are thought of in terms of exchange. Sexuality becomes a transfer point of money and power and a locus of control. It becomes a tactic, especially for women, who are in general terms unequal partners in the exchange. As Haitian women say, *"kom se karo te'm; se lajam'm"* ("my body is a piece of land; it is my money") (Lowenthal 1984, quoted in Charles 1994: 48). Sex becomes exchanged in terms of a generalized, delayed reciprocity, lest it be prostitution. Competition occurs between women for scarce resources in the form of men.

This occurs in an overarching Caribbean kinship system that, as Smith (1988) argues, puts a greater emphasis on consanguineal solidarity than on conjugal ties: "Ideally, conjugal partners imaginatively create "one love" between themselves, modeling their relations on kinship, which involves shared blood and the altruism shared blood should engender. But coupled lovers are not kin. Unions have an underlying pragmatic basis" (Sobo 1993: 201). This kinship system, entailing a "dual marriage" pattern whereby status equals marry (albeit later in life for the poor) but men of higher and women of lower status often enter extra-legal unions with each other (Smith 1988), is not only characteristic of working-class Afro-Trinidadians. Notwith-standing portrayals of the East Indian patriar-chal, patrilocal extended family and the Black female-headed one, differences between Black and East Indian family forms and mat-ing practices seem to be eroding (see, for instance, Abdulah 1988: 461; Miller 1994: 142–3, 156–7, 158, 159). This is especially so in urban and suburban areas of Trinidad where East Indians are seen by themselves and others to be "Creolizing."

SERIOUS PLAY IN THE FACTORY

When the situation is one of men and women working side by side or sharing a task that calls for team work, Eros may infiltrate the produc-tion line to evoke attachments of various quali-ties and durations of affection, ranging from the protracted attentions of true love to ephemeral ardencies of the opportune moment (Roy 1974: 46).

The Essential Utensils Ltd (EUL) factory is located in Diego Martin, a suburb of Trinidad and Tobago's capital, Port of Spain. Fifty-two of the sixty-three line workers are women, ranging in age from their late teens to their mid-forties. The rest of the line workers are young men in their late teens and early twen-ties. All eight supervisors are men, ranging in age from their early thirties to their early fifties. There is also an ethnic division of labour. The factory's husband-and-wife co-owners are White, most of the office workers are White, Chinese or "Mixed," and five of the supervisors are White, the rest being East Indian. Of the female workers, 71 percent are Black and 25 percent. are East Indian. Two young women are considered "Mixed." Of the male line workers, there are five East Indians and six Blacks (see Yelvington 1993a; 1993b; 1995).[6]. In the factory, the workers divide themselves up into peer groups based on gen-der, ethnicity and age for the purposes of socializing and for the exchange of goods and services through support networks. Women in their thirties and forties form one peer group.

Their workplace conversations revolve around issues of family and children. Most are in stable relationships based on common law or legal marriage and almost all have chil-dren. Women in their teens and twenties—those currently preferred in the factory's recruitment practices—form another peer group. Their workplace culture is character-ized by overt references to romance, sex and sexual horseplay. Most of these workers, even those who are married or have children, live in the households of older relatives. The Black and East Indian men form separate peer groups. The women workers are given tasks that require long periods of sitting at machines and workbenches. Although they are attached to the same departments, the young men are given tasks that call for them to move around the factory sometimes. The supervisors generally "lime" together at break times. Flirting occurs between the supervisors and the younger women workers. It also occurs between younger male and female workers. In both cases, flirting is for the most part—but certainly not always—initiated by the men. But the patterns of flirting are com-plicated by ethnicity. While the White super-visors and the young Black men flirt with both Black and East Indian women, the East Indi-an male supervisors and workers flirt almost exclusively with East Indian women. When the young women initiate flirting they do so with both young Black and East Indian men, as well as with the supervisors. Older women are not engaged in flirting, unless they are deemed to be not "respectable."

The interchanges between supervisors and workers both blur and demarcate the line between flirting and sexual harassment. While perhaps ultimately the definition of sexual harassment depends on those con-cerned, public discourse in Trinidad has been increasingly concerned with issues of work-place sexual harassment as the post-oil boom recession deepens and jobs become more scarce. During my fieldwork year (1986–87), Singing Sandra won the Calypso Queen title with the song "Die with my dignity," which told of a woman seeking a job in order to support her family but being met with supervisors sexual demands. Charges of sexual harassment in Trinidad have reached the highest and most visible levels ever. Even the leader of the official parliamentary opposition has been charged with sexual harassment. One man argued that the charges must be politically motivated, admitting that, after all, "most of us would be behind bars" if sexual harassment was always prosecuted" *(Economist* 1994: 54). In the factory, the supervisor–worker flirting idiom exhibits most clearly the power relations involved in sexuality-as-exchange relationships. Flirting, as defined above, is a means for the exercise of, and the resistance to, power.

Flirting's infatuation with power can be seen when comparing men's and women's flirting styles. Vishnu is a thirty-five-year-old unmarried toolmaker. He is not technically a supervisor but, given his age and the fact that he "limes" with the supervisors, he is shown the same kind of deference as the supervisors are shown. He is reviled by the women workers for his habit of coming up to them while they are working at their machines, draping his arm around their shoulders or perhaps pressing his body up against their back and talking to them. One day Vishnu leaned up against Rita, a young light-skinned "Mixed" woman, and spoke to her for about five minutes as she was operating her machine. That he chose to speak with Rita in this way was itself rare because Vishnu, like the other East Indian men, usually only flirts with East Indian women, although the fact that Rita was not Black was significant. I spoke to her afterwards. She told me that she did not like what Vishnu was doing, but reminded me that she was a new employee. She said that she did not want to "make trouble" and jeopardize her job, but wanted to make sure she had no "trouble" with Vishnu. So she said she was going to keep her feelings to herself. On one occasion, Winston chased the older Vishnu out of his department, berating him for bothering his "girls" and slowing up production. This led to an argument and a temporary chilling of Vishnu's and Winston's relationship.

Some women find themselves particular "targets" of the supervisors' attentions. Patricia seems to be a supervisor favorite. She is young, seen as attractive, and appears willing to respond in kind to the men's flirting. Johnny, a twenty-year-old Black worker, intimated that the older, more respectable, workers were offended by her precociousness: "Patricia have no respect. She act like she want to fuck down de place. She came over to me, in front of dese big women." Johnny himself, though, showed a willingness to flirt with Patricia. Connie, a twenty-five-year-old East Indian with long black hair, and who wears high-heeled shoes every day to work, is also an object of the supervisors' attentions. Even the male owner occasionally flirts with Connie, as his wife is hardly ever present on the factory floor.[7] Johnny told Connie half-jokingly that she was the "outside woman," or mistress, of the supervisors and the owner. The "outside woman," sometimes called a "deputy," as a woman who trades sex for economic goods, is a stock character in Trinidadian culture (see Miller 1994: 186–8). Throughout my fieldwork I was not aware of any supervisor–worker affairs, except for the short-lived dating relationship between Lloyd and Patricia in which, because of an absence of any subsequent bragging by Lloyd, I assume no sexual relations occurred.

What the women told me was that they had taken stock of their relative positions of influence and power within the factory hierarchy (they were at the bottom) and that they needed to play along with the supervisors' advances, to insinuate the possibility of a future sexual relationship, so that they could ensure smooth workplace relations and, ultimately, keep their jobs. Once Dolly, a twenty-one-year-old East Indian, was looking in Winston's desk for a cigarette. When he came over, she looked up at him and gave him an exaggerated smile. Without a word he smiled back knowingly, took a cigarette out of his pocket, and gave it to her. He told me later that he knew she was being nice to him just to get a cigarette, but shrugged his shoulders and asked rhetorically: "What you go do?"

Winston divulged to me once that Antigone, a twenty-five-year-old Black woman, had seemed to be expressing an interest in him when she asked him about his plans for Carnival. He told her that he was planning on retreating from the crowds and congestion and heading to Margarita Island, a Venezuelan resort. She then asked if she could come with him. Instead of a direct "yes," he replied by asking her "Are you going to sleep in the same room with me?" She replied, "Of course, why do you think I want to go?" "So I keepin' this real quiet," he told me after recounting the story, "I don't want everyone else to know." In the end, they never made the trip together. I do not know if Antigone was serious or just using innuendo and flirting as a workplace tactic, although I think it was the latter. What this also reveals is the role of boasting by men. It was important for Winston to boast to me about the prospect of the meeting and about the flirting exchange that set it up.

Flirting as accommodation to the supervisors stops short of actual sexual relations. The women were, in fact, concerned not to let such relationships develop. Maureen, a young East Indian, referred to her experiences in a previous job: "I been through it myself. The boss may think you look attractive and he want to *fren* ["friend," i.e. to establish a sexual relationship] wid you...I ain't doin'dat. I will fren wid you is one ting but I'm not workin by you too." The younger men, though not in a position of formal authority, nevertheless thought of sexuality as a point of material exchange even if they had little materially to offer in return. Terry, a nineteen-year-old East Indian, said to Patricia, who wanted a piece of the cake he was eating: "Give me a fuck and I'll give you a piece." Patricia, looking surprised and slightly annoyed, said, laughing, "Come now man, don't play dat."

Flirting initiated by the younger men is somewhat different from that between supervisors and the women workers, In such cases the indirection involved in flirting breaks down and communication becomes more direct. But the tension remains, just because the interaction is defined as flirting and the parties to it (especially the men) are not sure just how seriously to take apparent direct talk and promises. Paul and Johnny, two young Black men, were "talking rude" to Lucy, Elaine and Sybil, three young Black women. The topic was sex. Paul said that he wanted a woman with experience to be his "teacher." He turned to Lucy and asked if she was "experienced." She answered coyly with a "Maybe?" Wanting to know just how "experienced," Paul put his thumbs and forefingers together and made the shape of a circle and asked "It big so?," referring to her vagina. The implication was that the more sexually experienced, the "bigger" it would be. Lucy responded with a laugh: "what about you—how big is you?" Paul said "Come upstairs and I'll show yuh." While this kind of flirting is no doubt more direct, it remains flirting because there was no chance that Lucy would actually take Paul up on his offer. It does, however, have tangible effects. These kinds of interchanges occur many times daily. They have the combined result of sexualizing the younger women workers and of defining the work situation as one of sexual objectification. Both men and women become sexual objects, but in decidedly unequal ways.

When it is the women who initiate flirting, "sexy" looks are given along with suggestive body language. Stephanie, a twenty-five-year-old East Indian, was about to pick up parts from a box on the floor. She said to Terry, who was standing behind her, "Look Terry, I want to show you something." Wearing tight jeans, she then bent over showing Terry her buttocks and holding the pose for a few seconds. She then picked up the box. Terry just smiled. The young women flirt not only with the supervisors, but also with their male co-workers, in order to engage their attentions for instrumental purposes. The younger women in Terry's department ask him with dramatically whining voices to collect boxes of parts for them. The older workers in that department criticize the younger women for their behaviour. As Myra said, "He have them so. I does always tell him that. They can get for theyself if they had to. But they rely on him." At other times, women become involved in "bacchanal" and aggressively "heckle" (verbally bait and harass) men. On their mid-day break, Carole, 19, Margarita, 37, and Karen, 40, all of whom are Black, were looking out of an upstairs window when a young man got out of a delivery van and came over to urinate against the fence in front of the factory—not an uncommon sight in Trinidad. With his trousers unzipped, he looked up to see the women looking back at him. They exploded with laughter and, as he hurriedly did up his zipper, Carole yelled "You almost get stick!" Karen, in a rare lapse from respectability, called out "And it was almost out now!" He then ran across the street to urinate against a building. Carole yelled "Careful you don't lick down the wall wid dat!"

The older workers are scornful not only of the younger workers generally but of the older ones who do not behave respectably. They even blame the younger workers' low productivity and frequent mistakes on their horseplay—which is ironic given that the younger workers are preferred by the owners. The older women tend to engage in a discourse that upholds traditional notions of femininity and they emphasize maintaining the proper comportment for women of their status (although this should not be taken as capitulation and conformity, for respectability can also be a tactic of resistance; see Besson 1993). Daisy is a forty-five-year-old Black woman, the mother of four children. She said she does not like to go to parties any more because "I finish wid dat." I used to study that but that part of my life finished. Now I study Christ. You can't study both ... I used to wear pants [trousers]. Wid me it was pants, pants, pants. Then I realise that I should be wearing dresses and now I wearing dresses. I get more respect." Vera, 45, and Denise, 35, are not considered respectable because they often associate with the younger women. Johnny said:

Women get watch more than men. It not to say that men can't be respectable, but that women get watch for these things more than men do. A woman must act her age and be with the people her fucking age. See Vera? She don't hang wid people she age. She hang wid dem girls dere; dey cuss she and she hang wid dem.

While the conformity to traditional female behaviours that respectability entails has obvious disadvantages, it does offer the older women a sort of shield against the aggressive masculinity found in factory gender relations. I once saw a supervisor playfully slap Denise's behind and I thought that this would not happen to a "respectable" older worker. This male aggression is often manifested in mock fighting that seems to take place as a form of display for the benefit of the women workers. Jeremy and Brian, two young Black men, often wrestle with each other and, with the workers around them laughing and commenting, directly proceed to tickle some of the younger women. The association of flirting, sexuality, power and violence is brought even closer in the factory in a game the workers play called "hits." In this game, one person raps the knuckles of another. This alternates until one person is forced to concede because of the pain. On one occasion, Jeremy let Rita and Carole give him ten "hits" to the one he gave each of them. This was played out in an atmosphere of laugher, blushing and flirting.

The display and construction of a maleness where sexual and fighting prowess symbolically meet in flirting are perhaps more exaggerated in the younger workers, but are also definitely perceptible in the supervisors' flirtations and give insights into the ways in which masculinity is constructed through violence and control. The close association of sex and violence is evident in a number of cultural contexts worldwide (Harvey & Gow 1994). Violence seems to pervade relationships between women and men in the Caribbean. Sobo observes for Jamaica that sexual intercourse "is thought of as an exchange rather than a joint activity. It is also used for the expression of hostilities and ambivalences held toward the opposite sex. Inter-gender tensions and power struggles are symbolized in the treatment of bodies" (1993: 201). Violence between sexual partners has recently received grass-roots feminist attention (Morrow 1994). In Trinidad in 1994, the Caribbean Association for Feminist Research and Action rebuked three male psychiatrists who claimed that the newly-established Domestic Violence Act actually caused men to beat their women because of the threat that women might seek help under the Act's provisions (Women's International Network 1994; see also Alexander 1991). In the factory, while rather subtle and stylized methods of flirting are employed and valued, some flirting is not very subtle. Once, Robert, a nineteen-year-old Black man, was "sweet-talking" to Patricia who was sitting at a workbench. While he did so, he went around behind her and pulled the back of her T-shirt from her jeans. Startled, Patricia said "Boy!" To this, Robert feigned surprise and disingenuously asked "Wha'ppen?" Angrily, Patricia said "Get from around here!" To this Robert retorted "I'll do what de fuck I want!" and stormed off angrily. Later, he returned and tried to be nice to Patricia, and to pretend that everything was back to normal. But she was still very angry with him.

Violence in flirting ranges from the tacit to the overt. The younger women are targets of the men's flirting for several interrelated reasons. They are perhaps seen as sexually more attractive by the men. Few are involved in stable, long-term sexual relationships and are, therefore, possibly more vulnerable economically than the older workers. For these reasons sexuality and vulnerability are conflated. And their own flirting and non-"respectable" behaviour indicates to the men that they would possibly be receptive to sexual advances. Yet, they are adept at the "offer and refusal," to use Simmel's terms and, given the construction of masculinity as dominance and control, this frustrates the men, causing overt violence to enter flirting behaviours (see Moore 1994; Wade 1994). The undercurrent of violence is apparent in the use of the indirect "dropping words" style, which is associated with conflict, and with "sooting," which is confrontational as well. It is apparent in overtly "masculine" display and in games such as "hits" that are violent by definition.

There are wider power relationships to consider. Flirting in the factory recapitulates the discourses and practices of mating and of ethnic preference in Trinidad. These are, in turn, related to cultural biases, economic structure and to general attempts to acquire and convert "symbolic capital" (Bourdieu 1977: 171–83). The flirting relationships between the White supervisors and the younger Black and East Indian women tend to reproduce a history of White men's sexual access to Black and East Indian women under slavery and indenture. The present manifestation is the dual marriage system, referred to above, although this system does not necessarily entail interethnic mating. In a number of historical and ethnographic contexts a male-dominated discourse makes women represent the "purity" of the ethnic group. This is seen, for example, in the enforced isolation of White women in Caribbean slave societies (Bush 1981; Martínez–Alier 1989). In Trinidad, Blacks and East Indians see each other more often than not as political and economic competitors. In the factory, Black men flirt with Black and East Indian women. East Indian men flirt exclusively with East Indian women. From my point of view, the flirting styles themselves do not vary with ethnicity. While Trinidadians (of whatever ethnic affiliation) might assume that Black men and women employ more aggressive and overt styles, flirting styles in the factory, as we have seen, vary with age, sex, and position within the factory's formal hierarchy.

But, of course, this does not mean that flirting itself has nothing to do with ethnicity. Besides revealing a sometimes pervasive colonially-derived anti-Black aesthetic bias evidenced, for example, in the region's beauty contests in which light-skinned women with "European" features are habitually the winners (see Barnes 1994; Trinidad & Tobago 1973), here the flirting takes on the mantle of conflictual ethnic politics. Despite small recent increases, the incidence of interethnic marriage between Blacks and East Indians is historically low (Clarke 1993), although interethnic sexual relations occur on a wider scale. East Indian patriarchal discourse is preoccupied with the prevention of sexual relations and marriage between East Indian women and Black men (see Miller 1994: 198–200; Yelvington 1995: 178–85), although East Indian men are also discouraged from forming relationships with Black women. Among Blacks, there is no equivalent discourse but perhaps, on the contrary, encouragement to marry non-Blacks. A study published in 1979 revealed that 13 percent of Blacks had objections to Blacks marrying other Blacks while only 7 percent of Blacks had objections to Blacks marrying East Indians. Around 90 percent had no objections to Blacks marrying Whites or "Mixed" individuals. On the other hand, 53 percent of East Indians reported objections to East Indians marrying Blacks, while 90 percent had no objections to East Indians marrying Whites and/or "Mixed" individuals (Ryan et al. 1979: 63). By attempting to "conquer" East Indian women, Black men are, paradoxically, lowering the esteem of the East Indian group while even possibly improving, according to them, their own symbolic capital. By contrast, according to East Indian men, they would lose symbolic capital if they flirted with Black women because to mate with Blacks would depreciate the symbolic capital of East Indians without having a detrimental effect on Black esteem.

Despite ongoing transformations of East Indian family structure, the greater importance for East Indian men of the ethnicity of spouses relates to the historical shortage of East Indian women indentured workers, combined with colonial depictions of Blacks. East Indian men therefore "had" to emphasize ethnic endogamy. Given notions of Black women as more "independent" and thus potentially threatening to male control within the family, East Indian men are discouraged from considering Black women as potential mates. The stereotype of East Indian men using the cutlass or other weapons to control women has its basis in historical incidents of women's strategizing being met with violence and murder (Brereton 1979: 182; Wood 1968: 154). At the same time, the avoidance of Black women as mates is indicative of a masculinity uncomfortable, anxious and ambivalent in the face of "Creolization" (Sampath 1993), especially in relation to stereotypes of Black women as hyper-sexualized, independent and powerful, and of East Indian women as docile and domesticated. Yet, even though they experience a "diminished masculinity" (Cooper 1993: 165) different from that experienced by Blacks, an added dimension of East Indian men's flirting violence against East Indian women is their frustration with women who flirt with Black men.

The logic of Black masculinity is somewhat different. Through activities such as sports and the calypso, Black men depict themselves as being more masculine than East Indian men. The status of a "sweet man" or "saga boy" entails a willingness to seduce and subjugate women from other groups, and the more such exotic "conquests" the more status is achieved. The perception that Black men are more masculine may help explain why East Indian women flirt with Black men as much as with East Indian men. However, for the most part it is the men who initiate flirting. When the women respond, or when they initiate flirting, they seem to be trying to parry the advances of the men or to use their sexuality for instrumental purposes.

Along with its other characteristics, then, flirting involves violence. Mostly, to be sure, it is "symbolic violence" (Bourdieu 1977: 183–97; Krais 1993) as a mode of domination, involving the imposition of systems of symbolism and meaning to legitimize that domination. But this is not all. While the women may indeed experience the men's flirting as "legitimate" according to their normal expectations of men's behaviour, they also question this legitimacy by charging the men with sexual harassment. The men and women of the factory attempt to define flirting as concerned merely with sexual attraction. Yet, at the same time, they clearly employ flirting as a way of exercising power and playing out conflicts, using what can be called "transposed violence": a kind of force exerted when the ostensible meaning of an act disguises other, emergent meanings it may have. Flirting plays with sexual attraction while being a conduit for power relations, and these multiple meanings are fraught with contradiction and value conflict. The culturally "acceptable" and valorized practice of flirting shades into threat and coercion, which are less acceptable and more able to be resisted legitimately.

A THEORY OF FLIRTING

Flirting is both indicative of causal forces and, in a dialectical movement, partially responsible for their existence and efficacy. Flirters are not "bearers of structure." Rather, flirting is one tip of the structural iceberg, one *manifestation* of underlying, causal arrangements of power and knowledge to be explained by other kinds of theories. Social anthropologists may be inclined to analyse the foregoing description of flirting in terms of joking relationships. Radcliffe–Brown's depiction of joking relationships is, of course, well known. He extended his analysis to the realm of gender relations when he suggested that joking relations are expressions of potentially conflictual relationships. Specifically, joking relationships obtain between potential marriage or sexual partners and relations of avoidance obtain between those who are forbidden to mate (1952: 100). While this is true of the flirting in the EUL factory, Radcliffe–Brown's concept of joking relations can in no way encompass the complex structural realities that underlie behaviours in this ethnographic context. As Sharman (1969) has urged, the focus must be shifted to the analysis of the relationships themselves. Rather than a joking relationship between already given categories of people, representing and expressing various interests, flirting is a way

of constituting and constructing gendered, ethnic and "classed" subjects and subjectivities in the context of power inequalities which do not themselves stand outside of the constituting and constructing process. Like Radcliffe–Brown, I am concerned to move from a depiction of what flirting is to what flirting *does*. Flirting in the factory—and elsewhere in Caribbean society—is one way in which men control women. Flirting by the supervisors further entrenches their position of authority and therefore diminishes the younger women's status as workers. This tends to support the owners' strategies of hiring these relatively vulnerable workers. It is clear that in an industrial setting male supervisors have an interest in controlling female workers and encouraging docility, even if they do so unintentionally. The younger workers often behave in a rambunctious manner and let their horseplay stand in the way of their work. Through flirting, the supervisors attempt to keep the women's sexual horseplay in check with the implied threat that if it goes too far then it will turn into actual, inegalitarian, sexual relations. The young women lose respect for flirting with the men, which in turn ensures that they will be flirted with. Flirting by the younger male workers is no less harmful, because it serves further to objectify the younger women as sexually available and subordinate.

Flirting is part of a process in which younger women are eventually made to be "respectable" as they grow older, in order to fend off sexual advances of men. Flirting, with violent overtones, is responsible for enforcing respectability, which is both subordination to hegemonic values of passivity and piety and liberation from direct sexual harassment. Older, "respectable" women do not face such objectification because their respectability acts as a shield. In a way, the older women constrain themselves. Given their circumstances (a home, children) they do not "need" to be constrained. However, given that respectability entails traditional, colonial female stances, respectability guarantees objectification and subjugation by different means. At the same time, rather than directly upholding the values of authority, this may very well be the most effective way to resist authority. Women's flirting and "heckling," on the other hand, are behaviours in which women attempt to mitigate and resist men's control. In many ways, women's initiation of flirting ensures some measure of control over the situation. In contrast to Simmel, my efforts here are part of a project to develop what can be called a "political economy of meaning," indicative of the large and small processes involved in contestations over consciousness: systems of meaning can thus be analysed in terms of power relations. These power relations themselves are not given but constructed in pitched battles to decide meaning and interpretation. These battles are won and lost and the victor gets to determine the terms of the armistice, at least temporarily, when systems of meaning are created and enforced by groups with the most power. Analysing flirting thus becomes one way to analyse a society's fault lines by examining who may flirt with whom, when, and with what consequences. As Phillips writes, "Freud showed us—if we needed showing—that it is not more truthful to be serious" (1994: xi). Reality, with all its motivations and machinations, is not so much suspended in a game called flirting, but rather permeates it.

NOTES

Earlier versions of this article were presented at the Fourteenth Annual Conference of the Caribbean Studies Association, Bridgetown, Barbados, 23–26 May 1989, and the Seventh Biennial Southern Labor Studies Conference, Atlanta, Georgia, USA, 10–13 October 1991. I am grateful to the workers and owners of Essential Utensils Ltd for all their help and co-operation. I use pseudonyms for them and their factory in this article. I would like to thank Bridget Brereton, Barbara C. Cruz, John French, Daniel James, Shalini Puri, Daniel Miller and the anonymous readers for their comments on earlier drafts. I would also like to thank Simon Harrison for his thorough and useful editorial suggestions.

1. The *raspita* is the burnt part of the rice that remains stuck to the bottom of the pot. While not distinct to Cuba, *piropos* are what Cubans call the stylized, usually rhyming, sayings that men often utilize to comment to and/or about women, whom they do not know personally but whom they may pass in the street or in some other public place. Sometimes *piropos* are said directly to women, but, more often, they are said aloud apparently to no one but loudly enough for the woman in question to hear and in such a way that there is no doubt to whom *the piropo* is directed.

2. My participant-observation fieldwork was undertaken for my DPhil thesis at the University of Sussex. I worked alongside the workers (without pay) for a year (1986–87). While maintaining friendly relations with almost every worker in the factory, in my (perhaps) one mode as "detached observer," I chose not to become part of the flirting scene. My own stance emanated from a commitment to feminism, but also the safety of a postgraduate student who was never sure if he was doing things correctly.

3. As Miller (1994: 178) notes, if women do respond, on the other hand, the "sooter" may expect a conversation or the development of a liaison. One strategy for women is to have a stock answer that creates distance and to keep walking without turning around. Another is to hurl abuse back at the men once they are far away. Still another is to tease "limers." Sobo (1993: 180) reports on "rudies" (conspicuously sexually active women) in rural Jamaica using such situations to initiate sexual relationships.

4. Despite a discourse of Carnival as a national festival, it is still considered a Creole (i.e. non-East Indian) event. Yet the precedence for bawdiness in female peer groups is also found in the East Indian practice of *matikor*. *Matikor* is an all-female ceremony which precedes a wedding and involves female drunkenness, dancing in a sexually suggestive way, and singing insulting songs (Poynting 1987: 241–2). Miller (1994: 197) notes the "increasing syncretism between this and the act of wining."

5. Women's behaviour in Carnival has become a preoccupation of the "respectable" establishment. For example, Catholic Archbishop Anthony Pantin wrote about Carnival's good and bad points, the latter being mainly "women's skimpy costumes":

   I think it is absolutely disgraceful the way most of the women dress for Carnival. I am quite sure that many of them are married and I am really surprised that their husbands allow their wives to parade publicly in what is indecent attire . . . It is not surprising that skimpy costumes of vulgar and indecent behaviour, especially among the womenfolk *(Catholic News,* 27 February 1994, p. 16).

6. The factory could be seen as a throwback to the colonial ethnic division of labour, but a recent report shows the extent of this continuity (Centre for Ethnic Studies 1993).

7. While only in his late thirties, the factory owner possesses the criteria for respectability by virtue of class and ethnicity. Wilson argues that an emphasis on reputation decreases as class levels and age advance. Yet even ostensibly respectable men are interested in enhancing their masculine reputations if the situation is right. "'Big men" do engage in and boast about sexual exploits, but they usually do so quietly to avoid undermining the "respect" they command and to protect their wives' positions" (Sobo 1993: 178). On the other hand, Trinidadians struggle for respectability "in a land where no one can look back too far without finding a labourer or a crook, and sometimes a labourer who became a crook" (Naipaul 1981: 77), where class divisions are still taking form. In *The Middle Passage,* the problem Naipaul identifies is of persistent "transience" in the face of North Atlantic-defined "transcendence," to use Miller's (1994) terms. Trinidadians:

. . . can never completely identify themselves with what they read in magazines or see in films. Their frustration can only deepen, for their minds are closed to everything else. Reality is always separate from the ideal; but in Trinidad this fantasy is a form of masochism and is infinitely more cheating than the fantasy which makes the poor delight in films about rich or makes the English singer use an American accent. It is the difference between the Emily Post Institute advice on dating, published in the *Trinidad Guardian* ("The man must call for his date at her house"), and the calypso by Sparrow:

Tell your sister to come down, boy.
I have something here for she.
Tell she is Mr Benwood Dick,
The man from Sangre Grande.
She know me well. I give she already.
Mm. She must remember me. Go on, go on,
Tell she Mr Benwood come (1981: 65).

REFERENCES

Abdulah, N. 1988. Structure of the population: demographic developments in the independence years. In *Trinidad and Tobago: the independence experience 1962–1987* (ed.) S. Ryan. St. Augustine, Trinidad: Institute of Social and Economic Research, Univ. of the West Indies.

Abrahams, R.D. 1979. Reputation vs. respectability: a review of Peter J. Wilson's concept. *Revista/Review Interamericana* 9, 448–53.

—— 1983. *The man-of-words in the West Indies: performance and the emergence of creole culture.* Baltimore: The John Hopkins Univ. Press.

Alexander, M.J. 1991. Redrafting morality: the postcolonial state and the Sexual Offenses Bill of Trinidad and Tobago. In *Third world women and the politics of feminism* (eds) C.T. Mohanty et al. Bloomington: Indiana Univ. Press.

Allison, A. 1994. *Nightwork: sexuality, pleasure, and corporate masculinity in a Tokyo hostess club.* Chicago: Univ. of Chicago Press.

Austin, R.L. 1976. Understanding calypso content: A critique and an alternative explanation. *Carib. Q.* 22, 74–83.

Barnes, N.B. 1994. Face of the nation: race, nationalisms and identities in Jamaican beauty pageants. *Massachusetts Rev.* 35, 471–92.

Besson, J. 1993. Reputation and respectability reconsidered: a new perspective on Afro–Caribbean peasant women. In *Women and change in the Caribbean* (ed.) J.H. Momsen. Bloomington: Indiana Univ. Press; London: James Currey; Kingston: Ian Randle.

Bourdieu, P. 1977. *Outline of a theory of practice* (trans.) R. Nice. Cambridge: Univ. Press.

Brenneis, D. 1987. Talk and transformation. *Man* (N.S.) 22, 499–510.

Brereton, B. 1979. *Race relations in colonial Trinidad 1870–1900.* Cambridge: Univ. Press.

Bush, B.J. 1981. White "ladies," coloured "favorites" and black "wenches"; some considerations on sex, race and class factors in social relations in white creole society in the British Caribbean. *Slavery and Abolition* 2, 245–62.

—— 1990. *Slave women in Caribbean society 1650–1838.* London: James Currey; Bloomington: Indiana Univ. Press; Kingston: Heinemann.

Carbajo, A. 1968. El *millón catorce de dicharachos cubanos.* Miami Springs: Language Research Press.

Centre for Ethnic Studies 1993. *Employment practices in the public and private sectors in Trinidad and*

Tobago: 2 vols. St. Augustine, Trinidad: Centre for Ethnic Studies, Univ. of the West Indies.

Charles, C. 1994. Sexual politics and the mediation of class, gender and race in former slave plantation societies: the case of Haiti. In *Social construction of the past: representation as power* (eds) G.C. Bond & A. Gilliam. London: Routledge.

Chevannes, B. 1993. Sexual behaviour of Jamaicans: a literature review. *Social econ. Stud.* 42, 1–45.

Clark, C. 1993. Spatial pattern and social interaction among Creoles and Indians in Trinidad and Tobago. In *Trinidad ethnicity* (ed.) K.A. Yelvington. London: Macmillan; Knoxville: Univ. of Tennessee Press.

Cooper, C. 1993. *Noises in the blood: orality, gender and the "vulgar" body of Jamaican popular culture.* London: Macmillan.

Dann, G. 1987. *The Barbadian male: sexual attitudes and practice.* London: Macmillan.

Douglass, L. 1992. *The power of sentiment: love, hierarchy, and the Jamaican family elite.* Boulder: Westview Press.

Economist 1994. The politics of Trinidadian sex. 3 December, p. 54.

Elder, J.D. 1968. The male/female conflict in calypso. *Carib. Q.* 14, 23–41.

Eriksen, T.H. 1990. Liming in Trinidad: the art of doing nothing. *Folk* 32, 23–43.

Fisher, L.E. 1976. Dropping remarks and the Barbadian audience. *Am. Ethnol.* 3, 227–42.

Freilich, M. 1968. Sex, secrets, and systems. In *The family in the Caribbean* (ed.) S.N. Gerber, R. Piedras, Puerto Rico: Institute of Caribbean Studies, Univ. of Puerto Rico.

Hanly, E. 1991. Allure in Cuba, *Allure* July, 44–51.

Harvey, P.& P. Gow (eds) 1994. *Sex and violence: issues in representation and experience.* London: Routledge.

Jayawardena, C. 1963. *Conflict and solidarity in a Guianese plantation.* London: Athlone Press.

Krais, B. 1993. Gender and symbolic violence: female oppression in light of Pierre Bourdieu's theory of social practice. In *Bourdieu: critical perspectives* (eds) C. Calhoun *et al.* Chicago: Univ. of Chicago Press.

Lowenthal, I. 1984. Labor sexuality and the conjugal contract in rural Haiti. In *Haiti—today and tomorrow* (eds) C.R. Foster & A. Valdman. New York. Univ. Press of America.

Martinez–Alier, V. 1989 [1974]. *Marriage, class and colour in nineteenth-century Cuba: a study of mind attitudes and sexual values in a slave society.* Ann Arbor: Univ. of Michigan Press.

Mathurin, L. 1974. A historical study of women in Jamaica from 1655 to 1844. Thesis. University of the West Indies, Mona.

Mendes, J. 1986. *Cote ce cote la: Trinidad and Tobago dictionary.* Arima, Trinidad: John Mendes.

Miller, D. 1991. Absolute freedom in Trinidad. *Man* (N.S.) 26, 323–41.

——— 1994. *Modernity—an ethnographic approach: dualism and mass consumption in Trinidad.* Oxford Berg.

Mohammed, P. & C. Shepherd (eds) 1988. *Gender in Caribbean development.* St. Augustine, Trinidad: Institute of Social and Economic Research, Univ. of the West Indies.

Momsen, J.H. (ed.) 1993. *Women and change in the Caribbean.* Bloomington: Indiana Univ. Press; London: James Currey; Kingston: Ian Randle.

Moore, H. 1994. The problem of explaining violence in the social sciences. In *Sex and violence: issues in representation and experience* (eds) P. Harvey & P. Gow. London: Routledge.

Morrissey, M. 1989. *Slave women in the New World: gender stratification in the Caribbean.* Lawrence, KS. Univ. Press of Kansas.

Morrow, B.H. 1994. A grass-roots feminist response to intimate violence in the Caribbean. *West Stud. Inter. Forum* 17, 579–92.

Naipaul, V.S. 1981 [1962]. *The middle passage.* New York: Vintage Books.

Phillips, A. 1994. *On flirtation.* Cambridge, M.A.: Harvard Univ. Press.

Poynting, J. 1987. East Indian women in the Caribbean: experience and voice. In *India in the Caribbean* (eds) D. Dabydeen & B. Samaroo. London: Hansib/Univ. of Warwick.

Radcliffe–Brown, A.R. 1952. *Structure and function in primitive society.* London: Cohen & West.

Reddock, R.E. 1994. *Women, labour and politics in Trinidad and Tobago: a history.* London: Zed Books.

Rohlehr, G. 1985. "Man talking to man": calypso and social confrontation in Trinidad 1970 to 1984. *Carib. Q.* 31, 1–13.

——— 1988. Images of men and women in the 1930s calypsos: the sociology of food acquisition in the context of survivalism. In *Gender in Caribbean development* (eds) P. Mohammed & C. Shepherd. St. Augustine, Trinidad: Institute of Social and Economic Research, Univ. of the West Indies.

——— 1990. *Calypso and society in pre-independence Trinidad.* Port-of-Spain: Gordon Rohlehr.

Roy, D. 1974. Sex in the factory: informal heterosexual relationships between supervisors and work groups. In *Deviant behavior* (ed.) C. Bryant. Chicago: Rand McNally.

Ryan, S., E. Greene & J. Harewood 1979. *The confused electorate: a study of political attitudes and opinions in Trinidad and Tobago.* St. Augustine, Trinidad: Institute of Social and Economic Research, Univ. of the West Indies.

Ryan, S. & L.A. Barclay. 1992. *Sharks and sardines: Blacks in business in Trinidad and Tobago.* St. Augustine, Trinidad: Institute of Social and Economic Research, Univ. of the West Indies.

Safa, H.I. 1986. Economic autonomy and sexual equality in Caribbean society. *Social econ. Stud.* 36, 1–21.

—— 1995. *The myth of the male breadwinner: women and industrialization in the Caribbean.* Boulder: Westview Press.

Sampath, N.M. 1993. An evaluation of the "creolisation" of Trinidad East Indian adolescent masculinity. In *Trinidad ethnicity* (ed.) K.A. Yelvington. London: Macmillan; Knoxville: Univ. of Tennessee Press.

Schnepel, E.M. 1993. The other tongue, the other voice: language and gender in the French Caribbean. *Ethnic Groups* 10, 243–68.

Senior, O. 1991. *Working miracles: women's lives in the English-speaking Caribbean.* Bloomington: Indiana Univ. Press; London: James Currey; Mona, Jamaica: Institute of Social and Economic Research, Univ. of West Indies.

Sharman, A. 1969. "Joking" in Padhola: categorical relationships, choice and social control. *Man* (N.S.) 4, 103–17.

Simmel, G. 1950. *The sociology of Georg Simmel;* (trans. ed.) K.H. Wolff. New York: The Free Press.

—— 1984 [1911]. Flirtation. In *Georg Simmel: On women, sexuality, and love;* (trans., intro.) G. Oakes. New Haven: Yale Univ. Press.

Smith, R.T. 1988. *Kinship and class in the West Indies: a genealogical study of Jamaica and Guyana.* Cambridge: Univ. Press.

Sobo, E.J. 1993. *One blood: the Jamaican body.* Albany: State Univ. of New York Press.

Trinidad & Tobago 1973. *Report of the commission of enquiry into the Miss Trinidad and Tobago beauty contest 1971, and the organization of such contests and competitions in Trinidad and Tobago.* Report presented to the Acting Governor-General Sir Arthur H. McShine. Port of Spain: Government of Trinidad and Tobago.

Trouillot, M.R. 1992. The Caribbean region: an open frontier in anthropological theory. *Ann. Rev. Anthrop.* 21, 19–42.

Wade, P. 1994. Man the hunter: gender and violence in music and drinking contexts in Colombia. In *Sex and violence: issues in representation and experience* (eds) P. Harvey & P. Gow. London: Routledge.

Wilson, P.J. 1969. Reputation and respectability: a suggestion for Caribbean ethnography. *Man* (N.S.) 4, 70–84.

—— 1973. *Crab antics: the social anthropology of English-speaking Negro societies of the Caribbean.* New Haven: Yale Univ. Press.

Women's International Network. 1994. Women and violence: Trinidad and Tobago. *WIN News* 20, 38.

Wood, D. 1968. *Trinidad in transition.* London: Oxford Univ. Press.

Yelvington, K.A. 1993a. Gender and ethnicity at work in a Trinidadian factory. In *Women and change in the Caribbean* (ed.) J.H. Momsen. Bloomington: Indiana Univ. Press; London: James Currey; Kingston: Ian Randle.

—— 1993b. Ethnicity at work in Trinidad. In *The enigma of ethnicity: an analysis of race in the Caribbean and the world* (ed.) R. Premdas. St. Augustine, Trinidad: School of Continuing Studies, Univ. of the West Indies.

—— 1995. *Producing power: ethnicity, gender, and class in a Caribbean workplace.* Philadelphia: Temple Univ. Press.

Women's Intimate Friendships and Other Affairs: An Ethnographic Overview

Evelyn Blackwood

Anthropological evidence constitutes an important source for theorizing about women's sexualities. It allows us to go beyond European and American cultures and sexual categories to view sexuality from different perspectives. From a Western viewpoint sexuality appears to be an essential or core attribute of identity; Europeans and Americans tend to think that individuals have fixed sexual identities or orientations. The sexual practices and identities of the United States and Europe, however, often bear little resemblance to sexual relationships and practices in other cultures. The cultural evidence shows the richness and diversity of women's sexualities, and the importance of sociocultural factors in the construction of sexuality.

Social construction theory asserts that sexual acts only have meaning within the context of particular cultures and their beliefs about the self and the world. Human sexual potential takes its form through a number of social processes, including ideologies of religion or ritual, ethnicity, class, gender, family, and reproduction, as well as the material and social conditions of everyday life. These processes provide the interpretive context for sexual feelings, desires and longings. In this article I first take a number of case studies of women's same-sex relations in non-Western societies to illustrate the way particular sociocultural processes frame sexual desire within cultural schemas of meaning. Then I explore how cultural systems of gender construct different sexual beliefs and practices for men and women. In the third section I use two detailed examples of female sexualities, one from Suriname and one from West Sumatra,

From *Journal of Social Issues.* Reprinted by permission of Blackwell Publishers.

to argue that sexuality is neither a static category nor a fixed identity. I conclude the essay by exploring some broad patterns at work in framing women's sexualities across cultures.

CULTURAL CONTEXTSOF SEXUALITY

Female same-sex sexuality has been noted in a number of indigenous groups since the beginning of European imperialism (Blackwood 1986b; Blackwood and Wieringa 1999a).[1] The kinds of relationships that appear in the anthropological record include affective or intimate friendships between adult heterosexually married women, adolescent sex play, ritual same-sex practices, and erotic relations between a woman and a transgender female (a female-bodied man) (see Blackwood 1999).[2] In this section I discuss several case studies of women's same-sex relations to illuminate the sociocultural processes that construct particular sexualities. I take three different types of relationships—intimate friendship, erotic ritual practice, and adolescent sex play—to represent both the variety of sexualities as well as the complexities of the social processes involved.

Intimate Friendships

In Lesotho, a small country surrounded by the nation of South Africa, school girls have intimate friendships that they call mummy-baby relationships (Gay 1986). The "mummy-baby" relation is an institutionalized friendship between younger and older girls and women; it became popular throughout much of black southern African starting in the 1950s (Blacking 1978). Prior to this time, young women in rural communities were educated for adult life in initiation schools run by women. The neighboring Venda people organized an initiation school for a group of girls when they reached puberty. Each initiate was appointed a "mother," an older girl who helped her "child" through initiation. This practice established strong ties between the two age sets of young women, ties that were maintained through visits and exchanges of gifts for many years after (Blacking 1978). As a result of missionary efforts to stop this form of education, the schools are now virtually abandoned. The majority of young women attend public or boarding schools in neighboring towns or urban areas. Yet the bond between initiates serves as a cultural model for the mummy-baby relations of contemporary school girls.

In the contemporary mummy-baby relationship, two young women start a relationship by arranging private encounters and exchanging love letters and gifts. The older one, who becomes the mummy, might already have a boyfriend, or other babies, while the younger one, the baby, can only have one mummy. The mummies, being older, usually arrange when to get together and are the ones to give gifts to their babies. They are also a source of "advice on sex and protection from aggressively courting young men" (Gay 1986, 104). The couple treat the friendship like an affair, or romance; hugging, kissing and sexual relations are part of it (Gay 1986).[3] Many of the girls in these relationships are in their teens and only separated in age by a couple of years, but some young women who work or attend schools in distant towns establish relationships with older married women in those towns. For the girls who became mummies and babies to each other, their relationship is part of the romantic drama of growing up and learning the pleasures and responsibilities of relationships. As they become older, they may become mummies to their own babies, and they may begin to have boyfriends as well. Usually the intensity of mummy-baby relations ends with marriage, when a woman's attention is turned toward domestic responsibilities, but many women maintain the bonds of friendship with other women after marriage (Gay

1986). These adult friendships provide important emotional and economic ties for women within rural communities.

Mummy-baby relationships are constructed from a number of cultural sources. The similarities between mummy-baby relationships and those established in initiation schools mentioned earlier are quite strong. Older girls or women are relied on (and constructed) as an important source of friendship and social connection into adulthood. In a culture where it is taboo for a mother to talk about sexuality with a daughter, older girls in initiation schools and now "mummies" at school are the culturally sanctioned source for this information.

Cultural ideologies of sexuality constitute another element in the construction of mummy-baby relationships. Although in Lesotho men's sexuality is represented as being dominant and assertive, certain cultural practices define women as having agency in their own sexuality. In the past both married women and men had sexual partners other than their spouses (Nthunya 1997); their sexuality was not considered the sole property of their partner. Young girls were trained for adult sexual relations in initiation schools, and on their own practiced lengthening the labia, which women believe makes them "hotter." Although sexual ideology makes virginity important for Lesotho girls brought up under the influence of the Roman Catholic church, Gay argues that "female sensuality is both encouraged and restrained, but it is never denied" (Gay 1986, 101).

The mummy-baby relationship also draws on a tradition of rural women's special affective and gift exchange partnerships.[4] Women of an earlier generation in rural Lesotho established intimate friendships with other women called *motsoalle* (special friend) (Kendall 1999). These special friendships were long-term, loving, and erotic relationships that coexisted with heterosexual marriage. In this patrilineal country, in which family inheritance and property move from father to sons and women are legal minors, a woman at marriage moves to her husband's house and village. One woman, Nthunya, who had a *motsoalle*, was a poor, rural farmer most of her life (Nthunya 1997). When she married her husband, she moved to where her husband's family lived. She worked on their farm, raising sheep and growing maize. Her husband worked with her when he was home but was often away on road construction or other wage labor jobs. Together they had six children. During her marriage, she established a *motsoalle* relationship with another married woman, which she describes as follows:

> It's like when a man chooses you for a wife, except when a man chooses, it's because he wants to share the blankets with you. The woman chooses you the same way, but she doesn't want to share the blankets. She wants love only. When a woman loves another woman, you see, she can love her with a whole heart (Nthunya 1997, 69).

Their relationships was celebrated by gift-giving and feasting that involved the whole community. For the feast, a sheep was slaughtered, gifts were exchanged, and neighbors and kin from throughout the village came to eat, drink, and dance. This ritual feast publicly validated the commitment of the two women to each other. A relationship with a *motsoalle* was neither an alternative nor a threat to marriage. According to Nthunya, her husband and her *motsoalle's* husband were both supportive of their relationship. Such friendships had many benefits. Nthunya said, "In the old days friendship was very beautiful—men friends and women friends. Friendship was as important as marriage. Now this custom is gone; everything is changing" (Nthunya 1997, 72).

The poverty of Lesotho and the migration of husbands have often been used as explanations for women's intimate friendships in southern Africa. Such explanations assume that women are loving each other because they are deprived of heterosexual outlets. This deprivation thesis assumes that an underlying sexual urge must be satisfied even when husbands are absent. But the cultural context of Lesotho makes better sense of women's intimate friendships. As the preceding case suggests, sexuality for women of Lesotho is constructed through a number of sociocultural processes. These include the institution of women's friendships, which develop and maintain strong social networks for women, and the cultural tradition of age mates, in which groups of slightly older and more experienced girls provide advice, support, and protection for younger girls. Older girls are seen as appropriate sources of advice and guidance about heterosexual relations and also as appropriate partners in one's first romantic and sexual encounters. A cultural ideology of sexuality positions women as sexual actors and not the property of their spouses. These processes shape sexual intimacies with other girls as a way to develop and manage their own sexual feelings. Consequently, close emotional and intimate bonds between young women are constructed as part of growing up and an important source of social ties in adulthood.

Erotic Ritual Practices

The homoerotic ritual practices of aboriginal Australian women constitute another case that does not fall easily within a Western framework of sexual identities. Prior to interference from white Australians, aborigines were seminomadic, egalitarian foragers who lived in small camps. Their complex kinship system defined who was a potential marriage partner and who was not. Extramarital heterosexual relations as well as same-sex relations were the norm for both women and men (Roheim 1933).

Young girls were initiated into their adult roles at first menstruation through a process of training and ritual. Initiation ceremonies conveyed a number of messages about the configuration of tribal land, kinship categories, and proper social action. Included in these ceremonies were homoerotic dances between the women and the initiates. Earlier anthropologists, who were reluctant to discuss this aspect of initiation performances, described the movements of the women dancers as sexually suggestive, culminating in what was called "simulated intercourse" (Kaberry 1939). The intent of this performance was said to ensure heterosexual success (getting or keeping a husband or male lover). Since the 1950s such ceremonies are rarely performed in north Australia, but, according to Povinelli (1992), they continue to unnerve Anglo audiences and confuse young aboriginal women, who are now familiar with the Anglo gay identity. Older Belyuen women, however, are not troubled by the homoerotic "digging" (*yedabetj*) of the ritual performances. For them it is erotic play that initiates young women into the complex social and kin categories that circumscribe their lives as married adults (Povinelli 1992).[5]

For Australian aboriginal groups the social processes that produce erotic ritual play include a cultural ideology of women's sexuality in which women have agency, and beliefs in the power of ritual to influence and control human action. Adult women teach adolescent girls about proper kin relations and appropriate sexual partners through ritual practices between women; they also learn how to work magic for sexual success.

Adolescent Sex Play

Adolescent heterosexual play is well documented for many cultures. Its practice is closely tied to ideas about childhood, sexuality, and virginity. For girls it is more typical (or visible) in societies where virginity is not given heavy weight, such as the !Kung San of the Kalahari Desert of southern Africa. Few !Kung now live their nomadic foraging lifestyle, having been forced to settle in one place by colonial authorities and the postcolonial state, but one !Kung woman, Nisa, has recounted a life history that sheds light on adolescent sexual practices (Shostak 1983).

The egalitarian !Kung lived in small communities of kin that moved with the rains and availability of food. Each family had few possessions. The adult couple shared a small grass dwelling with their children, and in such close quarters waited until their children fell asleep to engage in sex. Adults insisted that they disapproved of childhood sex play (to disapproving missionaries, perhaps), but

when children played in their mock villages or in the bush, they played at the things their parents did, including keeping house and experimenting sexually. !Kung children and adolescents engaged in both heterosexual and homosexual play. Nisa recounted how she watched older girls play sexually with each other and then did the same with her girlfriends as she approached adolescence. The girls would use saliva to enhance the glide of genitals over genitals. As the girls got older, they were expected to play sexually with the boys, although Nisa describes herself as initially reluctant to do so. All the young girls Nisa knew later married men. For these !Kung women, however, marriage did not become the only locus of sexuality, since, according to Nisa, both men and women have sexual relations with partners other than their spouses. In adulthood the bonds of adolescence remain strong, providing women with loyal friends throughout their lifetimes.

The !Kung have constructed an adolescent phase of sexual experimentation that includes both same-sex and other-sex partners. This construction of sexuality is framed through several sociocultural processes, including ideologies of gender, family, and childhood. !Kung gender ideology is egalitarian, which means that in terms of families, neither marriage partner has exclusive sexual rights over the other. The learning period of childhood extends to developing adolescents, who are expected to engage in sexual play as a way to learn their sexual feelings and desires. Each of these factors combine to produce an adolescent sexuality in which experiences with both boys and girls are possible. Adolescence is constituted as a sexual "learning" period that precedes heterosexual marriage. In this period sexuality between young women is understood as part of their sexual exploration.

CONSTRUCTING MEN'S AND WOMEN'S SEXUALITIES

In this section I explore how gender ideologies construct men's and women's sexualities. By gender ideologies, I mean the set of ideas about men and women, their appropriate behaviors and attributes, and their relations to each other. These ideas in some cases structure very different sexualities for women and men. In the following examples from Papua New Guinea and patriarchal China, the sexual ideologies for men are quite distinct from those for women.

Among the Sambia of Papua New Guinea, for example, young boys are inseminated through oral sex with adult men during the initiation rituals of adolescence (Herdt 1981). This practice is understood as a means to ensure the proper development of masculine traits. According to Western definitions, such a practice would be considered "homosexual." In this Papua New Guinea culture, however, it is explicitly linked to notions of the efficacy of fluids for human development and the necessity of ritual insemination for the development of masculinity (Elliston 1995). Sambian boys are not said to go through a phase of homosexual behavior but rather to undergo ritual measures through sexual means to ensure masculinity and reproductive competence. Once properly inseminated to achieve their full masculinity, these young men are then ready for heterosexual marriage. In contrast, Sambian girls are thought to possess inherent femininity and reproductive competence, and hence, have no need to be given their femininity ritually. From all accounts, young girls do not engage in ritual "homosexual" practices. But although girls' sexual development is culturally unmarked, adult women's bodily fluids are seen as sexually dangerous and polluting to men (see also Clark 1997).

Another example of difference between men's and women's sexualities comes from China. During the nineteenth century in China the practice of marriage resistance and the creation of sisterhoods arose in the silk-producing province of Guangdon in south China (Sankar 1986; Topley 1975). Marriage, especially for young women in patriarchal China, was an oppressive institution. Men were entitled to control wives and family property. Due to the importance of reproducing the patrilineage and maintaining

ancestor worship, arranged marriages were the norm; often the young couple did not meet before they were married. The new wife went to live in the household of her husband and was at first considered little more than a servant under the strict supervision of her mother-in-law. In the province of Guangdon, marriage presented an especially frightening prospect since women not only married out of their village but in many cases into enemy territory (Sankar 1986). With the development of the silk industry in Guangdon in the mid-1800s, many young unmarried women went to work in the silk factories, earning money for themselves as well as their families. With their own income, some of these women were able to postpone marriage indefinitely. Fathers supported this delay since the daughters provided income to their families.

Through the institution of silk work a tradition of marriage resistance developed, culminating in the creation of intimate sisterhoods by those who refused to marry. A woman who refused to marry took a public vow to remain unwed and not engage in sexual relations with men. This vow established her adult status, freeing her parents from any obligation to arrange a marriage and securing her rights to ancestor worship in her natal house (Sankar 1986). Sisterhoods of six to eight women each were formed with such names as "Golden Orchid Association" or "Association for Mutual Admiration." The sisters lived in cooperative houses and established joint funds to be used for holidays, emergencies, retirement, or death. Some houses were "vegetarian halls" where the women led a religious life; others were called "spinster halls." These halls were not so strictly religious and vegetarian, but heterosexual contacts were not allowed in either (Honig 1985; Sankar 1986; Smedley 1976; Topley 1975). According to some of the studies of this institution, sisters had sexual relations with each other; "larger sisterhoods may have contained several couples or ménage à trois" (Sankar 1986; see also Topley 1975). The sisterhoods were banned as "feudal remnants" after the victory of the Red Army in 1949, and many sisters fled to Malaysia, Singapore,

Hong Kong and Taiwan. Wieringa (1987), who conducted interviews with sisters living in a Buddhist temple in Singapore, notes that the abbess and the nuns spoke freely of their sexual relations and described their choices to enter a "vegetarian life" as a positive decision.

These sisterhoods were not simply the result of oppressive marriage conditions. A number of other sociocultural factors were important in the development of the sisterhoods. It was the custom in this region for the patrilineal kin group to build a girls' house for their adolescent and unmarried daughters (Topley 1975). Houses that were built for unmarried older daughters became known as spinster houses. Women past the age of marriage were given a spinster ceremony through which they attained adult status. Younger sisters and brothers, who were waiting until their elder sibling married, were then allowed to marry. Each of these practices played a significant role in the construction of sisterhoods, although without the silk work, they were probably not significant enough on their own to produce sisterhoods.

In the cases of the Chinese sisterhoods and the Papua New Guinea Sambia, the absence of a mirror image to men's or women's (homo)sexual practices underscores the prominence of cultural gender ideologies in constructing sexual practices. In the Sambia case a cultural practice rooted in an ideology of gender antagonism and the efficacy of bodily fluids legitimates particular insemination practices between men and boys. In China patriarchal institutions ensuring control of women produced public resistance by women to oppressive marital and economic conditions, leading to the establishment of separatist sisterhoods.

In these cases, gender ideologies create different sexual roles, behaviors, meanings and desires for women and men. Consequently, men and women in these cultures see themselves differently as sexual actors. For Sambian men, men's sexuality must be carefully sustained and enhanced, while women are constantly reminded that their sexual organs and fluids are debilitating and even dangerous to

men. Historically in patriarchal China, men's sexual experiences and hence their desires were constructed broadly to include the practice of taking male consorts, particularly among upper-class men and royalty (Ng 1989). Women's sexual experiences were strictly limited to sexual relations with their husbands, unless they remained unmarried.

From these cases it is clear that gender ideologies are critical to the production of men's and women's sexualities. Gender ideologies construct what men and women are capable of sexually, limiting the heterosexual contacts of Sambian women, while prescribing frequent oral insemination for adolescent boys. It constructs what kinds of desires they are thought to have, as well as what kinds of experiences are actually possible, including the range of sexual partners permissible to Chinese men, the strict monogamy of Chinese wives, and the same-sex relations of unmarried Chinese women. By establishing certain ideas about who and what men and women are, gender ideologies create different possibilities for men's or women's understanding of their desires and their access to other sexual partners.

DECONSTRUCTING SEXUAL IDENTITIES

In the following section I will discuss in depth two cases of female same-sex relations that further complicate Western sexual categories. Studies of sexuality in Europe and America take for granted certain core assumptions about sexuality. Among those assumptions is the idea that individuals have fixed sexual object choices and sexual identities, defined typically as homosexual or heterosexual (with bisexual only recently getting attention). These assumptions turn out to have little cross-cultural reliability. Not all sexual practices across cultures fit neatly into the concept of sexual identities.

The following case concerns erotic attachments between women in Suriname, South America. The *mati* work, a widespread institution among Creole working-class women in Paramaribo, Suriname, is a sexual arrangement that is not based on a fixed notion of "sexual identity" (Wekker 1999).[6] *Mati*, although by no means a monolithic category, are women who have sexual relationships with men and with women; they may have a relationship with a man and a woman occurring at the same time or one at a time. While some *mati*, especially older women who have borne and raised their children, do not have sex with men any more, other, younger *mati* have a variety of arrangements with men, such as marriage, concubinage, or a visiting relationship. Women's relationships with women mostly take the form of visiting relationships, although a minority of women couples with their children live together in one household. These varied arrangements are made possible by the circumstance that most Creole, working-class women own or rent their own houses and are single heads of households (Wekker 1999).

The Afro-Surinamese folk religion, called Winti, provides the framework for the Creole concept of self and sexuality. Unlike the Western concept of the self as "unitary, authentic, bounded, static, trans-situational," the self in an Afro-Surinamese working-class universe is conceptualized as "multiplicitous, malleable, dynamic, and contextually salient" (Wekker 1999, 125). *Winti* religion pervades virtually all aspects of life, from before birth to beyond death. Within this framework both men and women are thought to be composed of male and female *winti,* gods. Both men and women are also deemed to be full sexual subjects, with their own desires and own possibilities to act on these desires. Sexual fulfillment per se is deemed important, while the gender of one's object choice is considered less important. According to one 84-year old *mati*, who had a variety of relationships with men in her life and bore a number of children, the "apples of her eye" throughout her long life were definitely women:

"I never wanted to marry or 'be in association with a man.' My 'soul.' / 'I' did not want to be under a man. Some women are like that. I am somebody who was not greedy on a man, my 'soul,' I,' wanted to be with women. It is your 'soul' that makes you so. It is more equal when you are with a woman; the same rights you have, I have too" (Wekker 1999, 284).

Thus, a *mati* is conceptualized as a woman, part of whose "I" desires and is sexually active with other women. Since the "I" is multiply and openly conceived, it is not necessary to claim a "truest, most authentic kernel of the self," a fixed sexual "identity" that is oriented to other women. Rather, *mati* work is seen as a particularly pleasing and joyous activity, not as an identity (Wekker 1999).

Surinamese *mati* (and Lesotho *motsoalle*) do not see themselves as "lesbians" in the Western sense; they have sex with each other, but their relations with men, including husbands and boyfriends, are also part of their sexuality. According to Wekker (1999), sexuality in this working-class cultural nexus is multiply constructed through ideas about the self, sexuality, gender, and religion.[7] But *mati* work is not a sexual identity nor a distinct category of persons. It is produced through an ideology of sexuality in which men and women are seen as sexual beings whose sexuality is fluid and multiple.

TOMBOIS IN WEST SUMATRA

Taking one final example from my own work on *tombois* among the Minangkabau in West Sumatra, Indonesia (Blackwood 1998), I look more closely at the relation between sexuality and gender identity, one's sense of being either a man or woman.[8] In Indonesia the term *tomboi* (derived from the English word "tomboy") is used for a female acting in the manner of men (I use "female" here to refer to the physical sex of the body). Although *tombois* have female bodies, they are locally understood as female-bodied men who are attracted to (normatively gendered) women. In this overview I briefly explain the cultural factors that produce the *tomboi* gender identity and how this identity complicates any simple understandings of gender or sexuality.

Tombois pride themselves on doing things like Minangkabau (and Indonesian) men. They play *koa*, a card game like poker, which is perceived as a men's game. They smoke as men do; rural women rarely take up smoking. They go out alone, especially at night, which is men's prerogative. Like men, they drive motorcycles; women ride behind (women do drive motorcycles but in a mixed couple the man always drives).

Tombois construct their desire for and relationships with women on a model of normative genders, emphasizing their masculinity and their partner's femininity. *Tombois* say that their lovers are always feminine women, women, that is, who adhere to the codes of femininity assigned to female bodies. Tombois and their partners call each other *papi* and *mami*, and refer to other female couples as *cowok* and *cewek*, Indonesian words that have the connotation of "guy" and "girl." Their use of gender-marked terms to describe partners in a relationship reflect *tombois'* understanding of themselves as situated within the category "man" (*laki-laki*).

Certain key social processes (cultural ideologies) in West Sumatra are involved in the production of the *tomboi* identity. Central to these is a gender ideology that constructs two genders as mutually exclusive and distinct categories. Typical of many Islamic cultures, the Minangkabau believe that men and women have different natures.[9] Men are said to be more aggressive and brave than women. Boys are admonished not to cry—crying is what girls do. Women are expected to be modest, respectful, and humble, especially young, unmarried women. The Minangkabau maintain physical segregation of the sexes in most public spaces and events. This gender ideology constructs differences in rights and privileges between men and women, without, however, constituting men as superior (see Blackwood 2000).

Another key social process is a kinship ideology that situates women as the producers and reproducers of their lineages. The Minangkabau have a matrilineal form of kinship in which inheritance and property passes from mothers to daughters. In the context of a rural kin-based society, heterosexual marriages are the key to the maintenance of vital social and kin ties because they construct an extended network of kin and in-laws. For Minangkabau women the continuation of this kinship network through marriage and children is critical to their own standing and influence both in their kin groups and in the community. Because daughters are essential to the continuation of the lineage, young women are carefully monitored by their elders to ensure that they marry and marry well. Daughters are not just reproducers, however; they are also the leaders of the next generation of kin. Consequently, there are no acceptable fantasies of womanhood in rural villages that do not include marriage and motherhood.

The restrictive definitions and expectations of masculinity and femininity attached to male and female bodies help produce gender transgressions in the following way. If a young girl plays too roughly and enjoys boys' activities when little, she is called *bujang gadis*, a term meaning "boy-girl," which distinguishes her as different. Identified as masculine by others, *tombois* make sense of their own gender behavior as being that of a boy. Because their behavior falls outside the bounds of proper femininity, *tombois* deny their female bodies and produce the only other gender recognized in this two-gender system, the masculine gender. The persuasiveness of the dominant gender ideology circulating in West Sumatra means that other forms of womanhood, such as a "masculine" woman or an unmarried woman working in men's jobs, are unimaginable. Consequently, some females appropriate a masculine gender identity because it is the most suitable model available. This case illustrates the way gender as well as sexuality is culturally produced. *Tomboi* identity is negotiated and produced in a cultural context in which Minangkabau kinship and community, as well as Islam and the Indonesian state, all have a voice.

THE SOCIAL PRODUCTION OF SEXUALITIES

My discussion of the cultural processes that construct same-sex sexualities is based on a small but growing number of case studies. There has been no systematic effort to compare the cases of women's same-sex relations cross-culturally.[10] The availability of adequate information is one problem. The difficulties of coding the various types of behavior documented even in this short essay raise other problems for statistical analyses. Despite the problems of formulating comparative analyses, some consistencies appear among the cases that allow for generalization about the social processes at work.

The broader patterns that appear in the cultural construction of sexuality can be connected to different types of gender ideologies, kinship systems, and class societies. Earlier attempts at comparative theories suggested that where men have greater control over women, or in societies stratified by class and gender, women's same-sex practices are subject to more oppression than men's (Rubin 1975) or limited to clandestine relations or marginalized groups (Blackwood 1986a). Both these suggestions rely on a "constraint" theory of sexuality by implying that without men's control, women's same-sex relations would flourish. Reworking this earlier attempt with a more constructionist approach, I would suggest that in strict patrilineal class societies, such as India and China, where inheritance and property rights belong to men, an ideology of women's inferiority and the need to control women's sexuality help to produce a sexuality oriented to reproduction and men's desires.

The Chinese example of patriarchy suggests that men's sexual prerogatives combined with their control of wives constructs exclusive same-sex relations of the sisterhoods

as both a resistance to marriage and a way to resolve the "threat" that an unmarried woman poses to men's control of their wives. Safeguards, such as chastity vows, were instituted to ensure that unmarried women with economic independence would not undermine marriage. For their part, women built on cultural expectations of close female bonds and the availability of economic resources to create sisterhoods and same-sex relationships.

In contrast, the cases of adolescent and ritual same-sex practices for the !Kung and Australian aborigines are produced in gender egalitarian, non-class societies. These societies have marriage requirements and prohibitions on certain forms of sexual relations. Yet, because they do not have the requirements about inheritance of property or rights of sexual access that are found in strict patrilineal societies, sexuality is constructed as something powerful, diverse, enjoyable, and explorable for both women and men. This is not to say that all non-class societies will produce multiple sexualities. In some societies same-sex relations may be culturally unintelligible (as certain groups have maintained to colonial superiors), but the evidence to back up such a statement with certainty is lacking. The important point is that many sociocultural processes work together to produce sexual meanings.

In sum, the cases presented here offer two important points. First, they provide evidence that the way sexuality is constructed—for instance, who is considered more sexually aggressive or more in need of sex—has everything to do with concepts of gender, selfhood, kinship (inheritance and property rights), and marriage. Second, they challenge the common assumption in the West that sexuality and sexual identity comprise stable, coherent categories. The cases mentioned above all show sexualities that fall outside of Western categories. If the very "nature" of sexuality derives from the cultural context, then what matters is how it is constructed in particular contexts, historical eras, or cultural domains. Consequently, careful ethnographic analysis that provides a cultural context for sexual practices will be the most productive way to further our understanding of women's sexualities.

NOTES

1. This discussion pertains to indigenous groups in Asia, Africa, the Pacific, Latin America, and native North America during colonial and postcolonial times. Because of space limitations I do not include material on white lesbians and lesbians of color in western Europe and the United States. For entry into the substantial scholarship on these groups, see Lewin 1996; Weston 1993.
2. Regarding the limitations of the anthropological record, see Blackwood and Wieringa 1999b.
3. The difficulties of categorizing something as a "sexual" relationship is exemplified in this case. Gay (1986) asked if young women in mummy-baby relationships make love like a man and a woman. Most women replied that the hugging and kissing of the mummy-baby relationship was different, distinguishing conceptually between what women do together sexually and what women and men do sexually.
4. This tradition appears to have died out after the 1950s (Kendall 1999). For a similar practice among Azande women, see Evans-Pritchard 1970.
5. For a similar ceremonial practice for women in the Solomon Islands in Melanesia, see Blackwood 1935.
6. Creoles, the second largest population group in Suriname, are the descendants of slaves brought from Africa and are mainly an urban group, also called Afro-Surinamese. They are distinguished culturally, psychologically, and ethnically from other blacks in Suriname, who are called the Maroons. The latter are the descendants of fugitive slaves who fled the plantations starting in the beginning of the seventeenth century (Wekker 1999).
7. Wekker also makes important connections between sexuality, colonial discourses, and colonial economic stratification that I do not have the space to discuss here.
8. For studies of other types of gender identities, such as the Native American two-spirit person, see Blackwood 1984b; Lang 1999.

9. Islam in West Sumatra is part of the everyday life of the Minangkabau, who generally see no conflict between *adat* (local customs, beliefs and laws) and Islam. The two have come to be mutually constructed (see Blackwood 2000).
10. In the research for my master's thesis (Blackwood 1984a) I surveyed a number of ethnographies, colonial records, and the Human Relations Area Files, and located reports of female same-sex practices in ninety-five indigenous cultures. This was not a comprehensive world survey and to my knowledge, no such survey has been done.

REFERENCES

Blacking, John. 1978. Uses of the Kinship Idiom in Friendships at Some Venda and Zulu Schools. In *Social System and Tradition in Southern Africa.* J. Argyle and E. Preston-Whyte, eds., pp. 101–117. Cape Town: Oxford University Press.

Blackwood, Beatrice. 1935. *Both Sides of Buka Passage.* Oxford: Clarendon Press.

Blackwood, Evelyn. 1984a. *Cross-Cultural Dimensions of Lesbian Relations.* Master's degree thesis, San Francisco State University.

———. 1984b. Sexuality and Gender in Certain Native American Tribes: The Case of Cross-Gender Females. *Signs: Journal of Women in Culture and Society* 10:27–42.

———. 1986a. Breaking the Mirror: The Construction of Lesbianism and the Anthropological Discourse in Homosexuality. In *The Many Faces of Homosexuality: Anthropological Approaches to Homosexual Behavior.* E. Blackwood, ed., pp. 1–17. New York: Harrington Park Press.

———, ed. 1986b. *The Many Faces of Homosexuality: Anthropological Approaches to Homosexual Behavior.* New York: Haworth.

———. 1998. Tombois in West Sumatra: Constructing Masculinity and Erotic Desire. *Cultural Anthropology* 13(4):491–521.

———. 1999. Indigenous Cultures. In *The Encyclopedia of Homosexuality.* B. Zimmerman, ed., Vol. 1 pp. 392–397. New York: Garland.

———. 2000. *Webs of Power: Women, Kin and Community in a Sumatran Village.* Lanham, MD: Rowman and Littlefield.

Blackwood, Evelyn, and Saskia E. Wieringa, eds. 1999a. *Female Desires: Same-Sex Relations and Transgender Practices Across Cultures.* New York: Columbia University Press.

———. 1999b. Sapphic Shadows: Challenging the Silence in the Study of Sexuality. In *Female Desires: Same-Sex Relations and Transgender Practices Across Cultures.* E. Blackwood and S.E. Wieringa, eds., pp. 39–66. New York: Columbia University Press.

Clark, Jeffrey. 1997. State of Desire: Transformations in Huli Sexuality. In *Sites of Desire, Economies of Pleasure: Sexualities in Asia and the Pacific.* L. Manderson and M. Jolly, eds., pp. 191–211. Chicago: University of Chicago Press.

Elliston, Deborah. 1995. Erotic Anthropology: "Ritualized Homosexuality" in Melanesia and Beyond. *American Ethnologist* 22(4):848–867.

Evans-Pritchard, E. E. 1970. Sexual Inversion among the Azande. *American Anthropologist* 72:1428–1434.

Gay, Judith. 1986. "Mummies and Babies" and Friends and Lovers in Lesotho. In *The Many Faces of Homosexuality: Anthropological Approaches to Homosexual Behavior.* E. Blackwood, ed., pp. 97–116. New York: Harrington Park Press.

Herdt, Gilbert. 1981. *Guardians of the Flute.* New York: McGraw-Hill.

Honig, Emily. 1985. Burning Incense, Pledging Sisterhood: Communities of Women Workers in the Shanghai Cotton Mills, 1919–1949. *Signs: Journal of Women in Culture and Society* 10(4):700–714.

Kaberry, Phyllis. 1939. *Aboriginal Woman, Sacred and Profane.* London: Routledge.

Kendall. 1999. Women in Lesotho and the (Western) Construction of Homophobia. In *Female Desires: Same-Sex Relations and Transgender Practices Across Cultures.* E. Blackwood and S.E. Wieringa, eds., pp. 157–180. New York: Columbia University Press.

Lang, Sabine. 1999. Lesbians, Men-Women, and Two-Spirits: Homosexuality and Gender in Native American Cultures. In *Female Desires: Same-Sex Relations and Transgender Practices Across Cultures.* E. Blackwood and S.E. Wieringa, eds., pp. 91–118. New York: Columbia University Press.

Lewin, Ellen, ed. 1996. *Inventing Lesbian Cultures in America.* Boston: Beacon.

Ng, Vivien W. 1989. Homosexuality and the State in Late Imperial China. In *Hidden from History: Reclaiming the Gay and Lesbian Past.* M. Duberman, M. Vicinus, and G.J. Chauncey, eds., pp. 76–89. New York: Meridian Books.

Nthunya, Mpho M'atsepo. 1997. *Singing Away the Hunger: The Autobiography of an African Woman.* Bloomington: Indiana University Press.

Povinelli, Beth. 1992. Blood, Sex, and Power: "Pitjawagaitj"/menstruation ceremonies and land politics in Aboriginal Northern Australia. Ninety-First Annual Meeting of the American Anthropological Association, San Francisco, 1992.

Roheim, Geza. 1933. Women and their Life in Central Australia. *Journal of the Royal Anthropological Institute of Great Britain and Ireland* 63:207–265.

Rubin, Gayle. 1975. The Traffic in Women: Notes on the Political Economy of Sex. In *Towards an Anthropology of Women.* R. Rapp, ed., pp. 157–211. New York: Monthly Review Press.

Sankar, Andrea. 1986. Sisters and Brothers, Lovers and Enemies: Marriage Resistance in Southern Kwangtung. *In The Many Faces of Homosexuality: Anthropological Approaches to Homosexual Behavior.* E. Blackwood, ed., pp. 69–83. New York: Harrington Park Press.

Shostak, Marjorie. 1983. *Nisa: The Life and Words of a !Kung Woman.* New York: Vintage Books.

Smedley, Agnes. 1976. *Portraits of Chinese Women in Revolution.* Westbury: The Feminist Press.

Topley, Marjorie. 1975. Marriage Resistance in Rural Kwangtung. In *Women in Chinese Society.* M. Wolf and R. Witke, eds., pp. 57–88. Stanford: Stanford University Press.

Wekker, Gloria. 1999. "What's Identity Got to Do with It?" Rethinking Identity in Light of the Mati Work in Suriname. In *Female Desires: Same-Sex Relations and Transgender Practices Across Cultures.* E. Blackwood and S.E. Wieringa, eds., pp. 119–138. New York: Columbia University Press.

Weston, Kath. 1993. Lesbian/Gay Studies in the House of Anthropology. *Annual Review of Anthropology* 22:339–67.

Wieringa, Saskia. 1987. *Uw Toegenegen Dora D.* Amsterdam: Furie.

VI

Equality and Inequality: The Sexual Division of Labor and Gender Stratification

In most societies certain tasks are predominantly assigned to men while others are assigned to women. In European and American cultures it used to be considered "natural" for men to be the family breadwinners; women were expected to take care of the home and raise the children. An underlying assumption of this division of labor was that men were dominant because their contribution to the material well-being of the family was more significant than that of women. Women were dependent on men and therefore automatically subordinate to them.

The "naturalness" of this division of labor has been called into question as women increasingly enter the labor force. However, has this significantly altered the status of women within their families and in the wider society? Or has it simply meant that women are now working a double day, performing domestic tasks that are negatively valued and not considered work once they get home from their "real" day's work? If employment enhances the social position of women, why is it that women still earn less than men earn for the same work? Why is there still a high degree of occupational segregation by gender? What precisely is the relationship between the economic roles of women and gender stratification? Cross-cultural research on the sexual division of labor attempts not only to describe the range of women's productive activities in societies with different modes of subsistence, but also to assess the implications of these activities for the status of women.

In many parts of the world women contribute significantly, if not predominantly, to subsistence. This is perhaps most apparent among hunting and gathering or foraging populations, and for this reason such groups have been labeled the most egalitarian of human societies. Hunters and gatherers used to form the bulk of the human population, but today only a small number remain. They are found in relatively isolated regions; they possess simple technology and therefore make little effort to alter the environment in which they live. They tend to be characterized by a division of labor whereby men hunt and women gather. Friedl (1975: 18) outlines four reasons for this division: the variability in the supply of game, the different skills required for hunting and gathering, the incompatibility between carrying burdens and hunting, and the small size of seminomadic foraging populations. Friedl (1975) further argues that in foraging societies in which gathering contributes more to the daily diet than hunting, women and men share equal status (see also Lee 1979; Martin and Voorhies 1975). Conversely, in societies in which hunting and fishing predominate (such as among the Inuit), the status of women is lower. It seems that female productive activities enhance the social position of women in society, but Sanday (1974) cautions that participation in production is a necessary but not sufficient precondition. Control over the fruits of their labor and a positive valuation of this labor are other factors to consider, as is the extent to which women are involved in at least some political activities. In addition, the absence of a sharp differentiation between public and private domains (Draper 1975) and the fact that there is no economic class structure and no well-defined male-held political offices (Leacock 1975) have been cited as explanations for the relative egalitarianism in foraging societies compared to more complex societies.

Despite the common assumption that men hunt and women gather, in some foraging societies the division of labor is not sharply defined. This often provides the basis for the highest degree of egalitarianism. Among the Tiwi, Australian aborigines who live on Melville Island off the coast of northern Australia, both men and women hunt and gather. Goodale (1971) demonstrates that resources and technology, rather than activities, are divided into male domains and female domains. Although the big game that Tiwi men hunt provides most of the meat to the group and therefore gives them a dominant position in the society, Tiwi women, who hunt and gather, provide more than half of the food consumed; they share in both the comradery and the spoils of their endeavors. As major provisioners, women are economic assets and a source of wealth and prestige for men in this polygynous society. Despite the fact that their opportunities for self-expression may be more limited than those of men, with age women acquire social status and can be politically influential. In general Goodale suggests that Tiwi culture emphasizes the equality of men and women in society.

Among the Agta Negritos of northeastern Luzon, the Philippines, women enjoy even greater social equality with their men than among the Tiwi. This is a society in which the division of labor and the battle of the sexes appear to be virtually absent. Agta women hunt game animals and fish just as men do. Not only do they make significant contributions to the daily food supply, but they also control the distribution of the foods they acquire, sharing them with their families and trading them in the broader community. The Griffins (in this book) argue that these roles are clearly the basis for female authority in decision-making within families and residential groups.

The Agta case challenges the widely held notion that in foraging societies pregnancy and child care are incompatible with hunting (Friedl 1978: 72). Agta women have developed methods of contraception and abortion to aid them in spacing their children. After becoming pregnant, they continue hunting until late in the pregnancy and resume hunting for several months after the birth of the child. There are always some women available to hunt, during which time children may be cared for by older siblings, grandparents, or other relatives. Reproduction is clearly not a constraint on women's economic roles in this society.

In horticultural societies, in which cultivation is carried out with simple hand-tool technology and slash-and-burn methods of farming, women also play important roles in production (Boserup 1970). One theory argues that the economic importance of female production in horticultural societies emerged from women's gathering activities in foraging groups. Horticultural societies vary in the degree to which men participate in crop cultivation as well as whether this cultivation is supplemented by hunting, fishing, and raising livestock. In addition, many horticultural societies are matrilineal (reckoning descent through the female line), and in these societies women tend to have higher status than in patrilineal societies. Lepowsky (in this book) points to gender egalitarianism among the horticultural and matrilineal people of the Pacific island of Vanatinai. In this society, men are not dominant over women either in practice or ideologically. Like men, women on this island can gain both prestige and power through engaging in exchange activities and the sponsorship of feasts where valuable goods are distributed. As a result of these activities, they can become "big women" as men can become "big men." Thus, Lepowsky argues that "the prominent positions of women in Vanatinai exchange and other activities outside of household and subsistence indicate as well as reinforce generally egalitarian relations between women and men. Vanatinai women have access to power both through their control of the economic capital of land and the subsistence and surplus production of yams and through their accumulation of symbolic capital in exchange and mortuary ritual" (1993:38).

Despite descent systems and economic roles that enhance the status and power of women among horticulturalists such as the people of Vanatinai, Friedl (1975) cautions that women's status is not universally high in such societies. Male control of valued property and male involvement in warfare (an endemic feature in many of these societies) can be mitigating factors that provide the basis for male dominance over women. For example, among horticulturalists in highland New Guinea, women raise staple crops but men raise prestige crops that are the focus of social exchange. This cultural valuation is the foundation for gender stratification that is then reinforced by gender ideologies of male superiority and a high degree of sexual antagonism between men and women (Brown and Buchbinder 1976; Herdt and Poole 1982; Strathern 1988). Among the Hua, for example, Meigs (1990) describes a "chauvinistic" ideology that is rooted in men's roles as warriors.

Among the Mundurucú, an Amazonian horticultural society who were also once involved in fierce warfare (Murphy and Murphy 1985), the division is such that men hunt, fish, and fell the forest area for gardens while women plant, harvest, and process manioc. In their daily tasks women form cooperative work groups, have authority, and are the equals of men. To the extent that their work "draws women together and isolates them from the immediate supervision and control of the men, it is also a badge of their independence" (Murphy and Murphy 1985: 237). However, according to a male-dominated ideology, women are subservient to men. Despite the contributions that Mundurucú women make to subsistence, what men do is assigned more value. As Murphy and Murphy state, "Male ascendancy does not wholly derive from masculine activities but is to a considerable degree prior to them" (234). Male domination among the traditional Mundurucú is symbolic. As the Mundurucú become increasingly drawn into a commercial economy based on the rubber trade, men, with their rights to rubber trees and to trading, may gain a more complete upper hand. "The women may well discover that they have traded the symbolic domination of the men, as a group, over the women, as a group, for the very real domination of husbands over wives" (238).

Although women's labor is clearly important in horticultural societies, it has been argued that it becomes increasingly insignificant relative to that of men with the development of intensive agriculture. Intensive agriculture is based on the use of the plow, draft animals, fertilizers, and irrigation systems. In a survey of 93 agricultural societies, Martin and Voorhies (1975: 283) demonstrate that 81 percent delegate farming to men who then achieve primacy in productive activities. One explanation for the decline in female participation in agriculture is that the female domestic workload tends to increase when root crops are replaced by cereal crops and when animal labor replaces manual labor (Martin and Voorhies 1975). Cereal crops require more extensive processing, and field animals must be cared for. Both these activities fall to women. In addition, the kin-based units of production and consumption become smaller, and this too adds to the burden on individual women.

Concomitant with the presumably declining importance of women in agricultural activities is a supposed decline in social status (Boserup 1970). Women's value is defined by their reproductive abilities rather than by their productive activities. It has been suggested that the lesser status of women in some agricultural societies, particularly those of Eurasia, compared to some horticultural societies, as in sub-Saharan Africa, is reflected in the contrast between systems of bridewealth and systems of dowry (Goody 1976). Bridewealth is a compensation to the bride's parents or her kin for the productive and reproductive rights of the bride; dowry, as a form of inheritance, provides a bride with land and other wealth and helps her to attract a husband (see Stone and James in this book).

Despite arguments describing a decline in women's status and their relegation to the domestic sphere in association with the emergence of intensive agriculture, cross-cultural data indicate that women in agricultural societies lead much more diverse and complex lives than some theories suggest. In northwestern Portugal women do most of the agricultural activity, inherit property equally, and are often the recipients of a major inheritance that generally includes the parental household (Brettell 1986). This division of labor has emerged because men have been assigned the role of emigrants. Another exception is rural Taiwan, where, despite the patriarchal and patrilineal character of Chinese society, women construct a familial network that gives them a good deal of power and influence in later life (Wolf 1972).

O'Hara (in this book) discusses the complex nature and meaning of women's work among present-day Irish farm families. In the traditional patriarchal Irish family (studied by Arensberg and Kimball in the 1930s) work was structured by gender and age. There was a strict division of labor that was considered "natural" and power was in the hands of men who were the primary heirs to property. Irish farm women today, according to O'Hara (1998:112) "have managed to lessen the constraints of patriarchy through becoming active partners in the farm business or through working off the farm." The women whom O'Hara studied, particularly those in the west of Ireland, clearly view the manual work they contribute to the farm as significant, if not vital, to the success of the enterprise. In addition, many Irish farm women contribute important nonmanual work, including keeping the books. According to O'Hara, a higher proportion of couples in the west of Ireland have joint bank accounts, and more women are involved in decision making, thereby lessening their subordination. They view themselves as being involved in a partnership and from it they reap personal satisfaction. However, O'Hara also describes women who, as farm helpers with less involvement in decision making and less access to farm income, view their role as one of continued subordination.

A final economic adaptation is that of pastoralism or herding. Some pastoralists are fully nomadic, moving their entire communities in accordance with the demands of the herd. Others are involved in cultivation and are therefore transhumant. They engage in seasonal migration. Among pastoralists the ownership, care, and management of herds are generally in the hands of men. Though there are exceptions, male domination of herding tends to be reflected in other aspects of social organization—the near universality of patrilineal descent and widespread patrilocal residence. Pastoral societies are also generally characterized by patriarchy and a dichotomization of the sexes, both symbolically and socially. Segregation of the sexes and gender stratification, in other words, are fundamental attributes of many pastoral societies.

The symbolic opposition between men and women is apparent among the Sarakatsani, a group of transhumant shepherds who live in the mountainous regions of the province of Epirus in Greece. According to Campbell (1964) the life of pastoral Sarakatsani revolves around three things: sheep, children (particularly sons), and honor. "The sheep support the life and prestige of the family, the sons serve the flocks and protect the honour of their parents and sisters, and the notion of honour presupposes physical and moral capacities that fit the shepherds for the hard and sometimes dangerous work of following and protecting their animals" (18). Gender ideology is embedded in these three valued items, especially in the parallel oppositions between sheep and goats on the one hand and men and women on the other. The practical division of labor parallels this symbolic opposition. Women give assistance in the care of animals and make major contributions to their families. The economic roles of husband and wife are complementary. Nevertheless, Sarakatsani husbands have ultimate authority over their wives; obedience to a husband is a moral imperative for a wife. As among the Mundurucú, ideology assigns women to a lesser status, in spite of their economic complementarity.

Rasmussen (in this book) reviews many of these aspects of men's and women's roles among pastoralists, but her essay focuses most closely on the Tuareg, a seminomadic, Islamic, socially stratified people who live in Niger, Mali, Burkina Faso, and Algeria. The Tuareg, in her view, offer variations to standard interpretations of gender in pastoral nomadic societies. For example, the frequent absence of Tuareg men from home (in raiding activities in the past and in separatist warfare against the central state governments of Mali and Niger more recently), as well as men's peaceful trading activities, have necessitated women's independence in work and the education of children. Tuareg women are not sequestered, they do not veil their faces (although Tuareg men do), and they do not engage in gestures of subservience to their husbands such as kneeling or bowing their heads. Men and women regularly meet and socialize in public and women regularly entertain male visitors (although not necessarily lovers) when their husbands are absent. Although Tuareg women are generally consulted by men about matters that affect the life of the camp or village, there are contexts in which women defer to men—before Islamic scholars, important chiefs, and elders on the patrilineal side. Much of the status of Tuareg women is sustained by their rights of ownership in livestock.

Rasmussen concludes with a discussion of the impact of increasing sedentarization on the roles of Tuareg men and women. Sedentarization has increased women's workloads and altered their bases of property. A shift to virilocal patterns of residence (living with the husband and his kin) has increasingly isolated women from the support of their own kin networks. And, for all Tuareg, sedentarization has reduced autonomy as it has opened new opportunities for work in cooperative agencies.

Generalizations are often made about the status of women according to different modes of adaptation. However, these readings demonstrate that there is a great deal of diversity within each subsistence strategy. For example, in foraging societies women may hunt as well as gather; in intensive agricultural and pastoral societies not all women are powerless, dependent, and relegated to the domestic sphere. Although women's contributions to subsistence are important to gender stratification, a number of other factors need to be considered. These include leadership roles in family and kinship units and in the wider community; inheritance of property; control of the distribution and exchange of valued goods; authority in child-rearing; and participation in ritual activities. In addition, the ideological definitions of women's roles and valuations of their economic activities are often powerful determinants of status.

To fully understand gender stratification, both ideology and participation in production must be taken into account. As Atkinson (1982: 248) states, "It is too facile to deny the significance of sexual stereotypes or to presume that women's influence in one context cancels out their degradation in another. Just as we know that women's status is not a unitary phenomenon across cultures, we need to be reminded that the intracultural picture is equally complex."

REFERENCES

Arensberg, Conrad M., and Solon T. Kimball. 1940. *Family and Community in Ireland.* Cambridge, Mass.: Harvard University Press.

Atkinson, Jane. 1982. "Review: Anthropology." *Signs* 8: 236–258.

Boserup, Esther. 1970. *Women's Role in Economic Development.* London: G. Allen and Unwin.

Brettell, Caroline B. 1986. *Men Who Migrate, Women Who Wait: Population and History in a Portuguese Parish.* Princeton: Princeton University Press.

———. 1995. *We Have Already Cried Many Tears: The Stories of Three Portuguese Migrant Women.* Prospect Heights, IL: Waveland Press.

Brown, Paula, and Georgeda Buchbinder (eds.). 1976. *Man and Woman in the New Guinea Highlands.* Washington, D.C.: American Anthropological Association.

Campbell, John K. 1964. *Honour, Family and Patronage.* Oxford: Oxford University Press.

Draper, Patricia. 1975. "!Kung Women: Contrasts in Sexual Egalitarianism in Foraging and Sedentary Contexts." In Rayna Reiter (ed.). *Toward an Anthropology of Women,* pp. 77–109. New York: Monthly Review Press.

Friedl, Ernestine. 1975. *Women and Men: An Anthropologist's View.* New York: Holt, Rinehart and Winston.

———. 1978. "Society and Sex Roles." *Human Nature* April: 68–75.

Goodale, Jane C. 1971. *Tiwi Wives: A Study of the Women of Melville Island, North Australia.* Seattle: University of Washington Press.

Goody, Jack. 1976. *Production and Reproduction.* Cambridge: Cambridge University Press.

Herdt, Gilbert, and Fitz Poole (eds.). 1982. "Sexual Antagonism, Gender, and Social Change in Papua New Guinea." *Social Analysis* (special issue), Volume 12.

Leacock, Eleanor. 1975. "Class, Commodity, and the Status of Women." In Ruby Rohrlich-Leavitt (ed.). *Women Cross-Culturally: Change and Challenge*, pp. 601–616. The Hague: Mouton.

———. 1978. "Women's Status in Egalitarian Society: Implications for Social Evolution." *Current Anthropology* 19(2): 247–275.

Lee, Richard. 1979. *The !Kung San.* Cambridge: Cambridge University Press.

Lepowsky, Maria. 1993. *Fruit of the Motherland: Gender in an Egalitarian Society.* New York: Columbia University Press.

Martin, M. Kay, and Barbara Voorhies. 1975. *Female of the Species.* New York: Columbia University Press.

Meigs, Anna. 1990. Multiple Gender Ideologies and Statuses. In Peggy Sanday and Ruth Goodenough (eds.). *Beyond the Second Sex: New Directions in the Anthropology of Gender*, pp. 99-112. Philadelphia: University of Pennsylvania Press.

Murphy, Yolanda, and Robert F. Murphy. 1985. *Women of the Forest.* New York: Columbia University Press.

O'Hara, Patricia. 1998. *Partners in Production? Women, Farm and Family in Ireland.* New York: Berghahn Books.

Sanday, Peggy Reeves. 1974. "Female Status in the Public Domain." In Michelle Z. Rosaldo and Louise Lamphere (eds.). *Woman, Culture, and Society*, pp. 189–206. Stanford: Stanford University Press.

Strathern, Marilyn. 1988. *The Gender of the Gift: Problems with Women and Problems with Society in Melanesia.* Berkeley: University of California Press.

Wolf, Margery. 1972. *Women and the Family in Rural Taiwan.* Stanford: Stanford University Press.

Woman the Hunter: The Agta

Agnes Estioko-Griffin and P. Bion Griffin

Among Agta Negritos of northeastern Luzon, the Philippines, women are of special interest to anthropology because of their position in the organization of subsistence. They are substantial contributors to the daily subsistence of their families and have considerable authority in decision making in the family and in residential groups. In addition, and in

Abridged with permission from Frances Dahlberg (ed.), *Woman the Gatherer* (New Haven: Yale University Press, 1981), pp. 121–140. Copyright © 1981 Yale University Press.

contradiction to one of the sacred canons of anthropology, women in one area frequently hunt game animals. They also fish in the rivers with men and barter with lowland Filipinos for goods and services.[1]

In this chapter, we describe women's roles in Agta subsistence economy and discuss the relationship of subsistence activities, authority allocation, and egalitarianism. With this may come an indication of the importance of the Agta research to the anthropology of women and of hunter-gatherers in general....

Women, especially women in hunting-gathering societies, have been a neglected domain of anthropological research. The recent volume edited by Richard Lee and Irven DeVore (1976) and the *!Kung of Nyae Nyae* (Marshall 1976) begin to remedy the lack but focus solely on the !Kung San of southern Africa. Other works are either general or synthetic (Friedl 1975; Martin and Voorhies 1975), or report narrowly bounded topics (Rosaldo and Lamphere 1974). Sally Slocum, writing in *Toward an Anthropology of Women* (Reiter 1975), has provided impetus for the Agta study. Slocum points out a male bias in studying hunter-gatherers, showing how approaching subsistence from a female view gives a new picture. From the insights of Slocum we have sought to focus on Agta women, to compare the several dialect groups, and to begin investigating the nature and implications of women as not "merely" gatherers but also hunters.

THE AGTA

The Agta are Negrito peoples found throughout eastern Luzon, generally along the Pacific coast and up rivers into the Sierra Madre interior.... Although perhaps fewer in numbers, they are also located on the western side of the mountains, especially on the tributary rivers feeding the Cagayan. In general terms, the Agta of Isabela and Cagayan provinces are not dissimilar to other present and past Philippine Negritos. (See Vanoverbergh 1925, 1929–30, 1937–38; Fox 1952; Garvan 1964; and Maceda 1964 for information on Negritos outside the present study area.) In the more remote locales, hunting forest game, especially wild pig, deer, and monkey, is still important. Everywhere, collection of forest plant foods has been eclipsed by exchange of meat for corn, rice, and cultivated root crops. Fishing is usually important throughout the dry season, while collection of the starch of the caryota palm (*Caryota cumingii*) is common in the rainy season. An earlier paper (Estioko and Griffin 1975) gives

some detail concerning the less settled Agta; both Bennagen (1976) and Peterson (1974, 1978a,b, n.d.) closely examine aspects of subsistence among Agta in the municipality of Palanan.

A brief review of Agta economic organization will be sufficient for later discussion of women's activities. Centuries ago all Agta may have been strictly hunter-gatherers. Since at least A.D. 1900 the groups near the towns of Casiguran (Headland and Headland 1974) and Palanan have been sporadic, part-time horticulturalists, supplementing wild plant foods with sweet potatoes, corn, cassava, and rice. The more remote, interior Agta, sometimes referred to as *ebuked* (Estioko and Griffin 1975), plant small plots of roots, a few square meters of corn, and a banana stalk or two. They usually plant only in the wet season, harvesting an almost immature crop when staples are difficult to obtain by trade. *Ebuked* neglect crop production, preferring to trade meat for grains and roots.

Lee and DeVore (1968:7) argue that women produce much of the typical hunter-gatherers' diet and that in the tropics vegetable foods far outweigh meat in reliability and frequency of consumption. The Dipagsanghang and Dianggu-Malibu Agta strikingly contradict this idea. They are superb hunters, eat animal protein almost daily, and, as noted above, may have both men and women hunting. (The Tasaday, to the south in Mindanao, may represent an extreme nonhunting adaptation, one in which plant food collection is very dominant [Yen 1976].) Hunting varies seasonally and by techniques used among various groups, but is basically a bow and arrow technology for killing wild pig and deer, the only large game in the Luzon dipterocarp forests. Monkey, although not large, is a reliable rainy season prey. Among Agta close to Palanan and Casiguran, hunting is a male domain. Many hunters pride themselves on skill with bow and arrow; less able hunters may use traps. Dogs to drive game are very desirable in the dry season when the forest is too noisy for daylight stalking of animals.

The collecting of wild plant food is not a daily task. Most Agta prefer to eat corn, cassava, and sweet potatoes, and neglect the several varieties of roots, palm hearts, and greens procurable in the forest.... Forest foods are difficult to collect, necessitate residence moves over long distances, and do not taste as good as cultivated foods. Emphasis of trade networks with lowland farmers favors deemphasis of forest exploitation of plants. Only in the rainy season do Agta actively process a traditional resource, the sago-like caryota palm. Fruits are often picked on the spur of the moment; seldom do parties leave camp solely for their collection.

Trade with farmers is practiced by all Agta known to us. Rumors of Agta "farther into the mountains" who never trade (or cultivate) seem to be without substance. In the report of the Philippine Commission (1908:334), evidence of lowland-Agta trade around 1900 indicates the *ibay* trade partner relationship to have some antiquity. As the lowlander population has increased since World War II, trade has also increased. Agta are more and more dependent on goods and foodstuffs gained from farmers; adjustments of Agta economic behavior continue to be made, with labor on farms being one aspect of change. Agta formerly simply traded meat for carbohydrates. Around Palanan they may now work for cash or kind when residing close to farmers' settlements. Hunting decreases as the demands of cultivation are met. A cycle is created, and further withdrawal from forest subsistence occurs. Farmers live in areas once solely owned by Agta. Debts to farmers increase with economic dependence; freedom of mobility and choice of activity decrease; and Agta in farming areas become landless laborers.

At the same time, Agta seek to get out of the cycle by emulating the farmers. Many Agta within ten kilometers of Palanan Centro are attempting to become farmers themselves. While the success rate is slow, the attempt is real. Again, when questioned by an early American anthropologist, Agta close to Palanan Centro claimed to be planting small rainy season plots with corn, roots, and upland rice (Worcester 1912:841). Living informants confirm the long practice of cultivation, but suggest a recent expansion of Agta fields and commitment to abandoning forest nomadism (especially over the last fifteen years). Around the areas of Disuked-Dilaknadinum and Kahanayan-Diabut in Palanan, Agta are well known for their interest in swidden cultivation. Even the most unsettled Agta farther upriver claim small fields and sporadically plant along the rivers well upstream of lowland farmsteads.

The horticultural efforts of the Agta appear less than is the case, since the social organization and settlement patterns are very different from those of the farmers. Agta throughout Isabela and Cagayan are loosely organized into extended family residential groups. A group, called a *pisan*, is seldom less than two nuclear families and very rarely more than five (in the dry season—perhaps slightly higher average during the wet season). The nuclear family is the basic unit of Agta society, being potentially self-sufficient under usual circumstances. The residential group is organized as a cluster of nuclear families united either through a common parent or by sibling ties. Non-kin friends may be visitors for several weeks, and any nuclear family is able to leave and join another group of relatives at will.

As is typical of hunting-gathering societies, no formal, institutionalized authority base exists. The nuclear family is the decision maker concerning residence, work, and relations with other people. Older, respected individuals, often parents and grandparents of group members, may be consulted, but their opinions are not binding. Often group consensus is desired; people who disagree are free to grumble or to leave.

The settlement pattern is determined, in part, by the seasonal cycle of rains and sunny weather, and by these influences on the flora and fauna exploited for food. Rainy season flooding restricts forest travel, brings hardships in exchange, but is compensated by good condition of the game animals. The dry season permits travel over greater distances and into the remote mountains. Predictable fish resources enhance the advantages of human dispersal; only the need to carry trade meats to farmers inhibits distant residence placement.

WOMEN'S ACTIVITIES

Women participate in all the subsistence activities that men do. Women trade with farmers, fish in the rivers, collect forest plant foods, and may even hunt game animals. Tasks are not identical, however; a modest sexual division of labor does exist. Furthermore, considerable variation is found among the groups of Agta of Isabella and Cagayan provinces. These differences may possibly be ascribed to degree of adjustment of Agta to lowland Filipino culture. Some differences may be due to unique culture histories and to little contact.

Although in Isabela most Agta women do not hunt with bow and arrows, with machetes, or by use of traps, most are willing to assist men in the hunt. Not uncommonly, women help carry game out of the forest. Since mature pig and deer are heavy and the terrain is difficult, this is no small accomplishment. Even in areas around Palanan and Casiguran, women are known to accompany men and dogs into the forest and to guide the dogs in the game drive. Some women are famous for their abilities to handle dogs; one informant, a girl about fifteen years of age, was especially skilled. In Palanan and Casiguran, women and men laugh at the idea of women hunting. Such a practice would be a custom of wild, uncivilized Agta (ebuked) far in the mountains, they say. Many of the attributes of ebuked seem to be old-fashioned customs still practiced by interior groups.

Two groups studied as part of the present research do have women who hunt. Among the Dipagsanghang Agta, several mature women claim to have hunting skills; they learned these in their unmarried teen years. They only hunt under extreme circum-stances, such as low food supplies or great distances from farmers and a supply of corn. All these Agta are found in southern Isabela between Dipagsanghang and Dinapiqui.

In the northernmost section of Isabela and well into Cagayan province, women are active and proficient hunters. While we have termed the Agta here as the Dianggu-Malibu group, we are actually referring to speakers of the southeast Cagayan dialect who live on the river drainage areas of the Dianggu and Malibu rivers.[2] Both the dialect and women who hunt are found over a considerably greater territory, according to informants, reaching north to Baggao, Cagayan, and at least to the Taboan River.

Among the Dianggu-Malibu women some variation, perhaps localized, perhaps personal, is found. On the Dianggu, some of the women questioned, and observed hunting, carried machetes and were accompanied by dogs. They claim to prefer the machete to the bow and arrow, allowing dogs to corner and hold pigs for sticking with the knife. Our sample of actual observations is too small to argue that only immature pigs are killed, but we do know that in the dry season adult male pigs are dangerous in the extreme. Dogs may be killed during hunts. Since Agta dogs are seldom strong animals, we wonder if mature pigs are acquired only occasionally. On the other hand, so many dogs are owned by these Agta that sheer numbers may favor large kills. We have observed two Agta women with as many as fifteen dogs. Other Dianggu women prefer the bow.

On the Malibu River, Agta women are expert bow and arrow hunters. On both of our brief visits to this group, women were observed hunting. They claim to use bows always, and they seek the full range of prey animals. Wild pig is most desired, while deer are often killed. Future work must quantify the hunting details, but women seem to vary slightly from men in their hunting strategies. Informants say they hunt only with dogs. On closer questioning they admit to knowing techniques that do not involve dogs—for example, they may climb trees and lie in wait for an animal to approach to feed on fallen fruit. Among all Agta, hunting practices vary considerably between the rainy and dry seasons. Our fieldwork in Malibu has been confined to the dry season, when dogs are important. In the rainy season solitary stalking is practiced. Field observations should eventually provide quantitative data on women hunting in this season; we must stress that our data are primarily from interview and brief observation. We have not resided among Cagayan Agta long enough to advance quantitatively based generalizations.

Women not only hunt but appear to hunt frequently. Like men, some enjoy hunting more than others. The more remotely located Agta seem most to favor hunting. Even among Agta certain males and females are considered lacking in initiative, a fault that may not be confined to hunting.

Informant data indicate that while women may make their own arrows, the actual blacksmithing of the metal projectile points is a male activity. More field research is necessary to confirm the universality of this detail. Other items of interest pertain to the composition of hunting parties. Most people in any one residence group are consanguineally or affinely related. We have observed several combinations of hunting parties. Men and women hunt together or among themselves. Often sisters, or mother and daughter, or aunt and niece hunt together. At Malibu, two sisters, co-wives of one male, hunt together, and either or both sisters join the husband to hunt. When young children exist, one of the two wives may stay at the residence while the husband and the other wife hunt and fish. Also, sisters and brothers cooperate on the hunt. A woman would not hunt with, for example, a cousin's husband unless the cousin were along.

The only real argument, in our opinion, that has been advanced to support the contention that women must gather and men hunt relates to childbearing and nurture. Among the Agta, during late pregnancy and for the first few months of nursing, a woman will not hunt. In spite of the small size of each residential group, however, some females seem always to be around to hunt, although one or more may be temporarily withdrawn from the activity. Women with young children hunt less than teenagers and older women. On the occasion of brief hunts—part of one day—children are cared for by older siblings, by grandparents, and by other relatives. Occasionally a father will tend a child. Only infants are closely tied to mothers.

Girls start hunting shortly after puberty. Before then they are gaining forest knowledge but are not strong. Boys are no different. We have no menopause data, but at least one woman known to us as a hunter must have passed childbearing age. She is considered an older woman, but since she is strong, she hunts. The pattern is typical of men also. As long as strength to travel and to carry game is retained, people hunt. Our best informant, a young grandmother, hunts several times a week.

Both Agta men and women fish. In fact, from early childhood until the infirmity of old age all Agta fish. If most adults are gone on a hunting trip for several days, the remaining adults and children must obtain animal protein by themselves. Only women in late pregnancy, with young infants, or into old age, withdraw from fishing, which makes considerable demands of endurance as well as skill. Some men excel at working in rough, deep, and cold waters. The everyday techniques for fishing are limited to underwater spear fishing. Glass-lensed wooden goggles, a heavy wire spear or rod varying according to size of fish sought, and an inner-tube rubber band complete the equipment. To fish, people simply swim underwater, seeking fish in the various aquatic environments known for each species. Girls in their teens are very capable at fishing. When fishing individually, women may be major contributors to the daily catch.

When group fishing is undertaken, a drive is conducted. In this operation, a long vine is prepared by attaching stones and banners of wild banana stalks. Two people drag the vine, one on each end and on opposite sides of the river, while the people in the water spear fish startled by the stones and stalks. Women join men in the drives, with older men and women dragging the vine while all able-bodied youths and adults work in the water.

Difficulty of fishing may be characterized as a gradient upon which men and women become less and less able as age and debilities increase. The elderly, when mobile, may still be productive, but instead of true fishing, their activities may be termed collecting. Both the coastal reef areas and freshwater rivers and streams have abundant shellfish, shrimp, and amphibians that may be caught by hand. Elderly women and grandchildren are especially eager to harvest these resources. Older men are not ashamed to follow suit, although the enthusiasm of others for the task seldom gives old men incentive. Men are much less eager to give up riverine fishing after middle age than are women. Clearly some emphasis on males securing protein is found among Agta. Women, however, seem to have traditionally been active in fishing. Interestingly, as a few Agta adopt lowland fishing technology, especially nets, women seldom participate. Like their female counterparts in lowland society, women are deemed not appropriate in net fishing.

One might expect that, on the basis of worldwide comparison, tropic hunters would really be gatherers, and that women would be the steady and substantial providers. Agta do not fit the generalizations now accepted. Few Agta women regularly dig roots, gather palm hearts, seek fruit, or pick greens. Most Agta daily consume domesticated staples grown by the farmers. Women are, however, very knowledgeable concerning flora and its use, and among the less settled Agta, young girls are still taught all traditional forest lore. Brides-to-be among these Agta are partially evaluated on the basis of their knowledge, skill, and endurance in collecting jungle plant foods.

Roots are collected by women whenever more desirable food is unobtainable, when several wild pigs have been killed and the men want to eat "forest food" with pig fat, or when a visit to relatives or friends calls for a special treat. The interior groups may actually combine meat and wild roots for weeks when camped so far from farmers that exchange for corn is impossible. Downriver Agta consider such a practice a real hardship, not to be willingly endured. Men are known to dig roots, even though they say it is women's work. On long-distance hunts men do not as a rule carry food, and they may occasionally dig roots to alleviate the all meat-fish diet.

As hunting is thought of as a "sort of" male activity among many Agta (in Isabela), processing the starch of the caryota palm is a female activity. Women cruise the forest searching for trees containing masses of the starch; they also chop down the trees, split the trunks, adze out the pith, and extract the flour. Often parties of women and girls work together, speeding up the laborious task. On occasion, men will assist. Extracting the flour starch is moderately heavy work, and tiring. Husbands may help when wives have a pressing need to complete a task quickly. Since much of the final product is given in gift form, the need for haste occurs frequently. Perhaps most important to note is the male participation. Sexual division of labor is tenuously bounded among all Agta. Emphases may exist, but a man can even build a house (i.e., tie the fronds to the frame—a female task).

As noted at the beginning, trade, exchange, and horticulture are not new to Agta. Informants, early photographs, and writings indicate that all but the most remote Agta were not "pure" hunter-gatherers after about A.D. 1900. Since the mountains have been a final retreat—from the earliest Spanish attempts to conquer the Cagayan Valley until the present—Agta must have been in contact with former farmers/revolutionaries in hiding. Keesing (1962), summarizing the peoples of northern Luzon, documents several societies of pagan swiddeners adjacent to or in Negrito territory. The Palanan River drainage area was inhabited by farmers before Spanish contact in the sixteenth century. Doubtless, Agta have participated in economic exchange and social intercourse for centuries. Agta now have institutionalized trade partnerships, at least in Palanan and Casiguran municipalities. Trade partners are called *ibay* (Peterson [1978*a,b*] discussed the *ibay* relationship in detail), and partnerships may last between two families over two or more generations. *Ibay* exchange meat for grains and roots, or meat for cloth, metal, tobacco, beads, and other goods. Services may be exchanged, especially in downriver areas. Fields may be worked by Agta, who then borrow a carabao, receive corn or rice, and satisfy any of a number of needs. What is important in relation to this chapter is that Agta women may engage in *ibay* partnerships. Among the lowland farmers almost all *ibay* are males. An Agta woman may be an *ibay* with a lowland man. According to our data, an Agta husband often is not also *ibay* with his wife's *ibay,* but he must treat the farmer as he would his own *ibay.* Of course Agta men and women trade with any farmer they choose, but such exchange is without the consideration given to an *ibay.* (Considerations include credit, acts of friendship, and first choice/best deal on goods.) Not only do women have *ibay,* but they very frequently are the most active agents of exchange. In areas where the trade rests mostly on meat and where men do most of the hunting, women are likely to carry out the dried meat and bring back the staple. They therefore gain experience in dealing with the farmers. We should note that many farmers attempt to cheat the Agta by shortchanging them on counts or weights, but they do so on the basis of gullibility or naiveté of the Agta, not on the basis of sex. Agta women are actually more aggressive traders than are men, who do not like confrontation.

Among the Dipagsanghang Agta, women seldom hunt today, and infrequently dig roots. They do carry out meat to trade. They seem to have an easier life, with emphasis on corn, rice, and roots instead of gathering wild foods. However, downriver, close to farmers, Agta women have reversed this trend, and are working harder and longer hours.[3] Intensification of the *ibay* relationship and need to own and cultivate land has forced women to

become horticulturalists and wage laborers for farmers. On their own family plots (family-owned, not male- or female-owned) they, together with adult males and youths, clear land, break soil, plant, weed, and harvest. When clearing virgin forest of large trees, women do not participate. They do clear secondary growth in fallowed fields.

In the families that reside close to Palanan ... men and women work almost daily in the fields of farmers. Women go to the forest to collect the lighter raw materials for house construction, mats, betel chews, medicines, and so on. Men follow a similar pattern, giving up hunting for field labor and a corn and sweet potato diet supplemented by small fish. Again we see a remarkable parallel in the activities of males and females.

Looking more closely at specialized women's activities, one may suggest increasing importance in downriver areas. Women have several domains that they use to gain cash or kind income. As just stated, income from labor in fields adds to the economic power of women. A small-scale traditional pursuit, shared by men and women, is the gathering of copal, a tree resin common to trees (*Agathis philippinensis*) found scattered in the Sierra Madre. Women often collect and carry the resin out to lowland "middlemen," who sell it to the depot in town. While corn and cash may be sought in exchange, cloth is desired in order to make skirts. Medicine and medical treatments for ailing children may be paid for by copal collection. Another example of entrepreneurship by females is a small-scale mobile variety store effort. After working in fields for cash and building a surplus, families may cross the Sierra Madre to the towns of San Mariano, Cauayan, and Ilagan. There Agta, often women, purchase in markets and stores goods for use and resale in Palanan. Palanan Centro itself has no real market, only several small general stores selling goods at highly marked up prices. Since no road reaches Palanan, all manufactured supplies must enter town by airplane from Cauayan or boat from Baler. Freight costs are high. Some Agta women are very eager to hike outside to get tobacco, which always commands a high price and a ready market.

DISCUSSION

The role of women in Agta economic activities has been reviewed. Assessment of an hypothesized egalitarian position of women may be more difficult, and rests on assertions and interpretations drawn from the economic roles. First, drawing in part from Friedl (1975), an argument can be made that women in Agta society have equality with men because they have similar authority in decision making. The authority could be based on the equal contribution to the subsistence resources. Working back, we see that among many Agta, women do contribute heavily to the daily food supply, do perform maintenance tasks with men, and may initiate food acquisition efforts through their own skills. They do control the distribution of their acquired food, sharing first with their own nuclear family and extended family, then trading as they see fit. They may procure nonfood goods as they desire. Men may do the same; generally spouses discuss what work to do, what needs should be satisfied, and who will do what. Whole residential groups frequently together decide courses of action. Women are as vocal and as critical in reaching decisions as are men. Further examples could strongly validate the hypothesis that women do supply a substantial portion of foods, and the assertion that women have authority in major decision making. Two questions arise. May we accept a causal relationship between percentage of food production and equality? Certainly there are cases to the contrary. According to Richard A. Gould (personal communication), Australian Aboriginal women in various areas collected the bulk of the food, yet remained less than equal (as we will define equality). Second, we may ask if Agta males and females are actually "equal."

Two avenues may suffice in answering this question. First, one might explore a defini-tion of equality, surely a culturally loaded concept. Since Agta women have authority or control of the economic gain of their own labor, they may be equal in this critical domain. Equality must surely be equated with decision-making power and control of one's own production. The second avenue of equality validation by the scientist may be to examine the female's control over herself in noneconomic matters. These could include selection of marriage partner, lack of premarital sexual intercourse proscription, spacing of children, ease of divorce, and polygyny rules.

In marriage, two forms are typical of Agta. One, the less common, is elopement by young lovers. While such marriages admittedly are fragile, elopement is not uncommon. In this case both partners must be willing. Rape and abduction are rare. Rape by Agta men is not known to the authors. Abduction must involve a slightly willing female, and is not done by young people. A mature man might abduct a married woman, crossing the mountains to a safe locale. To abduct a young girl would be difficult. Parents of eloping couples may be enraged, but usually reconcile themselves to the marriage. If the newlyweds stay together, no more is made of it.

The proper form of marriage is one arranged by customary meetings and discussions, as well as exchange of goods between two families. Often neither the bride nor the groom has had much say in the matter, although serious dislike by either would probably kill the negotiations before the marriage. Mothers are the most important in choosing who will marry whom. Even when their children are young, they are looking about for good partners. Word filters around when a young girl is marriageable, and efforts are made to get the appropriate young man and his family into negotiations before an undesirable family appears. Once any family with a prospective groom formally asks, a rejection is given only for strong and good reasons, since the denied family loses considerable face and may be angry enough to seek revenge.[4]

Criteria for choice of a marriage partner are varied. Often a young man in his early twenties marries a girl about fifteen. Girls entering marriage before puberty are not uncommon. In such cases the husband may help raise the girl until the time the marriage is consummated and full wifehood is recognized. Other combinations are seen. One much discussed case was the marriage of a woman in her forties to a man in his mid-twenties. The couple seemed very happy, with the wife paying rather special attention to her husband. The man's mother, a friend of the wife's, decided that the marriage was peculiar but acceptable.

Premarital female chastity is not an idea of much currency. Agta close to farmers will pay lip service to the idea, but should a girl become pregnant she will take a husband. There are no illegitimate Agta children, although an occasional rape of an Agta by a lowland male may produce a child. Since by the time a girl is fertile she likely will be married, illegitimacy is not the issue. Although some data are difficult to collect concerning sex, almost certainly girls are able to engage in sexual activity with relative ease; promiscuity is not favored in any circumstance. Males may have as little or great difficulty in engaging in sex as females. The Agta are widely dispersed in extended family groups; hence appropriate sexual partners are seldom seen. No homosexuality is known to exist.

Agta gossip suggests that many Agta, male and female, married and unmarried, constantly carry on extramarital sexual relations. This may be a function of gossip and a gross exaggeration. Whatever reality, neither males nor females seem to be especially singled out for criticism.

Women say they space their children. The practice certainly varies hugely from person to person, as does fecundity and luck in keeping children alive. The Agta use various herbal concoctions that supposedly prevent conception, cause abortions shortly after conception, and have several functions related to menstruation. These medicines are known to all Agta and are frequently used. Our census

data indicate that some women seem to be successful in spacing births. Other cases note high infant mortality yet no infanticide, female or male. All Agta abhor the idea.

Divorce is infrequent among Agta, with elopement being more prone to failure than are arranged marriages. Divorce does happen often enough, however, for us to look at the causes and relate them to an inquiry into female equality. First, either sex may divorce the other with equal ease. Agta have no possessions. Some gift giving between the two families establishes the marriage, but most of the gifts are food. Cloth, kettles, and minor items make up the rest. Return of marriage gifts is unlikely. Spouses simply take their personal possessions and return to the residential group of close relatives.

Causes for divorce are mainly laziness or improvidence, excessive adultery, or personality clashes and incompatibility, usually caused by a combination of the first two conditions. Skill and success in subsistence activities is of primary importance to marriage. While some Agta are less industrious and less skilled than others, all Agta expect a mate to work hard at all appropriate tasks. Should a male fail, divorce is likely. Occasionally, very young couples experience extra difficulties. These may be accentuated by displeased parents of either party.

Polygamy is not found in most of Isabela. Census data collected to date reveal only monogamy or serial monogamy. That is, spouses may be divorced or widow(er)ed several times in a lifetime. In Cagayan the data are incomplete but startling. Probably some of the strongest support for the equality of women hypothesis, when added to the facts of women as hunters, comes from a study of Agta polygamy. We noted earlier that two co-wives, sisters, hunted together in Malibu. South of Malibu at Blos, another husband and two sisters/co-wives arrangement was found. In the same residential unit we recorded a woman residing with her two co-husbands. They were not brothers; one was older than the wife, one younger. The other women considered this arrangement as humorous, but acceptable. An insight into the male sexual jealousy found in many societies worldwide is the comment of a Palanan Agta man. This old man, when told of the polyandrous marriage to the north, thought for a moment and commented, "Well, perhaps one man with two wives is OK, but a woman with two husbands? I find that totally bad." The women laughed at him.

NOTES

1. Although the authors have worked among the Agta about fourteen months, visits to the northerly group in the Dianggu-Malibu area have been brief. The practice of women hunting was first observed during a survey trip in 1972. We again visited the Dianggu group in 1975. In August 1978 we returned for one week to Dianggu and Malibu, where we verified in greater detail the subsistence activities of women. Data were collected using the Palanan Agta dialect and Ilokano.
2. Dianggu and Malibu are river names used by Agta and nearby Malay Filipinos. On the Board of Technical Surveys and Maps (Lobod Point, Philippines), the Dianggu is named the Lobod and the Malibu is named the Ilang.
3. Peterson (n.d.) argues that "downriver" Agta women are highly variable in their devotion to labor, older women being hardworking and young mothers not at all industrious.
4. Thomas Headland tells us that rejection of a prospective spouse may be a less serious matter among Casiguran Agta than among those we know.

REFERENCES

Bennagen, Ponciano. 1976. Kultura at Kapaligiran: Pangkulturang Pagbabago at Kapanatagan ng mga Agta sa Palanan, Isabela. M.A. thesis, Department of Anthropology, University of the Philippines, Diliman, Quezon City.

Briggs, Jean L. 1974. Eskimo women: makers of men. In *Many sisters: women in cross-cultural perspective,* ed. Carolyn J. Matthiasson, pp. 261–304. New York: Free Press.

Estioko, Agnes A., and P. Bion Griffin. 1975. The *Ebuked* Agta of northeastern Luzon. *Philippines Quarterly of Culture and Society* 3(4):237–44.

Flannery, Regina. 1932. The position of women among the Mescalero-Apache. *Primitive Man* 10:26–32.

———. 1935. The position of women among the eastern Cree. *Primitive Man* 12:81–86.

Fox, Robert B. 1952. The Pinatubo Negritos, their useful plants and material culture. *Philippine Journal of Science* 81:113–414.

Friedl, Ernestine. 1975. *Women and men: an anthropologist's view.* New York: Holt, Rinehart and Winston.

Garvan, John M. 1964. *The Negritos of the Philippines,* ed. Hermann Hochegger, Weiner beitrage zur kulturgeschichte und linguistik, vol. 14. Horn: F. Berger.

Goodale, Jane C. 1971. *Tiwi wives: a study of the women of Melville Island, north Australia.* Seattle, Wash.: University of Washington Press.

Gough, Kathleen. 1975. The origin of the family. In *Toward an anthropology of women,* ed. Rayna R. Reiter, pp. 51–76. New York: Monthly Review Press.

Hammond, Dorothy, and Alta Jablow. 1976. *Women in cultures of the world.* Menlo Park, Calif.: Benjamin/Cummings.

Harako, Reizo. 1976. The Mbuti as hunters—a study of ecological anthropology of the Mbuti pygmies. *Kyoto University African Studies* 10:37–99.

Headland, Thomas, and Janet D. Headland. 1974. *A Dumagat (Casiguran)–English dictionary.* Pacific Linguistics Series C. No. 28. Australian National University, Canberra: Linguistics Circle of Canberra.

Howell, F. Clark. 1973. *Early man,* rev. ed. New York: Time-Life Books.

Isaac, Glynn L. 1969. Studies of early culture in East Africa. *World Archaeology* 1:1–27.

———. 1971. The diet of early man: aspects of archaeological evidence from lower and middle Pleistocene sites in Africa. *World Archaeology* 2:278–98.

———. 1978. The food-sharing behavior of protohuman hominids. *Scientific American* 238(4):90–109.

Jenness, Diamond. 1922. *The life of the Copper Eskimos. Report of the Canadian Arctic Expedition 1913–1918,* vol. XII, pt. 9. Ottawa: Acland.

Keesing, Felix. 1962. *The ethnohistory of northern Luzon.* Stanford, Calif.: Stanford University Press.

Lancaster, Jane B. 1978. Carrying and sharing in human evolution. *Human Nature* 1(2):82–89.

Landes, Ruth. 1938. *The Ojibwa Woman.* New York: Columbia University Press.

Lee, Richard B., and Irven DeVore. 1968. Problems in the study of hunters and gatherers. In *Man the Hunter,* ed. Lee and DeVore. Chicago: Aldine.

————. 1976. *Kalahari hunter-gatherers: studies of the !Kung San and their neighbors.* Cambridge, Mass.: Harvard University Press.

Maceda, Marcelino M. 1964. *The culture of the mamanuas (northeast Mindanao) as compared with that of the other Negritos of Southeast Asia.* Manila: Catholic Trade School.

Marshall, Lorna. 1976. *The !Kung of Nyae Nyae.* Cambridge, Mass.: Harvard University Press.

Martin, M. Kay, and Barbara Voorhies. 1975. *Female of the species.* New York: Columbia University Press.

Peterson, Jean Treloggen. 1974. An ecological perspective on the economic and social behavior of Agta hunter-gatherers, northeastern Luzon, Philippines. Ph.D. dissertation, University of Hawaii at Manoa.

————. 1978*a.* Hunter-gatherer farmer exchange. *American Anthropologist* 80:335–51.

————. 1978*b.* The ecology of social boundaries: Agta foragers of the Philippines. *Illinois Studies in Anthropology No. 11.* University of Illinois, Urbana-Champaign, Ill.

————. n.d. Hunter mobility, family organization and change. In *Circulation in the Third World,* ed. Murray Chapman and Ralph Mansell Prothero. London: Routledge & Kegan Paul.

Philippine Commission. 1908. *8th Annual Report of the Philippine Commission: 1907.* Bureau of Insular Affairs, War Department. Washington, D.C.: Government Printing Office.

Quinn, Naomi. 1977. Anthropological studies on women's status. In *Annual review of anthropology,* ed. Bernard J. Siegel, pp. 181–225. Palo Alto, Calif.: Annual Reviews.

Reiter, Rayna R., ed. 1975. *Toward an anthropology of women.* New York: Monthly Review Press.

Rosaldo, Michelle Zimbalist, and Louise Lamphere, eds. 1974. *Woman, culture, and society.* Stanford, Calif.: Stanford University Press.

Slocum, Sally. 1975. Woman the gatherer: male bias in anthropology. In *Toward an anthropology of women,* ed. Rayna R. Reiter, pp. 36–50. New York: Monthly Review Press.

Tanner, Nancy, and Adrienne Zihlman. 1976. Women in evolution. Part I: Innovations and selection in human origins. *Signs: Journal of Women in Culture and Society* 1:585–608.

Tanno, Tadashi. 1976. The Mbuti net-hunters in the Ituri Forest, Eastern Zaire—their hunting activities and band composition. *Kyoto University African Studies* 10:101–35.

Turnbull, Colin M. 1965. *Wayward servants: the two worlds of the African pygmies.* Garden City, NY: Natural History Press.

Vanoverberg, Maurice. 1925. Negritos of northern Luzon. *Anthropos* 20:148–99.

————. 1929–30. Negritos of northern Luzon again. *Anthropos* 24:1–75, 897–911; 25:25–71, 527–656.

————. 1937–38. Negritos of eastern Luzon. *Anthropos* 32:905–28; 33:119–64.

Washburn, Sherwood L., and C. S. Lancaster. 1968. The evolution of hunting. In *Man the hunter,* ed. Richard B. Lee and Irven DeVore, pp. 293–303. Chicago: Aldine.

Worcester, Dean C. 1912. Head-hunters of northern Luzon. *National Geographic* 23(9):833–930.

Yen, D. E. 1976. The ethnobotany of the Tasaday: III. Note on the subsistence system. In *Further studies on the Tasaday,* ed. D. E. Yen and John Nance. Makati, Rizal: PANAMIN Foundation Research Series No. 2.

The Sexual Division of Labor on Vanatinai

Maria Lepowsky

THE SEXUAL DIVISION OF LABOR

The sexual division of labor for Vanatinai adults, young people, and children features a marked overlap between the tasks considered appropriate for men and for women, as predicted for egalitarian societies.[1] Both Vanatinai women and men tend and harvest yams, the most highly valued cultigen, sweet potato, taro, manioc, banana, and other garden crops, and individuals of both sexes know various forms of garden magic, including the magic used in the annual yam planting ritual.

A woman is referred to by both sexes as "the owner of the garden," *or ghuma tanuwagai*. Women and men together agree on where and when to clear land for a new yam garden and on how big it needs to be for subsistence and exchange purposes. Men cut tall forest trees to clear land for new gardens, but the work party is comprised of men and women, and the women cut the smaller trees and shrubs and supervise the burning of the forest cover. Men normally loosen the soil to form mounds for planting yams using eight-foot digging sticks, but I have observed women performing this task. Women generally do the actual preparation and planting of seed yams, and they take the major responsibility for maintaining the gardens.

Both sexes plan the nature and extent of the coming year's gardens and plant them, but women do most of the daily garden maintenance, although certain men too are renowned for their industry in gardening. Food is harvested, usually by individual women, when it is ready. Yams are the only annual crop, and the only root crop which it is possible to store for many months. They are

From Maria Lepowsky, *Fruit of the Motherland: Gender in an Egalitarian Society*, Columbia University Press, 1993.

harvested by both women and men along with the appropriate magic and may be stored in small yam houses constructed either in the garden or near the hamlet.

Men weed and harvest gardens according to individual temperament and household needs. Men have primary responsibility for working sago. They do most of the pounding of the sago pith to extract the starch, a major dietary staple, but again the work party is usually mixed, and women supervise the drying of cakes of sago starch over a low fire.

Both women and men forage for a wide variety of wild nuts, legumes, tubers, fruits, and leaves in the rain forest, although women generally spend more time foraging than most men. Foraging, and being in the forest, is considered more enjoyable than weeding gardens in the hot sun.

Both women and men collect shellfish, fish in the lagoon with monofilament line from shore or from a canoe, use derris root to stun and collect fish trapped in shallow pools in the coral, and fish in the inland streams for freshwater fish, prawns, and eel. Men fish with spears in the lagoon at low tide during the day and using torches of dead coconut leaf at night. More rarely, men hunt crocodiles at night with torches and spears, or spear dugong in the lagoon shallows. The amount of time a person spends fishing and collecting shellfish varies tremendously according to whether the individual likes to fish and not according to sex.

Both men and women care for domestic pigs. If a woman owns and raises a pig, it is she who decides whether or not to contribute for a memorial feast or other occasion to satisfy her personal exchange obligations.

Killing human beings with spears or greenstone axes was a former monopoly of men. Hunting with spears, for wild pig, dugong, and crocodile, is also an exclusively male activity. But Vanatinai women hunt as well, without using spears. They hunt opossum, flying foxes, and fruit bats by climbing forest trees or tall coconuts to sneak up on the slow-moving nocturnal marsupials. Women also hunt monitor lizards, which grow to four feet in length, by climbing tall mangrove trees or by setting traps for them.[2]

In many parts of the Pacific, women are not supposed to climb trees, but on Vanatinai women climb not only to hunt but to obtain coconuts or betel nuts. Women fish using a fishing line or derris root, a fish poison. Formerly both sexes fished using nets woven by men of the fibrous aerial root of the wild pandanus palm. Both women and men gather shellfish in streams and along the fringing reef. Both dive in the lagoon for giant Tridacna clams. More rarely women dive for the blacklip or goldlip pearlshell, which may be sold to traders, or for the red-rimmed oyster-like shells made by both men and women into the shell-disc necklaces that circulate throughout the Louisiade Archipelago and the kula ring as far as the Trobriand Islands.

Men do most of the work of building houses. Women participate by collecting sago leaves for roofing and by weaving sago leaves for one type of wall. They must also provide the builders with cooked food. A few men also make outrigger paddling canoes and, more rarely, sailing canoes, but both men and women paddle and sail them. Although men and male youths more frequently make up the crews of sailing canoes, some women are expert sailors and make trips on their own or with other women to gardens and water sources. Both sexes frequently paddle and pole canoes. In the East Calvados Islands, with their strong maritime orientation, women spend most of their time in garden work while men sail to trade, fish, and make sago on nearby islands.

Men carve ceremonial axe handles and lime spatulas of wood and delicate tortoise-shell lime spatulas. Both men and women manufacture shell-disc necklaces. Women weave pandanus sleeping mats, fine coconut-

leaf betel nut baskets, and coconut-leaf skirts. All these items circulate in interisland exchange and during mortuary feasts.

Daily cooking, washing, fetching water and firewood, and sweeping are primarily female tasks, but men occasionally perform each of them. Men and women both fetch water and firewood and cook during feasts and other communal occasions such as roofing or yam planting. Men butcher and boil pork, scrape coconut meat, and prepare the boiled sago and green coconut pudding. Women prepare the stone oven for roasting vegetable food.

It is always the woman's job to clean up pig droppings around the hamlet every morning, using a piece of sago bark and a coconut-rib broom. In many cases they are the owners of the pigs. An angry meeting of village men took place to complain when a teacher in the primary school at Griffin Point, who came from another part of Papua New Guinea, assigned both boys and girls to clean up pig droppings from the school grounds, and the job was afterward given only to the girls.

Women are responsible for sweeping the hamlet ground, or *bakubaku*, every morning, for cooking, for fetching water, fetching saltwater (for salting food), gathering firewood, washing dishes and clothes, and caring for children, a responsibility that is often delegated to older siblings or grandparents. Older brothers, fathers, mother's brothers, grandfathers, and other male relatives often play with children and carry them around, but they do this only when they feel like it.

Both men and women are tender and indulgent parents, but the care of young children is primarily the responsibility of women. Because a father and child belong to different lineages, his nurturing is perceived as a gift rather than an obligation of kinship. Men are frequently seen carrying around their offspring or maternal nieces or nephews, and they often take older boys and girls with them to the garden for the day or on gathering expeditions. People explain that the reason why a father's matrilineal kin must be compensated with valuables when someone dies is that the deceased excreted upon the father as an infant and the father cleaned it up uncomplainingly.

EXCHANGE AND THE LIFE CYCLE

Every individual from young adulthood to old age has obligations to contribute labor, food, pigs, or ceremonial valuables upon certain occasions, particularly to aid kin and affines who may be hosting or attending a mortuary feast. Death comes early to many people on Vanatinai, from infant and child mortality due to malaria, from childbirth, and from infectious diseases such as pneumonia and tuberculosis (Lepowsky 1990). Genealogies often show that half the offspring of one couple died in infancy or childhood, and young adults and middle-aged people occasionally die suddenly and mysteriously. It is likely therefore that by the time an individual reaches adulthood he or she will have lost several close kin or affines and participated in the year-long series of mourning restrictions and feasts.

Young people begin their exchange careers by producing foodstuffs and household goods for use at feasts, for less spectacular exchange purposes dictated by kin responsibilities, and for home consumption: yams and garden produce, sago, pigs, skirts, mats, and baskets. All of these objects may be generated by the labor of an industrious young man or woman, who by doing so gains a reputation as a hard worker and therefore as a desirable marriage partner.

The unmarried young in their teens and early twenties are also expected to work hard at the many tasks of the *zagaya* itself. Sometimes their kin or the host of a feast will reward their effort with a valuable such as a greenstone axe blade. Every worker is fed well and given uncooked food to take home afterward. Young adults may request ceremonial valuables from their matrilineal kin, father's kin, or parents' closest exchange partners to contribute to a ritual obligation such as a feast or bridewealth. They will be expected to

repay the debt with an equivalent valuable at a later time when asked. Another way in which a young person of either sex enters the ceremonial system is by raising a pig to maturity and contributing it to a feast or in exchange for valuables such as greenstone axe blades.

There is no difference in the obligations of men and women to provide food or valuables upon ceremonial occasions. When an exchange obligation arises, women as well as men may set off in quest of ceremonial valuables, leaving children, husbands, gardens, and household responsibilities behind.

A few adults refuse to participate at all in exchange. Some people of both sexes choose to contribute only the minimum expected by custom. Others strive to give more yams, more bundles of sago, more pigs, and more valuables and to host and organize more feasts for dead kin or affines, earning the title *gia*. The amount of energy that men and women expend in exchange-activities is largely a function of individual personality. But the offspring of big men and big women—people with successful exchange careers and generally people with rights to large tracts of good garden land—have an advantage. They will inherit the land, ceremonial valuables, and exchange partners of their parents and matrilineal kin.

They will also closely observe successful exchange activities and their nuances from an early age. The ten-year-old daughter of one big man had already circumnavigated Vanatinai on her father's sailing canoe three times, accompanying him on exchange expeditions and attending feasts. She had also visited several of the East Calvados Islands. By contrast, some middle-aged people from the Jelewaga area had never visited the eastern settlements of the island or any neighboring islands.

A reputation as a big man or big woman is not gained by any one act of generosity in exchange or even by hosting one memorial feast or *zagaya*. A cycle of personal exchange activities develops as an individual matures and takes on new social responsibilities. By their twenties many young people, married and unmarried, contribute ceremonial valuables as well as foodstuffs to feasts as individuals and develop their personal networks of exchange partners. But people in their thirties to early sixties tend to be most widely known for their wealth, skill, and knowledge about exchange. Not only the mothers but the fathers of young children are inhibited by the fear that envious sorcerers or witches may take revenge by injuring or killing their children. Parents of young children also refrain from extensive exchange activities because of their extra subsistence and child-care obligations.

Women on Vanatinai have the opportunity, if they wish, to build their personal reputations as *giagia* through exchange activities. If they do not choose to exert the effort, they, like Vanatinai men who do not choose to build their reputations through the exchange of valuables, may gain the respect of their peers by taking good care of their families, growing good gardens, or helping their neighbors through their skill in healing.

Mortuary and other exchanges on Vanatinai are a primary means of gaining prestige and symbolic capital available to both men and women, but it is up to the individual to decide whether regionwide renown and influence is worth the trouble. Experts in exchange, healing, or gardening must be "strong," whether they are male or female: willing to take risks and engage in persistent hard work beyond the demands of substinence. They must seek out and learn the magic or ritual knowledge without which they will not succeed, exposing not only themselves but their families to the risk of illness or death through the sorcery or witchcraft of envious competitors.

Vanatinai adults of both sexes show a wide range of personality differences, and they occupy their days with a variety of activities, accommodating the demands of subsistence, sharing with others, and maintaining their reputations as strong and reliable kinspeople and neighbors according to their personal desires and preferences. The degree of personal autonomy and privileges of women and men are largely symmetrical in freedom of movement, choosing marriage partners or divorcing them, launching careers as prominent exchangers of valuables, and acquiring supernatural knowledge and power. Their society values autonomy and tolerates idiosyncrasy and variation among women and men. It also values the same qualities of strength, wisdom, and generosity in both sexes.

NOTES

1. Sanday (1974, 1981) hypothesizes that where men and women contribute equally to subsistence, women's status will be higher and suggest that the mingling of the sexes in the tasks of daily life works against the rise of male dominance. Similarly Bacdayan (1977) sees "task interchangeability" between the sexes as an important correlation of high status of women in a particular society.
2. Female hunting is relatively rare worldwide, but it has been reported among foragers and horticulturists in various parts of the world, such as Australian aborigines of the Kimberleys and Melville Island (Kaberry 1939, Goodale 1971), the Agta of the Philippines (Estioko-Griffin and Griffin 1981, 1985) and the Ojibwa, Montagnais-Naskapi, and Rock Cree of Canada (Landes 1938, Leacock 1978, Brightman 1993).

REFERENCES

Bacdayan, Albert. 1977. "Mechanistic Cooperation and Sexual Equality Among the Western Bontoc." In Alice Schlegel, ed., *Sexual Stratification: A Cross-Cultural View.* New York: Columbia University Press.

Brightman, Robert. 1993. "Biology, Taboo, and Gender Politics in the Sexual Division of Foraging Labor." Department of Anthropology, Reed College, Manuscript.

Estioko-Griffin, Agnes, and P. Bion Griffin. 1981. "Woman the Hunter." In Frances Dahlberg, ed., *Woman the Gatherer.* New Haven, CT: Yale University Press.

Estioko-Griffin, Agnes, and P. Bion Griffin. 1985. "Woman Hunters: The Implications for Pleistocene Prehistory and Contemporary Ethnography." In Madeleine Goodman, ed., *Women in Asia and the Pacifica: Towards an East-West Dialogue*. Honolulu: Women's Studies Program, University of Hawaii.

Goodale, Jane. 1971. *Tiwi Wives*. Seattle: University of Washington Press.

Kaberry, Phyllis. 1939. *Aboriginal Woman: Sacred and Profane*. London: Routledge

Landes, Ruth. 1938. *The Ojibwa Woman*. New York: Columbia University Press.

Leacock, Eleanor. 1978. "Women's Status in Egalitarian Society: Implications for Social Evolution." *Current Anthropology* 19: 247–276.

Lepowsky, Maria. 1990. "Sorcery and Penicillin: Treating Illness on Papua New Guinea Island." *Social Science and Medicine* 30 (10): 1049–1063.

Sanday, Peggy. 1974. "Female Status in the Public Domain." In Michelle Rosaldo and Louise Lamphere, eds., *Woman, Culture and Society*. Stanford, Calif.: Stanford University Press.

Sanday, Peggy. 1981. *Female Power and Male Dominance: On the Origins of Sexual Inequality*. Cambridge: Cambridge University Press.

Divisions of Labour on Irish Family Farms

Patricia O'Hara

To the woman falls the first duty of the day. She must rake together such live ashes as remain in the slaked turf fire in the hearth, put down new sods for the fire, and rekindle the blaze. This done, she hangs the kettle on the hooks making ready for the first tea of the day. In the household the responsibility of day-to-day housekeeping belongs to the woman. Hers, too, is the care of the children. . . . But her work stretches beyond the house door. In the morning after breakfast she takes the milk buckets and milks the cows in the sheds in the haggard. This is merely one of the many trips she makes in and out of the kitchen doors for fuel, or water, to feed and tend the animals and the fowl. Her milking finished, she must bring the milk in and separate it... The whole process of the conversion of milk to butter is her charge... All the care of the calves, pigs, and fowl falls to her lot... Her work ends only with the separating that takes place when she brings her milk into the house. Even then, while the men may sit round the fire talking over the day's work or the affairs of the community, she is not idle... When the whole family has finally gone off to bed, it is she who must close up the house at night and slake the fire in the hearth. (Arensberg and Kimball, 1968: 37-39)

Arensberg and Kimball's detailed ethnographic description of rural life in the west of Ireland in the 1930s is a unique record of the working life of farm women on the small peasant farms of the time. The situation they describe would have been little different on smallholdings in other parts of the country. Farming was very much a family operation in which all able-bodied members were involved. Women were responsible for the farmyard economy of milking, rearing of young animals (usually pigs and calves), poultry, butter making and frequently the cultivation of vegetables as well. On the small tillage plots typical of smaller holdings, they helped with crop cultivation (potatoes, turnips, beet) and often at haymaking and harvesting. All self-provisioning—butter making, fruit preservation as well as cooking and baking—was their responsibility. In addition they usually bore large families and had complete responsibility for childcare and household work. Women's work involved an endless round of chores virtually unchanging with the seasons and physically exhausting.

From Patricia O'Hara, *Partners in Production? Women, Farm, and Family in Ireland*. New York: Berghahn Books, 1998.

Family work was structured around gender and age, a "concerted effort" within which there was a rigid division of labour between women and men (Arensberg and Kimball, 1968: 45). Animal husbandry, the buying and selling of animals, most fieldwork (e.g., ploughing, harrowing) and structural yard work (e.g., building, repairing) requiring heavy effort, was undertaken by the male "farmer" whose work was much more varied and less restricted in space than that of the farm wife. The division of labour and power was sustained by beliefs and values based on what were considered the "natural" attributes of each sex (1968: 48-49). Ridicule and derisiveness greeted those who breached sex-role boundaries, particularly when a man was seen to do a woman's work. Higher status and importance were attached to men's work, and they made all the major decisions related to the farm.

While Arensberg and Kimball have provided a valuable ethnographic description of familial arrangements on Irish family farms, their functionalist perspective (which portrayed the farm family as a harmonious haven of complementarity) led them to assume throughout that women themselves found this arrangement satisfactory and found "reward and pleasure" in their work roles (1968: 46). We have no evidence of whether, or how, women contested their roles or the kind of sanctions which might be brought to bear by the wife in the event of her husband failing to fulfil his work obligations or provide adequately for the family. It would appear that she had few, being herself without property or an independent source of income, so that it was in her interest to ensure the smooth operation and maximum profitability of the farm and the goodwill of her husband. Nevertheless the very separateness of work roles and the independent control of a regular proportion of the farm income (the butter and egg money) as well as their control and influence over the children, may have at least conferred on women a kind of domestic autonomy. For instance Bourke (1991: 8) has suggested that wives' power in the household

was considerable since they controlled the bulk of household expenditure which was spent on food. Refusal to cook a meal was also, she suggests, an important sanction used by women. A rigid division of labour may actually put limits on the exercise of patriarchal power, since women monopolise certain skills and knowledge (Connell, 1987: 125).

Whatever its limits, the Irish farm family as described by Arensberg and Kimball was strongly patriarchal with control of labour, property and succession in the hands of male farmers. The organisation of farm work was premised on a significant and constant input of the farm woman's labour. Her contribution to farm production was an essential part of her role as farm wife and was additional to her domestic and childcare responsibilities. Family farming as a social form therefore involved the incorporation of women's labour in farm production, and the well-being of the farm family was related to how effectively the farm wife executed her prescribed role. Her cooperation was assured by the fact that nothing less than her own and her children's present and future well-being depended on it. Reviewing Arensberg and Kimball's study, Hannan and Katsiaouni (1977: 20) observed that "the whole pattern of family interaction, both as to the allocation of task roles and of power is such as to maintain the superordinate-subordinate relationship between spouses." Indeed, Arensberg and Kimball's account of the internal structure of farm families is not unfamiliar to many contemporary farm wives, particularly those from smallholdings, who grew up in such circumstances and/or experienced them in the early days of their marriage....

The work of farm women on larger more prosperous farms in the east region in particular may not have been as arduous, mainly because of the presence of hired labour. Unfortunately, we do not have similar ethnographic evidence from these larger farms but we do know that hired farm and domestic labour was common (Breen, 1983; Fahey, 1990). Indeed one of the women from a relatively large farm in the present study suggested that her own life was much more difficult than that of her mother, observing that "my mother and grandmother were women of leisure with a lot of help." While the work of women may not have been so physically taxing as on smaller holdings, there is no reason to believe that the intrafamily authority system of male dominance was any different, although it may have been exercised somewhat differently.

FARM WOMEN AND FARM WORK

The conventional sociological distinctions between productive and reproductive work, and farm and domestic work are not easily recognized by farm women today. While they clearly see non-farm occupational waged work such as teaching or nursing as "work," their concept of unpaid work is rather indistinct. Consequently, by taking on normative definitions of work, they underestimate the work they do, either by not defining it as work at all, or by blurring the distinction between work and leisure. Women in the west for instance said that working on the bog was physically hard but that they really enjoyed being out in the fresh air, having all the family involved and getting the fuel in for the winter (incorporating concepts of leisure, family and farm household reproduction in one work task). Since the range of work done on a family farm does not fit into the conventional wage-labour work model, it tends to get treated in much the same way as domestic work—as being part of a way of life rather than a job/work in the conventional sense. Women often "talk down" the work that they do, comparing it to their mother's work which was much more difficult and physically taxing. In so far as they do make distinctions, the primary one is between "inside" and "outside" work. The latter can be "fieldwork" or "yardwork," or work on the bog which is thought of as farm work. "Inside work" includes both housework and childcare and household repairs and maintenance (such as decorating). Delphy and Leonard (1992: 202-3) have pointed

out that French farm women make the same inside/outside work distinction.

Manual Work

Sixty percent of farm women in the west and 40 percent of those in the east were regularly involved in manual work on the farm. Dairying and market gardening are the most labour intensive enterprises and it is on farms with these enterprises that women are most heavily involved in manual work. On dairy farms their work is usually in the yard and centered on the milking (including preparing the cows and washing up afterwards), feeding the calves, as well as herding, and checking cattle:

> I do a bit of everything—feed calves, take over if he's not here milking and washing. I can take over completely if he is away. The kids go for the cows morning and evening. H milks and I do the washing up most days. It depends on what I have to do inside, some days I might not be able to get out. I feed the calves, I think women are better at this, more patient and more used to children. Men will take them or leave them, women are more fussy about them. I'd also be involved in moving and changing stock, weighing lambs, sorting out cattle for the headage. (Dairy farm, W30)

Women on dairy farms are strongly aware of the importance of their work partly because it is so visible but also because they know that they are virtually indispensable to the smooth running of the enterprise. The time and work commitment involved in twice-daily milking seven days a week for most of the year means that family labour is virtually essential. (The only farm wife on a dairy farm who was not involved in farm work in any way was a teacher with seven young children and her husband had other help on the farm). As one farm wife said: "without my work he would have to work a lot slower and harder, he would have to be out earlier." Yet most do not do the actual milking on a regular basis but are more involved in the preparation and washing up afterwards. Avoiding milking can be a deliberate strategy, as in the case of one respondent whose husband has an off-farm job. She explains it this way:

> I love working on the farm and do all the work except milking. I said early on that I would never milk because I would be tied to it forever more. The problem with dairy farming is that you are always tied to the farm. There is never a break—you always have to come home to milk. Dairying is a long hard slog, there must be easier ways of making money. I'm not from a dairy farm and I thought [growing] potatoes was the hardest work until I got involved with cows. (Dairy farm, W15)

The predominant role of women on dairy farms is that of helper and the manual work that women do on these farms tends to be an extension of gender-specific household work—cleaning, tidying, feeding, organising. Care of young animals, mainly calves, is almost exclusively the woman's responsibility and women themselves see this as a gender-specific skill, attributing it to their greater patience and childcare experience.

> When my mother-in-law got sick the men couldn't cope with the calves so H said that I would have to come down to the yard and I did. I like doing it. I am not from a farm but I had watched her doing it. Women are better with calves, they have a maternal instinct, know when a calf is ill or cold like they would with children. Men wouldn't even see it. (Dairy farm, E24)
>
> I feed the calves. They say that women are better than men at rearing calves but me, I don't like to admit this. (Dairy farm, E6)
>
> Women are better at calf-rearing, especially dealing with sick calves. My husband wouldn't know. I'd make sure the calf would get its own milk, he wouldn't be as careful. There would be trouble if I didn't watch them and they might get scour or have to be put on medication. I wouldn't be blamed if the calf died but I'd be sorry. (Drystock farm, W7)

When farm families disengage from dairying, this is often precipitated by a wish to lessen the farm labour requirement, particularly when there is no other available family labour. Although this reduces the cleaning and tidying workload, women usually continue to look after the calves. On one farm where they had recently changed from dairying to drystock farming, the wife explained:

> We got out of dairying in April 1990. It was too time consuming, we wanted to take it a bit easier as we are here on our own now....I bring in the cows in the morning for suckling and put the calves on them. I'd be tending to sick calves....That's all the work I do now, although I might give him a hand during the day with herding or if the vet was coming, or dosing. In the past I did much more. (Drystock farm, W5)

Certainly farm women are very conscious of the labour requirements of dairy farming and few would envisage themselves being able to run a dairy farm on their own:

> I like farm work but I am doing less now than I used to. In the beginning there was no piped water and no machinery and H was away more...I often think that if anything happened to H, I wouldn't feel that I could continue on my own. I wouldn't be able to do the heavy work and if I had to pay someone, it wouldn't be feasible. I'd sell the stock and let the land. (Dairy farm, WI 2)

Market gardening too, makes huge labour demands on farm families, and in competitive market conditions family labour is a *sine qua non* of market gardening. The work is seasonal however, depending on the crop involved:

> I pick and grade tomatoes from April to September. During July and August it would be from 6:30 am to 8:30 pm and at other times six to seven hours. H's brother takes the tomatoes to the market two or three times a day. I work five-and-a-half days per week. I insist on taking a half day Saturday. (Market gardening, E3)

Another older woman, who now considers herself retired as she is over sixty, said:

> I am officially retired but I keep the books and I help out. I do all the grading [of vegetables] and select the staff in summer. I water plants, sow seed, all the easy jobs.... I worked all the time picking tomatoes, planting, grading. We had flowers—tulips, daffodils, chrysanthemums

. . . it was desperately hard work but we were young and we didn't mind it. We would be up at 6:00 am and often didn't finish until eleven at night. (Market gardening, E4)

In both dairying and market gardening the sheer urgency and physical demand of the manual work mean that the women involved are very conscious of their labour input. Because the family labour is so obviously crucial to the success of the enterprises, they have a sense of the teamwork involved in keeping the operation running smoothly and of the significance of their own contribution. Their involvement centres mainly around the yard and most have little direct input into what they call "fieldwork" except to help out in emergencies. Driving the tractor seems to be the critical boundary between yard and field work, with most women saying they would not drive the tractor except in an emergency. Unwillingness to drive the tractor may have its roots in culturally prescribed gender roles but it also appears to be a way of resisting incorporation into a whole range of heavy work which women prefer to avoid. As one woman put it:

I don't drive the tractor, although I suppose I would if I had to. My husband has said to me that it's a pity you don't drive the tractor. Whatever has to be done you just do it and that's it. It depends on what makes money. (Wl3)

The gender division of work then seems to occur primarily between yard and fieldwork, with women confining their manual work primarily to the yard. This is borne out by the work roles of the women on farms in the east on which tillage was the main enterprise. These farms are highly commercialised with two being run in partnership arrangements with the husband's brother(s). The third was run by a couple who had experienced severe financial difficulties over the past several years. None of these women had a significant involvement in manual work but two of them had a significant non-manual involvement as we shall see below.

Drystock farming was by far the most common main enterprise in both east and west, accounting for two-thirds of all the farms studied. The labour requirements on drystock farms vary greatly depending on the size and intensity of the farm operation. The work involvement of women on such farms is related to the labour demands of the enterprise and also to the availability of other family labour, including that of their husbands. It can range from primary responsibility for managing the farm operation to almost complete detachment from it. Extensive involvement is generally associated with the husbands' engagement in off-farm work or having an illness which restricts their labour input:

The system here is suckling cows and sheep. My husband got a heart attack seven weeks ago so I have been doing most of the farm work since then. My son helps with the heavy work in the evening. In the morning I milk a cow for the house and then let the calves to the cows, water and feed the cows. Then I count the stock and look at them.... I check the stock during the day. Some of the sheep are three miles away and if he is not fit to drive I go over on the bicycle to check them. In the evening I do the same chores as morning. I always did my share before H got sick but he would manage on his own if I couldn't get out. (Drystock farm, W4)

We have just cattle. I help with dosing, bring in the silage, check the stock to see if they are OK. Feeding them means going a mile and a half up the road as the farm is not here beside the house. (Drystock farm, E8, husband has off-farm job.)

I do everything and anything, I do the jobs as they come up and I have to do it. I feed calves, count cattle, sheep, help with lambing and so on. I like doing it, I would die in a town...The only job I don't do is drive the tractor....When the kids were small I didn't do as much because my father and mother-in-law were here. The farming was not as intensive then. I would say it is half and half between us as to the farm work. I put down housewife in the Census. I knew it was wrong, it's tradition I suppose. I don't know why. I suppose you feel you are downgrading your husband if you put down farmer. (Drystock farm, W6, husband has off-farm business.).

Women were more involved in manual work on drystock farms in the west than in the east for a variety of reasons. Firstly, fewer wives were themselves involved in off-farm paid work and so were available to work on the farm. Secondly, almost twice as many husbands in the west were involved in off-farm work and all but three of these were on drystock farms. Incidentally, on the three dairy farms where husbands were working off the farm, their work was either part-time or structured in such a way that they were available on the farm for much of the day. Thirdly, drystock farms in the west are smaller, less intensive and more reliant on the labour input of the immediate family; there are no adult children (sons) working full time on these farms and hired help is rarely employed and even then, only on a casual basis on the bigger holdings. Perhaps more significantly, women's involvement in farm work in the west represents the last vestiges of the small-farm economy described at the beginning of this chapter. The farmyard economy of egg production and butter production has disappeared, but for many women this has happened only in the present generation:

I had hens and loved them but they annoyed my husband around the dairy so we have not had them for fifteen years or so. I had ducks too, they were easy to rear and lovely to eat....I haven't made butter for years and I just used to make it for the house. As time went on we found that it didn't pay, you could buy butter cheaper. (W5)

I made butter when I was younger and sold it to the local shop, but I gave it up. I don't remember why, it was too much trouble I suppose. (W3)

We have no hens anymore ... they are dirty and a nuisance and they wouldn't lay half the time. I don't like free-range eggs now that I have got used to the others. (W1O)

The demise of the farmyard economy has not however pushed women on small holdings in the west back into the home but rather extended their involvement into other yard-based tasks with less rigid gender boundaries. They remain, however, in the private domain of farming, rarely engaging in public farm work such as attending livestock sales or open days, or representing the farm family at public meetings or in farming organisations. In fact very few of the women in either of the study areas were involved in organisations of any kind and those who were, tended to be those who were least involved in farm work.

The sense of engagement with the family farm (even on low-intensity drystock enterprises) which the accounts of women in the west convey, is in sharp contrast to several of those from the east, where the women are completely detached from the farm which they see as a business like any other. This is most common where wives come from non-farm backgrounds and/or have their own careers or businesses, but also on larger farms where labour is hired:

I do none [farm work] at all. The only thing I do is stand at the road when they are loading cattle or give a hand at herding but that is only three times a year or so. I never did any [farm] work, nor did H's mother. (Large drystock farm, E5)

I do no farm work and I never did any. I am the world's worst. I am interested in it I suppose, in that it is part of our lives, but I don't like animals and the smells and the dirt. I associate it with old farmhouses and the smells in them. I don't do account-keeping or any other work, I suppose it is lack of interest really. (Drystock farm, El 9, wife has own business.)

I don't do any, I just drive by. (Tillage, E21, wife has own business.)

Non-Manual Work

Almost all farm women are involved in non-manual farm work in some way. This can range from the fairly typical tasks of dealing with callers, awaiting deliveries, running errands or discussing the farm business, to total financial management for the whole farm operation. Generally non-manual work casts women in a supportive rather than managerial role. It is "inside work" in the same way as household work and childcare. Although it is farm work (in the sense that it would not be required if there were no farm) women often do not see it as such. The wife of a large tillage farmer in the east, herself from a non-farm background, described her involvement thus:

> I don't really do any farm work ... apart from standing at gates or something like that when I might be needed. I drive in summer, bringing teas and dinners to the fields and doing errands... I deal with callers, say when people come for hay and straw, and any other callers to the house and answer the phone ... if there is no one here for the phone it is bad. (Tillage, E1)

Being on call and available to help out when needed is typical of the non-manual role that many women play particularly on the larger farms and on farms where produce is being sold directly from the yard, as this requires that someone be available all the time. Even women who are in full-time paid work themselves sometimes take on this role:

> I make the phone calls and do all the errands and messages—the chemist, the vet and so on. I get the accounts ready for the IFAC [Irish Farm Accounts Cooperative] recorder and pay most of the bills or they would be left here otherwise. (Tillage and sheep, E1 5, Teacher)

Usually though, when women are in full-time paid work, they tend to have a lesser involvement in all farm work, but they are available as a reserve and in emergencies. As is the case with manual work, it is the women who are at home all the time or whose husbands have off-farm work who tend to have the greatest involvement. One woman working on a dairy farm described her work involvement (both manual and non-manual) as follows:

> I do about twenty to thirty percent of the work, just the handy work! I suppose if you were to include all the paper work, I do about fifty percent in all. Every year there is more paperwork for cattle. H says you would need to take a suitcase to the mart with all the papers. (Dairy farm, W30)

A majority of wives in both areas are involved in account-keeping and financial management. On low intensity drystock farms and on the more intensive farms where an accountant or a professional farm account service is used, this may simply be a matter of keeping track of bills and receipts but it means that wives have an intimate and ongoing knowledge of the farm finances. In the following example, the respondent has a full-time job, nevertheless it is she who keeps the farm accounts. In recent years they have experienced financial difficulties in farming and this has made her acutely aware of the need for proper financial management:

> I keep farm records for the accountant. I'd know better than H and I have to know what is going on, what money is there for food, the kids' education and so on. At the moment we don't know what to do, the accountant and our adviser are going to sort it out. I'd like to go without counting pennies for once. (Drystock farm, E22)

Other wives take on a more proactive managerial role in relation to the farm finances, usually explaining their involvement in terms of men's incompetence or unwillingness to take on the tedious work involved. This level of involvement is associated with commercialised farms where tight financial management is essential:

> I do all the books and when a problem arises I figure it out. Men haven't a clue [her husband and son]. When the accountant or IFAC ring up H puts them on to me. If I died in the morning I tell them they would end up in Mountjoy [prison], they are both the same. H only saw the accountant once when he had to... H was ill nine years ago and I had to do it then, so he left it to me. Women are better at balancing the books, they see further ahead. When there is any investment needed I'd be asked. (Dairy farm, E1 8)

> I don't do anything outside but do all the farm accounts and financial management for the farm, see the adviser, run errands etc. If they want a new tractor they come to me and Mum is supposed to find the money. . . There was a bank strike and when it was over everything was in a mess so I just took over. My husband just didn't want to bother. I'm better at it

and I have more education. A lot of women are keeping accounts, they are always there in the house and men want to be outside. I am the banker for the house and farm but it has its disadvantages, like the times when they want to buy things and I have to say no. I could always threaten to throw it there and say, "see for yourselves," but it would never come to that because they really don't want to have to do all that paperwork.... The men don't like keeping books, even the lads who have the Green Cert.[1] will leave it to me. (Large drystock farm, W3)

I do all the talking to the bank manager, H lacks confidence. He comes with me but he doesn't open his mouth.... I write all the cheques here and have learned to forge my husband's signature. I pay all the bills. It is an escape for him, he calls me his financial advisor but it means I have to face the music and I get all the hassle. (Market gardening, E1 3)

While these women clearly recognise their own competence in financial management, they also see that it is in their husbands' interest to hand over the tedium and stress involved in such work to someone else whom they can trust. Indeed the last woman quoted above was actually negotiating the sale of a part of the farm at the time of the interview, as the farm business was under severe financial pressure. It also allows the men to opt out of ongoing financial management but clearly demands a conjugal contract based on high levels of mutual trust and reciprocity. Although these wives, in having taken over the farm finances in this way, are acting in a managerial rather than secretarial role, they are a minority. Most women who are involved in account-keeping explain their involvement more in terms of it being a shared task, and see their own role as that of helper rather than manager. Those least likely to be involved in account-keeping are those who have their own off-farm jobs or businesses.

It is clear then that farm women are involved in a wide variety of farm work. Their degree of involvement is influenced by a complex of factors which are structured, inter alia, by the particular circumstances of the

[1] Certificate of vocational qualification in farming in Ireland.

family farm, the nature of the marital relationship and their own preferences. In general, women have a greater involvement in manual work on farms with more labour intensive systems such as dairying and market gardening where the success of the enterprise is essentially premised on the availability of family labour. But even on these farms, their involvement is in turn influenced by whether they are working off the farm; the availability of other labour; the patterns of involvement established from early in their marriage; and their own preferences. Women's work is carried out mainly in the farmyard and farmhouse rather than the fields, so that they are least likely to be involved in manual work on tillage farms. In general, women in the west conveyed a greater sense of engagement with farm work and farming as a livelihood. This reflects not only the differences in the nature of the farm economies between the two regions but also differences in the farm cultures, women's backgrounds, and off-farm work commitments of both spouses.

Having established the range of work performed by women on family farms, we now turn to the context in which such work is carried out. It is not so much the nature of the work which is important in understanding how farm women are subordinated, but rather the work relationship and how it is constituted. Do men/farmers control the work that women do? What rewards do women receive for their work? Do women always carry out such work in a subordinate relationship to their husbands or does negotiation involve a redistribution of power?

REWARDS FOR FARM WORK

Whatmore has argued that three of the most important dimensions of the patriarchal labour relations in the family farm are farm women's limited legal and financial interest in the family farm, their restricted involvement in farm decisionmaking and lack of control over the money generated from the farm business (1991: 82). Women on farms may do as much (or more) farm work as their husbands, or indeed be responsible for managing the farm as a business, and yet have no ownership rights to the family farm, no significant say in farm decision making and no control over the farm income. This too is the core of Delphy and Leonard's contention regarding women's work in the family, that is, that the essence of women's exploitation lies in the fact that they do not own what they produce within the family; the products of their labour belong to the head of household, i.e., in farm households, the farmer (1992: 89).

The patrilineal system of inheritance ensures that, with few exceptions, the only women who own land in their own right are widows and this is borne out in the present study. While a majority of farms in both east and west were owned solely by husbands, there are quite striking differences between the two areas in that the proportion in joint ownership was almost three times higher in the west. In the west 63 percent (19/30) of farms were registered in the husband's name only; 27 percent (8/30) were in joint names and, of the remaining three farms, two were owned by widows and the third had been transferred to a son. In the east, 83 percent (25/30) of the farms were owned solely by husbands and only 10 percent (3/30) were owned jointly, and the remaining two farms were owned by widows.

Involvement in decisionmaking reflects a somewhat similar pattern. On farms in the east, farm decisions were made by the couple jointly on 27 percent (8/30) of the farms, compared to 43 percent (13/30) in the west. A much higher proportion of couples in the west had joint bank accounts—two-thirds as opposed to one-third in the east. Thus, although the predominant situation is one of subordination, there are, especially in the west, a significant proportion of farms where wives have proprietary rights, are involved in joint decisionmaking, and have access to the couple's joint income. This is consistent with the earlier observation of a higher level of farm work involvement among women in the west.

While these regional differences are striking, differential rewards appear also to be influenced by the size of the farm operation, the system of farming, and wives' other work commitments. What is clear is that some women have evolved a conjugal arrangement with their husbands whereby, in relation to the operation of the farm at least, they have managed to negotiate a considerable lessening of their subordination. This situation is quite different from Delphy and Leonard's interpretation of the situation of wives on French family farms (1992: 205-7). There is considerably more variation than the straightforward patriarchal regime, characterised by complete male dominance and control over all farm decisions and money, that they describe.

What women say about farm work best captures this. Those who have negotiated a joint or sharing arrangement see themselves as being involved in a partnership, and use the terms "we'" and "ours" to refer to the farm as opposed to "his" or "theirs":

> Money is thrown up on the shelf and we help ourselves until it is gone. While it is there the two of us use it.... I don't think of it as payment. I say I'm an unpaid servant....Of course I'd like regular payment, who wouldn't, but not from the farm. It's not like that on a farm. (W6).
>
> I love working on the farm....The farm work is the least I could do because he is out working for most of the day. All the money we make here is shared and I consider it pay for the work I do. My husband appreciates it and sometimes tells me so. (W15)
>
> We work well together. The lads [her husband and brother-in-law] are inclined to say "we'll do this" and I'll say "let's think it through and look at all the options"...the three of us will talk it out and it will be a better decision. I think they do appreciate me, they will consult me on everything. (E3)
>
> I see us as partners, it is all joint. . . . We discuss farm decisions—like when H was buying a tractor, I said, do you need all the tractors, so we traded in two against a new one. The same with buying cattle, we discuss it. (E7)

These comments contrast with those of the farm wives who clearly perceive themselves to be in a subordinate role:

I don't mind farm work although sometimes I get sick of it. I like getting away from housework but dairying is an awful tie. No matter what time you get to bed you have to get up in the morning. . . . We really don't think of the money we get from the farm as payment for work. It really is different from a job where you have a wage coming in every week. I put down housewife in the Census, I don't know why really, I suppose I don't realise what I do. . . . The farmer's wife's work is not recognised, people don't realise what we do, the long hours, the hard work. Our work is taken for granted by everyone including husbands. Men have long hours too, all around the clock. It is a long day and there are ups and downs. (W1 8)

I am not the farm manager, I would always ask him. I would consult him first but I am involved in decisions and would call the vet and deal with him and other callers. . . . I would love to have been a farmer if I was a boy but my brother is at home now. In those days it was one of the boys who got the farm. (E II)

Other women perceive their subordinate role as being reinforced by ideological and institutional factors outside of the micro level of the farm family, whereby their work is not recognised and they are not considered as work units in the tax or social security system:

We each have an account. Most of the money goes into H's account and I have a small account for myself. I don't see the money in my account as payment, I regard the farm as a business. . . . I think there should be a tax allowance for the farmer's wife as they share the work also. I feel I'm doing as much for the farm as the others. (W3)

I don't like farm work, I do it because it is there . . . like having to milk. You are really tied with cows . . . I think the housewife should be entitled to some income, not dole. There are so many men on the dole, no one mentions the women. Their work is not recognised. People ask me if I am working and I say no. (W10)

I am completely unpaid [for the work on the farm]. I sometimes complain to them but when I look at the hours they work. . . . H is out in the yard at 6:30 a.m. every morning and sometimes doesn't come in until nine at night.

. . . People don't understand how hard you work in farming. . . . I think there should be something for the wife, there is no allowance for the wife's work in the tax system, they are not one unit of labour. It has nothing to do with money, it's about being recognised—I handle the money anyway. Ours is family money, they take what I give them. (E18)

All women are classed as equal nowadays, although I always felt I was equal to any man. I considered my father and my husband as the boss but I expected them to discuss things with me. . . . I put down housewife in the census, I don't know why. What else could I put down? Down the years it was the husband who was the farmer if the land was in his name. (E23)

The rewards for farm work are not then the same for all farm women. There is considerable variation in women's relationship to the family enterprise, the nature of the conjugal contract and their own understanding of that relationship.

REFERENCES

Arensberg, C. M., and S. T. Kimball. 1968. *Family and Community in Ireland.* Harvard: Harvard University Press (first edition 1940, reissued in 1968).

Bourke, J. 1991. "Women, Economics, and Power: Irish Women 1880-1914," *Irish Home Economics Journal,* 1(2):3-16.

Breen, R. 1983. "Farm Servanthood in Ireland, 1900–1940," *Economic History Review,* 36(1):87–102.

Connell, R. W. 1987. *Gender and Power.* Cambridge: Polity Press.

Delphy, C., and D. Leonard. 1992. *Familiar Exploitation: A New Analysis of Marriage in Contemporary Societies.* Cambridge: Polity Press.

Fahey, T. 1990. "Measuring the Female Labour Supply: Conceptual and Procedural Problems in Irish Official Statistics," *Economic and Social Review,* 21(2):163–91.

Hannan, D. E., and L. Katsiaouni. 1977. *Traditional Families? From Culturally Prescribed to Negotiated Roles in Farm Families.* Dublin: Economic and Social Research Institute.

Whatmore, S. 1991. *Farming Women: Gender Work and Family Enterprise.* London: Macmillan.

Pastoral Nomadism and Gender: Status and Prestige, Economic Contribution, and Division of Labor among the Tuareg of Niger

Susan Rasmussen

INTRODUCTION

Gender in Anthropology

This is a discussion of women's perceived economic contributions in relation to status, prestige, and division of labor in a traditionally pastoral nomadic, stockbreeding society, the Tuareg of the African Sahara and Sahel. I also offer a critique of some interpretations of gender and pastoralism in predominantly seminomadic communities moving toward sedentarization and migrant labor. First, I situate my own analysis in current approaches to gender in anthropology, and present an overview of studies of women's and men's roles in pastoral society. Following this section, I focus upon the Tuareg, a seminomadic, Islamic, socially stratified people who live in Niger, Mali, Burkina Faso, and Algeria, with an emphasis on data from my research among the Air Tuareg of northern Niger Republic.[1] I conclude with a brief discussion of socioeconomic and political transformations that impinge upon Tuareg gender, relations between the sexes, and issues raised for the future.

Gender is socially and culturally constructed, and can usefully be understood as a comparative, relational concept (Di Leonardo 1990; Butler 1990:6; Davison 1997). Critical to gender structuring are intertwined modalities: social variables such as ethnicity, class, religion, and age, among many (Ortner and Whitehead 1981; Di Leonardo 1990). Regional variations may also impinge on inter- and intragender identities and relationships (Meena 1992; Gaidzanwa 1985; Mannathoko 1992; Davison

Original material prepared for this text

1997). Each of these modalities, singly or in combination, interacts dialectically with gender in a given society at a specific point in time, altering the way women and men are perceived and how they perceive themselves and each other. Constructions of gender therefore depend heavily upon positionality.[2]

In recent years, a number of scholars have called for studies that treat gender dynamically, as occurring in processes generated by discrete locales and through particular histories; they assert that gender is not fixed either across time or in location (di Lauretis 1984; Scott 1988,1992; Kondo 1990; Probyn 1990; Butler 1992; Flax 1993; Barlow 1996). Thus although I use the term "women," I also try to make clear that the Tuareg women about whom I write do not constitute an undifferentiated category of "essentialized woman." They interact with men, and are defined by their age, social origins, occupations, kinship roles, and other locations in Tuareg society. I insist that specifics of time and place are critical; I aim to tease out the relationship of historical and social contexts to certain configurations of gender.[3] My point is not to argue for some timeless, quintessentially Tuareg sense of woman, but to show how gender and knowledge are constructed in a particular place and time, namely, of seminomadism: in a pastoralist nomadic community undergoing transitions whose directions are difficult to predict over the long term, but who now include some sedentary oasis gardening and migrant labor, within a larger, multiethnic nation-state experiencing ecological disaster, economic crisis, and political tensions.

Women and Men in Pastoral Nomadism

Some researchers (Barth 1961; Martin and Voorhies 1975:332–366) view pastoralism as one extreme on a continuum of dependence upon herd animals and cultivation for subsistence, in which segments of sedentary tilling communities may, during periods of scarce resources (i.e., droughts, overpopulation) come to depend increasingly on the products of their herd animals for subsistence. Much Tuareg data, however, contradicts this: in the difficulties of drought, many Tuareg have been pressured to become more sedentary, and to depend increasingly on products of their oasis gardens rather than herd animals for subsistence. Despite this, however, a pastoralist ideology persists. Many Tuareg yearn to return to pastoral nomadism but realize the necessity today for mixing subsistence modes of herding, oasis gardening, caravan and other itinerant trading, and migrant labor, and among the more specialized artisan social strata, arts/crafts production (Rasmussen 1992, 1994, 1996). Martin and Voorhies also observe that during periods of plenty, when the size of herds becomes cumbersome or provides the wherewithal for purchase of arable land, pastoral segments may be repatriated to villages. But among the Tuareg, exactly the opposite occurs: during periods of stress and deprivation when herds become greatly diminished or even depleted, population segments tend to be repatriated to villages.

Tuareg patterns therefore suggest the need to modify or refine some prevalent representations of the cyclical pattern of pastoralism (Martin and Voorhies 1975:334). They offer contradictions, or at least variations, of some previous interpretations of gender in pastoral nomadic societies, and show the need to deconstruct concepts in both pastoralist and gender studies. In a classic study, Martin and Voorhies (1975:351) acknowledge that it is difficult to point to any single pattern of economic adaptation or social juxtaposition of the sexes among pastoralists as a

whole, and correlations cannot always be converted to causal connections. Based upon their ethnological, cross-cultural and historical secondary data, these authors make several tentative generalizations. They note that the sexual division of labor seems related to the degree and nature of mobility required for the successful execution of subsistence activities (Martin and Voorhies 1975:352). They argue that gender variations among pastoralists are influenced by at least three factors: (1) their specific adaptation to a given environment (settlement pattern, interaction of herding and cultivation); (2) cultural history of society (common culture areas such as sedentary community origins in Africa south of the Sahara correlate with economic independence, the hoe, polygyny, and sexual freedom; those in the Middle East and of agricultural origins display the opposite pattern); and (3) recent diffusion of ideas rather than cultural origins (Islam, for example—although the Tuareg are an exception to other Muslim pastoralists, in demonstrating less emphasis on the patriarchal family and on gender inequalities) (Martin and Voorhies 1975:365–366).

From their study of fourty-four pastoral societies, Martin and Voorhies conclude that the female contribution to the diet of herders is small. Men do almost all herding and women dairy in only about one-third of societies. Men also do most of the cultivation in half of their sample, however, where cultivation is based on horticultural techniques, women are either the exclusive cultivators, or men and women share equally in cultivation (Martin and Voorhies 1975:339–343; O'Kelly and Carney 1986:66). Martin and Voorhies and O'Kelly and Carney suggest that among herders with a high dependence on crops, variations found in the gender division of labor may be a result of the influence of the parent cultural community out of which pastoral society developed. Hence it is instructive to acknowledge the cultures of neighbors. However, the reverse also holds true. Cultural flows are multidirectional, and Tuareg influences are also present in their neighboring sedentary farming cultures. Thus it is difficult to determine the direction of cultural and social influences, and it is not easy to generalize that all nomadic cultures with a horticultural background are more likely to share tasks, or that all those with an agricultural background are more likely to assign primary productive tasks to men.

O'Kelly and Carney (1986:66) argue that gender division of labor within many pastoral societies is "tipped toward male dominance" of economically productive tasks. These authors explain this in terms of the strength required to handle large animals. Males tend to be exclusive herders of large animals. Females may, however, herd smaller animals and serve as dairy maids for large and small species. Women and children contribute by gathering food, carrying water, and processing byproducts such as milk, wool, hides, and dung. But the lack of firm differentiation between domestic and public spheres encourages gender egalitarianism. Where women have some economic control, women's status may be raised. Boulding (1976:288–299) argues that women participate more fully in the total life of these societies than they do in settled agricultural communities. But Martin and Voorhies (1975) argue that male dominance of economic production gives rise to male dominance in the wider culture and social structure of pastoral societies. Lois Beck, on the other hand, found a flexible division of labor, economic interdependence between genders, and a low degree of gender segregation among the Qashqai of Iran (Beck in Beck and Keddie 1978:365–367). Furthermore, because of the small size of independent households of these pastoralists, males and females were partners in economically independent units, and neither males nor females formed strong separate solidarity groups.

Many authors agree that, however diverse the forms it takes, the division of labor among herders does not create a sharp dichotomy between domestic and public spheres. Women's tasks are more likely to take place in camp than men's tasks, but they do not isolate women in the household. Much women's work is done in cooperation with other women. Both men and women participate in collective work patterns with other members of the same gender. Camps are typically divided into women's spaces and men's spaces, but almost all activities are carried out in the open, avoiding development of private domestic spheres for women versus public spheres for men (O'Kelly and Carney 1986:67). Women's work may be household work, but it is public household work; public/domestic domains thus emerge as overly rigid and bound to western cultures.[4]

In many pastoral nomadic societies, ownership and control over the disposition of livestock appear to be predominantly in male hands. However, females are sometimes at least nominal owners of some livestock through inheritance, dowries, or purchase (O'Kelly and Carney 1986:68). But even owners of livestock cannot usually dispose freely of their animals: they are bound by an intricate web of kinship-based exchanges, which requires giving periodically large numbers of animals to close kin, as bridewealth to the bride's family, dowries to the groom, and as compensation for violation of certain rules, for example, homicide (Evans-Pritchard 1956; Hutchinson 1996) and adultery (Rasmussen 1998a). Furthermore, certain animals in a herd may be held jointly with others or in their interest, and are subject to many limitations on use and disposal. Males who control large herds thus do not necessarily derive significant economic power from these herds; rather, use rights are important considerations. But large herds bring prestige and influence to owners.

Other factors influencing gender are the defense needs and warfare practices of herders and patricentric kinship systems. In terms of Peggy Sanday's (1981:181) typology, many pastoralists appear to fall under the rubric of "real male dominance," because in most cases the environment is sufficiently dangerous for the society to depend on the strength and aggressiveness of their men for survival. Sanday argues that under such conditions of stress, for the sake of social and cultural survival, women "accept real male dominance." Once again, the Tuareg data suggest modifications of this hypothesis. Tuareg men's frequent absence from home in past raiding and more recent separatist warfare against the central state governments of Mali and Niger, and also men's peaceful trading, have encouraged, indeed necessitated women's independence in some domains of activity (education of children and work). However, some high-status men remain at home and control official political decisions. Thus a warrior aristocracy does not produce gender inequality in all respects; rather, there is a mixed bag here. In fact, some authors report legends of "warrior queens" in Tuareg and other pastoralist nomadic cultures (Boulding 1976:303–312; Rodd 1926:170). While difficult to verify, they suggest that women's elevated position in the class structure may modify their gender roles; thus class cross-cuts gender (Ortner and Whitehead 1981; Di Leonardo 1990).

The pastoral-nomadic/gender relationship is therefore complex, and defies facile generalizations or typologies. There are numerous cross-cultural contradictions and forces that tend toward both gender egalitarianism and male dominance. These suggest the importance of examining local cultures and histories.

THE TUAREG CASE

Tuareg Gender Roles and Relations Between the Sexes: Women's Status and Prestige

Tuareg pastoral nomads today are predominantly seminomadic and practice, to varying degrees, mixed subsistence patterns. Most Tuareg live in the central Sahara and along its borders, in the Sahel. More nomadic Tuareg herd camels, sheep, goats, cattle, and donkeys. They are Muslims of Berber origin. Most Tuareg of the Air Mountain region in Niger originated in the Fezzan and other areas of Libya. Eight politically distinct descent groups (drum groups) all speak mutually intelligible dialects of a Berber-derived language, Tamajaq, and are designated by geographic region. Two of these, Kel Ajjer and Kel Ahaggar, are the northern Tuareg in Algeria. The other six—Kel Adar, Kel Air, and Kel Geres, Iwllemmeden Kel Dennek, and Iwllemmeden Kel Ataram, and Kel Tademaket—live on the southern fringes of desert in Mali, Niger, and Burkina Faso, and are the southern Tuareg. Within the Kel Air are the political confederations of Kel Ewey, Kel Ferwan, and Kel Fadey, those groups emphasized in the present essay. Precolonial social organization was divided into free nobles, religious scholars, tributaries, smiths/artisans, and servile peoples. In most regions, slavery was abolished by the mid-twentieth century.

In general, many Tuareg women enjoy considerable rights and privileges. They are not sequestered, do not veil their faces (although Tuareg men do), and have much social and economic independence and freedom of movement. Separation of the sexes is relatively minimal. Men and women regularly meet and socialize in public. Women are singers and musicians, and organizers of many social events, such as drum playing and dance gatherings, which feature much flirting and courtship. Throughout their lives, many Tuareg women enjoy freedom of choice in sexual involvement and actively pursue romantic preferences (King 1903:280; Rodd 1926:174–175). They may regularly have male visitors, though not always lovers, when their husbands are absent (Rodd 1926:174–175); Nicolas 1946:225; Lhote 1955:335; Murphy 1964; Claudot-Hawad 1993).

Although many of these gender roles and relationships apply to most Tuareg, there is the need to refine and specify, rather than generalize, interpretation of some aspects of Tuareg women's status. Many Tuareg groups display variation in gender arrangements according to relative degrees of nomadism and sedentarization, devotion to official Islam, and regional and confederational differences, as well as age, kinship roles, and social stratum origins. The Kel Ewey *ineslemen* clans of maraboutique Islamic scholars, for example, attempt to control their women slightly more by placing greater emphasis upon virginity and application of Koranic inheritance laws. Even among these clans, however, women own property, are not secluded, and go about unveiled and relatively freely visit and receive male visitors, and although extramarital affairs are less tolerated, men, not women, are fined or punished in reprisals (Rasmussen 1994, 1998a, 1998b).

There are gender transformations over the life course: for example, age and marital status make a difference in women's status, prestige, and property ownership, as well as work and economic independence. Older women enjoy security as mothers-in-law and grandmothers. They specialize in herbal medicine, divination, and bone-setting healing specialties. Urbanization and nation-state policies also influence Tuareg women's status, roles, prestige, and economic bases of power. For example, much property in the Saharan town of Agadez is not independently owned by the married woman, but merged together with that of her husband in civic records.

There are, moreover, seasonal variations in residential spatial arrangements that symbolically convey gender-related socioeconomic processes. In seminomadic carvanning Air villages, the basic residential unit, *eghiwan,* is highly flexible, undergoing fission and fusion according to season and subsistence strategy. Men are often gone from five to seven months a year on caravan trade and migrant labor. Young, unmarried girls and older postchildbearing-age women often go out and establish temporary camps with their herds, intermittently for four months during the dry season; elderly women in the rainy season leave for several weeks to gather leaves and roots and grasses for sauces, and herbal healers are often absent on trips to collect medicines from trees on Mount Bagzan.

During the cold, dry caravanning season, women construct their tent doors to face outward, toward the compounds of their female relatives, the more matrifocal or matricentric space reflecting these women's greater cooperation and sharing at this time. In contrast, in the hot and rainy seasons while many men are at home, the women close these doors and construct doors opening onto the interior courtyard of the nuclear-household compound; the emphasis here is more patrifocal, and patricentric, reflecting greater focus within the nuclear household. Ties with maternal female kin become less emphasized during this time (women visit each other less, and do more housework such as cooking within their own kitchen while husbands are at home).

Most women prefer monogamous unions, and polygyny is a rare occurrence, except among some prominent chiefs, Islamic scholars, and prosperous, more sedentarized gardeners and merchants. I frequently heard women in monogamous marriages tease those who were co-wives about polygyny, and many women initiate divorce upon husbands' attempts to contract polygynous marriages. Polygynous men try to avoid co-wives' jealousy by installing wives in separate compounds and even distant villages. Co-wives never share cooking facilities or sleep in the same compound. A widow or divorcee may become a household head in advanced age; if younger, she usually returns to her parental household.

There is a tendency toward late marriages and preference for political marriages within the descent group or *tawsit* and chiefly among families in many noble groups. The idea in Tuareg marriage is an enduring relationship based upon romantic love. Tuareg often say they prefer to marry cross-cousins because the joking relationship that ordinarily obtains between them is conducive to a strong marital bond (Bernus 1981:149). On the other hand, some such marriages do not last because some Tuareg say close cousins continue to "feel like brother and sister" (Nicolaisen 1963; Murphy 1964). As the marriage stabilizes, the joking relationship is supposed to become a more serious relationship of mutual respect, with some aspects of a respect/reserve relationship in public between the spouses. Name avoidance does not entail wife-to-husband deference among the Tuareg as Schlegel (1975:167-168) inferred from the data available on Tuareg through the HRAF (Human Relations Area Files). The use of teknonymy and sobriquets is symmetric, applying to both sexes. The term for a new spouse is "friend," and later on, "wife" and "husband." Wife-to-husband deference is not a feature of Tuareg society, as it is among the Hausa, for example, where a wife ritually kneels when serving her husband. Tuareg women do not ritually kneel, bow their heads, or engage in any other extreme gestures of subservience to their husbands. Husbands, at least ideally, should regularly "defer" to their wives' wishes about as much as wives to husbands, in a mutual-respect relationship. One man, for example, commented that he had been considering polygyny, but had decided to refrain from taking a co-wife in deference to his wife's wishes, because he "respected" her. A woman may show her contempt for her husband's behavior by returning to her mother's camp, removing the tent and its contents, and leaving the man without a shelter. Direct expression of anger on the part of a man toward his wife is considered shameful.

The creation of a home and its furnishing in nomadic societies is usually part of the dowry institution: this occurs in the context of marriage. Tuareg women receive their nuptial tent as part of their dowry. It is constructed communally on the evening of the wedding by elderly female relatives of the bride, and torn down and reconstructed to be larger on each successive evening of the seven-day wedding ritual (Ramussen 1997). A tent thus comes into being with the wedding ritual, and is a metaphor for the institution of the family. Because descent is bilateral and the tent is matrilineally defined and transmitted, the tent also becomes a metaphor for matriliny and an allegory for maternity (Prussin 1995:92). A woman has the same status in her own tent as she has in her mother's; she is at home in both. Conversely, a man is a guest in his wife's tent.

The wedding tent, which after the marriage will be the tent of the newly married couple's residence, is erected near the camp of the bride's family. For seven days, this tent remains empty during the day, occupied by the couple only at night. The two spouses subsequently may choose to move with their tent to the husband's family camp. Since the tent is inherited matrilineally, it moves from one camp to another, as when the bride's relatives bring her tent to her husband's camp or village. An unmarried man usually lives in a straw and mat conical building called *tettrem*, or in more sedentarized communities, in an adobe mud house. These single men's buildings are located either within or just adjacent to their parents' compound. Traditionally, the only men who owned their own tent were noble drum-group chiefs. So Tuareg men and women do not inhabit tents in the same way. In general, only a married woman can have a tent. Thus the number of tents in a camp or village generally indicates the number of married women.

In Tuareg culture, the nuptial tent is therefore women's property, brought to the marriage as dowry, a central symbol in the wedding, and used as the married couple's sleeping room, but also much more: it symbolizes the traditional ideal of monogamy. Recently, however, many men have been constructing adobe mud houses that the married man owns. These houses now often stand next to the tent owned by a married woman within the married couple's household compound (Rasmussen 1994, 1996, 1997). The more nomadic Tuareg groups still count women as owners of compounds, as well as tents, in identifying the household compounds. But the semisedentarized Kel Ewey have begun to identify compounds by the names of husbands, as belonging to men, as they do the men's adobe mud houses in many of these compounds, standing next to the women's tents. These processes indicate some important changes in gender roles, status, and power upon sedentarization, which disrupts the property balance between the sexes. To what extent, then, does the tent confer women's control? The key issue, as Moore (1988:52-53) points out, is the relationship between women's productive and reproductive roles, in the descent and inheritance system.

Legal/Jural Rights, Property, Descent, and Inheritance

The Tuareg official political structure is male-dominated. Among the more nomadic groups, the camping group (*eghiwan*) is an extended family headed by a male elder (*amghar*). In more sedentarized, seminomadic groups this term *eghiwan* refers to the village or hamlet, which may include a number of families, many of whom are related, and today often also includes households whose members vary in occupation and degree of nomadism, sometimes combining or alternating between several different subsistence forms (for example, a man of diverse social stratum origins might practice caravan trade, herding, oasis gardening, and migrant labor within a single lifetime, in different seasons). Allied descent groups comprise a drum group or confederation under the power of a drum chief called *ettebel*, a legitimate male successor from the dominant noble group within it. The confederation is socially stratified into noble and vassal named groups.

Most Tuareg descent groups are bilateral, combining patrilineal influences from Islam with local matrilineal institutions. Many descent groups trace their origins matrilineally to female ancestresses or culture heroines, although some more devoutly Muslim groups and men in general tend to downplay these ancestresses and emphasize patrilineal descent and male ancestors or culture heroes. For example, many Kel Ewey Tuareg men and marabouts in rural Air communities where I conducted research mentioned Boulkhou, a patrilineal ancestor of the current *ettebel*, as their important founder. He had sunk the first well, built a mosque, and resisted enemies in battles in that region. By contrast, many women tended to emphasize Tagurmat, the female ancestor of the Kel Igurmaden descent group within the Kel Ewey confederation, who in a myth gave birth to twin daughters who founded the professions of herbalism and Islamic/Koranic healing. The Kel Fadey say their people descend from two sisters who came from the east, bringing with them livestock, herds, and a large wooden drum (the drum, kept by the chief's wife, is used to call the tribal sections together for political or military action) (Worley 1992:56). The Kel Fadey reckon their most important kinship connections through women (matrilineally), so a child's closest relationships are usually with his or her mother's people, especially the mother's brother. In the past, both property inheritance and succession to the chieftainship followed maternal lines, from a man to his sister's sons and daughters.

A recurring question in Tuareg ethnography has been the extent to which Tuareg practice matrilineal inheritance and descent and succession. In matriliny, theoretically, mothers and sisters of heirs enjoy status. A problem here is the use of the term to mean certain institutions, or "society" and "culture" in general (Oxby 1977). Also often ignored are variations among the different Tuareg groups and according to social context. Thus the issue becomes, which kin links are most important and what factors other than kinship are important in determining relationships between the generations and the sexes? Descent group (*tawsit*) allegiance is, in practice, through the mother. Ideally, however, political office passes from father to son in all groups but the Kel Geres, where it goes from maternal uncle to sister's son. Hence both matrilateral and patrilateral kin ties are important. There are also important criteria apart from kinship in political leadership: for example, wealth and personal qualities of leadership.

Women's property is passed down mainly from mother to daughter; men's, from father to son. Objects acquired by women before marriage include jewelry, blankets, a bed, other household items, and sometimes cloth and sandals. In the past, noble women brought a slave to their married household;

today, rural noble women still inherit an attached smith/artisan client family. Inheritance of livestock is predominantly Koranic: daughters receive one-third to one-half of sons' shares. Children are considered, among most Air Tuareg, more important heirs than spouses and siblings. If there are only daughters, a brother receives the son's share. The mother's brother is a less significant figure in some groups than in others, but everywhere the mother's brother/ sister's son tie features, at minimum, affection, and frequent gifts, and security in assistance. The sibling tie in fact sometimes competes with the husband-wife tie. Each spouse, regardless of postmarital residence, if possible spends much time during the day (for example, eating meals) at the residence of his/her own kin. Individuals often try to return to maternal kin in latter years of life. Women often refuse to follow husbands to remote places, for example, to start new gardens, and divorce often ensues (although this may be changing recently). Men are present with their sisters during the funeral sacrifice of meat in the event of their sisters' children's death. An older sister is described as "like a mother" to her younger brother; older brothers are supposed to take care of younger sisters, accompanying them on travel and assisting them in legal cases. Brothers and sisters are supposed to be allies, and brothers ideally should look out for sisters' legal and other interests. Often, brothers do support sisters upon the divorce, and also contribute to the support of widowed sisters' children. The father's sibling group is equated with the father, as a source of authority and possible conflict; the mother's sibling group, by contrast, is a source of love and aid, generosity, and support. A man has the right to take domestic animals from his true and classificatory mother's brothers. He must inform them of this act through a third party.

Some Tuareg say, "It is the stomach that colors the child." Another source of shared maternal identity is breast milk: those who are nursed by the same woman cannot marry. Possession by spirits not curable by Koranic verses is believed to be inherited matrilineally

from mother to daughter in breast milk. Formerly, matrilineal clans were associated with specific totems. Sultan Goma allotted land to noble women in these clans in order to prevent it from passing out of the clan's ownership (Nicolaisen 1963; Norris 1972,1975). Many Tuareg believe that the maternal nephew inherits intelligence from his maternal uncle. But Kel Ewey do not use separate kinship terms for a maternal versus paternal nephew; they refer to both as *tegazay*.

Nowadays, however, the concept of maternal kinship identity tends to be submerged in most legal practice. Koranic and patrilineal influence extend to naming, ideas about children's affiliation and identity, and marriage. Men refer to the offspring of a polygynous man and one of his co-wives as the "children of men." They tend to disparage an older form of naming a girl "daughter of" (*oult*) as "only done with an illegitimate child." Rural women are now called Madame plus the name of husband's father as surname, in postal addresses, clinic rosters, and school registration. Illegitimacy is considered shameful, antisocial, and greatly stigmatizing to the mother, A child belongs to the descent group or clan of his or her father. Men insist that the secret, Tamajaq name which older female relatives bestow on the child in the unofficial naming ritual the evening before the official Islamic naming by the father and marabout at the mosque, is "not important, it means nothing," but women dispute this, saying the latter name is as important to the child's identity as the Arabic, Koranic name. Women's property is sometimes subject to dispute and challenge in Koranic-based rulings by marabouts. For example, although a woman has the right to eject her husband from her tent, a woman's bridewealth is only reimbursed to the person the marabout rules is not at fault in divorce; many marabouts rule the woman at fault if she requests divorce to protest polygyny.

Nonetheless women's opinions are highly valued, and they are normally consulted by men on decisions that affect the life of the camp or village (Bernus 1981:146–147). Yet there are some contexts in which women defer to some men: namely, before Islamic scholars and important chiefs, and toward elders in general, particularly those on the patrilineal side. Female herbal medicine women, for example, referred patients to marabouts for diagnosis of illness, more often than vice versa. But women participate in public discussions over matters of concern to the group, represent themselves in legal cases, and exert great influence in the public sphere. For example, a smith/artisan woman in Agadez held a position as head of a smith/artisan women's cooperative, and also gave radio addresses on women's health issues.

Tuareg women generally enjoy a high degree of economic independence, since they own significant property in livestock. Under optimum conditions, therefore, livestock does constitute great security for women. But this can fluctuate according to climate and nation-state conditions. During droughts and armed conflicts, many herds were diminished, lost, or dispersed. Elderly women often survive off herds of donkeys, which are easy to care for (only requiring salt licks and free roaming for water) and which they sell off gradually at markets. A number of authors (Bernus 1981; Casajus 1987; Claudot-Hawad 1993; Keenan 1977; Lhote 1955; Murphy 1964), correctly I believe, have noted the importance of a custom among the Tuareg that allows women to acquire more property in livestock, and sometimes date palms, than they would normally have right to under Koranic law. This practice, known as *akh hudderan*, allows an individual to make a pre-inheritance gift of livestock to female relatives, usually daughters, sisters, and nieces, which they then own and control corporately. This property cannot be sold or otherwise disposed of.

Additionally, Tuareg women accumulate livestock through important gifts *(alkhalal)* from both parents and other relatives after birth, which form the basis of their own herds. Women may receive outright gifts of livestock from consanguine kin throughout their lives, and in all marriages after the first,

it is usually the wife herself who accepts the bridewealth *(taggalt)*. As a result of these gifts and pre-inheritance practices, therefore, some women under optimum conditions (of plentiful pasture, regular rainfall, cooperative male kin and spouses, and peace) may indeed become quite wealthy in livestock. Even in the recent droughts and warfare, some women manage to support themselves. In more prosperous and peaceful eras, it was not uncommon for a woman to be wealthier than her husband. But it is difficult to assess the extent to which women still enjoy these ideal property arrangements, in the light of recent upheavals. More nomadic nobles, in particular, have lost much property over the past twenty years. But these losses affect both sexes, not solely women. There are strong pressures to settle down and practice oasis gardening more extensively, and there is evidence that women's bases of property are increasingly altered by all these processes. In semisedentarized communities, for example, men's houses complicate property disputes on divorce. For example, after the divorce of Aghaly and Mariama (pseudonyms), Aghaly retained his mud house and Mariama her tent in the same compound on the same land. At first, the ex-husband did not want to leave his house. The couple took their case to the secular courts in Agadez, which ruled a compromise: each party changed the door on his or her respective structure, so that the buildings faced the exterior, rather than the interior courtyard. Aghaly ate his meals at his mother's home. This solution divided the property and also saved the divorced couple from daily interaction. Aghaly eventually moved back into his old house adjacent to his parents' compound in a neighboring village (Rasmussen 1996:18).

Some married women residing virilocally (with the husband's family) have very different spatial and social arrangements in their new home, which affect work and authority patterns. In initial postmarital uxorilocality (residence with the wife's family), most visiting and sharing of resources and work occurs between maternally related women (mothers and sisters and daughters); whereas in virilo-cal residence, the wife is more isolated from her own kin, and more dependent upon her husband and his family. She is also subject to a strict reserve relationship with her parents-in-law. She also obtains a bit less assistance with household tasks from her sisters-in-law than she would from her own sisters.

Sexual Division of Labor

Domestic work in more nomadic groups takes a minimum of women's time. Mothers can support pregnancy and breastfeed chil-dren while performing the physically demand-ing work of pastoralism, milking the livestock, and packing and moving the tents they own. One noble woman in a seminomadic village, the daughter of a local chief, has managed her own small store since 1997. Another woman has a small restaurant on a road from Agadez into the rural area. Older children usually watch small children and toddlers. Infants may be carried on the mother's back while she is working. There is little house cleaning to contend with. The tent needs to have the wall mats adjusted several times a day as the direction of the wind changes (Worley 1988:278), and it is swept out occasionally. Fresh clean sand is gathered at intervals for the tent floor. Grinding and sifting and crush-ing millet and other cereals is arduous work that all women, nowadays, do (in the past, slaves did this labor). In nomadic Kel Fadey camps, Worley reported that this task takes approximately two hours a day (Worley 1988: 278); in the seminomadic villages of the Kel Ewey Tuareg, I noticed, pounding millet took up far more of women's time, up to approxi-mately 90 percent of their day's work. In more sedentarized communities, therefore, women's time is taken up more extensively with food-processing work within the com-pound than is more nomadic women's time; these latter, by contrast, often circulate more widely away from the compound herding their own livestock at outlying pastures. Other cereal grains were traditionally crushed on a flat stone. Recently, several mills have been built in this area and women no longer crush

corn and wheat on flat stone as I had observed them do earlier in my research (in the 1970s and 1980s). In all Tuareg rural communities, women's communal work par-ties do mat and tent construction and repair, together in reciprocal gatherings called *gaya* (derived from Hausa).

Subsistence work regularly takes many women outside the village or camp for the collection of firewood, gathering of wild grains, berries, and other plants, and the daily drawing of water at a well, which may be sev-eral miles from the camp. Women view these tasks differently, however: some welcome tasks such as herding and gathering for the freedom they confer; others, however, view going to the well and herding as hot, arduous tasks. In semisedentarized communities around Mount Bagzan, some women are described as "housewives" (called by the French term *menageres*). These women have given up herding (though not always herd ownership), and have relegated this task to kinspersons. A few gardeners' wives have even given up their tents. Reasons given for this included scarcity of materials, and also no fur-ther need for a tent, in the presence of a hus-band's house. But most women still own and use tents, even alongside men's houses, and still own herds. Some women married to gar-deners are giving up herding and (if smiths) leatherwork, as well. Very few women individ-ually own gardens, which are traditionally inherited and owned mostly by men (though a few women have date-palms through matri-lineal *akh huderan* inheritance). Upon herds' depletion in drought, theft, or war, women are at a disadvantage because livestock herds are more difficult to reconstitute than oasis gardens. Traditionally, planting was done by men and harvesting done only by elderly women; recently, however, over the summer of 1998 I noticed some hints of change in these patterns. A development agency had established a women's garden cooperative, and some women had begun enclosing and gardening in this designated space, known as the "women's garden (enclosure)" (*afarag n tchidoden*). In order to prevent erosion, a fence was being constructed: each woman is paid an amount to participate in the work party, provide wood, and construct the fence. A female "president" supervises this project, in which the women take up a collection (250 CFA or approximately 50 cents each) from each household to build a well (cost: 25,000 CFA, approximately $50). When the well is completed, the project organization will give the group an animal. Women have also recently been involved in projects selling millet on the market in Agadez. It remains to be seen how extensively Tuareg women will pursue gardening tasks on these semisedentarized oases. This may constitute a significant departure from women's traditional work patterns, and become a new property base and source of economic power.

Many women who own animals, however, continue to herd small livestock—goats, sheep, and donkeys, and on occasion, camels when men are absent. Women milk the small livestock and process the milk into cheese and butter, consuming them within the household and also selling some of the surplus to travelers and other local residents. Women's subsistence work is considered critical in Tuareg pastoral production, and they must be capable of taking over some of the men's work on occasion when men are absent. In the 1960s, 1970s, and 1980s, for example, many young men left in exile from the droughts of 1973 and 1984, in search of jobs. In 1990, the Tuareg rebellion broke out. Therefore many young marriageable men became marginalized economically and politically, resisted some elders' efforts to arrange matches, or found it difficult to raise bridewealth to marry at all. A few men are beginning to sell Tuareg silver and leatherwork items abroad in international art fairs. Other men work on farms in Italy and Libya. Male migrant workers are forbidden by Libya to send or bring money home to Niger, however. So they must hide it, and/or wives must support their families on their own at home. Many women, not solely smith/artisans, do this by making basketry and embroidery for sale in craft shops in Niger and France,

though very few Tuareg women travel to France.

Smith/artisan men and women derive much income from arts and crafts. Metal and woodworking are smith men's work; most leatherworking is smith women's work. Women of diverse social origins tan hides, but mostly smith/artisan women cut and embroider them. Smith/artisan women in rural areas obtain cash and food gifts through leatherworking and rites-of-passage services for nobles. In Saharan towns, women smiths continue to do leatherwork, but with fewer raw materials, which cost more in the sedentarized setting, and also fewer customers, for demand there is lower than in rural communities where herders and gardeners need hide containers and implements, and tourists and functionaries buy more metal jewelry than leatherwork. Recently, some religious and human rights and aid organizations in France purchased millet while it was at a low price and gave it to Air Tuareg groups to store during the period of higher millet prices. These organizations also bring art objects made in workshops (by both men and women specialists) to sell in France at fairs. They sponsor women's basketry and weaving workshops, where artists modify traditional designs for sale in France.

CONCLUSIONS

Socioeconomic and Political Changes; Implications; Issues and Questions Raised for Future Trends

One of the key changes affecting the organization of nomadic pastoralism is the nomads' loss of autonomy after incorporation into sedentary nation-states, in the wake of the military advantage of sedentary states and revolutions in transportation technology during the past century (Barfield 1993:207). Upon sedentarization, there is disruption of traditional ties and undermining of important sources of defense and security. As men are increasingly obliged to travel as migrant laborers and children are sent to school, the workload of women extends from their traditional routines to a heavier involvement in supplementary tasks. In Niger, colonial and postcolonial eras saw pastoralist border zones farmed, depleting the soil and disrupting ecological and socioeconomic balance and relations between groups and lands. Mobility has been curtailed, censuses, schools and taxes imposed by colonial governments, and by postcolonial central state governments. Sometimes these have imposed a patrilineal bias. Tuareg are unique among pastoralists in the enduring significance their matrilineal institutions have for gender roles and relations between the sexes. Although these remain significant in the bilateral system, there is evidence that matriliny is under duress. This is shown by the transformations in property balance described in this article and elsewhere (Rasmussen 1994,1996,1997,1998). It is also shown in Gast's (1992: 151–172) description of Tuareg cultural encounters with more powerful neighbors: nation-state policies toward Tuareg nomads brought many workers, functionaries, soldiers, and tourists into rural Tuareg communities. Often, they were ignorant of and disrespectful toward traditional beliefs and practices; for example, they misunderstood evening festival and courtship customs as opportunities to seduce women, whereas traditionally, Tuareg cultural values emphasize music, poetry, flirting, visits, and conversation without necessarily including sexual intercourse. Some camps along routes became labeled by outsiders as places of license and prostitution (Gast 1996:169). In some respects, then, Tuareg women appear to have become the wards of men in encounters with outside males, and in national systems of registration/naming, food relief and medical distribution programs, taxation and census counts. However, as shown, there are also new opportunities—in new cooperative agencies and projects offering some benefits for women, as well as men.

The question raised is how nomadic pastoral Tuareg women actively respond to forces of sedentization, urbanization, and nationalism. Do they gain or lose? How? For example, women can use the urban setting to escape from an extended household ruled over by a mother-in-law. It is therefore hazardous to generalize too sweepingly about pastoralism, women, and gender, or to base observations solely upon structural as opposed to situational meanings and practices. Pastoral nomadic societies display a wide range of variation in economics, culture, and gender relations, and divergent transformations. Rather than building models and typologies, anthropologists need to deconstruct and refine pastoral and gender-related categories and processes.

NOTES

1. In these projects—on spirit possession, aging and the life course, herbal healers, and rural and urban smith/artisans, I gratefully acknowledge assistance from Fulbright Hays (1983,1998); Wenner Gren Foundation for Anthropological Research (1991,1995,1998); Social Science Research Council (1995); National Geographic Society for Research and Exploration (1995,1998); Indiana University (1983), and University of Houston (1991).

2. For example, Mohanty (1992) criticizes western feminists for essentializing women's experience regardless of race, class, or nationality. Mohanty faults western feminists for universalizing women's oppression, as well. She argues that western femininsts psychologize complex and often contradictory historical and cultural realities that mark differences among women. Differences among women need to be engaged rather than transcended. She also warns against globalizing women as victims; there is the need to acknowledge women's active agency. Yet feminists in these areas are diverse; they come from various schools of thought depending on their national and cultural orientations.

3. Despite very valuable work on women and gender in the Muslim world, there have been some tendencies to deploy "Islam" and "Muslim" as a gloss for very diverse cultural interpretations of official religion, their sharing of common themes notwithstanding. Mernissi's (1987) famous analysis of gender relations in Moroccan society is complemented and enriched by

perspectives from scholars on other Muslim societies in Africa, for example Afonja (1986).

4. Pastoralist societies therefore break down the assumed dichotomy of private/public or domestic/public domains, a tenacious concept in some early feminist anthropology (Rosaldo and Lamphere 1974) later critiqued in more recent anthropology of gender studies (Ong 1987).

5. These observations raise interesting issues. For example, traditionally, men's honor depended upon women's praise music upon their victorious return from battles; thus women control men's reputations. Women's praise songs of men often welcomed them after successful raids or migrant labor or caravan trade, but women could also mock and scorn men who returned less victorious or without money. Women still hold power over men's reputations, but many men have not returned victorious or wealthy in recent years. Some men have attempted to find social recognition through participation in the 1990–95 nationalist/separatist military conflict. Much new music of the Tuareg rebellion composed by both sexes, as well as women's traditional songs, perhaps is responding to these new predicaments and in effect, conveys men's and women's efforts to reconstruct social prestige and independent socioeconomic status in Tuareg gender-role relationships.

REFERENCES CITED

Afonja, S. 1986. Changing Modes of Production and the Sexual Division of Labor among the Yoruba. In *Women's Work*, E. Leacock and H. Safa, eds. South Hadley, MA: Bergin and Garvey.

Barfield, Thomas J. 1993. *The Nomadic Alternative.* Upper Saddle River, NJ: Prentice Hall.

Barlow, Tani. 1996. Theorizing Women: Funu, Guojia, Jiating. (Chinese Women, Chinese State, Chinese Family). In *Feminism and History*, Joan W. Scott, ed. Oxford: Oxford University Press.

Barth, Fredrik. 1961. *Nomads of South Persia: The Basseri Tribe of the Khamseh Confederacy.* Oslo: Oslo University Press.

Beck, Lois. 1978. Women among Qashqai Nomadic Pastoralist in Iran. In *Women in the Muslim World*, Lois Beck and Nikki Keddie, eds. Cambridge, MA.: Harvard University Press.

Bernus, Edmond. 1981. *Touaregs Nigeriens: Unité Culturelle et Diversité Regionale d'un Peuple Pasteur.*

Paris: Office de la Recherche Scientifique et Technique Outre-Mer.

Boulding, Elise. 1976. *The Underside of History.* Boulder, CO: Westview Press.

Butler, Judith. 1990. *Gender Trouble.* New York: Routledge Press.

Casajus, Dominique. 1987. *La Tente dans l'Essuf.* London and Paris: Cambridge.

Claudot-Hawad, Hélène 1993. *Les Touaregs: Portrait en Fragments.* Aix-en-Provence: Edisud.

Davison, Jean. 1997. *Gender, Lineage, and Ethnicity in Southern Africa.* Boulder, CO: Westview Press.

di Lauretis, Teresa. 1984. *Alice Doesn't: Feminism, Semiotics, Cinema.* Bloomington: Indiana University Press.

Di Leonardo, Michaela. 1990. *Gender at the Crossroads of Knowledge.* Berkeley: University of California Press.

Evans-Pritchard, E.E. 1956 *Nuer Religion*, Oxford: Oxford University Press.

Flax, Jane. 1993. *Disputed Subjects: Essays on Psychoanalysis, Politics, and Philosophy.* New York: Routledge.

Gaidzanwa, R. B. 1985. I*mages of Women in Zimbabwean Literature.* Harare: College Press.

Gast, Marcel. 1992. Relations Amoureuses chez les Kel Ahaggar. In *Amour, Phantasmes, et Sociétés en Afrique du Nord et au Sahara*, Tassadit Yacine, ed. Paris: L'Harmattan-Awal.

Hutchinson, Sharon. 1996. *Nuer Dilemmas.* Berkeley: Universityof California Press

Keenan, Jeremy. 1977. *Tuareg: People of Ahaggar.* New York: St. Martins Press.

King, William J. Harding. 1903. *A Search for the Masked Tawaraks.* London: Smith, Elder and Co.

Kondo, Dorinne. 1990. *Crafting Selves.* Chicago: University of Chicago Press.

Lhote, Henri. 1955. *Les Touaregs du Hoggar.* Paris: Payot.

Mannathoko, C. 1992. Feminist Theories and the Study of Gender in Southern Africa. In *Gender in Southern Africa*, R. Meena, ed. Harare: SAPES Books.

Martin, M. Kay, and Barbara Voorhies 1975. *Female of the Species.* New York: Columbia University Press.

Meena, R. 1992. Gender Research/Studies in Southern Africa: An Overview. In *Gender in Southern Africa: Conceptual and Theoretical Issues*, R. Meena, ed. Harare: SAPES Books.

Mernissi, Fatima. 1987. Beyond the Veil: Male-Female Dynamics in *Modern Muslim Society.* Bloomington: Indiana University Press.

Mohanty, C.T. 1992. Feminist Encounter: Locating the Politics of Experience. In *Destabilizing Theory: Contemporary Feminist Debates*, M. Barrett and A. Phillips, eds. Palo Alto: Stanford University Press.

Moore, Henrietta. 1988. *Feminism and Anthropology.* Minneapolis: University of Minnesota Press.

Murphy, Robert. 1964. Social Distance and the Veil. *American Anthropologist* 66:1257–1274.

Nicolaisen, Johannes. 1963. *Ecology and Culture of the Pastoral Tuareg.* Copenhagen: Royal National Museum.

Nicolas, Francis. 1946. *Tamesna: Les Ioullemmeden de l'Est, ou Tuareg Kel Dinnik, Cercle de T'awa— Colonie du Niger.* Paris: Imprimerie Nationale.

Norris, H.T. 1972. *Saharan Myth and Saga.* Oxford: Clarendon Press.

———. 1975. *The Tuaregs: Their Islamic Legacy and its Diffusion in the Sahel.* Warminster, England: Aris and Phillips.

O'Kelly, Charlotte G. and Larry S. Carney 1986. *Women and Men in Society: Cross-Cultural Perspectives on Gender Stratification.* Belmont, CA: Wadsworth Publishing Company.

Ong, Aihwa. 1987. *Spirits of Resistance and Capitalist Discipline: Factory Women in Malaysia.* Albany: State University of New York Press.

Ortner, Sherry. and Harriet Whitehead, eds. 1981. *Sexual Meanings.* Cambridge: Cambridge University Press.

Oxby, Clare. 1978. Sexual Division and Slavery in a Tuareg Community. Ph.D. dissertation, London School of Economics.

Probyn, Elspeth. 1990. Travels in the Postmodern: Making Sense of the Local. In *Feminism/Postmodernism*, Linda J. Nicholson, ed. New York: Routledge.

Prussin, LaBelle. 1995. *African Nomadic Architecture: Space, Place, and Gender.* Washington, DC: Smithsonian Institution Press.

Rasmussen, Susan. 1992. Disputed Boundaries: Tuareg Discourse on Class and Ethnicity. *Ethnology* 31: 351–366.

———. 1994. Female Sexuality, Social Reproduction, and Medical Intervention: Kel Ewey Tuareg Perspectives. *Culture, Medicine, and Psychiatry* 18:433–462.

———. 1995. *Spirit Possession and Personhood among the Kel Ewey Tuareg.* Cambridge: Cambridge University Press.

———. 1996. Tuareg Tent as Field Space and Cultural Symbol. *Anthropological Quarterly,* 69:14–27.

———. 1997. *The Poetics and Politics of Tuareg Aging: Life Course and Personal Destiny in Niger.* DeKalb, IL: Northern Illinois University Press.

———1998a. Within the Tent and at the Crossroads: Travel and Gender Identity among the Tuareg of Niger. *Ethos* 26:153–182.

———1998b. Only Women Know Trees: Medicine Women and the Role of Herbal Healing in Tuareg Culture. *Journal of Anthropological Research* 54:147–171.

Rodd, Francis, Lord of Rennell. 1926. People of the Veil. London: MacMillan and Co.

Rosaldo, Michele. and Louise Lamphere, eds. 1974. *Women, Culture, and Society.* Stanford: Stanford University Press.

Sanday, Peggy. 1981. *Female Power and Male Dominance: On the Origins of Sexual Inequality.* Cambridge: Cambridge University Press.

Schlegel, Alice. 1975. Three Styles of Domestic Authority: A Cross-Cultural Study. In *Being Female: Reproduction, Power, and Change*, Dana Raphael, ed. The Hague, Paris: Mouton Publishers.

Scott, Joan W. 1988. *Gender and the Politics of History.* New York: Columbia University Press.

Scott, Joan W. 1992. Experience. In *Feminists Theorize the Political*, Judith Butler and Joan W. Scott, eds. New York: Routledge.

Worley, Barbara. 1988. Bed Posts and Broad Swords: Tuareg Women's Work Parties and the Dialectics of Sexual Conflict. In *Dialectics and Gender: Anthropological Approaches*, Richard R. Randolph, David M. Schneider, and May N. Diaz, eds. Boulder: Westview Press.

———. 1992. Where All the Women Are Strong. *Natural History* 101 (11):54–64.

VII

Gender, Property, and the State

The relationship between sexual inequality, the emergence of class structures, and the rise of the state has been an enduring interest in anthropological studies of gender. The subordination of women appears to emerge as an aspect of state formation. According to Gailey (1987: 6), "Institutionalized gender hierarchy . . . is created historically with class relations and state formative processes, whether these emerge independently, through colonization, or indirectly through capital penetration." We are led to ask what relationship class and state formation have with the oppression of women and, when gender hierarchy occurs, why women are the dominated gender. How does the state have power to penetrate and reorganize the lives of its members, whether in Sumerian legal codes decreeing monogamy for women or in welfare laws in the United States that influence household composition? Eventually, studying state formation may help us understand the origins and interrelationships of class and patriarchy, and the social reproduction of inequality.

Much discussion of this subject has centered on Engels' book *The Origin of the Family, Private Property, and the State*, a nineteenth-century text in which Engels argues that the emergence of the concept of private property and its ownership by men, as well as the development of a monogamous family, led to the subordination of women. In Engels' scheme, prior to this, gender relations were egalitarian and complementary. All production was for use, and people worked together for the communal household. Thus, changes in gender relations were linked to changes in material conditions because the ownership of productive property (initially domestic animals) was concentrated in the hands of men. This thesis has been influential in many Marxist and feminist analyses of women's subordination. For example, Leacock notes, "There is sufficient evidence at hand to support in its broad outlines Engels' argument that the position of women relative to men deteriorated with the advent of class society" (1973: 30).

Following Engels, Leacock observes that in early communal society the division of labor between the sexes was reciprocal, and a wife and her children were not dependent on the husband. Further, "The distinction did not exist between a public world of men's work and a private world of women's household service. The large collective household was the community, and within it both sexes worked to produce the goods necessary for livelihood" (1973: 33). In this view the oppression of women was built on the transformation of goods for use into commodities for exchange; the exploitation of workers and of women was generated by this process, which involved the emergence of the individual family as an isolated unit, economically responsible for its members, and of women's labor as a private service in the context of the family. This led to the "world historical defeat of the female sex" (Engels 1973: 120; Silverblatt 1988: 430).

In a reanalysis of Engels, Sacks agrees that women's position declined with the elaboration of social classes but disputes Engels' emphasis on the role of private property in this process (Sacks 1982). Rather, Sacks links state formation and the decline in the centrality of kinship groups to the deterioration in women's status. She delineates two relationships defining women in noncapitalist societies: sisterhood and wifehood. "Sister" refers to women's access to resources based on membership in a kin group. This relation implies autonomy, adulthood, and possible gender symmetry. "Wife," on the other hand, refers to a relationship of dependency on the husband and his kin. Sacks suggests that the development of states undermined women's status by dismantling the kin group corporations that formed the basis for sister relations (Sacks 1982).

However, critics of Sacks' position have argued that the process of state formation may involve uneven and contradictory developments. For example, elite women in the Kingdom of Dahomey, West Africa, challenged state imperatives by means of control of marketing associations. Thus, Silverblatt rebuts Sacks' evolutionary paradigm, suggesting the inevitability of the decline in women's status with state formation; instead, she suggests that we acknowledge the complex history of the emergence of elite privilege in the rise of the state. In addition, elite women such as the royalty of Dahomey may or may not share the goals of peasant women. They may instead join with the male elite in suppressing the authority and power of peasant market women. This illustrates the potential contradictions of gender affiliation on one hand, and class position on the other.

Several anthropologists have observed that Engels lacked reliable ethnographic information and oversimplified the complexities of gender relations in kinship societies and in precapitalist states (Gailey 1987: 15). In a critique of Engels, Moore argues against his essentialist assumption that there is a "natural" division of labor in which men are concerned with productive tasks and women with domestic ones. She also disagrees that an inevitable relationship will transpire between property, paternity, and legitimacy, in which men "naturally" want to transmit property to genetic offspring (1988: 47–48).

While Rapp (in this book) agrees with these criticisms, she points out that Engels addresses many current concerns, such as the relationship between women's participation in production and female status, and the implications of the separation of the domestic-public domains for women's roles in society (see also Silverblatt 1988: 432).

She warns against overgeneralizing when trying to understand the origins of the state and ignoring the history and context in which political formations change. In her view, we must examine kinship structures that were supplanted with the rise of the state and replaced by territorial and class-specific politics. Kinship domains, formerly autonomous, were subjugated to the demands of emergent elites with repercussions for gender roles and relations.

Among the processes that we need to examine are the politics of kinship, the intensification of military complexes, the impact of trade on social stratification, and the changing content and role of cosmology. For example, in stratified societies the establishment of long-distance trade and tribute systems may affect elite marriage patterns, leading to the emergence of dowry and the exchange of women to cement male political alliances. Similar alliances are forged in societies that have experienced a rise in militarism. When economies change and demand increases for a traded commodity, exploitation of labor to produce it may also increase, and marriage systems that expand trading relations may be solidified through the exchange of women. Women themselves may be important figures in trading networks, as in West Africa and in Mesoamerica, where women are active in the marketplace.

Alternatively, the extension of the state into localized communities can significantly influence gender roles and relations. This occurs, for example, by undermining women's ritual responsibilities or by generating conflict between government policy and the respective interests of men and women (see Browner, this book). Finally, changes in political hierarchies were legitimated by cosmological explanations in early states such as those of the Inca and the Maya. For example, as Maya society became increasingly stratified, a category of elite rulers known as *ahaw* emerged. These rulers were legitimized by myths that established them as mediators between the natural and supernatural worlds and as protectors of the people. State ideology involved the celebration of both male and female forces, and the elite contained both men and women. Mothers of kings were always members of the high elite, and this class affiliation was also validated in myth (Schele and Freidel 1990, Freidel and Schele, this book).

Ortner examines the process of state formation, with particular regard to its effect on gender ideology (1978). She analyzes the widespread ideology that associates the purity of women with the honor and status of their families. This pattern is evident in Latin America and the Mediterranean, and in societies of the Middle East, India, and China. Broad similarities exist in these varied societies. Ortner questions why the control of female sexual purity is such a ubiquitous and important phenomenon. She notes that all modern cases of societies concerned with female purity occur in states or systems with highly developed stratification, and they bear the cultural ideologies and religions that were part of the emergence of these states. She argues that no prestate societies manifest the pattern linking female virginity and chastity to the social honor of the group. Thus, concern with the purity of women was, in Ortner's view, structurally, functionally, and symbolically linked to the historical emergence of state structures.

The rise of the state heralds a radical shift in ideology and practice, with the emergence of the patriarchal extended family in which the senior man has absolute authority over everyone in the household. Women are brought under direct control of men in their natal families and later by their husbands and affinal kin. Ideologically women are thought to be in danger, requiring male protection; they are idealized as mothers and for their purity.

One of the central questions in the analysis of the impact of state formation is the role of hypergamy (up-status marriage, usually between higher-status men and lower-status women). Ortner (1978) suggests that a significant development in stratified society involves the transformation of marriage from an essentially equal transaction to a potentially vertical one, where one's sister or daughter could presumably marry into a higher strata (wife of a nobleman, consort of a king). Hypergamy may help explain the ideal of female purity because concepts of purity and virginity may symbolize the value of a girl for a higher-status spouse. Thus "a virgin is an elite female among females, withheld, untouched, exclusive" (Ortner 1981: 32).

Hypergamous marriages often involve the exchange of significant amounts of property, particularly in the form of dowry. The relationship between dowry, inheritance, and female status has been explored in a number of societies with varying marriage patterns. Dowry has been described as a form of premortem inheritance, parallel to men's rights in property accrued through inheritance after death of parents or other legators. However, considering dowry as a form of inheritance prior to death and as part of a woman's property complex obscures an important difference between the clear legal inheritance rights that men possess and the dowry that women may or may not receive (McCreery 1976; see also Stone and James in this book). Women obtain dowry at the discretion of their parents or brothers, and dowry is not based on the same rights as other forms of inheritance to which men have access.

Although dowry has been viewed as a form of inheritance for women, the dowry system in northern India has taken a pernicious turn as brides are burned to death, poisoned, or otherwise "accidentally" killed by husbands and in-laws who believe that the women have brought inadequate dowries. Conservative estimates are that at least 2,000 women die each year as a result of dowry murders (Stone and James in this book). Legislation enacted in 1961 banning dowries, and in 1986 amending the penal code to introduce a new offense, now known as dowry death, has been ineffective, and the dowry system continues to be deeply embedded in local culture (Koman 1996). Although the bestowing of dowry in India is centuries old, dowry murders are a recent social problem. Stone and James argue that dowry deaths represent a response to a growing materialist consumerism sweeping India that has stimulated demands for larger and ever-increasing dowries. They analyze these murders in the context of a patrilineal and patrilocal society with strongly prescribed subservience of wives to husbands and in-laws, in which parents prefer to see a daughter dead, rather than divorced. Women's fertility, which may once have been a source of power, is increasingly less valued. Even a woman who gives birth to sons is not protected from the risk of wife-burning. Thus women's relative lack of economic power and the loss of their one traditional source of leverage, their fertility, have heightened their vulnerability to violence.

Although the status of Indian women as reflected in the exchange of property at marriage appears to be deteriorating, in other parts of the world women's legal status and property rights have improved through state-sponsored changes in the judicial system. For example, Starr (1984) examines how in Turkey the impact of capitalistic agriculture and settled village life profoundly affected gender relations and women's access to property. These changes occurred in the cultural context of Islamic notions of male dominance and female submission and legislation giving equal rights to women.

Ottoman family law gave women rights to divorce and some protection against polygamous marriage, but inheritance practices remained constrained by Islamic law, in which women were under the authority of their husbands, had the status of a minor, received half the share of the patrimony obtained by their brothers, and had no rights to children of a marriage. According to Ataturk's secular reforms in the 1920s, women's rights were expanded to full adult status, women received equal rights to paternal inheritance, protection was granted to widows, and other legislation was enacted promoting equality for women. At first these state-initiated rights were incongruent with cultural practices, but by the late 1960s women had begun to use the courts to protect their rights to property and their reputations. Starr points out that although Engels emphasized the negative impact of private owner-ship on women's status, in this case law and culture played a positive counterbal-ancing role resulting in women's emancipation.

In her cross-cultural exploration of the political experiences of contemporary women, Caldwell Ryan (in this book) illustrates the ways in which women engage, respond to, or resist the state. She notes that women's interaction with the state may take the shape of voting, seeking political office, participating in women's movements or other forms of collective action, or individual action in response to state policies. A global perspective on women's encounters with the state suggests that although some women have experienced an increase in formal political rights and "real" power, others have seen their gains eroded by such forces as religious fundamentalism and global economic crises. Major world religions including Chris-tianity, Hinduism, and Islam have experienced an increase in religious fundamen-talism in the last thirty years. Accordingly, Caldwell Ryan traces the impact of religious fundamentalism in Iran, Afghanistan, and India on the status of women in those countries. She shows that it is useful to consider the specific circumstances of national histories and identities rather than focusing solely on religious doctrine to analyze the impact of religious fundamentalism on women in particular states.

Similarly, global economic upheavals have negatively affected women's everyday lives as well as demonstrating their limited political power. Structural adjustment policies initiated by the World Bank and the International Monetary Fund, for example, have led to higher prices for food and a decline in public spending on health and social services, all leading to increased burdens for women, who have been forced to take on a greater responsibility for providing for their families in response to economic austerity measures. Caldwell Ryan's discussion underscores the links between women's political empowerment and economic autonomy. Ulti-mately, one catalyst for global gender equity is the emergent international feminist movement, which has succeeded in putting gender on the agenda of nearly every state. Thus such issues as girls' education, female labor, child custody, and women's inheritance and property rights have emerged as matters for national debate and political action.

If the state can shape family and gender relations directly through legislation such as that determining rights to property, it may also have more indirect impact. Allison (in this book) argues that in Japan, boxed lunches (obento), prepared by mothers for their children, are invested with a gendered state ideology. The state manipulates the ideological and gendered meanings associated with the box lunch as an important component of nursery school culture. Nursery schools, under state supervision, not only socialize children and mothers into the gendered roles they are expected to assume but also introduce small children to the attitudes and struc-tures of Japanese education. The obento, elaborately and artistically arranged, is intended to allow the mother to produce something of home and family to accom-pany the child into this new and threatening outside world. Embedded in the school's close scrutiny of obento production and consumption is a message to obey rules and accept the authority of the school, and by extension, of the state. The obento's message is also that mothers sustain their children through food and sup-port state ideology as well.

In all the works included in this chapter we see the enduring influence of the issues raised by Engels with regard to the relationship between gender, property rights, and state structures. However, cross-cultural data demonstrate that this relationship is much more complex and varied than Engels' original formulation. Equally, universal evolutionary paradigms that posit a uniform impact of the rise of the state on gender roles cannot do justice to the myriad ways in which specific cultural histories, diverse social hierarchies, and systems of stratification affect gender relations and ideology. Thus, Silverblatt (1988: 448) asks, "What of the challenges that women and men, caught in their society's contradictions, bring to the dominant order of chiefs and castes, an order they contour and subvert, even as they are contained by it? And what of the other voices, the voices that chiefs and rulers do not (or cannot or will not) express?" The complex histories of the relationship between any particular state and gender relations in it show that while state formation has contributed to the definition of womanhood, women have also contributed to the definition of states (Silverblatt 1988: 452).

REFERENCES

Engels, Frederick. 1973. *The Origin of the Family, Private Property and the State.* New York: International Publishers.

Gailey, Christine Ward. 1987. *Kinship to Kingship: Gender Hierarchy and State Formation in the Tongan Islands.* Austin: University of Texas Press.

Koman, Kathleen. 1996. "India's Burning Brides." *Harvard Magazine* 98 (3): 18–19.

Leacock, Eleanor Burke. 1973. "Introduction." In Frederick Engels (ed.). *The Origin of the Family, Private Property and the State*, pp. 7–57. New York: International Publishers.

McCreery, John L. 1976. "Women's Property Rights and Dowry in China and South Asia." *Ethnology* 15: 163–174.

Moore, Henrietta L. 1988. *Feminism and Anthropology.* Minneapolis: University of Minnesota Press.

Ortner, Sherry. 1978. "The Virgin and the State." *Feminist Studies* 4 (3): 19–35.

———1981. "Gender and Sexuality in Hierarchical Societies: The Case of Polynesia and Some Comparative Implications." In Sherry B. Ortner and Harriet Whitehead (eds.). *Sexual Meanings: The Cultural Construction of Gender and Sexuality*, pp. 359–410. Cambridge: Cambridge University Press.

Sacks, Karen. 1982. *Sisters and Wives: The Past and Future of Sexual Equality.* Urbana: University of Illinois Press.

Schele, Linda, and David Freidel. 1990. *A Forest of Kings.* New York: William Morrow.

Silverblatt, Irene. 1988. "Women in States." *Annual Review of Anthropology* 17: 427–461.

Starr, June. 1984. "The Legal and Social Transformation of Rural Women in Aegean Turkey. In Renee Hirschon (ed.). *Women and Property: Women as Property.* New York: St. Martin's Press, Inc.

Thinking about Women
and the Origin of the State

Rayna Rapp

While anthropologists vary widely in their assessment of the autonomy of women in prestate societies, there seems to be a general consensus that with the rise of civilization, women as a social category were increasingly subjugated to the male heads of their households (Gailey 1987; Leacock 1978; Rohrlich 1980; Sacks 1982; Sanday 1981; Silverblatt 1988). This consensus is based, implicitly or explicitly, on a formulation developed by Frederick Engels in *The Origin of the Family, Private Property, and the State*. Engels linked the growth of private productive property to the dismantling of a system of communal kinship that existed in prestate societies. In this process, he argued, marriage grows more restrictive, legitimacy of heirs more important, and wives generally become means of reproduction to their husbands. At the same time, reciprocal relations among kin are curtailed, unequal access to strategic productive resources gradually develops, and estates or classes arise out of formerly kin-based social organizations. In this analysis, the creation of a class hierarchy is intimately linked to the creation of the patriarchal family and to restrictions on women's autonomy.

Engels' analysis provides the foundation for many themes concerning women that are currently being investigated: the relation between the economic roles of women, their control of resources, and their social status; the relation between the mode of production and the mode of reproduction;[1] and the effects of the separation or merger of domestic and public spheres of activity on the lives of women.[2] However, a thesis central to

Revised by the editors with the permission and approval of the author.

Engels' analysis—the link between class oppression and gender oppression—has remained less well examined. Drawing on a growing body of theory and data concerning state formation that has been amassed in recent years by twentieth-century archaeologists,[3] this article examines Engels' theory about the relationship between the subjugation of women, social stratification, and the rise of the state.

Most of the early theoretical work on emergence of state society was reductive, and it often condensed a multiplicity of processes into overly simplistic models. These theories ranged from a concentration on the extraction of social surplus (surplus material resources or labor beyond that needed for subsistence) via increasing division of labor and more productive technology (Childe 1950, 1952); to a focus on the emergence of central political authority to administer irrigation-based societies (Wittfogel 1955, 1957); to the effects of population pressure and warfare within circumscribed environments (Carneiro 1970, Harner 1970).

All of these theories tend to see the state as an inevitable and efficient solution to a particular set of problems. They ignore the specific historical, political, and economic contexts in which societies change.[4] Finally, they underplay the importance of kinship as a domain within which resistance to state formation is situated.[5] Not uncoincidentally, it is within the kinship domain that women's subordination appears to occur.

In recent years, a new set of theoretical and systemic formulations that are more processual have been developed. Such formulations offer fascinating hints about the role of kinship structure, and possibly women, in stratification. Some of the processes examined in state formation—the politics of kinship, the changing content and role of religious systems, the intensification of military complexes, and the role of trade in stimulating or increasing social stratification—are most pertinent to our interests here. I will discuss each of these briefly, suggesting some of the lines of inquiry they direct us to pursue.

THE POLITICS OF KINSHIP

Many anthropologists have examined the internal tensions of ranked kinship systems (Kirchoff 1959; Sahlins 1958; Fried 1967). In highly ranked kinship systems, the role of women is of crucial importance. Women not only transmit status, but may be contenders for leadership positions, either directly or through their children. This seems to be the case in Polynesia and in parts of Africa. As Gailey (1987) shows for Tonga, the existence of elite, ranked women became more problematic as stratification increased.

We need to know more about marriage patterns in such systems. In archaeology, ethnology, and Western history, we find that elite marriages may be implicated in the politics of establishing and maintaining long-distance trade and tribute systems.[6] Dowry is associated with highly stratified systems and dowered, elite women may appear as pawns in a classic case of male alliances formed via their exchange.[7] Ortner (1978) suggests that in state-organized systems, marriage may shift from horizontal alliances between individuals of similar social and economic backgrounds to vertical alliances between individuals of different backgrounds. In the latter situation there is a marked tendency toward hypergamy whereby lower-status women marry upper-status men. Ortner links these structural properties of the marriage system with ideologies requiring sexual purity and the protection of women (but not of men).

Silverblatt (1987), in a study of the Inca elite, suggests that as the Incas extended their rule, they required conquered communities to send women to Cuzco to serve in the temples, courts, and as noblemen's wives. For the conquered communities, this practice represented a loss of autonomy in marriage patterns, and a burden. At the same time, it made possible upward mobility to the specific males who sent sisters and daughters to Cuzco. The women themselves gained a great deal of prestige, but lost any control they might have had in arranging their own marriages and living within their natal communities.

CHANGING COSMOLOGIES

Both Silverblatt and Ortner draw our attention to the relationship between women and the religious systems in early states. They remind us that religious systems were the glue that cemented social relations in archaic societies. Such systems were used, as in the Inca case, to underwrite and justify changes in political hierarchies.

Tension about female status is often found within these religious systems. Eliade (1960) claims that the ritual expression of sexual antagonism and the existence of bisexual and/or androgynous gods accompanies the social organizational changes associated with the neolithic period. Male gods are often superimposed on female and androgynous gods. Evidence for this layering over of female and/or androgynous figures comes from Mesoamerica (Nash 1980), Peru (Silverblatt 1987), and is, of course, a favorite theme of classicists for early Greek society (Arthur 1976; Pomeroy 1975).

Pagels (1976), working with second-century A.D. Gnostic texts, analyzes the symbol system of sects in which the early Christian god was bisexual, and the Holy Family consisted of mother, father, and son. Such sects were organized into non-hierarchical religious communities, in which offices were rotated, and women participated in both teaching and preaching—a far cry from the ascendant Christian cosmology and practice which became the mainstream tradition. Cosmological changes are ideological precipitates of structural tensions; it is clear that their form and content have a great deal to tell us about class and gender.

INTENSIFICATION OF WARFARE

As early states became increasingly militaristic, social organization was transformed.[8] Several case histories lead us to believe that under conditions of intense warfare, men were not only burdened by conscription, but were blessed with increasing power as household heads (Muller 1987; Rohrlich 1980). Elite males may gain land, political domains, and alliance-forming wives in the process. Yet, sweeping statements about male supremacy and warfare (Divale and Harris 1976) are overgeneralized, and some evidence seems to contradict the association of warfare and an elevation of male status at the expense of female autonomy.

In the ancient West, for example, the correlation often works the other way: Spartan women held offices, controlled their own property, and had a great deal of sexual freedom, allegedly because they kept society functioning while the men were at war. Moreover, producing soldiers was considered as important as training them. In Athens, women's access to public places and roles seems to have increased a great deal during times of warfare. In Rome, during the Second Punic War, women gained in inheritance settlements and held public offices formerly closed to them (Pomeroy 1975). In the medieval Franco-Germanic world, noblewomen attained approximate parity in politics and property-management during the years of the most brutal military crisis (McNamara and Wemple 1973).

All these examples concern elite women only; we know very little about the effects of warfare on laboring women, who probably suffered then, as they do now. Nonetheless, it is not clear that warfare degrades women's status; the specific context within which military organization and practice occurs must be taken into account. Blood and gore clearly are not universal variables in theorizing about women's subordination.

TRADE

The role of trade in increasing and/or spreading stratification is an intriguing one.[9] Foreign-trade goods may be spread in many ways: by middlemen, via migrations, through central trading centers, and in marriage exchanges, to name but a few. Several studies suggest that the social relationships that surround production and distribution, and which undergird trade, may generate class and gender inequality (Adams 1974; Kohl 1975; Wiley 1974; Gailey and Patterson 1987). We need to know who produces goods, who appropriates them, and who distributes them. As demand for a trade commodity increases, exploitation of labor to produce it may arise. Marriage systems may also be intensified to expand the reproduction of trading alliances. Certainly there are numerous ethnographic examples of polygyny as a means to increase access to goods that wives produce. There are also many instances of increasing class division linked to increasing bridewealth.

But the control, ownership, and distribution of valued resources after they are produced is not exclusively a male function. In Mesoamerica and the Andes, to this day, women are active in the marketplace. Silverblatt (1978) suggests that they were important traders in early Incan times. Adams (1966) records their existence in Mesopotamia. And of course, their presence is felt in stratified groups throughout Africa and the Caribbean as well (Mintz 1971). Under what conditions does long-distance trade pass into the hands of men, and when is it possible for women to continue to perform it? When women are traders, do they constitute an elite, class-stratified group? To the extent that trade is implicated in the intensification of production for exchange, women as producers, reproducers, and traders must be implicated too.

CONCLUSION: COLONIALISM, CAPITALIST PENETRATION, AND THE "THIRD WORLD"

As we come to identify the factors in state formation as they affect women, we must be careful to think in probabilistic rather than deterministic terms. We need to better understand the relative power of kinship and class, the interplay of household and public economic functions, the flexibility within religious systems, and the relative autonomy or subordination of women, in light of the possibilities open to each society. We should expect to find variations within state-making (and unmaking) societies over time, and between such societies, rather than one simple pattern.

Nowhere is this more evident than in analysis of the process of rapid penetration by patriarchal national states into the so-called Third World. While the history of such penetration varies from place to place and must be taken into account, certain patterns affecting the ways of life of women can be traced at a general level. Wherever women have been active horticulturalists of collective lands, the imposition of private property, taxation, labor migration, and cash cropping has had devastating effects. Their realm of productivity and expertise has been deformed and often destroyed (Blumberg 1976; Boserup 1970; Tinker 1976). Depending upon context, they may become either super-exploited, or underemployed, but always more dependent upon men.

The evidence also suggests a general pattern concerning political organization. Prior to colonial penetration, gender relations in indigenous cultures appear to have been organized along essentially parallel and complementary lines. Men and women had distinct but equally significant roles in production, distribution, and ritual activities.[10] Case histories from Africa, Asia, and the Americas suggest that patriarchal, colonizing powers rather effectively dismantled native work organizations, political structures, and ritual contexts. Leadership and authority were assigned to male activities, while female tasks and roles were devalued or obliterated. The complementary and parallel gender relations that characterized indigenous societies were destroyed. Several authors have gone so far as to argue that women, thus divested of their social organization and collective roles, have become like underdeveloped, monocrop regions. Once they lived in a diversified world; now they have been reduced to the role of reproducing and exporting labor power for the needs of the international world economy (Bossen 1973; Boulding 1975; Deere 1976).

State formation and penetration occurs over time; its form and force are highly variable, both within and between societies. Yet it is important to remember that the processes which began millennia ago are ongoing. Cumulatively, they continue to transform the lives of the masses of people who exist under their structures. It is a long way from the Sumerian law codes declaring monogamy for women to the welfare laws of the United States which affect parental relations and household structure. But in both cases, the power of the state to penetrate and reorganize the lives of its members is clear. As we seek to understand the complex, stratified societies in which we now operate, we are led to reflect on archaic societies in which the dual and intertwined processes of hierarchy we now retrospectively label "class" and "patriarchy" took their origins.

NOTES

1. Productive activities are those that generate income in cash, or other valued resources. Reproduction refers, broadly, to the set of activities encompassing domestic chores and other household activities such as childbearing, childrearing, and cooking.
2. For analyses implicitly or explicitly influenced by *Origins* see Brown 1975; Meillassoux 1975; Reiter 1975; Rubin 1975; Sacks 1974; Sanday 1974.
3. Summaries of the state formation literature may be found in Flannery 1972; Krader 1968; Service 1975; Webb 1975.

4. A less determinant and more processual perspective on stratification and state formation is set forth in Flannery 1972; Sabloff and Lamberg-Karlovsky 1975; and Tilly 1975. Such thinking also informs the corpus of Marxist historiography.

5. This has been a major thrust in Stanley Diamond's work (1951, 1974).

6. Such links are suggested in Flannery 1972; Wiley and Shimkin 1971; and by much of the literature on stratified chiefdoms (Sahlins 1958; Kirchoff 1959; and Fried 1967). In European history, we find instances in the international royal marriage patterns. See McNamara and Wemple (1973) for some of the implications of feudal marriage patterns.

7. See Arthur 1976; Ortner 1978; Goody and Tambiah 1973.

8. The temple and military complexes figure in the state formation schemes of Adams 1966; Steward 1955; and Wiley 1974 to name but a few.

9. The archaeology of trade is discussed in Sabloff and Lamberg-Karlovsky 1975, and is critically summarized in Adams 1974 and Kohl 1975. See also Wiley 1974.

10. Parallel and interarticulating forms of gender social organization are analyzed by Brown 1970; Silverblatt 1978; Siskind 1978; and Van Allen 1972.

REFERENCES

Adams, R. M. 1966. *The Evolution of Urban Society*. Chicago. Aldine.

———. 1974. "Anthropological Perspectives on Ancient Trade." *Current Anthropology* 15: 239–258.

Arthur, M. 1976. "Liberated Women: The Classical Era." In R. Bridenthal and C. Koontz (eds.). *Becoming Visible: Women in European History*. New York: Houghton and Mifflin.

Blumberg, R. 1976. "Fairy Tales and Facts: Economy, Fertility, Family and the Female." Unpublished paper.

Boserup, E. 1970. *Women's Role in Economic Development*. London: George Allen and Unwin.

Bossen, L. 1973. "Women in Modernizing Societies." *American Ethnologist* 2: 587–601.

Boulding, E. 1975. *Women, Bread, and Babies*. University of Colorado, Institute of Behavioral Sciences, Program on Research of General Social and Economic Development.

Brown, J. 1970. "A Note on the Economic Division of Labor by Sex." *American Anthropologist* 72: 1073–1078.

Brown, J. 1975. "Iroquois Women." In R. Reiter (ed.). *Toward an Anthropology of Women*. New York: Monthly Review Press.

Carneiro, R. J. 1970. "A Theory of the Origin of the State." *Science* 169: 733–738.

Childe, G. 1950. "The Urban Revolution." *Town Planning Review* 21 (3): 3–17.

Childe, G. 1952. "The Birth of Civilization." *Past and Present* 2: 1–10.

Deere, C. 1976. "Rural Women's Subsistence Production in the Capitalist Periphery." *Review of Radical Political Economics* 8: 9–18.

Diamond, S. 1951. *Dahomey: A Protostate in West Africa*. Ann Arbor: University of Michigan Press.

Diamond, S. 1974. *In Search of the Primitive: A Critique of Civilization*. New Brunswick, NJ: Transaction Books.

Divale, W., and M. Harris. 1976. "Population Warfare and the Male Supremacist Complex." *American Anthropologist* 78: 521–538.

Eliade, M. 1960. "Structures and Changes in the History of Religions." In C. Kraeling and R. Adams (eds.). *City Invincible*. Chicago: University of Chicago Press.

Flannery, K. 1972. "The Cultural Evolution of Civilizations." *Annual Review of Ecology and Systematics* 3: 399–426.

Fried, M. 1960. "On the Evolution of Social Stratification and the State." In S. Diamond (ed.). *Culture and History*. New York: Columbia University Press.

———. 1967. *The Evolution of Political Society*. New York: Random House.

Gailey, Christine Ward. 1987. *Kinship to Kingship: Gender Hierarchy and State Formation in the Tongan Islands*. Austin: University of Texas Press.

Gailey, Christine Ward, and Thomas C. Patterson. 1987. "Power Relations and State Formation." In Thomas C. Patterson and Christine W. Gailey (eds.). *Power Relations and State Formation*, pp. 1–26. Washington, DC: American Anthropological Association.

Goody, J., and S. Tambiah. 1973. *Bridewealth and Dowry*. Cambridge: Cambridge University Press.

Harner, M. 1970. "Population Pressure and Social Evolution of Agriculturalists." *Southwestern Journal of Anthropology* 26: 67–86.

Kirchoff, P. 1959. "The Principles of Clanship in Human Society." In M. Fried (ed.). *Readings in Anthropology* (Vol. 2). New York: Thomas Crowell.

Kohl, P. 1975. "The Archaeology of Trade." *Dialectical Anthropology* 1: 43–50.

Krader, L. 1968. *Formation of the State.* Englewood Cliffs: Prentice Hall.

Leacock, Eleanor. 1978. "Women's Status in Egalitarian Society: Implications for Social Evolution." *Current Anthropology* 19: 247–275.

McNamara, J., and S. Wemple. 1973. "The Power of Women through the Family in Medieval Europe: 500–1100." *Feminist Studies* 1: 126–141.

Meillassoux, C. 1975. *Femmes, greniers et capitaux.* Paris: Maspero.

Mintz, S. 1971. "Men, Women and Trade." *Comparative Studies in Society and History* 13: 247–269.

Muller, Viana. 1987. "Kin Reproduction and Elite Accumulation in the Archaic States of Northwest Europe." In Thomas C. Patterson and Christine W. Gailey (eds.). *Power Relations and State Formation.* pp. 81–97. Washington, DC: American Anthropological Association.

Nash, J. 1980. "Aztec Women: The Transition from Status to Class in Empire and Colony." In M. Etienne and E. Leacock (eds.). *Women and Colonization.* New York: Praeger.

Ortner, S. 1978. "The Virgin and the State." *Feminist Studies* 4 (3): 19–35.

Pagels, E. 1976. "What Became of God the Mother? Conflicting Images of God in Early Christianity" *Signs* 2: 293–303.

Pomeroy, S. 1975. *Goddesses, Whores, Wives and Slaves.* New York: Schoken Books.

Reiter, R. 1975. "Men and Women in the South of France." In R. Reiter (ed.). *Toward an Anthropology of Women.* New York: Monthly Review Press.

Rohrlich, Ruby. 1980. "State Formation in Sumer and the Subjugation of Women." *Feminist Studies* 6: 76–102.

Rubin, G. 1975. "The Traffic in Women." In R. Reiter (ed.). *Toward an Anthropology of Women.* New York: Monthly Review Press.

Sabloff, J., and C.C. Lamberg-Karlovsky. 1975. *Ancient Civilizations and Trade.* Albuquerque: University of New Mexico Press.

Sacks, K. 1974. "Engels Revisited." In Michelle Rosaldo and Louise Lamphere (eds.). *Woman, Culture and Society.* Stanford: Stanford University Press.

———. 1982. *Sisters and Wives: The Past and Future of Sexual Equality.* Urbana: University of Illinois Press.

Sahlins, M. 1958. *Social Stratification in Polynesia.* Seattle: University of Washington Press.

Sanday, Peggy. 1974. "Toward a Theory of the Status of Women." In Michelle Rosaldo and Louise Lamphere (eds.). *Woman, Culture and Society.* Stanford: Stanford University Press.

———. 1981. *Female Power and Male Dominance: On the Origins of Sexual Inequality.* Cambridge: Cambridge University Press.

Service, E. 1975. *Origins of the State and Civilization.* New York: Norton.

Silverblatt, Irene. 1978. "Andean Women in Inca Society." *Feminist Studies* 4 (3): 37–61.

———. 1987. *Moon, Sun, and Witches: Gender Ideologies and Class in Inca and Colonial Peru.* Princeton: Princeton University Press.

———. 1988. "Women in States." *Annual Review of Anthropology* 17: 427–461.

Siskind, J. 1978. "Kinship and Mode of Production." *American Anthropologist* 80: 860–872.

Steward, J. 1955. *The Theory of Culture Change.* Urbana: University of Illinois Press.

Tilly, C. 1975. "Reflections on the History of European State-Making." In C. Tilly (ed.). *The Formation of National States in Western Europe.* Princeton: Princeton University Press.

Tinker, I. 1976. "The Adverse Impact of Development on Women." In I. Tinker and M. Bramsen (eds.). *Women and World Development.* Washington, DC: Overseas Development Council.

Van Allen, J. 1972. "Sitting on a Man: Colonialism and the Lost Political Institutions of Igbo Women." *Canadian Journal of African Studies* 6: 165–181.

Webb, M. 1975. "The Flag Follows Trade." In J. Sabloff and C.C. Lamberg-Karlovsky (eds.). *Ancient Civilizations and Trade.* Albuquerque: University of New Mexico Press.

Wiley, G., 1974. "Precolumbian Urbanism." In J. Sabloff and C.C. Lamberg-Karlovsky (eds.). *Ancient Civilizations and Trade.* Albuquerque: University of New Mexico Press.

Wiley, G. and D. Shimkin. 1971. "The Collapse of the Classic Maya Civilization in the Southern Lowlands." *Southwestern Journal of Anthropology* 27: 1–18.

Wittfogel, K. 1955. "Oriental Society in Transition." *Far Eastern Quarterly* 14: 469–478.

———. 1957. *Oriental Despotism.* New Haven: Yale University Press.

Dowry, Bride-Burning, and Female Power in India

Linda Stone and Caroline James

Over the last two decades, the reports from India have shocked the world: married women murdered (usually burned to death) by their husbands and/or in-laws over the issue of inadequate dowry. These recent incidents of bride-burning are a shocking example of the new forms of violence against women which are arising in modern, or modernizing, settings in many areas of the world. In India, these events are occurring alongside the growth of feminist organizations, the expansion of educational and economic opportunities for women, and some societal questioning of traditional gender roles.

This article examines the bride-burning problem in India by looking at recent changes which have occurred not only with respect to dowry transactions, but also with respect to more traditional sources of female domestic power. It is not possible here to consider all of the complex factors which are contributing to the dowry murders in India, but we suggest, though necessarily tentatively, that along with the traditional lack of female control over family property and marriage arrangements, the problem may be further compounded by a new loss of female power in another important sphere, namely the power women could traditionally exercise through their fertility.

The article draws upon published accounts of bride-burning combined with material from interviews with a bride-burning survivor carried out by one of the authors (James). This case emerged not from research focused on bride-burning, but rather as part of a larg-

er study of literacy programs in adult education centers in Madhya Pradesh. In this study James (1988) found that many of the women who came to the adult education centers were fleeing dowry harassment or attempted burnings. The case we present here was selected for the depth and detail of information provided by the woman involved.

Before examining dowry murders, we offer some comments on dowry in India to place the issue in a broader cross-cultural perspective.

DOWRY IN INDIA

One feature of dowry systems in general which applies strongly to India is their association with socioeconomic stratification and the concerns of kin groups with maintaining or enhancing social status through marriage. In an historical treatment of dowry, Goody (1971, 1973, 1976) argued that in Eurasia, in contrast to Africa, intensive plow agriculture created differential wealth, promoting divisions between status groups. It then became important to perpetuate these divisions over the generations to insure that control over property remained within the status group. This was achieved in part by instituting "status group endogamy" through the mechanism of dowry marriage. Thus, "status group endogamy"

> . . . is not simply a question of the absence of marriage between groups . . . but of matching like for like, or getting an even better bargain. And the usual mechanism by which this is achieved is the matching of property, often by means of the dowry. . . . (Goody, 1973, p. 593)

Dowry, then, goes hand-in hand with a class system and with maintenance of the

Reprinted with permission from *Women's Studies International Forum* 18 (2): 125–135, by Linda Stone and Caroline James. (Oxford, England: Elsevier Science Ltd., Pergamon Imprint, 1995.)

superiority of higher groups over lower. Here marriages, at least among the upper classes, must be well-controlled and, by extension, so must courtship. The roles of matchmaker and chaperone become important in this Eurasian context, along with a high value placed on female virginity at marriage (Goody, 1976, p. 17). Women must be endowed with property in order to attract husbands of equal or higher rank, and their sexuality must be controlled in order to limit "... the possibility of conflicting claims on the estate in which a woman has rights" (Goody, 1976, p. 14). Schlegel (1991) has more recently confirmed the strong association between dowry transactions and cultural concerns with female premarital virginity, which, she argues, helps to prevent lower class males from claiming wealth through impregnating higher class females. Ultimately the whole complex of cultural values centering on female "purity" and the notion that the honor of male kin groups rests on the seclusion and sexual purity of its women (see Mandelbaum, 1988) is related to the institution of dowry as an instrument in preserving and perpetuating socioeconomic classes. As we shall see, both the themes of social status and female chastity recur through accounts of dowry murders.

There is, however, another common idea about dowry systems which does not apply well in India. This is the idea that dowry is a form of female property or wealth. Thus, Goody (1973) and others (e.g., Tambiah, 1973) have seen Eurasian dowry universally as "female inheritance"—women receive a portion of the family estate at marriage, rather than upon the death of the father or mother. This portion they receive as movable property rather than land which is left to sons. But many working in India, such as Miller (1981) and Sharma (1984), have convincingly shown that whereas this may be true in many areas of the world, in India dowry is property which passes from the bride's family to that of the groom, and that even if perceived to be "women's property" (*stridhan*) by some Indians themselves, in fact a bride does not have (and historically never had) genuine control over the use and

distribution of this property. Women in the Indian dowry system should be seen as vehicles of property transmission rather than as true inheritors.

Madhu Kishwar (1986), who has written several articles on dowry for the Indian feminist magazine *Manushi*, has argued that Indian dowry effectively functions to disinherit women and promote their economic dependency on men, which in her view is the real crux of the modern problem of dowry murders. Although current law permits daughters to inherit from the father's estate, more often women are upon marriage made to sign over these rights to their brothers. As for the dowry itself, Kishwar (1986) writes:

> In actuality, a woman is seldom allowed to have control even over things that are supposedly for her personal use. Gold and other jewelry are traditionally supposed to be a woman's personal security, but, in practice, the gold usually stays in the custody of her mother-in-law or husband. It is up to them to give her what they wish for her personal use and daily wear ... It is fairly common for certain items of her jewelry to be incorporated into her husband's sister's dowry. (pp. 6–7)

Moreover, Kishwar points out that were the point of Indian dowry to provide a daughter with some financial security, parents would give her productive assets such as land or a shop, rather than clothing and household goods, which depreciate in value.

Defining dowry as female inheritance, Goody (1976) saw it as a kind of economic "gain" for women. But the irony, to him, was that the system also entails a "loss" of women's control over their marriages or their sexual behavior:

> The positive control of marriage arrangements ... is stricter where property is transmitted to women. It is a commentary on their lot that where they are more propertied they are initially less free as far as marital arrangements go. (Goody, 1976, p. 21)

But in the Indian context, it would appear that women lose on all counts. This context (and the whole question of sources, or lack of sources, of female power) is important to bear in mind in any discussion of dowry murders. In India dowry not only serves to promote status group endogamy (hypergamy) to maintain a class system, but it is now actively manipulated to serve new ends of status-seeking among individual families. In this modern context, women as vehicles of property transmission not only lack control over both property and marriage arrangements, as was largely the case previously, but may in fact suffer considerable harassment, physical abuse, and even murder in connection with their roles as bringers of dowry.

DOWRY MURDERS

From what is known about dowry deaths, it is possible to see some patterns, although exceptions exist in every case. They appear to be largely, though not exclusively, occurring in Northwest India, and they are largely, though no longer exclusively, among Hindu groups. They occur most often in cases of arranged marriages (the most common form of marriage in India) but have occurred in cases of a "love match," and they occur predominantly among the urban middle-class (Kumari, 1989; van Willigen & Channa, 1991). It is difficult to know how widespread the problem is, but most conservative estimates are that at least 2000 women are victims of dowry deaths per year in India (Chhabra, 1986, pp. 12–13). The area showing the greatest problem is New Delhi, with an estimated two dowry deaths per day (Bordewich, 1986, p. 21). The number of reported cases increases yearly. It is not known to what extent the increase reflects an increase in reporting rather than an increase in the crime. However, it may be that the crime is still underreported since the number of hospital cases of severe burns in young married women exceeds reports of violence against women by burning (Kumari, 1989, p. 24).

The preponderance of cases of bride-burning in North India is significant. This is also the area in which Miller (1981) finds significantly more males than females in juvenile age groups. This she attributes to neglect of female children, who are an economic liability relative to males. In the Northern region, too, dowry marriages are more common. The expense of providing dowry for daughters is one reason which Miller finds for the relatively intense preference for sons and relative neglect of female children in the North.

Sharma suggests that North Indian dowry has dramatically inflated as India has shifted to a market, cash economy over the last 50 years: "... dowry used to be more or less conventionally determined and many items could be made in whole or part by members of the bride's family themselves (e.g. rugs, clothing, bedding)" (Sharma, 1984, p. 70). But now, especially among the urban middle classes, expectations of televisions, motor scooters, refrigerators, large sums of cash, and so on are usual. Many observers related modern dowry and dowry deaths to the frustration of the urban middle class, caught in a new consumerism, status-seeking, and rising expectations of a life style they cannot on their own earning power quite afford (Bordewich, 1986, pp. 24–25).

Sharma's (1984) work on dowry has also cleared up one confusion, namely how it is that marriageable women appear to be in great supply (everyone is anxious to marry off a daughter and even accused dowry murderers manage to secure new brides!) even though there are far more males than females in the marriageable age groups in the North. Hypergamy (marriage of women upward into higher status groups) was traditionally common in the North and with modern dowry is becoming more so. In addition, lessening of caste restrictions in modern marriages promotes more hypergamous competition. Dowry givers are thus competing upwards for scarce grooms at the top (Sharma, 1984, p. 72).

Dowry and dowry murders continue despite the fact that dowry transactions have been illegal in India since the Dowry Prohibition Act of 1961.[1] As a result of pressure by women's organizations, subsequent amendments to the Act have even strengthened the laws against dowry and dowry harassment (Ghadially & Kumar, 1988, pp. 175–176). However, what is actually dowry can be legally claimed as "voluntary gifts" at marriage. Dowry persists not only because the law is ineffective or difficult to enforce, nor because of the pressures and demands of the groom's family, but also because the families of brides, in spite of growing public awareness of the tragic consequences, continue to give dowry. This may be due to concerns that otherwise a daughter could not be married at all (universally considered an undesirable event in India), or that the family could not secure an appropriate match. Also, parents of the bride may continue to believe that a lavish dowry will help to secure their daughter's favorable treatment in her in-laws' home, after which they may "yield to extortion out of fear for their daughter's safety ..." (Bordewich, 1986, p. 24). Stein (1988) reports that many Indian women "still believe ... that not only can dowry be used to overcome disadvantages in the marriage market, such as dark skin color, but it gives them dignity and status" (p. 485).

From the reported cases of dowry murders, it appears that the difficulties usually start early in the marriage. A new bride is harassed and criticized for the pitiful dowry she has brought. She is encouraged to wrangle more and more from her family, yet her in-laws remain unsatisfied until, at some point, the situation explodes into an attempt on her life. One woman ("Sita") whose husband attempted to burn her, reported the following:

> I got married when I was 23 years old to a person whose family was not as wealthy as our family. My father [a businessman] gave $8,000 cash as dowry. [He] gave me expensive clothes like 500 saris, 10 golden jewelry sets and one diamond set, all the pots and pans necessary for the house, a television set, wardrobe, freezer, cooler fan, double bed, furniture and other things he thought would be useful in the house. More than that, he used to send things from time to time, like on festivals. One year of my

> marriage has not passed when my in-laws and husband started giving me trouble every day for more dowry. My mother-in-law started telling my husband, "Leave this woman and we will get you another one, at least the other party will give us more and better dowry than what these people have given us. What her parents have given us is nothing. Moreover, this girl is ugly and she is dark."

Sita's reference to the relative wealth of her family and her detailed description of her lavish dowry appear to reinforce the same materialistic values which evidently lie behind dowry harassment and murders. Later she spoke with bitter resentment about her husband's new wife who "... is using all my things, like all my expensive saris, jewelry and other things." Her account also suggests a blatant economic motive for dowry murder—that it frees the woman's in-laws to get a new bride and an additional dowry. A similar idea reported in an article by Bordewich (1986) is expressed by the father of an allegedly murdered bride:

> ... as soon as we agreed on the marriage they started troubling us. First they told us to buy diamond rings instead of mere gold ones ... Then they insisted on a sofa bed for fifteen thousand rupees, but I could only afford one that cost seven thousand. Whatever was in my means I did, but they were always displeased ... they demanded a stereo and tape-cassette system, and then they asked for saris for the boy's sisters ... and then for a gas stove. I gave them ... I had read that there were so many tortures and murders of young women over dowry and I was afraid of what might happen to [my daughter]. I told them I would pay whatever I could ... But they didn't even wait for the money to come. They probably realized they had gotten all they could from us. A few days later [my daughter] was dead ... There has never been an investigation ... Now they can marry their son to another girl and get another dowry. (p. 25)

The most common means of murder is soaking the bride in kerosene and setting her aflame, with a report to the police of a suicide or an accident in the kitchen. Sita describes how this was attempted on her:

[The winter my son was born] my mother-in-law started telling me not to wear so much gold jewelry at home, to remove it at night and keep it in the wardrobe. I did not understand why she was telling me this when she had not done so before. But I did what she asked. [Then] one evening my husband went into the kitchen and asked for a match box. My mother-in-law's sister-in-law gave him a match box which my husband then kept in the wardrobe very close to our bed. Then he left the house, saying he would be coming in late that night. That same evening, the electricity went off and my mother-in-law's sister-in-law came to get the match box to light a lamp. She found the match box in the wardrobe and took it. My husband came in very late that night when my son and I were sound asleep. Due to the cold, I had pulled the covers up over our heads. Suddenly I felt that the quilt was wet and cold, but I thought it was just due to being cold at night. But when I removed the quilt from my face, there was a strong smell of kerosene. I got up quickly and saw my husband getting into bed and covering himself, pretending he was sound asleep ... he had been looking for the match box which he could not find. You can imagine that if he could have found the match box, my son and I would not have survived. We would have been burned to ashes.

One theme recurrent in many dowry murder cases is the issue of the bride's "reputation" and sexual "purity," which, as we saw in Goody's (1976) discussions of dowry, serves as a link between the institution of dowry, family concerns with status, and the perpetuation of socio-economic classes. With respect to this issue, a woman facing dowry harassment is truly vulnerable as any suggestion of her "loose" character is an easy defense for her husband or in-laws. In the case above Sita reports that after fleeing from the bed,

I started crying loudly, then my husband and mother-in-law came and started telling me to leave the house. I told them I would not step out of the house until my parents came, because if I would have left the house, they would have told the police and everybody that I was the one who wanted to leave the husband and the house, that it was my fault and not anyone else's in the family. They would have

cooked up another story that I am a bad character and that that is why I left the house at that hour of the night (3:00 a.m.).

In a dowry murder case discussed by Kumari (1989), the husband accused of burning his young wife claimed that she had committed suicide because she could not forget her own "murky past" involving previous sexual activity (p. 64). Similarly, in newspaper accounts of dowry deaths it is common to find some innuendo of lapsed sexual behavior on the part of the victim.[2] Also illustrative is the following account, taken down by Bordewich (1986), from a woman who virtually sees a dowry murder:

... In the house across the street we could see a man beating his wife. I went out onto the balcony and saw that the neighbors had gathered in the street to watch ... A moment later I heard a scream ... and there in front of me was the woman, burning in the window. She tried to wrap herself in the curtains, but they went up in flames. I ran into the street, but none of the neighbors seemed disturbed. People were saying it was "just a domestic issue" or that the woman must have had "a loose moral character." The woman died soon afterward in the hospital. The husband was never charged. (p. 26)

DOWRY, FERTILITY, AND FEMALE POWER

Dowry murders must be viewed within the context of Indian culture, which is characterized by patrilineal descent, patrilocality, the joint family, and strongly prescribed subservience of wives to husbands and in-laws. In both the popular press and scholarly literature, discussions of dowry murders incorporate these and other elements of Indian cultural traditions and women's roles within them. Certainly the association of death, fire, and female chastity or purity has caught the attention of writers who have drawn parallels between modern bride-burning and the ancient upper caste custom of *sati*, or the burning of a widow alive on her husband's funeral pyre. This was considered a (theoretically self-willed) act of great religious merit, only to be performed by a chaste wife in a state of ritual purity (Stein, 1988, p. 464). Again, in Hindu mythology, Sita must prove her chastity to her husband, Rama, through passing unburned through fire, and in another myth Sati Devi proves her loyalty to her husband, Shiva, by leaping to her death into the ceremonial fire of her father who insulted him.

Whatever deeper meaning all this may have within the Indian consciousness, Stein (1988) rightly points out that both the ancient sati and modern bride-burning reflect one clear fact of Indian life: the unacceptability of the unmarried adult woman. Thus sati was a way to dispose of the widow, who in earlier times among high castes, could not remarry, but who could, if alive, remain in society as a threatening, uncontrolled sexual woman. In the modern context, the existence of an unmarried adult daughter, with all the same connotations of uncontrolled, dangerous sexuality, brings shame and dishonor to her parents whose duty it is to marry her off, and who receive religious merit for doing so. So great is the pressure to marry the daughter (and keep her married, a divorced woman being equally unacceptable and threatening in Indian society) that a woman's parents remain in a weak and vulnerable position with respect to dowry harassment. Stein (1988) concludes:

> ... marriage is still seen as the only way in which Indian women can be part of their own society, can function as social beings, even at the expense of their own personalities, and occasionally their lives.(p. 485)

The situation is compounded by another deep-rooted Indian tradition: the religious and social inferiority of the bride's family to that of the groom. In Hindu tradition a bride is a religious gift (*kanyadan,* gift of the virgin) and, as such, can only be given upward to those of higher rank, those to whom one must show perpetual deference and respect.

The inferior and subservient position of a wife to her husband is on another level shared by the family who gives her. Thus "the subordination and frequently oppressed position of the daughter-in-law is exacerbated by the exclusion and deference of her own kin" (Stein, 1988, p. 476).

Kishwar (1986) also refers to these relationships in her discussions of dowry deaths, highlighting the powerless position of a bride and her parents. For her, dowry harassment is but one of many techniques by which a groom and his family can humiliate a bride to "accept a subordinate position within the family and feel grateful for being allowed to survive at all in the marital home" (p. 4). She also affirms that marriage of the daughter and dowry are matters of status and family honor, so that "... most parents would rather see their daughters dead than have them get a divorce and return permanently to the parental home" (p. 5).

Chhabra (1986), noting the many cases of dowry deaths which involve the mother-in-law, discusses the role of the traditionally problematic relationship between a woman and her daughter-in-law in India in terms of modern dowry harassment. Participating in or encouraging dowry harassment is the mother-in-law's way of rejecting the new bride, whom she perceives as a threat to her son's support and loyalty to herself (pp. 6–10).

All of these sociocultural factors and many more are fundamental to accounting for dowry deaths and, along with the inability of police and the courts to alleviate the problem, go a long way toward explaining why these deaths persist. However, most of these cultural traditions, which have in various ways, degrees, and combinations deeply shaped Indian women's lives, have been around for centuries, whereas dowry murders are apparently quite new, becoming a recognized social issue in India in the 1970s (Kumari, 1989). The concept of "dowry death" was only legally established in India in the 1980s (van Willigen & Channa, 1991, p. 371).

What has changed in Indian society to bring about this form of violence against women? Along with the new socioeconomic issues already referred to, it is important to ask also whether women in this modern context have lost sources of power which previously gave them some leverage. Despite all the constraints on women and the general sense of powerlessness which any account of the traditional Hindu woman's life will give, it was still the case that a new bride did not endlessly suffer ill-treatment from and subservience to in-laws, but gradually transformed herself from lowly bride to respected mother, perhaps eventually to become a powerful mother-in-law herself.[3] Regardless of however lowly the position of the affinal women in this strongly patrilineal society, she was, at worst, a necessary evil since she alone held the power to reproduce the husband's lineage. In a more traditional scenario, the adept Hindu woman tried to please her husband not only to express a culturally required subservience but also in order to become pregnant, as this would ultimately be her way out of misery and toward a rising status within the husband's household. With each sign of successful fertility, and particularly with the birth of sons, her position improved. As with many areas of Asia, sons were desired to continue the patrilineage, serve as heirs, perform important funeral rituals for parents, and to provide security in old age. Economically they contributed to home-based production or could bring in cash income.

A woman's fertility was the key to what can be considered a "great transition" in her status and identity. Summarizing this for the whole of India, Mandelbaum (1970) wrote of the bride that

> ... the real relief comes when she becomes pregnant. Her mother-in-law can afford to relax a bit in her role as taskmistress; her husband is pleased; the men of the household are glad; there is an awakened interest in seeing that she eats well and rests easily. This first burgeoning also marks her first upward move in the family status hierarchy.... [then with childbirth] She is no longer the lowly probationer she was at first. If the child is a son, she has proved herself in

the most important way of all and her confidence is the more secure. The son is her social redeemer and thenceforth her importance in the family tends gradually to increase. (pp. 88–89)

Raising this issue shifts the focus somewhat away from dowry, over which women evidently never had much control, and toward other sources of female power which may be changing, at least among the urban middle classes of the North. In a sense, female fertility, or the high value placed on women's successful reproduction, may have served as a "safety valve" for women in the past. But once this fertility value diminishes, women's position is indeed insecure. One startling feature of the dowry murder cases is the high number of women murdered who had already produced children, even sons. In one study 36% of the dowry murder cases involved women who had already produced children; another 11% of the women were pregnant at the time of death (Ghadially & Kumar, 1988, p. 168). Although she does not give numbers, Stein (1988) notes of dowry murder victims that "... a surprising number of them are pregnant when they die" (pp. 474–475).

Even victims of dowry harassment seem surprised to realize that childbirth and particularly the birth of a son does not alleviate their situation. Sita, in the case discussed earlier, remarked that after being harassed over dowry, "I gave birth to a male child. [But even with this] they did not want to keep me or the child either. They cared only for the dowry." Similarly in the case of Suman, described in the Indian feminist magazine *Manushi,* it was reported that

> ... [The husband's] maltreatment of Suman continued to escalate. He pawned all her jewelry. Even the birth of her son did not improve the situation. When the son was a year old, Suman was once more beaten and thrown out of the house in the hope of pressuring her parents to give more dowry. (Kishwar, 1986, p. 8)

Demographic data from India supports the suggestion that the country's traditional strong value on high fertility may be changing. Fertility rates are declining and have been since the mid-1960s. An analysis of the 1981 census produced the following report:

> India, the second most populous country in the world, is experiencing the early stages of fertility transition. The unprecedented acceleration in the rate of growth of India's population, sparked off by declining mortality as early as 1921, has finally been arrested ... It is beyond doubt that a significant contribution to this phenomenon lately has been from declining fertility, of which there is ample cumulative evidence. (Rele, 1987, p. 513)

One reason for the decline is undoubtedly urbanization, which tends to dampen fertility since the "cost" of children increases while their economic benefits decline. The above report also shows that the pace of decline is accelerating and that although the decline is occurring in both rural and urban areas, urban fertility remains much lower than rural fertility. Other studies show that fertility rates are lower and declining faster among wealthier and more educated groups (Goyal, 1989). Along with fertility declines, some studies show declines in desired number of children, again most notable among urban, educated, and wealthier groups (Jejeebhoy & Kulkarni, 1989).

Could it be that changes in fertility values are taking place and that, however advantageous this may be for India's population problems, it may be a contributing factor to dowry murders? Demonstrating a significant change in fertility values (beyond merely showing a decline in fertility levels) and a definite connection with dowry murders would, of course, require much further research. Nevertheless, our inquiry into dowry murders, and discussion of the problem within the context of more traditional ways in which women acquired some domestic leverage, is suggestive. Previously through much of India a large joint family and the production of many sons was itself a source of prestige. Through successful reproduction, women could gain respect and greater security in the husband's household. In today's context, children and grandchildren, though undoubtedly still desired for all the same cultural reasons as before, become economically less important. At the same time a new urban consumerism and concern with material displays of wealth is widely reported in India and is directly referred to in all studies of dowry deaths. We suggest that insofar as these shifts in values may be occurring, they may diminish the domestic leverage women once exercised through reproduction.

WOMEN IN PRODUCTION AND REPRODUCTION

In his study of dowry systems, Goody (1976) incorporated the work of Boserup (1970), who distinguished systems of "female farming" (shifting cultivation), where women perform the major part of agricultural work, from "male farming" (plow agriculture) where male labor predominates. The latter is associated with private land ownership, a landless class of laborers, and dowry, as opposed to bridewealth marriages. Boserup saw the development of male farming in Asia, and the later shift to male farming in Africa, as detrimental to women since the diminution of their roles in production increased their economic and social marginalization.[4]

Boserup (1970) made the important point that in regions of female farming, women are valued both as workers and as child bearers, whereas in systems of male farming, they are valued as mothers only (p. 51). Applying these ideas to modern, urban India (where the valued economic activity is income-earning), it appears that a new problem facing women, at least among the middle classes, may be that women lack value, and therefore power, either as workers or as mothers. Of course middle class Indian women can and do make important contributions to household income, increasingly so in the modern context. But, as Sharma (1984) points out, we need to look at women's work in relation to the proportion of their economic potential relative to that of men:

> It might be possible to show that the expansion of dowry has been accompanied by a decline in women's capacity to contribute household income *compared with that of men,* even though there has been no absolute diminution of women's economic activity. New opportunities to earn cash wages in factories, in government employment and white collar occupations have expanded far more rapidly for men than for women ... .(pp. 67–68)

Boserup's critics (Beneria & Sen, 1981) claim that one problem with her analysis is that she ignored women's roles in reproduction. Their point is that women's reproductive roles in many cases hinder their full or equal participation in wage labor or other socially valued economic activities, whereas Boserup laid the blame on sexually biased cultural values and changes in technology. In fact, however, Boserup did address women's roles in reproduction, though not quite in the way her critics would have liked to have seen. Writing before 1970, she seems to have foreseen that changes in fertility values could occur and could negatively impact women. Speaking in general of societies with male farming systems, where women have been devalued as workers but are still valued as mothers, she wrote: "There is a danger in such a community that the propaganda for birth control, if successful, may further lower the status of women both in the eyes of men and in their own eyes" (Boserup, 1970, p. 51). Whereas it is unlikely that "propaganda for birth control" alone would have this effect, it may be that in India, urbanization and the growth of the consumer economy are bringing about the same result.

CONCLUSION

Many observers of the problem of dowry murders in India have contributed to showing a powerful link between this form of violence against women and women's relative lack of economic power. With the urbanization and consumerism characterizing India today, women have not shared in access to new economic opportunities with men. We suggest that at the same time, their one traditional source of leverage, their fertility, has possibly diminished in value. Regrettably, women are valued for the dowry they will bring; but so long as their valuation rests primarily in their being vehicles of property transmission, they will remain vulnerable to dowry harassment and murder.

NOTES

1. In India there has been a long history of anti-dowry movements, and only recently have they concerned dowry harassment and murder issues. For discussion see Kumari (1989).
2. This observation was made by Frank Myka (personal communication) in his review of cases of dowry murders in the *Hindustan Times* during 1989.
3. For discussion of these aspects of women's lives in Hindu Nepal see Bennett (1983).
4. Boserup's work was an early contribution to what has become a vast literature that links female subordination to women's roles in production and women's access to property. Many of the arguments put forth in this line of research follow, with modification, Engels' (1884) treatise on the origin of the family. Important current studies can be found in Leacock and Safa (1986). Modern studies have in general emphasized that both the development of the world capitalist system and international development projects in the Third World have had adverse consequences for women. Today, different positions are taken within this framework. For a review of the literature see Tiano (1987).

REFERENCES

Beneria, Lourdes, and Sen, Gita. (1981). "Accumulation, Reproduction, and Women's Role in Economic Development: Boserup Revisited." *Signs,* 7, 279–298.

Bennett, Lynn. (1983). *Dangerous Wives and Sacred Sisters: Social and Religious Roles of High Caste Women in Nepal.* New York: Columbia University Press.

Bordewich, Fergus M. (1986). "Dowry Murders." *Atlantic Magazine,* July, pp. 21–27.

Boserup, Ester. (1970). *Women's Role in Economic Development.* London: George Allen & Unwin, Ltd.

Chhabra, Sagari. (1986). *Dowry Deaths in India: A Double Bind Perspective.* Unpublished master's thesis, Washington State University, Pullman.

Engels, Fredrich. (1884). *The Origin of the Family, Private Property, and the State.* New York: International.

Ghadially, Rehana, and Kumar, Promod. (1988). "Bride-burning: The Psycho-Social Dynamics of Dowry Deaths." In Rehana Ghadially (Ed.), *Women in Indian Society* (pp. 167–177). New Delhi: Sage Publications.

Goody, Jack. (1971). "Class and Marriage in Africa and Eurasia." *American Journal of Sociology.* 76, 585–603.

———. (1973). "Bridewealth and Dowry in Africa and Eurasia." Jack Goody and S. J. Tambiah (Eds.), *Bridewealth and Dowry* (pp. 1–58). Cambridge: Cambridge University Press.

———, Jack. (1976). *Production and Reproduction.* Cambridge: Cambridge University Press.

Goyal, R. S. (1989). "Social Inequalities and Fertility Behavior." In S. N. Singh, M. K. Premi, P. S. Bhatia, and Ashish Bose (Eds.), *Population Transition in India* (Vol. 2, pp. 153–161). New Delhi: B. R. Publishing Corporation.

James, Caroline. (1988). *People and Projects in Development Anthropology: A Literacy Project in Madhya Pradesh, India.* Unpublished Ph.D. dissertation, Washington State University, Pullman.

Jejeebhoy, Shireen J., and Sumati Kulkami. (1989). "Demand for Children and Reproductive Motivation: Empirical Observations from Rural Maharashtra." In Singh, M. K. Premi, P. S. Bhatia, and Ashish Bose (Eds.), *Population Transition in India* (Vol. 2; pp. 107–121). New Delhi: B. R. Publishing Corporation.

Kishwar, Madhu. (1986). Dowry: "To Ensure Her Happiness or to Disinherit her?" *Manushi,* 34, 2–13.

Kumari, Rajana. (1989). *Brides are Not for Burning: Dowry Victims in India.* London: Sangam Books Ltd.

Leacock, Eleanor, Safa, Helen, and contributors. (1986). *Women's Work, Development and the Division of Labor by Gender.* Boston: Bergin and Garvey Publishers, Inc.

Mandelbaum, David, (1970). "Society in India," Vol 1: *Continuity and Change.* Berkeley: University of California Press.

———, (1988). *Women's Seclusion and Men's Honor.* Tucson: University of Arizona Press.

Miller, Barbara. (1981). *The Endangered Sex.* Ithaca: Cornell University Press.

Rele, J. R. (1987). "Fertility Levels and Trends in India." *Population and Development Review,* 13, 513–530.

Schlegel, Alice. (1991). "Status, Property and the Value on Virginity." *American Ethnologist,* 18, 719–734.

Sharma, Ursula. (1984). "Dowry in North India: Its Consequences for Women." Renee Hirschon (Ed.). *Women and Property—Women as Property* (pp. 62–73). New York: St. Martin's Press.

Stein, Dorothy. (1988). "Burning Widows, Burning Brides: The Perils of Daughterhood in India." *Pacific Affairs,* 61, 465–485.

Tambiah, S. J. (1973). "Dowry and Bridewealth and the Property Rights of Women in South Asia." In Jack Goody and S. J. Tambiah (Eds.), *Bridewealth and Dowry* (pp. 59–169). Cambridge, MA: Cambridge University Press.

Tiano, Susan. (1987). "Gender, Work and World Capitalism: Third World Women's Role in Development." In Beth B. Hess and Myra Marx Ferree (Eds.), *Analyzing Gender: A Handbook of Social Science Research* (pp. 216–243) Newbury Park: Sage Publications.

van Willigen, John, and V.C. Channa, (1991). "Law, Custom, and Crimes Against Women: The Problem of Dowry Death in India." *Human Organization,* 50, 369–376.

Encountering the State: Cross-Cultural Perspectives on Women's Political Experience
Josephine Caldwell Ryan

In 1987, a Kenyan woman named Wambui Otieno became involved in a protracted legal battle that pitted her against her husband's family (Nzomo 1997, Nzomo and Staudt 1994). Otieno, a Christian Kikuyu, had married a Luo man who, suspecting that his family might attempt to dispossess his wife after his death, had asked to be buried on his farm near Nairobi. The case was decided in favor of Otieno's husband's relatives, and he was buried in his natal village instead. The case had clear implications for women's rights in customary law, a fact that was not lost on Otieno. According to the *Washington Post* she "warned Kenyan women that if she did not have the right to bury her husband, then they may not have the right to inherit their husband's property" (May 25, 1987, cited in Nzomo 1997:242).

In Wambui Otieno's case, she did retain control over property rights, but this is not always the outcome. In sub-Saharan African countries with plural legal systems, disputes may be settled in courts of statutory law, customary law, and in some cases, Islamic law. Zambia, for example, has a dual legal system in which both customary law and statutory laws apply to inheritance. Statutory law, which gives more consideration to women's inheritance rights, is frequently ignored in favor of customary law that privileges male kinship ties over conjugal ties should the husband die intestate. The specifics of applicable customary law vary between ethnic groups, but in general, widows may be "inherited" as part of the estate or may be left destitute as a result of "property-grabbing" by the husband's family. New laws have attempted to address the problem by allowing men to designate women as heirs in their wills, but the problem

Original material prepared for this text.

persists. The Intestate Succession Act of 1989, for example, allows a woman to contest property-grabbing, yet a study by the Women in Southern Africa Research Trust has shown that most women do not take advantage of the law because of fear of witchcraft being worked against them by the husband's relatives (Munalula and Mwenda 1995:99).

The first case provides an example of a woman choosing to use a legal system to fight for her rights, while the second shows the failure of law to ensure that women's rights are protected even when that is the intent. This essay draws upon data from a variety of cultural contexts to illustrate ways in which women engage, respond to, or resist the state. Depending on their circumstances, women's interaction with the state may take the shape of formal participation (i.e., electoral politics), participation in women's movements or other forms of collective action with a political intent or effect, or individual responses to state policies that directly or indirectly affect quality of life for themselves and their families.

It is understood that the term "state" is not being considered as an impersonal, homogeneous force exclusively for evil or good but rather, as Waylen has observed, "a differentiated set of institutions, agencies, and discourses, and the product of a particular historical and political conjuncture (1998: 7). The term "political engagement" is also used in a broad sense. Since the 1970s Western feminist scholars have mounted a critique of male-dominated mainstream political practice and "politics" as an area of intellectual investigation. Deconstructing the androcentric biases inherent in the language and basic concepts of political science, they have argued for a broader definition of politics, one that would include activities of women not usually considered to be within the parameters of "conventional politics" (see for example volumes edited by Phillips 1998 and Randall and Waylen 1998, also Silverblatt 1988 and Waylen 1996). It is not the intention here to present a comprehensive survey of women's political activities or power; Silverblatt (1988: 452) is correct in her observation that "no uniform history of women in the state can account for the complex, often contradictory, histories of how women have engaged their particular political worlds."

CURRENT TRENDS AFFECTING WOMEN'S POLITICAL STATUS

With a few exceptions, women in contemporary states have the legal right to vote, but this does not mean it can always be exercised.[1] For example, Patience Ndetei, an elected member the Kenyan Parliament, made the following comments regarding the 1988 elections:

> My experience in the field was that a lot of women do not have the final say, especially at home as to whom they should vote for. I had a woman who was badly beaten by her husband and she had to run away from him simply because she was going to vote for me. . . . I confronted many other cases where women were not free (*Daily Nation*, April 30, 1988, cited in Nzomo 1997: 237).

Statistics on women's representation in politics indicate that in the last ten years there has been a dramatic increase in the number of women officeholders globally. The average percentage of women in national legislatures is nearly 11 percent, but this aggregate figure masks the real disparity between regions such as the Arab states, which have hovered around 3 percent for the last 25 years, and the Nordic states, which have seen an increase from 16.1 percent in 1975 to 36.4 percent in 1997. The opposite trend is present in the states that formerly comprised the Soviet Union and the Eastern bloc, which have seen female representation drop from an average of 23.3 percent in 1975 to 11.5 percent in

1997 (Inter-Parliamentary Union 1997, cited in Jaquette 1997).

Jane S. Jaquette notes that women's political participation and representation does not automatically result from having the right to vote, cannot be explained solely by cultural factors such as the degree of gender equality, and cannot be predicted by the level of economic development. In Japan, for example, less than 2 percent of legislators are women; in the U.S. women make up 11.2 percent of Congress. One mechanism for increasing women's political representation is the use of quota systems, adopted either by individual political parties, as in Mexico and Chile, or mandated by the state, as in Argentina, Taiwan, and Brazil. In Jaquette's view, if the present trends continue, women will soon achieve "critical mass" in many countries and be able to set the agenda for political change. Jaquette offers the following to account for the increase in female officeholders globally:

> Three interconnected reasons seem to stand out: First, the rise of the women's movement worldwide has heightened women's awareness of their political potential and developed new issues for which women are ready to mobilize. Second, a new willingness by parties and states to ease the constraints on women's access to politics, from increasing their recruitment pools to modifying electoral systems and adopting quotas. And third, as social issues supplant security concerns in the post-Cold War political environment, opportunities have opened for new styles of leadership and have reordered political priorities (1997: 27).

The editors of a detailed comparative study of women's political engagement in forty-three countries open their introduction on a slightly less optimistic note, stating that the major finding is that "in no country do women have political status, access, or influence equal to men's (Chowdhury et al. 1994: 3). Drawing on the findings from the individual case studies, they point to four major trends influencing the political participation of women at the national and subnational level: the rise of religious fundamentalism, the changing nature of nationalism, international economic forces, and the growth of international feminism (1994:4-10.)

RELIGIOUS FUNDAMENTALISM

Chowdhury et al. acknowledge an increase in religious fundamentalism in major world religions such as Christianity and Hinduism during the last three decades, but emphasize that Muslim fundamentalism has had the most significant impact (1994: 8). Two recent examples of Muslim fundamentalism linked to political power are the 1977–1979 Revolution in Iran, led by the party of the Ayatollah Khomeini, and the fall of the modernist People's Democratic Party of Afghanistan to fundamentalist Mujahideen revolutionaries in 1992. Both events resulted in immediate and dramatic shifts in the status of women in those countries.

In Iran, women's roles were dramatically restructured through a process of Islamicization after the 1979 Revolution, but as Parvin Paidar's study of gender and the political process in twentieth century Iran shows, women were granted legal and social rights "because they were mothers or potential mothers" (1995: 260). Ayatollah Khomeini adopted a policy of women's formal participation in national processes because:

> . . . the political imperatives of revolutionary Iran convinced him that the very survival of the Islamic Republic in its formative years depended upon the active participation of both men and women in society. This was why, contrary to many expectations, the establishment of a theocratic state did not result in outright prohibition of women from social activities (Paidar 1995: 303).

Valentine Moghadam's (1994) analysis shows that in Afghanistan, reform measures were introduced by the Marxist People's Democratic Party of Afghanistan (PDPA) which came to power in the Saur Revolution of 1978. These included campaigns to improve literacy rates and educational attainment for women, stop payment of bride price, the levirate, and coerced marriages, and end the exploitation of female labor. These measures met resistance because they posed a direct challenge to patriarchal values, economic practice, and the control of land. In the face of armed resistance and outside interference, the PDPA backed away from some of their original goals, and in the end the drive to raise the status of women failed. The Islamic opposition groups, known as the Mujahideen, received support from Pakistan, Saudia Arabia, Iran, and several other nations including the United States, and the result was a protracted period of internal conflict. In 1992 the Mujahideen assumed power; this signaled the beginning of a period of reversal of gains for women. Moghadam writes:

> Once they came to power, the Mujahideen factions began to fight each other, but the men all agreed on the question of women. Thus the very first order of the new government was that all women should wear veils (1994:230).

In 1996 a group of religious students, called the Taleban, formed an opposition army and captured the capital, Kabul, after a bloody two year campaign. Raised in refugee camps in the 1980s, the men of the Taleban espoused a particularly conservative doctrine of Islam, and according to Moghadam, had "no conception of modern governance, democratic or participatory rule, or women's rights" (1999:180). The oppression of women in Afghanistan is now a matter of world attention, resulting in campaigns by both feminist and human rights organizations, such as the Feminist Majority Foundation.[2]

Moghadam points out that the level of modernization in Iran prior to the revolution in Iran has helped to liberalize the roles of women. But as the Islamic Republic has become less restrictive, the tribal patriarchal context of politics in Afghanistan has led to a dismal situation for women as a result of religious fanaticism (Moghadam 1999:172). Thus, specific circumstances of national histories and identities must be considered in comprehending the political status of women in any particular context, rather than using Islam or Islamicization as the sole explanatory factor. Deniz Kandiyoti's (1988) concept of the "patriarchal bargain" is also useful in understanding why women may act in ways that maintain the status quo of patriarchy; women pay the price of a patriarchal bargain, and in return get some degree of protection. According to Kandiyoti, different systems offer different sorts of "patriarchal bargains" to women, each with different "rules of the game and different strategies for maximizing security and optimizing their life options" (1988: 277).

Swarup et al. (1994: 375–376) provide two singular examples of growing religious fundamentalism in India. In contrast to decades of legislative action that outlawed *sati* (the immolation of widows), ended child marriage, and prohibited dowry, in 1986 the Indian government introduced the Muslim Women's (Protection of Rights in Divorce) Act. This law was intended to pacify leaders of conservative factions of the Muslim community who were outraged by the outcome of the Shah Bano case in which the Indian Supreme Court awarded alimony to the wife of a Muslim lawyer who had already married a much younger woman. The husband claimed that the Indian government was meddling in matters of Islam set forth in the *Sharia*.[3] The 1986 Act affirmed the primacy of *Sharia* law for Muslim women, and was opposed by women's rights groups and many educated Muslims. In the following year, a young widow was burned on her husband's funeral pyre. The act was condemned by women's rights organizations and intellectuals, but thousands of Hindu men and women marched in support of *sati* as a matter of cultural and family right. The Indian government responded by enacting the Sati Prevention Measure of 1987, but pro-*sati* attitudes persist. Swarup et al. conclude:

> Thus, in the name of supporting traditional law and custom, Muslim and Hindu fundamentalists have tried to reinforce the loosening shackles of medieval paternalistic morality and preserve

male supremacy. Although fundamentalists have so far been only somewhat successful, their power is increasing. This resurgence, coupled with the desire of the central government to maintain political stability at all costs, means that the influence of progressive and secular women is likely to be less powerful on this issue than on others (1994:377).

Historically, religion has often been a contentious issue for global feminists. For example, untangling the relationship between patriarchy and religion and refuting stereotypic depictions of Muslim women is a central theme in the writings of Nawal El Saadawi. Trained as a physician and a gifted writer, El Saadawi's activism on behalf of women's rights and other political issues in Egypt resulted in her being fired from her post as Director of Public Health and jailed by the government of Anwar Sadat. In 1982 she founded the Arab Woman's Solidarity Foundation, whose motto is "Power of Women-Solidarity-Unveiling of the Mind" (El Saadawi 1997). A controversial figure at home and abroad, El Saadawi consistently affirms her identity as an Arab woman and a Muslim while simultaneously denouncing religious fundamentalism and its subordinating effects on women.

THE CHANGING NATURE OF NATIONALISM

Modern nationalism is complex and variable in terms of fundamental concepts and practices, and the resulting configurations have different effects on women's status and political options. Chowdhury et al. (1994:6–8) note that the dominant themes during the period of decolonizing and rebuilding following World War II were achieving and strengthening the political power of the nation-state. In the process of state building most women in the world achieved formal (though not actual) legal equality. In addition, state secularism resulted in more opportunities for women as it weakened the power of gender hierarchy associated with religious denominations. In recent decades, however, state-focused nationalism has been challenged by the growth of ethnic, regional, and communal forces. The expansion of the European Economic Community on the one hand and the disintegration of the former Soviet Union on the other are recent examples of the trends of universalism and particularism at work.

Nations formed through revolution, such as the former Soviet Union, or decolonization, such as many countries in sub-Saharan Africa, have had to deal with serious internal ethnic and communal conflicts, and "often with only a thin veneer of representative government to find solutions" (Chowdhury et al. 1994:7). The recent ethnic fighting in the fragmented former Yugoslavia is one outcome of the trend toward particularism, and in that case, the deliberate use of rape as a weapon of war stands out as a singular example of the risks it can entail for women's status. According to Ruth Siefert, about 60,000 women in Bosnia-Herzegovina were victims of this form of warfare (Siefert 1996: 35.)

Another dimension of nationalism in African states is the effect of the colonial heritage on women's status. In an important article on women's politics in Africa, Staudt wrote that anthropological studies had provided "a vision of extensive female power as well as formal female authority in select areas of Africa" (1981: 2). She pointed out that colonialism affected women in two ways: first, colonial policies rendered women invisible and ignored any political authority they had possessed; second, the form of nationalist movements and the position of women within them and the new governments themselves reflected the colonial overlay (Staudt 1981:5). The new socialist governments such as those of Angola, Ethiopia, Guinea, Mozambique, and Tanzania, were more likely to incorporate "emancipation ideology" in the state structures, explicitly mandating access to education and political participation for women, many of whom had participated in protests and guerilla movements in the nationalist cause. However, most failed to address women's roles in the domestic and subsistence spheres, which produced glaring contradictions, for example the inability of women in Tanzanian villages to access control over important resources, such as the control of land or money from crops they had farmed (Staudt 1981:8–10). Problems related to gender ideology and/or customary law persist into the present, as evidenced by a recent United Nations press release that describes women farmers as "invisible," noting that only 5 percent of the resources provided through extension services are available to women. On a more optimistic note, the press release also reports that in March 1999, Mozambique's parliament adopted a controversial land tenure law that stressed the equality of men and women in obtaining land titles (United Nations Africa Recovery 1999). As a participant at a 1998 leadership seminar held in Zimbabwe commented:

> In the African Women's Movement we have a troubled relationship with Nationalism. It is a relationship which binds us to certain loyalties, loyalties which are directly and indirectly connected by our subjective relationship with men who inherited the state at independence (Machipisa 1998).

In Africa and elsewhere, one of the most significant trends of the last two decades has been democraticization, a process that has significantly altered the political map of the world. The process has varied from region to region; in Latin America, dictatorships were replaced by popular sovereignty, while many European nations shook off the mantle of Soviet control. Women were participants in the transition in both cases, but there were differences too, as described by Jaquette and Wolchik:

> In Latin America, women organized to protest economic conditions and undermined the claims of authoritarian regimes that they were creating the necessary conditions for economic growth. In Central and Eastern Europe, women contributed to undermining support for the Communist regimes by fostering values in the home which were not approved by the

Communist leadership. In Latin America these strategies of resistance resulted in the mobilization of women around gender issues, whereas the reverse was true in Central and Eastern Europe, where women's movements have been slow to organize after the transitions. There some women expressed their desire to return to the home; others voiced open skepticism about the value of equality in labor force participation and politics, the core goals of Western feminism (1998:4).

In summary, women's political engagement is shaped partially by the form of any particular nation-state as well as the historical circumstances that produced it. It thus both reflects and creates particular forms of gender relations and inequity (Waylen 1998:7).

INTERNATIONAL ECONOMIC FORCES

The relationship between economic status and political power is extremely complex. In their recent volume on the history of women and development in Africa, Snyder and Tadesse (1995) identify educational opportunities and economic empowerment as the two most pressing areas that must be addressed in Africa to improve women's status.

While acknowledging the importance of women's machinery within the government to insure women's voices are heard and ultimately to transform the institution, they also underline the idea that economic autonomy is a prerequisite for political empowerment (1995:182–184).

It is beyond the scope of this essay to review the large body of literature on gender and economic development (see Lockwood, this volume). Development theories have shifted several times since World War II, both with respect to economic development in general and with respect to women in particular (for recent perspectives on the latter see Kabeer 1994, Marchand and Parpart 1995, Snyder and Tadesse 1995). Suffice it to say that by the mid 1970s it was clear that both planned and unplanned economic development was not benefiting women and men equally and that in some cases women were actually losing ground (Boserup 1970, Tinker 1990). Trends and crises in the global economy in the 1970s exacerbated flawed development strategies, resulting in mounting debt, runaway inflation, and declining standards of living. These problems and others were addressed by policies introduced by the World Bank and the International Monetary Fund to promote macroeconomic stabilization and force internal structural transformation beginning in 1979. Loans were granted with conditions attached to them, which frequently created major economic upheavals as a result of mandatory devaluation of currency and belt-tightening of national budgets. Although the results varied from country to country, the overall pattern was that "structural adjustment" policies decreased public spending on education, health, and food subsidies and had the result of increasing the burden on women, who frequently had to work longer hours to absorb the cost of basic necessities, frequently in the informal sector of the economy.

In Ghana, for example, one result of economic stress in the last two decades is that women have been forced to take on a greater responsibility for providing for their families' needs. Work in the informal sector provides an important survival strategy for poor women, who gain income from subsistence farming, petty trading, food processing, and soap making, but it is complicated by social and infrastructural obstacles. Women work up to sixteen hours a day in economic activities. Whereas men are more likely to be involved in cash-cropping activities, 90 percent of women are subsistence farmers, meaning that they engage in small-scale hoe cultivation for survival needs. Women also work their husbands' farms and are responsible for transporting and marketing the farm produce of their husbands' farms. Women in rural Ghana have access to communal land through their male relatives, but have low levels of production because of heavy demands on their own labor and lack of capital to invest in production. They may cooperate with other women to share labor, or join a local credit pool to obtain capital, but are largely bypassed by extension agents and state resources. Their subsistence production is not acknowledged in official statistics and they are harassed by tax collectors and other state officials (Okine 1993).

Okine reports that the principal economic activity of poor urban women is petty trading and hawking. Although there is an upper echelon of traders who are large-scale wholesalers, they account for a tiny percentage of all traders, most of whom start with little or no capital at all. Many are the sole providers for their households. Because all vending and trading without a license is illegal, petty traders have to be wary of the police in order to avoid having their goods confiscated.

Okine points out that the economic activities of Ghanaian working women could hardly be described as liberating, in contrast to the way the economic productivity has been framed in Western Europe, and also that women's economic contributions are not recognized by policy makers or given any sort of meaningful state support. From this she concludes that the cause of the "persistent impoverishment" of Ghanaian women is not a male-dominated society, but rather "a lack of political power" (Okine 1993:191). The message in Okine's analysis is that the Ghanaian government must make changes to stop the economic exploitation of women and that women's organizations must be politically aware so that women will mobilize to pressure government; this is fundamentally a top-down approach.

Daises and Sadden (1993) also focus on women of the Third World, but their perspective on the responses of women to austerity measures associated with economic reform is somewhat different. They borrow Scott's (1985) concept of "everyday forms of resistance" to emphasize the agency that exists even in mundane, unorganized action with clearly defined, short-term objectives. They suggest that "even defensive struggles can, in the right circumstances, develop into more extensive forms of struggle with a greater

capacity for expanding the room for maneuver and for changing the conditions within which struggle takes place" (Daises and Sadden 1993:11). They also discuss ways in which women use networks, associations, and diverse forms of protest to respond to austerity measures. One dramatic form of collective action is illustrated by "bread riots," which often develop from street protests over concerns about cost of living and increases in staple commodities. Women participated in a wave of bread riots that took place in the mid 1980s in the Middle East and several North African nations. The fact that such protests are spontaneous and based on immediate short-term objectives (economic relief) does not change the fact that they are political actions with the potential to change state policies.

WOMEN AND COLLECTIVE ACTION IN INTERNATIONAL FEMINISM

In September 1995, some 36,000 women from 189 nations met in Beijing, China for a much-anticipated United Nations Conference on Women, the fourth such conference to be held since 1975. Previous conferences had been held in Mexico City, Copenhagen, and Nairobi as part of the United Nations Decade on Women (1975–1985). In the two decades between the designation of 1975 as the Year of the Woman by the United Nations and the Beijing conference, a global institutional framework for empowering women was established, a complex process involving national governments, international agencies, nongovernmental organizations, activists, and scholars. In addition to creating the institutional structures for addressing gender issues at a global level, the process also involved reconciling a myriad of diverse national and regional identities and agendas, as well as exploring diverging conceptions of feminism.[4]

One result of the Beijing conference was the *Declaration and Platform for Action,* a sophisticated and comprehensive document that unequivocally situates gender inequality as a matter of human rights and social justice. It outlines a plan of action to create the conditions that will result in empowered girls and women achieving gender equity in all areas of life. It calls for national governments, the international community, and all segments of civil society to implement proposals and instruments from earlier conferences, such as the Convention on the Elimination of All Forms of Discrimination Against Women (CEDAW)[5] and to take immediate action in twelve "critical areas of concern." The increasing burden of poverty on women, inequality in access to equal and adequate education and training, inequality in economic structures and policies, and inequality between women and men in the sharing of power and decision making are among those so identified. In addition to putting gender issues on the global agenda, the Beijing document is testimony that the international women's movement has come of age. As the authors of a recent analysis of the events leading up to the Beijing conference note,

> The Beijing process marks a turning point in the development of the women's movement. It demonstrated the strength of coordinated action, the political creativity of the movement and its ability to appropriate and permeate both national and global spheres. In doing so, the women's movement manifested itself as a political movement with a global character (Lycklama a Nijeholt et al 1998: 43.)

An explicit agenda for creating gender equity is needed because even when communities have a strong tradition of single sex organizing (see Van Allen, this volume), it does not necessarily mean that women will use their mutual aid or social organizations effectively to express their political will (Staudt 1981). According to Staudt and Parpart, the overall picture for women in Africa is that despite high levels of organizational affiliation, "their gains in pressuring states have been minimal" (1989:8). Snyder and Tadesse point out that in Africa there has been an increase in professional women's organizations[6] and growth in coordinating

organizations, but that "coalitions between grassroots women and educated women are still infrequent despite the great potential they hold for exerting pressure on governments to meet the immediate needs of rural women and to enact national policies that place human development and food security first" (1995:187).

Maxine Molyneaux has made a distinction between women's movements that are based on "practical" gender interests and address short-term, immediate concerns as opposed to those based on "strategic" interests; the latter derive "deductively from an analysis of women's subordination and from the formulation of a more satisfactory set of arrangements" (1985, cited in Waylen 1996: 20–22). Activities motivated by practical gender interests are diverse and take many forms, ranging from the "bread riots" discussed previously to communal kitchens, human rights campaigns, urban women's centers, and the like. Feminist movements involve women coming together self-consciously as women to press gender issues and are thus based on "strategic" gender interests. There is overlap between the two categories, but the scheme assists in understanding why women's movements do not necessarily involve a feminist consciousness.

The political participation of women in Argentina provides examples of both kinds of women's movements (Feijoo 1998). Although they were not enfranchised until 1947, Argentinean women were active in trade unions, anarchist and socialist movements, and other organizations. Before the 1976 military takeover, the women in various class and ethnic categories had been exposed to and had interacted with a variety of political ideologies, including international feminism in the 1970s, which resulted in the establishment of explicitly feminist organizations. The 1976 takeover introduced a period of state terrorism aimed at eliminating all dissident forces. Students, activists, and other "leftist" elements who posed a threat of popular mobilization were kidnapped and tortured, resulting in the "disappearance" of over 30,000 people (Feijoo

1989: 31–33). In response, women, generally mothers in their forties and fifties, engaged in increasingly large public demonstrations in the Plaza de Mayo, the main government square in Buenos Aires. Because they were acting in the role of mothers looking for their children, the military did not apply the usual punishments for subversion (Waylen 1996: 109). After the transition to democracy, however, the Madres distanced themselves from active political participation. Still their example was a model for similar movements in other Latin American dictatorships as well as for groups within Argentina seeking to cope with the difficult economic times that accompanied the transition.

In the process of constitutional reorganization, a quota law was passed requiring that 30 percent of upper level positions on party tickets be filled with women candidates; this has dramatically increased the formal participation of women. There has also been a resurgence of feminist organizing. It is thus ironic that as a result of the tendencies of President Menem to support the most conservative factions of women's organizations that the Argentinean delegation to the Beijing conference opposed policies favoring women's reproductive rights and "even questioned the use of the term 'gender'" (Feijoo 1989:43).

Further evidence of the overlap between practical and strategic gender interests in women's organizing is provided by Scarpaci's (1993) study of poor Chilean women under the Pinochet dictatorship (1973–1990). He interviewed members of a sewing cooperative formed to provide income from sewing tapestries and appliques to offset the costs of filing appeals on behalf of family members who had been detained by the state security forces. One finding was that the collective expanded to include literacy campaigns as well as discussion of women's issues. According to one member:

> When I began working I realized that I contribute to my household. I contribute economically and therefore I don't find it fair that my husband should get upset because I participate

in the [cooperative] and that he tells me I should do the wash and other things. I get upset, damn it, because I don't think only women should do these household chores (Scarpaci 1993:41).

In this case, it appears that a feminist consciousness was being produced through interaction in an organization that began as a response to a "practical" gender issue.

Understanding women's political motivation and mode of participation is no easier in countries with a longer history of liberal democracy, as in modern Japan. In a book remarkable for its innovative methodology as well as fresh thinking on the subject of women's political participation, Robin LeBlanc (1999) steps aside from the conventional studies of voter turnout and party platforms, waving on the "taxi" of political analysis and choosing a "bicycle" methodology to understand what citizenship means to Japanese housewives. LeBlanc was instructed by Japanese housewives how to ride a bicycle along paths and back alleyways quite different from the routes taxis took. In the process, she came to see the geography of her surroundings differently, and developed an awareness of the presence and activities of women from a new perspective. She notes that what one sees in the world of politics also depends on the social "transportation," or identity, one has. Ethnographic methods allowed LeBlanc to "follow" the paths Japanese housewives use as they confront the political system, producing information that would have been inaccessible from the "taxi" of formal political studies. Thus she provides a unique view into how Japanese women, alienated from the male world of elite politics and very conscious of themselves as "housewives," experience citizenship in a non-Western liberal democracy.

For example, she finds that participating in consumer cooperatives and volunteering "against" politics in activist causes are avenues through which housewives engage in collective action. She explores the interface between the public label of "housewife" and participation in the politics of the Netto party, which itself is the political wing of one such cooperative. Acknowledging that "bicycle citizenship" has its limitations in the present configuration of Japanese elite politics, she argues that this mode of citizenship is a facet of political organization that needs to be explored in other contexts as well.

THE GAP BETWEEN RHETORIC AND REALITY

As the foregoing discussion indicates, there are no easy generalizations about the nature or degree of political power of women. The last 25 years have been characterized by unprecedented global social, economic, and political change. Given that the obstacles to women's formal political participation have been removed (on paper at least) in most of the world's nations, does this mean that real political equity is in the near future for women?

Where women are disadvantaged educationally or struggle under entrenched patriarchal world views, political empowerment will not come easily. In Zimbabwe, for example, legislation was passed in the last two decades that permitted women to vote and made both men and women legally of age at 18. It also reformed divorce law for civil marriage, although marriage under customary law, which includes traditions of succession and inheritance, is also recognized. Before the years of structural adjustment, women also benefited from literacy campaigns and public health initiatives. Some state policies are less positive, such as the "clean up" campaigns that ostensibly target prostitutes. According to Jacobs, the 1983 campaign was directed against "younger, better-off-than-average women who appeared to be beyond 'traditional' patriarchal controls; that is, women for whom some employment opportunities have opened up recently" (1989:168).

The failure of the land tenure programs to consider gender as a factor has also had negative impact on women. The biggest such project in sub-Saharan Africa, Zimbabwe's

program to redistribute land to landless poor, takes two forms: in Model A projects, plots of land are distributed to heads of households, while in Model B projects, individuals own land communally. Jacobs found that resettlement benefited women in that it led to increased household incomes, but that women were excluded from holding title to individual plots. Unmarried women or widows can apply, but only small numbers actually receive title to the twelve acre plots. In case of divorce, a woman loses her right to remain on the land. One benefit that resettled women have that separates them from other Zimbabwean women is that rulings by resettlement officials have allowed wives, rather than brothers of the deceased, to inherit land. Thus, in Zimbabwe, gender ideology emphasizes the value of women who are rural producers, but state policy does not forbid their exclusion from the means of production. Polygyny rates are up in the resettlement areas, suggesting that junior wives are being used as laborers. Also, like urban women, resettlement women fear divorce because it will lead to poverty and loss of their children. For this reason, they are not likely to assert their demands (Jacobs 1998:129).

CONCLUSION

Nearly five years after the Beijing conference, this overview of trends affecting women's political engagement shows that the goals and strategies of women's political struggles are diverse and that the results of their efforts show uneven progress. It is also clear that the growth of an international feminist movement, a measurable trend to include "women's rights machinery" in national governments, and even increased numbers of female officeholders, will not bring women political power by themselves. There are new tools, such as the growing international communications network, but "cybersisterhood" cannot reach those who lack access to computers.

Although she is speaking about Zambian women, Munachonga's observation that "discrepancies between formal support for women's development and actual practice will not disappear easily, because the attitudes underpinning this reality are not amenable to legislation," applies to politically disadvantaged women everywhere (1989: 140). She sees long-term political education, requiring the concerted efforts of women, as the only solution. The truth of Munachonga's assessment can be seen in the current controversy in Zimbabwe surrounding the Magaya vs. Magaya case, in which Venia Magaya, age 52, was disinherited of her father's estate in favor of her younger half-brother. In March 1999 the Supreme Court ruled that according to customary law women's rights to inheritance, ownership of property, and custody of children are inferior to men's. Infuriated by the ruling, women's groups are calling for constitutional reform (Bald 1999). There is no doubt that women in Zimbabwe, who were crucial in that country's struggle for independence, have the potential to reshape political and social institutions. The question in Zimbabwe and around the globe is simply, how long will it take to create gender equity?

NOTES

1. The government of Kuwait recently rejected a measure that would have given women the right to vote (*New York Times*, December 1, 1999).
2. The Feminist Majority Foundation has mounted a large-scale education and petition drive to raise global awareness of the situation in Afghanistan. See their homepage at *www.feminist.org*.
3. All Muslims are subject to the Sharia, the code of divine law derived from the Quran, teachings of the Prophet Mohammed, and other sources. The Sharia contains guidelines and rules for all aspects of a Muslim's life.
4. This process continues into the present. A recent issue of Women's Studies International Forum is devoted to the interface of local feminisms and the implication for global feminisms (Flew et al. 1999).
5. CEDAW was adopted in 1979, the U.N. General Assembly and is an international bill of rights for women. It defines what constitutes discrimination

against women and sets up an agenda for national action to end it. An Optional Protocol to the Convention sets up procedures to make claims and to investigate cases of grave or systematic violations of women's rights is in process. (See the web site for United Nations Division for the Advancement of Women, *www.un.or/womenwatch/daw*).
6. Snyder and Tadesse cite a figure of 30,000 such groups in Kenya alone (1995:195).

REFERENCES

Bald, Margaret. 1999. "Second-Class Citizens." *World Press Review* 46(8):21.

Boserup, Esther. 1970. *Women's Role in Economic Development*. New York: St. Martin's Press.

Chowdhurry, Najma, and Barbara J. Nelson, with Kathryn A. Carver, Nancy J. Johnson, and Paula L. O'Loughlin. 1994. "Redefining Politics: Patterns of Women's Political Engagement from a Global Perspective." In Barbara J. Nelson and Najma Chowdhurry (eds.), *Women and Politics Worldwide*, pp. 3–24. New Haven: Yale University Press.

Daines, Victoria, and David Seddon. 1993. "Confronting Austerity: Women's Responses to Economic Reform." In Meredith Turshen and Briavel Holcomb (eds.), *Women's Lives and Public Policy: The International Experience*, pp. 3–32. Westport, Conn.: Praeger Publishers.

El Saadawi, Nawal. 1997. *The Nawal El Saadawi Reader*. London: Zed Books.

Feijoo, Maria del Carmen. 1998. "Democratic Participation and Women in Argentina. In Jane S. Jaquette and Sharon L. Wolchik (eds.), *Women and Democracy: Latin America and Central and Eastern Europe*, pp. 29–46. Baltimore: The Johns Hopkins Press.

Flew, Fiona, with Barbara Bagilhole, Jean Carabine, Natalie Fenton, Celia Kitzinger, Ruth Lister and Sue Wilkenson. 1999. Introduction: Local Feminisms, Global Futures. *Women's Studies International Forum* 22(4): 393–453.

Jacobs, Susan. 1989. "Zimbabwe: State, Class, and Gendered Models." In Jane L. Parpart and Kathleen A. Staudt (eds.), *Women and the State in Africa*, pp. 161–184. Boulder, Colorado: Lynne Rienner Publishers.

———. 1998. "The Gendered Politics of Land Reform: Three Comparative Studies". In Vicky Randall and Georgina Waylen (eds.), *Gender,*

Politics, and the State, pp. 121–142. London: Routledge.

Jacquette, Jane S. 1997. "Women in Power: From Tokenism to Critical Mass." *Foreign Policy*, Fall 1997, pp. 23–37.

——— and Sharon L. Wolchik. 1998 "Women and Democratization in Latin America and Central and Eastern Europe: A Comparative Introduction." In Jacquette, Jane S., and Sharon L. Wolchik, (eds.), *Women and Democracy: Latin America and Central and Eastern Europe*, pp. 1–28. Baltimore, MD: John Hopkins University Press.

Kabeer, Nalia. 1994. *Reversed Realities: Gender Hierarchies in Development Thought*. London: Verso.

Kandiyoti, Deniz. 1988. "Bargaining with Patriarchy." *Gender and Society* 2(3):274–290.

LeBlanc, Robin M. 1999. *Bicycle Citizens: The Political World of the Japanese Housewife*. Berkeley: University of California Press.

Lycklama a Nijeholt, Joke Sweibel, and Virginia Vargas. 1998. The Global Institutional Framework: The Long March to Beijing." In Geertje Lycklama a Nijeholt, Virginia Vargas, and Saskia Wieringa (eds.), *Women's Movements and Public Policy in Europe, Latin America, and the Caribbean*, pp. 25–48. New York: Garland Publishing, Inc.

Machipisa, Lewis. 1998. "Rights-Africa: Women Groups Prepare for the Next Millennium." November 23, 1998. Interpress Service. *http://www.oneworld.org/ips2/nov98/16_48_060.html*

Marchand, Marianne H., and Jane L. Parpart (eds). 1995. *Feminism/Postmodernism/Development*. London: Routledge.

Moghadam, Valentine M. 1994. "Revolution, Islamist Recation, and Women in Afghanistan." In Mary Ann Tétrault (ed.), *Women and Revolution in Africa, Asia, and the New World*, pp. 211–235. Columbia, SC: University of South Carolina Press.

———. 1999. "Revolution, Religion, and Gender Politics: Iran and Afghanistan Compared. In *Journal of Women's History*, 10(4):172–195.

Molyneux, M. 1985. "Mobilization Without Emancipation? Women's Interest, the State and Revolution in Nicaragua." *Feminist Studies* 11(2):227–254.

Munachonga, Monica L. 1989. "Women and the State: Zambia's Development Policies and Their Impact on Women." In Jane L. Parpart and Kathleen A. Staudt (eds.), *Women and the State in Africa*, pp. 130–142. Boulder: Lynne Rienner Publishers.

Munalula, Margaret Mulela, and Winnie Sithole Mwenda. 1995. "Case Study: Women and Inheritance Law in Zambia." In Margaret Jean Hay and Sharon Stichter (eds.), *African Women South of the Sahara*, pp. 93–100. New York: Longman.

Nzomo, Maria. 1997. "Kenyan Women in Politics and Public Decision-Making." In Gwendolyn Mikell (ed.), *African Feminism: The Politics of Survival in Sub-Saharan Africa*, pp. 232–254. Philadelphia: University of Pennsylvania Press.

———, and Kathleen Staudt. 1994. "Man-Made Political Machinery in Kenya: Political Space for Women?" In Barbara J. Nelson and Najma Chowdhurry (eds.), *Women and Politics Worldwide*, pp. 416–433. New Haven: Yale University Press.

Okine, Vicky. 1993. "The Survival Strategies of Poor Families in Ghana and the Role of Women Therein." In Joycelin Massiah (ed.), *Women in Developing Economies: Making Visible the Invisible*, pp. 167–194. Providence, RI: Berg Publishers.

Paidar, Parvin. 1995. *Women and the Political Process in Twentieth-Century Iran*. Cambridge: Cambridge University Press.

Parpart, Jane L., and Kathleen A. Staudt. 1989. "Women and the State in Africa." In Jane L. Parpart and Kathleen A. Staudt (eds.), *Women and the State in Africa*, pp. 1–19. Boulder: Lynne Rienner Publishers.

Phillips, Anne. Ed. 1998. *Feminism and Politics*. New York: Oxford University Press.

Randall, Vicky, and Georgina Waylen (eds.) 1998. *Gender, Politics and the State*. London: Routledge.

Siefert, Ruth. 1996. "The Second Front: The Logic of Sexual Violence in Wars." *Women's Studies International Forum* 19(1–2): 35-43.

Silverblatt, Irene. 1988. "Women in States." *Annual Review of Anthropology* 17:427–461.

Scarpaci, Joseph L. 1993. "Empowerment Strategies of Poor Urban Women under the Chilean Dictatorship." In Meredith Turshen and Brian Holcomb (eds.), *Women's Lives and Public Policy*, pp. 33–50. Westport, Connecticut: Greenwood Press.

Scott, J.C. 1985. *Weapons of the Weak: Everyday Forms of Peasant Resistance*. New York and London: Yale University Press.

Snyder, Margaret C. and Mary Tadesse. 1995. *African Women and Development: A History*. London: Zed Books.

Staudt, Kathleen. 1981. "Women's Politics in Africa." *Studies in Third World Societies*, 16:1–28. Williamsburg, VA: College of William and Mary.

————, (ed.). 1990. *Women, International Development, and Politics*. Philadelphia: Temple University Press.

Swarup, Hem Lata, Niroj Sinha, Chitra Ghosh, and Pam Rajput. 1994. "Women's Political Engagement in India: Some Critical Issues." In Barbara Nelson and Najma Chowdhury (eds), *Women and Politics Worldwide*, pp. 363–379. New Haven: Yale University Press.

Tinker, Irene (ed.). 1990. *Persistent Inequalities: Women and World Development*. New York: Oxford University Press.

United Nations. 1995. Report of the Fourth World Conference on Women, Beijing, 4–15 September 1995. A/CONF./177/20.

United Nations. 1999. "Women Farmers, the 'Invisible' Producers. *Africa Recovery*, vol. 11, no. 2.

Waylen, Georgina. 1996. *Gender in Third World Politics*. Boulder, Colorado: Lynne Rienner Publishers, Inc.

————. 1998. "Gender, Feminism, and the State: An Overview". In Vicky Randall and Georgina Waylen (eds.), *Gender, Politics and the State*, pp. 1-16. London: Routledge.

Japanese Mothers and Obentōs:
The Lunch-Box as Ideological State Apparatus

Anne Allison

INTRODUCTION

Japanese nursery school children, going off to school for the first time, carry with them a boxed lunch (*obentō*) prepared by their mothers at home. Customarily these *obentōs* are highly crafted elaborations of food: a multitude of miniature portions, artistically designed and precisely arranged, in a container that is sturdy and cute. Mothers tend to expend inordinate time and attention on these *obentōs* in efforts both to please their children and to affirm that they are good mothers. Children at nursery school are taught in turn that they must consume their entire meal according to school rituals.

Food in an *obentō* is an everyday practice of Japanese life. While its adoption at the nursery school level may seem only natural to Japanese and unremarkable to outsiders, I will argue in this article that the *obentō* is

Reprinted with permission from *Anthropological Quarterly* 64: 195–208, 1991. Copyright © The Catholic University of America.

invested with a gendered state ideology. Overseen by the authorities of the nursery school, an institution which is linked to, if not directly monitored by, the state, the practice of the *obentō* situates the producer as a woman and mother, and the consumer, as a child of a mother and a student of a school. Food in this context is neither casual nor arbitrary. Eaten quickly in its entirety by the student, the *obentō* must be fashioned by the mother so as to expedite this chore for the child. Both mother and child are being watched, judged, and constructed; and it is only through their joint effort that the goal can be accomplished.

I use Althusser's concept of the Ideological State Apparatus (1971) to frame my argument. I will briefly describe how food is coded as a cultural and aesthetic apparatus in Japan, and what authority the state holds over school in Japanese society. Thus situating the parameters within which the *obentō* is regulated and structured in the nursery school setting, I will examine the practice both of making and eating *obentō* within the context of one nursery school in Tokyo. As an anthropologist and mother of a child who attended this school for fifteen months, my analysis is based on my observations, on discussions with other mothers, daily conversations and an interview with my son's teacher, examination of *obentō* magazines and cookbooks, participation in school rituals, outings, and Mothers' Association meetings, and the multifarious experiences of my son and myself as we faced the *obentō* process every day.

I conclude that *obentōs* as a routine, task, and art form of nursery school culture are endowed with ideological and gendered meanings that the state indirectly manipulates. The manipulation is neither total nor totally coercive, however, and I argue that pleasure and creativity for both mother and child are also products of the *obentō*.

CULTURAL RITUAL AND STATE IDEOLOGY

As anthropologists have long understood, not only are the worlds we inhabit symbolically constructed, but also the constructions of our cultural symbols are endowed with, or have the potential for, power. How we see reality, in other words, is also how we live it. So the conventions by which we recognize our universe are also those by which each of us assumes our place and behavior within that universe. Culture is, in this sense, doubly constructive: constructing both the world for people and people for specific worlds.

The fact that culture is not necessarily innocent, and power not necessarily transparent, has been revealed by much theoretical work conducted both inside and outside the discipline of anthropology. The scholarship of the neo-Marxist Louis Althusser (1971), for example, has encouraged the conceptualization of power as a force which operates in ways that are subtle, disguised, and accepted as everyday social practice. Althusser differentiated between two major structures of power in modern capitalist societies. The first, he called, (Repressive) State Apparatus (SA), which is power that the state wields

and manages primarily through the threat of force. Here the state sanctions the usage of power and repression through such legitimized mechanisms as the law and police (1971: 143–5).

Contrasted with this is a second structure of power—Ideological State Apparatus(es) (ISA). These are institutions which have some overt function other than a political and/or administrative one: mass media, education, health and welfare, for example. More numerous, disparate, and functionally polymorphous than the SA, the ISA exert power not primarily through repression but through ideology. Designed and accepted as practices with another purpose—to educate (the school system), entertain (film industry), inform (news media), the ISA serve not only their stated objective but also an unstated one—that of indoctrinating people into seeing the world a certain way and of accepting certain identities as their own within that world (1971: 143–7).

While both structures of power operate simultaneously and complementarily, it is the ISA, according to Althusser, which in capitalist societies is the more influential of the two. Disguised and screened by another operation, the power of ideology in ISA can be both more far-reaching and insidious than the SA's power of coercion. Hidden in the movies we watch, the music we hear, the liquor we drink, the textbooks we read, it is overlooked because it is protected and its protection—or its alibi (Barthes 1957: 109–111)—allows the terms and relations of ideology to spill into and infiltrate our everyday lives.

A world of commodities, gender inequalities, and power differentials is seen not therefore in these terms but as a naturalized environment, one that makes sense because it has become our experience to live it and accept it in precisely this way. This common-sense acceptance of a particular world is the work of ideology, and it works by concealing the coercive and repressive elements of our everyday routines but also by making those routines of the everyday familiar, desirable, and simply our own. This is the critical element of Althusser's notion of ideological power: ideology is so potent because it becomes not only ours but us—the terms and machinery by which we structure ourselves and identify who we are.

JAPANESE FOOD AS CULTURAL MYTH

An author in one *obentō* magazine, the type of medium-sized publication that, filled with glossy pictures of *obentōs* and ideas and recipes for successfully recreating them, sold in the bookstores across Japan, declares, "... the making of the *obentō* is the one most worrisome concern facing the mother of a child going off to school for the first time (*Shufunotomo* 1980: inside cover). Another *obentō* journal, this one heftier and packaged in the encyclopedic series of the prolific women's publishing firm, *Shufunotomo*, articulates the same social fact: "First-time *obentōs* are a strain on both parent and child" (*"hajimete no obentō wa, oya mo ko mo kinchoˉshimasu"*) (*Shufunotomo* 1981: 55).

An outside observer might ask: What is the real source of worry over *obentō*? Is it the food itself or the entrance of the young child into school for the first time? Yet, as one look at a typical child's *obentō*—a small box packaged with a five or six-course miniaturized meal whose pieces and parts are artistically arranged, perfectly cut, and neatly arranged—would immediately reveal, no food is "just" food in Japan. What is not so immediately apparent, however, is why a small child with limited appetite and perhaps scant interest in food is the recipient of a meal as elaborate and as elaborately prepared as any made for an entire family or invited guests.

Certainly, in Japan much attention is focussed on the *obentō*, investing it with a significance far beyond that of the merely pragmatic, functional one of sustaining a child with nutritional foodstuffs. Since this investment beyond the pragmatic is true of any food prepared in Japan, it is helpful to examine culinary codes for food preparation that

operate generally in the society before focussing on children's *obentōs*.

As has been remarked often about Japanese food, the key element is appearance. Food must be organized, re-organized, arranged, re-arranged, stylized, and re-stylized to appear in a design that is visually attractive. Presentation is critical: not to the extent that taste and nutrition are displaced, as has been sometimes attributed to Japanese food, but to the degree that how food looks is at least as important as how it tastes and how good and sustaining it is for one's body.

As Donald Richie has pointed out in his eloquent and informative book *A Taste of Japan* (1985), presentational style is the guiding principle by which food is prepared in Japan, and the style is conditioned by a number of codes. One code is for smallness, separation, and fragmentation. Nothing large is allowed, so portions are all cut to be bite-sized, served in small amounts on tiny individual dishes, and are arranged on a table (or on a tray, or in an *obentō* box) in an array of small, separate containers.[1] There is no one big dinner plate with three large portions of vegetable, starch, and meat as in American cuisine. Consequently the eye is pulled not toward one totalizing center but away to a multiplicity of de-centered parts.[2]

Visually, food substances are presented according to a structural principle not only of segmentation but also of opposition. Foods are broken or cut to make contrasts of color, texture, and shape. Foods are meant to oppose one another and clash: pink against green, roundish foods against angular ones, smooth substances next to rough ones. This oppositional code operates not only within and between the foodstuffs themselves, but also between the attributes of the food and those of the containers in or on which they are placed: a circular mound in a square dish, a bland colored food set against a bright plate, a translucent sweet in a heavily textured bowl (Richie 1985: 40–41).

The container is as important as what is contained in Japanese cuisine, but it is really the containment that is stressed, that is, how food has been (re)constructed and (re)arranged from nature to appear, in both beauty and freshness, perfectly natural. This stylizing of nature is a third code by which presentation is directed; the injunction is not only to retain, as much as possible, the innate naturalness of ingredients—shopping daily so food is fresh and leaving much of it either raw or only minimally cooked—but also to recreate in prepared food the promise and appearance of being "natural." As Richie writes, "... the emphasis is on presentation of the natural rather than the natural itself. It is not what nature has wrought that excites admiration but what man has wrought with what nature has wrought" (1985: 11).

This naturalization of food is rendered through two main devices. One is by constantly hinting at and appropriating the nature that comes from outside—decorating food with seasonal reminders, such as a maple leaf in the fall or a flower in the spring, serving in-season fruits and vegetables, and using season-coordinated dishes such as glassware in the summer and heavy pottery in the winter. The other device, to some degree the inverse of the first, is to accentuate and perfect the preparation process to such an extent that the food appears not only to be natural, but more nearly perfect than nature without human intervention ever could be. This is nature made artificial. Thus, by naturalization, nature is not only taken in by Japanese cuisine, but taken over.

It is this ability both to appropriate "real" nature (the maple leaf on the tray) and to stamp the human reconstruction of that nature as "natural" that lends Japanese food its potential for cultural and ideological manipulation. It is what Barthes calls a second order myth (1957: 114–7): a language which has a function people accept as only pragmatic—the sending of roses to lovers, the consumption of wine with one's dinner, the cleaning up a mother does for her child—which is taken over by some interest or agenda to serve a different end—florists who can sell roses, liquor companies who can market wine, conservative politicians who

campaign for a gendered division of labor with women kept at home. The first order of language ("language-object"), thus emptied of its original meaning, is converted into an empty form by which it can assume a new, additional, second order of signification ("metalanguage" or "second-order semiological system"). As Barthes points out however, the primary meaning is never lost. Rather, it remains and stands as an alibi, the cover under which the second, politicized meaning can hide. Roses sell better, for example, when lovers view them as a vehicle to express love rather than the means by which a company stays in business.

At one level, food is just food in Japan—the medium by which humans sustain their nature and health. Yet under and through this code of pragmatics, Japanese cuisine carries other meanings that in Barthes' terms are mythological. One of these is national identity: food being appropriated as a sign of the culture. To be Japanese is to eat Japanese food, as so many Japanese confirm when they travel to other countries and cite the greatest problem they encounter to be the absence of "real" Japanese food. Stated the other way around, rice is so symbolically central to Japanese culture (meals and *obentōs* often being assembled with rice as the core and all other dishes, multifarious as they may be, as mere compliments or side dishes) that Japanese say they can never feel full until they have consumed their rice at a particular meal or at least once during the day.[3]

Embedded within this insistence on eating Japanese food, thereby reconfirming one as a member of the culture, are the principles by which Japanese food is customarily prepared: perfection, labor, small distinguishable parts, opposing segments, beauty, and the stamp of nature. Overarching all these more detailed codings are two that guide the making and ideological appropriation of the nursery school *obentōs* most directly: 1) there is an order to the food: a right way to do things, with everything in its place and each place coordinated with every other, and 2) the one who prepares the food takes on the responsibility of producing food to the standards of perfection and exactness that Japanese cuisine demands. Food may not be casual, in other words, nor the producer casual in her production. In these two rules is a message both about social order and the role gender plays in sustaining and nourishing that order.

SCHOOL, STATE, AND SUBJECTIVITY

In addition to language and second order meanings I suggest that the rituals and routines surrounding *obentōs* in Japanese nursery schools present, as it were, a third order, manipulation. This order is a use of a currency already established—one that has already appropriated a language of utility (food feeds hunger) to express and implant cultural behaviors. State-guided schools borrow this coded apparatus: using the natural convenience and cover of food not only to code a cultural order, but also to socialize children and mothers into the gendered roles and subjectivities they are expected to assume in a political order desired and directed by the state.

In modern capitalist societies such as Japan, it is the school, according to Althusser, which assumes the primary role of ideological state apparatus. A greater segment of the population spends longer hours and more years here than in previous historical periods. Also education has not taken over from other institutions, such as religion, the pedagogical function of being the major shaper and inculcator of knowledge for the society. Concurrently, as Althusser has pointed out for capitalist modernism (1971: 152, 156), there is the gradual replacement of repression by ideology as the prime mechanism for behavior enforcement. Influenced less by the threat of force and more by the devices that present and inform us of the world we live in and the subjectivities that world demands, knowledge and ideology become fused, and education emerges as the apparatus for pedagogical and ideological indoctrination.

In practice, as school teaches children how and what to think, it also shapes them for the roles and positions they will later assume as adult members of the society. How the social order is organized through vectors of gender, power, labor, and/or class, in other words, is not only as important a lesson as the basics of reading and writing, but is transmitted through and embedded in those classroom lessons. Knowledge thus is not only socially constructed, but also differentially acquired according to who one is or will be in the political society one will enter in later years. What precisely society requires in the way of workers, citizens, and parents will be the condition determining or influencing instruction in the schools.

This latter equation, of course, depends on two factors: 1) the convergence or divergence of different interests in what is desired as subjectivities, and 2) the power any particular interest, including that of the state, has in exerting its desires for subjects on or through the system of education. In the case of Japan, the state wields enormous control over the systematization of education. Through its Ministry of Education (Monbushō), one of the most powerful and influential ministries in the government, education is centralized and managed by a state bureaucracy that regulates almost every aspect of the educational process. On any given day, for example, what is taught in every public school follows the same curriculum, adheres to the same structure, and is informed by textbooks from the prescribed list. Teachers are nationally screened, school boards uniformly appointed (rather than elected), and students institutionally exhorted to obey teachers given their legal authority, for example, to write secret reports (*naishinsho*), that may obstruct a student's entrance into high school.[4]

The role of the state in Japanese education is not limited, however, to such extensive but codified authorities granted to the Ministry of Education. Even more powerful is the principle of the *"gakureki shakkai"* (lit. academic pedigree society) by which careers of adults are determined by the schools they attend as youths. A reflection and construction of the new economic order of post-war Japan,[5] school attendance has become the single most important determinant of who will achieve the most desirable positions in industry, government, and the professions. School attendance is itself based on a single criterion: a system of entrance exams which determines entrance selection and it is to this end—preparation for exams—that school, even at the nursery school level, is increasingly oriented. Learning to follow directions, do as one is told, and *"ganbaru"* (Asanuma 1987) are social imperatives, sanctioned by the state, and taught in the schools.

NURSERY SCHOOL AND IDEOLOGICAL APPROPRIATION OF THE *OBENTŌ*

The nursery school stands outside the structure of compulsory education in Japan. Most nursery schools are private; and, though not compelled by the state, a greater proportion of the three to six-year old population of Japan attends preschool than in any other industrialized nation (Tobin et al.1989; Hendry 1986; Boocock 1989).

Differentiated from the *hoikuen,* another pre-school institution with longer hours which is more like daycare than school,[6] the *yochien* (nursery school) is widely perceived as instructional, not necessarily in a formal curriculum but more in indoctrination to attitudes and structure of Japanese schooling. Children learn less about reading and writing than they do about how to become a Japanese student, and both parts of this formula— Japanese and student—are equally stressed. As Rohlen has written, "social order is generated" in the nursery school, first and foremost, by a system of routines (1989: 10, 21). Educational routines and rituals are therefore of heightened importance in *yochien,* for whereas these routines and rituals may be the format through which subjects are taught in higher grades, they are both form and subject in the *yochien.*

While the state (through its agency, the Ministry of Education) has no direct mandate over nursery school attendance, its influence is nevertheless significant. First, authority over how the *yochien* is run is in the hands of the Ministry of Education. Second, most parents and teachers see the *yochien* as the first step to the system of compulsory education that starts in the first grade and is closely controlled by Monbushō. The principal of the *yochien* my son attended, for example, stated that he saw his main duty to be preparing children to enter more easily the rigors of public education soon to come. Third, the rules and patterns of "group living" (shūdan-seikatsu), a Japanese social ideal that is reiterated nationwide by political leaders, corporate management, and marriage counselors, is first introduced to the child in nursery school.[7]

The entry into nursery school marks a transition both away from home and into the "real world," which is generally judged to be difficult, even traumatic, for the Japanese child (Peak 1989). The *obentō* is intended to ease a child's discomfiture and to allow a child's mother to manufacture something of herself and the home to accompany the child as s/he moves into the potentially threatening outside world. Japanese use the cultural categories of *soto* and *uchi; soto* connotes the outside, which in being distanced and other, is dirty and hostile; and *uchi* identifies as clean and comfortable what is inside and familiar. The school falls initially and, to some degree, perpetually, into a category of *soto.* What is ultimately the definition and location of *uchi,* by contrast, is the home, where family and mother reside.[8] By producing something from the home, a mother both girds and goads her child to face what is inevitable in the world that lies beyond. This is the mother's role and her gift; by giving of herself and the home (which she both symbolically represents and in reality manages)[9], the *soto* of the school is, if not transformed into the *uchi* of home, made more bearable by this sign of domestic and maternal hearth a child can bring to it.

The *obentō* is filled with the meaning of mother and home in a number of ways. The first is by sheer labor. Women spend what seems to be an inordinate amount of time on the production of this one item. As an experienced *obentō* maker, I can attest to the intense attention and energy devoted to this one chore. On the average, mothers spend 20–45 minutes every morning cooking, preparing, and assembling the contents of one *obentō* for one nursery school-aged child. In addition, the previous day they have planned, shopped, and often organized a supper meal with leftovers in mind for the next day's *obentō*. Frequently women[10] discuss *obentō* ideas with other mothers, scan *obentō* cookbooks or magazines for recipes, buy or make objects with which to decorate or contain (part of) the *obentō*, and perhaps make small food portions to freeze and retrieve for future *obentō*.[11]

Of course, effort alone does not necessarily produce a successful *obentō*. Casualness was never indulged, I observed, and even mothers with children who would eat anything prepared *obentōs* as elaborate as anyone else's. Such labor is intended for the child but also the mother: it is a sign of a woman's commitment as a mother and her inspiring her child to being similarly committed as a student. The *obentō* is thus a representation of what the mother is and what the child should become. A model for school is added to what is a gift and a reminder from home.

This equation is spelled out more precisely in a nursery school rule—all of the *obentō* must be eaten. Though on the face of it this is petty and mundane, the injunction is taken very seriously by nursery school teachers and is one not easily realized by very small children. The logic is that it is time for the child to meet certain expectations. One of the main agendas of the nursery school, after all, is to introduce and indoctrinate children into the patterns and rigors of Japanese education (Rohlen 1989; Sano 1989; Lewis 1989). And Japanese education, by all accounts, is not about fun (Duke 1986).

Learning is hard work with few choices or pleasures. Even *obentōs* from home stop once the child enters first grade.[12] The meals there are institutional: largely bland, unappealing, and prepared with only nutrition in mind. To ease a youngster into these upcoming (educational, social, disciplinary, culinary) routines, *yochien obentōs* are designed to be pleasing and personal. The *obentō* is also designed, however, as a test for the child. And the double meaning is not unintentional. A structure already filled with a signification of mother and home is then emptied to provide a new form: one now also written with the ideological demands of being a member of Japanese culture as well as a viable and successful Japanese in the realms of school and later work.

The exhortation to consume one's entire *obentō*[13] is articulated and enforced by the nursery school teacher. Making high drama out of eating by, for example, singing a song; collectively thanking Buddha (in the case of Buddhist nursery schools), one's mother for making the *obentō*, and one's father for providing the means to make the *obentō*; having two assigned class helpers pour the tea, the class eats together until everyone has finished. The teacher examines the children's *obentōs*, making sure the food is all consumed, and encouraging, sometimes scolding, children who are taking too long. Slow eaters do not fare well in this ritual, because they hold up the other students, who as a peer group also monitor a child's eating. My son often complained about a child whose slowness over food meant that the others were kept inside (rather than being allowed to play on the playground) for much of the lunch period.

Ultimately and officially, it is the teacher, however, whose role and authority it is to watch over food consumption and to judge the person consuming food. Her surveillance covers both the student and the mother, who in the matter of the *obentō*, must work together. The child's job is to eat the food and the mother's to prepare it. Hence, the responsibility and execution of one's task is not only shared but conditioned by the other. My son's teacher would talk with me daily about the progress he was making finishing his *obentōs*. Although the overt subject of discussion was my child, most of what was said was directed to me; what I could do in order to get David to consume his lunch more easily.

The intensity of these talks struck me at the time as curious. We had just settled in Japan and David, a highly verbal child, was attending a foreign school in a foreign language he had not yet mastered; he was the only non-Japanese child in the school. Many of his behaviors during this time were disruptive: for example, he went up and down the line of children during morning exercises hitting each child on the head. Hamada-sensei (the teacher), however, chose to discuss the *obentōs*. I thought surely David's survival in and adjustment to this environment depended much more on other factors, such as learning Japanese. Yet it was the *obentō* that was discussed with such recall of detail ("David ate all his peas today, but not a single carrot until I asked him to do so three times") and seriousness that I assumed her attention was being misplaced. The manifest reference was to box-lunches, but was not the latent reference to something else?[14]

Of course, there was another message, for me and my child. It was an injunction to follow directions, obey rules, and accept the authority of the school system. All of the latter were embedded in and inculcated through certain rituals: the nursery school, as any school (except such non-conventional ones as Waldorf and Montessori) and practically any social or institutional practice in Japan, was so heavily ritualized and ritualistic that the very form of ritual took on a meaning and value in and of itself (Rohlen 1989: 21, 27–8). Both the school day and school year of the nursery school were organized by these rituals. The day, apart from two free periods, for example, was broken by discrete routines—morning exercises, arts and crafts, gym instruction, singing—most of which were named and scheduled. The school year was also segmented into and marked by three annual events—sports day (*undōkai*) in the fall, winter assembly (*seikatsu happyōkai*) in

December, and dance festival (*bon odori*) in the summer. Energy was galvanized by these rituals, which demanded a degree of order as well as a discipline and self-control that non-Japanese would find remarkable.

Significantly, David's teacher marked his successful integration into the school system by his mastery not of the language or other cultural skills, but of the school's daily routines—walking in line, brushing his teeth after eating, arriving at school early, eagerly participating in greeting and departure ceremonies, and completing all of his *obentō* on time. Not only had he adjusted to the school structure, but he had also become assimilated to the other children. Or restated, what once had been externally enforced now became ideologically desirable; the everyday practices had moved from being alien (soto) to familiar (uchi) to him, from, that is, being someone else's to his own. My American child had to become, in some sense, Japanese, and where his teacher recognized this Japaneseness was in the daily routines such as finishing his *obentō*. The lesson learned early, which David learned as well, is that not adhering to routines such as completing one's *obentō* on time leads to not only admonishment from the teacher, but rejection from the other students.

The nursery school system differentiates between the child who does and the child who does not manage the multifarious and constant rituals of nursery school. And for those who do not manage there is a penalty which the child learns either to avoid or wish to avoid. Seeking the acceptance of his peers, the student develops the aptitude, willingness, and in the case of my son—whose outspokenness and individuality were the characteristics most noted in this culture—even the desire to conform to the highly ordered and structured practices of nursery school life. As Althusser (1971) wrote about ideology: the mechanism works when and because ideas about the world and particular roles in that world that serve other (social, political, economic, state) agendas become familiar and one's own.

Rohlen makes a similar point: that what is taught and learned in nursery school is social order. Called *shūdanseikatsu* or group life, it means organization into a group where a person's subjectivity is determined by a group membership and not "the assumption of choice and rational self-interest" (1989: 30). A child learns in nursery school to be with others, think like others, and act in tandem with others. This lesson is taught primarily through the precision and constancy of basic routines: "Order is shaped gradually by repeated practice of selected daily tasks ... that socialize the children to high degrees of neatness and uniformity" (p. 21). Yet a feeling of coerciveness is rarely experienced by the child when three principles of nursery school instruction are in place: 1) school routines are made "desirable and pleasant" (p. 30), 2) the teacher disguises her authority by trying to make the group the voice and unit of authority, and 3) the regimentation of the school is administered by an attitude of "intimacy" on the part of the teachers and administrators (p. 30). In short, when the desires and routines of the school are made into the desires and routines of the child, they are made acceptable.

MOTHERING AS GENDERED IDEOLOGICAL STATE APPARATUS

The rituals surrounding the *obentō* consumption in the school situate what ideological meanings the *obentō* transmits to the child. The process of production within the home, by contrast, organizes its somewhat different ideological package for the mother. While the two sets of meanings are intertwined, the mother is faced with different expectations in the preparation of the *obentō* than the child is in its consumption. At a pragmatic level the child must simply eat everything in the lunch box, whereas the mother's job is far more complicated. The onus for her is getting the child to consume what she has made, and the general attitude is that this is far more the mother's responsibility (at this nursery

school, transitional stage) than the child's. And this is no simple or easy task.

Much of what is written, advised, and discussed about the *obentō* has this aim explicitly in mind: that is, making food in such a way as to facilitate the child's duty to eat it. One magazine advises:

> The first day of taking *obentō* is a worrisome thing for mother and "*boku*" (child)[15] too. Put in easy-to-eat foods that your child likes and is already used to and prepare this food in small portions (*Shufunotomo* 1980: 28).

Filled with pages of recipes, hints, pictures, and ideas, the magazine codes each page with "helpful" headings:

- First off, easy-to-eat is step one.
- Next is being able to consume the *obentō* without leaving anything behind.
- Make it in such a way for the child to become proficient in the use of chopsticks.
- Decorate and fill it with cute dreams (*kawairashi yume*).
- For older classes (*nenchō*), make *obentō* filled with variety.
- Once he's become used to it, balance foods your child likes with those he dislikes.
- For kids who hate vegetables. . . .
- For kids who hate fish. . . .
- For kids who hate meat . . . (pp. 28–53).

Laced throughout cookbooks and other magazines devoted to *obentō*, the *obentō* guidelines issued by the school and sent home in the school flier every two weeks, and the words of Japanese mothers and teachers discussing *obentō*, are a number of principles: 1) food should be made easy to eat: portions cut or made small and manipulable with fingers or chopsticks, (child-size) spoons and forks, skewers, toothpicks, muffin tins, containers, 2) portions should be kept small so the *obentō* can be consumed quickly and without any left-overs, 3) food that a child does not yet like should be eventually added so as to remove fussiness (*sukikirai*) in food habits, 4) make the *obentō* pretty, cute, and visually changeable by presenting the food attractively and by adding non-food objects such as silver paper, foil, toothpick flags, paper napkins, cute handkerchiefs, and variously shaped containers for soy sauce and ketchup, and 5) design *obentō*-related items as much as possible by the mother's own hands including the *obentō* bag (*obentōfukuro*) in which the *obentō* is carried.

The strictures propounded by publications seem to be endless. In practice I found that visual appearance and appeal were stressed by the mothers. By contrast, the directive to use *obentō* as a training process—adding new foods and getting older children to use chopsticks and learn to tie the *furoshiki*[16]—was emphasized by those judging the *obentō* at the school. Where these two sets of concerns met was, of course, in the child's success or failure completing the *obentō*. Ultimately this outcome and the mother's role in it, was how the *obentō* was judged in my experience.

The aestheticization of the *obentō* is by far its most intriguing aspect for a cultural anthropologist. Aesthetic categories and codes that operate generally for Japanese cuisine are applied, though adjusted, to the nursery school format. Substances are many but petite, kept segmented and opposed, and manipulated intensively to achieve an appearance that often changes or disguises the food. As a mother insisted to me, the creation of a bear out of miniature hamburgers and rice, or a flower from an apple or peach, is meant to sustain a child's interest in the underlying food. Yet my child, at least, rarely noticed or appreciated the art I had so laboriously contrived. As for other children, I observed that even for those who ate with no obvious "fussiness," mothers' efforts to create food as style continued all year long.

Thus much of a woman's labor over *obentō* stems from some agenda other than that of getting the child to eat an entire lunch-box. The latter is certainly a consideration and it is the rationale as well as cover for women being scrutinized by the school's authority figure—the teacher. Yet two other factors are important. One is that the *obentō* is but one aspect of the far more expansive and continuous commitment a mother is expected to make

for and to her child. "*Kyōiku mama*" (education mother) is the term given to a mother who executes her responsibility to oversee and manage the education of her children with excessive vigor. And yet this excess is not only demanded by the state even at the level of the nursery school; it is conventionally given by mothers. Mothers who manage the home and children, often in virtual absence of a husband/father, are considered the factor that may make or break a child as s/he advances towards that pivotal point of the entrance examinations.[17]

In this sense, just as the *obentō* is meant as a device to assist a child in the struggles of first adjusting to school, the mother's role generally is perceived as being the support, goad, and cushion for the child. She will perform endless tasks to assist in her child's study: sharpen pencils and make midnight snacks as the child studies, attend cram schools to verse herself in subjects her child is weak in, make inquiries as to what school is most appropriate for her child, and consult with her child's teachers. If the child succeeds, a mother is complimented; if the child fails, a mother is blamed.

Thus at the nursery school level, the mother starts her own preparation for this upcoming role. Yet the jobs and energies demanded of a nursery school mother are, in themselves, surprisingly consuming. Just as the mother of an entering student is given a book listing all the pre-entry tasks she must complete, for example, making various bags and containers, affixing labels to all clothes in precisely the right place and with the size exactly right, she will be continually expected therafter to attend Mothers' Association meetings, accompany children on fieldtrips, wash the clothes and indoor shoes of her child every week, add required items to a child's bag on a day's notice, and generally be available. Few mothers at the school my son attended could afford to work in even part-time or temporary jobs. Those women who did tended either to keep their outside work a secret or be reprimanded by a teacher for insufficient devotion to their child. Motherhood, in other words, is institutionalized through the child's school and such routines as making the *obentō* as a full-time, kept-at-home job.[18]

The second factor in a woman's devotion to over-elaborating her child's lunch-box is that her experience doing this becomes a part of her and a statement, in some sense, of who she is. Marx writes that labor is the most "essential" aspect to our species-being and that the products we produce are the encapsulation of us and therefore our productivity (1970: 71–76). Likewise, women are what they are through the products they produce. An *obentō* therefore is not only a gift or test for a child, but a representation and product of the woman herself. Of course, the two ideologically converge, as has been stated already, but I would also suggest that there is a potential disjoining. I sensed that the women were laboring for themselves apart from the agenda the *obentō* was expected to fill at school. Or stated alternatively, in the role that females in Japan are highly pressured and encouraged to assume as domestic manager, mother, and wife, there is, besides the endless and onerous responsibilities, also an opportunity for play. Significantly, women find play and creativity not outside their social roles but within them.

Saying this is not to deny the constraints and surveillance under which Japanese women labor at their *obentō*. Like their children at school, they are watched by not only the teacher but each other, and perfect what they create, partially at least, so as to be confirmed as a good and dutiful mother in the eyes of other mothers. The enthusiasm with which they absorb this task then is like my son's acceptance and internalization of the nursery school routines; no longer enforced from outside it becomes adopted as one's own.

The making of the *obentō* is, I would thus argue, a double-edged sword for women. By relishing its creation (for all the intense labor expended, only once or twice did I hear a mother voice any complaint about this task), a woman is ensconcing herself in the ritualization and subjectivity (subjection) of being a mother in Japan. She is alienated in the sense that others will dictate, inspect, and manage her work. On the reverse side, however, it is precisely through this work that the woman expresses, identifies, and constitutes herself. As Althusser pointed out, ideology can never be totally abolished (1971: 170); the elaborations that women work on "natural" food produce an *obentō* which is creative and, to some degree, a fulfilling and personal statement of themselves.

Minami, an informant, revealed how both restrictive and pleasurable the daily rituals of motherhood can be. The mother of two children—one, aged three and one, a nursery school student, Minami had been a professional opera singer before marrying at the relatively late age of 32. Now, her daily schedule was organized by routines associated with her child's nursery school: for example, making the *obentō*, taking her daughter to school and picking her up, attending Mothers' Association meetings, arranging daily play dates, and keeping the school uniform clean. While Minami wished to return to singing, if only on a part-time basis, she said that the demands of motherhood, particularly those imposed by her child's attendance at nursery school, frustrated this desire. Secretly snatching only minutes out of any day to practice, Minami missed singing and told me that being a mother in Japan means the exclusion of almost anything else.[19]

Despite this frustration, however, Minami did not behave like a frustrated woman. Rather she devoted to her mothering an energy, creativity, and intelligence I found to be standard in the Japanese mothers I knew. She planned special outings for her children at least two or three times a week, organized games that she knew they would like and would teach them cognitive skills, created her own stories and designed costumes for afternoon play, and shopped daily for the meals she prepared with her children's favorite foods in mind. Minami told me often that she wished she could sing more, but never once did she complain about her children, the chores of child-raising, or being a mother. The attentiveness displayed otherwise in her mothering was exemplified most fully in Minami's *obentōs*. No two were ever alike, each had at least four or five parts, and she kept trying out new ideas for both new foods and new designs. She took pride as well as pleasure in her *obentō* handicraft; but while Minami's *obentō* creativity was impressive, it was not unusual.

Examples of such extraordinary *obentō* creations from an *obentō* magazine include: 1) ("donut *obentō*"): two donuts, two wieners cut to look like a worm, two cut pieces of apple, two small cheese rolls, one hard-boiled egg made to look like a rabbit with leaf ears and pickle eyes and set in an aluminum muffin tin, cute paper napkin added, 2) (wiener doll *obentō*): a bed of rice with two doll creations made out of wiener parts (each consists of eight pieces comprising hat, hair, head, arms, body, legs), a line of pink ginger, a line of green parsley, paper flag of France added, 3) (vegetable flower and tulip *obentō*): a bed of rice laced with chopped hard-boiled egg, three tulip flowers made out of cut wieners with spinach precisely arranged as stem and leaves, a fruit salad with two raisins, three cooked peaches, three pieces of cooked apple, 4) (sweetheart doll *obentō*—*abekku ningyō no obentō*): in a two-section *obentō* box there are four rice balls on one side, each with a different center, on the other side are two dolls made of quail's eggs for heads, eyes and mouth added, bodies of cucumber, arranged as if lying down with two raw carrots for the pillow, covers made of one flower—cut cooked carrot, two pieces of ham, pieces of cooked spinach, and with different colored plastic skewers holding the dolls together (*Shufunotomo* 1980: 27, 30).

The impulse to work and re-work nature in these *obentōs* is most obvious perhaps in the strategies used to transform, shape, and/or disguise foods. Every mother I knew came up with her own repertoire of such techniques, and every *obentō* magazine or cookbook I examined offered a special section on these devices. It is important to keep in mind that these are treated as only flourishes: embellishments added to parts of an *obentō* composed of many parts. The following is a list from one magazine: lemon pieces made into butterflies, hard boiled eggs into *daruma* (popular Japanese legendary figure of a monk without his eyes), sausage cut into flowers, a hard-boiled egg decorated as a baby, an apple piece cut into a leaf, a radish flaked into a flower, a cucumber cut like a flower, a *mikan* (nectarine orange) piece arranged into a basket, a boat with a sail made from a cucumber, skewered sausage, radish shaped like a mushroom, a quail egg flaked into a cherry, twisted *mikan* piece, sausage cut to become a crab, a patterned cucumber, a ribboned carrot, a flowered tomato, cabbage leaf flower, a potato cut to be a worm, a carrot designed as a red shoe, an apple cut to simulate a pineapple (pp. 57–60).

Nature is not only transformed but also supplemented by store-bought or mother-made objects which are precisely arranged in the *obentō*. The former come from an entire industry and commodification of the *obentō* process: complete racks or sections in stores selling *obentō* boxes, additional small containers, *obentō* bags, cups, chopstick and utensil containers (all these with various cute characters or designs on the front), cloth and paper napkins, foil, aluminum tins, colored ribbon or string, plastic skewers, toothpicks with paper flags, and paper dividers. The latter are the objects mothers are encouraged and praised for making themselves: *obentō* bags, napkins, and handkerchiefs with appliqued designs or the child's name embroidered. These supplements to the food, the arrangement of the food, and the *obentō* box's dividing walls (removable and adjustable) furnish the order of the *obentō*. Everything appears crisp and neat with each part kept in its own place: two tiny hamburgers set firmly atop a bed of rice; vegetables in a separate compartment in the box; fruit arranged in a muffin tin.

How the specific forms of *obentō* artistry—for example, a wiener cut to look like a worm and set within a muffin tin—are encoded symbolically is a fascinating subject. Limited here by space, however, I will only offer initial suggestions. Arranging food into a scene recognizable by the child was an ideal mentioned by many mothers and cookbooks. Why those of animals, human beings, and other food forms (making a pineapple out of an apple, for example) predominate may have no other rationale than being familiar to children and easily reproduced by mothers. Yet it is also true that this tendency to use a trope of realism—casting food into realistic figures—is most prevalent in the meals Japanese prepare for their children. Mothers I knew created animals and faces in supper meals and/or *obentōs* made for other outings, yet their impulse to do this seemed not only heightened in the *obentō* that were sent to school but also played down in food prepared for other age groups.

What is consistent in Japanese cooking generally, as stated earlier, are the dual principles of manipulation and order. Food is manipulated into some other form than it assumes either naturally or upon being cooked: lines are put into mashed potatoes, carrots are flaked, wieners are twisted and sliced. Also, food is ordered by some human rather than natural principle; everything must have neat boundaries and be placed precisely so those boundaries do not merge. These two structures are the ones most important in shaping the nursery school *obentō* as well, and the inclination to design realistic imagery is primarily a means by which these other culinary codes are learned by and made pleasurable for the child. The simulacrum of a pineapple recreated from an apple therefore is less about seeing the pineapple in an apple (a particular form) and more about reconstructing the apple into something else (the process of transformation).

The intense labor, management, commodification, and attentiveness that go into the making of an *obentō* laces it, however, with many and various meanings. Overarching all is the potential to aestheticize a certain social order, a social order which is coded (in cultural and culinary terms) as Japanese. Not only is a mother making food more palatable to her nursery school child, but she is creating food as a more aesthetic and pleasing social structure. The *obentō*'s message is that the world is constructed very precisely and that the role of any single Japanese in that world must be carried out with the same degree of precision. Production is demanding; and the producer must both keep within the borders of her/his role and work hard.

The message is also that it is women, not men, who are not only sustaining a child through food but carrying the ideological support of the culture that this food embeds. No Japanese man I spoke with had or desired the experience of making a nursery school *obentō* even once, and few were more than peripherally engaged in their children's education. The male is assigned a position in the outside world where he labors at a job for money and is expected to be primarily identified by and committed to his place of work.[20] Helping in the management of home and raising of children has not become an obvious male concern or interest in Japan, even as more and more women enter what was previously the male domain of work. Females have remained at and as the center of home in Japan and this message too is explicitly transmitted in both the production and consumption of entirely female-produced *obentō*.

The state accrues benefits from this arrangement. With children depending on the labor women devote to their mothering to such a degree, and women being pressured as well as pleasurized in such routine maternal productions as making the *obentō*—both effects encouraged and promoted by institutional features of the educational system heavily state-run and at least ideologically guided at even the nursery school level—a gendered division of labor is firmly set in place. Labor from males, socialized to be compliant and hard-working, is more extractable when they have wives to rely on for almost all domestic and familial management. And females become a source of cheap labor, as they are increasingly forced to enter the labor market to pay domestic costs (including those vast debts incurred in educating children) yet are increasingly constrained to low-paying part-time jobs because of the domestic duties they must also bear almost totally as mothers.

Hence, not only do females, as mothers, operate within the ideological state apparatus of Japan's school system that starts semi-officially, with the nursery school, they also operate as an ideological state apparatus unto themselves. Motherhood is state ideology, working through children at home and at school and through such mother-imprinted labor that a child carries from home to school as with the *obentō*. Hence the post-World War II conception of Japanese education as being egalitarian, democratic, and with no agenda of or for gender differentiation, does not in practice stand up. Concealed within such cultural practices as culinary style and child-focussed mothering, is a worldview in which the position and behavior an adult will assume has everything to do with the anatomy she/he was born with.

At the end, however, I am left with one question. If motherhood is not only watched and manipulated by the state but made by it into a conduit for ideological indoctrination, could not women subvert the political order by redesigning *obentō*? Asking this question, a Japanese friend, upon reading this paper, recalled her own experiences. Though her mother had been conventional in most other respects, she made her children *obentō*s that did not conform to the prevailing conventions. Basic, simple, and rarely artistic, Sawa also noted, in this connection, that the lines of these *obentō*s resembled those by which she was generally raised: as gender-neutral, treated as a person not "just as a girl," and being allowed a margin to think for herself. Today she is an exceptionally independent woman who has created a life for herself in America, away from homeland and parents, almost entirely on her own. She loves Japanese food, but the plain *obentō*s her mother made for her as a child, she is newly appreciative of now, as an adult. The *obentō*s fed her, but did not keep her culturally or ideologically attached. For this, Sawa says today, she is glad.

NOTES

Acknowledgments The fieldwork on which this article is based was supported by a Japan Foundation Postdoctoral Fellowship. I am grateful to Charles Piot for a thoughtful reading and useful suggestions for revision and to Jennifer Robertson for inviting my contribution to this issue. I would also like to thank Sawa Kurotani for her many ethnographic stories and input, and Phyllis Chock and two anonymous readers for the valuable contributions they made to revision of the manuscript.

1. As Dorinne Kondo has pointed out, however, these cuisinal principles may be conditioned by factors of both class and circumstance. Her *shitamachi* (more traditional area of Tokyo) informants, for example, adhered only casually to this coding and other Japanese she knew followed them more carefully when preparing food for guests rather than family and when eating outside rather than inside the home (Kondo 1990: 61–2).

2. Rice is often, if not always, included in a meal: and it may substantially as well as symbolically constitute the core of the meal. When served at a table it is put in a large pot or electric rice maker and will be spooned into a bowl, still no bigger or predominant than the many other containers from which a person eats. In an *obentō* rice may be in one, perhaps the largest, section of a multi-sectioned *obentō* box, yet it will be arranged with a variety of other foods. In a sense rice provides the syntactic and substantial center to a meal yet the presentation of the food rarely emphasizes this core. The rice bowl is refilled rather than heaped as in the preformed *obentō* box, and in the *obentō* rice is often embroidered, supplemented, and/or covered with other foodstuffs.

3. Japanese will both endure a high price for rice at home and resist American attempts to export rice to Japan in order to stay domestically self-sufficient in this national food *qua* cultural symbol. Rice is the only foodstuff in which the Japanese have retained self-sufficient production.

4. The primary sources on education used are Horio 1988; Duke 1986; Rohlen 1983; Cummings 1980.

5. Neither the state's role in overseeing education nor a system of standardized tests is a new development in post-World War II Japan. What is new is the national standardization of tests and, in this sense, the intensified role the

state has thus assumed in overseeing them. See Dore (1965) and Horio (1988).

6. Boocock (1989) differs from Tobin et al. (1989) on this point and asserts that the institutional differences are insignificant. She describes extensively how both yōchien and hoikuen are administered (yōchien are under the authority of Monbushō and hoikuen are under the authority of the Kōseishō, the Ministry of Health and Welfare) and how both feed into the larger system of education. She emphasizes diversity: though certain trends are common amongst preschools, differences in teaching styles and philosophies are plentiful as well.

7. According to Rohlen (1989), families are incapable of indoctrinating the child into this social pattern of shūndanseikatsu by their very structure and particularly by the relationship (of indulgence and dependence) between mother and child. For this reason and the importance placed on group structures in Japan, the nursery school's primary objective, argues Rohlen, is teaching children how to assimilate into groups. For further discussion of this point see also Peak 1989; Lewis 1989; Sano 1989; and the *Journal of Japanese Studies* issue [15(1)] devoted to Japanese preschool education in which these articles, including Boocock's, are published.

8. For a succinct anthropological discussion of these concepts, see Hendry (1987: 39–41). For an architectural study of Japan's management and organization of space in terms of such cultural categories as uchi and soto, see Greenbie (1988).

9. Endless studies, reports, surveys, and narratives document the close tie between women and home; domesticity and femininity in Japan. A recent international survey conducted for a Japanese housing construction firm, for example, polled couples with working wives in three cities, finding that 97% (of those polled) in Tokyo prepared breakfast for their families almost daily (compared with 43% in New York and 34% in London); 70% shopped for groceries on a daily basis (3% in New York, 14% in London), and that only 22% of them had husbands who assisted or were willing to assist with housework (62% in New York, 77% in London) (quoted in *Chicago Tribune* 1991). For a recent anthropological study of Japanese housewives in English, see Imamura (1987). Japanese sources include

Juristo zōkan sōgō tokushu 1985; *Mirai shakan* 1979; *Ohirasōri no seifu kenkyūkai* 3.

10. My comments pertain directly, of course, to only the women I observed, interviewed, and interacted with at the one private nursery school serving middle-class families in urban Tokyo. The profusion of obentō -related materials in the press plus the revelations made to me by Japanese and observations made by other researchers in Japan (for example, Tobin 1989; Fallows (1990), however, substantiate this as a more general phenomenon.

11. To illustrate this preoccupation and consciousness: during the time my son was not eating all his obentō many fellow mothers gave me suggestions, one mother lent me a magazine, his teacher gave me a full set of obentō cookbooks (one per season), and another mother gave me a set of small frozen food portions she had made in advance for future obentōs.

12. My son's teacher, Hamada-sensei, cited this explicitly as one of the reasons why the obentō was such an important training device for nursery school children. "Once they become ichinensei (first-graders) they'll be faced with a variety of food, prepared without elaboration or much spice, and will need to eat it within a delimited time period."

13. An anonymous reviewer questioned whether such emphasis placed on consumption of food in nursery school leads to food problems and anxieties in later years. Although I have heard that anorexia is a phenomenon now in Japan, I question its connection to nursery school obentōs. Much of the meaning of the latter practice, as I interpret it, has to do with the interface between production and consumption, and its gender linkage comes from the production end (mothers making it) rather than the consumption end (children eating it). Hence while control is taught through food, it is not a control linked primarily to females or bodily appearance, as anorexia may tend to be in this culture.

14. Fujita argues, from her experience as a working mother of a daycare (hoikuen) child, that the substance of these daily talks between teacher and mother is intentionally insignificant. Her interpretation is that the mother is not to be overly involved in, nor too informed about, matters of the school (1989).

15. "Boku" is a personal pronoun that males in Japan use as a familiar reference to themselves. Those in close relationships with

males—mothers and wives, for example—can use *boku* to refer to their sons or husbands. Its use in this context is telling.

16. In the upper third grade of the nursery school (*nenchō* class; children aged five to six) my son attended, children were ordered to bring their *obentō* with chopsticks and not forks and spoons (considered easier to use) and in the traditional *furoshiki* (piece of cloth which enwraps items and is double tied to close it) instead of the easier-to-manage *obentō* bags with drawstrings. Both *furoshiki* and chopsticks (*o-hashi*) are considered traditionally Japanese and their usage marks not only greater effort and skills on the part of the children but their enculturation into being Japanese.

17. For the mother's role in the education of her child, see, for example, White (1987). For an analysis, by a Japanese of the intense dependence on the mother that is created and cultivated in a child, see Doi (1971). For Japanese sources on the mother-child relationship and ideology (some say pathology) of Japanese motherhood, see Yamamura (1971); Kawai (1976); Kyūtoku (1981); *Sorifu seihonen taisaku honbuhen* (1981); *Kadeshobo shinsha* (1981). Fujita's account of the ideology of motherhood at the nursery school level is particularly interesting in this connection (1989).

18. Women are entering the labor market in increasing numbers yet the proportion to do so in the capacity of part-time workers (legally constituting as much as thirty-five hours per week but without the benefits accorded to full-time workers) has also increased. The choice of part-time over full-time employment has much to do with a woman's simultaneous and almost total responsibility for the domestic realm (*Juristo* 1985: see also Kondo 1990).

19 As Fujita (1989: 72–79) points out, its mothers are treated as a separate category of mothers, and non-working mothers are expected, by definition, to be mothers full time.

20. Nakane's much quoted text on Japanese society states this male position in structuralist terms (1970). Though dated, see also Vogel (1963) and Rohlen (1974) for descriptions of the social roles for middle-class, urban Japanese males. For a succinct recent discussion of gender roles within the family, see Lock (1990).

REFERENCES

Althusser, Louis. 1971. *Ideology and Ideological State Apparatuses (Notes toward an investigation in Lenin and philosophy and other essays)*. New York: Monthly Review.

Asanuma, Kaoru. 1987. *"Ganbari" no Kozo (Structure of "Ganbari")*. Tokyo: Kikkawa Kobunkan.

Barthes, Roland. 1957. *Mythologies*. Trans. by Annette Lavers. New York: Noonday Press.

Boocock, Sarane Spence. 1989. Controlled diversity: An overview of the Japanese preschool system. *The Journal of Japanese Studies* 15(1): 41–65.

Chicago Tribune. 1991. Burdens of Working Wives Weigh Heavily in Japan. January 27, Section 6, p. 7.

Cummings, William K. 1980. *Education and Equality in Japan*. Princeton NJ; Princeton University Press.

Doi, Takeo, 1971. *The Anatomy of Dependence: The Key Analysis of Japanese Behavior*. Trans. by John Becker. Tokyo: Kodansha Int'l. Ltd.

Dore, Ronald P. 1965. *Education in Tokugawa Japan*. London: Routledge and Kegan Paul.

Duke, Benjamin. 1986. *The Japanese School: Lessons for Industrial America*. New York: Praeger.

Fallows, Deborah. 1990. "Japanese Women." *National Geographic* 177(4): 52–83.

Fujita, Mariko. 1989. "It's All Mother's Fault": Childcare and the Socialization of Working Mothers in Japan. *The Journal of Japanese Studies* 15(1): 67–91.

Greenbie, Barrie B. 1988. *Space and Spirit in Modern Japan*. New Haven, CT: Yale University Press.

Hendry, Joy. 1986. *Becoming Japanese: The World of the Pre-School Child*. Honolulu: University of Hawaii Press.

———. 1987. *Understanding Japanese Society*. London: Croom Helm.

Horio, Teruhisa. 1988. *Educational Thought and Ideology in Modern Japan: State Authority and Intellectual Freedom*. Trans. by Steven Platzer. Tokyo: University of Tokyo Press.

Imamura, Anne E. 1987. *Urban Japanese Housewives: At Home and in the Community*. Honolulu: University of Hawaii Press.

Juristo zōkan Sōgōtokushu. 1985. Josei no Gensai to Mirai (The present and future of women). 39.

Kadeshobo shinsha. 1981. *Hahaoya (Mother)*. Tokyo: Kadeshobo shinsha.

Kawai, Hayao. 1976. *Bosei shakai nihon no Byōri (The Pathology of the Mother Society—Japan)*. Tokyo: Chuo Koronsha.

Kondo, Dorinne K. 1990. *Crafting Selves: Power, Gender, and Discourses of Identity in a Japanese Workplace*. Chicago, IL: University of Chicago Press.

Kyū toku, Shigemori. 1981. *Bogenbyo͞ (Disease Rooted in Motherhood)*. Vol. II. Tokyo: Sanma Kushuppan.

Lewis, Catherine C. 1989. From Indulgence to Internalization: Social Control in the Early School Years. *Journal of Japanese Studies* 15(1): 139–157.

Lock, Margaret. 1990. Restoring Order to the House of Japan. *The Wilson Quarterly* 14(4): 42–49.

Marx, Karl, and Frederick Engels. 1970 (1947). *Economic and Philosophic Manuscripts*, ed. C.J. Arthur. New York: International Publishers.

Mirai shakan. 1979. Shufu to onna (Housewives and Women). Kunitachishi Komininkan Shimindaigaku Semina - no Kiroku. Tokyo: Miraisha.

Mouer, Ross and Yoshio Sugimoto. 1986. *Images of Japanese Society: A Study in the Social Construction of Reality*. London: Routledge and Kegan.

Nakane, Chie, 1970. *Japanese Society*. Berkeley: University of California Press.

Ohirasōri no Seifu kenkyūkai. 1980. Katei Kiban no Jujitsu (The Fullness of Family Foundations). (Ohirasōri no Seifu Kenkyūkai - 3). Tokyo: Okurashō Insatsukyōku.

Peak, Lois. 1989. "Learning to Become Part of the Group: The Japanese Child's Transition to Preschool Life." *The Journal of Japanese Studies* 15(1): 93–123.

Ritchie, Donald. 1985. *A Taste of Japan: Food Fact and Fable, Customs and Etiquette, What the People Eat*. Tokyo: Kodansha International Ltd.

Rohlen, Thomas P. 1974. *The Harmony and Strength: Japanese White-Collar Organization in Anthropological Perspective*. Berkeley: University of California Press.

——. 1983. *Japan's High Schools*. Berkeley: University of California Press.

——. 1989. "Order in Japanese Society: Attachment, Authority and Routine." *The Journal of Japanese Studies* 15(1): 5–40.

Sano, Toshiyuki. 1989. "Methods of Social Control and Socialization in Japanese Day-Care Centers. *The Journal of Japanese Studies* 15(1):125–138.

Shufunotomo Besutoserekushon shiri-zu. 1980. Obentō 500 sen. Tokyo: Shufunotomo Co., Ltd.

Shufunotomohyakka shiri-zu. 1981. 365 nichi no obentō hyakka. Tokyo: Shufunotomo Co.

Sōrifu Seihonen Taisaku Honbuhen, 1981. Nihon no kodomo to hahaoya (Japenese mothers and chldren): Kokusaihikaku (international comparisons). Tokyo: Sōrifu Seishonen Taisaku Honbuhen.

Tobin, Joseph J., David Y. H. Wu, and Dana H. Davidson. 1989. *Preschool in Three Cultures: Japan, China, and the United States*. New Haven, CT: Yale University Press.

Vogel, Erza. 1963. *Japan's New Middle Class: The Salary Man and His Family in a Tokyo Suburb*. Berkeley: University of California Press.

White, Merry. 1987. *The Japanese Educational Challenge: A Commitment to Children*. New York: Free Press.

Yamamura, Yoshiaki. 1971. *Nihonjin to Haha: Bunka Toshite No Haha no Kannen Ni Tsuite no Kenkyu (The Japanese and Mother: Research on the Conceptualization of Mother as Culture)*. Tokyo: Toyo-shuppansha.

VIII

Gender, Household, and Kinship

The study of kinship has been central to cross-cultural research. Marriage customs, systems of descent, and patterns of residence have been described and compared in a range of societies around the world. At the heart of traditional studies of kinship is the opposition between the domestic domain on the one hand and the public, political, and jural domain on the other. Anthropologists, particularly those working in Africa, studied kinship in this latter domain. They delineated large corporate descent groups called lineages that managed property and resources and that were the basic building blocks of political organization (Fortes 1949, 1953). Marriage, for some kinship theorists, is a political transaction, involving the exchange of women between men who wish to form alliances (Levi-Strauss 1969; see also Ortner 1978). A woman, from this perspective, is a passive pawn with little influence over kinship transactions. She is viewed "in terms of the rights her kin have to her domestic labor, to the property she might acquire, to her children, and to her sexuality" (Lamphere 1974: 98). The dynamic, affective, and even interest-oriented aspects of women's kinship are essentially ignored in an approach that is rooted in androcentric principles: Women have the children; men impregnate the women; and men usually exercise control (Fox 1967).

Recent critiques of the traditional study of kinship have pointed out that it is "no longer adequate to view women as bringing to kinship primarily a capacity for bearing children while men bring primarily a capacity for participation in public life" (Collier and Yanagisako 1987: 7). A gendered approach to kinship takes a number of different directions but focuses on the status of men and women in different kinship systems and on the power (defined as the ability to make others conform to one's desires and wishes) that accrues to women through their manipulation of social relations (Maynes et al. 1996). Cross-cultural variations in the status of men and women have been examined in relation to rules of descent and postmarital residence (Martin and Voorhies 1975; Friedl 1975). Among horticulturalists, for example, women have higher status in societies characterized by matrilineal descent (descent through the female line from a common female ancestor) and matrilocal residence (living with the wife and her kin after marriage) than in societies characterized by patrilineal descent (descent through the male line from a common male ancestor) and patrilocal residence (living with the husband and his kin after marriage). In matrilineal systems, descent group membership, social identity, rights to land, and succession to political office are all inherited through one's mother.

When matrilineality is combined with matrilocal residence, a husband marries into a household in which a long-standing domestic coalition exists between his wife and her mother, sisters, and broader kin relations (Friedl 1975). These women cooperate with one another in work endeavors and provide mutual support. Although in a matrilineal system a man retains authority over his sisters and her children, the coalitions formed by kin-related women can provide them with power and influence both within and beyond the household (Brown 1970; Lamphere 1974) and also with a degree of sexual freedom. The important issue for women's status, as Schlegel (1972: 96) has argued, is not the descent system per se but the organization of the domestic group.

In this book, Menon discusses a classic anthropological case of matrilineality—the Nayar of South India. The Nayar are perhaps best known for their marriage system, which could be both polygynous (a man with several wives) or polyandrous (a woman with several husbands). Traditional Nayar women went through two forms of marriages, one the *tali-tying* (the tali is a gold ornament), and the other the *sambandam*, or joining together with one or more visiting husbands (See Gough 1961 for further discussion). Both these ceremonies legitimized reproduction for the matrilineal descent group or *taravad*. Menon (this book) focuses not only on the status and roles of women within the traditional matrilineal *taravads*, but also on how a slow shift from matriliny to patriliny (itself the result of broader social and economic changes) has opened other avenues for women. Among modern-day Nayar, *tali-tying* no longer exists, marriages are monogamous, and couples live in nuclear family households. While some authors have suggested that the status and autonomy accorded Nayar women under the traditional system has declined with these changes, Menon argues that both class and kinship position influenced the relative autonomy of women within the *taravad* just as they do in the new monogamous and nuclear family system.

In contrast to matrilineal and matrilocal systems, in patrilineal and patrilocal societies women do not have their own kin nearby. A woman enters her husband's household as a stranger. Separated from her own kin, she cannot forge lateral alliances easily. However, other opportunities are open to women that enhance their power and status in patrilineal and patrilocal societies. Taiwanese women, for example, marry into the households of their husbands (Wolf 1972). A Taiwanese wife must pay homage to her husband's ancestors, obey her husband and mother-in-law, and bear children for her husband's patrilineage. According to Wolf (1972: 32), "A woman can and, if she is ever to have any economic security, must provide the links in the male chain of descent, but she will never appear in anyone's genealogy as that all-important name connecting the past to the future."

After a Taiwanese wife gives birth to a son, her status in the household begins to change, and it improves during her life course as she forges what Wolf calls a uterine family—a family based on the powerful relationship between mothers and sons. The subordination of conjugal to intergenerational relationships that is exemplified by the Taiwanese case, as well as the opportune ways in which women take advantage of filial ties to achieve political power within and beyond the household, are apparent in other societies around the world—for example, in sub-Saharan Africa (Potash 1986).

When a Taiwanese wife becomes a mother-in-law she achieves the greatest power and status within her husband's household. Wolf (1972: 37) concludes that "the uterine family has no ideology, no formal structure, and no public existence. It is built out of sentiments and loyalties that die with its members, but it is no less real for all that. The descent lines of men are born and nourished in the uterine families of women, and it is here that a male ideology that excludes women makes its accommodations with reality." Similarly, Hausa trading women in West Africa are able to compensate for an ideology that keeps them in residential seclusion by depending on their children to distribute their goods, provide information on the world outside the household, and help with child care and cooking (Schildkrout 1983).

Wolf's research on Taiwanese women substantiates Lamphere's (1974: 99) observation that "the distribution of power and authority in the family, the developmental cycle of the domestic group, and women's strategies are all related." By "strategies" Lamphere is referring to the active ways in which women use and manipulate kinship to their own advantage. The strategic use of kinship is a mechanism for economic survival among the African-American families of a Midwestern town described by Stack (in this book). The households of these families are flexible and fluid; they are tied together by complex networks of female kinship and friendship. If the boundaries of the household are elastic, the ties that unite kin and friends are long-lasting. Through these domestic networks, women exchange a range of goods and services including child care. They rely on one another and through collective efforts keep one another afloat. When one member of the network achieves a degree of economic success she can choose to withdraw from kin cooperation to conserve resources. However, by reinitiating gift-giving and exchange, at some point she can easily reenter the system. Stack's research shows one example of a strategy pursued by many families in the United States who must cope with urban poverty and the constant threat of unemployment.

A similar approach is shown in research on Afro-Caribbean families, who also live in conditions of economic uncertainty and stress. This research has generated a vigorous debate about a complex of characteristics, including female-headed households, women's control of household earnings and decision making, kinship networks linked through women, and the absence of resident men. This complex of characteristics has been referred to as matrifocality. Drawing on data from her research in Jamaica, Prior (in this book) reviews the concept of matrifocality, a concept first introduced by Raymond Smith in 1956 to describe the central position and power of the mother within the household. Rather than viewing these households as disorganized or pathological results of slavery and colonialism, anthropologists recently have stressed their adaptive advantages (Bolles and Samuels 1989) for women who are both mothers and economic providers. Furthermore, as Prior suggests, the composition of households in the Caribbean is fluid; they can be female-headed at one point in time and nuclear at another. Arguing against a widely held conception within anthropology, Prior suggests that fathers and male partners are by no means marginal to the household.

Prior points out that very little work has been done on the relations between men and women in such households because men were always assumed to be absent. One neglected aspect of male–female household relations is domestic violence. Such violence often emerges because the expectations that women hold for men, whether they are monetary contributions to the household or fidelity, are not fulfilled. The potential for violence that can erupt when women challenge men about these unfulfilled obligations can undercut the power that women otherwise maintain within the household.

Women-centered families like those of African-Americans and Afro-Caribbeans have been described for other parts of the world (Tanner 1974). Both Brettell (1986) and Cole (1991) find such families among populations in northern Portugal and link them to a long history of male emigration. Whether in agriculture or in fishing, many women in northern Portugal must fulfill both male and female roles within the household.

In this region women often inherit significant property and there is a tendency for matrilocal residence or neolocal residence near the wife's kin. This matrilateral bias is also apparent among Japanese-American immigrants in the urban United States (Yanagisako 1977). Manifested in women-centered kin networks, this bias influences patterns of co-residence, residential proximity, mutual aid, and affective ties. Rather than stressing the economic reasons for the maintenance of kinship ties, Yanagisako draws attention to the role of women as kin keepers who foster and perpetuate channels of communication and who plan and stage elaborate family rituals.

The social and ritual importance of kinship is precisely what di Leonardo (in this book) focuses on in her discussion of the female world of cards and holidays. The Italian-American women she describes work in the labor market and at home, but they are also engaged in "kin work." Kin work is women's work and involves maintaining contact through all kinds of mechanisms with family members who are deemed important. Unlike child care and house cleaning, it is a task that has to be carried out by the woman herself. Though it is often burdensome, women undertake kin work, according to di Leonardo, because through it they can set up a chain of valuable and long-term obligations within a wide circle of social relations.

Although di Leonardo identifies other parts of the developed world in which women have greater kin knowledge than men and work hard at maintaining kinship networks (for example, Lomnitz and Perez-Lizaur 1987), several questions are open to further empirical investigation. For example, why does kin work take on ritual significance in some societies, and why is it culturally assigned to women in some contexts and to men in others? Di Leonardo interprets the emergence of gendered kin work in association with a relative decline in importance of the domain of public male kinship that is found, for example, in African societies characterized by a powerful principle of descent. The shift, she suggests, is part of the process of capitalist development. Enloe (1990) has taken these arguments much further by demonstrating how both global politics and global economics are engendered. Without kin work, for example, Hallmark (the card manufacturer) would be out of business.

Collier and Yanagisako (1987) have argued that gender and kinship are mutually constructed and should be brought together into one analytic field (see also Stone 1997). Kinship and gender are closely allied because they are both based in, but not exclusively determined by, biology and because what it means to be a man or a woman is directly linked to the rules of marriage and sexuality that a culture constructs. As Lindenbaum (1987: 221) has observed, "Relations of kinship are in certain societies, relations of production. If kinship is understood as a system that organizes the liens we hold on the emotions and labors of others, then it must be studied in relation to gender ideologies that enmesh men and women in diverse relations of productive and reproductive work. The variable constructions of male and female that emerge in different times and places are central to an understanding of the character of kinship."

REFERENCES

Bolles, A. Lynn and Deborah d'Amico Samuels. 1989. "Anthropological Scholarship on Gender in the English-Speaking Caribbean." In Sandra Morgen (ed.). *Gender and Anthropology*, pp. 171–188. Washington, DC: American Anthropological Association.

Brettell, Caroline B. 1986. *Men Who Migrate, Women Who Wait: Population and History in a Portuguese Parish*. Princeton: Princeton University Press.

Brown, Judith K. 1970. "Economic Organization and the Position of Women Among the Iroquois." *Ethnohistory* 17: 151–167.

Collier, Jane Fishburne and Sylvia Junko Yanagisako. 1987. *Gender and Kinship: Essays Toward a Unified Analysis*. Stanford: Stanford University Press.

Cole, Sally. 1991. *Women of the Praia: Work and Lives in a Portuguese Coastal Community*. Princeton: Princeton University Press.

Enloe, Cynthia. 1990. *Bananas, Beaches and Bases: Making Feminist Sense of International Politics*. Berkeley: University of California Press.

Fortes, Meyer. 1949. *The Web of Kinship Among the Tallensi*. London: International African Institute, Oxford University Press.

———. 1953. "The Structure of Unilineal Descent Groups." *American Anthropologist* 55: 25–39.

Fox, Robin. 1967. *Kinship and Marriage: An Anthropological Perspective*. Harmondsworth: Penguin.

Friedl, Ernestine. 1975. *Women and Men: An Anthropologist's View*. New York: Holt, Rinehart and Winston.

Gough, Kathleen. 1961. "Nayar: Central Kerala." In David M. Schneider and Kathleen Gough (eds.) *Matrilineal Kinship*, pp 298–384. Berkeley: University of California Press.

Lamphere, Louise. 1974. "Strategies, Cooperation, and Conflict Among Women in Domestic Groups." In Michelle Z. Rosaldo and Louise Lamphere (eds.). *Woman, Culture, and Society*, pp. 97–112. Stanford: Stanford University Press.

Levi-Strauss, Claude. 1969. *The Elementary Structures of Kinship*. Boston: Beacon Press.

Lindenbaum, Shirley, 1987. "The Mystification of Female Labors." In Jane Fishburne Collier and Sylvia Junko Yanagisako (eds.). *Gender and Kinship: Essays Toward a Unified Analysis*. Stanford: Stanford University Press.

Lomnitz, Larissa and Marisol Perez-Lizaur. 1987. *A Mexican Elite Family, 1820–1980*. Princeton: Princeton University Press.

Martin, M. Kay and Barbara Voorhies. 1975. *Female of the Species*. New York: Columbia University Press.

Maynes, Mary Jo, Ann Waltner, Birgitte Soland, and Ulrike Strasser. 1996. *Gender, Kinship, Power: A Comparative and Interdisciplinary History*. New York: Routledge.

Ortner, Sherry. 1978. "The Virgin and the State." *Feminist Studies* 4 (3): 19–35.

Potash, Betty (ed.). 1986. *Widows in African Societies*. Stanford: Stanford University Press.

Schildkrout, Enid. 1983. "Dependence and Autonomy: The Economic Activities of Secluded Hausa Women in Kano." In Christine Oppong (ed.). *Female and Male in West Africa*. Winchester, MA: Allen and Unwin.

Schlegel, Alice. 1972. *Male Dominance and Female Autonomy: Domestic Authority in Matrilineal Societies*. New Haven: Human Relations Area Files.

Smith, Raymond. 1956. *The Negro Family in British Guiana: Family Structure and Social Status in the Villages*. London: Routledge and Kegan Paul.

Stone, Linda. 1997. *Kinship and Gender: An Introduction*. Boulder, CO.: Westview Press.

Tanner, Nancy. 1974. "Matrifocality in Indonesia and Africa and Among Black Americans." In Michelle Z. Rosaldo and Louise Lamphere (eds.). *Woman, Culture, and Society*, pp. 129–156. Stanford: Stanford University Press.

Wolf, Margery. 1972. *Women and the Family in Rural Taiwan*. Stanford: Stanford University Press.

Yanagisako, Sylvia Junko. 1977. "Women-Centered Kin Networks in Urban Bilateral Kinship." *American Ethnologist* 2: 207–226.

Male Authority and Female Autonomy: A Study of the Matrilineal Nayars of Kerala, South India

Shanti Menon

In the winter of 1990, I was travelling on a train from Trichur to Madras in South India. My travelling companion was a middle-aged Nayar businessman, a widower. We got into a discussion about my research in Kerala. He was surprised that I was even considering studying Nayar women on the subject of female empowerment. "You are wasting your time," he said, with an arrogance that is typical of upper class Nayar men.

> Our women are really very well off, they are treated with great respect and they wield a lot of power. You should be studying the lower castes. Their women are treated like cattle. The men treat them like pieces of property which they own. They are not like us. That is the difference between matrilineality and patrilineality. Our women are in a very fortunate situation.

Later that evening he talked about his attempts to arrange a marriage for his son.

> All we want is a girl with a college degree and from an upper middle-class family. We want a girl who will stay at home and take care of things. I can't believe how difficult that is. Today, the moment a girl has a college degree she wants to go out and work. And once she starts earning some money she becomes very headstrong and self-willed. She starts placing her interests before that of the men in the household, and that's when the problems start. I know a lot of marriages that are breaking up because of this reason. We want to avoid that. Today girls are very different from what they were when I was young.

From Mary Jo Maynes, Ann Waltner, Birgitte Soland, and Ulrike Strassed, eds. *Gender, Kinship and Power: A Comparative and Interdisciplinary History.* New York: Routledge.

I found it interesting that he did not see the contradiction between the two sets of statements that he had made, a tension between beliefs and practices that characterizes the situation of women within the Nayar matrilineal kinship system. In this paper I propose to explore these tensions and the relationship between the dominant discourse on gender and kinship on the one hand and women's agency on the other. As Foucault (1978) states, "where there is power, there is resistance and yet, or rather consequently, this resistance is never in a position of exteriority in relation to power." I argue, through a narration of women's experiences, that Nayar matrilineality, like patrilineal kinship systems, operates within the structures of patriarchy. Nayar women covertly contest and disrupt this script in their everyday lives. They do not, however, openly challenge it.

In the public domain, Nayar women's speech and actions are framed within the terms of the dominant discourse. Scott (1990, p. 4) states that "situations of domination produce a public transcript in close conformity with how the dominant group would wish to have things appear. The dominant never control the stage absolutely, but their wishes normally prevail. In the short run, it is in the interest of the subordinate to produce a more or less credible performance, speaking the lines and making the gestures he knows are expected of him." This is a tactic that Nayar women adopt in their dealings with men. The "hidden transcript" is revealed in their private behavioral practices, at variance with their speech and actions in the public sphere.

In the first section of this article, I will describe the Nayar matrilineal kinship system and the transformation of this institution. In the second section, I will narrate, through Nayar women's "voices," their experiences of living within this kinship system, and what the changes mean in the context of their lives. In the final section, I will analyze women's contestation and disruption of the dominant gender and kinship ideology.

The accounts of women's lives are based on my fieldwork in Alanthara village in Trichur District, Central Kerala. Situated three miles from Trichur town, the district headquarters, Alanthara has expanded considerably over the past thirty years. Traditionally, the village has been an agricultural community. The land reform laws of the 1960s, which included a limit on the size of landholdings and redistribution of excess land among the landless laborers, brought radical changes in the economic pattern in the village. Tenant farming was abolished, and tenants were given the rights to the land that they cultivated. The Nayar households in the village, most of whom were landowners, lost a significant part of their holdings. Today agriculture is no longer a viable primary source of income for most families. Many of the young men work in urban areas, either within the state or outside. The expanding economy in the Middle East, following the oil boom, has provided laboring jobs for several young men in the village. The large sums of money that they send home to their families have drastically affected not only the class structure within the village but also the quality of life that people lead and their expectations and aspirations for the future.

I spent one year living in the village and talking with women from the "old" families. "Old" is a term used by the villagers when speaking of established families who have lived in the village for two generations or more, as opposed to those who have moved into the village in the recent past. In narrating the accounts of Nayar women's lives, I speak from my specific location as a Nayar woman whose family has lived in Alanthara for generations. Though I did not grow up in the village, I have strong ties with the place; it is my "home" in India.

Though the experiences narrated in these accounts are true for many Nayar women living in rural Central Kerala, they cannot be extended to Nayar women living in other regions in the state. Women's experiences within the matrilineal tradition vary across the state depending on socioeconomic and cultural factors.

NAYAR MATRILINEALITY IN CENTRAL KERALA

The Nayars of Central Kerala, a dominant caste group, traditionally "exemplified an extremely matrilineal form of social organization" (Moore 1986, p. 523). This was reflected primarily in their laws of inheritance and marriage systems. The Nayars lived in matrilineal joint families called *taravads*. A traditional *taravad* usually consisted of a set of matrilineally related kin, both male and female. This would include sisters and brothers, the sisters' children and their daughters' children. The property was owned communally by all the members of the family but it was managed by the most senior male member of the family, called the *karanavan*. He had no right to sell or give the property away; this could only be done with the consent of all the members of the *taravad*, but his authority regarding the management of the property and decisions taken within the *taravad* was absolute. Descent was traced through the female line, and property passed from a mother to her children, both male and female. A son had no right to pass his inheritance on to his children. On his death it reverted back to his *taravad*.

The marriage system *(sambandham)* of the matrilineal Nayars was characterized by loose marital ties, expressed in serial and simultaneous polyandry and polygyny and hypergamy, that is to say both men and women had multiple spouses, and women married men of a higher caste or class. Hypergamy was encouraged by the *taravad* because such a union raised its "prestige." The men lived in their own *taravads*, with their mothers and sisters, and visited their wives in the evening. They had no rights or responsibilities over their children. A woman's children were the responsibility of her *taravad*. There were no fathers or in-laws in a *taravad,* and little importance was attached to a relationship between husband and wife or father and children (Mencher 1965).

In the second half of the nineteenth century, the "impact of a cash economy, western style education, improved communication and a British inspired system of law" (Jeffrey 1976, p. xiv) led to major social and political changes. This in turn led to a popular demand for laws changing traditional matrilineal practices. A series of legislative measures stretching from 1896 to 1976, relating to personal and inheritance laws, slowly eroded matrilineal practices in Central Kerala (Jeffrey 1990). The changes were a result of "massive economic, ideological and legislative pressures (Mies 1980, p. 89) aimed at bringing the group in line with the dominant patrilineal system that existed in the rest of India. This has resulted in a redefinition of Nayar women's positions. In the following section of this paper, I narrate women's accounts of their experiences within this rapidly changing system. In doing so, my intention is not to reproduce the workings of the matrilineal system, but to explore ways in which matrilineality and patrilineality mirror one another. I examine women's locations within matrilineal kinship groups and the implications of these locations for the degree of autonomy that women exercise both within private spaces and in the public domain.

WOMEN'S VOICES AND THE "EXPERIENCE" OF MATRILINEALITY

Though legislation has effectively abolished matrilineal practices in Kerala, the Nayars, like my travelling companion on the train, still regard themselves and are seen by other castes as a matrilineal group. Though they occupy a subordinate position within the

kinship group, Nayar women do not experience some of the oppressive situations faced by women in patrilineal kinship groups. Kandiyoti (1988, p. 278) describes the control and manipulation of women under "classic" Indian patriarchy:

> Girls are given away in marriage at a very young age into households headed by their husband's father. There, they are subordinate not only to all the men but also to the more senior women, especially their mother-in-law . . . The young bride enters her husband's household as an effectively dispossessed individual who can establish her place in the patriliny only by producing male offspring. The patrilineage totally appropriates both women's labor and progeny and renders their work and contribution to production invisible.

Nayar women in Alanthara do not face similar situations. A woman owns property, and is never placed in a subservient position in her husband's home. A girl is not seen as a burden on her family, and there are no social pressures on her to bear sons. Her *taravad* is always her "home," and provides a great deal of security:

> It makes a difference when we are living in our own homes, we have greater autonomy because it is our place. The men may have more power than the women, often they only *seem* to take all the decisions in the family. What many people do not realize is that very often it is the women "within" the home who are the real decision makers, the men merely carry them out. But as we all know, it is important to project the men as the "real" figures of authority, to the world at large. This is necessary for the prestige of the *taravad.* However, being on our own ground gives us great strength. We have the freedom to speak freely without bothering about formal niceties. We have to deal with people related to us by blood, our mothers, our brothers, they are all "ours." That is not so with our husband's families. It is easier to deal with our own, to express needs and opinions and take actions that are related to our life. It is different with a set of people who we are connected with by marriage ties. Our strength lies in our own home. (Girija, age twenty-eight)

The *taravad* provides women with a space from which they can challenge the dominant gender ideology and exercise a certain degree of autonomy.

The Nayars are not a homogenous group, and a woman's influence within her kinship group is mediated by the socioeconomic class in which her *taravad* is situated. Women from landowning families are far more dependent on and controlled by the men in their *taravads* than women who are members of less affluent *taravads*. This is often ignored by writers when discussing the situation of Nayar women within the matrilineal kinship system. In 1901, the Cochin Census Commissioner, M. Sankara Menon (a Nayar), wrote:

> The condition of women under this complicated system requires to be specially noticed. The two sexes are nearly on a par as to inheritance of property. Again conjugal freedom also being not all on one side, the relations of the sexes appear to be more rational than amongst most other communities . . . . Further, the woman is free to enjoy the pleasures of social life, as it seldom falls to her lot to be worried with the miseries of domestic seclusion. (Fuller 1976, p. 6)

This picture was almost never completely accurate. The *karanavan* had considerable authority over all the members of the *taravad,* and women's movements outside the taravad and their sexuality were controlled. The extent of autonomy wielded by Nayar women is mediated both by their family organization and by their locations within a hierarchical class structure. Following Dyson and Moore (1983, p. 45) 1 define female autonomy as women's:

> capacity to manipulate [their] personal environment. Autonomy indicates the ability . . . to obtain information and to use it as the basis for making decisions about [their] private concerns and those of [their] intimates. Autonomy, in other words, relates directly to human agency.

In the traditional Nayar extended family, like in the patrilineal extended family, the oldest male member, the *karanavan,* was in a position of authority. Upper-class Nayar women, like the women in the other dominant castes and classes in patrilineal India, lived very circumscribed lives, controlled by their male kin. Kalyaniamma, a seventy-three-year-old matriarch of one of the leading *taravads* in Alanthara, described what it was like for her to live and grow up in a rural, landowning, upper-class *taravad.*

> I grew up in a joint family which included my grandmother, my mother, my mother's brother who was the karanavan of the *taravad,* and the five of us children—my four siblings and I. For many years my uncle's wife and their children also lived in our *taravad.* This was very unusual, but then the social practices had slowly begun to change at this time.
>
> My uncle, the *karanavan,* managed all the affairs of the household, including the finances. He would give the women money to run the household, and they were accountable to him for every *paise* that they spent.
>
> Though we women had some degree of freedom within the house, we were in charge of running the household and seeing to it that everything worked smoothly, our lives were very restricted. Most of the time we were confined to the physical space within the *taravad.* We had no access to the front of the house, and as a young girl I was not allowed to meet with male visitors to the *taravad.* The only time we went out of the *taravad* was to visit the temples, and at this time we were closely supervised by the older women. On rare occasions we visited the homes of other members of the family, but this did not happen often. We did not go to the stores, that was absolutely out. Everything that we wanted, including our clothes, was bought for us by the men. We had no choice but to like the clothes that they bought for us. No one asked us for an opinion anyway, and we never thought to give one. It was not our place. It is so different today. Women move around and there aren't as many restrictions as there were when I was young. My daughters had greater control over their lives when they were young than I ever did. That may have been because the *taravad* had broken up at the time they were growing up, and they lost their father when they were very young. It is easier dealing with a woman than negotiating with an autocratic male. (Kalyaniamma, age seventy-three)

The women in Kalyaniamma's *taravad* had a limited degree of autonomy in the management of "domestic" affairs, but on the whole their lives were controlled by the *karanavan*. The transformation of matrilineality within a brief time span is reflected in her description of the differences between her life and that of her daughters.

Kalyaniamma belongs to an affluent, landowning family in the village, a family that has the financial resources that enables it to seclude its women physically. Her kinswoman, Gowriamma, a member of a distant and less affluent branch of the same *taravad*, had greater autonomy in the management of her affairs. Her relatively lower class status placed far fewer social constraints on her life than that experienced by Kalyaniamma:

My father died when I was around thirteen years old. My mother became mentally unstable, and we were very badly off financially. The *karanavans* in the main *taravad* helped us quite a bit, but there was only so much that they could do, after all they had their own responsibilities. So my brother and I started working. I went out to work. That was quite unusual, in these parts at least. There were very few Nayar women in the job force; it is not like it is today. Today a lot of Nayar women are employed. When I was young only women from poor families went out to work. Families that had some income and could maintain a minimum standard of living, families where the members had something to eat everyday, and clothes to wear, in such families, the women stayed at home, they did not go out to work. I went to work because I had to; I had no choice, but I was an exception. Even many educated Nayar women stayed at home. The families felt that it was a matter of the *taravad* honor, it was a disgrace to send the women out of the home. I have been managing this household from a very young age, after all I helped to raise my siblings. I make all the decisions in this family. I am used to it, I cannot live any other way. (Gowriamma, age sixty-five)

Kalyaniamma and Gowriamma belong to different branches of the same *taravad*. The difference in their class positions influenced the control that each woman had over her life. There were far fewer physical and social constraints in Gowriamma's life than there were in Kalyaniamma's.

Women who lived in small *taravads* where there was no *karanavan* in residence also had a greater degree of autonomy. This fact was alluded to by all the women with whom I spoke:

It is easier for women to live together without men, especially when it is mother and daughters. The house is ours, and it is a very warm and supportive environment. (Janakiamma, age sixty-five)

My father died when I was very young and I lived here with my mother. My uncles did not live with us. We had a very close relationship, I could discuss everything with her. We made all the decisions regarding the household together . . . There are all the little things that women share with each other, especially mothers and daughters. It is a special relationship. In many respects my life was a lot easier than that of women in some of the other *taravads* where the *karanavans* took all the decisions and the women were expected to follow directions. I had a great deal of freedom. (Sharadaamma, age sixty-five)

Within the matrilineal tradition, the Nayars were both polygynous and polyandrous. Theoretically this meant that a woman could form and break alliances with men. However, in practice this, like the other aspects of her life, was mediated by her class position. For upper-class Nayar women, whose lives were strictly regulated by a set of rigid social codes, the opportunity to form independent relationships with men was practically nonexistent. The *karanavan* controlled the alliances that were formed. It is very likely that, similar to patrilineal kinship systems, women were used in forging male kinship networks and to further the interests of the male members of the *taravad*. The social control of women, through control of their sexuality, differs by class, and has different implications for women depending on their class status. Kalyaniamma describes the situation in her *taravad* in these words:

My mother and my grandmother had *sambandham* relationships. The trend shifted with our generation—we had monogamous marriages. There were monogamous marriages even in my mother's time, but in our *taravad* my mother and grandmother had polyandrous unions . . . . I have heard it said that after the five of us, my brothers, sister and I, were born our uncles decided that there were enough children in the *taravad.* They felt that the children were depleting the resources of the *taravad,* that they could not afford to economically support any more children. So they stopped the men from visiting my mother. That was the end of her *sambandham* relationships . . . . Our marriages were all arranged by the family. At this time it had become customary for the boy and girl to meet before the marriage was settled. I remember my husband came to visit us and I did meet with him before we were married. Of course the decision to accept the proposal was taken by the older members of the family, my grandmother and my uncle. I was not asked or expected to express an opinion. (Kalyaniamma, age seventy-three)

In this case, the men in the *taravad* had rights over their female kin, and they exercised rights to form social links and build power networks. The women had control over the marriage arrangements, and their dependence on the *taravad* left them with no choices or alternative courses of action.

Gowriamma, on the other hand, was economically independent. She worked to support her siblings, and the absence of a male authority figure gave her greater freedom. She had two children out of wedlock, and has been living with a man whom she has not married. Though this is common knowledge in the village, she is not ostracized, and is accepted by all the Nayar families.

Stolcke (1981) argues that in caste and lineage societies, where members' positions are determined by birth, marriage patterns and rules of inheritance either partially or totally define a person's social condition. Class and caste supremacy is maintained by endogamous marriages and the control of women's sexuality in them. Though the Nayars were hypergamous, marriage between individuals of widely different social classes was frowned upon. For example, Janakiamma, whose family owned a small store in the village, wanted to marry Raghu, a member of one of the landowning families. The idea was met with stiff opposition by both families:

Raghu and I wanted to marry each other but the families were absolutely against it. His family belonged to a higher social class. Even though we are both Nayars, the *karanavan* in his *taravad* made it known to the *karanavan* in our *taravad* that they would not accept our marriage. We lived in a joint family at that time, and my uncle made all the decisions in the family. He did not want to do anything that would antagonize Raghu's family, after all their status was higher than ours. So I was married off to a man working in Madras, I suppose they thought that was far enough to keep us apart. (Janakiamma, age sixty-five)

A marriage alliance not only brings two individuals together, but also links families and establishes genealogical status. For a couple to challenge this arrangement would lead to a disruption of class hierarchies, and was therefore actively discouraged.

Janakiamma returned to the village a few years later. Her *taravad* had split up by this time and they were no longer under the control of her uncle. She and Raghu started a relationship that lasted till his death a few years ago. Speaking about this she said:

I think women today have a lot more freedom than when I was young. I feel that if it had been today, we would not have to go through all that we did, we would have gone ahead and got married, and the families would have eventually come around. My mother was sympathetic but she was powerless, there was little that she could do . . . . In a way I think the system today is much better. It is easier to talk with and persuade a husband, rather than a brother. I think most women have some degree of power over men in a situation where they are sexually involved, and that is not the case with brothers. There is always a distance and it is impossible to talk with them beyond a point. (Janakiamma, age sixty-five)

It is significant that Janakiamma recognizes that, with the changing times, the control of women has passed from brothers to husbands. Women still do not have the autonomy, within the kinship system, to negotiate relationships for themselves, unless they step out of the sphere of male influence. Today, marriages are still arranged among the Nayars, but many more women have the freedom to refuse a match, and they are no longer governed by a tradition that demanded silence and absolute obedience to the will of the *karanavan*:

> Today marriage proposals are discussed with the young girls, and they have the freedom to turn down an alliance that they do not want. There is a lot of pressure on couples today to make a marriage work, and I think with a little bit of give and take most marriages can be made to work out. There are very few options for women if they walk out of a marriage, it is less socially acceptable to do so. It was easier to walk away from a marriage when I was young than it is today. (Janakiamma, age sixty-five)

The shift from matrilineality to patrilineality and monogamous marriages has meant that the "ownership" of a woman has passed from her *taravad* to her husband. It has also brought with it social and cultural pressures on women to adapt and conform to the patrilineal and patriarchal image of the "ideal" Indian woman, one who is loyal and submissive to her husband. It is no longer considered "respectable" for a woman to divorce her husband, and it is difficult for a woman to remarry, whether she is divorced or widowed.

Women from lower socioeconomic families are still in a vulnerable position and are often "used" to enhance the status of their *taravads*. Sudha was married at the age of eighteen to a young man in the village who is mentally retarded. She did not want the marriage, but was powerless to do anything about it. With little education and a job as a housemaid, she was pressured by her family to accept the match because:

> My family thought this marriage would get them out of the circle of poverty. Sunil's is an old *taravad,* and the marriage would raise our status. Everyone told me not to be selfish and think only of myself. So my life was sacrificed in the larger interests of the family. (Sudha, age twenty-eight)

The marriage alliance enabled Sudha's family to establish kinship connections that would have been impossible any other way. A few years later, her *taravad* was able to capitalize on this connection when they arranged a marriage for her younger sister to a man who belonged to a higher socioeconomic class. Sudha's better economic situation enabled her to pay some of the wedding expenses.

The shift towards patrilineality and the nuclear family has resulted in a different kind of control over women's sexuality. As Kalyaniamma describes it:

> Today if a woman is widowed, her chances of remarrying are very limited. That was not an issue when I was a child. By the time I was an adolescent there was also a stigma attached to unmarried women who had children. I think it went hand in hand with the spread of monogamous marriages. The women were not ostracized or anything, but people talked about it very disparagingly. Now of course, it is very difficult. It would be really hard on a woman if she has an illegitimate child, no matter to which class she belongs. (Kalyaniamma, age seventy-three)

Janakiamma's relationship with Raghu attracted some comment, but was accepted by the people in the village. Today, a woman in a similar situation would be ostracized irrespective of her caste and class situation.

Today polyandry and polygyny are nonexistent in Kerala. Male role definitions have shifted, and the husband, rather than the brother, is central to a woman's life. With the shift in the location of power, a woman's relationship with her husband and his family has taken on a significance that was absent within the *taravad* system:

> When my daughters come home for the vacations, they spend more time with their husbands' families than they do here. That is a big change in our residence patterns. We do not say

anything. Times have changed, and we feel that once the girls are married they ought to follow the wishes of their husbands . . . . And since the men stay in their homes, they expect their wives to do the same. (Veena, age forty-two)

This change in residence patterns has further weakened the Nayar matrilineal kinship system.

The social and economic changes that have resulted in the slow shift from matriliny to patriliny have also opened up new avenues for women. Today Nayar women are no longer constrained by the rigid traditions and practices that existed in the *taravad*. They have greater access to the world outside the four walls of their home, and increasing numbers are joining the work force.

MALE AUTHORITY AND FEMALE AUTONOMY

The narratives in the previous section are expressions of the "public" discourse on gender and kinship. They provide only a partial picture of individual women's lives within the matrilineal system. Women's agency and their subversion of the dominant discourse are obscured in this picture. It hides the fact that within their separate sphere women create a space from which they can resist male authority in subtle and silent ways. This resistance is never articulated; it is a shared secret among women. To voice it would be to bring out into the open, to make public the contradictions within which they operate—contradictions which they accept as part of their everyday lives.

The fact that Nayar women lived in *taravads* with related kin made it easy for women to forge bonds and work together to subvert male authority. For example, Janakiamma and Raghu could not influence the *karanavans* in both their *taravads* to arrange their marriage. However, in spite of all the restrictions on her movement, Janakiamma frequently met with Raghu, and at one time the two of them even contemplated eloping. When I asked her how she did this, she laughed and said:

There are ways and ways. Do you really believe that the men know everything that goes on in a household? The women do. The women would have liked to arrange this marriage, my mother was sympathetic but there was little that she could do. Marriages are negotiated between two families and the women were helpless... After my marriage ended, I returned home. My uncles had moved out of the *taravad* by then, and there was only my mother and I. It was easy for Raghu and I to start a relationship. My mother was very supportive, and we did not have to fear anyone. (Janakiamma, age sixty-five)

The strategies women employ to undermine the dominant ideology lurk in the background and are embedded within the contradictions in their narratives. For example, when talking about the control of resources in her *taravad*, Kalyaniamma said:

In our families it is the men who control the money. They keep the money with them and give it out to the women to run the household. In many instances the women had to account to the men for the money that they spent. My mother did not have to do that. But we had to ask the men for money. (Kalyaniamma, age seventy-three)

Later, when we discussed decision-making within the household, she presented a very different picture:

I am in charge of everything in this household. I control the money, I make the decisions. I think in most *taravads* it is the women who make the decisions. Of course, the men like to think that they do, and we let it seem that way (laughs), but when you get down to the bottom of it, it is the women who are in control. (Kalyaniamma, age seventy-three)

In this instance Kalyaniamma informally subverted the authority of the men in the family. She recognized that this has to be done covertly and within the private space of the family. The men accept this fact, as long as their authority is not publicly challenged and both sides pretend that it is the men who are in charge of affairs. As Scott (1991,

p. 779) points out, the fact that women's power can only be exercised within the private domain of the household "reaffirms men's official rule as powerholders [and] is a tribute . . . to men's continued control of the public transcript."

Women also employ strategies of submission and silence in order to negotiate positions of autonomy for themselves. Neeta, a young woman who works as a clerk in a government office, described the financial arrangements in her family in these words:

> My husband makes almost all the decisions in the household, and I go along with him . . . . It is not really as difficult as it sounds. I hand my paycheck to him every month, he controls the money and the expenses for the household. I like it that way, it saves me a lot of bother. (Neeta, age twenty-seven)

In this statement she lays out the traditional position that places men in control of household resources. Later, talking about her job, she says:

> I do not think I could ever give up my job. I enjoy the independence it gives me . . . . I do not have to depend on anyone for money, I do not have to ask someone for every little thing that I need.
>
> I: But you told me earlier that you handed your paycheck to your husband?
>
> N: I do that, but I do not give him everything. I keep some money aside for my use and give him the rest. This money is mine to do with as I please. I do not spend it on the household or on the children; that has to come out of the money in the bank. I am sure that my husband knows that I do not give him all my salary, but he has never asked me about it and I see no need to discuss it with him. There are some things that are best not spoken about, we all know that don't we? (laughs) (Neeta, age twenty-seven)

In this instance Neeta has created a space for herself by not directly confronting her husband's authority. In this situation her submission and silence are temporary holding positions rather than markers of oppression.

My intention in this paper is not to argue that Nayar women are able to resist or counteract all forms of male domination. However, I would like to contradict the suggestion made by some writers (Mies 1980; Liddle and Joshi 1986) that matrilineal kinship systems gave women a considerable degree of autonomy. As these narratives show, women's lives are made up of overlapping and intersecting layers within which they negotiate specific positions, depending on their class locations and the particular historical moment.

Dorothy Smith (1987) argues that our view of the world is not built upon our experiences. Instead it is constructed on the silence of women, by men who occupy positions of power. In this paper, I have attempted to represent the voices of a few Nayar women, to capture some of the tensions of their experiences as they have lived and articulated them. However, "it is not individuals who have experience, but subjects who are constituted through experience" (Scott 1991, p. 779). The evidence presented in these separated yet related narratives offers complex yet partial insights into individual women's lives. Their subversion of the dominant gender and kinship ideology that places them in subordinate positions is embedded in silence and contradictions. They do not offer any critique of their situation or directly challenge male authority. Instead they work around it, and in so doing perpetuate gender hegemonies. In many significant ways, patrilineality and matrilineality, at least as practiced among the Nayars, are two sides of the same coin, particularly with regard to the power relationships within which women are located. Women's resistance to these power relationships may take on new meanings within changing contexts as matrilineality is further transformed and redefined by historical forces and dominant ideologies.

NOTE

The fieldwork on which this paper is based was carried out in Alanthara village, Trichur District,

Kerala during 1990 and 1991. It was supported by a grant from the American Institute of Indian Studies, Chicago. I would like to thank Sari Biklen, Susan Wadley, Jyotsna Singh and Deborah Neff for comments on earlier drafts of this article.

REFERENCES

Dyson, Tim, and Mick Moore. "On Kinship Structure, Female Autonomy, and Demographic Behavior in India." *Population and Development Review*, Vol. 9, No. I (March 1983): 35–60.

Foucault, Michel. *The History of Sexuality Vol. 1: An Introduction.* New York: Random House, 1978.

Fuller, C.J. *The Nayars Today.* Cambridge: Cambridge University Press, 1976.

Jeffrey, Robin. *The Decline of Nayar Dominance.* New York: Holmes & Meier Publishers Inc., 1976.

Jeffrey, Robin. "Matriliny, Women, Development—and a Typographical Error." *Pacific Affairs* 63 (Fall 1990): 373–377.

Kandiyoti, Deniz. "Bargaining with Patriarchy." *Gender and Society,* Vol. 2, No. 3 (September 1988):274–290.

Liddle, Joanna, and Rama Joshi. *Daughters of Independence.* London: Zed Books Ltd., 1986.

Mencher, Joan P. "The Nayars of South Malabar." In *Comparative Family Systems,* ed. M.F. Nimkoff. Boston: Houghton Mifflin Company, 1965, pp. 163–191.

Mies, Maria. *Indian Women and Patriarchy. Conflicts and Dilemmas of Working Women.* New Delhi: Concept Publishing Company, 1980.

Moore, Melinda A. "A New Look at the Nayar Taravad." *Man* (N.S.) 20 (1986): 523–541.

Omvedt, Gail. "'Patriarchy': the Analysis of Women's Oppression," *The Insurgent Sociologist.* Vol. 13, No. 3 (1986): 30–50.

Scott, James C. *Domination and the Art of Resistance.* New Haven: Yale University Press, 1990.

Scott, James W. "A New Look at the Nayar Taravad," *Man* (N.S.) 20 (1986): 523–541.

Scott, Joan W. "The Evidence of Experience." *Critical Inquiry* 17 (1991): 773-797.

Smith, Dorothy. *The Everyday World as Problematic. A Feminist Sociology.* Boston: Northeastern University Press, 1987.

Stolcke, Verena. "Women's Labours: The Naturalisation of Social Inequality and Women's Subordination." In *Of Marriage and the Market: Women's Subordination Internationally and its Lessons,* eds. Kate Young, Carol Wolkowitz and Roslyn McCullagh. London and New York: Routledge, 1981, pp.159–177.

Domestic Networks: "Those You Count On"

Carol Stack

In The Flats the responsibility for providing food, care, clothing, and shelter and for socializing children within domestic networks may be spread over several households. Which household a given individual belongs to is not a particularly meaningful question, as we have seen that daily domestic organization depends on several things: where people sleep, where they eat, and where they offer

their time and money. Although those who eat together and contribute toward the rent are generally considered by Flats residents to form minimal domestic units, household changes rarely affect the exchanges and daily dependencies of those who take part in common activity.

The residence patterns and cooperative organization of people linked in domestic networks demonstrate the stability and collective power of family life in The Flats. Michael Lee grew up in The Flats and now has a job in Chicago. On a visit to The Flats, Michael described the residence and domestic organization of his kin. "Most of my kin in The Flats lived right here on Cricket Street, numbers sixteen, eighteen, and twenty-two, in these three apartment buildings joined together. My mama decided it would be best for me and my three brothers and sister to be on Cricket Street too. My daddy's mother had a small apartment in this building, her sister had one in the basement, and another brother and his family took a larger apartment upstairs. My uncle was really good to us. He got us things we wanted and he controlled us. All the women kept the younger kids together during the day. They cooked together too. It was good living."

Yvonne Diamond, a forty-year-old Chicago woman, moved to The Flats from Chicago with her four children. Soon afterward they were evicted. "The landlord said he was going to build a parking lot there, but he never did. The old place is still standing and has folks in it today. My husband's mother and father took me and the kids in and watched over them while I had my baby. We stayed on after my husband's mother died, and my husband joined us when he got a job in The Flats."

When families or individuals in The Flats are evicted, other kinsmen usually take them in. Households in The Flats expand or contract with the loss of a job, a death in the family, the beginning or end of a sexual partnership, or the end of a friendship. Welfare workers, researchers, and landlords have long known that the poor must move frequently. What is much less understood is the relationship between residence and domestic organization in the black community.

The spectrum of economic and legal pressures that act upon ghetto residents, requiring them to move—unemployment, welfare requirements, housing shortages, high rents, eviction—are clear-cut examples of external pressures affecting the daily lives of the poor. Flats residents are evicted from their dwellings by landlords who want to raise rents, tear the building down, or rid themselves of tenants who complain about rats, roaches, and the plumbing. Houses get condemned by the city on landlords' requests so that they can force tenants to move. After an eviction, a landlord can rent to a family in such great need of housing that they will not complain for a while.

Poor housing conditions and unenforced housing standards coupled with overcrowding, unemployment, and poverty produce hazardous living conditions and residence changes. "Our whole family had to move when the gas lines sprung a leak in our apartment and my son set the place on fire by accident," Sam Summer told me. "The place belonged to my sister-in-law's grandfather. We had been living there with my mother, my brother's eight children, and our eight children. My father lived in the basement apartment 'cause he and my mother were separated. After the fire burned the whole place down, we all moved to two places down the street near my cousin's house."

When people are unable to pay their rent because they have been temporarily "cut off aid," because the welfare office is suspicious of their eligibility, because they gave their rent money to a kinsman to help him through a crisis or illness, or because they were laid off from their job, they receive eviction notices almost immediately. Lydia Watson describes a chain of events starting with the welfare office stopping her sister's welfare checks, leading to an eviction, co-residence, overcrowding, and eventually murder. Lydia sadly related the story to me. "My oldest sister was cut off aid the day her husband got out of jail. She and her husband and their three children were evicted from their apartment and they came to live with us. We were in crowded conditions already. I had my son, my other sister was there with her two kids, and my mother was about going crazy. My mother put my sister's husband out 'cause she found out he was a dope addict. He came back one night soon after that and murdered my sister. After my sister's death my mother couldn't face living in Chicago any longer. One of my other sisters who had been adopted and raised by my mother's paternal grandmother visited us and persuaded us to move to The Flats, where she was staying. All of us moved there—my mother, my two sisters and their children, my two baby sisters, and my dead sister's children. My sister who had been staying in The Flats found us a house across the street from her own."

Overcrowded dwellings and the impossibility of finding adequate housing in The Flats have many long-term consequences regarding where and with whom children live. Terence Platt described where and with whom his kin lived when he was a child. "My brother stayed with my aunt, my mother's sister, and her husband until he was ten, 'cause he was the oldest in our family and we didn't have enough room—but he stayed with us most every weekend. Finally my aunt moved into the house behind ours with her husband, her brother, and my brother; my sisters and brothers and I lived up front with my mother and her old man."

KIN-STRUCTURED LOCAL NETWORKS

The material and cultural support needed to absorb, sustain, and socialize community members in The Flats is provided by networks of cooperating kinsmen. Local coalitions formed from these networks of kin and friends are mobilized within domestic networks; domestic organization is diffused over many kin-based households which themselves have elastic boundaries.

People in The Flats are immersed in a domestic web of a large number of kin and friends whom they can count on. From a social viewpoint, relationships within the community are "organized on the model of kin relationships" (Goodenough 1970, p. 49). Kin-constructs such as the perception of parenthood, the culturally determined criteria which affect the shape of personal kindreds, and the idiom of kinship, prescribe kin who can be recruited into domestic networks.

There are similarities in function between domestic networks and domestic groups which Fortes (1962, p. 2) characterizes as "workshops of social reproduction." Both domains include three generations of members linked collaterally or otherwise. Kinship, jural and affectional bonds, and economic factors affect the composition of both domains and residential alignments within them. There are two striking differences between domestic networks and domestic groups. Domestic networks are not visible groups, because they do not have an obvious nucleus or defined boundary. But since a primary focus of domestic networks is child-care arrangements, the cooperation of a cluster of adult females is apparent. Participants in domestic networks are recruited from personal kindreds and friendships, but the personnel changes with fluctuating economic needs, changing life styles, and vacillating personal relationships.

In some loosely and complexly structured cognatic systems, kin-structured local networks (not groups) emerge. Localized coalitions of persons drawn from personal kindreds can be organized as networks of kinsmen. Goodenough (1970, p. 49) correctly points out that anthropologists frequently describe "localized kin groups," but rarely describe kin-structured local groups (Goodenough 1962; Helm 1965). The localized, kin-based, cooperative coalitions of people described in this chapter are organized as kin-structured domestic networks. For brevity, I refer to them as domestic networks.

RESIDENCE AND DOMESTIC ORGANIZATION

The connection between households and domestic life can be illustrated by examples taken from cooperating kinsmen and friends mobilized within domestic networks in The Flats. Domestic networks are, of course, not centered around one individual, but for simplicity the domestic network in the following example is named for the key participants in the network, Magnolia and Calvin Waters. The description is confined to four months between April and July 1969. Even within this short time span, individuals moved and joined other households within the domestic network.

THE DOMESTIC NETWORK OF MAGNOLIA AND CALVIN WATERS

Magnolia Waters is forty-one years old and has eleven children. At sixteen she moved from the South with her parents, four sisters (Augusta, Carrie, Lydia, and Olive), and two brothers (Pennington and Oscar). Soon after this she gave birth to her oldest daughter, Ruby. At twenty-three Ruby Banks had two daughters and a son, each by a different father.

When Magnolia was twenty-five she met Calvin, who was forty-seven years old. They lived together and had six children. Calvin is now sixty-three years old; Calvin and Magnolia plan to marry soon so that Magnolia will receive Calvin's insurance benefits. Calvin has two other daughters, who are thirty-eight and forty, by an early marriage in Mississippi. Calvin still has close ties with his daughters and their mother who all live near one another with their families in Chicago.

Magnolia's oldest sister, Augusta, is childless and has not been married. Augusta has maintained long-term "housekeeping" partnerships with four different men over the past twenty years, and each of them has helped her raise her sisters' children. These men have maintained close, affectional ties with the family over the years. Magnolia's youngest sister, Carrie, married Lazar, twenty-five years her senior, when she was just fifteen. They stayed together for about five years. After they separated Carrie married Kermit, separated from him, and became an alcoholic. She lives with different men from time to time, but in between men, or when things are at loose ends, she stays with Lazar, who has become a participating member of the family. Lazar usually resides near Augusta and Augusta's "old man," and Augusta generally prepares Lazar's meals. Ever since Carrie became ill, Augusta has been raising Carrie's son.

Magnolia's sister Lydia had two daughters, Lottie and Georgia, by two different fathers, before she married Mike and gave birth to his son. After Lydia married Mike, she no longer received AFDC benefits for her children. Lydia and Mike acquired steady jobs, bought a house and furniture, and were doing very well. For at least ten years they purposely removed themselves from the network of kin cooperation, preventing their kin from draining their resources. They refused to participate in the network of exchanges which Lydia had formerly depended upon; whenever possible they refused to trade clothes or lend money, or if they gave something, they did not ask for anything in return. During this period they were not participants in the domestic network. About a year ago Lydia and Mike separated over accusations and gossip that each of them had established another sexual relationship. During the five-month-period when the marriage was ending, Lydia began giving some of her nice clothes away to her sisters and nieces. She gave a couch to her brother and a TV to a niece. Anticipating her coming needs, Lydia attempted to reobligate her kin by carrying out the pattern which had been a part of her daily life before her marriage. After Lydia separated from her husband, her two younger children once again received AFDC. Lydia's oldest daughter, Lottie, is over eighteen and too old to receive AFDC, but Lottie has a three-year-old daughter who has received AFDC benefits since birth.

Eloise has been Magnolia's closest friend for many years. Eloise is Magnolia's first son's father's sister. This son moved into his father's household by his own choice when he was about twelve years old. Magnolia and Eloise have maintained a close, sisterly friendship. Eloise lives with her husband, her four children, and the infant son of her oldest daughter, who is seventeen. Eloise's husband's brother's daughter, Lily, who is twenty, and her young daughter recently joined the household. Eloise's husband's youngest brother is the father of her sister's child. When the child was an infant, that sister stayed with Eloise and her husband.

Billy Jones lives in the basement in the same apartment house as Augusta, Magnolia's sister. A temperamental woman with three sons, Billy has become Augusta's closest friend. Billy once ran a brothel in The Flats, but she has worked as a cook, has written songs, and has attended college from time to time. Augusta keeps Billy's sons whenever Billy leaves town, has periods of depression, or beats the children too severely.

Another active participant in the network is Willa Mae. Willa Mae's younger brother, James, is Ruby's daughter's father. Even though James does not visit the child and has not assumed any parental duties toward the child, Willa Mae and Ruby, who are the same age, help each other out with their young children.

Calvin's closest friend, Cecil, died several years ago. Cecil was Violet's husband. Violet, Cecil, and Calvin came from the same town in Mississippi and their families have been very close. Calvin boarded with Violet's family for five years or so before he met Magnolia. Violet is now seventy years old. She lives with her daughter, Odessa, who is thirty-seven, her two sons, Josh, who is thirty-five and John, who is forty, and Odessa's three sons and daughter. Odessa's husband was killed in a fight several years ago and ever since then she and her family have shared a household with Violet and her two grown sons. Violet's sons Josh and John are good friends with Magnolia, Ruby, and Augusta and visit them frequently. About five years ago John brought one of his daughters to live with his mother and sister because his family thought that the mother was not taking proper care of the child; the mother had several other children and did not object. The girl is now ten years old and is an accepted member of the family and the network.

Chart 1 shows the spatial relations of the households in Magnolia and Calvin's domestic network in April 1969. The houses are scattered within The Flats, but none of them is more than three miles apart. Cab fare, up to two dollars per trip, is spent practically every day, and sometimes twice a day, as individuals visit, trade, and exchange services. Chart 2 shows how individuals are brought into the domestic network.

The following outline shows residential changes which occurred in several of the households within the network between April and June 1969.

APRIL 1969

Household Domestic Arrangement

1. Magnolia (38) and Calvin (60) live in a common-law relationship with their eight children (ages 4 to 18).
2. Magnolia's sister Augusta and Augusta's "old man," Herman, share a two-bedroom house with Magnolia's daughter Ruby (22) and Ruby's three children. Augusta and Herman have one bedroom, the three children sleep in the second bedroom, and Ruby sleeps downstairs in the living room. Ruby's boyfriend, Art, stays with Ruby many evenings.
3. Augusta's girlfriend Billy and Billy's three sons live on the first floor of the house. Lazar, Magnolia's and Augusta's ex-brother-in-law, lives in the basement alone, or from time to time, with his ex-wife Carrie. Lazar eats the evening meal, which Augusta prepares for him, at household #2.
4. Magnolia's sister Lydia, Lydia's "old man," Lydia's two daughters, Georgia and Lottie, Lydia's son, and Lottie's three-year-old daughter live in Lydia's house.
5. Willa Mae (26), her husband, her son, her sister Claudia (32), and her brother James (father of Ruby's daughter) share a household.
6. Eloise (37), her husband Jessie, their four children, their oldest daughter's (17) son, and Jessie's brother's daughter Lily (20), and Lily's baby all live together.
7. Violet (70), her two sons, Josh (35) and John (40), her daughter Odessa (37), and Odessa's three sons and one daughter live together. Five years ago John's daughter (10) joined the household.

CHART 1 Spatial Relations in Magnolia and Leo's Domestic Network

JUNE 1969

Household Domestic Arrangement

1. Household composition unchanged.
2. Augusta and Herman moved out after quarreling with Ruby over housekeeping and cooking duties. They joined household #3. Ruby and

Art remained in household #2 and began housekeeping with Ruby's children.
3. Billy and her three sons remained on the first floor and Lazar remained in the basement. Augusta and Herman rented a small, one-room apartment upstairs.
4. Lottie and her daughter moved out of Lydia's house to a large apartment down the street,

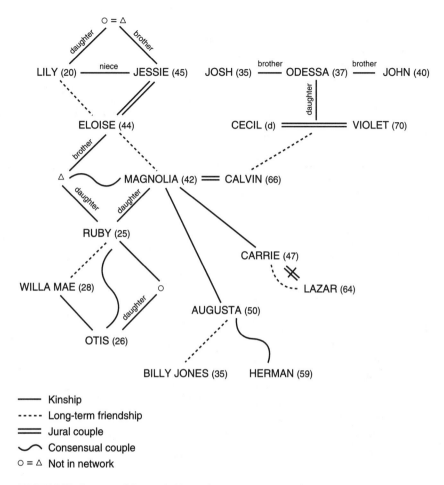

CHART 2 Kin-Structured Domestic Network

which they shared with Lottie's girl friend and the friend's daughter. Georgia moved into her boyfriend's apartment. Lydia and her son (17) remained in the house with Lydia's "old man."

5. James began housekeeping with a new girl friend who lived with her sister, but he kept most of his clothes at home. His brother moved into his room after returning from the service. Willa Mae, her husband, and son remained in the house.

6. Household composition unchanged.

7. Odessa's son Raymond is the father of Clover's baby. Clover and the baby joined the household which includes Violet, her two sons, her daughter, Odessa, and Odessa's three sons and one daughter and John's daughter.

Typical residential alignments in The Flats are those between adult mothers and sisters, mothers and adult sons and daughters, close adult female relatives, and friends defined as kin within the idiom of kinship. Domestic organization is diffused over these kin-based households.

Residence patterns among the poor in The Flats must be considered in the context of domestic organization. The connection between residence and domestic organization is apparent in examples of a series of domestic and child-care arrangements within Magnolia and Calvin's network a few years ago. Consider the following four kin-based residences among Magnolia and Calvin's kin in 1966.

Household Domestic Arrangement

1. Magnolia, Calvin, and seven young children.
2. Magnolia's mother, Magnolia's brother, Magnolia's sister and her sister's husband, Magnolia's oldest daughter, Ruby, and Ruby's first child.
3. Magnolia's oldest sister, Augusta, Augusta's "old man," Augusta's sister's (Carrie) son, and Magnolia's twelve-year-old son.
4. Magnolia's oldest son, his father, and the father's "old lady."

Household composition *per se* reveals little about domestic organization even when cooperation between close adult females is assumed. Three of these households (1, 2, 3) were located on one city block. Magnolia's mother rented a rear house behind Magnolia's house, and Magnolia's sister Augusta lived in an apartment down the street. As we have seen, they lived and shared each other's lives. Magnolia, Ruby, and Augusta usually pooled the food stamps they received from the welfare office. The women shopped together and everyone shared the evening meal with their men and children at Magnolia's mother's house or at Magnolia's. The children did not always have a bed of their own or a bed which they were expected to share with another child. They fell asleep and slept through the night wherever the late evening visiting patterns of the adult females took them.

The kinship links which most often are the basis of new or expanded households are those links children have with close adult females such as the child's mother, mother's mother, mother's sister, mother's brother's wife, father's mother, father's sister, and father's brother's wife.

Here are some examples of the flexibility of the Blacks' adaptation to daily, social, and economic problems (Stack 1970, p. 309).

Relational Link	Domestic Arrangement
Mother	Viola's brother married his first wife when he was sixteen. When she left him she kept their daughter.
Mother's mother	Viola's sister Martha was never able to care for her children because of her nerves and high blood. In between husbands, her mother kept her two oldest children, and after Martha's death, her mother kept all three of the children.
Mother's brother	A year after Martha's death, Martha's brother took Martha's oldest daughter, helping his mother out since this left her with only two children to care for.
Mother's mother	Viola's daughter (20) was living at home and gave birth to a son. The daughter and her son remained in the Jackson household until the daughter married and set up a separate household with her husband, leaving her son to be raised by her mother.
Mother's sister	Martha moved to Chicago into her sister's household. The household consisted of the two sisters and four of their children.
Father's mother	Viola's sister Ethel had four daughters and one son. When Ethel had a nervous breakdown, her husband took the three daughters and his son to live with his mother in Arkansas. After his wife's death, the husband took the oldest daughter, to join her siblings in his mother's home in Arkansas.
Father's mother	When Viola's younger sister, Christine, left her husband in order to harvest fruit in Wisconsin, Christine left her two daughters with her husband's mother in Arkansas.
Father's sister	When Viola's brother's wife died, he decided to raise his two sons himself. He kept the two boys and never remarried

although he had several girl friends and a child with one. His residence has always been near Viola's and she fed and cared for his sons.

The basis of these cooperative units is mutual aid among siblings of both sexes, the domestic cooperation of close adult females, and the exchange of goods and services between male and female kin (Stack 1970). R.T. Smith (1970, p. 66) has referred to this pattern and observes that even when lower-class Blacks live in a nuclear family group, what is "most striking is the extent to which lower-class persons continue to be involved with other kin." Nancie Gonzalez (1970, p. 232) suggests that "the fact that individuals have simultaneous loyalties to more than one such grouping may be important in understanding the social structure as a whole."

These co-residential socializing units do indeed show the important role of the black female. But the cooperation between male and female siblings who share the same household or live near one another has been underestimated by those who have considered the female-headed household and the grandmother-headed household (especially the mother's mother) as the most significant domestic units among the urban black poor.

The close cooperation of adults arises from the residential patterns typical of young adults. Due to poverty, young females with or without children do not perceive any choice but to remain living at home with their mother or other adult female relatives. Even if young women are collecting AFDC, they say that their resources go further when they share goods and services. Likewise, jobless males, or those working at part-time or seasonal jobs, often remain living at home with their mother or, if she is dead, with their sisters and brothers. This pattern continues long after men have become fathers and have established a series of sexual partnerships with women, who are living with their own kin, friends, or alone with their children. A result of this pattern is the striking fact that households almost always have men around:

male relatives, by birth or marriage, and boyfriends. These men are often intermittent members of the households, boarders, or friends who come and go; men who usually eat, and sometimes sleep, in the households. Children have constant and close contact with these men, and especially in the case of male relatives, these relationships last over the years.

The most predictable residential pattern in The Flats is that men and women reside in one of the households of their natal kin, or in the households of those who raised them, long into their adult years. Even when persons temporarily move out of the household of their mother or of a close relative, they have the option to return to the residences of their kin if they have to.

GENEROSITY AND POVERTY

The combination of arbitrary and repressive economic forces and social behavior, modified by successive generations of poverty, make it almost impossible for people to break out of poverty. There is no way for those families poor enough to receive welfare to acquire any surplus cash which can be saved for emergencies or for acquiring adequate appliances or a home or a car. In contrast to the middle class, who are pressured to spend and save, the poor are not even permitted to establish an equity.

The following examples from Magnolia and Calvin Waters' life illustrates the ways in which the poor are prohibited from acquiring any surplus which might enable them to change their economic condition or life style.

In 1971 Magnolia's uncle died in Mississippi and left an unexpected inheritance of $1,500 to Magnolia and Calvin Waters. The cash came from a small run-down farm which Magnolia's uncle sold shortly before he died. It was the first time in their lives that Magnolia or Calvin ever had a cash reserve. Their first hope was to buy a home and use the money as a down payment.

Calvin had retired from his job as a seasonal laborer the year before and the family was on welfare. AFDC allotted the family $100 per month for rent. The housing that the family had been able to obtain over the years for their nine children at $100 or less was always small, roach-infested, with poor plumbing and heating. The family was frequently evicted. Landlords complained about the noise and often observed an average of ten to fifteen children playing in the household. Magnolia and Calvin never even anticipated that they would be able to buy a home.

Three days after they received the check, news of its arrival spread throughout their domestic network. One niece borrowed $25 from Magnolia so that her phone would not be turned off. Within a week the welfare office knew about the money. Magnolia's children were immediately cut off welfare, including medical coverage and food stamps. Magnolia was told that she would not receive a welfare grant for her children until the money was used up, and she was given a minimum of four months in which to spend the money. The first surplus the family ever acquired was effectively taken from them.

During the weeks following the arrival of the money, Magnolia and Calvin's obligations to the needs of kin remained the same, but their ability to meet these needs had temporarily increased. When another uncle became very ill in the South, Magnolia and her older sister, Augusta, were called to sit by his side. Magnolia bought round-trip train tickets for both of them and for her three youngest children. When the uncle died, Magnolia bought round-trip train tickets so that she and Augusta could attend the funeral. Soon after his death, Augusta's first "old man" died in The Flats and he had no kin to pay for the burial. Augusta asked Magnolia to help pay for digging the grave. Magnolia was unable to refuse. Another sister's rent was two months overdue and Magnolia feared that she would get evicted. This sister was seriously ill and had no source of income. Magnolia paid her rent.

Winter was cold and Magnolia's children and grandchildren began staying home from school because they did not have warm winter coats and adequate shoes or boots. Magnolia and Calvin decided to buy coats, hats, and shoes for all of the children (at least fifteen). Magnolia also bought a winter coat for herself and Calvin bought himself a pair of sturdy shoes.

Within a month and a half, all of the money was gone. The money was channeled into the hands of the same individuals who ordinarily participate in daily domestic exchanges, but the premiums were temporarily higher. All of the money was quickly spent for necessary, compelling reasons.

Thus random fluctuations in the meager flow of available cash and goods tend to be of considerable importance to the poor. A late welfare check, sudden sickness, robbery, and other unexpected losses cannot be overcome with a cash reserve like more well-to-do families hold for emergencies. Increases in cash are either taken quickly from the poor by the welfare agencies or dissipated through the kin network.

Those living in poverty have little or no chance to escape from the economic situation into which they were born. Nor do they have the power to control the expansion or contraction of welfare benefits (Piven and Cloward 1971) or of employment opportunities, both of which have a momentous effect on their daily lives. In times of need, the only predictable resources that can be drawn upon are their own children and parents, and the fund of kin and friends obligated to them.

REFERENCES

Fortes, Meyer. 1962. "Marriage in Tribal Societies." *Cambridge Papers in Social Anthropology,* No. 3. Cambridge: Cambridge University Press.

Gonzalez, Nancie. 1970. "Toward a Definition of Matrifocality." In *Afro-American Anthropology: Contemporary Perspectives,* eds. N. E. Whitten and John F. Szwed. New York: The Free Press.

Goodenough, Ward H. 1962. "Kindred and Hamlet in Lakalai, New Britain." *Ethnology* 1:5–12.

———. 1970. *Description and Comparison in Cultural Anthropology.* Chicago: Aldine Publishing Company.

Helm, June. 1965. "Bilaterality in the Socio-Territorial Organization of the Arctic Drain Age Dene." *Ethnology,* 4:361–385.

Piven, Frances Fox and Richard A. Cloward. 1971. *Regulating the Poor: The Functions of Public Welfare.* New York: Vintage Books.

Smith, Raymond T. 1970. "The Nuclear Family in Afro-American Kinship." *Journal of Comparative Family Studies* 1(1):55–70.

Stack, Carol B. 1970. "The Kindred of Viola Jackson: Residence and Family Organization of an Urban Black American Family." In *Afro-American Anthropology: Contemporary Perspectives,* eds. N. E. Whitten and John F. Szwed. New York: The Free Press, pp. 303–312

Matrifocality, Power, and Gender Relations in Jamaica

Marsha Prior

Anthropologists have long recognized kinship units in which women maintain considerable control over the household earnings and decision making. While numerous studies have provided pertinent data and have contributed to the theory of social organization, the subject of female-focused kinship units has always been controversial, subject to bias, and confusing. The variations in terminology and a preoccupation with the origin of these units is responsible for much of the confusion. In addition, two biases, prevalent throughout the twentieth century, have influenced our understanding and acceptance of female-focused units. One bias has been the predominant view that nuclear families are "normal"; the other bias is the failure to recognize the full extent of female roles in society. The unfortunate result of this is that very little is known about the dynamics within and between female-focused kinship units.

The term *matrifocal,* which is most commonly used to refer to households composed of a key female decision maker, was coined by R.T. Smith in 1956. Recognition of such households precedes the usage of this term, however. As early as the 1930s scholars noted

that African-American and African-Caribbean households were not composed of nuclear families as were the majority of middle-class households in the United States and Great Britain. Observers were struck by the authoritative role of women in these households and the limited role of the father in the family. Mothers controlled the earnings brought into the household and made key decisions. Fathers were either absent or did not appear to play a major role in economic contributions and in household decision making. However, attempts to address this situation reveal more the attitudes and biases prevalent at that time—many of which remain with us today—than any real insight as to the nature of such units. These *maternal families,* as they were often called during this early period, were viewed by scholars as deviant structures (Mohammed 1988). The high rate of illegitimacy and instability among mating partners was cited as proof that these families were disorganized and detrimental to the well-being of their members (Henriques 1953; Simey 1946; see also Moynihan 1965).

The bias toward nuclear family organization that dominated early studies stems from nineteenth-century evolutionists who viewed the nuclear family as a superior system of

Original material prepared for this text.

kinship organization and from Malinowski who argued that nuclear families are universal (Collier, Rosaldo, and Yanigisako 1982). Thus, societies that exhibited large numbers of non-nuclear households were considered abnormal, and it was essential that their development be explained.

Scholars naturally turned to the common characteristics of these female-focused societies, noting that they were former slave societies from Africa. One explanation, suggested by Frazier (1939), held that maternal families were an adaptive strategy to the slave system that defined slaves as individual property who could be traded to another plantation at any time. Nuclear families would have been torn apart with frequent trading of adult slaves. Plantation owners were less likely, though, to tear apart mother-child dyads, at least until the child reached adolescence. Thus, the stable unit in a slave system was a household consisting of mothers and their children. The other explanation common during this time period, argued that the maternal family stemmed from the traditional African system that survived in spite of the Africans' forced migration and subsequent integration into the slave system (Herskovits 1941). These two theories enjoyed a lively debate until the mid-1950s when scholars moved away from historical explanations and emphasized the role of present social or economic conditions.

M.G. Smith (1962) argued that family structure in the West Indies was determined by the already existing mating systems that vary somewhat throughout the region. Clarke (1957), R.T. Smith (1956), and Gonzalez (1960) focused more on the effect that the current economic system had on household organization. The prevalent household structure found among African descendants in the United States and the Caribbean was viewed as an adaptive strategy to poverty, unemployment, or male migration. Nuclear families with only two working adults per household are believed by some to be at risk in socioeconomic environments in which poverty conditions exist, unemployment is high, and adult men must migrate to find work (see Durant-Gonzalez 1982; Gonzalez 1970:242). Thus, in such societies we are more likely to see households composed of a mother, a grandparent, and children; a mother and children; adult siblings and their children; or adult siblings, their children, and a grandparent.

The emphasis placed on the socioeconomic environment marked a new trend in matrifocal studies whereby the relationship between men and women took a more prominent position. However, the studies placed more emphasis on the "marginal" or absent man than on the ever-present woman and were criticized for ignoring the wide range of roles and tasks performed by women. Furthermore, Smith noted (1962:6) specific ethnographic data were used to generalize about matrifocal societies throughout the Caribbean. This proved to be problematic in understanding matrifocal societies theoretically, and it generated confusion as scholars used different terms to refer to similar types of kinship and household organizations.

R.T. Smith used the term *matrifocal* to refer to the type of structure he originally witnessed among lower class British Guianese (1956). Taking a developmental approach, Smith noted that matrifocal households arise with time after a man and woman begin to cohabit. Early in the cycle the woman is economically dependent on the male partner. Her primary role is to provide care for the children, but as the children grow older and earn money for small tasks and labor it is the mother who controls their earnings. The father, meanwhile, has been unable to make significant contributions to the household economy due to his overall low status within a society that maintains prejudicial hiring policies. Smith's concept of matrifocality focuses on two criteria—the salience of women in their role as mothers and the marginality of men (i.e., their inability to contribute economically to the household) (1956; 1973; 1988).

The study of household structure conducted by Gonzalez on the Garifuna (Black Carib) of Guatemala was not intended, nor originally identified, as a study on matrifocality per se, but Gonzalez did not note the effect that male emigration had on household structure (1960). Gonzalez observed that households were comprised of members who were related to each other consanguineally (through blood); no two members of the household were bound by marriage. These consanguineal households developed in response to a socioeconomic environment that encouraged men to migrate as they sought employment (see also Gonzalez 1984 for comments regarding the applicability of dividing households into consanguineal and affinal types).

The terms and definitions for the household structures observed by R.T. Smith and Gonzalez were created to fit specific ethnographic data. They were later applied by various scholars to other societies that exhibited similar structures, which created confusion (see Kunstadter 1963; Randolph 1964; M.G. Smith 1962:6; and R.T. Smith 1973:126) and was exacerbated by the use of other terms to rectify the problem (e.g., the use of matricentric or female-headed). Thus, in the literature we see these terms used interchangeably to refer to structures in which women control household earnings and decision making and men are viewed as marginal, though the impetus behind such household formation may differ from one society to the next. The whole concept became so clouded with terms and biases that Gonzalez astutely noted that depending on which scholar one is reading, matrifocality can suggest (1) that women are more important than the observer had expected, (2) that women maintain a good deal of control over money in the household, (3) that women are the primary source of income, or (4) that there is no resident male (1970:231–232).

Recent authors have criticized the emphasis on men's marginality and the focus on women's domestic tasks that arose in the study of matrifocality (Barrow 1988; Mohammed 1988; Tanner 1974). Concentration on women's *domestic* tasks ignores the full extent of women's networks, their access to resources, control over resources, relations with men, and relationship between household and society, all of which are important considerations when discussing matrifocality. Male marginality is problematic in part because the term is difficult to define. Does it mean that the father does not live in the household? Has he migrated out of the community? Does he contribute sporadically, or not at all, to the household economy? Is he not around to make household decisions?

As Tanner has remarked, matrifocality should not be defined in "negative terms" (i.e., by the absence of the father). Instead, we should focus on the role of women as mothers, and note that in matrifocal systems mothers have at least some control over economic resources and are involved in decision making. According to Tanner, however, matrifocality goes beyond these two criteria. To be matrifocal a society must culturally value the role of mother—though not necessarily at the expense of fathers. In matrifocal societies the woman's role as mother is central to the kinship structure, but Tanner does not limit this role to domestic tasks. As mothers women may participate in cultivation, petty marketing, wage labor, in rituals, and so forth (1974). This broader definition allows us to recognize matrifocal units within a variety of kinship systems. Matrifocal units can exist in matrilineal or patrilineal societies, within nuclear families, and in bilateral systems. In any society with an emphasis on the mother-child dyad where this unit is culturally valued and where the mother plays an effective role in the economy and decision making of the unit, that unit can be defined as matrifocal (Tanner 1974:131–132).

Tanner's definition finally allows us to avoid some of the problems that previous studies encountered and permits us to further address issues pertinent to matrifocal units. We can examine gender relations within the context of gender hierarchies and the broader socioeconomic environment of which matrifocal households are a part. One area that has received little attention is the relationship between physical violence against women and matrifocality. Violence against women and matrifocality seem to contradict each other due to the assumptions regarding power and the authoritative role of women in matrifocal households.

Women, having access to and control over resources and authority to make household decisions, are viewed as powerful. This view has been particularly evident in studies of women in the Caribbean where a large number of matrifocal households exist (Massiah 1982). Caribbean women are frequently portrayed as powerful, autonomous individuals (Ellis 1986; Powell 1982, 1986; Safa 1986). Although Caribbean women's control and power over resources and decisions is not to be discounted, fieldwork in a low-income community in Jamaica suggests that matrifocality and physical violence against women are not mutually exclusive. To understand the relationship between these two phenomena requires knowledge of sociocultural elements that affect both gender relations and matrifocal household organization.

The community of study is a low-income urban neighborhood approximately 0.05 square miles located in the parish of St. Andrew, Jamaica. During the time at which data were collected, 1987 to 1988, there were an estimated 210 households with a population of 1,300. The majority of the households were of wooden construction, many without electricity, and very few with running water. Some of the wealthier residents maintained houses constructed of concrete. No telephones were present in any household because telephone lines were not available.

Within the community a variety of household organizational units were observed. Nuclear families based on common-law marriage, legal marriage, or coresidency existed. There were also single female-headed households, single male-headed households, and a variety of extended and collateral arrangements. Finally, there were households whose membership included kin and nonkin (i.e., a friend or acquaintance may reside in the household). This range in domestic organization demonstrates that household member-

ship may vary in response to economic and social conditions.

What makes these arrangements more interesting is that the households are subject to change. During the course of the fieldwork households altered their membership; thus, a nuclear arrangement would shift to single female-headed with children as the father moved out, and it might have shifted again if a grandmother or sister moved in. Regardless of the various household arrangements, matrifocality was observed. Women certainly maintained control over the economic resources and were responsible for many household decisions. Women as mothers were structurally central to the kinship units, and mothers were culturally valued as indicated by both male and female informants.

Although Caribbean women are portrayed as powerful and autonomous, male–female relations, as anywhere in the world, are based on some form of interdependence. Within this community social and economic status are intricately tied to gender relations. Both genders support the basic notion that women are to provide sexual services and domestic labor for men, and men are to provide women with money and gifts. However, the relationships are not a simple equation whereby women provide sexual services and domestic labor in exchange for money. Women often spoke of sexual activity as something that they desired and enjoyed, and men felt free to request money from women with whom they have had relations (especially if she is the mother to any of his children). Nevertheless, there is an understanding that if a woman will not provide sexual services or domestic labor or if the man does not provide cash or gifts from time to time, the relationship will end. These expectations played key roles in understanding gender relations and the behavior of men and women.

In addition to these expectations, adult status is primarily attained by the birth of a child. At this socioeconomic level higher educational degrees, prestigious employment, and ownership of cars and houses are out of most community members' reach. Both men and women view the birth of a child as an opportunity to announce their own adult status. Thus, children are normally desired and are a source of pride for both the mother and father.

The instability that marks male–female relationships is recognized by community members and can be related to cultural values as well as to the socioeconomic environment that encourages men and women to seek more resourceful partners. Male and female informants readily acknowledged the shifting allegiances between men and women. Men were known to keep several girlfriends at one time, and marriage, common-law or legal, was no guarantee that monogamy will follow. Women also admitted to keeping an eye out for a better partner and said they would initiate a change if they so desired. Couples tended to set up visiting relationships whereby the couple did not coreside. Children, of course, may be born from these unions. If a Jamaican woman of this socioeconomic class married at all, it was more likely to occur after the age of thirty (see Brody 1981:253–255).

As households were observed and data collected through the course of fieldwork, it became apparent that fathers and male partners were not marginal to the households. Whether or not they resided in the same household as the woman, they could potentially be very influential. It also became clear that in certain situations female control over household issues could be jeopardized. A brief look at some of the households and the gender relations among men and women will demonstrate these points.

MARY'S HOUSEHOLD

Mary is a twenty-seven-year-old mother occupying a one-room wooden house—no electricity or running water—with four children. The two oldest children were fathered by one man; the youngest two were fathered by another. Sexual relations with the first father had ceased several years ago; however, Mary does maintain sexual relations with the younger children's father, though he keeps other girlfriends.

Mary's primary source of income stems from sporadic petty marketing. When Mary has the capital to invest in goods, she sells clothing and shoes in a downtown Kingston stall that is rented by her mother. Mary is very much involved in politics; she attends meetings, distributes literature, and talks to anyone about her party's political candidates and officials. She was able to work for a few months as an enumerator during a national campaign to register voters. Mary depends on contributions from the two fathers of her children. The first father rarely comes to visit, but he is in the National Guard, draws a steady paycheck, and consistently sends money for the children.

The father of her two youngest children, who works as a cook and a driver, is usually good about bringing money but has, on occasion, lapsed. Such lapses can be a severe stress on Mary's limited household budget and were the source of domestic violence on one occasion. Earl, the father of Mary's youngest children, had promised to bring some money. When he showed up at her doorstep she asked for the money, and he told her that he didn't have any. This made her angry so she began yelling at him, and a fight ensued. They began hitting each other with their fists, but the fight escalated when Earl picked up a shovel and hit Mary on the wrist. Mary fought back by taking a cutlass and striking him on the shoulder. Earl then left the premises, and Mary sought medical treatment for the pain in her wrist.

This was the first and only act of violence between the two in a seven-year period. Mary stated that they rarely even quarrel. Though not typical, the violence demonstrates the economic dependence of Mary on the contributions of the fathers and the stress that can surface when she is threatened by the lack of such contributions. Mary admitted that she was extremely angry when he told her that he had no money to give her because he had promised earlier that he would bring her some. She was convinced that he had the money to give but was holding out on her.

DORA'S HOUSEHOLD

Dora, twenty-eight years old, lives under similar circumstances as Mary and has had comparable experience regarding fathers and money. Dora is the mother of three children. Two live with her; one stays with relatives in the country. Dora's one-room house has neither electricity nor running water.

The father of Dora's first two children provides some money to the household. Dora is almost totally dependent on these contributions because she is confined to the house and cannot work due to a crippling disease. Ned, the father of her youngest child, provides nothing to the household, which is a continuous source of grief to Dora. Dora is quiet and normally avoids conflict. Her one attempt to address Ned's negligence resulted in violence, as had Mary's. Dora had decided that because Ned did not provide clothes or money for their son, Michael, he did not deserve to see the child. She packed up Michael's belongings and sent him over to Ned's sister's house for a short while, believing that the sister would feed Michael and buy him some clothes. When Ned arrived to take Michael for a visit to his own house, he questioned the child's whereabouts and became angry when Dora told him that he had been sent to Ned's sister's house. Ned began hitting Dora. She struck back once but relented when Ned punched her in the side and ran off. She did not see him again for several days. This incident occurred six months prior to our interview, and Dora has not asked Ned for anything since and vows that she never will.

RITA'S HOUSEHOLD

Rita lives in a household consisting of six members, including herself. Two of her four children, a granddaughter, a friend of her daughter, and Rita's boyfriend occupy a three-room apartment without electricity or running water. Rita is thirty-nine years old. Her boyfriend, Tom, is 40 and has lived with her for four years. They have no common children.

Rita runs a successful neighborhood bar, giving her control over the major portion of the household budget. She receives some financial contribution from the father of one daughter. Rita and Tom have established a reciprocal relationship regarding money. She does expect him to contribute from his earnings as a taxi driver when he is able, but she may be just as likely to provide Tom with money when he is in need. Rita is aware of Tom's other girlfriends and realizes that a good deal of his earnings go to entertaining these women. With her own successful business Rita is less financially dependent on her male partner than other women. She does look to Tom, however, for companionship and emotional support. The time he spends with other women is reluctantly accepted, though on one occasion his infidelities did result in conflict. One night, as he came home late, Rita began cursing Tom and made derogatory remarks about Tom's other girlfriend. Tom responded by punching Rita. She fought back for a few minutes then they both simply let it go. In the past year Rita has avoided comment on Tom's affairs and is determined to put up with it, for now at least, because she is not ready to end the relationship. Rita's attitude is that most men do this, so there is little point in severing this relationship to find another boyfriend who will do the same.

HANNAH'S HOUSEHOLD

Thirty-six-year-old Hannah is an articulate and ambitious woman. She lives in a two-room house with seven other people (five of her six children live with her along with a friend her age and a friend of one of her daughters).

Hannah worked as a domestic but lost her job during my stay in the community. She did have a job lined up, cleaning the office of a dentist.

Hannah's first three children were fathered by one man; her fourth child was fathered by another man; and her last two children were fathered by a third man. The first man to father her children is now sick and unable to work. He does not provide any financial support to Hannah's household. The other two fathers help out every now and then, but the support is not enough for her to rely on. She rarely sees any of her children's fathers now, but Hannah did relate an incident involving the last father, Gerald, that occurred nearly five years prior to our interview. At the time of the incident Hannah and Gerald were still intimately involved but did not coreside. Hannah had grown dissatisfied with the relationship because Gerald provided no support for herself or his children. Thus, she had decided to break off the relationship. When Gerald learned of her decision he became angry and abusive. One night after everyone had gone to bed, he came to her house, began yelling at her, and proceeded to destroy some of her belongings: He broke a lamp and smashed a small table. Another night he came to her window, tore off the screen, and began yelling at her again. He threw a bucket of water on her and the children and threw stones. Hannah, not wanting the children to get hurt, went outside to confront him, and he began physically assaulting her. Hannah managed to grab a broken bottle and cut him with it. Gerald then left the premises, never bothering her much afterwards.

SUMMARY

Although women in matrifocal households often maintain control over resources and decision making within the household, the previous data indicate that the power associated with such control and authority can be compromised. Power, as defined by Adams, is the control over one's environment and the ability to control the environment of others based on access and control of resources that are of value to the other (1975:12). In the cases cited above the interdependence between men and women and the access that men have to certain resources must be addressed to understand female power and domestic violence.

As indicated previously, both genders view women as exercising control over sexual services and domestic labor, and men have access to some (though not all) of the economic resources that women need. At this socioeconomic level men may not be able to contribute significantly to the household economy. Nevertheless, women view men as a source of monetary and material needs and feel they have the right to demand these resources. Though women are constantly seeking ways to earn money and often don't want to rely on contributions from male partners, many, again due to the socioeconomic environment, are dependent on male contributions, no matter how small. The data suggest that while men are dependent on women, they can more easily circumvent the control that female partners have over desired resources than women can circumvent the resources that men control. In this culture it is acceptable for men to have more than one female partner. While women complain of this it is expected and negates the control that individual women can exert. Women, on the other hand, may try to circumvent male control over economic resources, but they are also subjected to an economic system that exploits the lower class for their cheap labor and that offers high unemployment. In addition to this interdependence these women are members of a culture that may value women *as mothers*, but women in general do not necessarily enjoy a high status. In other words the *mother* role is valued, but women are overall subordinate to men (Henry and Wilson 1975). Male informants felt it was their right to physically coerce or punish women as they saw fit, but a man would almost never physically abuse his own mother.

In relating the cases cited previously the intent is not to suggest that the women were weak, powerless, and always dominated by men. Women often fought back and worked to become as independent as possible. These cases are also not intended to promote negative images of men. I recount incidences of abuse to demonstrate the extreme to which men can affect matrifocal households, but I must emphasize that male influence can also be positive and rewarding for members of the household. Fathers were observed visiting their children, taking them to the health clinic, and providing money, food, and clothing.

The data collected from this study remind us that, in spite of a long interest in matrifocality, we still have much to learn. We must rid ourselves of biases that narrow our focus. Just as it was wrong to assume that men are marginal, that women perform only domestic tasks, and that the nuclear family is "normal," we must not assume that women in matrifocal societies are *always* powerful or that they consistently enjoy a high status within that society. The power that women exert must be documented and integrated into the overall cultural context that would also note gender relations, the socioeconomic environment, the political environment, and cultural values. Only then can studies on matrifocality provide us with a better understanding of human behavior.

REFERENCES

Adams, Richard N. 1975. *Energy and Structure: A Theory of Social Power.* Austin: University of Texas Press.

Barrow, Christine. 1988. Anthropology, the Family and Women in the Caribbean. In Patricia Mohammed and Catherine Shepherd (eds.). *Gender in Caribbean Development,* pp. 156–169. Mona, Jamaica: University of West Indies.

Brody, Eugene B. 1981. *Sex, Contraception, and Motherhood in Jamaica.* Cambridge, MA: Harvard University Press.

Clarke, Edith. 1957. *My Mother Who Fathered Me.* London: George Allen & Unwin.

Collier, Jane, Michelle Rosaldo, and Sylvia Yanagisako. 1982. Is There a Family? New Anthropological Views. In Barrie Thorne (ed.). *Rethinking the Family: Some Feminist Questions,* pp. 25–39. New York: Longman.

Durant-Gonzalez, Victoria. 1982. The Realm of Female Familial Responsibility. In Joycelin Massiah (ed). *Women and the Family,* pp. 1–27. Cave Hill, Barbados: University of the West Indies, Institute of Social and Economic Research.

Ellis, Pat. 1986. Introduction: An Overview of Women in Caribbean Society. In Pat Ellis (ed.). *Women of the Caribbean,* pp. 1–24. Kingston: Kingston Publishers.

Frazier, E. Franklin. 1939. *The Negro Family in the United States.* Chicago: Chicago University Press.

Gonzalez, Nancie L. 1960. Household and Family in the Caribbean. *Social and Economic Studies* 9: 101–106.

———. 1970. Toward a Definition of Matrifocality. In Norman E. Whitten, Jr. and John F. Szwed (eds.). *Afro-American Anthropology,* pp. 231–244. New York: The Free Press.

———. 1984. Rethinking the Consanguineal Household and Matrifocality. *Ethnology* 23(1): 1–12.

Henriques, Fernando M. 1953. Family and Colour in Jamaica. London: Eyre and Spottiswoode.

Henry, Frances and Pamela Wilson. 1975. The Status of Women in Caribbean Societies: An Overview of Their Social, Economic and Sexual Roles. *Social and Economic Studies* 24(2): 165–198.

Herskovits, Melville J. 1941. *The Myth of the Negro Past.* New York: Harper & Brothers.

Kunstadter, Peter. 1963. A Survey of the Consanguine or Matrifocal Family. *American Anthropologist* 65: 56–66.

Massiah, Joycelin. 1982. Women Who Head Households. In Joycelin Massiah (ed.). *Women and the Family,* pp. 62–130. Cave Hill, Barbados: University of West Indies, Institute of Social and Economic Research.

Mohammed, Patricia. 1988. The Caribbean Family Revisited. In Patricia Mohammed and Catherine Shepherd (eds.). *Gender in Caribbean Development,* pp. 170–182. Mona, Jamaica: University of West Indies.

Moynihan, Daniel P. 1965. The Negro Family: The Case for National Action. U.S. Department of Labor, Washington, D.C.

Powell, Dorian. 1982. Network Analysis: A Suggested Model for the Study of Women and the Family in the Caribbean. In Joycelin Massiah (ed.). *Women and The Family*, pp. 131–162. Cave Hill, Barbados: University of the West Indies, Institute of Social and Economic Research.

———. 1986. Caribbean Women and Their Response to Familial Experiences. *Social and Economic Studies* 35(2): 83–130.

Randolph, Richard R. 1964. The "Matrifocal Family" as a Comparative Category. *American Anthropologist* 66: 628–31.

Safa, Helen. 1986. Economic Autonomy and Sexual Equality in Caribbean Society. *Social and Economic Studies* 35(3): 1–21.

Simey, Thomas. 1946. *Welfare Planning in the West Indies*. Oxford: Clarendon Press.

Smith, M.G. 1962. *West Indian Family Structure*. Seattle: University of Washington Press.

Smith, Raymond T. 1956. *The Negro Family in British Guiana: Family Structure and Social Status in the Villages*. London: Routledge and Kegan Paul.

———. 1973. The Matrifocal Family. In Jack Goody (ed.). *The Character of Kinship*, pp. 121–144. London: Cambridge University Press.

———. 1988. *Kinship and Class in the West Indies: A Genealogical Study of Jamaica and Guyana*. New York: Cambridge University Press.

Tanner, Nancy. 1974. Matrifocality in Indonesia and Africa and Among Black Americans. In Michelle Zimbalist Rosaldo and Louise Lamphere (eds.). *Woman, Culture, and Society*, pp. 129–156. Stanford: Stanford University Press.

The Female World of Cards and Holidays: Women, Families, and the Work of Kinship[1]

Micaela di Leonardo

> Why is it that the married women of America are supposed to write all the letters and send all the cards to their husbands' families? My old man is a much better writer than I am, yet he expects me to correspond with his whole family. If I asked him to correspond with mine, he would blow a gasket.
>
> *Letter to Ann Landers*

> Women's place in man's life cycle has been that of nurturer, caretaker, and helpmate, the weaver of those networks of relationships on which she in turn relies.
> Carol Gilligan, *In a Different Voice*[2]

Feminist scholars in the past fifteen years have made great strides in formulating new understandings of the relations among gender, kinship, and the larger economy. As a result of this pioneering research, women are newly visible and audible, no longer submerged within their families. We see households as loci of political struggle, inseparable parts of the larger society and economy, rather than as havens from the heartless world of industrial capitalism.[3] And historical and cultural variations in kinship and family forms have become clearer with the maturation of feminist historical and social-scientific scholarship.

Two theoretical trends have been key to this reinterpretation of women's work and family domain. The first is the elevation to visibility of women's nonmarket activities—housework, child care, the servicing of men, and the care of the elderly—and the definition of all these activities as *labor*, to be enumerated alongside and counted as part of overall social reproduction. The second theoretical trend is the nonpejorative focus on women's domestic or kin-centered networks. We now see them as the products of conscious strategy, as crucial to the functioning of kinship systems, as sources of women's autonomous power and possible primary sites of emotional fulfillment, and, at times, as the vehicles for actual survival and/or political resistance.[4]

Recently, however, a division has developed between feminist interpreters of the "labor" and the "network" perspectives on women's lives. Those who focus on women's work tend to envision women as sentient, goal-oriented actors, while those who concern themselves with women's ties to others tend to perceive women primarily in terms of nurturance, other-orientation—altruism. The most celebrated recent example of this division is the opposing testimony of historians Alice Kessler-Harris and Rosalind Rosenberg in the Equal Employment Opportunity Commission's sex discrimination case against Sears Roebuck and Company. Kessler-Harris argued that American women historically have actively sought higher-paying jobs and have been prevented from gaining them because of sex discrimination by employers. Rosenberg argued that American women in the nineteenth century created among themselves, through their domestic networks, a "women's culture" that emphasized the nurturance of children and others and the maintenance of family life and that discouraged women from competition over or heavy emotional investment in demanding, high-paid employment.[5]

I shall not here address this specific debate but, instead, shall consider its theoretical background and implications. I shall argue that we need to fuse, rather than to oppose, the domestic network and labor perspectives. In what follows, I introduce a new concept, the work of kinship, both to aid empirical feminist research on women, work, and family and to help advance feminist theory in this arena. I believe that the boundary-crossing nature of the concept helps to confound the self-interest/altruism dichotomy, forcing us from an either-or stance to a position that includes both perspectives. I hope in this way to contribute to a more critical feminist vision of women's lives and the meaning of family in the industrial West.

In my recent field research among Italian-Americans in Northern California, I found myself considering the relations between women's kinship and economic lives. As an anthropologist, I was concerned with people's kin lives beyond conventional American nuclear family or household boundaries. To this end, I collected individual and family life histories, asking about all kin and close friends and their activities. I was also very interested in women's labor. As I sat with women and listened to their accounts of their past and present lives, I began to realize that they were involved in three types of work: housework and child care, work in the labor market, and the work of kinship.[6]

By kin work I refer to the conception, maintenance, and ritual celebration of cross-household kin ties, including visits, letters, telephone calls, presents, and cards to kin; the organization of holiday gatherings; the creation and maintenance of quasi-kin relations; decisions to neglect or to intensify particular ties; the mental work of reflection about all these activities; and the creation and communication of altering images of family and kin vis-à-vis the images of others, both folk and mass media. Kin work is a key element that has been missing in the synthesis of the "household labor" and "domestic network" perspectives. In our emphasis on individual women's responsibilities within households and on the job, we reflect the common picture of households as nuclear units, tied perhaps to the larger social and economic system, but not to *each other.* We miss the point of telephone and soft drink advertising, of women's magazines' holiday issues, of commentators' confused nostalgia for the mythical American extended family: it is kinship contact *across households,* as much as women's work within them, that fulfills our cultural expectation of satisfying family life.

Maintaining these contacts, this sense of family, takes time, intention, and skill. We tend to think of human social and kin networks as the epiphenomena of production and reproduction: the social traces created by our material lives. Or, in the neoclassical tradition, we see them as part of leisure activities, outside an economic purview except insofar as they involve consumption behavior. But the creation and maintenance of kin and quasi-kin networks in advanced industrial societies is *work;* and, moreover, it is largely women's work.

The kin-work lens brought into focus new perspectives on my informants' family lives. First, life histories revealed that often the very existence of kin contact and holiday celebration depended on the presence of an adult woman in the household. When couples divorced or mothers died, the work of kinship was left undone; when women entered into sanctioned sexual or marital relationships with men in these situations, they reconstituted the men's kinship networks and organized gatherings and holiday celebrations. Middle-aged businessman Al Bertini, for example, recalled the death of his mother in his early adolescence: "I think that's probably one of the biggest losses in losing a family—yeah, I remember as a child when my Mom was alive . . . the holidays were treated with enthusiasm and love ... after she died the attempt was there but it just didn't materialize." Later in life, when Al Bertini and his wife separated, his own and his son Jim's participation in extended-family contact decreased rapidly. But when Jim began a relationship with Jane Batemen, she and he moved in with Al, and Jim and Jane began to invite his kin over for holidays. Jane single-handedly planned and cooked the holiday feasts.

Kin work, then, is like housework and child care: men in the aggregate do not do it. It differs from these forms of labor in that it is harder for men to substitute hired labor to accomplish these tasks in the absence of kinswomen. Second, I found that women, as the workers in this arena, generally had much greater kin knowledge than did their husbands, often including more accurate and extensive knowledge of their husbands' families. This was true both of middle-aged and younger couples and surfaced as a phenomenon in my interviews in the form of humorous arguments and in wives' detailed additions to husbands' narratives. Nick Meraviglia, a middle-aged professional, discussed his Italian antecedents in the presence of his wife, Pina:

NICK: My grandfather was a very outspoken man, and it was reported he took off for the hills when he found out that Mussolini was in power.

PINA: And he was a very tall man; he used to have to bow his head to get inside doors.

NICK: No, that was my uncle.

PINA: Your grandfather too, I've heard your mother say.

NICK: My mother has a sister and a brother.

PINA: *Two* sisters!

NICK: You're right!

PINA: Maria and Angelina.

Women were also much more willing to discuss family feuds and crises and their own roles in them; men tended to repeat formulaic statements asserting family unity and respectability. (This was much less true for younger men.) Joe and Cetta Longhinotti's statements illustrate these tendencies. Joe responded to my question about kin relations: "We all get along. As a rule, relatives, you got nothing but trouble." Cetta, instead, discussed her relations with each of her grown children, their wives, her in-laws, and her own blood kin in detail. She did not hide the fact that relations were strained in several cases; she was eager to discuss the evolution of problems and to seek my opinions of her actions. Similarly, Pina Meraviglia told the following story of her fight with one of her brothers with hysterical laughter: "There was some biting and hair pulling and choking ... it was terrible! I shouldn't even tell you...." Nick, meanwhile, was concerned about maintaining an image of family unity and respectability.

Also, men waxed fluent while women were quite inarticulate in discussing their past and present occupations. When asked about their work lives, Joe Longhinotti and Nick Meraviglia, union baker and professional, respectively, gave detailed narratives of their work careers. Cetta Longhinotti and Pina Meraviglia, clerical and former clerical, respectively, offered only short descriptions focusing on factors of ambience, such as the "lovely things" sold by Cetta's firm.

These patterns are not repeated in the younger generation, especially among younger women, such as Jane Batemen, who have managed to acquire training and jobs with some prospect of mobility. These younger women, though, have *added* a professional and detailed interest in their jobs to a felt responsibility for the work of kinship.[7]

Although men rarely took on any kin-work tasks, family histories and accounts of contemporary life revealed that kinswomen often negotiated among themselves, alternating hosting, food-preparation, and gift-buying responsibilities—or sometimes ceding entire task clusters to one woman. Taking on or ceding tasks was clearly related to acquiring or divesting oneself of power within kin networks, but women varied in their interpretation of the meaning of this power. Cetta Longhinotti, for example, relied on the "family Christmas dinner" as a symbol of her central kinship role and was involved in painful negotiations with her daughter-in-law over the issue: "Last year she insisted—this is touchy. She doesn't want to spend the holiday dinner together. So last year we went there. But I still had my dinner the next day ... I made a big dinner on Christmas Day, regardless of who's coming—candles on the table, the whole routine. I decorate the house myself too . . . well, I just feel that the time will come when maybe I won't feel like cooking a big dinner—she should take advantage of the fact that I feel like doing it now." Pina Meraviglia, in contrast, was saddened by the centripetal force of the developmental cycle but was unworried about the power dynamics involved in her negotiations with daughters- and mother-in-law over holiday celebrations.

Kin work is not just a matter of power among women but also of the mediation of power represented by household units.[8] Women often choose to minimize status claims in their kin work and to include numbers of households under the rubric of family. Cetta Longhinotti's sister Anna, for example, is married to a professional man whose parents have considerable economic resources, while Joe and Cetta have low incomes and no other well-off kin. Cetta and Anna remain close, talk on the phone several times a week, and assist their adult children, divided by distance and economic status, in remaining united as cousins.

Finally, women perceived housework, child care, market labor, the care of the elderly, and the work of kinship as competing responsibilities. Kin work was a unique category, however, because it was unlabeled and because women felt they could either cede some tasks to kinswomen and/or could cut them back severely. Women variously cited the pressures of market labor, the needs of the elderly, and their own desires for freedom and job enrichment as reasons for cutting back Christmas card lists, organized holiday gatherings, multifamily dinners, letters, visits, and phone calls. They expressed guilt and defensiveness about this cutback process and, particularly, about their failures to keep families close through constant contact and about their failures to create perfect holiday celebrations. Cetta Longhinotti, during the period when she was visiting her elderly mother every weekend in addition to working a full-time job, said of her grown children, "I'd have the whole gang here once a month, but I've been so busy that I haven't done that for about six months." And Pina Meraviglia lamented her insufficient work on family Christmases, "I wish I had really made it traditional ... like my sister-in-law has special stories."

Kin work, then, takes place in an arena characterized simultaneously by cooperation and competition, by guilt and gratification. Like housework and child care, it is women's work, with the same lack of clear-cut agreement concerning its proper components: How often should sheets be changed? When should children be toilet trained? Should an aunt send a niece a birthday present? Unlike housework and child care, however, kin work, taking place across the boundaries of normative households, is as yet unlabeled and has no retinue of experts prescribing its correct forms. Neither home economists nor child psychologists have much to say about nieces' birthday presents. Kin work is thus more easily cut back without social interference. On the other hand, the results of kin work—frequent kin contact and feelings of intimacy—are the subject of considerable cultural manipulation as indicators of family happiness. Thus, women in general are subject to the guilt my informants expressed over cutting back kin-work activities.

Although many of my informants referred to the results of women's kin work—cross-household kin contacts and attendant ritual gatherings—as particularly Italian-American, I suggest that in fact this phenomenon is broadly characteristic of American kinship. We think of kin-work tasks such as the preparation of ritual feasts, responsibility for holiday card lists, and gift buying as extensions of women's domestic responsibilities for cooking, consumption, and nurturance. American men in general do not take on these tasks any more than they do housework and child care—and probably less, as these tasks have not yet been the subject of intense public debate. And my informants' gender breakdown in relative articulateness on kinship and workplace themes reflects the still prevalent occupational segregation—most women cannot find jobs that provide enough pay, status, or promotion possibilities to make them worth focusing on—as well as women's perceived power within kinship networks. The common recognition of that power is reflected in Selma Greenberg's book on nonsexist child rearing. Greenberg calls mothers "press agents" who sponsor relations between their own children and other relatives; she advises a mother whose relatives treat her disrespectfully to deny those kin access to her children.[9]

Kin work is a salient concept in other parts of the developed world as well. Larissa Adler Lomnitz and Marisol Pérez Lizaur have found that "centralizing women" are responsible for these tasks and for communicating "family ideology" among upper-class families in Mexico City. Matthews Hamabata, in his study of upper-class families in Japan, has found that women's kin work involves key financial transactions. Sylvia Junko Yanagisako discovered that, among rural Japanese migrants to the United States, the maintenance of kin networks was assigned to women as the migrants adopted the American ideology of the independent nuclear family household. Maila Stivens notes that urban Australian housewives' kin ties and kin ideology "transcend women's isolation in domestic units."[10]

This is not to say that cultural conceptions of appropriate kin work do not vary, even within the United States. Carol B. Stack documents institutionalized fictive kinship and concomitant reciprocity networks among impoverished black American women. Women in populations characterized by intense feelings of ethnic identity may feel bound to emphasize particular occasions—Saint Patrick's or Columbus Day—with organized family feasts. These constructs may be mediated by religious affiliation, as in the differing emphases on Friday or Sunday family dinners among Jews and Christians. Thus the personnel involved and the amount and kind of labor considered necessary for the satisfactory performance of particular kin-work tasks are likely to be culturally constructed.[11] But while the kin and quasi-kin universes and the ritual calendar may vary among women according to race or ethnicity, their general responsibility for maintaining kin links and ritual observances does not.

As kin work is not an ethnic or racial phenomenon, neither is it linked only to one social class. Some commentators on American family life still reflect the influence of work done in England in the 1950s and 1960s (by Elizabeth Bott and by Peter Willmott and Michael Young) in their assumption that working-class families are close and extended, while the middle class substitutes friends (or anomie) for family. Others reflect the prevalent family pessimism in their presumption that neither working- nor middle-class families have extended kin contact.[12] Insofar as kin contact depends on residential proximity, the larger economy's shifts will influence particular groups' experiences. Factory workers, close to kin or not, are likely to disperse when plants shut down or relocate. Small businesspeople or independent professionals may, however, remain resident in particular areas—and thus maintain proximity to kin—for generations, while professional employees of large firms relocate at their firms' behest. This pattern obtained among my informants.

In any event, cross-household kin contact can be and is effected at long distance through letters, cards, phone calls, and holiday and vacation visits. The form and functions of contact, however, vary according to economic resources. Stack and Brett Williams offer rich accounts of kin networks among poor blacks and migrant Chicano farmworkers functioning to provide emotional support, labor, commodity, and cash exchange—a funeral visit, help with laundry, the gift of a dress or piece of furniture.[13] Far different in degree are exchanges such as the loan of a vacation home, a multifamily boating trip, or the provision of free professional services—examples from the kin networks of my wealthier informants. The point is that households, as labor- and income-pooling units, whatever their relative wealth, are somewhat porous in relation to others with whose members they share kin or quasi-kin ties. We do not really know how class differences operate in this realm; it is possible that they do so largely in terms of ideology. It may be, as David Schneider and Raymond T. Smith suggest, that the affluent and the very poor are more open in recognizing necessary economic ties to kin

than are those who identify themselves as middle class.[14]

Recognizing that kin work is gender- rather than class-based allows us to see women's kin networks among all groups, not just among working-class and impoverished women in industrialized societies. This recognition in turn clarifies our understanding of the privileges and limits of women's varying access to economic resources. Affluent women can "buy out" of housework, child care—and even some kin-work responsibilities. But they, like all women, are ultimately responsible, and subject to both guilt and blame, as the administrators of home, children, and kin network. Even the wealthiest women must negotiate the timing and venue of holidays and other family rituals with their kinswomen. It may be that kin work is the core women's work category in which all women cooperate, while women's perceptions of the appropriateness of cooperation for housework, child care, and the care of the elderly varies by race, class, region, and generation.

But kin work is not necessarily an appropriate category of labor, much less gendered labor, in all societies. In many small-scale societies, kinship is the major organizing principle of all social life, and all contacts are by definition kin contacts.[15] One cannot, therefore, speak of labor that does not involve kin. In the United States, kin work as a separable category of gendered labor perhaps arose historically in concert with the ideological and material constructs of the moral mother/cult of domesticity and the privatized family during the course of industrialization in the eighteenth and nineteenth centuries. These phenomena are connected to the increase in the ubiquity of productive occupations *for men* that are not organized through kinship. This includes the demise of the family farm with the capitalization of agriculture and rural-urban migration; the decline of family recruitment in factories as firms grew, ended child labor, and began to assert bureaucratized forms of control; the decline of artisanal labor and of small entrepreneurial enterprises as large firms took greater and greater shares of the commodity market; the decline of the family firm as corporations—and their managerial work forces—grew beyond the capacities of individual families to provision them; and, finally, the rise of civil service bureaucracies and public pressure against nepotism.[16]

As men increasingly worked alongside of non-kin, and as the ideology of separate spheres was increasingly accepted, perhaps the responsibility for kin maintenance, like that for child rearing, became gender-focused. Ryan points out that "built into the updated family economy ... was a new measure of voluntarism." This voluntarism, though, "perceived as the shift from patriarchal authority to domestic affection," also signaled the rise of women's moral responsibility for family life. Just as the "idea of fatherhood itself seemed almost to wither away" so did male involvement in the responsibility for kindred lapse.[17]

With postbellum economic growth and geographic movement, women's new kin burden involved increasing amounts of time and labor. The ubiquity of lengthy visits and of frequent letter-writing among nineteenth-century women attests to this. And for visitors and for those who were residentially proximate, the continuing commonalities of women's domestic labor allowed for kinds of work sharing—nursing, childkeeping, cooking, cleaning—that men, with their increasingly differentiated and controlled activities, probably could not maintain. This is not to say that some kin-related male productive work did not continue; my own data, for instance, show kin involvement among small businessmen in the present. It is, instead, to suggest a general trend in material life and a cultural shift that influenced even those whose productive and kin lives remained commingled. Yanagisako has distinguished between the realms of domestic and public kinship in order to draw attention to anthropology's relatively "thin descriptions" of the domestic (female) domain. Using her typology, we might say that kin work as gendered labor comes into

existence within the domestic domain with the relative erasure of the domain of public, male kinship.[18]

Whether or not this proposed historical model bears up under further research, the question remains, Why do women do kin work? However material factors may shape activities, they do not determine how individuals may perceive them. And in considering issues of motivation, of intention, of the cultural construction of kin work, we return to the altruism-versus-self-interest dichotomy in recent feminist theory. Consider the epigraphs to this article. Are women kin workers the nurturant weavers of the Gilligan quotation, or victims, like the fed-up woman who writes to complain to Ann Landers? That is, are we to see kin work as yet another example of "women's culture" that takes the care of others as its primary desideratum? Or are we to see kin work as another way in which men, the economy, and the state extract labor from women without a fair return? And how do women themselves see their kin work and its place in their lives?

As I have indicated previously, I believe that it is the creation of the self-interest/altruism dichotomy that is itself the problem here. My women informants, like most American women, accepted their primary responsibility for housework and the care of dependent children. Despite two major waves of feminist activism in this century, the gendering of certain categories of unpaid labor is still largely unaltered. These work responsibilities clearly interfere with some women's labor force commitments at certain life-cycle stages; but, more important, women are simply discriminated against in the labor market and rarely are able to achieve wage and status parity with men of the same age, race, class, and educational background.[19]

Thus for my women informants, as for most American women, the domestic domain is not only an arena in which much unpaid labor must be undertaken but also a realm in which one may attempt to gain human satisfactions—and power—not available in the labor market. Anthropologists Jane Collier and Louise Lamphere have written compellingly on the ways in which varying kinship and economic structures may shape women's competition or cooperation with one another in domestic domains.[20] Feminists considering Western women and families have looked at the issue of power primarily in terms of husband–wife relations or psychological relations between parents and children. If we adopt Collier and Lamphere's broader canvas, though, we see that kin work is not only women's labor from which men and children benefit but also labor that women undertake in order to create obligations in men and children and to gain power over one another. Thus Cetta Longhinotti's struggle with her daughter-in-law over the venue of Christmas dinner is not just about a competition over altruism, it is also about the creation of future obligations. And thus Cetta's and Anna's sponsorship of their children's friendship with each other is both an act of nurturance and a cooperative means of gaining power over those children.

Although this was not a clear-cut distinction, those of my informants who were more explicitly antifeminist tended to be most invested in kin work. Given the overwhelming historical shift toward greater autonomy for younger generations and the withering of children's financial and labor obligations to their parents, this investment was in most cases tragically doomed. Cetta Longhinotti, for example, had repaid her own mother's devotion with extensive home nursing during the mother's last years. Given Cetta's general failure to direct her adult children in work, marital choice, religious worship, or even frequency of visits, she is unlikely to receive such care from them when she is older.

The kin-work lens thus reveals the close relations between altruism and self-interest in women's actions. As economists Nancy Folbre and Heidi Hartmann point out, we have inherited a Western intellectual tradition that both dichotomizes the domestic and public domains and associates them on exclusive axes such that we find it difficult to see self-interest in the home and altruism in the workplace.[21] But why, in fact, have women fought for better jobs if not, in part, to support their children? These dichotomies are Procrustean beds that warp our understanding of women's lives both at home and at work. "Altruism" and "self-interest" are cultural constructions that are not necessarily mutually exclusive, and we forget this to our peril.

The concept of kin work helps to bring into focus a heretofore unacknowledged array of tasks that is culturally assigned to women in industrialized societies. At the same time, this concept, embodying notions of both love and work and crossing the boundaries of households, helps us to reflect on current feminist debates on women's work, family, and community. We newly see both the interrelations of these phenomena and women's roles in creating and maintaining those interrelations. Revealing the actual labor embodied in what we culturally conceive as love and considering the political uses of this labor helps to deconstruct the self-interest/altruism dichotomy and to connect more closely women's domestic and labor-force lives.

The true value of the concept, however, remains to be tested through further historical and contemporary research on gender, kinship, and labor. We need to assess the suggestion that gendered kin work emerges in concert with the capitalist development process; to probe the historical record for women's and men's varying and changing conceptions of it; and to research the current range of its cultural constructions and material realities. We know that household boundaries are more porous than we had thought—but they are undoubtedly differentially porous, and this is what we need to specify. We need, in particular, to assess the relations of changing labor processes, residential patterns, and the use of technology to changing kin work.

Altering the values attached to this particular set of women's tasks will be as difficult as are the housework, child-care, and occupational-segregation struggles. But just as feminist research in these latter areas is complementary and cumulative, so researching kin work should help us to piece together the home, work, and public-life landscape—to see the female world of cards and holidays as it is constructed and lived within the changing political economy. How female that world is to remain, and what it would look like if it were not sex-segregated, are questions we cannot yet answer.

NOTES

Many thanks to Cynthia Costello, Rayna Rapp, Roberta Spalter-Roth, John Willoughby, and Barbara Gelpi, Susan Johnson, and Sylvia Yanagisako of *Signs* for their help with this article. I wish in particular to acknowledge the influence of Rayna Rapp's work on my ideas.

1. Acknowledgment and gratitude to Carroll Smith-Rosenberg for my paraphrase of her title, "The Female World of Love and Ritual: Relations between Women in Nineteenth-Century America," *Signs: Journal of Women in Culture and Society* 1, no. 1 (Autumn 1975): 1–29.
2. Ann Landers letter printed in *Washington Post* (April 15, 1983); Carol Gilligan, *In a Different Voice* (Cambridge, Mass.: Harvard University Press, 1982), 17.
3. Heidi I. Hartmann, "The Family as the Locus of Gender, Class, and Political Struggle: The Example of Housework," *Signs* 6, no. 3 (Spring 1981): 366–94; and Christopher Lasch, *Haven in a Heartless World: The Family Besieged* (New York: Basic Books, 1977).
4. Representative examples of the first trend include Joann Vanek, "Time Spent on Housework," *Scientific American* 231 (November 1974): 116–20; Ruth Schwartz Cowan, "A Case Study of Technological and Social Change: The Washing Machine and the Working Wife," in *Clio's Consciousness Raised*, ed. Mary Hartmann and Lois Banner (New York: Harper & Row, 1974), 245–53; Ann Oakley, *Women's Work: The Housewife, Past and Present* (New York: Vintage, 1974); Hartmann; and Susan Strasser, *Never Done: A History of American Housework* (New York: Pantheon

Books, 1982). Key contributions to the second trend include Louise Lamphere, "Strategies, Cooperation and Conflict among Women in Domestic Groups," in *Woman, Culture and Society,* ed. Michelle Zimbalist Rosaldo and Louise Lamphere (Stanford, Calif.: Stanford University Press, 1974), 97–112; Mina Davis Caulfield, "Imperialism, the Family and the Cultures of Resistance," *Socialist Revolution* 20 (October 1974): 67–85; Smith-Rosenberg; Sylvia Junko Yanagisako, "Women-centered Kin Networks and Urban Bilateral Kinship," *American Ethnologist* 4, no. 2 (1977): 207–26; Jane Humphries, "The Working Class Family, Women's Liberation and Class Struggle: The Case of Nineteenth Century British History," *Review of Radical Political Economics* 9 (Fall 1977): 25–41; Blanche Weisen Cook, "Female Support Networks and Political Activism: Lillian Wald, Crystal Eastman, Emma Goldman," in *A Heritage of Her Own*, ed. Nancy F. Cott and Elizabeth H. Pleck (New York: Simon & Schuster, 1979); Temma Kaplan, "Female Consciousness and Collective Action: The Case of Barcelona, 1910–1918," *Signs* 7, no. 3 (Spring 1982): 545–66.
5. On this debate, see Jon Weiner, "Women's History on Trial," *Nation* 241, no. 6 (September 7, 1985): 161, 176, 178–80; Karen J. Winkler, "Two Scholars' Conflict in Sears Sex-Bias Case Sets Off War in Women's History," *Chronicle of Higher Education* (February 5, 1986), 1, 8; Rosalind Rosenberg, "What Harms Women in the Workplace," *New York Times* (February 27, 1986); Alice Kessler-Harris, "Equal Employment Opportunity Commission vs. Sears Roebuck and Company: A Personal Account," *Radical History Review* 35 (April 1986): 57–79.
6. Portions of the following analysis are reported in Micaela di Leonardo, *The Varieties of Ethnic Experience: Kinship, Class and Gender among California Italian-Americans* (Ithaca, N.Y.: Cornell University Press, 1984), chap. 6.
7. Clearly, many women do, in fact, discuss their paid labor with willingness and clarity. The point here is that there are opposing gender tendencies in an identical interview situation, tendencies that are explicable in terms of both the material realities and current cultural constructions of gender.
8. Papanek has rightly focused on women's unacknowledged family status production, but what is conceived of as "family" shifts and varies (Hanna Papanek, "Family Status Production:

The 'Work' and 'Non-Work' of Women," *Signs* 4, no. 4 [Summer 1979]: 775–81).

9. Selma Greenberg, *Right from the Start: A Guide to Nonsexist Child Rearing* (Boston: Houghton Mifflin Co., 1978), 147. Another example of indirect support for kin work's gendered existence is a recent study of university math students, which found that a major reason for women's failure to pursue careers in mathematics was the pressure of family involvement. Compare David Maines et al., *Social Processes of Sex Differentiation in Mathematics* (Washington, D.C.: National Institute of Education, 1981).

10. Larissa Adler Lomnitz and Marisol Pérez Lizaur, "The History of a Mexican Urban Family," *Journal of Family History* 3, no. 4 (1978): 392–409, esp. 398; Matthews Hamàbata, Crested Kimono Power and Love in the Japanese Business Family (Ithaca, N.Y.: Cornell University Press, 1990); Sylvia Junko Yanagisako, "Two Processes of Change in Japanese-American Kinship," *Journal of Anthropological Research* 31 (1975): 196–224; Maila Stivens, "Women and Their Kin: Kin, Class and Solidarity in a Middle-Class Suburb of Sydney, Australia," in *Women United, Women Divided*, ed. Patricia Caplan and Janet M. Bujra (Bloomington: Indiana University Press, 1979), 157–84.

11. Carol B. Stack, *All Our Kin: Strategies for Survival in a Black Community* (New York: Harper & Row, 1974). These cultural constructions may, however, vary within ethnic/racial populations as well.

12. Elizabeth Bott, *Family and Social Network,* 2d ed. (New York: Free Press, 1971): Michael Young and Peter Willmott, *Family and Kinship in East London* (London: Routledge & Kegan Paul, 1957), and *Family and Class in a London Suburb* (London: Routledge & Kegan Paul, 1960). Classic studies that presume this class difference are Herbert Gans, *The Urban Villagers: Group and Class in the Life of Italian-Americans* (New York: Free Press, 1962); and Mirra Komarovsky, *Blue-Collar Marriage* (New York: Random House, 1962). A recent example is Ilene Philipson, "Heterosexual Antagonisms and the Politics of Mothering," *Socialist Review* 12, no. 6 (November–December 1982): 55–77. Edward Shorter, *The Making of the Modern Family* (New York: Basic Books, 1975), epitomizes the pessimism of the "family sentiments" school. See also Mary Lyndon

Shanley. "The History of the Family in Modern England: Review Essay," *Signs* 4, no. 4 (Summer 1979): 740–50.

13. Stack; and Brett Williams, "The Trip Takes Us: Chicano Migrants to the Prairie" (Ph.D. diss., University of Illinois at Urbana-Champaign, 1975).

14. David Schneider and Raymond T. Smith, *Class Differences and Sex Roles in American Kinship and Family Structure* (Englewood Cliffs, N.J.: Prentice-Hall, Inc., 1973), esp. 27.

15. See Nelson Graburn, ed., *Readings in Kinship and Social Structure* (New York: Harper & Row, 1971), esp. 3–4.

16. The moral mother/cult of domesticity is analyzed in Barbara Welter, "The Cult of True Womanhood, 1820–1860," *American Quarterly* 18, no. 2 (Summer 1966): 151–74; Nancy Cott, *The Bonds of Womanhood: "Women's Sphere" in New England, 1780–1835* (New Haven, Conn.: Yale University Press, 1977); and Ruth Bloch, "American Feminine Ideals in Transition: The Rise of the Moral Mother, 1785–1815," *Feminist Studies* 4, no. 2 (June 1978): 101–26. The description of the general political-economic shift in the United States is based on Harry Braverman, *Labor and Monopoly Capital: The Degradation of Work in the Twentieth Century* (New York: Monthly Review Press, 1974); Peter Dobkin Hall, "Family Structure and Economic Organization: Massachusetts Merchants, 1700–1850," in *Family and Kin in Urban Communities, 1700–1950*, ed. Tamara K. Hareven (New York: New Viewpoints, 1977), 38–61; Michael Anderson, "Family, Household and the Industrial Revolution," in *The American Family in Social-Historical Perspective*, ed. Michael Gordon (New York: St. Martin's Press, 1978), 38–50; Tamara K. Hareven, *Amoskeag: Life and Work in an American Factory City* (New York: Pantheon Books, 1978); Richard Edwards, *Contested Terrain: The Transformation of the Workplace in the Twentieth Century* (New York: Basic Books, 1979); Mary Ryan, *The Cradle of the Middle Class: The Family in Oneida County, New York, 1790–1865* (Cambridge: Cambridge University Press, 1981); Alice Kessler-Harris, *Out to Work: A History of Wage-earning Women in the United States* (New York: Oxford University Press, 1982).

17. Ryan, 231–32.

18. Sylvia Junko Yanagisako, "Family and Household: The Analysis of Domestic Groups," *Annual Review of Anthropology* 8 (1979): 161–205.

19. See Donald J. Treiman and Heidi I. Hartmann, eds., *Women, Work and Wages: Equal Pay for Jobs of Equal Value* (Washington, D.C.: National Academy Press, 1981).

20. Lamphere (n. 4 above); Jane Fishburne Collier, "Women in Politics," in Rosaldo and Lamphere, eds. (n. 4 above), 89–96.

21. Nancy Folbre and Heidi I. Hartmann, "The Rhetoric of Self-Interest: Selfishness, Altruism, and Gender in Economic Theory," in *The Consequences of Economic Rhetoric,* ed. Arjo Klamer and Donald McCloskey (New York: Cambridge University Press, 1988).

IX

Gender, Ritual, and Religion

In many non-western societies women's ritual roles are central and indispensable to community cohesion and well-being. In contrast, in Anglo-European cultures women's religious activities tend to be secondary and marginal because of the pre-eminence of men in both organizational hierarchies and doctrine. Anthropological research has long recognized that religious systems reflect, support, and carry forward patterns of social organization and central values of a society. What has not been sufficiently recognized is the interrelationships of men and women in the perpetuation of social life through religious activities.

The study of the ritual activities of women has often been embedded in analyses of life cycle events, such as the Nkang'a girl's puberty ritual among the Ndembu of Central Africa (Turner 1968: 198) or pregnancy and childbirth rituals in Asia (Jacobson 1989; Laderman 1983). With the exception of these areas of research, the study of women and religion has often been neglected, despite the fact that women are prominent in religious activities. As a result of a renewed interest in the study of gender in various cultures, scholars have begun to explore how the religious experience of women is different from that of men; whether and how women become ritual specialists; what religious functions they perform and the degree to which these are private or public; and finally, what implications these ritual activities have for women's prestige and status.

This has led, in some cultural contexts, to an attempt to formulate a more complete ethnographic picture. For example, in the literature on Australian aborigines, where there is a good deal of debate about gender roles, a number of ethnologists have asserted that the dominance of senior men is sustained by their control of sacred knowledge and that their position is recognized by both men and women in the culture (Warner 1937; White 1975; Bern 1979). This viewpoint has been challenged by Diane Bell (1981, 1983), who notes that male anthropologists have underestimated and under-reported the religious life of Australian aboriginal women. She argues that "Both men and women have rituals that are closed to the other, both men and women allow the other limited attendance at certain of their rituals, and, finally, there are ceremonies in which both men and women exchange knowledge and together celebrate their membership in one society and their duty to maintain the law of their ancestors" (1981: 319).

Bell focuses in particular on the love rituals of women, rituals that originally were viewed by ethnologists as magic and therefore deviant, unimportant, and marginal to the central decision-making realm of men. In contrast, Bell suggests that in the celebration of these rituals, used by women to establish and maintain marriages of their own choosing, "Women clearly perceived themselves as independent opera-tors in a domain where they exercised power and autonomy based on their dream-ing affiliations with certain tracts of land. These rights are recognized and respected by the whole society" (1981: 322). The love rituals of Australian aborigi-nal women are, in short, by no means peripheral to the society. They are under-written by Dreamtime Law and feared by men who are often unaware that they are being performed and unable to negate their power. Through their rituals some Australian aboriginal women have, as Hamilton (1981) suggests, a mechanism with which to challenge the ideology of male superiority that is expressed in male ritual.

Mathews (1985) provides us with another example of an important arena of reli-gious activity—the civil-religious hierarchy or cargo system in Mesoamerica—that has long been considered a public and exclusively male arena. If women were men-tioned at all in studies of the cargo system, it was for their peripheral roles in food preparation. Based on her research in the state of Oaxaca in Mexico, Mathews begins by pointing out that an application of the domestic-public model (see Sec-tion III) to an understanding of these religious ceremonies obscures the significant ritual roles of women because it places the cargo system in the public sphere of activity and fails to acknowledge the importance of the household unit. Rather than oppose men and women within a rigid domestic-public model, Mathews empha-sizes the parallel and interdependent roles of men and women in the execution of cargo. Male cargo holders (*mayordomos*) organize and coordinate the activities of men, and female cargo holders (*mayordomas*) organize and coordinate the activities of women. At the end of their year of responsibility, both share in the prestige gained from service.

If Oaxacan women have an important and prestige-conferring role within the religious sphere of cargo activity, similar opportunities are denied them within the civil sphere. Thus Mathews explores the impact of the penetration of the state (see Section VII) on the lives of women. A sexual divide-and-rule state policy, she argues, makes men into social adults and women into domestic wards whose dealings with the public sphere become restricted. Prestige in local institutions is undermined by its absence in extracommunity institutions, and as civil offices assume increasing importance at the expense of cargo offices, the position of women is eroded.

In contrast to the underestimation of women's religious roles in the literature on Australian aborigines and the Mesoamerican cargo system, studies of sub-Saha-ran Africa have long recognized that the ritual life of women is both significant and highly elaborated. In this region, women are involved in complex ceremonies of initiation; they are engaged in witchcraft and divination (Mendonsa 1979; Ngubane 1977); they act as spirit mediums and healers (Green 1989; Sargent 1989); they lead and participate in possession cults (Berger 1976); and they form their own secret societies (MacCormack 1979).

Boddy (in this book) discusses the role of women in the zar spirit possession cult of northern Sudan. In particular she emphasizes how zar serves as a cultural resource mobilized by individuals, particularly women, under certain conditions. Boddy argues that the Sudanese women in the village of Hofiriyat where she con-ducted her research view themselves in a complementary rather than inferior or sub-ordinate position vis-à-vis men. This complementarity in gender relations is reflected in the dialectical relationship between zar and Islam. "If women are constrained by their gender from full participation in Islam, men are constrained by theirs from full participation in the zar (Boddy 1989:60). Zar is not, in Boddy's view, a "peripheral cult" (Lewis 1971).

In a range of cultural contexts, anthropologists have argued that women use spirit possession and trance as an outlet for the stress that results from their social and material deprivation and subordination (Broch 1985; Hamer and Hamer 1966; Lewis 1966, 1986; Morsy 1979; Pressel 1973). As Danforth (1989: 99) argues with regard to firewalking (Anastenaria) in northern Greece, "Through these rituals women seek to address the discrepancies that characterize the relationship between an official ideology of male dominance and a social reality in which women actually exercise a significant degree of power. Spirit possession...provides a context for the resolution of conflict often associated with gender roles and gender identity." Boddy views the zar cult in more nuanced terms. Although she acknowledges that some of her informants use zar to improve their subordinate status, she emphasizes that women are more susceptible to spirit attack (as illness episode) "as a function of their femininity." Zar is a form of feminist discourse for women with marital or fertility problems. Close to 50 percent of Hofriyati women who were ever or are married have succumbed to possession. "Spirits, villagers assert, rarely trouble themselves with the unwed" (Boddy 1989:166).

Discourse, in the form of sexually explicit funerary songs and dances performed by women, is also the subject of McIntosh's analysis (in this book) of death rituals among the Giriama of Kenya. McIntosh begins by noting that many ritual forms, particularly in sub-Saharan Africa, lend themselves to unruliness, turning the normative social world upside down (see also Davis 1971, 1975). But, she asks, does such ritual behavior really pose a threat to patriarchal orders and how can it be understood from an insider's perspective? Have these perceptions changed in conjunction with the arrival of Western lifestyles and tourism? McIntosh argues that in a gender-neutral sense the sexual license of funerary songs is a mechanism by which the Giriama can confront the power of death. Grief and sexual expression are assimilated such that a funeral becomes like a wedding: "the last wedding of the deceased." However, the persistence of this "tradition" occurs in a society where women's sexuality is still controlled by a set of popular expectations about female modesty and yet simultaneously challenged by the growth of a "sex safari" industry. The obscenities expressed by women in the funerary rituals are thus viewed with ambivalence—innocuous tradition on the one hand; a training ground for real sexual promiscuity and misconduct on the other. Today women are frequently derided for, if not prohibited by their husbands from participating in these unruly rituals.

In Africa, and elsewhere around the world, anthropologists have identified female religious practitioners (healers and shamans) who are often conceived of as women apart. They frequently transcend local cultural definitions of womanhood and are recognized as having extraordinary characteristics. Laurel Kendall (1985) notes that Korean women who become *mansin* (shamans) stand above the social and economic constraints generally imposed on a proper Korean wife and mother. The mansin occupies an ambiguous status similar to that of other "glamorous but morally dubious female marginals, the actress, the female entertainer, and the prostitute." Though not always accorded respect, the mansin wears the costumes and speaks with the authority of the gods. Mansin and their rituals are, in Kendall's view, "integral components of Korean family and village religion. Within this religious system, women and shamans perform essential ritual tasks that complement men's ritual tasks" (1985: 25). Korean housewives come to the mansin for therapeutic answers to a range of personal and household problems; for divinations about the future and prospects for the coming year; and for female solidarity and a "venting of the spleen" (Kendall 1985: 25). Women's rituals in Korea, like those in some other parts of the world, are both practical and expressive. As Mernissi (1978) suggests, based on her research in Morocco, female devotional societies provide a tightly knit community of supporters and advisers. The Christian Science movement founded in America by Mary Baker Eddy in the late nineteenth century was a healing religion that also offered middle-class women a "socially acceptable alternative to the stifling Victorian stereotypes then current" (Fox 1989: 98).

Mama Lola, the Vodou priestess (*manbo*) described by Brown (in this book) is a ritual specialist, diviner, and healer working in New York who, when she is possessed, "acts out the social and psychological forces that define and often contain the lives of contemporary Haitian women." Through ritual, Mama Lola empowers her clients. This phenomenon of psychological empowerment is characteristic of other religious systems; it is described by Danforth (1989) in his discussion of the New Age Firewalking cult in the United States and by Wadley (1989) in her analysis of the active control over their lives that north Indian village women gain through their ritual activities.

Mama Lola maintains a very personal relationship with two female spirits. To one she stands in the role of child to a spiritual mother, thereby metaphorically expressing an important bond within Haitian culture and society that is manifested in her own relationship with her daughter Maggie. This ritually embedded mother–child metaphor can be found in other parts of the world where women healers meet the physical and emotional needs of their patients just as mothers meet the needs of their children (Wedenoja 1989; Kerewsky-Halpern 1989). If one of Mama Lola's female spirits represents the nurturing side of women in relation to their children, the other represents the romantic side in relation to men.

In Haitian Vodou the diverse roles of women are projected into the religious sphere. This is equally true of other religious traditions. In Catholic cultures values about ideal womanhood are sanctified by the image of the Virgin Mary, who represents submission, humility, serenity, and long suffering (Stevens 1973). In Mexico, for example, Eve and the Virgin Mary are contrasting images that "encode the cycle of reproduction within the domestic group. When a woman is nursing and sexually continent she resembles the Virgin. When she submits to sex, she is more like Eve" (Ingham 1986: 76). Hindu goddesses are also multifaceted; they are mothers, mediators, and protectresses. According to Preston (1985: 13), there is a connection "between the role of women in Indian life and the special position of female deities in the Hindu pantheon. Though Indian women are supposed to be absolutely devoted to their husbands who are respected as embodiments of the deity, women may also reign supreme in their own domains as mothers of their children." In Dinaan Hinduism the Great Goddess takes several forms, some good and some evil. Babb (1975: 226) suggests that these two aspects reflect an opposition in male and female principles: "When female dominates male, the pair is sinister; when male dominates female the pair is benign."

Of importance, then, to some students of the relationship between gender and religion is the question of how women are portrayed in religious symbolism and doctrine. One of the most intriguing representations of women in religious thought is the Shaker conception of a female God. The Shakers were a millenarian Christian group who arrived on the shores of America in the late eighteenth century. As Procter-Smith (in this book) points out, long before recent feminists began to refer to God as "she," the Shakers believed in God the mother to complement God the father and conceived of their leader, Ann Lee, as a manifestation of the second coming of Christ in female form.

This millennial thinking empowered women and permitted the eradication of women's subordination. Shaker men and women shared spiritual authority and the leadership roles that were specified by this authority. Long before Engels (see Section VII), the Shakers appear to have recognized that property, marriage, and sexuality may undermine the status of women, and they therefore worked to eliminate these phenomena both ideologically and practically from their way of life. They upheld celibacy and the communal ownership of property. Procter-Smith observes, however, that the Shakers were not fully successful in their efforts. A patriarchal and hierarchical model persisted, as did a division of labor that followed broader societal patterns for what men and women do. To this Setta (1989: 231) has added the observation that Shaker theology was dominated by men while women were the spirit mediums, a distinction in her view that parallels a frequent human division "between men as scholars and thinkers and women as vehicles for religious experience."

Shakerism in its original form had much in common with some of the female-oriented religious cults described by anthropologists working in other parts of the world. It too was based in spirit possession and other forms of ecstatic behavior. It too was organized around the metaphor of mother who gives birth to, nurtures, and protects her child believers. It too provided an outlet for women who were otherwise constrained by the social institutions of nineteenth-century American society.

In this book, we have taken the approach that what it means to be male and female (i.e., gender) is learned and shaped within a cultural context. Religious symbols are a powerful mechanism by which culturally appropriate gender messages are transmitted. As Bynum observes, "It is no longer possible to study religious practice or religious symbols without taking gender—that is, the cultural experience of being male or female—into account" (1986: 1–2). In addition, through participation and leadership in ritual, women may enhance their social position. Involvement in religious activities may also generate a sense of female or community solidarity through membership in a congregation or participation in ritual functions.

REFERENCES

Babb, Lawrence. 1975. *The Divine Hierarchy.* New York: Columbia University Press.

Bell, Diane. 1981. "Women's Business Is Hard Work: Central Australian Aboriginal Women's Love Rituals." *Signs* 7: 314–337.

———. 1983. *Daughters of the Dreaming.* London: George Allen and Unwin.

Berger, Iris. 1976. "Rebels or Status-Seekers? Women as Spirit Mediums in East Africa." In Nancy J. Hafkin and Edna G. Bay (eds.). *Women in Africa,* pp. 157–182. Stanford: Stanford University Press.

Bern, J. 1979. "Ideology and Domination: Toward a Reconstruction of Australian Aboriginal Social Formation." *Oceania* 50: 118–132.

Boddy, Janice. 1989. *Wombs and Alien Spirits: Women, Men, and the Zar Cult in Northern Sudan.* Madison: University of Wisconsin Press.

Broch, Harald Meyer. 1985. "'Crazy Women Are Performing in Sombali': A Possession-Trance Ritual on Bonerate, Indonesia." *Ethos* 13: 262–282.

Bynum, Caroline Walker. 1986. "Introduction: The Complexity of Symbols." In Caroline Walker Bynum, Steven Harrell, and Paula Richman (eds.). *Gender and Religion: On the Complexity of Symbols,* pp. 1–20. Boston: Beacon.

Danforth, Loring M. 1989. *Firewalking and Religious Healing: The Anastenaria of Greece and the American Firewalking Movement.* Princeton: Princeton University Press.

Davis, Natalie Zemon. 1971. "The Reasons of Misrule: Youth Groups and Charivaris in Sixteenth-Century France." *Past and Present* 50:41–75

———. 1975. "Women on Top." In Natalie Zemon Davis, *Society and Culture in Early Modern France,* pp. 124–151. Stanford: Stanford University Press.

Fox, Margery. 1989. "The Socioreligious Role of the Christian Science Practitioner." In Carole Shepherd McClain (ed.). *Women as Healers: Cross-Cultural Perspectives,* pp. 98–114. New Brunswick, NJ: Rutgers University Press.

Green, Edward C. 1989. "Mystical Black Power: The Calling to Diviner-Mediumship in Southern Africa." In Carole Shepherd McClain (ed.). *Women as Healers: Cross-Cultural Perspectives,* pp. 186–200. New Brunswick, NJ: Rutgers University Press.

Hamer, J. and I. Hamer. 1966. "Spirit Possession and its Socio-Psychological Implications among the Sidamo of Southwest Ethiopia." *Ethnology* 5: 392–408.

Hamilton, Annette. 1981. "A Complex Strategical Situation: Gender and Power in Aboriginal Australia." In N. Grieve and P. Grimshaw (eds.). *Australian Women: Feminist Perspectives,* pp. 69–85. Melbourne: Oxford University Press.

Ingham, John. 1986. *Mary, Michael and Lucifer.* Austin: University of Texas Press.

Jacobson, Doranne. 1989. "Golden Handprints and Red-Painted Feet: Hindu Childbirth Rituals in Central India." In Nancy Auer Falk and Rita M. Gross (eds.). *Unspoken Worlds: Women's Religious Lives,* pp. 59–71. Belmont, CA: Wadsworth Publishing Co.

Kendall, Laurel. 1985. *Shamans, Housewives, and Other Restless Spirits: Women in Korean Ritual Life.* Honolulu: University of Hawaii Press.

Kerewsky-Halpern, Barbara. 1989. "Healing with Mother Metaphors: Serbian Conjurers' Word Magic." In Carole Shepherd McClain (eds.). *Women as Healers: Cross-Cultural Perspectives,* pp. 115–135. New Brunswick, NJ: Rutgers University Press.

Laderman, Carol. 1983. *Wives and Midwives: Childbirth and Nutrition in Rural Malaysia.* Berkeley: University of California Press.

Lewis, L. M. 1966. "Spirit Possession and Deprivation Cults." *Man* 1: 307–329.

———. 1971. *Ecstatic Religion: An Anthropoligical Study of Spirit Possession and Shamanism.* Baltimore: Penguin Books.

———. 1986. *Religion in Context: Cults and Charisma.* Cambridge: Cambridge University Press.

MacCormack, Carol P. 1979. "Sande: The Public Face of a Secret Society." In Bennetta Jules-Rosette (ed.). *New Religions of Africa,* pp. 27–39. Norwood, NJ: Ablex.

Mathews, Holly F. 1985. "'We are Mayordomo': A Reinterpretation of Women's Roles in the Mexican Cargo System." *American Ethnologist* 12 (2): 285–301.

Mendonsa, Eugene L. 1979. "The Position of Women in the Sisala Divination Cult." In Bennetta Jules-Rosette (ed.). *The New Religions of Africa,* pp. 57–67. Norwood, NJ: Ablex.

Mernissi, Fatima. 1978. "Women, Saints and Sanctuaries." *Signs* 3: 101–12.

Morsy, Soheir. 1979. "Sex Roles, Power, and Illness." *American Ethnologist* 5: 137–150.

Ngubane, H. 1977. *Body and Mind in Zulu Medicine: An Ethnography of Health and Disease In Nyuswa-Zulu Thought and Practice.* New York: Academic Press.

Pressel, Ester. 1973. "Umbanda in Sao Paulo: Religious Innovations in a Developing Society." In Erika Bourguignon (ed.). *Religion, Altered States of Consciousness and Social Change,* pp. 264–318. Columbus: Ohio State University Press.

Preston, James J. 1985. *Cult of the Goddess: Social and Religious Change in a Hindu Temple.* Prospect Heights, IL: Waveland. (Orig pub. 1980.)

Sanday, Peggy. 1974. "Female Status in the Public Domain." In Michelle Z. Rosaldo and Louise Lamphere (eds.). *Woman, Culture, and Society,* pp. 189–206. Stanford: Stanford University Press.

Sargent, Carolyn. 1989. "Women's Roles and Women Healers in Contemporary Rural and Urban Benin." In Carole Shepherd McClain (ed.). *Women as Healers: Cross-Cultural Perspectives,* pp. 204–218. New Brunswick, NJ: Rutgers University Press.

Setta, Susan M. 1989. "When Christ Is a Woman: Theology and Practice in the Shaker Tradition." In Nancy Auer Falk and Rita M. Gross (eds.). *Unspoken Worlds: Women's Religious Lives,* pp. 221–234. Belmont, CA: Wadsworth.

Stevens, Evelyn. 1973. "Marianismo: The Other Face of Machismo in Latin America." In Ann Pescatello (ed.). *Female and Male in Latin America,* pp. 89–101. Pittsburgh: University of Pittsburgh Press.

Turner, Victor. 1968. *Drums of Affliction.* Oxford: Clarendon Press.

Wadley, Susan S. 1989. "Hindu Women's Family and Household Rites in a North Indian Village." In Nancy Auer Falk and Rita M. Gross (eds.). *Unspoken Worlds: Women's Religious Lives,* pp. 72–81. Belmont, CA: Wadsworth.

Warner, William Lloyd. 1937. *A Black Civilization: A Study of an Australian Tribe.* New York: Harper & Row.

Wedenoja, William. 1989. "Mothering and the Practice of 'Balm' in Jamaica." In Carole Shepherd McClain (ed.). *Women as Healers: Cross-Cultural Perspectives,* pp. 76–97. New Brunswick, NJ: Rutgers University Press.

White, I. 1975. "Sexual Conquest and Submission in the Myths of Central Australia." In L. Hiatt (ed.). *Australian Aboriginal Mythology,* pp. 123–142. Canberra: Australian Institute of Aboriginal Studies.

Spirit Possession and Gender Complementarity: Zâr in Rural Northern Sudan

Janice Boddy

July 20, 1976, 4:00 P.M. The door to my hôsh *bangs open. Asia ducks beneath the lintel, lifts the water container from her head, and pours its contents into my* zîr. *Her face is seamed with sweat.* "Allaaah!*" she exclaims, "the land is hot today!* Shufti, ya *Janice, I've heard they are drumming in Goz. Do you want to go?"*

Of course!—a zâr *is on. But the walk in this heat is a long one, and my leg has been badly swollen for several days.*

This chapter is excerpted from Janice Boddy, *Women, Men and the Zâr Cult in Northern Sudan* (University of Wisconsin Press, 1989) and adapted for this volume.

"Sadig is borrowing camels from his cousin. You must ride."

Moments later I am teetering sidesaddle, following the equally inexpert Sadig along a trail that hems some withered fields of maize. My camel munches lazily at each low acacia, and I am soon covered in scratches from their thorns. Prodding seems only to anger the beast, and I fear a painful bite; it would have been faster to walk. Still beyond sight of Goz we are reached by the deep bass of drumming, fitful through the sultry air. The camels perk, raise their heads, start trotting toward the sound.

Goz is a newish settlement, an odd assortment of square thatched huts, thorn corrals, and a couple of half-completed mud-brick hôshs. *The drumming* comes from one of these. Hofriyati[1] arriving by foot have preceded my arrival; the zâr has just begun. Ideally a zâr should take place in the room of a house, if capacious, but because of the heat, today's has been mounted in the yard.

A litany of greetings over, I am seated near the dancing grounds an open area (mîdân) bounded on three sides by palm-fiber ground mats. Here sit several dozen chanting women: the spirit-possessed. Now and then one rises to her knees and begins to move her upper body in time with the sonorous beat. In the center of the mîdân stands the shaykha—zâr practitioner or "priestess"—a forceful, brawny woman in an electric-pink pullover, tôb[2] tied loosely at her waist. She is arguing with a woman just as brash as she, who, between expletives, puffs furiously on a cigarette. I learn that the shaykha speaks not to the woman but to her spirit, in an effort to diagnose the source of the woman's complaint. Observing from the side is a tall, very black, incongruously muscled figure clad in a tôb, large wristwatch, and hairnet—the shaykha's reputedly transvestite assistant from south of Shendi. In contrast, the "ayâna—"sick woman" and focus of the ceremony—is frail, elderly. She rests quietly on a pillow next to the musicians, facing the front of the hôsh, arms and legs curled tight against her white-tôbed body.

The shaykha concludes her discussion, sits down, and starts to drum. Using only the tips of her fingers, she beats a large earthen dallûka stretched with goat hide, its whitened flanks boldly adorned with mauve geometric designs. Another dallûka responds in shifted accents, joined half a second later by the nugarishan, a tall brass mortar that rings, when struck, like a cowbell, only deeper. A fourth woman beats a complementary rhythm on an inverted aluminum washtub or tisht. The result is a complicated syncopation, its underlying pattern one long beat, three short. The sound is less soothing than cacophonous, yet endlessly repeated and accompanied by reiterative chants, the effect is indeed soporific. The chants, I learn, are called "threads"—khuyût (singular is khayt)—and when sung they are said to be "pulled."

The rhythm intensifies; the ayâna rises to dance. Now visible over her tôb is a red sash attached to a reddish waist cloth in the style of a Sam Browne belt. She is possessed, my companions say, by

Khawâja (Westerner) spirits: a doctor, lawyer, and military officer—all of these at once. Yet it is the lattermost she appears to manifest in dance. Her tôb is folded cowl-like over her head, obscuring her face; she flourishes a cane—hooked, as in vaudevillian burlesque. Her dance is a slow, rhythmic walk crisscrossing a chimeric square, feet first moving side to side, then forward and back. With a leap of the imagination she is an officer of the desert corps conducting drill. Every so often she bends rigidly at the hip and, cane pressed to her forehead, bobs her torso up and down. I am told that her spirits have requested the white tôb, cane, cigarettes, "European" belt, and yet to be purchased, a radio.

The band takes up the chant of another zâr. The ayâna sits; the shaykha leaves her drum and starts to dance, tôb covering her head. Suddenly, the tôb is thrown off. She turns on her heel, goose-steps the length of the mîdân, stops before me, abruptly pulls herself to attention. She salutes me three or four times, stiffly, eyes glazed and staring, a grin playing wildly on her face. Her left hand grips a sword within its sheath; with her right she grasps my own with unusual strength and pumps it "Western style" in time to the drums. I am shaken by this treatment and by thoughts of her sword. The chant sounds like a military march: I recognize the British Pasha spirit, Abu Rîsh Ya Amîr ad-Daysh ("Owner of Feathers, O Commander of the Army"). The drums desist. At once my hand is released. The shaykha's features assume a more dignified composure and she returns to the center of the mîdân.

Evening falls. Women rise to dance—or "descend" (nazal), as the zâr step is called—throughout the night. Others respond to the spirits' chants from a kneeling position, bobbing up and down from the waist, tôbs covering their heads like so many Halloween ghosts. One who stands has mounted a zâr in the past: she has "slaughtered" (dabahat, for dhabahat) for the spirits, thus confirming relations with those by which she is possessed. A woman who remains sitting or kneeling has yet to sacrifice; though acknowledged to be possessed, and perhaps even aware of the types of zayran that bother her, she remains somewhat uncertain of her spirits and limited to kneeling at their ceremonies until she undertakes a cure. Yet she is no less an adept for this.

In the waning, eerie light I see a woman—spirit—performing a strange pantomime with a sword, crouching low, sweeping the flat of the weapon back and forth along the ground. She dashes through these postures with skill and grace; I am reminded of a hunter flushing game, or a soldier wary of enemies lying hidden in dense vegetation.

At the start of another chant a tall older woman dressed in red lights a cigarette. She struts down the mîdân, smoking, walking stick held perpendicular to the ground at the end of an outstretched arm, pompous, indifferent, mandarinlike. Some chants later she reappears, transmogrified. Now she and the transvestite stage a sword fight closely resembling the men's dance of a nearby desert people. The combatants leap at each other with apparent abandon, landing within inches of the audience, their sharp unsheathed blades swooping dangerously from aloft. Spectators shrink in terror at their bravado. The two are possessed, I learn, by zâyran of the Arab (Nomad) species.

Occasionally during the evening's drumming, the shaykha dances around the ayâna, encircling her with her arms, coaxing a seemingly reluctant spirit to enter its host and fully reveal itself before the assembly. But the ayâna has not risen since her foray into the mîdân at the start. She sits, silently watching.

I notice at the end of each chant that several who have "descended"—standing or kneeling— begin to scratch themselves, and hiccup and burp indiscriminately. Zaineb tells me these reactions signify the spirit's departure from the body of its host, of a woman's leaving trance.

July 24, 5:30 PM. Last day of the ceremony. The sacrificial ram is led into the mîdân, and a red and gold cloth—a garmosîs or bridal shawl—is placed over its back and head. The musicians play a chant. Incense is freshly lit, and the brazier thrust beneath the shawl. The animal is forced to inhale the smoke, then led from the mîdân and slaughtered by the ayâna's son. Blood spurting from its throat is collected in a bowl and placed before the drums. The ayâna crosses seven times over the carcass before it is dragged off to be butchered. With the others I now step forward to deposit a few piasters in the victim's congealing blood. Someone whispers an invitation to drink araki (liquor)…being

khawâja (a westerner) I am expected to imbibe. The possessed anoint themselves with blood, some also take a sip; the shaykha daubs it on herself and the ayâna's feet and arms. Drumming and chanting recommence. Still wearing her stigmata of the zâr the ayâna rises to dance.

A woman "descends" with a prayer shawl round her neck, holding its fringed ends in her hands, rocking to and fro as she paces the mîdân. The gesture echoes that of men at a zikr, a "remembrance" ceremony of the Islamic (sûfî) fraternities from whose membership women are excluded.

Later another woman (Zaineb's cousin and sister-in-law) dances briskly wearing trousers of a European cut; she is possessed, I learn, by the Airplane Captain zâr.

Later still, an older lady performs the local "pigeon dance," concluding with a shabâl[3] to the dancer in the Mediterranean head scarf. She has been seized by Muna, Sitt ash-Shabâl, a southern prostitute zâr given to mimicking village women when appearing in their midst.

An unwed girl now rises, snatches up the bridal shawl, and flings it over her head. She shuffles forward, out of time with the chant. Onlookers gasp. This is the costume of Lulîya, the Ethiopian prostitute fond of Hofriyati weddings whose thread was sung some time ago; it is unlikely that She[4] would return so soon, and uninvited. The audience tries to dissuade the girl without success. It is not right, they say, for an unmarried girl to dance so like a bride, in public. Has she no shame? Beside me a woman snaps, "That virgin is not possessed (mazûr). She just wants a husband!"

Night falls; a pressure lamp is placed on a low table near the musicians. The mîdân is a pond of light shallowing to darkness at its sides. Dancers cast weird shadows on the sand, eyes in faces lit from below appear enormous, wild. Drums throb without flagging; redolent smoke of incense clouds the evening. The atmosphere is tense, intoxicating, eerie.

A piercing cry—a uniformed schoolgirl nine or ten years old has sprawled forward into the mîdân, upheld on all four limbs, body jerking rapidly up and down from the shoulders. Immediately, she is led off by some older women, told it is not proper for a child to behave this way at a zâr. But she does not stop. Outside the mîdân the women try to calm her.

Now she is sobbing and has gone quite limp. When efforts to revive her fail she is dragged, resisting, back into the center. She balks at attempts to bring her to the shaykha *and is deposited before the drums. The* shaykha *approaches; the girl cringes. The* shaykha *censes her, covers her with a white* tôb, *and asks, "What do you want? Who are you?" No response.*

Onlookers taunt the intrusive zâr, *trying vainly to garner its sympathy: "Ah, her father is poor! Her mother is blind! Her brother is ill!" The* shaykha *sends for the girl's father. He is brought into the* mîdân *and made to give his daughter's spirit ten piasters (about twenty-five cents). Still there is no word from the* zâr; *the girl remains limp, appearing deeply entranced.*

It is getting late. Smells of cooking waft through the mîdân, *and laughter from the kitchen. More drumming and dancing are called for. The* shaykha *requests certain threads to test for various species of* zayran, *hoping the presumptuous spirit will be drawn to identify itself. She blows into the schoolgirl's ears and behind her neck, she pulls at her limbs, whips her softly with a length of rope, beats her lightly with an iron spear. She censes her, rolls her head along the girl's body. She takes the girl in her arms and dances to and fro, blowing a whistle to the incessant beat. She leads the girl around the* mîdân *and is twice successful in getting her to move briefly of her own accord. At last the girl jogs back and forth through the open space, one arm pumping like the wheel of a locomotive, the other, raised and crooked at elbow, sounding an imagined alarm. The* shaykha *blows her pipe whistle in accompaniment. The troublesome spirit is identified:* Basha-t-Adil *the* Khawâja *railway engineer.*

Still the episode continues. For over an hour the shaykha *tries every technique in her repertoire, aiming to convince the implacable* zâr *to abandon his newfound host and refrain from bothering her again until she is a woman and married. Finally the* shaykha *guides the girl out of the* mîdân *and out of the* hôsh. *They cross the threshold, the* khashm al-bayt,[5] *backwards, facing the assembly; they remain in the path for several minutes, then return as they had left facing the* mîdân. *The girl, now calmed and weeping softly, is brought to sit near me—a human* khawâja—*but placed with her back to the ritual.*

Soon the sacrificial meal is served and proceedings brought to a close. It is almost 2:00 A.M. The ayâna *is now formally well, though tomorrow she must eat the head meat of the ram in a private ceremony followed by a procession to the Nile. Several people approach the* ayâna, *touch her right shoulder and say* 'Insha 'allâh byinf'ik, *"God willing, it is benefiting you." In the company of my neighbors I return, exhausted, to Hofriyat.*

ZÂR AND ZAYRAN

Smoking, wanton dancing, flailing about, burping and hiccuping, drinking blood and alcohol, wearing male clothing, publicly threatening men with swords, speaking loudly lacking due regard for etiquette: these are hardly the behaviors of Hofriyati women for whom dignity and propriety are leading concerns. But in the context of a *zâr* they are common and expected. The ceremony is rich in complex imagery and movement. Yet it has none of the solemn pageantry of a Mass, nor the predictable, repetitive manipulation of symbols which I, raised as a Catholic, might have found familiar. The tone of a *zâr* resembles neither the subdued formality of a Muslim Friday prayer, nor the unorchestrated ceremoniousness of life cycle rites in Hofriyat. It is closer in character to *zikrs* of the Qadriya and Khatmiya *sûfî* orders in Sudan, but lacks their cohesion and transcendent focus. What is singular about a *zâr* is its spontaneity, its imagination, whose basis nonetheless is a comprehensive repertoire of symbols and spirit roles—a resource on which participants draw for inspiration. Moves are lightly choreographed—improvisations on well-known themes; "players" are interchangeable, costumes readily borrowed and exchanged. But during the performance, neither players' bodies nor their costumes belong to village women—they belong, instead, to *zayran*. *Zâr* rituals are always fraught with tension and surprise, for at any moment a woman might be "seized" by a spirit that Hofriyati did not before know existed, or she did not know she had.

How is all of this to be understood? What is this phenomenon; who or what are these spirits that so dramatically appear in women's bodies?

THE POSSESSION CONCEPT[6]

Zâr refers to a type of spirit, the illness such spirits can cause by possessing humans, and the rituals necessary to their pacification. The cult is found throughout the northern Sudan and variations of the same name appear in Egypt, Ethiopia, Somalia, (where it is called *sâr*), Arabia, and southern Iran.[7]

In writing of spirit "possession" in Hofriyat, I am using indigenous terms. When someone is considered to be affected by a *zâr*, people say of her, *inda rih, inda zâr,* or *inda dastûr*[8]—"she has a spirit." Alternatively, they say she is *mazûr* or *madastîr*—"with spirit," possessed. *Zâr* influence, being possessed of and by a spirit, is considered an affliction and expressed as illness. A spirit causes its novice host to suffer; however initial misery should be surpassed by a more positive concern on the part of the spirit for its host's well-being as their relationship progresses. Once possessed, always possessed: *zayran* never wholly abandon those they have chosen as their hosts.

Someone diagnosed as *zâr* possessed is liable to be affected by her spirit(s) at any time. *Zayran* are able to infiltrate the bodies of their hosts at will, a move which villagers say always coincides with the latter's entrancement. According to Hofriyati, possession trance (*ghaybîya* or *ghaybûba*) is a state induced by the spirit's forceful entry into the body, which displaces or shifts the person's human self to another perceptual plane. It is, as Bourguignon (1973: 12–13) suggests, "a radical discontinuity of personal identity"; yet in contrast to her model, the distortion of perception this entails pertains not only to the self but to other entities as well.

Still, trance is only one manifestation of possession in Hoftiyat, for *zayran* affect their hosts in countless additional ways (see also Constantinides 1972, 1977; Cloudsley

1983:81). They are always near, or in local parlance "above" *(fôg)*, their human hosts, whence they might influence people's perceptions and behaviors in the course of daily life. Further, despite the acknowledged powers of *zayran,* possession trance rarely occurs unpremeditatedly, outside of ritual contexts. Here one is not diagnosed as possessed because she becomes entranced; rather, she becomes entranced because she is possessed. Schoolgirl mishaps notwithstanding, the possessed rarely enter trance spontaneously; this is something one must learn to do in the course of a curing ceremony in order to negotiate an appropriate relationship with instrusive *zayran.* As adepts put it, one must learn how not to resist a spirit's attempts to enter the human world through the medium of her body. The implicit link to ideas about sexual intercourse in Hoftiyat is striking and reiterated in the fact that a woman should be married before she becomes possessed.

Thus trance is in no way aberrant; it is a practiced behavior which the possessed are expected to display under certain conditions. Although an integral part of possession therapy and relapse prophylaxis, it is not consistently evinced by the possessed during ceremonies, and when evinced, it is variable in apparent depth and duration from one episode or individual to the next. Since it is considered inappropriate to be entered by a spirit (or a husband) while menstruating, a woman at a *zâr* signals *zayran* of her condition by tying a knot in her braids, so constraining the spirits' activity. Moreover, because it must conform to prescribed patterns of "spiritness," trance performance requires skill and considerable control. Thus it is not, as some would assert, a spontaneous neurological manifestation of nutritional deficiency which (at least originally) is accounted for after the fact as possession (e.g., Kehoe and Giletti 1981). Such models betray their foundation in a Western rationalism which derogates any mode of consciousness other than that of critical self-awareness. In the search for reductive biological explanations as to why trance should occur, trance itself is misconstrued, parted from its cultural context. Here an essential point is missed. For villagers the system of meaning—possession—is both logically and contextually prior to the behavior—trance—through which it finds expression (cf. Lambek 1981:7).

This is not to deny that biological factors might affect the proclivity to enter trance or the ease with which the behavior is learned. Some of the possessed initially experience difficulty in becoming lost from themselves and allowing their spirits to assume control; others do not. Here perhaps one's nutritional status plays a role. Still, it must be stressed that Hofriyati generally enter trance *after* having been diagnosed as possessed or, if undiagnosed, when attending a spirit ritual. And in either case, an individual's trance behavior is learned (cf. Bourguignon 1973:4–15, 1976: 37 ff.), shaped by her knowledge of *zayran* and their provenance. It may be novel and unexpected, but must be consistent with villagers' understanding of spirits to be accepted as legitimate possession and not considered dissimulation or idiosyncratic madness. The few women who do enter trance spontaneously—apparently uninduced, in nonceremonial situations—are hardly neophytes. Rather, they are long-term adepts of the *zâr* who, in the course of their possession careers, have become progressively more skilled at alternating modes of consciousness and allowing the spirits to exhibit themselves through their bodies (see also Besmer 1983:24).

According to Hofriyati, the fact that possession trance typically must be induced and is rare apart from public ritual has less to do with human ability or volition than with spirit caprice. Humans convoke *zayran* through ritual drumming and singing, and normally the spirits—for whom access to the human world is a principal motive for possession—are willing to oblige. Indeed, they regard such invitations as their due, in partial fulfillment of bargains struck with humans, and are likely to become disgruntled and dangerous when neglected or put off. If the possessed take care to mollify them, spirits ought to respond by confining their appearance to ritual contexts where they can frolic and be entertained. Yet none of this is certain. Spirits are willful, and for sport or revenge might "descend" into their hosts without benefit of prior summons. So despite the controlled nature of possession trance and spirit display, the startling possibility exists that at any moment a woman might not be who she usually is.

In Hofriyat possession is a matter of fact. Here the reality of spirits and their powers goes unchallenged, even by villagers who have no firsthand experience of them and regardless of how hotly they dispute the proper therapy for possession affliction, discussed later. Clearly, Hofriyati, like the rest of us, face doubts concerning their beliefs from time to time. But cosmological mavericks they are not. Doubts, like beliefs, are grounded in a social context. *Zayran* are immanent in the world of Hofriyat; sceptic and zealot, both, are canopied by their existence.

THE POSSESSED

In Hofriyat, as elsewhere in Sudan, possession activity is mainly, but not exclusively, the province of women.[9] Somewhat more than 40 percent of Hofriyati women ever married and over the age of fifteen (N = 129 [1977] and 135 [1984]) claim a *zâr* affliction. Marital status is a significant factor in possession illness: spirits, villagers assert, rarely trouble themselves with the unwed—with women whose fertility has yet to be activated.[10] Most affected are those between the ages of thirty-five and fifty-five, two-thirds of whom have spirits. This proportion is due to a cumulative effect: once possessed a woman is always possessed thereafter.

By contrast, only a handful of men from the entire village area are publicly acknowledged to be possessed. In Hofriyat itself only four men (about 5 percent of the resident adult male population) are considered adepts of the *zâr*; three have undergone the requisite ceremonies, one when only thirteen years of age. Two men born in the village but now living elsewhere are known to have spirits, and I obtained information concerning ten others from the vicinity, five of whom were deceased prior to fieldwork. During my six-year absence from the village, only one man had become possessed, in contrast to sixteen women. In 1984, several male acquaintances privately declared themselves to be possessed and confessed admiration for the *zâr,* but would not publicly seek to confirm their afflictions for fear of losing face.

Why is this the case? Why, assuming that possession is a public idiom for the articulation and interpretation of experience,[11] should there exist sexual disproportion among those who acknowledge having spirits? An obvious approach is to ask whether the range of experience that possession constructs is more common to Hofriyati women than to men. This I think to be the case, mainly because possession is closely linked to fertility with which women are identified and for which they bear responsibility. I do not agree with I. M. Lewis (1971, 1986) on this issue, who, arguing from a sociological perspective, suggests that *zâr* possession is a strategy which women use in an oblique attempt to redress the effects of their subordinate social status. Lewis holds that since spirits demand desiderata which husbands must provide if their wives are to regain well-being, possession can be seen as a measure of gender conflict: it is a strategic evocation of shared beliefs by women wishing to mitigate their subordination to men.

The perspective is illuminating, but presents a number of difficulties. First, it places unwarranted emphasis on the assumed intentionality of women and thus insidiously underestimates the factuality of spirits in the Sudanese world. Words like *strategy* imply volition, which may certainly be present and, if so, motivated by status considerations in some cases of possession but certainly not in all. Moreover, Lewis's deprivation hypothesis appears to presume that women seek the same status held by men, which , since men have deprived them of it, was originally within

their purview. Such assumptions fail to bear scrutiny in Hofriyat, where the social worlds of men and women are largely separate and distinct, a condition due not to happenstance or the prevailing wills of men, but to cultural design. Wilson's (1967) critique of the model tries to address this problem by shifting the locus of proposed status competition from intersex to intrasex relations and, in so doing, is sympathetic to the Sudanese context. However, it shares with Lewis's theory the drawback of a conflict orientation to social interaction that is firmly rooted in Western premises of individualism,[12] whose validity in non-Western cultures must be open to debate (cf Morsy 1978; Boddy 1988). Even granting that status may be a consideration in certain episodes of possession illness, the sociological argument cannot account for the *zâr* in its entirety. It glosses over the issue of belief and is therefore unable to explain or interpret possession forms (for example, the characteristics of spirits, the nature and variety of possession symptoms) and processes (such as the reevaluation of one's past that acquiring a spirit entails). Such factors, however important to the possessed, are implicitly deemed incidental when the investigator's focus is competition.[13] The social status model is unidimensional, at once too general in application and too narrow in concern to deal adequately with the complexities of *zâr.*

It is imperative to ask why so many scholars —among them Kehoe and Giletti (1981)— are committed to viewing possession as a consequence of women's deprivation rather than their privilege, or perhaps their inclination. Such explanations consistently mislocate the question of why women should be more susceptible to possession than men. Especially in his early work, Lewis (1971:77), for example, suggests that joining a *zâr* coterie enables women to express solidarity vis-à-vis men, who are seen as their oppressors. Men have Islam, which excludes women from active participation; hence women, who are socially peripheral, must resort to the equally peripheral cult of *zâr* both to mitigate their subordination and to express religious fervor (Lewis

1971:66–99; see also Lewis 1986:23–50, 102–5). This is a classic but unhappily androcentric portrayal of women, who are forever seen as reacting to men rather than acting for themselves within a specific cultural context.

To avoid such pitfalls, we need to examine closely how the sexes in Hofriyat conceive of their interrelations both collectively and individually. Judging from my informants, some women—by no means all or only those who are possessed—clearly feel subordinate to men, resent their positions, and are not consistently above vituperation. However, their feelings seem to derive less from their status as women than from the specific actions of individual men, notably husbands. And the problem these men pose is not that they deny women, as a class, an elevated social position, but that they sometimes—often inadvertently—thwart individual women's legitimate attempts to achieve it. The reverse can also be said for women, who may frustrate the status aspirations of men. Both sexes are active participants in the social life of Hofriyat, bisected as it is into gender-distinct yet partially overlapping spheres. If men are central and women peripheral with respect to Islam and external relations, women are central and men peripheral when it comes to physical, social, and cultural reproduction: the worldliness of village life. Although men and women are subject to different constraints, the actions of each bear consequence for those of the other.

Indeed, whatever consciousness women have of themselves as a group is hardly one of inferiority and wholescale subordination to men, but of complementarity. As villagers see it, the sexes are engaged—not in a war—but in a dialectical relationship of qualitatively disparate yet socially equivalent parts, each commanding certain resources but reliant on the other for fulfillment. They do not conceive of themselves as locked in a struggle between classes, hierarchically understood. Although a Marxist critique might legitimately consider this to be a mystification of political realities, it cannot be ignored if we are truly concerned with the meaning of *zâr* to women and men in Hofriyat. Political relations are mystified for both within the Hofriyati universe of meaning.

When properly situated in the framework of sexual complementarity, the question of why women as a category should be more likely than men to interpret certain experiences as possession expands to two: Why women? Why not men? As Kapferer (1983:98) astutely argues with respect to women's preponderance in Sri Lankan exorcisms, such questions cannot be resolved by focusing on the possessed's motives and intentions alone, independent of the cultural constructs that inform them. We need to consider the qualities that define the sexes in Hofriyat, the typifications each sex holds of the other, the components of gender identity (see also Nelson 1971). Only then might we have a basis for deciding whether a particular incidence of possession constitutes attempted cross-sex or intrasex status manipulation, or something else—an expression of psychological or social disturbance (cf. Crapanzano 1973, 1977b, 1980; Obeyesekere 1970,1981; Kapferer 1983, 1986), cross-sex communication (cf. Lambek 1980, 1981), religious experience (cf. Constantinides 1972, 1977; Lewis 1986), a form of play, dramatic allegory, or all of these and more. Its cultural underpinnings—idioms of the everyday world, prosaic conceptualizations of gender—empower possession as a form of social discourse.

Thus put, a focus on the articulatory potential of possession instead of on the status aspirations of individuals possessed changes the tenor of the analytic enterprise. It widens the interpretive net and does not attempt to simplify matters where simplicity belies the facts. Rather, it makes possible a variety of explanations at different levels of analysis and experience, all of them immanent in the *zâr* as a system of meaning, all of them potentially relevant to any specific episode of possession.

Returning to Hofriyati gender constructs and the *zâr*, both sexes allege that women are naturally more vulnerable to spirit attack as a function of their femininity.[14] Spirits are attracted to women—and married women in particular—for it is they who use henna, perfumes, soaps, and scented oils; wear gold jewelry and diaphanous wraps, all human finery which spirits are known to covet. The proclivities of *zayran* are symmetrical to those of Hofriyati women: both are regarded as consumers of goods provided by men.

Although many questions remain to be addressed, this goes some way toward explaining why women interpret certain experiences and illness episodes as possession. It also suggests why, in this sexually polarized community, men do not. But here more remains to be said. A common characterization of women that they do not completely share is that because they are wanting in '*agl*, (reason or social sense), they lack sufficient moral strength to uphold the tenets and ideals of Islam. According to local religious authorities it is reprehensible and abhorrent—though not, strictly speaking, *haram* (forbidden)—for Muslims to traffic with spirits. They say that each individual has the responsibility to steer a proper course of spirit avoidance, something women find more difficult to do than men. Women's perceived inability to resist and so deny *zayran* access to earthly pleasures is put down to their inherent moral frailty, notwithstanding that they are more likely to encounter *jinn* than men. Just as the public identity of women accounts for their greater participation in the *zâr* so the public identity of men as pious Muslims accounts, in part, for their forbearance (see also Lambek 1981:62–64).

The last is solely a masculine perspective. Women see no incompatibility between the *zâr* and Islam: to them possession ritual is part of a general religious enterprise (cf. Constantinides 1972:98). Hofriyati culture therefore contains conflicting interpretations of the relationship between possession and Islam. These, in turn, have divergent implications for the handling of troublesome spirits.

EXORCISM VERSUS ACCOMMODATION

Where men hold the reputedly orthodox view that intrusive spirits can and must be dislodged from the body by force, women maintain that *zayran* cannot be got rid of at all.[15] Adepts insist that if one's illness is caused by a *zâr*, no amount of Islamic or even Western medicine will effect a cure. Attempts to exorcise the spirit serve merely to exacerbate the patient's condition. Symptom remission alone can be achieved, and only if the afflicted agrees to hold a propitiatory ceremony on behalf of the as yet unnamed *zâr*. During this ceremony, often held long after her initial illness has dissipated, the possessed enters into a contractual relationship with the spirit(s) responsible for her lapse from health. There, in response to drumming and singing chants associated with the various named *zayran*, she ideally enters trance: a spirit's chant is an invitation to "descend" *(nazal)* and enter the body of its host, where its identity can be affirmed and its demands revealed.[16] In return for certain offerings, acquisitions, and observances, the invasive spirit agrees to restore, and refrain from further jeopardizing, its host's well-being.

Henceforward, human host and possessive *zâr* are joined in continuous but unequal partnership. The spirit remains above her, able to exert its influence or infiltrate her body at will. To some extent the possessed can rely on the spirit's compliance in maintaining her health, but only so long as she regularly attends the ceremonies of others, abstains from traditional mourning behavior, associates herself with clean and sweet-smelling things, and is not given over to strong emotion. A violation of these provisions renders her vulnerable to relapse. Yet the curing rite has opened communications between the two entities, and it is hoped that any future problems can be dealt with expeditiously. From the spirit's perspective, contracts with humans are infinitely renegotiable, so if the possessed wishes to allay further attack from her *zâr*, she must take scrupulous care to mollify it. If all goes well, what begins as an uneasy truce between a willful spirit and its initially reluctant host might graduate to positive symbiosis as their relationship stabilizes and matures. Alleviating the symptoms of possession illness is a matter of establishing reciprocal obligations between spirit and host; their relationship should become, like that between partners in a marriage, one of complementarity, exchange, and mutual accommodation.

Although the majority of men denounce the propitiation of *zayran*, this is not because they deny that such spirits exist. In Hofriyat, *zayran* comprise a distinct class of *jinn*,[17] mischievous invisible beings that populate a world that is parallel to our own and contiguous with it but imperceptible to humans most of the time. Typical of their exceptional attributes, *jinn* can transform themselves into animals, assume human form (but incompletely so, for their feet are always hooved), or take possession of live human bodies at will. *Jinn* are mentioned in the Quran (Suras 6, 17, 18, 34, 37, 46, 55, 72, and 114); they are a constant if often low-key part of both men's and women's daily lives.

Further, should a man become ill there is a chance that the diagnosis will be possession regardless of its feminine associations. Men recognize the powers of *zayran* and acknowledge that even the most pious among them occasionally succumbs to spirit attack. But this is where their public support for the cult stops: most insist that, despite a practiced resistance, *zayran*, like other *jinn*, must eventually capitulate to the powerful exorcistic techniques of Islamic medicine. In the company of their fellows they decry as un-Islamic women's ceremonial attempts to assuage and socialize the spirits.

In face of such weighty opposition the *zâr* cult thrives, and its rites are attended even by the most submissive and religious of wives. For women, *zâr* falls squarely within the purview of Islam. And when arguing their position with men (something I witnessed only twice), women said that Allah expects the afflicted to seek respite from their suffering—clearly, it is better to be healthy than "broken" by spirits or overzealous efforts to dislodge them. Perhaps men are right that involvement in the cult imperils one's prospect of a pleasurable afterlife, but then, is Allah not merciful?

Men, for their part, though publicly adamant that only exorcism is correct in the eyes of Islam, are privately not so intractable (cf. Barclay 1964:206; Constantinides 1982). Often hesitant, concerned, uncertain that Islamic medications will effect a cure or fearing reprisals of a powerful spirit if it is put off, most do not interfere when their womenfolk conduct propitiatory ceremonies, and provide money to meet the spirits' demands. Here perhaps, as Lewis (1971: 88) suggests, men tacitly recognize the contradiction between the formal ideology of male supremacy and the social (and cultural) importance of women. Intriguing, too, in the light of the ethnographic situation in Hofriyat, is Lewis's more recent view that woman's participation in the *zâr* might offer men "the privilege of vicarious participation in what they ostensibly condemn as superstition and heresy. Thus, if there is a dual spiritual economy [male and female], its two branches are interdependent and complementary" (Lewis 1986:106). It seems plausible that just as men's religious devotions count also for their womenfolk (1986:106), so women's *zâr* devotions might count indirectly for their men. As noted earlier, several male informants confided in 1984 that they believe themselves incurably possessed by *zayran*. These men enjoy listening to spirit rituals from afar or watching *bi shubbak* ("through a window"), but do not openly attend for fear of ridicule. Such peripheral and vicarious participation echoes that of women at a *zikr*—the "dervish" rite of Islamic fraternities whose membership in Sudan is exclusively male.

GLOSSARY

dallûka	large pottery drum used in weddings and zâr ceremonies
hôsh	house yard and/or wall that encloses it
shabâl	woman's gesture of flicking her hair at an approaching man in the context of a wedding dance; said to confer luck
shaykha	female curer of the zâr cult
zâr	a type of spirit, the illness it can cause, and the ritual by which the illness is assuaged; more generally, the "cult" that surrounds such spirits

zikr   remembrance: ceremony of the Islamic
        fraternities
zîr   large water jar

NOTES

1. Hofriyat is a pseudonym for the Sudanese village where I began conducting field work in 1976. "Hofriyati" refers to the people of the village, all of whom speak Arabic and profess Islam. The village is located on the Nile, a little over 120 miles (200 km) north and east of Khartoum.
2. A woman's modesty garment, consisting of some nine meters of cloth wound around the body and covering the head.
3. A flick of the hair, a movement said to confer luck on the recipient.
4. I use an initial capital letter (e.g. He, She) when referring to a specific spirit in order to indicate its sex while distinguishing it from its human host.
5. Literally, mouth of the house.
6. For a discussion of the cult's possible origins see Boddy 1989 and Constantinides 1991.
7. On northern Sudan see Constantinides 1977, 1982, 1991; Kenyon 1991, 2000. On *zar* in Egypt see Al-Guindi 1978; Kennedy 1978; Saunders 1977; in Ethiopia, Leiris 1958; Young 1975; in Somolia, where it is better known as *sar*, Lewis 1971, 1986; in Arabia, Trimingham 1965:258; and in southern Iran, Modarressi 1968.
8. This term literally means "statute" or "constitutional law," and colloquially, "permission" (Wehr 1976:281). In northern Sudan, however, the term also refers to a door jamb (Constantinides 1977:65–66, n. 6) or a bolt (Hillelson 1930: 35). The reference to doorways is significant, and discussed in Boddy 1989.
9. See Barclay (1964:196–206); Cloudsley (1983:67–87); Constantinides (1972, 1977); Trimingham (1965:174–77); Zenkovsky (1950).
10. For a discussion of the relationship between female fertility and possession see Boddy 1989.
11. See Crapanzano 1977. This point is more fully developed in Boddy 1989.
12. Although the fluctuating kinship networks of Hofriyati are individualistic this is not to say that the individual is the focal social unit in Hofriya. Hofriyati women and men are always subordinate to a range of collective interests: family, lineage, village, religious group, etc.
13. Lewis (1971:30, 1983) certainly does not consider other factors unimportant, yet they do not figure into his analysis to the same extent as does the question of cross-sex competition.
14. See Kapferer (1983:100–110) for a similar view of the susceptibility of Sri Lankan women.
15. Interestingly, this is similar to the situations of men and women in a marriage: although men may divorce an unwanted wife at will, women must accommodate themselves to the marriage, however unhappy.
16. Spirits are hardly inanimate or genderless, as my use of the impersonal pronoun implies. But when not referring to specific spirits and possession episodes, I use the neuter form to avoid confusion between humans and *zayran*.
17. However, the classification of spirits varies somewhat from area to area in Sudan, and in some places (though not in Hofriyat or its environs) *zayran* and *jinn* are considered different forms of spirit being. On this issue see Constantinides (1972:102–4), and Trimingham (1965:177 ff.).

REFERENCES:

Al-Guindi, Fadwa. 1978. The Angels of the Nile: A Theme in Nubian Ritual. In *Nubian Ceremonial Life*, edited by John Kennedy, pp. 104–113. Berkeley: University of California Press.

Barclay, Harold. 1964. *Buurri al-Lamaah: A Suburban Village in Sudan*. Ithaca, NY: Cornell University Press.

Besmer, Fremont E. 1983. *Horses, Musicians, and Gods: The Hausa Cult of Possession-Trance*. South Hadley, Mass: Bergin and Garvey.

Boddy, Janice. 1988. Spirits and Selves in Northern Sudan. The Cultural Therapeutics of Possession and Trance. *American Ethnologist* 15(1): 4-27.

———. 1989. *Wombs and Alien Spirits: Women, Men and the Zâr Cult in Northern Sudan*. Madison: University of Wisconsin Press.

Bourguignon, Erika. 1973. Introduction: A Framework for the Comparative Study of Altered States of Consciousness. In *Religion, Altered States of Consciousness, and Social Change*, edited by Erika Bourguignon, pp. 3–35. Columbus: Ohio State University Press.

———. 1976. *Possession*. San Francisco: Chandler and Sharp.

Brown, Karen M. 1990. *Mama Lola: A Vodou Priest-ess in Brooklyn.* Berkeley: University of California Press.

Cloudsley, Ann. 1983. *Women of Omdurman: Life, Love, and the Cult of Virginity.* London: Ethno-graphica.

Constantinides, Pamela. 1972. Sickness and the Spirits: A Study of the "Zâr" Spirit Possession Cult in Northern Sudan. Ph.D. dissertation, University of London.

———. 1977. "Ill at Ease and Sick at Heart": Sym-bolic Behavior in a Sudanese Healing Cult. In *Symbols and Sentiments,* edited by Ian M. Lewis, pp. 185–205. Bloomington: Indiana University Press.

———. 1982. Women's Spirit Possession and Urban Adaptation in the Muslim Northern Sudan. In *Women United, Women Divided: Com-parative Studies of Ten Contemporary Cultures,* edit-ed by P. Caplan and D. Bujra, pp. 141–76. New York: John Wiley.

———1991. "The History of *Zâr* in the Sudan." In I. M. Lewis, Ahmed al-Safi and Sayyid Hurreiz, Edi-tors. *Women's Medicine: The Zâr-Bori Cult in Africa and Beyond,* pp. 83–99. Edinburgh: International African Institute, Edinburgh University Press.

Crapanzano, Vincent. 1973. *The Hamadsha: A Study in Moroccan Ethnopsychiatry.* Berkeley: University of California Press.

———. 1977a. Mohammed and Dawua: Possession in Morocco. In *Case Studies of Spirit Possession,* edited by Vincent Crapanzano and Vivian Gar-rison, pp. 141-76. New York: John Wiley.

———. 1977b. Introduction to *Case Studies of Spirit Possession,* edited by Vincent Crapanzano and Vivian Garrison, pp. 1-39. New York: John Wiley.

———. 1980. *Tuhami: Portrait of a Moroccan.* Chica-go: University of Chicago Press.

Hillelson, S. 1930. *Sudan Arabic, English Arabic Vocabulary.* 2nd ed. London: Sudan Govern-ment.

Kapferer, Bruce. 1983. *A Celebration of Demons: Exor-cism and the Aesthetics of Healing in Sri Lanka.* Bloomington: Indiana University Press.

———. 1986. Performance and the Structure of Meaning and Experience. In *The Anthropology of Experience,* edited by V. W. Turner and E. M. Bruner, pp188–206. Chicago: University of Illi-nois Press.

Kehoe, Alice B., and Dody H. Giletti. 1981. Women's Preponderance in Possession Cults: The Calcium Deficiency Hypothesis Extended. *American Anthropologist* 83(3): 549–61.

Kennedy, John G. 1978. *Nubian Ceremonial Life,* edited by John Kennedy. Berkeley: University of California Press.

Kenyon, Susan. 1991. Five Women of Sennar. New York: Oxford University Press.

———. 2000. " [title to follow]" In Heike Behrend and Ute Luig, editors. *Spirit Possession, Moderni-ty, and Power in Africa.* Madison: University of Wisconsin Press.

Lambek, Michael. 1980. Spirits and Spouses: Pos-session as a System of Communication among the Malagasy Speakers of Mayotte. *American Eth-nologist* 7(2):318–31.

———. 1981. *Human Spirits: A Cultural Account of Trance in Mayotte.* New York: Cambridge Univer-sity Press.

Leiris, Michel. 1958. *La Possession et ses aspects théâ-traux chez les Ethiopiens de Gondar.* L'Homme: Cahiers d'ethnologie, de géographie et de lin-guistique. Paris: Plon.

Lewis, I. M. 1971. *Ecstatic Religion: An Anthropologi-cal Study of Spirit Possession and Shamanism.* Balti-more, Md.: Penguin Books.

———. 1986. *Religion In Context: Cults and Charis-ma.* Cambridge: University of Cambridge Press.

Modaressi, Tahgi. 1968. The Zar Cult in South Iran. In *Trance and Possession States,* edited by Raymond Prince, pp. 149–55. Montreal: R. M. Bucke Memorial Society.

Morsy, Soheir. 1978. Sex Roles, Power, and Illness in an Egyptian Village. *American Ethnologist,* 5:137–50.

Nelson, Cynthia. 1971. Self, Spirit Possession, and World-View: An Illustration from Egypt. *Interna-tional Journal of Psychiatry* 17:194–209.

Obeyesekere, Gananath. 1970. The Idiom of Pos-session. *Social Science and Medicine* 4:97–111.

———. 1981. *Medusa's Hair: An Essay on Personal Symbols and Religious Experience.* Chigago: Uni-versity of Chicago Press.

Saunders, Lucie Wood. 1977. Variants in Zar Expe-rience in an Egyptian Village. In *Case Studies in Spirit Possession,* edited by Vincent Crapanzano and Vivian Garrison, pp. 177–91. New York: John Wiley.

Trimingham, J. Spencer. 1965. *Islam in the Sudan.* 1949. Reprint. London: Oxford University.

Vantini, Giovanni. 1981. *Christianity in the Sudan.* Bologna, Italy: EMI Press.

Wehr, Hans. 1976. *A Dictionary of Modern Written Arabic.* 3rd ed. Edited by J. Milton Cowan. Itha-ca, N.Y.: Spoken Language Services.

Wilson, Peter. 1967. Status Ambiguity and Spirit Possession. *Man,* n.s. 2:366–78.

Young, Allan. 1975. Why Amhara Get Kureynya: Sickness and Possession in an Ethiopian Zar Cult. *American Ethnologist* 2(3):567–84.

Zenkovsky, Sophie. 1950. Zar and Tambura as Practiced by the Women of Omdurman. *Sudan Notes and Records.* 31(1): 65–81.

"Tradition" and Threat: Women's Obscenity in Giriama Funerary Rituals

Janet McIntosh

INTRODUCTION

It is midday in the Giriama village outside the town of Malindi, Kenya, and women are gathering on one side of a well-swept clearing framed by mud and thatch huts. They sit with their legs stretched before them, comparing their finery—flamboyant *leso* cloths; clean, bright polyester blouses from town; and the customary bustles of grass and cotton that accentuate their hips. My black skirt and T-shirt seem dull by comparison, but as always the women greet me warmly, seating me on a woven mat on the earth next to them. We are assembling to mark the passing of a young woman who died in childbirth; her body lies in the center of the clearing, cradled by a bed of woven sisal ropes. Her mother and three elderly women flank the bed, waving small handkerchiefs in desultory motions to chase off the flies. They have not slept since the tragic night before, but some of them are capable of laughter as well as tears, and occasionally break into a low-key song and dance, swishing their handkerchiefs rhythmically. Other female kin are out of sight, gathered in a nearby hut where they will receive well-wishers during the next five days of ceremony. And at the other side of the homestead the men carry out their tasks: six or seven take turns digging a grave, while others decide where they will buy the planks to build a coffin. Most sit on mats, drinking from small gourds of palm wine, discussing local politics, and comparing the jobs they have lost and gained in town.

Original material prepared for this text.

Word has gone out through the neighboring communities that a funeral has begun, and the crowd swells to about two hundred as the afternoon wears on. When a male song leader arrives and positions himself near the corpse, ten or fifteen enthusiastic women gather around him. At his cue, several of them begin to jangle winnowing trays laden with broken glass, creating a silvery percussive effect. The rest break into song and dance, shuffling in a circle, shimmying their hips emphatically, and punctuating their movement now and then by falling forward and catching themselves with a well placed step. Some of their songs speak to death and decay: "Fly away, housefly. You can't land on this body, because it's covered with rashes." But many of the lyrics are teasing and a little startling: "Mother's clothes are falling off," quips one song. As the singers warm to their task, the lyrics become graphic:

> May I screw you? May I screw you?
> An unmarried non-virgin will be screwed
> A man's wife is maize meal and meat
> I will die and stop screwing

One by one, women and girls from the surrounding crowd join in, and the circle widens to accommodate them. Soon they put aside the winnowing trays, clapping with enthusiasm as they sing and shuffle around the corpse and its tenders, who continue to whisk the flies away. From time to time the dancers stop in their tracks and face the center of the circle, clapping loudly. Several women leap into the middle and begin to gyrate their pelvises, inching up to the others to simulate sexual contact and intercourse. Normal decorum is abandoned; a seventy-year-old woman grinds against a thirty-year-old male song leader, while a young woman simulates sex with her mother-in-law. A woman with gray hair organizes a stunt, placing a giant wooden pestle upside down by the head of the corpse, climbing onto it and moving her pelvis in quick circles, barely keeping her balance. I turn to my neighbor, a married woman holding a baby, and remark: "I have talked to many people about your funerals, but I still wonder why the women perform these songs and dances."

"It's just our tradition," she says with a gentle smile, adding: "They are trying to distract the bereaved people from their pain." I ask why she doesn't join in. "My husband doesn't like me to," she replies, "He thinks the women who do the dances have no respect for their men." Another woman inside the circle, an unmarried forty-something, mimes a sex act with more zeal than most. A young man from the village passes me and whispers in my ear snidely: "That one is a prostitute; she keeps a lot of men happy." Another song begins:

> Mr. Charo Baya knows how to screw
> Finish fast; I want to get home and cook!
> My husband doesn't screw me that way.
> Charo Baya you've won me—Your penis is big;
> my hips can't hold you.

As the dancing grows louder and more exuberant, three giggling teenagers pull me into the fray and prod me before them, daring me to perform the dance moves. An old woman glares at us from just outside the circle; like some other elders, she objects to the participation of young unmarried women, and I wonder if her ire is directed partly at me. I clap and step my way around the corpse until shyness gets the better of me and I withdraw to the margins, craning my neck to take in the scene. I can see the men still clustered on their side of the homestead, drinking,

talking, and observing the grave-diggers, who sweat profusely as they struggle to complete their job before nightfall. A few young men stand on the edge of the dancing circle, looking on with small gourds of palm wine in their hands, ogling and occasionally lunging at the women they admire the most. One of the men plunges in and is set on by two women who gyrate against his side and back until he extricates himself, laughing. The circle closes again, a riot of stepping, clapping women, who seem to delight as each new song ups the ante of bawdy suggestion.

A Giriama funeral in the Malindi area is a momentous event, a protracted ritual far longer, more expensive, and better attended than any other rite in Giriama custom. Social life is magnified during these gatherings: men gain and lose prestige in displays of generosity; commerce in food, palm wine, and property quickens; old friends strike up new relations; and enemies settle their grudges, sometimes violently. Above all, women's funerary songs and dances escalate into lewd rebellions that, like the above scenario, far outstrip normal expectations for female behavior. What does this sexual performance by women signify? Is it considered mere "tradition," a benign ritual release, as the young woman above and many others wanted me to believe? Or do the currents of disapproval— her husband's denunciation of the dancing women, the passing young man's whisper, and the old woman's stare—suggest another level of interpretation, one that takes the rebellious overtones of the songs and dances more seriously?

These questions have a precedent in a broader literature that explores the relationship between gender, power, and ritual. Much of this literature emphasizes the unique opportunity that ritual offers subordinate groups, particularly women, to violate custom and express discontent. Ritual spirit possession, for example, has been heralded as a means of "[expressing] dissatisfaction with existing patterns" (Bourguignon 1973: 33), especially in cultures where other avenues of

redress are not available (Lewis 1971). Possession can also open a space for violations of
sexual protocol redolent of those in Giriama
funerals; in Danforth's account of possession
by St. Constantine among Anastenaridien
Greeks, possessed women engage in "flamboyant, demonstrative, even flirtatious behavior that is considered more appropriate for
men" (1989: 100). By becoming "symbolically male" through possession, Danforth says,
such women garner publicity while enhancing their power and status beyond the domestic sphere (100). Whereas spirit possession
partakes of its own special devices—including
the appropriation of the agency and powers
of the possessing spirit—other types of ritual
offer women additional opportunities for misbehavior. In numerous sub-Saharan African
rituals, for example, normative arrangements
are turned upside-down and subordinate
groups, women in particular, may temporarily take on the roles of their social superiors
(Gluckman 1963). Ritual form, then, seems to
lend itself to unruliness like that in Giriama
women's funerary song and dance.

While it may provide a useful emotional
outlet for women's frustrations, the enduring
question is whether unruly ritual behavior
poses a substantial threat to patriarchal
orders. When there is no possessing spirit
from which to borrow prestige, do the exceptional events within a ritual confer any new
powers on the participants? Do ritual acts
really challenge the tenets of social life once
the ritual moment has passed? Social theorists
have tended to address this issue in general
terms. Mary Douglas, for example, sees ritual
misbehavior as universally beguiling and
potentially threatening to the status quo: "We
seek to create order," she writes, "[yet] we do
not simply condemn disorder. We recognise
that it is destructive to existing patterns; also
that it has potentiality. It symbolizes both danger and power" (Douglas 1966: 94). In his
analysis of medieval carnivals, Mikhael
Bakhtin interprets ritual bawdiness as a
moment of freedom that just might have
enduring effects; a "true feast of becoming,
change, and renewal" (Bakhtin 1962: 18).

Although such readings credit unruly ritual
with liberating potential, others doubt that it
poses a genuine threat or challenge to the
powers that be. According to Gluckman, a ritual of rebellion that takes place within a
strong social structure is but an ineffectual
gesture; a form of "instituted protest [that] in
complex ways renews the unity of the system"
(1954: 3).

In this article, I approach the question of
ritual power from a somewhat different angle.
Rather than asking whether Giriama women's
funerary songs and dances actually change
the social system, I instead explore how Giriama themselves perceive them. And in a parallel to the tension between theorists like
Douglas and Gluckman, I detect two conflicting interpretations of funerary obscenity
among Giriama in the Malindi area. At one
level, the women's performance is publicly
couched as Gluckman might have predicted:
a harmless "tradition" and a salubrious tool of
emotional healing. Yet another, less formal
discourse implies that the songs and dances
threaten the sexual dignity of Giriama
women. Although Douglas might locate this
threat in some generic danger inherent to
unruly ritual, "danger" is always construed in
light of tensions specific to a given social
moment. In fact, I argue, Giriama women's
funerary songs have long been obscene, yet
the current disapproval among Giriama in
Malindi is distinctly colored by a development
that is both modern and local: the arrival of
Western lifestyles and tourism on the Kenya
coast, and the corresponding emergence of a
fraught sexual ethos in society-at-large.

GIRIAMA, PAST AND PRESENT

The Giriama are the largest of nine related
Bantu groups called the Mijikenda, who live
in a 5,000-square mile strip in the coastal hinterland of eastern Kenya. According to Mijikenda oral history, their people dwelled as
subsistence farmers for centuries while based
in fortified villages called *kaya* that were governed by male elders and organized by sacred

spaces, age-set rituals, and semi-secret societies termed *mwanza*. The *kaya* dispersed in the nineteenth century, and since then Mijikenda culture has been subject to forces that threaten older ways of life. But like all self-told histories, Mijikenda accounts are both reflections of the past and "statements of what informants feel it should be" (Willis 1993: 44). *Kaya* are often invoked as part of a nostalgic call for unity and "authenticity" in moments of social, economic, and political insecurity (Parkin 1991; Mazrui 1997), yet stories of isolated life in the *kayas* obscure the fact that for centuries, coastal Mijikenda have interacted with wealthier town-dwelling Arab and Swahili Muslims in fluid economic, religious, and even kin relations. And in the colonial and post-colonial eras, Mijikenda have endured difficult integration into a multicultural coastal economy of Europeans, Asians, Arabs, Swahili, and upcountry Kenyans. Today, cash is increasingly important for the essentials of life in and near Malindi, making wage labor a virtual necessity, yet many Giriama who seek jobs are hampered by lack of training and employer prejudice. Education is perceived as a key to wealth, but school fees are out of reach for many Giriama families. Now as then, few Mijikenda own land or large businesses, and other ethnic groups on the coast regard them as a low-status, "backward" people. Such economic and ideological pressures have resulted in numerous Giriama conversions to Islam or Christianity, yet aggressive assertions of Giriama "tradition" still play a role in local and governmental politics. And rituals such as funerals remain popular despite Muslim and Christian censure.[1]

SEX AND DEATH IN FUNERARY RITUAL

The two major funerary song-and-dance types for Giriama women in the Malindi area, termed *kifudu* and *kihoma*, are considered "traditional," yet oral histories indicate that both originated outside of Giriama funerals. *Kifudu* songs are accompanied by the rhythmic shaking of shells or broken glass in a broad winnowing tray, and the dances involve much shimmying of the breasts and hips. According to Giriama elders, *kifudu* emerged from a women's fertility cult called *mwanza wa kifudu* that dates back to the *kaya* era. In the *mwanza wa kifudu,* women kept sacred clay pots that were named after their deceased former custodians and believed to have a life force of their own. Since *kifudu* pots could either protect or destroy women's health and reproductive capacities, they were supplicated at every new moon: removed from their shrines to be spoken to, sung and danced to, and "played" by blowing air over their openings. The supplicatory songs and dances were called *kifudu cha tsongo,* and, according to anthropologist Monica Udvardy, were characterized by "obscene or ludicrous" lyrics and correspondingly "suggestive movements" (Udvardy 1990b: 142). These songs were imported into the funerals of members of the *mwanza wa kifudu* but at some point, for unknown reasons, they were generalized to funerals at large. The propitiation of *kifudu* pots still takes place in some Giriama homesteads further inland, but in many areas, including Malindi, the tradition has dwindled, and the *kifudu* fertility medicines have been dispersed among and reinterpreted by individual diviner/healers (Thompson 1990).[2] Yet *Kifudu* songs endure, and some women still compose new ones that address two major themes: death and grief, and bawdy sexual antics. *Kifudu* songs are customarily sung by post-menopausal women (Udvardy 1990a: 145), but in the Malindi area the sanctions for their performance have been blurred, and young women and even pubescent girls participate, to the dismay of some elders.

The second variety of funerary song, called *kihoma*, is said to be more obscene than *kifudu*. *Kihoma* involves a slightly different dance style accompanied by vigorous clapping and, unlike *kifudu*, is totally prohibited after the corpse has been buried. Men as well as women compose these songs, and the lyrics discuss graphic sexual themes from both male and female points of view.[3] In some Giriama groups, men occasionally dance to *kihoma* songs as well, but among Giriama close to Malindi, women and girls dominate the dancing almost exclusively. Giriama informants claim that *kihoma* songs originated with another Mijikenda group, the Chonyi, and some elders suggest they have been popularized in recent years by young funeral participants who are excessively zealous about their sexual content. But while elders distinguish between *kifudu* and *kihoma* and decry the changes in funerary performance, most youth are only dimly aware of the songs' histories, and are hard-pressed to categorize individual songs as either *kifudu* or *kihoma*. I will return to the subject of how elders regard changes in funerary songs below, for their disapproval signals more holistic changes in Giriama life.

Leaving these controversies aside for the moment, I want to explore Giriama explanations for why sexual songs should be performed at funerals in the first place. Anthropologists van Gennep (1960) and Victor Turner (1967) have written at length about the "liminal" phase in rites of passage, in which normal social rules are suspended and ritual participants behave in unorthodox ways. In many sub-Saharan funerals, liminality takes the specific form of inversion: a reversal of ordinary hierarchies and taboos.[4] In Giriama funerals, the visibility of the corpse defines the boundaries of the liminal phase; Giriama say that its uncanny presence opens behavioral possibilities that are curtailed off from everyday experience.[5] And, in keeping with the sub-Saharan funerary theme of inversion, *kifudu* and *kihoma* song and dance upend customary expectations with implications of female promiscuity, female sexual aggression, incest, adultery, and homosexuality.[6] Yet funerary inversions in other African cultures include all kinds of reversals, including turning clothing inside out, moving in a counterclockwise direction, and slandering local rulers. So why should sexual license be the inversion of choice for Giriama? Giriama explain that sex has an antithetical relation to death, a tension that lends sexual imagery a special emotional charge. The funerary songs and dances, they say, "mock" death by confronting its power with defiant expressions of sexual pleasure. For those who remember that *kifudu* performances emerge from a fertility cult, the songs and dances also invoke reproductive capacity, the continuation of life even in the presence of its end. And the ecstatic and ridiculous elements of the songs and dances are said to "change the minds" of the bereaved, distracting them from their grief by presenting them with images pleasurable, extreme, and, sometimes, silly.[7] Witty double-entendres such as the line: "I'll bury something in you!" instantaneously defuse the miseries of death and burial by rhetorically transforming the death rite into a sexual encounter.

Yet there is another, more paradoxical relationship between death and sexual permissiveness at these funerals, in which they are not so much juxtaposed as aligned.[8] The dancing circle where the corpse lies is referred to as a "bad place" with negative supernatural overtones, and this "bad place," say informants, is a place in which "bad things can happen." The corpse, then, is both a signal that existential normalcy has vanished and a prompt to wreak further havoc, as the *kifudu* and *kihoma* songs and dances do with their dissolute symbolism. One Giriama man aligns the destruction of death with the disgrace of sexual abandon; when I asked him to explain *kifudu* and *kihoma* to me, he replied: "Someone has died! Things have already turned to shit, so why not let everything run to ruin?" Other informants assimilate grief and sexual expression on the emotional level, saying: "When someone has died, and your grief is so bad, what can you do but laugh and celebrate?" Such utterances surely have performative elements, as expressions of wishful thinking that might help to create the kind of celebration they describe and in so doing help the bereaved to forget their sorrow. But they also contain an implicit theory, a strange emotional geometry in which extreme grief passes beyond sorrow and travels full circle to the giddy version of joy seen in *kifudu* and *kihoma* performances. This paradox is echoed in the expression of some funeral participants: "A funeral is like a wedding; the last wedding of the deceased."

GENDER, SEXUALITY, AND CHANGE IN GIRIAMA LIFE

The sexual content of *kifudu* and *kihoma* songs and dances appears to play an important role in processing and transforming the emotions that accompany death, but it is also a pivotal site for complex and changing gender relationships among Giriama in the Malindi area. Before discussing local interpretations of women's funerary performances, I offer here a brief history of the shifting gender dynamics that underlie them. Since the nineteenth century, the patriarchal household arrangements of the *kaya* era have undergone considerable change in many Giriama communities, yet the theme of male dominance persists. Homesteads in the *kaya* model are made up of several polygynous households headed by a senior man who makes decisions about property allocation, conflicts, and patrilineal rituals. Parents and other elders oversee marital arrangements, including bride-price transactions, and women's rights to resources are severely constrained by a patrilineal inheritance system. These structures endure in some Giriama communities, but in others, economic changes and cultural contact have destabilized older ways of life. In the small villages flanking Malindi town, for example, household arrangements have an improvisational feel. Young men may split off from their father's homestead in search of economic opportunities closer to town, squatting on land owned by Muslims or upcountry Kenyans with other Mijikenda hopefuls, and building one or two huts for their wife or wives. In cases of divorce or abandonment, some women choose to live on their own, supporting themselves and their children rather than returning to their natal homestead. But shifting household arrangements have not

greatly enhanced women's economic opportunities. Although men venture into town to seek wage labor, and may aspire to private investments and property ownership, women rarely accumulate capital or property of their own, tending to remain close to home as they raise children and till the family's small subsistence farm plot. For income they may sell domestic animals, firewood, thatch, deep-fried goods, and the surplus from their small farming plots, but such enterprises rarely yield a large profit. A significant number of women become professional diviner-healers, an increasingly popular choice that can lead to prestige and a limited degree of financial power (Thompson 1990). Yet even such creative pursuits do not weaken the pervasive gender ideology that limits girls' and women's prospects. Many parents prefer to spend their limited school fee money on their sons, a pattern that perpetuates both economic and ideological inequities. One man justifies the limitations on girls' education with the assertion that "our women are pure womanhood in its natural state." In Giriama discourse, this "natural state" is deemed servile, irresponsible, and capricious, while men, by contrast, are considered strong, brave, and more intellectual (McIntosh 1996; Thompson 1990).

The sexual customs that emerged from the *kaya* era have also changed in the Malindi area, yet a powerful residue of sanctions and proscriptions remains. According to *kaya* custom, sexual courtship and behavior should be highly discreet. Sex itself must be engaged in with care because it is believed to be linked to supernatural powers. Ritual sexual intercourse, for example, is said to bring prosperity and purification when performed at moments of significant social transition (Udvardy 1990a, 1990b). Termed "*mathumia*," these rites between spouses can mark the "coming out" ceremony of a newborn, the circumcision of a son, and the various training phases of a diviner-healer. They may sanction a child's marriage arrangement, or purify individuals in a compromised state (a widow, for example, should have ritual intercourse with another man if her husband dies an inauspicious death). Senior males are pivotal figures in *mathumia* rites; when an individual in a homestead dies, for example, or when a homestead relocates, the senior male must perform *mathumia* with his first wife before other homestead members can resume normal sexual relations. When a couple violates *mathumia* restrictions, their children are believed susceptible to illness and death. Udvardy suggests that *mathumia* rites underscore the "mutual dependence of the genders for the prosperous enactments of creation, recreation, and transformation" (Udvardy 1990a: 87), but, she adds, the rites often depend on the leadership of male homestead heads, and therefore re-inscribe their seniority. Meanwhile, the Giriama belief in women's "greater potential to cause disorder" (Thompson 1990) generates additional constraints for female sexuality. Unmarried girls are expected to protect their chastity, and married women (not men) who are unfaithful may inflict their children with a supernaturally borne illness termed *kirwa*.

With cultural contact and change, Giriama communities everywhere have altered some or all of these customs, yet women's sexuality is still policed by popular expectation. Christianity and Islam, of course, do not recognize *mathumia* or *kirwa* beliefs, but both portray premarital sex and overt expressions of sexuality as sinful, particularly among women. Among Giriama who do not consider themselves Muslim or Christian, *kirwa* beliefs and *mathumia* proscriptions are followed only erratically by members of the younger generation. In fact, popular expectations in Malindi operate primarily by means of secular ideologies. Whereas today's men are said to be more sexually aggressive than in the past, women are still expected to resist advances, defining their decency through modesty. In conversation this theme occasionally appears through trope of hunting: men play the role of predator, women of prey, and the ones with integrity elude capture until they can run no more. And while they may desire sex, women are constrained by an unwritten rule

of silence: unlike men, women should not initiate sexual liaisons verbally. "A woman can say it [express desire] with her body," my informants tell me, "but not with her mouth." The female body's language, furthermore, should be subtle and indirect: a glance, a fleeting half-smile, or a slight, sinuous motion. The burden of sexual comportment, hence, has largely shifted from both sexes (as seen in *mathumia* proscriptions) to women and girls alone.

If sexual *expectations* continue their policing function, sexual *behavior* in Malindi town constantly threatens to violate these proscriptions. While Giriama communities everywhere are faced with sexual changes, Malindi's economic and cultural situation has created exceptional tensions. In recent decades, numerous upcountry Kenyans have moved to the coast for economic opportunities, bringing versions of modernity in tow, including nuclear family structure, consumerist aspirations, and "Western" sexual behavior with demonstrative premarital passion. The last twenty years have also brought a high volume of European and American tourists, who flock to the palm-lined beaches of the Indian Ocean in a display of wealth, hedonism, and exposed flesh. Malindi has become a popular "sex safari" destination, with visitors of both sexes searching for an exotic fling. This clientele has lured many young African men and women into hustling and prostitution in Malindi's casinos, hotels, and beaches. Even Giriama who rarely enter town are aware of the changing sexual habits in urban centers, reading about them in the newspapers, and noting the sexual lyrics of the urban-based music that pumps from young men's boom boxes. And the practice of exchanging sex for cash has filtered into the surrounding villages, where some women have begun to solicit local clients, often because of economic need. In one village on the outskirts of Malindi town, a sixty-year-old Giriama man was recently arrested for paying a thirteen-year-old girl for sex; she capitulated, she said, because her single mother had no source of income for food. Several elder women told me stories of schoolgirls selling their bodies to teachers and other students—narratives that entwine the elders' anxieties about the lures of prostitution and the perils of a Western-style education. Even Giriama women who do not sell sex are also said to be changing their sexual habits. One Giriama man in his late thirties, for example, told me that he had recently propositioned a woman for sexual relations, but was so shocked and revolted when she accepted on the spot (rather than putting him off time and again as he expected) that he withdrew the suggestion. Evidently, expectations of female modesty are alive in Giriama ideology in the Malindi area, but are constantly challenged and changed. This tension sets the stage for local interpretations of funerary songs.

WOMEN'S RITUAL LICENSE: CONFLICTING INTERPRETATIONS

On the face of it, *kifudu* and *kihoma* performances offer Giriama women a unique opportunity to express their desires and decry male power while asserting their own self-worth. At a funeral, any woman—old, young, married or single—can intone a sexual invitation ("May I screw you?") and exult in the imagined pleasures of adultery ("Charo Baya knows how to screw!") While they flout conventions verbally, the women enact further obscenities with their bodies by dancing suggestively and simulating sexual intercourse with partners normally forbidden to them. But *kifudu* and *kihoma* performances do not simply play with expressions of desire; they also enact women's rivalry with and resentment against men. Whereas Giriama men compete with other men during funerary "prestige competitions" (Parkin 1972: 81), women bond with one another in their funerary songs, directing antagonism and rivalry outward toward men and toward women from neighboring areas. Sexual derision is a popular weapon: "My husband doesn't know how to screw me," complains one lyric. Another song mocks jealous husbands while belittling

their genitalia: "A jealous husband will not grow fat/He only has thin legs and long testicles." Still another song degrades women from a rival community, then berates an elderly man for being an inept provider: "You don't clothe me or feed me, grandfather. You know, you're just yoghurt." In a way, these songs are the symbolic antithesis of *mathumia*: they desacralize sex, they flout the order of sexual custom, they put a thumb in the eye of male elders, and they stress antagonism between genders rather than interdependence. In a culture where women's power, sexual autonomy, and general worth are constrained and demeaned, these full-throated testimonies of anger, sexual agency, and pride are surely emotionally significant gestures of resistance.

But can we assume that onlookers, and the singers themselves, understand the women's words and actions as an important and enduring statement of rebellion? *Kifudu* and *kihoma* take place within a ritual frame, and like all rituals, this one sets up an extra-ordinary and perplexing relationship between the ritual participants and what they are saying and doing. In his exploration of this relationship, Gluckman analyses numerous rituals of rebellion that flout the existing power structure through blasphemy, humor, and obscenity (Gluckman 1954; 1965). Using ethnographic evidence from Zulu and other African cultures, he concludes that participation in such rituals does not constitute a threat to the status quo. In fact, he argues, such rituals often emerge from a strong social order, and further solidify it:

> The acceptance of the established order as right and good, and even sacred, seems to allow unbridled license, very rituals of rebellion, for the order itself keeps this rebellion within bounds. Hence to act the conflicts, whether directly or by inversion or in other symbolical forms, emphasizes the social cohesion within which the conflicts exist (1965: 125).

The "ritual of rebellion," then, is a kind of cage for disorder, particularly in societies where social structure is already strong. If anything, Gluckman implies, rebellion is less likely after such rituals, for rebellious impulses are restricted to a socially sanctioned time and place, and thus reminded of their impotence.

At the same time that the ritual context brackets antisocial behavior, ritual form can also defuse subversive messages by virtue of the fact that most ritual behaviors are secondhand. Anthropologist Lila Abu-Lughod makes a related observation in her account of Egyptian Bedouin women's poetry (Abu-Lughod 1986). Bedouin women recite poetry to express feelings of grief and self-pity that would normally be unacceptable because in Bedouin culture, stoicism and emotional self-control are considered essential to social dignity. Abu-Lughod suggests that a poem is an acceptable medium of expression because it offers the woman who recites it a kind of alibi: if the woman reciting the poem did not author it, she cannot be fully credited with the sentiments in the text. As a result, a woman performing poetry is exempt from normal critiques of emotional expression, being evaluated instead by a "different set of standards regarding conformity to societal ideals" (207). While Abu-Lughod's analysis does not directly concern ritual, we can extrapolate her analysis to ritual form, in which participants' acts and utterances have a pre-scripted, second-hand quality similar to that of poetic recitation.

If we combine Gluckman's and Abu-Lughod's accounts, we can interpret ritual as doubly qualified to defuse potentially subversive messages. First, ritual is sharply bracketed from everyday life by a special space, time, and behavioral protocol; its boundaries might be likened to quotation marks that set it off from the continuous stream of ordinary happenings. Second, the content of ritual does not spring anew from the agency and opinions of ritual participants, but instead is derivative of rituals past, and as such, resembles reported speech more than first-hand utterance. If these devices are central to local interpretations of *kifudu* and *kihoma*, we might expect the performances to pose no

threat to Giriama social order, and the singers themselves to be treated no differently for participating. And indeed, this is a common account of *kifudu* and *kihoma* among Giriama near Malindi. In interviews, I asked numerous informants whether women's funerary songs are permissible given the overarching expectation of female sexual modesty, and was repeatedly told that the songs are "just tradition," and hence do not constitute a genuine rebellion against social expectations. This reassurance was often delivered in a quick and patterned fashion, rather like a stock response designed to strip the performances of any significance beyond their generic status as "tradition," and, perhaps, to preclude further inquiry by this probing outsider.[9] These stock dismissals of *kifudu* and *kihoma* may have a protective function for the Giriama community at large, for they emphasize that such behaviors are restricted to the ritual frame and hence pre-empt accusations that their non-ritual social habits are primitive and debased. And women defend their performances as "just tradition" with special alacrity, guarding their most privileged moment of expression by denying that real expression is involved at all.

But are Giriama women's funerary utterances and actions completely absolved by the ritual context? Are women really free to say and do anything in ritual without consequence? Despite the public sanction for *kifudu* and *kihoma*, unofficial currents of ambivalence and disapproval run through the Giriama communities near Malindi town. In informal contexts such as casual conversations, gossip sessions, and whispered asides like that of the man who passed me during the funeral, men of all ages and elder women voice anxiety about *kifudu* and *kihoma* performances today. A number of young men say that although they might be tempted to sleep with a woman who enjoys performing the songs and dances, they would not marry her—implying that the free sexual expression in the performances is sexually attractive, but suggests inferior virtue. Still other men, like the husband of the woman I spoke to at the funeral above, forbid their wives to participate in the singing and dancing at all, seeming to fear either that stigma will attach to their wives, or that the performance might augur actual promiscuity. Meanwhile, older women complain that the young girls who participate in funerary songs and dances "don't respect their elders anymore" and are prone to promiscuity and prostitution. In such discussions, *kifudu* and *kihoma* are portrayed not as meaningless ritual behaviors, but instead as a kind of training ground for real sexual misconduct. Apparently, Giriama detect the seeds of genuine danger and resistance described by Douglas and Bakhtin, and fear that these might escape the ritual boundary, putting down roots in ordinary life.

Where does this tension between stock approval of funerary obscenity and informal disapproval emerge from? The moralizing forces of Islam and Christianity doubtless contribute to the discourse of danger, since both religions construe Giriama rituals as heathenistic and corrupt. But those who regard the rituals with suspicion include numerous Giriama who do not call themselves converts—in fact some of them, including some elderly women, openly despise the influence of world religions on their milieu. Although Mary Douglas might ascribe their disapproval of funerary ritual to the inherent dangers of "disorder," she may undervalue the ways in which culturally specific anxieties define "disorder" as "dangerous." Interestingly, Gluckman anticipates the importance of context in construals of unruly ritual, though he deals with it only indirectly. Where there is little threat of misconduct outside of the ritual context, he says, ritual rebellion will not affect the extant social order. But, he predicts, "where the [social] relationships involved are weak, there cannot be license in ritual" (1965: 132). Gluckman does not explain the concept of "weak relationships" in great detail, but the fraught sexual issues in the Malindi area surely bring Giriama society under this rubric. While the homestead breaks apart, women and girls are loosed from the mast, and through a kind of *bricolage* of the examples

that surround them, improvise new sexual identities. Male homestead heads in the Malindi area no longer orchestrate sexual conduct through *mathumia*, and as supernatural proscriptions for sexual transgression fade, fears of adultery mount. Women's potential promiscuity spells a drop in male control over female sexuality (and, by implication, paternity), giving men reason for discomfort.[10] Meanwhile, the elders' authority is shunted to the side, making both elder men and elder women uncomfortable as they watch old hierarchies of respect and resource distribution crumble.[11]

As these social anxieties grow, the membrane surrounding the ritual becomes permeable in two directions. Sexual threats run from the outside in, as growing numbers of girls join the obscene dancing circles—a violation of previous ritual guidelines that the elders link to their exposure to promiscuity and prostitution in daily life. In turn, the portrayal of sexual dissolution in the ritual threatens, in the popular imagination, to spill beyond its bounds and influence daily behavior. Since the acts and utterances in funerary songs and dances have begun to speak of possible rather than unlikely behavior, the ritual content is no longer totally dismissed as a benign kind of reported speech. Instead, currents of suspicion frame the ritual content as a first-hand report of the unruly desires of women participants. Thus ritual participants are caught between two interpretations of their actions: although they are partially absolved by the protective cloak of tradition, they also risk the labels of promiscuity or unmarriagability. In funerary ritual today, an expressive space for women is offered with one hand and revoked with the other.

I would like to return briefly to a subject I mentioned earlier: the elder women's claim that funerary songs are now revoltingly obscene compared to the gentler, more graceful performances of their youth. Although this complaint may have an element of truth, I do not take it entirely at face value. First, I witnessed some of the same elderly women who complain about funerary obscenity participating in the lewdest songs and dances with delight; evidently, the style was not as alien to them as they suggested. Secondly, early missionary and colonial reports of *kifudu* song and dance suggest that it was obscene long before these women were young. Ludwig Krapf, the first missionary to East Africa, mentions "immoralities and abominations" practiced at a *mwanza wa kifudu* ceremony he witnessed in 1847, noting that "[these] are well known to every one" (Krapf 1968 [1860]: 162). The colonial officer Arthur Champion, writing around 1914, describes one *kifudu* dance as "demoniacal" and "frenz[ied]" (26), and relates that "[another] dance performed by two old women over the grave was of an extremely sensual character. This unseemly dance produced great mirth amongst the mourners" (Champion 1967: 28). Although these accounts are colored by an overarching colonialist horror toward African rites, and although they do not rule out the possibility that the rituals contain more brazen material now than then, they do suggest that overtly sexual material in funerary songs and dances is not new. It is possible, then, that the elder women's complaints are about something more than obscenity *within* ritual. Although the obscene signifiers within funerary ritual may not have changed significantly, the social context for their interpretation has changed, lending the sexual phenomena signified in the ritual a more real and threatening cast. The elder women's nostalgia, then, may not be for another kind of song, but for another way of life altogether.

CONCLUSION

Sex is considered "appropriate" subject matter at a Giriama funeral for gender-neutral reasons. It symbolizes the extremity of life's borders, it distracts the mourners from their misery, and it mocks the despair and the finality of death. Yet in their songs and dances, women magnify these sexual elements and direct them at male targets, giving funerary

rituals acute significance for Giriama gender politics. Through these ritual moments women assert female unity and pride, vent their complaints about male power, and convey their joy in breaking through the sexual decorum normally expected of them.

Given all of this, what should we make of the original tension between Douglas' and Gluckman's accounts of ritual license? Gluckman's insistence that rituals of rebellion are benign is echoed by Giriama themselves when they attest that their funerals are "just tradition." But although the protective ritual frame may render their acts partially permissible, the women's fulminating grievances do not go unacknowledged. Douglas' suggestion that ritual disorder spells "danger" also circulates among Malindi-based Giriama as an interpretive possibility. Thus, for the ambivalent onlooker at a funeral, an archetypical expression of Giriama "tradition" threatens to encourage, if not serve as a catalyst for a transformation in the gendered order.

As I have suggested, the perceived "danger" in women's funerary songs stems not simply from the presence of disorder in the ritual, but largely from changes in the surrounding social context that influence the interpretation of that disorder. The new sexual options in Malindi both vex the patriarchal order and challenge the "official" notion that ritual can successfully contain its own subversive strains. But I don't mean to imply that Malindi is the only site of such contests over ritual meaning. Giriama everywhere interact with other cultures, creating local social tensions that could challenge the security of the ritual frame—a pattern that may reach into the past as well. Although elders idealize the virtuous sexual codes of their youth, their memories are shaped by nostalgia, raising the possibility that sexual behavior has long run up against customary expectations, and that a double discourse about women's funerary performances has obtained for some time. We might, in fact, expand this argument outward, into a general suggestion. Perhaps Gluckman idealizes the "official" discourses of social unity in the African societies he studies, and in so doing, over-looks the changes, tensions, and fault lines elemental to *all* societies. If this is the case, if no society is so intact, then disorderly ritual moments *are* potentially as uniformly "dangerous" as Mary Douglas posits—only the degree and shape of danger will be locally construed, and presumably construed differently by various groups within a given society. The mere presence of "danger" in ritual, then, should not encourage theoreticians to leap to a universally triumphant narrative of female ritual unruliness, for such a leap would overlook the nuance and force of local interpretations of the ritual and its relationship to everyday life. In the Giriama case, such interpretations limit the practical efficacy of women's ritual gestures, for either the ritual gestures are not taken seriously or they are taken seriously and met with the sort of redress we have seen (derision or prohibition). What women can accomplish through unruly ritual, then, remains an open question that can only be addressed case by case, with close attention to the local anxieties that define the perplexing relationship between the mundane social world and the exhilarating alternatives encoded in ritual.

ACKNOWLEDGMENTS. I would like to thank Jennifer Dickinson, Rachel Heiman, Larry Hirschfeld, Penelope Papailias, and Gaye Thompson for their valuable feedback on a draft of this essay. Gaye Thompson provided rich insights into Giriama society, as did Kainga Kalume Tinga. My research assistant, Maxwell Phares Kombe, supported me with astonishing patience and intelligence, for which I will always be grateful. The people who assisted me along the way are far too numerous to name but they include many Giriama, Swahili, and Europeans who welcomed me, talked to me, and tolerated me, often with kindness and good humor. Thanks are also due to the Malindi Museum Society and Fort Jesus Museum, Mombasa for their interest and support. This research was carried out with a grant from the Fulbright-Hays Foundation.

NOTES

1. Although Giriama have partially internalized the message that they are "backward," they counter it with themes of rebellion against the groups who have scorned them. A number of funerary songs, which I do not present here, are laced with expressions of defiance against Muslims, Christians, and upcountry tribes. The strategic use of a stigmatized "tradition" as a tool of vengeance has important implications for Giriama political ideology, but these are beyond the scope of this article.

2. Udvardy notes that despite their importance, the *kifudu* secret societies are "not much talked about" (1990b: 151) by comparison to men's cults, lending them a "muted" quality common to female-dominated institutions (Ardener 1977). Perhaps this relative silence has facilitated their rapid transformation and quick disappearance from memory. Most Giriama under thirty in Malindi know *kifudu* as funerary song and dance only, not as a secret society—despite the fact that the *kifudu* society is still active several kilometers West of the town.

3. The dual narrative perspective of funerary songs is important to their significance, but it introduces complexities beyond the scope of this article. Briefly, I think that the songs' narrative volatility helps to construct the "ritual alibi" I discuss later in this article, by making the songs seem more like reported speech than first person expression. Yet, clearly, this alibi is not sufficient to defuse all suspicion toward the women who participate.

4. A survey of texts on East Africa, conducted over forty years ago, found more than 600 sources describing inversions in connection with death rituals (Berglund 1957).

5. Kihoma songs must cease the instant the corpse has been buried, suggesting that the visibility of the corpse defines the boundaries of the liminal period. This seems a fitting criterion, given that a corpse appears to embody liminality itself: the dead person is neither here nor there, for breath and mind have vanished, yet the flesh, bafflingly, remains.

6. Despite the fact that women may dance against one another in a sexually suggestive way at funerals, I found no evidence that lesbian sex is a Giriama cultural category. While they are aware that female–female sexual relations can occur among their Swahili and Arab

neighbors, they have no term for it in their mother tongue. Informants tell me that if a woman loves another woman, she will sexualize the relationship not through direct contact but by arranging an affair between her husband and the female object of her affection. Homosexual sex between men, on the other hand, is acknowledged and condemned.

7. In a village about fifty kilometers Southwest of Malindi, Udvardy reports that Giriama considered funerary songs "entertainment for the departing spirit...the songs must be sung to accompany the spirit, so that it knows it is not alone and need not be sad" (Udvardy 1990a: 145–146). In Malindi, however, the emphasis is entirely on the emotions of those still living. This discrepancy may reflect a gradual move away from customary ancestor propitiation in Malindi; those who decline to consider the departing spirit set a precedent for neglecting the ancestral spirit as well.

8. The alignment of sex and death has been suggested too by Western avant-garde theorists such as Georges Bataille (1897-1962), who posited a fundamental kinship between sex and death in the human psyche. According to Bataille (1962), sex and death are conceptually aligned for existential reasons: both can dissolve the social self, lifting the boundary between individual subjectivity and the rest of the world. Bataille's theory emerges from a particular moment in Western history—after Renaissance writers had construed orgasm as a "small death"; after de Sade made his mark with his sex- and violence-ridden fiction; and after Freud suggested that orgasm resolves both life and death instincts—so should be applied with caution to other cultural contexts. Yet it does seem that numerous cultures have drawn some kind of symbolic equivalence between sex and death, suggesting that their sign qualities lend them to symbolic interplay.

9. The category of "tradition" has strategic dimensions in numerous colonial and post-colonial contexts. It may, for example, be used to protect or decry a given cultural practice; to sanction new forms of authority; or to confer an aura of unquestionability upon an otherwise contentious act. For more on such processes, see Hobsbawm and Ranger (1983).

10. It is worth noting that male objections to funerary songs primarily address their obscene contents, and not the contents that articulate a female–male rivalry. I suggest this discrepancy

emerges from the fact that at the economic and political levels, patriarchy among Giriama remains intact and so is not threatened by the songs that express rivalry per se. Male control over female sexuality, on the other hand, *is* under threat. Men's disapproval of funerary performances, then, is correspondingly focused on female sexual expression.

REFERENCES

Abu-Lughod, Lila. 1986. *Veiled Sentiments: Honor and Poetry in a Bedouin Society.* Berkeley: University of California Press.

Ardener, Edwin. 1977. "Belief and the Problem of Women," in Shirley Ardener, ed., *Perceiving Women.* New York: John Wiley and Sons.

Bakhtin, M. M. 1962. *Rabelais and his World.* Transl. Helene Iswolsky. Cambridge: MIT Press.

Bourguignon, Erika, Ed. 1973. *Religion, Altered States of Consciousness, and Social Change.* Columbus: Ohio State University Press.

Bataille, Georges. 1962. *Death and Sensuality: A Study of Eroticism and the Taboo.* New York: Walker and Company.

Berglund, A. I. 1957. *Some African Funerary Inversions.* Unpublished M.A. Thesis. Uppsala: Department of Cultural Anthropology, Library of the African Research Programme.

Champion, A. M. 1967. *The Agiriama of Kenya.* London: Royal Anthropological Institute.

Danforth, Loring M. 1989. *Firewalking and Religious Healing: The Anastenaria of Greece and the American Firewalking Movement.* Princeton: Princeton University Press.

Douglas, Mary. 1966. *Purity and Danger: An Analysis of the Concepts of Pollution and Taboo.* London: Routledge.

Gluckman, Max. 1954. *Rituals of Rebellion in South-East Africa.* Manchester: Manchester University Press.

———. 1965. *Custom and Conflict in Africa.* Oxford: Basil Blackwell.

Hobsbawm, Eric and Terence Ranger. 1983. *The Invention of Tradition.* Cambridge: Cambridge University Press.

Krapf, J. Lewis. 1968. *Travels, Researches, and Missionary Labors during an 18 Years' Residence in Eastern Africa.* Missionary Researches and Travels Nr. 2. London: Frank Cass and Co.

Lewis, I.M. 1971. *Ecstatic Religion: A Study of Shamanism and Spirit Possession.* London: Routledge.

Mazrui, Alamin M. 1997. *Kayas of Deprivation, Kayas of Blood: Violence, Ethnicity, and the State in Coastal Kenya*. Nairobi: Human Rights Commission.

McIntosh, Janet S. 1996. Professed Disbelief and Gender Identity on the Kenya Coast. In Natasha Warner et al.,eds. *Gender and Belief Systems*. Berkeley, California: Berkeley Women and Language Group, University of California.

Parkin, David J. 1972. *Palms, Wine, and Witnesses: Public Spirit and Private Gain in an African Farming Community*. London: Intertext Books.

———. 1991. *Sacred Void: Spatial Images of Work and Ritual among the Giriama of Kenya*. Cambridge: Cambridge University Press.

Thompson, Sally Gaye. 1990. *Speaking "Truth" to Power: Divination as a Paradigm for Facilitating Change among Giriama in the Kenyan Hinterland*. Unpublished Doctoral dissertation in Anthropology, presented to the School of African and Oriental Studies, University of London.

Turner, Victor. 1967. *The Forest of Symbols*. Ithaca, NY: Cornell University Press.

Udvardy, Monica. 1990a. *Gender and the Culture of Fertility among the Giriama of Kenya*. Unpublished Doctoral dissertation in Anthropology, presented to the University of Uppsala, Sweden.

———. 1990b. "Kifudu: A Female Fertility Cult among the Giriama." In Anita Jacobson-Widding and Walter van Beek, eds., *The Creative Communion: African Folk Models of Fertility and the Regeneration of Life*. Uppsala: Academiae Ubsaliensis. Distributed by Almquist and Wiksell International, Stockholm, Sweden.

van Gennep, Arnold. 1960. *The Rites of Passage*. Transl. Monika B. Vizedom and Gabrielle L. Caffee. Chicago: University of Chicago Press.

Willis, Justin. 1993. *Mombasa, the Swahili, and the Making of the Mijikenda*.Oxford: Clarendon Press.

Mama Lola and the Ezilis: Themes of Mothering and Loving in Haitian Vodou

Karen McCarthy Brown

Mama Lola is a Haitian woman in her mid-fifties who lives in Brooklyn, where she works as a Vodou priestess. This essay concerns her relationship with two female *lwa*, Vodou spirits whom she "serves." By means of trance states, these spirits periodically speak and act through her during community ceremonies and private healing sessions. Mama Lola's story will serve as a case study of how the Vodou spirits closely reflect the lives of those who honor them. While women and men routinely and meaningfully serve both male and female spirits in Vodou, I will focus here on only one strand of the complex web of relations between the "living" and the Vodou spirits, the strand that connects women and female spirits. Specifically I will demonstrate how female spirits, in their iconography and possession-performance, mirror the lives of contemporary Haitian women with remarkable specificity. Some general discussion of Haiti and of Vodou is necessary before moving to the specifics of Mama Lola's story.

Vodou is the religion of 80 percent of the population of Haiti. It arose during the eighteenth century on the giant sugar plantations of the French colony of Saint Domingue, then known as the Pearl of the Antilles. The

Reprinted with permission from Nancy Falk and Rita Gross (eds.), *Unspoken Worlds: Women's Religious Lives* (Belmont, Calif.: Wadsworth Publishing Co.), pp. 235–245. The main ideas in this article are developed further in a chapter of *Mama Lola: Vodou Priestess in Brooklyn* (Berkeley: University of California Press, 1991).

latter name was earned through the colony's veneer of French culture, the renowned beauty of its Creole women, and most of all, the productivity of its huge slave plantations. Haiti is now a different place (it is the poorest country in the Western hemisphere) and Vodou, undoubtedly, a different religion from the one or ones practiced by the predominantly Dahomean, Yoruba, and Kongo slaves originally brought there. The only shared language among these different groups of slaves was French Creole, yet they managed before the end of the eighteenth century to band together (most likely through religious means) to launch the only successful slave revolution during this immoral epoch. As contemporary Haitian history has made amply clear, a successful revolution did not lead to a free and humane life for the Haitian people. Slave masters were quickly replaced by a succession of dictators from both the mulatto and black populations.

Haitians started coming to the United States in large numbers after François Duvalier took control of the country in the late 1950s. The first wave of immigrants was made up of educated, professional people. These were followed by the urban poor and, most recently, the rural poor. All were fleeing dead-end lives in a society drenched in corruption, violence, poverty, and disease. There are now well over one-half million Haitians living in the U.S.

Alourdes, the name by which I usually address Mama Lola, came to New York in 1963 from Port-au-Prince, the capital of Haiti and a city of squalor and hopelessness where she had at times resorted to prostitution to feed three small children. Today, twenty-five years later, Alourdes owns her own home, a three-story row house in the Fort Greene section of Brooklyn. There she and her daughter Maggie run a complex and lively household that varies in size from six people (the core family, consisting of Alourdes, Maggie, and both their children) to as many as a dozen. The final tally depends on how many others are living with them at any given time. These may be recent arrivals from Haiti, down-on-their-luck friends and members of the extended family, or clients and members of the extended family, or clients of Alourdes's Vodou healing practice.

Maggie, now in her thirties, has been in the United States since early adolescence and consequently is much more Americanized than her mother. She is the adult in the family who deals with the outside world. Maggie does the paperwork which life in New York requires and negotiates with teachers, plumbers, electricians, and an array of creditors. She has a degree from a community college and currently works as a nurse's aide at a New York hospital.

Most of the time Alourdes stays at home where she cares for the small children and carries on her practice as a *manbo,* a Vodou priestess. Many Haitians and a few others such as Trinidadians, Jamaicans, and Dominicans come to her with work, health, family, and love problems. For diagnostic purposes, Alourdes first "reads the cards." Then she carries out healing "work" appropriate to the nature and severity of the problem. This may include: counseling the client, a process in which she calls on her own life experience and the shared values of the Haitian community as well as intuitive skills bordering on extrasensory perception; administering baths and other herbal treatments; manufacturing talismans; and summoning the Vodou spirits to "ride" her through trance-possession in order that spiritual insight and wisdom may be brought to bear on the problem.

Vodou spirits (Haitians never call them gods or goddesses) are quite different from deities, or even saints, in the way that we in North America usually use those terms. They are not moral exemplars, nor are their stories characterized by deeds of cosmic or even heroic proportion. Their scale (what makes them larger than life though not other than it) comes, on the one hand, from the key existential paradoxes they contain and, on the other, from the caricature-like clarity with which they portray those pressure points in life. The *lwa* are full-blown personalities who preside over some particular social arena, and the roles they exemplify contain, as they do for the living who must fill them, both positive and negative possibilities.

Trance-possession within Vodou is somewhat like improvisational theater.[1] It is a delicate balancing act between traditional words and gestures which make the spirits recognizable and innovations which make them relevant. In other words, while the character types of the *lwa* are ancient and familiar, the specific things they say or do in a Vodou ritual unfold in response to the people who call them. Because the Vodou spirits are so flexible and responsive, the same spirit will manifest in different ways in the north and in the south of Haiti, in the countryside and in the cities, in Haiti and among the immigrants in New York. There are even significant differences from family to family. Here we are considering two female spirits as they manifest through a heterosexual Haitian woman who has lived in an urban context all her life and who has resided outside of Haiti for a quarter of a century. While most of what is said about these spirits would apply wherever Vodou is practiced, some of the emphases and details are peculiar to this woman and her location.

Vodou is a combination of several distinct African religious traditions. Also, from the beginning, the slaves included Catholicism in the religious blend they used to cope with their difficult lives. Among the most obvious borrowings were the identifications of African spirits with Catholic saints. The reasons why African slaves took on Catholicism are complex. On one level it was a matter of habit. The African cultures from which the slaves were drawn had traditionally been open to the religious systems they encountered through trade and war and had routinely borrowed from them. On another level it was a matter of strategy. A Catholic veneer placed over their own religious practices was a convenient cover for the perpetuation of these frequently outlawed rites. Yet this often cited and too often politicized explanation points to only one level of the strategic value of Catholicism. There was something deep in the slaves' religious traditions that very likely

shaped their response to Catholicism. The Africans in Haiti took on the religion of the slave master, brought it into their holy places, incorporated its rites into theirs, adopted the images of Catholic saints as pictures of their own traditional spirits and the Catholic calendar as descriptive of the year's holy rhythms, and in general practiced a kind of cultural judo with Catholicism. They did this because, in the African ethos, imitation is not the sincerest form of flattery but the most efficient and direct way to gain understanding and leverage.

This epistemological style, exercised also on secular colonial culture, was clearly illustrated when I attended Vodou secret society[2] ceremonies in the interior of Haiti during the 1983 Christmas season. A long night of thoroughly African drumming and dancing included a surprising episode in which the drums went silent, home-made fiddles and brass instruments emerged, and a male and female dancer in eighteenth-century costume performed a slow and fastidious *contradans*. So eighteenth-century slaves in well-hidden places on the vast sugar plantations must have incorporated mimicry of their masters into their traditional worship as a way of appropriating the masters' power.

I want to suggest that this impulse toward imitation lies behind the adoption of Catholicism by African slaves. Yet I do not want to reduce sacred imitation to a political maneuver. On a broader canvas this way of getting to know the powers that be by imitating them is a pervasive and general characteristic of all the African-based religions in the New World. Grasping this important aspect of the way Vodou relates to the world will provide a key for understanding the nature of the relationship between Alourdes and her female spirits. When possessed by her woman spirits, Alourdes acts out the social and psychological forces that define, and often confine, the lives of contemporary Haitian women. She appropriates these forces through imitation. In the drama of possession-performance, she clarifies the lives of women and thereby empowers them to make the best of the choices and roles available to them.

Sacred imitation is a technique drawn from the African homeland, but the kinds of powers subject to imitation shifted as a result of the experience of slavery. The African religions that fed into Haitian Vodou addressed a full array of cosmic, natural, and social forces. Among the African spirits were those primarily defined by association with natural phenomena such as wind, lightning, and thunder. As a result of the shock of slavery, the lens of African religious wisdom narrowed to focus in exquisite detail on the crucial arena of social interaction. Thunder and lightning, drought and pestilence became pale, second-order threats compared with those posed by human beings. During the nearly 200 years since their liberation from slavery, circumstances in Haiti have forced Haitians to stay focused on the social arena. As a result, the Vodou spirits have also retained the strong social emphasis gained during the colonial period. Keeping these points in view, I now turn to Alourdes and two female Vodou spirits she serves. They both go by the name Ezili.

The Haitian Ezili's African roots are multiple.[3] Among them is Mammy Water, a powerful mother of the waters whose shrines are found throughout West Africa. Like moving water, Ezili can be sudden, fickle, and violent, but she is also deep, beautiful, moving, creative, nurturing, and powerful. In Haiti Ezili was recognized in images of the Virgin Mary and subsequently conflated with her. The various manifestations of the Virgin pictured in the inexpensive and colorful lithographs available throughout the Catholic world eventually provided receptacles for several different Ezilis as the spirit subdivided in the New World in order to articulate the different directions in which women's power flowed.

Alourdes, like all Vodou priests or priestesses, has a small number of spirits who manifest routinely through her. This spiritual coterie, which differs from person to person, both defines the character of the healer and sets the tone of his or her "temple." Ezili

Dantor is Alourdes's major female spirit, and she is conflated with Mater Salvatoris, a black Virgin pictured holding the Christ child. The child that Dantor holds (Haitians usually identify it as a daughter!) is her most important iconographic detail, for Ezili Dantor is above all else the woman who bears children, the mother par excellence.

Haitians say that Ezili Dantor fought fiercely beside her "children" in the slave revolution. She was wounded, they say, and they point to the parallel scars that appear on the right cheek of the Mater Salvatoris image as evidence for this. Details of Ezili Dantor's possession-performance extend the story. Ezili Dantor also lost her tongue during the revolution. Thus Dantor does not speak when she possesses someone. The only sound the spirit can utter is a uniform "de-de-de." In a Vodou ceremony, Dantor's mute "de-de-de" becomes articulate only through her body language and the interpretive efforts of the gathered community. Her appearances are thus reminiscent of a somber game of charades. Ezili Dantor's fighting spirit is reinforced by her identification as a member of the Petro pantheon of Vodou spirits, and as such she is associated with what is hot, fiery, and strong. As a Petro spirit Dantor is handled with care. Fear and caution are always somewhere in the mix of attitudes that people hold toward the various Petro spirits.

Those, such as Alourdes, who serve Ezili Dantor become her children and, like children in the traditional Haitian family, they owe their mother high respect and unfailing loyalty. In return, this spiritual mother, like the ideal human mother, will exhaust her strength and resources to care for her children. It is important to note here that the sacrifice of a mother for her children will never be seen by Haitians in purely sentimental or altruistic terms. For Haitian women, even for those now living in New York, children represent the main hope for an economically viable household and the closest thing there is to a guarantee of care in old age. The mother–child relationship among Haitians is thus strong, essential, and in a not unrelated way, potentially volatile. In the countryside, children's labor is necessary for family survival. Children begin to work at an early age, and physical punishment is often swift and severe if they are irresponsible or disrespectful. Although in the cities children stay in school longer and begin to contribute to the welfare of the family at a later age, similar attitudes toward childrearing prevail.

In woman-headed households, the bond between mother and daughter is the most charged and the most enduring. Women and their children form three- and sometimes four-generation networks in which gifts and services circulate according to the needs and abilities of each. These tight family relationships create a safety net in a society where hunger is a common experience for the majority of people. The strength of the mother–daughter bond explains why Haitians identify the child in Ezili Dantor's arms as a daughter. And the importance and precariousness of that bond explain Dantor's fighting spirit and fiery temper.

In possession-performance, Ezili Dantor explores the full range of possibilities inherent in the mother–child bond. Should Dantor's "children" betray her or trifle with her dignity, the spirit's anger can be sudden, fierce, and uncompromising. In such situations her characteristic "de-de-de" becomes a powerful rendering of women's mute but devastating rage. A gentle rainfall during the festivities at Saut d'Eau, a mountainous pilgrimage site for Dantor, is readily interpreted as a sign of her presence but so is a sudden deluge resulting in mudslides and traffic accidents. Ezili's African water roots thus flow into the most essential of social bonds, that between mother and child, where they carve out a web of channels through which can flow a mother's rage as well as her love.

Alourdes, like Ezili Dantor, is a proud and hard-working woman who will not tolerate disrespect or indolence in her children. While her anger is never directed at Maggie, who is now an adult and Alourdes' partner in running the household, it can sometimes

sweep the smaller children off their feet. I have never seen Alourdes strike a child, but her wrath can be sudden and the punishments meted out severe. Although the suffering is different in kind, there is a good measure of it in both Haiti and New York, and the lessons have carried from one to the other. Once, after Alourdes disciplined her ten-year-old, she turned to me and said: "The world is evil.... You got to make them tough!"

Ezili Dantor is not only Alourdes's main female spirit, she is also the spirit who first called Alourdes to her role as priestess. One of the central functions of Vodou in Haiti, and among Haitian emigrants, is that of reinforcing social bonds. Because obligations to the Vodou spirits are inherited within families, Alourdes's decision to take on the heavy responsibility of serving the spirits was also a decision to opt for her extended family (and her Haitian identity) as her main survival strategy.

It was not always clear that this was the decision she would make. Before Alourdes came to the United States, she had shown little interest in her mother's religious practice, even though an appearance by Ezili Dantor at a family ceremony had marked her for the priesthood when she was only five or six years old. By the time Alourdes left Haiti she was in her late twenties and the memory of that message from Dantor had either disappeared or ceased to feel relevant. When Alourdes left Haiti, she felt she was leaving the spirits behind along with a life marked by struggle and suffering. But the spirits sought her out in New York. Messages from Ezili and other spirits came in the form of a debilitating illness that prevented her from working. It was only after she returned to Haiti for initiation into the priesthood and thus acknowledged the spirits' claim on her that Alourdes's life in the U.S. began to run smoothly.

Over the ten years I have known this family, I have watched a similar process at work with her daughter Maggie. Choosing the life of a Vodou priestess in New York is much more difficult for Maggie than it was for her mother. To this day, I have yet to see Maggie move all the way into a trance state. Possession threatens and Maggie struggles mightily; her body falls to the floor as if paralyzed, but she fights off the descending darkness that marks the onset of trance. Afterwards, she is angry and afraid. Yet these feelings finally did not prohibit Maggie from making a commitment to the *manbo's* role. She was initiated to the priesthood in the summer of 1982 in a small temple on the outskirts of Port-au-Prince. Alourdes presided at these rituals. Maggie's commitment to Vodou came after disturbing dreams and a mysterious illness not unlike the one that plagued Alourdes shortly after she came to the United States. The accelerated harassment of the spirits also started around the time when a love affair brought Maggie face to face with the choice of living with someone other than her mother. Within a short period of time, the love affair ended, the illness arrived, and Maggie had a portentous dream in which the spirits threatened to block her life path until she promised to undergo initiation. Now it is widely acknowledged that Maggie is the heir to Alourdes's successful healing practice.

Yet this spiritual bond between Alourdes and Maggie cannot be separated from the social, economic, and emotional forces that hold them together. It is clear that Alourdes and Maggie depend on one another in myriad ways. Without the child care Alourdes provides, Maggie could not work. Without the check Maggie brings in every week, Alourdes would have only the modest and erratic income she brings in from her healing work. These practical issues were also at stake in Maggie's decision about the Vodou priesthood, for a decision to become a *manbo* was also a decision to cast her lot with her mother. This should not be interpreted to mean that Alourdes uses religion to hold Maggie against her will. The affection between them is genuine and strong. Alourdes and Maggie are each other's best friend and most trusted ally. In Maggie's own words: "We have a beautiful relationship . . . it's more than a twin, it's like a Siamese twin.... She is my soul." And in Alourdes's: "If she not near

me, I feel something inside me disconnected."

Maggie reports that when she has problems, Ezili Dantor often appears to her in dreams. Once, shortly after her arrival in the United States, Maggie had a waking vision of Dantor. The spirit, clearly recognizable in her gold-edged blue veil, drifted into her bedroom window. Her new classmates were cruelly teasing her, and the twelve-year-old Maggie was in despair. Dantor gave her a maternal backrub and drifted out the window, where the spirit's glow was soon lost in that of a corner streetlamp. These days, when she is in trouble and Dantor does not appear of her own accord, Maggie goes seeking the spirit. "She don't have to talk to me in my dream. Sometime I go inside the altar, just look at her statue . . . she says a few things to me." The image with which Maggie converses is, of course, Mater Salvatoris, the black virgin, holding in her arms her favored girl child, Anaise.

It is not only in her relationship with her daughter that Alourdes finds her life mirrored in the image of Ezili Dantor. Ezili Dantor is also the mother raising children on her own, the woman who will take lovers but will not marry. In many ways, it is this aspect of Dantor's story that most clearly mirrors and maps the lives of Haitian women.

In former days (and still in some rural areas) the patriarchal, multigenerational extended family held sway in Haiti. In these families men could form unions with more than one woman. Each woman had her own household in which she bore and raised the children from that union. The men moved from household to household, often continuing to rely on their mothers as well as their women to feed and lodge them. When the big extended families began to break up under the combined pressures of depleted soil, overpopulation, and corrupt politics, large numbers of rural people moved to the cities.

Generally speaking, Haitian women fared better than men in the shift from rural to urban life. In the cities the family shrank to the size of the individual household unit, an arena in which women had traditionally been in charge. Furthermore, their skill at small-scale commerce, an aptitude passed on through generations of rural market women, allowed them to adapt to life in urban Haiti, where the income of a household must often be patched together from several small and sporadic sources. Urban women sell bread, candy, and herbal teas which they make themselves. They also buy and re-sell food, clothing, and household goods. Often their entire inventory is balanced on their heads or spread on outstretched arms as they roam through the streets seeking customers. When desperate enough, women also sell sex. They jokingly refer to their genitals as their "land." The employment situation in urban Haiti, meager though it is, also favors women. Foreign companies tend to prefer them for the piecework that accounts for a large percentage of the jobs available to the poor urban majority.

By contrast, unemployment among young urban males may well be as high as 80 percent. Many men in the city circulate among the households of their girlfriends and mothers. In this way they are usually fed, enjoy some intimacy, and get their laundry done. But life is hard and resources scarce. With the land gone, it is no longer so clear that men are essential to the survival of women and children. As a result, relationships between urban men and women have become brittle and often violent. And this is so in spite of a romantic ideology not found in the countryside. Men are caught in a double bind. They are still reared to expect to have power and to exercise authority, and yet they have few resources to do so. Consequently, when their expectations run up against a wall of social impossibility, they often veer off in unproductive directions. The least harmful of these is manifest in a national preoccupation with soccer; the most damaging is the military, the domestic police force of Haiti, which provides the one open road toward upward social mobility for poor young men. Somewhere in the middle of this spectrum lie the drinking and gambling engaged in by large numbers of poor men.

Ezili Dantor's lover is Ogou, a soldier spirit sometimes pictured as a hero, a breathtakingly handsome and dedicated soldier. But just as often Ogou is portrayed as vain and swaggering, untrustworthy and self-destructive. In one of his manifestations Ogou is a drunk. This is the man Ezili Dantor will take into her bed but would never depend on. Their relationship thus takes up and comments on much of the actual life experience of poor urban women.

Ezili Dantor also mirrors many of the specifics of Alourdes's own life. Gran Philo, Alourdes's mother, was the first of her family to live in the city. She worked there as a *manbo*. Although she bore four children, she never formed a long-term union with a man. She lived in Santo Domingo, in the Dominican Republic, for the first years of her adult life. There she had her first two babies. But her lover proved irrational, jealous, and possessive. Since she was working as hard or harder than he, Philo soon decided to leave him. Back in Port-au-Prince, she had two more children, but in neither case did the father participate in the rearing of the children. Alourdes, who is the youngest, did not know who her father was until she was grown. And when she found out, it still took time for him to acknowledge paternity.

In her late teens, Alourdes's fine singing voice won her a coveted position with the Troupe Folklorique, a song and dance group that drew much of its repertoire from Vodou. During that period Alourdes attracted the attention of an older man who had a secure job with the Bureau of Taxation. During their brief marriage Alourdes lived a life that was the dream of most poor Haitian women. She had a house and two servants. She did not have to work. But this husband, like the first man in Philo's life, needed to control her every move. His jealousy was so great that Alourdes was not even allowed to visit her mother without supervision. (The man should have known better than to threaten that vital bond!) Alourdes and her husband fought often and, after less than two years, she left. In the years that followed, there were times when Alourdes had no food and times when she could not pay her modest rent but, with pride like Ezili Dantor's, Alourdes never returned to her husband and never asked him for money. During one especially difficult period Alourdes began to operate as a Marie-Jacques, a prostitute, although not the kind who hawk their wares on the street. Each day she would dress up and go from business to business in downtown Port-au-Prince looking for someone who would ask her for a "date." When the date was over she would take what these men offered (everyone knew the rules), but she never asked for money. Alourdes had three children in Haiti, by three different men. She fed them and provided shelter by juggling several income sources. Her mother helped when she could. So did friends when they heard she was in need. For a while, Alourdes held a job as a tobacco inspector for the government. And she also dressed up and went out looking for dates.

Maggie, like Alourdes, was married once. Her husband drank too much and one evening, he hit her. Once was enough. Maggie packed up her infant son and returned to her mother's house. She never looked back. When Maggie talks about this marriage, now over for nearly a decade, she says he was a good man but alcohol changed him. "When he drink, forget it!" She would not take the chance that he might hit her again or, worse, take his anger and frustration out on their son.

Ezili Dantor is the mother—fierce, proud, hard-working, and independent. As a religious figure, Dantor's honest portrayal of the ambivalent emotions a woman can feel toward her lovers and a mother can feel toward her children stands in striking contrast to the idealized attitude of calm, nurture, and acceptance represented by more standard interpretations of the Holy Mother Mary, a woman for whom rage would be unthinkable. Through her iconography and possession-performances, Ezili Dantor works in subtle ways with the concrete life circumstances of Haitian women such as Alourdes and Maggie. She takes up their lives, clarifies

the issues at stake in them, and gives them permission to follow the sanest and most humane paths. Both Alourdes and Maggie refer to Ezili Dantor as "my mother."

Vodou is a religion born of slavery, of wrenching change and deep pain. Its genius can be traced to long experience in using the first (change) to deal with the second (pain). Vodou is a religion in motion, one without canon, creed, or pope. In Vodou the ancient African wisdom is preserved by undergoing constant transformation in response to specific life circumstances. One of the things which keeps Vodou agile is its plethora of spirits. Each person who serves the spirits has his or her own coterie of favorites. And no single spirit within that group can take over and lay down the law for the one who serves. There are always other spirits to consult, other spirit energies to take into account. Along with Ezili Dantor, Alourdes also serves her sister, Ezili Freda.

Ezili Freda is a white spirit from the Rada pantheon, a group characterized by sweetness and even tempers. Where Dantor acts out women's sexuality in its childbearing mode, Freda, the flirt, concerns herself with love and romance. Like the famous Creole mistresses who lent charm and glamour to colonial Haiti, Ezili Freda takes her identity and worth from her relationship with men. Like the mulatto elite in contemporary Haiti who are the heirs of those Creole women, Freda loves fine clothes and jewelry. In her possession-performances, Freda is decked out in satin and lace. She is given powder and perfume, sweet smelling soaps and rich creams. The one possessed by her moves through the gathered community, embracing one and then another and then another. Something in her searches and is never satisfied. Her visits often end in tears and frustration.[4]

Different stories are told about Freda and children. Some say she is barren. Others say she has a child but wishes to hide that fact in order to appear fresher, younger, and more desirable to men. Those who hold the latter view are fond of pointing out the portrait of a young boy that is tucked behind the left elbow of the crowned Virgin in the image of Maria Dolorosa with whom Freda is conflated. In this intimate biographical detail, Freda picks up a fragment from Alourdes's life that hints at larger connections between the two. When Alourdes was married she already had two children by two different men. She wanted a church wedding and a respectable life, so she hid the children from her prospective in-laws. It was only at the wedding itself, when they asked about the little boy and girl seated in the front row, that they found out the woman standing before the altar with their son already had children.

Alourdes does not have her life all sewn up in neat packages. She does not have all the questions answered and all the tensions resolved. Most of the time when she tells the story of her marriage, Alourdes says flatly: "He too jealous. That man crazy!" But on at least one occasion she said: "I was too young. If I was with Antoine now, I never going to leave him!" When Alourdes married Antoine Lovinsky she was a poor teenager living in Port-au-Prince, a city where less than 10% of the people are not alarmingly poor. Women of the elite class nevertheless structure the dreams of poor young women. These are the light-skinned women, who marry in white dresses in big Catholic churches and return to homes that have bedroom sets and dining room furniture and servants. These are the women who never have to work. They spend their days resting and visiting with friends and emerge at night on the arms of their men dressed like elegant peacocks and affecting an air of haughty boredom. Although Alourdes's tax collector could not be said to be a member of the elite, he provided her with a facsimile of the dream. It stifled her and confined her, but she has still not entirely let go of the fantasy. She still loves jewelry and clothes and, in her home, manages to create the impression, if not the fact, of wealth by piling together satin furniture, velvet paintings, and endless bric-a-brac.

Alourdes also has times when she is very lonely and she longs for male companionship. She gets tired of living at the edge of poverty and being the one in charge of such a big and ungainly household. She feels the pull of the images of domesticity and nuclear family life that she sees every day on the television in New York. Twice since I have known her, Alourdes has fallen in love. She is a deeply sensual woman and this comes strongly to the fore during these times. She dresses up, becomes coquettish, and caters to her man. Yet when describing his lovable traits, she always says first: "He help me so much. Every month, he pay the electric bill," and so forth. Once again the practical and the emotional issues cannot be separated. In a way, this is just another version of the poor woman selling her "land." And in another way it is not, for here the finances of love are wound round and round with longing and dreams.

Poor Haitian women, Alourdes included, are a delight to listen to when their ironic wit turns on what we would label as the racism, sexism, and colonial pretense of the upper-class women Freda mirrors. Yet these are the values with power behind them both in Haiti and in New York, and poor women are not immune to the attraction of such a vision. Ezili Freda is thus an image poor Haitian women live toward. She picks up their dreams and gives them shape, but these women are mostly too experienced to think they can live on or in dreams. Alourdes is not atypical. She serves Freda but much less frequently than Dantor. Ezili Dantor is the one for whom she lights a candle every day; she is the one Alourdes turns to when there is real trouble. She is, in Alourdes' words, "my mother." Yet I think it is fair to say that it is the tension between Dantor and Freda that keeps both relevant to the lives of Haitian women.

There is a story about conflict between the two Ezilis. Most people, most of the time, will say that the scars on Ezili Dantor's cheek come from war wounds, but there is an alternative explanation. Sometimes it is said that because Dantor was sleeping with her man, Maria Dolorosa took the sword from her heart and slashed the cheek of her rival.

A flesh-and-blood woman, living in the real world, cannot make a final choice between

Ezili Dantor and Ezili Freda. It is only when reality is spiced with dreams, when survival skills are larded with sensuality and play, that life moves forward. Dreams and play alone lead to endless and fruitless searching. And a whole life geared toward survival becomes brittle and threatened by inner rage. Alourdes lives at the nexus of several spirit energies. Freda and Dantor are only two of them, the two who help her most to see herself clearly as a woman.

To summarize the above discussion: The Vodou spirits are not idealized beings removed from the complexity and particularity of life. On the contrary, the responsive and flexible nature of Vodou allows the spirits to change over space and time in order to mirror people's life circumstances in considerable detail. Vodou spirits are transparent to their African origins and yet they are other than African spirits. Ancient nature connections have been buried deep in their iconographies while social domains have risen to the top, where they have developed in direct response to the history and social circumstances of the Haitian people. The Vodou spirits make sense of the powers that shape and control life by imitating them. They act out both the dangers and the possibilities inherent in problematic life situations. Thus, the moral pull of Vodou comes from clarification. The Vodou spirits do not tell the people what should be; they illustrate what is.

Perhaps Vodou has these qualities because it is a religion of an oppressed people. Whether or not that is true, it seems to be a type of spirituality with some advantages for women. The openness and flexibility of the religion, the multiplicity of its spirits, and the detail in which those spirits mirror the lives of the faithful makes women's lives visible in ways they are not in the so-called great religious traditions. This visibility can give women a way of working realistically and creatively with the forces that define and confine them.

NOTES

1. I use terms such as possession-performance and theater analogies in order to point to certain aspects of the spirits' self-presentation and interaction with devotees. The terms should not be taken as indicating that priestesses and priests simply pretend to be spirits during Vodou ceremonies. The trance states they enter are genuine, and they themselves will condemn the occasional imposter among them.
2. In an otherwise flawed book, E. Wade Davis does a very good job of uncovering and describing the nature and function of the Vodou secret societies. See *The Serpent and the Rainbow* (New York: Simon and Schuster, 1985).
3. Robert Farris Thompson traces Ezili to a Dahomean "goddess of lovers." *Flash of the Spirit: African and Afro-American Art and Philosophy* (New York: Random House, 1983), p. 191.
4. Maya Deren has drawn a powerful portrait of this aspect of Ezili Freda in *The Divine Horsemen: The Living Gods of Haiti* (New Paltz, N.Y.: Documentext, McPherson and Co., 1983), pp. 137–45.

FURTHER READINGS

Brown, Karen McCarthy. "The Center and the Edges: God and Person in Haitian Vodou." *The Journal of the Interdenominational Theological Center* 7, no. 1 (Fall 1979).

———. "Olina and Erzulie: A Woman and a Goddess in Haitian Vodou." *Anima*, Spring 1979.

———. "Systematic Forgetting, Systematic Remembering: Ogou in Haiti." In *Africa's Ogun: Old World and New.* ed. by Sandra T. Barnes. Bloomington, Ind.: University of Indiana Press, 1988.

———. "Alourdes: A Case Study of Moral Leadership in Haitian Vodou." In *Saints and Virtues,* ed. by John S. Hawley. Berkeley, Calif.: University of California Press, 1987.

———. "Afro-Caribbean Spirituality." In *Caring and Curing: Health and Medicine in the Western Religious Traditions,* ed. by Lawrence Eugene Sullivan. New York: Macmillan Press, 1988.

———. "The Power to Heal: Reflections on Women, Religion and Medicine." In *Shaping New Vision: Gender and Values in American Culture.* Ann Arbor, Mich.: UMI Press, 1987.

Deren, Maya. *Divine Horsemen: The Living Gods of Haiti.* New Paltz, N.Y.: Documentext, McPherson and Co., 1983.

Metraux, Alfred. *Voodoo in Haiti.* New York: Schocken Books, 1972.

Thompson, Robert Farris. *Flash of the Spirit: African and Afro-American Art and Philosophy.* New York: Random House, 1983.

Blessed Mother Ann, Holy Mother Wisdom: Gender and Divinity in Shaker Life and Belief

Marjorie Procter-Smith

Can Christians speak of God the Creator and God the Savior in any terms but male? "I believe in God, the Father Almighty, maker of heaven and earth; and in Jesus Christ his only Son, our Lord." "Glory be to the Father and to the Son and to the Holy Ghost." These phrases, recited or sung by generations of Christians, make it clear that the traditional Christian emphasis rests on a male God and his divine male son. Centuries of Christian doctrine, ritual, prayer, and song have repeated and developed the Father-Son imagery so thoroughly that it is difficult for many to imagine Christianity using any other language. When some contemporary feminists propose calling God Mother or imagining a woman Christ, they are often ridiculed or accused of abandoning the Christian tradition.

But in fact 200 years ago a Christian sect known as the Shakers spoke of God as Mother and believed that their founder, Ann Lee, was the second coming of Christ in female form. This essay discusses who the Shakers were, why they used female language for God, and how that language related to the roles and lives of women in the community.

WHO ARE THE SHAKERS?

In 1774, nine English passengers disembarked at New York harbor after a seventy-nine-day voyage from Liverpool. The passengers were Ann Lee, a prophetess and religious leader from Manchester in England, and her eight followers (six men and two

Original material prepared for this text.

women). These voyagers had been members of a group known in England as "Shaking Quakers." One of many small sects who prophesied the imminent end of the world and return of Christ to earth, the Shaking Quakers were chiefly known in England for disrupting church services with their ecstatic speech, singing, and prophesying.

When Ann Lee joined the group, they were guided by a charismatic woman, Jane Wardley. However, sometime around 1770, Ann Lee had an extraordinary religious experience, which propelled her into prominence among them. She later described this experience in language borrowed from her own experience of childbirth:

> Thus I labored, in strong cries and groans to God, day and night, till my flesh wasted away, and I became like a skeleton, and a kind of down came upon my skin, until my soul broke forth to God; which I felt as sensibly as ever a woman did a child, when she was delivered of it.[1]

As a result of this experience of new birth, Lee was favored with ecstatic visions of God and Jesus, Heaven and Hell. In the course of these visions, it was revealed to Lee by Jesus Christ that the "sin which is the root of all evil" is sexual intercourse, even within lawful marriage. Ann Lee's witness against "the doleful works of the flesh," an insistence on absolute celibacy, became one of the central tenets of Shaker faith and a foundation for the development of Shaker community life.

Armed with these powerful heavenly visions, Lee claimed authority as leader of the group and convinced her followers of the necessity of resettling in America, where new missionary fields lay open to them. Once in America, Ann Lee and her small group settled in the wilderness of New York state in a village called Niskeyuna (now Watervliet, New York, near Albany) and began to gather new believers in Lee's message.

Lee taught that perfection was possible in this life, provided one "took up a full cross," which meant, practically speaking, willingness to confess all known sins to a Shaker leader (either Mother Ann or someone designated by her); to accept a celibate life, regardless of marital status; and to live a sinless life after the manner of Christ.

The term "Shaker" was a derisive one, given by non-Shakers who observed the ecstatic religious behavior of Ann Lee and her followers. Typical Shaker worship included shouting, leaping, dancing, whirling about, singing in unknown tongues, and falling into trances. Prophetic announcements and gestures were common, and Shaker worshippers thereby gained access to the spiritual world.

Lee's visions, however, were exceptional. To the observer, she appeared strange, otherworldly, and perhaps a bit frightening. One early follower remembered seeing Lee

> sit in her chair, from early in the morning, until afternoon, under great operations and power of God. She sung in unknown tongues, the whole of the time; and seemed to be wholly divested of any attraction to material things. All her sensations appeared to be engaged in the spiritual world.[2]

Lee reported that her visions during such periods included face-to-face conversations with God and with Jesus, visions of Heaven and the saints, and harrowing views of the suffering of the damned in Hell. In particular she described her relationship with Jesus as especially intimate:

> I have been walking in fine valleys with Christ, as with a lover.... Christ is ever with me, both in sitting down and rising up; in going out and coming in. If I walk in groves and valleys, there he is, with me; and I converse with him as one friend converses with another, face to face.[3]

She also referred to Christ as her husband, her "Lord and Head," who preempts the authority of any human man. Lee's earthly husband, who had accompanied her to America, had not found Shaker doctrine and life satisfactory and apparently left the group early on.

At first Lee and the other leaders of the group advised new converts to return to their families and live in peace and holiness with them, an evangelical strategy that often seemed to work, because many of the first converts to Shakerism in America were members of a few large New England families. However, by 1782 or so necessity was conspiring with religious disposition to encourage the development of communal living, at least in a rather informal way. Clusters of Believers (as Shakers preferred to call themselves) began pooling their financial resources to provide support for poorer families and to provide food and lodging for traveling Shaker missionaries and visitors who gathered to hear the Shaker message.

When Ann Lee died in 1784 the remaining leaders recognized that for their movement to survive they needed to establish a more formal order and structure for living the Shaker life. Lee's successor, James Whittaker, began the process of organizing Believers into communities on the basis of common ownership of property and goods, or "joint interest." This process of "gathering into order" was continued by Whittaker's successor, Joseph Meacham, and his associate and successor, Lucy Wright.

Shaker communities, organized into units called "families," were constructed in part to replace the natural families that celibate Shakers were required to give up. All members were called "brother" or "sister," with those in leadership designated as "elders" and "eldresses." Each family had two elders and two eldresses who held spiritual authority over the brothers and sisters; two deacons and two deaconesses who were responsible for the material well-being of the family (providing for food, clothing, upkeep of buildings and grounds, and so forth); and several trustees, who handled all business dealings with the "World," as non-Shakers were called.[4]

Overall, there have been eighteen major Shaker communities and several smaller and short-lived ones. During the middle of the nineteenth century the Shakers reached their peak membership of perhaps as many as 6,000.[5] Membership began to decline soon after this, however, and now only a very few individuals remain.[6]

SHAKER RELIGIOUS LANGUAGE

Shakerism grew in a religious environment in which many Christians believed in the imminent return of Jesus Christ to earth. This millennialism, as it is called, predisposed people to expect miraculous signs of various kinds. For example, on May 19, 1780, settlers clearing land in New England burned off brush and trees, and the resulting smoke hid the sun, making the day as dark as night. Terrified New Englanders, seeing birds and farm animals go to sleep as if it were night and remembering apocalyptic Biblical prophecy about the sun becoming "black as sackcloth," cried, "The day of judgment is come!" During Ann Lee's missionary journey through New England between 1781 and 1783 she and some of her followers saw a particularly spectacular display of the Northern Lights. One commented that the lights were "a sign of the coming of the Son of Man in the clouds of heaven." Although Ann Lee rejected this interpretation, clearly Shakers shared the general disposition of people to look for "signs and portents."

Likewise, millennialist expectations predisposed people to look for prophets and visionists. In such a milieu, then, Ann Lee's extraordinary visions and prophecies, her singing in unknown tongues, and astonishing messages about sin and perfection aroused intense interest. The extravagant singing and dancing in Shaker gatherings and the charismatic presence of Ann Lee combined to convince many New Englanders that the Second Coming was upon them.

In this religious context, believers concluded that Ann Lee had been the instrument of initiating the millennial church and had opened to the world the possibility of a life of Gospel perfection. The official name of the Shakers was the United Society of Believers in Christ's Second Appearing, also sometimes called the Millennial Church.

Some of the earliest Shaker theological works are explicit that Ann Lee herself is the one "in whom Christ did visibly make his second appearance."[7] Ann Lee and Jesus Christ are described in parallel terms as embodiments of the Christ-Spirit:

> The man who was called Jesus and the woman who was called Ann, are verily the two foundation pillars of the Church of Christ.[8]

Fundamental to this interpretation of Ann Lee as parallel to Jesus is Lee's own claim to have been married to Christ.

Another important element in the development of Shaker religious language is the title by which most Believers addressed Ann Lee during her life and remembered her after her death: "Mother" Ann. Perhaps because Lee was older than many of her American converts and because of the emotional attachment Believers felt for Ann Lee, the title of "Mother" became synonymous with Ann Lee, and Shaker documents routinely assume that the reader will know that any reference to "Mother" is a reference to Ann Lee.

Although Lee is often remembered as a rather stern mother who chastised her errant children and spoke sharply to them, she is represented predominantly as a loving mother who gave birth to her children in the faith, who labored over them and for them, and who guided them in the faith. A Shaker hymn expresses this idea:

> Born by our Mother, we were led,
> By her our infant souls were fed;
> And by her suff'rings and her toils
> She brought salvation to our souls.[9]

Thus, Jesus and Mother Ann were Believers' "Gospel Parents," as described in this hymn:

Our Father and our Mother
Have borne us in the birth,
Their union is together,
Redeemed from the earth:
We children born, are not forlorn,
But like our Parents dear,
We've overcome the wicked one,
And reign in Zion here.[10]

Having worked out the theological significance of Ann Lee as Mother and as Second appearing of Christ, Shakers turned their thoughts to the question of God. Unlike the theological development of an understanding of Ann Lee, which was based on personal experience of her as their spiritual mother, the Shaker doctrine of God was largely based on intellectual conviction.

The reasoning went something like this: If Ann Lee is our Mother and she is the female embodiment of the Christ-Spirit, then she holds a parallel position to Jesus as the first and male embodiment of the Christ-Spirit. If Jesus as the Christ reveals God the Father to humankind, then Mother Ann must also reveal God, and the God she reveals must necessarily be God the Mother. A major Shaker theological work puts it this way:

The first appearing of Christ, in the simplest terms of language, is the Revelation of the Father, and the second appearing of Christ is the Revelation of the Mother; but for the subject under consideration we have preferred the title, "The Revelation of the Holy Ghost," as the most forcible and striking of all other scripture terms.[11]

This Mother-Holy Ghost God whom Ann Lee was said to reveal was later called Holy Mother Wisdom, who was said to reign with God the Father in heaven, as described in this hymn:

Long ere this fleeting world began
Or dust was fashioned into man,
There *Power* and *Wisdom* we can view,
Names of the *Everlasting Two*.
The Father's high eternal throne

Was never fill'd by one alone:
There Wisdom holds the Mother's seat
And is the Father's helper-meet.[12]

Shaker theologians regarded their dual Father-Mother God as logically superior to the trinitarian God of more traditional Christian theology. "As every individual on the world sprang from a father and a mother, the conclusion is self-evident, that the whole sprang from one joint parentage," argued Shaker theologian Benjamin Seth Youngs in 1808. It makes more sense, he reasoned, to talk about a God who is male and female than a God who is all male. Ridiculing "defective" trinitarian doctrine, Youngs wrote:

First the Father, second the Son, and third the Holy Ghost; He proceeding from Father and Son ... without the attribute of either Mother or Daughter ... and [they] finally look for the mystery of God to be finished in the odd number of three males.... Where then is the correspondent cause of the woman's existence?[13]

The cause of woman's existence, Shakers believed, had been revealed by Mother Ann, a Mother God, who shared God the Father's throne and represented "wisdom" to God the Father's "power."

Beginning in the 1830s a period of intense internal revival affected all the Shaker communities and brought the image of God the Mother into prominence in Shaker experience. Beginning with trance-like experiences similar to the ecstatic worship of the earliest days of Shakerism, the revival swept through all of the communities and lasted for more than ten years. Believers once again sang heavenly songs in unknown tongues, leaped and whirled about uncontrollably, and fell into trances in which they saw and spoke to long-dead Shaker leaders, including Mother Ann, Father William Lee (Ann Lee's brother), Father Joseph (Meacham), and others. This period became known as "Mother Ann's Work," because it was believed that Mother Ann, seeing the loss of vitality in the faith of her children, had sent them this revival.

Most notably, certain Believers claimed to have been chosen as "instruments" of various heavenly beings, usually angels, who delivered messages from Mother Ann and other heavenly denizens to Believers. For the most part these claims were accepted by the leadership and by the members, and their messages were received with great respect and awe.[14] A disproportionate number of these instruments were women.

During the height of the revival, between 1840 and 1843, Holy Mother Wisdom made a series of visits to the communities in the person of a female instrument. Sometimes the visits lasted several days and included individual interviews by Holy Mother Wisdom of each member of the community. These visits were carefully prepared for by periods of fasting, prayer, confessions of sin, and intensive cleaning of the grounds and buildings. The visit normally concluded with Holy Mother Wisdom bestowing her "mark" on the forehead of each Believer or granting them some similar spiritual blessing. One contemporary observer remembered Holy Mother Wisdom concluding the visit with these words: "Around thy head I place a golden band. On it is written the name of me, Holy Mother Wisdom! the Great Jehovah! the Eternal God! Touch not mine anointed!"[15]

SHAKER WOMEN

Shaker women had before them the example of Ann Lee. On the one hand, she was extraordinarily gifted: prophetess, visionary, bride, and companion of Christ; teacher; judge; and loving but strict spiritual mother. On the other hand she shared the experiences of many of the women who were drawn to Shakerism: She was poor and illiterate; she had been married to a man she described as "very kind, according to nature," and had given birth to four children and had seen them all die in infancy; she had suffered persecution for her religious beliefs; and she had struggled to make a living and survive in a new land. Lee's exceptional ability to infuse with religious meaning her own struggles and sufferings as a woman provided a rich resource to her female followers who shared many of her experiences.

Later theological speculation interpreted Ann Lee as the Second Christ, an object not only of loving memory but also a figure of cosmic significance: one of the two "foundation pillars" of the Church, the Daughter of God, the Mother of All Living, the Revelation of God the Mother. Shaker women had not only the memory of a spiritually powerful woman who was like them in many ways, but they also had access to a positive, powerful female Christ and a loving Mother God.

The loving Mother God came to be known as Holy Mother Wisdom and was presented to them materially in the form of a woman visionist. During the visitations of Holy Mother Wisdom each woman and man in the community received at the hands of a woman a gift directly from God, the mark of Holy Mother Wisdom, and heard from the mouth of a woman words of judgment or blessing. Although female instruments did not always speak only in the name of Holy Mother Wisdom or Mother Ann, the strength of the communities' belief in these figures legitimated women's exercise of their prophetic gifts in general.

Shaker women's more temporal gifts were also legitimated by Shaker community structures. The development of a centralized and tightly structured leadership after the "gathering into order" might have excluded women, after the pattern of many other religious movements founded by women. Indeed leadership did not automatically pass to other women on Ann Lee's death. On the contrary Lee was succeeded by two men before a pattern of female leadership was established with the appointment by Joseph Meacham of Lucy Wright as "Mother" of the entire sect alongside himself as "Father."

At first there was considerable resistance to Mother Lucy's leadership from male Shakers who were offended by the idea of a woman in a position of religious authority over them, and many people left the community in protest. However, the pattern of dual male and female leadership was established and remained the norm for all Shaker communities. This requirement gave Shaker women greater access to positions of religious leadership than women in most other Christian groups. Appointment to eldress of a community meant the opportunity to exercise temporal and spiritual leadership, greater responsibility, and chances to travel to other communities.

At the same time along with the advantages of the Shaker theological and communal system for woman came some disadvantages. The theological interpretation of Holy Mother Wisdom, for example, depended a great deal on popular nineteenth-century views of "women's sphere" and the "cult of True Womanhood."[16] Holy Mother Wisdom was described by one Shaker writer as "endless love, truth, meekness, long forbearance, and loving kindness . . . the Mother of all Godliness, meekness, purity, peace, sincerity, virtue, and chastity."[17] Although in theory such virtues were to apply to all Shakers, in fact they were associated with women primarily, even divine women.

The Shaker communal system provided opportunities for leadership for women, but it did so in the context of a strictly hierarchical system in which leaders were not elected but appointed by their superiors, and virtually absolute obedience to the leaders was expected. Work in the communities was rigidly divided, with women largely confined to traditional "women's work": food preparation, clothing manufacture and maintenance, and household maintenance. This pragmatic division of labor was interpreted as being of divine origin, and Shaker women were advised that true freedom for them lay in remaining within "woman's sphere."

CONCLUSIONS

It is striking how many contemporary feminist religious issues are found in the history of Shakerism. Contemporary feminists have challenged mainstream religious groups to expand women's opportunities for religious leadership, to reconsider the use of exclusively male language about God and Christ, and to develop religious language that draws on women's experience. From an examination of Shaker history we may see a Christian group that struggled to preserve women's religious leadership, that worshipped God as Mother as well as Father, and that drew some of its central religious terms from women's traditional childbearing and household work.

Most radical of the Shakers' ideas about women and religion, and most startlingly contemporary, is their grasp of the connection between an exclusively male representation of God and a male-dominated society. Antoinette Doolittle, editor of the Shaker journal *Shaker and Shakeress* from 1873 to 1875, observed, "As long as we have all male Gods in the heavens we shall have all male rulers on the earth."[18] They also insisted that the recognition of the female in deity was essential to women's social and religious emancipation, and they were unflinching in their criticism of male-centered theology and church.

However, their answer to their critique of male-centered religion was a highly dualistic system based on the fundamental difference between men and women. In this oppositional system women's "sphere" was diametrically opposed to that of men, and it left women in the same place reserved for them by conventional wisdom. Although redeemed Shaker women were spiritually superior to all unredeemed women and men, women by nature were understood to be more sinful than men. Indeed, this greater sinfulness of women necessitated, in part, the Second Coming of Christ in female form. A Shaker hymn says,

> As disobedience first began
> In Eve, the second part of man
> The second trumpet could not sound
> Til second Eve her Lord had found.[19]

"Second Eve" here refers to Ann Lee, whose Lord is Christ.

The questions these limitations of the Shaker system raise are several and are now being dealt with in contemporary feminist critiques of religion. First, there is the question of valorizing women's traditional experience. Such valorization recognizes that the work women have done for eons—care of children, care of households, concern for maintenance of human relationships—is the work of world-construction and world-maintenance, and as such it is religious work. The risk of such valorization, as the Shaker history shows, is that it reinforces the cultural notion that such work is women's sole work and that it is solely women's work. Such a view restricts women's access to other kinds of work and suggests that men need not concern themselves with such work, a bifurcation that feminism has taken some pains to correct.

Second, the Shaker story raises questions about essentialism. Is there some essential female character or virtue? Some Shaker theologians assumed that there was such a thing and that they knew what it was. Both arguments that female character is essentially flawed or sinful and that female character is essentially nurturant, loving, and caring claim such knowledge, and both views can be found not only in Shakerism but in other religions as well. Some contemporary feminists have challenged such claims about women, insisting instead that while women share some oppressions in common as women, women's experiences are diverse and complex and cannot be simplified into claims of innate evil or innate goodness.

Third, the Shakers demonstrate both the difficulties of preserving and perpetuating strong female leadership and the value of having the example of a female founder as a living memory in the community's life. The Shaker's most effective method of ensuring the continuation of female leadership, however, was their ideological system, which demanded equal leadership by men and women and recruited and developed strong women for leadership positions. Without such structural demands even the memory of Ann Lee would not have sufficed to preserve women's religious leadership.

NOTES

1. *Testimonies of the Life, Character, Revelations and Doctrines of our Ever Blessed Mother Ann Lee, and the Elders With Her* (Hancock, MA: J. Talcott and J. Deming, Junrs., 1816), p. 47.
2. Ibid., p. 200.
3. Ibid., p. 211.
4. For further information on the Shakers' business dealings, see Edward Deming Andrews, *The Community Industries of the Shakers* (University of the State of New York, 1933; New York State Museum Handbook No. 15).
5. The actual peak population of Shaker communities is disputed. Compare Edward Deming Andrews, *The People Called Shakers* (New York: Dover Publications, 1953), p. 224; Priscilla J. Brewer, *Shaker Communities, Shaker Lives* (Hanover, NH: University Press of New England, 1986), p. 156; and William Sims Bainbridge, "Shaker Demographics 1840–1900: An Example of the Use of U.S. Census Enumeration Schedule," *Journal For the Scientific Study of Religion* 21 (1982), p. 355.
6. At present the Shaker communities of Sabbathday Lake, Maine, and Canterbury, New Hampshire, are the only occupied communities.
7. *Testimonies* (1816), p. 2.
8. Benjamin Seth Youngs, *The Testimony of Christ's Second Appearing* (Albany: The United Society, 1810, Second Edition), p. 440.
9. Seth Y. Wells, compiler, *Millennial Praises* (Hancock, MA: Josiah Talcott, 1813), p. 105.
10. Ibid., p. 35.
11. Youngs, p. 537.
12. Wells, p. 1.
13. Youngs, p. 454.
14. Shaker manuscript collections such as those found at the Western Reserve Historical Society, the Shaker Museum at Old Chatham, New York, and the Archives and Manuscript Division of the New York Public Library have large numbers of recorded gift drawings and messages from this period, most of them by women.
15. David R. Lamson, *Two Years' Experience Among the Shakers* (West Boylston, MA: Published by the author, 1848), p. 95.
16. See Barbara Welter, "The Cult of True Womanhood," *American Quarterly* 18 (1966), pp. 151–174.

17. Paulina Bates, *The Divine Book of Holy Wisdom* (Canterbury, NH: n.p., 1849), p. 661.
18. "Address of Antoinette Doolittle, Troy, NY, March 24, 1872," *The Shaker* 2.6 (June 1872), p. 43.
19. Wells, p. 250.

REFERENCES

Andrews, Edward Deming. 1953. *The People Called Shakers.* New York: Dover Publications.
Foster, Lawrence. 1984. *Religion and Sexuality: The Shakers, the Mormons, and the Oneida Community.* Urbana: University of Illinois Press.

Garrett, Clarke. 1989. *Spirit Possession and Popular Religion: From the Camisards to the Shakers.* Baltimore: Johns Hopkins.
Humez, Jean. 1981. *Gifts of Power: The Writings of Rebecca Jackson, Black Visionary, Shaker Eldress.* Amherst: University of Massachusetts Press.
Mercadante, Linda. 1990. *Gender, Doctrine, and God: The Shakers and Contemporary Theology.* Nashville: Abingdon Press.
Patterson, Daniel W. 1979. *The Shaker Spiritual.* Princeton: Princeton University Press.
Procter-Smith, Marjorie. 1985. *Women in Shaker Community and Worship.* Lewiston, NY: Edwin Mellen Press.
Sasson, Diane. 1983. *The Shaker Spiritual Narrative.* Knoxville: University of Tennessee.

X

Gender, Politics, and Reproduction

All human reproductive behavior is culturally patterned. This cultural patterning includes menstrual beliefs and practices; restrictions on the circumstances in which sexual activity may occur; beliefs and practices surrounding pregnancy, labor, and the postpartum period; understanding and treatment of infertility; and the significance of menopause. Although research on human biological reproduction has been dominated by medical concerns such as normal and abnormal physiological functioning, an increasing anthropological literature emphasizes the centrality of reproduction to global social, political, and economic processes (Ginsburg and Rapp 1995; Sargent and Brettell 1996). Biological reproduction refers to the production of human beings, but this process is always a social activity, leading to the perpetuation of social systems and social relations. The ways in which societies structure human reproductive behavior reflect core social values and principles, informed by changing political and economic conditions (Browner and Sargent 1990: 215).

Much of the available anthropological data on reproduction prior to 1970 is to be found within ethnographies devoted to other subjects. For example, Montagu (1949) analyzed concepts of conception and fetal development among Australian aborigines, and Malinowski (1932) wrote about reproductive concepts and practices among the Trobriand Islanders. Several surveys of ethnographic data on reproduction were compiled, such as Ford's (1964) study of customs surrounding the reproductive cycle or Spencer's (1949–1950) list of reproductive practices around the world.

In the past twenty years anthropologists have sought to use cross-cultural data from preindustrial societies to help resolve women's health problems in the industrialized world (Davis-Floyd and Sargent 1997; Jordan 1978). For example, comparative research on birth practices has raised questions regarding the medicalization of childbirth in the United States. Anthropologists have also involved themselves in international public health efforts to improve maternal and child health around the world. In addition, anthropological research has helped clarify the relationship between population growth and poverty. While some analysts have held the view that overpopulation is a determinant of poverty and the poor must control their fertility to overcome impoverishment, others argue the reverse: People have many children because they are poor (Rubinstein and Lane 1991: 386).

Concern with population growth has often focused on women as the potential users of contraceptives, although women's personal desires to limit fertility may not be translated into action because of opposition from husbands, female relations, or others with influence or decision-making power. In this area of research anthropologists have an important contribution to make in examining such factors as cultural concepts regarding fertility and family size, the value of children, dynamics of decision making within the family and community, and the relationship between women's reproductive and productive roles.

Since the 1970s anthropological interest has turned to the linkages between cultural constructions of gender, the cultural shaping of motherhood, and reproductive beliefs and practices. In many societies throughout the world the relationship between women's status and maternity is clear: A woman attains adult status by childbearing, and her prestige may be greatly enhanced by bearing numerous male children (Browner and Sargent 1990: 218). Thus, in the Middle East a woman is "raised for marriage and procreation [and] acquires her own social status only by fecundity" (Vieille 1978: 456), while in parts of Africa pressures to be prolific weigh heavily on women (Sargent 1982).

In much of the world infertility is dreaded by men and women alike but is a particular burden to women (Browner and Sargent 1990: 219). Such pressure to reproduce is especially intense in agrarian societies, which have a high demand for labor. However, in many hunter-gatherer and horticultural societies, motherhood and reproduction are less emphasized. As Collier and Rosaldo observe, "Contrary to our expectation that motherhood provides women everywhere with a natural source of emotional satisfaction and cultural value, we found that neither women nor men in very simple societies celebrate women as nurturers or women's unique capacity to give life" (1981: 275).

Just as beliefs and practices regarding fertility are culturally patterned, birth itself is a cultural production (Jordan 1978). As Romalis notes, "The act of giving birth to a child is never simply a physiological act but rather a performance defined by and enacted within a cultural context" (1981: 6). Even in advanced industrial societies such as the United States, childbirth experiences are molded by cultural, political, and economic processes (Oakley 1980; Martin 1987; Michaelson et al. 1988). Studying the cultural patterning of birth practices can illuminate the nature of domestic power relations and the roles of women as reproductive health specialists, and it can increase our understanding of the relations between men and women cross-culturally.

Davis-Floyd (in this book) illustrates how gender ideology is revealed in the management of American pregnancy and birth. Childbirth in the United States is standardized, and it is usually highly technological. Davis-Floyd argues that core beliefs in American society about science, technology, and patriarchy shape American birth. Through the routinizing of high-tech childbirth, a message is conveyed to American women that their bodies are defective machines and that they must therefore rely on more efficient machines to give birth. Drawing on centuries-old Western European notions of nature, culture, and society, today's dominant medical model regards the male body as the ideal body-machine, while the female body is considered abnormal and inherently inadequate. Hospital birth "rituals" work to transform the birthing woman into an "American mother," who has been socialized through the birth experience to accept core values of the society. Thus birth is a cultural rite of passage, in which the patriarchal status quo is reproduced and reaffirmed.

Although reproduction is culturally patterned, not all individuals in a society share reproductive goals. As Browner (in this book) points out, reproductive behavior is influenced by the interests of a woman's kin, neighbors, and other members of the community, and these interests may conflict. Government policies regarding the size and distribution of population may differ from the interests of reproducing women. Women's goals in turn may not be shared by their partners or other individuals and groups in the society. Browner examines the ways in which access to power in a society determines how conflicts concerning reproduction are carried out and dealt with by analyzing population practices in a Chinantec-Spanish-speaking township in Oaxaca, Mexico.

In this community the government's policy to encourage fertility reduction was imposed on a pre-existing conflict between the local community as a whole, which encouraged increased fertility, and women of the community, who sought to limit family size. Women and men manifested very different attitudes concerning fertility desires: Women sought much smaller families than men. As children increasingly attended school their economic benefits appeared slight to their mothers. Further, women viewed pregnancy as stressful and debilitating. Yet despite these negative views, women felt they could not ignore pressures to reproduce.

Such pressure came from community men, who valued a large population for the defense and well-being of the collectivity, and from women, who, while not desiring more children themselves, wanted other women to bear children in the interests of the group. In spite of the ease of obtaining government contraceptives, women rejected their use. In this cultural, political, and economic context, local women experienced conflict between personal desires to have few children and local pressures to be prolific.

Personal desires for children together with a pronatalist culture and advances in reproductive technology have generated consumer demand for surrogate motherhood in the United States, according to Ragoné's research (in this volume). Ragoné explores surrogates' stated motivations for becoming surrogate mothers as well as the details of their actual experiences. She describes surrogates' explanations as a cultural script reflecting widely accepted ideas about reproduction, motherhood, and family. In contrast to popular opinion, surrogates deny being motivated by financial gain. Rather, they conceptualize surrogacy as a "gift," a priceless donation to the commissioning couple. The apparent "commodification" of women's bodies represented in surrogate motherhood remains a troubling issue, however. In addition, the recent shift from traditional surrogacy (in which the surrogate contributes an ovum) to gestational surrogacy, where the surrogate gestates the couples' embryos, raises important questions about what constitutes "real" parenthood. Surrogacy challenges the Euro-American emphasis on genetic relatedness and the biological basis of kinship, and creates potential conflicts surrounding the claims of different kinds of biological and nonbiological mothers and fathers. Thus surrogacy poses profound challenges to our understandings of kinship, family, and reproduction.

Ginsburg (1987) also discusses reproduction as a domain of contested meanings, using the example of abortion in American culture. She suggests that the focus of this conflict of interests is the relationship between reproduction, nurturance, sex, and gender. Using life histories of pro-life and pro-choice activists in Fargo, North Dakota, she reveals how different historical conditions affect reproductive decisions. The activist protesters in Fargo vie for the power to define womanhood in light of a basic American cultural script in which, in the context of marriage, pregnancy results in childbirth and motherhood. Ginsburg argues that the struggle over abortion rights is a contest for control over the meanings attached to reproduction in America and suggests that "female social activism in the American context operates to mediate the construction of self and gender with larger social, political, and cultural processes."

Similarly, Whitbeck argues that controversy over abortion rights in the United States must be understood in relation to a cultural context that neglects women's experiences and the status of women as "moral individuals." Rather, American culture regards women and women's bodies as "property to be bartered, bestowed, and used by men" (Whitbeck 1983: 259). Concern with restricting access to abortions derives from the interest of the state or others in power to control women's bodies and their reproductive capacity (Whitbeck 1983: 260).

Ginsburg's research shows that pro-choice activists in Fargo cluster in a group born in the 1940s and influenced by the social movements of the 1960s and 1970s. These movements offered a new vision of a world defined not only by reproduction and motherhood, but filled with broader possibilities. Right-to-life women comprised one cohort born in the 1920s and a second cohort born in the 1950s. Many of these women experienced their commitment to the right-to-life movement as a sort of conversion, occurring at the time they moved out of the paid work force to stay home with children. Women's life histories indicate that embracing a pro-life or pro-choice position "emerges specifically out of a confluence of reproductive and generational experiences." Reproduction, often defined in American culture as a biological domain, takes on meaning within a historically specific set of cultural conditions.

Whereas Ginsburg discusses how abortion activists seek to define American womanhood in relation to cultural ideals of motherhood and nurturance, Gruenbaum (in this book) shows that cultural expectations of marriage and motherhood in Sudan form the context for the deeply embedded practice of female circumcision. Female circumcision is reported to exist in at least twenty-six countries, and estimates of the number of women of all ages who have been circumcised in Africa reach 100 million; other estimates suggest that as many as 5 million children are operated on each year (Kouba and Muasher 1985; Sargent 1991; Toubia 1994). The various forms of female circumcision present serious risks, such as infection and hemorrhage at the time of the procedure, and future risks to childbearing; therefore, social scientists, feminists, and public health organizations have opposed the practices. However, as Gruenbaum observes, female circumcision "forms part of a complex sociocultural arrangement of female subjugation in a strongly patrilineal, patriarchal society" and continues to be most strongly defended by women, who carry out the practice.

Women in Sudan derive status and security as wives and mothers. Virginity is a prerequisite for marriage, and in this context clitoridectomy and infibulation, the major forms of circumcision, are perceived as protecting morality. Thus, these practices persist because they are linked to the important goal of maintaining the reputation and marriageability of daughters. Forty years of policy formulated by the Sudanese government and by international health organizations emphasizing the physically dangerous dimensions of female circumcision and prohibiting the most extensive forms of the practice have not resulted in its elimination.

As Gruenbaum notes, clitoridectomy and infibulation are considered by Sudanese men and women to enhance a woman's ability to please her husband sexually, while attenuating inappropriate sexual desire outside marriage. Insofar as women are dependent on husbands for social and economic support and have few opportunities for educational advancement or viable employment, female circumcision is unlikely to be eradicated on medical grounds.

Miller's discussion of female infanticide and child neglect in North India (in this book) is also set in a strongly patrilineal, patriarchal society and dramatically illustrates the links between gender ideology, reproduction, and health. In North India family survival depends on the reproduction of sons for the rural labor force, and preference for male children is evident in substantial ethnographic data documenting discrimination against girls. In this region preferences for male children result in celebrations at the birth of a boy, while a girl's birth goes unremarked. Sex-selective child care and female infanticide also indicate cultural favoring of male children.

Reports of female infanticide in India have occurred since the eighteenth century. There is evidence that a few villages in North India have never raised one daughter. In spite of legislation prohibiting female infanticide, the practice has not totally disappeared, although Miller argues that direct female infanticide has been replaced by indirect infanticide or neglect of female children. Indirect female infanticide is accomplished by nutritional and health care deprivation of female children, a phenomenon also discussed by Charlton (1984). Miller argues that the strong preference for sons in rural North India is related to their economic and social functions.

The preference for male children has important repercussions in the increasing demand for abortion of female fetuses following amniocentesis. For example, in one clinic in North India 95 percent of female fetuses were aborted following prenatal sex determination. Thus, new reproductive technologies such as amniocentesis are seen to be manipulated by patriarchal interests. Miller suggests that, ultimately, understanding the patriarchal culture of north India may help promote more effective health care and enhanced survival chances for female children.

The readings in this section illustrate the ways in which human reproductive behavior is socially constructed and influenced by economic and political processes (Ginsburg and Rapp 1991). Rather than perceiving reproductive health in a narrow biological or purely personal framework, cross-cultural research suggests that women's health needs should be addressed in the context of their multifaceted productive, reproductive, and social roles. Consequently, decisions about such reproductive health issues as family size and composition are never left to the individual woman, but are influenced by kin, community, and state interests. These interests are often contested with the introduction of new reproductive technologies enabling sophisticated prenatal testing, treatment for infertility, and surrogate mothering. As these technologies increasingly spread throughout the world, their availability will raise important questions regarding cultural definitions of parenting, concepts of personhood, and gender roles and relations.

REFERENCES

Browner, Carole and Carolyn Sargent. 1990. "Anthropology and Studies of Human Reproduction." In Thomas M. Johnson and Carolyn Sargent (eds.). *Medical Anthropology: Contemporary Theory and Method,* pp. 215–229. New York: Praeger Publishers.

Charlton, Sue Ellen M. 1984. *Women in Third World Development.* Boulder, CO: Westview Press.

Collier, Jane F. and Michelle Z. Rosaldo. 1981. "Politics and Gender in Simple Societies." In Sherry B. Ortner and Harriet Whitehead (eds.). *Sexual Meanings: The Cultural Construction of Gender and Sexuality,* pp. 275–329. Cambridge: Cambridge University Press.

Davis-Floyd, Robbie and Carolyn Sargent. 1997. "Introduction: The Anthropology of Birth." In Robbie Davis-Floyd and Carolyn Sargent (eds.). *Childbirth and Authoritative Knowledge*, pp. 1–51. Berkeley: University of California Press.

Ford, Clellan Stearns. 1964. "A Comparative Study of Human Reproduction." *Yale University Publications in Anthropology* No. 32: Human Relations Area Files Press.

Ginsberg, Faye. 1987. Procreation Stories: Reproduction, Nuturance, and Procreation in Life Narratives of Abortion Activists. *American Ethnologist* 14(4): 623–636.

Ginsburg, Faye and Rayna Rapp. 1991. "The Politics of Reproduction." *Annual Review of Anthropology* 20: 311–43.

——— (eds.). 1995. *Conceiving the New World Order: The Global Politics of Reproduction*. Berkeley: University of California Press.

Jordan, Brigitte. 1978. *Birth in Four Cultures*. Montreal: Eden Press Women's Publications.

Kouba, Leonard J. and Judith Muasher. 1985. "Female Circumcision in Africa: An Overview." *African Studies Review* 28 (1): 95–110.

Malinowski, Bronislaw. 1932. *The Sexual Life of Savages in Northwestern Melanesia*. London: Routledge and Kegan Paul.

Martin, Emily. 1987. *The Woman in the Body: A Cultural Analysis of Reproduction*. Boston: Beacon Press.

Michaelson, Karen, et al. 1988. *Childbirth in America: Anthropological Perspectives*. South Hadley, MA: Bergin and Garvey.

Montagu, M. F. Ashley. 1949. "Embryology from Antiquity to the End of the 18th Century." Ciba Foundation Symposium 10 (4): 994–1008.

Oakley, Ann. 1980. *Women Confined: Towards a Sociology of Childbirth*. New York: Schocken Books.

Romalis, Shelly (ed.). 1981. *Childbirth: Alternatives to Medical Control*. Austin: University of Texas Press.

Rubinstein, Robert A. and Sandra D. Lane. 1991. "International Health and Development." In Thomas M. Johnson and Carolyn Sargent (eds.). *Medical Anthropology: Contemporary Theory and Method*, pp. 367–391. New York: Praeger Publishers.

Sargent, Carolyn. 1982. *The Cultural Context of Therapeutic Choice*. Dordrecht, Holland: D. Reidel Publishing Company.

———. 1991. "Confronting Patriarchy: The Potential for Advocacy in Medical Anthropology." *Medical Anthropology Quarterly* 5 (1): 24–25.

Sargent, Carolyn F. and Caroline B. Brettell (eds.). 1996. *Gender and Health: An International Perspective*. Upper Saddle River, NJ: Prentice Hall, Inc.

Spencer, Robert. 1949–1950. "Introduction to Primitive Obstetrics." Ciba Foundation Symposium 11 (3): 1158–88.

Toubia, Nahid, M.D. 1994. "Female Circumcision as a Public Health Issue. *The New England Journal of Medicine* 331(11): 712–716.

Vieille, Paul. 1978. "Iranian Women in Family Alliance and Sexual Politics." In Lois Beck and Nikki Keddie (eds.). *Women in the Muslim World*, pp. 451–472. Cambridge: Harvard University Press.

Whitbeck, Caroline. 1983. "The Moral Implications of Regarding Women as People: New Perspectives on Pregnancy and Personhood." In William B. Bondeson et al. (eds.). *Abortion and the Status of the Fetus*, pp. 247–272. Dordrecht, Holland: D. Reidel Publishing.

Gender and Ritual: Giving Birth the American Way

Robbie E. Davis-Floyd

Although the array of new technologies that radically alter the nature of human reproduction is exponentially increasing, childbirth is still an entirely gendered phenomenon. Because only women have babies, the way a society treats pregnancy and childbirth reveals a great deal about the way that society treats women. The experience of childbirth is unique for every woman, and yet in the United States childbirth is treated in a highly standardized way. No matter how long or short, how easy or hard their labors, the vast majority of American women are hooked up to an electronic fetal monitor and an IV (intravenously administered fluids and/or medication), are encouraged to use pain-relieving drugs, receive an episiotomy (a surgical incision in the vagina to widen the birth outlet in order to prevent tearing) at the moment of birth, and are separated from their babies shortly after birth. Most women also receive doses of the synthetic hormone pitocin to speed their labors, and they give birth flat on their backs. Nearly one-quarter of babies are delivered by Cesarean section.

Many Americans, including most of the doctors and nurses who attend birth, view these procedures as medical necessities. Yet anthropologists regularly describe other, less technological ways to give birth. For example, the Mayan Indians of Highland Chiapas hold onto a rope while squatting for birth, a position that is far more beneficial than the flat-on-your-back-with-your-feet-in-stirrups (lithotomy) position. Mothers in many low-technology cultures give birth sitting, squatting, semi-reclining in their hammocks, or on their hands and knees, and are nurtured through the pain of labor by experienced midwives and supportive female relatives. What then might explain the standardization and technical elaboration of the American birthing process?

One answer emerges from the field of symbolic anthropology. Early in this century, Arnold van Gennep noticed that in many societies around the world, major life transitions are ritualized. These cultural *rites of passage* make it appear that society itself effects the transformation of the individual. Could this explain the standardization of American birth? I believe the answer is yes.

I came to this conclusion as a result of a study I conducted of American birth between 1983 and 1991. I interviewed over 100 mothers, as well as many of the obstetricians, nurses, childbirth educators, and midwives who attended them.[1] While poring over my interviews, I began to understand that the forces shaping American hospital birth are invisible to us because they stem from the conceptual foundations of our society. I realized that American society's deepest beliefs center on science, technology, patriarchy, and the institutions that control and disseminate them, and that there could be no better transmitter of these core values and beliefs than the hospital procedures so salient in American birth. Through these procedures, American women are repeatedly told, in dozens of visible and invisible ways, that their bodies are defective machines incapable of giving birth without the assistance of these other, male-created, more perfect machines.

RITES OF PASSAGE

A *ritual* is a patterned, repetitive, and symbolic enactment of a cultural belief or value; its primary purpose is alignment of the belief sys-

Copyright © 1994 Robbie E. Davis-Floyd.

447

tem of the individual with that of society. A *rite of passage* is a series of rituals that move individuals from one social state or status to another as, for example, from girlhood to womanhood, boyhood to manhood, or from the womb to the world of culture. Rites of passage transform both society's perception of individuals and individuals' perceptions of themselves.

Rites of passage generally consist of three stages, originally outlined by van Gennep: (1) *separation* of the individuals from their preceding social state; (2) a period of *transition* in which they are neither one thing nor the other; and (3) an *integration* phase, in which, through various rites of incorporation, they are absorbed into their new social state. In the year-long pregnancy/childbirth rite of passage in American society, the separation phase begins with the woman's first awareness of pregnancy; the transition stage lasts until several days after the birth; and the integration phase ends gradually in the newborn's first few months of life, when the new mother begins to feel that, as one woman put it, she is "mainstreaming it again."

Victor Turner, an anthropologist famous for his writings on ritual, pointed out that the most important feature of all rites of passage is that they place their participants in a transitional realm that has few of the attributes of the past or coming state. Existing in such a non-ordinary realm, he argues, facilitates the gradual psychological opening of the initiates to profound interior change. In many initiation rites involving major transitions into new social roles (such as military basic training), ritualized physical and mental hardships serve to break down initiates' belief systems, leaving them open to new learning and the construction of new cognitive categories.

Birth is an ideal candidate for ritualization of this sort, and is, in fact, used in many societies as a model for structuring other rites of passage. By making the naturally transformative process of birth into a cultural rite of passage, a society can ensure that its basic values will be transmitted to the three new members born out of the birth process: the new baby, the woman reborn into the new social role of mother, and the man reborn as father. The new mother especially must be very clear about these values, as she is generally the one primarily responsible for teaching them to her children, who will be society's new members and the guarantors of its future.

THE CHARACTERISTICS OF RITUAL

Some primary characteristics of ritual are particularly relevant to understanding how the initiatory process of cognitive restructuring is accomplished in hospital birth. We will examine each of these characteristics in order to understand (1) how ritual works; (2) how the natural process of childbirth is transformed in the United States into a cultural rite of passage; and (3) how that transformation works to cement the patriarchal status quo.

Symbolism

Above all else, ritual is symbolic. Ritual works by sending messages in the form of symbols to those who perform and those who observe it. A *symbol* is an object, idea, or action that is loaded with cultural meaning. The left hemisphere of the human brain decodes and analyzes straightforward verbal messages, enabling the recipient to either accept or reject their content. Complex ritual symbols, on the other hand, are received by the right hemisphere of the brain, where they are interpreted holistically. Instead of being analyzed intellectually, a symbol's message will be *felt* through the body and the emotions. Thus, even though recipients may be unaware of incorporating the symbol's message, its ultimate effect may be extremely powerful.

Routine obstetric procedures are highly symbolic. For example, to be seated in a wheelchair upon entering the hospital, as many laboring women are, is to receive through their bodies the symbolic message that they are disabled; to then be put to bed is to receive the symbolic message that they are sick. Although no one pronounces, "You are disabled; you are sick," such graphic demonstrations of disability and illness can be far more powerful than words. Suzanne Sampson told me:

> I can remember just almost being in tears by the way they would wheel you in. I would come into the hospital, on top of this, breathing, you know, all in control. And they slap you in a wheelchair! It made me suddenly feel like maybe I wasn't in control any more.

The intravenous drips commonly attached to the hands or arms of birthing women make a powerful symbolic statement: They are umbilical cords to the hospital. The cord connecting her body to the fluid-filled bottle places the woman in the same relation to the hospital as the baby in her womb is to her. By making her dependent on the institution for her life, the IV conveys to her one of the most profound messages of her initiation experience: In American society, we are all dependent on institutions for our lives. The message is even more compelling in her case, for *she* is the real giver of life. Society and its institutions cannot exist unless women give birth, yet the birthing woman in the hospital is shown, not that *she* gives life, but rather that the *institution* does.

A Cognitive Matrix

A *matrix* (from the Latin *mater,* mother), like a womb, is something from within which something else comes. Rituals are not arbitrary; they come from within the belief system of a group. Their primary purpose is to enact, and thereby, to transmit that belief system into the emotions, minds, and bodies of their participants. Thus, analysis of a culture's rituals can lead to a profound understanding of its belief system.

Analysis of the rituals of hospital birth reveals their cognitive matrix to be the *technocratic model* of reality which forms the philosophical basis of both Western biomedicine and American society. All cultures develop technologies. But most do not supervalue their technologies in the particular way that we do. This point is argued

clearly by Peter C. Reynolds (1991) in his book *Stealing Fire: The Mythology of the Technocracy* (a *technocracy* is a hierarchical, bureaucratic society driven by an ideology of technological progress). There he discusses how we "improve upon" nature by controlling it through technology. The technocratic model is the paradigm that charters such behavior. Its early forms were originally developed in the 1600s by Descartes, Bacon, and Hobbes, among others. This model assumes that the universe is mechanistic, following predictable laws that the enlightened can discover through science and manipulate through technology, in order to decrease their dependence on nature. In this model, the human body is viewed as a machine that can be taken apart and put back together to ensure proper functioning. In the seventeenth century, the practical utility of this body-as-machine metaphor lay in its separation of body, mind, and soul. The soul could be left to religion, the mind to the philosophers, and the body could be opened up to scientific investigation.

The dominant religious belief systems of Western Europe at that time held that women were inferior to men—closer to nature and feebler both in body and intellect. Consequently, the men who developed the idea of the body-as-machine also firmly established the male body as the prototype of this machine. Insofar as it deviated from the male standard, the female body was regarded as abnormal, inherently defective, and dangerously under the influence of nature.

The metaphor of the body-as-machine and the related image of the female body as a defective machine eventually formed the philosophical foundations of modern obstetrics. Wide cultural acceptance of these metaphors accompanied the demise of the midwife and the rise of the male-attended, mechanically manipulated birth. Obstetrics was thus enjoined by its own conceptual origins to develop tools and technologies for the manipulation and improvement of the inherently defective, and therefore anomalous and dangerous, process of birth.

The rising science of obstetrics ultimately accomplished this goal by adopting the model of the assembly-line production of goods as its template for hospital birth. Accordingly, a woman's reproductive tract came to be treated like a birthing machine by skilled technicians working under semiflexible timetables to meet production and quality control demands. As one fourth-year resident observed:

> We shave 'em, we prep 'em, we hook 'em up to the IV and administer sedation. We deliver the baby, it goes to the nursery, and the mother goes to her room. There's no room for niceties around here. We just move 'em right on through. It's hard not to see it like an assembly line.

The hospital itself is a highly sophisticated technocratic factory; the more technology the hospital has to offer, the better it is considered to be. Because it is an institution, the hospital constitutes a more significant social unit than an individual or a family. Therefore it can require that the birth process conform more to institutional than personal needs. As one resident explained,

> There is a set, established routine for doing things, usually for the convenience of the doctors and the nurses, and the laboring woman is someone you work around, rather than with.

The most desirable end-product of the birth process is the new social member, the baby; the new mother is a secondary by-product. One obstetrician commented, "It was what we were all trained to always go after—the perfect body. That's what we were trained to produce. The quality of the mother's experience—we rarely thought about that."

Repetition and Redundancy

Ritual is marked by repetition and redundancy. For maximum effectiveness, a ritual concentrates on sending one basic set of messages, repeating it over and over again in different forms. Hospital birth takes place in a series of ritual procedures, many of which convey the same message in different forms. The open and exposing hospital gown, the ID bracelet, the intravenous fluid, the bed in which she is placed—all these convey to the laboring woman that she is dependent on the institution.

She is also reminded in myriad ways of the potential defectiveness of her birthing machine. These include periodic and sometimes continuous electronic monitoring of that machine, frequent manual examinations of her cervix to make sure that it is dilating on schedule, and, if it isn't, administration of the synthetic hormone pitocin to speed up labor so that birth can take place within the required 26 hours.[2] All three of these procedures convey the same messages over and over: *Time is important, you must produce on time, and you cannot do that without technological assistance because your machine is defective.* In the technocracy, we supervalue time. It is only fitting that messages about time's importance should be repeatedly conveyed during the births of new social members.

Cognitive Reduction

In any culture, the intellectual abilities of ritual participants are likely to differ, often markedly. It is not practical for society to design different rituals for persons of different levels of intellectual ability. So ritual utilizes specific techniques, such as rhythmic repetition, to reduce all participants to the same narrower level of cognitive functioning. This low level involves thinking in either/or patterns that do not allow for consideration of options or alternative views.

Four techniques are often employed by ritual to accomplish this end. One is the *repetition* already discussed above. A second is *hazing,* which is familiar to undergraduates who undergo fraternity initiation rites but is also part of rites of passage all over the world. A third is *strange-making*—making the commonplace appear strange by juxtaposing it with the unfamiliar. Fourth is *symbolic inversion*—metaphorically turning things upside-down and inside-out to generate, in a phrase coined by Roger Abrahams (1973), "The power attendant upon confusion."

For example, in the rite of passage of military basic training, the initiate's normal patterns of action and thought are turned topsy-turvy. He is made strange to himself: His head is shaved, so that he does not even recognize himself in the mirror. He must give up his clothes, those expressions of his past individual identity and personality, and put on a uniform identical to that of the other initiates. Constant and apparently meaningless hazing, such as orders to dig six ditches and then fill them in, further breaks down his cognitive structure. Then through repetitive and highly symbolic rituals, such as sleeping with his rifle, the basic values, beliefs, and practices of the Marines are incorporated into his body and his mind.

In medical school and again in residency, the same ritual techniques that transform a youth into a Marine are employed to transform college students into physicians. Reduced from the high status of graduate to the lowly status of first-year medical student, initiates are subjected to hazing techniques of rote memorization of endless facts and formulas, absurdly long hours of work, and intellectual and sensory overload. As one physician explained:

> You go through, in a six-week course, a thousand-page book. You have pop quizzes in two or three courses every day the first year. We'd get up around 6, attend classes till 5, go home and eat, then head back to school and be in anatomy lab working with a cadaver, or something, until 1 or 2 in the morning, and then go home and get a couple of hours sleep, and then go out again.

Subjected to such a process, medical students often gradually lose any broadminded goals of "helping humanity" they had upon entering medical school. A successful rite of passage produces new professional values structured in accordance with the technocratic and scientific values of the dominant medical system. The emotional impact of this cognitive narrowing is aptly summarized by a former resident:

> Most of us went into medical school with pretty humanitarian ideals. I know I did. But the whole process of medical education makes you inhuman.... you forget about the rest of life. By the time you get to residency, you end up not caring about anything beyond the latest techniques and most sophisticated tests.

Likewise, the birthing woman is socialized by ritual techniques of cognitive reduction. She is made strange to herself by being dressed in a hospital gown, tagged with an ID bracelet, and by the shaving or clipping of her pubic hair, which symbolically de-sexualizes the lower portion of her body, returning it to a conceptual state of childishness. (In many cultures, sexuality and hair are symbolically linked.) Labor itself is painful, and is often rendered more so by the hazing technique of frequent and very painful insertion of someone's fingers into her vagina to see how far her cervix has dilated. This technique also functions as a strange-making device. Since almost any nurse or resident in need of practice may check her cervix, the birthing woman's most private parts are symbolically inverted into institutional property. One respondent's obstetrician observed, "It's a wonder you didn't get an infection, with so many people sticking their hands inside of you."

Cognitive Stabilization

When humans are subjected to extremes of stress and pain, they may become unreasonable and out of touch with reality. Ritual assuages this condition by giving people a conceptual handle-hold to keep them from "falling apart" or "losing it." When the airplane starts to falter, even passengers who don't go to church are likely to pray! Ritual mediates between cognition and chaos by making reality appear to conform to accepted cognitive categories. In other words, to perform a ritual in the face of chaos is to restore order to the world.

Labor subjects most women to extremes of pain, which are often intensified by the alien and often unsupportive hospital environment. They look to hospital rituals to relieve the distress resulting from their pain and fear. They utilize breathing rituals taught in hospital-sponsored childbirth education classes for cognitive stabilization. They turn to drugs for pain relief, and to the reassuring presence of medical technology for relief from fear. LeAnn Kellog expressed it this way:

> I was terrified when my daughter was born. I just knew I was going to split open and bleed to death right there on the table, but she was coming so fast, they didn't have any time to do anything to me. . . . I like Cesarean sections, because you don't have to be afraid.

When you come from within a belief system, its rituals will comfort and calm you. Accordingly, those women in my study who were in basic agreement with the technocratic model of birth before going into the hospital (70%) expressed general satisfaction with their hospital births.

Order, Formality, and a Sense of Inevitability

Its exaggerated and precise order and formality set ritual apart from other modes of social interaction, enabling it to establish an atmosphere that feels both inevitable and inviolate. To perform a series of rituals is to feel oneself locking onto a set of "cosmic gears" that will safely crank the individual through danger to safety. For example, Trobriand sea fishermen described by anthropologist Bronislaw Malinowski (1954) regularly performed an elaborate series of rituals on the beach before embarking. The fishermen believed that these rituals, when carried out with precision, would obligate the gods of the sea to do their part to bring the fishermen safely home. Likewise, obstetricians, and many birthing women, feel that correct performance of standardized procedures ought to result in a healthy baby. Such rituals generate in humans a sense of confidence that

makes it easier to face the challenge and caprice of nature.

When women who have placed their faith in the technocratic model are denied its rituals, they often react with fear and a feeling of being neglected:

> My husband and I got to the hospital, and we thought they would take care of everything. I kept sending my husband out to ask them to give me something for the pain, to check me, but they were short-staffed and they just ignored me until the shift changed in the morning.

Hospital rituals such as electronic monitoring work to give the laboring woman a sense that society is using the best it has to offer—the full force of its technology—to inevitably ensure that she will have a safe birth.

However, once those "cosmic gears" have been set into motion, there is often no stopping them. The very inevitability of hospital procedures makes them almost antithetical to the possibility of normal, natural birth. A "cascade of intervention" occurs when one obstetric procedure alters the natural birthing process, causing complications, and so inexorably "necessitates" the next procedure, and the next. Many of the women in my study experienced such a "cascade" when they received some form of pain relief, such as an epidural, which slowed their labor. Then pitocin was administered through the IV to speed up the labor, but pitocin very suddenly induced longer and stronger contractions. Unprepared for the additional pain, the women asked for more pain relief, which ultimately necessitated more pitocin. Pitocin-induced contractions, together with the fact that the mother must lie flat on her back because of the electronic monitor belts strapped around her stomach, can cause the supply of blood and oxygen to the fetus to drop, affecting the fetal heart rate. In response to the "distress" registered on the fetal monitor, an emergency Cesarean is performed.

Acting, Stylization, Staging

Ritual's set-apartness is enhanced by the fact that it is usually highly stylized and self-consciously acted, like a part in a play. Most of us can easily accept this view of the careful performances of TV evangelists, but it may come as a surprise that those who perform the rituals of hospital birth are often aware of their dramatic elements. The physician becomes the protagonist. The woman's body is the stage upon which he performs, often for an appreciative audience of medical students, residents, and nurses. Here is how one obstetrician played to a student audience observing the delivery he was performing:

> "In honest-to-God natural conditions babies were *sometimes* born without tearing the perineum and without an episiotomy, but without artificial things like anesthesia and episiotomy, the muscle is torn apart and if it is not cut, it is usually not repaired. Even today, if there is no episiotomy and repair, those women quite often develop a rectocoele and a relaxed vaginal floor. This is what I call the saggy, baggy bottom." (Laughter by the students. A student nurse asks if exercise doesn't help strengthen the perineum.) "No, exercises may be for the birds, but they're not for bottoms.... When the woman is bearing down, the leveator muscles of the perineum contract too. This means the baby is caught between the diaphragm and the perineum. Consequently, anesthesia and episiotomy will reduce the pressure on the head, and hopefully, produce more Republicans." (More laughter from the students) (Shaw 1974: 90).

Cognitive Transformation

The goal of most initiatory rites of passage is cognitive transformation. It occurs when the symbolic messages of ritual fuse with individual emotion and belief, and the individual's entire cognitive structure, reorganize around the newly internalized symbolic complex. The following quote from a practicing obstetrician presents the outcome for him of such transformative learning:

> I think my training was valuable. The philosophy was one of teaching one way to do it, and that was the right way.... I like the set hard way. I like the riverbanks that confine you in a direction.... You learn one thing real well, and that's *the* way.

For both nascent physicians and nascent mothers, cognitive transformation of the initiate occurs when reality as presented by the technocratic model, and reality as the initiate perceives it, become one and the same. This process is gradual. Routine obstetric procedures cumulatively map the technocratic model of birth onto the birthing woman's perceptions of her labor experience. They align her belief system with that of society.

Take the way many mothers come to think about the electronic fetal monitor, for example. The monitor is a machine that uses ultrasound to measure the strength of the mother's contractions and the rate of the baby's heartbeat through electrodes belted onto the mother's abdomen. This machine has become *the* symbol of high technology hospital birth. Observers and participants alike report that the monitor, once attached, becomes the focal point of the labor.[3] Nurses, physicians, husbands, and even the mother herself become visually and conceptually glued to the machine, which then shapes their perceptions and interpretations of the birth process. Diana Crosse described her experience this way:

> As soon as I got hooked up to the monitor, all everyone did was stare at it. The nurses didn't even look at me anymore when they came into the room—they went straight to the monitor. I got the weirdest feeling that *it* was having the baby, not me.

This statement illustrates the successful conceptual fusion between the woman's perceptions of her birth experience and the technocratic model. So thoroughly was this model mapped on to her psyche that she began to feel that the machine was having the baby, that she was a mere onlooker. Soon after the monitor was in place, she requested a Cesarean section, declaring that there was "no more point in trying."

Consider the visual and kinesthetic images that the laboring woman experiences—herself in bed, in a hospital gown, staring up at an IV pole, bag, and cord, and down at a steel bed and a huge belt encircling her waist. Her entire sensory field conveys one overwhelming message about our culture's deepest values and beliefs: Technology is supreme, and the individual is utterly dependent upon it.

Internalizing the technocratic model, women come to accept the notion that the female body is inherently defective. This notion then shapes their perceptions of the labor experience, as exemplified by Merry Simpson's story:

> It seemed as though my uterus had suddenly tired! When the nurses in attendance noted a contraction building on the recorder, they instructed me to begin pushing, not waiting for the *urge* to push, so that by the time the urge pervaded, I invariably had no strength remaining but was left gasping and dizzy.... I felt suddenly depressed by the fact that labor, which had progressed so uneventfully up to this point, had now become unproductive.

Note that she does not say "The nurses had me pushing too soon," but "My uterus had tired," and labor had "become unproductive." These responses reflect her internalization of the technocratic tenet that when something goes wrong, it is her body's fault.

Affectivity and Intensification

Rituals tend to intensify toward a climax. Behavioral psychologists have long understood that people are far more likely to remember, and to absorb lessons from, those events that carry an emotional charge. The order and stylization of ritual, combined with its rhythmic repetitiveness and the intensification of its messages, methodically create just the sort of highly charged emotional atmosphere that works to ensure long-term learning.

As the moment of birth approaches, the number of ritual procedures performed upon the woman will intensify toward the climax of birth, whether or not her condition warrants such intervention. For example, once the woman's cervix reaches full dilation (10 cm), the nursing staff immediately begins to exhort the woman to push with each contraction, whether or not she actually feels the urge to push. When delivery is imminent, the woman must be transported, often with a great deal of drama and haste, down the hall to the delivery room. Lest the baby be born *en route,* the laboring woman is then exhorted, with equal vigor, *not* to push. Such commands constitute a complete denial of the natural rhythms of the woman's body. They signal that her labor is a mechanical event and that she is subordinate to the institution's expectations and schedule. Similar high drama will pervade the rest of her birthing experience.

Preservation of the Status Quo

A major function of ritual is cultural preservation. Through explicit enactment of a culture's belief system, ritual works both to preserve and to transmit the culture. Preserving the culture includes perpetuating its power structure, so it is usually the case that those in positions of power will have unique control over ritual performance. They will utilize the effectiveness of ritual to reinforce both their own importance and the importance of the belief and value system that legitimizes their positions.

In spite of tremendous advances in equality for women, the United States is still a patriarchy. It is no cultural accident that 99 percent of American women give birth in hospitals, where only physicians, most of whom are male, have final authority over the performance of birth rituals—an authority that reinforces the cultural privileging of patriarchy for both mothers and their medical attendants.

Nowhere is this reality more visible than in the lithotomy position. Despite years of effort on the part of childbirth activists, including many obstetricians, the majority of American women still give birth lying flat on their backs. This position is physiologically dysfunctional. It compresses major blood vessels, lowering the mother's circulation and thus the baby's oxygen supply. It increases the need for forceps because it both narrows the pelvic outlet and ensures that the baby, who must follow the curve of the birth canal, quite literally will be born heading upward, against gravity. This lithotomy position completes the process of symbolic inversion that has been in motion ever since the woman was put into that "upside-down" hospital gown. Her normal bodily patterns are turned, quite literally, upside-down—her legs are in the air, her vagina totally exposed. As the ultimate symbolic inversion, it is ritually appropriate that this position be reserved for the peak tranformational moments of the initiation experience—the birth itself. The doctor—society's official representative—stands in control not at the mother's head nor at her side, but at her bottom, where the baby's head is beginning to emerge.

Structurally speaking, this puts the woman's vagina where her head should be. Such total inversion is perfectly appropriate from a social perspective, as the technocratic model promises us that eventually we will be able to grow babies in machines—that is, have them with our cultural heads instead of our natural bottoms. In our culture, "up" is good and "down" is bad, so the babies born of science and technology must be delivered "up" toward the positively valued cultural world, instead of down toward the negatively valued natural world. Interactionally, the obstetrician is "up" and the birthing woman is "down," an inversion that speaks eloquently to her of her powerlessness and of the power of society at the supreme moment of her own individual transformation.

The episiotomy performed by the obstetrician just before birth also powerfully enacts the status quo in American society. This procedure, performed on over 90 percent of first-time mothers as they give birth, expresses the value and importance of one of our technocratic society's most fundamental markers—the straight line. Through episiotomies, physicians can deconstruct the vagina (stretchy, flexible, part-circular and part-formless, feminine, creative, sexual, non-linear), then reconstruct it in accordance with our cultural belief and value system. Doctors are taught (incorrectly) that straight cuts heal faster than the small jagged tears that sometimes occur during birth. They learn that straight cuts will prevent such tears, but in fact, episiotomies often cause severe tearing that would not otherwise occur (Klein 1992; Shiono et al. 1990; Thorp and Bowes 1989; Wilcox et al. 1989[4]). These teachings dramatize our Western belief in the superiority of culture over nature. Because it virtually does not exist in nature, the line is most useful in aiding us in our constant conceptual efforts to separate ourselves from nature.

Moreover, since surgery constitutes the ultimate form of manipulation of the human body-machine, it is the most highly valued form of medicine. Routinizing the episiotomy, and increasingly, the Cesarean section, has served both to legitimize and to raise the status of obstetrics as a profession, by ensuring that childbirth will be not a natural but a surgical procedure.

Effecting Social Change

Paradoxically, ritual, with all of its insistence on continuity and order, can be an important factor not only in individual transformation but also in social change. New belief and value systems are most effectively spread through new rituals designed to enact and transmit them; entrenched belief and value systems are most effectively altered through alterations in the rituals that enact them.

Nine percent of my interviewees entered the hospital determined to avoid technocratic rituals in order to have "completely natural childbirth," yet ended up with highly technocratic births. These nine women experienced extreme cognitive dissonance between their previously held self-images and those internalized in the hospital. Most of them suffered severe emotional wounding and short-term post-partum depression as a result. But 15 percent did achieve their goal of natural childbirth, thereby avoiding conceptual fusion with the technocratic model. These women were personally empowered by their birth experiences. They tended to view technology as a resource that they could choose to utilize or ignore, and often consciously subverted their socialization process by replacing technocratic symbols with self-empowering alternatives. For example, they wore their own clothes and ate their own food, rejecting the hospital gown and the IV. They walked the halls instead of going to bed. They chose perineal massage instead of episiotomy, and gave birth like "primitives," sitting up, squatting, or on their hands and knees. One of them, confronted with the wheelchair, said "I don't need this," and used it as a luggage cart. This rejection of customary ritual elements is an exceptionally powerful way to induce change, as it takes advantage of an already charged and dramatic situation.

During the 1970s and early 1980s, the conceptual hegemony of the technocratic model in the hospital was severely challenged by the natural childbirth movement which these 24 women represent. Birth activists succeeded in getting hospitals to allow fathers into labor and delivery rooms, mothers to birth consciously (without being put to sleep), and mothers and babies to room together after birth. They fought for women to have the right to birth without drugs or interventions, to walk around or even be in water during labor (in some hospitals, Jacuzzis were installed). Prospects for change away from the technocratic model of birth by the 1990s seemed bright.

Changing a society's belief and value system by changing the rituals that enact it is possible, but not easy. To counter attempts at change, individuals in positions of authority often intensify the rituals that support the status quo. Thus a response to the threat posed by the natural childbirth movement was to intensify the use of high technology in hospital birth. During the 1980s, periodic electronic monitoring of nearly all women became standard procedure, the epidural rate shot up to 80 percent, and the Cesarean rate rose to nearly 25 percent. Part of the impetus for this technocratic intensification is the increase in malpractice suits against physicians. The threat of lawsuit forces doctors to practice conservatively—that is, in strict accordance with technocratic standards. As one of them explained.

Certainly I've changed the way I practice since malpractice became an issue. I do more C-sections ... and more and more tests to cover myself. More expensive stuff. We don't do risky things that women ask for—we're very conservative in our approach to everything.... In 1970 before all this came up, my C-section rate was around 4 percent. It has gradually climbed every year since then. In 1985 it was 16 percent, then in 1986 it was 23 percent.

The money goes where the values lie. From this macro-cultural perspective, the increase in malpractice suits emerges as society's effort to make sure that its representatives, the obstetricians, perpetuate our technocratic core value system by continuing through birth rituals to transmit that system. Its perpetuation seems imperative, for in our technology we see the promise of our eventual transcendence of bodily and earthly limitations—already we replace body parts with computerized devices, grow babies in test tubes, build space stations, and continue to pollute the environment in the expectation that someone will develop the technologies to clean it up!

We are all complicitors in our technocratic system, as we have so very much invested in it. Just as that system has given us increasing control over the natural environment, so it has also given not only doctors but also women increasing control over biology and birth. Contemporary middle-class women *do* have much greater say over what will be done to them during birth than their mothers, most of whom gave birth during the 1950s and 1960s under general anesthesia. When what they demand is in accord with technocratic values, they have a much greater chance of getting it than their sisters have of achieving natural childbirth. Even as hospital birth still perpetuates partriarchy by treating women's bodies as defective machines, it now also reflects women's greater autonomy by allowing them conceptual separation from those defective machines.

Epidural anesthesia is administered in about 80 percent of American hospital births.

So common is its use that many childbirth educators are calling the 1990s the age of the "epidural epidemic." As the epidural numbs the birthing woman, eliminating the pain of childbirth, it also graphically demonstrates to her through lived experience the truth of the Cartesian maxim that mind and body are separate, that the biological realm can be completely cut off from the realm of the intellect and the emotions. The epidural is thus the perfect technocratic tool, serving the interests of the technocratic model by transmitting it, and of women choosing to give birth under that model, by enabling them to use it to divorce themselves from their biology:

> Ultimately the decision to have the epidural and the Cesarean while I was in labor was mine. I told my doctor I'd had enough of this labor business and I'd like to ... get it over with. So he whisked me off to the delivery room and we did it. (Elaine)

For many women, the epidural provides a means by which they can actively witness birth while avoiding "dropping into biology." Explained Joanne, "I'm not real fond of things that remind me I'm a biological creature—I prefer to think and be an intellectual emotional person." Such women tended to define their bodies as tools, vehicles for their minds. They did not enjoy "giving in to biology" to be pregnant, and were happy to be liberated from biology during birth. And they welcomed advances in birth technologies as extensions of their own ability to control nature.

In dramatic contrast, six of my interviewees (6 percent), insisting that "I am my body," rejected the technocratic model altogether. They chose to give birth at home under an alternative paradigm, the *holistic model*. This model stresses the organicity and trustworthiness of the female body, the natural rhythmicity of labor, the integrity of the family, and self-responsibility. These homebirthers see the safety of the baby and the emotional needs of the mother as one. The safest birth for the baby will be the one that provides the most nurturing environment for the mother.[5] Said Ryla,

> I got criticized for choosing a home birth, for not considering the safety of the baby. But that's exactly what I was considering! How could it possibly serve my baby for me to give birth in a place that causes my whole body to tense up in anxiety as soon as I walk in the door?

Although homebirthers constitute only about 2 percent of the American birthing population, their conceptual importance is tremendous, as through the alternative rituals of giving birth at home, they enact—and thus guarantee the existence of—a paradigm of pregnancy and birth based on the value of connection, just as the technocratic model is based on the principle of separation.

The technocratic and holistic models represent opposite ends of a spectrum of beliefs about birth and about cultural life. Their differences are mirrored on a wider scale by the ideological conflicts between biomedicine and holistic healing, and between industrialists and ecological activists. These groups are engaged in a core value struggle over the future—a struggle clearly visible in the profound differences in the rituals they daily enact.

CONCLUSION

Every society in the world has felt the need to thoroughly socialize its citizens into conformity with its norms, and citizens derive many benefits from such socialization. If a culture had to rely on policemen and make sure that everyone would obey its laws, it would disintegrate into chaos, as there would not be enough policemen to go around. It is much more practical for cultures to find ways to socialize their members from the *inside*, by making them *want* to conform to society's norms. Ritual is one major way through which such socialization can be achieved.

American obstetrical procedures can be understood as rituals that facilitate the internalization of cultural values. These procedures are patterned, repetitive, and profoundly symbolic, communicating messages concerning our culture's deepest beliefs about the necessity for cultural control of natural processes. They provide an ordered structure to the chaotic flow of the natural birth process. In so doing, they both enhance the natural affectivity of that process and create a sense of inevitability about their performance. Obstetric interventions are also transformative in intent. They attempt to contain and control the process of birth, and to transform the birthing woman into an American mother who has internalized the core values of this society. Such a mother believes in science, relies on technology, recognizes her biological inferiority (either consciously or unconsciously), and so at some level accepts the principles of patriarchy. She will tend to conform to society's dictates and meet the demands of its institutions, and will teach her children to do the same.

Yet it is important to note that human beings are not automatons. Human behavior varies widely even within the restraints imposed by particular cultures, including their rituals. As July Sanders sums it up:

> It's almost like programming you. You get to the hospital. They put you in this wheelchair. They whisk you off from your husband, and I mean just start in on you. Then they put you in another wheelchair, and send you home. And then they say, well, we need to give you something for the depression. [Laughs] Get away from me! That will help my depression!

Through hospital ritual procedures, obstetrics deconstructs birth, then inverts and reconstructs it as a technocratic process. But unlike most transformations effected by ritual, birth does *not* depend upon the performance of ritual to make it happen. The physiological process of labor itself transports the birthing woman into a naturally transitional situation that carries its own affectivity. Hospital procedures take advantage of that affectivity to transmit the core values of American society to birthing women. From society's perspective, the birth process will not be

successful unless the woman and child are properly socialized during the experience, transformed as much by the rituals as by the physiology of birth. In the latter half of this century, women have made great strides in attaining equality with men on many cultural fronts. Yet, as I noted at the beginning, the cultural treatment of birth is one of the most revealing indicators about the status of women in a given society. In the United States, through their ritual transformation during birth, women learn profound lessons about the weakness and defectiveness of their bodies and the power of technology. In this way, every day in hospitals all over the country, women's status as subordinate is subtly reinforced, as is the patriarchal nature of the technocracy.

NOTES

1. The full results of this study appear in Davis-Floyd 1992.
2. In Holland, by way of contrast, most births are attended by midwives who recognize that individual labors have individual rhythms. They can stop and start; can take a few hours or several days. If labor slows, the midwives encourage the woman to eat to keep up her strength, and then to sleep until contractions pick up again (Beatriz Smulders, Personal Communication, 1994; Jordan 1993).
3. As is true for most of the procedures interpreted here as rituals, there is no scientific justification for the routine use of the electronic fetal monitor: Numerous large-scale studies have shown no improvement in outcome (Leveno et al. 1986; Prentice and Lind 1987; Sandmire 1990; Shy et al. 1990). What these studies do show is that a dramatic increase in the rate of Cesarean section accompanies routine electronic monitoring. Most commonly, this increase is due both to the occasional malfunctioning of the machine, which sometimes registers fetal distress when there is none, and to the tendency of hospital staff to overreact to fluctuations on the monitor strip.
4. See Goer 1995: 274–284 for summaries and interpretations of these studies and others concerning electronic fetal monitoring.

5. For summaries of studies that demonstrate the safety of planned, midwife-attended home birth relative to hospital birth, see Davis-Floyd 1992, Chapter 4, and Goer 1995.

REFERENCES

Abrahams, Roger D. 1973. "Ritual for Fun and Profit (or The Ends and Outs of Celebration)." Paper delivered at the Burg Wartenstein Symposium No. 59, on "Ritual: Reconciliation in Change." New York: Wenner-Gren Foundation for Anthropological Research.

Davis-Floyd, Robbie E. 1992. *Birth as an American Rite of Passage*. Berkeley: University of California Press.

Goer, Henci. 1995. *Obstetric Myths Versus Research Realities: A Guide to the Medical Literature*. Westport, CT: Bergin and Garvey.

Jordan, Brigitte. 1993. *Birth in Four Cultures: A Cross-Cultural Investigation of Birth in Yucatan, Holland, Sweden and the United States* (4th edition revised). Prospect Heights: Waveland Press.

Klein, Michael et al. 1992. "Does Episiotomy Prevent Perineal Trauma and Pelvic Floor Relaxation?" *Online Journal of Current Clinical Trials* 1 (Document 10).

Leveno K. J., F. G. Cunningham, S. Nelson, M. Roark, M. L. Williams, D. Guzick, S. Dowling, C. R. Rosenfeld, A. Buckley. 1986. "A Prospective Comparison of Selective and Universal Electronic Fetal Monitoring in 34,995 Pregnancies." *New England Journal of Medicine* 315 (10): 615–619.

Malinowski, Bronislaw. 1954. (orig. pub. 1925). "Magic, Science, and Religion." In *Magic, Science and Religion and Other Essays,* pp. 17–87. New York: Doubleday/Anchor.

Prentice, A. and T. Lind. 1987. "Fetal Heart Rate Monitoring During Labor—Too Frequent Intervention, Too Little Benefit." *Lancet* 2: 1375–1877.

Reynolds, Peter C. 1991. *Stealing Fire: The Mythology of the Technocracy*. Palo Alto, CA: Iconic Anthropology Press.

Sandmire, H. F. 1990. "Whither Electronic Fetal Monitoring?" *Obstetrics and Gynecology* 76 (6): 1130–1134.

Shaw, Nancy Stoller. 1974. *Forced Labor: Maternity Care in the United States*. New York: Pergamon Press.

Shiono, P., M. A. Klebanoff, and J. C. Carey. 1990. "Midline Episiotomies: More Harm Than Good?" *American Journal of Obstetrics and Gynecology* 75 (5): 765–770.

Shy, Kirkwood, David A. Luthy, Forrest C. Bennett, Michael Whitfield, Eric B. Larson, Gerald van Belle, James P. Hughes, Judith A. Wilson, Martin A. Stenchever. 1990. "Effects of Electronic Fetal Heart Rate Monitoring, as Compared with Periodic Auscultation, on the Neurologic Development of Premature Infants." *New England Journal of Medicine* 322 (9): 588–593.

Thorp J. M. and W. A. Bowes. 1989. "Episiotomy: Can Its Routine Use Be Defended?" *American Journal of Obstetrics and Gynecology* 160 (5Pt1): 1027–1030.

Turner, Victor. 1979. (orig. pub. 1964). "Betwixt and Between: The Liminal Period in Rites de Passage." In W. Lessa and E. Z. Vogt (eds.). *Reader in Comparative Religion,* pp. 234–243. 4th edition. New York: Harper and Row.

van Gennep, Arnold. 1966 (orig. pub. 1908). *The Rites of Passage*. Chicago: University of Chicago Press.

Wilcox, L. S. et al. 1989. "Episiotomy and Its Role in the Incidence of Perineal Lacerations in a Maternity Center and a Tertiary Hospital Obstetric Service." *American Journal of Obstetrics and Gynecology* 160 (5Pt1): 1047–1052.

The Politics of Reproduction in a Mexican Village

Carole H. Browner

Although women in all societies bear children in private, or with only a select few present, human reproduction is never entirely a personal affair. Kin, neighbors, and other members of the larger collectives of which women are a part seek to influence reproductive behavior in their groups. Their concerns, however, about who reproduces, how often, and when frequently conflict quite sharply with the desires of the reproducers themselves.[1] At the state level, governments develop policies with which they try to shape the size, composition, and distribution of their populations. These policies inevitably seek to influence the reproductive activities of individuals. They may be directed toward the fertility of the whole society or selectively imposed on particular classes, subcultures, or other internal groups,[2] but they are usually promoted without much consideration for the individual women who bear and raise the children, and, as a result, they may not be embraced by their target groups. Further, state-initiated population policies are sometimes challenged by internal groups whose objectives differ from those of the state.[3]

It is surprising that conflicts between the reproductive desires of a society's fecund women and the demographic interests of other individuals, groups, and political entities are rarely explored. After a comprehensive review of research in demography, population studies, and the anthropology and sociology of reproduction, Rosalind Pollack Petchesky reports, "Utterly lacking [in these fields] is any sense that the methods and goals of reproduction, and control over them, may themselves be a contested area within [a] cul-

ture."[4] Also absent from this research is the recognition that differential access to a society's sources of power determines how conflicts over reproduction are conducted and resolved, and even whether resolution ever occurs.

The following account analyzes the relationship between the population practices in one indigenous community in Mexico and the Mexican government's recent effort to reduce population growth. It shows that the government's fertility-reducing policy was superimposed on a long-standing local conflict between this community's women, who wished to limit the size of their own families, and the community as a whole, which wanted all of its female members to reproduce abundantly. Despite their apparent concordance with the goals of the state, the women refused the government's contraceptive services. They continued to have many children instead. The discussion will consider both why these indigenous rural women did not act on the fertility desires they expressed and why the demographic policies of Mexico have met uncertain success; for the two are outcomes of the same phenomenon: an overriding cultural prohibition in that community against any kind of fertility control.

BACKGROUND

The data presented here were collected in 1980–81 in a community I will call San Francisco, a Chinantec-Spanish-speaking *municipio* (township) located five hours by bus from the capital of the state of Oaxaca. The *municipio* was made up of a *cabecera* (head town) and a number of *ranchos* (hamlets) spread over a fifty-kilometer range. A year's participant observation was combined with interviews from a sample selected from the 336 adult women who lived in San Francisco. This sample consisted of 180 women selected to represent the age, residence, and linguistic background of the women. The husbands of the married women were also interviewed, a total of 126 men.

Historically, an important element in women's attempts to control their fertility was the use of medicinal plants. In addition to learning the respondents' reproductive desires and attitudes toward childbearing and child rearing, one aim of the interviews was to determine how the knowledge and use of such plants for management of reproduction and the maintenance of reproductive health were distributed and what might be the social implications of this distribution of knowledge before and after the Mexican government's introduction of modern birth control techniques. Demographic, economic, and health data were also obtained.

The *municipio* consisted of just over three hundred families of subsistence farmers who lived dispersed over its 18,300 hectares. Nearly two-thirds of the households (65 percent) cultivated the community's abundant communal landholdings in the tropical lowlands thirty miles east of the *cabecera,* or three hours from there by bus. The remainder used private plots located either in the *cabecera* or in the highland territory that individual Franciscanos purchased in 1930 from a neighboring *municipio,* or they farmed in both places. About a third of the families (32 percent) lived permanently on lowland ranches while most of the rest divided their time between the town center and the lowlands. Although only 5 percent of the households worked solely for wages, another 80 percent reported cash income from at least occasional wage labor.

Most full-time *rancho* residents had regular contact with the *cabecera.* Men made the trip several times each year to attend mandatory town assemblies. Men were also required to reside in the head town during their terms of civil and/or religious community service (*cargos*), which required several years of full-time

commitment over the course of their lifetimes. Women had no formal reason for regular visits to the *cabecera,* but they sometimes went during holidays. In addition, they were expected to help their husbands carry out *cargo* responsibilities and often moved with them to the *cabecera* during their husbands' terms of office.

Until about 1965, the *municipio* fit the model of a closed corporate peasant community,[5] maintaining only sporadic contact with the world outside. Since that time, San Francisco's isolation had been sharply reduced by mandatory primary education, the construction of the Oaxaca-Tuxtepec highway and a feeder road connecting the *cabecera* in it, and a growing stream of migrants leaving the area for Oaxaca City, Mexico City, and the United States. Nevertheless, for many residents, daily life was much as it had always been: 42 percent of the women interviewed and 16 percent of the men had never been more than a few miles outside the community.

WOMEN'S ATTITUDES TOWARD PREGNANCY AND CHILDREN

Women in San Francisco expressed sharply negative attitudes about childbearing and child rearing, an unexpected finding that is contrary to the results of most other studies of peasants' attitudes toward fertility in Latin America.[6] While most research has suggested that peasant women want fewer children than they actually have, it has also suggested that, among these women, three to five children is considered the ideal family size and childlessness is considered a great misfortune. In San Francisco, a very different picture emerged. Among my study population, it was not unusual for women to volunteer that they would have preferred to remain childless or to have far smaller families than they did have. (Sixty of the 180 women interviewed had five or more children.) Sixty-three percent believed that there were women in their community who would choose childlessness if they could. As one informant explained, "The women without children, they're the smart ones"; and yet, as we shall see, choosing childlessness was socially very problematic.[7]

The differences in fertility desires between women and men in San Francisco underscored the women's negative attitudes. Respondents were asked whether they wanted to have more children. The majority of both sexes who still considered themselves of childbearing age said they wanted no more (see table 1), but women were satisfied with far smaller families than were men. The overwhelming majority of the women (80 percent) who had at least one living child said they were content with their present family size. Moreover, of the small number of childless women ($N = 9$), one-third indicated that they were satisfied to remain so. However, most of the men who were satisfied with family size had at least four children (60 percent), and of the childless men ($N = 6$), none indicated that he was satisfied.

Women with large families said they resented the demands of child care and the limitations it placed on them. Many saw children as a burden. They considered them too much work, too hard to raise, a source of problems, "war," and domestic strife. They viewed children as pesky disturbances who kept them

tied to the house. One woman told me, "[The people of the community] want us to have many children. That's fine for them to say. They don't have to take care of them and keep them clean. My husband sleeps peacefully through the night, but I have to get up when the children need something. I'm the one the baby urinates on; sometimes I have to get out of bed in the cold and change both our clothes. They wake me when they're sick or thirsty, my husband sleeps through it all."

This resentment was balanced to some extent by the women's perception of advantages associated with children. They particularly valued the physical and emotional companionship of their children, in part because the women were extremely reluctant to be at home alone, especially at night. They feared ghosts, phantoms, and spirits and worried about drunks reputed to harass solitary women. Women also tried to avoid going alone on errands out of town, for they feared wild animals and unknown men. They always sought out a child—their own or someone else's—if no other companion could be found.

Overall, however, most Franciscanas did not perceive much practical advantage in rearing large families. There was little economic benefit seen, for the women considered their

TABLE 1 Fertility Goals of Adults in a Mexican Municipio, 1980

LIVING CHILDREN (N)	WOMEN				MEN			
	NO	YES	TOTAL	YES (%)	NO	YES	TOTAL	YES (%)
0	3	6	9	67	0	6	6	100
1	7	4	11	36	3	3	6	50
2	9	4	13	31	5	5	10	50
3	16	7	23	30	10	13	23	57
4	11	3	14	21	13	2	15	13
5	11	3	14	21	6	4	10	40
6+	31	1	32	3	23	1	24	4
Totals	88	28	116	24	60	34	94	36

Note—Number of responses to the question. "Do you want more children?" by number of living children. The remaining responses among women and men are: Women ($N = 180$): too old, 47; no husband, 8; ambiguous, 3; missing data, 6. Men ($N = 126$): too old, 25; ambiguous, 3; missing data, 4. (The response "no wife" was not possible since all men in the sample were the husbands of women interviewed.)

offspring lazy or too busy with other activities to be of much help. Since mandatory school attendance was strictly enforced in San Francisco, and children were encouraged by school authorities to attend frequent after-school activities, mothers often felt saddled with chores that their children should have done. Although women hoped their offspring would care for them in their old age, the expectation that they would actually do so was changing as children left the village to find employment elsewhere. Interestingly, mothers expressed greater support for their children's migration than did fathers.[8] Nevertheless, the women felt disappointed when they realized that they had been forgotten at home.

In addition to resenting the hard work of raising children and the frustrations of its uncertain rewards, the women in this sample saw frequent pregnancies as physically stressful and even debilitating. In their view, much of a woman's blood supply during pregnancy was devoted to nourishing the developing fetus. This left their own bodies unbalanced and susceptible to the large number of disorders that could be caused by penetration of cold and *aire* (air, winds). They also saw parturition as a threat to their health, believing that, during childbirth, the womb—and the rest of the body—must "open" to expel the newborn and that this process increased the body's already heightened vulnerability to *aire*.

Postpartum complications were common among Franciscanas. Of the 180 interviewed, two-thirds reported at least one. They ranged from conditions the women considered relatively minor, such as facial swelling and backaches, to such serious conditions as uterine prolapse and uncontrolled bleeding. Emotional complications were sometimes mentioned as well. For instance, one woman reported that, after the birth of her second child, she was unable to tolerate criticism from her husband's relatives, with whom she and her family then lived. "I wanted to get up and run and run, I had no idea to where," she told me. In addition to the complications of pregnancy per se, women also feared that frequent childbirth and short birth intervals caused menstrual hemorrhaging, exhaustion, and early death. There are no reliable data on postpartum mortality for this particular population, but examples existed in the memories of all women interviewed.

The women's illness experiences that were not related to pregnancy reinforced their understanding that frequent pregnancies harmed their general health. Those who had had four or more pregnancies were significantly more likely than the rest to report at least one serious illness ($\chi^2 = 7.06$, $P < .001$). Even when age was controlled for, this pattern occurred. Women with four or more pregnancies were also significantly more likely to report a greater number of minor health problems overall, including headaches, backaches, breast problems, and *coraje* (anger sickness; $\chi^2 = 6.38$, $P < .025$). Again with age controlled for, women who had had four or more pregnancies were less healthy overall than women who had had fewer pregnancies.

THE CASE FOR LARGE FAMILIES

Despite the desires of many Franciscanas to have few (or no) children, they did not think that they could actually do so. The pressures on them to reproduce were simply too great to ignore. These pressures came most often and overtly from the community's men, who argued that a populous community was vital to the defense of the collectivity and its interests. Women were another source of pressure. Although most wanted few children themselves, they felt that other women were obligated by the needs of the collectivity to bear many children.

Maintaining a sufficient population base was a constant source of concern. San Francisco was surrounded by communities that coveted its comparatively large landholdings. It needed a sizable male population to defend its borders in case of armed attack by neighboring enemy communities who still threatened the *municipio*. One particularly bloody battle in the 1950s claimed the lives of thirteen Franciscanos. Residents also felt threatened by indications that the federal government might resettle members of other communities or ethnic groups onto San Francisco's lands or allocate territory to other *municipios* that were litigating for it because, unlike many rural *municipios,* San Francisco had more land than its population required. Residents were also concerned about the regional government's proposals to consolidate San Francisco with neighboring *municipios* because it was considered far too small to remain independent. The most likely of these plans would combine San Francisco with its most hated and feared enemy.

A number of endogenous factors also threatened the community's population base. Despite the presence in the *cabecera* of two government health centers, disease continued to take a significant toll. The rate of infant mortality in the state was one of Mexico's highest. On average, deaths from all causes in San Francisco had not declined during the past fifteen years.[9] Migration from the community to the state and national capitals and to the United States was also taking increasing numbers of the most able-bodied women and men. In the past two decades, the state of Oaxaca had experienced Mexico's highest rate of out-migration, suffering a net population loss of 290,000 between 1960 and 1970 alone. Because this trend had continued, Oaxaca's population had grown more slowly than that of any other Mexican state.[10] San Francisco had been acutely affected by these broader demographic trends. Of the women interviewed whose children were grown, nearly two-thirds reported having at least one child who resided outside the *municipio,* and more than one-fourth reported that all their grown children lived elsewhere.

Half of San Francisco's adult population was now over forty years old. As a result of this aging trend, an increasing proportion of the population were experiencing declining physical strength and productivity, which residents felt boded ill for the community's future. One concrete and very important manifestation of these difficulties was the inability of the *municipio* to find enough men to fill the annual eighteen-man quota for civil and religious *cargo* positions. Moreover, there had been increasing pressure for independence from San Francisco on the part of some of the lowland *rancho* subcommunities (*agencias*); two had already won semiautonomous status from the regional government, and at least one of these was continuing to press for even greater independence.[11] All of these trends led residents of San Francisco to worry about the collectivity's future and to seek ways to diminish the impact of depopulation.

THE BIRTH CONTROL TREE

Although some of the reasons for the depopulation of San Francisco were new, concern about the size and strength of the collectivity was not. The conflict between the collective desire for a large and populous community and individual women's wishes to have few children had had a long, dramatic history in the *municipio.*

On many occasions during my fieldwork, men told me how, some twenty years before, they had cut down a tree whose bark was used by women as a contraceptive. They needed to eliminate the tree, they said, because so many women were refusing to bear children. This is the story the men told: Not far from the town center and just off a popular path to the lowland hamlets was a tree without a name. Its bark turned red when stripped from its trunk and was said to prevent conception. The large old tree was the only one of its kind known to the people of San Francisco. "Who knows where the seed came from," said one elderly resident; "strange it was the only one." Women who wished to avoid pregnancy brewed tea from the bark and drank it prior to intercourse. This would "burn" their wombs and render them temporarily sterile. This tea was dangerous and powerful, "like poison," some said. It could kill an incautious user. Women who drank the tea several times grew emaciated and weak. Even if they subsequently wished to bear children, as many as eight years might pass before a pregnancy.

Some said the users went secretly at night to get bark from the tree. Others thought that itinerant peddler women from an enemy town secretly sold Franciscanas strips of the dried bark along with other wares. Said one man, "It was they who deceived our women into not wanting children because they didn't want our town to grow."

A group of San Francisco's men were at work one day cutting back brush from the path that passed near the tree. They could see it from where they worked, almost stripped of its bark from frequent use. "Let's get rid of it," one of them said quietly; "we must have more children in this town." The others quickly agreed. "So," explained one who had been there, "we cut down the tree and tore its roots right out." They used the trunk to restore a nearby bridge in disrepair and returned home tired but satisfied with their work. (In an alternate version of the story, the men saw the tree, were angered, and stripped it entirely of its bark, causing it to die.)

I asked some of the men who said they were responsible for the act why they had killed the tree. "We were angry," one told me. "The women weren't having babies. They were lazy and didn't want to produce children." Another said that the women "had stopped making children. We were working hard with our men's work, but they weren't doing any of their women's work." One who said he remembered the incident explained that "the town was small and we wanted it to grow. We wanted a big town and we needed more people. But the women wouldn't cooperate." A woman I interviewed saw the men's motives differently. "The men depended on the women," she said. "They couldn't have their children by themselves. But the women were walking free. The men pulled out the tree to control the women so they'd have children for them."

My research in San Francisco led me to ask often about the birth control tree. Every man I asked had heard of it although none could tell me its name or show me one like it. These

days, they explained, people seldom passed the spot where it had grown because a better road to the lowlands had been built. After weeks of asking, I nearly concluded that the tree was only a myth. Persistence finally led me to a woman who said her husband could show me the tree. He was more than reluctant to comply. "What if people found out that it has grown back?" he said. "What if they began to use it again? Then what would happen to the town?"

I continued to press him. Finally, he said he would not show me the tree but would take my field assistant's nine-year-old son to see it. The boy could later lead me to the spot. During the same period, one of the men who said he had participated in the destruction of the tree agreed to see if it had possibly regenerated. During different weeks, each of the two informants independently led me to the same clump of *Styrax argenteus*. As the second man showed me the abundant young growth, he expressed surprise that several had grown where only one had been.

The women I asked about the tree were consistently less informative than the men. While all the men knew of the birth control tree, the majority of women said they had never even heard of it, let alone used it to avoid pregnancy. The men did not believe the women were as ignorant as they claimed. I asked one man how the men had learned of the tree if the women had used it only in secret. He replied, "Of course the women think they have their secrets. But we men were able to find out. They have no secrets from us."

THE WOMEN'S RESPONSES TO PRESSURES TO REPRODUCE

There are several morals to this story, but the inevitability of negative reactions to behaviors that place individual interests above those of the collectivity is a very important one. In San Francisco, married women with few or no children were seen as selfish and socially negligent regardless of whether their low fertility was natural or willfully induced. Such women were particularly vulnerable to gossip, much of which centered on their fertility behavior. They were sharply and repeatedly criticized for causing miscarriages and using contraceptives. Some were even accused of infanticide. All of their acts were carefully monitored by relatives and other interested parties to detect any efforts to avoid pregnancy. For example, lemon juice was widely regarded as a contraceptive and an abortifacient.[12] After failing to conceive during her first year of marriage, one woman fell subject to her mother-in-law's constant gossip and criticism for avoiding her reproductive responsibilities by eating too much of the fruit. Another woman determinedly broke her young daughter of the habit of enjoying lemons, for she feared that they would damage her daughter's fertility.

Women with small families were susceptible to gossip about marital infidelity, which diminished the social status of their husbands as well. As a middle-aged mother of six explained, "The women who are most likely to go with other men are the ones who don't have much work to do. They have time for sex. But if you have a lot of kids like I do, you have to work very hard all the time. The tiredness takes over at the end of the day and you don't have time to think about the husbands of other women. You don't have time to go out looking for men." The targets of such gossip attributed it to envy of the relative wealth and freedom they enjoyed as a result of having small families—and they adamantly denied that their low fertility was due to contraceptives.

Contraceptives were, however, readily available at the town's two government-run health centers; one even provided the services free of charge. The Mexican government's interest in lowering its national birth rate had led it since 1972 to promote family planning aggressively.[13] The walls of both clinics were decorated almost exclusively with posters demonstrating the benefits of small families and *paternidad responsable* (responsible parenthood).[14] They were written in simple language with humorous illustrations. The text of a typical one read: "What will happen when

we are more? We will have less money . . . less food . . . less education . . . less space . . . less clothing . . . less peace. You can avoid these problems if you plan your family. Now planning is easier! Consult the family doctor at the Social Security Clinic although you may not be insured. *The consultation is free.*"[15] Each clinic assigned its staff monthly inscription quotas for new contraceptive users. Health center personnel were expected to undertake house-to-house campaigns to introduce fecund women to modern birth control techniques.

Overwhelmingly, Franciscanas rejected these government services. For the period between January 1980 and February 1981, records from the two clinics indicated that thirteen Franciscanas initiated contraceptive use—only 7 percent of women between the ages of eighteen and forty-five. These women used contraceptives for an average of just 3.5 months before stopping, and only one continued using contraceptives for longer than six months.

When I asked several who said they wanted no more children why they did not seek the means to avoid pregnancy, they revealed an extreme reluctance to engage in socially disapproved behavior. Some indicated they would never consider obtaining birth control from government clinics because they would be ashamed to be publicly "registered" as a user of contraceptives. This same fear of community censure led women to avoid other means of fertility control and even the kinds of behavior that could be construed as attempts at fertility limitation. When I naively asked one of the town midwives if she had ever been asked to perform an abortion, she looked at me and said, "They wouldn't dare." Similarly, a Franciscana suffering from menstrual delay was afraid to inquire locally for a remedy. Even though she was convinced that she was not pregnant, she was sure she would be accused of abortion if she took a remedy to induce menstrual bleeding.

The women responded to these pressures to reproduce not simply by refusing to use contraceptives but also by denying they knew anything whatsoever about ways to limit fertility. It seemed they felt that merely possessing information would be interpreted as evidence of their malevolent intentions. When I asked women the direct question, "Do you know of any herbs or other remedies that can be used to avoid pregnancy?" only 11 percent mentioned specific techniques such as the infamous birth control tree. Another 6 percent said they believed that ways existed but knew of none themselves. The remaining 83 percent said they believed there were no traditional ways to avoid getting pregnant. An even larger proportion (86 percent) said they knew no ways to induce an abortion. Even Franciscanas who considered themselves authorities on a great many subjects pleaded ignorance when it came to birth limitation.

Denial, however, did not necessarily imply ignorance. Probes revealed that 60 percent who had initially said they knew no ways to limit births had at least heard of the existence of techniques for fertility limitation. The vast majority of these respondents named modern rather than traditional methods and the responses were often quite oblique. For example, to the questions, "Is there *anything* that can be done to not have children if one doesn't want to have them? If so, what things?" typical responses were: "Yes, in the health center"; "I know the doctor has some"; "They say there are pills, medicines." Other replies explicitly identified the government as the source of contraceptives, shifting the question away from indigenous techniques for birth limitation to methods made available from outside the community. For example, "These days the government doesn't allow people to have so many children. It gives them medicines so they won't"; and "There used to be lots of herbs. Now, the government sends us doctors."

Yet none of the affirmative responses to the questions about knowledge of birth control could be interpreted as endorsements of contraceptive use. No respondent seemed to regard the available fertility-limiting techniques as liberating or as helping them to achieve their expressed goals of having small families. In fact, when responding

affirmatively to the probe concerning their knowledge of contraceptives, the women would frequently volunteer a disclaimer in an apparent effort to dissociate themselves even further from the information, even though the probe did not concern their own experiences with contraceptives. For instance: "Well, yes, I have heard that there are medicines available, but I haven't tried them"; "Yes, there are remedies in the health center, but I haven't looked into it"; and, "They say there are medicines in the health center, but I myself haven't used any." Even most of those few in my study population (four out of six women) whose health center records revealed a history of contraceptive use strenuously denied use when directly asked during interviews.

Others told me with extreme caution what they knew about contraception. Some who during interviews had denied all knowledge of contraceptive methods subsequently came to my house to tell me about plants or other techniques that had previously "escaped" their memories. Even knowledge that seemed to me benign was very reluctantly conveyed if it pertained to birth limitation. For example, after initially denying she knew any remedies to induce an abortion, one woman reconsidered and whispered, "I don't know if this would really work, but some say that it can: carrying heavy loads, carrying heavy tumplines of firewood every day, doing a lot of laundry. It's said this can make one abort." Although this idea might be inferred from the circumstances under which miscarriages were observed to have occurred, women carefully guarded even this much knowledge, for they feared it would be incriminating.

IMPLICATIONS OF THE RESEARCH

These data shed light on the context in which a national population planning program was experienced in a rural indigenous community. The context was political, economic, civic, and cultural. On the part of the Mexican government, the decision to promote family planning among indigenous populations was politically delicate, for many Mexican nationalists regard the preservation of their Indian cultural heritage as fundamental to their cultural identity as Mexicans, and aggressive programs to limit the growth of indigenous groups may be perceived as cultural genocide.[16] However, because economic development could not keep pace, the need to check population growth proved more pressing than the state's concerns with the politics of ethnic preservation. Terry L. McCoy has shown, moreover, that the recognition that the government could be destabilized by unchecked growth among less than fully loyal social classes and cultural groups provided significant impetus for the Mexican population policy.[17] In Mexico, as in other developing countries, such policies are used to further state consolidation.

A reduction in San Francisco's rate of population growth was, as we have seen, the last thing the male guardians of the collectivity wanted. While appreciating the value of birth control for the nation in the abstract, and in some cases even wishing for relatively small families themselves, the men unambivalently rejected family planning for the people of San Francisco. In contrast, the women were caught between their desires to have very few children and inexorable local social pressures to be prolific. Because of this pressure, government family planning services could not help the women achieve their own fertility goals. In fact, the existence of these services may have made it even more difficult for the women to practice covert fertility limitation: with the availability of modern contraceptives in the community, women fell under even more suspicion than before.

It has all too often been assumed that women's reproductive goals could be understood by analyzing those of the larger collectivities of which they are a part. However, when collectivities have specific fertility goals, it is reasonable to expect that these goals will conflict with the reproductive desires of at least some of the female members of the group. The extent to which women successfully implement their individual fertility goals depends on a number of factors that vary according to the characteristics of the particular society in which they live. These include the nature of the gender-based power relations and the extent to which women feel they can support one another in controversy. In stratified societies, issues related to social class and ethnicity also play a part, and women may be torn by conflicting sets of interests.[18] Studies that fail to consider *both* these broad sociopolitical conditions and the interests and desires of individual women will understate the complexity, misrepresent the realities, and yield questionable conclusions about reproductive policy and reproductive behavior.

NOTES

Support for this research was generously provided by grants from the National Science Foundation (BNS-8016431), National Institute for Child Health Development (HD-04612), and the Wenner-Gren Foundation for Anthropological Research (3387). Arthur J. Rubel provided truly valuable assistance during all phases of this research, including the production of this report. Judith Friedlander's suggestions also contributed importantly to the manuscript.

1. Burton Benedict, "Social Regulation of Fertility," in *The Structure of Human Populations,* ed. G. A. Harrison and A. J. Boyce (Oxford: Clarendon Press, 1972), 73–89; Carole Browner, "Abortion Decision Making: Some Findings from Colombia," *Studies in Family Planning* 10, no. 3 (1979): 96–106; Thomas K. Burch and Murray Gendall, "Extended Family Structure and Fertility: Some Conceptual and Methodological Issues," in *Culture and Population: A Collection of Current Studies,* ed. Steven Polgar (Cambridge, Mass.: Schenkman Publishing Co.; Chapel Hill, N.C.: Carolina Population Center, 1971), 87–104; Ronald Freedman, "The Sociology of Human Fertility: A Trend Report and Bibliography," *Current Sociology* 10/11, no. 2 (1961–62): 35–121; Frank Lorimer, *Culture and Human Fertility: A Study of the Relation of Cultural Conditions to Fertility in Nonindustrial and Transitional Societies* (Paris: Unesco, 1958); John F. Marshall, Susan Morris, and Steven

Polgar, "Culture and Natality: A Preliminary Classified Bibliography," *Current Anthropology* 13, no. 2 (April 1972): 268–78; Moni Nag, *Factors Affecting Human Fertility in Nonindustrial Societies: A Cross-cultural Study* (New Haven, Conn.: Human Relations Area Files Press, 1976); Steven Polgar, "Population History and Population Policies from an Anthropological Perspective." *Current Anthropology* 13, no. 2 (April 1972): 203–11.

2. Bernard Berelson, *Population Policy in Developed Countries* (New York: McGraw-Hill Book Co., 1974); J. C. Caldwell, "Population Policy: A Survey of Commonwealth Africa," in *The Population of Tropical Africa,* ed. John C. Caldwell and Chukuka Okonjo (New York: Columbia University Press, 1968), 368–75; Leslie Corsa and Deborah Oakley, *Population Planning* (Ann Arbor: University of Michigan Press, 1979), chap. 5, 155–94; William L. Langer, "Checks on Population Growth, 1750–1850," *Scientific American* 226, no. 2 (1972): 92–99; Benjamin White, "Demand for Labor and Population Growth in Colonial Java," *Human Ecology* 1, no. 3 (1973): 217–39.

3. Ad Hoc Women's Studies Committee Against Sterilization Abuse, *Workbook on Sterilization and Sterilization Abuse* (Bronxville, N.Y.: Sarah Lawrence College, 1978); Toni Cade, "The Pill: Genocide or Liberation?" in *The Black Woman,* ed. Toni Cade (New York: New American Library, 1970), 162–69; Lucinda Cisler, "Unfinished Business: Birth Control and Women's Liberation," in *Sisterhood Is Powerful: An Anthology of Writings from the Women's Liberation Movement,* ed. Robin Morgan (New York: Vintage Books, 1970), 245–89; Sally Covington, "Is 'Broader' Better? Reproductive Rights and Elections '84," *Taking Control: The Magazine of the Reproductive Rights National Network* 1, no. 1 (1984): 6–8; Boston Women's Health Book Collective, *Our Bodies, Ourselves: A Book by and for Women* (New York: Simon & Schuster, 1971); Reproductive Rights National Network, "Caught in the Crossfire: Third World Women and Reproductive Rights," *Reproductive Rights Newsletter* 5, no. 3 (Autumn 1983): 1–13; Helen Rodriguez-Trias, *Sterilization Abuse* (New York: Barnard College, Women's Center, 1978).

4. Rosalind Pollack Petchesky, *Abortion and Woman's Choice: The State, Sexuality, and Reproduction Freedom* (New York and London: Longman, Inc., 1984), esp. 10.

5. Eric R. Wolf, "Types of Latin American Peasantry: A Preliminary Discussion," *American Anthropologist* 57 (1955): 452–71, and "Closed Corporate Peasant Communities in Mesoamerica and Central Java," *Southwestern Journal of Anthropology* 13 (1957): 1–18.

6. Clifford R. Barnett, Jean Jackson, and Howard M. Cann, "Childspacing in a Highland Guatemala Community," in Polgar, ed. (n. 1 above), 139–48; Paula H. Hass, "Contraceptive Choices for Latin American Women," *Populi* 3 (1976): 14–24; Jenifer Oberg, "Natality in a Rural Village in Northern Chile," in Polgar, ed., 124–38; Michele Goldzieher Shedlin and Paula E. Hollerbach, "Modern and Traditional Fertility Regulation in a Mexican Community: The Process of Decision-Making," *Studies in Family Planning* 12, no. 6/7 (1981): 278–96. John Mayone Stycos, *Ideology, Faith, and Family Planning in Latin America: Studies in Public and Private Opinion on Fertility Control* (New York: McGraw-Hill Book Co., 1971).

7. It should be noted that the women's professed negative attitudes toward childbearing and child rearing generally were not apparent in their behavior toward their children.

8. C. H. Browner, "Gender Roles and Social Change: A Mexican Case," *Ethnology* 25, no. 2 (April 1986): 89–106.

9. Arthur J. Rubel, "Some Unexpected Health Consequences of Political Relations in Mexico" (paper presented at the eighty-second annual meeting of the American Anthropological Association, Chicago, 1983).

10. Consejo Nacional de Población México (CONAPO), *México Demográfico: Breviario* (Mexico City: CONAPO, 1979), 52, 78. More recent statistics on out-migration are not available.

11. Anselmo Hernandez Lopez, personal communication, Oaxaca, Mexico, 1981.

12. C. H. Browner and Bernard Ortiz de Montellano, "Herbal Emmenagogues Used by Women in Columbia and Mexico," in *Plants Used in Indigenous Medicine: A Biocultural Approach,* ed. Nina Etkin (New York: Docent Publishers, 1986), 32–47.

13. Victor Urquidi et al., *La explosión humana* (Mexico City: Litoarte, 1974); Frederick C. Turner, *Responsible Parenthood: The Politics of Mexico's New Population Policies* (Washington, D.C.: American Enterprise Institute for Public Policy Research, 1974).

14. This official slogan of the government's population control program was chosen to emphasize

the concrete advantages of small families to individual couples rather than the macrodemographic benefits of a reduced national birth rate (Terry L. McCoy, "A Paradigmatic Analysis of Mexican Population Policy," in *The Dynamics of Population Policy in Latin America,* ed. Terry L. McCoy [Cambridge, Mass.: Ballinger Publishing Co., 1974], 377–408, esp. 397).

15. Mexico City: Instituto Mexicano de Seguro Social (IMSS); italics in original. In the mid-1960s, the government's Social Solidarity Program (*Solidaridad Social*) extended the social security health system to cover the health needs of some rural areas. Family planning services were part of the coverage.

16. [Gonzalo] Aquirre Beltrán, *Obra polémica* (Mexico City: Instituto Nacional de Antropología e Historia, 1976); Luis Leñero Otero, *Valores ideológicos y las políticas de población en México* (Mexico City: Editorial Edicol, 1979), 115–17.

17. McCoy, 377–408.

18. Floya Anthias and Nira Yuval-Davis, "Contextualizing Feminism: Gender, Ethnic and Class Divisions," *Feminist Review* 15 (Winter 1983): 62–75, esp. 70–71.

Surrogate Motherhood: Rethinking Biological Models, Kinship, and Family

Heléna Ragoné

In the wake of publicity created by the Baby M Case[1] it seems unlikely that anyone in the United States can have remained unfamiliar with surrogate motherhood or can have failed to form an opinion. The Baby M Case raised, and ultimately left unanswered, many questions about what constitutes motherhood, fatherhood, family, reproduction, and kinship. When I began my field research in 1987, surrogate mother programs and directors had already become the subject of considerable media attention, a great deal of it sensationalized and negative in character. Much of what has been written about surrogate motherhood, has, however, been largely speculative or polemic in nature. Opinions have ranged from the view that surrogate motherhood is symptomatic of the dissolution of the American family[2] and the sanctity of motherhood, to charges that it reduces or assigns women to a breeder class structurally akin to prostitution (Dworkin 1978), or that it constitutes a form of commercial baby selling (Annas 1988; Neuhaus 1988).

Data for this chapter derive from nine years of ongoing ethnographic research. Twenty-eight formal interviews with traditional surrogates and twenty-six with gestational surrogates were conducted, as well as twenty-six interviews with individual members of couples (i.e., individuals who had enlisted the services of traditional as well as gestational surrogates) and five interviews with ovum donors. Aside from these formal interviews I also engaged in countless conversations with surrogates, observing them as they interacted with their families, testified before legislative committees, worked in surrogate programs, and socialized at program gatherings with directors and others. The opportunity to observe the daily workings of the surrogate mother programs provided me with invaluable data on the day-to-day operations of such programs. I attended the staff meetings of one such program on a regular basis and observed the consultations in which prospective couples and

Original material prepared for this text.

surrogates were interviewed singly by such members of the staff as the director, a psychologist, a medical coordinator, or the administrative coordinator.

In addition to these formal interviews I conducted thousands of hours of participant observation and was able to observe numerous consultations between program staff, intending couples, and prospective surrogate mothers. I have attempted, whenever possible, to select individuals from the various phases of the traditional and gestational surrogacy process: those individuals who have not yet been matched, those who are newly matched and are attempting "to get pregnant," those who have confirmed pregnancies, and those who have recently given birth, as well as those for whom several years have elapsed since the birth of their child. My decision to interview individuals in all stages of the process has been motivated by my wish to assess what, if any, shifts individuals might experience as they go through the process.

Historically there have been three profound shifts in the Western conceptualization of the categories of conception, reproduction, and parenthood. The first occurred in response to the separation of intercourse from reproduction through birth control methods (Snowden et al. 1983), a precedent that may have paved the way for surrogate motherhood in the 1980s (Andrews 1984:xiii). A second shift occurred in response to the emergence of assisted reproductive technologies (ARTs) and to the subsequent fragmentation of the unity of reproduction, when it became possible for pregnancy to occur without necessarily having been "preceded by sexual intercourse" (Snowden et al. 1983:5). The third shift occurred in response to further advances in reproductive medicine that called into question the "organic unity of fetus and mother" (Martin 1987:20). It was not, however, until the emergence of reproductive medicine that the fragmentation of motherhood became a reality; with that historical change what was once the "single figure of the mother is dispersed among several potential figures, as the functions of maternal procreation—aspects of her physical parenthood—become dispersed" (Strathern 1991:32).

TRADITIONAL SURROGACY

There are two types of surrogate mother programs: "open" programs, in which surrogate and couple select one another and interact throughout the insemination and the pregnancy, and "closed" programs, in which couples select their surrogates from biographical and medical information and a photograph of the surrogate is provided to them by programs. After the child is born in a "closed" program, the couple and surrogate meet only to finalize the step-parent adoption. Due to advances in reproductive medicine and to consumer demand, there are now also two types of surrogacy: traditional surrogacy in which the surrogate contributes an ovum to the creation of the child, and gestational or in-vitro fertilization (IVF) surrogacy where the surrogate gestates the couples' embryos.

Studies of the surrogate population tend to focus, at times exclusively, on surrogates' stated motivations for becoming surrogate mothers (Parker 1983). Their stated reasons include the desire to help an infertile couple start a family, financial remuneration, and a love of pregnancy (Parker 1983:140). Soon after I began my own research, I observed a remarkable degree of consistency or uniformity in surrogates' responses to questions about their initial motivations for becoming surrogates. It was as if they had all been given a script in which they espoused many of the motivations earlier catalogued by Parker: motivations that also, as I will show, reflect culturally accepted ideas about reproduction, motherhood, and family.

I also began to uncover several areas of conflict between professed motivations and actual experiences, discovering, for example, that although surrogates claim to experience "easy pregnancies" and "problem-free labor," it was not unusual for surrogates to have experienced miscarriages, ectopic pregnancies, and related difficulties, For example, Jeannie, age 36, divorced with one child, described the ectopic pregnancy she experienced while she was a traditional surrogate in this manner: "*I almost bled to death: I literally almost died for my couple.*" Nevertheless, she was again inseminated a second time for the same couple. As this and other cases demonstrate, even when their experiences are at odds with their stated motivations, surrogates tend not to acknowledge inconsistencies between their initially stated motivations and their subsequent experiences. This reformulation of motivations can be seen in the following instance. Fran, age 27, divorced with one child, described the difficulty of her delivery in this way: "*I had a rough delivery, a C-section, and my lung collapsed because I had the flu but it was worth every minute of it. If I were to die from childbirth, that's the best way to die. You died for a cause, a good one.*" As both these examples illustrate, some surrogates readily embrace the idea of meaningful suffering, heroism, or sacrifice, and although their stated motivations are of some interest they do not adequately account for the range of shifting motivations uncovered in my research.

One of the motivations most frequently assumed to be primary by the casual observer is remuneration and I took considerable pains in trying to evaluate the influence of monetary rewards on surrogates. In all programs, surrogates receive between $10,000 and $15,000 (for three to four months of insemination and nine months of pregnancy, on average), a fee that has changed only nominally since the early 1980s. As one program psychologist explained, the amount paid to surrogates is intentionally held at an artificially low rate so as to screen out women who might be motivated by monetary gain alone. One of the questions I sought to explore was whether surrogates were denying the significance of remuneration in order to cast their actions in the more culturally acceptable light of pure altruism, or whether they were motivated, at least in part, by remuneration and in part by other factors with the importance of remuneration decreasing as the pregnancy

progressed, the version of events put forth by both program staff and surrogates.

The opinion popular among both scholars and the general population, that surrogates are motivated primarily by financial gain, has tended to result in oversimplified analyses of surrogate motivations. More typical of surrogate explanations for the connection between the initial decision to become a surrogate and the remuneration received are comments such as those expressed by Fran. "*It [surrogacy] sounded so interesting and fun. The money wasn't enough to be pregnant for nine months.*" Andrea, age 29, who was married with three children, said "*I'm not doing it for the money. Take the money: that wouldn't stop me. It wouldn't stop the majority.*" Sarah, age 27, who attended two years of college, and was married with two children, explained her feelings about remuneration in the following way: "*What's $10,000 bucks? You can't even buy a car. If it was just for the money you will want the baby. Money wasn't important. I possibly would have done it for expenses, especially for the people I did it for. My father would have given me the money not to do it.*

The issue of remuneration proved to be of particular interest in that, although surrogates do accept monetary compensation for their reproductive work, its role is a multifaceted one. The surrogate pregnancy, unlike a traditional pregnancy, is viewed by the surrogate and her family as work; as such, it is informed by the belief that work is something that occurs only within the context of a paid occupation (Ferree 1984:72). It is interesting to note that surrogates rarely spend the money they earn on themselves. The majority of surrogates I interviewed spent their earnings on home improvement, gifts for their husbands, a family vacation, or simply to pay off "family debts."

One of the primary reasons that most surrogates do not spend the money they earn on themselves alone appears to stem from the fact that the money serves as a buffer against and/or reward to their own families, particularly to their husbands who must make a number of compromises as a result of the surrogate arrangement. One of these compromises is obligatory abstention from sexual intercourse with their wives from the time insemination takes place until a pregnancy has been confirmed (a period that lasts on average from three to four months in length, but that may be extended for as long as one year).

The devaluation of the amount of the surrogate payment by the surrogates themselves as insufficient to compensate for "nine months of pregnancy" serves several important purposes. First, this view is representative of the cultural belief that children are "priceless" (Zelizer 1985); in this sense surrogates are merely reiterating a widely held cultural belief when they devalue the amount of remuneration they receive. For example, when the largest and one of the most well-established surrogate mother programs changed the wording of its advertising copy from "Help an Infertile Couple" to "Give the Gift of Life," the vastly increased volume of response revealed that the program had discovered a successful formula with which to reach the surrogate population. With surrogacy, the gift is conceptualized as a child, a formulation that is widely used in Euro-American culture—for example, in blood donation (Titmuss 1971) and organ donation (Fox and Swazey 1992).

The gift formulation holds particular appeal for surrogates because it reinforces the idea that having a child for someone is an act for which one cannot be compensated. As I have already mentioned, the gift of life narrative is further enhanced by some surrogates to include the near-sacrifice of their own lives in child birth (Ragoné 1996, 1999). Fran, whose dismissal of the importance of payment I have already quoted, also offered another, even more revealing account of her decision to become a surrogate mother: "*I wanted to do the ultimate thing for somebody, to give them the ultimate gift. Nobody can beat that, nobody can do anything nicer for them.*" Stella, age 38, married with two children, noted that the commissioning couples "*consider it [the baby] a gift and I consider it a gift.*" Carolyn, age 33, married with two children, discussed her feelings about

remuneration and having a surrogate child in these terms: "*It's a gift of love. I have always been a really giving person, and it's the ultimate way to give. I've always had babies so easily. It's the ultimate gift of love.*" For Euro-Americans it is "gift relations" rather than economic exchanges that characterize the family (Carrier 1990:2). Thus, when surrogates minimize or dismiss the importance of money, they are on the one hand reiterating cultural beliefs about the pricelessness of children, and they are on the other hand suggesting that the exchange of a child for money is not a relationship of reciprocity but of kinship.

Once a surrogate enters a program, she also begins to recognize just how important having a child is to the commissioning couple. She sees with renewed clarity that no matter how much material success the couple has, their lives are emotionally impoverished because of their inability to have a child. In this way the surrogate's fertility serves as a leveling device for perceived, if unacknowledged, economic differences, and many surrogates begin to see themselves as altruistic or heroic figures who can rectify the imbalance in a couple's life. The surrogate's sense of place and her social network are greatly enlarged as she receives telephone calls from the program, rushes to keep doctor's appointments, meets with prospective couples, (she may even be flown to other cities to meet couples), and later on attends (in the open programs) monthly or semi-monthly surrogate support-group meetings. In some programs she may attend individual therapy sessions. She is often taken out socially by her couple, she may receive gifts from them for herself and her children, be telephoned regularly by them or receive cards and letters from them, and she attends holiday parties and other social events hosted by the program. Her sense of importance is also enhanced when she tells others about her new and unusual work. Once a surrogate meets, selects, and is selected by her couple and begins insemination—another rite of passage that confers additional status upon her— the couple becomes central to her life, adding an important steady source of social interaction and stimulation.

The entire surrogate experience serves to alter the balance of power in the surrogate's personal life, giving her entrée to a more public role and creating new and exciting demands upon her time. From the moment she places a telephone call to a surrogate mother program to the moment she delivers a child, the balance of power in a surrogate's personal life is altered radically. Her time can no longer be devoted exclusively to the care and nurture of her own family because she has entered into a legal and social contract to perform an important and economically rewarded task: helping an infertile couple to begin a family of their own. Unlike other types of employment, this activity cannot be regarded as unfeminine, selfish, or nonnurturant.

In this sense, we can see how surrogacy assists surrogates in their efforts to transcend the limitations of their domestic roles by highlighting "their differences from men ... [b]y accepting and elaborating upon the symbols and expectations associated with their cultural definition" (Rosaldo 1974:37), for example, motherhood. The gravity of the task provides the surrogate with an opportunity to do more than care for her family alone, and surrogates often report feeling that they are undertaking a task laden with importance, a project that fills them with a sense of pride and self-worth. Sally, age 33, married with two children and a full-time homemaker, discussed how surrogacy provided her with a feeling of unique accomplishment: "*Not everyone can do it. It's like the steelworkers who walk on beams ten floors up; not everyone can do it, not everyone can be a surrogate.*"

GESTATIONAL SURROGATES

From 1987 to 1993 over 95 percent of all surrogacy arrangements were traditional. As of 1994 a profound shift occurred with 50 percent of all surrogacy arrangements gestational and as of 1999 that percentage continues to increase at the largest surrogate mother program

(which is also the largest ovum donation program). With the advent of gestational surrogacy, however, reproduction is not only separated from sexual intercourse and motherhood but from pregnancy as well. In addition, gestational surrogacy creates three discernible categories of motherhood where there was previously only one: (1) the biological mother, the woman who contributes the ovum (traditionally assumed to be the "real mother"); (2) the gestational mother, the woman who gestates the embryos but who bears no genetic relationship to the child; and (3) the social mother, the woman who raises or nurtures the child.

The growing prevalence of gestational surrogacy is, in part, guided by recent legal precedents in which a surrogate who does not contribute an ovum toward the creation of a child has a significantly reduced possibility of being awarded custody in the event that she reneges on her contract and attempts to retain custody of the child. However, although legal factors have certainly contributed to the meteoric rise in the rates of gestational surrogacy, it should be remembered that for couples the ability to create a child genetically related to both parents is the primary reason that gestational surrogacy continues to grow in popularity.

But not all gestational surrogate arrangements involve the couple's embryos; numerous cases involve the combination of donor ova and the intending father's semen. Why then do couples pursue gestational surrogacy when traditional surrogacy provides them with the same degree of biogenetic linkage to the child, has a higher likelihood of being successful, and costs less? Several reasons are cited by the staff of the largest surrogate mother program. The primary reason is that many more women are willing to donate ova than are willing to serve as surrogate mothers. This surrogate program is now also the largest ovum donation program in the U.S. with over 300 screened donors on file. The second reason, as previously mentioned, is that the U.S. courts would, in theory, be less likely to award custody to a gestational surrogate than to a traditional surrogate who contributed her own ovum to the creation of the child.[3] But perhaps most importantly, when commissioning couples choose donor ova/gestational surrogacy, they sever the surrogate's genetic link to and/or claim to the child. By contrast, with traditional surrogacy the adoptive mother must emphasize the importance of nurturance and social parenthood, while the surrogate mother deemphasizes her biogenetic tie to the child.

An additional reason, and one of critical importance, is that couples from certain racial, ethnic and religious groups (e.g., Japanese, Taiwanese, and Jewish) could find women who were willing to donate their ova, but were rarely able to locate women who were willing to serve in the capacity of surrogate. Thus, couples from particular ethnic/racial/religious groups who are seeking donors from those groups often pursue ovum donation/gestational surrogacy.[4]

The gestational surrogate's articulated ideas about relatedness (or more accurately, the presumed lack thereof) also produce a shift in emphasis away from potentially problematic aspects of gestational surrogacy, such as race and ethnicity. Unlike traditional surrogate arrangements in which the majority of couples and surrogates are Euro-American, it is not unusual for gestational surrogates and commissioning couples to come from diverse racial, ethnic, religious and cultural backgrounds. In fact, approximately 30 percent of all gestational surrogate arrangements at the largest program now involve surrogates and couples matched from different racial, ethnic, and cultural backgrounds. I have, over the last four years, interviewed a Mexican-American gestational surrogate who was carrying a child for a Japanese couple; an African-American gestational surrogate who had attempted several embryo transfers unsuccessfully for both a Japanese couple and a Euro-American couple; a Euro-American gestational surrogate who had delivered twins for a Japanese couple; and a Taiwanese couple looking for an Asian American ovum donor and gestational surrogate.

When I questioned Carole, an African-American gestational surrogate (who at twenty-nine was single, with one child, and had yet to sustain a gestational pregnancy) about the issue of racial difference (between herself and her couple), she stated: *"I had friends who had a problem because [they thought] I should help blacks. And I told them, Don't look at the color issue. If a white person offered to help you, you wouldn't turn them down."* However, the following statement by Carole reveals that the issue of racial difference is further nuanced as a positive factor, one that actually facilitates the surrogate/child separation process: *My mom is happy the couple is not black because she was worried I would want to keep it [the baby]. The first couple I was going to go with was black. I don't want to raise another kid.*

When I questioned Linda, a thirty-year old Mexican-American woman pregnant with a child for a couple from Japan, about this issue, her reasoning illustrated how beliefs concerning racial difference can be used by surrogates (and couples) to resolve any conflicting feelings about the child being related to a surrogate by virtue of having been carried in her body: *No, I haven't [thought of the child as mine], because she's not mine, she never has been. For one thing, she is totally Japanese, It's a little hard for me. In a way she will always be my Japanese girl; but she is theirs."* In this quote, we can see how Linda recapitulates one of the initial motivations cited by gestational surrogates, the desire to bear a child for an infertile couple while highlighting the lack of physical and racial resemblance, or biogenetic tie. *"If I was to have a child, it would only be from my husband and me. With AI [traditional surrogacy], the baby would be a part of me. I don't know if I could let a part of me . . . . AI was never for me; I never considered it."*

Carole and Linda are aware, of course, as are other gestational surrogates, that they do not share a genetic tie with the children they produce as gestational surrogates. But concerns such as Carole's about raising an African-American couple's child reveal how racial resemblance raises certain questions about relatedness even when there is no genetic tie.[5] Although she knows that the child is not genetically hers, certain boundaries become blurred for her when an African-American couple is involved whereas with a Euro-American couple the distinction between genetic/nongenetic or self/other is clear. Cultural conceptions such as this about the connection between race and genetics deserve further exploration.

Not surprisingly, the shift from traditional to gestational surrogacy has attracted a different population of women. Overall, women who elect to become gestational surrogates tend to articulate the belief that traditional surrogacy, even though less medically complicated[6] is not an acceptable option for them because they are uncomfortable with the prospect of contributing their own ovum to the creation of a child. They also cannot readily accept the idea that a child who is genetically related to them would be raised by someone else. In other words, they explicitly articulate the opinion in traditional surrogacy (where the surrogate contributes an ovum) that the surrogate is the mother of the child, whereas in gestational surrogacy (where she does not contribute an ovum) she is not. They are nonetheless interested in participating in gestational surrogacy because it provides them with access to the world of surrogacy.[7] This often includes, interestingly enough, women who have been voluntarily sterilized (tubal ligations). For example, Barbara, age 30, married with three children, a Mormon and a two-time gestational surrogate (now planning a third pregnancy) stated: *"The baby is never mine. I am providing a needed environment for it to be born and go back to mom and dad. It's the easy kind of babysitting."*

Oddly enough, the beliefs of IVF surrogates run contrary to current legal opinion as expressed in the findings of both Britain's Warnock Report and the Australian Waller Commission's report that "when a child is born to a woman following the donation of another's egg the women giving birth should, for all purposes, be regarded in law as the mother of that child" (Shalev 1989:117). It should be noted that the opinion expressed in both the Warnock Report and the Waller

Commission contradicts not only the views expressed by IVF surrogates but also by commissioning couples who choose gestational surrogacy precisely because it eliminates the issue of genetic relatedness for them. It also contradicts Euro-American kinship ideology, specifically the continued emphasis on the importance of biogenetic relatedness.[8] However, this effort to expand our definition of biological relatedness, which has until recently depended on a genetic component, runs contrary to the Euro-American emphasis on biogenetic relateness, in which genetic parents are legally and socially considered the "real" parents. This fragmentation or dispersal of parenthood, a byproduct of reproductive technologies, has resulted in what Marilyn Strathern has describes as the "claims of one kind of biological mother against other kinds of biological and nonbiological mothers" (1992:32) and fathers.

How then to account for the gestational surrogate's motivations? Should a gestational surrogate's maternal rights be "modeled on the law of paternity, where proof of genetic parentage establishes ... parentage, or ... on the nine month experience of pregnancy as establishing the preponderant interest of ... parentage" (Hull 1990:152). It is of fundamental importance to gestational surrogates to circumvent the biogenetic tie to the child, and they do so in spite of the greatly increased degree of physical discomfort and medical risk they face in IVF procedures (as compared to risks associated with traditional surrogacy, which are the same as those faced in traditional pregnancy).[9] Any effort, legal or ethical, to argue that pregnancy is a determining factor in parenthood not only fails to consider Euro-American kinship ideology but perhaps most importantly neglects to consider the position of the gestational surrogate and commissioning couple.

The medical procedures commonly encountered by gestational surrogates [the self-administration of hormonal medications] can cause considerable discomfort. In the following example, Barbara discussed her experience: *"After a while you dread having to do it; I had lumps from all those injections. Two times a day and twice a week, three injections a day. If you don't do it, the pregnancy would be lost … You are just [as] concerned with the pregnancy as if it's your own, sometimes more.*" Vicky, age 33, Euro-American, married with three children, who had given birth three weeks earlier, explained how she was able to sustain her motivation and commitment throughout the difficult medical procedures: "*It was hard, but it needed to be done for the baby's sake. All the shots [were] on a daily basis. I didn't mind it at all, but it had to be at a certain time. It was like a curfew. Sure it was painful, but it does go away.*"

The sentiments expressed by Barbara and Vicky are similar to those expressed by traditional surrogates who have experienced difficult, sometimes life-threatening pregnancies and deliveries. Both cast these experiences in terms of meaningful or heroic suffering (Ragoné 1996). The vastly increased physical discomfort and scheduling difficulties are, however, a price that gestational surrogates are willing to endure in order to circumvent what they regard as the problematic biogenetic tie. Barbara expressed a belief shared by many gestational surrogates about their pregnancies when she stated: "*I separate AI [artificial insemination] and IVF completely, almost to the point I don't agree with AI. I feel like that person is entering into an agreement to produce a child to give to someone else. I feel it is* her baby *she is giving away*" [emphasis mine]. In a similar fashion, Lee, age 31, married with two children, Euro-American, who was waiting for an embryo transfer, discussed the differences between traditional (AI) and gestational surrogacy. "*Yes, it's [the fetus] inside my body, but as far as I am concerned, I don't have any biological tie. The other way [AI], I would feel that there is some part of me out there.*"

This view of surrogacy differs in several important ways from the one expressed by traditional surrogates, who advance the idea that the term "parent" should be applied only to individuals who actually choose to become engaged in the process of raising a child, regardless of the degree of relatedness. They

achieve this perspective in part by separating motherhood into two components: biological motherhood and social motherhood. Only social motherhood is viewed by traditional surrogates as "real" motherhood; in other words, nurturance is held to be of greater importance than biological relatedness. In this respect, it is the gestational surrogate, not the traditional surrogate, who tends to subscribe to a decidedly more traditional rendering of relatedness.

It was perhaps impossible to predict with any degree of certainty that advances in reproductive medicine coupled with an increase in consumer demand would produce such a profound shift in the rates of traditional (AI) and gestational surrogacy. Assistive reproductive technologies, e.g., surrogate motherhood, ovum donation, and sperm donation, have called into question what was once understood to be the "natural" basis of parenthood. As we have seen, traditional surrogates underplay their own biological contribution in order to bring to the fore the importance of the social, nurturant role played by the adoptive mother. In this way motherhood is reinterpreted as primarily an important social role in order to sidestep problematic aspects of the surrogate's biogenetic relationship to the child and the adoptive mother's lack of a biogenetic link. For traditional surrogates nurture takes precedence and ascendancy over nature; motherhood is understood as a social construct rather than a biological phenomenon. Gestational surrogates however, interestingly remain committed to the genetic model of parenthood,[10] reasoning that "real" parenthood is in fact genetic.

Many of the early theories about the future of surrogacy focused, at times exclusively, upon its potential for exploitation, but they failed to take into consideration the fact that both fertility and infertility must be contextualized: both are embedded in a series of personal, social, historical, and cultural processes and practices. Within surrogates' statements, assessments, and questions is testimony to the plasticity and resilience of family, which in spite of these seemingly odd changes, persists.

ACKNOWLEDGMENTS

I owe a very special thank you to Dr. Sydel Silverman of the Wenner Gren Foundation for Anthropological Research for her support. An additional thank you is also owed to the University of Massachusetts–Boston for ongoing support in the form of Faculty Development Grants. I am especially indebted to the women and men who have shared their experiences with me over the last ten years; their belief in and commitment to this research has made it an engaging and rewarding experience. I would also like to extend very special and heartfelt thanks to the directors, psychologists, and surrogate program staff who have over the years generously given of their time and their expertise.

NOTES

1. A couple, Elizabeth and William Stern, contracted with a surrogate, Mary Beth Whitehead, to bear a child for them because Elizabeth Stern suffered from multiple sclerosis, a condition that can be exacerbated by pregnancy. Once the child was born, however, Whitehead refused to relinquish the child to the Sterns, and in 1987, William Stern, the biological father, filed suit against Whitehead in an effort to enforce the terms of the surrogate contract. The decision of the lower court to award custody to the biological father and to permit his wife to adopt the child was overturned by the New Jersey Supreme Court, which then awarded custody to William Stern, prohibiting Elizabeth Stern from adopting the child while granting visitation rights to Mary Beth Whitehead. These decisions mirrored public opinion about surrogacy (Hull 1990: 154).
2. See Rapp (1978: 279) and Gordon (1988:3) for a historical analysis of the idea of the demise of the American family.
3. In June 1993, the California Supreme Court upheld the decisions of both the lower court and the court of appeals with respect to gestational surrogacy contracts. In Anna Johnson v

Mark and Crispina Calvert, Case #SO 23721, a case involving an African American gestational surrogate, a Filipina American mother and a Euro-American father, the gestational surrogate and commissioning couple both filed custody suits. Under California law, both of the women could, however, claim maternal rights: Johnson, by virtue of being the woman who gave birth to the child; and Calvert, who donated ovum, because she is the child's genetic mother. In rendering their decision, however, the court circumvented the issue of relatedness, instead emphasized the "intent" of the parties as the ultimate and decisive factor in any determination of parenthood. The court concluded that if the genetic and birth mother are not one and the same person then "she who intended to procreate the child—that is, she who intended to bring about the birth of a child that she intended to raise on her own—is the natural mother under California law."
4. Why women from certain cultural groups are willing to donate ova but not serve as surrogates is a subject of considerable interest. Since gestational surrogates reason that they (unlike traditional surrogates and ovum donors,) do not part with any genetic material, they are able to deny that the child(ren) they produce are related to them. Given the parameters of Euro-American kinship ideology, additional research will be required to ascertain why ovum donors do not perceive their donation of genetic material as problematic.
5. During the course of the interview, I specifically asked her what her feelings and ideas were about having a child for a couple from another racial background (I also asked this question of all the surrogates who were matched with couples from different racial backgrounds).
6. Gestational surrogates often complain about the discomfort they experience as a result of having to self-inject two or three times per day for as long as three to four months of the pregnancy. They report that progesterone is especially painful, since it is oil-based and has a tendency to pool and lump under the skin. Even though the largest of the surrogate programs claims to inform gestational surrogates about the need to self-administer shots, several gestational surrogates reported that they had not anticipated either the frequency or the discomfort of the injections.

7. I have discussed elsewhere in great detail the system of rewards that makes surrogate motherhood attractive to this group of women (Ragoné 1994; 1996, 1999).

8. While there are in fact observable differences in family patterns within the U.S., most notably among poor and working poor African-Americans whose alternative models of mothering/parenting may stem from "West African cultural values" as well as "functional adaptations to race and gender oppression" (Collins 1988: 119; Stack 1974), we should not lose sight of the fact that such perceived differences in family patterns do not necessarily weaken Euro-American kinship ideology. They continue to privilege the biogenetic model of family.

9. Aside from studies of the increased rates of multiple births there are few longitudinal studies on the effects of infertility treatments. Research does, however, suggest that infertility patients have an increased risk of ovarian cancer (Jensen, Riis, et al. 1987). The question remains: although an infertile women knowingly accepts the risks associated with infertility treatments, do surrogacy and ovum donation programs provide their populations with adequate information about the possibility of long-term risk?

10. Once a gestational surrogate has begun to develop a relationship with her couple and has experienced several unsuccessful embryo transfers, she may begin to reformulate or revise her initial beliefs concerning relatedness and family. An unsuccessful gestational surrogate may, for example, opt to become what is referred to in surrogate-mother programs as a "cross-over," someone who chose initially to participate in gestational surrogacy but then decided to become a traditional surrogate.

REFERENCES

Andrews, Lori. 1984. *New Conceptions: A Consumer's Guide to the Newest Infertility Treatments.* New York: Ballatine.

Annas, George. 1988. "Fairy Tales Surrogate Mothers Tell." In *Surrogate Motherhood: Politics and Privacy.* Larry Gostin, ed., pp.43–55. Bloomington: Indiana University Press.

Carrier, James. 1990. Gifts in a World of Commodities: The Ideology of the Perfect Gift in American Society. *Social Analysis* 29:19–37.

Collins, Patricia Hill. 1988. *Black Feminist Thought: Knowledge, Consciousness and the Politics of Empowerment.* New York: Routledge.

Dworkin, Andrea. 1978. *Right-Wing Women.* New York: Perigee Books.

Ferree, Myra. 1984. Sacrifice, Satisfaction and Social Change: Employment and the Family. In *My Troubles are Going to Have Trouble with Me.* Karen Sacks and Dorothy Remy, eds., pp.61–79. New Brunswick, NJ: Rutgers University Press.

Fox, Renee and Judith Swazey.1992. *Spare Parts: Organ Replacement in American Society.* New York and Oxford: Oxford University Press.

Gordon, Linda. 1988.*Heroes of Their Own Lives.* New York: Viking.

Hull, Richard. 1990.Gestational Surrogacy and Surrogate Motherhood: In *Ethical Issues in the New Reproductive Technologies,* Richard Hull, ed., pp.150–155. Belmont, CA: Wadsworth Publishers.

Jensen, P., Riis, B., Rodbro, P., Stram, V., and Christiansen, C. 1987. Climacteric symptoms after oral and percutaneous hormone replacement therapy. *Matvritas* 9: 207–215.

Martin, Emily. 1987.*The Woman in the Body: A Cultural Analysis of Reproduction.* Boston: Beacon Press.

Neuhaus, Robert. 1988. Renting Women, Buying Babies and Class Struggles. *Society* 25(3):8–10.

Parker, Phillip. 1983.Motivation of Surrogate Mothers: Initial Findings. *American Journal of Psychiatry* 1 40:117–119.

Ragoné, Heléna. 1994. *Surrogate Motherhood: Conception in the Heart.* Boulder, CO, and Oxford: Westview Press/Basic Books:.

———. 1996. Chasing the Blood Tie: Surrogate Mothers, Adoptive Mothers and Fathers. *American Ethnologist* 23(2): 352–365.

———. 1998. Incontestable Motivations. In *Reproducing Reproduction: Kinship, Power, and Technological Innovation.* Sarah Franklin and Heléna Ragoné, eds., Philadelphia: University of Pennsylvania Press.

———. 1999. The Gift of Life: Surrogate Motherhood, Gamete Donations and Constructions of Altruism. In *Transformative Mothering: On Giving and Getting, in a Consumer Culture.* Linda Layne (eds.), pp132–176. New York: New York University Press.

———. 2000. Of Likeness and Difference: How Race is Being Transfigured by Gestational Surrogacy. In *Ideologies and Technologies of Motherhood: Race, Class, Sexuality and Nationalism.* Heléna Ragoné and France Winddance Twine, eds. New York and London: Routledge.

Rapp, Rayna. 1978. Family and Class in Contemporary America: Notes Toward an Understanding of Ideology. *Science and Technology* 42(3)278–300.

Rosaldo, Michelle. 1974. Woman, Culture and Society: A Theoretical Overview. In *Woman, Culture and Society*, M. Rosaldo and L. Lamphere, eds. Stanford, CA: Stanford University Press.

Shalev, Carmel. 1989. *Birth Power: The Case for Surrogacy*. New Haven: Yale University Press.

Snowden, R. Mitchell, G. and E. Snowden.1983. *Artificial Reproduction: A Social Investigation*. London: Allen and Unwin.

Stack, Carol. 1974. *All Our Kin*. New York: Harper & Row

Strathern, Marilyn. 1991.The Pursuit of Certainty: Investigating Kinship in the Late Twentieth Century. Distinguished Lecture. Society of the Anthropology of Europe.

———. 1992. *Reproducing the Future: Anthropology, Kinship and the New Reproductive Technologies*. Manchester: Manchester University Press.

Titmus, Richard. 1971. *The Gift Relationship: From Human Blood to Social Policy*. New York: Pantheon Books.

Warnock, Mary. 1984. *The Warnock Report: Report of the Committee of Inquiry into Human Fertilisation and Embryology*. London: Her Majesty's Stationery Office.

Zelizer, Viviana. 1985. *Pricing the Priceless Child*. New York: Basic Books.

The Movement Against Clitoridectomy and Infibulation in Sudan: Public Health Policy and the Women's Movement

Ellen Gruenbaum

Sudan is one of the countries where the most severe form of female circumcision persists and is practiced widely among both Muslims and Coptic Christians, in both urban and rural communities. Only the largely non-Muslim Southern Region is free of the practice, except among people of northern origin.

The most common form of the operation is referred to as pharaonic circumcision, consisting of the removal of all external genitalia—the clitoris, the clitoral prepuce, the labia minora and all or part of the labia majora—and infibulation (stitching together of the opening), so as to occlude the vaginal opening and urethra. Only a tiny opening is left for the passage of urine and menses. A modified version, Sunna circumcision, is less common, and consists of excision of the pre-

puce of the clitoris, generally also with partial or total excision of the clitoris itself (clitoridectomy), but without infibulation.

The operations customarily are performed by traditional or government-trained midwives on girls in the 5–7 year age range; the girls, however, may be older or younger, since it is common to circumcise two or three sisters at the same time. These occasions are ones of celebration, with new dresses, bracelets, and gifts for the girls. An animal may be slaughtered and a special meal prepared for the many guests and well-wishers who are expected to drop in. In wealthy families, musical entertainment is often arranged for an evening party. The girls themselves, though they may be fearful of the operation, look forward to the first occasion at which they will be treated as important people.

The origin of the practice is unknown, though its existence in the ancient civilizations of the Nile Valley in Egypt and Sudan has been documented. The practice survived the spread of Christianity to the ruling groups of the Nile Valley kingdoms in Sudan in the 6th century. Waves of Arab migration, intermarriage with the indigenous people, and the influence of Islamic teachers resulted in Islam's becoming the dominant religion of northern Sudan by about 1500. Pharaonic circumcision, along with other non-Islamic beliefs such as veneration of ancestors or saints and spirit possession cults, was successfully incorporated into the Sudanese Islamic belief system. The practice is deeply embedded in Sudanese cultures; and it should be recognized that the symbolic significance and cultural concomitants of female circumcision undoubtedly play important roles in individual repetition of the custom, as the work of Janice Boddy (1979) has shown.

Still, to say that it is a "custom" is not a sufficient explanation for the persistence of this damaging practice. Numerous physically harmful effects have been documented in the medical literature (Verzin 1975, Cook 1976, Shandall 1967). At the time of circumcision, girls may suffer from hemorrhage, infections, septicemia, retention of urine, or shock; deaths may result from these complications. The infibulated state may also result in retention of menses or difficulties in urination (due to scar tissue), and may be related to an apparently high prevalence of urinary tract and other chronic pelvic infections (Boddy 1979, Toubia 1981). At first intercourse, infibulation presents a barrier which is painfully torn unless cut open by husband, midwife, or doctor. Childbirth is complicated by the inelastic scar tissue of infibulation, which must be cut open by the birth attendant and restitched after delivery. Vasicovaginal fistulae, which can result from such obstructed labor, are by no means rare in Sudan. Such a fistula—a passage between the urinary bladder and the vagina created by damage to tissue between the two organs—results in a most embarrassing condition for the woman, who cannot retain her urine and therefore leaks constantly (Toubia 1981).

Why, then, in light of these physically harmful, even life-threatening, consequences, do women continue to perform these operations on their daughters? Much of the literature has gone no further than the observation that it is "customary," or as one Sudanese writer has put it, "the implicit and explicit message being that it is something we inherited from an untraceable past which has no rational meaning and lies within the realm of untouchable sensitivity of traditional people" (Toubia 1981:4).

Social scientists and feminists writing on the subject have pointed out that female circumcision forms part of a complex sociocultural arrangement of female subjugation in a strongly patrilineal, patriarchal society (*cfb.,* Assaad 1980, Hayes 1975, El Saadawi 1980b). The fact that it is women who carry out the practice, and who are its strongest defenders, must be analyzed in terms of their weaker social position.

Women in Sudan generally must derive their social status and economic security from their roles as wives and mothers. Among most cultural groups in northern Sudan, female virginity at marriage is considered so important that even rumors questioning a girl's morality may be enough to besmirch the family honor and to bar her from the possibility of marriage. In this context, clitoridectomy and infibulation serve as a guarantee of morality. Sudanese women hold that clitoridectomy helps to attenuate a girl's sexual desire so that she is less likely to seek premarital sex; infibulation presents a barrier to penetration. Any girl known to have been "properly" circumcised in the pharaonic manner can be assumed to be a virgin and therefore marriageable, while doubts can be raised about those who are not circumcised or have had only the modified Sunna circumcision.

Attempts to formulate policies against the practice have seldom recognized the significance of the linkage between the operations and the social goal of maintaining the reputations and marriageability of daughters in a strongly patriarchal society. In addition, the economic and social status of midwives, the group chiefly responsible for performing the operations, has seldom been seriously considered. Instead, government policies have tended to emphasize simple legal prohibitions; propaganda against the apparent ideological supports of the practice; spreading information on some of the physically harmful aspects of female circumcision; and tacit acceptance of a compromise policy of modification and "modernization" of the practice.

Some policies resulting from these emphases are undoubtedly useful. Certainly the recommendations of the 1979 Khartoum Conference (Seminar on Traditional Practices Affecting the Health of Women, sponsored by the Eastern Mediterranean Regional Office of the World Health Organization) are to be commended and supported. These recommendations included a call for clear national policies for the abolition of the practice in the countries where it persists; the passage of legislation in support of such policies; the intensification of general education on the dangers and undesirability of the practice; and intensification of educational programs for birth attendants and other practitioners to enlist their support. Because there is such strong social motivation for continuing the practice in Sudan, however, I would argue that the proposed public health education approach would have only a weak or slow effect. Policy on female circumcision requires rethinking.

In the following sections, I draw upon my experience in Sudan, where I carried out research on rural health services and lectured at the University of Khartoum. My goal here is twofold: to consider the reasons for failure of past anticircumcision policies, and to provide a critique of current policy efforts. In addition, I hope to provide insights into what is necessary for the development of viable policies.

ABOLITION EFFORTS IN SUDAN

The first efforts to eliminate the practice of clitoridectomy and infibulation in Sudan came during the British colonial period (1898–1956). When a British midwife was brought in to organize a midwifery training school in 1920, efforts were made to dissuade the traditional midwives enrolled in the training program from continuing the practice. But persuasion and example apparently had little effect.

In 1946, an edict was promulgated prohibiting pharaonic circumcision. This attempt to impose the colonialists' values on the culture of a subject people by force of law also failed completely, and was even met with violent resistance. Residents of the town of Rufa'a still talk about "our Revolution"—the day in 1946 when they tore the government prison to the ground to free a midwife who had been arrested for circumcising a girl. Government troops fired on the crowd, and injured some; yet even this failed to stem popular resistance to the British and to their attempts to outlaw the entrenched custom.

Resistance to the government ban did not require rebellion. Since the activity took place outside the purview of the foreign government, the practice simply continued as before. In fact, historically, the government seldom attempted the sort of enforcement that led to the Rufa'a "Revolution."

Another approach used by the British against the practice was propaganda. In 1945, the Sudan Medical Service issued and circulated a pamphlet, written in both English and Arabic, that condemned pharaonic circumcision and urged the Sudanese to abandon the practice. It was signed by the highest ranking British and Sudanese doctors, and was endorsed by Sudanese religious leaders. The Mufti of Sudan provided an authoritative Islamic legal opinion stating that female circumcision was not obligatory under Islam; and another endorsing religious leader advocated the substitution of Sunna circumcision (clitoridectomy). Thus, while the backing of the religious leaders was something less than total opposition to female circumcision, their opposition to the pharaonic form is important. (Few Sudanese queried in villages where I worked, however, were aware that the religious leaders had ever spoken against female circumcision.)

During this same period, the mid-1940s, several educated Sudanese women—teachers and midwives—undertook speaking tours in the provinces to publicize the bad effects of pharaonic circumcision. An Arabic poster used during the campaign declared that the Sunna circumcision came from the Prophet Mohammed, and should therefore replace the pharaonic form, ascribed to "Pharaoh the enemy of God" (Hall and Ismail 1981:93–95).

Today, after three decades of illegality, pharaonic circumcision of girls continues to be widely performed in both rural and urban areas. It is openly celebrated, with feasting and gift-giving. Midwives speak freely of their participation in the perpetuation of the practice. To my knowledge there have been no government efforts in recent years to enforce the legal prohibition.

There has, however, been some change in the methods used in performing the operations, although this has not been uniform. The dangerously unhygienic traditional methods, such as performing the operation over a hole in the ground, using knives for cutting, thorns and leg binding for infibulation, and plain water for cleansing, have been supplanted by the availability of better equipment and knowledge of more hygienic methods. The government-trained village midwife whose practice I observed did the operations on a wood and rope bed covered with a plastic sheet. She used xylocaine injections for local anesthesia, new razor blades, suture needles, dissolving sutures when available, and prophylactic antibiotic powder. Her equipment was sterilized with boiling water before use. After this initial use, however, she returned the instruments to the same bowl of previously boiled water, and did not resterilize them before using them in a second girl's operation. The midwife purchases most of the necessary supplies and medications out of her earnings; some of the basic equipment necessary for childbirth attendance is provided by the government, however, and some supplies are obtained informally through the local government health center.

CURRENT POLICY EFFORTS

In more recent years, opponents—ordinarily resorting to medical and psychological arguments against pharaonic circumcision—have recognized that complete eradication of the practice is an unrealistic short-term objective. While continuing to advocate eventual eradication, policymakers have tended to attempt to mitigate the effects by substituting the less drastic Sunna form of circumcision. This opinion, held unofficially by the government health service's leaders and many medical doctors with whom I spoke in the late 1970s, has meant that many doctors are willing to perform such operations themselves. They assume that, in terms of medical safety, it is better for them to perform clitoridectomies in their offices.[1]

As policy positions, both the eradication goal and the "modification" compromise are problematic. The view that the practice should or could be "eradicated," as if it were a disease, is a particularly medical view. While it is reasonable that arguments against circumcision stress physical risks, the problem nevertheless is one that is not necessarily amenable to medical solutions. The medical view implies not only that the practice is "pathological," but that its solution might lie in some sort of campaign-style attack on the problem. Social customs, however, are not "pathologies"; and such a view is a poor starting point for change, since it is not one necessarily shared by the people whose customs are under attack. While these people may be open to the view that a practice such as this may be harmful in some ways, to approach it as an evil or pathological situation is to insult those who believe strongly in it and consider it a means of promoting cleanliness and purity, and is unlikely to foster consideration of change. Furthermore, the decades of emphasis on medical reasons for discontinuing the practice have not in fact resulted in its abandonment. For example, in a study of medical records of 2526 women in Khartoum and Wad Medani, Mudawi (1977a) found only seven to be uncircumcised; twelve had been clitoridectomised only, and the remainder had been infibulated.[2] A questionnaire sample survey of about 10,000 women in Sudan found that 82 percent were infibulated (El Dareer 1979).

Another problem with the strategy of promoting a modified form of circumcision as a transitional program relates to the unfortunate ideological linkage of the modified type. Among Sudanese who practice pharaonic circumcision, it is widely believed that the practice is commanded by Islam. While this interpretation is disavowed by many Islamic scholars, the belief that both male and female circumcision were commanded by the Prophet Mohammed persists.[3] This widespread belief serves as strong ideological support for a practice known to predate Islam (Diaz and Mudawi 1977) and which is perpetuated largely because of its important social functions.

The use of the term "Sunna circumcision" for the less drastic operation, which many reformers are encouraging as the most feasible short-term alternative, has unfortunately reinforced the ideological linkage with Islam. To describe a practice as "Sunna" is to consider it religious law.[4] Since Sudanese Muslims are adherents of the Sunni branch of Islam (i.e., "those who follow the Sunna"), they do not want to say their practice is incongruent with Sunni tradition. The linguistic root of the words Sunni and Sunna is the same, and although "Sunna circumcision" does not literally imply linkage to Sunni Islam, they are commonly associated. Indeed, the ideological linkage between the term "Sunna circumcision" and the religion has been reinforced even by an eminent Sudanese gynecologist, Dr. Suliman Mudawi, who writes that, "The Sunna circumcision, or clitoridectomy, is the legal operation recommended by Islam, consisting of the excision of the glans clitoris and sometimes a small portion of the clitoris itself" (Mudawi 1977b).

Thus, now that the term "Sunna circumcision" is widely known, many people profess to practice it—since they wish to be regarded as faithful Sunnites—even when the operation is performed as before with infibulation after removal of clitoris and labia. Reform efforts advocating a modified operation, therefore, may have resulted in a change in nomenclature, rather than widespread change in the operations. Thus, reports that pharaonic circumcision with infibulation is gradually being abandoned in Sudan, which are based on questionnaire interviews or anecdotal material (e.g., Clark and Diaz 1977, Cook 1976), may be misleading, since some of those who say they have adopted the Sunna form simply may have begun calling pharaonic circumcision by another name.

In spite of the importance of ideological supports, it would not be sufficient to attack the presumed religious reasons. Change efforts must take into consideration the socioeconomic relations in which Sudanese women are enmeshed, and the social dilemmas to which families that try to change the practice would be exposed. After all, where a most significant aspect of marriage is control of female reproductive capacity, and where circumcision has come to be the mechanism for guaranteeing the perfect condition of that capacity, to dispense with circumcision is to violate a basic condition of an essential social relation. Thus, a religious scholar's testimony that female circumcision is not necessary for religious reasons would not be sufficient for a mother to risk her daughter's marriageability. Similarly, awareness of medical and psychological[5] hazards may be only weakly deterrent; a daughter's marriageability would scarcely be risked because of a psychological notion that she may suffer bad dreams or never experience orgasm. Marriage and children are more vital, closer to the meaning of life and to a woman's economic survival, than transitory emotional feelings.

While most women are economically active, either in subsistence production, wage employment, trade, or production of commodities, economic well-being—indeed, survival in many of the harsher rural areas—requires large family production units. A husband and children are necessary to a woman's economic security; not only do children contribute their labor at an early age to the family's economic production—especially in rural areas—but also they are security for old age. Commonly, women are to some degree dependent on their husbands for access to land or domestic animals, their labors, and/or their wages. A husband dissatisfied with his wife—either personally or because of reproductive inadequacy—is considered more likely to take a second wife. Although polygyny frequently enhances the prestige and wealth of the husband, it commonly weakens the individual woman's economic position and, if the other wife or wives bear children, lessens her own children's inheritance. Under Islamic law,[6] a divorced woman has no right to child custody after the age of seven for boys and the age of nine for girls, regardless of the reasons for divorce or on whose initiative the marriage was ended. Men have the right to unilateral divorce, but women do not. With these constraints it is not surprising that most women put considerable effort into pleasing their husbands and protecting their reputations, so as to safeguard their marriages.

Efforts to please husbands and safeguard virtue take many forms. Beautification methods, while pleasurable for a woman herself and usually done in pleasant camaraderie with other women, are primarily directed toward husbands, with the most sensuous techniques being reserved for married women. Even poor rural women spend considerable time and effort on the arts of decorative henna staining of hands and feet, removal of body hair, sauna-like incensing of the body, careful selection of clothing and ornaments, and decorative hair plaiting. They also prepare special scented substances for massaging their husbands.

Beyond these, the enhancement of a woman's ability to please her husband is considered to be most importantly achieved by clitoridectomy and infibulation. One midwife I spoke with claimed that clitoridectomy allowed for longer intercourse, pleasing to the man. This belief presupposes that a woman experiencing more sexual stimulation

would be less patient, and can hardly be credited as a major factor in perpetuating clitoridectomy. On the other hand, the attenuation of *inappropriate* sexual desire, before marriage and extramaritally, should be considered one of the major goals of the practice.

It is infibulation, and especially reinfibulation, that is alleged to contribute most significantly to the sexual pleasure of men. Following childbirth, the midwife restitches the long incision made for the delivery of the baby. A tighter reinfibulation is expected to result in greater pleasure for the husband when intercourse is resumed following the customary forty-day postpartum recovery period. One reinfibulation I witnessed, performed by a government-trained midwife following a woman's thirteenth childbirth, left a completely smooth vulva, the urethral opening completely concealed, and only a pin-sized opening to the vagina. A number of women told me that such tight reinfibulation gives husbands greater sexual pleasure, the tightness lasting approximately three months after resumption of sexual intercourse. They claimed that husbands were more generous in their gifts (clothes, jewelry, perfumes) when the reinfibulation is very tight. It was clear, too, that such marital sexual satisfaction is considered important in avoiding the possibility of the husband exercising his legally guaranteed rights to unilateral divorce or polygynous marriage.

The attitudes of women toward the practice of clitoridectomy and infibulation are often contradictory. Occasionally, I encountered Sudanese women who were surprised to learn that American and European women are not circumcised. Others realized that Europeans did not circumcise women, but believed that all Muslims did. Although they found it hard to believe that Saudi Arabian women are not circumcised, such information did nothing to undermine their faith in the importance of the practice. To my comment that American women are left "natural," they replied, "But circumcision *is* natural for us."

There was, however, recurrent ambivalence expressed in many of the conversations I had on this topic. Without questioning the necessity of circumcision, a woman might sigh and say, "Isn't it difficult?" When discussing repeated reinfibulation with one small group of urban women (which included a new mother who had just been reinfibulated a few days before), I was urged, "Be sure and put all this in your report, about how difficult it is for us."

DEVELOPING VIABLE POLICY ALTERNATIVES

That women perpetuate practices painful and dangerous to themselves and their daughters and that inhibit their own sexual gratification must be understood in the context of their social and economic vulnerability in a strongly patriarchal society. Public health policymakers must allow for the fact that the circumcision of girls is a deeply rooted social custom. Even among urban-dwelling, educated families, there are those who would take their daughters back to the relatives in a rural village for circumcision, to ensure a traditional, thorough operation.

Although harmful sequelae have brought female circumcision to the attention of medical professionals, it is argued here that medical opinion can have little relevance in changing the situation. While more research into the psychological and medical hazards of circumcision could be useful for convincing influential educated people to back efforts toward change, the medical model and the efforts of the medical services system are limited in terms of policy development. Effective change can only come in the context of a women's movement oriented toward the basic social problems affecting women, particularly their economic dependency, educational disadvantages, and obstacles to employment (e.g., the dearth of child day-care facilities for urban workers). To improve women's social and economic security, marital customs must be challenged, and new civil laws are needed to offer additional protection to married and divorced women concerning child custody, rights in marital property, and financial support, going beyond the present provisions of Islamic and customary law. Further, general health conditions are very poor and must be improved. With an infant mortality rate conservatively estimated at 140 per 1000 (Sudan, Ministry of Health, 1975a:6), and with a high prevalence of numerous disabling and life-threatening illnesses, especially dangerous to children, it is not surprising that Sudanese women—particularly in rural areas—seek to give birth to large numbers of children. The crude birth rate is approximately 49 per 1000 (Sudan, Ministry of Health 1975a:5). Thus, basic health issues are important concerns of women.

The implications of reducing women's dependency through improvement of their economic opportunities are far-reaching. Any policy that would threaten the form or importance of the family and its functions would obviously excite widespread reaction. At the same time, Sudan's current laws and social values already offer some advantages to women in promising productive roles. Educated women are expected to hold full-time jobs and to have the right to the same pay and benefits as men in comparable jobs, although there are social barriers to women's participation in certain occupations. While many struggles remain to be fought on this front, the fact that wide networks of people benefit from each person employed in a stable job means that families generally back the educated woman who wants to work. Frequently, child care can be provided by relatives during working hours, and there is a general acceptance of the principle of equal pay for equal work. In addition, the government (the largest employer of the educated) gives eight weeks' paid maternity leave, often additional unpaid leave with position held, and makes special allowances for the needs of nursing mothers.

While these offer a good basis for developing women's position, many problems prevent women from taking full advantage of the opportunities that do exist. Working women complain (or, more often, do not complain, but simply carry on) that they must still perform all the usual housework after coming home, and are still expected to make time for all the traditional visiting and hospitality. Women college students find their neighbors and relatives consider them snobbish if they do not take the time for such visiting, regardless of the demands of their studies. This is especially hard on women medical students who must keep odd hours, and often spend the night at the hospital during their clinical training.

The family continues to be an extremely important factor, however, in the lives of even the most advantaged, educated, employed women. Since childbearing is expected to begin immediately after marriage, the employed woman most commonly depends on her mother or another female relative to provide child care. Family members become dependent on her income, and she may find herself locked into the necessity of working even when other social obligations make it difficult. Should her marriage falter and her husband divorce her, she may not only lose his support but custody of her children as well. Clearly, additional social services would help overcome these problems. For example, while government-sponsored child care centers presently exist in some towns, many women workers find them unavailable or too costly. Some form of social security benefits could reduce women's vulnerability to divorce and loss of support and child custody. But state subsidy of such services outside the family currently is neither a feasible nor a desired alternative in Sudan, where government policy favors investment in economic development over expansion of social service expenditures.

A full discussion of development strategies and their implications for women's position in the society would be outside the scope of this paper. It is important to realize, however, that while women share in the desire for economic development in their poor country, just as they desire increased incomes for their families and themselves, current development policies offer little to women. Sudan's development has been of the peripheral capitalist pattern of uneven development (O'Brien 1980). Investment has gravitated toward the center of the country in the most highly productive centers of primary products for export or import substitution. All too frequently, foreign investments have been self-serving, emphasizing high technology that the developed countries want to sell, or the production of products that the investors want to import. The high technology emphasis, which appeals to scheme managers and government officials seeking to "modernize," results in jobs for men rather than women, and sometimes even undercuts existing productive roles of women (see Sørbø 1977).

Sudanese and other Middle Eastern women have demonstrated their interest in changing their lot by the formation of women's organizations such as the Sudanese Women's Union. The Union has a history of militant action, as when Sudanese women took to the streets in the popular uprising that overthrew the military regime in 1964. While the issues such women's groups have chosen to address have long included modifying or abolishing circumcision, they have addressed themselves more urgently to other problems. In the 1950s and 1960s for example, the women's organization in Sudan was concerned with nationalist issues: the achievement of national independence, avoidance of control by U.S. imperialist interests, and the development of democratic government. In the early 1970s, the women's union was restructured under the ruling party (under Nimeiri's government, which came to power in a coup d'etat in 1969), and most of the communist and other politically radical women were purged or barred from leadership. Since then, the thrust of the organization has also changed somewhat. In the urban and "modern" sector rural areas (such as the Gezira Irrigation Scheme), the primary activities of the Union as they touch the lives of the ordinary women center on cultural and educational activities—embroidery classes, crafts shows, and the like and support for the ruling party; eradication of circumcision has not been a high priority.

The majority of women in the country, who live outside the towns and agricultural schemes or in the poor neighborhoods and rural villages in those areas, have not by and large been recruited into such organizations. Yet these women, too, have a number of very basic concerns: improved incomes, education for their children, clean water, and basic health services. Organizing these rural women, however, has proven difficult. In a prosperous village in the Gezira Irrigated Scheme, for example, the membership of the local branch of the Women's Union has not met in two years. One divorced woman, a Union member, tried to organize women in that village to take an active part in improving village sanitation. She was unable to mobilize support, however, even though a fully staffed health center (which should share responsibility for public health) is located in the village. Further, though this woman is part of the mandated one-third female membership of the village People's Council, she and the other women members are not ordinarily informed of meetings. Her participation as an individual in development is also blocked. Although she is literate, she is not highly enough educated to qualify for a white-collar job; and her brother has opposed her working in agriculture, a position that would threaten the prestige of the family.

This is not to say that women's organizations and programs are everywhere ineffective. In fact there is much enthusiasm in Gezira villages for the literacy campaigns and home economics courses offered by the Gezira Scheme's Social Development Department. But if the woman just mentioned must face such obstacles even in a relatively well off village that has resources to devote to local projects, the problems of the more remote and poorer villages, where literacy campaigns and women's organizations have not penetrated at all, are far greater.

Since, as history demonstrates, circumcisions can continue with or without governmental sanction, it is impossible to conceive of any efforts to change the custom having an effect unless they are supported by women themselves. These changes will come only as the result of many other societal changes, especially those that enable women to be less economically dependent on men and thus less oriented toward pleasing husbands.

POLICY CONTRIBUTIONS

To assert that changes in female circumcision must come from the women themselves and their social movement is not to say that policymakers have nothing to contribute. Indeed, there are several key areas where public policy and specifically health policy could contribute significantly.

First, further research is appropriate. Much of the writing thus far has been based on case studies, anecdotal material, or haphazard sampling (e.g., Assaad 1980, Hayes 1975). It would be useful to relate the place of circumcision and its celebration to the social position of women in societies where the practice is common. Studies should focus particularly on the significance of marriage, the importance of virginity and its relation to the maintenance of family "honor" (e.g., segregation of sexes, chaperoning, infibulation, manner of dress), and the economic participation of women and form of economic organization (especially whether the organization of production continues to emphasize family production units). Whether more clinical medical articles, describing the operations and their sequelae, would add anything to arguments against the practice is uncertain, although more information on the treatment of complications could be useful. Epidemiological studies of the apparently high rates of urinary and vaginal infections associated with circumcision also would be in order. Although I am aware of no data on a relationship between the operations and infertility or low fertility, such a relationship has nevertheless been suggested (*cf.*, Hosken 1980; Hayes 1975); Hayes (1975), in fact, considered lowered fertility a "latent function" of female circumcision. Certainly infertility might be expected in cases of obstructed intercourse (Sudan Medical Service 1945), and in association with the medical complications of circumcision. The existence of a demonstrable relationship between circumcision and infertility could provide a powerful argument against the operations in countries such as Sudan with strong pronatalist values.

Second, policies that promote the opportunities of women in education and employment could be beneficial in two ways. First, reducing women's dependence on marriage and motherhood as the only economically viable social roles could separate circumcision from basic economic survival and thus weaken support for it. Second, education and employment could be expected to enhance women's ability to act as a group by enabling them to become more involved in shaping their own destiny through access to political and economic power and greater opportunities for organizing themselves. Women then would be better able to influence and implement policies according to their own priorities. The realization of such opportunities may require not only that additional social security and other support services be provided but, in addition, that economic development policies be challenged. The high technology strategies which have so often resulted in skilled jobs for men while undermining women's traditional productive roles and ignoring the possibility of their involvement in new areas, may need to be revised.

The Role of Midwives

A particularly important locus of policy concerns should be the role of midwives, since they are the principal practitioners of circumcision. It is not enough to recommend that they be educated as to its harmful effects; it must also be recognized that fees, together with gifts such as soap, perfume, meat from the celebration slaughter and other foods, constitute important elements of a midwife's income. Government-trained midwives, if they are paid at all, receive only a very small monthly retainer fee from the local government. This is not paid in all areas and is too small to be considered even a meager salary. Untrained, traditional midwives receive no benefits from the government at all; even basic equipment for childbirth attendance is supplied only to the trained midwives, and both groups must purchase their own drugs and supplies, unless acquired informally through local health services facilities of the government. The fee-for-service payment system means that the midwife's income is directly dependent on the number of births attended and circumcision performed.

The current drive for the development of Primary Health Care for the achievement of WHO's goal of "Health for All by the Year 2000" could very usefully seek out midwives to be Community Health Workers. The additional training would benefit their midwifery practices, and whatever status individual midwives already have achieved as respected community members concerned with health could enhance their influence as health care providers. Further, since barriers to the effective health care of women by male health care providers now prevent women from receiving needed care, more female providers would fill a real need.[7]

Providing midwives with a wider role and some other income might help them heed educational efforts against circumcision by reducing the conflicts of interest with respect to income. Difficulties inherent in the training of midwives (involving a full year's study away from family, especially hard for married women and mothers) have been overcome. The same could be expected for Community Health Workers, whose training period is shorter. Such a strategy could help to achieve primary health care goals while improving midwifery at less cost than training and supporting two separate specialized individuals. Since midwives, as women, have access to

women and children even in the most traditional communities, they could be expected
to be very effective in promoting maternal
and child health goals.

PERSPECTIVES ON
INTERNATIONAL POLICYMAKING

Such recommendations should be considered
in the context of the social dynamics of an
underdeveloped country. The dependency
relations between a country such as Sudan
and the more powerful capitalist financial
centers has surely played as much a part in
molding priorities in social and health policy
as have religion and cultural tradition.

Social scientists who seek to design rational, sensible, and culturally sensitive public
health policies, must ask themselves several
questions. What would be necessary to ensure
the adoption of their proposals? What are the
interests of the social classes with access to the
most political power in a country? What
image of their country do the relevant national ministries, organizations, and occupational
groups wish to portray? What sort of research
or program priorities might they want to
block? Which would they prefer to support?

Similarly, international organizations and
the aid missions of developed countries are
limited by their own hidden agendas.[8] For
example, USAID projects ordinarily must be
demonstrated to have some beneficial effect
on U.S. trade, U.S. geopolitical strategies, or
other U.S. interests; beneficial effects on the
people or the economies of the developing
countries are desirable, but secondary. To
suppose that an aid mission might withhold
support from such programs as primary
health care until serious work against female
circumcision is undertaken is to pretend that
aid missions are moral entities instead of
international political and economic tools.
For aid to be accepted by the host government, its terms ordinarily must be beneficial
to the interests of ruling groups or to governmental stability. Aid must not, therefore,
make the nation or the government appear

backward, discriminatory, or as having anything less than the best interests of the entire
populace at heart.

While international bodies such as the United Nations organizations are less likely to have
such strongly political agendas, and can be
assumed to be genuinely oriented to abstract
goals such as peace and health, they, too, suffer from an inability to be critical of host governments. Programs must be invited and
collaborative, although these organizations'
apparently neutral political position gives
them somewhat more leeway to provide guidance without seeming offensively imperialistic.

I believe it is a mistake to insist, as some
outspoken critics do, that aid missions, international organizations, and even nongovernmental and church groups take firm stands
"to prevent the operations" (Hosken 1980).
Such agencies and organizations would have
no political interest in taking such a controversial stand except where host governments
might ask them to do so as part of an indigenous movement against the practice. But
even if the necessary forces could be mobilized in the developed countries to force the
adoption of such a policy and such agencies
and organizations *did* adopt this stance, a
"backlash" phenomenon would all too likely
follow. Heavy-handedness on the part of the
developed countries is generally unwelcome
in fiercely nationalistic underdeveloped
countries such as Sudan. Thus, while its external relationships may be those of dependency
and its economic system capitalist (including
some state-capitalist structures and some use
of "socialist" ideology), there is no loyalty to a
particular power which extends beyond
national interests or economic constraints.
Even Saudi Arabia, with its stranglehold control of the supply of much of Sudan's energy
and investment capital and its influential role
in religious leadership of the Islamic countries, has thus far been able to impose only
temporary or partial social programs—such
as the crackdown on prostitution in Khartoum in 1976–77. The Nimeiri government,
however, has stalled on such issues as the abolition of alcohol or imposition of an Islamic

constitution, which might prove either widely unpopular or which might jeopardize the government's control over the largely non-Muslim south.

Policy research must be placed in this context. It is clear that the movement against clitoridectomy and infibulation must receive its primary momentum for national movements in which women themselves play a leading role. Thus, policy researchers should keep in mind that it is not appropriate merely to expose practices and make recommendations to outside organizations. Wherever possible, indigenous women and women's organizations should be involved in all stages of the research, from formulation of the problem to development of policy. Only in this way will such indigenous movements be sure to benefit from the research.

NOTES

1. In support of this point, one Sudanese doctor recently stated that before the Khartoum Conference in 1979, the medical profession's official policy "was not total abolition of female circumcision, but the promotion of clitoridectomy under more hygienic circumstances as a substitute for infibulation" (Toubia 1981).
2. It is ironic that this same author, a senior Sudanese gynecologist, has said, "Although the habit is still practised in some parts of the Sudan it is gratifying to note that it is gradually dying out." He is further quoted as saying. "The most effective line of attack was a medical one" (quoted in Toubia 1981:3).
3. The sayings attributed to the Prophet Mohammed on this subject do not, however, endorse infibulation. "Reduce but do not destroy," is often quoted by reformers. Another saying, handed down by Um Attiya, is, "Circumcise but do not go deep, this is more illuminating to the face and more enjoyable to the husband" (Sudanese Medical Service 1945, in Foreword by the Mufti of the Sudan).
4. While "Sunna" may be translated as "rule" or "tradition," the Islamic ideology asserts that Islam is not simply a religion, but a "way of life." Hence, it is not uncommon for Sudanese Muslims to assume linkages between cultural traditions and religious beliefs, and to assume that their shared beliefs and practices are rooted in formal Islamic doctrine. In his statement against pharaonic circumcision in 1945, the Mufti of Sudan cited a religious authority who believed that "male circumcision was a Sunna and female circumcision was merely preferable" (Sudanese Medical Service 1945). This usage implies a greater obligation for that which is termed "Sunna." Therefore, to attach the term "Sunna" to female circumcision is to imply that *some* form of circumcision is expected by religious law.
5. The psychological effects of female circumcision have only recently received any systematic attention in Sudan (*see,* e.g., Baashar et al. 1979).
6. All matters concerning marriage, divorce, custody and inheritance in Sudan are governed by customary rather than civil law. A system of *shari'a* courts exists for the administration of Islamic law for cases where the individuals involved are Muslims.
7. It is interesting to note that in Sudan, where the great majority of primary health care workers at all levels are male, government statistics show males outnumbering females in 89 out of the 93 categories of treated illnesses that are not female-specific conditions (Sudan, Ministry of Health 1975a).
8. Dr. Nawal el Saadawi, an Egyptian physician and novelist who has written extensively on women in Arab societies, has criticized the "'them' helping 'us'" approach of some foreign groups: "That kind of help, which they think of as solidarity, is another type of colonialism in disguise. So we must deal with female circumcision ourselves. It is our culture, we understand it, when to fight against it and how, because this is the process of liberation" (El Saadawi 1980a).

REFERENCES

Assaad, Marie Bassili. 1980. "Female Circumcision in Egypt: Social Implications, Current Research, and Prospects for Change," *Studies in Family Planning* 11(1):3–16.

Baashar, T. A., et al. 1979. "Psycho-social Aspects of Female Circumcision. Seminar on Traditional Practices Affecting the Health of Women." World Health Organization, Regional Office for the Eastern Mediterranean.

Boddy, Janice. 1979. Personal Communication. [Based on her PhD research, University of British Columbia.]

Clark, Isobel and Christina Diaz. 1977. "Circumcision: A Slow Change in Attitudes," *Sudanow* (March 1977):43–45.

Cook, R. 1976. "Damage to Physical Health from Pharaonic Circumcision (Infibulation) of Females: A Review of the Medical Literature." World Health Organization, September 30, 1976.

Diaz, Christina and Suliman Mudawi. 1977. "Circumcision: The Social Background," *Sudanow* (March 1977):45.

El Dareer, Asma. 1979. "Female Circumcision and Its Consequences for Mother and Child." Contributions to the ILO African Symposium on the World of Work and the Protection of the Child. Yaoundé, Cameroun.

El Saadawi, Nawal. 1980a. "Creative Women in Changing Societies: A Personal Reflection," *Race and Class* 22(2):159–182.

———. 1980b. *The Hidden Face of Eve: Women in the Arab World*. London: Zed Press.

Hall, Marjorie and Bakhita Amin Ismail. 1981. *Sisters Under the Sun: The Story of Sudanese Women*. London: Longmans.

Hayes, Rose Oldfield. 1975. "Female Genital Mutilation, Fertility Control, Women's Roles and the Patrilineage in Modern Sudan," *American Ethnologist* 2(4):617–633.

Hosken, Fran P. 1980. *Female Sexual Mutilations: The Facts and Proposals for Action*. Lexington, MA: Women's International Network News.

Mudawi, Suliman. 1977a. "Circumcision: The Operation," *Sudanow* (March 1977):43–44.

———. 1977b. "The Impact of Social and Economic Changes on Female Circumcision." Sudan Medical Association Congress Series, No. 2.

O'Brien, John J. 1980. "Agricultural Labor and Development in Sudan." PhD dissertation, University of Connecticut.

Shandall, A. A. 1967. "Circumcision and Infibulation of Females," *Sudan Medical Journal* 5:178–212.

Sørbø, Gunnar M. 1977. *How to Survive Development: The Story of New Halfa*. Khartoum: Development Studies and Research Centre Monograph Series No. 6.

Sudan Medical Service. 1945. *Female Circumcision in the Anglo-Egyptian Sudan*. Khartoum: Sudan Medical Service, March 1, 1945.

Sudan Ministry of Health. 1975a. *Annual Statistical Report*. Khartoum: Ministry of Health.

———. 1975b. *National Health Programme 1977/78–1983/84*. Khartoum: Ministry of Health.

Toubia, Nahid F. 1981. "The Social and Political Implications of Female Circumcision: The Case of Sudan." MSc Proposal, University of College of Swansea, Wales.

Verzin, J. A. 1975. "Sequelae of Female Circumcision," *Tropical Doctor* (Oct., 1975).

Female Infanticide and Child Neglect in Rural North India

Barbara D. Miller

INTRODUCTION

Sitting in the hospital canteen for lunch every day, I can see families bringing their children

From Nancy Scheper-Hughes (ed.), *Child Survival*, pp. 95–112. Reprinted by permission of Kluwer Academic Publishers. Copyright © 1987 by D. Reidel Publishing Company, Dordrecht, Holland.

into the hospital. So far, after watching for five days, I have seen only boys being carried in for treatment, no girls (author's field notes, Ludhiana Christian Medical College, November 1983).

When the hospital was built, equal-sized wards for boys and girls were constructed. The boys' ward is always full but the girls' ward is underutilized (comment of a hospital administrator, Ludhiana Christian Medical College, November 1983).

In one village, I went into the house to examine a young girl and I found that she had an advanced case of tuberculosis. I asked the mother why she hadn't done something sooner about the girl's condition because now, at this stage, the treatment would be very expensive. The mother replied, "then let her die, I have another daughter." At the time, the two daughters sat nearby listening, one with tears streaming down her face (report by a public health physician, Ludhiana Christian Medical College, November 1983).

When a third, fourth, or fifth daughter is born to a family, no matter what its economic status, we increase our home visits because that child is at high risk (statement made by a public health physician, Ludhiana Christian Medical College, November 1983).

These quotations, taken from field notes made during a 1983 trip to Ludhiana, the Punjab, India are indicative of the nature and degree of sex-selectivity in health care of children there. Ethnographic evidence gleaned from the work of other anthropologists corroborates that intrahousehold discrimination against girls is a fact of life in much of the northern plains region of India (Miller 1981: 83–106). The strong preference for sons compared to daughters is marked from the moment of birth. Celebration at the birth of a son, particularly a first son, has been documented repeatedly in the ethnographic literature (Lewis 1965: 49; Freed and Freed 1976: 123, 206; Jacobson 1970: 307–309; Madan 1965: 63; and Aggarwal 1971: 114). But when a daughter is born, the event goes unheralded and anthropologists have documented the unconcealed disappointment in families which already have a daughter or two (Luschinsky 1962: 82; Madan 1965: 77–78; Minturn and Hitchcock 1966: 101–102). The extreme disappointment of a mother who greatly desires a son, but bears a daughter instead, could affect her ability to breastfeed successfully; "bonding" certainly would not be automatically assured between the mother and the child; and the mother's disappointed in-laws would be far less supportive than if the newborn were a son (Miller, 1986).

A thorough review of the ethnographic literature provides diverse but strongly suggestive evidence of preferential feeding of boys in North Indian villages (Miller 1981: 93–94), as well as preferential allocation of medical care to boys. Sex ratios of admissions to northern hospitals are often two or more boys to every one girl. This imbalance is not due to more frequent illness of boys, but rather to sex-selective parental investment patterns.

The practice of sex-selective child care in northern India confronts us with a particularly disturbing dilemma that involves the incongruity between Western values that insist on equal life chances for all, even in the face of our universal failure to achieve that goal, versus North Indian culture which places strong value on the survival of sons rather than daughters. Public health programs in North India operate under the guidance of the national goal of "equal health care for all by the year 2000" which was declared by many developing nations at the Alma Ata conference in 1978. Yet the families with whom they are concerned operate with a different set of goals less concerned with the survival of any one individual than with the survival of the family. In rural North India the economic survival of the family, for sociocultural reasons, is dependent on the reproduction of strong sons and the control of the number of daughters who are financial burdens in many ways.

The chapter examines a variety of data and information sources on the dimensions and social context of female infanticide and daughter neglect in rural North India, an area where gender preferences regarding offspring are particularly strong. I review what is known about outright female infanticide in earlier centuries and discuss the situation in North India today, examining the empirical evidence and current theoretical approaches to the understanding of son preference and daughter disfavor. The next section considers the role of a public health program in the Punjab. In conclusion I address the issue of humanist values concerning equal life chances for all versus North Indian patriarchal values promoting better life chances for boys than girls, and the challenge to anthropological research of finding an appropriate theoretical approach to the study of children's health and survival.

INFANTICIDE: BACKGROUND

I consider infanticide to fall under the general category of child abuse and neglect which encompasses a range of behaviors. As I have written elsewhere:

> ... it is helpful to distinguish forms of neglect from those of abuse ... abuse is more "active" in the way it is inflicted; it is abuse when something is actually *done* to harm the child. In the case of neglect, harm comes to the child because something is *not done* which should have been. Thus, sexual molestation of a child is abusive, whereas depriving a child of adequate food and exercise is neglectful. One similarity between abuse and neglect is that both, if carried far enough, can be fatal (Miller 1981: 44–45).

Infanticide, most strictly defined, is the killing of a child under one year of age. Infanticide would be placed at one extreme of the continuum of effects of child abuse and neglect—it is fatal. At the opposite end of the continuum are forms of child abuse that result in delayed learning, slowed physical growth and development patterns, and disturbed social adjustment. Outright infanticide can be distinguished from indirect or "passive" infanticide (Harris 1977); in the former the means, such as a fatal beating, are direct and immediate, while in the latter, the means, such as sustained nutritional deprivation, are indirect.

Infanticide is further delineated with respect to the ages of the children involved. Most broadly defined, infanticide applies to the killing of children under the age of twelve months (deaths after that age would generally be classified as child *homicide,* although the definition and, hence, duration of childhood is culturally variable). *Neonaticide* usually pertains to the killing of a newborn up to twenty-four hours after birth and is sometimes given a separate analysis (Wilkey et al. 1982). The induced *abortion* of a fetus is sometimes categorized as a prenatal form of infanticide that has been termed *"feticide"* in the literature.[1]

The discussion in this chapter encompasses both infanticide and child homicide, that is non-accidental deaths to minors from the time of birth up to the age of about fifteen or sixteen when they would become adults in the rural Indian context. For convenience, I will use the term infanticide to apply to the entire age range.

I have asserted (1981: 44) that where infanticide is systematically sex-selective, it will be selective against females rather than males. There are few cases of systematic male-selective infanticide in the literature that I reviewed. Some more recent work on the subject, however, has begun to reveal a variety of patterns. For example, a study conducted on several villages in a delta region of Japan using data from the Tokugawa era (1600–1868) reveals the existence of systematic infanticide which was sex-selective, but selective against males almost as frequently as females, depending on the particular household composition and dynamics (Skinner 1984).

Obviously all household strategies concerning the survival of offspring are not based solely on gender considerations, and it is doubtful that we can ever come close to a good estimation of just "how much" gender-based selective differential in the treatment of children exists, and how much of this is biased against females. Nevertheless, one part of the world where female-selective infanticide is particularly apparent is in North India, and across India's northwestern border through Pakistan . . . to the Near East, and perhaps in a diminished form also in North Africa. Looking toward the East from India, it seems that Southeast Asia is largely free of the son preference/daughter disfavor syndrome, as opposed to China where one result of the one-child policy . . . was the death of thousands of female infants.

FEMALE INFANTICIDE IN
PRE-TWENTIETH CENTURY INDIA

The British discovery of infanticide in India occurred in 1789 among a clan of Rajputs in the eastern part of Uttar Pradesh, a northern state.[2] All of the infanticide reported by British district officers and other observers was direct female infanticide. A lengthy quotation from a mid-nineteenth century description by a British magistrate in the Northwest Provinces of India demonstrates how open was the knowledge of the practice of female infanticide at that time:

> There is at Mynpoorie an old fortress, which looks far over the valley of the Eesun river. This has been for centuries the stronghold of the Rajahs of Mynpoorie, Chohans whose ancient blood, descending from the great Pirthee Raj and the regal stem of Neem-rana, represents *la crème de la crème* of Rajpoot aristocracy. Here when a son, a nephew, a grandson, was born to the reigning chief, the event was announced to the neighboring city by the loud discharge of wall-pieces and matchlocks; but centuries had passed away, and no infant daughter had been known to smile within those walls.
>
> In 1845, however, thanks to the vigilance of Mr. Unwin [the district collector], a little grand-daughter was preserved by the Rajah of that day. The fact was duly notified to the Government, and a letter of congratulations and a dress of honour were at once dispatched from head-quarters to the Rajah.
>
> We have called this incident, the giving of a robe of honour to a man because he did not destroy his grand-daughter a *grotesque* one; but it is very far from being a ridiculous incident. When the people see that the highest authorities in the land take an interest in their social or domestic reforms, those reforms can give an impetus which no lesser influences can give them. The very next year after the investiture of the Rajah, the number of female infants preserved in the district was *trebled!* Fifty-seven had been saved in 1845; in 1846, one hundred and eighty were preserved; and the number has gone on steadily increasing ever since (Raikes 1852: 20–21).

A review of the secondary literature on female infanticide in British India reveals its practice mainly in the Northwest, and among upper castes and tribes. Not all groups practiced female infanticide, but there are grim reports that a few entire villages in the northwestern plains had never raised one daughter.[3] On the basis of juvenile (under ten years of age) sex ratios for districts in the Northwest Provinces, 1871, I have estimated crudely that for nineteenth-century Northwest India it would not be unreasonable to assume that one-fourth of the population preserved only half the daughters born to them, while the other three-fourths of the population had balanced sex ratios among their offspring (Miller 1981: 62). This assumption yields a juvenile sex ratio of 118 (males per 100 females) in the model population, which is comparable to current juvenile sex ratios in several districts of northwestern Indian and Pakistan (Miller 1981, 1984). It seems clear that female infanticide in British India was widespread in the Northwest rather than of limited occurrence.

The British investigated the extent and causes of female infanticide, and in 1870 passed a law against its practice. Other policy measures, based on their assessment of the causes of the practice, included subsidizing the dowries of daughters that were "preserved" by prominent families, and organizing conferences in order to enlighten local leaders and their followers about the need to prevent infanticide (Cave Browne 1857).

There are two areas of ignorance about the wider context of the historic practice of female infanticide in India. First, we know little about the apparent and gradual transition from direct to indirect infanticide. It appears that either deep-seated social change and/or British policy against the practice of female infanticide succeeded in bringing about the near-end of direct female infanticide by the beginning of this century. In the twentieth century we hear little about female infanticide in census reports, district gazetteers, or anthropological descriptions of rural life. What is needed is a careful tracing of the situation from roughly 1870 when the practice was outlawed to the present time in order to plot the dynamics of change from outright to indirect infanticide. Second, we need to know much more about the sociocultural determinants of female infanticide in British India. The British pointed to two causal factors— "pride and purse." The pride of upper castes and tribes is said to have pushed them to murder female infants rather than give them away as tribute to a more dominant group, or even as brides which is viewed as demeaning in rural North India today. By "purse" is meant dowry, and most groups that practiced infanticide did have the custom of giving large dowries with daughters.[4] But there is some contradictory evidence. In the undivided Punjab, it has been documented for the early twentieth century that dowry was not widely given among the rural Jats, a caste which nonetheless exhibited very high sex ratios (i.e., males over females) among its juvenile population. In fact, the Jats, a landed peasant caste, often secured brides through brideprice, which should have provided an economic incentive for parents to preserve daughters (Darling 1929; see also the discussion in Miller 1984). Further exploration of archival materials for the nineteenth century would help illuminate this matter.

FEMALE INFANTICIDE AND NEGLECT: THE CURRENT CONTEXT

It is beyond doubt that systematic indirect female infanticide exists today in North India. It is possible that outright infanticide of neonates is also practiced, though nearly impossible to document due to the extreme privacy of the birth event and the great ease with which a neonate's life may be terminated.[5] This section of the paper is concerned with indirect female infanticide, which is accomplished by nutritional and health-care deprivation of children, and which results in higher mortality rates of daughters than sons.[6]

There is a strong preference for sons in rural North India and there are several strong sociocultural reasons for this preference. Sons are economic assets: they are needed for farming, and for income through remittances if they leave the village. Sons play important roles in local power struggles over rights to land and water. Sons stay with the family after their marriage and thus maintain the parents in their old age; daughters marry out and cannot contribute to the maintenance of their natal households. Sons bring in dowries with their brides; daughters drain family wealth with their required dowries and the constant flow of gifts to their family of marriage after the wedding. Sons, among Hindus, are also needed to perform rituals which protect the family after the death of the father; daughters cannot perform such rituals.

Elsewhere I have argued that extreme son preference is more prevalent in North India than in the South and East, and that it is more prevalent among upper castes and classes than lower castes and classes (Miller 1981). By extension, daughter neglect would follow the same pattern. Some of the key research questions include: how extensive is daughter disfavor in different regions and among various social strata in India? How serious are its consequences in terms of mortality and in health status of the survivors (not to mention more difficult to diagnose conditions such as emotional and cognitive development)? Are these patterns changing through time? At this point, scattered studies help illuminate some aspects of these questions, but there is no study that addresses them all systematically either for one locale or for India as a whole.

First, let us consider the question of the extent of the practice in India. In a recent publication, Lipton (1983) suggests that fatal discrimination against daughters in India is a very localized, and thus minor, problem. But my all-India analysis (1981), using juvenile sex ratios as a surrogate measure of child mortality, shows that while the most afflicted area encompasses only two or three states of India, there are seriously unbalanced sex ratios among children in one-third of India's 326 rural districts, an area spanning the entire northwestern plains.[7] Simmons et al. (1982)

provide results from survey data on 2064 couples in the Kanpur region of Uttar Pradesh (a state in northern India) which reveal that reported infant and child mortality rates for girls aged one month up to three years of age are much higher than the rates for boys. This finding is similar to, though less astonishing than, Cowan and Dhanoa's (1983) report that in a large sub-population carefully monitored in Ludhiana district, the Punjab, 85 percent of all deaths to children aged 7–36 months were female. Another dependable database that has been carefully analyzed by Behrman (1984) and Behrman and Deolalikar (1985) concerns an area of India where juvenile sex ratios are not notably unbalanced, south-central India in the area between Andhra Pradesh and Maharashtra. The authors have found that there is a noticeable nutrient bias in favor of boys in the intrahousehold allocation of food. This unequal distribution has a seasonal dimension: in the lean season boys are more favored over girls in the distribution of food in the family, while in the surplus season distribution appears quite equal.

Class/caste variations in juvenile sex ratios are also important. Simmons et al. (1982) unfortunately do not present findings on class or caste patterns. They mention that education of the parents is a positive influence on child survival in the first year of life, less so in the second and third. If parental education can be used as a crude indicator of class status, then it would seem that survival for both boys and girls would be more assured in better-off families. Demographic data from the Ludhiana area of Punjab state have been analyzed for class differences by Cowan and Dhanoa (1983). Among upper class, landed families (termed "privileged" by Cowan and Dhanoa), there is a large disparity between survival rates for male and female children and also in the nutritional status of those surviving (Table 1). These disparities are mirrored, though less severe, in the lower class, landless population. Cowan and Dhanoa found that birth order strongly affects the survival and status of daughters. Second-born and third-born daughters are classified by health care personnel as "high risk" infants, as are high birth order children of both sexes born to very large families, regardless of socioeconomic status. The extent of fatal daughter disfavor in this relatively affluent state of India is severe, and it contributes to Punjab's having infant (up to one year of age) mortality rates higher that those of poorer states where daughter discrimination is less severe (Miller 1985).

Caldwell et al.'s data on a cluster of villages in Karnataka (southern-central-India), with a total population of more than 5000, revealed "surprisingly small" differences in infant and child mortality by economic status, father's occupation and religion (1983:197). (This area of the country is

TABLE 1 Prevalence of 2nd/3rd Degree Malnutrition in 911 Children in Second and Third Year of Life, Ludhiana, the Punjab

	NUMBER	SEX RATIO[a]	WITH 2ND/3RD DEGREE MALNUTRITION[b]	RATIO OF MALE TO FEMALE MALNOURISHED
Privileged males	231	111.0	2	1:6.5
Privileged females	208		13	
Under-privileged males	244	102.5	11	1:2.6
Under-privileged females	228		29	
TOTAL	911	106.5	55	1:3.2

[a]Sex ratio refers to the number of males per hundred females.
[b]The numbers in this column were read from a graph and may be off by a small margin.
Source: Cowan and Dhanoa (1983: 352)

characterized by balanced juvenile sex ratios at the district level.) The authors do not mention whether there are any sex differentials in child survival and health. Infant mortality rates are, however, much lower in households with an educated mother than those where the mother has little education. Girls tend to receive less food than boys, and family variables are mentioned as being involved in this matter.

Another report from a region with balanced juvenile sex ratios, a two-village study in West Bengal reported on by Sen and Sengupta (1983), produced some provocative findings. The authors did not look at mortality but rather at levels of undernourishment in children below five years of age according to caste and land ownership status of the household. Results were surprising: the village with a more vigorous land redistribution program had a greater nutritional sex bias, even among children in families who had benefited from the redistribution. In the second village, children in poor families had higher nutritional standards and a lower male-female differential than their counterparts in the first village.

Rosenzweig and Schultz (1982) used a subsample of rural households in India, presumably nationwide, and found that boys have significantly higher survival rates relative to girls in landless rather than in landed households. Horowitz and Keshwar report that survey data from a Punjab village (northern India) demonstrate more pronounced son preference among the propertied peasant castes, although the phenomenon is "nearly" as strong among agricultural laborers (1982: 12); they do not provide health or survival statistics, but use data on stated preferences of parents.

The preceding review indicates that, while we do not possess an ideal picture of the extent and nature of daughter disfavor, there is evidence that its practice does exist widely in India and does tend to exhibit class/caste patterns—though the exact nature of these is in dispute. We know very little about the question of change through time since few good

sources of longitudinal data exist, and those that do exist have not been examined for sex disparity information as yet.

SEX-SELECTIVE ABORTION

Several years ago a Jain woman in her sixth month of pregnancy came to Ludhiana Christian Medical Hospital for an amniocentesis test. The results of the test showed that genetic defects such as Down's syndrome or spina bifida were not present in the fetus. The test indicated that the fetus was female. The woman requested an abortion and was refused. She went to a clinic in Amritsar, another major city in the Punjab, and had the abortion done (report by a physician, Ludhiana, November 1983).

This anecdote was told to me at Ludhiana Christian Medical College as an explanation why Ludhiana CMC no longer performs amniocentesis. There were so many requests for abortion of female fetuses following amniocentesis that the hospital made a policy decision not to provide such services.[8] Today a person with intent to abort a female fetus in Ludhiana must take the train about 90 miles to Amritsar where the service is available. An especially poignant aspect of the anecdote is the information that the woman was a Jain. Jainism supports nonviolence toward all life forms. Orthodox Jains sometimes wear cloths over their mouths so as not to swallow a fly, and Jains do not plow the earth for fear of inadvertently cutting in half a worm. But the Jain woman in the anecdote was willing to abort a female fetus in the sixth month of gestation, so strong was the cultural disfavor toward the birth of daughters.

At this time I do not have access to data on the number of female fetuses aborted each year in India, nor to data on the social characteristics of those people who seek to abort their female fetuses. Nonetheless, several considerations are important: how can we estimate the extent of the practice? What are the social and economic characteristics of those families seeking to abort female fetuses? What are the demographic characteristics of the families seeking sex-selective abortion? There are some clues.

In 1980 an article published in *Social Science and Medicine* provided some evidence of the extent of the phenomenon based on clinic records in a large city of western India (Ramanamma and Bambawale 1980). In one hospital, from June 1976 to June 1977, 700 individuals sought prenatal sex determination. Of these fetuses, 250 were determined to be male and 450 were female.[9] While all of the male fetuses were kept to term, fully 430 of the 450 female fetuses were terminated. This figure is even more disturbing in light of the fact that western India is characterized by a less extreme son preference than the Northwest.

There is an eager market in India for sex-selective abortion, although the cost of the service may make it prohibitive for the poorest villagers. A report in *Manushi* (1982) states that the service is available in Chandigarh, the Punjab, for only 500 rupees.[10] Another report mentions that the charge was 600 rupees at a clinic in Amritsar, the Punjab (*Washington Post* 1982). A recent visitor to Ahmedabad, Gujarat, reports a charge of only 50 rupees in a clinic there (Everett 1984). Whether the charge is 50 rupees or 500 rupees, the cost is minor compared to the benefits reaped from the possibility of having a son conceived at the next pregnancy, or compared to the money that would have been needed to provide a dowry for the girl were she to survive.

DETERMINANTS OF SON PREFERENCE AND DAUGHTER DISFAVOR

Why does son preference exist, and why does it often exist in tandem with the practices of sex-selective abortion, female infanticide, and female neglect? Anthropologists have proposed "explanations" for the practice of female infanticide in simple societies, but less work has been done for complex civilizations. Recent problems in China, provoked by the

one-child policy, have attracted attention to the subject, but little scholarly thinking, with few exceptions. . . . A range of hypothesized causal factors has been suggested to account for female infanticide in the past few years. They can be divided into ecologic/economic determinants, social structural determinants and sociobiological determinants.

From the broadest population ecology perspective, Harris (1977) proposes that female infanticide, and by extension sex-selective abortion, will most likely occur when a society has reached a crisis level in its population/resources ratio, or right after that crisis when the society has moved into a necessarily expendable portion of the population in relation to resources. This theory has explanatory power for some cases, but we might bear in mind that infanticide is only one of many possible strategies for ameliorating a high population/resources ratio. Other options include migration, and the reduction of natural population growth through delayed marriage, abstinence, abortion, and other forms of birth control both traditional and modern.

My interpretation, based on the case of North India, gives more emphasis to economic demand factors. I have hypothesized that labor requirements for males versus females (themselves ecologically, agriculturally and culturally defined) are key in determining households' desires regarding number and sex of offspring (Miller 1981, 1984). Although I take the sexual division of labor as primary, I view it as creating a secondary and very powerful determinant in the domestic marriage economy. In the case of India, the contrast between dowry marriages and bridewealth marriages illustrates the "mirroring" of the sexual division of labor in marriage costs: generally where few females are employed in the agricultural sector, large dowries prevail, but where female labor is in high demand, smaller dowries or even bridewealth are the main form of marriage transfers.

Other more orthodox economic approaches stress rational decision-making on the part of the family based on perceived "market opportunities" of offspring (Rosenzweig and Schultz 1982) or intrafamily resource allocation systems (Simmons et al. 1982). Sen and Sengupta propose that land distribution patterns are an important determinant of sex differentials in children's nutritional status (1983).

The major exponents of a social structural theory are Dyson and Moore (1983). They identify the patriarchal nature of North Indian society as the basis for the neglect of daughters and other manifestations of low female status. They do not seek to explain why society in North India is strongly patriarchal—that is simply a given.

Dickemann, who studied female infanticide cross-culturally and particularly in stratified societies such as traditional northern India and China, provides a sociobiological interpretation for female infanticide (1979, 1984). Her early observation of the connection between hypergynous marriage systems and female infanticide was a particularly important contribution (1979). Dickemann views sex ratio manipulation among offspring as one reproductive strategy that will, under alternate resource conditions, result in maximum reproductive success for the family. She has recently stated that:

> Like other acts of reproductive management, infanticide-pedicide seems to be best understood at present, in all species, as one parameter of interindividual and interfamilial competition for the proportional increase in genes in the next generation ... (1984: 436).

In terms of the explanatory power of evolutionary models with respect to the cause of violent mistreatment of human offspring, however, Hrdy and Hausfater (1984: xxxi) agree with Lenington (1981) that "only a portion of such cases" will be thus explained.

PUBLIC HEALTH AND PATRIARCHY

Ten years ago when I began my research on fatal neglect of daughters in rural India the problem was not widely accepted by scholars

in the West or in India as a serious one.[11] Today the practice of fatal daughter disfavor is more widely recognized by scholars as a serious social issue. Current concern in India about the growing recourse to sex-selective abortion, using information on sex of the fetus derived from amniocentesis, adds a new and important dimension to problems of female survival and the ethics of abortion (Ramanamma and Bambawale 1980; Kumar 1983).

Operating within such a patriarchal system, could any health care program seeking to provide equal health care for all have any success? There is controversy concerning the impact of health care programs in alleviating sex differences in child survival in patriarchal cultures, particularly North India. Some writers suggest that a simple increase in health care services will improve the situation for girls (Minturn 1984). Others have found evidence that increased services will be diverted to priority children, most often boys, and that only secondarily will low priority children, most often girls, benefit.[12] Finally, the introduction of new medical technologies—such as amniocentesis—can be manipulated to advance patriarchal priorities (Miller 1986).

Focus on the Punjab

The Punjab, India's wealthiest state, is located in the northwestern plains region adjacent to Pakistan. Its economy is agricultural with wheat the major food crop, but there is a well-developed industrial sector also. Within the Punjab, Ludhiana district is usually recognized as the most "developed" district. Ludhiana district also stands out because it houses one of the best medical colleges and community health programs in India, Ludhiana Christian Medical College. Ludhiana, and the Punjab district, are squarely in the area in northwestern India where juvenile sex ratios are the most masculine and excess female child mortality the greatest (Miller 1985).

Since the early 1970s, Ludhiana CMC has been monitoring the reproductive and health status of the surrounding population—first as a pilot project in three rural locations and one urban location, and later in the entire block of Sahnewal (an administrative subdivision of the district), with a population of about 85,000. The monitoring is part of a decentralized, comprehensive basic health care program that focuses on the welfare of mothers and children and includes both health care delivery at village centers and home-based educational programs. For each of the nearly 14,000 families in Sahnewal block, the CMC Ludhiana program maintains family folders containing information on all family members and their health status. Mortalities are carefully recorded in each folder and also in Master Registers kept in 49 village centers throughout the block. Some analysis of these data has been performed (Cowan and Dhanoa 1983) which provides startling figures on sex differentials of mortality for children aged 7–36 months in which female deaths constituted 85 percent of the total (1983: 341).

Cowan and Dhanoa note that one important result of their intensive home-based visiting approach in the rural Punjab is a reduction in the percentage of female child deaths (1983: 354). There is no doubt that their approach can be effective for saving the lives of high-risk children, though it requires great effort and entails much surveillance of private life. Two questions arise from this finding: a related result of increased survival for girls is an increase in the percentage of malnourished girls—girls' lives have been saved, but the quality of those lives may not be at all equal to that of males. Would even more intensive home visiting help alleviate this problem? Furthermore, some would argue that the death of unwanted children might be preferable to their extended mistreatment and suffering (Kumar 1983. . .).

We have not estimated the unit health care costs by sex and priority of the child, but the cost of saving the life of a low priority female child must far outweigh the cost of saving and improving the life of a high priority male. It is not unthinkable that the time will arrive when, with fiscal stringency the watchword of the day, the cost of intensive health care and survival monitoring for girls becomes a barrier to programs such as the one at Ludhiana CMC. Two arguments can be developed to counter policies which would limit special efforts to equalize life chances between boys and girls. First, one might look to the broader social costs of a society in which the sex ratio is seriously unbalanced. It cannot be proven that unbalanced sex ratios invariably lead to social disturbances, but there is much cross-cultural evidence to support this (Divale and Harris 1976). A balanced sex ratio does not guarantee social tranquility, but it could minimize some sources of social tension. Second, in a strongly son-preferential culture, women bear many children in the attempt to produce several sons. The pattern of selective care which promotes son survival to the detriment of daughter survival is built on "over-reproduction" and much child wastage. Mothers bear a physical burden in this system. The Ludhiana program seeks to keep children alive and wanted, and to promote family planning after a certain number and sex composition of children have been born in a household; this goal should reduce the physical burden on mothers created by extended childbearing.

HUMANISTIC VALUES, PATRIARCHAL VALUES, AND ANTHROPOLOGY

This chapter discusses an extreme form of sex-selective child care, one which is not universally found throughout the world though it is not limited to rural North India. Strong preference for sons which results in life-endangering deprivation of daughters is "culturally" acceptable in much of rural North India with its patriarchal foundation. It is not acceptable from a Western humanistic or altruistic perspective ... nor from that of an emergent, international feminist "world view." But, how can anthropological research, with its commitment to nonethnocentric reporting of cultural behavior, contribute to an amelioration of the "worldview conflicts" that create inappropriate public health programs targeted at high-risk children, that sometimes only prolong the suffering of these disvalued ones?

... [P]erhaps positivistic anthropology and Western altruism can work together. First, let me hasten to soften the hard edges of the "conflict" in world views that Cassidy 1987 has constructed: there is no such thing as purely objective and nonethnocentric anthropological research and there is, increasingly, less and less culturally uninformed altruism being foisted on the Third World. All anthropologists, as Schneider so clearly states (1984), have their own unavoidable, culturally-influenced presuppositions and biases through which they choose subjects for research and through which they analyze their data. The best an anthropologist can do is state the nature of his/her presuppositions at the outset: mine, influenced by my white, middle class, American upbringing, are based on the precept that human life, its duration and quality, is something to which all persons should have equal access, although I am fully aware of the fact that scarcity (real or culturally defined) results in priorities about the quality of life that certain groups will receive. Thus I define female infanticide and skewed sex ratios as a social "problem." As an applied anthropologist I believe that socio-behavioral data can provide the key to successful public programs which seek to ameliorate the "problem."

My experience, though too brief, in working with Dr. Betty Cowan and Dr. Jasbir Dhanoa (two "altruists") in Ludhiana convinced me that there is hope for a realistic solution to the conflict between altruism and, in this case, extreme patriarchy, in the sensitive applications of social science knowledge and research. The public health program at Ludhiana is perhaps never going to dilute the force of Indian patriarchy, but knowledge about the patriarchal culture can help promote more effective health care. For instance, the Ludhiana hospital built equal-sized wards for boys and girls, on the Western model. But families bring their boys in for health care in much greater numbers than their girls; the girls' ward is relatively empty while the boys' ward is overflowing. Health care practitioners thus realized the need for very decentralized health care rather than only hospital-based services, including frequent home visiting, if health care was to reach girls.

Anthropologists can provide important information to health care intervenors which will allow those intervenors to be more effective in delivering their services. The most important issue in the Ludhiana area still to be resolved is the impact of class and caste stratification on female survival. Health care practitioners see daughter disfavor largely as a result of poverty. My own research would question poverty as the principal determinant in Ludhiana because there is a marked disparity in survival of boys and girls in the propertied class as well as in the unpropertied class. Although the larger picture is unclear because of lack of data across North India, it is obvious that policy implications differ greatly depending on class/caste dimensions of village life. If health care programs are to be targeted to "high-risk" groups, anthropologists can help by providing data on the nature of these groups and the potential implications of intervention in their lives.

NOTES

Much of my recent research on this subject has been supported by grants from the Wenner-Gren Foundation for Anthropological Research. I am grateful for the Foundation's support which enabled me to visit two hospitals in India during November 1983 in order to learn about their community health programs: Ludhiana Christian Medical College in the Punjab and Vellore Christian Medical College in Tamil Nadu. While in India, I received help from many people, but I especially want to thank Dr. Betty Cowan, Principal of Ludhiana CMC, and Dr. P.S. Sundar Rao, Chief of the Biostatics Department at Vellore CMC. An earlier version of this chapter was presented at a seminar sponsored by the Department of Anthropology and the Asian Studies Program at the University of Pittsburgh in March 1985, and I am grateful for the comments I received from those who attended. Finally, I must thank The Metropolitan Studies Program, The Maxwell School, Syracuse University, for support of my work

1. A discussion of abortion and infanticide from a Western philosophical view is provided in Tooley (1983).
2. We know very little about the practice of female infanticide in India before the British era. The discussion that follows is extracted in large part from Miller (1981: 49–67).
3. Critics are quick to point out that without daughters, villages will not "survive." But in the case of North India, marriage is village exogamous, particularly for Hindus; that is, brides must come from a village other than the groom's. Villages without daughters would "survive" because they would bring in daughters-in-law. More anecdotally, the Community Health Program at Ludhiana CMC was started by a woman physician who was the third daughter of the Grewal lineage to be preserved; even without daughters, the Grewal lineage has "survived" for centuries.
4. Another effect, largely urban and upper-class, of the dowry system in North India is the murder of young wives by their in-laws in order to procure a second bride with her dowry (Sharma 1983).
5. Knowledgeable physicians who have worked with the community health care program in the rural areas surrounding Ludhiana, the Punjab, know that there is a preponderance of female neonatal deaths as compared to those of males. They are averse to labelling this as due to infanticide since an autopsy may well not reveal an intentional death as opposed to a stillbirth or an unintentional death. The physicians do know that neonatal deaths constitute a serious problem, and one that is the hardest for them to deal with due to the secrecy surrounding births in rural India.
6. A detailed discussion of the dynamics of son preference in India can be found in Miller (1981), and a comparison between Pakistan and Bangladesh in Miller (1984).
7. This pattern in Northwest India extends over the Indian border into Pakistan . . . .
8. The central government of India has banned prenatal sex determination tests in govern-

ment hospitals throughout the country for the same reason.
9. The preponderance of females in the sample is probably due to sheer accident.
10. In 1984–85, one dollar equaled approximately twelve rupees.
11. There are some notable exceptions to this generalization (Bardhan 1974; Chandrasekhar 1972; Dandekar 1975; Visaria 1961), although none of these scholars emphasized the major role of sex-differential survival of children in creating the preponderance of males over females.
12. Srilatha (1983) reports that in a large study area in Tamil Nadu, South India, infant and child mortality rates have declined significantly in the last ten years, but the decline was dramatic for boys and only slight for girls. The implication is that improved health services may be differentially allocated to boys and girls in this area of India.

REFERENCES

Aggarwal, Partap C. 1971. *Caste, Religion and Power. An Indian Case Study.* New Delhi: Shri Ram Centre for Industrial Relations.

Bardhan, Pranab K. 1974. "On Life and Death Questions," *Economic and Political Weekly* 10(32–34): 1293–1303.

Behrman, Jere R. 1984. "Intrahousehold Allocation of Nutrients in Rural India: Are Boys Favored? Do Parents Exhibit Inequality Aversion?" Unpublished manuscript, University of Pennsylvania, Department of Economics. (Revised 1985.)

Behrman, Jere R. and Anil B. Deolalikar. 1985. "How Do Food and Product Prices Affect Nutrient Intakes, Health and Labor Force Behavior for Different Family Numbers in Rural India?" Paper presented at the 1985 Meetings of the Population Association of America, Boston.

Caldwell, J.C., P.H. Reddy, and Pat Caldwell. 1983. "The Social Component of Mortality Decline: An Investigation in South India Employing Alternative Methodologies." *Population Studies* 37: 185–205.

Cassidy, Clare Manod. 1987. World-view Conflict and Toddler Malnutrition: Change Agent Dilemmas. In *Child Survival: Anthropological Perspective on the Treatment and Maltreatment of*

Children. Nancy Scheper-Hughes (ed.), pp. 293–324. Boston: D. Reidel.

Cave Browne, John. 1857. *Indian Infanticide: Its Origin, Progress, and Suppression.* London: W.H. Allen.

Chandrasekhar, S. 1972. *Infant Mortality, Population Growth and Family Planning in India.* Chapel Hill, NC: University of North Carolina Press.

Cowan, Betty and Jasbir Dhanoa. 1983. "The Prevention of Toddler Malnutrition by Home-based Nutrition Education." In *Nutrition in the Community: A Critical Look at Nutrition Policy, Planning, and Programmes.* D.S. McLaren (ed.), pp. 339–356. New York/London: John Wiley and Sons.

Dandekar, Kumudini. 1975. "Why Has the Proportion of Women in India's Population Been Declining?" *Economic and Political Weekly* 10(42): 1663–1667.

Darling, Malcolm Lyall. 1929. *Rusticus Loquitur or the Old Light and the New in the Punjab Village.* London: Oxford University Press.

Dickemann, Mildred. 1979. "Female Infanticide, Reproductive Strategies, and Social Stratification: A Preliminary Model." In *Evolutionary Biology and Human Social Behavior: An Anthropological Perspective.* N.A. Chagnon and W. Irons (eds.), pp. 321–367. North Scituate, MA: Duxbury Press.

———. 1984. "Concepts and Classification in the Study of Human Infanticide: Sectional Introduction and Some Cautionary Notes" In *Infanticide: Comparative and Evolutionary Perspectives.* Glenn Hausfater and Sarah Blàffer Hrdy (eds.), pp. 427–439. New York: Aldine Publishing Company.

Divale, William and Marvin Harris. 1976. "Population, Warfare, and the Male Supremacist Complex." *American Anthropologist* 78: 521–538.

Dyson, Tim and Mick Moore. 1983. "Gender Relations, Female Autonomy and Demographic Behavior: Regional Contrasts within India." *Population and Development Review* 9(1): 35–60.

Everett, Jana. 1984. Personal communication. (Dr. Everett is a political scientist at the University of Colorado, Denver.)

Freed, Stanley A. and Ruth S. Freed. 1976. "Shanti Nagar: The Effects of Urbanization in a Village in North India: 1. Social Organization," *Anthropological Papers of the American Museum of National History.* Vol. 53: Part 1. New York: The American Museum of Natural History.

Harris, Marvin. 1977. *Cannibals and Kings: The Origins of Cultures.* New York: Random House.

Horowitz, B. and Madhu Keshwar. 1982. "Family Life—The Unequal Deal." *Manushi* 11: 2–18.

Hrdy, Sarah Blaffer and Glenn Hausfater. 1984. "Comparative and Evolutionary Perspectives on Infanticide: Introduction and Overview." In *Infanticide: Comparative and Evolutionary Perspectives.* Glenn Hausfater and Sarah Blaffer Hrdy (eds.), pp. xii–xxxv. Aldine Publishing Company.

Jacobson, Doranne. 1970. "Hidden Faces: Hindu and Muslim Purdah in a Central Indian Village." Unpublished doctoral dissertation, Columbia University.

Kumar, Dharma. 1983. "Male Utopias or Nightmares?" *Economic and Political Weekly,* January 15: 61–64.

Lenington, S. 1981. "Child Abuse: The Limits of Sociobiology," *Ethnology and Sociobiology* 2: 17–29.

Lewis, Oscar. 1965. *Village Life in Northern India: Studies in a Delhi Village.* New York: Random House.

Lipton, Michael. 1983. "Demography and Poverty." World Bank Staff Working Papers, Number 623. Washington, DC: The World Bank.

Luschinsky, Mildred S. 1962. "The Life of Women in a Village of North India: A Study of Role and Status." Unpublished doctoral dissertation, Cornell University.

Madan, T.N. 1965. *Family and Kinship: A Study of the Pandits of Rural Kashmir.* New York: Asia Publishing House.

Manushi. 1982. "A New Form of Female Infanticide." 12: 21.

Miller, Barbara D. 1981. *The Endangered Sex: Neglect of Female Children in Rural North India.* Ithaca, NY: Cornell University Press.

———. 1984. "Daughter Neglect, Women's Work and Marriage: Pakistan and Bangladesh Compared." *Medical Anthropology* 8(2): 109–126.

———. 1985. "The Unwanted Girls: A Study of Infant Mortality Rates," *Manushi* 29: 18–20.

———. 1986. "Prenatal and Postnatal Sex-Selection in India: The Patriarchal Context, Ethical Questions and Public Policy." Working Paper No. 107 on Women in International Development (East Lansing, MI: Office of Women in International Development, Michigan State University).

Minturn, Leigh. 1984. "Changes in the Differential Treatment of Rajput Girls in Khalapur: 1955–1975," *Medical Anthropology* 8(2): 127–132.

Minturn, Leigh and John T. Hitchcock. 1966. *The Rajputs of Khalapur, India. Six Cultures Series,* Volume III. New York: John Wiley and Sons.

Raikes, Charles. 1852. *Notes on the North-Western Provinces of India*. London: Chapman and Hall.

Ramanamma, A. and Usha Bambawale. 1980. "The Mania for Sons: An Analysis of Social Values in South Asia," *Social Science and Medicine* 14B: 107–110.

Rosenzweig, Mark R. and T. Paul Schultz. 1982. "Market Opportunities, Genetic Endowments, and Intrafamily Resource Distribution: Child Survival in Rural India," *American Economic Review* 72(4): 803–815.

Schneider, David M. 1984. *A Critique of the Study of Kinship*. Ann Arbor, MI: The University of Michigan Press.

Sen, Amartya and Sunil Sengupta. 1983. "Malnutrition of Children and the Rural Sex Bias," *Economic and Political Weekly Annual Number*, May: 855–864.

Sharma, Ursula. 1983. "Dowry in North India: Its Consequences for Women," In *Women and Property, Women as Property*. Renee Hirschon (ed.), pp. 62–74. London: Croom Helm.

Simmons, George B., Celeste Smucker, Stan Bernstein, and Eric Jensen. 1982. "Post Neo-Natal Mortality in Rural India: Implications of an Economic Model," *Demography* 19(3): 371–389.

Skinner, G. William. 1984. "Infanticide as Family Planning in Tokugawa Japan." Paper prepared for the Stanford-Berkeley Colloquium in Historical Demography, San Francisco.

Srilatha, K.V. 1983. Personal communication. (Dr. Srilatha is an epidemiologist, Senior Training and Research Officer, Rural Unit for Health and Social Assistance, Vellore Christian Medical College, Tamil Nadu, India).

Tooley, Michael. 1983. *Abortion and Infanticide*. Oxford: Oxford University Press.

Visaria, Pravin M. 1961. *The Sex Ratio of the Population of India. Census of India 1961*, Vol. 1, Monograph No. 10. New Delhi: Office of the Registrar General.

Washington Post. August 25. 1982. "Birth Test Said to Help Indians Abort Females."

Wasserstrom, Jeffrey. 1984. "Resistance to the One-Child Family," *Modern China* 10(3): 345–374.

Wilkey, Ian, John Pearn, Gwynneth Petrie, and James Nixon. 1982. "Neonaticide, Infanticide and Child Homicide," *Medicine, Science and the Law* 22(1): 31–34.

XI

Colonialism, Development, and the Global Economy

We live today in a global world based on complex political and economic relationships. There are few places that remain untouched by international markets, the mass media, geopolitics, or economic aid. However, the global world, particularly the global economy, is not a new phenomenon. It has its roots in the sixteenth century, when the powerful countries of Western Europe began to colonize populations in Asia, Africa, and the Americas. Part of this process involved the extraction of raw materials such as gold, sugar, rubber, and coffee, and the exploitation of the labor of indigenous populations for the profit of the colonizing nations.

Although most of the colonized world achieved independence by the 1960s, the economic domination of the capitalist world system that was initiated during the colonial period has not been significantly altered. In the late twentieth century an imbalanced relationship between the countries of the industrial, or "developed," world and the developing, or Third World, remains. How have the men and women of the developing world experienced the continuing impact of the penetration of capitalism and the integration of their societies into the global economy?

This question has been addressed in particular with regard to women, and two opposing views have been formulated. Chaney and Schmink (1980), in a review of studies on women and modernization, describe a minority position suggesting that women in the Third World are downtrodden and that capitalist development can help them improve their situation. Those who hold this opinion emphasize that women's economic and social status can be enhanced by an increase in female labor-force participation. Another perspective, stimulated by Ester Boserup's argument that in the course of economic development women experience a decline in their relative status within agriculture (1970: 53), suggests that colonialism and development have introduced "a structure and ideology of male domination" (Leacock 1979: 131). In many parts of the world, originally egalitarian gender relationships have been replaced by more hierarchical ones, and women have consequently been marginalized and removed from the positions of economic and political decision making that they held in the precolonial period.

Researchers have demonstrated the negative effects of colonialism and capitalist penetration in a number of different historical contexts. Silverblatt (1980: 160), for example, portrays the Spanish conquest of the Andes as a "history of the struggle between colonial forces which attempted to break down indigenous social relations and reorient them toward a market economy and the resistance of the indigenous people to these disintegrating forces." Her focus is on the impact of this struggle on the lives of Andean women.

In the pre-Inca and Inca periods Andean women had status and power that were manifested in their customary usufruct rights to land and in their ability to organize labor. After the conquest, Spanish law came up against Andean custom with regard to the property rights of women. In addition, "The Spanish system...ignored the deeply embedded Andean conception of the household embodying the necessary complementarity of male and female labor" (Silverblatt 1980: 168). The result of Spanish colonialism in the Andes was the strengthening of patrilineal and patrilocal ties at the expense of matrilineal and matrilocal ties. Women became both politically and religiously disenfranchised. Indeed, women who continued to practice traditional religion were persecuted. Despite this persecution, the religious practices survived and became a very important mechanism of cultural resistance and defense (Silverblatt 1980: 179).

The Spanish conquest of the Americas was a religious enterprise as much as a political and economic enterprise. In other parts of the world this religious dimension was also present. Grimshaw (1989), for example, presents a historical analysis of the efforts of Christian missionary wives to introduce native Hawaiian women to western notions of femininity, particularly the values of piety, purity, submissiveness, and domesticity that were given new meaning with the rise of the "cult of true womanhood" in nineteenth-century America. Missionary wives were horrified by the lack of education and relaxed sexuality of their Hawaiian female counterparts and set out to teach them a set of new ideas about marriage, child care, family, and religion. All these were founded in the gendered division of labor and society that predominated in their own cultural tradition. In the process, in Grimshaw's view, they attacked several aspects of traditional Hawaiian culture that gave women some measure of autonomy. The work of these missionary wives was by no means easy because they faced a kinship system that emphasized relationships among a wide network of kin rather than the exclusive relationship between husband and wife. Though the education that was provided to Hawaiian women helped them adjust to the world into which they were progressively integrated, Grimshaw notes that many other aspects of Hawaiian society—especially the notions of masculinity and femininity—were ultimately resistant to change in an economic system that could not be easily transformed into a carbon copy of that on the American continent.

Van Allen (in this book) also deals with the impact of Christianity on native populations, in her discussion of Igbo gender relations in Nigeria from the late nineteenth century to the 1970s. Here too an ideology of male domination was inculcated in mission schools. This ideology in turn sustained new economic and political structures that were introduced as part of the colonial system of government. In the traditional dual-sex political system of the Igbo, both men and women had access to political participation and public status, though the opportunities for wealth and power were always greater for men. For women, group solidarity and associations provided a basis for their power and activity in what were clearly public decision-making processes. When the British arrived they immediately attempted to alter a system that was characterized by "diffuse authority, fluid and informal leadership, shared rights of enforcement, and a more or less stable balance of male and female power." Operating with their own set of cultural assumptions about the appropriate roles for men and women, the British established a political structure in which women could not easily participate. The ultimate result, says Van Allen, was a social system that concentrated national political power in the hands of a small, educated, wealthy male elite. This eventually culminated in the "Aba Riots" (in British terms) or "Women's War" (in the Igbo language) of 1929. In this action Igbo women were using a traditional mechanism to express their frustrations, but the British interpreted their actions as instigated by men and failed to recognize that the roots of the women's demonstration lay in Igbo political structures that gave equal voice to men and women.

Although the Igbo were ultimately not very successful in their protest efforts, Etienne and Leacock (1980) suggest that in other historical contexts women resisted colonization and acted to defend themselves. This was true, for example, of Seneca women in Pennsylvania and New York who withstood the attempts of Quakers to put agricultural production in the hands of men, to individualize land tenure, and to deny them political participation (Rothenberg 1980). A similar resistance to change has been documented for several other North American Indian groups (Grumet 1980). According to Weiner (1980: 43), the colonial period did not diminish the economic power of women in the Trobriand Islands in Melanesia "because no one ever knew that banana leaves had economic value." Women's wealth withstood a number of western incursions and, as a result, "served to integrate new kinds of Western wealth, as well as individual economic growth, into the traditional system."

The impact of culture contact and colonialism on the lives of women in the developing world has not been uniform. Indeed, Silverblatt (1980) stresses class distinctions—elite Inca women had different experiences from peasant women. However, it is evident that one aspect of colonialism was the imposition of European and American ideas about the appropriate roles of men and women. Programs designed to stimulate economic development in Third World societies continue to perpetuate culturally rooted assumptions about gender and the division of labor, particularly the definition of men as breadwinners and women as homemakers (Charlton 1984). Based on these assumptions, development planners, often with the support of local elites, direct their efforts at providing new skills and technology to men, even when women are the ones involved in subsistence production and trade (Chaney and Schmink 1980). As Schrijvers (1979: 111-112) has observed, "If women got any attention, it was as mothers and housekeepers in family-planning projects and in training programs for home economics.... Male-centered development programs often resulted in new divisions of labor between the sexes, by which the dependency of women on men greatly increased."

Lockwood (in this book) reviews the literature on the differential effects of the penetration of capitalism and development around the world, which sometimes work to the benefit of women and sometimes to their detriment. More specifically, she explores the relationships among gender ideology, women's control of material resources, family and kinship structures, and capitalist development. Based on a comparative analysis of two Tahitian cases where development programs were introduced in the 1960s, she argues that a gender ideology that empowers women is not sufficient to counter the increasing dependence on men that often results from developmental change. Rather, women must also control strategic resources in order to maintain status and power in both household and community in the face of capitalist penetration.

Like Lockwood, Wilson-Moore (in this book) shows that under certain conditions development programs can have a positive impact on women and their families. She explores the viability of homestead gardening as an economic strategy for women in Bangladesh where both men and women are involved in gardening, but use different methods and cultivate different crops. Women's gardens can be an effective foundation for the nutritional well-being of family members and do not necessarily have to compete with those of men. Development, in Wilson-Moore's view, is as much about feeding as it is about profit, and any program that is introduced should take into account the importance of subsistence as well as cash cropping in the context of the complementary gender roles in the local social system.

Agribusiness and multinational industrial production are other forms of global capitalism that bring mixed benefits for women in developing countries. Arizpe and Aranda (1981) argue that strawberry agribusiness, although a major employer for women in Zamora, Mexico, does not enhance women's status or create viable new opportunities for women. These researchers examine why women comprise such a high proportion of the employees in this business and cite cultural factors that constrain opportunities for women and continue to define women's work as temporary and supplementary. Employers take advantage of these constraints— they permit them to keep wages low and work schedules flexible. Arizpe and Aranda's conclusions support those of other researchers who point to a range of phenomena that make a female labor force attractive to multinational business and industry. "Women's socialization, training in needlework, embroidery and other domestic crafts, and supposedly 'natural' aptitude for detailed handiwork, gives them an advantage over men in tasks requiring high levels of manual dexterity and accuracy; women are also supposedly more passive—willing to accept authority and less likely to become involved in labour conflicts. Finally, women have the added advantage of 'natural disposability'—when they leave to get married or have children, a factory temporarily cutting back on production simply freezes their post" (Brydon and Chant 1988: 172).

As with agribusiness, the internationalization of capitalist production has led to the relocation in developing countries of many labor-intensive and export-oriented manufacturing and processing plants owned by multinational corporations. Many of these have provided new opportunities for employment, primarily for women. For example, in some electronics factories in Southeast Asia, women make up 80 percent to 90 percent of the labor force (Brydon and Chant 1988). However, just as with the assessment of the impact of development schemes on the lives of women in the developing world, there are two opposing views about the effect of multinationals. Some emphasize the benefits of jobs that provide women with greater financial stability (Lim 1983), while others see multinationals perpetuating or even creating new forms of inequality as they introduce young women to a new set of individualist and consumerist values. The sexually segregated work force remains in place within paternalistic industrial contexts that encourage turnover and offer no opportunities for advancement (Nash and Fernandez-Kelly 1983).

Fernandez-Kelly (1984) analyzes workers' responses to the international political and economic system at the levels of household and factory along the Mexican side of the U.S.–Mexico border, where more than 100 assembly plants (maquiladoras) have been established. These industries primarily employ women. By working herself in the apparel industry, Fernandez-Kelly documented hiring practices and working conditions of factory women. Low wages, oppressive working conditions, lack of job mobility, and insecure job tenure make maquiladoras a precarious option, selected by women with few alternatives. Factory workers also suffer from the contradictions between idealized notions of women's roles and their actual involvement in wage labor, which causes conflict over mores and values.

In this book, Cairoli describes how young unmarried Moroccan women employed in the export garment industry in Fez, Morocco reconcile some of the contradictions between the cultural values and role expectations for women and the reality of their industrial employment. Inspired by Aihwa Ong's (1991:280) emphasis on the "experiential and interpretive dimensions of work relations," Cairoli discusses how these female laborers transform their workplace into an interior domestic space, operating in it as they would in their own household. "They model their position in the factory hierarchy on their role in the household and so are able not only to accept the domination of the factory, but to find in that domination their own sources of personal self-worth and power." Factory owners become like fathers who guard the virtue of their female workers. Fellow garment workers are like sisters and thus the authority of a female supervisor is akin to the authority of the eldest sister. As in the Moroccan home, female space in the factory is separated from male space.

Zimmer-Tamakashi (in this book) presents a somewhat different point of view, describing a situation where the introduction of wage labor and the shift from household to factory industry have problematic social implications, particularly for gender relations. She discusses the sexual politics of Papua New Guinea's educated elite, and the sexual competition among men of different tribal and national backgrounds. In a situation where men have access to cash and women have become more dependent on them, cases of domestic violence have increased. Women are experiencing a growing sense of gender oppression, and rape and violence against women have become "women's issues" largely ignored by male politicians. Those women who themselves enter the cash economy may experience more autonomy, but this too may generate domestic violence from men motivated by a fear of women's independence and their own economic uncertainty.

Although Cairoli's work, coupled with that of Ong (1987), show examples of adaptation and resistance in the face of global capitalism, in the final analysis, much of the work on women in development tends to support Leacock's (1979) rather pessimistic assessment. Real development, from her perspective, "would mean bringing an end to the system whereby the multinational corporations continue to 'underdevelop' Third World nations by consuming huge proportions of their resources and grossly underpaying their workers" (1979: 131). This will require a truly international effort. The gendered approach to colonialism and development has demonstrated the close relationship between capitalist penetration, patriarchal gender ideologies, and the sexual division of labor. This relationship has been present since the early days of colonialism and has been perpetuated by a global economy that has created an international division of labor often oppressing both men and women, but especially women. As Chaney and Schmink (1980: 176) put it, development policies and programs frequently lead "not only to the degradation of the physical environment but also of the social environment, as various groups are systematically excluded from the tools of progress and their benefits."

REFERENCES

Arizpe, Lourdes and Josefina Aranda. 1981. "The 'Comparative Advantages' of Women's Disadvantages: Women Workers in the Strawberry Export Agribusiness in Mexico." *Signs* 7: 453–473.

Boserup, Esther. 1970. *Woman's Role in Economic Development*. New York: St. Martin's Press.

Brydon, Lynne and Sylvia Chant. 1988. *Women in the Third World: Gender Issues in Rural and Urban Areas*. New Brunswick, NJ: Rutgers University Press.

Chaney, Elsa M. and Marianne Schmink. 1980. "Women and Modernization: Access to Tools." In June Nash and Helen I. Safa (eds.). *Sex and Class in Latin America*, pp. 160–182. South Hadley, MA: J.F. Bergin Publishers.

Charlton, Sue-Ellen M. 1984. *Women in Third World Development*. Boulder CO: Westview Press.

Etienne, Mona and Eleanor Leacock. 1980. "Introduction." In Mona Etienne and Eleanor Leacock (eds.). *Women and Colonization: Anthropological Perspectives*, pp. 1–24. New York: Praeger.

Fernandez-Kelly, Maria Patricia. 1984. "Maquiladoras: The View From the Inside." In Karen Brodkin Sacks and Dorothy Remy (eds.) *My Toubles are Going to Have Trouble With Me*, pp .229–246. New Brunswick, NJ: Rutgers Press.

Grimshaw, Patricia. 1989. "New England Missionary Wives, Hawaiian Women and the Cult of True Womanhood," In Margaret Jolly and Martha MacIntyre (eds.), *Family and Gender in the Pacific: Domestic Contradictions and the Colonial Impact*, pp. 191–44. Cambridge: Cambridge University Press

Grumet, Robert Steven. 1980. "Sunksquaws, Shamans, and Tradeswomen: Middle Atlantic Coastal Algonkian Women During the 17th and 18th Centuries." In Mona Etienne and Eleanor Leacock (eds.). *Women and Colonization: Anthropological Perspectives*, pp. 43–62. New York: Praeger.

Leacock, Eleanor. 1979. "Women, Development, and Anthropological Facts and Fictions." In Gerrit Huizer and Bruce Mannheim (eds.). *The Politics of Anthropology: From Colonialism and Sexism Toward a View from Below*, pp. 131–142. The Hague: Mouton.

Lim, Linda Y. C. 1983. "Capitalism, Imperialism, and Patriarchy: The Dilemma of Third-World Women Workers in Multinational Factories." In June Nash and Maria Patricia Fernandez-Kelly (eds.). *Women, Men and the International Division of Labor*, pp. 70–91. Albany: State University of New York.

Nash, June and Maria Patricia Fernandez-Kelly (eds.). 1983. *Women, Men and the International Division of Labor*. Albany: State University of New York.

Ong, Aihwa. 1987. *Spirits of Resistance and Capitalist Discipline: Factory Women in Malaysia*. Albany: State University of New York Press.

———. 1991. "The Gender and Labor Politics of Post-Modernity." *Annual Review of Anthropology* 20:279–309.

Rothenberg, Diane. 1980. "The Mothers of the Nation: Seneca Resistance to Quaker Intervention." In Mona Etienne and Eleanor Leacock (eds.). *Women and Colonization: Anthropological Perspectives*, pp. 63–87. New York: Praeger.

Schrijvers, Joke. 1979. "Viricentrism and Anthropology." In Gerrit Huizer and Bruce Mannheim (eds.). *The Politics of Anthropology: From Colonialism and Sexism Toward a View from Below*, pp. 97–115. The Hague: Mouton.

Silverblatt, Irene. 1980. "Andean Women Under Spanish Rule." In Mona Etienne and Eleanor Leacock (eds.). *Women and Colonization: Anthropological Perspectives*, pp. 149–185. New York: Praeger.

Weiner, Annette. 1980. "Stability in Banana Leaves: Colonization and Women in Kiriwina, Trobriand Islands." In Mona Etienne and Eleanor Leacock (eds.). *Women and Colonization: Anthropological Perspectives*, pp. 270–293. New York: Praeger.

"Aba Riots" or Igbo "Women's War"? Ideology, Stratification, and the Invisibility of Women

Judith Van Allen

The events that occurred in Calabar and Owerri provinces in southeastern Nigeria in November and December of 1929, and that have come to be known in Western social-science literature as the "Aba Riots," are a natural focus for an investigation of the impact of colonialism on Igbo women.[1] In the development and results of that crisis can be found all the elements of the system that has weakened women's position in Igboland—and in much of the rest of Africa as well.[2] The "Aba Riots" are also a nice symbol of the "invisibility" of women: "Aba Riots" is the name adopted by the British; the Igbo called it *Ogu Umunwanyi*, the "Women's War" (Uchendu 1965: 5; Okonjo 1974: 25, n. 40). This is more than a word game. In politics, the control of language means the control of history. The dominant group and the subordinate group almost always give different names to their conflicts, and where the dominant group alone writes history, its choice of terminology will be perpetuated. Examples of this manipulation of language abound in American history, as any examination of standard textbooks will reveal.

Calabar and Owerri provinces covered roughly the southeast and southwest quarters of Igboland, the traditional home of the Igbo peoples. In November of 1929, thousands of Igbo women from these provinces converged on the Native Administration centers—settlements that generally included the headquarters and residence of the British colonial officer for the district, a Native Court building and a jail, and a bank or white trader's store (if such existed in the district).[3] The women chanted, danced, sang songs of ridicule, and demanded the caps of office (the official insignia) of the Warrant Chiefs, the Igbo chosen from each village by the British to sit as members of the Native Court. At a few locations the women broke into prisons and released prisoners. Sixteen Native Courts were attacked, and most of these were broken up or burned. The "disturbed area" covered about 6,000 square miles and contained about two million people. It is not known how many women were involved, but the figure was in the tens of thousands. On two occasions, British District Officers called in police and troops, who fired on the women and left a total of more than 50 dead and 50 wounded. No one on the other side was seriously injured.[4]

The British "won," and they have imposed their terminology on history; only a very few scholars have recorded that the Igbo called this the "Women's War." And in most histories of Nigeria today one looks in vain for any mention that women were even involved. "Riots," the term used by the British, conveys a picture of uncontrolled, irrational action, involving violence to property or persons, or both. It serves to justify the "necessary action to restore order," and it accords with the British picture of the outpouring of Igbo from their villages as some sort of spontaneous frenzy, explained by the general "excitability" of these "least disciplined" of African peoples (Perham 1937:219). "Aba Riots," in addition, neatly removes women from the picture. What we are left with is "some riots at Aba"—not by women, not involving complex organization, and not ranging over most of southeastern Nigeria.

To the British Commissions of Enquiry established to investigate the events, the Igbo as a whole were felt to be dissatisfied with the general system of administration. The women simply were seen as expressing this underlying general dissatisfaction. The British explanation for the fact that women rather than men "rioted" was twofold: the women were aroused by a rumor that they would be taxed at a time of declining profits from the palm products trade; and they believed themselves to be immune from danger because they thought British soldiers would not fire on women (Perham 1937:213–217). The possibility that women might have acted because as women they were particularly distressed by the Native Administration system does not seem to have been taken any more seriously by the Commissions than women's demands in testimony that they be included in the Native Courts (Leith-Ross 1939:165).

The term "Women's War," in contrast to "Aba Riots," retains both the presence and the significance of the women, for the word "war" in this context derived from the pidgin English expression "making war," an institutionalized form of punishment employed by Igbo women and also known as "sitting on a man." To "sit on" or "make war on" a man involved gathering at his compound at a previously agreed-upon time, dancing, singing scurrilous songs detailing the women's grievances against him (and often insulting him along the way by calling his manhood into question), banging on his hut with the pestles used for pounding yams, and, in extreme cases, tearing up his hut (which usually meant pulling the roof off). This might be done to a man who particularly mistreated his wife, who violated the women's market rules, or who persistently let his cows eat the women's crops. The women would stay at his hut all night and day, if necessary, until he repented and promised to mend his ways (Leith-Ross 1939: 109; Harris 1940: 146–48).[5]

"Women's War" thus conveys an action by women that is also an extension of their traditional method for settling grievances with men who had acted badly toward them.

Understood from the Igbo perspective, this term confirms the existence of Igbo women's traditional institutions, for "making war" was the ultimate sanction available to women for enforcing their judgments. The use of the word "war" in this specifically Igbo sense directs attention to the existence of those female political and economic institutions that were never taken into account by the British, and that still have not been sufficiently recognized by contemporary social scientists writing about the development of nationalist movements.

Conventionally, Western influence has been seen as "emancipating" African women through (1) the weakening of kinship bonds; (2) the provision of "free choice" in Christian monogamous marriage; (3) the suppression of "barbarous" practices (female circumcision, ostracism of mothers of twins, slavery); (4) the opening of schools; and (5) the introduction of modern medicine, hygiene, and (sometimes) female suffrage. What has not been seen by Westerners is that for some African women—and Igbo women are a striking example—actual or potential autonomy, economic independence, and political power did not grow out of Western influences but existed already in traditional "tribal" life. To the extent that Igbo women have participated in any political action—whether anticolonial or nationalist struggles, local community development, or the Biafran war—it has been not so much because of the influence of Western values as despite that influence.

TRADITIONAL IGBO POLITICAL INSTITUTIONS

In traditional Igbo society, women did not have a political role equal to that of men. But they did have a role—or more accurately, a series of roles—despite the patrilineal organization of Igbo society. Their possibilities of participating in traditional politics must be examined in terms of both structures and values. Also involved is a consideration of what it means to talk about "politics" and "political roles" in a society that has no differentiated, centralized governmental institutions.

Fallers (1963) suggests that for such societies, it is necessary to view "the polity or political system ... not as a concretely distinct part of the social system, but rather as a functional aspect of the whole social system: that aspect concerned with making and carrying out decisions regarding public policy, by whatever institutional means." Fallers's definition is preferable to several other functionalist definitions because it attempts to give some content to the category "political." Examples will make this clear. Let us take a society that has no set of differentiated political institutions to which we can ascribe Weber's "monopoly of the legitimate use of physical force within a given territory," and yet that holds together in reasonable order; we ask the question, What are the mechanisms of social control? To this may be added a second question, based on the notion that a basic governmental function is "authoritative allocation": What are the mechanisms that authoritatively allocate goods and services? A third common notion of politics is concerned with power relationships, and so we also ask, Who has power (or influence) over whom?

The problem with all of these approaches is that they are at the same time too broad and too narrow. If everything in a society that promotes order, resolves conflicts, allocates goods, or involves the power of one person over another is "political," then we have hardly succeeded in distinguishing the "political" as a special kind of activity or area or relationship. Igbo women certainly played a role in promoting order and resolving conflicts (Green 1947: 178–216; Leith-Ross 1939: 97, 106–9), but that does not make them political actors. In response to each of those broad definitions, we can still ask, Is this mechanism of social control or allocation, or this power relationship, a *political* mechanism or relationship? In answering that question, Fallers provides some help. It is their relationship to public policy that makes mechanisms, relationships, or activities "political."

There are many different concepts of "public" in Western thought. We will consider only two, chosen because we can possibly apply them to Igbo politics without producing a distorted picture. There seem to be actions taken, and distinctions made, in Igbo politics and language that make it not quite so ethnocentric to try to use these Western concepts. One notion of "public" relates it to issues that are of concern to the whole community; ends served by "political functions" are beneficial to the community as a whole. Although different individuals or groups may seek different resolutions of problems or disputes, the "political" can nevertheless be seen as encompassing all those human concerns and problems that are common to all the members of the community, or at least to large numbers of them. "Political" problems are shared problems that are appropriately dealt with through group action— their resolutions are collective, not individual. This separates them from "purely personal" problems. The second notion of "public" is that which is distinguished from "secret," that is, open to everyone's view, accessible to all members of the community. The settling of questions that concern the welfare of the community in a "public" way necessitates the sharing of "political knowledge"— the knowledge needed for participation in political discussion and decision. A system in which public policy is made publicly and the relevant knowledge is shared widely contrasts sharply with those systems in which a privileged few possess the relevant knowledge—whether priestly mysteries or bureaucratic expertise—and therefore control policy decisions.

Traditional Igbo society was predominantly patrilineal and segmental. People lived in "villages" composed of the scattered compounds of relatively close patrilineal kinsmen; and related villages formed what are usually referred to as "village groups," the largest functional political unit. Forde and Jones (1950: 9, 39) found between 4,000 and 5,000 village groups, ranging in population from several hundred to several thousand persons. Political power was diffuse, and leadership was fluid and informal. Community decisions were made and disputes settled through a variety of gatherings (villagewide assemblies; women's meetings; age grades; secret and title societies; contribution clubs; lineage groups; and congregations at funerals, markets, or annual rituals) as well as through appeals to oracles and diviners (Afigbo 1972: 13–36).[6] Decisions were made by discussion until mutual agreement was reached. Any adult present who had something to say on the matter under discussion was entitled to speak, so long as he or she said something that the others considered worth listening to; as the Igbo say, "A case forbids no one." Leaders were those who had "mouth"; age was respected, but did not confer leadership unless accompanied by wisdom and the ability to speak well. In village assemblies, after much discussion, a small group of elders retired for "consultation" and then offered a decision for the approval of the assembly (Uchendu 1965: 41–44; Green 1947: chaps. 7–11; Harris 1940: 142–43).

In some areas, the assemblies are said to have been of all adult males; in other areas, women reportedly participated in the assemblies, but were less likely to speak unless involved in the dispute and less likely to take part in "consultation." Women may have been among the "arbitrators" that disputants invited to settle particular cases; however, if one party to the dispute appealed to the village as a whole, male elders would have been more likely to offer the final settlement (Green 1947: 107, 112–13, 116–29, 169, 199). Age grades existed in most Igbo communities, but their functions varied; the predominant pattern seems to have been for young men's age grades to carry out decisions of the village assembly with regard to such matters as clearing paths, building bridges, or collecting fines (Uchendu 1965: 43). There was thus no distinction among what we call executive, legislative, and judicial activities, and no political authority to issue commands. The settling of a dispute could merge into a discussion of a new "rule," and acceptance by the disputants and the

group hearing the dispute was necessary for the settlement of anything. Only within a family compound could an individual demand obedience to orders; there the compound head offered guidance, aid, and protection to members of his family, and in return received respect, obedience, and material tokens of good will. Neither was there any distinction between the religious and the political: rituals and "political" discussions were interwoven in patterns of action to promote the good of the community; and rituals, too, were performed by various groups of women, men, and women and men together (Afigbo 1972; Meek 1957: 98–99, 105; Uchendu 1965: 39–40).

Matters dealt with in the village assembly were those of common concern to all. They could be general problems for which collective action was appropriate (for example, discussion might center on how to make the village market bigger than those of neighboring villages); or they could be conflicts that threatened the unity of the village (for example, a dispute between members of different families, or between the men and the women) (Harris 1940: 142–43; Uchendu 1965: 34, 42–43). It is clear, then, that the assembly dealt with public policy publicly. The mode of discourse made much use of proverbs, parables, and metaphors drawn from the body of Igbo tradition and familiar to all Igbo from childhood. Influential speech involved the creative and skillful use of this tradition to provide counsel and justification—to assure others that a certain course of action was both a wise thing to do and a right thing to do. The accessibility (the "public" nature) of this knowledge is itself indicated by an Igbo proverb: "If you tell a proverb to a fool, he will ask you its meaning." Fools were excluded from the political community, but women were not.[7]

Women as well as men thus had access to political participation; for women as well as for men, public status was to a great extent achieved, not ascribed. A woman's status was determined more by her own achievements than by those of her husband. The resources available to men were greater, however; thus, although a woman might rank higher among women than her husband did among men, very few women could afford the fees and feasts involved in taking the highest titles, a major source of prestige (Meek 1957: 203). Men "owned" the most profitable crops and received the bulk of the money from bridewealth. Moreover, if they were compound heads, they received presents from compound members. Through the patrilineage, they controlled the land. After providing farms for their wives, they could lease excess land for a good profit. Men also did more of the long-distance trading, which had a higher rate of profit than did local and regional trading, which was almost entirely in women's hands (Green 1947: 32–42).

Women were entitled to sell the surplus of their own crops. They also received the palm kernels as their share of the palm produce (they processed the palm oil for the men to sell). They might also sell prepared foods, or the products of women's special skills (processed salt, pots, baskets). All the profits were theirs to keep (Leith-Ross 1939: 90–92, 138–39, 143). But these increments of profit were relatively low. Since the higher titles commonly needed to ensure respect for village leaders required increasingly higher fees and expenses, women's low profits restricted their access to villagewide leadership. Almost all of those who took the higher titles were men, and most of the leaders in villagewide discussions and decisions were men (Green 1947: 169; Uchendu 1965: 41). Women, therefore, came out as second-class citizens. Though status and the political influence it could bring were "achieved," and though there were no formal limits to women's political power, men by their ascriptive status (membership in the patrilineage) acquired wealth that gave them a head start and a lifelong advantage over women. The Igbo say that "a child who washes his hands clean deserves to eat with his elders" (Uchendu 1965: 19). What they do not say is that at birth some children are given water and some are not.

WOMEN'S POLITICAL INSTITUTIONS

Though women's associations are best described for the south—the area of the Women's War—their existence is reported for most other areas of Igboland, and Forde and Jones made the general observation that "women's associations express their disapproval and secure their demands by collective public demonstrations, including ridicule, satirical singing and dancing, and group strikes" (1950: 21).

Two sorts of women's associations are relevant politically: those of the *inyemedi* (wives of a lineage) and of the *umuada* (daughters of a lineage). Since traditional Igbo society was predominantly patrilocal and exogamous, almost all adult women in a village would be wives (there would also probably be some divorced or widowed "daughters" who had returned home to live). Women of the same natal village or village group (and therefore of the same lineage) might marry far and wide, but they would come together periodically in meetings often called *ogbo* (an Igbo word for "gathering"). The *umuada's* most important ritual function was at funerals of lineage members, since no one could have a proper funeral without their voluntary ritual participation—a fact that gave women a significant measure of power. The *umuada* invoked this power in helping to settle intralineage disputes among their "brothers," as well as disputes between their natal and marital lineages. Since these gatherings were held in rotation among the villages into which members had married, they formed an important part of the communication network of Igbo women (Okonjo 1974: 25; Olisa 1971: 24–27; Green 1947: 217–29).

The companion grouping to the *umuada* was the *inyemedi,* the wives of the lineage, who came together in villagewide gatherings that during the colonial period came to be called *mikiri* or *mitiri* (the Igbo version of the English "meeting"). *Mikiri* were thus gatherings of women based on common residence rather than on common birth, as in the case of *ogbo*.

The *mikiri* appears to have performed the major role in daily self-rule among women and to have articulated women's interests as opposed to those of men. *Mikiri* provided women with a forum in which to develop their political talents and with a means for protecting their interests as traders, farmers, wives, and mothers (Green 1947; Leith-Ross 1939; Harris 1940; Okonjo 1974). In *mikiri*, women made rules about markets' crops, and livestock that applied to men as well as women; and they exerted pressure to maintain moral norms among women. They heard complaints from wives about mistreatment by husbands, and discussed how to deal with problems they were having with "the men" as a whole. They also made decisions about the rituals addressed to the female aspect of the village's guardian spirit, and about rituals for the protection of the fruitfulness of women and of their farms. If fines for violations or if repeated requests to husbands and elders were ignored, women might "sit on" an offender or go on strike. The latter might involve refusing to cook, to take care of small children, or to have sexual relations with their husbands. Men regarded the *mikiri* as legitimate; and the use of the more extreme sanctions—though rare—was well remembered.

Though both *ogbo* and *mikiri* served to articulate and protect women's interests, it is probably more accurate to see these groups as sharing in diffused political authority than to see them as acting only as pressure groups for women's interests. Okonjo [1976] argues ... that traditional Igbo society had a "dual-sex political system"; that is, there was a dual system of male and female political-religious institutions, each sex having both its own autonomous sphere of authority and an area of shared responsibilities. Thus, women settled disputes among women, but also made decisions and rules affecting men. They had the right to enforce their decisions and rules by using forms of group ostracism similar to those used by men. In a society of such diffuse political authority, it would be misleading to call only a village assembly of men a "public"

gathering, as most Western observers unquestioningly do; among the Igbo, a gathering of adult women must also be accepted as a public gathering.

COLONIAL "PENETRATION"

Into this system of diffuse authority, fluid and informal leadership, shared rights of enforcement, and a more or less stable balance of male and female power, the British tried to introduce ideas of "native administration" derived from colonial experience with chiefs and emirs in northern Nigeria. Southern Nigeria was declared a protectorate in 1900, but ten years passed before the conquest was effective. As colonial power was established in what the British perceived as a situation of "ordered anarchy," Igboland was divided into Native Court Areas that violated the autonomy of villages by lumping together many unrelated villages. British District Officers were to preside over the courts, but they were not always present because there were more courts than officers. The Igbo membership was formed by choosing from each village a "representative" who was given a warrant of office. These Warrant Chiefs also constituted what was called the Native Authority. The Warrant Chiefs were required to see that the orders of the District Officers were executed in their own villages, and they were the only link between the colonial power and the people (Afigbo 1972: 13–36, 207–48).

In the first place, it was a violation of Igbo concepts to have one man represent the village; and it was even more of a violation that he should give orders to everyone else. The people obeyed the Warrant Chief when they had to, since British power backed him up. In some places Warrant Chiefs were lineage heads or wealthy men who were already leaders in the village. But in many places they were simply ambitious, opportunistic young men who put themselves forward as friends of the conquerors. Even where the Warrant Chief was not corrupt, he was still, more than anything else, an agent of the British. The people avoided using Native Courts when they could do so, but Warrant Chiefs could force cases into the Native Courts and fine people for infractions of rules. Because he had the ear of the British, the Warrant Chief himself could violate traditions and even British rules and get away with it (Anene 1967: 259; Meek 1957: 328–30).

Women suffered particularly under the arbitrary rule of Warrant Chiefs, who reportedly took women to marry without allowing them the customary right to refuse a particular suitor. They also helped themselves to the women's agricultural produce and domestic animals (Onwuteaka 1965: 274). Recommendations for reform of the system were made almost from its inception both by junior officers in the field and by senior officers sent out from headquarters to investigate. But no real improvements were made. An attempt by the British in 1918 to make the Native Courts more "native" by abolishing the District Officers' role as presiding court officials had little effect, and that mostly bad. Removing the District Officers from the courts simply left more power in the hands of corrupt Warrant Chiefs and the increasingly powerful Court Clerks. The latter, intended to be "servants of the court," were able in some cases to dominate the courts because of their monopoly of expertise—namely, literacy (Meek 1957: 329; Gailey 1970: 66–74).

THE WOMEN'S WAR

In 1925, the British decided to introduce direct taxation in order to create the Native Treasury, which was supposed to pay for improvements in the Native Administration, in accordance with the British imperial philosophy that the colonized should pay the costs of colonization. Prices in the palm trade were high, and the tax—on adult males—was set accordingly. Taxes were collected without widespread trouble, although there were "tax riots" in Warri Province (west of the Niger) in 1927.

In 1929, a zealous Assistant District Officer in Bende division of Owerri Province, apparently acting on his own initiative, decided to "tighten up" the census registers by recounting households and property. He told the Chiefs that there was no plan to increase taxes or to tax women. But the counting of women and their property raised fears that women were to be taxed, particularly because the Bende District Officer had lied earlier when the men were counted and had told the men that they were not going to be taxed. The women, therefore, naturally did not believe these reassurances. The taxation rumor spread quickly through the women's communication networks, and meetings of women took place in various market squares, which were the common places for women to have large meetings. In the Oloko Native Court Area—one of the areas of deception about the men's tax—the women leaders, Ikonnia, Nwannedie, and Nwugo, called a general meeting at Orie market. Here it was decided that as long as only men were approached in a compound and asked for information the women would do nothing. If any woman was approached, she was to raise the alarm; then the women would meet again to decide what to do. But they wanted clear evidence that women were to be taxed (Afigbo 1972; Gailey 1970: 107–8).

On November 23, an agent of the Oloko Warrant Chief, Okugo, entered a compound and told one of the married women, Nwanyeruwa, to count her goats and sheep. She replied angrily, "Was your mother counted?" at which "they closed, seizing each other by the throat" (Perham 1937: 207). Nwanyeruwa's report to the Oloko women convinced them that they were to be taxed. Messengers were sent to neighboring areas, and women streamed into Oloko from all over Owerri Province. They "sat on" Okugo and demanded his cap of office. They massed in protest at the District Office and succeeded in getting written assurances that they were not to be taxed. After several days of mass protest meetings, they also succeeded in getting Okugo arrested, tried, and convicted of "spreading news likely to cause alarm" and of physical assault on the women. He was sentenced to two years' imprisonment (Gailey 1970: 108–13).

News of this victory spread rapidly through the market-*mikiri-ogbo* network, and women in many areas then attempted to get rid of their Warrant Chiefs and the Native Administration itself. Nwanyeruwa became something of a heroine as reports of her resistance spread. Money poured in from grateful women from villages scattered over a wide area but linked by kinship to Nwanyeruwa's marital village. Nwanyeruwa herself, however, was "content to allow" leadership in her area to be exercised by someone else. The money collected was used not for her but for delegates going to meetings of women throughout southern Igboland to coordinate the Women's War.

The British ended the rebellion only by using large numbers of police and soldiers—and, on one occasion, Boy Scouts. Although the shootings in mid-December and the growing numbers of police and soldiers in the area led the women to halt most of their activities, disturbances continued into 1930. The "disaffected areas"—all of Owerri and Calabar provinces—were occupied by government forces. Punitive expeditions burned or demolished compounds, took provisions from the villages to feed the troops, and confiscated property in payment of fines levied arbitrarily against villages in retribution for damages (Gailey 1970: 135–37).

During the investigations that followed the Women's War, the British discovered the communication network that had been used to spread the rumor of taxation. But that did not lead them to inquire further into how it came to pass that Igbo women had engaged in concerted action under grassroots leadership, had agreed on demands, and had materialized by the thousands at Native Administration centers dressed and adorned in the same unusual way—all wearing short loincloths, all carrying sticks wreathed with palm fronds, and all having their faces smeared with charcoal or ashes and their heads bound with young ferns. Unbeknownst to the British, this was the dress and adornment signifying "war," the sticks being used to invoke the power of the female ancestors (Harris 1940: 143–45, 147–48; Perham 1937: 207ff; Meek 1957: ix).

The report of the Commission of En-quiry exonerating the soldiers who fired on the women cited the "savage passions" of the "mobs"; and one military officer told the Commission that "he had never seen crowds in such a state of frenzy." Yet these "frenzied mobs" injured no one seriously, which the British found "surprising"; but then the British did not understand that the women were engaged in a traditional practice with traditional rules and limitations, only carried out in this instance on a much larger scale than in precolonial times.[8]

REFORMS—BUT NOT FOR WOMEN

The British failure to recognize the Women's War as a collective response to the abrogation of rights resulted in a failure to ask whether women might have had a role in the traditional political system that should be incorporated into the institutions of colonial government. Because the women—and the men—regarded the investigations as attempts to discover whom to punish, they volunteered no information about women's organizations. But would the British have understood those organizations if they had? The discovery of the market network had suggested no further lines of inquiry. The majority of District Officers thought that the men had organized the women's actions and were secretly directing them. The women's demands that the Native Courts no longer hear cases and that "all white men should go to their own country"—or at least that women should serve on the Native Courts and a woman be appointed a District Officer—were in line with the power of women in traditional Igbo society but were regarded by the British as irrational and ridiculous (Gailey 1970: 130ff; Leith-Ross 1939: 165; Perham 1937: 165ff).

The reforms instituted in 1933 therefore ignored the women's traditional political role, though they did make some adjustments to traditional Igbo male and male-dominated political forms. The number of Native Court Areas was greatly increased, and their boundaries were arranged to conform roughly to traditional divisions. Warrant Chiefs were replaced by "massed benches," which allowed large numbers of judges to sit at one time. In most cases it was left up to the villages to decide whom and how many to send. Though this benefited the women by eliminating the corruption of the Warrant Chiefs, and thus made their persons and property more secure, it provided no outlet for collective action, their real base of power (Perham 1937: 365ff).

In 1901 the British had declared all jural institutions except the Native Courts illegitimate, but it was only in the years following the 1933 reforms that Native Administration local government became effective enough to make that declaration at all meaningful. The British had also outlawed "self-help"—the use of force by anyone but the government to punish wrongdoers. And the increasingly effective enforcement of this ban eliminated the women's ultimate weapon: "sitting on a man." In attempting to create specialized political institutions on the Western model, with participation on the basis of individual achievement, the British created a system in which there was no place for group solidarity, no possibility of dispersed and shared political authority or power of enforcement, and thus very little place for women (Leith-Ross 1939: 109–10, 163, 214). As in the village assemblies, women could not compete with men for leadership in the reformed Native Administration because they lacked the requisite resources. This imbalance in resources was increased by other facets of British colonialism—economic "penetration" and missionary influence. All three—colonial government, foreign investment, and the church—contributed to the growth of a system of political and economic stratification that made community decision-making less

"public" in both senses we have discussed and that led to the current concentration of national political power in the hands of a small, educated, wealthy, male elite. For though we are here focusing on the political results of colonialism, they must be seen as part of the whole system of imposed class and sex stratification.

MISSIONARY INFLUENCE

Christian missions were established in Igboland in the late nineteenth century. They had few converts at first, but by the 1930s their influence was significant, though generally limited to the young (Leith-Ross 1939: 109–18; Meek 1957: xv). A majority of Igbo eventually "became Christians," for they had to profess Christianity in order to attend mission schools. Regardless of how nominal their membership was, they had to obey the rules to remain in good standing, and one rule was to avoid "pagan" rituals. Women were discouraged from attending meetings where traditional rituals were performed or where money was collected for the rituals, which in effect meant all *mikiri, ogbo,* and many other types of gatherings (Ajayi 1965: 108–9).

Probably more significant, since *mikiri* were losing some of their political functions anyway, was mission education. The Igbo came to see English and Western education as increasingly necessary for political leadership—needed to deal with the British and their law—and women had less access to this new knowledge than men had. Boys were more often sent to school than girls, for a variety of reasons generally related to their favored position in the patrilineage, including the fact that they, not their sisters, would be expected to support their parents in their old age. But even when girls did go, they tended not to receive the same type of education. In mission schools, and increasingly in special "training homes" that dispensed with most academic courses, the girls were taught European domestic skills and the Bible, often in the vernacular. The missionaries' avowed purpose in educating girls was to train them for Christian marriage and motherhood, not for jobs or for citizenship. Missionaries were not necessarily against women's participation in politics; clergy in England, as in America, could be found supporting women's suffrage. But in Africa their concern was the church, and for the church they needed Christian families. Therefore, Christian wives and mothers, not female political leaders, were the missions' aim. As Mary Slessor, the influential Calabar missionary, said: "God-like motherhood is the finest sphere for women, and the way to the redemption of the world."[9] As the English language and other knowledge of "book" became necessary to political life, women were increasingly cut out and policy-making became less public.

ECONOMIC COLONIALISM

The traditional Igbo division of labor—in which women owned their surplus crops and their market profits, while men controlled the more valuable yams and palm products and did more long-distance trading—was based on a subsistence economy. Small surpluses could be accumulated, but these were generally not used for continued capital investment. Rather, in accord with traditional values, the surplus was used for social rather than economic gain: it was returned to the community through fees and feasts for rituals for title-taking, weddings, funerals, and other ceremonies, or through projects to help the community "get up." One became a "big man" or a "big woman" not by hoarding one's wealth but by spending it on others in prestige-winning ways (Uchendu 1965: 34; Meek 1957: 111).

Before the Pax Britannica, Igbo women had been active traders in all but a few areas (one such was Afikpo, where women farmed but did not trade).[10] The ties of exogamous marriage among patrilineages, the cross-cutting networks of women providing channels for communication and conciliation, and the ritual power of female members of patrilineages all enabled the traditional system to deal with conflicts with relatively little warfare (Anene 1967: 214ff; Green 1947: 91, 152, 177, 230–32). Conflict also took the nonviolent form of mutual insults in obscene and satirical songs (Nwoga 1971: 33–35, 40–42); and even warfare itself was conducted within limits, with weapons and actions increasing in seriousness in inverse proportion to the closeness of kinship ties. Women from mutually hostile village groups who had married into the same patrilineage could if necessary act as "protectors" for each other so that they could trade in "stranger" markets (Green 1947: 151). Women also protected themselves by carrying the stout sticks they used as pestles for pounding yams (the same ones carried in the Women's War). Even after European slave-trading led to an increase in danger from slave-hunters (as well as from head-hunters), Igbo women went by themselves to their farms and with other women to market, with their pestles as weapons for physical protection (Esike 1965: 13).

The Pax increased the safety of short- and especially of long-distance trading for Igbo women as for women in other parts of Africa. But the Pax also made it possible for European firms to dominate the market economy. Onwuteaka argues that one cause of the Women's War was Igbo women's resentment of the monopoly British firms had on buying, a monopoly that allowed them to fix prices and adopt methods of buying that increased their own profits at the women's expense (1965: 278). Women's petty trading grew to include European products, but for many women the accumulated surplus remained small, often providing only subsistence and a few years' school fees for some of their children—the preference for sending boys to school further disadvantaging the next generation of women (Mintz 1971: 251–68; Boserup 1970: 92–95). A few women have become "big traders," dealing in £1000 lots of European goods, but women traders remain for the most part close to subsistence level. Little is open to West African women in towns except trading, brewing, or prostitution, unless they are among the tiny number who have special vocational or professional training (for example, as dressmakers, nurses, or teachers) (Boserup 1970: 85–101, 106–38). The "modern" economic sector, like the "modern" political sector, is dominated by men, women's access being limited "by their low level of literacy and by the general tendency to give priority to men in employment recruitment to the modern sector" (Boserup 1970: 99).

Women outside urban areas—the great majority of women—find themselves feeding their children by farming with their traditional digging sticks while men are moving into cash-cropping (with tools and training from "agricultural development programs"), migrant wage-labor, and trading with Europeans (Boserup 1970: 53–61, 87–99; Mintz 1971: 248–51). Thus, as Mintz suggests, "while the economic growth advanced by Westernization has doubtless increased opportunities for (at least some) female traders, it may also and simultaneously limit the range of their activities, as economic changes outside the internal market system continue to multiply" (p. 265). To the extent that economic opportunities for Africans in the "modern" sector continue to grow, women will become relatively more dependent economically on men and will be unlikely to "catch up" for a very long time, even if we accept education as the key. The relative stagnation of African economic "growth," however, suggests that the traditional markets will not disappear or even noticeably shrink, but will continue to be needed by the large numbers of urban migrants living economically marginal lives. Women can thus continue to subsist by petty trading, though they cannot achieve real economic independence from men or gain access to the resources needed for equal participation in community life.

It seems reasonable to see the traditional Igbo division of labor in production as interwoven with the traditional Igbo dispersal of political authority into a dual or "dual-sex" system. It seems equally reasonable to see the disruptions of colonialism as producing a new, similarly interwoven economic-political pattern—but one with stronger male domination of the cash economy and of political life.

To see this relationship, however, is not to explain it. Even if the exclusion of women from the colonial Native Administration and from nationalist politics could be shown to derive from their exclusion from the "modern" economic sector, we would still need to ask why it was men who were offered agricultural training and new tools for cash-cropping, and who are hired in factories and shops in preference to women with the same education. And we would still need to ask why it was chiefly boys who were sent to school, and why their education differed from that provided for girls.

VICTORIANISM AND WOMEN'S INVISIBILITY

At least part of the answer must lie in the values of the colonialists, values that led the British to assume that girls and boys, women and men, should be treated and should behave as people supposedly did in "civilized" Victorian England. Strong male domination was imposed on Igbo society both indirectly, by new economic structures, and directly, by the recruitment of only men into the Native Administration. In addition, the new economic and political structures were supported by the inculcation of sexist ideology in the mission schools.

Not all capitalist, colonialist societies are equally sexist (or racist); but the Victorian society from which the conquerors of Igboland came was one in which the ideology that a woman's place is in the home had hardened into the most rigid form it has taken in recent Western history. Although attacked by feminists, that ideology remained dominant throughout the colonial period and is far from dead today. The ideal of Victorian womanhood—attainable, of course, only by the middle and upper classes, but widely believed in throughout society—was of a sensitive, morally superior being who was the hearthside guardian of Christian virtues and sentiments absent in the outside world. Her mind was not strong enough for the appropriately "masculine" subjects: science, business, and politics.[11] A woman who showed talent in these areas did not challenge any ideas about typical women: the exceptional woman simply had "the brain of a man," as Sir George Goldie said of Mary Kingsley (Gwynn 1932: 252).[12] A thorough investigation of the diaries, journals, reports, and letters of colonial officers and missionaries would be needed to prove that most of them held these Victorian values. But a preliminary reading of biographies, autobiographies, journals, and "reminiscences," plus the evidence of statements about Igbo women at the time of the Women's War, strongly suggests that the colonialists were deflected from any attempt to discover or protect Igbo women's political and economic roles by their assumption that politics and business were not proper, normal places for women.[13]

When Igbo women forced the colonial administrators to recognize their presence during the Women's War, their brief "visibility" was insufficient to shake these assumptions. Their behavior was simply seen as aberrant and inexplicable. When they returned to "normal," they were once again invisible. This inability to "see" what is before one's eyes is strikingly illustrated by an account of a visit by the High Commissioner, Sir Ralph Moor, to Aro Chukwu after the British had destroyed (temporarily) the powerful oracle there: "To Sir Ralph's astonishment, the women of Aro Chukwu solicited his permission to reestablish the Long Juju, which the women intended to control themselves" (Anene 1967: 234). Would Sir Ralph have been "astonished" if, for example, the older men had controlled the oracle before its destruction and the younger men had wanted to take it over?

The feminist movement in England during the colonial era did not succeed in making the absence of women from public life noted as a problem that required a remedy. The movement did not succeed in creating a "feminist" consciousness in any but a few "deviants," and such a consciousness is far from widespread today; for to have a "feminist" consciousness means that one notices the "invisibility" of women. One wonders where the women are—in life and in print. That we have not wondered is an indication of our own ideological bondage to a system of sex and class stratification. What we can see, if we look, is that Igbo men have come to dominate women economically and politically: individual women have become economic auxiliaries to their husbands, and women's groups have become political auxiliaries to nationalist parties. Wives supplement their husbands' incomes but remain economically dependent; women's "branches" have provided votes, money, and participants in street demonstrations for political parties but remain dependent on male leaders for policymaking. Market women's associations were a vital base of support for the early National Council for Nigeria and the Cameroons (NCNC), the party that eventually was to become dominant in Igbo regions (although it began as a truly national party). And though a few market-women leaders were ultimately rewarded for their loyalty to the NCNC by appointment to party or legislative positions, market women's associations never attained a share in policymaking that approached their contribution to NCNC electoral success (Bretton 1966: 61; MacIntosh 1966: 299, 304–9; Sklar 1963: 41–83, 251, 402). The NCNC at first had urged female suffrage throughout the country, an idea opposed by the Northern People's Congress (NPC), dominated by Moslem emirs. Soon, however, the male NCNC leadership gave up pushing for female suffrage in the north (where women have never yet voted) in order to make peace with the NPC and the British and thus insure for themselves a share of power in the postindependence government. During the period between independence in 1960 and the 1966 military coups that ended party rule, some progress was made in education for girls. By 1966, consequently, female literacy in the East was more than 50 percent in some urban areas and at least 15 percent overall—high for Africa, where the overall average is about 10 percent and the rural average may be as low as 2 percent (MacIntosh 1966: 17–37; *West African Pilot,* April 29, 1959; Pool 1972: 238; UNESCO 1968).

Exhortations to greater female participation in "modern life" appeared frequently in the newspapers owned by the NCNC leader, Nnamdi Azikiwe, and a leadership training course for women was begun in 1959 at the Man O' War Bay Training Centre, to be "run on exactly the same lines as the courses for men, with slight modifications," as the *Pilot* put it. The motto of the first class of 22 women was, "What the men can do, the women can" (Van Allen 1974b: 17–20). But there was more rhetoric than reality in these programs for female emancipation. During the period of party politics, no women were elected to regional or national legislatures; those few who were appointed gained favor by supporting "party first," not "women first." Perhaps none of this should be surprising, given the corruption that had come to dominate national party politics (MacIntosh 1966: 299, 612–14; Sklar 1963: 402; Van Allen 1974b: 19–22).

BIAFRA AND BEYOND

On January 15, 1966, a military coup ended the Igbos' relationship with the NCNC: all political parties, and therefore their women's branches, were outlawed. A year and a half later—after the massacres of more than 30,000 Easterners in the North, the flight of more than a million refugees back to the East, a countercoup, and the division of the Igbo-dominated Eastern Region into three states—Biafra declared herself an independent state. In January 1970 she surrendered; the remaining Igbo are now land-locked, oilless, and under military occupation by a Northern-dominated military government.[14] Igbo women demonstrated in the streets to protest the massacres, to urge secession, and, later, to protest Soviet

involvement in the war (Ojukwu 1969: 91, 143, 145–46, 245). During the war, the women's market network and other women's organizations maintained a distribution system for what food there was and provided channels for the passage of food and information to the army (Uzoma 1974: 8ff; Akpan 1971: 65–67, 89, 98–99, 128–30). Women joined local civilian-defense militia units and in May 1969 formed a "Women's Front" and called on the Biafran leadership to allow them to enlist in the infantry (Uzoma 1974: 5–8; Ojukwu 1969: 386).

During and after the war, local civilian government continued to exist more or less in the form that evolved under the "reformed" Native Administration. The decentralization produced by the war has by some reports strengthened these local councils, and the absence of many men has strengthened female participation (Peters 1971: 102–3; Adler 1969: 112; Uzoma 1974: 10–12). Thus, at tragic human cost, the war may have made possible a resurgence of female political activity. If this is so, women's participation again stems much more from Igbo tradition than from Western innovation.

It remains to be seen whether Igbo women, or any African women, can gain real political power without the creation of a "modern" version of the traditional "dual-sex" system (which is what Okonjo argues is needed) or without a drastic change in economic structures so that economic equality could support political equality for all women and men, just as economic stratification now supports male domination and female dependence. What seems clear from women's experiences—whether under capitalism, colonialism, or revolutionary socialism—is that formal political and economic equality are not enough. Unless the male members of a liberation movement, a ruling party, or a government themselves develop a feminist consciousness and a commitment to male-female equality, women will end up where they have always been: invisible, except when men, for their own purposes personal or political, look for female bodies.

NOTES

1. This paper is a revised version of papers presented at the 1971 African Studies Association meeting and at the 1974 UCLA African Studies Center Colloquium on "Women and Change in Africa: 1870–1970." I am grateful to Terrence O. Ranger, who organized the UCLA colloquium, and to the other participants (particularly Agnes Aidoo, Jim Brain, Cynthia Brantley, Temma Kaplan, and Margaret Strobel) for their encouragement, useful criticisms, and suggestions.

2. Today the Igbo, numbering about 8.7 million, live mainly in the East-Central State of Nigeria, with some half million in the neighboring Mid-Western State. The area in which they live corresponds approximately to Igboland at the time of the colonial conquest.

3. A number of Ibibio women from Calabar were also drawn into the rebellion, but the mass of the participants were Igbo.

4. Perham 1937: 202–12. Afigbo 1972 and Gailey 1970 give more detailed accounts of the Women's War than does Perham; all three, however, base their descriptions on the reports of the two Commissions of Enquiry, issued as Sessional Papers of the Nigerian Legislative Council (Nos. 12 and 28 of 1930), on the Minutes of Evidence issued with No. 28, and on intelligence reports made in the early 1930's by political officers. Afigbo, an Igbo scholar, provides the most extensive and authoritative account of the three, and he is particularly good on traditional Igbo society.

5. Similar tactics were also used against women for serious offenses (see Leith-Ross 1939: 97).

6. Though there is variation among the Igbo, the general patterns described here apply fairly well to the southern Igbo, those involved in the Women's War. The chief exceptions to the above description occur among the western and riverain Igbo, who have what Afigbo terms a "constitutional village monarchy" system, and among the Afikpo of the Cross River, who have a double-descent system and low female participation in economic and political life (P. Ottenberg 1959 and 1965). The former are more hierarchically organized than other Igbo but are not stratified by sex, having a women's hierarchy parallel to that of the men (Nzirimo 1972); the latter are strongly stratified by sex, with the senior men's age grade dominating community decision-making. Afikpo women's age grades are weak; there is no *mikiri* or, because of the double-descent system, *ogbo* (these terms are defined later in this paper ... Afikpo women have not traditionally been active in trade; and female status among the Afikpo is generally very low. Afikpo Igbo, unlike almost all other Igbo, have a men's secret society that has "keeping women in their place" as a major purpose (P. Ottenberg 1959 and 1965).

7. I rely here chiefly on Uchendu 1965 and personal conversations with an Igbo born in Umu-Domi village of Onicha clan, Afikpo division. Some of the ideas about leadership were suggested by Schaar 1970. His discussion of what "humanly meaningful authority" would look like is very suggestive for studies of leadership in "developing" societies.

8. A few older men criticized the women for "flinging sand at their chiefs," but Igbo men generally supported the women though they nonetheless considered it "their fight" against the British. It is also reported that both women and men shared the mistaken belief that the women would not be fired upon because they had observed certain rituals and were carrying the palm-wrapped sticks that invoked the power of the female ancestors. The men had no illusions of immunity for themselves, having vivid memories of the slaughter of Igbo men during the conquest (Perham 1937: 212ff; Anene 1967: 207–24; Esike 1965: 11; Meek 1957: x).

9. For the missionaries' views and purposes, see Ajayi 1965, Basden 1927, Bulifant 1950, Maxwell 1926, and Livingstone n.d.

10. It is an unfortunate accident that the Afikpo Igbo, with their strong sexual stratification, have been used as examples of "the Igbo" or of "the effect of colonialism on women" in widely read articles. Simon Ottenberg's "Ibo Receptivity to Change" is particularly misleading, since it is about "all" Igbo. There is one specific mention of women: "The social and economic independence of women is much greater in some areas than in others." True, but the social and economic independence of women is much greater in virtually *all* other Igbo groups than it is in Afikpo, where the Ottenbergs did fieldwork. There are said to be "a variety of judicial techniques" used, but all the examples given are of men's activities. There is a list of non-kinship organizations,

but no women's organizations are listed. Sanday's otherwise useful and thought-provoking article (1973) both takes the Afikpo as "the" Igbo and exaggerates the amount of change in female status that female trading brought about. Phoebe Ottenberg, Sanday's ultimate source on Afikpo women, described the change in female status as existing "chiefly on the domestic rather than the general level," with the "men's position of religious, moral, and legal authority . . . in no way threatened" (1959: 223). For examples of precolonial female trading in Igboland and elsewhere, see Little 1973 (particularly p. 46, n. 32); Uchendu 1965; Van Allen 1974b: 5–9; Dike 1956; and Jones 1963.

11. The fact that Englishwomen of the "lower classes" had to work in the fields, in the mills, in the mines, or on the street did not stop the colonialists from carrying their ideal to Africa, or from condemning urban prostitution there (just as they did at home) without acknowledging their contribution to its origin or continuation.

12. Mary Kingsley, along with other elite female "exceptions" who influenced African colonial policy (e.g., Flora Shaw Lugard and Margery Perham), held the same values that men did, at least in regard to women's roles. They did not expect ordinary women to have political power any more than men expected them to, and they showed no particular concern for African women.

13. For examples of this attitude among those who were not missionaries, see Anene 1967: 222–34; Crocker 1936; Meek 1957; Kingsley 1897; Perham 1960; and Wood 1960.

14. The attitude of the Northern emirs who now again dominate the Nigerian government is perhaps indicated by their order in June 1973 that single women get married or leave Northern Nigeria because Moslem religious authorities had decided that the North African drought was caused by prostitution and immorality. Landlords were ordered not to let rooms to single women, and many unmarried women were reported to have fled their home areas *(Agence France-Presse,* as reported in *The San Francisco Chronicle,* June 23, 1973). In late 1975 the military government appointed a 50-man body to draft a constitution for Nigeria's return to civilian rule. As of this writing women's protests have produced no changes in its membership.

REFERENCES

Adler, Renate. 1969. "Letter from Biafra," *The New Yorker,* Oct. 4.

Afigbo, A. E. 1972. *The Warrant Chiefs: Indirect Rule in South-Eastern Nigeria, 1891–1929.* London.

Ajayi, J. F. Ade. 1965. *Christian Missions in Nigeria, 1841–1891: The Making of a New Elite.* Evanston, Ill.

Akpan, Ntieyong U. 1971. *The Struggle for Secession, 1966–1970.* London.

Anene, J. C. 1967. *Southern Nigeria in Transition, 1885–1906.* New York.

Basden, G. T. 1927. *Edith Warner of the Niger.* London.

Boserup, Ester. 1970. *Woman's Role in Economic Development.* New York.

Bretton, Henry L. 1966. "Political Influence in Southern Nigeria," in Herbert J. Spiro, ed., *Africa: The Primacy of Politics.* New York.

Bulifant, Josephine C. 1950. *Forty Years in the African Bush.* Grand Rapids, Mich.

Crocker, W. R. 1936. *Nigeria: A Critique of British Colonial Administration.* London.

Dike, K. Onwuka. 1956. *Trade and Politics in the Niger Delta, 1830–1885.* London.

Esike, S. O. 1965. "The Aba Riots of 1929." *African Historian* (Ibadan), 1, no. 3.

Fallers, Lloyd Ashton. 1963. "Political Sociology and the Anthropological Study of African Politics," *Archives Européennes de Sociologie.*

Forde, Daryll, and G. I. Jones. 1950. *The Ibo- and Ibibio- Speaking Peoples of South-Eastern Nigeria.* London.

Gailey, Harry A. 1970. *The Road to Aba.* New York.

Green, M. M. 1947. *Igbo Village Affairs.* London.

Gwynn, Stephen. 1932. *The Life of Mary Kingsley.* London.

Harris, J. S. 1940. "The Position of Women in a Nigerian Society," *Transactions of the New York Academy of Sciences.* New York.

Jones, G. I. 1963. *The Trading States of the Oil Rivers.* London.

Kingsley, Mary H. 1897. *Travels in West Africa.* London.

Leith-Ross, Sylvia. 1939. *African Women: A Study of the Ibo of Nigeria.* London.

Little, Kenneth. 1973. *African Women in Towns.* London.

Livingstone, W. P. n.d. *Mary Slessor of Calabar.* New York.

MacIntosh, John P., ed. 1966. *Nigerian Government and Politics.* London.

Maxwell, J. Lowry. 1926. *Nigeria: The Land, the People and Christian Progress.* London.

Meek, C. K. 1957. *Law and Authority in a Nigerian Tribe.* London.

Mintz, Sidney W. 1971. "Men, Women, and Trade," *Comparative Studies in Society and History,* 13.

Nwoga, D. I. 1971. "The Concept and Practice of Satire among the Igbo," *Conch,* 3, no. 2.

Nzirimo, Ikenna. 1972. *Studies in Ibo Political Systems: Chieftaincy and Politics in Four Niger States.* Berkeley, Calif.

Ojukwu, C. Odumegwu. 1969. *Biafra.* New York.

Okonjo, Kamene, 1974. "Political Systems with Bisexual Functional Roles—The Case of Women's Participation in Politics in Nigeria." Paper presented at the Annual Meeting of the American Political Science Association, Chicago.

———. 1976. "The Dual-Sex Political System in Operation: Igbo Women and Community Politics in Midwestern Nigeria," In Nancy J. Hafkin, and Edna Bay, eds., *Women in Africa: Studies in Social and Economic Change.* Stanford.

Olisa, Michael S. O. 1971. "Political Culture and Political Stability in Traditional Igbo Society," *Conch, 3, no. 2.*

Onwuteaka, J. C. 1965. "The Aba Riot of 1929 and Its Relation to the System of 'Indirect Rule,'" *The Nigerian Journal of Economic and Social Studies,* November.

Ottenberg, Phoebe V. 1959. "The Changing Economic Position of Women Among the Afikpo Ibo," in W. R. Bascom and M. J. Herskovits, eds., *Continuity and Change in African Cultures.* Chicago.

———. 1965. "The Afikpo Ibo of Eastern Nigeria," in James L. Gibbs, Jr., ed., *Peoples of Africa.* New York.

Ottenberg, Simon. 1959. "Ibo Receptivity to Change," in W. R. Bascom and M. J. Herskovits, eds., *Continuity and Change in African Cultures.* Chicago.

Perham, Margery. 1937. *Native Administration in Nigeria.* London.

———. 1960. *Lugard: The Years of Authority, 1898–1945.* London.

Peters, Helen. 1971. "Reflections on the Preservation of Igbo Folk Literature," *Conch,* 3, no. 2.

Pool, Janet E. 1972. "A Cross-Comparative Study of Aspects of Conjugal Behavior Among Women of Three West African Countries," *Canadian Journal of African Studies,* 6, no. 2.

Sanday, Peggy R. 1973. "Toward a Theory of the Status of Women," *American Anthropologist, 75, no. 5.*

Schaar, John H. 1970. "Legitimacy in the Modern State," in Philip Green and Sanford Levinson, eds., *Power and Community.* New York.

Sklar, Richard. 1963. *Nigerian Political Parties.* Princeton, N.J.

Uchendu, Victor C. 1965. *The Igbo of Southeast Nigeria.* New York.

United Nations Economic and Social Council (UNESCO). 1968. "Problems of Plan Implementation: Development Planning and Economic Integration in Africa."

Uzoma, Chinwe. 1974. "The Role of Women in the Nigerian/Biafran Civil War as Seen Through My Experiences Then." Unpublished personal communication to Judith Van Allen.

Van Allen, Judith. 1972. "'Sitting on a Man': Colonialism and the Lost Political Institutions of Igbo Women," *Canadian Journal of African Studies,* 6, no. 2.

———. 1974a. "African Women—Modernizing into Dependence?" Paper presented at the conference on "Social and Political Change: The Role of Women," sponsored by the University of California, Santa Barbara, and the Center for the Study of Democratic Institutions.

———. 1974b. "From Aba to Biafra: Women's Associations and Political Power in Eastern Nigeria." Paper presented at the UCLA African Studies Center Colloquium on Women and Change in Africa, 1870–1970.

———. 1974c. *"Memsahib, Militante, Femme Libre: Political and Apolitical Styles of African Women,"* in Jane Jaquette, ed., *Women in Politics.* New York.

Wood, A. H. St. John. 1960. "Nigeria: Fifty Years of Political Development among the Ibos," in Raymond Apthorpe, ed., *From Tribal Rule to Modern Government.* Lusaka, Northern Rhodesia.

The Impact of Development on Women: The Interplay of Material Conditions and Gender Ideology

Victoria S. Lockwood

During the colonial era, European nations expanded their cultural, economic, and political hegemony over much of the non-western world (see Wolf 1982). To gain access to the material wealth of their colonies, the Europeans established conditions under which native populations had little choice but to produce crops or other commodities for markets, or to work for wages on European plantations or in mines. As these processes escalated and other western interventions intensified, capitalist relations of production began to subsume indigenous economies in most parts of the world.

Since that time, capitalism has proven a versatile, dynamic, and ever-expanding political economic system. Today, even the most remote and isolated village has been touched and transformed by it. The general terms often applied to that transformation—"development" and "modernization"—describe not only the processes of market integration (and shifts to capitalist production relations), but also the dynamic restructuring of social institutions, social relations, and world view that accompanies it.

Although there is great diversity in how this structural and ideological transformation has taken place around the world, research focused on gender issues in development has identified several important themes. First, men and women rarely participate in development the same way; in other words, they do not have access to the same kinds of development-generated opportunities and choices. Second, men and women

Original material prepared for this text.

rarely share equally in the various "costs" and "benefits" of development. Indeed, a growing number of studies suggest that women's social, economic, and political position relative to that of men actually deteriorates with capitalist development, or that, at best, its effects on women are highly mixed (Boserup 1970; Etienne and Leacock 1980; Nash 1977; Fernandez-Kelly 1981; Charleton 1984; Bossen 1975, 1984; Caulfield 1981; Afonja 1981).

At the same time, a number of cases in which women's position and status have improved show that there are important exceptions to this general trend. In other words, it is clear that, "The changes brought about by colonialism, or, later, capitalist productive relations, are not *automatically* detrimental to women" (Rapp 1979: 505, cited in Di Leonardo 1991: 15; my emphasis). Thus, "... we must be wary of simplistically portraying men as the winners and women as the losers" (Moore 1988: 79). As the rapidly growing body of literature on women and development points out, the situation is much more complex than that.

The highly variable impact of development on non-western women raises a number of important questions. How, specifically, does development (capitalist integration) differentially affect men and women, and why does women's position frequently deteriorate? And, in those cases where women's position has improved, is it possible to identify particular material/structural or ideological factors that have contributed in the development process to maintaining women's position or to promoting gender equity?

My goal in this article is twofold: first, to discuss these questions in the context of recent research; and second, to present a comparative case study of two rapidly modernizing, neighboring Tahitian islands[1] that sheds light on these issues.

VARIABILITY IN DEVELOPMENT'S IMPACT ON WOMEN

Most scholars agree that it is difficult to generalize about the impact of development on non-western women. As Moore (1988: 74) notes, "Women are not a homogeneous category, and the circumstances and conditions of their lives in the varying regions of the world are very different." Nevertheless, it is possible to identify the factors that play a major role in shaping how women in any particular society are affected by integration into capitalist markets and production systems. These factors interact in highly complex ways to shape the choices and options—the "opportunity structures"—open to women.

But first, in order to understand how men and women—even husbands and wives in the same family—can differentially experience development, it is important to remember that families are internally stratified units and that family members do not necessarily share the same priorities or goals (see Wilk 1989). Gender and age differences structure patterns of unequal access to authority, decision-making prerogatives, and control over family activities and resources. Those that do have access— most often senior males or male heads of households—may be in a favored position to participate in new and prestigious economic activities (e.g., commercial agriculture). In contrast, other family members, such as wives, may find that "modernization" simply means working longer hours at devalued household tasks that bring in little or no money, and having less say over the affairs of their families.

Forms of Capitalist Integration

One of the key factors affecting women's position is the *manner* in which different communities participate in capitalist markets and are integrated into global capitalism (see Mukhopadhyay and Higgins 1988). In rural areas, previously subsistence-based families may begin producing cash crops for local or export markets, become involved in other kinds of commodity production (i.e., crafts), or seek jobs in nearby towns. If jobs are available, families may abandon agriculture wholly or in part. As they become more dependent on money and imported foods and the cost of living increases, some rural villagers leave the countryside, migrating to nearby cities in search of wage work. Sometimes the search for work ultimately takes rural migrants to foreign industrialized nations where they are absorbed into the low-skilled, low-paid urban work force.

Each of these forms of capitalist integration has different implications for men and women depending on how the sexual division of labor is renegotiated to reflect new economic conditions; that renegotiation will be shaped by ideological notions of the types of work "appropriate" for men and women. Cash-crop agriculture may be defined as the domain of men, while women continue to produce food crops. Women may specialize in the production and sale of crafts if craft production was a female activity before market integration. If men migrate to find wage jobs, women may be left at home to feed and support families. If families migrate, men may find work in the city, but women who cannot find jobs may resort to street peddling or other marginal activities in the urban informal sector.

Degree of Structural Transformation

The *degree* to which a particular society has been incorporated into capitalist relations of production also plays a role in shaping how women are affected by development. Some communities have resisted or avoided full incorporation and maintained pre-capitalist institutions and values (see, for example, Rodman 1993; Petersen 1993); this is true in many rural "peasant" communities in the Third World where families produce for markets or hold wage jobs, yet simultaneously maintain kin-based relations of production and property ownership. In other communities, pre-capitalist institutions have largely been replaced by capitalist relations of production; this is true in areas of the most extensive commercial and missionary intervention.

These structural changes include shifts from kin- or family-based systems of property ownership to individual ownership. Land and labor become commodified and production becomes oriented to market sales and making money; wealth accumulation becomes a major goal. Those who are able to accumulate capital become an elite who are in a position to concentrate control over land and the other means of production. These processes result in the formation of class structures and the promotion of individualistic, competitive, and profit-oriented value systems characteristic of capitalist societies.

The impact of development on women will, in part, be shaped by how far this structural transformation has advanced. If, for example, increasing pressure on land has caused a system of land tenure to shift from matriclan ownership to individual ownership, women may find that they have lost control over land while men who participate in cash-cropping or other market-oriented activities are increasingly gaining individual control. On the other hand, where communities have resisted this shift to individual ownership, women may find that their property rights have not diminished.

Existing Systems of Gender, Family, and Social Relations

Another critical factor shaping the impact of development on women is the local system of gender and family relations, including patterns of gender stratification and ideology. There is great diversity in these systems around the world ranging from the relatively egalitarian, horticultural societies of island New Guinea (Lepowsky 1993), to the highly gender stratified and segregated Islamic societies of the Middle East (see Abu-Lughod 1986). Variability in gender structures is accompanied by fundamental differences in how different societies conceive of femaleness and maleness, and in what they perceive to be the basic mental and physical capabilities of men and women. Gender ideology, as well as family and kinship structures, will play a major role in determining the kinds of behaviors and socioeconomic roles that are considered appropriate (and consistent with family responsibilities) for women.

THE WESTERN GENDER BIAS IN DEVELOPMENT

Appreciating the complexity of forces that shape the options open to men and women as their communities develop explains little, however, about the frequently negative impact of development on women. If development were in fact a gender-neutral phenomenon, one would expect that the *relative* social, economic, and political position of men and women would remain the same—both men's and women's situations would either improve or deteriorate in more or less the same ways. But this rarely happens. Numerous studies now point to several important processes of gender discrimination embedded in western-style, capitalist development, processes that have contributed to women's deteriorating position in many developing regions. In some cases, development has introduced forms of gender bias that did not previously exist in non-western communities; in others, introduced gender biases have intensified existing gender asymmetries.

Women and "Modernization"

Prior to the 1970s and the surge of scholarly interest in women's issues, it was widely (and ethnocentrically) assumed that modernization ("westernization") promoted more egalitarian gender relations, and greater rights and freedoms for women. In an influential article, Laurel Bossen (1975) noted, "The Western industrialized nations [were] thought to be closest to an ideal of modern egalitarian treatment for women ... Hence modern changes that [brought] societies closer to the Western pattern and standard [were] presented as advantageous to women" (1975: 587). Evidence of women's increasing equality included legal freedoms; the right to vote, run for office, and own property; as well as greater participation in the wage labor force. The latter was thought to promote female economic independence from "traditional family structures." In contrast, women in rural developing areas were thought to be "servile, dependent, and decidedly inferior to ... men" (1975: 587).

Bossen effectively argues that neither the egalitarian view of western gender relations nor the servile, inferior view of Third World women reflects reality. Although western women may possess certain legal rights, they do not enjoy full equality with men, nor are they as socially valued or esteemed as men. At the same time, research in less technologically sophisticated, non-western cultures has shown that, in some cases, women may be highly valued and possess many of the same socioeconomic and political prerogatives as men (see Lepowsky 1993 on the Vanatinai of New Guinea; Geertz 1961 on the Javanese; Kluckhohn and Leighton 1946 on the Navajo; and Etienne and Leacock 1980). Thus, as Bossen (1975: 589) notes "... it does not follow that the greater wealth and superior technology controlled by modern societies corresponds to greater equality among its members, female or otherwise."

"Modernized Patriarchy"

The gender biases that characterize western capitalist societies—and which were more severe in the Victorian era—were first introduced in many non-western regions during the colonial era. They have continued to reappear, however, as one "subtext" of many western-designed or oriented development programs.

One of these gender biases is a structural feature of western, capitalist relations of production in which the formal economic ("productive") and domestic/reproductive spheres are artificially distinguished, and the latter is devalued. In capitalist societies, "The concept of labor [is] reserved for activity that produces surplus value" (i.e., cash-earning activities) (Mies 1982a: 2; see also Sacks 1974). Thus, "work" becomes commodity or cash-crop production, or wage employment, activities that were typically dominated by men after their introduction; men, then, become associated with a formal, "productive" sphere that is often physically (spatially) separated from the activities of the household/domestic sphere.

Many of the typical activities of women—giving birth to and caring for children, maintaining the household and its affairs, production for family use/consumption—are not defined as "productive" in capitalist systems because they generate nothing of monetary value, and thus women do not "work." Thus much of the work that women do perform in the domestic domain becomes "invisible." An important example of this is that agricultural development efforts in Africa and elsewhere have frequently focused on men, even though "invisible" women farmers actually produce 50 percent of the world's food for direct consumption (Escobar 1995: 172–173).

Capitalist enterprises benefit from the structural separation of the productive and domestic domains because, since women do no work, they do not have to be compensated for their labor; they also benefit in that women (and sometimes children) serve as a relatively inexpensive, available, and easily dismissed pool of labor. If the demand for labor increases in the capitalist system or families cannot support themselves on one income, women may move into wage labor, but they are typically paid less than men. The rationale of capitalist employers is that women are "temporary" (and less skilled) workers who really belong at home with the children.

This capitalist economic rationale for the devaluation and domestication of women was reinforced during the colonial era (and since) by patriarchal, Victorian-era notions of appropriate male/female activities and relations, and by notions of female inferiority (physically and intellectually). In the Society Islands, for example, English missionaries believed that cultivation (previously practiced by both Tahitian men and women) was "unsuitable to [the female] sex" and that pre-contact women's other economic activities were "derogatory to the female and inimical to an improvement in morals"; they decided that "men should dig, plant, and prepare the food, and the women make cloth, bonnets, and attend to the householdwork" (Ellis 1981, III: 392–393, cited in Thomas 1987). Being relegated to making bonnets at home was quite a step down, particularly for high-ranking Tahitian women, who had figured prominently in the affairs and sociopolitical machinations of their chiefdoms—and sometimes even led warriors into battle—before the arrival of the Europeans (Oliver 1974; Lockwood 1988).

The model of Christian family life advanced by missionaries and colonial officials provided a supporting ideological framework for the structural separation of the male-dominated productive domain and the devalued, female domestic domain. The Bible describes the moral and correct family as consisting of a male head of family who is father and provider, and a female wife and mother who is his helpmate and subordinate. Women's financial dependence on the male "breadwinner" is a cornerstone of their secondary status.

Western gender biases not only domesticated non-western women, they frequently also introduced a "value structure that defines women's primary task in society as biological and social reproduction"; when this occurs in conjunction with a system—capitalism—that "allocates higher rewards to production roles in the public domain ... men [achieve] an edge over women" (Afonja 1986: 134). That edge frequently supported patriarchal gender and family systems.

Relegation to a devalued, "nonproductive" domestic sphere was frequently accompanied in many cases by women's loss of control over productive resources and property; these

were vested in the male "breadwinner" and head of the family. And that loss of control had a critical, negative impact on women's social position, authority, and status. In capitalist systems, control over the means of production (resources, capital, technology) is the material basis of differential authority and power; this is true not only in the community at large, but also in the internally stratified family. Following Schlegel (1977), "power" can be defined as the ability to control one's own and others' persons and activities, as well as the ability to make the decisions and shape the affairs/policies of the family or social group. Where women do not participate in productive activities or control resources or income, they are not only financially dependent on men, they are also relatively powerless and politically subordinate to men (see Freidl 1975, 1991).

By introducing structures and ideologies that privilege men and "domesticate" women, western-style development has frequently limited the options available to women and contributed to a decline in their status in the family and community.[2] In these cases, development becomes more than simply a means for promoting market integration or raising the standard of living, it becomes a vehicle for institutionalizing "modernized" patriarchy (Escobar 1995: 177).

Contemporary Negative Trends for Women

Several of the major trends in Third World development today reflect these gender biases. In rural areas, the devaluation and domestication of women has contributed to the *feminization of subsistence agriculture.* When new cash crops and technologies were introduced (during the colonial era and more recently), it was typically assumed that men were the farmers, and new opportunities, credits, and modern technology were made available to them. In many areas of Africa and Latin America where women had in fact been the major farmers, women were pushed into subsistence cultivation for family consumption. Defined as part of the "domestic" domain, subsistence production became both deval-ued and "invisible." As women assumed "the burden for providing for 'family' consump-tion" ... they were "often prevented from engaging in cash-crop production themselves, and the frequent bias of government schemes and incentives in favour of male farmers (and the cash crops they produce) lead to further discrimination and disadvantage for women" (Moore 1988: 75). The cost to women of the feminization of subsistence agriculture was often exacerbated by changes in land tenure and other systems of property rights that effectively negated women's rights and insti-tutionalized systems of individual (often male) ownership and inheritance.

Women are frequently pushed into subsis-tence production not only by male domina-tion of cash-crop production (and of resources and technology), but also by male domination of most wage jobs and by male out-migration. In rural areas, where jobs are available on plantations or on commercial farms, women are typically hired as lowly-paid domestics, while men have access to the high-er-paying and more prestigious jobs. When men migrate from rural areas to towns in search of wage work, rural women are fre-quently left at home with the double burden of caring for the house and children, and ful-filling familial subsistence needs.

Not only does subsistence production become devalued and invisible in the domes-tic domain, but women's other productive—and even cash-earning—activities frequently do as well. In many developing regions, women have found ways to earn small amounts of cash income by producing mar-ketable crafts or other commodities (i.e., pre-pared foods) in their homes ("cottage industries").

In the Yucatan, for example, Mayan women weave hammocks (Littlefield 1978), and in India women make lace (Mies 1982b). But these women's situation is much like that of other poor, female commodity producers who work out of their homes. They are dependent on outside suppliers who bring them the raw materials for their craft, and

they are exploited by commercial middlemen and exporters who pay them little yet reap large profits for themselves. Because women have few income-earning options outside the domestic domain and are largely bound to this domain by gender and family structures, they are unable to alter the conditions of that exploitation. Because this work is frequently defined as "domestic activity women do in their spare time," instead of as productive labor (Moore 1988: 84 citing Mies 1982b), these contributions to family livelihood are devalued and become invisible.

It is important to note that in both the cases where rural women seek wage jobs or produce commodities at home, the prevailing perception that women are domestics who make no productive contributions to the fam-ily has little to do with reality. Indeed, the entire artificial conceptualization of a female "domestic" domain in opposition to a formal, male "productive" domain is largely a myth in most developing regions (see Lamphere in this volume). Nevertheless, the "myth" remains strong and western gender ideology supports it. The dual beneficiaries are men, whose dominant position as "provider" and head of the family remains intact and unthreatened, and capitalist enterprises, which hire female "domestics" cheaply.

Another major trend in Third World devel-opment has been the *feminization of the indus-trial labor force*. It has been estimated that 80 percent of the workers in world market facto-ries (typically owned by western multination-al corporations) are young women (13–25 years old) (Moore 1988: 100; see also Nash and Fernandez-Kelly 1983). Young women are hired because of their "... apparently innate capacities for the work—'nimble fin-gers'—their docility, their disinclination to unionize, and the fact that women are cheap because, while men need an income to sup-port a family, women do not" (Moore 1988: 101). Women are also paid less (as noted above), and hired at the lowest levels (skilled and management positions go to men), because they are seen as temporary workers. It appears that wage earning and financial contributions to families frequently do enhance young women's personal autonomy (see Ong 1987; Kung 1994). But often there are also significant social costs, and rarely does women's position improve in the male-dominated family.

These cases suggest that even though women's income earning is a *potential* material foundation for enhanced authority and status in the household, that potential may not be realized. Young female Taiwanese factory workers, for example, turn over their wages to their fathers, the heads of patriarchal Chinese families (Kung 1994). And in other cases, women's income may be so meager (due to low wages) or devalued that it is seen only as a "domestic supplement." Thus gender ideologies and family structures may redefine or "mystify" women's actual productive and income contributions—effecitvely negating them.

MAINTAINING WOMEN'S POSITION: THE INTERPLAY OF MATERIAL CONDITIONS AND GENDER IDEOLOGY

The relatively smaller number of cases in which women's position has not deteriorated illustrates how key material factors, supported by prevailing gender ideology and family systems, have worked to enhance women's autonomy, authority, and power in the family and community. In rural Java, for example, shifts to an export agricultural economy during the Dutch colonial period (and since) were not associated with major changes in the sexual division of labor, or in women's relatively high status and economic independence (Stoler 1977). Both men and women played important roles in labor-intensive, wet rice cultivation, and women were also significantly involved in trading activities. Through agricultural wage labor and trading, women became significant income earners in the household: "... women clearly control family finances and dominate the decision-making process" in the domestic domain, but Stoler

notes that the domestic and public domains actually merge and overlap (1977: 85). In poorer households, women's income gives them both independence and authority in the family; in wealthier households, women's earnings could become the "material basis for social power" (84); where they are able to buy land or expand lucrative trading operations, women achieved both economic and political power.

Similarly, women in male-dominated Yoruba society (Nigeria) have achieved economic independence by participating in commercial enterprises and trade, and by owning houses (Barnes 1990). In this society where marriages are brittle and women do not inherit property from husbands, owning a house is an important form of social security for women. Income from commercial enterprises is used to purchase a house; the house then generates capital from rents. By owning the house, Yoruba women achieve the status of senior authority figure in the household. This is possible because even though Yoruba gender and family structures strongly favor men, women and men "are [seen as] equally capable of performing society's valued and essential tasks" (Barnes 1990: 255). Thus, when a woman owns a house, she is able to undermine the conditions that promote her structural subordination and achieve some social power. Female "home owners" also achieve political clout in their urban neighborhoods and sometimes become community leaders.

All the cases that have been cited in which development-related socioeconomic change did not promote women's increasing subordination have two significant characteristics in common. First, women were able to exert control over strategic productive resources (usually through ownership), and/or they were able to earn *and* control cash income (capital). And second, prevailing gender ideologies *supported* (did not redefine or negate) female participation in production and income earning, as well as female control over the products of their labor, including income. Whether women's productive efforts take place in the "formal" public domain or in the domestic domain (or in that large amorphous area where the two domains are actually one in many cases), they are socially defined as "producers," and they *control* key resources and income.

The cases of rural Tahitian women on the islands of Tubuai and Rurutu (Austral Islands, French Polynesia) show how different forms of market integration may have strikingly different consequences for women (even in the same society). They also show how women's control of resources and income plays a critical role in shaping their differential authority, decision making, and "power" in the household and community.

DIFFERENT OUTCOMES FOR WOMEN ON NEIGHBORING TAHITIAN ISLANDS

Rurutu and Tubuai are neighboring islands in rural French Polynesia. They are culturally similar, sharing the relatively homogeneous, Neo-Tahitian sociocultural patterns that coalesced in the region following centuries of French colonial and Christian missionary intervention. They have also both experienced the intense French government efforts to "modernize" and develop its overseas Pacific territory over the last three decades. In addition, the islands are similar in their geographic and population sizes (about 2,000 people; 300 households).

The push for regional development began in the early 1960s. In the rural outer islands, development programs were aimed at modernizing agriculture by transforming Tahitian taro farmers and fishermen into export producers for the rapidly growing Papeete market. Various heavily subsidized projects were implemented on different islands; they included copra and coffee production, European vegetable cultivation, and other kinds of commodity production (e.g., crafts).

Rural modernization also included the building of schools and clinics, rural electrification and telephone services (late 1980s), and integration of rural populations into the

French family welfare and legal systems. Each rural island was designated a "municipality" and provided with a budget to employ a significant number of islanders on the government payroll (as road or maintenance workers, clerks, teachers, or secretaries). In the absence of commercial and tourist development on these remote islands, there are few other kinds of jobs. Today, about 45 percent of all families on Rurutu and Tubuai include an employed member, usually the male household head; about 25 percent of all jobs are held by women. Despite income earning from jobs or commodity production, most families continue to rely on agriculture/fishing to fulfill their subsistence needs.

Through their various cash-earning activities, as well as government social programs, many rural Tahitian families have achieved relatively high incomes and a level of material affluence unknown in many parts of the "developing" world (see discussion later in this chapter). At the same time, however, the cost of living in this import-dependent society is extremely high, and consumption standards are constantly rising. Consequently, and despite their high incomes, cash is ever-scarce and highly coveted. Most families today pursue any and all economic activities possible to generate cash income.

Pre-Modernization Gender Relations and Stratification

Before the introduction of development programs in the 1960s, rural families on both Tubuai and Rurutu mainly cultivated gardens (taro and other root crops, coconuts, bananas) and fished to fulfill subsistence needs. Small amounts of cash were earned through copra production or vanilla cultivation, or from sporadic sales of manioc starch, fresh foods, or pandanus craft items to passing schooners. Land was owned jointly by cognatic groups of kin; both men and women inherited rights in the land owned by their parents and grandparents.

Patterns of Tahitian domestic organization and gender relations reflected French colonial and Christian missionary efforts to transform

Tahitians in their own images. As noted earlier, missionaries specifically sought to bring Tahitian society more into line with Victorian-era mores and practices (Thomas 1987). In accord with those patterns, as well as with Christian precepts, men were defined as the "breadwinners," "providers," and heads of their families. Men performed most agricultural labor and fished. Women's appropriate (and moral) domain was the household, where they spent their time caring for children, doing the housework, and weaving pandanus mats (and making bonnets) (Ellis 1981, III: 392–393, cited in Thomas 1987). Islanders today sometimes describe women's domain as "interior" (household) and men's domain as "exterior," the fields and ocean.

Men dominated cash-earning opportunities where they were available. Men processed copra and planted vanilla gardens, and controlled the cash earnings (see Lockwood 1988; Oliver 1981). Although women's efforts were concentrated in the household itself, they also worked in their husbands' gardens, fished from the reef, and performed many other kinds of "productive" labor. Nevertheless, a general pattern of male authority and preeminence (and female subordination) in the household was promoted by Christian teachings and the Bible, and by male control of increasingly coveted cash income. Although wives were usually in charge of daily expenditures for food and other necessities, husbands dispersed these monies to their wives as they saw fit.

Despite these structural changes, Tahitians somehow failed to become indoctrinated in Victorian-era attitudes about women's relative inferiority. Although Tahitians were (and are) devout believers in the familial/domestic prescriptions of the Bible, their own understandings of the nature of men and women differed substantially from those of the French and the missionaries. Most importantly, they did not have a belief in individuals' superiority or inferiority based on gender criteria.[3] This was reflected in a psychological study of Tahitian men and women conducted in the early 1960s (Levy 1973). Levy (1973:

236) concluded that in the Tahitian world view, women and men are seen to be much alike in their capabilities and talents, and to have no major personality, behavioral, or intellectual differences. He note that Tahitians acknowledged that men's and women's *lives* were different—because of women's role in reproduction and because they perform different tasks—but that's all.

Indeed, one of the major themes of Tahitian gender ideology is male/female interdependence, and not hierarchy (superiority/inferiority) as in many western societies. Thus, although Tahitian women were economically and politically subordinate in the post-contact, male-dominated household, they were not (and are not today), treated as inferiors. In contemporary communities, women receive a great deal of respect and admiration from both men and other women for their roles as managers of the family and domestic domain, and for their devoted care of their children (see Langevin 1990). Despite their "domesticity," they are outspoken at community meetings and exhibit little deference to men.

Rural Development: Differing Paths for Tubuai and Rurutu

The economic profiles of Tubuai and Rurutu began to diverge in the early 1960s when government development planners charted different courses for each island. Tubuai was chosen as a major target for agricultural development, specifically European green vegetable and potato cultivation. It also became the administrative center for the five Austral Islands, and the site for the one high school in the group. A small airstrip was built to facilitate transport and contact with Tahiti.

Today, Tubuai Islanders are heavily involved in commercial agriculture, as well as other kinds of commodity production and export; these activities are largely the domain of men, although women are needed to perform substantial amounts of secondary labor in agricultural fields. Tubuai is today the regional potato producer, exporting over 1,200 tons (metric) to Papeete each year; it also exports about 550 tons of vegetables annually. The commodification of land and labor, shifts to individual land ownership (from the previous kin-based system), and the spread of new ethics of wealth accumulation and consumerism are increasingly observable. Of all of the Austral Islands, Tubuai is the most developed and affluent; in 1994, average familial income was about $2,000/month (Lockwood 1993). It is also the most westernized as measured in the number of islanders who have attended the French-staffed high school and who aspire to a western material lifestyle.

In the mid-1980s and despite the fact that they were not "farmers," Tubuai women began to sign up with the Agricultural Service in large numbers to plant potatoes. Women's access to land was assured by their own familial lands, and they also had access to the same financial subsidies and credits as male farmers. By the early 1990s, 43 percent of all potato farmers were women (Lockwood 1993).

Tubuai women had always earned small amounts of money from selling crafts or a few vegetables to other families, and a few held jobs as teachers, secretaries, or maintenance workers. But, for most women, potato cultivation was the first opportunity to earn significant amounts of income of their own; most women—who typically cultivate on a smaller scale than men—earn between $1,000 and $1,500 during the three-month potato season. Because Tahitians believe that income earned by an individual belongs to that individual, wives are able to make their own independent decisions about how their money will be expended. Indeed, many female potato farmers explain that they decided to plant potatoes to have their own money to do as they like; women's money is, however, almost always used to buy food, clothes, and other items for their families.

Thus by the early 1990s, Tubuai women were adopting new "modern" socioeconomic roles and breaking down barriers in the traditional sexual division of labor that defined women as "domestics." They had also achieved a level of financial autonomy.

The Island of Rurutu

The island of Rurutu's development trajectory has been significantly different. Because of its rugged interior terrain, agricultural development projects were not promoted, although in recent years limited efforts have been made to expand the potato project and green vegetable cultivation there. (In 1990, islanders exported about 35 tons of onions and 60 tons of taro, tarua, and bananas.) A small airstrip was built on the island, and government services and jobs were created much as on Tubuai.

Most families on Rurutu earn money from the craft production of their female members and craft items are Rurutu's major export. Crafts include pandanus mats, satchels, and hats, Tahitian quilts (*tifaifai*), and shell and flower necklaces—items once made exclusively for household use. Rurutu women produce crafts as part of their domestic work in their own households, or while participating in a *pupu,* a cooperative work group of ten to twenty women who usually belong to the same church. Their reputation for fine craft production extends throughout the territory.

Rurutu women have organized cooperatives to help sell their crafts, and these are supported and subsidized by various government programs. (Craft cooperatives are present on most outer islands, but they are most highly developed on Rurutu.) Women are active agents in making arrangements to sell their items in Papeete though relatives, or if necessary, through a retailer at the central urban market. The minimal use of non-kin middlemen means that female producers retain almost all of the market price of their products. In the early 1990s, Rurutu's annual craft exports were valued at about $400,000 (one-third the value of Tubuai's potato crop).

How Rurutu women came to specialize in craft production to an extent that far exceeds that of other rural islands, however, is not clear (and informants could not explain it). As noted earlier, most rural

Tahitian women weave mats and make quilts for household use. This specialization probably began to emerge in the pre-development decades; at that time, the populations of neighboring islands earned small amounts of cash selling copra, coffee, or manioc starch. Rurutu families had little of these items to sell; they could, however, sell mats and hats to the local Chinese family-owned general stores for export to Papeete. Thus, in the absence of other significant options, it is likely that women launched themselves into commercial craft production and in so doing, they became central agents in the generation of their families' incomes.

Although Rurutu is integrated into regional markets through craft and other kinds of small-scale production, it is today less "westernized" than Tubuai. As commercial agriculture is little developed, the traditional, family-based system of land ownership is not threatened by the kinds of changes taking place on Tubuai. Ethics of familial sharing and participation in cooperative work groups (*pupus*) are widespread on Rurutu, but have generally disappeared on Tubuai. Because families do not participate in potentially lucrative vegetable exports, most make significantly less money than Tubuai families (the average monthly income is $1,500). Consequently, there is less western-style consumerism. And because until recently, Rurutu children were required to board at the Tubuai high school in order to attend it, fewer Rurutu Islanders have received as many years of formal French education as Tubuai Islanders.

And clearly, on Rurutu, there has been little change in the traditional division of labor. The division between the female's "interior" world and the male's "exterior" world is strictly maintained. Interestingly, it is women who chastise other women who violate these "proper" roles by "doing men's work" in the gardens; women are highly protective of their domain. Compare to more "modern" Tubuai women, then, Rurutu women appear to be both "traditional" and domestic.

THE GENDER CONSEQUENCES OF DIFFERENT DEVELOPMENT PATHS[4]

Although Rurutu women may not be doing anything "new," they have achieved an important role in income generation (and control) that is unparalleled on the more modernized Tubuai. Careful examination of household budgets and income on both islands revealed that women on Rurutu are indeed significant "providers." On Rurutu, women bring in more than 50 percent of all income in almost half of all families (45.5 percent). In other words, it is almost equally likely in Rurutu families that the wife/mother is the breadwinner as it is that the husband/father is the breadwinner. On Tubuai, women are the breadwinners in only 26 percent of all families.[5]

And in this society where women *retain control* of the income they generate, Rurutu women are given credit for their productivity. This was summed up by one Rurutu man who said that women today differed from those of his grandmother's generation because they helped to "provide" for the family (the male role). I had not heard Tubuai women described this way, although they are certainly involved in many productive activities. It became clear that a general ethic of women as "providers" existed on Rurutu that was not articulated on Tubuai.

Rurutu women's status as "providers" was reflected in a subtle shift away from the typical pattern of husbands as heads of families to "joint husband/wife" family heads. In 49 percent of all Rurutu families the husband was declared head of the family, while in 41 percent, husbands and wives were joint household heads. In comparison, Tubuai had a much higher proportion of male household heads (68 percent) and husbands and wives were "joint" heads in only 25 percent of all families.[6] Rurutu women also played a greater role than Tubuai women in decision making about household budgets and expenditures.[7]

There were also significant differences between the two islands in how women and men were perceived and valued. Informants were asked to compare men and women in terms of various characteristics including intelligence, who worked harder, and several other personality traits. They were also asked who was "superior": men, women, or both (equal). Tubuai and Rurutu islanders generally agreed on most of the characteristics of men and women, with the exception of intelligence and superiority. On Rurutu, the majority of informants (58 percent) thought that women were more intelligent, while on Tubuai, the majority (64 percent) thought that men and women were equally intelligent.[8] (Only 29 percent of Tubuai Islanders thought that women were more intelligent.) And, on both Rurutu and Tubuai, the majority thought that men and women were "equal" (56 percent and 82 percent respectively); but on Rurutu, 23 percent of all informants thought that women were superior, whereas this was true of only 2 percent of all Tubuai informants. (It is also interesting to note that no one thought men worked hardest; both sets of islanders thought either women worked hardest, or that men and women worked equally hard.)

The higher valuation of Rurutu women can also be seen in women's greater political participation on the island. In 1994, three women served on the 16-member, island municipal council; one woman had been elected as a district mayor (the island has three districts). On Tubuai, islanders could remember no woman ever serving on the municipal council, and no woman has ever been elected mayor or district mayor.

There was also a tendency for both male and female Rurutu Islanders to extol the virtues of women to a greater extent than on Tubuai, although women were clearly held in high regard on both islands. When asked to compare the thoughts and mentality of men and women, Rurutu informants (male and female) described women as more expressive and outgoing (men were reserved), as better organizers, and generally as "seeing farther" than men. Women were described as more active in church and community groups than

men, and they tended to take on the organizational roles in those activities. Both men and women described men's thoughts as centered on their taro gardens and fishing; once these tasks were successfully accomplished, men relaxed or got together with other men to drink; they were described as having "few concerns" other than farming and fishing. Women, however, were described as constantly thinking about how to make ends meet, how to generate the money that was needed for a household purchase, or how to organize the next church event. They "saw further" in that they were constantly contemplating the future needs of their families.

It should be noted that although Rurutu women's economic roles and income generation have promoted greater gender equity in familial authority and decision making and in community leadership than on Tubuai, they are not associated with other differences in family organization, fertility, or gender-based land-use patterns. On both islands, most families are nuclear in structure (about two-thirds of all families), have an average household size of five to six people, and produce approximately five children. Between 20 and 30 percent of all families reside on and cultivate the wife's land (most familial); the rest utilize the husband's land.

CONCLUSION

As the discussion has shown, many of the western gender biases described above were introduced into Tahitian society, promoting the structural domestication of women, including their economic dependence on male "providers" and heads of families. But at the ideological level, Tahitians never accepted notions of male superiority and female inferiority, continuing to see men and women in a largely egalitarian, interdependent way that afforded mutual respect for both. Consequently, and despite other kinds of changes in their society, women never lost their rights to own and control land and other resources, they were never divested of the right to control the income they earned, and they were given credit for the productive contributions they made regardless of their "domesticity."

On Rurutu, development introduced conditions under which women would oftentimes become the breadwinners in their families. That critical role has been translated into enhanced authority and decision-making prerogatives for women, and a higher social valuation. In contrast, although Tubuai women are economically active and "development-oriented," their financial contributions to the household remain minimal compared to those of men (in most cases). Thus, in the "quest for money," Tubuai women are not seen as "provisioners"; they also remain financially dependent on husbands in the majority of cases. Consequently, men are still defined as the heads of households in most families. And although women's social esteem and status is generally high on Tubuai, it is not as high as on Rurutu.

The cases of Tubuai and Rurutu highlight the interplay of both material conditions and gender ideology in shaping how capitalist development affects women. They suggest that a gender ideology that "empowers" women (i.e., Tahitian women's generally high status) is *not* sufficient—in and of itself—to ensure that women will not be subordinate to, and dependent on, men in developing regions of the world. The Rurutu data reinforce the conclusion drawn from other cases where women's position has not deteriorated: Women's control of strategic material resources and capital—the material basis of "power" in all capitalist systems—is a *necessary* condition for achieving a position of relative authority and power in both the household and community. It is important to note, however, that the extent to which women are able to control resources and capital will in part be determined by prevailing gender ideologies and family structures. Thus one can conclude that where women in developing regions are able to produce a strong material base, and where gender ideology empowers them to control it for their own ends, they will be in a position to achieve greater gender equity with men.

NOTES

1. In 1994–1995, a comparative study of the differential impact of capitalist development on women was undertaken on the neighboring Tahitian islands of Tubuai, Rurutu, and Raivavae. Two other anthropologists, Jeanette Dickerson-Putman and Anna Laura Jones, contributed to the project. The study was funded by a gratefully acknowledged grant from the National Science Foundation (SBR-9311414).

2. Women's relative lack of opportunity compared to men can also be seen in their strikingly lower rates of literacy and educational attainment (particularly in Latin America, the Middle East, and Africa) (see Moore 1988), as well as in higher rates of female morbidity and mortality (Charleton 1984).

3. Pre-contact Tahitians (both male and female) were ranked relative to one another in terms of the amount of *mana*, or supernatural power, they possessed (see Oliver 1974). *Mana*, and thus social rank, was determined by birth and genealogical distance from high-ranking chiefs; males and females were ranked in this highly stratified society by these criteria and not by gender. High-ranking women clearly dominated lower-ranking men.

4. In this comparative study, 164 Tubuai households and 181 Rurutu households were included (approximately 55–60 percent of all island households). These households were chosen to be representative of the populations at large in terms of two criteria: 1) major household economic activity/socioeconomic status (income), and 2) stage in the developmental cycle of the family (young, middle, elderly families). Informants included male and female household heads, as well as couples.

5. Tubuai households (N = 139): In 103 (74 percent) women earn less than half of all income; in 36 (26 percent) women earn more than half of all income. Rurutu households (N = 134): In 73 (54.5 percent) women earn less than half of all income; in 61 (45.5 percent) women earn more than half of all income. This is a statistically significant difference: Chi-square = 11.47; $p < .00071$; df = 1. (Families of single male or female heads were not included.)

6. For Tubuai (N = 134 households), husbands were declared head of the family in 91 households (68 percent), husbands and wives were joint heads in 34 households (25 percent), and wives were declared the head in 9 households (7 percent). For Rurutu (134 households), husbands were declared head in 66 households (49 percent), husbands and wives were joint heads in 55 households (41 percent), and wives were declared the head in 13 households (10 percent). The difference between the two islands is statistically significant (Chi-square = 9.66; p < .0079; df = 2). (Households of single household heads were not included in the analysis.)

7. Although on both islands the predominant pattern is for either wives, or husbands and wives together, to oversee day-to-day household expenditures, this is more often true on Rurutu (82 percent of all families) than on Tubuai (74 percent). Similarly, wives contribute to decision-making about large consumer purchases in 87 percent of all Rurutu families, but in 75 percent of Tubuai families.

8. Tubuai informants (N = 58): Most intelligent—women (17 or 29 percent; men (4 or 2 percent), both (37 or 64 percent). Rurutu informants (N = 33): Most intelligent—women (19 or 58 percent), men (2 or 6 percent), both (12 or 36 percent). The difference between the two islands is statistically significant (Chi-square = 7.20, p < .0272; df = 2).

REFERENCES

Abu-Lughod, Lila. 1986. *Veiled Sentiments: Honor and Poetry in a Bedouin Society.* Berkeley: University of California Press.

Afonja, Simi. 1986. "Changing Modes of Production and the Sexual Division of Labor Among the Yoruba." In E. Leacock and H. Safa (eds). *Women's Work: Development and the Division of Labor by Gender.* S. Hadley: Bergin & Garvey.

Barnes, Sandra. 1990. "Women, Property and Power." In P. Sanday and R. Goodenough (eds.). *Beyond the Second Sex,* pp. 253–280. Philadelphia: University of Pennsylvania Press.

Boserup, Ester. 1970. *Women's Role in Economic Development.* London: George Allen and Unwin.

Bossen, Laurel. 1975. "Women in Modernizing Societies." *American Ethnologist* 2 (4): 587–601.

———. 1984. *The Redivision of Labor: Women and Economic Choice in Four Guatemalan Communities.* Albany: State University of New York Press.

Caulfield, Mina. 1981. "Equality, Sex, and the Mode of Production." In G. Berreman (ed.). *Social Inequality: Comparative and Developmental Approaches,* pp. 201–219. New York: Academic Press.

Charleton, Sue Ellen. 1984. *Women in Third World Development.* Boulder: Westview.

Di Leonardo, Michaela, ed. 1991. *Gender at the Crossroads of Knowledge: Feminist Anthropology in the Postmodern Era.* Berkeley: University of California Press.

Escobar, Arturo. 1995. *Encountering Development: The Making and Unmaking of the Third World.* Princeton, NJ: Princeton University Press.

Etienne, M. and E. Leacock, eds. 1980. *Women and Colonization: Anthropological Perspectives.* Cambridge: J.F. Bergin.

Fernandez-Kelly, Maria P. 1981. "The Sexual Division of Labor, Development, and Women's Status." *Current Anthropology* 22 (4): 414–419.

Friedl, Ernestine. 1975. *Women and Men: An Anthropologist's View.* Prospect Heights, IL: Waveland Press.

———. 1991. "Society and Sex Roles." In E. Angeloni (ed.). *Annual Editions, Anthropology 91/92,* pp. 112–116. Guilford, CT: Dushkin Publishing.

Geertz, Hildred. 1961. *The Javanese Family.* New York: Free Press.

Kluckhohn, C. and D. Leighton. 1946. *The Navaho.* Cambridge, MA: Harvard University Press.

Kung, Lydia. 1994. *Factory Women in Taiwan.* New York: Columbia University Press.

Langevin, Christine. 1990. *Tahitiennes de la Tradition a l'Integration Culturelle.* Paris: Editions L'Harmattan.

Lepowsky, Maria. 1993. *Fruit of the Motherland: Gender in an Egalitarian Society.* New York: Columbia University Press.

Levy, Robert. 1973. *Tahitians: Mind and Experience in the Society Islands.* Chicago: University of Chicago Press.

Littlefield, Alice. 1978. "Exploitation and the Expansion of Capitalism: The Case of the Hammock Industry of Yucatan." *American Ethnologist* 5 (3): 495–508.

Lockwood, Victoria. 1988. "Capitalist Development and the Socioeconomic Position of Tahitian Peasant Women." *Journal of Anthropological Research* 44 (3): 263–285.

————. 1989. "Tubuai Women Potato Planters and the Political Economy of Intra-Household Gender Relations." In R. Wilk (ed.). *The Household Economy: Reconsidering the Domestic Mode of Production,* pp. 197–220. Boulder, CO: Westview.

————. 1993. *Tahitian Transformation: Gender and Capitalist Development in a Rural Society.* Boulder, CO: Lynne Rienner.

Mies, Maria. 1982a. "The Dynamics of the Sexual Division of Labor and the Integration of Rural Women into the World Market." In L. Beneria (ed.). *Women and Development: The Sexual Division of Labor in Rural Societies,* pp. 1–28. New York: Praeger.

————. 1982b. *The Lace Makers of Narsapur.* London: Zed Press.

Moore, Henrietta. 1988. *Feminism and Anthropology.* Minneapolis: University of Minneapolis Press.

Mukhopadhyay, C. and P. Higgins. 1988. "Anthropological Studies of Womens' Status Revisited: 1977–1987." *Annual Review of Anthropology* 17: 461–495.

Nash, June. 1977. "Women and Development: Dependency and Exploitation." *Development and Change* 8: 161–182.

Nash, June and Maria Fernandez-Kelly, eds. 1983. *Women and Men and the International Division of Labor.* Albany: State University of New York Press.

Oliver, Douglas. 1974. *Ancient Tahitian Society.* (3 vols.) Honolulu: University of Hawaii Press.

————. 1981. *Two Tahitian Villages: A Study in Comparison.* Honolulu: The Institute for Polynesian Studies.

Ong, Aihwa. 1987. *Spirits of Resistance and Capitalist Discipline: Factory Women in Malaysia.* Albany: State University of New York Press.

Petersen, Glenn. 1993. "Some Pohnpei Strategies for Economic Survival." In *Contemporary Pacific Societies: Studies in Development and Change,* V. Lockwood, et al., eds., pp. 185–196. Englewood Cliffs, N.J.: Prentice-Hall.

Rapp, Rayna. 1979. "Anthropology: Review Essay." *Signs* 4 (3): 497–513.

Rodman, Margaret. 1993. "Keeping Options Open: Copra and Fish in Rurual Vanuatu." In *Contemporary Pacific Societies: Studies in Development and Change,* V. Lockwood, et al., eds., pp. 171–184. Englewood Cliffs, N.J.: Prentice-Hall.

Sacks, Karen. 1974. "Engels Revisited: Women, the Organization of Production and Private Property." In *Woman, Culture and Society,* M. Rosaldo and L. Lamphere, eds., pp. 207–222. Stanford: Stanford University Press.

Schlegel, Alice. 1977. *Sexual Stratification: A Cross-Cultural View.* New York: Columbia University Press.

Stoler, Ann. 1977. "Class Structure and Female Autonomy in Rural Java." *Signs* 3: 74–89.

Strathern, Marilyn. 1984. "Domesticity and the Denigration of Women." In O'Brien, D. and S. Tiffany (eds.). *Rethinking Women's Roles: Perspectives from the Pacific.* Berkeley: University of California Press.

Thomas, Nicholas. 1987. "Complementarity and History: Misrecognizing Gender in the Pacific." *Ocenia* 57 (4): 261–270.

Wilk, Richard, ed. 1989. *The Household Economy: Reconsidering the Domestic Mode of Production.* Boulder: Westview Press.

Wolf, Eric. 1982. *Europe and the People Without History.* Berkeley: University of California Press.

Doing Their Homework: The Dilemma of Planning Women's Garden Programs in Bangladesh

Margot Wilson-Moore

Recently a number of development agencies in Bangladesh (for example, CARE, CIDA, Helen Keller International, the Mennonite Central Committee, Save the Children, UNICEF, USAID) have planned and implemented independent projects or program components directed specifically toward homestead gardening as an alternative to field crop production. For the growing cadre of marginal and landless farmers with little or no cultivable land outside of the household, homestead gardening constitutes a subsistence strategy with considerable potential for improving family nutrition and cash generation.

Traditionally a complement to field crop production, homestead gardens provide a much-needed supply of nutritious, interesting, and vitamin-rich foods for home consumption. In addition, the sale of homestead garden produce makes substantial amounts of cash available for rural farm families. The discussion that follows considers homestead gardening within the broad context of international development in Bangladesh and more particularly in relation to the burgeoning literature on the role of women in development. This discussion focuses specifically on homestead gardening as a viable development strategy for rural women.

International development aid constitutes a major influence for change today. In Bangladesh millions of foreign aid dollars comprise a large proportion of the national budget. Since 1974 to 1975, Bangladesh has received not less than $700 million from the

United States each year in international aid, and these donations represent two-to three-and-one-half times the total revenue budget generated in-country. However, the results in terms of quantifiable improvements are relatively few, and despite these substantial foreign aid contributions Bangladesh continues to demonstrate a negative balance of payments (greater than $5 million in 1984 to 1985) and a negative balance of trade ($135 million US in 1984 to 1985).

Environmental stress, population pressure, illiteracy, and historical explanations such as exploitation and isolation have been espoused as general causes for the persistent poverty in Bangladesh. Similarly, behavioral causes, such as a closely structured hierarchy and system of patronage, rugged individualism, and failure of Bangladeshis to "trust" one another and work cooperatively, have been offered as causes of the destitution and privation that characterize daily life in Bangladesh (Maloney 1986).

Whatever the causes, pervasive poverty and widespread destitution are commonplace, and in terms of standard "development" criteria, such as per capita income, literacy rate, mortality and fertility rates, economic diversification, and physical and social infrastructure, Bangladesh can only be termed a development failure. Historically, vast transfers of resources out of the area have significantly depleted the resource base while more recent problems of overpopulation, land fragmentation, and environmental disasters have drawn the attention of the international aid community.

Women's issues have received considerable attention from the international donor

Original material prepared for this text.

544

community in recent years, but to understand the "state of the art" of women and development research[1] in Bangladesh, it is necessary to trace its roots in broader issues of development theory and feminism. Early development theory tended to overlook the special needs of women, anticipating perhaps a "trickle-down" of benefits from men toward whom most programs are directed. Feminist critiques of development theory revolve primarily around this issue—the failure of development theory to address the problems of women directly. Women are either categorized with men or ignored altogether. Women are routinely subsumed within the rubric of more general development processes that are expected to address the issues of both men and women.

A variety of critiques of development theory exist (for an in-depth discussion see Jaquette 1982; Barnes-McConnell and Lodwick 1983; Wilson-Moore 1990), and the ongoing dialogue among these critiques has generated a vast and critical literature addressing the issue of women and development in the Third World. The feminist critique of development theory is firmly grounded in feminist thought, and the theoretical perspectives that have emerged in feminist development theory clearly reflect theoretical underpinnings in feminist theory. Feminist theoretical models predict relationships between various spheres of women's lives[2] and generate research questions and information useful, indeed imperative, for appropriate development planning for women.

Too often, however, women and development researchers fail to incorporate feminist theory into their research designs or neglect to articulate the underlying feminist assumptions that influence their work. Theorizing is, in large part, left to feminist academicians who usually rely on ethnographic (rather than development) literature for constructing and testing their models. As a result feminist theory, women, and development research have progressed, in recent years, along separate and divergent paths. Despite the actuating influence of feminist theory on

women and development research and their common concerns with the situation of women, discourse between these two bodies of literature is remarkably scant.

Women and development research tends to be of a highly practical nature, concentrating on the immediate and pragmatic problems faced by women in developing nations. Resources and institutional support are then directed toward these identified needs. A women's component may be incorporated into existing development programs, or alternatively projects may be designed specifically and solely for women. Often, however, development programs do not meet the needs of the women for whom they are designed. Many focus on "individual solutions," such as education to improve women's opportunities for urban wage employment, increase their access to innovative technology, or improve their subsistence production skills. Too often the systemic constraints on Third World people in general and on women in particular, such as high rates of unemployment and lack of child-care facilities, are overlooked.

The role of women in socioeconomic development has been the subject of much interest in Bangladesh (cf. Hossain, Sharif, and Huq 1977; Islam 1986) and has focused the attention of the aid community on those development issues particular to women, especially those at the lowest economic levels who are often the poorest of the poor. Khan et al. (1981) have shown that in 1981 326 government and nongovernment programs for women were registered with the Ministry of Women's Affairs. The majority provide training in knitting, sewing, embroidery, handicrafts, and garment-making. Unfortunately, however, although directed toward poor and destitute women, the income-generating potential of these skills is minimal (Khan et al. 1981:24) and the emphasis on low payment and domestic-like work only serves to perpetuate women's subordinate status and economic circumstance.

In 1986 Schaffer found that the focus of more than 100 development projects directed specifically toward women had expanded to include self-help and income generation, family planning and health, education and literacy, agriculture development projects, rural employment and industry, and female leadership training. The majority of these projects focus on integrating women into existing programs, although a few "women only" projects exist. Most donor agencies philosophically support development activities for women (Schaffer 1986:4); however, a number of cultural attitudes toward women constrain them. The view of women's work as minimal and unimportant is compounded by the women's own perception of their work as noneconomic and therefore without value.

Beyond this, religious proscriptions that predicate family honor on women's virtue and legislate women's appropriate place as inside the household necessitate development on an outreach basis (providing inputs and training to women in their own homes), while effectively preventing agencies from recruiting female staff to provide that outreach service.

Initially, little specific information was available about women in Bangladesh, and the resulting imperative for more and better data regarding women's roles, statuses, and activities generated a predominantly descriptive focus in the early research. This is especially true in the rural areas where early village studies (cf. Raper 1970; Zaidi 1970) provided only brief references to women's activities. Other village studies followed (cf. Arens and Van Beurden 1980; BRAC 1983; Chowdhury 1978; Hartmann and Boyce 1983; Mukherjee 1971), but still little direct reference was made to women.

More recently a number of authors have commented on the "invisibility" of women's economic contribution in Bangladesh (cf. Chen 1986; Huq 1979; Islam 1986; Smock 1977; Wallace et al. 1987). Women's labor routinely includes postharvest processing of field crops, such as rice, jute, mustard seed, lentils, and millet; care of animals; homestead gardening; and minor household maintenance, to name only a few. Because the labor of rural women takes place primarily inside

the household, it often goes unnoticed. Nevertheless, their economic contribution is substantial (Chen 1986; Wallace et al. 1987). The importance of these kinds of studies is in shifting the focus away from the view of women as dependent and helpless. Instead, they are recognized as actors, engaged in economic pursuits in both rural and urban areas. As such they cease to be "welfare cases" and become instead an appropriate target for "mainstream" development processes.

In addition to their traditional domestic roles increasing numbers of women from landless and marginal families are being forced by economic circumstance to leave their homes to seek wage labor. At the same time technology, especially mechanized rice processing, is displacing rural women from their traditional roles in postharvest processing of field crops (Begum 1989). Cooperative programs are encouraging and supporting female entrepreneurs, but the success of these schemes often accrues from their constituting an extension of existing female roles that do not "encroach upon the traditional domain of men ... [and are] not conceived as a threat to men's interests" (Begum 1989: 527).

Homestead gardening as a development strategy for women fits easily within these dictates because it neither encroaches on nor threatens men's traditional subsistence activities. Homestead gardening is an integral part of women's work in Bangladesh (cf. Chen 1983; Hannan 1986; Hassan 1978; Huq 1979; Hussain and Banu 1986; Scott and Carr 1985) and provides an opportunity for women to make sizable contributions to the rural farm family in terms of nutritious food for consumption as well as income generated from the sale of excess produce.

Homestead gardening is *not* the exclusive purview of women, although much of the research to date suggests that it is (Chen 1986; Huq 1979). This misconception is likely a result of research bias toward women. In Bangladesh women's issues have become a primary concern of development planners, and as a result women's roles are often considered without reference to other members of the community and to men in particular. The result is a misrepresentation of women as the principle, even exclusive, actors in certain sectors of the subsistence economy; in this case as the cultivators of homestead gardens. By contrast data from my own research (Wilson-Moore 1989, 1990) show that both men and women are involved in vegetable cultivation, although some clear differences exist between what men and women do in the garden.

Men and women grow different crop varieties at different times of the year—men in winter, women in summer. The fact that the crops grown by women tend to be more indigenous in nature and those cultivated by men more likely to be imported varieties may be an artifact of men's more active participation in the public sphere. Because men are active in the marketplace, they may simply be exposed to new varieties of vegetables most often and are therefore more predisposed to experimentation. In a similar vein it may be argued that women are in some sense a reservoir of traditional information and cultivation patterns, reflective of a time before imported varieties and development inputs were available.

A clear distinction also exists between male and female patterns of vegetable cultivation in which men's patterns are reminiscent of field crop production patterns characterized by monocropping and the rows and beds of European gardens. Women's gardens, by contrast, have a jumbled appearance and may represent the indigenous patterns commonly in practice prior to outside influence (for a discussion of cross-cultural gardening traditions see Brownrigg 1985).

Women's gardens are found inside or immediately adjacent to the household. Requirements for housing, cooking, stabling of animals, and postharvest processing and storage of field crops necessitate that individual plants or small clusters of plants be scattered throughout the homestead, dotted around the central courtyard and household structures. Small plots may be located around

the periphery of larger homesteads, usually immediately outside of the circle of infacing buildings.

Gourds are encouraged to grow over trellises, along the walls, and across the roofs of buildings. Other climbing plants may be trained to grow up the trunks of nearby trees. Shade-loving plants are grown under the cover of fruit and fuelwood trees, and those more tolerant of direct sun are planted in the clear places.

Plant species are highly diverse. Because there are no beds or rows, tall and medium height trees, smaller bushy shrubs, upright plants, creepers, and root crops form the horizontal layers characteristic of this type of garden. Weeding is infrequent, and it is often difficult to differentiate the homestead garden from the surrounding undergrowth. In fact an untrained observer might not recognize this type of homestead garden at all.

Husbands often fail to recognize the gardening efforts of their wives, even when the proof was crawling across the roofs and walls of the homestead and into the cooking pot at meal times. That men fail to acknowledge women's productive labor in gardens may lie partially in more general societal attitudes toward women as producers (they are not seen as such) but also in the scattered appearance of their homestead gardens, which prevents their immediate recognition by uninterested, or uninitiated, observers, be they husband, anthropologist, or development worker.

Women cultivate vegetable varieties that spring up readily, can be produced from seed preserved from the previous year, and are well-adapted to the seasonal vagaries of the climate, flourishing inside and around the homestead with a minimum of care or input. Women often stagger the planting times so that everything does not mature at once. In fact related women in separate households may coordinate their planting times, as well as the varieties planted, to maximize their production through sharing.

Vegetable gardens cultivated by women tend to have a high diversity of plant species but a small number of plants of any particular type. Accordingly, the quantities are smaller yet more varied, and they are intended for family consumption. High diversity and low volume production is the predominant characteristic of women's gardening patterns in Bangladesh and throughout Asia, a strategy well-suited to fulfilling family consumption needs.

It is no coincidence that the vegetables grown most commonly in homestead gardens are the ones villagers prefer to eat. These vegetables can be eaten on a daily basis without becoming unappetizing. Alternatively the diversity of vegetables produced in the homestead garden also helps to offset the boredom of eating the same food every day. In fact villagers prefer to have a variety of foods, even if that means eating something that they dislike from time to time.

In this way the garden acts as a living larder, providing fresh produce on a daily basis. As individual plants become ripe the women harvest them and prepare them for consumption. If more vegetables become ripe than can be consumed within the household at one time, they may be given away, traded with neighbors, or sent to the market for sale.

Homestead gardening as a development strategy for women is predicated on a view of women's production as valuable and essential to the nutritional and economic welfare of the rural farm family. Furthermore, the minimal overlap between men's and women's gardening patterns ensures that as a development strategy homestead gardening also does not compete with men's traditional activities in field crop cultivation or vegetable production. Thus, homestead gardening conforms to two primary stipulations (Begum 1989; Schaffer 1986) for success and would seem an ideal development strategy for women.

Unfortunately, these stipulations do not necessarily guarantee a positive result, and outcomes of garden programming may prove surprising if the planners have not "done their homework" prior to implementation. In this regard Brownrigg has (1985) emphasized the necessity of in-depth locally based research and observes that when such

research is omitted or conducted in a cursory manner programs often fail to meet the needs of the target population. Barnett (1953) has argued that acceptance of innovation is based on the ability of recipient populations to analyze new ideas and technologies and to identify some similarity with existing culture traits. Accordingly, the more identifiable an innovation is, the more easily it can be matched with a trait already existing in the cultural lexicon, and the more readily it will be adopted.

Social science, and anthropology in particular, has much to contribute. Participant observation is a field methodology well-suited to producing detailed information about existing indigenous practices; information often not available through any other means; and information appropriate, perhaps imperative, for planners who wish to build on and enhance those existing practices. By focusing on extant patterns planners can effectively determine which goals are attainable and which populations are most appropriately targeted.

In the context of Bangladesh, for example, homestead garden programs intended to improve family nutrition and increase consumption of vitamin-rich vegetables are most appropriately directed toward women because their production is intended, in the first instance, for home consumption. If, on the other hand, program goals include increasing family income through sale of garden produce, men may constitute a more appropriate target group because their vegetable production is traditionally intended for the market. Finally, a program goal of increased access to cash for women requires careful consideration because women's limited access to the market and ramifications of cash generation on family nutrition are two important, potentially negative, dimensions of income-generating schemes for women.

Women routinely remain secluded within the household in Bangladesh. As a result, marketing of women's garden produce constitutes something of a dilemma. Produce must be transported and sold by a male family member or neighbor. Women are able to retain control over the cash generated in this way by providing a shopping list (for household essentials such as oil or kerosene) when they turn over the produce for sale. Accordingly, the money is recycled back into the family budget on a daily basis and does not accumulate. It fails to be assigned a "value" by men or women and as a result goes unrecognized. That this particular economic contribution fails to affect women's status in any appreciable way has been discussed elsewhere (Wilson-Moore 1989).

Beyond the lack of recognition that greets women's economic enterprise in the garden, Boserup (1970) has shown that when women's economic activities become profitable (especially in terms of cash generation), men tend to take them over (see also Chaney and Schmink 1976). Male takeovers of the income-generating component of women's homestead gardening and the displacement of women from their traditional roles in vegetable production necessitates only a small shift in production activities. However, the ramifications in terms of family nutritional well-being may be far-reaching. Rural farm families depend on women's homestead production for a ready supply of varied and vitamin-rich vegetable foods, a complement nutritionally and aesthetically to the masebhate (rice and fish) mainstays of the Bangladeshi diet.

Redirecting women's vegetable production toward the market would necessitate a change in production technique, disrupting the traditional patterns of women's homestead garden production and interfering with that ready supply of vegetable foods. The traditional pattern that produces small quantities of diverse vegetable foods intended for consumption within the homestead would have to be replaced by high-output, low-diversity cropping. Furthermore, there is little evidence to suggest that rural families would use the cash earned in this way to "buy back" or replace vegetable foods in the diet. Rather, high-status processed foods such as tea, white sugar, white flour, and bread are more apt to make an appearance when cash becomes available for their purchase.

Maintaining a balance between growing vegetable crops in large volume for sale and in sufficient variety for home consumption represents a problem in terms of the space and time constraints of homestead production. However, the existing, complementary yet rarely overlapping patterns of men's and women's traditional vegetable production seems well-suited to the respective cash generation and consumption needs of the family. Accordingly, planners concerned with pervasive poverty and widespread nutritional deficiency diseases in Bangladesh may wish to consider the benefits of developing each of these gardening strategies as they mutually, yet independently, support the rural farm family.

NOTES

1. Throughout this paper the terminology women and development has been used as a generic term for women's development in an effort to avoid more specific references such as women in development (WID) or development for women. These advocate, in the first case, the incorporation of a women's component into existing programs and, in the second, separate programming by women for women (see Jaquette 1982; Barnes-McConnell and Lockwick 1983; Wilson-Moore 1990 for a more comprehensive discussion of these terms).

2. For example, see Boserup (1970), Friedl (1975), and Sanday (1973, 1974) for models that predicate women's status on women's participation in the work force and their economic contribution to the family.

REFERENCES

Arens, Jenneke and Jos Van Beurden. 1980. *Jhagrapur: Poor Peasants and Women in a Village in Bangladesh*. Calcutta: Orient Longman.

Barnes-McConnell, Pat and Dora G. Lodwick. 1983. *Working with International Development Projects: A Guide for Women–in–Development*. East Lansing: Michigan State University, Office of Women in International Development.

Barnett, Homer. 1953. *Innovation: The Basis of Culture Change*. New York: McGraw-Hill.

Begum, Kohinoor. 1989. "Participation of Rural Women in Income-Earning Activities: A Case

Study of a Bangladesh Village," *Women's Studies International Forum* 12(5):519–528.

Boserup, Ester. 1970. *Women's Role in Economic Development.* New York: St. Martin's Press.

BRAC (Bangladesh Rural Advancement Committee). 1983. *Who Gets What and Why: Resource Allocation in a Bangladesh Village.* Dhaka: BRAC Publication.

Brownrigg, Leslie. 1985. *Home Gardening in International Development: What the Literature Shows.* Washington, DC: League for International Food Education.

Chaney, Elsa and Marianne Schmink. 1976. "Women and Modernization: Access to Tools." In June Nash and Helen Safa (eds.). *Sex and Class in Latin America.* New York: Praeger.

Chen, Martha Alter. 1986. *A Quiet Revolution: Women in Transition in Rural Bangladesh.* Cambridge: Schenkman Publishing.

Chowdhury, Anwarullah. 1978. *A Bangladesh Village: A Study of Social Stratification.* Dhaka: Centre for Social Studies.

Friedl, Ernestine. 1975. *Women and Men: An Anthropologist's View.* New York: Holt, Rinehart and Winston.

Hannan, Ferdouse H. 1986. *Past, Present and Future Activities of Women's Desk.* Comilla: Bangladesh Academy for Rural Development.

Hartmann, Betsy and James K. Boyce. 1983. *A Quiet Violence: Views from a Bangladesh Village.* London: Oxford University Press.

Hassan, Nazmul. 1978. *Spare Time of Rural Women: A Case Study.* Dhaka: University of Dacca, Institute of Nutrition and Food Science.

Hossain, Monowar, Raihan Sharif, and Jahanara Huq (eds.). 1977. *Role of Women in Socio-Economic Development in Bangladesh.* Dhaka: ABCO Press.

Huq, Jahanara. 1979. "Economic Activities of Women in Bangladesh: The Rural Situation." In Women for Women (eds.). *The Situation of Women in Bangladesh,* pp. 139–182. Dhaka: BRAC Printers.

Hussain, S. and S. Banu. 1986. *BARD Experiences in Organization of Women in their Involvement in Agricultural Related Activities.* Comilla: Bangladesh Academy for Rural Development.

Islam, Shamima. 1986. "Work of Rural Women in Bangladesh: An Overview of Research." Paper presented at workshop on women in agriculture. Comilla: Bangladesh Academy for Rural Development.

Jaquette, Jane S. 1982. "Women and Modernization Theory: A Decade of Feminist Criticism," *World Politics* 34(2):267–284.

Khan, Salma, Jowshan Rahman, Shamima Islam, and Meherunnessa Islam. 1981. *Inventory for Women's Organizations in Bangladesh.* Dhaka: UNICEF.

Maloney, Clarence. 1986. *Behavior and Poverty in Bangladesh.* Dhaka: University Press Limited.

Mukherjee, Ramkrishna. 1971. *Six Villages of Bengal.* Bambay: Popular Prakashan.

Raper, Arthur. 1970. *Rural Development in Action: The Comprehensive Experiment at Comilla, East Pakistan.* Ithaca: Cornell University Press.

Sanday, Peggy. 1973. "Toward a Theory of the Status of Women," *American Anthropologist* 75(5): 1682–1700.

———. 1974. "Female Status in the Public Domain." In Michelle Z. Rosaldo and Louise Lamphere (eds.). *Woman, Culture, and Society,* pp. 189–206. Stanford, CA: Stanford University Press.

Sattar, Ellen. 1979. "Demographic Features of Bangladesh with Reference to Women and Children." In Women for Women (eds.), *The Situation of Women in Bangladesh,* pp. 1–22. Dhaka: BRAC Printers.

Schaffer, Teresita C. 1986. *Survey of Development Project and Activities for Women in Bangladesh.* Dhaka: Provatee Printers.

Scott, Gloria L. and Marilyn Carr. 1985. *The Impact of Technology Choice on Rural Women in Bangladesh: Problems and Opportunities.* Washington, DC: World Bank Working Paper No. 731.

Smock, Audrey Chapman. 1977. "Bangladesh: A Struggle with Tradition and Poverty." In Janet Z. Giele and Audrey C. Smock (eds.). *Women: Roles and Status in Eight Countries,* pp. 83–126. New York: John Wiley and Sons.

Wallace, Ben J., Rosie M. Ahsan, Shahnazz H. Hussain, and Ekramul Ahsan. 1987. *The Invisible Resource: Women and Work in Rural Bangladesh.* Boulder: Westview Press.

Wilson-Moore, Margot. 1989. "Women's Work in Homestead Gardens: Subsistence, Patriarchy, and Status in Northwest Bangladesh," *Urban Anthropology* 18(203):281–297.

———. 1990. "Subsistence, Patriarchy, and Status: Women's Work in Homestead Gardens in Northwest Bangladesh." Ph.D. dissertation, Southern Methodist University, Dallas, Texas.

Zaidi, S. M. Hafeez. 1970. *The Village Culture in Transition: A Study of East Pakistan Rural Society.* Honolulu: East-West Press.

Factory as Home and Family: Female Workers in the Moroccan Garment Industry

M. Laetitia Cairoli

My factory is better . . . because every girl in it is like a daughter of the owner.

Thus, one Fez clothing factory worker explained why she had remained at her job for four years, despite the notoriously low pay and constant overtime demanded there. In the past two decades the Moroccan garment industry has developed into one of the country's most significant export trades and Moroccan females have become the labor power for clothing manufacture. Although their role in the garment factories is widely regarded as exploitative and demeaning, the workers themselves continue to use the idiom of family to describe their relationships to factory owners, administrators, supervisors, and their fellow workers. In the course of a year of ethnographic research in the city of Fez, I began an exploration of how garment factory workers make sense of their labor on the shop floor.

Inside one Fez garment factory, where I worked during a three-month period, I observed workers as they sought to impose their own assumptions and values upon the factory system and thereby render their labor meaningful. Nearly all of Morocco's garment factory workers are female and most are unmarried.[1] They confront the factory with a set of cultural values that order their social world, central to which is their identity as kinswoman, a self-perception workers believe to be ordained by Islam. Despite their engagement with the factory, workers continue to perceive themselves first and foremost as daughters, sisters, and perhaps wives and mothers in a patriarchal family. As such, they presume that their rightful place. is in the private sphere of the home, which is

Reproduced by permission of the Society for Applied Anthropology from *Human Organization* vol. 57, no. 2, 1998.

the arena of their most noble efforts. Thus, they transform the workshop floor into an interior space, recast factory staff into family, and operate in the factory as they would in the household. In this way they retain their prized identity as kinswoman, even within the factory, and they convert factory labor into work that is significant to them.[2] In doing so, however, they render themselves more amenable to the factory's exploitation.

There are, of course, limits to the workers' re-creation of the factory: for Moroccan females, the garment factory is a new kind of public space with characteristics unlike the private arena of the home. In some instances, workers find that their efforts to impose the blueprint of home and family on the factory fall short, and they confront what they recognize to be foreign work regimes and excessive domination. When this occurs, workers resist. I do not see this behavior as contradictory; rather, I assert that the workers' ability to comply with factory domination (which occurs far more frequently than does resistance) is rooted in their conversion of factory into home. Here I explore how this transformation is enacted.

THE "GLOBAL FACTORY"

Any study of Moroccan female garment workers must be set in the context of the recent literature on the phenomenon of women's participation in factory production. Over the past two decades, this scholarship has explored the effects of global capitalism on the definitions and meanings of gender. Two central questions have been posed: the first concerns the impact of women's participation in industrialization on the women themselves, on the men, on the family, and on the local culture. The second question is whether this impact—and the very participation of women in factories worldwide—is intrinsic to factory technology itself and/or capitalism, or if it results from local culture (Warren and Borque 1989). Researchers have sought to understand whether women's participation in these new forms of labor marks their liberation from local . . . "patriarchy," or marks a new kind of enslavement to the demands of foreign capital. Those arguing the former possibility have pointed to ways in which factory work provided women an escape from the confines of home and new opportunities for personal autonomy (Lim 1983; Salaff 1981). Other researchers have emphasized, instead, the exploitation in modern production systems that is particularly detrimental to female status (Nash and Fernandez-Kelly 1983).

The literature on women and technology has demonstrated that women's entry into capitalist wage work affects the nature of gender roles and relations in complex and contradictory ways. As Nash (1981) notes, female participation in new forms of capitalist wage labor intensities existing forms of gender subordination, while simultaneously decomposing and recomposing them. The roots of these transformations are found both in local patriarchies and in global capitalism. While the literature on women in the global factory has illuminated critical aspects of gender transformations which accompany the movement of global capital, much of the early research was limited in scope.

A particular weakness in the literature is its relative lack of detailed cultural analysis of what Ong (1991:280) calls the "experiential and interpretive dimensions of work relations." Much of the earliest research overlooked the unique ways in which workers transform capitalist work regimes and formulate their own kinds of meanings. This limitation in the literature was partly a result of the analysts' perspective on the nature of capitalism. Characterizing the capitalist system as powerful and deterministic, theorists often assumed that the methods and relations of production associated with high-tech factories would occur wherever these factories were established (Blim 1992). Theorists would then analyze the new industrialization as an effect of a standard logic, or as the result of the intersection of capitalism and a local patriarchal system.

More recent conceptualizations of the global capitalist system stress the flexibility of capitalist processes and allow for a new interpretation of the effects of industrialization (Blim 1992; Ong 1991). Capitalism (including its associated technology) is no longer seen as a homogenizing agent that flattens local systems into replicas of each other. Instead, capitalism is now understood to merge with indigenous values and practices and thus to proliferate new kinds of labor processes and relations.

If this particular perspective on capitalism is adopted, the phenomenon of the factory, and the lives of its workers, can be studied as a cultural process linked to other local cultural forms, rather than as a consequence of capitalist production (Calagione and Nugent 1992). With this perspective, the local particulars in the worker's experience of industrialization become central; indeed, they become the focus of the study. Here, I follow this approach and discuss the Moroccan clothing factory as another expression of specifically Moroccan cultural values. Workers experience their labor according to Moroccan categories already familiar to them, and use their own cultural meanings to interpret the garment factory. The Fez garment factory is thoroughly "Moroccanized" despite imported technology and systems of production.

Inside the factory, the garment workers struggle to retain a notion of themselves as family members, specifically as daughters (or sometimes as wives) in patriarchal households. They have accepted a notion of themselves as subservient and dutiful long before they enter the garment factory. They model their position in the factory hierarchy on their role in the household and so are able not only to accept the domination of the factory, but to find in that domination their own sources of personal self-worth and power. Thus, workers transform colleagues into loyal sisters and factory owners into concerned fathers, They are able to accept the constraints that the factory imposes by assimilating the owners' dominance into other, more acceptable forms of relationships. This remolding of relationships formed inside the factory to fit the prototypes of ties formed outside ultimately makes the workers available for increased exploitation. Persons with authority in the factory capitalize on workers' interpretations of their roles to maximize production and ultimately increase profit.

RESEARCH METHODS

I conducted the fieldwork for this study in the city of Fez from August 1994 to August 1995. The fieldwork involved intensive ethnography, which included formal interviews of Fez factory owners, formal and informal interviews of workers and their families, two random surveys carried out in separate garment factories in the city, and three months of participant observation inside one of those garment factories. The factory where I worked, which I call "Confection," employs some 150 workers and has been in operation for some six years. It is typical in size and operation of garment factories in Fez. At Confection 1 worked in the packaging department, where finished garments are tagged and prepared for shipment. This experience provided me a position from which to observe everyday work routines, the nature of the work process, staff hierarchies, and personal interactions inside the factory. It was through "acting like a worker" that I began to understand something of what factory work means to Moroccan factory girls.

THE ECONOMIC CONTEXT
OF GARMENT PRODUCTION

Today clothing manufacture is one of Morocco's chief export industries, and garments account for a quarter of the country's exports (Leymarie and Tripier 1992). Conservative estimates suggest that Morocco's garment factories employ close to a quarter of the country's factory workers: some 95,000 of the country's total 444,000 industrial workers produce garments. Virtually all of these workers are female (Ministère du Commerce 1994).[3]

The importance of the garment industry to the Moroccan economy is a recent phenomenon. Before the 1980s, garment manufacture was relatively insignificant. Between 1981 and 1991 the production of garments more than quadrupled (Leymarie and Tripier 1992) and, although males had formerly predominated in the garment factories, it was females who were hired, en masse, to staff the new enterprises.[4] The boom in the Moroccan garment business, and the concomitant employment of females, was fueled by several factors. These included the government economic readjustment program, trade agreements with the European Economic Community, and the movement of European production "off-shore."

The Moroccan government economic readjustment program, instituted in 1983, was a primary catalyst of the new trend (Leymarie and Tripier 1992). Before the institution of the readjustment program, Moroccan industry consisted largely of state-owned, high-tech enterprises with little capacity for generating employment. These included such industries as phosphate mining and production of thread and cloth. The program sought to replace such industries with private, low capital, labor-intensive ones. This change in Moroccan industry marked a shift in the gender of the country's work-force. As Morocco turned to light manufacturing for export, including garment production, food processing and electronics manufacturing, females flooded into factories. This employment of female factory workers is characteristic of export-oriented industries across the globe (Nash and Fernandez-Kelly 1983; Rothstein and Blim 1992; Ong 1987, 1991, Nash 1981).

European sub-contractors (predominantly French), motivated by favorable trade conditions and the desire for "off-shore" production sights, became involved in the industry in the late 1970s. They sought out Moroccan enterprises that could supply them with low cost labor, they sent in raw materials needed for production and export the final products. These subcontractors encouraged the wide scale employment of females, enjoying greater profits because women would accept far lower wages than the salaries men demanded (Joekes 1982a, 1982b, 1985). Thus, the nature and structure of the Moroccan garment industry is defined by the relationship between the European contractors and private Moroccan industrialists.

Moroccan garment factories are generally small, family-owned businesses with staffs of 50 employees or less, flexible enough to respond to a foreign, somewhat volatile, market. Because of their relatively small size they can, and often do, elude government regulation. The garment factories commonly do not heed Moroccan labor law, which in part accounts for their poor working conditions. The factories open and close rapidly and unexpectedly, with fluctuations in the external market. Thus, Moroccan females labor in an industry that provides them insecure positions and relatively poor conditions (Leymarie and Tripier 1992).

Originally, Morocco's garment factory workers, like all Moroccan factory hands, were predominantly male. Before the 1980s, female garment factory workers did unskilled work on the margins of production, but they did not operate sewing machines. Today, however, women and girls fill nearly all positions in the garment factories. The wide-scale employment of females as garment factory workers takes on new meanings in the Moroccan context.

The Social Context of Garment Production

In my research I found that garment factory workers are, for the most part, unmarried young girls who live at home with their parents and unmarried siblings. This fact is widely recognized in Morocco. The workers are generally daughters of lower class households which, in comparison with others of their class, are relatively poor and suffer high rates of male unemployment. (I herein refer to the households where garment workers live as "factory households"). The vast majority of garment workers contribute all or at least part of their earnings to household support and are significant wage-earners.[5]

Despite their positions as breadwinners, factory workers retain a fierce hold on the value of the patriarchal family. Both in word and action, they revere the traditional hierarchy that establishes males as protectors and females as dependents. Garment workers speak of factory labor as a temporary aberration they must tolerate until a successful marriage places them in the position of non-working wife and mother (married workers. a minority, are often young and as yet childless; workers with children generally work because they are destitute).

In their homes, garment workers enact the rituals of subservience that confirm and reinforce their positions as daughters, or sometimes as wives, in either case female and junior members of the household. In spite of their engagement with the factory, workers strive to maintain their identity as kinswoman because this identity is more central to them than their self-perception as workers.[6]

Local ideologies of gender, to which workers adhere, reinforce the patriarchal structure of factory households. Male authority in the family is legitimized by an ideology that defines women as economically dependent, subservient, and in need of control. According to the Moroccan gender code, a woman's proper role is that of wife and mother, a position that is essentially non-economic and properly played out in the privacy of the domestic sphere. Men appropriately take the position of breadwinner and operate in the economic sphere outside the home. Thus, women are symbolically associated with the home and with private, interior domestic space. A family's honor is embedded in its ability to keep women inside and protected, thus maintaining the divide between male and female that is at once a separation between inside and outside, private and public, kin and non-kin, home and business.[7]

The favored portrayal of female activities as home-bound, kin-related and non-economic obscures the fact that Moroccan women have always been active in the economy (Beneria 1984, Davis 1983). Today, the economic participation of Moroccan females represents 36% of national economic activity (Direction de la Statistique 1994), although it goes largely unrecognized., Still, the above-described gender code retains its position as an ideal, rooted in the popular understanding of Islam. The mass entry of Fez's women into the garment factories blatantly contradicts the pervasively held Moroccan notions of family and gender. In this article, I explore how factory workers live with this contradiction.

The Factory in Fez

Fez is an ancient city, revered among Moroccans as a spiritual capital and regarded as a bulwark of Islam and Muslim society. Traditionally, Fez has been an important artisanal center. Today it is a textile town. At independence, the Moroccan government established its largest public cloth spinning and weaving factories in Fez, which were (and are today) staffed by men. During the 1980s garment manufacturing emerged as the city's principal industry and today the sewing factories of Fez employ more than a third of all Fez factory workers, nearly all of them women (Ministère du Commerce 1995a, 1995b). This is a vivid contrast to the situation that existed less than three decades ago, when the town's textile enterprises were the province of men.

Industrial enterprises are scattered throughout the city of Fez, although most industry is located in three industrial quarters. Small factories and artisanal workshops producing for the local market and the tourist trade are found in the ancient medina. Other modest-sized factories exist in the city's newer sections, including the Ville Nouvelle and the recently developed urban periphery. The bulk of Fez's industry, including the largest and most "modern" factories, many of which produce for export, is located in the city's industrial quarters. These include the oldest and largest, Quartier Industriel Sidi Brahim, the industrial quarter of Doukkarat, and the most recently created quarter in Ben Souda. Three-quarters of Fez's factory workers labor in these districts (Fejjal 1987).

The majority of Fez's garment factories are privately owned by a class of Moroccan elite, known as the *Fassi*. The term "Fassi" is used throughout the country to describe a group of influential families originally native to the city of Fez, who control much of Morocco's wealth and political power. The Fassi are at the top of the local class structure, which includes a middle level of educated bureaucrats and a lower level made up of the majority of city dwellers, who are relatively poor and uneducated. This lower class is the class with which garment workers identify.

THE LABOR PROCESS AND FACTORY STAFF

The labor process in Fez garment factories involves six separate steps, which precede and follow upon the actual sewing of the garments. They include, in sequential order: the intake and inventory of fabric and supplies imported from Europe; the cutting of the fabric; the actual sewing of the garments, carried out by workers seated in rows ("sewing lines"); the ironing of finished products; the final inspection of completed garments; and packaging and shipment. This production sequence is carried out in the same manner, using the same kind of technology, in garment factories throughout the world.

These production talks are carried out by factory staff who labor in a hierarchy of authority. At the top of this hierarchy are the factory owners, who are either upper-class Moroccans (generally the above-described Fassi) or Europeans; in both cases, those at the top owners of the factory hierarchy are most frequently men.[8]Owners generally leave the daily direction of the factory to be handled by administrators, the garment manufacturing technicians who plan and supervise production. Like the owners, these individuals are upper-class Moroccan men (often of the owner's family) or Europeans.[9] A workshop director, generally a Moroccan man, oversees the management of all factory staff on the workshop floor. Next in the hierarchy are the workshop supervisors, who manage each particular production process; there are, for instance, one or two line supervisors for each sewing line. These supervisors are generally Moroccan males or females, of the same class as the workers. Finally, at the bottom of the factory hierarchy, are the mass of factory workers, who are Moroccan females of the lower class.

On the margins of production are the factory mechanics, transport bus drivers, secretaries and maids. The mechanics and bus drivers are Moroccan lower-class men, the former considered relatively skilled. The secretaries are Moroccan females who, because they are literate and not engaged in manual work, hold relatively high status within the factory. The maids, unskilled and impoverished females in a demeaned occupation, occupy the lowest position in the hierarchy.

Factory staff rely on familiar and valued models of relationships to interact with each other and with those who control them. I will explore how local assumptions about home and family, assumptions that are themselves infused with ideas about gender, inform the workers' attempts to transform factory relations into meaningful intercourse.

Factory as Home and Family

I like this factory very, very much. The people here are nice, it is like a family. There are hardly any men working here ... so it is like being in your own house ... If I ever left this job, I would go straight back home.

The gendering of the workshop floor as female transforms what might have been a public and immoral space into a private and acceptable one. As Emen, a seven-year employee of the Confection expressed it above, the fact that garment factories hire (nearly) only females makes the work that goes on in them somewhat more respectable. The factory is a private space, like a house, because it is a female space, a space free from the threat of illicit sexuality. Whatever transpires inside the factory is less morally questionable because the shop floor is imagined to be a private rather than a public arena. As one worker explained with pride, "one girl passes her cloth to another girl, and we are at ease, because we are all girls."

Garment factory workers are generally demeaned by Fez inhabitants for their participation in factory labor. Factory labor is in itself poorly regarded because it is manual labor, neither autonomous nor artisanal, and participation in factory work connotes a low class status. But for females, it suggests as well a lack of family honor and the real or potential loss of personal virtue. Girls who engage in factory labor are assumed to be related to males who are unable to appropriately support and protect them. The glaring presence of factory girls on the streets of Fez is often cited as proof of the inability of families to control and monitor their daughters. In response to such deprecating images, garment workers take refuge in the fact that they work in a safe, protected, all-female environment.

The actual physical construction of the factories and the way workers approach and understand factory space expresses the notion of factory as home. The factories producing for export, situated in Fez's three industrial districts, are large, low-lying structures that look like warehouses. Rows of narrow windows parallel the factory roofs but are almost unnoticeable from outside. The windows are generally too high for a passerby to see inside and, unlike the male-staffed cement and construction factories (where metal doors are often left open and interior courtyards are visible to the outside), the garment factories in the same districts housing Moroccan girls are shut tight to the stranger's eye. They look at first glance as if they are unoccupied.

Large metal doors mark the entrance to the factories and a guardian sits directly behind these doors. The doors open into a courtyard where the trucks that transport materials to and from Europe load and unload. The factory men—the guardian, mechanics and drivers—often remain in this open, transitional space. On arrival workers file through the courtyard and directly into the workshop. This is an area separate from the courtyard, located behind it, or up a flight of stairs. Once they have arrived inside the factory, workers may not leave the building without permission (often written) from their supervisors. At the Confection factory, workers who became ill during the work day required written authorization to get past the guardian and walk out of the building. Even if a worker wished to quit the job permanently, she could not leave the premises with written permission. The factory is a private space, tightly enclosed and closely monitored.

Altogether, then, the garment factory is a concrete structure built around an open courtyard, monitored by a male guardian, in which women remain protected from view and separate from males present. This description of place is reminiscent of the traditional Fez household (Mernissi 1994), in which a male slave prevented the entrance of strangers, and where women remained protected inside, carrying out the labor specific to them. While such households may have existed only rarely and for the wealthy few, the notion of the home as a private, enclosed and specifically female space remains a Moroccan ideal. The female garment factory is modeled on this prototype.

Unlike Moroccan female bureaucrats who wear European business suits, or university students who wear western style skirts or jeans on campus,[10] garment factory workers do not don "professional" or western dress to go to work. They travel to, and from the factory in the modest jellaba, a long, loose fitting robe worn in public spaces by traditional Moroccan women. Their retention of the jellaba sig-

nals identification with conventional Moroccan womanhood, as opposed to "modern" working women or with university girls (two other groups of women in transition.) Inside the factories, workers are dressed in the informal clothing of Moroccan women wear in the privacy of the home: baggy, pajama-like dresses or skirts or blue jeans in distinctive Moroccan combinations of style and color (in some factories workers must wear regulation smocks). Most wear plastic sandals on their bare feet, as they would at home. In summer the workshops can be stiflingly hot, and workers who take pains to dress modestly in the public arena of the streets labor in a minimum of clothing in the factory, as if confident that they are not exposed to a stranger's view.

Inside this production center imagined as domestic space, factory owners and workers alike assert that they work together a "as a family;" owners claim to treat workers "as daughters." Workers identify the owners in a protective role that their fathers might hold, and assert that all fellow garment workers are "sisters."[11] Even where workers recognize the discontinuities between ties formed inside the factory and those formed at home, the analogy to family life is implicit. For example, one worker, who detested the factory, claimed she would prefer to stay at home because her mother, as she said, "would never yell at (her) the way this administrator does."

The factory is the home and family is the idiom through which factory personnel think about their relations to each other. The gendered dimension of family relationships is evident in the way female factory workers approach owners, co-workers and supervisors, male and female.

In using the metaphor of family, workers quite consciously help owners in their achievement of production goals. Despite a skill hierarchy among them, they treat each other as "sisters" and thus with relative equality. Workers vehemently assert that they support each other in the accomplishment of factory tasks. Repeatedly, I was told stories of lines of machine operators who had stayed late in order to help one of their slower members, or of individual machine operators who had fallen behind in their own tasks in order to assist an inexperienced newcomer. Workers emphasized their willingness to work well with each other, taking pride in their ability to behave in a sisterly fashion. At Confection (as at many other Fez factories) workers ate lunch together from communal plates, just as they would at home, making evident their attempts to replicate the atmosphere of the home inside the factory.

The sisterly relations among workers is perhaps most evident in the way they interact with their supervisors, particularly in their defiance of factory demands. Females are increasingly being placed in supervisory positions inside Fez factories and the majority of sewing line supervisors today are female. At Confection, workers were relatively free in directly challenging female supervisors; they seemed to fear these supervisors less than they feared supervisory males.

Disputes between workers and female supervisors were not uncommon and often took the form of loud and sudden outbursts of resistance from workers in response to unbearable production pressures. Before such exchanges became problematic, however, the defiant worker's co-workers would often intervene, attempting to assuage the stressed worker's feelings and encourage her compliance. In one such case, I watched as a put-upon worker argued with her supervisor, refusing to complete a particular task. When the other workers tried to calm this worker and urge her compliance, the worker asked, "Why should she be allowed to boss me?" In response, her colleague asserted, "If Hakima cannot boss us, then who will?" The annoyed worker ultimately complied.

Co-workers had reminded the rebellious worker of the validity of the hierarchy among them, one not foreign to the mode of control used within the family. An age-hierarchy among siblings is accepted in traditional Moroccan homes, and it is recognized that the eldest sister has the authority to lead her younger sisters in the housework. Verbalization of defiance and argument is not uncom-

mon among siblings in a household. Neither is the eventual cooperation attained through a common acknowledgement of, and respect for, a universally recognized hierarchy, The authority of the female supervisor gains validity because it is reminiscent of the authority of the eldest sister. This argument, like others between workers and their female supervisors, is reminiscent of arguments between sisters in a household. Arguments with male supervisors take on a different tone, as discussed below. First, however, it is necessary to discuss the position of males in the factory.

Workers and workshop-level supervisors are today nearly exclusively female. Still, there are some males present inside the factories and on the workshop floor. The men may be the factory owners, high level administrators, the workshop director, supervisors, or the male service workers (who include the factory transport drivers, guardians, and mechanics). It is now rare to find men on the sewing lines; three was the greatest number of male sewing machine operators I could identify in any Fez factory, and most have none.

In general, the factory men attempt to separate themselves from the females. Factory guardians and transport drivers generally remain in the courtyard, separate from the workshop floor and the females there. The mechanics' duties compel them to be present on the workshop floor amidst the females. At Confection, they did not dally on the floor and remained in a separate room when possible. The factory men took lunch together, eating only after the mass of workers had left the lunch room. Just as men in Moroccan homes often remove themselves after meals to retreat to the all-male public cafes and street corners, men in the factory did not linger with women in a space that was clearly female.

The men present on the workshop floor are most often the workshop director and the supervisors directing the labor of the female machine operators. As noted above, the majority of line supervisors in Fez factories today are female; still, most factories retain at least several men in the position of sewing line supervisor. Almost all factories have retained men in the position of cutting supervisor (a post requiring technical training largely unavailable to lower-class Moroccan females). All the Fez factories I visited retained a male as workshop director, the position of greatest authority on the workshop floor. Workshop directors are always men, one informant explained, because "a man can make the girls afraid, but a woman cannot."

This hierarchy of gender authority on the factory floor reflects the hierarchy within the domestic sphere, where women carry out the daily labor and men retain the authority, The organization and use of space inside the factory makes explicit a gender hierarchy taken for granted. The few men who are present on the workshop floor (either administrators, supervisors or mechanics) are free to move about the factory at will. The female workers, however, are not permitted to leave their positions without authorization; a pass is required even to use the restroom. Workers must remain in place until production quotas are met and often do not know when the workday will end. Officially, they are not permitted to speak while they work.[12]

Thus, the very few males present on the workshop floor are upright figures standing and moving with relative self-control across a space in which females are fixed. It appears that males control females in an otherwise all-female space. The apparent immobilization of women in fixed places inside the factory parallels the limits placed on their freedom of movement in the culture generally. It also reiterates the local gender ideology that defines women as subservient and men as in control.

Given this presumed hierarchy of authority between male and female, the female garment workers directly confront male supervisors less often than female supervisors. In one case I observed a young packaging worker carrying heavy boxes down a staircase while the male workshop supervisor stood by, watching her without assisting. When the task was done the worker complained to her colleagues that the supervisor had done nothing to help. One colleague responded, "What business does a man have working in this factory?" and the other coworkers agreed that a man has no compelling interest in factory work. The demeaned labor in the garment factory is not worthy of a man's time or energy. It is common in Moroccan households to watch females toil while males relax, and factory families invariably defend this as natural. Just as a girl would not expect her father, or even her brother, to help her carry out her household tasks, so a garment factory worker ought not to expect assistance from males on the workshop floor. Garment factory work is degraded work and it is the work of females.

Nonetheless, workers do occasionally resist the authority of men in the factory; they are, however, sanctioned for it. In one case at Confection, a sewing line operator asked her male supervisor for permission to use the restroom. When he refused her, she stood up to leave her seat nonetheless. He slapped her and she, in return, slapped him. She was fired for her deed. In explaining to me why the worker was forced to leave, one girl said, "In Morocco a man can hit a woman but a woman must never, ever, hit a man. Even if he hits her, she must not hit him back." These customs prevail on the shop floor.

Factory owners, almost always male, are removed from everyday interactions on the shop floor, and thus are not engaged in the quotidian labor process. According to the dominant metaphor, factory owners are fathers and the mass of females who toil on the workshop floor, daughters. Cast in the role of fathers, owners take their positions as guardians of female virtue seriously. They provide transportation so that workers can travel to and from the factory in the protected space of factory vans (which are frequently all-female spaces; male workers often travel separately). In this way, owners curb the workers' wanderings on the streets of Fez, like fathers protecting their chastity.[13] In many factories, owners required the workers to remain inside while awaiting the arrival of the company vans, thereby preventing their unnecessary exposure on the street. At Confection the owner instituted a rule forbidding workers from travelling to and from the factory on public transportation and requiring all workers to commute in the company vans. The rule was put in place when the owner discovered that young men were frequenting the local streets in the early evening, hoping to socialize with workers leaving the factory.

Thus, the owners' control of workers reaches beyond service inside the factory. The owners' efforts to monitor female comportment on the streets of Fez were approved by community members and workers as well. Owners themselves used the idiom of family to characterize their relations with workers. One owner described himself as the workers' "father, brother, uncle, friend." He reported that he gave extra money to the neediest workers, and he claimed to buy many of them the rams needed for the ritual annual sacrifice, Although it was impossible to corroborate his story, owners cultivated the loyalty of workers by presenting themselves as concerned and watchful fathers.

Typically, workers verbalized feelings of fondness and respect for the factory owners. Concerning the above-mentioned transportation regulations at Confection, many workers defended the restrictions placed on their movements outside the factory, claiming that such controls helped maintain their reputations and assure the community that they were honorable girls. In a similar way, I found that Moroccan girls who chafed at the restrictions their fathers and brothers placed upon them would nonetheless defend these men against criticism and readily portray their influence as a form of protection or an expression of concern. Thus, workers justified the owners' increased control just as they might justify the limits placed on them by male kin as the men's attempt to guard and shelter them, Workers, perceiving themselves as "daughters," were compelled by a sense of family obligation to comply with the limits imposed on them.

This rich and meaningful basis for relationship binds girls to the factory in a sort of moral obligation that many workers acknowledge. Work becomes a commitment to the father and, through fulfilling it, a worker demonstrates her high moral standing as a female, and as a member of the community. One worker at a Fez garment factory described the working of overtime as a kind of moral obligation, a burden necessary to bear. "If the boss needs us to stay and work till seven o'clock in the evening, we must stay. We have to help him keep his commitments with people overseas." She explained how a fellow worker got fired: one evening when they were working overtime, the girl just got up from her machine and said to the owner, "Just give me my money for my hours worked." She then left the factory without waiting to be certain the export truck was ready to go, unwilling to help the owner meet his deadlines. "One must not speak like that," the first worker said, criticizing the actions of her colleague. "It sounds hard, as if you do not trust that the boss will give you what he owes you." Although workers frequently see little of the factory owners, the relationship between worker and owner is phrased as highly personalized and based on trust.

Another worker described an incident that forced her to miss the seven-day naming ceremony for her sister's first-born child, which she sorely regretted. In recounting how this had come to pass, she emphasized the cooperative and dutiful quality of her own response:

> On the day of the naming ceremony, I went to the director and said, "Today is the seventh-day naming ceremony for my sister's first child, I want to leave early to attend." The director pleaded with me "Please, we cannot let you go early today. Please, don't go. You understand we need you, don't you?" I answered, "Yes, no problem."

In continuing, the worker explained that she could have feigned illness in order to be released from the factory that day, but she would not do so because she was an honest and trustworthy person. Although I prompted her, the worker would express no resentment or anger at this sequence of events. According to her interpretation, she was never forbidden to leave the factory but rather was begged to stay and help. And to this appeal she responded. She missed her sister's party because she was obliged to answer a higher duty.

This worker's description of loyalty to the factory is a familiar form of discourse among workers, and it precisely parallels the way in which relations with family are described., For instance, another worker described to me her premature departure from school, which came about when her father approached her and (by her account) said, "my little daughter... you can see the situation we are in. Please, can you leave school and try to get work to help us?" The worker emphasized that her father had never commanded her but rather had pleaded with her. As she recounted his words, the worker imitated her father's begging voice and placed her fingertips over her mouth and kissed them, mimicking the gesture her father had used to signal a request.

Within the family, workers do not experience authority simply as a gripping hold on their liberties and personal autonomy. Instead, in submitting to authority, they perceive themselves as providing a needed response to a call for service. The assistance they provide to the owners, and to their male kin as well, is in some ways a source of personal power, for it is these females alone who can answer the males' call for assistance. They interpret their own compliance as a moral obligation, and in cooperating they display their own good character and worthiness as daughters or wives.[14]

As the worker/owner relationship gets carried out in terms of the code associated with father/daughter, parent/child or possibly husband/wife, what might appear as domination or exploitation of workers by owners often gets reconfigured into something more acceptable. By thinking in terms of the family model, workers can experience owners and administrators not as dominating, but as begging or pleading for their cooperation and assistance. In cooperating with the owner,

they assert their own moral rectitude as loyal, principled individuals who understand the importance of preserving the social tie above all else.

CONCLUSION

It is young unmarried women who staff the garment factories of Morocco. Fez locals, and Moroccans generally, claim that the low pay, long hours, and unpaid overtime associated with garment factory labor are accepted by these young girls because they work "only for clothes and make-up." As daughters (or sometimes wives), workers are presumed to be supported by family males; they are believed to contribute minimally, at most, to household support. As noted above, contrary to public opinion, research indicates that garment factory workers are an important source of household support.

Nonetheless, the local understanding of women's participation in low-paid factory labor coincides with Marxist feminist explanations of female employment on the global assembly line (Elson and Pierson 1981). From both perspectives, it is women's role in reproduction, and their position as dependent daughters, wives, and/or mothers, that explains their vulnerability to and acceptance of low-wage work.

Here, I have attempted to explore how Moroccan understandings of home, family and gender render females willing workers on the garment factory shop floor. Workers transform the public space of the factory into the private space of the home in an attempt to assuage the contradiction inherent in their presence inside the factory, outside the home, in a role ideologically reserved for men. They behave inside this "home" as kinswoman, using the assumptions and practices associated with family to regulate their comportment inside factory walls. They approach owners much like fathers, and supervisors like parents or elder sisters. They treat each other like siblings. They accept factory hierarchies based on their understanding of, and reverence for, the patriarchal family and the gender order it endorses.

Local meanings and values thus mediate the workers' approach to the factory. Their transformation of factory into a home allows them to accommodate the owners' power with little resistance. They willingly accept the factory administration's power as they would accept the authority of their own fathers, in their role as daughters, or that of their husbands in the role of wife. In this way, the owners are able to appropriate labor at a low cost without risking resistance. To some extent, workers and their families are willing accomplices in the factory's exploitation, because this exploitation gets phrased in terms that are not only accepted, but revered.

NOTES

1. Here, the word "workers" refers to the female garment factory workers of Fez. I refer to the workers as "girls" rather than women because the vast majority of them are unmarried and thus defined, in Morocco, as girls, or *binet.* The residents of Fez, Moroccans generally, and the workers themselves refer to garment factory workers as girls.
2. Here I contrast the idea of "labor" with that of "work" as in Comaroff and Comaroff (1987) and Walman (1979).
3. The accuracy of these numbers is questionable. The figures are based on government census materials and reflect only the factories officially registered with the government. It is widely understood in Morocco, however, that many industrial operations are unregistered and "hidden." Factory owners prefer to keep their operations unnoticed by the government to avoid the financial and legal implications that are inherent in official recognition. Even where the factory itself is recognized by the government, many of its workers may not be. Factory owners often regard even permanent, full-time employees as seasonal workers, temporary staff, or apprentices, and thus deny them the work papers that would ensure them the benefits prescribed by law. Obviously, government data cannot account for such employees. One economist in Morocco suggested that government figures be doubled to arrive at a more accurate count of industrial workers in Fez. During one year in Fez, I met few garment workers who held work registration papers. None of the 150 workers in the factory where I worked had working papers.
4. Moroccan men were slowly replaced by women in the garment industry. Throughout the 1980s females were hired to replace departing males in existing factories and most workers hired in new factories were female. Females were frequently hired to replace males involved in labor unrest. Fez factory owners recounted that males working in Fez garment factories before the general workers strike of 1990 were replaced by females. Morocco suffers high rates of unemployment, and mate joblessness has not been alleviated by the boom in the garment industry.
5. According to my survey research, 76% of workers surveyed were never-married females, 16% were married and 8% were divorced., Nearly all of the workers surveyed (92%) were between the ages of 13 and 25. Never-married and divorced workers (84% of the total) almost invariably lived as daughters in their natal households (divorced young women return to their natal homes when possible). Married workers lived either in their husband's natal home or in a separate conjugal home. The majority of married workers were newly married women who had worked in the factory before marriage. Most of the married workers who continued working after having children were destitute women whose husbands were unable to work, Workers earned anywhere from 300 to 800 dirhams per month, and 89%of workers reported contributing some or all of their salary to the family. These salaries were considered significant in lower class households in which men found difficulty securing steady work.
6. Although I am not in any way suggesting a privileged relationship between Islam and women's subjugation to factory labor, other researchers have investigated women's participation in wage labor with focus on the Muslim context. (Hijab 1988; Ibrahim 1985; Macleod 1991; Ong 1987; and White 1994).
7. Abu Lughod (1986) provides a complex exploration of the notion ofhonor, and an early, comprehensive collection on the notion of honor isfound in Peristiany (1966). See Dwyer 1978, Mernissi 1987, Sabbah 1984 and Combs-Schilling 1989 for discussions of specifically

Moroccan notions of honor as they pertain to gender and gender relations.

8. Related women—the wives and sometimes daughters of the owners—are prominent in the operation of a few Fez factories. But it is most frequently men who play the day-to-day role of factory owner and administrator.

9. It is interesting to note that many of the European technical directors are female while Moroccan technical directors are almost exclusively male.

10. There is a growing number of university students who today dress in distinctively Islamic robes, but I do not consider them here.

11. This situation is reinforced by the fact that many workers are related to each other through biological kinship. High level factory staff are often relatives of the factory owner (Fejjal 1987) so that there is a sense in each factory that this is a family enterprise. Personal ties are key in the recruitment of new workers: factory owners and administrators give the relatives and friends of trusted workers preference in hiring. It is common for sisters, cousins, even mother and daughter to work in the same factory, either at the same time or sequentially. At Confection, 10% of the workers had sisters or cousins working contemporaneously with them; others reported that their relatives had worked there previously. Nearly 20% of the workers surveyed had sisters who worked in other garment factories in Fez. Biological kin ties among the workers help contribute to making the idiom of family a reality.

12. Moroccans, men in particular, characterize women as "full of empty talk." Their propensity to be engaged in meaningless speech is prohibited on the factory floor.

13. There are economic reasons for providing transport as well: for many workers, the cost of public transportation to and from the factory would represent such a large percentage of the salary as to make working purposeless. The father of one former worker laughed wryly when he explained that his daughter's month of factory work had actually cost the family money; the girl's salary did not cover her bus fare to and from the factory. (She was considered an apprentice, which explains her absurdly low salary).

14. Abu Lughod (1986) explores the dimensions of the authority relationship between Bedouin men and women.

REFERENCES

Abu Lughold, Lila. 1986. Veiled Sentiments. Berkely: University of California Press.

Beneria, Lourdes. 1984. Women and Rural Development: Morocco. Cultural Survival Quarterly 8(2):30–32.

Blim, Michael L. 1992. Introduction: The Emerging Global Factory and Anthropology. In Anthropology and the Global Factory: Studies of the New Industrialization in the Late Twentieth Century. M.L. Blim and F.A. Rothstein, eds., pp. 1–30. New York: Bergin and Garvey.

Calagione, John and Daniel Nugent. 1992. Workers' Expressions: Beyond Accommodation and Resistance on the Margins of Capitalism. In Worker's Expressions: Beyond Accommodation and Resistance. J. Calagione and D. Nugent, eds., pp. 1–34. Albany: SUNY Press.

Comaroff, John L. and Jean Comaroff. 1987. The Madman and the Migrant: Work and Labor in the Historical Consciousness of a South African People. American Ethnologist 14(2): 191–209.

Combs-Schilling, M. Elaine. 1989. Sacred Performances: Islam, Sexuality and Sacrifice. New York: Columbia University Press.

Davis, Susan S. 1983. Patience and Power: Women's Lives in a Moroccan Village. New York: Schenkman.

Dwyer, Daisy H. 1978. Images and Self-Images: Male and Female in Morocco. New York: Columbia University Press.

Direction de la Statistique de Maroc. 1994. Femme et Condition Feminine au Maroc. Rabat: Les Editions Guessous.

Elson, Diane and Ruth Pierson. 1981. The Subordination of Women and the Internationalisation of Factory Production. In Of Marriage and the Market: Women's Subordination in International Perspective. Kate Yound, ed., pp. 144–166. London: CSE Books.

Fejjal, Ali. 1987. Industrie et Industrialisation à Fes. Revenue de Geographie Marocaine Nouvelle Serie 11(2): 55–70.

Fernandez-Kelly, Maria P. 1983. For We Are Sold, I and My People: Women and Industry in Mexico's Frontier. Albany: State University of New York Press.

Hijab, Nadia. 1988. Womanpower: The Arab Debate on Women at Work. Cambridge: Cambridge University Press.

Ibrahim, Beth. 1985. Cairo's Factory Women. In Women and the Family in the Middle East.

Elizabeth Fernea, ed., pp. 293–299. Austin: University of Texas Press.

Joekes, Susan. 1982a. The Multifibre Arrangement and Outward Processing: The Case of Morocco and Tunisia. In EEC and the Third World. C. Stevens, ed., pp. 102–112. London: Hodder and Soughton.

———1982b. Female-led Industrialization and Women's Jobs in Third World Export Manufacturing: The Case of the Moroccan Clothing Industry. Brighton: Institute of Development Studies Research Reports No. 15.

———1985. Working for Lipstick? Male and Female Labour in the Clothing Industry in Morocco. In Women, Work and Ideology in the Third World. H. Afshar, ed., pp. 183–214. London: Tavistock Publications.

Leymarie, Serge and Jean Tripier. 1992. Maroc: Le Prochain Dragon? Casablana: Editions Eddif Maroc.

Lim, Linda Y.C. 1993. Capitalism, Imperialism and Patriarchy: The Dilemma of Third-World Women Workers in Multinational Factories. In Women, Men, and the International Division of Labor. June Nash and M.P. Fernandez-Kelly, eds., pp. 205–223. Albany: State University of New York Press.

Macleod, Arlene E. 1991. Accommodating Protest: Working Women, the New Veiling, and Change in Cairo. New York: Columbia University Press.

Mernissi, Fatima. 1987. Beyond the Veil: Male-Female Dynamics in a Modern Muslim Society. Bloomington: Indiana University Press.

———1994. Dreams of Trespass: Tales of a Harem Girlhood. New York: Addison-Wesley Publishing Company.

Ministère du Commerce de L'Industrie et de la Privatisation. 1994. Situation des Industries de Transformation. Rabat: Dèlegation de Commerce et de l'Industrie de la Wilaya de Fes.

Nash, June. 1981. Ethnographic Aspects of the World Capitalist System. Annual Review of Anthropology 10:393–424.

Nash, June and Maria P. Fernandez-Kelly eds., 1983. Women, Men and the International Division of Labor. Albany: State University of New York Press.

Ong, Aibwa. 1987. Spirits of Resistance and Capitalist Discipline: Factory Women in Malayisia. Albany: State University of New York Press.

———1991. The Gender and Labor Politics of Postmodernity. Annual Review of Anthropology 20:279–309.

Perisiany, J.G. 1966. Honor and Shame: The Values of Mediterranean Society. Chicago: University of Chicago Press.

Rothstein, Francis A. and Michael L. Blim, eds., 1992. Anthropology and the Global Factory: Studies of the New Industrialization in the Late Twentieth Century. New York: Bergen and Garvey.

Sabbah, Fatna. 1984. Woman in the Muslim Unconscious. New York: Oxford Pergamon Press.

Salaff, Janet. 1981. Working Daughters of Hong Kong: Filial Piety or Power in the Family? New York: Cambridge University Press.

Wallman, Sandra, ed. 1979. The Social Anthropology of Work. London: Academic Press.

Warren, Kay B. and Susan C. Bourque. 1989. Women, Technology and Development Ideologies: Frameworks and Findings. In Gender and Anthropology. S. Morgen, ed., pp. 382–411. Washington: American Anthropological Association.

White, Jenny B. 1994. Money Makes Us Relatives: Women's Labor in Urban Turkey. Austin: University of Texas Press.

"Wild Pigs and Dog Men": Rape and Domestic Violence as "Women's Issues" in Papua New Guinea

Laura Zimmer-Tamakoshi

INTRODUCTION

Male violence against women is a concern of feminists in both developed and developing countries (Counts, Brown & Campbell 1992; Davies 1994). Leaders in many developing countries, however, have been slow in recognizing the extent and nature of the problem. This is in part because of insufficient research and cultural norms allowing for a "certain amount of wife-beating" and forced sex within marriage (United Nations 1989). It is also the result of women's weaker political presence in developing countries and male resentment over a few women's gains in economic and social independence. Nevertheless, prompted by alarm over increased violence against women, concern over the deleterious effects of violence on women's participation in development, and negative images of Papua New Guinea in the world press, in 1982 the Papua New Guinean government directed its Law Reform Commission to begin research into domestic violence. The resulting, and for a developing country, unprecedented publications revealed that a majority of Papua New Guinean wives have been hit by their husbands, most more than once a year, with urban wives suffering a higher level of violence than their rural counterparts (Toft, ed. 1985, 1986a, 1986b; Toft and Bonnell 1985). Less systematically researched, rape is also a concern as Papua New Guinea tops the United States with a reported rate of 45 rapes per 100,000 persons versus 35 per 100,000 in the United States and well above the lower inci-

Original material prepared for this text.

dences of reported rapes in Japan and other industrial and non-industrial nations (Herman 1989: 23). In 1990 there were, 1,896 rapes reported in Papua New Guinea, a country with less than 4 million in population (Dinnen 1993). Such statistics do not capture the severity of the problem, however, as most of these rapes were committed by three or more rapists (with more than 15, 20, or 40 males participating in any particular gang rape), and, as in the United States and elsewhere, many rapes are unreported, especially those committed by the victims' husbands, lovers, dates, or close relatives (Dinnen 1996; Finkelhor and Yllo 1985; Russell 1984; Toft 1985; Toft 1986a; Zimmer 1990).

This chapter examines violence against women in Papua New Guinea, reviewing past and present patterns of rape and domestic violence and adding to a multidimensional theory concerning the prevalence and increase of such violence. Although traditional attitudes toward violence contribute to its acceptance, recent research has targeted the psychological and economic pressures of development and inequality as fueling violence against women, particularly as they have different effects on the circumstances and attitudes of males and females. Josephides (n.d.), for example, argues that in Papua New Guinea, "Much of men's violence towards women is motivated by a fear that women are gaining a new kind of independence," and that men's violence is an attempt to terrify and control the women. Both Josephides and Bradley (1994), who worked at the Papua New Guinea Law Reform Commission from 1986 to 1990, see the violence as stemming not only from men's insecurities about their wives' potential independence but also their own uncertain situations and the effects of urban lifestyles (including alcohol abuse and reduced social support networks) on male–female relations. Other factors are increased eroticism and sexual conflicts as old taboos disappear and men (and sometimes women) place greater demands on their spouses and sexual partners (Jenkins 1994; Rosi and Zimmer-Tamakoshi 1993).

Supporting these arguments with cases and other material, I also develop a needed political dimension to better understand violence against women in Papua New Guinea (and elsewhere, as I discuss in the concluding section of this chapter). While individuals commit violence and it is individuals who experience the traumas and dislocations of change and development, the intersection of sex and class politics also informs and fuels sexual and domestic violence. With a small number of Papua New Guineans enjoying an elite lifestyle and under pressure from the "grassroots" to bring about an economic miracle on their behalf, elite women have become targets of disaffection not only from men and women in the lower classes but also from men in their own class. Feeling harassed on all sides, by unsympathetic constituents and, from their perspective, "demanding" or *bikhet* (uncontrollable, conceited) wives and girlfriends, many elite males have taken the path of least resistance and higher political capital, scapegoating elite women and using violence to assert control over them (Rosi and Zimmer-Tamakoshi 1993; Zimmer-Tamakoshi 1993b and 1995). Thus, I not only contend, along with others, that 1) women's opportunities for self-expression and economic independence threaten the self-esteem and security of men who do not have such opportunities and 2) that such men use violence against women to assert or regain a sense of dominance. I also argue that 3) violence against women is rife among Papua New Guinea's elite (a fact demonstrated by the Law Reform Commission reports) even when one excludes what Josephides has referred to in person as anti-feminist *rascals*

(or criminals) some of who are members of elite society (as has been reported by Dinnen 1993; Harris 1988; and Zimmer-Tamakoshi n.d.) and 4) that the violence is partly motivated by class and sexual tensions that paint elite females as symbols of all that is wrong with contemporary Papua New Guinean society. Finally, violence against women does not occur in isolation from other forms of violence. Political tensions in Papua New Guinea are grounded in a weak state that is unable to ensure even basic services to its population or to control public disturbances such as tribal conflicts over land. As has been argued for Papua New Guinea (A. Strathern 1993) and other parts of the world (Riches 1986), expressions of conflict such as the resumption of tribal warfare in the New Guinean highlands have strategic value in the context of a weak state. In a weak state violence may be a rational means of social advantage when there are no higher-level powers strong enough or interested enough in interfering with lower-level clashes. In the case of violence against women, men who want to can assert their dominance over women with little fear of resistance as long as there is widespread envy or fear of those women, and state officials charged with protecting them are unable or unwilling to do so.

WILD PIGS AND DOG MEN

Rape and domestic violence are not common in every New Guinean society (see Goodale 1980 and Mitchell 1992), but, fearing violence, most Papua New Guinean women walk in groups when going to and from their gardens or to office, school, or marketplace. Because husbands and boyfriends are likely perpetrators of violence against them, women also seek the protective company of family and friends when they are at home. Women's fear of violence, especially sexual violence, is fanned with vivid stories of past attacks on women and fresh accounts in the daily press. Around village hearths in the night, women and girls listen to the hushed and often admonitory tones of older persons telling them tales (captured in early anthropological monographs) of gang rape and mutilation of women's genitals as ways men "used to" punish errant wives and daughters (Meggitt 1964: 204, 207; Newman 1964: 266; Read 1952: 14); how wife-swapping or preying on other men's wives were tolerated as long as neither was too blatant an attack on a man's self-esteem (Berndt 1962: 160, Brown 1969: 94; Langness 1969: 45 and 1974: 204; Read 1954: 866); and how rape did and does occur in the varied contexts of women being found alone on a garden path or at work in their gardens, in war, and when a man tires of his lover, wishes to end an adulterous affair or lessen his culpability in either case by instigating a gang rape of the woman (Berndt 1962: 168). Outside the highlands, Tolai women shudder when they hear how Tolai men's cults once celebrated masculinity with the sexual abuse of widows and other women without male protection (Bradley 1982, 1985; Parkinson 1907: 473). And in West New Britain, Lakalai women do not mourn changes in the men's ceremonial season, which once included the casual rape of women in their own villages (Chowning 1985: 85).

Although many men's cults and their predations on women have died out as Christianity has taken over (Bradley 1985 and Chowning 1985), violence against women continues. Today, the contexts in which violence occurs are more but there are parallels in the circumstances of some of the victims and the motivations of their attackers. Finding a woman alone on a garden path is now varied in cases like one in 1983 in which a former rugby league star and two other assailants beat and raped a three-months-pregnant woman when they found her alone on the Daulo Pass where she was stranded after the vehicle in which she was a passenger broke down (PNG *Post Courier* 1984a). Tiring of his lover, a young man may arrange to have her gang-raped as did a young man in the city of Lae when he forced his girlfriend to have sex with his friends after he had sex with her (PNG *Post Courier* 1984c). Another traditional

form of violence—humiliating the enemy by raping their women—was echoed in the same month when a man was held by two assailants and forced to watch while a third man raped his wife in Rabaul village (PNG *Post Courier* 1984g). In the same month, a gang of about 15 youths, all under the age of 20, raped a nine-year-old girl, her mother, and another woman while the women's husbands were beaten and held at knife-point. The gang then broke into a nearby house and stole $6,000 worth of cash and goods (PNG *Post Courier* 1984b, d, e, f, g). The gangs' actions replicated attacks against the enemies' women in warfare, but in this instance there was the added twist that some of the younger rapists were trying to prove their right to membership in the gang by raping white women (see Harris 1988 on *rascal* gang entry requirements). Echoes of using rape and beatings to punish errant wives or daughters abound in the case of "Bill and Maria" (Case 2 below) in which "Bill" (all names are pseudonyms for obvious reasons) rapes his wife in a public carpark as a means of asserting his dominance and punishing her independence.

In many traditional Papua New Guinean societies, particularly in the Highlands, violence against women was part of a sociopolitical context in which political eminence was achieved through the control and distribution of wealth, and older men and women controlled access to land and marriage, two main ingredients in the acquisition of wealth. Marriage was important for both males and females for it was through marriage that one acquired a helpmate, produced children, and paid off one's debts to society. For men of ambition, marrying several women was virtually the only means of becoming a "Big Man," as women's gardening and pig-raising activities and daughters' brideprices brought men the necessary "wealth" (pigs, yams, shells) to fund networks of supporters and to outgive competitors within and outside their clans. To marry at all required the support of older men and women, who gathered together the brideprice. The process of attracting brideprice supporters began during a man's childhood and youth, when he and his peers participated in lengthy initiations designed to test and strengthen their obedience and relationships to their supporters. During initiation, young men were told many falsehoods about women as a way of keeping them away from women until their elders were ready to support their marriages. Such fabrications included depictions of women, particularly young women, as dangerous and untrustworthy creatures who were to be feared and avoided if possible (Counts 1985; Dickerson-Putman n.d.; Faithorn 1976; Gelber 1986; Zimmer-Tamakoshi 1996a). Boys learned that "over-indulgence in sexual relations with women depletes a man's vital energies leaving his body permanently exhausted and withered" (Meggitt 1964: 210) and that contact of any kind with women causes a man "to accumulate debilitating dirt in his body" (Newman 1964: 265). Young women's powers of seduction were portrayed as so great that young men were warned not to look at a young woman because "if you look at her, and she looks at you, then you will copulate" (Berndt 1962: 103; Read 1954: 867; Langness 1967: 165).

Part of the ideology initiates learned included notions of male superiority and dominance over women. Men's superiority was said to reside in their greater capacity for self-control. Initiates were taught that mature men do not act "like wild pigs" having sex indiscriminately or like "women" acting on whim and self-interest rather than promoting the social good (Gelber 1986, Chapter Two; Lindenbaum 1976: 56). Young men who were disrespectful of or doubted their elders' injunctions risked permanent bachelorhood as they depended on older men and women for brideprice help (Bowers 1965; Glasse 1969: 26; Waddell 1972: 46), and few prospective in-laws would allow their daughters to marry "dog men," men with inordinant desires for sex who spent their lives "sniffing" after other men's wives and destroying the village peace.

Promoting male solidarity, notions of male superiority allowed for effective regulation of access to and control over women. In most Papua New Guinean societies, the importance of female labor to men was such—and still is—that men have variously portrayed women as men's "hands" (Lindenbaum 1976: 59), "tradestores" (M. Strathern 1972: 99), "tractors" (Langness 1967: 172), and "capital assets" (Cook 1969: 102). Recent ethnographies suggest it was more young women's sexuality and labor than older women's that was at issue, as older women had rewards and reasons of their own to support their husbands' activities and to promote the well-being of their children's clans as well as their own (Counts 1985; Dickerson-Putman n.d.; M. Strathern 1980; Zimmer-Tamakoshi 1996a). Just as parents warned sons against the dangers of women, so too did they warn daughters against unregulated association with young men. They also taught their daughters that safety lay in cooperating with their elders to achieve fruitful marriages and honorable lives. Women—young or old—who rebelled against such beliefs or interfered with men's activities and plans, risked beatings and punitive rapes (Berndt 1962; Josephides 1985; Meggitt 1964; Read 1954; and M. Strathern 1972). Believing women to be weak-willed, husbands justified beating their wives fairly regularly as a way of getting them to fulfill their obligations to them. Also believing women to be by nature deceitful and seductive, men readily blamed rape victims for bringing the rapes on themselves. Women were thus wise to build large networks of supporters in their own and their husbands' groups who might rise to their defense in the case of rape or an overzealous wife-beater.

Today, introduced notions of women's inferiority and men's right to dominate them, men's greater access to cash incomes and women's increasing dependence on men, the weakening of parents' economic control over sons and daughters (especially those living and working in urban areas), and opportunities (primarily through education) for a few women to achieve both economic and social independence all contribute to an increasing incidence of violence against women in

Papua New Guinea. Grafted onto old beliefs, the views of some Christian missions—that women be subservient to and mindful at all times of their husbands' and, much less so, their parents' wishes—and foreign media portrayals of women as erotic sex objects, docile housewives, or man-eaters, further alienate young Papua New Guineans from one another as women are shrouded in further mystifications. During my first year of fieldwork with a group of Highlanders known as the Gende, an urban gang member bragged to me about his sexual exploits which included kidnapping and raping young girls and even a married woman. In response to my shocked expression, he assured me that "They liked it! It was like it is in a James Bond movie—sexy! The woman fights with James Bond and tries to kill him and then he forces her to have sex with him and she is his woman from then on. Sometimes he kills her if she is a really bad woman." When I asked if he had killed anyone, he said he had killed the one woman because he feared she would tell her husband that he had raped her (which he denied, insisting that it wasn't rape and that "She liked it! I'm sexy!").

In the material realm, men's control of economic resources has tightened in both village and town as the proceeds from most cash crops are controlled by men, men dominate the job market, and men's educational opportunities are greater than women's. Women's dependence on men is greatest among urban women. One result of this dependence is that urban husbands—especially prosperous ones—are more likely to fight with their wives, to cheat on them, and to abuse them both physically and sexually (Ranck and Toft 1986; Rosi and Zimmer-Tamakoshi 1993; Zimmer-Tamakoshi 1993a). Several Gende women I know left husbands who beat them, drank too much, and wasted their salaries on other women, saying they'd rather marry a village husband who worked with them in the gardens and not against them in town. In the case of low-income husbands who are less attractive to other women, a wife's threat to return to the village to find another husband

is taken very seriously, and such a husband is less likely even than a villager to beat his wife (Ranck and Toft 1986; Zimmer-Tamakoshi 1996b).

The weakening of parental control over the beliefs and actions of the younger generation and its relationship to violence against women can be illustrated in the experience of another Gende woman. This young woman's husband, also Gende, grew up in Port Moresby and is more western in his outlook on life than she is. Jealous of his womanizing and pressured by her relatives to get him to pay off the remaining brideprice he owes them, she has stayed in town, playing cards most of the time her husband is working and being the butt of his anger or lust whenever he is home. Although she usually suffers his abuse quietly, on one occasion he forced her to have sex during her period, a heinous act in the eyes of more traditional Gende. Hysterical and threatening suicide, the young woman cut off one of her fingers with an axe, thereby demonstrating her shame. A parallel experience occurred a generation before to the girl's aunt. Married to a migrant but living in the village, the aunt was forced by her young husband—on a rare visit home—to have sex during her period. Ashamed and angry, the aunt moped around the village for a day and then left for her garden house—several miles distant from the village—where she hung herself. Unsuspecting, her family did not find her until it was too late. When the women cleaned her body for burial, they discovered menstrual blood mixed with semen smeared over her lower body and skirt as well as bruises on her arms and chest where her husband had apparently held her down forcefully. Although such actions would have resulted in the young man's death in the past, the aunt's husband stayed in town, away from the girl's parents and male relatives, hiding behind the power of Australian colonial law and her parents' belief that the young man would be more useful to them if he continued working and paid them a large compensation payment for their daughter's death.

How far outside the normal realm of parental control (and protection) young persons can get is illustrated in "Violet's" case. In this case, parental pressures and absence are only part of the story. Other factors responsible for "Violet's" fate are her naive hopes for love and romance, and a sociocultural environment in which many young men no longer fear women so much as see them as sexual prey.

Case 1—"Violet"

I have written elsewhere on the motives and circumstances of young village women moving to town in the hope of attracting suitors who can pay the large brideprices expected by the women's families and fulfill women's dreams of a prosperous lifestyle (Zimmer-Tamakoshi 1993a). Living with younger kinsmen, married sisters, or even non-relatives, these girls are poorly chaperoned and often end up victims of sexual assault and bondage. One such victim was Violet. When she first came to Port Moresby, Violet stayed with an older sister and brother-in-law in a house provided by the company her brother-in-law worked for. Violet spent her days looking after her sister's children while her sister worked as a checker in a local supermarket. Evenings, Violet attended the local movie theater with girlfriends or stayed home to watch T.V. with her sister's family. As soon as she moved in with her sister, Violet became the target of her brother-in-law's unwanted sexual advances. On numerous occasions, feigning illness in order to spend the day at home and threatening to kill her if she revealed what he was doing, Violet's brother-in-law had sex with Violet. When Violet became pregnant, her sister wanted to send her back to the village, but Violet feared the censure and disappointment of her parents. Violet obtained an illegal abortion and moved in with a girlfriend.

Supporting herself by prostitution and frequenting the notorious "Pink Pussycat" and other cocktail lounges, Violet continues to hope that she will one day meet and marry a "nice man" who will take her out of her misery. The types of men Violet is most likely to meet, however, are married men looking for an evening's distraction or university students preying on naive husband-hunters. The violent and sexually-charged atmosphere of both the University and the city are well-known to anyone who has spent time in either location. In a paper on the situations of women students at the University of Papua New Guinea, Joan Oliver reported that "women students had a pervasive fear of attack, harassment, threats, bashings, rape and breaking into rooms by male students or strangers" (1987: 159; see also Still and Shea's report of 1976). She further reported that because of their fears many women either drop out of school or become engaged to male protectors who not infrequently soon have the women pregnant (1987: 170).

With the proportion of female students at UPNG hovering at 10 percent, male students are in keen competition with one another for the friendship of female classmates. The competition works itself out along divisions of language and region as, for example, Chimbu *wantoks* (persons who speak Chimbu) jealously attempt to guard all Chimbu girls for themselves and Papuans (from southern Papua New Guinea) fight off any non-Papuans who might try to have a relationship with a Papuan girl. Since having sex with a female student risks reprisal from her campus *wantoks*—but not the police!—many University men satisfy their sexual desires by visiting Port Moresby's night spots and bringing back girls like Violet to the University playing fields and dorms where they have sex with them—often forced. These escapades may also bring reprisals, of course, as happened when a gang of University students raped a young girl from a nearby squatter settlement on the University football field while her younger brother was made to watch. Class antagonism as well as ethnic outrage was evident as men and boys from the settlement stalked the campus paths and housing areas for weeks after threatening to rape female students and teachers at UPNG for what the "spoiled, *bikhet* school boys" had done.

MERI WANTOK AND MERI UNIVERSITI

As suggested in the previous paragraph, a broad set of factors that seems conducive to high levels of violence against women in Papua New Guinea is the extra-local politics of sexuality. This set of factors includes the intersections of elite and urban sexual politics with nationalist and class interests and rhetoric. In a paper on nationalism and sexuality in Papua New Guinea, I argued that the practice of holding educated women, or *meri universiti*, responsible for all that is wrong with contemporary Papua New Guinean society is both a political maneuver to ease class and inter-ethnic tensions and jealousies in Papua New Guinea's culturally diverse society (Zimmer-Tamakoshi 1993b) and a satisfying fiction for the majority of Papua New Guineans who feel left out of "progress" and "development." Symbolizing privilege and, in some instances, sexual freedom (or anarchy), *meri universiti* and *skull meri* (school girls) are both envied for their perceived opportunities and hated as selfish betrayers of their cultural roots, while "grassroots" women and more circumspect elite women who show (or appear to show) greater concern for their kin and language groups are accorded respect as *meri wantok* and *meri bilong ples*.

There is as much diversity within the elite as without, particularly between educated men and women. Unlike their male counterparts, who come from all parts of the nation, Papua New Guinea's small class of educated elite women come almost entirely from coastal and off-shore island areas that have been long involved with the outside world. As a result, they are more likely than their male peers to come from educated and economically privileged backgrounds, and as a group they are more western in demeanor and appearance than most Papua New Guinean women. Another difference between educated men and women (and between educated women and the majority of Papua New Guinea's population) is that many educated elite women come from matrilineal societies

in which women's status tends to be higher relative to many patrilineal societies and women are freer in their relations with men. On one occasion, when I was having dinner at the Bird of Paradise hotel in Goroka, I was surprised to learn that the couple at the table beside me were married (but not to each other!), were travelling together throughout the Highlands on government business, and that their spouses on Bougainville Island were satisfied with the phone calls the pair made at each stop on their tour of duty. It was difficult to imagine such easy professionalism in a partnership involving a Highlands man and woman. Rumors and jealous spouses would prevent this as Highlanders (and many other Papua New Guineans) believe it is impossible for men and women to be together for long without engaging in sex. Unusual, such behavior becomes a focus of the anger and jealousies that exist between the sexes and between class, ethnic, and racial groupings in Papua New Guinea.

Increasing the distance between elite men and themselves some elite women have opted for marriage with non-Papua New Guineans or to forgo marriage entirely. Several examples are two of the three women to ever sit as members of National Parliament and a former president of the National Council of Women, all married to or in long-term relationships with white, expatriate males. Such high-profile interracial relationships on the part of women embarrass the male leadership as the majority of Papua New Guineans see them as signs of elite immorality and weakness (e.g. elite men's inability to control their women) and collaboration of the elite with outsiders and former colonials. There have been attempts to control elite women's freedoms at all levels of Papua New Guinean society from the government down, including public censure, violence, and the refusal of full citizenship rights to foreign spouses and recurrent threats to disenfranchise the children of mixed marriages.

An example of the public scapegoating of elite or educated women is the "mini-skirt debate." The "mini-skirt debate" began back in the early seventies—prior to Papua New Guinea's independence in 1975—with Tolai religious and political leaders in East New Britain calling for a campaign against immodest dress and claiming that school girls and young women were provoking an increasing incidence of rape and STDs in East New Britain by wearing provocative western-style clothing and makeup. The debate entered the pages of Papual New Guinea's *Post Courier* where it has continued off and on for years. The response of young women to men's condemnation of their dress is summed up in one early letter to the editor signed "Four Tolai Girls" (PNG *Post Courier* 1973a). As quoted in Hogan (1985: 56–57):

[The young women] had no doubts that the banning of mini-skirts would have wider implications. For its writers, wearing mini-skirts signified that they wanted greater control over their lives. They accused the initiators of the circular of having political motivations—of using the issue of public morality for their own political purposes ... and [of knowing] that with education women would be able to judge the decisions of men.

Three male Tolai students at the University of Papua New Guinea added their opinions to the debate by writing that the four Tolai girls were blindly following the dictates of western culture and wanting "to keep on 'pleasing' and 'praising' the colonial administration without stopping and asking themselves a single question" (PNG *Post Courier* 1973b).

The political advantages of focusing on the behaviors of a few elite women and suggesting that they are the root cause of problems both for women and the country as a whole are the obvious appeal to the masses, the small cost of blaming persons who do not constitute a large constituency, and the ease of following a time-honored tradition of blaming women for problems that men create or holding them up as suspicious characters bent on interfering in men's relations with one another. The anti-colonial sentiment and racial undercurrents in elite men's

condemnation of elite women is also a popular cause in a nation that is trying to unite a diversity of regions and language groups into one strong nation (see Lindstrom 1992).

Two cases that illustrate the sexual politics of Papua New Guinea's educated elite and the sexual competition among men of different tribal and national backgrounds are the cases of "Bill and Maria" and "Lita." Although their cases are well-known to me, I can only sketch in the barest of details here in this brief chapter. Readers who wish to read more detailed cases are referred to Susan's Toft's harrowing account of marital violence of two couples living in Port Moresby (1985) and Andrew Strathern's grisly report on sadistic rape in Hagen (1985).

Case 2—"Bill and Maria"

I have written about Bill and Maria in a paper on love and marriage among the educated elite in Port Moresby (Rosi and Zimmer-Tamakoshi 1993). I described how this young couple—both highlanders, both finishing their education at UPNG and the parents of two young children—were suffering severe pressures and tensions in their marriage, with the result that they fought often and violently. Much of the tension was caused by in-laws: Maria's father demanding a large brideprice for his educated daughter, and Bill's village-based family critical of Maria's lack of traditional skills and anxious that the couple pay most of the brideprice and childwealth payments themselves. Raised on a government station and exposed in her religious and educational experience to western ideas about appropriate and desirable marital relations, Maria was hurt and angered by Bill's drinking, numerous infidelities, and by his toying with the idea of marrying a second wife back in the highlands to raise pigs for exchange purposes.

What I did not discuss in that paper was the fact that Bill ended most arguments with his wife by raping her, sometimes in public places. On one occasion, after coming home drunk and disheveled in the early morning hours, Bill dragged Maria out of bed and raped her—spread-eagled over a car hood in a University parking lot—while loudly accusing her of being the cause of all his troubles, of having affairs with other men, and of dressing and behaving too provocatively to be a good wife. While there was little truth to his accusations, his use of these particular criticisms to justify his brutality reveals important contradictions in the lives of educated men, contradictions arising from the complex politics of sexuality in contemporary Papua New Guinea. On many occasions, Bill expressed pride in Maria's education and her poise in social situations involving both Papua New Guineans and expatriates. At one large garden party, for example, at which scores of University professors and students had gathered, Bill and Maria joined easily into the festivities, eating, drinking, dancing, and talking with the other guests—together and singly. As the evening progressed, however, Bill began following Maria around, demanding that she join the group of women who were sitting on woven mats on the perimeter of the night's action. These women—the wives of older and more conservative faculty and staff—were dressed modestly in *meri wantok* fashion in form-hiding *meri blouses* and ankle-length *laplaps,* and spent the evening quietly talking with one another and tending small children they had brought with them to the party. Also on the fringes, but drinking heavily, were some of Bill's male relatives—several students and several older men who did maintenance work at the university. These men ogled skimpily dressed expatriate women and the more daring *meri universiti* at the same time they criticized Bill for allowing Maria to wear a short, tight skirt and form-revealing blouse.

At the University club and at parties, I many times heard men slander particular women, their clothing choices, and their alleged sexual habits. If the women were not related to the men, they would also discuss ways of going about seducing or raping the woman. Add to this the disapproving and often envious statements of men's lesser-educated kin—telling their more advantaged brothers to avoid marrying women who waste

money on makeup and fancy clothes like spoiled white women at the same time as they express their desire to have sex with such women—and a situation arises in which it seems impossible for men like Bill to have it both ways—a wife who is attractive in new and sophisticated ways but one who does not attract the desire or censure of men who are her husband's associates, friends, relatives, or enemies.

Case 3—"Lita"

Further illuminating the sexual side of interethnic and interracial politics in urban Papua New Guinea, Lita's case is interesting because she is one of a small number of Papua New Guinean women who have discarded traditional relationships in order to express themselves in new and unusual ways. Pretty, bright, and poised in the presence of men of all ages and nationalities, Lita was engaged to a middle-aged expatriate when I first met her in one of the classes I was teaching at UPNG. Spurning her age-mates and vocal about her preference for white men—whom she claimed were gentler and more supportive of women's interests (for similar sentiments see the case of "Barbara" in Rosi and Zimmer-Tamakoshi 1993)—Lita accepted the gifts and attentions of her lover while at the same time playing the field at local discos and bars frequented by expatriate and Papua New Guinean businessmen and leaders.

Halfway through the semester, Lita began a secret love affair with one of her teachers at UPNG—an expatriate who was much younger than her fiance. When the affair became public knowledge and both expatriate lovers were spying on the other and attempting to engage the sympathies and help of Lita's friends, Lita's *wantoks* abducted her from her apartment, severely beat her and raped her, warning her to cease having affairs with either man and to choose someone from her own ethnic and racial background to marry. When I learned about the attack from some of Lita's classmates, I was dismayed by their lack of sympathy for her. Saying that she should not have embarrassed her *wantoks* and other

Papua New Guineans by choosing white lovers over black, the majority felt she had only gotten what she deserved and that she was lucky her *wantoks* had not killed her.

Lita's social background is similar to Maria's in that both women were raised in urban or peri-urban settings by parents who are employed in the government sector and who—in their commitment to a more western, or "modern" ethic—have raised their daughters to expect more egalitarian and open relations with men than is the norm in most parts of Papua New Guinea. Unfortunately for both young women, most of their *wantoks* do not agree and feel that the young women's "immodest" and "loose" behavior is injurious to ethnic and racial pride. Furthermore, both young women's *wantoks* are for the most part far less prosperous than either young woman's family, and there are economic and class tensions to contend with. When Lita informed her parents she was engaged to a foreigner, they at first protested it would never work. Promised a large brideprice, however, they and many of their village *wantoks* allowed that the marriage might be a good idea. Lita's *wantoks* at UPNG, however, took her engagement as an insult to them as more suitable partners, and when she compounded the insult by having affairs with two expatriates at the same time, it was too much to bear. In Maria's case, while her father and brothers have threatened to have her husband arrested for his repeated brutality, her *wantoks* side with Bill, contending that Maria is at least partly to blame for his behavior and that her husband and father should see to it that she conform to the clothing and behavioral norms of most highlanders rather than some small segment of PNG and expatriate society.

RAPE AND DOMESTIC VIOLENCE AS "WOMEN'S ISSUES"

As the foregoing suggests, violence against women has long been accepted in many Papua New Guinean societies as a legitimate means of controlling women and expressing or affecting men's relations with other men. From studies done in the 1980s by the Law Reform Commission (Toft, ed. 1985, 1986b) and other ethnographic sources we know that in the past both women and men agreed to men's right to chastise women with beatings and sometimes rape. Today, when some women's increased opportunities for self-expression and economic independence are perceived as threatening men's relations and the general good, many men and even many women consider violence to be an acceptable "comeuppance" for young women like Maria and Lita, and a means of preserving ethnic and national unity and pride. Nevertheless, there has been a sea change in women's attitudes toward violence against them and not only amongst elite women. Since the Second World War and the expansion of Papua New Guinea's towns and cities, urban dwellers have voiced their concerns over high rates of urban crime and domestic violence. Urban women have been especially concerned with the ever-present threat of pack rape and domestic violence associated with urban men's greater alcohol consumption, male sexual jealousy, and money problems (Toft 1986a: 12–14). In 1981, the National Council of Women passed a resolution stating that crimes against women seemed to be increasing and that there were inadequate controls to protect women. The Council then requested the government to investigate the problem, and on August 18, 1982, the Papua New Guinea Minister for Justice passed to the Law Reform Commission a Reference on Domestic Violence (Toft, ed. 1986a). The ensuing studies revealed many things about the nature, extent, and causes of domestic violence in Papua New Guinea as well as changing attitudes toward violence against women. Positive correlations were shown to exist, for example, between a decreasing acceptance of domestic violence and a person's sex, degree of urbanization, and levels of education and income (Toft 1986a: 23–26). Significantly, both urban low-income women and elite women are far less prepared than rural women to admit fault in failing to meet obligations to their husbands or to believe they "deserve" occasional beatings. Although the majority of urban men—especially educated men—also say it is unacceptable to hit wives, their apparent change in attitude is not reflected in their behavior.

Statistics are a weak measure of reality, however, and it is in case studies that we learn the depth of experience and motivations behind women's change of attitudes. In a study of two cases of marital violence in Port Moresby, Toft (1985) shows how men's violence against women interferes with the women's abilities, needs, and desires to function well in urban environments. One informant, "Rose," was regularly hit by her husband, who also phoned her at work in jealous piques and sometimes beat her so badly she could not work or take care of their young children. In a paper on Gende women in town, I make the point that while many urban women are technically unemployed, they fulfill many obligations to their village kin and in-laws and must be free to move about the urban environment without fear (Zimmer-Tamakoshi 1996b). Women in low-income households, for example, are almost always in town to protect their husbands' incomes from dissipation (e.g., alcohol, cards, prostitutes) and to see that their children get a better education than is always possible in the village. To achieve these ends, women meet husbands at their place of work on pay day for the handing over of the pay packet, they search the urban markets and stores for bargains to make their husbands' small incomes pay for both household and extra-household exchange demands, and they do without their school-age children's help in the daily round of collecting firewood and water for use in substandard squatter settlements at the edge of town. Such women have little patience with violent husbands whose utility to them is marginal at best. Women with more education have potentially greater opportunities to live life differently than their mothers' generation. Often, however, their desires and potential are not realized as violence, and fear of

violence, keeps them out of work. Female graduates of Papua New Guinea's teachers' colleges, for example, rarely teach for more than a year or so after graduating, even though they express, during their training, a strong desire and ability to be career teachers. A major constraint against their fulfilling their self-expectations is the threat of male violence against them, causing many to flee into early marriages and the comparative safety of compliance with men's wishes (Wormald and Crossley 1988).

Women's growing sense of gender oppression and their anger over their wasted potential reveals itself in diverse and often unusual ways. Young women like "Violet," impregnated by her brother-in-law and more or less abandoned by her family, may turn to prostitution to earn a living and make men pay for what they would otherwise take anyway. In urban contexts where women and girls have few options, "selling their bodies" to husbands or customers makes economic sense however much self-violence its represents (see also Borrey 1994). Cases like "Donna's" (see below), in which women are packraped because they represent a threat to men's interests or, as in this case, a threat to Papua New Guinean pride, are more and more seen as deliberate assaults against women as a whole and not individual women.

Case 4—"Donna"

Donna was a successful Filipina business woman married to one of the expatriate lecturers at UPNG and living on campus in one of the homes provided for UPNG faculty and their families. Resentment against expatriate women is high in Papua New Guinea, because most expatriate women live enviable lifestyles and many fill full- or part-time positions in the work force that Papua New Guineans feel should be given to Papua New Guinean workers, especially male workers. Openly critical of what she felt were lax working habits on the part of her Papua New Guinean employees, Donna earned even more enmity than usual.

Sometime in the late 1980s, Donna and her husband were eating dinner when a gang of rascals broke through their dining room windows, beat the husband, and abducted Donna. Taking Donna by car to a remote location, the gang raped her and then left her, naked and badly injured. After crawling and stumbling back to the University, Donna left the country to be joined soon after by her husband. Newspapers and gossip revealed that Donna had been the victim of a pay-back rape for her racial slurs and her successful competition against Papua New Guinean businessmen. Although her rape shocked the University community, particularly the expatriates, many persons—expatriate and Papua New Guinean, male and female—blamed Donna for being too outspoken and too obviously successful for a female expatriate business woman.

As time went on, however, public outcry began to divide itself along sexual rather than racial lines, and all women were more fearful as they went about their daily activities. In another much-reported case in the city of Lae, several Papua New Guinean men raped and then murdered a respected and well-liked white helicopter pilot when the man she was trying to sell her car to drove her to a secluded place where he was joined by the other men. During the trial, there were demonstrations throughout Papua New Guinea in favor of a strong penalty—"Death," "Katim bol bilong ol" ("cut their balls off!")—and when the defendants were let off with light sentences there was a spontaneous demonstration of several thousand women in Port Moresby protesting "men's disregard for women."

Although in the mid-1980s Papua New Guinea's male-dominated government supported the Law Reform Commission studies and a subsequent public awareness campaign on violence against women, rape and domestic violence are now "women's issues" in Papua New Guinea and no longer even a small part of male politicians' rhetoric. This shift became brutally apparent in 1987 when an all-male Parliament booed Rose Kekedo and other women from the floor when they tried to present the Law Reform Commis-

sion's interim report on domestic violence (The Times of Papua New Guinea 1992). In 1987 and since there have been no women in Papua New Guinea's Parliament. Papua New Guinea has never had more than a few women in higher government positions, and at most there have been only three Papua New Guinean women in Parliament at the same time (1977–1982). Significantly, none of these women ever felt the need to run a feminist campaign, until recently that is. Since 1987, as the numbers of female candidates and winners continues to shrink (Wormald 1992), female leaders such as former Parliamentarians Josephine Abaijah and Nahau Rooney have taken public positions on women's issues, focusing most on the concerns of "grassroots" women as crucial to Papua New Guinea's future and, of course, their own re-election. Rape and domestic violence top the list of concerns, however, as they affect all women (Waram 1992a and 1992b). Women's organizations have joined the campaign against violence with women leaders in Port Moresby choosing the theme "Violence Against Women" for their May 1993 International Women's Day Celebration (The Times of Papua New Guinea 1993b) and provincial women's leaders in East New Britain embarking on a campaign against violence and making plans to open a women's crisis center by 1994 (The Times of Papua New Guinea 1993a).

Similar situations exist in other Pacific countries where violence against women is less prevalent but nonetheless serious and feared by women who see it destroying their families and any hopes they have for establishing new opportunities and relationships for themselves (Dominy 1990; Lateef 1990; Ralston 1993; Trask 1989; Zimmer-Tamakoshi 1993b and 1995). Women in Vanuatu and the Solomon Islands have been especially vocal, decrying the effects of colonialism and modernity on their societies (most notably alcohol abuse, consumerism, gambling, and class and sex inequalities), but, above all, the impact of male dominance on women's hopes and aspirations (see Billy, Lulei, and

Sipolo 1983; Griffen 1976; Molisa 1983, 1987, 1989). Asserting what it is that women want, Vanuatu poet and feminist Grace Mera Molisa both unites and speaks for women throughout the Pacific in her poem "Colonised People" (1987: 9–13), part of which is reprinted here:

> Women too
> have a right
> to be Free.
>
> Free to think
> Free to express
> Free to choose
> Free to love
> and be loved
> as Woman Vanuatu.

She does not, however, any more than my argument has, lay the blame for women's plight simply on the shoulders of men. While she blasts male leaders for scapegoating female politicians who threaten their grasp of power in "Hilda Lini" (1987: 26–27), she also condemns women for envying other women's successes and going along with men's definitions of things in "Delightful Acquiescence" (1989: 24):

> Half of Vanuatu
> is still colonised
> by her self.
>
> Any woman
> showing promise
> is clouted
> into acquiescence.

REFERENCES

Berndt, Ronald M. 1962. *Excess and Restraint: Social Control among a New Guinea Mountain People.* Chicago: University of Chicago Press.

Billy, A., H. Lulei, and J. Sipolo, eds. 1983. *"Mi Mere": Poetry and Prose by Solomon Islands Women Writers.* Honiara.

Borrey, Anou. 1994. "Youth, Unemployment, and Crime." Paper presented at the National Employment Summit, 11–12 May, Port Moresby.

Bowers, Nancy. 1965. "Permanent Bachelorhood in the Upper Kaugel Valley of Highland New Guinea." *Oceania* 36: 27–37.

Bradley, Christine. 1982. "Tolai Women and Development." University College of London. Unpublished Ph.D. Thesis.

———. 1985. "Attitudes and Practices Relating to Marital Violence Among the Tolai of East New Britain." In Susan Toft (ed). *Domestic Violence in Papua New Guinea,* pp. 32–71. Port Moresby: Papua New Guinea Law Reform Commission Monograph No. 3.

———. 1994. "Why Male Violence Against Women is a Development Issue: Reflections from Papua New Guinea." In Miranda Davies (ed). *Women and Violence,* pp. 10–26. London: Zed Books, Ltd.

Brown, Paula. 1969. "Marriage in Chimbu." In R.M. Glasse and M.J. Meggitt (eds.). *Pigs, Pearlshells, and Women: Marriage in the New Guinea Highlands,* pp. 77–95. New Jersey: Prentice Hall, Inc.

Chowning, Ann. 1985. "Kove Women and Violence: The Context of Wife-Beating in a West New Britain Society." In Susan Toft (ed.). *Domestic Violence in Papua New Guinea,* pp. 72–91. Port Moresby: Papua New Guinea Law Reform Commission Monograph No. 3.

Cook, E. A. 1969. "Marriage Among the Manga." In R.M. Glasse and M.J. Meggitt (eds.). *Pigs, Pearlshells, and Women: Marriage in the New Guinea Highlands,* pp. 96–116. New Jersey: Prentice Hall, Inc.

Counts, Dorothy Ayres. 1985. *"Tamparonga:* 'The Big Women' of Kaliai." In J.K. Brown, Virginia Kerns, and Contributors. *In Her Prime: A New View of Middle-Aged Women,* pp. 49–64. South Hadley, MA: Bergin and Garvey Publishers, Inc.

Counts, Dorothy Ayers, Judith K. Brown, and Jacquelyn C. Campbell, eds. 1992. *Sanctions and Sanctuary: Cultural Perspectives on the Beating of Wives.* Boulder: Westview Press.

Davies, Miranda, ed. 1994. *Women and Violence: Realities and Responses Worldwide.* London: Zed Books Ltd.

Dickerson-Putman, Jeanette. 1996. "From Pollution to Empowerment: Women, Age, and Power Among the Bena Bena of the Eastern Highlands." In J. Dickerson-Putman (ed). *Women, Age, and Power: The Politics of Age Difference Among Women in Papua New Guinea and Australia.* Pacific Studies 19 (4): 41–70

Dinnen, Sinclair. 1993. "Big Men, Small Men and Invisible Women." *Australian and New Zealand Journal of Criminology* (March 1993) 26: 19–34.

———. 1996. "Law, Order, and State." In Laura Zimmer-Tamakoshi (ed.). *Modern PNG Society.* Bathurst, Australia: Crawford House Press.

Dominy, Michelle. 1990. "Maori Sovereignty: A Feminist Invention of Tradition." In J. Linnekin and L. Poyer (eds.). *Cultural Identity and Ethnicity in the Pacific,* pp. 237–257. Honolulu: University of Hawaii Press.

Faithorn, Elizabeth. 1976. "Women as Persons: Aspects of Female Life and Male-Female Relations Among the Kafe." In P. Brown and G. Buchbinder (eds.). *Man and Woman in the New Guinea Highlands,* pp. 86–95. Washington, DC: American Anthropological Association.

Finkelhor, David and Kersti Yllo. 1985. *License to Rape: Sexual Abuse of Wives.* New York: Holt, Rinehart, and Winston.

Gelber, Marilyn G. 1986. *Gender and Society in the New Guinea Highlands: An Anthropological Perspective on Antagonism Toward Women.* Boulder, CO: Westview Press, Inc.

Glasse, R. M. 1969. "Marriage in South Fore." In R.M. Glasse and M.J. Meggitt (eds.). *Pigs, Pearlshells, and Women: Marriage in the New Guinea Highlands,* pp. 16–37. Englewood Cliffs, NJ: Prentice Hall, Inc.

Goodale, Jane C. 1980. "Gender, Sexuality, and Marriage: A Kaulong Model of Nature and Culture." In C. MacCormack and M. Strathern (eds.). *Nature, Culture and Gender,* pp. 119–142. Cambridge: Cambridge University Press.

Griffen, V., ed. 1976. *Women Speak Out! A Report of the Pacific Women's Conference, October 27–November 2.* Suva.

Harris, Bruce. 1988. *The Rise of Rascalism—Action and Reaction in the Evolution of Rascal Gangs.* Port Moresby: Papua New Guinea Institute of Applied Social and Economic Research.

Herman, Dianne F. 1989. "The Rape Culture." In Jo Freeman (ed.). *Women: A Feminist Perspective,* pp. 20–44. Mountain View, California: Mayfield Publishing Company.

Hogan, Evelyn. 1985. "Controlling the Bodies of Women: Reading Gender Ideologies in Papua New Guinea." In Maev O'Collins et al. *Women in Politics in Papua New Guinea,* pp. 54–71. Working Paper No. 6. Canberra Department of Political and Social Change, Australian National University.

Jenkins, Carol (and The National Sex and Reproduction Research Team). 1994. *National Study of Sexual and Reproductive Knowledge and Behaviour in Papua New Guinea.* Papua New Guinea Institute of Medical Research Monograph 10.

Josephides, Lisette. 1985. *The Production of Inequality: Gender and Exchange Among the Kewa.* London: Tavistock.

———. n.d. "Gendered Discourses of Tradition and Change." Unpublished paper.

Langness, L. 1967. "Sexual Antagonism in the New Guinea Highlands: A Bena Bena Example." *Oceania* 37: 61–177.

———. 1969. "Marriage in Bena Bena." In R.M. Glasse and M.J. Meggitt (eds.). *Pigs, Pearlshells, and Women: Marriage in the New Guinea Highlands,* pp. 38–55. Englewood Cliffs, NJ: Prentice Hall, Inc.

———. 1974. "Ritual, Power, and Male Dominance." *Ethos* 2: 189–212.

Lateef, S. 1990. "Current and Future Implications of the Coups for Women in Fiji." *The Contemporary Pacific* 2 (1): 113–130.

Lindenbaum, Shirley. 1976. "A Wife is the Hand of Man." In P. Brown and G. Buchbinder (eds.). *Man and Woman in the New Guinea Highlands,* pp. 54–62. Washington, DC: American Anthropological Association.

Lindstrom, Lamont. 1992. *Pasin Tumbuna: Cultural Traditions and National Identity in Papua New Guinea.* Culture and Communications Working Paper. Honolulu: Institute of Culture and Communications, East-West Center.

Meggitt, Mervyn J. 1964. "Male-Female Relationships in the Highlands of Australian New Guinea." *American Anthropologist* 66: 204–224.

Mitchell, William E. 1992. "Why Wape Men Don't Beat Their Wives: Constraints Toward Domestic Tranquility in a New Guinea Society." In Counts, Brown, and Campbell (eds.). *Sanctions and Sanctuary: Cultural Perspectives on the Beating of Wives,* pp. 89–98. Boulder: Westview Press.

Molisa, Grace Mera. 1983. *Black Stone.* Suva.

———. 1987. *Colonised People.* Port Vila, Vanuatu.

———. 1989. *Black Stone II.* Port Vila, Vanuatu.

Newman, Philip L. 1964. "Religious Belief and Ritual in a New Guinea Society." *American Anthropologist* 66: 257–272.

Oliver, Joan. 1987. "Women Students at the University of Papua New Guinea in 1985." In S. Stratigos and P.J. Hughes (eds). *The Ethics of Development: Women as Unequal Partners in Development,* pp. 156–172. Port Moresby: University of Papua New Guinea Press.

Parkinson, R. 1907. *Thirty Years in the South Seas* (trans. by N.C. Barry from *Dreissig Jahre in der Sudsee*). Stuttgart: Strecker and Schroder. Typescript in the Papua New Guinea Collection, University of Papua New Guinea.

PNG Post Courier. 1973a. "Four Tolai Girls." June 13.

———. 1973b. "Three Mataungan Students." June 28.

———. 1984a. "Gang Rapist Jailed for Seven Years." April 13, p. 9.

———. 1984b. "Pack Rape! Horror Attack on Two Families." October 4, p. 1.

———. 1984c. "Two More Attacks." October 23, p. 2.

———. 1984d. "Another Youth is Charged." October 25, p. 2.

———. 1984e. "Badili Horror: Sixth Youth Charged." October 26, p. 2.

———. 1984f. "Badili Attack Man Charged." October 30, p. 2.

———. 1984g. "Young Girl Raped." October 31, p. 2.

Ralston, Caroline. 1993. "Maori Women and the Politics of Tradition: What Roles and Power Did, Do, and Should Maori Women Exercise?" *The Contemporary Pacific* 5 (1): 23–44.

Ranck, Stephen and Susan Toft. 1986. "Domestic Violence in an Urban Context with Rural Comparisons." In S. Toft (ed.). *Domestic Violence in Urban Papua New Guinea*, pp. 3–51. Law Reform Commission of Papua New Guinea, Occasional Paper No. 19.

Read, Kenneth E. 1952. "Nama Cult of the Central Highlands, New Guinea." *Oceania* 23: 1–25.

———. 1954. "Marriage Among the Gahuka-Gama of the Eastern Central Highlands, New Guinea." *South Pacific* 7: 864–871.

Riches, David, ed. 1986. *The Anthropology of Violence.* Oxford: Basil Blackwell.

Rosi, Pamela and Laura Zimmer-Tamakoshi. 1993. "Love and Marriage Among the Educated Elite in Port Moresby." In R. Marksbury (ed.). *The Business of Marriage: Transformations in Oceanic Matrimony*, pp. 175–204. The University of Pittsburgh Press.

Russell, Diana E. H. 1984. *Sexual Exploitation.* Beverly Hills, CA: Sage Publications.

Still, K. and J. Shea. 1976. *Something's Got to be Done So We Can Survive in This Place: The Problem of Women Students at UPNG.* Education Research Unit Research Report 20. Port Moresby: University of Papua New Guinea.

Strathern, A. 1985. "Rape in Hagen." In S. Toft (ed.). *Domestic Violence in Papua New Guinea*, pp. 134–140. Law Reform Commission of Papua New Guinea Monograph No. 3.

———. 1993. "Violence and Political Change in Papua New Guinea." *Pacific Studies* 16 (4): 41–60.

Strathern, M. 1972. *Women in Between: Female Roles in a Male World, Mt. Hagen, New Guinea.* London: Seminar Press.

———. 1980. "No Nature, No Culture: The Hagen Case." In C. MacCormack and M. Strathern (eds.). *Nature, Culture and Gender*, pp. 174–222. Cambridge: Cambridge University Press.

The Times of Papua New Guinea. 1992. "The Status of Women in Papua New Guinea." 9 January, p. 19.

———. 1993a. "East New Britain Women Embark on Campaign Against Violence." 4 March, p. 5.

———. 1993b. "Women Celebrate Their Day on Monday." 4 March, p. 2.

Toft, Susan. 1985. "Marital Violence in Port Moresby: Two Urban Case Studies." In S. Toft (ed.). *Domestic Violence in Papua New Guinea*, pp. 14–31. Papua New Guinea Law Reform Commission Monograph No. 3.

Toft, Susan, ed. 1985. *Domestic Violence in Papua New Guinea.* Papua New Guinea Law Reform Commission Monograph No. 3.

———. 1986a. *Domestic Violence in Urban Papua New Guinea.* Papua New Guinea Law Reform Commission Occasional Paper No. 19.

———. 1986b. *Marriage in Papua New Guinea.* Papua New Guinea Law Reform Commission Monograph No. 4.

Toft, Susan and S. Bonnell, eds. 1985. *Marriage and Domestic Violence in Rural Papua New Guinea.* Papua New Guinea Law Reform Commission Occasional Paper No. 18.

Trask, Haunani-Kay. 1989. "Fighting the Battle of Double Colonization: The View of an Hawaiian Feminist." *Ethnies* 8–9–10 (1): 61–67.

United Nations. 1989. *Violence Against Women in the Family.* Vienna: Centre for Social Development and Humanitarian Affairs.

Waddell, Eric. 1972. *The Mound Builders: Agricultural Practices, Environment and Society in the Central Highlands of New Guinea.* Seattle: University of Washington Press.

Waram, Ruth. 1992a. "Violence: A Crime Against Women." *Papua New Guinea Post Courier* 13 February, 24–25.

———. 1992b. "Women's Day Snubbed, While Many Centres Go Without Celebrations." *Papua New Guinea Post Courier* 26 March, 25 and 28.

Wormald, Eileen. 1992. "1992 National Election— Women Candidates in the Election." *The Times of Papua New Guinea* 28 May, 23–26.

Wormald, Eileen and Anne Crossley, eds. 1988. *Women and Education in Papua New Guinea and the South Pacific.* Port Moresby: University of Papua New Guinea Press.

Zimmer, Laura J. 1990. "Sexual Exploitation and Male Dominance in Papua New Guinea." In a special issue on *Human Sexuality. Point* 14: 250–267.

Zimmer-Tamakoshi, Laura. 1993a. "Bachelors, Spinsters, and 'Pamuk Meris.'" In R. Marksbury (ed.). *The Business of Marriage: Transformations in Oceanic Matrimony,* pp. 83–104. University of Pittsburgh Press.

———. 1993b. "Nationalism and Sexuality in Papua New Guinea." *Pacific Studies* 16 (4): 61–97.

———. 1995. "Passion, Poetry, and Cultural Politics in the South Pacific." In R. Feinberg and L. Zimmer-Tamakoshi (eds.). *Politics of Culture in the Pacific Islands,* special issue *Ethnology* 34 (2 & 3): 113–128.

———. 1996a. "Empowered Women." In W. Donner and J. Flanagan (eds.). *Social Organization and Cultural Aesthetics: Essays in Honor of William H. Davenport,* pp. 84–101. University of Pennsylvania Press.

———. 1996b. "Papua New Guinean Women in Town: Housewives, Homemakers, and Household Managers." In L. Zimmer-Tamakoshi (ed.). *Modern PNG Society.* Bathurst, Australia: Crawford House Press.

———. n.d. "Patterns of Culture in the Tower of Babel: Letters from Port Moresby, Papua New Guinea." Accepted for publication in *Journal de la Societe des Oceanistes.*

Film List

GENERAL FILMS

The Gender Tango. Films for the Humanities & Sciences. 1997. 47 minutes.

Looks at the way that women define themselves and are defined by others. Includes sections on a young beauty contest contestant in the U.S., a Latin American woman who sells cosmetics "hut to hut" in the Amazon; a woman who masqueraded as a man to gain acceptance in the male-dominated world of jazz music; and two contrasting aboriginal societies: in one, women are seen as evil and polluting and in the other , they are treated as valuable, powerful members of the tribe.

Cross-Cultural Comparisons: Gender Roles. Western Illinois University (distributed by Insight Media). 1995. Two volumes, 60 minutes each.

Compares gender roles in several countries. The first part discusses Hindu, Chinese, and Islamic gender roles, examining cultural practices that give men authority over women. The second part focuses on societies that have tried to remedy gender inequalities with specific policies and changes in law. Examples from China, the former Soviet Union, and Sweden are presented.

Gender Matters. A production for the Open University by the BBC. 1992. 24 minutes.

Examines gender subordination, probing its effects on both individuals and societies. Profiling individual women, it looks at their varied roles and proposes that future development policies focus on changing existing forms of control while maintaining cultural sensitivity.

In My Country: An International Perspective on Gender. Utah Valley State College. 1993. Two volumes, 91 minutes total.

This video is designed to be used as a resource for studying cultural attitudes related to gender. Divided into sections by topic, it covers division of household labor, types of discipline for boys and girls, marriage decisions, control of money, and society's view on rape, care of the elderly, and attitudes towards homosexuals. Features interviews with people from Zaire, El Salvador, St. Vincent, England, Taiwan, Sweden, Lebanon, Japan, India, China, the Fiji Islands, and Mexico.

BIOLOGY, GENDER, AND HUMAN EVOLUTION

Jane Goodall Studies of the Chimpanzee. "Tool Using.". National Geographic Society. 1978. 24 minutes.

Describes how young chimpanzees play with objects and how this play prepares them for making and using tools as adults.

Among the Wild Chimpanzees. National Geographic Society. 1984. 59 minutes.

Features Jane Goodall as researcher and examines infant chimpanzee development and behavior, male–female dominance, and hunting.

Brain Sex: Brain Architecture and the Sexes. Discovery Communications. 1992. 3 volumes, 52 minutes each.

This series examines differences between male and female learning patterns, appetites, expectations, and behaviors, exploring how fetal sex hormone levels affect later behavior. It considers evidence that men and women use different parts of the brain to carry out similar functions, probes evolution's role in shaping gender differences, and looks at differences in attitudes towards love and sex. Series titles include: 1. *Sugar and Spice: The Facts Behind Sex Differences; 2. Anything You Can Do, I Can Do Better: Why the Sexes Excel Differently;* and, *3. Love, Love Me Do: How Sex Differences Affect Relationships.*

Sex and Gender with Evelyn Fox Keller. PBS Video. 1990. 30 minutes.

Evelyn Fox Keller, a theoretical physicist and feminist historian of science, describes how gender plays a significant role in Western scientific theory and method.

The Long-Haired Warriors. University of California Extension Center for Media and Independent Learning. 1998. 60 minutes.

This documentary introduces a number of Vietnamese women who were active in the National Liberation Front and shows the major role played by Vietnamese women in the Vietnamese Conflict and the historical precedents for same. In this video, Vietnamese women tell of their war experiences during the Vietnamese Conflict; their active participation, their involvement, the tortures they endured, the effects of the Vietnamese Conflict to this day.

The Dream Becomes Reality? Nation Building and the Continued Struggle of the Women of the Eritrean People's Liberation Front : A Documentary. University of California Extension Center for Media and Independent Learning. 1995. 43min.

Features 6 Etritrean women who participated in the 30-year military struggle for independence from Ethiopia. During the war these women fought and worked in various aspects of the revolutionary media as members of the Eritrean People's Liberation Front. Now in post-war Eritrea the women speak about the war, the gender egalitarianism among the liberation forces, and their thoughts about the current situation of women in post-war Eritrea. Includes significant background on the liberation struggle.

DOMESTIC WORLDS
AND PUBLIC WORLDS

Kypseli: Women and Men Apart—A Divided Reality. University of California, Berkeley. 1976. 40 minutes.

Examines gender roles in a Greek peasant village.

Afghan Women. University of California, Berkeley. 1975. 17 minutes.

Examines the role of women in a rural community in northern Afghanistan.

Some Women of Marrakech. Granada Disappearing World Series. Thomas Howe Associates. 1976. 55 minutes. Re-edited for Odyssey, 1981.

Discusses the importance of marriage and family for women in Morocco and shows the impact of religion and class on women's lives.

Women, Work and Babies. NBC production. 1985. 60 minutes.

Discusses gender ideology in the United States and problems of working mothers.

The Double Day. IWFP. Cinema Guild. 1975. 51 minutes.

Discusses burdens of working women in Latin America.

Clotheslines. Filmmaker's Library. 1981. 32 minutes.

Shows the love-hate relationship that women have with cleaning the family clothes.

Not Baking. University of California. 1995. 9 minutes.

A woman explores her inability to bake. Archival footage demonstrates the tremendous force of America's baking tradition.

Power Plays. Corporation for Community College Television. 1988. 30 minutes.

Explores the relationship of gender to conjugal power, both traditionally and as it exists today. It shows how conjugal power varies in different socioeconomic strata and considers how relative conjugal power varies between public and private spheres. It also discusses factors that increase equality between spouses and describes alternatives to power politics in a marriage.

Defying the Odds: Women Around the World Create New Roles. Filmakers Library. 1996. 29 minutes.

This film was produced for the Beijing Women's Conference and focuses on the lives of four women of diverse ages and backgrounds who have broken ground in new fields. They are questioning age-old traditions as they forge careers in their respective societies.

The Double Shift Films for the Humanities & Sciences. 1996. 47 minutes.

Most women who have careers and raise families do a "double shift"—they hold one job for which they are paid and another for which they are not. This program examines that reality and whether or not women can ever be equal in this situation.

A Man in a Woman's World. Huby's Ltd. 1997. 18 minutes.

This video explores the stereotypes that surround men who choose an occupation traditionally filled by women. Men explain the challenges and rewards of working in such traditionally female dominated jobs as nurse or flight attendant.

The Double Burden: Three Generations of Working Mothers. New Day Films. 1992. 56 minutes.

Portrays the lives of three families—one Mexican-American, one Polish-American, and one African-American—each with three generations of women who have worked outside the home while raising families.

THE CULTURAL CONSTRUCTION
OF GENDER AND PERSONHOOD

A Man, When He is a Man. Women Make Movies. 1982. 66 minutes.

Set in Costa Rica, this film illuminates the social climate and cultural traditions that nurture machismo and allow the domination of women to flourish in Latin America.

Sexism in Language: Thief of Honor, Shaper of Lies. University of California. 1995. 29 minutes.

Analyzes the gender bias that permeates everyday language.

Small Happiness. Women of a Chinese Village. New Day Films. VHS Video cassette. 1984. 58 minutes.

Provides historical perspective on marriage, birth control, work, and daily life.

The Women's Olamal: The Organization of a Maasai Fertility Ceremony. Documentary Educational Resources. 1984. 115 minutes.

Presents a picture of women's lives in the male-dominated society of the Maasai in Kenya.

Maasai Manhood. ISHI. 1983. 53 minutes.

Describes a male initiation ritual among the pastoral Maasai of Kenya.

Rivers of Sand. University of California, Berkeley. 1975. 83 minutes.

Portrays male supremacy among the Hamar of Ethiopia, including male initiation.

Killing Us Softly III. Cambridge Documentary Films. 1999. 30 minutes.

Details psychological and sexual themes in American advertising. In this film, Kilbourne updates the classic film and looks at how the image of women in advertising has changed over the last 20 years.

Slim Hopes. Media Education Foundation. 1995. 30 minutes.

Offers a new way to think about eating disorders such as anorexia and bulimia and provides a critical perspective on the social impact of advertising. New film by Jean Kilbourne.

Beyond Macho. Films for the Humanities and Sciences. 1985. 26 minutes.

Explores roles for men that have evolved in response to feminism and economic changes in the United States through an examination of the lives of two men, one a nurse and the other a "house-husband."

Men and Masculinity. OASIS. 1990. 30 minutes.

Covers the thirteenth National Conference on Men and Masculinity and discusses a broad range of men's movement issues in the United States, including antipornography activism, challenges to homophobia, and domestic violence.

Stale Roles and Tight Buns. OASIS. 1988. 29 minutes.

Uses advertising images to show how men are stereotyped in the media and how myths develop that limit men's and women's roles.

Becoming a Woman in Okrika. Filmakers Library. 1990. 27 minutes.

A coming-of-age ritual in a village in the Niger Delta.

Surname Viet Given Name Nam. Women Make Movies. 1989. 108 minutes.

Explores the multiplicity of identities of Vietnamese women in Vietnam and in California.

Faces of Change: Andean Women. University of California, Berkeley. 1975. 19 minutes.

Describes cultural ideals of female subservience among Aymara.

The Smell of Burning Ants. Film Arts Foundation. 1995. 21 minutes.

The film depicts the often painful aspects of male socialization in the west.

Juggling Gender. Women Make Movies. 1992. 27 minutes.

Through a focus on a bearded lesbian performer, the film explores the fluidity of gender and the construction of gender identity.

The Gay Gene. Films for the Humanities & Sciences. 1998. 29 minutes.

Focuses on the science behind the controversial genetic research into the so-called "gay gene." A geneticist explains how the study was carried out, from the initial interviews with gay men and their families, to the plotting of family trees, the extraction of DNA, and the analysis of samples in the lab. The program also considers the findings of the research: that homosexuality is, in part, genetically determined. It discusses whether these finds will advance the cause of gay rights and promote tolerance and understanding in society at large.

Multiple Genders: Mind and Body in Conflict. Films for the Humanities & Sciences. 1997/1998. 40 minutes.

Looks at whether or not there are only two sexes. A transsexual doctor contends that there are more and that transsexuals and hermaphrodites at least constitute two others. A theologian addresses the moral implications of multisexual orientation, while a physician and polygendered people ask: Is sex the same as gender? Are inter-sexes mistakes or parts of nature?

Barbie Nation: An Unauthorized Tour. New Day Films. PBS. 1998. 54 minutes.

Plumbs the cult of the Barbie Doll, telling the Barbie stories of diverse men, women and children. It is about the creation of femininity and the marking—and subversion—of femininity's icon.

Tough Guise: Media Images & the Crisis in Masculinity. Wellesley Centers for Women. 1999. 40 minutes.

Although femininity has been widely examined, the dominant role of masculinity has until recently remained largely invisible. *Tough Guise* is the first program to look systematically at the relationship between the images of popular culture and the social construction of the masculine identities in the United States in the late 20th century.

Growing Up and Liking It: The Menstruation Myth. Filmakers Library. 1991. 28 minutes.

The monthly menstruation cycle, a natural occurrence that from time immemorial has made women the object of taboo and superstition, is the subject of this video. We meet women of varying ages and cultural backgrounds who share with us the vivid and often disturbing memories coming of age.

CULTURE AND SEXUALITY

Women Like Us. Women Make Movies. 1990. 49 minutes.

Portrays older lesbian women in Great Britain, their feelings and lifestyles, and discusses the implications of sexual orientation for family and work relations.

On Being Gay. TRB Productions. 1986. 80 minutes.

Through a monologue by Brian McNaught, this film addresses myths about homosexuality and such topics as growing up gay in a straight world, Bible-based bigotry, stereotypes, transvestitism, transsexualism, and AIDS.

Metamorphosis: Man into Woman. Filmakers Library. 1990. 58 minutes.

Features a transsexual confronting gender stereotypes in society.

Man Oh Man—Growing Up Male in America. New Day Films, Inc. 1987. 19 minutes.

Focuses on being a man in contemporary American society, with an emphasis on the difficulties of living up to cultural ideals of manhood.

Choosing Children. Cambridge Documentary.

Explores three situations in which lesbians have had children.

Masai Manhood. Films Incorporated Video. 1983. 52 minutes.

Focuses on the lives of Masai men and the Eunoto ceremony that marks their transition from warrior to elder.

De Mujer a Mujer. Women Make Movies. 1995. 46 minutes.

Latina women discuss their experiences and feelings about sexuality and maturation.

Sex and Money. Filmakers Library. 1989. 50 minutes.

Focuses on transsexual individuals in the United States and the Netherlands. Dr. John Money addresses differences between gender identity and gender roles. Contains explicit sexual material.

Friends and Lovers. World Cultures on Film and Video, University of California. 1994. 28 minutes.

Gay men discuss their feelings about intimacy in an age of AIDS and challenge our assumptions about relationships and sexuality.

The Remarkable Case of John/Joan. Canadian Broadcasting Corporation. Filmakers Library. 1997. 30 minutes.

Eight-month-old John was the victim of an accident during circumcision which left him with almost no penis. The next year when he was almost two it was decided to have his testicles removed and bring him up as a girl following the theory that environment was more important in creating sexual identity than biology. When he was an adolescent John learned the truth about his birth and having been miserable as a girl he underwent reconstructive surgery to return himself to being a man.

Honored by the Moon. Women Make Movies. 1989/1990. 15 minutes.

Addresses issues of homophobia within the American Indian community. Native American lesbians and gay men speak of their unique historical and spiritual role.

Beauty Before Age: Growing Old in Gay Culture. New Day Films. 1997. 22 minutes.

Explores the power of youth and beauty in the gay community. A diverse group of men, ages 19 to 77, navigate their fears of becoming old, undesirable, and alone. Offers a male perspective on a traditionally female issue, and illuminates the larger societal obsession with physical appearance.

Sexuality in MesoAmerica: Machismo and Marianismo. Cinema Guild. 1996. 33 minutes.

Describes how machismo and marianismo shape sexual behavior and identity in Mesoamerica. Shows the historical and cultural antecedents of these models, illustrates how they are integrated in different social sectors, and explores how they are being redefined by contemporary revolutionary movements.

I'm not A Common Woman(Yo No Soy Una Qualquiera). Women Make Movies. 1989. 20 minutes.

In Argentina, "qualquiera" means many things: a nobody, a thing, a Jane Doe. However in slang its meaning is clear—whore. This video exploits the double entendre to its fullest, creating a provocative portrait of Latin machismo and female resistance.

Sunflowers. University of California Extension Center for Media and Independent Learning. 1997. 50 minutes.

Portrait of a spirited community of gay men in a rural town in the Philippines. The Sunflowers, as they are called locally, have since 1975 performed in drag the town's most important annual Christian festival.

EQUALITY AND INEQUALITY: THE SEXUAL DIVISION OF LABOR AND GENDER STRATIFICATION

Hunters and Gatherers

N!ai: The Story of a !Kung Woman. Penn State University. 1980. 59 minutes.
   Features the biography of a !Kung woman from early childhood to middle age and the impact of colonial penetration on her life.
The Warao. University of California, Berkeley. 1978. 57 minutes.
   Ethnographic account of division of labor among the Warao of the Orinoco River Delta in Venezuela.
Before We Knew Nothing. World Cultures on Film and Video, U. of California. 1989. 62 minutes.
   An exploration of the roles and activities of Ashaninka women in the Amazon rain forest.

Horticulturalists

Seasons of the Navajo. PBS Video. Peace River Films. 1984. 60 minutes.
   Presents one family's kinship with the earth through seasons, touching briefly on Navajo matriliny and women's work and craft responsibilities.
The Trobriand Islanders of Papua New Guinea. Films Incorporated Video. 1990. 52 minutes.
   Focuses on the distribution of women's wealth after a death and the month of celebration following the yam harvest.
Guardians of the Flutes: The Secrets of Male Initiation. Filmakers Library. 1994. 55 minutes.
   Deals with the Sambia people, a warlike tribe whose secret rituals of initiation are aimed at making their warriors courageous and bold.

Agriculturalists

Luisa Torres. Chip Taylor Communications. 1980. 28 minutes.
   The recollections of a Hispanic woman in northern New Mexico; discusses division of labor, marriage, use of medicinal plants, and other aspects of daily life.
Kheturni Bayo: North Indian Farm Women. Penn State. 1980. 19 minutes.

Examines the roles and the duties of the women in a typical extended family of land-owning peasants in Gujarat, India.
Seed and Earth. Filmakers Library. 1994. 36 minutes.
   Portrays everyday life in rural West Bengal. Shows how gender and age determine work, ritual, and leisure activities.
The Ladies of the Lake: A Matriarchial Society. Filmakers Library. 1998. 20 minutes.
   Looks at a rare matriarchal community in southwest China. The Mosuo culture has survived both the time of the concubines and the cultural revolution but is now being threatened by Beijing's one-child-per-family policy. In this culture power is handed from the matriarch to the most intelligent daughter.

Pastoralists

Masai Women. Thomas Howe Associates. 1983. 52 minutes.
   Examines the role of women among pastoralists in Kenya.
Women of the Toubou. University of California, Berkeley. 1974. 25 minutes.
   Examines gender roles among nomads of the Sahara.
Boran Women. University of California, Berkeley. 1975. 18 minutes.
   Shows women's daily work in Kenyan society, including caring for cattle, milk storage, and child care.
Deep Hearts. University of California, Berkeley. 1980. 53 minutes.
   Documentary on the Bororo Fulani in Niger, Africa. Focuses on ritual dances in which men compete in a beauty contest.
Hamar Trilogy. Filmakers Library. 1994/1991/1994 55 minutes each.
   Trilogy focuses on the Hamar, an isolated people of southwestern Ethiopia whose traditional lifestyle has barely been touched by war and the famine in the north. The films concentrate on the powerful and outspoken Hamar women. Titles include: *The Women Who Smile; Two Girls Go Hunting;* and *Our Way of Loving.*

Miscellaneous

Asante Market Women. Penn State. 1983. 52 minutes.
   Power of Ghanaian market women from a matrilineal and polygynous society.
From the Shore. Indiana University. 1989.
   Explores the formation of a fishing cooperative among women in the coastal village of Shimoni,

Kenya, in defiance of the traditional roles of women.

Maids and Madams. Filmakers Library. 1985. 52 minutes.

Describes the plight of Black female domestic servants in South Africa and analyzes the relationship between gender, class, and apartheid.

A Kiss on the Mouth. Women Make Movies. 1987. 30 minutes.

Examines female prostitution in urban Brazil.

My Husband Doesn't Mind if I Disco. World Cultures on Film and Video, University of California. 1995. 28 minutes.

The negotiation of role and gender ideology in Tibet.

Mamma Benz: An African Market Woman. (Also titled: *God Gave Her a Mercedes Benz.*) Filmakers Library. 1992/1993. 48 minutes.

The markets of Africa are dominated by strong older women. They control the price and determine who can buy their goods. These women rule the markets and are treated with deference. This film focuses on one of these women who presides over the cloth market in Lomé, Togo.

A Little for my Heart and a Little for My God: A Muslim Women's Orchestra. Filmakers Library. 1993. 60 minutes.

Since in Algeria women are traditionally not allowed to mix with men, female orchestras customarily entertain gatherings of women. This film is a portrait of one of these orchestras. (In French with English subtitles.)

GENDER, PROPERTY, AND THE STATE

No Longer Silent. International Film Bureau. 1986. 57 minutes.

Analyzes dowry deaths in India, as well as the cultural preference for boys and female infanticide.

Modern Brides. South Asian Area Center, University of Wisconsin. 1985. 30 minutes.

Features two young women, one with an arranged marriage and one with a "love match," and discusses the bride's capacity to work as a substitute for dowry.

Las Madres: The Mothers of Plaza de Mayo. Direct Cinema Ltd. 1986. 64 minutes.

Focuses on Argentinean mothers who, beginning in 1977, defied laws against civil demonstrations to protest the disappearance of their children under the military dictatorship.

Donna: Women in Revolt. Women Make Movies. 1980. 65 minutes.

An examination of the history and development of Italian feminism through the personal stories of women involved in the women's rights movement at the turn of the century, the resistance during World War II, and of present day feminists.

Weaving the Future: Women of Guatemala. Women Make Movies. 1988. 28 minutes.

A perspective on women in Guatemala's liberation struggle, exploring the pivotal role of women in building a just society amid political strife and poverty.

Gabriella. Women Make Movies. 1988. 67 minutes.

Examines the work of a mass organization of diverse women's groups in the Philippines.

Women of Niger: Between Fundamentalism and Democracy. Women Make Movies. 1993. 26 minutes.

Niger is a traditionally Islamic country where women are not allowed to vote for themselves and those who speak out about their rights have been physically attacked and excommunicated. Muslim Fundamentalism clashes with the country's struggle for democracy, of which women are among the most ardent defenders. This film deals with human rights and the impact of fundamentalism on women.

Our Honor and His Glory: Honor Killing in the Palestine Zone. Filmakers Library. 1997. 28 minutes.

In some areas of North Africa, the Middle East, and Asia, honor is deemed of such importance that a father, a brother or a cousin is entitled by tribal custom to kill a woman, often a young girl, who is suspected of having sullied the family's honor. This film documents two cases in Palestinian villages.

Keep Her Under Control: Law's Patriarchy in India. University of California Extension Center for Media and Independent Learning. 1998. 52 minutes.

This film explores the role of women in a Muslim-dominated village in Rajasthan, in northern India. It focuses on the story of a single woman who refuses to live by the moral and legal codes of the village's Islamic patriarchy.

GENDER, HOUSEHOLD, AND KINSHIP

Dadi's Family. Odyssey. 1981. 58 minutes.

Describes family tensions in a patrilineal joint household in northern India.

A Wife Among Wives. University of California, Berkeley. 1981. 70 minutes.

Turkana women discuss polygyny.

Tobelo Marriage. University of California, Berkeley. 1990. 106 minutes.

Chronicles a marriage ritual in Eastern Indonesia, including exchange of valuables, negotiations, and preparatory activities.

Asian Heart. Filmakers Library. 1987. 38 minutes.

Deals with marriage brokering between clients from Denmark and Filipino "mail order brides."

A Village in Baltimore. Doreen Moses. 1730 21st St. N.W. Washington, DC 20009. 1981. 63 minutes.

Conveys the problems and conflicts of changing identities and traditions among Greek immigrants in the United States, focusing on dowry, marriage, and other social events.

All Dressed in White. University of California. 1994. 18 minutes.

Explores the complex relationships among religion, ethnicity, and gender by investigating one key symbol: the wedding dress. Based on stories of four women in a Catholic Indian family from Goa who have migrated to Singapore and then to California.

Chronicle of a Savanna Marriage. Filmakers Library. 1997. 56 minutes.

Follows the marriage of one girl for 15 years starting from when she was promised to her future husband through her circumcision, marriage, and the addition of additional wives to the household.

Not Without My Veil: Among the Women of Oman. Filmakers Library. 1993. 29 minutes.

Examines the view of Muslim women as oppressed and confined. The practice of wearing the traditional veil symbolizes this for many westerners, but this video shows a different reality. It shows these women as educated, professional women who choose to wear the veil as a symbol of their origins and their identities.

Just Mom and Me: Single Motherhood. Filmakers Library. 2000. 60 minutes.

This film interweaves the stories of five single mothers in vastly different circumstances. Filmed over three years, this is a realistic portrayal of the financial and emotional challenges of single parenting. It also gives voice to the children who reflect on the realities of not having a father in the home.

Single Dads. Huby's; Distributed by The School Co. 1997. 18 minutes.

Are single dads treated differently from single moms? Are there government and community resources available to single dads? This program focuses on the special challenges of being a single father, looking at how single fathers balance family and job responsibilities.

The Polygamists. Films for the Humanities & Sciences. 1998. 52 minutes.

This documentary takes place in Mant, Utah and follows several of the 450 families who practice plural marriage in the town.

Because This is About Love: A Portrait of Gay and Lesbian Marriage. Filmakers Library. 1991. 28 minutes.

The stories of five lesbian and gay couples.

Fighting Grandpa. Greg Pak. Filmakers Library. 1999. 21 minutes.

The filmmaker tells the story of his Korean immigrant grandmother's seventy-year struggle with her husband. Forced to give up her dream of becoming a nurse she is left with their four children for ten years while her husband studied in the U.S., and finally brought to America to endure her husband's parsimonious ways, she had every right to be bitter. But when her husband dies, her stoicism gives way to piercing grief that confounds the filmmaker and his family. Showing that the relationships of their immigrant forebears could only dimly be understood by today's generations.

A Day Will Come: Change and Tradition in Pakistani Marriage. Filmakers Library. 2000. 28 minutes.

Follows the engagement of two children of a middle class family in Quetta, Pakistan. The two engagements could not be more different because one of the engagements is a traditional, arranged marriage to a woman that the groom has never met, while the second engagement is a love match.

Saheri's Choice: Arranged Marriages in India. Films for the Humanities & Sciences. 1998. 25 minutes.

Examines the custom of arranged marriages in India. It follows the story of one girl and her family as they confront the reality of an impending marriage that was arranged when the girl was barely six. An overview of the custom shows it to be widely practiced by all castes although many Indians view it negatively. This is a candid glimpse into contemporary Indian society.

GENDER, RITUAL, AND RELIGION

Out of Order. Icarus Films. 1983. 88 minutes.

Presents personal narratives of six women in various stages of convent life.

Behind the Veil: Nuns. Wombat Productions. 1984. 115 minutes.

Examines the history of women in the Christian Church.

The Living Goddess. University of California, Berkeley. 1979. 30 minutes.

Studies the Newar of Nepal, focusing on a ritual cult in which young virgin girls are thought to embody the spirits of goddesses.

The Shakers. University of California, Berkeley. 1974. 29 minutes.

Traces the growth and decline of the Shaker community.

A Sense of Honor. Films Incorporated. 1984. 55 minutes.

Made by an Egyptian anthropologist, the film describes the impact of Islamic fundamentalism on the lives of women in Egypt.

Rastafari: Conversations Concerning Women. Eye in I Filmworks. 1984. 60 minutes.

Examines the roles and relations of men and women in the Jamaican Rastafarian movement.

A Veiled Revolution. Icarus. 1982. 27 minutes.

Attempts to discern the reasons behind the movement in Egypt by young educated women to resume wearing traditional Islamic garb.

An Initiation Kut For A Korean Shaman. Laurel Kendall and Diana Lee and the Center for Visual Anthropology. University of Hawaii Press. 1991. 36 minutes.

Portrays the initiation of Chini, a young Korean woman demonstrating her ability to perform as a shaman and shouting out the spirit's oracles.

Mammy Water: In Search of Water Spirits in Nigeria. University of California. 1991. 59 minutes.

Focuses on the worship of a local water goddess by the Ibibio-, Ijaw-, and Igbo-speaking people of southeastern Nigeria.

Hidden Faces. Women Make Films. 1990. 52 minutes.

The conflict between feminist ideals and Islamic values and traditions of the veil and clitoridectomy.

Beyond the Veil: Are Iranian Women Rebelling? Films for the Humanities & Sciences. 1997. 22 minutes.

In this program a female reporter dons the *hijah*—"modest dress"—and goes undercover to find out how Iranian women feel about the government-enforced dress code and about their diminished role in Iranian society.

Who Will Cast the First Stone? Cinema Guild. 1989. 52 minutes.

Examines the impact of Islamization on women in Pakistan, in particular the Hudood Ordinances under which adultery, rape, or extramarital sex are considered a crime against the state, punishable by stoning to death.

Rights of Passage: Four Stories of Survival. Filmakers Library. 1994. 30 minutes.

This film gives the stories of four young women coming of age in different parts of the world and looks at what can be the personal cost of this transition.

Daughters of the Nile (Dochters van de Nijl). Distributed by Filmakers Library. 1992. 46 minutes.

This film about Egypt's women captures their separate and subordinate life under the Islamic code. Men and women speak about their traditions, expectations, and patterns of life.

Monday's Girls. California Newsreel. 1994. 50 minutes.

Follows two young Nigerian women's different experiences of a traditional rite of passage. Young virgins spend five weeks in "fattening rooms," emerging to dance before the villagers and to be married. One of the women is eager to take part while the other, who returns from the city at her father's request, is not certain she wants to.

GENDER, POLITICS, AND REPRODUCTION

No Longer Silent. International Film Bureau. 1986. 57 minutes.

Discusses dowry deaths in India, as well as the cultural preference for boys and female infanticide.

Rites. Filmakers Library. 1990. 52 minutes.

Considers three major contexts in which female "genital mutilation" occurs: cosmetic, punitive, and rite of passage. Particularly emphasizes the health risks and psychological consequences of female circumcision.

China's One-Child Policy. Nova Special. 1985. 60 minutes.

A documentary on China's population policy, its implementation, unpopularity, and its relation to gender ideology.

Nyamakutaù: The One Who Receives: An African Midwife. Filmakers Library. 1989. 32 minutes.

Portrays a traditional African midwife who incorporates pharmaceuticals with local practices to improve health standards in her village.

Birth and Belief in the Andes of Ecuador. University of California. 1995. 28 minutes.

A portrait of women in four Andean communities, documenting their beliefs and practices surrounding childbirth and infant care. Cultural construction of the female body, ideas about conception, motives for post-partum seclusion, and gender differences in the "natures" and needs of infants are all shown to be part of this ethnomedical system.

On the Eighth Day. Women Make Movies. 1992. Two parts, 51 minutes each.

A two-part film series which explores the social, economic, and political influences and impacts of new reproductive and genetic technologies.

Something Like War. Women Make Movies. 1991. 52 minutes.

The film explores the intersection of the reality of women's lives and the family planning project enforced by the government.

Birth Stories. Cinema Guild. 1994. 30 minutes.

Blends women's personal stories of pregnancy and birth with footage of actual birth. The program captures the full spectrum of women's emotional reactions, from amazement to resentment, providing amusing but illuminating insights into a common experience that is still poorly understood and appreciated.

Whose Bodies, Whose Rights. University of California Extension Center for Media and Independent Learning. 1996. 56 minutes.

Explores the growing debate over male circumcision in America, showing that the practice has only the flimsiest medical rational and is primarily a repressive social custom based on medical and cultural myths.

Fire Eyes: Female Circumcision. Filmakers Library. 1994. 60 minutes.

Presents an African viewpoint on the culturally explosive issue of female circumcision. Testimony from doctors details the various forms of female circumcision and the ob/gyn problems that result, and several women who have experienced it speak out about their experiences and their views on the practice for their daughters.

Gift of a Girl: Female Infanticide. Filmakers Library. 1997. 24 minutes.

Explores the complexity of female infanticide in southern India and shows steps that are being taken to eradicate the practice.

Abortion: Stories From the North and South. Cinema Guild. 1984. 55 minutes.

Filmed in Ireland, Japan, Thailand, Peru, Columbia, and Canada, this cross-cultural survey shows how abortion transcends race religion and social class, and how differences in the practice and perception of abortion are mainly in the degree of secrecy and danger accompanying it.

La Operacion. Cinema Guild. 1982. 40 minutes.

Examines the controversial use of female sterilization as a means of population control in Puerto Rico, which has the highest incidence of sterilization in the world.

COLONIALISM, DEVELOPMENT, AND THE GLOBAL ECONOMY

Women at Risk. Filmakers Library. 1991. 56 minutes.
Presents portraits of women refugees in Asia, Africa, and Latin America.

The Global Assembly Line. New Day Films. 1986. 58 minutes.

A portrayal of the lives of working women and men in the "free trade zones" of developing countries and North America. Focuses on Mexico and the Philippines.

Bringing It All Back Home. Women Make Movies. 1987. 48 minutes.

Analyzes how the patterns of international capital investment and the exploitation of Third World women workers in free-trade zones is being brought home to the First World, as Britain's declining industrial regions have been designated "enterprise zones" to attract the multinationals.

Women Under Siege. Icarus. 1982. 26 minutes.

Illustrates women's lives and political goals in a Palestinian refugee camp near the Israeli border.

A State of Danger. Women Make Movies. 1989. 28 minutes.

Offers a perspective on the Intifada, presenting women's testimonies on their experiences with the Israeli military.

Hell to Pay. Women Make Movies. 1988. 52 minutes.

Presents an analysis of the international debt situation through the eyes of the women of Bolivia.

Holding Our Ground. International Film Bureau, Inc. 1988. 51 minutes.

Features women and children in the Philippines who pressure the government for land reform, establish their own money lending system, and build shelters for street children.

Maria's Story. Filmakers Library. 1990. 53 minutes.

Portrays an FMLN guerilla, Maria Serrano, who has been living in the countryside for 11 years. Discusses her role in the revolution as well as the impact of the revolution on her family.

Time of Women. Women Make Movies. 1988. 20 minutes.

A portrait of the life of women in an Ecuadorian village where men are absent as migrants. The film looks at the impact of national economic policies on these rural women.

Fair Trade. Indiana University. 1989.

Profiles Tanzanian women and their struggle to become small entrepreneurs, and looks at the impact of development organizations and the aid that they extend to women through capital loans.

Where Credit Is Due. Indiana University. 1989.

Features the problem that Kenyan women have with the banking system, which generally refuses loans to women, and describes the Kenya Women's Finance Trust as an example of a credit cooperative for women borrowed from rural traditions of Women's support groups.

Once This Land Was Ours. Women Make Movies. 1991. 19 minutes.

The feminization of poverty in rural agricultural India.

Troubled Harvest. Women Make Movies. 1990. 30 minutes.

This documentary traces the female workers' experience with the fruit industry in Mexico and Latin America.

Modern Heroes, Modern Slaves. Filmakers Library. 1997. 45 minutes.

Starting from the case of Flor Contemplacion, a Philippine maid hanged in Singapore for killing her abusive employer, this film shows the human and sometimes tragic side of this organized labor trade: failed marriages, family break ups, and exploitation and abuse at the hands of unscrupulous employers.

Behind the Smile. Filmakers Library. 1993. 46 minutes.

Hundreds of thousands of young Thai women leave their rural homes and work in the factories of Bangkok. This film explores the lives of these young women who live in crowded dormitories or shacks with few possessions, homesick for their families.

In Danku the Soup is Sweeter: Women and Development in Ghana. Filmakers Library. 1992. 30 minutes.

In this village in the north of Ghana, as in many African villages, women carry the burden of caring for the children, raising food, and trying to make a better life for their families. Through a special project, the women were given access to credit for the first time. This aid allowed them to become "entrepreneurs" and the film follows two women in their new enterprises as they struggle to make their enterprises work and to pay back their loans.

Water for Tonoumassé. Filmakers Library. 1987. 28 minutes.

Shows the efforts of a group of a group of villagers to get clean water by drilling a well nearby instead of making a daily eight-hour trek to get water from a contaminated source. It chronicles the success of this project in which women played a key role.

Sisters and Daughters Betrayed: The Trafficking of Women and Girls and the Fight to End It. University of California Extension Center for Media and Independent Learning. 1995. 28 minutes.

Sex trafficking is a global—and especially Asian—crisis of growing dimensions. Millions of women and young girls have been illegally transported from rural to urban areas and across national borders for the purpose of prostitution. This video explores the social and economic forces that drive this lucrative underground trade, and the devastating effect it has on women's lives..

Daughters of Ixchel: Maya Thread of Change. University of California Extension Center for Media and Independent Learning. 1993. 29 minutes.

Explores the lives of Maya women today, portrays their ancient weaving processes, and examines the economic, political, and cultural forces that are profoundly affecting the women and their weaving.

The Women's Bank of Bangladesh. Films for the Humanities & Sciences. 1997. 47 minutes.

Describes the philosophy, development, and function of the Grameen Bank, then follows three women who have taken out loans to fund their cottage industries. Islamic leaders and most males oppose the bank as being contrary to Islamic law, but the bank's founder defends the bank and its policy saying that women in the region are more competitive in business than men.

Women of the Earth: Australian Aborigines. Films for the Humanities & Sciences. 1998. 56 minutes.

Portrays Australia's Aborigines through the eyes of aboriginal women. Archival footage, excellent narration, and storytelling by the women themselves reveal the tribes' struggle for land rights, and the even greater struggle to retain their traditional lifestyles and customs in a world that is fast disappearing.